Communications
in Computer and Information Science   1332

More information about this series at http://www.springer.com/series/7899

Haiqin Yang · Kitsuchart Pasupa ·
Andrew Chi-Sing Leung ·
James T. Kwok · Jonathan H. Chan ·
Irwin King (Eds.)

Neural
Information Processing

27th International Conference, ICONIP 2020
Bangkok, Thailand, November 18–22, 2020
Proceedings, Part IV

 Springer

Editors
Haiqin Yang [ID]
Department of AI
Ping An Life
Shenzhen, China

Andrew Chi-Sing Leung [ID]
City University of Hong Kong
Kowloon, Hong Kong

Jonathan H. Chan [ID]
School of Information Technology
King Mongkut's University
of Technology Thonburi
Bangkok, Thailand

Kitsuchart Pasupa [ID]
Faculty of Information Technology
King Mongkut's Institute
of Technology Ladkrabang
Bangkok, Thailand

James T. Kwok [ID]
Department of Computer Science
and Engineering
Hong Kong University of Science
and Technology
Hong Kong, Hong Kong

Irwin King [ID]
The Chinese University of Hong Kong
New Territories, Hong Kong

ISSN 1865-0929   ISSN 1865-0937 (electronic)
Communications in Computer and Information Science
ISBN 978-3-030-63819-1   ISBN 978-3-030-63820-7 (eBook)
https://doi.org/10.1007/978-3-030-63820-7

Preface

This book is a part of the five-volume proceedings of the 27th International Conference on Neural Information Processing (ICONIP 2020), held during November 18–22, 2020. The conference aims to provide a leading international forum for researchers, scientists, and industry professionals who are working in neuroscience, neural networks, deep learning, and related fields to share their new ideas, progresses, and achievements. Due to the outbreak of COVID-19, this year's conference, which was supposed to be held in Bangkok, Thailand, was organized as fully virtual conference.

The research program of this year's edition consists of four main categories, Theory and Algorithms, Computational and Cognitive Neurosciences, Human-Centered Computing, and Applications, for refereed research papers with nine special sessions and one workshop. The research tracks attracted submissions from 1,083 distinct authors from 44 countries. All the submissions were rigorously reviewed by the conference Program Committee (PC) comprising 84 senior PC members and 367 PC members. A total of 1,351 reviews were provided, with each submission receiving at least 2 reviews, and some papers receiving 3 or more reviews. This year, we also provided rebuttals for authors to address the errors that exist in the review comments. Meta-reviews were provided with consideration of both authors' rebuttal and reviewers' comments. Finally, we accepted 187 (30.25%) of the 618 full papers that were sent out for review in three volumes of Springer's series of *Lecture Notes in Computer Science* (LNCS) and 189 (30.58%) of the 618 in two volumes of Springer's series of *Communications in Computer and Information Science* (CCIS).

We would like to take this opportunity to thank all the authors for submitting their papers to our conference, and the senior PC members, PC members, as well as all the Organizing Committee members for their hard work. We hope you enjoyed the research program at the conference.

November 2020

Haiqin Yang
Kitsuchart Pasupa

Organization

Honorary Chairs

Jonathan Chan   King Mongkut's University of Technology Thonburi,
                                        Thailand
Irwin King   Chinese University of Hong Kong, Hong Kong

General Chairs

Andrew Chi-Sing Leung   City University of Hong Kong, Hong Kong
James T. Kwok   Hong Kong University of Science and Technology,
                                        Hong Kong

Program Chairs

Haiqin Yang   Ping An Life, China
Kitsuchart Pasupa   King Mongkut's Institute of Technology Ladkrabang,
                                      Thailand

Local Arrangements Chair

Vithida   King Mongkut University of Technology Thonburi,
  Chongsuphajaisiddhi   Thailand

Finance Chairs

Vajirasak Vanijja   King Mongkut's University of Technology Thonburi,
                                      Thailand
Seiichi Ozawa   Kobe University, Japan

Special Sessions Chairs

Kaizhu Huang   Xi'an Jiaotong-Liverpool University, China
Raymond Chi-Wing Wong Hong Kong University of Science and Technology,
                                      Hong Kong

Tutorial Chairs

Zenglin Xu   Harbin Institute of Technology, China
Jing Li   Hong Kong Polytechnic University, Hong Kong

Proceedings Chairs

Xinyi Le   Shanghai Jiao Tong University, China
Jinchang Ren   University of Strathclyde, UK

Publicity Chairs

Zeng-Guang Hou   Chinese Academy of Sciences, China
Ricky Ka-Chun Wong   City University of Hong Kong, Hong Kong

Senior Program Committee

Sabri Arik   Istanbul University, Turkey
Davide Bacciu   University of Pisa, Italy
Yi Cai   South China University of Technology, China
Zehong Cao   University of Tasmania, Australia
Jonathan Chan   King Mongkut's University of Technology Thonburi,
                               Thailand
Yi-Ping Phoebe Chen   La Trobe University, Australia
Xiaojun Chen   Shenzhen University, China
Wei Neng Chen   South China University of Technology, China
Yiran Chen   Duke University, USA
Yiu-ming Cheung   Hong Kong Baptist University, Hong Kong
Sonya Coleman   Ulster University, UK
Daoyi Dong   University of New South Wales, Australia
Leonardo Franco   University of Malaga, Spain
Jun Fu   Northeastern University, China
Xin Geng   Southeast University, China
Ping Guo   Beijing Normal University, China
Pedro Antonio Gutiérrez   Universidad de Córdoba, Spain
Wei He   University of Science and Technology Beijing, China
Akira Hirose   The University of Tokyo, Japan
Zengguang Hou   Chinese Academy of Sciences, China
Kaizhu Huang   Xi'an Jiaotong-Liverpool University, China
Kazushi Ikeda   Nara Institute of Science and Technology, Japan
Gwanggil Jeon   Incheon National University, South Korea
Min Jiang   Xiamen University, China
Abbas Khosravi   Deakin University, Australia
Wai Lam   Chinese University of Hong Kong, Hong Kong
Chi Sing Leung   City University of Hong Kong, Hong Kong
Kan Li   Beijing Institute of Technology, China
Xi Li   Zhejiang University, China
Jing Li   Hong Kong Polytechnic University, Hong Kong
Shuai Li   University of Cambridge, UK
Zhiyong Liu   Chinese Academy of Sciences, China
Zhigang Liu   Southwest Jiaotong University, China

Wei Liu	Tencent, China
Jun Liu	Xi'an Jiaotong University, China
Jiamou Liu	The University of Auckland, New Zealand
Lingjia Liu	Virginia Tech, USA
Jose A. Lozano	UPV/EHU, Spain
Bao-liang Lu	Shanghai Jiao Tong University, China
Jiancheng Lv	Sichuan University, China
Marley M. B. R. Vellasco	PUC of Rio de Janeiro, Brazil
Hiroshi Mamitsuka	Kyoto University, Japan
Leandro Minku	University of Birmingham, UK
Chaoxu Mu	Tianjin University, China
Wolfgang Nejdl	L3S Research Center, Germany
Quoc Viet Hung Nguyen	Griffith University, Australia
Takashi Omori	Tamagawa University, Japan
Seiichi Ozawa	Kobe University, Japan
Weike Pan	Shenzhen University, China
Jessie Ju Hyun Park	Yeungnam University, Japan
Kitsuchart Pasupa	King Mongkut's Institute of Technology Ladkrabang, Thailand
Abdul Rauf	Research Institute of Sweden, Sweden
Imran Razzak	Deakin University, Australia
Jinchang Ren	University of Strathclyde, UK
Hayaru Shouno	The University of Electro-Communications, Japan
Ponnuthurai Suganthan	Nanyang Technological University, Singapore
Yang Tang	East China University of Science and Technology, China
Jiliang Tang	Michigan State University, USA
Ivor Tsang	University of Technology Sydney, Australia
Peerapon Vateekul	Chulalongkorn University, Thailand
Brijesh Verma	Central Queensland University, Australia
Li-Po Wang	Nanyang Technological University, Singapore
Kok Wai Wong	Murdoch University, Australia
Ka-Chun Wong	City University of Hong Kong, Hong Kong
Raymond Chi-Wing Wong	Hong Kong University of Science and Technology, Hong Kong
Long Phil Xia	Peking University, Shenzhen Graduate School, China
Xin Xin	Beijing Institute of Technology, China
Guandong Xu	University of Technology Sydney, Australia
Bo Xu	Chinese Academy of Sciences, China
Zenglin Xu	Harbin Institute of Technology, China
Rui Yan	Peking University, China
Xiaoran Yan	Indiana University Bloomington, USA
Haiqin Yang	Ping An Life, China
Qinmin Yang	Zhejiang University, China
Zhirong Yang	Norwegian University of Science and Technology, Norway

De-Nian Yang	Academia Sinica, Taiwan
Zhigang Zeng	Huazhong University of Science and Technology, China
Jialin Zhang	Chinese Academy of Sciences, China
Min Ling Zhang	Southeast University, China
Kun Zhang	Carnegie Mellon University, USA
Yongfeng Zhang	Rutgers University, USA
Dongbin Zhao	Chinese Academy of Sciences, China
Yicong Zhou	University of Macau, Macau
Jianke Zhu	Zhejiang University, China

Program Committee

Muideen Adegoke	City University of Hong Kong, Hong Kong
Sheraz Ahmed	German Research Center for Artificial Intelligence, Germany
Shotaro Akaho	National Institute of Advanced Industrial Science and Technology, Japan
Sheeraz Akram	University of Pittsburgh, USA
Abdulrazak Alhababi	Universiti Malaysia Sarawak, Malaysia
Muhamad Erza Aminanto	University of Indonesia, Indonesia
Marco Anisetti	University of Milan, Italy
Sajid Anwar	Institute of Management Sciences, Pakistan
Muhammad Awais	COMSATS University Islamabad, Pakistan
Affan Baba	University of Technology Sydney, Australia
Boris Bacic	Auckland University of Technology, New Zealand
Mubasher Baig	National University of Computer and Emerging Sciences, Pakistan
Tao Ban	National Information Security Research Center, Japan
Sang Woo Ban	Dongguk University, South Korea
Kasun Bandara	Monash University, Australia
David Bong	Universiti Malaysia Sarawak, Malaysia
George Cabral	Rural Federal University of Pernambuco, Brazil
Anne Canuto	Federal University of Rio Grande do Norte, Brazil
Zehong Cao	University of Tasmania, Australia
Jonathan Chan	King Mongkut's University of Technology Thonburi, Thailand
Guoqing Chao	Singapore Management University, Singapore
Hongxu Chen	University of Technology Sydney, Australia
Ziran Chen	Bohai University, China
Xiaofeng Chen	Chongqing Jiaotong University, China
Xu Chen	Shanghai Jiao Tong University, China
He Chen	Hebei University of Technology, China
Junjie Chen	Inner Mongolia University, China
Mulin Chen	Northwestern Polytechnical University, China
Junying Chen	South China University of Technology, China

Chuan Chen	Sun Yat-sen University, China
Liang Chen	Sun Yat-sen University, China
Zhuangbin Chen	Chinese University of Hong Kong, Hong Kong
Junyi Chen	City University of Hong Kong, Hong Kong
Xingjian Chen	City University of Hong Kong, Hong Kong
Lisi Chen	Hong Kong Baptist University, Hong Kong
Fan Chen	Duke University, USA
Xiang Chen	George Mason University, USA
Long Cheng	Chinese Academy of Sciences, China
Aneesh Chivukula	University of Technology Sydney, Australia
Sung Bae Cho	Yonsei University, South Korea
Sonya Coleman	Ulster University, UK
Fengyu Cong	Dalian University of Technology, China
Jose Alfredo Ferreira Costa	Federal University of Rio Grande do Norte, Brazil
Ruxandra Liana Costea	Polytechnic University of Bucharest, Romania
Jean-Francois Couchot	University of Franche-Comté, France
Raphaël Couturier	University Bourgogne Franche-Comté, France
Zhenyu Cui	University of the Chinese Academy of Sciences, China
Debasmit Das	Qualcomm, USA
Justin Dauwels	Nanyang Technological University, Singapore
Xiaodan Deng	Beijing Normal University, China
Zhaohong Deng	Jiangnan University, China
Mingcong Deng	Tokyo University, Japan
Nat Dilokthanakul	Vidyasirimedhi Institute of Science and Technology, Thailand
Hai Dong	RMIT University, Australia
Qiulei Dong	Chinese Academy of Sciences, China
Shichao Dong	Shenzhen Zhiyan Technology Co., Ltd., China
Kenji Doya	Okinawa Institute of Science and Technology, Japan
Yiqun Duan	University of Sydney, Australia
Aritra Dutta	King Abdullah University of Science and Technology, Saudi Arabia
Mark Elshaw	Coventry University, UK
Issam Falih	Paris 13 University, France
Ozlem Faydasicok	Istanbul University, Turkey
Zunlei Feng	Zhejiang University, China
Leonardo Franco	University of Malaga, Spain
Fulvio Frati	Università degli Studi di Milano, Italy
Chun Che Fung	Murdoch University, Australia
Wai-Keung Fung	Robert Gordon University, UK
Claudio Gallicchio	University of Pisa, Italy
Yongsheng Gao	Griffith University, Australia
Cuiyun Gao	Harbin Institute of Technology, China
Hejia Gao	University of Science and Technology Beijing, China
Yunjun Gao	Zhejiang University, China

Xin Gao	King Abdullah University of Science and Technology, Saudi Arabia
Yuan Gao	Uppsala University, Sweden
Yuejiao Gong	South China University of Technology, China
Xiaotong Gu	University of Tasmania, Australia
Shenshen Gu	Shanghai University, China
Cheng Guo	Chinese Academy of Sciences, China
Zhishan Guo	University of Central Florida, USA
Akshansh Gupta	Central Electronics Engineering Research Institute, India
Pedro Antonio Gutiérrez	University of Córdoba, Spain
Christophe Guyeux	University Bourgogne Franche-Comté, France
Masafumi Hagiwara	Keio University, Japan
Ali Haidar	University of New South Wales, Australia
Ibrahim Hameed	Norwegian University of Science and Technology, Norway
Yiyan Han	Huazhong University of Science and Technology, China
Zhiwei Han	Southwest Jiaotong University, China
Xiaoyun Han	Sun Yat-sen University, China
Cheol Han	Korea University, South Korea
Takako Hashimoto	Chiba University of Commerce, Japan
Kun He	Shenzhen University, China
Xing He	Southwest University, China
Xiuyu He	University of Science and Technology Beijing, China
Wei He	University of Science and Technology Beijing, China
Katsuhiro Honda	Osaka Prefecture University, Japan
Yao Hu	Alibaba Group, China
Binbin Hu	Ant Group, China
Jin Hu	Chongqing Jiaotong University, China
Jinglu Hu	Waseda University, Japan
Shuyue Hu	National University of Singapore, Singapore
Qingbao Huang	Guangxi University, China
He Huang	Soochow University, China
Kaizhu Huang	Xi'an Jiaotong-Liverpool University, China
Chih-chieh Hung	National Chung Hsing University, Taiwan
Mohamed Ibn Khedher	IRT SystemX, France
Kazushi Ikeda	Nara Institute of Science and Technology, Japan
Teijiro Isokawa	University of Hyogo, Japan
Fuad Jamour	University of California, Riverside, USA
Jin-Tsong Jeng	National Formosa University, Taiwan
Sungmoon Jeong	Kyungpook National University, South Korea
Yizhang Jiang	Jiangnan University, China
Wenhao Jiang	Tencent, China
Yilun Jin	Hong Kong University of Science and Technology, Hong Kong

Wei Jin	Michigan State University, USA
Hamid Karimi	Michigan State University, USA
Dermot Kerr	Ulster University, UK
Tariq Khan	Deakin University, Australia
Rhee Man Kil	Korea Advanced Institute of Science and Technology, South Korea
Sangwook Kim	Kobe University, Japan
Sangwook Kim	Kobe University, Japan
DaeEun Kim	Yonsei University, South Korea
Jin Kyu Kim	Facebook, Inc., USA
Mutsumi Kimura	Ryukoku University, Japan
Yasuharu Koike	Tokyo Institute of Technology, Japan
Ven Jyn Kok	National University of Malaysia, Malaysia
Aneesh Krishna	Curtin University, Australia
Shuichi Kurogi	Kyushu Institute of Technology, Japan
Yoshimitsu Kuroki	National Institute of Technology, Kurume College, Japan
Susumu Kuroyanagi	Nagoya Institute of Technology, Japan
Weng Kin Lai	Tunku Abdul Rahman University College, Malaysia
Wai Lam	Chinese University of Hong Kong, Hong Kong
Kittichai Lavangnananda	King Mongkut's University of Technology Thonburi, Thailand
Xinyi Le	Shanghai Jiao Tong University, China
Teerapong Leelanupab	King Mongkut's Institute of Technology Ladkrabang, Thailand
Man Fai Leung	City University of Hong Kong, Hong Kong
Gang Li	Deakin University, Australia
Qian Li	University of Technology Sydney, Australia
Jing Li	University of Technology Sydney, Australia
JiaHe Li	Beijing Institute of Technology, China
Jian Li	Huawei Noah's Ark Lab, China
Xiangtao Li	Jilin University, China
Tao Li	Peking University, China
Chengdong Li	Shandong Jianzhu University, China
Na Li	Tencent, China
Baoquan Li	Tianjin Polytechnic University, China
Yiming Li	Tsinghua University, China
Yuankai Li	University of Science and Technology of China, China
Yang Li	Zhejiang University, China
Mengmeng Li	Zhengzhou University, China
Yaxin Li	Michigan State University, USA
Xiao Liang	Nankai University, China
Hualou Liang	Drexel University, USA
Hao Liao	Shenzhen University, China
Ming Liao	Chinese University of Hong Kong, Hong Kong
Alan Liew	Griffith University, Australia

Chengchuang Lin	South China Normal University, China
Xinshi Lin	Chinese University of Hong Kong, Hong Kong
Jiecong Lin	City University of Hong Kong, Hong Kong
Shu Liu	The Australian National University, Australia
Xinping Liu	University of Tasmania, Australia
Shaowu Liu	University of Technology Sydney, Australia
Weifeng Liu	China University of Petroleum, China
Zhiyong Liu	Chinese Academy of Sciences, China
Junhao Liu	Chinese Academy of Sciences, China
Shenglan Liu	Dalian University of Technology, China
Xin Liu	Huaqiao University, China
Xiaoyang Liu	Huazhong University of Science and Technology, China
Weiqiang Liu	Nanjing University of Aeronautics and Astronautics, China
Qingshan Liu	Southeast University, China
Wenqiang Liu	Southwest Jiaotong University, China
Hongtao Liu	Tianjin University, China
Yong Liu	Zhejiang University, China
Linjing Liu	City University of Hong Kong, Hong Kong
Zongying Liu	King Mongkut's Institute of Technology Ladkrabang, Thailand
Xiaorui Liu	Michigan State University, USA
Huawen Liu	The University of Texas at San Antonio, USA
Zhaoyang Liu	Chinese Academy of Sciences, China
Sirasit Lochanachit	King Mongkut's Institute of Technology Ladkrabang, Thailand
Xuequan Lu	Deakin University, Australia
Wenlian Lu	Fudan University, China
Ju Lu	Shandong University, China
Hongtao Lu	Shanghai Jiao Tong University, China
Huayifu Lv	Beijing Normal University, China
Qianli Ma	South China University of Technology, China
Mohammed Mahmoud	Beijing Institute of Technology, China
Rammohan Mallipeddi	Kyungpook National University, South Korea
Jiachen Mao	Duke University, USA
Ali Marjaninejad	University of Southern California, USA
Sanparith Marukatat	National Electronics and Computer Technology Center, Thailand
Tomas Henrique Maul	University of Nottingham Malaysia, Malaysia
Phayung Meesad	King Mongkut's University of Technology North Bangkok, Thailand
Fozia Mehboob	Research Institute of Sweden, Sweden
Wenjuan Mei	University of Electronic Science and Technology of China, China
Daisuke Miyamoto	The University of Tokyo, Japan

Kazuteru Miyazaki	National Institution for Academic Degrees and Quality Enhancement of Higher Education, Japan
Bonaventure Molokwu	University of Windsor, Canada
Hiromu Monai	Ochanomizu University, Japan
J. Manuel Moreno	Universitat Politècnica de Catalunya, Spain
Francisco J. Moreno-Barea	University of Malaga, Spain
Chen Mou	Nanjing University of Aeronautics and Astronautics, China
Ahmed Muqeem Sheri	National University of Sciences and Technology, Pakistan
Usman Naseem	University of Technology Sydney, Australia
Mehdi Neshat	The University of Adelaide, Australia
Quoc Viet Hung Nguyen	Griffith University, Australia
Thanh Toan Nguyen	Griffith University, Australia
Dang Nguyen	University of Canberra, Australia
Thanh Tam Nguyen	Ecole Polytechnique Federale de Lausanne, France
Giang Nguyen	Korea Advanced Institute of Science and Technology, South Korea
Haruhiko Nishimura	University of Hyogo, Japan
Stavros Ntalampiras	University of Milan, Italy
Anupiya Nugaliyadde	Murdoch University, Australia
Toshiaki Omori	Kobe University, Japan
Yuangang Pan	University of Technology Sydney, Australia
Weike Pan	Shenzhen University, China
Teerapong Panboonyuen	Chulalongkorn University, Thailand
Paul S. Pang	Federal University Australia, Australia
Lie Meng Pang	Southern University of Science and Technology, China
Hyeyoung Park	Kyungpook National University, South Korea
Kitsuchart Pasupa	King Mongkut's Institute of Technology Ladkrabang, Thailand
Yong Peng	Hangzhou Dianzi University, China
Olutomilayo Petinrin	City University of Hong Kong, Hong Kong
Geong Sen Poh	National University of Singapore, Singapore
Mahardhika Pratama	Nanyang Technological University, Singapore
Emanuele Principi	Università Politecnica delle Marche, Italy
Yiyan Qi	Xi'an Jiaotong University, China
Saifur Rahaman	International Islamic University Chittagong, Bangladesh
Muhammad Ramzan	Saudi Electronic University, Saudi Arabia
Yazhou Ren	University of Electronic Science and Technology of China, China
Pengjie Ren	University of Amsterdam, The Netherlands
Colin Samplawski	University of Massachusetts Amherst, USA
Yu Sang	Liaoning Technical University, China
Gerald Schaefer	Loughborough University, UK

Rafal Scherer	Czestochowa University of Technology, Poland
Xiaohan Shan	Chinese Academy of Sciences, China
Hong Shang	Tencent, China
Nabin Sharma	University of Technology Sydney, Australia
Zheyang Shen	Aalto University, Finland
Yin Sheng	Huazhong University of Science and Technology, China
Jin Shi	Nanjing University, China
Wen Shi	South China University of Technology, China
Zhanglei Shi	City University of Hong Kong, Hong Kong
Tomohiro Shibata	Kyushu Institute of Technology, Japan
Hayaru Shouno	The University of Electro-Communications, Japan
Chiranjibi Sitaula	Deakin University, Australia
An Song	South China University of Technology, China
mofei Song	Southeast University, China
Liyan Song	Southern University of Science and Technology, China
Linqi Song	City University of Hong Kong, Hong Kong
Yuxin Su	Chinese University of Hong Kong, Hong Kong
Jérémie Sublime	Institut supérieur d'électronique de Paris, France
Tahira Sultana	UTM Malaysia, Malaysia
Xiaoxuan Sun	Beijing Normal University, China
Qiyu Sun	East China University of Science and Technology, China
Ning Sun	Nankai University, China
Fuchun Sun	Tsinghua University, China
Norikazu Takahashi	Okayama University, Japan
Hiu-Hin Tam	City University of Hong Kong, Hong Kong
Hakaru Tamukoh	Kyushu Institute of Technology, Japan
Xiaoyang Tan	Nanjing University of Aeronautics and Astronautics, China
Ying Tan	Peking University, China
Shing Chiang Tan	Multimedia University, Malaysia
Choo Jun Tan	Wawasan Open University, Malaysia
Gouhei Tanaka	The University of Tokyo, Japan
Yang Tang	East China University of Science and Technology, China
Xiao-Yu Tang	Zhejiang University, China
M. Tanveer	Indian Institutes of Technology, India
Kai Meng Tay	Universiti Malaysia Sarawak, Malaysia
Chee Siong Teh	Universiti Malaysia Sarawak, Malaysia
Ya-Wen Teng	Academia Sinica, Taiwan
Andrew Beng Jin Teoh	Yonsei University, South Korea
Arit Thammano	King Mongkut's Institute of Technology Ladkrabang, Thailand
Eiji Uchino	Yamaguchi University, Japan

Nhi N.Y. Vo	University of Technology Sydney, Australia
Hiroaki Wagatsuma	Kyushu Institute of Technology, Japan
Nobuhiko Wagatsuma	Tokyo Denki University, Japan
Yuanyu Wan	Nanjing University, China
Feng Wan	University of Macau, Macau
Dianhui Wang	La Trobe University, Australia
Lei Wang	Beihang University, China
Meng Wang	Beijing Institute of Technology, China
Sheng Wang	Henan University, China
Meng Wang	Southeast University, China
Chang-Dong Wang	Sun Yat-sen University, China
Qiufeng Wang	Xi'an Jiaotong-Liverpool University, China
Zhenhua Wang	Zhejiang University of Technology, China
Yue Wang	Chinese University of Hong Kong, Hong Kong
Jiasen Wang	City University of Hong Kong, Hong Kong
Jin Wang	Hanyang University, South Korea
Wentao Wang	Michigan State University, USA
Yiqi Wang	Michigan State University, USA
Peerasak Wangsom	CAT Telecom PCL, Thailand
Bunthit Watanapa	King Mongkut's University of Technology Thonburi, Thailand
Qinglai Wei	Chinese Academy of Sciences, China
Yimin Wen	Guilin University of Electronic Technology, China
Guanghui Wen	Southeast University, China
Ka-Chun Wong	City University of Hong Kong, Hong Kong
Kuntpong Woraratpanya	King Mongkut's Institute of Technology Ladkrabang, Thailand
Dongrui Wu	Huazhong University of Science and Technology, China
Qiujie Wu	Huazhong University of Science and Technology, China
Zhengguang Wu	Zhejiang University, China
Weibin Wu	Chinese University of Hong Kong, Hong Kong
Long Phil Xia	Peking University, Shenzhen Graduate School, China
Tao Xiang	Chongqing University, China
Jiaming Xu	Chinese Academy of Sciences, China
Bin Xu	Northwestern Polytechnical University, China
Qing Xu	Tianjin University, China
Xingchen Xu	Fermilab, USA
Hui Xue	Southeast University, China
Nobuhiko Yamaguchi	Saga University, Japan
Toshiyuki Yamane	IBM Research, Japan
Xiaoran Yan	Indiana University, USA
Shankai Yan	National Institutes of Health, USA
Jinfu Yang	Beijing University of Technology, China
Xu Yang	Chinese Academy of Sciences, China

Feidiao Yang	Chinese Academy of Sciences, China
Minghao Yang	Chinese Academy of Sciences, China
Jianyi Yang	Nankai University, China
Haiqin Yang	Ping An Life, China
Xiaomin Yang	Sichuan University, China
Shaofu Yang	Southeast University, China
Yinghua Yao	University of Technology Sydney, Australia
Jisung Yoon	Indiana University, USA
Junichiro Yoshimoto	Nara Institute of Science and Technology, Japan
Qi Yu	University of New South Wales, Australia
Zhaoyuan Yu	Nanjing Normal University, China
Wen Yu	CINVESTAV-IPN, Mexico
Chun Yuan	Tsinghua University, China
Xiaodong Yue	Shanghai University, China
Li Yun	Nanjing University of Posts and Telecommunications, China
Jichuan Zeng	Chinese University of Hong Kong, Hong Kong
Yilei Zhang	Anhui Normal University, China
Yi Zhang	Beijing Institute of Technology, China
Xin-Yue Zhang	Chinese Academy of Sciences, China
Dehua Zhang	Chinese Academy of Sciences, China
Lei Zhang	Chongqing University, China
Jia Zhang	Microsoft Research, China
Liqing Zhang	Shanghai Jiao Tong University, China
Yu Zhang	Southeast University, China
Liang Zhang	Tencent, China
Tianlin Zhang	University of Chinese Academy of Sciences, China
Rui Zhang	Xi'an Jiaotong-Liverpool University, China
Jialiang Zhang	Zhejiang University, China
Ziqi Zhang	Zhejiang University, China
Jiani Zhang	Chinese University of Hong Kong, Hong Kong
Shixiong Zhang	City University of Hong Kong, Hong Kong
Jin Zhang	Norwegian University of Science and Technology, Norway
Jie Zhang	Newcastle University, UK
Kun Zhang	Carnegie Mellon University, USA
Yao Zhang	Tianjin University, China
Yu Zhang	University of Science and Technology Beijing, China
Zhijia Zhao	Guangzhou University, China
Shenglin Zhao	Tencent, China
Qiangfu Zhao	University of Aizu, Japan
Xiangyu Zhao	Michigan State University, USA
Xianglin Zheng	University of Tasmania, Australia
Nenggan Zheng	Zhejiang University, China
Wei-Long Zheng	Harvard Medical School, USA
Guoqiang Zhong	Ocean University of China, China

Binghui Zhang
Shihong Zhang   South China University of Technology, China
Xiaojun Xuan   Southwest Jiaotong University, China
Hao Zhou   Central South University, China
Yingjiang Zhou   Harbin Engineering University, China
                       Beijing University of Posts and Telecommunications,
                       China
Dong Zeng   Sichuan University, China
Zhi Yuan   The University of Manchester, UK

Contents – Part IV

Human Activity Recognition

Image Processing and Computer Vision

Natural Language Processing

Recommender Systems

**The 13th International Workshop on Artificial Intelligence
and Cybersecurity**

Data Mining

A Hybrid Representation of Word Images for Keyword Spotting

Hongxi Wei[1,2,3]($\boxtimes$), Jing Zhang[1,2,3], and Kexin Liu[1,2,3]

[1] School of Computer Science, Inner Mongolia University, Hohhot 010021, China
cswhx@imu.edu.cn
[2] Provincial Key Laboratory of Mongolian Information Processing Technology,
Hohhot, China
[3] National and Local Joint Engineering Research Center of Mongolian Information
Processing Technology, Hohhot, China

Abstract. In the task of keyword spotting based on query-by-example, how to represent word images is a very important issue. Meanwhile, the problem of out-of-vocabulary (OOV) is frequently occurred in keyword spotting. Therefore, the problem of OOV keyword spotting is a challenging task. In this paper, a hybrid representation approach of word images has been presented to accomplish the aim of OOV keyword spotting. To be specific, a sequence to sequence model has been utilized to generate representation vectors of word images. Meanwhile, a CNN model with VGG16 architecture has been used to obtain another type of representation vectors. After that, a score fusion scheme is adopted to combine the above two kinds of representation vectors. Experimental results demonstrate that the proposed hybrid representation approach of word images is especially suited for solving the problem of OOV keyword spotting.

Keywords: Keyword spotting · Word image representation · Score fusion · Out-of-vocabulary

1 Introduction

As far as historical document images, optical character recognition (OCR) is usually not so robust due to low image quality and handwriting deformations. In the domain of historical document image retrieval, keyword spotting can be taken as an alternative approach when OCR is hard or infeasible. The process of keyword spotting is to obtain relevant word images from a word image collection that are similar to a given query keyword through image matching without utilizing OCR [1]. According to the way of providing query keywords, keyword spotting can be divided into two categories [2,3]: *query-by-string* (QBS) and *query-by-example* (QBE).

In the QBS based approaches, a query keyword is represented by an ASCII string [4]. Hence, the QBS based approaches always require a mapping from textual strings to word images. This mapping can be generated through the

© Springer Nature Switzerland AG 2020
H. Yang et al. (Eds.): ICONIP 2020, CCIS 1332, pp. 3–10, 2020.
https://doi.org/10.1007/978-3-030-63820-7_1

supervised learn-ing manner on a word image collection with textual annotations. When such annotated data are unavailable or inadequate, the QBE based approaches are competent for the task of keyword spotting. To be specific, an example image of the query keyword should be provided and then used for retrieving on a collection of word images [5].

In this study, we focus on realizing keyword spotting in the way of QBE. Hence, learning efficient representation for word images is an essential issue in our research. In early study of keyword spotting, profile features were firstly used for representing word images and images were matched by dynamic time warping (DTW). The disadvantage of DTW is time-consuming and inefficient to real time matching. After that, Bag-of-Visual-Words (BoVW) technology was utilized to convert word images into fixed-length vectors [6]. Various distances (e.g. Euclidean distance, Minkowski distance, cosine, etc.) were applied to measure similarities between word images. On the basis of BoVW, Wei et al. [7] proposed visual language model (VLM) to represent word images. Therein, each word image was treated as a probability distribution of visual words and query likelihood model was employed to rank word images. Nevertheless, the visual words in BoVW and VLM are independent, which results in not only missing spatial orders between neighboring visual words but also lacking semantic information of visual words.

To solve the above problems, a latent Dirichlet allocation (LDA) based topic model has been adopted to obtain semantic relatedness between visual words [8]. Furthermore, GloVe has been applied to capture deeply semantic information of visual words [9]. In this manner, each visual word was mapped into an embedding vector (named visual word embeddings) within semantic space. Afterwards, translation language model (TLM) [10] and word mover's distance (WMD) [11] were utilized to calculate similarities between word images, respectively. Because visual words are generated from local descriptors (such as SIFT) by a certain clustering algorithm, these visual words based representation approaches, including LDA, TLM and WMD, still make use of low-level image features.

In recent years, deep neural networks especially convolutional neural networks (CNN) have been attracted much more attention and shown superior performance in various computer vision tasks as well as for keyword spotting [12]. When a word image is fed into a well-trained CNN, and then the activations of the fully-connected layer are usually extracted as the representation vector (called CNN embedding vector) of the corresponding word image. By this way, cosine or Euclidean distance is competent for measuring similarity between word images depending on their embedding vectors. In this study, such embedding vectors will be used for representing word images.

In learning based representation approaches, the amount of vocabulary in training set is often far less than the complete vocabulary of a certain language. Therefore, unseen vocabularies in training samples might be taken as query keywords at the retrieval stage or appear in documents that will be retrieved. As a result, the problem of out-of-vocabulary is occurred frequently in keyword spotting.

In this paper, we concentrate on the task of OOV keyword spotting in historical document images. On the one hand, word images can be converted into the corresponding representation vectors by a seq2seq model. Such a representation vector contains contexts of neighboring frames within one word image. On the other hand, CNN embedding vectors of word images can be extracted from a classic CNN model (e.g. VGG16) after effectively training. These vectors involve deep features of word images. Finally, a score fusion scheme is employed to rank word images, where the fused scores (i.e. similarities) are calculated from seq2seq embedding vectors and CNN embedding vectors, respectively.

2   Learning Based Word Image Representation

In order to attain to the aim of OOV keyword spotting in the way of QBE, we propose a learning based method for representing word images. Specifically, historical document images should be segmented into word images to form a collection of word images. Thus, word images are treated as the handling objects in our study. Afterwards, two kinds of deep neural networks are used to learn efficient representation for word images, severally. The former is a seq2seq model with attention mechanism and the latter is a CNN model with classic architecture. In the retrieval phase, similarities from the two deep models are fused together to formulate a ranked list of word images. The details of the proposed method are presented in the following subsections.

2.1   Seq2seq Embedding Vectors

We have designed a seq2seq model with attention mechanism to capture relationships between a word image and its letters for solving the problem of OOV, which is composed of an encoder, a decoder, and an attention network is adopted to connect between the encoder and the decoder. The encoder consists of a deep neural network (DNN) and a bi-directional LSTM (BLSTM). The DNN is taken as a feature extractor and the BLSTM is used for transforming an input sequence of frames into a list of vectors. To generate input sequences, each normalized word image is segmented into multiple frames with equal size. And the adjacent two frames are overlapped half a frame. For a given sequence of frames, such as $(x_1, x_2, ..., x_N)$, the corresponding list of vectors $(h_1, h_2, ..., h_N)$ can be generated by the following formula.

$$h_i = \overrightarrow{h_i} + \overleftarrow{h_i} \tag{1}$$

Where $\overrightarrow{h_i}$ and $\overleftarrow{h_i}$ denote output vectors of the ith frame of a word image from forward LSTM and backward LSTM, separately. N is the length of the input sequence of frames.

The attention network is composed of a hidden layer and a softmax layer to form a feed forward neural network. The generated list of vectors by the encoder is fed into such an attention network where parts of input vectors are enhanced and the rest are faded. By this way, the decoder can choose the most relevant states for the current output letter and filter out irrelevant states depending on the outputs of the attention network. Our decoder is implemented as a combination of a LSTM with 64 memory cells and a softmax layer.

When the proposed seq2seq model is fine-trained, the outputs of the encoder using (1) will be considered as seq2seq embedding vectors of word images. Using such embedding vectors, *Euclidean distance* can be regarded as score (denoted by $Score_{seq2seq}$) of similarity between two word images, which is calculated on their embedding vectors (denote by $\vec{w}$ and $\vec{q}$) as follows.

$$Score_{seq2seq}(\vec{w}, \vec{q}) = \sqrt{\sum_{i=1}^{M}(w_i - q_i)^2} \qquad (2)$$

Where w_i and q_i denote the ith element of the seq2seq embedding vectors $\vec{w}$ and $\vec{q}$, respectively. M denotes the dimension of the seq2seq embedding vector.

2.2 CNN Embedding Vectors

We employ a CNN model with VGG16 architecture for generating the corresponding embedding vectors of word images. There are 16 layers in total, including 13 convolutional layers, 2 fully-connected layers (denoted by FC1 and FC2) and one softmax output layer. Therein, all convolution filters are set to 3 × 3 with a stride of one pixel. The second, fourth, seventh, tenth and thirteenth convolutional layers are followed by a max-pooling layer, severally. For each max-pooling layer, its kernel size is 2 × 2 with a stride of two pixels, which makes the output of the corresponding convolutional layer reduce to a half. As the VGG16 was designed for natural images as input, we modified the number of neurons in FC1 and FC2. And they are both set to 1024 in this study.

Generally, the activations of the fully-connected layer (i.e. FC1 or FC2) are extracted as CNN embedding vectors of word images. Since there are two fully-connected layers, a comparison between FC1 and FC2 has been performed and the better one has been determined (see Sect. 3). Using such embedding vectors, similarity score (denoted by $Score_{CNN}$) between two word images can be calculated on the corresponding embedding vectors. By comparing and analyzing, cosine is chosen for measuring similarity between word images in this study. The formula of $Score_{CNN}$ is presented as below.

$$Score_{CNN}(\vec{u}, \vec{v}) = \frac{\sum_{i=1}^{N}(u_i \cdot v_i)}{\sqrt{\sum_{i=1}^{N} u_i^2} \cdot \sqrt{\sum_{i=1}^{N} v_i^2}} \qquad (3)$$

Where u_i and v_i denote the ith element of the CNN embedding vectors $\vec{u}$ and $\vec{v}$, severally. N is the length of the embedding vector.

2.3 Score Fusion Scheme

When a query keyword image is provided, cosines and Euclidean distances are adopted for measuring similarities between a word image and the query keyword image in CNN embedding representation and seq2seq embedding representation, respectively. For fusing these two kinds of scores, Euclidean distance (i.e. $Score_{seq2seq}$) needs to be scaled into the range from 0 to 1 by the following equation.

$$
\begin{aligned}
Norm(Score_{seq2seq}(word_j)) = & \left[\max_{1 \leqslant i \leqslant C} S_{seq2seq}(word_i) - S_{seq2seq}(word_j) \right] \\
& / \left[\max_{1 \leqslant i \leqslant C} S_{seq2seq}(word_i) - \min_{1 \leqslant i \leqslant C} S_{seq2seq}(word_i) \right]
\end{aligned}
\tag{4}
$$

Where $S_{seq2seq}(word_j)$ means Euclidean distance calculated by Eq.(2) between the jth word image and the provided query keyword image; $\max_{1 \leqslant i \leqslant C}(\cdot)$ and $\min_{1 \leqslant i \leqslant C}(\cdot)$ are the maximum score and the minimum score according to the provided query keyword image, separately; C is the number of word images for being retrieved. Hence, the final scores for ranking word images are as follows.

$$
\begin{aligned}
Score_{Final}(word_j) = & (1 - \lambda) \cdot Score_{CNN}(word_j) \\
& + \lambda \cdot Norm(Score_{seq2seq}(word_j))
\end{aligned}
\tag{5}
$$

Where $Score_{Final}(word_j)$ denotes the final score between the jth word image and the provided query keyword image, and $\lambda(0 < \lambda < 1)$ is a fusion coefficient. By using Eq. (5), a ranked list of word images can be produced in descending order of these scores to attain the aim of the QBE based keyword spotting.

3 Experimental Results

3.1 Dataset

To evaluate the performance of the proposed representation method for word images, a set of historical Mongolian documents has been collected, which consists of 100 pages. These documents have been scanned into colored TIF format with 600 dpi. Through a series of preprocessing steps, a collection of Mongolian word images has been formed. After removing non-words (e.g. over-segmentation or under-segmentation), the total number of Mongolian word images is 20,948. Each word image has been given text annotation manually. In our dataset, there are 48 letters and the amount of vocabulary is 1,423 by analyzing these textual annotations.

We split this dataset into four folds in class level, where three folds contain 356 vocabularies and the other fold contains 355 vocabularies. In this way, test set is completely OOV. In our experiment, *4-fold cross validation* is performed for evaluating performance and standard *mean average precision* (MAP) is used as evaluation metric. In this study, all word images are normalized into the same size. Specifically, the height and width are set to 310 pixels and 50 pixels, separately.

3.2 Performance of Seq2seq Embedding Vectors

In this experiment, $Score_{seq2seq}$ is used for measuring similarity between two word images. Since the height of the frame is an important factor affecting the performance, we tested various frame heights and overlap sizes in this experiment. To be specific, the frame heights are decreased from 8 pixels to 2 pixels with an interval of 2 pixels and the overlapping sizes are half a frame consistently. The comparative results are shown in Table 1. Specially emphasizing, **FxHy** denotes that the frame height is x pixels and y pixels are overlapped between two adjacent frames.

Table 1. The comparative results of seq2seq embedding vectors (%).

Fold	F8H4	F6H3	F4H2	F2H1
Fold1	74.98	77.80	82.23	80.16
Fold2	78.98	78.87	82.11	85.08
Fold3	74.91	77.94	79.76	79.08
Fold4	77.80	80.72	83.50	84.59
Avg	**76.67**	**78.83**	**81.90**	**82.23**

The best performance for OOV keyword spotting can be attained to **82.23%**, when the frame height is set to 2 pixels. It indicates that the smaller of the frame height the higher performance can be gained.

3.3 Performance of CNN Embedding Vectors

We obtain CNN embedding vectors of word images from the activations of the fully-connected layer in the utilized VGG16 model. Since there are two fully-connected layers in VGG16, a comparison between the two fully-connected layers has been performed. The detailed results are listed in Table 2. In this experiment, $Score_{CNN}$ is used for calculating similarity between two word images. From Table 2, we can see that the performance of the first fully-connected layer (FC1) is consistently better than the second one (FC2).

3.4 Performance of Score Fusion Scheme

In this experiment, the proposed score fusion scheme is used to rank word images according to Eq.(5). By comparison, the best performance (**87.55%**) is obtained

Table 2. The comparative results between FC1 and FC2 (%).

Method	Fold1	Fold2	Fold3	Fold4	Avg
FC1	**84.48**	**85.98**	**80.03**	**83.27**	**83.44**
FC2	83.25	84.76	78.92	82.70	82.41

Table 3. The comparative results between baselines and our proposed method (%).

Method	Fold1	Fold2	Fold3	Fold4	Avg
BoVW [6]	40.40	51.43	42.25	43.62	44.43
AVWE [9]	59.57	66.83	60.76	58.63	61.45
RNN [9]	54.54	62.05	53.30	60.82	57.68
AVWE-SC [5]	63.25	65.06	63.99	64.71	64.25
AVWE+RNN [9]	75.05	79.43	75.39	75.83	76.43
Seq2seq (F2H1)	80.16	85.08	79.08	84.59	82.23
CNN (FC1)	84.48	85.98	80.03	83.27	83.44
Seq2seq+CNN (F2H1+FC1, $\lambda = 0.7$)	**88.02**	**90.35**	**84.62**	**87.21**	**87.55**

by combining F2H1 with FC1 when λ is set to 0.7. The performance of the score fusion scheme is superior to not only seq2seq embedding vectors but also CNN embedding vectors.

Additionally, we have tested the performance of several baselines on our dataset. The comparative results are given in Table 3. The representations of word images by seq2seq and CNN are obviously superior to various baselines. Meanwhile, the proposed score fusion scheme between seq2seq and CNN attains the best performance on our dataset. It demonstrates that our proposed method can solve the problem of OOV effectively for keyword spotting.

4   Conclusion

To attain the aim of OOV keyword spotting by means of QBE, seq2seq embedding vectors are presented to represent word images. It can obtain the relationships between frames and letters within one word image. Moreover, the activations of the fully-connected layers with VGG16 architecture were used for representing word images as well. It can generate the holistic representation of word images. Afterwards, a score fusion scheme has been utilized, which can significantly improve the performance of OOV keyword spotting. Therefore, seq2seq embedding vectors and CNN embedding vectors are complementary with each other.

Acknowledgments. This study is supported by the Natural Science Foundation of Inner Mongolia Autonomous Region under Grant 2019ZD14, the Project for Science and Technology of Inner Mongolia Autonomous Region under Grant 2019GG281, the

Program for Young Talents of Science and Technology in Universities of Inner Mongolia Autonomous Region under Grant NJYT-20-A05, and the Natural Science Foundation of China under Grant 61463038 and 61763034.

References

1. Giotis, A.P., Sfikas, G., Gatos, B., Nikou, C.: A survey of document image word spotting techniques. Pattern Recogn. **68**(8), 310–332 (2017)
2. Gurjar, N., Sudholt, S., Fink, G.A.: Learning deep representations for word spotting under weak supervision. In: Proceedings of the 13th International Workshop on Document Analysis Systems (DAS'18), pp. 7–12. IEEE (2018)
3. Wei, H., Gao, G.: A keyword retrieval system for historical Mongolian document images. Int. J. Doc. Anal. Recogn. (IJDAR) **17**(1), 33–45 (2013). https://doi.org/10.1007/s10032-013-0203-6
4. Wilkinson, T., Lindstrom, J., Brun, A.: Neural Ctrl-F: segmentation-free query-by-string word spotting in handwritten manuscript collections. In: Proceedings of 2017 IEEE International Conference on Computer Vision (ICCV'17), pp. 4433–4442. IEEE (2017)
5. Wei, H., Zhang, H., Gao, G.: Word image representation based on visual embeddings and spatial constraints for keyword spotting on historical documents. In: Proceedings of the 24th International Conference on Pattern Recognition (ICPR'18), pp. 3616–3621. IEEE (2018)
6. Aldavert, D., Rusinol, M., Toledo, R., Llados, J.: A study of bag-of-visual-words representations for handwritten keyword spotting. Int. J. Doc. Anal. Recogn. **18**(3), 223–234 (2015)
7. Wei, H., Gao, G.: Visual language model for keyword spotting on historical Mongolian document images. In: Proceedings of the 29th Chinese Control and Decision Conference (CCDC'17), pp. 1737–1742. IEEE (2017)
8. Wei, H., Gao, G., Su, X.: LDA-based word image representation for keyword spotting on historical mongolian documents. In: Hirose, A., Ozawa, S., Doya, K., Ikeda, K., Lee, M., Liu, D. (eds.) ICONIP 2016. LNCS, vol. 9950, pp. 432–441. Springer, Cham (2016). https://doi.org/10.1007/978-3-319-46681-1_52
9. Wei, H., Zhang, H., Gao, G.: Representing word image using visual word embeddings and RNN for keyword spotting on historical document images. In: Proceedings of the 18th International Conference on Multimedia and Expo (ICME'17), pp. 1368–1373. IEEE (2017)
10. Wei, H., Zhang, H., Gao, G.: Integrating visual word embeddings into translation language model for keyword spotting on historical mongolian document images. In: Zeng, B., Huang, Q., El Saddik, A., Li, H., Jiang, S., Fan, X. (eds.) PCM 2017. LNCS, vol. 10736, pp. 616–625. Springer, Cham (2018). https://doi.org/10.1007/978-3-319-77383-4_60
11. Wei, H., Zhang, H., Gao, G., Su X.: Using word mover's distance with spatial constraints for measuring similarity between mongolian word images. In: Liu, D., Xie, S., Li, Y., Zhao, D., El-Alfy, E.S. (eds.) Neural Information Processing. ICONIP 2017. Lecture Notes in Computer Science, vol 10637. Springer, Cham (2017). https://doi.org/10.1007/978-3-319-70093-9_20
12. Krishnan, P., Dutta, K., Jawahar, C.: Deep feature embedding for accurate recognition and retrieval of handwritten text. In: Proceedings of the 15th International Conference on Frontiers in Handwriting Recognition (ICFHR'16), pp. 289–294. IEEE (2016)

A Simple and Novel Method to Predict the Hospital Energy Use Based on Machine Learning: A Case Study in Norway

Kai Xue[1,2,5], Yiyu Ding[2], Zhirong Yang[2,3], Natasa Nord[2],
Mael Roger Albert Barillec[2], Hans Martin Mathisen[2], Meng Liu[1,5], Tor Emil Giske[4],
Liv Inger Stenstad[4], and Guangyu Cao[2(✉)]

[1] School of Civil Engineering, Chongqing University, Chongqing 400045, China
{xuek1213,liumeng2033}@126.com
[2] Norwegian University of Science and Technology (NTNU), 7041 Trondheim, Norway
{yiyu.ding,zhirong.yang,natasa.nord,hans.m.mathisen,
guangyu.cao}@ntnu.no, mrbarill@stud.ntnu.no
[3] Aalto University, 00076 Helsinki, Finland
[4] Operating Room of the Future at St. Olavs Hospital, St. Olavs Hospital, Trondheim, Norway
{Tor.Emil.Giske,Liv-Inger.Stenstad}@stolav.no
[5] National Centre for International Research of Low-Carbon and Green Buildings,
Ministry of Science and Technology, Chongqing University, Chongqing 400045, China

Abstract. Hospitals are one of the most energy-consuming commercial buildings in many countries as a highly complex organization because of a continuous energy utilization and great variability of usage characteristic. With the development of machine learning techniques, it can offer opportunities for predicting the energy consumptions in hospital. With a case hospital building in Norway, through analyzing the characteristic of this building, this paper focused on the prediction of energy consumption through machine learning methods (ML), based on the historical weather data and monitored energy use data within the last four consecutive years. A deep framework of machine learning was proposed in six steps: including data collecting, preprocessing, splitting, fitting, optimizing and estimating. It results that, in Norwegian hospital, Electricity was the most highly demand in main building by consuming 55% of total energy use, higher than district heating and cooling. By means of optimizing the hyper-parameters, this paper selected the specific parameters of model to predict the electricity with high accuracy. It concludes that Random forest and AdaBoost method were much better than decision tree and bagging, especially in predicting the lower energy consumption.

Keywords: Machine learning · Energy prediction · Hospital building

Supported by the Norwegian University of Science and Technology (NTNU), the St. Olavs Hospital in Norway, the China Scholarship Council (CSC), the National Key R&D Program of China (No. 2018YFD1100704) and the Graduate Scientific Research and Innovation Foundation of Chongqing (No. CYB17006).

H. Yang et al. (Eds.): ICONIP 2020, CCIS 1332, pp. 11–22, 2020.
https://doi.org/10.1007/978-3-030-63820-7_2

1 Introduction

As the buildings has become one of the largest energy consumers in the world, the energy saving in building is of great significance for the prediction of energy [1]. From the perspective of function, technology, economy, management and procedures, a hospital can be defined as a highly complex organization, where a continuous energy utilization is required, including electricity, heating and cooling [2]. Some researchers highlighted that hospitals are the second most energy-consuming commercial buildings in many countries, after the food service [3].

As for a special requirement with a clean air and infection control, hospital building require a continuous power to support reliable services 24 h per day. At a survey from the European Union, hospital buildings are responsible for 10% of the total energy use, with occupying about 7% of the non-residential buildings in whole EU [4]. According to the detailed running data of a large number of devices in a Norway hospital, Tarald Rohde [5] concluded that the majority of large medical imaging equipment devices are in use only during daytime. In this article, the usage patterns of these equipment showed great variability between day and night, as well as weekday and weekend, which need to be concerned mostly. The same results were indicated in the study of K.B. Lindberg [6] through monitoring over 100 non-residential buildings from all over Norway. It mentioned that hospital building need to estimate separately for working and weekends because of the different heating load pattern.

In the past time, there have been many studies on short-term load forecasting [7], often using statistical models [8], state-space methods [9], fuzzy systems [10] and artificial neural networks (ANN) [11]. A lot of literatures mentioned by K.B. Lindberg [6], calculate the heat load of the building by a simplified electric equivalent or by a detailed building simulation model based on assumptions on the building's characteristics. However, according to Richalet et al. [12], a methodology for load and energy predictions should be based on measured energy data (i.e. statistical models), because the real behaviors of the building can differ significantly from its design due to various operation of the building's energy system.

Nowadays as described in the literature of Wenqiang Li et al., with the development of machine learning techniques, more new models will be invented, and the rapid developments in big data can offer opportunities for the effective use of these models for prediction. As a data-driven model, machine learning mainly relies on the operating data of building HVAC systems, and is more common in predicting building energy consumption [13].

Recently, there are a lot of researchers have utilized the machine learning method to predict energy consumption based on weather station data for case building or HVAC system. By using machine learning Liu, J.-Y. et al. build a predict model between indoor temperature and three parameters (outdoor dry-temperature, passenger flow and supply air temperature) in subway station. Through setting different time delays in time-series prediction, it was found that Support vector regression (SVR) obtained better accuracy than Back propagation neural network (BPNN) and Classification and regression tree (CART), which reflect the data mining models had the best prediction accuracy as well as highest efficiency [14]. R. Sendra-Arranz et al. used the Recurrent neural networks

(RNN) model by receiving the 6 input variables, including three outdoor weather parameters (the outdoor temperature, the relative humidity and the irradiance) and three indoor variables (the indoor CO_2 level, the indoor temperature of the house and the reference temperature set by the user) to predict the forecasted power consumption in a self-sufficient solar house implemented with the ANN Python's library Pytorch. The model with highest accuracy of the predictions reaches a test Pearson correlation coefficient of 0.797 and normalized root mean square error (NRMSE) of 0.13 [15].

Additionally, because the working time for HVAC system produces a lot of running data, many of literatures have focused on the equipment to predict the energy consumption and even make the work of fault detection, diagnosis, and optimization to improve the efficiency of system based on the mature and rich data acquisition system. A machine learning algorithm applied by Tao Liu et al., namely Deep Deterministic Policy Gradient (DDPG), is firstly used for short-term HVAC system energy consumption prediction through three weather data parameters (Outdoor temperature, relative humidity and wind speed). The results demonstrate that the proposed DDPG based models can achieve better prediction performance than common supervised models like BP Neural Network and Support Vector Machine [16]. In order to obtain a better model, Yao Huang et al. proposed the ensemble learning methods to select 10 original variables for the energy consumption prediction model for residential buildings with GSHP, including system operating parameters and meteorological parameters. Four machine learning methods are contained, which are ELM method, MLR method, XGB method and SVR method respectively. Results showed that the proposed prediction model based on ensemble learning could reduce the MAE of the testing set prediction result, which ranged from 29.1% to 70% [17]. In addition, focused on a fan-coil, Yaser I. Alamin et al. collected a historical dataset from the CIESOL building in Spain, including the impulse air velocity and the current indoor air temperature in one period from 2013.05−2014.04. In order to predict and assess the fan-coil power demand, an ANN model was obtained. The results developed a model called RBFANN which is very simple and the computational resources for its application are tiny and easily available at modern automation systems [18].

Specially, for hospital building, A. Bagnasco et al. proposed a multi-layer perceptron ANN, based on a back propagation training algorithm, to forecast the electrical consumption in Turin, by taking the inputs of loads, type of the day (e.g. weekday/holiday), time of the day and weather data. The good performances achieved (MAPE and PE5% mean value respectively close to 7%, and 60%) in this work suggests that a similar approach could be applied to forecast the energy loads in other building categories (i.e. domestic, industrial). However, this article only predicts the electrical load which has seasonal variation [2].

Recently, the machine learning methods were relatively mature in energy prediction area with more accurate and quick prediction by adjusting parameters using easier features. However, most of literature use deep learning method for example ANN, which is relative complex, and in order to achieve more precisely, it needs to integrate other optimization algorithm, as a result of taking a lot of time. Therefore, this paper focused on the hospital energy consumption prediction to build a simple method based on machine learning method, with the following three issues posed to be solved:

- What's the characteristic on hospital energy in Norway?
- How to predict the energy consumption using the novel machine learning method?
- Which is the best model among the selected machine learning methods and what's the best parameters?

2 Method Development

2.1 Data Collection

The data set is included by two parts: the meteorological data and the hourly energy consumption data monitored by energy meters of hospital building. The meteorological data was used as the input parameters to predict the energy consumption, including outdoor temperature, outdoor relative humidity, wind speed, global radiation and longwave radiation. All meteorological data were collected from the Norwegian Centre for Climate Services (NCCS) through a weather station about 4 km away from the hospital. The energy data were downloaded from the hospital energy management system which kept the same interval, and as the output of prediction. All the HVAC devices, for example the pump, ventilation, heat pump et al., have been monitored by installing the electric meter by the hospital technician. Meanwhile, the data were uploaded on the system as an interval of 15 min. This paper downloaded the dataset from 2016.01.01 to 2020.01.01 in St. Olavs hospital in Trondheim, Norway, shown in Table 1.

Table 1. Original data description.

Model variable	No.	Variable name	Unit	Resolution	Range	Type
Input	1	Date and time	/	15 min	2016.01–2020.01	String
	2	Outdoor Temperature	°C	1 h	−25 − 25	Numerical
	3	Relative humidity	%	1 h	0 − 100	Numerical
	4	Wind speed	m/s	1 h	0 − 15	Numerical
	5	Global radiation	W/m²	1 h	0 − 800	Numerical
	6	Longwave radiation	W/m²	1 h	0 − 500	Numerical
Output	7	Electricity consumption	kWh	15 min	0−500	Numerical

2.2 Model Development

The method of machine learning used in this paper was decision tree and its optimization algorithm.

(1) Decision Tree

The decision tree methodology is one of the most commonly used data mining methods. It uses a flowchart-like tree structure to segregate a set of data into various predefined classes, thereby providing the description, categorization, and generalization of given datasets. As a logical model, decision tree shows how the value of a target variable can be predicted by using the values of a set of predictor variables. More details about this algorithm can be found in literature [19].

(2) Ensemble algorithms

Ensemble algorithms are aimed to construct a set of classifiers or regressors to build a more robust and higher-performance classifier or regressor. Bagging and boosting are the two main ensemble methods, which can be merged with basic learners [20]. The base models in the article were established by the front Decision tree.

a. *Bagging-decision tree*

Bagging, namely bootstrap aggregating, was proposed by Breiman to obtain an aggregated predictor. Bagging sequentially combines the weak learners to reduce the prediction errors [21]. What's more, Bagging can be used with any base classification techniques and votes classifiers generated by different bootstrap samples. The core of the Bagging algorithm is the majority voting over results from a substantial number of bootstrap samples [22].

b. *Random Forest*

In contrast to the bagging mentioned above, Random Forest (RF) selects only a few features randomly during each training, thereby achieving a lower error level and requiring less running time than when all the features are used [21].

c. *AdaBoost*

Boosting is one of the most powerful machine learning algorithms developed in the past few years. The idea of the boosting algorithm is that it generates a series of basic learners by re-weighting the samples in the training sets. AdaBoost, with an exponential loss function is the most widely used forms in boosting. More details about this algorithm can be found in literature [23].

2.3 Data Preprocessing

According to the machine learning, data preprocessing is a vital process which may even occupy 80% of whole work described in some articles, especially for the site measurement data for HVAC system [17]. Usually, for the most machine learning method, the extension of data processing decides the accuracy of model's prediction. There were two steps to preprocess the raw data set.

Step1: data cleaning. Through analysis of the data distribution, it processed the missing values, null values and abnormal values which were very general in data collection meters before prediction using pandas, a very useful toolkit in Python.

Step2: feature analysis. Since the data set existed a diversity type as list in Table 1, it was necessary to apply the original data in order to train model correctly. For the string such as data and time, this paper converted the time information to the periodic data including "month", "day", "hour". Therefore, it can be manually encoding by using sin/cos function to transform this data to the period between 2*pi and −2*pi. While for "year", only four category values, it needs to be transformed into the numeric value. Through this way, it can be created a binary column for each category and returns a sparse matrix using the model in scikit-learning, a machine learning package in Python. For the other input parameters in Table 1, it calculated the daily average and daily variance data as new features for five input parameters to analysis the seasonal characteristic more intuitively. In addition, in order to remove the mean and scale to unit variance, each variable was standardized before training [24]. In total, through this preprocessing method, including data standardization, data encoding, the model input has been derived 25 features to achieve a more accuracy prediction. The process of data preprocessing showed in Fig. 1.

2.4   Fit Model and Hyper-Parameters Optimization

Before predict model, the data set was divided randomly into training data and testing data. The first 75% of data was selected as training, while the remaining 25% was used for testing data. After the data division, scikit-learn was utilised to fit the training data. In addition, cross validation and grid search technique were used to select the best combination of hyper-parameters in each predict method [16]. The hyper-parameters to be optimized are detailed in Table 2.

Table 2. Hyper-parameters optimization.

Model	Hyper-parameters	Values
Decision tree	min_samples_leaf	2, 4, 6, 8, 10, 12, 14, 16, 18, 20
	max_depth	4,8,12,16,20
Bagging	n_estimators	50,100
	max_samples	100,200
Random forest	n_estimators	10,30,60,90,120
	max_features	1,3,5,7, 'auto'
AdaBoost	n_estimators	20,50,80
	loss	'linear', 'square', 'exponential'

2.5 Evaluation Index of Model Performances

In this paper, the MSE (Mean squared error), MAE (Mean absolute error) and R2 score (coefficient of determination) was applied to assess the performance of the predictive model. The index was formulated as below:

$$MSE = \frac{1}{N}\sum_1^N Y_i - P_i^2 \tag{1}$$

$$MAE = \frac{1}{N}\sum_1^N |Y_i - P_i| \tag{2}$$

$$R^2 = 1 - \left(\sum_1^N Y_i - P_i^2 / \sum_1^N Y_i - \bar{Y}^2\right) \tag{3}$$

where, $Y_i, P_i, \bar{Y}$ represent the measured value, predicted value and average measured value, respectively. In the best prediction, the predicted values exactly match the measured values, which results in $R^2 = 1.0$.

In addition, visualization method based on Python such as boxplot representation were used to compare the energy distribution of the predicted results in different periods.

2.6 The Framework of Machine Learning to Predict

According to the previous description, a six-step framework of the prediction process was created clearly in Fig. 1.

3 Case Study

The University hospital of St. Olav (see Fig. 2) opened on 1 February 2010, and it is integrated with the Norwegian University of Science and Technology. St. Olavs is the local hospital with the number of beds close to 1000 for the population of Trøndelag, Norway. It contains about 20 clinics and departments, including Lab Center (25556 m^2), Gastro Center (31500 m^2), Acute, Heart and Lung Center (40093 m^2), Woman-Child Center (31427 m^2), Knowledge Center (17354 m^2), Movement Center (19304 m^2), with an area of nearly 250000 m^2. The hospital has built a very detailed energy management system to collect energy data in order to maintain the HVAC system.

Figure 3 illustrated the compositions of the three kinds of energy demands per m^2 in each of the six main hospital buildings during the year of 2019. For the total energy consumption, it showed that Lab Centre and Gastro Centre are much higher than the others, since these two centers were special than other, not only in running time, but also some equipment. It was also found that all of the buildings have a larger energy consumption compared with the demand of Guidance of Hospital in Building Technical Regulations, Norway (TEK17), which set a limited value of 225 kWh/m^2 [25]. Therefore, it reflected a large potential of saving energy in hospital building. On the other hand, almost, in Norwegian hospital, electricity was the most highly demand in main building, with 55% rate on average, higher than District heating and cooling. The knowledge center was a relative balanced demand in energy consumption.

4 Results

According to the description in Sect. 2.1, five parameters were contained in data set from 2016 to 2020. This section explored the data set and compared the results between the predicted and actual energy consumption. In order to compare the actual data and predicted data, this paper selected four specific time period in the data set. The counts and information were listed in Table 3.

(1) **Compare the Actual Data and Predict Data**

Table 4 showed the actual and predicted data in the four different machine learning methods. Firstly, it can be easy to see that the weekday electricity was high obviously than weekend, about 50kWh high in average. This result was decided by the schedule in hospital staff and patient. In Norway, people preferred to enjoy the weekend time, unlike some countries which have heavily work in weekday. The decrease of medical activity brought the decline of Energy-using devices. Similarly, the winter was higher than summer, about 25 kWh in average, which effected by a longer winter period compared with other countries.

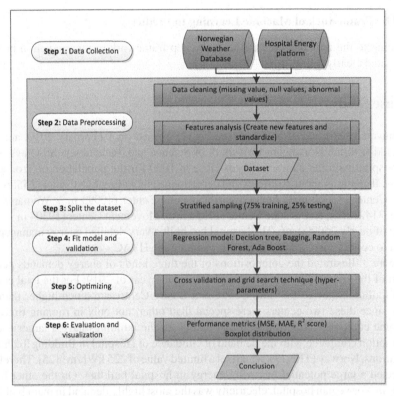

Fig. 1. The flow chart of predict energy by machine learning.

Fig. 2. The case study building.

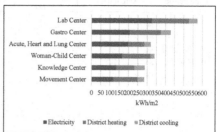

Fig. 3. Several main buildings energy consumption.

Table 3. The counts of different time period.

Time period	Counts/hours	Selected Days	Year
Weekend	10032	Saturday, Sunday	2016−2020
Weekday	25009	Monday, Tuesday, Wednesday, Thursday, Friday	
Summer	2976	July	
Winter	2976	January	

Secondly, for different models, decision tree and AdaBoost were much more accuracy, not only in the higher electricity (weekday and winter) and lower electricity (weekend), but also the electricity distribution such as the box plot showed. However, for decision tree, it indicated a worse prediction in outlier data, for example the weekend data. In addition, Bagging method was the bad estimator which make the prediction data higher than the actual data in weekend, while for weekday, the prediction data was lower. On behalf of the traditional predict method, such as the linear regression, it always achieved a simpler and quicker predict in the data trend with a normal distribution in errors between actual and predict data. Indeed, this way show good results when the data presented a regular distribution. However, when the dataset changed more complex for example the time-series dataset. The ML methods made each predicted value as close to the actual value as possible, thus, it can up to a smaller error.

(2) Evaluation of Result

This paper also uses three metrics (the MSE, MAE and R^2 score) to estimate the predicted results in train data and test data through comparing all of the actual data and predicted data, see Fig. 4. It showed that Random forest and AdaBoost method were much better than decision tree and bagging, especially in test data. Through optimizing the hyper-parameters, it can obtain the best estimator (n_estimators: 90; max_features: 5) for Random forest method, while for AdaBoost method, the value of best estimator

Table 4. Compared the predict and actual results of electricity using four ML methods

Note: DT, BAG, RF, AB represented the predicted results using the machine learning methods of decision tree, bagging, random forest, adaboost, respectively.

was (n_estimators: 80; loss: linear). According to the MSE and MAE, a better predict result occurred in the training dataset, except for the method of Bagging. For regression problems, the averaging method is usually used in the Bagging algorithm, and the regression results obtained by some weak learners are arithmetic averaged to obtain the final model output, which make a close value between training and testing dataset. However, because of a larger variance in whole year produced in electricity data between weekday and weekend, the algorithm of Bagging has a weakness predict results in this sort of dataset.

5   Conclusions

The machine learning method was proposed in this paper to predict the hospital building energy consumption in the cold Nordic climate. Four methods were utilized to predict the electricity consumption. The main conclusions are as follows:

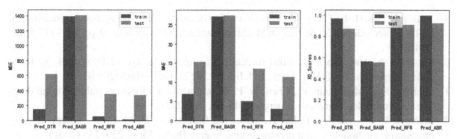

Fig. 4. The MSE (left), MAE (center) and R^2 score (right) of different model.

(a) A result can be found that all of the buildings have a larger energy consumption compared with the demand of Guidance of Hospital in Building Technical Regulations, Norway, which set a limited value of 225 kWh/m². Electricity was the most highly demand in main building in Norwegian hospital, with 55% rate in average, higher than district heating and cooling.

(b) Because of the fluctuation characteristic of energy consumption, the predicted data need to match not only the higher actual data, but also the small data such as night energy consumption. For electricity consumption, it showed that Random forest and AdaBoost method were much better than decision tree and bagging. Decision tree and bagging had a worse prediction in weekend and weekend data.

(c) This paper has selected the best combination of hyper-parameters in each prediction method: for electricity, it recommends to use Random forest (n_estimators: 90; max_features: 5) and AdaBoost (n_estimators: 80; loss: linear).

References

1. Ürge-Vorsatz, D., Cabeza, L.F., Serrano, S., Barreneche, C., Petrichenko, K.: Heating and cooling energy trends and drivers in buildings. Renew. Sustain. Energy Rev. **41**, 85–98 (2015)
2. Bagnasco, A., Fresi, F., Saviozzi, M., Silvestro, F., Vinci, A.: Electrical consumption forecasting in hospital facilities: an application case. Energy Building **103**, 261–270 (2015)
3. González, A.G., Sanz-Calcedo, J., Salgado, D.: Evaluation of energy consumption in german oshpitals: benchmarking in the public sector. Energies **11**, 2279 (2018)
4. Dobosi, I., Tanasa, C., Kaba, N.-E., Retezan, A., Mihaila, D.: Building energy modelling for the energy performance analysis of a hospital building in various locations. E3S Web of Conferences **111**, p. 06073 (2019)
5. Rohde, T., Martinez, R.: Equipment and energy usage in a large teaching hospital in norway. J. Healthc. Eng. **6**, 419–434 (2015)
6. Lindberg, K., Bakker, S., Sartori, I.: Modelling electric and heat load profiles of non-residential buildings for use in long-term aggregate load forecasts. Utilities Policy **58**, 63–88 (2019)
7. Chen, Y., Luh, P., Rourke, S.: Short-term load forecasting: similar day-based wavelet neural networks. IEEE Trans. Power Syst. **25**(1), 322–330 (2008)
8. Yan, J., Tian, C., Huang, J., Wang, Y.: Load forecasting using twin gaussian process model. In: Proceedings of 2012 IEEE International Conference on Service Operations and Logistics, and Informatics, pp. 36–41. IEEE (2012)

9. Yanxia, L., Shi, H.-F.: The hourly load forecasting based on linear Gaussian state space model. In: 2012 International Conference on Machine Learning and Cybernetics **2**, pp. 741–747. IEEE (2012)
10. Khosravi, A., Nahavandi, S.: Load forecasting using interval type-2 fuzzy logic systems: optimal type reduction. IEEE Trans. Ind. Inform. **10**(2), 1055–1063 (2013)
11. Jetcheva, J.G., Majidpour, M., Chen, W.-P.: Neural network model ensembles for building-level electricity load forecasts. Energy Build. **84**, 214–223 (2014)
12. Richalet, V., Neirac, F.P., Tellez, F., Marco, J., Bloem, J.J.: HELP (house energy labeling procedure): methodology and present results. Energy Build. **33**(3), 229–233 (2001)
13. Li, W., Gong, G., Fan, H., Peng, P., Chun, L.: Meta-learning strategy based on user preferences and a machine recommendation system for real-time cooling load and COP forecasting. Appl. Energy **270**, 115144 (2020)
14. Liu, J.Y., Chen, H.X., Wang, J.Y., Li, G.N., Shi, S.B.: Time Series Prediction of the Indoor Temperature in the Subway Station Based on Data Mining Techniques. Kung Cheng Je Wu Li Hsueh Pao/Journal of Engineering Thermophysics **39**(6), 1316–1321 (2018)
15. Sendra-Arranz, R., Gutiérrez, A.: A long short-term memory artificial neural network to predict daily HVAC consumption in buildings. Energy Building **216**, 109952 (2020)
16. Liu, T., Xu, C., Guo, Y., Chen, H.: A novel deep reinforcement learning based methodology for short-term HVAC system energy consumption prediction. Int. J. Refrig **107**, 39–51 (2019)
17. Huang, Y., Yuan, Y., Chen, H., Wang, J., Guo, Y., Ahmad, T.: A novel energy demand prediction strategy for residential buildings based on ensemble learning. Energy Procedia **158**, 3411–3416 (2019)
18. Alamin, Y.I., Álvarez, J.D., del Mar Castilla, M., Ruano, A.: An Artificial Neural Network (ANN) model to predict the electric load profile for an HVAC system. IFAC-PapersOnLine **51**(10), 26–31 (2018)
19. Yu, Z., Haghighat, F., Fung, B.C.M., Yoshino, H.: A decision tree method for building energy demand modeling. Energy Buildings **42**(10), 1637–1646 (2010)
20. Gong, B., Ordieres-Meré, J.: Prediction of daily maximum ozone threshold exceedances by preprocessing and ensemble artificial intelligence techniques: Case study of Hong Kong. Environ. Model Softw. **84**, 290–303 (2016)
21. Breiman, L.: Machine Learning, Volume 45, Number 1 - SpringerLink. Mach. Learn. **45**, 5–32 (2001)
22. Wu, Z., et al.: Using an ensemble machine learning methodology-Bagging to predict occupants' thermal comfort in buildings. Energy Buildings **173**, 117–127 (2018)
23. Ridgeway, G.: Generalized boosted models: a guide to the GBM package. Comput. **1**, 1–12 (2005)
24. Scikit-learn. https://scikit-learn.org/. Accessed 2020
25. Directorate, T.B.Q.: https://dibk.no/byggereglene/byggteknisk-forskrift-tek17/10/innledning. Accessed 2020

An Empirical Study to Investigate Different SMOTE Data Sampling Techniques for Improving Software Refactoring Prediction

Rasmita Panigrahi[1]([✉]), Lov Kumar[2], and Sanjay Kumar Kuanar[1]

[1] GIET University, Gunupur, Odisha, India
{rasmita,sanjay.kuanar}@giet.edu
[2] BITS Pilani Hyderabad, Hyderabad, India
lovkumar505@gmail.com

Abstract. The exponential rise in software systems and allied applications has alarmed industries and professionals to ensure high quality with optimal reliability, maintainability etc. On contrary software companies focus on developing software solutions at the reduced cost corresponding to the customer demands. Thus, maintaining optimal software quality at reduced cost has always been the challenge for developers. On the other hand, inappropriate code design often leads aging, smells or bugs which can harm eventual intend of the software systems. However, identifying a smell signifier or structural attribute characterizing refactoring probability in software has been the challenge. To alleviate such problems, in this research code-metrics structural feature identification and Neural Network based refactoring prediction model is developed. Our proposed refactoring prediction system at first extracts a set of software code metrics from object-oriented software systems, which are then processed for feature selection method to choose an appropriate sample set of features using Wilcoxon rank test. Once obtaining the optimal set of code-metrics, a novel ANN classifier using 5 different hidden layers is implemented on 5 open source java projects with 3 data sampling techniques SMOTE, BLSMOTE, SVSMOTE to handle class imbalance problem. The performance of our proposed model achieves optimal classification accuracy, F-measure and then it has been shown through AUC graph as well as box-plot diagram.

Keywords: Software refactoring prediction · Code smell · Artificial Neural Network

1 Introduction

In the last few years, software has emerged as one of the most important form of technology to meet major decision-centric computational demands pertaining to business, Defence, communication, industrial computing and real-time control,

© Springer Nature Switzerland AG 2020
H. Yang et al. (Eds.): ICONIP 2020, CCIS 1332, pp. 23–31, 2020.
https://doi.org/10.1007/978-3-030-63820-7_3

security, healthcare, scientific research etc. Undeniably, the existence of modern human life can't be expected without software computing environment. The efficacy and unavoidable significance of software technologies have broadened the horizon for scientific, social as well as business communities to exploit it for optimal decision-making purposes. Being a significant need of modern socio-economic and scientific needs, software industry has taken a broadened shape inviting gigantically large-scale business communities to explore better technologies for better and enhanced productivity. Refactoring is the rework of existing code into well-designed code, and therefore assessing a code for its refactoring probability can be of utmost significance to ensure quality-software solution. Refactoring can help developers identifying bugs, improper design and vulnerability to strengthen the quality of the software product by means of enhanced logic-programme and complexity-free development. Though, authors have made different efforts to deal with refactoring problem such as analyzing structural elements, graphs, code metrics etc, identifying an optimal signifier has always remained a challenge. Recently, authors found that among the major possible solutions, exploiting software code-metrics can be vital to assist method-level refactoring proneness estimation. Refactoring can be defined as the modification of non-functional parameters without altering its desired output. Refactoring can be method level, class level, variable level, etc. Our work is all about the method level refactoring. We have considered seven different method level refactoring operations for our analysis such as: Extract Method, Inline Method, Move Method, Pull up Method, Push down Method, Rename Method and Extract and Move method.

In this paper a multi-purposive effort is made which intends to identify most suitable code-metrics and classification environment to perform method-level refactoring prediction or assessment. As a solution in this research a novel refactoring prediction model is developed for real-time software systems which obtains a set of source code metrics from software system by source meter tool. The obtained features are further processed to get the optimal code metrics by appropriate feature selection technique. After getting the significant features one of the statistical test will be conducted to select appropriate set of significant features (i.e. Wilcoxon test). This paper implements Artificial Neural Network for refactoring prediction at method level as well as to improve the prediction different SMOTE data sampling techniques are used with an empirical study.

- Q1: Whether the model gives any different results depending upon a different number of layers.
- Q2: which data sampling technique gives the optimal solution?
- Q3: All features or significant features give a good result.

2   Related Work

Martin Fowler has published a book "Refactoring: Improving the design of code" on1999. After its publication it has become the challenge for every researcher.

Earlier Mens and Tourwe [1] have done the survey on refactoring activities, tools support and supporting techniques. They have focused on the necessity of refactoring, code refactoring and design refactoring. Specifically, authors have shared their viewpoint on the impact of refactoring towards to software quality. Rosziati lbrahim et al. [2] has proposed a tool named as DART(Detection and refactoring tool) to detect the code smell and implement its corresponding refactoring activities without altering the system's functionality. Over the years empirical studies have recognized a correlation between code quality and refactoring operations. Kumar et al. [3] worked on a class-level refactoring prediction by applying machine learning algorithm named Least Squares Support Vector Machines (LSSVM) with different kernels and principal component analysis (PCA) as a feature extraction technique. To deal with data imbalance issue, authors applied synthetic minority over-sampling (SMOTE) technique. Employing different software metrics as refactoring-indicator authors performed refactoring prediction, where LSSVM with radial basis function (RBF) was found performing than the other state-of-art methods.

3   Study Design

This section presents the details regarding various design setting used for this research.

3.1   Experimental Data Set

There was a repository known as tera-PROMISE, which is publicly assessable by any researcher. The tera-promise repository contains open source projects related to software engineering, effort estimation, faults, source code analysis. Our data set has been downloaded from the tera-PROMISE repository, which makes our work easy. The tera-PROMISE repository is the standardized repository, which is manually validated by Kedar [4] and shared the data set publicly. We have taken five open source java projects which are present in GitHub Repository with subsequent releases.

3.2   Research Contribution

The presented work in this paper shows a novel and something different research contributions. In this paper, we are computing source code metrics at the method level. Basing up on the existing work, our study is on refactoring prediction at method level on 5 open source java projects (i.e. Antr4, titan, junit, mct, oryx) using Artificial Neural Network with 5 different hidden layers (ANN+1HL, ANN+2HL, ANN+3HL, ANN+4HL, ANN+5HL) and to improve the efficiency of software prediction different data sampling techniques (i.e. SMOTE, BLSMOTE, SVSMOTE).

4 Research Methodology

This section describes the model followed by an experiment implementing the Artificial Neural Network with 5 different hidden layers for refactoring prediction at method level with 3 different data sampling techniques. Figure 1 shows the outline of the proposed model for refactoring prediction at the method level by considering 5 open source java projects. Figure 2 identifies that the approach which we have proposed contains a multi step. 1st of all data set has to be collected from the tera-PROMISE repository. The source meter tool is implemented for source code metrics calculation. Significant features are to be selected through the Wilcoxon rank test, and Min-Max normalization is to carried for feature scaling, and then Data imbalance issues can be sorted through 3 data sampling techniques. ANN classifier is used for training the model, and lastly, the performance of the model is evaluated through different performance parameters (i.e., AUC, Accuracy, and F-measure). During the first phase, the data has to be pre-processed, where significant features are to be extracted by the Wilcoxon rank-sum test. Model building is the second phase, which consists of data normalization that may cause data balancing. Data unbalance issues can be solved by 3 data sampling techniques (i.e., SMOTE, BLSMOTE, and SVSMOTE).

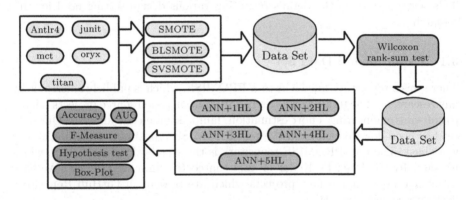

Fig. 1. Proposed model for refactoring prediction at the method level

5 Experimental Results

In this paper, we have used the ANN technique for refactoring prediction at the method level, and then it's performance has been improved by SVSMOTE data sampling technique and this has been represented in 3 performance measures (AUC, ACCURACY, F-measure). If we will talk about the performance in terms of ACCURACY of ANN gives likely same result irrespective of number of hidden layers. Like this, the performance of ANN in terms of AUC and F-measure gives the same type of result irrespective of a number of hidden layers. From the above table we can conclude that increasing or decreasing number of hidden layers of ANN technique does not affect to its performance. Table 3 focuses on the ANN technique's performance in 3 different performance measures (ACCURACY, AUC) (Table 1).

Table 1. Performance Value: Classification Techniques

			Accuracy					AUC				
			1HL	2HL	3HL	4HL	5HL	1HL	2HL	3HL	4HL	5HL
ORG	AM	antlr4	98.85	98.47	98.85	98.73	98.6	0.95	0.91	0.95	0.98	0.7
ORG	AM	JUnit	99.38	99.43	99.38	99.47	99.43	0.5	0.59	0.53	0.65	0.43
ORG	SG	antlr4	98.51	98.66	98.57	98.7	98.73	0.66	0.74	0.69	0.62	0.64
ORG	SG	JUnit	99.03	99.38	99.38	99.29	99.38	0.66	0.74	0.6	0.46	0.52
SMOTE	AM	antlr4	99.71	99.31	86.28	90.13	79.88	1	1	0.95	0.96	0.89
SMOTE	AM	JUnit	81.03	81.18	81.27	80.67	77.79	0.89	0.9	0.88	0.89	0.86
SMOTE	SG	antlr4	77.05	79.03	78.38	80.73	81.06	0.85	0.86	0.87	0.88	0.89
SMOTE	SG	JUnit	65.45	67.42	66.78	66.33	71.82	0.78	0.79	0.78	0.77	0.81

5.1 Artificial Neural Network Classifier Results

In this paper we have focused on ANN classifier with 5 different hidden layers. In consideration of ANN classifier with its five hidden layers performance, we get all the hidden layers performance is likely the same depending upon different performance measures (AUC, Accuracy, F-measures). AUC performance of all the hidden layers of ANN is coming within a range .75 to .8, which is less than the mean AUC value. Accuracy performance of ANN with all hidden layers is in a range 80 to 85%, which is more than the mean accuracy. When we are considering F-measure performance, all are achieving more than .8, and that is more than their mean F-measure value. Figure 2 shows the performance of the ANN classifier in the form of the Box-plot diagram.

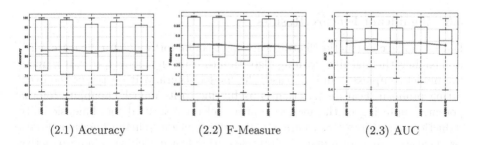

(2.1) Accuracy   (2.2) F-Measure   (2.3) AUC

Fig. 2. Performance evaluation of ANN with different Hidden layer

5.2   Data Imbalance Issue Results

Classifier building is very difficult if data is imbalanced. There is a technical test for the researcher to build an efficient model for refactoring prediction when data is unbalanced. This problem can be solved by an efficient technique i.e. Synthetic minority over sampling (SMOTE). SMOTE combines both the under-sampled as well as over-sampled. BLSMOTE is another over sampling technique which considers only boarder-line samples. SVSMOTE is one kind of over-sampling technique which uses SVM (support vector Machine) algorithm for the samples which is near to boarder-line. The performance of the sampling techniques (SMOTE, BLSMOTE, SVSMOTE) has been shown through the Box-plot diagram in Fig. 3. In the diagram we can see that SMOTE and SVSMOTE perform well that is more then its mean F-measure, But BLSMOTE gives 0.76 result which is less than mean F-measure performance. The performance result in terms of AUC of all the three imbalancing technique gives less than the mean AUC value. SVSMOTE gives the better performance the other SMOTE techniques. **Research answer Q2:-** From the experiment, we obtained that ORG means original data, and out of all three sampling techniques, SVSMOTE outperforms well.

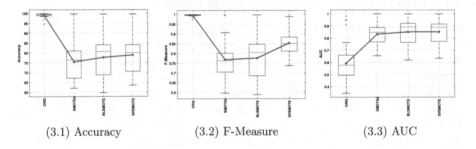

(3.1) Accuracy   (3.2) F-Measure   (3.3) AUC

Fig. 3. Performance evaluation of data imbalance issue

5.3   Significant Feature Results

During model construction feature selection is an important factor. Feature selection enables the machine learning algorithm to train the model faster. It reduces the model complexity and increases the model accuracy. It decreases the overfitting problem. Feature selection is useful due to its unlock capability for the potential uplifting of the model. Feature selection is used for dimensionality reduction to improve the accuracy and performance in a high dimensional data set. Feature importance plays a vital role during feature selection in a predictive modelling project. Feature importance means to class of techniques to assign the score to input featuresfor a predictive model. In this work we have focused two types of considerations with all features and significant features. We have got the experimental result that significant features gives well performance as compare to all features. We have measured the model's performance in terms of AUC, Accuracy and F-measure in this article. During F-measure computation we have found that significant features and all features give the result, which is more than the mean F-measure value. Where as AUC computation all features gives the result of less than the mean AUC value. Both all features and significant features give same result as mean Accuracy. All the performances of all features and significant features have been shown on Fig. 4 in terms of box-plot diagram. **Research Answer Q3:** - Model Proposed gives good results with significant features as a comparison to all features.

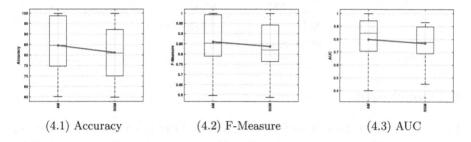

(4.1) Accuracy   (4.2) F-Measure   (4.3) AUC

Fig. 4. Performance of all feature and significant features

5.4 Statistical Description of Significance Test Results

The learning efficiency, allied classification capacity makes ANN a potential solution for major Artificial Intelligence (AI) purposes or decision-making purposes. In this article, ANN, with its five different hidden layers, was used as a classifier. The statistical description of the performance of ANN with 5 different layers has been represented in Table 2. ANN with different layers does not effect on the model's performance. During the significance test of data sampling techniques, all the benefits in Table 2 are less than 0.5. It means a very less number of samples are imbalanced. So, it gives the optimal result for refactoring prediction at the method level. Table 3 provides the effect that significant features give a good result, so the model is accepted (Table 4).

Table 2. Statistical Significance test of ANN with different Hidden Layer

	ANN-1HL	ANN-2HL	ANN-3HL	ANN-4HL	ANN-5HL
ANN-1HL	1.00	0.61	0.96	0.88	0.72
ANN-2HL	0.61	1.00	0.68	0.77	0.42
ANN-3HL	0.96	0.68	1.00	0.88	0.72
ANN-4HL	0.88	0.77	0.88	1.00	0.62
ANN-5HL	0.72	0.42	0.72	0.62	1.00

Table 3. Statistical Significance test of SMOTE with its versions

	ORG	SMOTE	BLSMOTE	SVSMOTE
ORG	1.00	0.00	0.00	0.00
SMOTE	0.00	1.00	0.13	0.11
BLSMOTE	0.00	0.13	1.00	1.00
SVSMOTE	0.00	0.11	1.00	1.00

Table 4. Statistical Significance test of features

	AM	SGM
AM	1	0.027961344
SGM	0.027961344	1

6   Conclusion

In this paper, an explorative effort was made to identify an optimal computing environment for refactoring prediction purposes that, as a result, could help to achieve cost-efficient and reliable software design. In the proposed method, different code-metrics features, including object-oriented code metrics, were taken into consideration to characterize each code-class as refactoring prone or non-refactoring. With this motive obtaining a large number of code-metrics which describes different programming aspects or code-characteristics such as coupling, cohesion, complexity, depth, dependency, etc. A set of metrics were obtained, which were subsequently processed for significant feature selection. The proposed model intended to retain only significant features for eventual classification and to achieve a feature selection method was applied. On the other hand, realizing the data imbalance problem, three different sampling methods, including SMOTE, BLSMOTE, SVSMOTE in conjunction with original samples, provided sufficient training data for classification. This research introduced a classification algorithm, including ANN, with its five different hidden layers. Thus, as a contributing solution, this research recommends implementing ANN with any number of hidden layers that will give us the same type of results. ANN is used to achieve optimal and automatic refactoring prediction systems that, as a result, can help firms or developers to design software with better quality, reliability, and cost-efficiency.

References

1. Mens, T., Tourwé, T.: A survey of software refactoring. IEEE Trans. Softw. Eng. **30**(2), 126–139 (2004)
2. Ibrahim, R., Ahmed, M., Nayak, R., Jamel, S.: Reducing redundancy of test cases generation using code smell detection and refactoring. Journal of King Saud University-Computer and Information Sciences, **32**(3), pp. 367–374 2018

3. Kumar, L., Sureka, A.: Application of lssvm and smote on seven open source projects for predicting refactoring at class level. In: 2017 24th Asia-Pacific Software Engineering Conference (APSEC), pp. 90–99. IEEE (2017)
4. Kádár, I., Hegedus, P., Ferenc, R., Gyimóthy, T.: A code refactoring dataset and its assessment regarding software maintainability. In: 2016 IEEE 23rd International Conference on Software Analysis, Evolution, and Reengineering (SANER), 1, pp. 599–603. IEEE (2016)

Prediction Model of Breast Cancer Based on mRMR Feature Selection

Junwen Di and Zhiguo Shi[✉]

School of Computer and Communication Engineering, University of Science and Technology Beijing, Beijing 100083, China
szg@ustb.edu.cn

Abstract. In real life, there are a lot of unbalanced data, and there are great differences in the data volume in category distribution, especially in the medical data where this problem is more prominent because of the prevalence rate. In this paper, the P-mRMR algorithm is proposed based on the mRMR algorithm to improve the feature selection process of unbalance data, and to process the attributes with more missing values and integrate the missing values into feature selection while selecting features specific to the characteristics of more missing values in the data set, so as to reduce the complexity of the data pre-processing. In the experiments, the AUC, confusion matrix and probability of missing value are used to compare the algorithms. The experiment shows that the features selected by the improved algorithm have better results in the classifiers.

Keywords: Feature selection · mRMR · Unbalanced data · Disease prediction

1 Introduction

The method of on-the-spot questionnaires is adopted to obtain some data on women in three provinces in China, including personal information, living habits, physical health and other aspects. This article is based on the data set collected by this project for processing and analysis. However, category of the data set collected by the project is not balanced. The number of people who had been diagnosed with breast cancer is far lower than those who have not, at 1:100. The result of traditional data processing method is more biased towards the majority class, and is not friendly to the minority class, but for unbalanced data, the minority class are more important. Therefore, the processing of unbalanced data sets needs to seek new methods and discrimination methods.

Most raw data sets contain a large number of features, some of which are irrelevant or repetitive, and we collectively refer to these features as useless features. The existence of useless features makes the data set bloated, increases

Supported by National Key R&D Program of China (No. 2018YFC0810601), National Key R&D Program of China (No. 2016YFC0901303), National Natural Science Foundation of China (No. 61977005).

H. Yang et al. (Eds.): ICONIP 2020, CCIS 1332, pp. 32–40, 2020.
https://doi.org/10.1007/978-3-030-63820-7_4

the burden of classification tasks, reduces the efficiency, and may have a negative impact on the classification results. Therefore, we need to conduct feature selection. Feature selection, i.e. selecting the smallest feature subset from the original feature set to maximize the evaluation criteria, can reduce the acquisition time of the original data, and reduce the storage space of the data, improve the interpretability of the classification model, obtain the classification model more quickly, improve the classification performance, and help to visualize the data and knowledge.

Based on the above problems, an improved feature selection method based on mRMR is proposed in this paper. In the process of feature selection, we change the preference of feature selection algorithm to the majority class by adjusting the weight of the degree of correlation between category and feature, and take into account the influence of missing values on feature selection when calculating the redundancy among features. According to the characteristics of breast cancer data set collected, this paper only gives a discussion to the binary classification problems.

2 Related Work

In recent years, the research on feature selection of unbalanced data mainly focuses on two aspects: data and feature selection algorithm optimization. However, both oversampling and undersampling will affect the distribution of data, which may result in the bias of subsequent feature selection and classification results.

At the algorithm level, by improving the existing feature selection algorithm, the problem of data unbalance can be solved algorithmically to reduce the influence of data unbalance on feature selection. The common methods for feature selection algorithms are filtering, wrapping and embedding method. Kira et al. proposed the classical Relief algorithm, which is a feature selection algorithm based on distance measurement [18]. Battiti et al. Proposed the mutual information-based MIFS (Mutual Information Feature Selection) algorithm. Which uses greedy strategy to select a feature set with strong correlation with categories and low redundancy with selected features [1]. Specific to unbalanced data, Moayedikia et al. introduces a method of feature selection that uses symmetric uncertainty and coordinated search, SYMON, to measure the dependence of features on class labels by symmetric uncertainty. This helps identify powerful features when retrieving the least frequent class labels [15]. Peng et al. Proposed the mRMR (Max-relevance and Min-redundancy) algorithm, which uses the average mutual information of candidate features and selected features as the estimated value of redundancy, and removes the redundancy feature while the feature reaches the maximum correlation [9]. In this paper, we improve the mRMR algorithm.

3 Improved mRMR Algorithm

3.1 mRMR Algorithm

mRMR uses mutual information as a metric. Mutual information is the amount of information contained in a random variable about another random variable, or the uncertainty that a random variable decreases because it knowns another random variable. Assuming that there is a random variable X and another random variable Y, their mutual information is shown in formula (1).

$$I(X;Y) = H(X) - H(X \mid Y) \tag{1}$$

In terms of probability, mutual information is derived from the joint probability distribution $p(x,y)$ of random variables X and Y and the marginal probability distribution $p(x)$ and $p(y)$, as shown in formula (2).

$$I(x;y) = \sum_{x,y} p(x,y) \log \frac{p(x,y)}{p(x)p(y)} \tag{2}$$

The mRMR algorithm takes into account not only the correlation between features and class labels, but also the correlation between features.

The correlation between feature set S and class C is defined by the mean value of all mutual information values between each feature and class c, as shown in the formula (3).

$$D(S,C) = \frac{1}{|S|} \sum_{f_i \in S, c_j \in C} I(f_i; c_j) \tag{3}$$

The redundancy of all features in set S is defined by the average value of all mutual information values between feature f_i and feature f_h, as shown in formula (4).

$$R(S) = \frac{1}{|S|^2} \sum_{f_i, f_h \in S} I(f_i; f_h) \tag{4}$$

$$mRMR = \max \left[\frac{1}{|S|} \sum_{f_i \in S, c_j \in C} I(f_i; c_j) - \frac{1}{|S|^2} \sum_{f_i f_h \in S} I(f_i; f_h) \right] \tag{5}$$

Finally, the feature set with maximum correlation and minimum redundancy is selected according to formula (5).

3.2 Probability-Based Optimization Algorithm P-mRMR

It can be seen from formula (2) that the mutual information is obtained by the joint probability distribution $p(x,y)$ of random variable X and Y and the marginal probability distribution $p(x)$ and $p(y)$, so the proportion of class variables is very important when calculating the mutual information between features and class variables. However, inthe data set, the minority class accounts for a low proportion, so when calculating the mutual information, the minority class has little influence on the result of the final feature selection, which is not conducive to the selection of feature subsets that is biased towards the minority class classification. In this paper, we improve the mRMR algorithm and screen the missing values by probability. For high-dimensional data sets, the calculation of probability is very simple, and will not result in too long running time due to complex computation. And for unbalanced data sets, the improvement using probabilities is simple but effective. The probability is selected as the coefficient to improve the calculation method of mutual information, and adjust the weights of different classes when calculating the maximum correlation. For the binary classification problem, set the minority class are a positive example c_0, and the majority class as a negative example, the probability of the positive example is $p_{(c_0)}$ and the probability of the negative example is $p_{(c1)}$.

$$\begin{cases} p_{(c_0)} = count\,(c_0)\,/n \\ p_{(c_1)} = count\,(c_1)\,/n \\ \quad p_{(c_0)} + p_{(c_1)} = 1 \end{cases} \tag{6}$$

The probability of the negative example $p_{(c_1)}$ is taken as the weight of the positive example c_0, and the probability of the positive example $p_{(c_0)}$ as the weight of the negative example c_1, and then the mutual information between each feature f_i and the class label is shown in formula (7).

$$D'\,(f_i) = I\,(f_i; c_0) * p_{(c_1)} + I\,(f_i; c_1) * p_{(c_0)} \tag{7}$$

For sparse matrices, there are a large number of missing values in the data set. Since there may be important data in the feature, features containing missing values that cannot be easily deleted, but using mutual information to calculate the values containing a large number of missing values and class labels will show that there is a strong correlation between them, and this correlation is wrong and should not exist. Therefore, when calculating the inter-feature redundancy, this paper considers the missing values. By calculating the proportion of missing data in each feature value and adding it to the calculation of inter-feature redundancy, we obtain the measurement sum of the degree of redundancy and missing degree of each feature, such as formula (8), in which $\sum_{f_h \in S} I\,(f_i; f_h)$ is the sum of the mutual information between a feature f_i and other features in the feature set. The greater the mutual information between a feature and other features, the higher the degree of redundancy between the feature and other features, $p_{(f_i, null)}$ is the probability of missing a value in the feature f_i.

$$R'\,(f_i) = \sum_{f_h \in S} I\,(f_i; f_h) + p_{(f_i,\ null\ )} \tag{8}$$

According to the formula (5), the mRMR algorithm finally selects an optimal feature subset S from the feature set, and sets the selection process of the optimal subset as the single variable feature selection to calculate the difference value of correlation degree between features and class labels, the redundancy between the feature and other feature, and the degree of feature loss, and select the k feature with the largest results as the optimal feature subset, which greatly reduces the time complexity of the feature selection algorithm.

$$P - mRMR = max_k \left[D' \left(f_i \right) - R' \left(f_i \right) \right] \qquad (9)$$

4   Experimental Analysis

4.1   Introduction to Data Set

The survey subjects of the data used in this experiment are selected from women of Han nationality who are 25–70 years old and have lived in Shandong, Jiangsu, Hebei Province and Tianjin for more than 2 years and have lived there for at least 6 months during the survey period. Long-term migrant workers were excluded from the study. Subsequently, counties or districts were randomly selected from each province [9].

According to the disease characteristics of breast cancer, the project designed 20 data sheets with 1,484 fields covering living habits, family conditions and personal information. This experiment selected the history of menstruation, childbearing history, personal diseases and examination and treatment history, family history, smoking, diet, drinking, tea, physical condition, sleep scale, attitude and cognition of breast cancer, psychological scale, a total of 12 questionnaires and 829 fields, and 382 attributes are left to be processed after manual deletion of the meaningless, repetitive attributes with chaotic feature values. The data set has 54,799 data, of which 583 are in the minority class and 54,216 are in the majority class.

In this paper, the sklearn package in python was used to calculate the mutual information of the data set, and four classifiers, namely, the Balanced-BaggingClassifier, BalancedRandomForestClassifier [6], RUSBoostClassifier [17] and EasyEnsembleClassifier [13] were used to classify the data in order to avoid the biased results of a single classifier.

4.2   Experimental Results

In this paper, four feature selection algorithms are selected to compare with the improved P-mRMR, including mRMR, f_classif, mutual_info_classif, and chi2. With AUC as the index of classification evaluation, the classification effect is shown in Fig. 1. The X-axis represents the percentage of the number of selected features, and the Y-axis represents the value of AUC.

As can be seen from Fig. 1, the effect of the feature selection algorithm on the RUSBoostClassifier shows an unstable trend. According to the analysis, it is because the RUSBoostClassifier integrates random undersampling in the learning of AdaBoost. The search mechanism used in the Adaboost algorithm is the backtracking method. When training the weak classifier, the local best weak classifier was obtained by greedy algorithm every time, and it cannot guaranteed

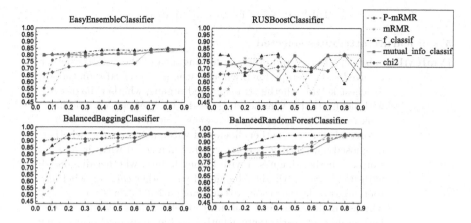

Fig. 1. The AUC index of classifier after feature selection

that the weighted one selected is the best of all. Because the classification effect of RUSBoostClassifier is not stable, the classification effects of only the other three classifiers are analyzed below. Compared with the mRMR algorithm, P-mRMR has better performance. When 10% of features are selected, the performance difference between the two algorithms is the biggest. When 60% of features are selected, the performance of the two algorithms tends to be the same. From

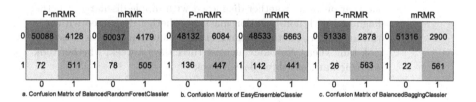

Fig. 2. Confusion Matrix

Fig. 1, it can be concluded that 60% of the feature ratio has better classification effect, and P-mRMR and mRMR have similar classification effect. For the analysis on the confusion matrix and selection features of the P-mRMR algorithm and mRMR algorithm on the classifier when 60% of features are selected, the majority class is set as 0, and the minority class is set as 1, then the confusion matrix is shown in Fig. 2. From Fig. 2, it can be concluded that the classification accuracy of P-mRMR algorithm is always higher than that of mRMR algorithm, and the BalancedBaggingClassifier has the best classification effect. According to the experimental, the repetition rate of attribute of the features selected by different algorithms is lower when 10% of the features are selected, so 5% of features are selected to compare and analyze the characteristics of features selected by each algorithm. Due to space limitations, we compare only the features selected in P-mRMR and f-classify.

Table 1. 5% of Feature attributes

5% of feature attributes selected	
P-mRMR	Whether received radiotherapy for angioma of chest wall, whether received radiotherapy for thymoma, whether received radiotherapy for chest keloid, whether transplanted organs, whether diagnosed with nephropathy, whether diagnosed with liver cancer, whether took toremifene at least 3 days a weak, whether diagnosed with colorectal cancer, whether diagnosed with gastric cancer, whether diagnosed with gastric cancer, whether diagnosed with thyroid cancer, whether diagnosed with kidney failure, whether diagnosed with lung cancer, whether diagnosed with other cancers, whether took anatrazole /letrazole/ exemestane at least 3 days a week, whether took tamoxifen/ Nolvadex at least 3 days a week, whether had a bilateral ovariectomy, whether had an unilateral ovariectomy, whether diagnosed with endometriosis
f-classif	Whether took anatrazole/ letrozole/ exemestane at least three days a week, whether diagnosed with a benign breast tumor, whether had a breast biopsy (acupuncture), whether had a breast biopsy (surgery), whether received radiotherapy for a tumor or cancer, whether diagnosed with uterine cancer, whether diagnosed with galactoma, whether received breast or ovary operation or puncture, whether remembered the time of last menstrual, Whether received radiotherapy for a disease, whether had complete unilateral or bilateral mastectomy, whether the menstruation have stopped for one year or more, whether diagnosed with nipple discharge, whether diagnosed with non-lactation mastitis, whether diagnosed with ovarian cancer, whether diagnosed with lactation mastitis, whether took tamoxifen/ Nolvadex at least three days a week, whether took tamoxifen at least three days a week

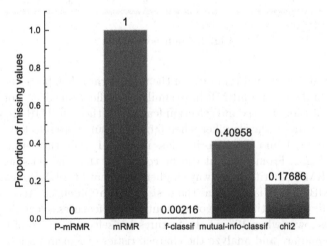

Fig. 3. The proportion of missing values of the features selected by different feature selection algorithms

As can be seen from Table 1 and Fig. 3, the features selected by mRMR, f-classif, mutual_info_clasif, chi2 algorithm have a large number of missing values, and it means that most people will not encounter the situation described by the features, which is not conducive to the establishment of disease model. And the f-classif algorithm, which performs well in the AUC curve, has redundancy in the feature selection results, such as "whether received radiotherapy for a disease" or "whether received radiotherapy for a thymoma" and other attributes.

5 Conclusion

In this paper, we propose a P-mRMR algorithm based on the mRMR algorithm, and realize the improvement of the feature selection bias towards the majority class and the existence of a large number of missing values in the mRMR algorithm. Through the experimental analysis, by using AUC as evaluation index, the result of P-mRMR algorithm is better than that of mRMR algorithm on classifiers, and the attributes with a lot of missing values are removed, which makes the classification model more universal for most people.

However, the purpose of the mRMR algorithm is to find the feature of maximum correlation and minimum redundancy, so the feature selected by the algorithm is not the optimal solution, and will not show the best performance on the classifier, and the P-mRMR algorithm which inherits the mRMR has the same problem. In addition, in the process of removing the attributes with missing values, features with a lot of missing values but important information can not be retained. Moreover, the improved P-mRMR algorithm has not been verified on other data sets. In the process of weight selection, it should be adjusted according to the distribution characteristics of different data sets, and it needs to be improved later.

References

1. Battiti, R.: Using mutual information for selecting features in supervised neural net learning. IEEE Trans. Neural Netw. 5(4), 537–550 (1994)
2. Bolón-Canedo, V., Sánchez-Maroño, N., Alonso-Betanzos, A., Benítez, J., Herrera, F.: A review of microarray datasets and applied feature selection methods. Inf. Sci. 282, 111–135 (2014)
3. Bolón-Canedo, V., Seth, S., Sánchez-Maroño, N., Alonso-Betanzos, A., Principe, J.C.: Statistical dependence measure for feature selection in microarray datasets. In: European Symposium on ESANN (2012)
4. Chawla, N.V., Bowyer, K.W., Hall, L.O., Kegelmeyer, W.P.: Smote: synthetic minority over-sampling technique. J. Artif. Intell. Res. 16(1), 321–357 (2011)
5. Chawla, N.V., Japkowicz, N., Kotcz, A.: Editorial: special issue on learning from imbalanced data sets. AM Sigkdd Explor. Newsl. 6(1), 1–6 (2004)
6. Chen, C., Breiman, L.: Using random forest to learn imbalanced data. University of California, Berkeley (2004)
7. Chen, H., Li, T., Fan, X., Luo, C.: Feature selection for imbalanced data based on neighborhood rough sets. Inf. Sci. 483, 1–20 (2019)

8. Guyon, I., Elisseeff, A.: An introduction to variable and feature selection. J. Mach. Learn. Res. **3**(6), 1157–1182 (2003)
9. Peng, H., Long, F., Ding, C.: Feature selection based on mutual information criteria of max-dependency, max-relevance, and min-redundancy. IEEE Trans. Pattern Anal. Mach. Intell. **27**(8), 1226–1238 (2005)
10. Li, A., Wang, R., Xu, L.: Shrink: a breast cancer risk assessment model based on medical social network. In: 2017 IEEE 37th International Conference on Distributed Computing Systems (ICDCS), pp. 1189–1196. IEEE (2017)
11. Li, D.C., Liu, C.W., Hu, S.C.: A learning method for the class imbalance problem with medical data sets. Comput. Biol. Med. **40**(5), 509–518 (2010)
12. Li, J., et al.: Feature selection: a data perspective. AM Comput. Surv. **50**(6), 1–45 (2016)
13. Liu, X.Y., Wu, J., Zhou, Z.H.: Exploratory undersampling for class-imbalance learning. IEEE Trans. Syst. Man Cybern. B **39**(2), 539–550 (2009)
14. Mafarja, M.M., Mirjalili, S.: Hybrid binary ant lion optimizer with rough set and approximate entropy reducts for feature selection. Soft Comput. **23**(15), 6249–6265 (2018). https://doi.org/10.1007/s00500-018-3282-y
15. Maldonado, S., Weber, R., Famili, F.: Feature selection for high-dimensional class-imbalanced data sets using support vector machines. Inf. Sci. **286**, 228–246 (2014)
16. Moayedikia, A., Ong, K.L., Boo, Y.L., Yeoh, W.G., Jensen, R.: Feature selection for high dimensional imbalanced class data using harmony search. Eng. Appl. Artif. Intell. **57**, 38–49 (2017)
17. Seiffert, C., Khoshgoftaar, T.M., Van Hulse, J., Napolitano, A.: Rusboost: a hybrid approach to alleviating class imbalance. IEEE Trans. Syst. Man Cybern. A Syst. Hum. **40**(1), 185–197 (2010)
18. Urbanowicz, R.J., Melissa, M., La, C.W., Olson, R.S., Moore, J.H.: Relief-based feature selection: introduction and review. J. Biomed. Inform. **85**, 189–203 (2017)
19. Wasikowski, M., Chen, X.W.: Combating the small sample class imbalance problem using feature selection. IEEE Trans. Knowl. Data Eng. **22**(10), 1388–1400 (2010)
20. Yan-Xia, L.I., Yi, C., You-Qiang, H.U., Hong-Peng, Y.: Review of imbalanced data classification methods. Control Decis. **34**(04), 673–688 (2019)
21. Yin, L., Ge, Y., Xiao, K., Wang, X., Quan, X.: Feature selection for high-dimensional imbalanced data. Neurocomput. **105**, 3–11 (2013)
22. Zhang, C., Wang, G., Zhou, Y., Yao, L., Wang, X.: Feature selection for high dimensional imbalanced class data based on f-measure optimization. In: 2017 International Conference on Security, Pattern Analysis, and Cybernetics (SPAC), pp. 278–283. IEEE(2018)

Clustering Ensemble Selection
with Analytic Hierarchy Process

Wei Liu[1], Xiaodong Yue[1,2(✉)], Caiming Zhong[3], and Jie Zhou[4]

[1] School of Computer Engineering and Science, Shanghai University,
Shanghai 200444, China
ldachuan@outlook.com, yswantfly@shu.edu.cn
[2] Shanghai Institute for Advanced Communication and Data Science,
Shanghai University, Shanghai, China
[3] College of Science and Technology, Ningbo University, Ningbo 315211, China
zhongcaiming@nbu.edu.cn
[4] College of Computer Science and Software Engineering, Shenzhen University,
Guangdong 518060, China
jie_jpu@163.com

Abstract. Existing clustering ensemble selection methods adopt internal and external evaluation indexes to measure the quality and diversity of base clusterings. The significance of base clustering is quantified by the average or weighted average of multiple evaluation indexes. However, there exist two limitations in these methods. First, the evaluation of base clusterings in the form of linear combination of multiple indexes lacks the structural analysis and relative comparison between clusterings and measures. Second, the consistency between the final evaluation and the multiple evaluations from different measures cannot be guaranteed. To tackle these problems, we propose a clustering ensemble selection method with Analytic Hierarchy Process (AHPCES). Experimental results validate the effectiveness of the proposed method.

Keywords: Clustering ensemble selection · Analytic hierarchy process · Multiple clustering evaluation indexes

1 Introduction

Clustering ensemble selection creates the final clustering by evaluating and selecting a subset of base clusterings, and it performs as good as even better than full clustering ensemble [6,13,17,18]. Quality and diversity of base clustering are two critical issues of clustering ensemble selection. A subset of base clusterings of both high quality and diversity will produce a precise ensemble result.

Most existing clustering ensemble selection methods adopt internal and external evaluation indexes to measure the quality and diversity of base clusterings. The significance of base clustering is directly quantified by the average

© Springer Nature Switzerland AG 2020
H. Yang et al. (Eds.): ICONIP 2020, CCIS 1332, pp. 41–49, 2020.
https://doi.org/10.1007/978-3-030-63820-7_5

(or weighted average) of multiple evaluation indexes [18]. However, there exist the following problems in these methods. First, the final evaluation of base clusterings is obtained by the linear combination of multiple indexes, which is a single level evaluation assemble and lacks the structural analysis and relative comparison between clusterings and measures. Second, the consistency between the final evaluation of base clusterings and the multiple evaluations from different measures cannot be guaranteed.

To tackle the problems above, we propose a clustering ensemble selection method based on Analytic Hierarchy Process (AHPCES) [15] in this paper. AHP is a structured technique for organizing and analyzing complex group decisions. As to the characteristics of AHP for group decision making, we apply it to formulate the clustering ensemble selection process. Specifically, we design an analytic hierarchy process to evaluate base clusterings, which achieves the hierarchical ensemble of the weights of evaluations from base clustering level to criteria level. Considering the significances of evaluation measures and integrating the weights of base clusterings under multiple measures in hierarchy, AHP-based method can generate more reasonable and consistent evaluations of base clustering results which facilitates the selective clustering ensemble.

The rest of this paper is organized as follows. Section 2 introduces the proposed method in detail, which includes comparison matrix construction, weight computation and algorithm implementation. In Sect. 3, experiment results validate the effectiveness of the AHP-based selection for clustering ensemble.

2   Clustering Ensemble Selection with AHP

The framework of the proposed AHPCES consists of three levels. On the bottom level of base clusterings, all the base clusterings are measured with multiple evaluation indexes under the criteria of quality and diversity; On the second level of evaluation index, multiple evaluation indexes are grouped and composed to form the overall evaluation of base clusterings in the aspects of quality and diversity respectively; On the top level of criteria, the final significance of base clusterings is obtained by integrating the significances of the criteria of quality and diversity. The detailed computation of the base clustering significance is introduced below.

On the top level, the significance of a clustering result C_i is obtained by

$$sig(C_i) = \lambda_q \cdot q_{C_i} + \lambda_d \cdot d_{C_i},$$
$$\lambda_q, \lambda_d \in [0,1] \text{ and } \lambda_q + \lambda_d = 1 \tag{1}$$

in which the weights λ_q and λ_d denote the significances of the criteria of clustering quality and diversity and we set $\lambda_q = 0.7, \lambda_d = 0.3$ as default. q_{C_i} and d_{C_i} denote the evaluations of the quality and diversity of the clustering C_i.

On the second level of evaluation index, given L quality measures and T diversity measures, q_{C_i} and d_{C_i} are obtained by

$$q_{C_i} = \sum_{l=1}^{L} wq_l \cdot q_{C_i}^l, \ d_{C_i} = \sum_{t=1}^{T} wd_t \cdot d_{C_i}^t \tag{2}$$

where $0 \leq wq_l, wd_t \leq 1$ and $\sum_{l=1}^{L} wq_l = \sum_{t=1}^{T} wd_t = 1$. $q_{C_i}^l$ and $d_{C_i}^t$ denote the evaluations of the clustering C_i with the lth quality measure and the tth diversity measure respectively, wq_l and wd_t are the normalized significance weights of the measures.

On the bottom level of base clustering results, adopting L quality and T diversity measures to evaluate M base clusterings, we suppose $\{q_{C_i}^1, ..., q_{C_i}^l, ..., q_{C_i}^L\}$ are L quality evaluations and $\{d_{C_i}^1, ..., d_{C_i}^t, ..., d_{C_i}^T\}$ are T diversity evaluations of a clustering C_i, $1 \leq i \leq M$ and normalize all the evaluations to $[0, 1]$. The pairwise comparison of clusterings C_i and C_j in quality can be formulated by

$$L(i,j)_q^l = q_{C_i}^l - q_{C_j}^l, \; q_{C_i}^l \geq q_{C_j}^l \text{ and } 1 \leq l \leq L \tag{3}$$

and the pairwise comparison of clusterings in diversity can be formulated by

$$L(i,j)_d^t = d_{C_i}^t - d_{C_j}^t, \; d_{C_i}^t \geq d_{C_j}^t \text{ and } 1 \leq t \leq T \tag{4}$$

Based on the pairwise comparison, given an evaluation measure, we can construct a comparison matrix of all the clusterings.

Definition 1. *Pairwise-Comparison Matrix of Clustering Results.* *Given* M *clusterings and an evaluation measure, the pairwise comparison of clusterings* C_i *and* C_j *is* $L(i,j)_{q|d}^{l|t}$ *denoted by* $L(i,j)$. *Suppose a mapping* $f : L(i,j) \rightarrow [1,9]$ *ranks continuous pairwise comparison into 9 levels through sorting and partitioning all the values, the comparison matrix of clusterings is constructed as follows.*

$$\mathbf{P} = [\mathbf{P}(i,j)\,|1 \leq i,j \leq M]$$
$$= \begin{pmatrix} 1 & f(L(1,2)) & \cdots & f(L(1,M)) \\ \vdots & \vdots & \ddots & \vdots \\ 1/f(L(1,M)) & 1/f(L(2,M)) & \cdots & 1 \end{pmatrix} \tag{5}$$

For convenience, we use $\mathbf{P}_q^l$ to denote the comparison matrix of the lth quality measure and $\mathbf{P}_d^t$ to denote the matrix of the tth diversity measure.

According to the AHP theory, the elements of the comparison matrix indicate the levels of relative importance between the different clustering results. '1 | 9' means 'equal | extreme importance'. Moreover, because $\mathbf{P}(i,j) \cdot \mathbf{P}(j,i) = 1$, the comparison matrix $\mathbf{P}$ is a positive reciprocal matrix. Referring to [15], we can further define the consistent comparison matrix of clusterings.

Definition 2. *Consistent Comparison Matrix.* *If the pairwise-comparison matrix* $\mathbf{P} = [\mathbf{P}(i,j)\,|1 \leq i,j \leq M]$ *is a positive reciprocal matrix, it is consistent if and only if the following relationship holds.*

$$\mathbf{P}(i,k) \cdot \mathbf{P}(k,j) = \mathbf{P}(i,j), \; 1 \leq i,j \text{ and } k \leq M. \tag{6}$$

A comparison matrix $\mathbf{P}$ is 'perfectly consistent', if $\mathbf{P}$ satisfies the $C.R. = 0$. A comparison matrix $\mathbf{P}$ is 'near consistent', if the consistent ratio $0 \leq C.R. \leq 0.1$. The ratio $C.R. = \frac{C.I.}{R.I.}$, $R.I.$ is a random index whose value depends on M and $C.I. = \frac{\lambda_{\max}-M}{M-1}$, in which $\lambda_{\max}$ is the maximum eigenvalue of the matrix. If a comparison matrix is consistent (or near), the principle eigenvector of the matrix is the consistent low-rank representation of all the pairwise comparisons [15]. The experiments will validate the consistency of the constructed comparison matrix.

Due to the principal eigenvector of a consistent comparison matrix $\mathbf{P}$ is a necessary representation of the priorities derived from the pairwise comparisons, we can calculate the evaluations of clusterings through the eigendecomposition of the comparison matrix. The elements of the obtained principal eigenvector represent the significance of the corresponding clustering results, which are consistent to the pairwise comparisons. For the $M \times M$ pairwise comparison matrix $\mathbf{P}_q^l$ of the lth quality measure, we normalize the element sum of the principle eigenvector $\mathbf{q}^l$ to one and obtain the quality weights of M clustering results.

$$\mathbf{P}_q^l \cdot \mathbf{q}^l = \lambda_{\max} \cdot \mathbf{q}^l, \ \mathbf{q}^l = \{q_{C_1}^l, \cdots, q_{C_M}^l\} \text{ and } \sum_{i=1}^{M} q_{C_i}^l = 1 \qquad (7)$$

For multiple L quality measures, the principle eigenvectors of L comparison matrices lead to L groups of quality weights $\{\mathbf{q}^1, ..., \mathbf{q}^L\}$ as the overall quality evaluation of the clustering results. In a similar way, we can calculate the diversity weights of clustering results $\mathbf{d}^t = \{d_{C_1}^1, \cdots, d_{C_M}^T\}$ through the eigendecomposition of comparison matrices of diversity measures $\mathbf{P}_d^t, 1 \leq t \leq T$.

Besides constructing the comparison matrices to compute the weights of clustering results $q_{C_i}^l$ and $d_{C_i}^t$, we should also construct comparison matrices to calculate the significance weights of evaluation measures, i.e. wq_l, wd_t. In this paper, we adopt four internal indexes as the quality measures ($L = 4$) and three external indexes as the diversity measures ($T = 3$). The internal indexes include Calinski Harabasz index (CHI) [3], Davies-Bouldin index (DBI) [5], Compactness (CP) and Separation (SP). The external indexes include Cluster Accuracy (CA), Adjusted Rand index (ARI) and Normalized Mutual Information (NMI). Referring to [14], we can construct a 4×4 comparison matrix $\mathbf{P}_{eq}$ for quality measures and a 3×3 comparison matrix $\mathbf{P}_{ed}$ for diversity measures.

$$\mathbf{P}_{eq} = \begin{pmatrix} & \text{DB} & \text{CH} & \text{CP} & \text{SP} \\ \text{DB} & 1 & 3 & 8 & 9 \\ \text{CH} & 1/3 & 1 & 7 & 8 \\ \text{CP} & 1/8 & 1/7 & 1 & 3 \\ \text{SP} & 1/9 & 1/8 & 1/3 & 1 \end{pmatrix}, \ \mathbf{P}_{ed} = \begin{pmatrix} & \text{CA} & \text{NMI} & \text{ARI} \\ \text{CA} & 1 & 2 & 3 \\ \text{NMI} & 1/2 & 1 & 2 \\ \text{ARI} & 1/3 & 1/2 & 1 \end{pmatrix} \qquad (8)$$

Similar to the calculation of weights of clusterings, the significance weights of evaluation measures are computed through eigendecomposition of $\mathbf{P}_{eq}$ and $\mathbf{P}_{ed}$.

$$\mathbf{P}_{eq} \cdot \mathbf{eq} = \lambda_{\max} \cdot \mathbf{eq}, \ \mathbf{P}_{ed} \cdot \mathbf{ed} = \lambda_{\max} \cdot \mathbf{ed} \qquad (9)$$

Clustering Ensemble Selection with Analytic Hierarchy Process 45

Algorithm 1. Clustering Ensemble Selection with AHP (AHPCES)

Input: M base clustering results $\mathbf{C} = \{C_1, C_2, \cdots, C_M\}$;

1: Construct $\mathbf{P}_{eq}$, $\mathbf{P}_{ed}$ and compute $\mathbf{eq} = \{wq_1, \cdots, wq_L\}$, $\mathbf{ed} = \{wd_1, \cdots, wd_T\}$;
2: **for** $l = 1$ to L **do**
3:     Construct $\mathbf{P}_q^l$ and compute $\mathbf{q}^l = \{q_{C_1}^l, \cdots, q_{C_M}^l\}$;
4: **end for**
5: **for** $t = 1$ to T **do**
6:     Construct $\mathbf{P}_d^t$ and compute $\mathbf{d}^t = \{d_{C_1}^t, \cdots, d_{C_M}^t\}$;
7: **end for**
8: Construct $\mathbf{Q} = \{\mathbf{q}^1, ..., \mathbf{q}^L\}$ and $\mathbf{D} = \{\mathbf{d}^1, ..., \mathbf{d}^T\}$;
9: Compute $\mathbf{Q} \cdot \mathbf{eq} = \{q_{C_1}, q_{C_2}, ..., q_{C_M}\}$ and $\mathbf{D} \cdot \mathbf{ed} = \{d_{C_1}, d_{C_2}, ..., d_{C_M}\}$;
10: Compute the significance of clustering results $sig(C_i) = \lambda_q \cdot q_{C_i} + \lambda_d \cdot d_{C_i}, 1 \le i \le M$;

11: Rank the clustering results according to their significances.

Table 1. Description of Data Sets

Data sets	Instance	Class	Sources	Data sets	Instance	Class	Sources
DS1(S1)	5000	15	[7]	DS7(D31)	3100	31	[1]
DS2(Jain)	373	2	[11]	DS8(Heart)	270	2	[1]
DS3(Flame)	240	2	[8]	DS9(Wine)	178	3	[1]
DS4(Spiral)	312	3	[4]	DS10(Ecoli)	336	8	[1]
DS5(Pathbased)	300	3	[4]	DS11(Australian Credit Approval)	690	2	[1]
DS6(Aggregation)	788	7	[9]				

where $\mathbf{eq} = \{wq_1, \cdots, wq_L\}$, $\sum_{l=1}^{L} wq_l = 1$ and $\mathbf{ed} = \{wd_1, \cdots, wd_T\}$, $\sum_{t=1}^{T} wd_t = 1$. The normalized principal eigenvectors $\mathbf{eq}$ and $\mathbf{ed}$ provide the comparative significance weights of the evaluation measures in quality and diversity respectively.

As introduced above, synthesizing the weights of clustering results and evaluation measures as shown in Formulas (1) and (2), we can quantify the overall evaluation of clustering results under multiple measures and thereby select the significant clusterings for ensemble. The process of clustering ensemble selection based on AHP is presented in Algorithm 2.

3 Experimental Results

We implement three experiments to validate AHPCES. In these experiments, we adopt kmeans to generate 50 base clusterings, set the selection ratio ranges from 20% to 60%, use LinkCluE [10] as the consensus function and adopt three external criteria (CA, ARI, NMI) and three internal criteria (SC, DI, CHI) to evaluate the clusterings, high evaluation values indicate the high performances of the clusterings. All the experiments are performed on 11 data sets. The detailed descriptions of the data sets are shown in Table 1.

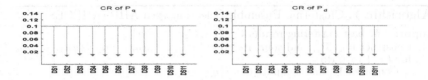

Fig. 1. Consistency ratios of comparison matrices.

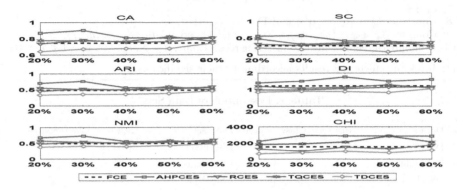

Fig. 2. Comparison of different clustering selection strategies.

3.1 Test of Comparison Matrix Consistency

In the first experiment, in order to demonstrate the consistency of the constructed pairwise comparison matrices of clustering quality and diversity (see Sect. 2), we compute the consistency ratio $C.R.$ of all the pairwise comparison matrices for the base clusterings on each data set.

Figure 1 shows the average consistency ratio of the quality and diversity comparison matrices $C.R. \leq 0.1$ (namely near consistent), which indicates that the principal eigenvectors of comparison matrices can be used to quantify the significance of base clusterings in quality and diversity.

3.2 Test of AHP-based Clustering Selection

In the second experiment, we implement two tests to verify the AHPCES. In the first test, we compare AHPCES with four clustering selection strategies, which include Full Clustering Ensemble (FCE), Random Clustering Ensemble Selection (RCES), Top-k Quality Clustering Ensemble Selection (TQCES) and Top-k Diversity Clustering Ensemble Selection (TDCES).

Figure 2 shows the average evaluations on all the data sets against the selection ratios ranging from 20% to 60%. We can find that, under the same selection proportions, AHPCES achieves the most precise ensemble results than the other selection strategies, which means the AHPCES is more effective to select the significant base clusterings for ensemble.

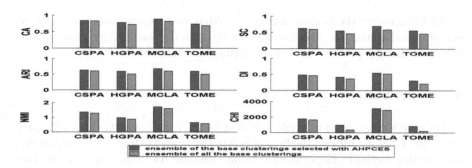

Fig. 3. Comparison of ensemble with/without AHPCES on four consensus functions.

Table 2. Comparison of elegant clustering ensemble selection methods

Criterion	Method			
	AHPCES	CAS	ACES	SELSCE
CA	0.8904(30%)	0.6607(50%)	0.7871(30%)	0.7628(50%)
ARI	0.7701(30%)	0.3588(60%)	0.5845(30%)	0.5421(50%)
NMI	0.7519(30%)	0.4238(60%)	0.5920(30%)	0.5647(50%)
SC	0.5337(30%)	0.3382(60%)	0.4049(30%)	0.3615(50%)
DI	1.6723(50%)	0.9082(20%)	1.2681(20%)	1.2538(30%)
CHI	2933(40%)	1890(40%)	1935(20%)	1341(50%)

In the second test, we adopt four consensus functions to ensemble the clusterings selected by AHPCES and the full clusterings without selection. The consensus functions include CSPA, HGPA, MCLA [16] and TOME [19]. With different consensus functions, Fig. 3 shows the comparison between the ensemble results with AHPCES and without selection. We can find that, for all the consensus functions, the AHPCES can improve the full ensemble results, which validates the robustness of the AHP strategy for base clustering selection.

3.3 Overall Evaluation

In the final experiment, we expect to overall evaluate the proposed AHPCES method through comparing with three elegant clustering ensemble selection methods. The methods for comparison include Cluster and Selection algorithm (CAS) [6], Adaptive Cluster Ensemble Selection algorithm (ACES) [2] and Selective Spectral Clustering Ensemble algorithm (SELSCE) [12]. Because of the limitation of paper length, we just present the average evaluations generated by different selection strategies on all the data sets.

Table 2 presents the comparison between AHPCES and other clustering ensemble selection methods. We show the max average value evaluated by each criterion and attach the corresponding selected proportion. It is obvious that

AHPCES achieves the best performances. Abundant experiments indicate that our proposed method is effective to select the qualified and diverse base clusterings, and thereby produce precise clustering ensemble results.

4 Conclusions

we propose a clustering ensemble selection method with analytic hierarchy process (AHPCES) to address the limitations of the most existing clustering ensemble selection methods. Experimental results validate AHPCES can generate reasonable and consistent evaluations of base clusterings for selective ensemble. Our future work will focus on the theoretical analysis of the consistency of pairwise comparison matrices and try to improve the construction of the comparison matrices of evaluations indexes.

Acknowledgment. This work was supported by National Natural Science Foundation of China (Nos. 61976134, 61991410, 61991415) and Open Project Foundation of Intelligent Information Processing Key Laboratory of Shanxi Province (No. CICIP2018001).

References

1. Asuncion, A., Newman, D.: UCI machine learning repository (2007)
2. Azimi, J., Fern, X.: Adaptive cluster ensemble selection. In: Twenty-First International Joint Conference on Artificial Intelligence, **9**, pp. 992–997 (2009)
3. Caliński, T., Harabasz, J.: A dendrite method for cluster analysis. Commun. Stat. Theory Methods **3**(1), 1–27 (1974)
4. Chang, H., Yeung, D.Y.: Robust path-based spectral clustering. Pattern Recogn. **41**(1), 191–203 (2008)
5. Davies, D.L., Bouldin, D.W.: A cluster separation measure. IEEE Trans. Pattern Anal. Mach. Intell. **2**, 224–227 (1979)
6. Fern, X.Z., Lin, W.: Cluster ensemble selection. Stat. Anal. Data Min. ASA Data Sci. J. **1**(3), 128–141 (2008)
7. Fränti, P., Virmajoki, O.: Iterative shrinking method for clustering problems. Pattern Recogn. **39**(5), 761–775 (2006)
8. Fu, L., Medico, E.: Flame, a novel fuzzy clustering method for the analysis of dna microarray data. BMC Bioinform. **8**(1), 3 (2007)
9. Gionis, A., Mannila, H., Tsaparas, P.: Clustering aggregation. ACM Trans. Knowl. Discov. from Data (TKDD) **1**(1), 4 (2007)
10. Iam-on, N., Garrett, S., et al.: Linkclue: a matlab package for link-based cluster ensembles. J. Stat. Softw. **36**(9), 1–36 (2010)
11. Jain, A.K., Law, M.H.C.: Data clustering: a user's dilemma. In: Pal, S.K., Bandyopadhyay, S., Biswas, S. (eds.) PReMI 2005. LNCS, vol. 3776, pp. 1–10. Springer, Heidelberg (2005). https://doi.org/10.1007/11590316_1
12. Jia, J., Xiao, X., Liu, B., Jiao, L.: Bagging-based spectral clustering ensemble selection. Pattern Recogn. Lett. **32**(10), 1456–1467 (2011)
13. Jie, Z., Zhihui, L., Duoqian, M., Can, G., Xiaodong, Y.: Multigranulation rough-fuzzy clustering based on shadowed sets. Inf. Sci. **507**, 553–573 (2018)

14. Liu, Y., Li, Z., Xiong, H., Gao, X., Wu, J., Wu, S.: Understanding and enhancement of internal clustering validation measures. IEEE Trans. Cybern. **43**(3), 982–994 (2013)
15. Saaty, T.L.: Decision-making with the ahp: why is the principal eigenvector necessary. Eur. J. Oper. Res. **145**(1), 85–91 (2003)
16. Strehl, A., Ghosh, J.: Cluster ensembles-a knowledge reuse framework for combining multiple partitions. J. Mach. Learn. Res. **3**(Dec), 583–617 (2002)
17. Yue, X., Miao, D., Cao, L., Wu, Q., Chen, Y.: An efficient color quantization based on generic roughness measure. Pattern Recogn. **47**(4), 1777–1789 (2014)
18. Zhao, X., Liang, J., Dang, C.: Clustering ensemble selection for categorical data based on internal validity indices. Pattern Recogn. **69**, 150–168 (2017)
19. Zhong, C., Yue, X., Zhang, Z., Lei, J.: A clustering ensemble: two-level-refined co-association matrix with path-based transformation. Pattern Recogn. **48**(8), 2699–2709 (2015)

Deep Learning for In-Vehicle Intrusion Detection System

Elies Gherbi[1,2(✉)], Blaise Hanczar[2], Jean-Christophe Janodet[2],
and Witold Klaudel[1]

[1] Institute of research systemX, 91120 Palaiseau, France
elies.gherbi@systemX.fr, {elies.gherbi,witold.klaudel}@irt-systemX.fr
[2] IBISC, Univ Evry, Université Paris-Saclay, Saint-Aubin, France
{blaise.hanczar,jeanchristophe.janodet}@univ-evry.fr

Abstract. Modern and future vehicles are complex cyber-physical systems. The connection to their outside environment raises many security problems that impact our safety directly. In this work, we propose a Deep CAN intrusion detection system framework. We introduce a multivariate time series representation for asynchronous CAN data which enhances the temporal modelling of deep learning architectures for anomaly detection. We study different deep learning tasks (supervised/unsupervised) and compare several architectures, in order to design an in-vehicle intrusion detection system that fits in-vehicle computational constraints. We conduct experiments with many types of attacks on an in-vehicle CAN using SynCAn Dataset.

Keywords: Intrusion detection system · In-vehicle security · Deep learning · Anomaly detection · Time series

1 Introduction

Future applications like autonomous transportation require various technologies that allow the vehicles to interact with other vehicles (VANETs), pedestrians and road infrastructure. These controllers make the vehicles more and more connected with the external world, which allow new functionalities but also dramatically increase the security risk.

In this work, we focus on the CAN bus, which is *de facto* standard for in-vehicle communication. In-vehicle networks technologies must ensure a set of requirements, some of which are time-critical and safety-related. CAN protocol uses broadcast communication techniques. Each node in the network can send and receive a packet to/from the bus [1]. CAN bus contains several vulnerabilities. It does not include the different security criteria in its design. It lacks security facilities like message authentication, that prevents an unauthorized node from joining the communication and broadcast malicious messages to other nodes. It also lacks encryption because it would make overhead for real-time communication. These weaknesses of the protocol are as many possibilities left to hackers to attack, as shown in the cyber-security literature [1,14]. Several attacks scenarios have been demonstrated on vehicles. *E.g.*, [12] has performed four different tests on the control window lift, warning light, airbag control system and central gateway.

We focus on anomaly detection based intrusion detection using the advances in deep-learning architectures to handle the CAN data structure. To do so, we define three levels for the in-vehicle IDS framework: 1) CAN data level, 2) sequence modelling level and 3) detection level.

This research aims to propose a general in-vehicle IDS using deep learning; we propose a representation for CAN data, and experiments several deep learning architectures for sequence modelling. We finally get an anomaly detection IDS that meets both the needs and the constraints of in-vehicles systems.

2 Background and Related Works

CAN Data. Any CAN message is composed of several fields: an ID and a 64-bit payload. The ID is unique and defines the content (set of signals encoded in a range of several bits) and the priority of the message [6]. A timestamp is added whenever the message is captured. From those characteristics, many representation and feature can be derived as time interval, sequence, time-frequency. Notice that the payload signals are encoded, so it is hard to obtain the signals values without the constructor specifications. CAN Intrusion Detection Systems generally intervene at two levels: either the flow level or the payload level. In flow-based approaches, a flow is a group of packets sharing common properties during a specific period. In payload-based approaches, the payload represents the information carried by the packet. This information is exchanged between the ECUs, and their interpretation reflects the behaviour of the vehicle.Notice that some attacks may highly impact the communication flow, like flooding attack, and will be more easily detected at the flow level. On the other hand, other types of attacks are not visible in the communication flow and be detected only at the payload level. To the best of our knowledge, the actual IDS are either flow based or payload based, while our proposition is based on both.

CAN Intrusion Detection System. We here focus on anomaly-based approaches only. The method starts by defining a model (*profile*) that specifies the actual normal behaviour of the system. Any behaviour that does not conform to the normal profile is considered as an anomaly. The anomaly-based IDS have many advantages: there is no need to maintain a database of signatures, and they can detect unknown attacks since at least from a theoretical standpoint, each attack compromises the normal behaviour of a system.

With the advances of deep learning for time series, many deep learning architectures have been used to solve sequential modelling problems, and anomaly detection based CAN IDS is one of them. In [19], the authors propose a deep convolutional network classifier IDS, a supervised approach designed to learn about traffic patterns and detect different malicious behaviours. They reduce the unnecessary complexity in the architecture of inception-resnet. They have tested their model on different types of attacks using bit-level CAN dataset where each input consists in 29 sequential CAN IDS. In [8], the authors tackle a large dataset with an extensive type of attacks (SynCAN dataset). They propose a deep learning architecture that handles the structure of CAN data; It is composed of independent recurrent neural networks, one for each ID in the input. The goal of those separated LSTM is to learn about the state of each ID. The whole state of the network is represented by a joint vector of the outputs of all separated LSTM. The second part of the architecture takes the joint latent vector as an input for an autoencoder (fully connected network) that enables unsupervised learning; The task of the autoencoder is to reconstruct the signals for each possible input message based on the joint vector. The attack detection occurs by observing the deviation between the signal value of a message at the current time step with its reconstruction. [16] proposes an IDS by analyzing bit-level CAN message, using LSTM to predict the next message based on the history size of 10 messages; If the distance between the predicted message and the actual message is bigger than a threshold, then the message is an anomaly.

We note that, in the literature, many dimensions can be considered to design the CAN IDS. The used data highly impacts the type of detectable attacks, as well as the design of the model that must learn about a broad range of situations to ensure that the model encompasses the exhaustive space of normality, and decreases the false positive rate. There is also another dimension, which is the In-Vehicle context, where the memory and computation power is limited, so the practical feasibility of any given CAN IDS needs to be evaluated in front of the constraints of the in-vehicle context.

3   In-Vehicle Intrusion Detection System

We propose a new IDS for vehicle described through 3 levels: 1) the CAN data level resumed in a feature matrix, 2) the time sequence modelling level and 3) the anomaly detection level. Notice that the training and update of the models are performed offline and outside from the vehicle; Only the exploitation of the models is embedded in the vehicle, which performs inference and detection.

3.1   Feature Matrix Construction

The first step is to transcript the flow of CAN messages, sent separately and asynchronously at irregular moments, into a Multirate Multivariate times series (MMTS) which contains both payload and flow information. The CAN data is composed of different messages broadcasted from different ECUs. The stream S of messages is represented by a sequence of N messages $S = \{V_1, ..., V_N\}$. We denote $V_i = \{id_i, P_i, t_i\}$ the i-th message captured by the IDS. $id_i \in \{1, ..., m\}$ is the ID of the ECU that sent the message, m is the number of ECU, P_i is the payload contained in the message and $t_i \in [0, t_N]$ is the time of reception. The payload P_i contains a vector of size n_{id} containing the signal sent from ECU id. The number of variables n_{id} extracted from each payload depends on the ECU.

Although deep learning models can be trained with this type of sequences, this representation is clearly not optimal for the learning of neural networks. The two main problems of this representation is that the payload variables from the same ECU are not split around the sequence and the time interval between two messages is not constant.

We change the messages flow representation S into a multivariate time series representation T. The time range of the messages flow is discretized into K time stamps of constant time Δ. The time series $T = \{t_1, ..., t_K\}$ is a series of time points, each time point represents the set of messages received during the corresponding time stamp $t_k = \{V_t | t \in [(k-1)\Delta, k\Delta[\}$. This time series is then represented by a matrix $M_{\sum_{id=1}^{m}(n_{id}+1) \times K}$ where each column represents a time point and the rows represent the variables contained in the payloads of all ECU. For each time point we could have received several messages from the same ECU and have different values for the same variables; In these cases we keep the last received values since we want to take our decision on the most recent available information. We also add to this matrix a row for each ECU indicating the number of messages received from this ECU. This representation regroups both payload and flow features, which enables the model to detect both attacks on payload and flow in the in-vehicle communication system.

3.2   CAN Sequence Modelling

Many DNNs architectures are used for time series modelling tasks. In this work, we review 4 types of sequence modelling architectures: FCN, CNN, LSTM and TCN. We compare their ability to learn the hierarchical representation vector of the CAN matrix to perform anomaly detection. This vector is either given by the bottleneck of the autoencoders in the unsupervised task, or the final layer of the architectures in the supervised task.

Fully-Connected Network (FCN): FCN is a standard architecture for deep learning models [2]. FCN is a generic architecture usable for any type of data. All the neurons in layer l_i receive the signal from every neuron in the layer l_{i-1} and send their output to every neurons of the layer l_{i+1} with $i \in [1, L]$ (L number of layers in the architecture). The elements of the time series are treated independently from each other, thus the temporal dimension of the data is ignored with this architecture.

Recurrent Neural Network (LSTM): Recurrent neural networks are explicitly devoted to sequence modelling [9]. They avoid the long-term dependency vanishing problem using cells state that is used as an internal memory. At each time, the network learn which information to add, to forget and to update into the cells state. Based on the cells state, inputs, previous hidden state, the LSTM learn a vector representation (hidden state) of the time series a the current time.

1D Convolutional Neural Network (CNN): In the context of time series, convolution is a sliding filter over the time series. The time series exhibits only one dimension. Thus this convolution will result in a moving average with a sliding window. Therefore, applying several filters results in learning several discriminative features which are useful for sequence modelling. Besides, the same convolution is used to find the result for all timestamps $t \in [1, T]$ (weight sharing). This is a valuable property, as it enables the model to learn filters that are invariant across the time dimension. 1D CNN for time series is characterized with a causal convolution; It means that the output at time t is convolved only with elements from time t or earlier in the previous layers. This characteristics ensures that the sequence input must have a one-to-one causal relationship in chronological order. The result of convolution can be considered as a time series whose dimension is equal to the number of these filters used. 1D CNN has another layer with pooling operation, which achieves dimension reduction of feature maps while preserving most information.

Temporal Convolution Network (TCN): TCN with dilated convolution is designed to combine simplicity and very long term memory [3]. There are many differences with 1D CNN described above. In addition to the causal convolution, the architecture can take a sequence of any length and map it to an output sequence with the same length. To achieve this, zero padding of length (kernel size - 1) is added. Moreover, the TCN architecture can look very far into the past using a combination of residual layers and dilated convolution. The dilated convolution [15] enables an exponentially sizeable receptive field using dilation factor d and the filter size k. When using dilated convolutions, we increase d exponentially with the depth of the network, allowing a very large history using deep networks.

3.3   Anomaly Detection

Unsupervised IDS. In this work, the autoencoder aims to reconstruct the input sequence (a multivariate time series). Formally, given a sequence $T = (t_1, ..., t_K)$ where $T_i \in \mathbb{R}^n$ and n is the number of variables, the autoencoder aims at predicting $\hat{T} = (\hat{t}_1, ..., \hat{t}_K)$ at each time (sequence-to-sequence problem). The autoencoder that performs a nonlinear mapping from the current state to its identity, is decomposed into two parts: the encoder and the decoder. The encoder projects the temporal pattern dependencies and trends of the time series in latent space h. The latent vector is given by $h^i = f(T.W^i + b^i)$, where W^i and b^i respectively denote the weight matrix and bias up to the bottleneck i-th layer. The decoder, considered as the transposed network of the encoder, uses the information of latent space h to reconstruct the input sequence: $\hat{T} = f(h^i.W_d^i + b_d)$. The mean square loss error (MSE) is used to perform an end-to-end learning objective: $L(T, \hat{T}) = \frac{1}{K} \Sigma_i^n (t_i - \hat{t}_i)^2$. At the inference phase, the MSE is used as an anomaly score. The idea is that the autoencoder learnt to reconstruct only the normal data and will obtain a high MSE on the anomaly.

Supervised IDS. Supervised IDS use a FCN to make anomaly prediction from the vector representation of the time series learnt from sequence modeling level. In this case, we suppose that the training dataset contains labelled attack examples and these attacks form an homogeneous class. These requirements generally hold when we construct a model that aims to detect well-known types of attack. Formally, we assume that there are 2 classes: Normal (0) and Anomaly (1). The learning set is a collection of pairs $\{(T_1, Y_1), ..., (T_K, Y_K)\}$ where T_i is a multivariate sequence and $Y_i \in \{0, 1\}$ is the corresponding label. The classifier training is performed by minimization of the cross entropy between the true class and predicted class. Notice that the classes are highly unbalanced, the anomaly is much smaller than the normal class, the classes are therefore weighted in the cross entropy in function on their prior. At the inference phase, the MLP returns the probability of anomaly.

4 Experiments and Results

4.1 SynCAN Dataset

SynCAN is a synthetic dataset proposed in [8]. The data consists of 10 different message IDs. We evaluate our model on the following types of attack: *Plateau* (a signal is overwritten to a constant value), *Continuous* (a signal is overwritten so that it slowly drifts away), *Playback* (a signal value is overwritten over a period of time with a recorded time series), *Suppress* (the attacker prevents an ECU from sending messages), and *Flooding* (the attacker sends messages of a particular ID with high frequency to the CAN bus).

We set five seconds as an estimated time-frame for the intrusion detection system to monitor the vehicle. Thus, the sampling window is fixed to $\Delta = 50ms$, and each sequence is composed of $K = 100$ consecutive elements. From a general standpoint, K and Δ are hyperparameters which depend on the domain expert requirement (the maximum memory size, forensic analysis and safety protocol to enable the prevention actions). The feature matrix size is (100*30) where 30 is the sum of 20 signal features and 10 occurrence features. We scale the data between [0, 1] using min-max normalization.

A sequence is labelled normal if all elements in the sequence are normal. If a sequence contains at least one anomaly, the sequence is considered as an anomaly. SynCAN database is a collection of $\sim 2'000'000$ normal sequences. 70% of them are used for training and 10% for validation. The last 20% are mixed with anomalous sequences to build the test data. We have 5 test databases, one per attack, made of 70% normal examples and 30% anomalous examples.

4.2 Results

We use 4 different architectures (FCN, CNN, TCN, LSTM) with 2 experiment settings: unsupervised anomaly detection and supervised anomaly detection. We have trained the models on 500 epochs, with a batch size 100. We used ADAM as the optimizer for the gradient descent with learning rate decay.[1]

In Table 1, we show the metrics on the unsupervised task using autoencoders with different architectures. All architectures show excellent performances for all types of attack. TCN is slightly better on most attack cases and comparable with LSTM on *Plateau* attack. Notice that on the *Suppress* attack, the models perform worse than on the other attacks, while the CNN collapses with a lot of false positive. It shows that *Suppress* attack is unobtrusive. Moreover, in representation matrix M, there is no explicit mention to the missing values. Nevertheless, TCN and LSTM still have good results, thus can implicitly retrieve the information in the learning stage from the representation matrix.

Table 1. Autoencoder-based architectures results

	TCN			LSTM			CNN			FCN		
	Precis.	Recall	F1	Precis.	Recall	F1	Precis.	Recall	F1	Precis.	Recall	F1
Continues	**0.997**	**0.991**	**0.994**	0.991	0.988	0.990	0.996	0.988	0.992	0.993	0.978	0.985
Plateau	0.995	0.984	0.990	**0.996**	**0.985**	**0.991**	0.993	0.979	0.986	0.990	0.981	0.987
Suppress	**0.986**	**0.957**	**0.971**	0.984	0.954	0.969	0.951	0.554	0.700	0.951	0.862	0.904
Flooding	0.995	0.986	0.991	0.996	0.988	0.991	**0.996**	**0.989**	**0.992**	0.996	0.988	0.991
Playback	**0.996**	**0.989**	**0.992**	0.996	0.986	0.991	0.994	0.989	0.991	0.995	0.988	0.991

In Table 2, we show the experiments on the supervised task (Binary classifier). TCN is still slightly better than the others, and close to the CNN. Notice that for LSTM architecture, the results are not as good as in unsupervised setting. Indeed, we have reduced the rate of normal data in the training set in order to rebalance the data and help the model not to learn from the normal features only. LSTMs are more data-hungry than CNN and TCN. It shows that TCN needs less data than LSTM for CAN data modelling.

In Table 3, we conduct the same experiment but we eliminate the occurrence features from representation matrix M. We notice for the *Flooding* attack, the performances of all the models decreases dramatically. Indeed this attack impacts the flow of the CAN data, and this information is encoded through the occurrences in the matrix. We also observe that the performances are slightly worse on the *Playback* and *Plateau* attacks. Therefore, payload-based attacks are also easier to detect when the occurrence features are present in the matrix. Hence full matrix, with both signal features and occurrence features, contributes to detect both payload and flow-based attacks.

Finally, in Table 4, we have compared the models in terms of training time and size of parameters. The latter reflects the memory needed by the IDS to work. Remind that the IDS are embedded in vehicle where memory resources is strongly limited. TCN is good both in terms of training time and model size. TCN benefits from filters shared weight, so it dramatically reduces the number of parameters. When the size of the input data is increasing, the number of

---

[1] See https://github.com/anonymeEG/Deep-Learning-4-IDS for implementation.

Table 2. Classification using the occurrence matrix representation

	TCN			CNN			LSTM			FCN		
	Precis.	Recall	F1	Precis.	Recall	F1	Precis.	Recall	F1	Precis.	Recall	F1
Continues	**0.996**	**0.986**	0.990	0.995	0.991	0.995	0.959	0.933	0.948	0.89	1.00	0.94
Plateau	**0.997**	**0.998**	0.997	0.991	0.953	0.971	0.984	0.953	0.968	0.87	1.00	0.93
Suppress	**0.999**	**0.999**	**0.999**	0.998	0.998	0.999	0.992	0.999	0.995	0.86	1.00	0.92
Flooding	**0.999**	**0.999**	**0.999**	0.999	0.999	0.999	0.999	0.999	0.999	0.87	1.00	0.93
Playback	**0.997**	0.988	0.992	0.997	0.995	**0.995**	0.994	0.989	0.991	0.89	1.00	0.94

Table 3. Classification using the standard sampling without occurrence features

	TCN			CNN			LSTM		
	Precision	Recall	F1	Precision	Recall	F1	Precision	Recall	F1
Continues	0.995	0.994	**0.994**	0.983	0.990	0.986	0.945	0.957	0.950
Plateau	0.973	0.978	0.975	0.995	0.998	**0.996**	0.959	0.984	0.971
Suppress	0.986	0.996	0.990	0.990	0.971	0.980	0.939	0.969	0.953
Flooding	0.985	0.978	0.981	0.971	0.915	0.928	0.927	0.972	0.913
Playback	0.992	**0.998**	0.994	0.992	0.772	0.868	0.935	0.924	0.929

Table 4. Models characteristics vs. computational resources

Models	Training time	Number of parameters	Model size (32-bits floats)
FCN	8022 s	75238	0,3 MB
CNN	10011 s	9518	0.03 MB
TCN	7969 s	3822	0.01 MB
LSTM	92714 s	2920	0.01 MB

parameters does not explode exponentially. Unlike LSTM, TCN convolutions can be done in parallel since the same filter is used in the layer. Therefore, in both training and inference phase, even though the series is long, it can be processed as a whole, whereas with LSTM, they must be processed sequentially.

5 Conclusion

In this paper, we introduce a novel in-vehicle intrusion detection system based on a large series of experiments which validate the different levels of the system: 1) At the data level, we use a representation matrix to structure the CAN data information that groups both flow and payload information. 2) At the sequence modelling level, we use a TCN architecture, since we have shown that it performs well with respect to the detection metrics and computational resources consumption. 3) At the detection level, we jointly use a classifier and an autoencoder, so the IDS can deal with both known and unknown attacks. Notice that our results were established by using the SynCAN Dataset, which is the only available public dataset as far as we know.

The in-vehicle system has many components, and we have implicitly assumed that the monitoring of the data was centralized. Nonetheless, in new secured in-vehicle architectures, the parts of the system are isolated, so the CAN data topology changes, and we need to think about a distributed framework for IDS. Another important issue concerns the compression of deep learning models to better fit the embedded capacity of the in-vehicle system.

References

1. Avatefipour, O., Malik, H.: State-of-the-art survey on in-vehicle network communication (can-bus) security and vulnerabilities. CoRR (2018)
2. Bagnall, A.J., Bostrom, A., Large, J., Lines, J.: The great time series classification bake off: an experimental evaluation of recently proposed algorithms. extended version. CoRR abs/1602.01711 (2016)
3. Bai, S., Kolter, J.Z., Koltun, V.: An empirical evaluation of generic convolutional and recurrent networks for sequence modeling. CoRR abs/1803.01271 (2018)
4. Dupont, G., den Hartog, J., Etalle, S., Lekidis, A.: Network intrusion detection systems for in-vehicle network - technical report. CoRR (2019)
5. Seo, E., Song, H.M., Kim, H.K.: Gids: gan based intrusion detection system for in-vehicle network. In: 2018 16th (PST) (2018)
6. Farsi, M., Ratcliff, K., Barbosa, M.: An overview of controller area network. Comput. Control Eng. J. 10(3), 113–120 (1999)
7. Martinelli, F., Mercaldo, F., Nardone, V., Santone, A.: Car hacking identification through fuzzy logic algorithms. In: 2017 (FUZZ-IEEE), pp. 1–7 (2017)
8. Hanselmann, M., Strauss, T., Dormann, K., Ulmer, H.: An unsupervised intrusion detection system for high dimensional CAN bus data. CoRR (2019)
9. Hochreiter, S., Schmidhuber, J.: Long short-term memory. Neural Comput. 9(8), 1735–1780 (1997)
10. Hoppe, T., Kiltz, S., Dittmann, J.: Security threats to automotive CAN networks - practical examples and selected short-term countermeasures. Reliab. Eng. Syst. Saf. 96(1), 11–25 (2011)
11. Kang, M.J., Kang, J.W.: Intrusion detection system using deep neural network for in-vehicle network security. PLoS ONE 11, 1–17 (2016)
12. Koscher, K., et al.: Experimental security analysis of a modern automobile. In: 31st IEEE S&P (2010)
13. Moore, M.R., Bridges, R.A., Combs, F.L., Starr, M.S., Prowell, S.J.: A data-driven approach to in-vehicle intrusion detection. In: CISRC '2017 (2017)
14. Nilsson, D.K., Larson, U., Picasso, F., Jonsson, E.: A first simulation of attacks in the automotive network communications protocol flexray. In: CI- SIS'2008 (2008)
15. Oord, V., et al.: A generative model for raw audio (2016)
16. Pawelec, K., Bridges, R.A., Combs, F.L.: Towards a CAN IDS based on a neural-network data field predictor. CoRR (2018)
17. Song, H.M., Woo, J., Kim, H.K.: In-vehicle network intrusion detection using deep convolutional neural network. Veh. Commun. 21, 100198 (2020)
18. Young, C., Olufowobi, H., Bloom, G., Zambreno, J.: Automotive intrusion detection based on constant CAN message frequencies across vehicle driving modes. In: AutoSec (2019)
19. Song, H., Woo, J., Kang, H.: Automotive intrusion In-vehicle network, Controller area network (CAN), Intrusion detection, Convolutional neural network. VC (2020)

Efficient Binary Multi-view Subspace Learning for Instance-Level Image Retrieval

Zhijian Wu, Jun Li[✉], and Jianhua Xu

School of Computer Science and Technology, Nanjing Normal University,
Nanjing 210023, Jiangsu, China
{192235022,lijuncst,xujianhua}@njnu.edu.cn

Abstract. The existing hashing methods mainly handle either the feature based nearest-neighbour search or the category-level image retrieval, whereas a few efforts are devoted to instance retrieval problem. Besides, although multi-view hashing methods are capable of exploring the complementarity among multiple heterogeneous visual features, they heavily rely on massive labeled training data, and somewhat affects the real-world applications. In this paper, we propose a binary multi-view fusion framework for directly recovering a latent Hamming subspace from the multi-view features. More specifically, the multi-view subspace reconstruction and the binary quantization are integrated in a unified framework so as to minimize the discrepancy between the original multi-view high-dimensional Euclidean space and the resulting compact Hamming subspace. In addition, our method is amenable to efficient iterative optimization for learning a compact similarity-preserving binary code. The resulting binary codes demonstrate significant advantage in retrieval precision and computational efficiency at the cost of limited memory footprint. More importantly, our method is essentially an unsupervised learning scheme without any labeled data involved, and thus can be used in the cases when the supervised information is unavailable or insufficient. Experiments on public benchmark and large-scale datasets reveal that our method achieves competitive retrieval performance comparable to the state-of-the-art and has excellent scalability in large-scale scenario.

Keywords: Instance retrieval · Multi-view fusion · Multi-view subspace reconstruction · Binary quantization

1 Introduction

In recent years, Deep Convolutional Neural Network (DCNN) has demonstrated unrivalled superiority and achieved state-of-the-art performance in many

This work was supported by the Natural Science Foundation of China (NSFC) under Grants 61703096, 61273246 and the Natural Science Foundation of Jiangsu Province under Grant BK20170691.

H. Yang et al. (Eds.): ICONIP 2020, CCIS 1332, pp. 59–68, 2020.
https://doi.org/10.1007/978-3-030-63820-7_7

computer vision tasks [1,2]. In instance retrieval, the compact image features extracted from the top layer of DCNN network are considered as desirable alternative to the previous shallow hand-crafted model. Massive works in the literature take advantage of the off-the-shelf deep features generated from the activations of the upper layers of a pre-trained DCNN architecture [3,4]. In particular, massive efforts are devoted to exploring the intrinsic complementarity between the hand-crafted shallow features and the deep features for multiple feature fusion [5,6], since shallow hand-crafted features inherit certain desirable property from local invariant descriptors, and play a supplementary role in multi-view feature fusion.

Due to the rapid growth of image volume, fast retrieval in a large database has emerged as a necessary research topic [7]. The cost of finding the exact nearest neighbors is prohibitively high in the case that the target database is very large or that computing the distance between the query item and the database item is computationally expensive. Instead of exact exhaustive search, a practical and feasible strategy is to make use of the Approximate Nearest Neighbor (ANN) technique or hashing based method for accelerating the search and matching process [8]. Particularly, Hashing methods transform the high-dimensional features to a compact low-dimensional binary codes for efficient representations. Benefiting from the resulting binary codes, fast image search can be carried out via binary pattern matching or Hamming distance evaluation, which dramatically reduces the computational cost and further optimizes the efficiency of the search. To further improve retrieval performance, a variety of multi-view hashing methods have also emerged to model the correlation between multiple features in binary quantization [9,10].

As mentioned in [11], the vast majority of the deep hashing methods focus on category-level image retrieval, since the binary codes generated from high-level deep features severely suffers from the lossy encoding, and thus the discriminative power of visual representation with hashing codes fails to meet the demand of instance level image retrieval. Although multi-view hashing methods can well preserve the diverse characteristics of multi-view data, most of them are supervised methods that requires the training process with sufficient labeled data [11,12]. In practice, the existing instance-specific training data is either unavailable or insufficient for instance retrieval, making the supervised multi-view hashing methods heavily relying on the training data infeasible.

In this paper, we propose a novel unified binary multi-view subspace learning (BMSL) framework to project the original multi-view features into a common latent hamming space and generate a compact binary code. More specifically, the proposed method simultaneously minimizes the multi-view subspace reconstruction and binary quantization error by rotating the projection matrix while learning the subspace, so as to ensure that the projected subspace and the binary codes are both optimal due to the principle that rotation does not change the projection relationship. Since both multi-view reconstruction and binary quantization within our framework are built on efficient l_2 estimator, our method leads itself to fast iterative optimization. Besides, our method does not rely on labeled data and thus can be used as efficient unsupervised multi-view hashing in large-scale instance retrieval scenarios. To the best of our knowledge, this is the first attempt to address the unsupervised instance retrieval problem with a unified binary multi-view subspace learning framework.

The rest of this paper is organized as follows. We elaborate our method in details in Sect. 2. Next, we present the experimental evaluations in Sect. 3. Finally, our work is concluded and summarized in Sect. 4.

2   Our Binary Multi-view Subspace Learning Method

2.1   Formulation

There are two main modules in our framework: multi-view data fusion based on subspace learning and binary quantization built on rotation transformation. For the first component, given the original multi-view data $\{Z_v\}_{v=1}^m \in \mathbb{R}^{D_v \times n}$, we seek to uncover the underlying subspace $X \in \mathbb{R}^{d \times n}$ such that the original multi-view features can be recovered from this subspace via view-specific generation matrix $\{P_v\}_{v=1}^m \in \mathbb{R}^{D_v \times d}$. m is the number of data views while n is the number of images. D_v indicates the view-specific feature dimensionality while d is the dimension of the latent subspace. Mathematically, we have:

$$E_v = \sum_{v=1}^m \|Z_v - P_v X\|_F^2 \tag{1}$$

where E_v is denoted as the view-dependent reconstruction error.

In terms of the binary quantization, the encoding process can be represented as $B = sgn(X^T)$ where $B \in \{-1, 1\}^{n \times d}$. Thus, the resulting binary subspace B can be reconstructed with the quantization loss$\|B - X^T\|$, while $X^T = Z_v^T W$ where W is actually $(P_v^{-1})^T$. Rotating W with any orthogonal matrix $R \in \mathbb{R}^{d \times d}$, we have $\tilde{W} = WR$ with the original projection maintained. Thus, we can orthogonally transform the subspace representation X^T in such a way as to minimize the quantization loss.

$$Q_v = \|B - X^T R\|_F^2 \tag{2}$$

where Q_v is denoted as the binary quantization error.

Thus, in order to simultaneously minimize the multi-view reconstruction error and binary quantization loss, our method is formulated as follows:

$$\min_{P_v, X, B, R} \sum_{v=1}^m \|Z_v - P_v X\|_F^2 + \lambda \sum_{v=1}^m \|P_v\|_F^2 + \beta \|X\|_F^2 + \gamma \|B - X^T R\|_F^2 \tag{3}$$

$$s.t. \quad B \in \{-1, 1\}^{n \times d}, \quad R^T R = I$$

where λ, β and γ are tuning parameters controlling the trade-off between respective regularization terms. As can be seen from Eq. (3), our approach integrates multi-view subspace projection and binary encoding into a unified model. More importantly, since the orthogonal transformation does not change the mapping relationship in the process of binary encoding, both the subspace projection and the binary coding are guaranteed to be optimal in our unified framework.

2.2 Optimization

The formulation in Eq. (3) requires simultaneous optimization of the four parameters: the view-dependent generation matrix P_v, the low-dimensional subspace embedding X, the orthogonal rotation matrix R and the binary codes B. To solve this problem, we design an iterative algorithm to alternate the optimization of the four variables for minimizing the overall error:

P_v **update by fixing** X, B, R. After removing the irrelevant terms, the formulation in Eq. (3) is reduced to:

$$\min_{P_v} \|Z_v - P_v X\|_F^2 + \lambda \|P_v\|_F^2 \tag{4}$$

Let:

$$\mathcal{L} = \min_{P_v} \|Z_v - P_v X\|_F^2 + \lambda \|P_v\|_F^2 \tag{5}$$

Thus, we take the derivative of L w.r.t. P_v and set the derivative to 0, leading to the close-form solution as follows:

$$P_v = Z_v X^T (X X^T + \lambda I)^{-1} \tag{6}$$

X **update by fixing** P_v, B, R. With the irrelevant terms discarded, the formulation in Eq. (3) is simplified as:

$$\min_X \|Z_v - P_v X\|_F^2 + \beta \|X\|_F^2 + \gamma \|B - X^T R\|_F^2 \tag{7}$$

Analogously, we take the derivative of L w.r.t. X and set the derivative to 0 for obtaining the following close-form solution:

$$X = \left(\sum_{v=1}^m P_v^T P_v + \beta I + \gamma R R^T\right)^{-1} \left(\sum_{v=1}^m P_v^T Z_v + \gamma R B^T\right) \tag{8}$$

B **update by fixing** P_v, X, R. While updating B, we only maintain the terms regarding B, and thus the problem is reduced to:

$$\min_B \|B - X^T R\|_F^2 \tag{9}$$

Expanding Eq. (9), we have:

$$\begin{aligned} &\min_B \|B\|_F^2 + \|X^T\|_F^2 - 2tr(B R^T X) \\ &= \min_B nd + \|X^T\|_F^2 - 2tr(B R^T X) \end{aligned} \tag{10}$$

Since $n \cdot d$ is constant while the projected data matrix X is fixed, minimizing Eq. (10) is equivalent to maximizing

$$tr(B R^T X) = \sum_{i=1}^n \sum_{j=1}^d B_{ij} \tilde{X}_{ij} \tag{11}$$

Table 1. Comparison of different baselines on Holidays and UKBench.

Datasets	CNN	SERVE-RSIFT	SERVE-LCS
Holidays (mAP%)	**74.27**	53.65	68.62
UKBench (4×Recall@4)	**3.55**	3.22	3.29

where $\tilde{X}_{ij}$ denotes the elements of $\tilde{X} = X^{\mathrm{T}}R$. To maximize this formulation with respect to B, we have $B_{ij} = 1$ whenever $\tilde{X}_{ij} \geq 0$ and -1 otherwise.

R update by fixing P_v, X, B. Similar to the above-mentioned steps, we remove the irrelevant terms and rewrite Eq. (3) as follows:

$$\min_{R} \left\| B - X^{\mathrm{T}}R \right\|_F^2 \tag{12}$$

The objective function shown in Eq. (12) is in spirit the classic orthogonal Procrustes problem [13]. In our method, Eq. (12) is minimized by computing the SVD of the $n \times n$ matrix $B^{\mathrm{T}}X^{\mathrm{T}}$ as $S\Omega\hat{S}^{\mathrm{T}}$ and letting $R = \hat{S}S^{\mathrm{T}}$.

We alternate the above four steps and iteratively repeat the process until minimizing Eq. (3) is converged.

3   Experiments

3.1   Datasets

1. **INRIA Holidays** [14]. It contains 1,491 images divided into 500 query groups depending on the specific query topic. The first image in each group is used as the query, and the rest as the related ground-truth images. In terms of the performance measure, we compute average precision (AP) for each query group and obtain mean average precision (mAP) by averaging all AP scores for the overall evaluation.
2. **UKBench** [15]. This dataset includes 10,200 images of 2,550 query groups, whilst each group consists of four images that contain the same target or scene. Each image in the database is used as query image in turn, and the remaining images in the same group are related ground truths. For evaluation, 4×Recall@4 is computed as the number of ground-truth images among the top returned four images.
3. **Flickr100k** [16]. This large dataset has a total of 100,071 images collected from Flickr by searching for popular Flickr tags. This dataset is typically merged with other datasets to evaluate the large-scale scalability of retrieval algorithms in large-scale scenarios.

3.2 Experiments Setting

In our experiments, three heterogeneous image signatures are used, namely CNN, SERVE-LCS and SERVE-RSIFT [17]. Besides, we also make use of the VLAD+ feature for the subsequent evaluation in large-scale retrieval scenario. As for the CNN feature, we directly use the 4096-dimensional description of 33th-layer activation of the pre-trained VGG-16 model [18] as the feature representation. Besides, we employ the two SERVE signatures in [17] producing respective image representations with 4,096 and 6,144 dimensions. In terms of VLAD+, we reproduce the method in [19] and also use a vocabulary of 256 visual words for producing 16,384 dimensional representation.

Since our method works in an unsupervised fashion, we empirically set the two parameters λ and β to 0.5. Besides, to compromise between the multi-view reconstruction error and the binary quantization loss, parameter γ was set to 0.001. In implementation, we set the subspace dimension and the binary code length as 256 for compact representation and efficient retrieval.

Table 2. The performance of our method on Holidays and UKBench.

Datasets	BMSL-CSR	BMSL-CSL	BMSL-CSRSL
Holidays (mAP%)	80.33	81.15	**84.7**
UKBench (4×Recall@4)	3.53	3.57	**3.64**

3.3 Results

Baselines. We first present the performance of three baseline retrieval methods in which the three individual features are respectively combined with efficient cosine similarity, which are denoted as CNN, SERVE-RSIFT and SERVE-LCS accordingly. The retrieval results of different baselines on the two datasets are shown in Table 1. It can be observed that CNN reveals unrivaled performance advantage against the conventional hand-crafted features, which implies the deep feature plays a dominant role in multi-view fusion.

The Performance of the Proposed Algorithm. We evaluate our method BMSL for multi-view features fusion. In implementation, we use different combinations of multiple heterogeneous features. To explore the complementarity between deep feature and the hand-crafted features, the three sets of multi-view features involved in our experiments include: CNN & SERVE-RSIFT, CNN & SERVE-LCS and CNN, SERVE-RSIFT & SERVE-LCS. The corresponding methods using the three feature sets are denoted as **BMSL-CSR**, **BMSL-CSL**, and **BMSL-CSRSL** respectively.

Table 2 shows the performance of our algorithm on the two benchmark datasets. It can be observed that our method significantly improves the baseline

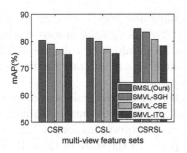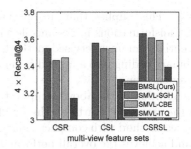

Fig. 1. Comparison of different unsupervised multi-view hashing approaches on the Holidays (left) and UKBench (right).

Table 3. Comparison of our method with the state-of-the-arts.

Method	Feature dimension	Holidays	UKBench
CRB-CNN-16 [20]	512	**85.4**	3.56
GoogLeNet [21]	128	83.6	–
SPoC [4]	256	80.2	**3.65**
Ours	256	84.7	3.64

performance even with compact binary codes. On Holidays dataset, our BMSL-CSRSL method combines the three signatures to obtain the highest mAP at 84.7%, which outperforms the three baselines by 10.43%, 31.05% and 16.08%, respectively. Analogous performance boosts are also observed on UKBench.

Comparative Studies. In order to further demonstrate the advantages of our method, we compared our approach with the other classic unsupervised multi-view hashing methods:

1. **SMVL-SGH**: We firstly utilize SMVL algorithm [5] to produce a low-dimensional embedded representation. Next, we directly make use of the graph hashing based SGH algorithm [22] to transform the resulting subspace representations to generate the binary code.
2. **SMVL-CBE**: We encode the subspace representation resulting from SMVL into the binary codes by using the CBE algorithm [23]. CBE method achieves efficient hashing by using circulant projections.
3. **SMVL-ITQ**: In this method, we separately perform SMVL for producing the latent subspace and ITQ [13] for generating compact binary codes.

For the sake of consistency, we adopt the same setup of multi-view features as our method. Figure 1 illustrates that our approach consistently achieves superior performance on both datasets. For instance, when combining all three features, our method achieves 84.7% mAP score on Holidays and significantly exceeds the other competing methods reporting respective scores at 83.35%, 80.64% and

77.96%. This implies that unsupervised hashing methods are more prone to lossy transformations in instance-level retrieval. Although the proposed scheme is essentially an unsupervised method, it integrates multi-view subspace learning and binary coding into a unified framework, and thus can mitigate the limitation of lossy encoding.

In addition to the above comparative studies, we also compare our algorithm with the state-of-the-arts on the two benchmarks. As presented in Table 3, the proposed method with compact binary codes even outperforms some CNN methods and achieves the overall performance on par with the state-of-the-arts. This indicates that the proposed method can make full use of the complementarity between deep and hand-crafted features, and significantly improve the retrieval efficiency with improved performance.

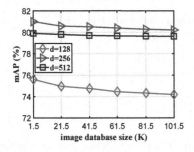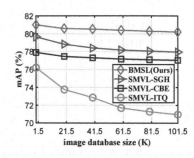

Fig. 2. Large-scale evaluations of our approach with varying feature dimensions (left) and the other competing methods on the Holidays + Flickr100k (right).

Scalability to Large Database. In order to evaluate the scalability of our approach, we merge the Holidays with Flickr100k for large-scale evaluations. Figure 2 illustrates the performance of our approach with varying features dimensions and the other competing methods with $d = 256$ when the distractor images are incrementally added to Holidays. It is shown that our method achieves the highest accuracy when the feature dimension is set as 256 in large-scale scenario. Besides, the competing methods exhibits significantly degraded performance with the distractor images added incrementally, whereas our approach is hardly affected with the increasing distractor images. This substantially demonstrates the promising scalability of our approach.

4   Conclusions

In this paper, we have proposed a binary multi-view subspace learning method for multi-view fusion in instance retrieval. We integrate the multi-view subspace reconstruction and binary quantization into a unified framework and the resulting binary codes can be used for compact representation and efficient matching.

To our knowledge, this is the first attempt to address the instance retrieval problem by using a unified binary multi-view subspace learning method. Since our approach is an unsupervised method, it substantially benefits the cases when the instance-specific training data is either unavailable or insufficient. The evaluations on the public benchmarks and large-scale datasets reveal that the proposed method achieves promising performance on par with the state-of-the-arts with desirable scalability.

References

1. Krizhevsky, A., Sutskever, I., Hinton, G.E.: Imagenet classification with deep convolutional neural networks. In: NIPS, pp. 1097–1105 (2012)
2. Razavian, A.S., Azizpour, H., Sullivan, J., Carlsson, S.: CNN features off-the-shelf: an astounding baseline for recognition. In: CVPRW, pp. 512–519 (2014)
3. Wan, J., et al.: Deep learning for content-based image retrieval: a comprehensive study. In: ACM MM, pp. 157–166 (2014)
4. Yandex, A.B., Lempitsky, V.: Aggregating local deep features for image retrieval. In: ICCV, pp. 1269–1277 (2015)
5. Li, J., Yang, B., Yang, W., Sun, C., Zhang, H.: When deep meets shallow: subspace-based multi-view fusion for instance-level image retrieval. In: ROBIO, pp. 486–492 (2018)
6. Zhou, W., Li, H., Sun, J., Tian, Q.: Collaborative index embedding for image retrieval. IEEE TPAMI 40(5), 1154–1166 (2018)
7. Strecha, C., Bronstein, A.M., Bronstein, M.M., Fua, P.: LDAHash: improved matching with smaller descriptors. IEEE TPAMI 34(1), 66–78 (2012)
8. Zhang, J., Peng, Y.: SSDH: semi-supervised deep hashing for large scale image retrieval. IEEE TCSVT 29(1), 212–225 (2019)
9. Liu, X., Huang, L., Deng, C., Lu, J., Lang, B.: Multi-view complementary hash tables for nearest neighbor search. In: ICCV, pp. 1107–1115 (2015)
10. Zhu, L., Lu, X., Cheng, Z., Li, J., Zhang, H.: Deep collaborative multi-view hashing for large-scale image search. IEEE TIP 29, 4643–4655 (2020)
11. Zheng, L., Yang, Y., Tian, Q.: SIFT meets CNN: a decade survey of instance retrieval. IEEE TPAMI 40(5), 1224–1244 (2018)
12. Wang, J., Zhang, T., Song, J., Sebe, N., Shen, H.T.: A survey on learning to hash. IEEE TPAMI 40(4), 769–790 (2018)
13. Gong, Y., Lazebnik, S.: Iterative quantization: a procrustean approach to learning binary codes. In: CVPR, pp. 817–824 (2011)
14. Jegou, H., Douze, M., Schmid, C.: Hamming embedding and weak geometric consistency for large scale image search. In: Forsyth, D., Torr, P., Zisserman, A. (eds.) ECCV 2008. LNCS, vol. 5302, pp. 304–317. Springer, Heidelberg (2008). https://doi.org/10.1007/978-3-540-88682-2_24
15. Nister, D., Stewenius, H.: Scalable recognition with a vocabulary tree. In: CVPR, pp. 2161–2168 (2006)
16. Philbin, J., Chum, O., Isard, M., Sivic, J., Zisserman, A.: Object retrieval with large vocabularies and fast spatial matching. In: CVPR, pp. 1–8 (2007)
17. Li, J., Xu, C., Gong, M., Xing, J., Yang, W., Sun, C.: SERVE: soft and equalized residual vectors for image retrieval. Neurocomputing 207, 202–212 (2016)
18. Simonyan, K., Zisserman, A.: Very deep convolutional networks for large-scale image recognition. In: ICLR, pp. 1–14 (2015)

19. Arandjelović, R., Zisserman, A.: All about VLAD. In: CVPR, pp. 1578–1585 (2013)
20. Alzubi, A., Amira, A., Ramzan, N.: Content-based image retrieval with compact deep convolutional features. Neurocomputing **249**, 95–105 (2017)
21. Ng, J.Y., Yang, F., Davis, L.S.: Exploiting local features from deep networks for image retrieval. In: CVPRW, pp. 53–61 (2015)
22. Jiang, Q., Li, W.: Scalable graph hashing with feature transformation. In: IJCAI, pp. 2248–2254 (2015)
23. Yu, F.X., Kumar, S., Gong, Y., Chang, S.: Circulant binary embedding. In: ICML, pp. 946–954 (2014)

Hyper-Sphere Support Vector Classifier with Hybrid Decision Strategy

Shuang Liu[1] and Peng Chen[2(✉)]

[1] Dalian Minzu University, Dalian 116600, China
dlnuliushuang@qq.com
[2] Dalian Neusoft University of Information, Dalian 116023, China
44531347@qq.com

Abstract. If all bounding hyper-spheres for training data of every class are independent, classification for any test sample is easy to compute with high classification accuracy. But real application data are very complicated and relationships between classification bounding spheres are very complicated too. Based on detailed analysis of relationships between bounding hyper-spheres, a hybrid decision strategy is put forward to solve classification problem of the intersections for multi-class classification based on hyper-sphere support vector machines. First, characteristics of data distribution in the intersections are analyzed and then decision class is decided by different strategies. If training samples of two classes in the intersection can be classified by intersection hyperplane for two hyper-spheres, then new test samples can be decided by this plane. If training samples of two classes in the intersection can be approximately linearly classified, new test samples can be classified by standard optimal binary-SVM hyper-plane. If training samples of two classes in the intersection cannot be linearly classified, new test samples can be decided by introducing kernel function to get optimal classification hyper-plane. If training examples belong to only one class, then new test samples can be classified by exclusion method. Experimental results show performance of our algorithm is more optimal than hyper-sphere support vector machines with only one decision strategy with relatively low computation cost.

Keywords: Hyper-sphere support vector classifier · Intersection region · Hybrid decision strategy · Classification hyper-plane · Multi-class classification

1 Introduction

Support Vector Machine (SVM) is originally put forward to solve binary classification problem with the idea of maximum-margin hyper-plane separating training samples. The classification hyper-plane is restricted with support vectors, which are used for the decision of a new test sample. Many researchers have successfully applied SVM in many fields [1,2]. To solve multi-class classification

© Springer Nature Switzerland AG 2020
H. Yang et al. (Eds.): ICONIP 2020, CCIS 1332, pp. 69–77, 2020.
https://doi.org/10.1007/978-3-030-63820-7_8

problem in real applications, binary SVM needs to be extended or combined together to complete the complex classification task. There are many methods extending binary SVM to multi-class classification [3–5], such as one-against-one, one-against-all, hierarchy SVM classifiers, or DAG SVM classifiers. But because at least $k(k-1)/2$ quadratic programming (QP) optimization problems needs to be combined together to solve k class classification problem, computation cost for these methods is relatively high.

For multi-class classification problem, sphere-structured SVM is one special solution [6]. Based on one-class SVM, hyper-sphere SVM classifier tries to construct a minimum bounding hyper-sphere restricting all training samples of one class within it as much as possible. The bounding hyper-sphere for each class is restricted with its center and its radius. Similar to binary SVM, this method maximizes the gap between different hyper-spheres by the smallest radius. New test samples are classified depending on the bounding hyper-spheres they falls into. Since this method needs no combination of further computation and solves multi-class classification problem with direct computation of all hyper-spheres together, its computation complexity is less than all the above mentioned combination methods. Sphere-structured SVM has been studied a lot since its presentation. To get good performance for hyper-sphere SVM, Liu et al. [7,8] proposed one fuzzy hyper-sphere SVM and one multiple sub-hyper-spheres SVM for multi-class classification. Most of these research focused on one decision rule and few researchers adopted two or more decision rules.

As mentioned above, each training data is bounded within a bounding hyper-sphere. If all bounding hyper-spheres for training data of every class are independent and new test sample falls inside only one hyper-sphere, its classification decision is easy to compute. But real application data are very complicated and relationships between different classification bounding hyper-spheres are very complicated too. When hyper-spheres for each class are intersected or not independent, it is difficult for one simple decision function to get the right classification result. Classification accuracy of test samples falling inside the intersection will influence the final classification performance. Based on the analysis of data distributions for such samples in the intersections, a hybrid decision strategy is put forward in this paper. Section 2 introduces statistical analysis of the intersection data distribution, mathematical description of our hyper-sphere SVM and implementation details of the proposed method. Section 3 discusses the experimental results and Sect. 4 gives the conclusions.

2   Our Method

2.1   Mathematical Description of Hyper-Sphere Support Vector Classifier

Similar with mathematic description of the original binary SVM, mathematic principles of hyper-sphere SVM is as follows. Supposing there is a set of n-dimensional training samples of m classes, the task is to compute the minimum bounding hyper-sphere for each class. Here, the minimum bounding hyper-sphere refers to the smallest hyper-sphere that encloses all the training samples of one class. Referenced by binary SVM, slack variables ξ_{ki} are introduced by permitting isolated points and a non-linear mapping function ϕ is introduced by transforming the training samples into a high dimensional feature space to solve nonlinear separation problems. So seeking the minimum bounding hyper-sphere for each class is to find the minimum bounding hyper-sphere enclosing all the training examples of that class. This process can be computed by solving the following constrained quadratic optimization problem in Eq. (1).

$$\min_{c_k, R_k} R_k^2 + C_k \sum_{i=1}^{m} \xi_{ki}$$

$$s.t. \tag{1}$$

$$\|\phi(\boldsymbol{x_i}) - c_k\|^2 \leq R_k^2 + \xi_k$$
$$\xi_i \geq 0, i = 1, \cdots, l_k$$

For class k, its minimum bounding hyper-sphere S_k is characterized by its center c_k and radius R_k. And C_k is the penalty factor and $\xi_{ki} \geq 0$ are slack variables.

By introducing Lagrange multipliers, Lagrange polynomial can be written as Eq. (2).

$$L(R_k, c_k, \xi_i, \alpha_i, \beta_i) = R_k^2 + C_k \sum_{i=1}^{l_k} \xi_{ki} - \sum_{i=1}^{l_k} \alpha_i \left(R_k^2 + \xi_{ki} - \|\phi(\boldsymbol{x_i}) - c_k\|^2 \right) - \sum_{i=1}^{l_k} \beta_i \xi_{ki}$$
$$\tag{2}$$

By taking the partial directives of L with respect to R_k,c_k and ξ_i and substituting them back to Eq. (2), the original optimization problem becomes its dual optimization problem in the following format as Eq. (3).

$$\min_{\alpha_i} \sum_{i,j=1}^{l_k} \alpha_i \alpha_j K(\boldsymbol{x_i}, \boldsymbol{x_j}) - \sum_{i=1}^{l_k} \alpha_i K(\boldsymbol{x_i}, \boldsymbol{x_i})$$

$$s.t. \tag{3}$$

$$\sum_{i=1}^{l_k} \alpha_i = 1$$

$$0 \leq \alpha_i \leq C_k, i = 1, \cdots, l_k$$

In Eq. (3), the kernel trick is adopted to compute inner products in the feature space, that is, $K(\boldsymbol{x_i}, \boldsymbol{x_j}) = \phi(\boldsymbol{x_i}) \cdot \phi(\boldsymbol{x_j})$. Support vectors are the vectors $\boldsymbol{x_i}$ with $\alpha_i > 0$. The Lagrange multipliers get the solutions after solving Eq. (3). So the center can be computed by Eq. (4) and the resulting decision function can be computed as Eq. (5). Then the radius R_k can be computed by equating $f_k(\boldsymbol{x})$ to zero for any support vector. For class k, its minimum bounding hyper-sphere S_k is obtained by the solution of its center and radius.

$$c_k^2 = \sum_{i,j=1}^{l_k} \alpha_i \alpha_j K(\boldsymbol{x}_i, \boldsymbol{x}_j) \tag{4}$$

$$f_k(\boldsymbol{x}) = sgn(R_k^2 - \sum_{i,j=1}^{l_k} \alpha_i \alpha_j K(\boldsymbol{x}_i, \boldsymbol{x}_j)) + 2\sum_{i=1}^{l_k} K(\boldsymbol{x}_i, \boldsymbol{x}) - K(\boldsymbol{x}, \boldsymbol{x})) \tag{5}$$

Based on Eq. (5), the new point $\boldsymbol{x}$ falls inside of the hyper-sphere if $f_k(\boldsymbol{x}) > 0$. $\boldsymbol{x}$ falls outside of the hyper-sphere if $f_k(\boldsymbol{x}) < 0$ and $\boldsymbol{x}$ lies on the hyper-sphere if $f_k(\boldsymbol{x}) = 0$.

2.2   Analysis of Data in the Intersection of Hyper-Spheres

Ideally, all hyper-spheres are independent and each test sample is correctly classified by one hyper-sphere decision function. But it can happen that two or more hyper-spheres intersect, that is, one sample falls inside several hyper-spheres. Or a new test sample falls outside of all hyper-spheres. How to correctly classify these data points influence the accuracy performance of the resulting classifier. In Fig. 1, the minimum bounding sphere for class 1 and class 2 are S_1 and S_2. S_1' of class 1 belongs to sphere S_2 and S_2' of class 1 belongs to sphere S_1. $\boldsymbol{x}_1$ belongs to S_1' and $\boldsymbol{x}_2$ belongs to S_2' and they are both support vectors. For example, $\boldsymbol{x}_2$ is a support vector of class 2, so $\boldsymbol{x}_2$ belongs to class 2. But based on the decision function, $f_2(\boldsymbol{x}_2) = 0$ and $f_1(\boldsymbol{x}_2) > 0$, so $\boldsymbol{x}$ belongs to class 1. Obviously, it is the wrong classification result. So when two or more hyper-spheres intersect, only Eq. (5) is used as decision rule may lead to wrong decision results.

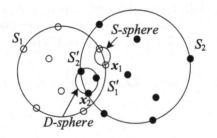

Fig. 1. Illustration of two hyper-spheres intersecting.

To solve this problem, one sub-hyper-sphere support vector machine is put for-ward to classify samples in the intersections in [9]. In the research, same error data hyper-sphere (data points belong to the same class of the mother hyper-sphere) and different error data hyper-sphere (data points belong to different class of the mother hyper-sphere) are introduced. The decision process is completed by them. In Fig. 1, S-sphere and D-sphere are same error data sub-hyper-sphere and different error data hyper-sphere for class 1. If a new test sample lies in the intersection, S-sphere and D-sphere are used as the classification rule to get the right class.

But by introducing multiple QP optimization problems again, its computation complexity increases. To reduce computation complexity of QP optimization problem, new decision rules are put forward in this paper. Given the training data set, there will be three cases for position of the new test sample, that is, inside one hyper-sphere or in the intersections or outside of all spheres after computing hyper-spheres for all classes. It is easy to get decision class for the inclusion case. If a new test sample x_2 falls outside of all spheres, Eq. (6) is adopted as its class j decision $(j = 1, \cdots, m)$.

$$min(\frac{d_{xj}^2}{R_j^2} - 1), where\ d_{xj}^2 = \|\phi(x) - c_j\|^2 = K(x, x) - 2\sum_{i=1}^{l_k} \alpha_i K(x, x_i) + \sum_{i,j=1}^{l_k} \alpha_i \alpha_j K(x_i, x_j)$$
(6)

If a new test sample belongs to the intersections, there are three cases for different data distribution as following.

(1) For the first case, the intersection hyper-plane can separate samples of two classes directly. Intersection hyper-plane is easy to get from subtraction of two spheres equations.

(2) For the second case, intersection hyper-plane cannot separate samples of two classes directly, so binary optimal plane is used as separation plane for linear and nonlinear cases as shown in Fig. 2.

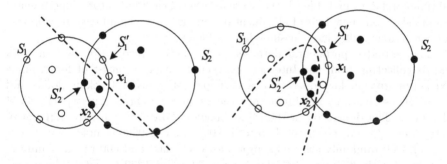

Fig. 2. Case of binary classification plane as separation plane for linear (left) and nonlinear (right) data.

(3) For the third case, there is only one class data in the intersection. For this case, exclusion method is adopted as the decision rule.

As can be seen from the reference [6,9], training time complexity for the sphere-structured SVM is $O(n^2)$. Testing time for the sphere-structured SVM is decided by its decision process. For our new hybrid hyper-sphere SVM, its training time complexity is $O(n^2)$. In testing phase, time complexity may be $O(1)$ for case of only one class data in the intersection, $O(n)$ for case of binary classification plane as separation plane and $O(n^2)$ for case of nonlinear classification plane as separation plane. The average time complexity is lower than that of sub-hyper-sphere SVM with $O(n^2)$.

2.3   Implementation Details of the Proposed Method

The proposed hyper-sphere support vector classifier with hybrid decision strategy follows three steps to complete classification process, which are listed as Algorithm 1. And testing process is described as Algorithm 2. Suppose there are m classes needs to be classified.

3   Experimental Results and Analysis

In this section some experimental results are given to verify the efficiency of the new improved classification rule and compare it with hyper-sphere SVMs and sub-hyper-sphere SVMs. The first experimental datasets IRIS and glass come from the UCI [10] Repository of machine learning databases. The second data comes from one real application of action recognition in videos.

For three classes of IRIS data set, all samples are randomly grouped as three parts and one part with number 15 is used as test, the other two 135 as training set. For glass data set, a subset with three classes is selected and the same data pre-processing is adopted as paper [6]. For hyper-sphere SVMs and sub-hyper-sphere SVMs [9], $C = 100, \sigma = 1.25$ is used. For our new approach, RBF kernel with parameter optimization search are used to get the best classification accuracy. Experimental results are shown in Table 1. All experiments were done for 10 times and data in Table 1 is the average value of each indicator. Experimental results show our new hybrid classification rule is effective and easy to compute for the simple multi-class classification problems.

The second experimental data set is one action recognition system from videos collecting from the Internet. Extracted features consist of foregrounds extraction, morphology operations and shape feature, KLT tracking points and so on. These features are input into the proposed hybrid hyper-sphere SVM classifiers. The dimension of the input image is 20 dimensions, the number of categories is 6, and the size of data set is 9000. Among 9000 samples, data1 consists of 3000 randomly selected samples for each class and 600 testing samples, and data2 with 3000 and 600, data3 with 7800 and 1200 as data1.The experiment was repeated 10 times and the average value was selected as the final experimental result. The accuracy of our method is 86.15, 90.11 and 92.15 for three datasets respectively. For the other two methods, the highest accuracy is fuzzy hyper-sphere SVM, the values are 85.04, 89.19 and 90.67 for three datasets and 83.98, 88.30, 89.33 for sub-sphere SVM. Performance of our new method is better than the other two methods.

Algorithm 1: Training Process for our HSSVM classifier with hybrid decision strategy

---

Step1 reads training data for each class.

for $k=1$ *to* m **do**
  QP optimization problems are solved based on SMO algorithm, Lagrange multipliers are obtained by QP solving, and sphere model is obtained based on Lagrange multipliers;
end

Step2 computes position relations between any two spheres.

for $i=1$ *to* m **do**
  for $j=i+1$ *to* m **do**
    $D_{i,j} = \|c_i - c_j\|^2$ (Euclidean distance between center of the i-th and j-th sphere);
    if $|R_i - R_j| \leq D_{i,j} \leq |R_i + R_j|$ **then**
      hyper-sphere S_i, S_j intersects and saves in SR_i;
    end
    if $D_{i,j} > |R_i - R_j|$ **then**
      hyper-sphere S_i, S_j are independent and saves SR_d;
    end
  end
end

Step3 sets decision rules for each pair of spheres in SR_i. For class j, its corresponding hyper-sphere is S_j. Here, S_j' is the intersection of S_i and S_j. C_j is data set of different error samples in S_j' and A_j is data set of same error samples in S_j'.

if $|C_j| = 0 \,\|\, |A_j| = 0$ **then**
  all data in the intersection be-longs to one class and saves it as the exclusion file; If new test sample falls in the intersection, its class decision is the class with number of training samples larger than zero;
end

if $|C_j| \neq 0$ *and* $|A_j| \neq 0$ **then**
  if $|C_j| > 1$ *and* $|A_j| > 1$ **then**
    intersecting plane is computed for two spheres S_i and S_j. If samples of two classes can be separated directly by the intersecting plane, it is saved as decision classification plane. If data of two classes falls in two sides of the intersecting plane, this intersecting plane is saved as decision plane;
  end
  if *samples of two classes can not be separated directly by the intersecting plane* **then**
    binary optimal SVM plane by introducing slack variables or map function is computed and saved as the decision plane;
  end
  if $|C_j| == 1$ *and* $|A_j| == 1$ **then**
    two spheres are tangent and two classes are saved as classification result;
  end
end

Algorithm 2: Testing Process for our HSSVM classifier with hybrid decision strategy

---

//computes classification results for test samples
for i=1 *to* M **do**
    for j=1 *to* m **do**
        distance d_{ij}^2 between sample i and S_j is computed;
        if $d_{ij}^2 - R_j^2 \leq 0$ **then**
        | sample i falls inside of S_j;
        else
        | sample i falls outside of the sphere;
        end
    end
    number N of hyper-spheres containing sample i is counted;
    if $N == 1$ **then**
    | sample i falls inside only one sphere, it belongs to this class;
    end
    if $N == 0$ **then**
    | i falls outside of all spheres, use Eq.(6) as decision rule;
    end
    if $N > 1$ **then**
        Suppose sample i falls inside $S_j, j = 1, \cdots, r$;
        for j=1 *to* r **do**
            for e=j+1 *to* r **do**
                if $S_j, S_e \in SR_i$ **then**
                    if *binary optimal plane exists* **then**
                    | this binary optimal plane is used as decision plane;
                    end
                    if *binary optimal plane exists* **then**
                    | exclusion method is adopted as decision rule;
                    end
                    if $i \in$ *spherical surface of* S_j, S_e **then**
                    | sample i belongs to two classes;
                    end
                end
            end
        end
    end
end

Table 1. Comparison result for IRIS classification.

Iris/glass	Training time	No. of Support Vector	Accuracy
Traditional hyper-sphere SVM	4.56 s/5.89 s	45/54	96.68%/62.15%
Sub-hyper-sphere SVM	5.78 s/7.35 s	56/68	97.78%/65.96%
New hybrid hyper-sphere SVM	3.556 s/4.785 s	37/42	99.86%/68.75%

4 Conclusions

To improve classification performance of traditional hyper-sphere SVM, one hybrid decision strategy for hyper-sphere support vector classifier is put forward in this paper. To get high classification performance for test samples and decreases computation complexity of QP optimization problems, four decision rules are discussed and detailed algorithm is given. Results on benchmark data and real application data show our hybrid decision rule leads to better generalization accuracy than the existing methods, decreasing computation complexity and saving training time.

Acknowledgement. This research was funded by the Natural Science Foundation of Liaoning Province, China (grant no. 2019-ZD-0175).

References

1. Mohanty, S.: Speaker identification using SVM during oriya speech recognition. Int. J. Image, Graph. Signal Process. **10**, 28–36 (2015)
2. Sun, A., Lim, E.P., Liu, Y.: On strategies for imbalanced text classification using SVM: a comparative study. Decis. Support Syst. **48**(1), 191–201 (2009)
3. Hsu, C.W., Lin, C.J.: A comparison of methods for multi-class support vector machines. IEEE Trans. Neural Netw. **13**(2), 415–425 (2002)
4. Vural, V., Dy, J.G.: A hierarchical method for multi-class support vector machines. In: ACM International Conference on Machine Learning, pp. 831–838 (2004)
5. Chmielnicki, W., Stapor, K.: Combining one-versus-one and one-versus-all strategies to improve multiclass SVM classifier. In: Proceedings of the 9th International Conference on Computer Recognition Systems, pp. 37–45 (2016)
6. Zhu, M., Wang, Y., Chen, S., Liu, X.: Sphere-structured support vector machines for multi-class pattern recognition. In: Wang, G., Liu, Q., Yao, Y., Skowron, A. (eds.) RSFDGrC 2003. LNCS (LNAI), vol. 2639, pp. 589–593. Springer, Heidelberg (2003). https://doi.org/10.1007/3-540-39205-X_95
7. Liu, S., Chen, P., Li, K.Q.: Multiple sub-hyper-spheres support vector machine for multi-class classification. Int. J. Wavelets Multiresolut. Inf. Process. **12**(3), 1450035 (2014)
8. Liu, S., Chen, P., Yun, J.: Fuzzy hyper-sphere support vector machine for pattern recognition. ICIC Express Lett. **9**(1), 87–92 (2015)
9. Wu, Q., Jia, C.Y., Zhang, A.F.: An improved algorithm based on sphere structure SVMs and simulation. J. Syst. Simul. (Chinese) **20**(2), 345–348 (2008)
10. UCI repository of machine learning databases. http://www.ics.uci.edu/mlearn/. Accessed 1 May 2020

Knowledge Graph Embedding Based on Relevance and Inner Sequence of Relations

Jia Peng[1,2], Neng Gao[1], Min Li[1,2(✉)], and Jun Yuan[1,2]

[1] SKLOIS, Institute of Information Engineering, CAS, Beijing, China
{pengjia,gaoneng,minli,yuanjun}@iie.ac.cn
[2] School of Cyber Security, University of Chinese Academy of Sciences,
Beijing, China

Abstract. Knowledge graph Embedding can obtain the low-dimensional dense vectors, which helps to reduce the high dimension and heterogeneity of Knowledge graph (KG), and enhance the application of KG. Many existing methods focus on building complex models, elaborate feature engineering or increasing learning parameters, to improve the performance of embedding. However, these methods rarely capture the influence of intrinsic relevance and inner sequence of the relations in KG simultaneously, while balancing the number of parameters and the complexity of the algorithm. In this paper, we propose a concatenate knowledge graph embedding method based on relevance and inner sequence of relations (KGERSR). In this model, for each $< head, relation, tail >$ triple, we use two partially shared gates for head and tail entities. Then we concatenate these two gates to capture the inner sequence information of the triples. We demonstrate the effectiveness of the proposed KGERSR on standard FB15k-237 and WN18RR datasets, and it gives about 2% relative improvement over the state-of-the-art method in terms of $Hits@1$, and $Hits@10$. Furthermore, KGERSR has fewer parameters than ConmplEX and TransGate. These results indicate that our method could be able to find a better trade-off between complexity and performance.

Keywords: Knowledge graph embedding · Relations relevance · Inner sequence · Cascade model

1 Introduction

KG simulates human understanding of various things and their relations in the real world to construct structured and semantic knowledge representation. Because of the large amount data in real-world KG, an efficient and scalable solution is crucial. KGE is a feature extraction process, mapping a complex network which includes nodes, content, and relations into low-dimensional vector spaces.

Supported by the National Key Research and Development Program of China.

Many KGE methods have been proposed [1,11,13] to learn low-dimensional vectors of entities and relations. In fact, an entity may have multiple aspects which may be related to different relations [8]. Therefore, many independent models [6,8], have been proposed recently and usually outperform dependent models on public datasets. However, current methods always assume the independence between relations and try to learn unique discriminate parameter set for each relation, which leads to a sharp increase in parameters and high time complexity.

Meanwhile, the sequence information in triple should also be taken into account. Although the translation-based model considers the order to some extent by the formula $h + r \approx t$, it is still under exploit to inherent sequence information of the triples.

To optimize embedding performance by considering the relevance and inner sequence, we explore knowledge graphs embedding from two perspectives. On one hand, there is a certain potential connection between the relations, which is neither completely independent nor completely consistent for one entity. On the other hand, the triple should be considered as a sequence, which includes the order information. Based on those ideas, we develop a novel partial layer concatenate mechanism and propose an efficient knowledge graph embedding method based on relevance and inner sequence of relations (KGERSR). It uses a shared concatenate sigmoid layer: one part is two shared filters for discriminating specific relation information of all kinds of relations; the other part is a uniform sequence holder that preserves the inner sequence information of the triple.

We evaluate our method on knowledge graph completion, and the experiments show that our model is comparable to or even outperforms state-of-the-art baselines. The main contributions of this paper are summarized as follows:

- We found that the relations in the heterogeneous KG are not completely independent, while each relation contributes differently to the embedding of one aspect of the entity. Therefore, we propose a scalable and efficient model KGERSR with two gates to discriminate the inherent relevance of relations.
- Besides, the inner sequence of relations needs to be considered in the embedding of the entity. We develop a layer concatenate mechanism to capture the inner sequence information of the triples.
- In order to find a balance between complexity and accuracy, we propose an shared parts of parameter matrix which can preserve correlation and inner sequence information, using three parameter matrices. The complexity is as same order as transE.
- Experiments show that KGERSR delivers some improvements compared to state-of-the-art baselines, and reduces parameters. These results indicate that our method is a good way to further optimize embedding in a real KG.

2   Related Work

Translational Distance Models is one of the representative methods of KG Embedding model. TransE [1] is the earliest translational distance model. It represents both entities and relations as vectors in the same space. Despite its simplicity and efficiency, TransE has flaws in dealing with 1-to-N, N-to-1, and N-to-N relations [8,14], so that they do not do well in dealing with some complex properties. To overcome the disadvantages of TransE in dealing with complex relations, some method such as transH [14] and transR [8] are proposed, which introduce relation-specific entity embeddings strategy. Those methods need a large-scale of parameters and high time complexity, which prevent them from applying on large-scale KG.

Some works take the relevence of relations into account, assuming the relations fit some sort of random distribution, and modeling them as random variables. KG2E [4] represents entities and relations as random vectors drawn from multivariate Gaussian distributions. TransG [15] also models entities with Gaussian distributions, and it believes that a relation can have multiple semantics, hence it should be represented as a mixture of Gaussian distributions. However, once the entities and relations of the actual KG do not conform to the assumed distribution, the effect of those models will be weakened.

There are many methods based on semantic matching models that also consider the correlation between relations to reduce learning parameters. DistMult [16] introduces a vector $\mathbf{r}$ and requires $\mathbf{M}_r = diag(\mathbf{r})$. The scoring function is hence defined as $f_r(h,t) = \mathbf{h}^\top diag(\mathbf{r})\mathbf{t}$. This score captures pairwise interactions between only the components of h and t along the same dimension, and reduces the number of parameters to $\mathcal{O}(d)$ per relation. However, this oversimplified model can only deal with symmetric relations which is clearly not powerful enough for general KG. ComplEx [13] extends DistMult by introducing complex-valued embeddings so as to better model asymmetric relations.

In the KG, the sequence of relations can also reflect the semantic relation between entities. Lin proposed a representation learning method Path-based TransE (PTransE)[9]. Given a path p linking two entities h and t, p can be calculated using the addition, multiplication, or RNN of all r_i on the path. Guu et al. [3] proposed a similar framework, the idea of which is to build triples using entity pairs connected not only with relations but also with relation paths. Those models considering relational paths can greatly improve the discrimination of knowledge representation learning and improve performance on tasks such as knowledge graph completion. However, they both had to make approximations by sampling or pruning to deal with the huge number of paths.

3   Our Model

3.1   Motivation

Relations of KG are relevant for each entity. <Arnold Schwarzenegger, isGovernor, California> and <Arnold Schwarzenegger, isMemberOf, Republican> jointly infer to <Arnold Schwarzenegger, is, Politician>. Therefore, we should not completely separate the relations, or embedding together indiscriminately.

By building the learning network, the model can automatically learn the intrinsic relevance between the relations, and let the related work together to express the characteristics of one aspect of the entity.

Additionally, KG is a directed graph, which head entity and tail entity have inner sequence connected by relation. The entities connected by the order relations will affect each other. Consequently, as mentioned before, path in a triple can also reflect the semantic relation between entities. A model capable of capturing sequence information should be proposed. Although the translation-based models handle the path information, which have preserved a certain information of the sequence, they still under exploit to inherent sequence information of the triples.

We should consider retaining the relevance of the relations while retaining the sequence information. So, we combine the ideas of LSTM [5] and RNN [12]. For the relevance of relations, we hope that related relations work and irrelevant relations are ignored, so we design two shared gates for head and tail entities embedding with relations, which draw on the core idea of LSTM. For sequence of relations, we consider the triples as a sequence combining by $[h, r]$ and $[r, t]$. So we develop a recurrent discriminate mechanism to retain the sequence information which draw on the core idea of RNN.

3.2   KGE with Relevance and Sequence of Relations

The framework of KGERSR is shown as Fig. 1 and the detailed descriptions are as follow:

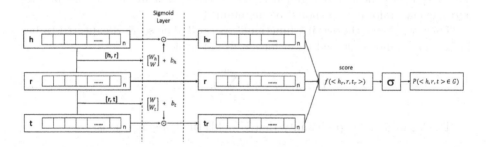

Fig. 1. The KGERSR architecture.

- We map every entity and relation into continues vector with same dimension R^m. Then we get original h, r, t embedding vectors.
- We input both entity embedding and relation embedding into the concatenate sigmoid layer consisted by parameter matrix, which determined by entity and relation together.
- Then we set two shared gates, σ_h and σ_t for head and tail entities respectively. Those two gates partially shared one recurrent parameter matrix W between $[h, r]$ and $[r, t]$.

- We realize non-linear and adaptive relation-specific discrimination through multiplying the different parts of concatenate layer output and entity embedding element-wise.
- We capture the inherent sequence property through multiplying the shared part of concatenate layer output and entity embedding element-wise.
- Last, we build a scoring function useing discriminated information of heads and tails. Based on the score, we can determine whether the triple is valid.

Each triple is composed of two entities and their relation. We define $h, t, r \in R^m$ as their embeddings respectively. The parameters of concatenate layer are denoted as W_h, W_t, $W \in R^{m \times m}$ and b_h, $b_t \in R^m$. W_h and W_t record the relevance between the relations, respectively. W is first affected by $[h, r]$ and then by $[r, t]$, so that W can record the inner sequence of the whole triple. The discriminated vectors of entities are defined as

$$h_r = [h] \odot \sigma([W_h, W] \cdot \begin{bmatrix} h \\ r \end{bmatrix} + [b_h]) \tag{1}$$

$$t_r = [t] \odot \sigma([W, W_t] \cdot \begin{bmatrix} r \\ t \end{bmatrix} + [b_t]) \tag{2}$$

The sigmoid function $\sigma(\bullet)$ is applied in a element-wise manner. $[,]$ means the concatenate operation. $\odot$ means the element-wise product.

In practice, we enforce constraints on the norms of the embeddings. That is to say, $\forall h, t, r$, we have $||h||_2 = 1$, $||r||_2 = 1$, $||t||_2 = 1$, $||h_r||_2 = 1$ and $||t_r||_2 = 1$. The output of concatenate sigmoid layers describes how much relation-specific and sequence information should be maintained.

Then, we define the scoring function f as Eq. 3. The score is expected to be higher for a valid triple and lower for an invalid triple.

$$f(< h, r, t >) = \sum_{k=1}^{m} h_{rk} r_k t_{rk} \tag{3}$$

The log-odd of the probability that G holds the triple is true is:

$$P(< h, r, t > \in G) = \sigma(f(< h, r, t >)) \tag{4}$$

3.3 Training

We use the Adam optimizer [7] to minimize the loss function [13] with L_2 regularization on weight matrix W_h, W_t and W of concatenate layer.

$$L = \sum_{<h,r,t> \in \{G \cup G'\}} log(1 + exp(-Y_{hrt} f(< h, r, t >)))$$
$$+ \frac{\lambda}{2}(||W_h||_2^2 + ||W_t||_2^2 + ||W||_2^2) \tag{5}$$

where $Y_{hrt} = 1$ if $< h, r, t > \in G$, and $Y_{hrt} = -1$ otherwise. G' is a collection of invalid triples generated by replacing entities or relations in training triples randomly. We use $\eta = \frac{|G'|}{|G|}$, which is an important hyperparameter, to represent negative samples per training sample. G' is defined as

$$G' = \{< h', r, t > |h' \in E\} \cup \{< h, r, t' > |t' \in E\} \cup \{< h, r', t > |r' \in R\}$$

(6)

In practice, we initialize the embeddings, weight matrices and weight vectors of gates through sampling from a truncated standard normal distribution. We use Adam optimizer with a constant range of learning rates for each epoch to carried out the training process which is stopped based on model's performance.

3.4 Complexity Analysis

The parameter number of our method is $\mathcal{O}(N_e m + N_r n + 3m^2 + 2m)(m = n)$, and the time complexity is $\mathcal{O}(m^2)$. N_e, N_r represent the number of entities, relations respectively. m, n are the dimension of entity and relation embedding space, respectively. The parameter complexity of KGERSR is almost the same as TransE in an epoch, because $m \ll N_r \ll N_e$ among existing KG. The discriminate parameters brought by the filters can be ignored compare to embedding parameters. Besides, KGERSR do not need any hyper parameter or pre-training to prevent overfitting. This makes KGERSR can be trained easier, so that it can be used to process the real-world KG.

4   Experiments

4.1   Knowledge Graph Completion Results

Knowledge graph completion aims to predict the missing h or t for a relation fact triple $< h, r, t >$. In this task, we need to filter out the correct triples from hybrid triples.

In this task, we use two datasets: WN18RR and FB15K-247, shown as Table 1. Since the datasets are same, we directly copy experimental results of several baselines. For those two datasets, we traverse all the training triples for at most 1000 rounds. We report MRR which is the mean reciprocal rank of all correct entities) and $(Hits@K)$ which is the proportion of correct entities ranked in top K as our evaluation metrics.

Table 1. Statistics of datasets

Dataset	#Rel	#Ent	#Train	#Valid	#Test
WN18RR	11	40943	86835	3034	3134
FB15K-237	237	14541	272115	17535	20466

We select the hyper parameters of KGERSR via grid search according to the MRR on the validation set. On WN18RR, the best configurations are: $\lambda = 0.01$, $\alpha = 0.01$, $m = 200$, $B = 120$ and $\eta = 25$. On FB15K-237,the best configurations are: $\lambda = 0.1$, $\alpha = 0.1$, $m = 200$, $B = 500$ and $\eta = 25$. Table 2 shows the evaluation results on knowledge graph completion.

From Table 2, we observe that KGERSR outperforms all of baselines in some metric and achieves comparable results in other metric. On more relational but sparse data set FB15K-237, our method outperforms 2.3% higher at MRR and 1.9% higher at $Hits@1$ than previous best result. Besides, on less relational but dense data set WN18RR, our method achieves comparable results in MRR and $Hits@1$ than previous best results.

Table 2. Experimental results of knowledge graph completion

Model	WN18RR			FB15K-237		
	MRR	Hits@10(%)	Hits@1(%)	MRR	Hits@10(%)	Hits@1(%)
TransE-2013 [1]	0.266	50.1	39.1	0.294	46.5	14.7
DistMult-2015 [16]	0.43	49.0	39	0.241	41.9	15.5
ComplEX-2016 [13]	0.44	51.0	41	0.247	42.8	15.8
ConvE-2018 [2]	0.43	52.0	40.0	0.325	50.1	23.7
ConvKB-2018 [10]	0.248	**52.5**	–	0.396	51.7	–
TransGate-2019 [17]	0.409	51.0	39.1	0.404	**58.1**	25.1
RKGE-2019 [18]	0.44	**53.0**	**41.9**	0.477	55.4	44.2
KGERSR	**0.45**	48.3	40.9	**0.488**	56	**45.02**

The results indicate that our model is able to achieve more improvements on more relational but sparse graph FB15K-237. The promotion of less relational but dense data set WN18RR is relatively limited. That is to say, our model can perform better in more relational graph. That result shows that the relational relevance part in our model plays a more critical role in KG completion task. The improvement on the indicator $Hits@1$ is obvious, which shows that our algorithm has great ability on precise link prediction. In general, the results demonstrate that our method has a certain generalization. At the same time, the proposed method using concatenate gates which takes into account the relevance and sequence of relations can more fully capture the essential characteristics of entities and relations in KG.

4.2   Parameter Efficiency

We further investigate the influence of parameters on the performance and the sensitivity to parameters of our model. Experiments below focus on FB15K-237, with the best configurations obtained from the previous experiment. Training was stopped using early stopping based on filtered MRR on the validation set. For the negative samples, embedding size and batch size parameters, we select the parameter values in the corresponding interval one by one, and view the changes in MRR and the corresponding training time. The result shown in Fig. 2.

- We let negative samples(η) vary in $\{1, 5, 10, 25, 50, 100\}$. It can be observed from Fig. 2(a) that generating more negative samples clearly improves the results. When η exceeds 25, the growth rate of indicators such as MRR, $Hits@1$ and $Hits@10$ slows down, and the results are basically flat, while the corresponding training time still increases linearly. So considering the training time, we choose $\eta = 25$ as the optimal parameter.
- We let embedding size(m) vary in $\{50, 100, 200, 300\}$. It can be observed from Fig. 2(b) that the embedding size improves the model performance from 50 to 200 interval, but the performance of $Hits@10$ decreases from 55.4% to 55.3% when $m = 300$. Simultaneously, the training time of the model also increases accordingly. In other words, blindly increasing the size of the matrix does not guarantee the effectiveness of the model. The reason may be that increasing the embedding size make some triples trained less inadequately, which makes it impossible to learn accurate embedding results. So considering the model performance, we choose $m = 200$ as the optimal parameter.

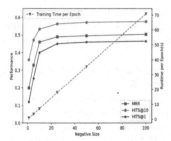
(a) Performance and Epoch Time Effected by Negative Size

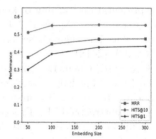
(b) Performance Effected by Negative Size

Fig. 2. Performance of the different parameter size

5   Conclusion and Future Work

In this paper, in order to find a balance between complexity and accuracy, we propose an shared parts of parameter matrix which can preserve correlation and sequence information, using three parameter matrices. Experiments show that KGERSR outperforms of state-of-the-art baselines in some indicators and achieves comparable results in other indicators. These results indicate that our method is a good way to further optimize embedding in the real KG.

In the future, we will conduct further study from the following aspects: (1) Add information such as text and attributes to further increase the accuracy of knowledge embedding. (2) We will use some sophisticated methods like RNNs to further optimize KGERSR methods. (3) The connection between triples is closer to the graph model.

References

1. Antoine, B., Nicolas, U., Alberto, G.D., Jason, W., Oksana, Y.: Translating embeddings for modeling multi-relational data. In: Neural Information Processing Systems (NIPS), pp. 1–9 (2013)
2. Dettmers, T., Minervini, P., Stenetorp, P., Riedel, S.: Convolutional 2d knowledge graph embeddings. Proc. AAAI, 1811–1818 (2017)
3. Guu, K., Miller, J., Liang, P.: Traversing knowledge graphs in vector space. In: Proceeding of Empirical Methods Natural Language Process, pp. 318–327 (2015)
4. He, S., Liu, K., Ji, G., Zhao, J.: Learning to represent knowledge graphs with gaussian embedding. In: The 24th ACM International Conference on Information and Knowledge Management (CIKM), pp. 623–632, October 2015
5. Hochreiter, S., Schmidhuber, J.: Long short-term memory. Neural Comput. **9**(8), 1735–1780 (1997)
6. Ji, G., Kang, L., He, S., Zhao, J.: Knowledge graph completion with adaptive sparse transfer matrix. In: AAAI Conference on Artificial Intelligence (2016)
7. Kingma, D., Ba, J.: Adam: a method for stochastic optimization. In: International Conference on Learning Representations (2015)
8. Lin, Y., Liu, Z., Sun, M., Liu, Y., Zhu, X.: Learning entity and relation embeddings for knowledge graph completion. Proc. AAAI, 2181–2187, January 2015
9. Lin, Y., Liu, Z., Luan, H., Sun, M., Rao, S., Liu, S.: Modeling relation paths for representation learning of knowledge bases. Comput. Sci. (2015)
10. Nguyen, D.Q., Nguyen, T.D., Nguyen, D.Q., Phung, D.Q.: A novel embedding model for knowledge base completion based on convolutional neural network. Proc. NAACL (2018)
11. Socher, R., Chen, D., Manning, C.D., Ng, A.: Reasoning with neural tensor networks for knowledge base completion. In: Lake Tahoe (2013)
12. Socher, R., et al.: Recursive deep models for semantic compositionality over a sentimenttreebank. In: Proceedings of EMNLP, pp. 1631–1642 (2013)
13. Trouillon, T., Welbl, J., Riedel, S., Gaussier, É., Bouchard, G.: Complex embeddings for simple link prediction. In: Proceedings of ICML, pp. 2071–2080 (2016)
14. Wang, Z., Zhang, J., Feng, J., Chen, Z.: Knowledge graph embedding by translating on hyperplanes. In: AAAI Conference on Artificial Intelligence (2014)
15. Xiao, H., Huang, M., Zhu, X.: Transg: a generative model for knowledge graph embedding. In: Proceedings of the 54th Annual Meeting of the Association for Computational Linguistics, vol. 1: Long Papers, pp. 2316–2325 (2016)
16. Yang, B., Yih, S.W.T., He, X., Gao, J., Deng, L.: Embedding entities and relations for learning and inference in knowledge bases. In: Proceedings of the International Conference on Learning Representations (ICLR), May 2015
17. Yuan, J., Gao, N., Xiang, J.: Transgate: Knowledge graph embedding with shared gate structure. In: Proceedings of the AAAI Conference on Artificial Intelligence, vol. 33, pp. 3100–3107, July 2019
18. Yuan, J., Gao, N., Xiang, J., Tu, C., Ge, J.: Knowledge graph embedding with order information of triplets. In: Yang, Q., Zhou, Z.-H., Gong, Z., Zhang, M.-L., Huang, S.-J. (eds.) PAKDD 2019. LNCS (LNAI), vol. 11441, pp. 476–488. Springer, Cham (2019). https://doi.org/10.1007/978-3-030-16142-2_37

MrPC: Causal Structure Learning in Distributed Systems

Thin Nguyen[1(✉)], Duc Thanh Nguyen[2], Thuc Duy Le[3], and Svetha Venkatesh[1]

[1] Applied Artificial Intelligence Institute (A2I2), Deakin University,
Melbourne, Australia
`thin.nguyen@deakin.edu.au`
[2] School of Information Technology, Deakin University, Melbourne, Australia
[3] School of Information Technology and Mathematical Sciences,
University of South Australia, Adelaide, Australia

Abstract. PC algorithm (**PC**) – named after its authors, Peter and Clark – is an advanced constraint based method for learning causal structures. However, it is a time-consuming algorithm since the number of independence tests is exponential to the number of considered variables. Attempts to parallelise **PC** have been studied intensively, for example, by distributing the tests to all computing cores in a single computer. However, no effort has been made to speed up **PC** through parallelising the conditional independence tests into a cluster of computers. In this work, we propose **MrPC**, a robust and efficient **PC** algorithm, to accelerate **PC** to serve causal discovery in distributed systems. Alongside with **MrPC**, we also propose a novel manner to model non-linear causal relationships in gene regulatory data using kernel functions. We evaluate our method and its variants in the task of building gene regulatory networks. Experimental results on benchmark datasets show that the proposed **MrPC**gains up to seven times faster than sequential **PC** implementation. In addition, kernel functions outperform conventional linear causal modelling approach across different datasets.

Keywords: Causality · Explainable AI · Causal structure learning · Distributed systems

1 Introduction

PC is an important algorithm in learning causal structures for observational data [1,8]. However, the algorithm is also well-known for its high computational complexity as the number of independence tests is exponential to the number of considered variables in the worst case. This limits the applicability of the **PC** algorithm in practice. To address this issue, parallelising the algorithm is often applied, such as in [4], where the authors distributed the independence tests as tasks fed into a multi-core computer. However, there is no method speeding the **PC** algorithm in distributed systems, for example, on a cluster of computers.

© Springer Nature Switzerland AG 2020
H. Yang et al. (Eds.): ICONIP 2020, CCIS 1332, pp. 87–94, 2020.
https://doi.org/10.1007/978-3-030-63820-7_10

1.1   Related Work

There have been several causal discovery and causal inference methods that use **PC** as the core component and therefore they will be benefited from an efficient **PC**. Some methods have been proposed to improve the efficiency of **PC** by introducing heuristic methods, but they rather compromise the accuracy [7]. Meanwhile, others [4] aimed to parallelise the conditional independence tests into different cores of a computer, limiting the scale of the parallelisation.

Advances in cluster computing can help parallelise the conditional independence tests in **PC** algorithm into a set of connected computers. Among the most popular architectures is MapReduce [2], a distributed computing programming model, designed to enable and simplify parallel programming. The framework has been implemented and extended in several distributed systems, including Apache Spark [9], where RDD (Resilient Distributed Dataset) is proposed to keep data in-memory for faster computation.

To verify the independence/dependence of variables from coincident data, conditional independence tests are conducted. Conventionally, independence tests are performed via correlation matrices [6], which implicitly impose a linear relationship between the factors. However, this assumption is not always true in reality and unknown generally.

1.2   Contributions

In this paper, we investigate learning causal structures in distributed systems. The contributions of our work are two-fold as follows.

- First, we propose **MrPC** to perform the **PC** algorithm [1] on Apache Spark [9], a cluster computing framework supporting parallel, distributed computation and storage on multiple computers. Extending MapReduce and equipping it with in-memory computing capacity, Apache Spark speeds up the execution of iterative jobs. This framework fits well the task of distributed computation of independence tests for **PC** algorithm.
- Second, we propose to estimate conditional independence between variables using kernel functions. Kernel functions allow to capture non-linear and complex relationships. We investigate various kernel types and prove that conventional correlation metric used in causal discovery is a special case.

To evaluate our method, we firstly experimented **MrPC** on six datasets provided in [4] to examine how a distributed algorithm could help speed up the **PC** algorithm. Experimental results showed that on the same computing infrastructure, **MrPC** can gain up to seven times faster than **PC-stable** [1], a sequential **PC** implementation. We then investigated how kernel functions work in capturing gene regulatory networks of *Escherichia coli* (*E. coli*) and *Saccharomyces cerevisiae* (*S. cerevisiae*), provided in the DREAM5 network inference challenge [5]. We found that kernel functions perform better than conventional correlation metric on both the datasets.

2   Proposed Method

2.1   Distributed Computation

The **PC** algorithm [8] has two main steps. In the first step, it learns from data a skeleton graph, which contains only undirected edges. The orientation of the undirected edges is performed in the second step to form an equivalence class of Directed Acyclic Graphs (DAGs). As the first step of the **PC** algorithm contributes to most of the computational costs, we only focus on the modification of this step in this paper.

The skeleton learning step of the **PC** algorithm starts with a complete, undirected graph and deletes recursively edges based on either marginal, $I(X, Y)$, or conditional, $I(X, Y|\mathbb{S})$, independence tests. For example, the edge between two causal factors X and Y is removed if we can find a set of other factors that does not include X and Y, and when conditioning on $\mathbb{S}$, X and Y are independent. In the worst case, the running time of the **PC** algorithm, is exponential to the number of nodes (variables), and thus it is inefficient when applying to high dimensional datasets.

In this paper, we model the dependency between two causal factors as an edge in a graph, where each node represents a causal factor. Under Spark, a MapReduce-enabled framework, to perform parallel computations of conditional independences, each edge being tested for conditional independence is considered as a single element in the *mappers* and is parallelly distributed to the *mappers* via executers (*Map* operations). The executers run the tests and return whether the input edges are independent in the current graph. The driver aggregates and summarises all the outputs from the *mappers*, updates the learning causal structures and decides the next step (*Reduce* operations).

The original **PC** algorithm [8] have the benefit of lesser number of tests, in comparison with **PC-stable** [1], as it updates the learning graph after every independence test. However, the structures returned by the original version [8] are dependent on the order of the couples of variables to be tested. To achieve order-independent structures, **PC-stable** [1] proposed to update the graph after completing all the tests at a level, which is a number of factors conditioned on. We parallel **PC-stable** [1] to use up the capacity of computing systems, their cores and all computers in the cluster, which is unused in the original approach. We summarise our parallel implementation of **PC-stable** algorithm in Algorithm 1, **MrPC** (abbreviated for **MapReduce PC**).

2.2   Kernel-Based Relation

Independence tests, either marginal or conditional, for the input variables are often conducted via correlations/partial correlations which are calculated from correlation matrices. Conventionally, a correlation matrix of factors implies a linear relationship between the factors. However, this assumption is neither always held in reality nor applied for all kinds of data distributions. Inspired by the work in [10], in this paper, we propose to calculate the correlation between

Algorithm MrPC()

   Input   : A dataset where each sample is encoded by V features and the significant level α.

   Output: A graph G encodes the conditional independence among V features in the dataset.

   $G =$ fully connected graph of V nodes

   $l = 0$: number of variables to be conditioned on

   while *True* **do**

      continued = False

      The driver ships all edges of current graph G to every executor.

      The executors process each edge (X,Y) by the function independenceTest(X,Y) and send tuples (X,Y,independence,continued) back to the driver

      The driver updates:

            removes from G the edge (X,Y) with independence=True

            sets *continued*=True if there exists a tuple with *continued*=True

      l += 1

      if *continued* = *False* **then**

         | break

      end

   end

1   **return**

Procedure independenceTest(X, Y)

   independence = False

   continued = False

   $\mathbb{N} = neighbor(X) \setminus \{Y\}$

   if $|\mathbb{N}| \geq l$ **then**

      if $|\mathbb{N}| > l$ **then**

         | *continued* = True

      end

      for $\mathbb{Z} \subseteq \mathbb{N}$ *and* $|\mathbb{Z}| = l$ **do**

         if $I(X, Y | \mathbb{Z})$ **then**

            independence = True

            break

         end

      end

   end

1   **return** X,Y,independence,continued

Algorithm 1: MrPC (MapReduce PC).

causal factors using kernel functions. Suppose that we have a dataset including N samples. Suppose that there are d different factors involved in each sample, i.e., each sample is encoded by a vector $\mathbf{f}_i = [f_{i,1}, f_{i,2}, ..., f_{i,d}] \in \mathbb{R}^d$. We can construct a matrix M with d rows and N columns for the dataset as follow,

$$M = \begin{pmatrix} f_{1,1} & f_{2,1} & \cdots & f_{N,1} \\ \cdots & \cdots & \cdots & \cdots \\ f_{1,d} & f_{2,d} & \cdots & f_{N,d} \end{pmatrix} \tag{1}$$

Based on M, we define a vector $\bar{\mathbf{f}} \in \mathbb{R}^d$ which contains the mean values of factor types over N samples and a vector $\mathbf{v} \in \mathbb{R}^d$ which contains the variance values of factor types. Then, we define a centric-normalised matrix $\hat{M}$ which is obtained by translating M by $\bar{\mathbf{f}}$ and normalising its k-th row by $\sqrt{v_k}$. In particular, we compute

$$\hat{M} = \begin{pmatrix} \frac{f_{1,1}-\bar{f}_1}{\sqrt{v_1}} & \frac{f_{2,1}-\bar{f}_1}{\sqrt{v_1}} & \cdots & \frac{f_{N,1}-\bar{f}_1}{\sqrt{v_1}} \\ \cdots & \cdots & \cdots & \cdots \\ \frac{f_{1,d}-\bar{f}_d}{\sqrt{v_d}} & \frac{f_{2,d}-\bar{f}_d}{\sqrt{v_d}} & \cdots & \frac{f_{N,d}-\bar{f}_d}{\sqrt{v_d}} \end{pmatrix} \qquad (2)$$

Finally, we define a kernel-based correlation matrix C of $d \times d$ in which each element $C_{i,j}$ is the result of a kernel function K applied on rows i and j of $\hat{M}$. In particular, let $\hat{M}(i)$ and $\hat{M}(j)$ respectively denote the i-th and j-th row of $\hat{M}$, $C_{i,j}$ is calculated as,

$$C_{i,j} = K\left(\hat{M}(i), \hat{M}(j)\right) = \left\langle \Phi\left(\hat{M}(i)\right), \Phi\left(\hat{M}(j)\right) \right\rangle \qquad (3)$$

where $\Phi(\mathbf{x})$ is an implicit function that maps a vector $\mathbf{x}$ in a low dimensional space $\mathcal{L}$ (for example, of d dimensions) to a high dimensional space $\mathcal{H}$ and $\langle \cdot, \cdot \rangle$ is the inner product of two vectors. There are several kernel functions proposed in the literature [3]. In this paper, we investigate common kernel functions including polynomial, sigmoidal, and Gaussian radial basis function (RBF).

Polynomial Kernel

$$K\left(\hat{M}(i), \hat{M}(j)\right) = \left\langle \hat{M}(i), \hat{M}(j) \right\rangle^p \qquad (4)$$

where p is the degree of the kernel. Note that when $p = 1$, $K\left(\hat{M}(i), \hat{M}(j)\right)$ induces to the conventional correlation of two factors types i and j. This shows that the polynomial kernel is a generalised form of the conventional correlation, which only captures linear relationships. Indeed, when $p = 1$, we have,

$$K\left(\hat{M}(i), \hat{M}(j)\right) = \frac{\frac{1}{N}\sum_{k=1}^{N}\left(f_{i,k} - \bar{f}_i\right)\left(f_{j,k} - \bar{f}_j\right)}{\sqrt{v_i}\sqrt{v_j}} = Corr(i,j) \qquad (5)$$

where $Corr(i,j)$ is the correlation between variables i and j.

Gaussian Radial Basis Function (RBF) Kernel

$$K\left(\hat{M}(i), \hat{M}(j)\right) = \exp\left(-\frac{\left\|\hat{M}(i) - \hat{M}(j)\right\|_2^2}{2\sigma^2}\right) \qquad (6)$$

where $\|\cdot\|_2$ is the L_2- norm and σ is a user parameter set to 0.1 in our experiments.

Sigmoidal Kernel

$$K\left(\hat{M}\left(i\right),\hat{M}\left(j\right)\right) = \tanh\left(\left\langle \hat{M}\left(i\right),\hat{M}\left(j\right)\right\rangle\right) \qquad (7)$$

where $\tanh\left(z\right) = \frac{e^z - e^{-z}}{e^z + e^{-z}}$.

Finally, we compute the partial correlations $\rho_{i,j}$ for every pair of factors as,

$$\rho_{i,j} = \frac{C_{i,j}^{-1}}{\sqrt{C_{i,i}^{-1} C_{j,j}^{-1}}} \qquad (8)$$

where C^{-1} is the inverse matrix of C.

3   Experiments

3.1   MrPC (distributed) V. PC-stable (sequential)

In the first experiment, we evaluated **MrPC** on six benchmark datasets provided in [4]. On each dataset, we also compared the running time of **MrPC** with that of the sequential approach **PC-stable** in [1]. The same parameter setting was used in both approaches, such as the significant level (α) is set to 0.01 in both settings. Also, the same computing infrastructure was used in both approaches.

Table 1. Running time (in minutes) of **MrPC** v. the sequential version (**PC-stable** [1]) on six datasets [4].

Dataset	#samples	#variables	PC-stable	MrPC	Ratio
NCI-60	47	1,190	4.57	1.66	2.75
BR51	50	1,592	31.34	10.64	2.95
MCC	88	1,380	25.73	9.63	2.67
Scerevisiae	63	5,361	79.15	22.65	3.49
Saureus	160	2,810	197.71	57.97	3.41
DREAM5-Insilico	805	1,643	1301.32	177.11	7.35

The running time needed for the **PC** algorithm by **MrPC** and the sequential approach **PC-stable** [1] is shown in Table 1. On six datasets experimented, **MrPC** performs between 2.75 and 7.35 times faster than the **PC-stable** [1]. Through experiments, we found that the gain is less on small datasets as the majority of running time is spent for Spark's initialisation, for example, locating and distributing resources to computing elements (executors). However, on larger datasets, the same amount of time and computation is spent for preprocessing but this amount is much smaller than the total running time, as the number of independence tests often increases with the size of the datasets. In summary, the larger the dataset is, the more benefit **MrPC** gains, and as shown in Table 1, the speed is improved up to seven times on DREAM5-Insilico dataset.

Table 2. Performance of different kernel functions in capturing gene regulatory networks of for *E. coli* and *S. cerevisiae* [5]. The best performances are in bold, the worst are in italics.

Kernel	AUROC	AUPR
Correlation	*0.50233*	*0.01402*
Polynomial ($p = 2$)	0.50836	0.01689
Polynomial ($p = 3$)	**0.51813**	**0.02892**
RBF	0.50349	0.01436
Sigmoidal	0.50238	0.01404

a.*E. coli* dataset.

Kernel	AUROC	AUPR
Correlation	*0.49918*	*0.01720*
Polynomial ($p = 2$)	0.50069	0.01749
Polynomial ($p = 3$)	0.50055	0.01747
RBF	**0.50102**	**0.01756**
Sigmoidal	0.49922	0.01720

b. *S. cerevisiae* dataset.

3.2 Kernel Functions

In the second experiment, we implemented **MrPC** with different kernel functions and compared these kernels with the conventional correlation computation, in building gene regulatory networks (GRN) for *E. coli* and *S. cerevisiae*. We conducted the experiment on the datasets provided in the DREAM5 network inference challenge [5], which aimed to reconstruct GRN from high-throughput data. Area under receiver operating characteristic (AUROC) and area under the precision-recall (AUPR) curves were used as performance measures [5].

We report the performance of the proposed **MrPC**with different kernels in building GRN for *E. coli* and for *S. cerevisiae* in Table 2(a) and Table 2(b) respectively. Experimental results show that, cubic polynomial kernel ($p = 3$) performs best on *E. coli* dataset in both AUROC and AUPR measures (see Table 2(a)). The second place also belongs to polynomial kernel but square polynomial kernel ($p = 2$). We found that both cubic and square polynomial kernels outperform the conventional correlation, which is proven as a case of polynomial kernels with $p = 1$. RBF kernel takes the third place while sigmoidal kernel slightly outperforms the conventional correlation. We note that this ranking is consistent in both AUROC and AUPR measures.

On *S. cerevisiae* dataset (see Table 2(b)), RBF kernel shows superior performance and achieves the first place. Cubic and square polynomial kernels perform similarly yet surpass the conventional correlation. Like *E. coli* dataset, there is slight difference in the performance of sigmoidal kernel and the conventional correlation on *S. cerevisiae* dataset. However, it is still clear to see the improvement of sigmoidal kernel compared with the conventional correlation.

4 Conclusion

Discovering causal links for observational data is an important problem with implications in causal discovery research. **PC** is a well-known tool for that task but is also a time-consuming algorithm. In an attempt to parallelise **PC**, thanks to advancements in distributed/cluster computing, we propose **MrPC** to accelerate **PC** for causal discovery in distributed systems. In addition, equipped with

MrPC, we propose to model non-linear causal relationships by using kernel functions to build gene regulatory networks from gene expression data. Experimental results on benchmark datasets show that the proposed **MrPC** is faster than sequential **PC** implementation, and kernel-based modelling outperforms conventional linear causal modelling in constructing gene regulatory networks.

References

1. Colombo, D., Maathuis, M.H.: Order-independent constraint-based causal structure learning. JMLR **15**(1), 3741–3782 (2014)
2. Dean, J., Ghemawat, S.: MapReduce: simplified data processing on large clusters. Commun. ACM **51**(1), 107–113 (2008)
3. Hofmann, T., Schölkopf, B., Smola, A.J.: Kernel methods in machine learning. Ann. Stat. **36**(3), 1171–1220 (2008)
4. Le, T., Hoang, T., Li, J., Liu, L., Liu, H., Hu, S.: A fast PC algorithm for high dimensional causal discovery with multi-core PCs. IEEE/ACM Trans. Comput. Biol. Bioinform. **16**(5), 1483–1495 (2019)
5. Marbach, D., et al.: Wisdom of crowds for robust gene network inference. Nat. Methods **9**(8), 796 (2012)
6. Shimizu, S., Hoyer, P.O., Hyvärinen, A., Kerminen, A.: A linear non-Gaussian acyclic model for causal discovery. JMLR **7**, 2003–2030 (2006)
7. Silverstein, C., Brin, S., Motwani, R., Ullman, J.: Scalable techniques for mining causal structures. Data Min. Knowl. Disc. **4**(2–3), 163–192 (2000)
8. Spirtes, P., Glymour, C.N., Scheines, R., Heckerman, D.: Causation, Prediction, and Search. MIT Press, Cambridge (2000)
9. Zaharia, M., Chowdhury, M., Franklin, M.J., Shenker, S., Stoica, I.: Spark: cluster computing with working sets. In: Proceedings of the USENIX Conference on Hot Topics in Cloud Computing, pp. 10 (2010)
10. Zhang, K., Peters, J., Janzing, D., Schölkopf, B.: Kernel-based conditional independence test and application in causal discovery. In: Proceedings of UAI, pp. 804–813 (2011)

Online Multi-objective Subspace Clustering for Streaming Data

Dipanjyoti Paul[(✉)], Sriparna Saha, and Jimson Mathew

Indian Institute of Technology Patna, Patna, India
{dipanjyoti.pcs17,sriparna,jimson}@iitp.ac.in

Abstract. This paper develops an online subspace clustering technique which is capable of handling continuous arrival of data in a streaming manner. Subspace clustering is a technique where the subset of features that are used to represent a cluster are different for different clusters. Most of the streaming data clustering methods primarily optimize only a single objective function which limits the model in capturing only a particular shape or property. However, the simultaneous optimization of multiple objectives helps in overcoming the above mentioned limitations and enables to generate good quality clusters. Inspired by this, the developed streaming subspace clustering method optimizes multiple objectives capturing cluster compactness and feature relevancy. In this paper, we consider an evolutionary-based technique and optimize multiple objective functions simultaneously to determine the optimal subspace clusters. The generated clusters in the proposed method are allowed to contain overlapping of objects. To establish the superiority of using multiple objectives, the proposed method is evaluated on three real-life and three synthetic data sets. The results obtained by the proposed method are compared with several state-of-the-art methods and the comparative study shows the superiority of using multiple objectives in the proposed method.

Keywords: Multi-objective optimization · Subspace clustering · Streaming data · ICC-index · PSM-index · Overlapping objects

1 Introduction

Subspace clustering (SC) [6] is a special case of traditional clustering where each cluster in subspace partitioning is represented by a different subset of features (called subspace feature set). Again, in SC, there is a possibility that an object is relevant to more than one subspace feature sets which indicates that an object can be a part of more than one cluster. Again, nowadays a huge number of data samples are being continuously generated by different application domains. For instance, in social media networks, such as, in Twitter, whenever a new tweet is posted or in Facebook or Instagram whenever a new message or photo is posted, it is considered as a new sample and in each and every minute, a large number

© Springer Nature Switzerland AG 2020
H. Yang et al. (Eds.): ICONIP 2020, CCIS 1332, pp. 95–103, 2020.
https://doi.org/10.1007/978-3-030-63820-7_11

of such samples are generated. Due to this continuous generation, clustering method on streaming data requires updating the model in time to time.

In streaming data, the arrival of the data is a continuous process and so the updation of the model. The updation of the model should be fast enough to properly follow the stream. In case of streaming data, the subspace clustering model has to undergo several challenges such as; *cluster drift* [7], the clusters change their positions/structures/properties in feature space; *cluster inflation/deflation* [7], size of the cluster may increase/decrease; *cluster appearing/disappearing*, a new cluster may appear or an existing cluster may disappear; *subspace modifications*, an updation is required for the subspace feature set; *overlapping objects modification*, some non-overlapping objects may get overlapped and vice-versa.

The first streaming data clustering method developed is offline K-means [9]. CluStream [2] is developed based on a two-phase scheme concept i.e., online and offline. DenStream [10] and SDStream [11] are the density-based streaming data clustering approaches. DenStream forms clusters based on the reachability of the micro-clusters by checking their distances between each other. SDStream is an extension of DenStream method where it applies the sliding window. DENGRIS [12] and D-Stream [4] are the grid-based streaming data clustering approaches. In order to capture the dynamic behaviour of the streaming data, D-stream uses a time-dependent decaying factor in density computation. However, DENGRIS applies sliding window protocol to consider the most recent objects.

The proposed method is a center-based meta-heuristic evolutionary clustering technique. The method is capable of generating subspace clusters for streaming data by optimizing multiple objectives [5,6]. The objective functions that we have considered are two cluster validity indices, ICC-index [5] and modified version of PSM-index [5]. However, the mutation operators are defined in this paper in such a way that they are capable of adapting to the new environment quickly. The mutation operators are *exogenous genetic material uptake* [5] and a newly defined *translocation and duplication divergence (TDID)*. In streaming data, whenever a stream data arrives, the streaming method updates the model by keeping a global picture of the data arrived till the time. Therefore, whenever a chunk of data arrives, the method clusters the chunk based on the current model, and then the model may get updated based on some criteria. So, when there is a concept drift, i.e., the distribution of the data changes, there is a possibility that the model needs to be updated. The developed algorithm is tested with a few real-life and synthetic data sets. It is also compared with a few previous streaming data clustering methods and the comparison shows the superiority of using multiple objectives in the proposed method.

2 Proposed Algorithm

The proposed method develops a subspace clustering algorithm for streaming data. It uses the multi-objective optimization framework in order to cluster the stream while adapting to the new environment quickly and efficiently.

2.1 Problem Formulation

The task of the developed method is to generate subspace clusters and update the model continuously on the arrival of the stream. The problem is defined as:

– Given
- The data stream $D = \{d_1, d_2, \ldots\}$ arriving continuously infinite times, can also be represented in the form of horizons such as $\{H_1, H_2, \ldots\}$. These objects are represented by the feature set $F = \{f_1, f_2, \ldots, f_F\}$ of size $|F|$.
- A set of objectives represented by r validity indices such as $\{V_1, V_2, \ldots, V_r\}$ are used to optimize the clusters.

– Find
- Partition each arriving horizon H_j into C subspace clusters such as $\{C_1, C_2, \ldots, C_C\}$, where each cluster is represented by a subset of feature set, $F_i \subseteq F$; $i \in [1, C]$.
- The subspace cluster $C_i = \{d_1^i, d_2^i, \ldots, d_{n_i}^i\}$ is represented by subspace feature $F_i = \{f_1^i, f_2^i, \ldots, f_{k_i}^i\}$ where n_i: size of the cluster i, d_j^i: jth element of cluster i, k_i: size of the subspace feature i and f_j^i: jth feature of subspace feature i i.e., F_i.
- The generated clusters will either be overlapping or non-overlapping, i.e., $\cup_{i=1}^{C} C_i = H$, H is the horizon size and $C_i \cap C_j \neq \phi$ for some $i \neq j$.

2.2 Model Representation

The proposed method is a center-based meta-heuristic online data clustering technique. The model consists of a phenotype (P) and a genotype (G) and both of them can be represented by a 2-dimensional zero matrix consisting of N_{max} rows and F columns, i.e., of size $N_{max} * F$. The rows of the phenotype refer to the phenotypic traits or the core points, i.e., the coordinates of the cluster centers along different dimensions. Whereas, the genotype refers to the number of genes associated with each of the coordinate values.

When a new data stream H_{t+1} arrives, based on some criteria, the streaming method either updates the model, M_t or not, i.e., $M_{t+1} = M_t$. More precisely, when there is a change in the distribution of the stream data, i.e., when concept drift occurs, most of the time the model gets updated. The updation of a model indicates the change in the cluster centers, subspace feature sets, size of the clusters as well as, change in the number of clusters. Again, when the model needs to be updated, the updation is done on the existing model, M_t, i.e., on the existing centers at the time 't' by keeping a global picture of the streaming data. The overview of the proposed streaming method is shown in Fig. 1.

Initialization: At the very beginning, a phenotype is created by selecting a cluster center randomly and updating its coordinate (by uniformly selecting an object from the initial horizon along a particular feature) based on some probability. The corresponding genotype (G) value is also increased by one. Next, another center is selected uniformly and the same process is followed. The process is repeated until the weight of the genotype becomes $\alpha * N_{max}$ where $\alpha \in \{1, 2,..\} \mid 10 * (\alpha - 1) < |F| \leq 10 * \alpha$. However, at any point 't', the mean and the variance of an incoming horizon can be computed as $\mu_t = \frac{(t-1)*\mu_{t-1}+(\mu_C)_t}{t}$ and $\sigma_t = \frac{(t-1)*\sigma_{t-1}+(\sigma_C)_t}{t}$ [8]. μ_{t-1} and σ_{t-1} are the mean and the variance till time $(t-1)$. μ_{Ct} and σ_{Ct} are the mean and the variance of the current data stream.

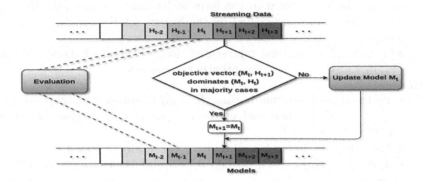

Fig. 1. Overview of proposed multi-objective streaming subspace clustering technique

2.3   Mutation Operators

The mutation operators in streaming data clustering are defined in such a way that the model could be able to adapt quickly in order to keep track of the stream data. The mutation operators that are defined in this approach are *exogenous genetic material uptake* and *translocation and duplication divergence (TDID)* and are applied in the same order.

Exogenous Genetic Material Uptake. The change of environment takes place on the arrival of streaming data and therefore some bacteria may reach *competent* state, uptaking external DNA that carries useful biological functions. This results in the addition of direct environmental information and it will either create a new core point or update an existing one in the phenotype or it may also delete an existing core point. The detailed operation can be found in [5].

Translocation and Duplication Divergence (TDID) This mutation is based on the duplication and translocation divergence operator. At each event, either the translocation-deletion (TD) or duplication-inversion (ID) divergence operator is performed and the number of such events to be performed can be determined by the binomial law $\beta(\mu_d, C)$; μ_d is the divergence operator rate. Let an existing cluster 'c' be chosen uniformly and a subset of features $f' \subseteq F_c$ (size $= \eta$, a random integer in the interval $[1; |F_c|]$) is selected for duplication and deletion. $|F_c|$ is the size of the subspace feature $|F_c|$ of cluster 'c'. Next, a number δ is uniformly chosen from the interval $\{-\eta, ..., -1, 1, ..., \eta\}$ (excluding 0). If the value δ is positive, TD divergence is performed otherwise ID divergence.

To perform any of the two divergences, i.e., to perform any of these four operations, say 'u' be the number of features selected either to perform duplicate or inverse or translocate or deletion operation. In each case, firstly a subset of features selected sequentially of size u_1 (random integer from [1; u]) is considered and then another subset of features of size u_2 (a random integer from [1; u-u_1]) are selected. The process will continue until all the features in 'u' are used for execution. Therefore, for both the TD and ID divergence operators, η is divided into two equal parts, η_1 and η_2. The first η_1 features are used to perform either duplication or translocation and the remaining η_2 features are used either for inversion or deletion, respectively. In case of deletion, an existing center is selected and the corresponding coordinate values along the feature $f \in f'$ are replaced by zero. The gene count is also replaced by zero. For duplication, if there already exists a non-zero value $(f \in f')$, it is replaced with the mean of the existing and the new values otherwise just replaced with the new co-ordinate. The gene count in the genotype (G) will simply increase by one. However, for translocation, the co-ordinate values of a center along the features are sequentially selected and moved to some other positions in the same center. The gene count of the selected position is marked with zero and the count of the moved positions is increased by one. Similarly, for inversion, the selected position will simply be reversed and the corresponding gene count is also reversed.

2.4 Objective Functions

Objective functions that have used in this approach are represented in the form of validity indices such as ICC-index and modified version of PSM-index [5].

Intra-cluster Compactness (ICC-index): Intra-cluster Compactness deals with the compactness within a cluster. However, it is defined as $ICC(H, P) = \left[\frac{1}{C} * \sum_{i=1}^{C} \frac{1}{\lceil n_i \rceil} \sum_{s \in m_i} dis(d_s, C_i) \right]$. The term C is the total number of clusters produced. n_i is the size of the cluster 'i' and $dis(d_s, C_i) = \sum_{f \in F_i} |d_{s,f} - C_{i,f}| + \sum_{f \in F \setminus F_i} |d_{s,f} - \mu_f|$ is the Manhattan distance between an object (d_s) to its cluster center (C_i). μ_f is the mean distance value between objects to the original cluster center. H is the horizon size and m_i is the membership degree.

Paul-Saha-Mathew (PSM) Index: PSM-index is primarily defined to optimize the subspace feature set. This index can be computed by merging the modified objectives, *Feature Per Cluster* (FPC) [5] & *Feature Non-redundancy* (FNR) [5].

Feature Per Cluster: In subspace clustering, the size of the subspace feature used to represent a cluster should neither be too high nor too low. In the proposed method the optimal size of the subspace feature is considered as near to the mean value of the minimum (1) and maximum ($|F|$) possible subspace feature size. Therefore, the optimal range of (FPC) is $\pm\epsilon_1$ to the mean value and is defines as: $FPC(P) = \left[\frac{\sum_{i=1}^{C}|F_i|}{C} - \frac{|F|+1}{2}\right] \pm \epsilon_1$.

Feature Non-redundancy: This objective is to avoid the subspace feature sets representing clusters having large number of features in common. It is not that FNR doesn't support intersecting subspace but minimizes the redundancy. The range of optimal FNR value is defined by a factor ϵ_2 as $FNR(P) = \left[\frac{1}{C_{C_2}}\sum_{i=1}^{C-1}\sum_{j=i+1}^{C}|(|F_i| \cap |F_j|)|\right] \pm \epsilon_2$. ϵ_1 and ϵ_2 are the two parameters used to define the optimal ranges of FPC and FNR, respectively.

The normalized PSM-index is defined as $PSM(P) = \left[\frac{2*FPC(P)+FNR(P)}{|F|}\right]$. In the proposed method, the objective is to minimize both the objective functions in order to achieve good subspace clustering.

2.5   Generation of Subspace Clusters

Every time a stream data arrives, clustering is performed on the stream. Each object of the stream has to be assigned to a particular cluster, i.e., to find the membership degree. The membership function of an object that is considered here is the modified version of the function used in Fuzzy C-means [3]. Here, Manhattan distance is used for distance calculation. The fuzzy membership μ_{ij} of an object 'j' with respect to a cluster 'i' is computed as $\mu_{ij} = \left[\sum_{k=1}^{C}\left[\frac{dis(d_j,C_i)}{dis(d_j,C_k)}\right]^{(\frac{2}{t}-1)}\right]^{-1}$. We obtain the fuzzy membership values of an object with respect to all the cluster centers. The membership degree, m_{ij} of an object 'j' is computed based on the difference between the maximum of fuzzy values of 'j' with respect to all centers to the fuzzy value with respect to cluster 'i'. If the difference is less than a threshold value then $m_{ij} = 1$ otherwise '0'. The threshold is defined as $[\gamma * C]^{-1}$. C is the number of clusters and γ is the minimization factor.

3   Data Sets and Experimental Setup

This section describes the data sets used to test the proposed method, various evaluation metrics and a few existing streaming clustering methods.

3.1   Data Sets Used and Parameter Settings

The proposed method is tested with three real-life and three synthetic data sets. The real-life data sets used in this method are selected from [8], such as *Forest Cover Type*, *Network Intrusion* and *Iris*. In order to make a fair comparison, only the top 100 (*Covertype*) and 200 (*NetIntrusion*) chunks of size 1000 arriving in the form of a stream are considered for testing except *iris* where chunk size is

50. The synthetic data sets that have used are *SynFullDyn*, *SynDriftDyn* and SynClusterNbDyn [7], generated by following the same procedure as in [1].

The proposed method always maintains $N = 10$ number of solutions and maximum possible number of clusters is $N_{max} = 20$ for real and 30 for synthetic data sets. Again, when the model also needs to be updated, it iterates $I = 10$ times. Moreover, the parameters ϵ_1 and ϵ_2 are defined as $\epsilon_1 = i$ and $\epsilon_2 = j$, i, j $\in \{1, 2, \ldots\}$ such that $10 * (i - 1) \leq F < 10 * i$ and $5 * (j - 1) \leq F < 5 * j$. Again, for a fair comparison, the horizon size for synthetic data sets is taken as 200. The divergence operator rate $\mu_d = 0.005$, minimization factor $\gamma = 8$ (synthetic data sets) and $\gamma = 4$ for real data sets except *NetIntrusion* where it is 12.

3.2 Comparing Methods and Evaluation Metrics

The proposed method is tested on various real-life and synthetic data sets and in order to compare its performance on these real-life data sets a few benchmark approaches have been considered. The comparing methods are CluStream [2], HPStream [1] and DFPS-Clustering [8] etc.

The performance of the streaming data clustering algorithms can be evaluated by Accuracy [7], CE (Clustering Error) [7], SSCE (Subspace CE) [7] and two statistical score measures, namely Rand-index (RI) [8] and Kappa-index (KI) [8]. SSCE is specifically designed to evaluate subspace clustering methods. Moreover, more the values of these metrics, the better are the results.

4 Experimental Results

In this section we show the results obtained by the proposed method and its comparison with various other algorithms.

The results are evaluated every time on the arrival of a stream data in the form of a horizon with respect to the metrics, Accuracy, RI-index and KI index. However, the results reported in Table 1 are the average of the scores obtained at different time stamps. Comparing all the clustering methods with respect to different evaluation metrics, the following observations can be made.

- The proposed algorithm performs better in comparison to other algorithms in the majority of the cases considering *RI-index* as an evaluation metric.
- With respect to *accuracy*, the proposed method provides the best results.
- Moreover, with respect to *KI-index* also, the proposed method is superior as it reports a better score for the majority of the data sets.

We have also reported the metric values obtained for real-data sets at different time stamps of the incoming horizon and are represented in the form of a graph for the metrics, *Accuracy* (Fig. 2(a)), *RI-index* (Fig. 2(b)) and *KI-index* (Fig. 2(c)), respectively, as shown in Fig. 2. Proposed method is also tested on some synthetic data sets to test its performance. Superiority of the proposed method is also observed from the obtained results with respect to synthetic data sets.

Table 1. Comparison amongst the proposed method and other methods for the real-life streaming data sets with respect to the metrics, *Accuracy, RI and KI index*

Metrices	Data Sets	STREAM	CluStream	HPStream	DFPS-clustering	**MOO-Stream**
RI-index	*Iris*	0.9089	0.9206	–	0.9282	**0.933**
	CoverType	0.5987	0.6243	–	0.6495	0.628
	NetIntrusion	0.8624	0.8848	–	0.9211	**0.962**
KI-index	*Iris*	0.8873	0.8923	–	0.9015	**0.921**
	CoverType	0.0604	0.0856	–	0.1132	**0.221**
	NetIntrusion	0.8283	0.8474	–	**0.9004**	0.854
Accuracy	*Iris*	–	–	–	–	**0.999**
	CoverType	–	0.69	0.71	–	**0.781**
	NetIntrusion	–	0.935	0.953	–	**0.988**

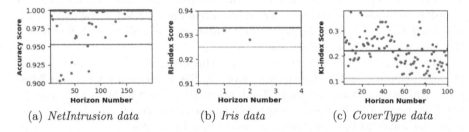

(a) *NetIntrusion data*   (b) *Iris data*   (c) *CoverType data*

Fig. 2. Metric scores with respect to different streaming horizons for real datasets and comparison of the proposed method (blue) with DFPS (orange) and HPStream (green) (Color figure online)

5   Conclusions and Future Works

In this paper, we have developed a multi-objective based subspace clustering technique which can handle streaming data. The multi-objective optimization based framework and the developed new mutation operator helps to adapt the model quickly to the new environment when streaming data arrives. The proposed method is tested with a few real-life and synthetic data sets and based on the comparison, it can be claimed that the proposed method provides better results in most of the cases and it is superior than state-of-the-art techniques.

In future, the proposed approach can be tested on some more data sets. Also, the clustering method can be extended to apply in a multi-view framework.

Acknowledgement. Dr. Sriparna Saha would like to acknowledge the support of Early Career Research Award of Science and Engineering Research Board (SERB) of Department of Science & Technology India to carry out this research.

References

1. Aggarwal, C C., Han, J., Wang, J., Yu, P.S.: A framework for projected clustering of high dimensional data streams. In: Proceedings of the Thirtieth International Conference on Very Large Data, vol. 30, pp. 852–863 (2004)
2. Aggarwal, C.C., Philip, S.Y., Han, J., Wang, J.: A framework for clustering evolving data streams. In: Proceedings 2003 VLDB Conference, pp. 81–92 (2003)
3. Bezdek, J.C., Ehrlich, R., Full, W.: FCM: the fuzzy c-means clustering algorithm. Comput. Geosci. **10**, 191–203 (1984)
4. Chen, Y., Tu, L.: Density-based clustering for real-time stream data. In: Proceedings of the 13th ACM SIGKDD International Conference on Knowledge Discovery and Data Mining, pp. 133–142 (2007)
5. Paul, D., Saha, S., Mathew, J.: Improved subspace clustering algorithm using multi-objective framework and subspace optimization. Expert Syst. Appl. 113487 (2020)
6. Paul, D., Saha, S., Mathew, J.: Fusion of evolvable genome structure and multi-objective optimization for subspace clustering. Pattern Recogn. **95**, 58–71 (2019)
7. Peignier, S.: Subspace clustering on static datasets and dynamic data streams using bio-inspired algorithms. Ph.D. Thesis, University de Lyon, INSA Lyon (2017)
8. Yan, X., Razeghi, J.M., Homaifar, A., Erol, B.A., Girma, A., Tunstel, E:. A novel streaming data clustering algorithm based on fitness proportionate sharing. In: IEEE Access, pp. 184985–185000 (2019)
9. Guha, S., Mishra, N., Motwani, R., o'Callaghan, L.: Clustering data streams. In: Proceedings 41st Annual Symposium on Foundations of Computer Science, pp. 359–366 (2000)
10. Cao, F., Estert, M., Qian, W., Zhou, A.: Density-based clustering over an evolving data stream with noise. In: Proceedings of the 2006 SIAM International Conference on Data Mining, pp. 328–339 (2006)
11. Ren, J., Ma, R.: Density-based data streams clustering over sliding windows. In: Sixth International Conference on Fuzzy Systems and Knowledge Discovery, vol. 5, pp. 248–252 (2009)
12. Amini, A., Wah, T.Y., Teh, Y.W.: DENGRIS-stream: a density-grid based clustering algorithm for evolving data streams over sliding window. In: International Conference on Data Mining and Computer Engineering, pp. 206–210 (2012)

Predicting Information Diffusion Cascades Using Graph Attention Networks

Meng Wang and Kan Li[(✉)]

School of Computer Science and Technology, Beijing Institute of Technology,
Beijing 100081, China
{3120181036,likan}@bit.edu.cn

Abstract. Effective information cascade prediction plays a very important role in suppressing the spread of rumors in social networks and providing accurate social recommendations on social platforms. This paper improves existing models and proposes an end-to-end deep learning method called CasGAT. The method of graph attention network is designed to optimize the processing of large networks. After that, we only need to pay attention to the characteristics of neighbor nodes. Our approach greatly reduces the processing complexity of the model. We use realistic datasets to demonstrate the effectiveness of the model and compare the improved model with three baselines. Extensive results demonstrate that our model outperformed the three baselines in the prediction accuracy.

Keywords: Social network · Information cascade prediction · Graph attention network

1 Introduction

The emergence of online social platforms, such as Twitter, Weibo, Facebook, Instagram, WeChat, QQ, has changed our daily lives. Information diffusion cascade occurs when people see the tweets of others on the platforms and then retweet the information that the others have written. Cascade information can play an important role in addressing the issue of controlling and predicting information diffusion. Along with this growth of the messages on these platforms, however, there are increasing concerns over complex and dynamic information diffusion cascade prediction.

Much work so far has focused on information diffusion cascade prediction. It mainly falls into four main categories: feature-based method, generative process method and deep learning-based methods. Information diffusion cascade prediction still has many challenges: (1) lack of knowledge of dynamic network graph structure when real social networks are constantly changing. This greatly affects the general type of the model. (2) the accuracy of the information diffusion cascade prediction take into account not only structural information but also temporal information.

© Springer Nature Switzerland AG 2020
H. Yang et al. (Eds.): ICONIP 2020, CCIS 1332, pp. 104–112, 2020.
https://doi.org/10.1007/978-3-030-63820-7_12

Here, we introduce an attention and temporal model called CasGAT to predict the information diffusion cascade, which can handle network structure predictions in different time periods. It only deals with the relationship between nodes and neighbor nodes in the graph, without first acquiring the structural features of the entire graph. Therefore, it can handle tasks including evaluating models on completely invisible graphs during training. In addition, CasGAT uses deep learning methods, graphical attention networks and time decay to enhance our framework.

In the rest of this paper, Sect. 2 reviews the related work. In Sect. 3, we describe the main aspects of CasGAT methodology in details. Experimental evaluations quantifying the benefits of our approach are presented in Sect. 4 and Sect. 5 concludes the paper and outlines directions for future work.

2   Related Work

In this section, we briefly review the research on the Information diffusion cascade prediction. In general, existing method of information diffusion cascade prediction falls into three main categories.

2.1   Feature-Based Method

As for early adopts and network structure, the properties of featured-based methods energetically depends on the quality of the hand-crafted features. These features are mainly extracted from temporal features [8,10], structural features [1,12], content features [5,11] and features defined by early adopters [4,6]. Faced with complex problems and massive data, it is difficult for people to systematically design and measure Effectively capture complex features of relevant information.

2.2   Generation Process Method

The generation process method focuses on modeling the strength function independently for each message arrival. Generally, they observe each event and learn the parameters by maximizing the probability of the event occurring within the observation time window. Shen et al. [9] used the enhanced Poisson process to model three factors in the social network (the influence of nodes, the decay process of information heat, and the "rich get rich" mechanism). These methods show enhanced interpretability, but the implicit information in cascade dynamics cannot be fully utilized to obtain satisfactory predictions.

2.3   Deep Learning-Based Method

Deep learning-based methods are inspired by the latest success of deep learning in many fields, and cascade prediction using deep neural networks has achieved significant performance improvements. The first proposed information cascade predictor (DeepCas) based on deep learning [7] converts a cascade graph into a sequence of nodes by random walk, and automatically learns the representation of each graph. Cao et al. [2] proposed a process based on deep learning, which inherits the high interpretability of the Hawkes process and has the high predictive power of deep learning methods. However, due to the low efficiency of cascading sampling bias and local structure embedding, they lack good learning ability in cascading structure information and dynamic modeling.

3   Model

The information cascade is affected by many factors. The overview of the architecture is shown in Fig. 1. The model takes a cascade graph as the input and predicts the information increment size as the outputs. Next, we focus on the detailed methods one by one.

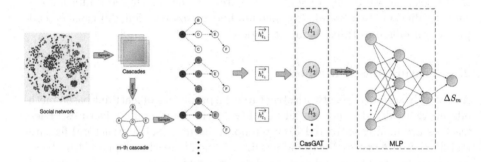

Fig. 1. The overview of our model architecture.

3.1   Basic Definitions

We denote a social network (e.g., weibo network) as $\mathcal{G} = (\mathcal{V}, \mathcal{E})$, where $\mathcal{V}$ is the set of all users of $\mathcal{G}$, $\mathcal{E} \subseteq \mathcal{V} \times \mathcal{V}$ is the set of all relationships between users. Suppose we have M pieces of message in the social network, let $C = \{C_m, (1 \leq m \leq M)\}$ be the set of M information cascades. We use $g_{t_i}^i = \left(v_{t_i}^i, e_{t_i}^i\right)$ to represent the cascade path for the i-th information diffusion of the message m at t_i, where $v_{t_i}^i$ represents the subset of V, $e_{t_i}^i$ represents the relationship between the users in $v_{t_i}^i$. The objective problem of this paper can be expressed as: given a set of information cascades $C_m(t)$ observed on a given social network information cascade $C = (C_1, C_2, \ldots, C_M)$, we want to predict the increment size ΔS_m of each information cascade C_m for a fixed time window Δt, i.e., $\Delta S_m = \left|S_m^{T+\Delta t}\right| - \left|S_m^T\right|$.

3.2   Cascade Embedding

Each information cascade on every social media almost consists of a sequence of retweets, so the big cascade is becoming a big problem when processing the original graph cascade. There are different ways to represent cascaded input. In our approach, the cascade C_m represents the propagation path of the message m. We can get the cascade graph $G_{t_i}^i$ which is represented as a set of cascade paths that are sampled through the $G_{t_i}^i = \left\{ g_{t_1}^i, g_{t_2}^i, g_{t_3}^i, \ldots, g_T^i \right\}, t_i \in [0, T)$. Each cascade graph not only contains the structure information between the users, but also carries the temporal information. $G_{t_i}^i$ consists of a set of matrices.

3.3   Graph Attention Layer

This part of our model is based on graph attention network. In our approach, we use the method called feature decomposition to compute the eigenvectors of the above matrix in $G_{t_i}^i$. And we get the set of node features, $\mathbf{h} = \{\overrightarrow{h_{t_1}^i}, \overrightarrow{h_{t_2}^i}, \overrightarrow{h_{t_3}^i}, \ldots, \overrightarrow{h_T^i}\}$ as the input of graph attention layer. In order to get the corresponding conversion between the input and output, we need to perform linear transformation at least once according to the input features to get the output features, so we need to train a weight matrix $\mathbf{W}$ for all bytes. The attention coefficients

$$e_{uv} = f(W\overrightarrow{h_u^i}, W\overrightarrow{h_v^i}) \tag{1}$$

indicate the importance of node v's features to node u. In order to make the attention coefficient easier to calculate and compare, we introduced softmax function to regularize all adjacent nodes of u:

$$\alpha_{uv} = softmax_v(e_{uv}) = \frac{\exp(e_{uv})}{\sum_{k \in V} \exp(e_{uk})} \tag{2}$$

Combining the above formulas (1) and (2), sorting them together can get the complete attention mechanism as follows:

$$\alpha_{uv} = softmax_v(e_{uv}) = \frac{\exp\left(LeakyReLU\left(\overrightarrow{f}^T\left[W\overrightarrow{h_u^i}\|W\overrightarrow{h_v^i}\right]\right)\right)}{\sum_{k \in V} \exp\left(LeakyReLU\left(\overrightarrow{f}^T\left[W\overrightarrow{h_u^i}\|W\overrightarrow{h_k^i}\right]\right)\right)} \tag{3}$$

where $.^T$ represents transposition and $\|$ is the concatenation operation
    The outputs of this layer are represented:

$$h_{struc} = \boldsymbol{h} = \sigma\left(\sum_{v \in V} \alpha_{uv}\overrightarrow{h_v^i}\right) \tag{4}$$

The output characteristics of this node are related to all the nodes adjacent to it, which are obtained after their linear and nonlinear activation.

3.4   Temporal Embedding

In our model, we will embed time. We use the most common LSTM (Long short-term memory) to model temporal embedding. Below we will talk about the specific implementation of these aspects. LSTM is a special kind of RNN. We use the most common LSTM (Long Short Term Memory) to model temporal embeddings. LSTM is a special RNN that can selectively memorize past information through a memory unit. The specific implementation method is as follows:

$$
\begin{aligned}
f_t &= \sigma \left(W_f \cdot \left[h_{t-1}, g_t^i \right] + b_f \right) \\
i_t &= \sigma \left(W_i \cdot \left[h_{t-1}, g_t^i \right] + b_i \right) \\
\tilde{C}_t &= \tanh \left(W_C \cdot \left[h_{t-1}, g_t^i \right] + b_C \right) \\
C_t &= f_t * C_{t-1} + i_t * \tilde{C}_t \\
o_t &= \sigma \left(W_o \left[h_{t-1}, g_t^i \right] + b_o \right)
\end{aligned}
\tag{5}
$$

where g_t^i is a matrix representation of the cascade path, and f_t, i_t, o_t are respectively the input gate, forget gate and output gate. The hidden state is then updated by:

$$
h_t = o_t * \tanh \left(C_t \right)
\tag{6}
$$

Finally, we get the collection of the m messages $h_{tem} = h = \{ \overrightarrow{h_1}, \overrightarrow{h_2}, \overrightarrow{h_3}, \dots, \overrightarrow{h_M} \}$.

3.5   Time-Delay Function and Output Layer

Social networking is a very dynamic process. For example, when a Weibo has just been published, it has the greatest influence, and then its effect will become smaller and smaller over time. This is why we have to add the time decay factor. Current methods have power-law functions ($\phi(t) = (t+c)^{-(1+\theta)}$) and exponential functions ($\phi(t) = e^{-\theta t}$) to simulate. In our model, we use a non-parametric method to make a more appropriate representation of the time decay factor. We assume that the overall observation time window is $[0, T)$, and then split the observation time window into l disjoint time intervals $\{[t_0 = 0, t_1), [t_1, t_2), \dots [t_{l-1}, t_l = T)\}$. We need to learn the discrete variable of time decay effect $\lambda_j, j \in (1, 2, \dots, l)$. For different cascade paths, we all add time decay parameters to get a new representation:

$$
h_t' = \lambda_m (h_{tem} + h_{struc})
\tag{7}
$$

and the m-th cascade path can be represented by:

$$
h'(C_m) = \sum_{t=1}^{T} h_t'
\tag{8}
$$

The final output of our model consists of a multi-layer perceptron (MLP), expressed as follows:

$$
\Delta S_i = \mathbf{MLP} \left(h'(C_i) \right)
\tag{9}
$$

4 Experiments

In this section, we will present the details of experiments conducted on real-world datasets and the results analysis between our proposed model and baseline.

4.1 Dataset

The dataset is from Sina Weibo, one of the most popular microblogging platform in China. This dataset is provided by Cao [2]. In Sina Weibo, the network is composed of the relationship among a big group of users. The relationship contains the retweets, likes and comments. In this paper, we concentrate on the retweets of messages. Compared to likes and comments, retweet is the most direct way to form a cascade. The crawl time of dataset is from 0:00 on June 1, 2016 to 24:00 on June 1, 2018. It remains 119,313 messages in total. We filter out the message before 6 am and after 9 pm. And the length T of observation time window, we consider three settings, i.e., T = 1 h, 2 h and 3 h. Finally, we sort all the rest cascades by publishing time, replacing the first 70% as the training set, the middle 15% as the verification set, and the last 15% as the test set.

4.2 Baselines and Variants of Our Model

For a comprehensive comparison, we considered a variety of the latest alternatives in the methods mentioned above. The baselines are DeepCas [7], Deep-Hawkes [2] and CasCN [3]. In addition to comparing with existing baseline, we also compared with some variants of CasGAT. Here are a few variants of our model: CasGAT-GCN, CasGAT-GRU, CasGAT-Time.

4.3 Evaluation Metric

For the information cascade prediction problem, we choose standard evaluation metrics—MSLE (mean square log-transformed error) in our experiments. The smaller MSLE, the better prediction performance. Specifically, MSLE is the metric for evaluating the linking accuracy, defined as:

$$MSLE = \frac{1}{M} \sum_{i=1}^{M} \left(\log \Delta S_i - \log \Delta \widetilde{S}_i \right)^2 \tag{10}$$

where M is the total number of the messages, ΔS_i is the prediction result and $\Delta \widetilde{S}_i$ is the actual result.

mSLE is the median of $\left(\log \Delta S_i - \log \Delta \widetilde{S}_i \right)^2$ which can effectively reduce the impact of outliers, defined as:

$$mSLE = median_{i=1...M} \left(\log \Delta S_i - \log \Delta \widetilde{S}_i \right)^2 \tag{11}$$

Table 1. The performance of baseline model and CasGAT on Sina Weibo dataset

Observation Time	1 h		2 h		3 h	
Evaluation Metric	mSLE	MSLE	mSLE	MSLE	mSLE	MSLE
DeepCas	0.918	3.693	0.857	3.276	0.906	3.212
DeepHawkes	0.736	2.501	0.689	2.384	0.694	2.275
CasCN	0.638	2.375	0.615	2.243	0.542	2.098
CasGAT	**0.606**	**2.253**	**0.547**	**2.093**	**0.503**	**1.936**

4.4   Result

In this section, we compare the performance of our model with the three baselines. The results are illustrated in Table 1.

Table 1 summarizes the performance comparison between CasGAT and three baselines on the Sina Weibo dataset. Generally speaking, the proposed CasGAT model performs relatively well in the information cascade prediction on the public Sina Weibo dataset. It is superior to traditional methods, such as feature-based methods and generation methods, and superior to the latest deep learning methods. MSLE and mSLE are statistically significantly reduced.

To study and prove the effectiveness of each component of our model, we introduced three variants of CasGAT. These variants are all modified models for a part of our model framework. The experimental results are shown in Table 2, from which we can see that the original CasGAT caused a certain reduction in prediction error compared to other variants. Through comparison with CasGAT-Time, we find that the time decay effect is essential for cascade size prediction. Similarly, CasGAT-GCN and CasGAT-GRU also reduce prediction performance to some extent. Among them, the error of CasGAT-GRU variant is smaller than the original model within 1 h, but the error of the original model is still small in the subsequent time.

Table 2. The performance of CasGAT and its variants on Sina Weibo dataset

Observation time	1 h		2 h		3 h	
Evaluation Metric	mSLE	MSLE	mSLE	MSLE	mSLE	MSLE
CasGAT-GCN	0.618	2.292	0.574	2.186	0.525	1.994
CasGAT-GRU	**0.601**	**2.249**	0.550	2.138	0.516	1.952
CasGAT-Time	0.927	2.641	0.845	2.598	0.701	2.336
CasGAT	0.606	2.253	**0.547**	**2.093**	**0.503**	**1.936**

In summary, structural and time information are two key components in CasGAT. These two factors play an indispensable role in improving prediction accuracy.

5 Conclusion

We propose a new information cascade propagation model based on deep learning - CasGAT. Our model uses structure and temporal information to achieve information cascade prediction. The model mainly adds a graph attention mechanism, which greatly reduces the complexity of modeling graphs. We put our focus on neighbor nodes instead of the entire graph, which can further improve our prediction performance. In the future, we will increase our efforts to expand the model's perception capabilities and extend the model to more effective data sets.

Acknowledgments. This research was supported by Beijing Natural Science Foundation (No. L181010, 4172054), National Key R & D Program of China (No. 2016YFB0801100), and National Basic Research Program of China (No. 2013CB329605).

References

1. Bao, P., Shen, H.W., Huang, J., Cheng, X.Q.: Popularity prediction in microblogging network: a case study on Sina Weibo. In: Proceedings of the 22nd International Conference on World Wide Web, pp. 177–178 (2013)
2. Cao, Q., Shen, H., Cen, K., Ouyang, W., Cheng, X.: DeepHawkes: bridging the gap between prediction and understanding of information cascades. In: Proceedings of the 2017 ACM on Conference on Information and Knowledge Management, pp. 1149–1158 (2017)
3. Chen, X., Zhou, F., Zhang, K., Trajcevski, G., Zhong, T., Zhang, F.: Information diffusion prediction via recurrent cascades convolution. In: 2019 IEEE 35th International Conference on Data Engineering (ICDE), pp. 770–781. IEEE (2019)
4. Cui, P., Jin, S., Yu, L., Wang, F., Zhu, W., Yang, S.: Cascading outbreak prediction in networks: a data-driven approach. In: Proceedings of the 19th ACM SIGKDD International Conference on Knowledge Discovery and Data Mining, pp. 901–909 (2013)
5. Hong, L., Dan, O., Davison, B.D.: Predicting popular messages in Twitter. In: Proceedings of the 20th International Conference Companion on World Wide Web, pp. 57–58 (2011)
6. Lerman, K., Galstyan, A.: Analysis of social voting patterns on digg. In: Proceedings of the First Workshop on Online Social Networks, pp. 7–12 (2008)
7. Li, C., Ma, J., Guo, X., Mei, Q.: DeepCas: an end-to-end predictor of information cascades. In: Proceedings of the 26th International Conference on World Wide Web, pp. 577–586 (2017)
8. Pinto, H., Almeida, J.M., Gonçalves, M.A.: Using early view patterns to predict the popularity of YouTube videos. In: Proceedings of the Sixth ACM International Conference on Web Search and Data Mining, pp. 365–374 (2013)
9. Shen, H., Wang, D., Song, C., Barabási, A.L.: Modeling and predicting popularity dynamics via reinforced Poisson processes. In: Twenty-Eighth AAAI Conference on Artificial Intelligence (2014)
10. Szabo, G., Huberman, B.A.: Predicting the popularity of online content. Commun. ACM **53**(8), 80–88 (2010)

11. Tsur, O., Rappoport, A.: What's in a hashtag? Content based prediction of the spread of ideas in microblogging communities. In: Proceedings of the fifth ACM International Conference on Web Search and Data Mining, pp. 643–652 (2012)
12. Weng, L., Menczer, F., Ahn, Y.Y.: Predicting successful memes using network and community structure. In: Eighth International AAAI Conference on Weblogs and Social Media (2014)

PrivRec: User-Centric Differentially Private Collaborative Filtering Using LSH and KD

Yifei Zhang[1,2], Neng Gao[1]($\boxtimes$), Junsha Chen[1,2], Chenyang Tu[1],
and Jiong Wang[1,2]

[1] SKLOIS, Institute of Information Engineering, CAS, Beijing, China
{zhangyifei,gaoneng,chenjunsha,tuchenyang,wangjiong}@iie.ac.cn
[2] School of Cyber Security, University of Chinese Academy of Sciences,
Beijing, China

Abstract. The collaborative filtering (CF)-based recommender systems provide recommendations by collecting users' historical ratings and predicting their preferences on new items. However, this inevitably brings privacy concerns since the collected data might reveal sensitive information of users, when training a recommendation model and applying the trained model (i.e., testing the model). Existing differential privacy (DP)-based approaches generally have non-negligible trade-offs in recommendation utility, and often serve as centralized server-side approaches that overlook the privacy during testing when applying the trained models in practice. In this paper, we propose PrivRec, a user-centric differential private collaborative filtering approach, that provides privacy guarantees both intuitively and theoretically while preserving recommendation utility. PrivRec is based on the locality sensitive hashing (LSH) and the teacher-student knowledge distillation (KD) techniques. A teacher model is trained on the original user data without privacy constraints, and a student model learns from the hidden layers of the teacher model. The published student model is trained without access to the original user data and takes the locally processed data as input for privacy. The experimental results on real-world datasets show that our approach provides promising utility with privacy guarantees compared to the commonly used approaches.

Keywords: Information security · Neural collaborative filtering · Differential privacy · Locality sensitive hashing · Knowledge distillation

1 Introduction

Collaborative filtering (CF) leverages the historical interactions between users and items to predict their preferences on a new set of items [12]. It provides recommendations by modeling users' preferences on items based on their historical user-item interactions (e.g., explicit five-star rating and implicit 0–1 feedback

© Springer Nature Switzerland AG 2020
H. Yang et al. (Eds.): ICONIP 2020, CCIS 1332, pp. 113–121, 2020.
https://doi.org/10.1007/978-3-030-63820-7_13

on items) [5]. However, the direct collecting and modeling on the original data might reveal personally sensitive data and brings privacy concerns, since a neural model generally overfits on specific training examples in the sense that some of these examples are implicitly memorized.

Recently, many researches focus on DP-based recommendation approaches. Differential privacy (DP) has emerged as a strong privacy notion with a provable privacy guarantee. McSherry et al. [8] applied differential privacy theory to recommender systems for the first time, and Nguyên et al. [9] applied local differential privacy (LDP) to help users to hide their own information even from first-party services during the data collection process. However, existing DP-based models generally focus on the training data privacy but overlook the data privacy in practice while applying trained models (namely during testing). A DP-based CF model needs to be retrained when applying it on new users that are not in the training data, which is computationally expensive. Intuitively, an LDP-based method can protect user privacy during testing by applying random response from the client side. However, LDP can only guarantee the accuracy of the statistical result while avoiding individual record disclosure, leading to the fact that a single input from the client is often flooded with too much random noises, which reduces the recommendation utility.

In this work, we propose PrivRec, a user-centric differentially private collaborative filtering approach, that preserves recommendation utility. PrivRec leverages a user-centric privacy enhancing algorithm to privately model users from the client sides, which protects the data privacy of both training data and the data during testing. Specifically, an LSH-based user data modeling process is applied to generate user representations with intuitive privacy, and the Laplace mechanism is leveraged to provide theoretical privacy. Moreover, a knowledge distillation architecture is applied for further privacy guarantee, as the released model does not have the access of the original sensitive user information in the training data. Our contributions can be summarized as follows:

- We propose PrivRec, a user-centric differentially private collaborative filtering approach that protects user privacy, while retaining recommendation utility.
- We address the challenge of the privacy-enhanced client-side utility-preserving user modeling with a locality sensitive hashing-based user representation algorithm that applies Laplace mechanism.
- We prevent the privacy disclosure from the potential overfitting of the models by introducing the knowledge distillation architecture. The released student model is trained without any access to the original sensitive data.
- Experimental results on two real-world datasets demonstrate that PrivRec outperforms other neural collaborative filtering-based methods on retaining recommendation utility with privacy guarantees.

2   Preliminaries

2.1   Differential Privacy

Differential privacy (DP) [3] has become the *de facto* standard for privacy preserving problems. Local differential privacy (LDP) is a special case of DP where
the random perturbation is performed by the users on the client side.

Definition 1. *A randomized mechanism $\mathcal{M}$ satisfies ϵ-differential privacy (ϵ-
DP) if for any adjacent sets d, d' differing by only one record for any subset S
of outputs $S \subseteq R$,*

$$\Pr[\mathcal{M}(d) \in S] \le e^{\epsilon} \cdot \Pr[\mathcal{M}(d') \in S], \tag{1}$$

where $\Pr$ *denotes the probability and* ϵ *is positive. Lower values of* ϵ *indicates
higher degree of privacy.*

Laplace Mechanism is the most commonly used tool in differential privacy
and has been applied in a number of works on differential privacy analysis [8,15].

Definition 2. *For a real-valued query function* $q : \mathcal{D}^n \to R$ *with sensitivity* Δ,
the output of Laplacian mechanism will be,

$$\mathcal{M}(d) = q(d) + Lap(\frac{\Delta}{\epsilon}), \tag{2}$$

where $Lap(\Delta)$ *is a random variable drawn from the probability density function*

$$Lap(x) = \frac{1}{2\Delta}e^{-\frac{|x|}{\Delta}}, \forall x \in R. \tag{3}$$

2.2   Locality Sensitive Hashing

Locality Sensitive Hashing (LSH) [4] is an effective approach for approximate
nearest neighbor search and has been applied in many privacy-preserving tasks
[14]. The main idea of LSH is to find a hashing function or a family of hashing
functions such that a hash collision occurs on similar data with higher probability
than others, i.e., it is likely that, (i) two neighboring points are still neighbors
after hashing, and (ii) two non-neighboring point are still not neighbors after
hashing. For data in domain S with distance measure D, an LSH family is
defined as:

Definition 3. *A family of hashing functions* $\mathcal{H} = \{h : S \to U\}$ *is called
(d_1, d_2, p_1, p_2)-sensitive, if for any $x, y \in S$,*

$$\text{If } D(x, y) \le d_1, \text{then } \Pr[h(x) = h(y)] \ge p_1, \tag{4}$$

$$\text{If } D(x, y) \ge d_2, \text{then } \Pr[h(x) = h(y)] \le p_2. \tag{5}$$

MinHash. Minwise hashing [2] is the LSH for resemblance similarity, which is usually leveraged to measure text similarity. MinHash applies a random permutation (i.e., hashing function) $\pi : \Omega \to \Omega$ on the given set S, and stores only the minimum value of the results of the permutation mapping. Specifically, a permutation mapping randomly shuffles all possible items of the input, and returns the corresponding indices of input items. Formally, the result of MinHash (namely *signature*) is defined as,

$$h_{\pi}^{min}(S) = \min(\pi(S)). \tag{6}$$

Given sets S_1 and S_2, the probability of that the two sets have the same signature is shown as,

$$\Pr(h_{\pi}^{min}(S_1) = h_{\pi}^{min}(S_2)) = \frac{|S_1 \bigcap S_2|}{|S_1 \bigcup S_2|}, \tag{7}$$

By applying multiple independent MinHash permutations, the probability of the two sets having the same MinHash signature is an unbiased estimate of their Jaccard similarity [13].

2.3   Knowledge Distillation

Knowledge Distillation (KD) is introduced by Hinton et al. [6], to transfer "knowledge" from one machine learning model (the *teacher*) to another (the *student*). The main idea of KD is that the student model can learn the distilled information directly from the teacher model, in order to reduce the amount of parameters while retain the performance. Specifically, the teacher model is trained on the original training data with ground-truth labels, and then the student model is fed with the same input but set the outputs of hidden layers in the teacher model as targets.

3   Threat Model

We are addressing two major privacy threats, *training data privacy* and *privacy in practice*. The training data privacy is the common problem since the identity-revealing user representations are stored in the first-party service providers or memorized by the potential overfitting of machine learning models. The potential data breach brings privacy threats on the training data. When applying a trained machine learning model, the privacy in practice is often overlooked. Consider a client-server scenario, a client-side user is faced with one of the following problems: (i) if the user is an existing user whose historical data are in the training set, it is expected to send its identifier (e.g., user ID, cookies) so that the server can retrieve the corresponding representations, which reveals its identity; (ii) if the user is a new user, it cannot get personalized recommendations since they are not modeled, or it has to send its historical data for the server to infer its preferences, which brings threats of privacy disclosure.

4   Design of PrivRec

4.1   Framework

Our approach follows the teacher-student knowledge distillation (KD) structure. We illustrate the visualized framework of PrivRec in Fig. 1. It consists of two parts: the teacher model and the student model. We leverage a multi-layer perceptron (MLP) to perform neural collaborative filtering (NCF) by predicting the interaction between a user and an item. It is the prototype of many recent researches on CF-based neural recommender systems [1,5,7,11]. Next, we will present the specifics of the PrivRec.

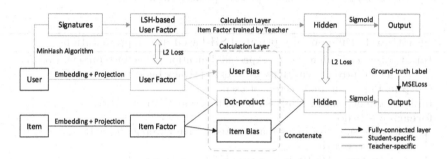

Fig. 1. The general framework of our approach. The teacher-only modules are replaced with the student-only modules in the student model.

4.2   Components

Teacher. The teacher model is a naive NCF model trained on the training data without any privacy constraints. Consider a user u and an item v, the network structure is described as follows. The model takes the identifiers u and v as input and embeds them to the d_u and d_v-dimensional latent spaces with embedding layers $emb_u : u \rightarrow p_u$ and $emb_v : v \rightarrow p_v$. Then, p_u and p_v are projected to matrix factorization spaces with the same dimension d_m, denoted as $m_u : p_u \rightarrow f_u$ and $m_v : p_v \rightarrow f_v$. The calculation layer concatenates the summed dot-product of the factors $dot(f_u, f_v)$ and the results of two bias layers $bias : f \rightarrow b$ for the two factors. Finally, the result of the calculation layer is passed to a regression layer composed by a fully-connected layer with the sigmoid activation for the final prediction $\sigma : l_{u,v} \rightarrow \hat{r}_{u,v}$. Overall, the teacher learns the latent representation of users and items for the prediction. The teacher model is not published for privacy of the training data. Formally, we have:

$$f_u = m_u(emb_u(u)), \quad f_v = m_v(emb_v(v)), \tag{8}$$

$$\hat{r}_{u,v} = \sigma(calc(f_u, f_v)) = \sigma(cat(dot(f_u, f_v), bias(f_u), bias(f_v))). \tag{9}$$

Student. The structure of the student model is similar with the teacher's, but takes different inputs and targets. It is this model that be published to the deployment environment in practice. We reuse the item embeddings p_v in the teacher model, since they do not reveal user-specific information. The user embedding layer is replaced by a differentially private locality sensitive hashing(LSH)-based representation procedure described in Algorithm 1. The MinHash functions are *publicly available* and identical for all user, so that the permutations stay unchanged both in server-side training process and in client-side practice. The hashing signatures are arranged into a vector, where each entry represents a perspective of the user data. Accordingly, the user representation can be computed completely on the client side with the publicly available LSH permutations and the user's private positive item set.

Algorithm 1: Differentially private LSH-based user representation.

Input: User set U, item set V, expected dimention of vector representation K, global privacy sensitivity Δ, overall privacy budget ϵ.
Output: Representation vectors of users.
Initialize k independent MinHash random permutations $\pi = \{\pi_1, \pi_2, \cdots, \pi_K\}$;
foreach $u \in U$ **do**
 Select the subset of items that u rated over its average $S_u = \{u|r_{u,v} > \bar{r}_u\}$;
 foreach $\pi_i \in \pi$ **do**
  Generate a MinHash signature $h_i^{min}(u) = \min(\pi_i(S_u))$;
  $h_i^{min}(u) = h_i^{min}(u) \mod 2$; // *A hashing result itself has no numerical significance for additive noises. A "mod 2" operation is leveraged to binarize the signatures, so that applying Laplace mechanism on MinHash signatures will not completely invalidate the user representation.*
  $h_i^{min}(u) = h_i^{min}(u) + Lap(\frac{\Delta}{\epsilon})$;
 Concatenate the k signatures $h_u = [h_1^{min}(u), h_2^{min}(u), \cdots, h_k^{min}(u)]$;
 A fully-connected layer FC is applied on h_u;
 Append h_u as u's representation vector to result;
Return the user representation vectors.

The remaining difference between the teacher model and the student model is that the student is not trained on the ground-truth labels. Instead, it learns from the output of the teacher's user factorization layer f_u and the last hidden output l_u, v. The LSH-based user representation sig_u obtained from the above algorithm is projected to a fully-connected layer as the student's user factor $fc : sig_u \to f'_u$, and the output of the calculation layer is $l'_{u,v}$.

We summarize the working process of the student model as follows. (i) It projects user u's identifier into a latent space with the LSH-based algorithm for the MinHash signatures sig_u as Algorithm 1; (ii) The signatures are fed into a fully-connected layer to get the student's user factor $fc : sig_u \to f'_u$; (iii) the item v's factor f_v is obtained from the teacher model; (iv) the factors f'_u and f_v are passed to the calculation layer; (v) finally, the regression layer is applied to produce the final prediction.

Detailed privacy analysis of PrivRec is omitted due to page limit. Please refer to the extended version on arXiv.

5 Experiments

5.1 Experimental Settings

Datasets. We conduct our experiments on the commonly used MovieLens 1M dataset of movie ratings and the Jester dataset of joke ratings. We filter out the invalid data, including the users and items with no ratings in the dataset, and the users that rate equally on all items.

Metric. To measure the effectiveness of knowledge distillation . The recommendation utility is measured as the accuracy of rating prediction. We adopt mean absolute error $\mathrm{mae}(y_{predict}, y_{truth}) = E|y_{predict} - y_{truth}|$ as the metric of the recommendation accuracy. A lower mae indicates a more precise rating prediction on collaborative filtering.

Baselines. We evaluate our model by comparing with several widely used baseline methods. Specifically, neural collaborative filtering models with following pretrained user representations are considered:

- NCF: The original Neural Collaborative Filtering method that models users and items into representation vectors. It is the prototype of our teacher model without privacy constraints.
- SVD: Singular Value Decomposition, a matrix factorization method, is one of the most popular collaborative filtering methods. It takes user-item interaction matrix as input, and returns the low-dimensional representations of users.
- LDA: Latent Dirichlet Allocation is an unsupervised learning algorithm for natural language processing initially, and discover topics based on contents. We employ LDA to learn a user's latent preference as its representation.
- LSH: Locality Sensitive Hashing is the prototype of our LSH-based user representation. It applies multiple MinHash signatures on a user's historical data as the user's representation vector.
- DP-SVD, DP-LDA and DP-LSH: We apply the differentially private Laplace mechanism on the baselines above to explore the utility preservation of our LSH-based differentially private user representation.

5.2 Results

We compare our PrivRec with the mentioned baselines for the neural collaborative filtering recommender systems. As shown in Fig. 2(a), by comparing the first six methods in the legend ([DP-]SVD, [DP-]LDA, [DP-]LSH), we observe that Laplace mechanism significantly degrades the recommendation service utility of SVD and LDA, while LSH-based method is having less trade-off in applying differential privacy. This demonstrates that the LSH-based user representation implies more user preferences than traditional methods after introducing the same amount of noises. According to the last three methods in the legend (DP-LSH, NCF, PrivRec), the knowledge distillation (KD) architecture of our PrivRec substantially improves the recommendation utility of the DP-LSH method. PrivRec shows comparable averaged recommendation utility with the baselines, with the same privacy budget of differential privacy and intuitively stronger privacy within its knowledge distillation training process.

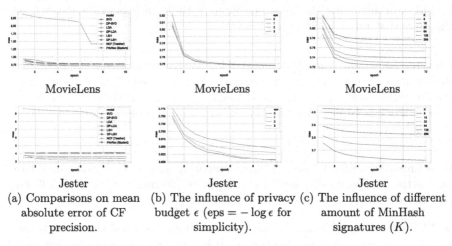

MovieLens	MovieLens	MovieLens
Jester	Jester	Jester
(a) Comparisons on mean absolute error of CF precision.	(b) The influence of privacy budget ϵ (eps $= -\log \epsilon$ for simplicity).	(c) The influence of different amount of MinHash signatures (K).

Fig. 2. Experimental results.

Further experimental results on the influence of the noise scale and the amount of MinHash signatures are shown in Figs. 2(b) and (c). The influence on ϵ is measured with the averaged result on different K, and vice versa. A greater eps indicates smaller ϵ, which introduces more noises into MinHash signatures and provides stronger guarantee on user privacy, while slightly downgrading prediction accuracy. A larger K implies more facets of hashing and more information of user data, and further reduces rating prediction error.

6   Conclusion

In this work, we focus on both training data privacy and the privacy in practice during testing in neural collaborative filtering. The proposed PrivRec is an early effort to protect user privacy in practice from the client side. It manages to model a user locally and privately with a LSH-based algorithm and the DP principle. PrivRec shows promising results with privacy guarantees on NCF. In the future, we will extend it to more variety of recommender systems.

Acknowledgments. This work is supported by the National Key Research and Development Program of China.

References

1. Bai, T., Wen, J.R., Zhang, J., Zhao, W.X.: A neural collaborative filtering model with interaction-based neighborhood. In: Proceedings of the 2017 ACM on Conference on Information and Knowledge Management, pp. 1979–1982 (2017)
2. Broder, A.Z., Charikar, M., Frieze, A.M., Mitzenmacher, M.: Min-wise independent permutations. J. Comput. Syst. Sci. **60**(3), 630–659 (2000)
3. Dwork, C., McSherry, F., Nissim, K., Smith, A.: Calibrating noise to sensitivity in private data analysis. In: Halevi, S., Rabin, T. (eds.) TCC 2006. LNCS, vol. 3876, pp. 265–284. Springer, Heidelberg (2006). https://doi.org/10.1007/11681878_14
4. Gionis, A., Indyk, P., Motwani, R., et al.: Similarity search in high dimensions via hashing. VLDB **99**, 518–529 (1999)
5. He, X., Liao, L., Zhang, H., Nie, L., Hu, X., Chua, T.S.: Neural collaborative filtering. In: Proceedings of the 26th International Conference on World Wide Web, pp. 173–182. International World Wide Web Conferences Steering Committee (2017)
6. Hinton, G., Vinyals, O., Dean, J.: Distilling the knowledge in a neural network. arXiv preprint arXiv:1503.02531 (2015)
7. Liu, Y., Wang, S., Khan, M.S., He, J.: A novel deep hybrid recommender system based on auto-encoder with neural collaborative filtering. Big Data Min. Anal. **1**(3), 211–221 (2018)
8. McSherry, F., Mironov, I.: Differentially private recommender systems: building privacy into the NetFlix prize contenders. In: Proceedings of the 15th ACM SIGKDD International Conference on Knowledge Discovery and Data Mining, pp. 627–636. ACM (2009)
9. Nguyên, T.T., Xiao, X., Yang, Y., Hui, S.C., Shin, H., Shin, J.: Collecting and analyzing data from smart device users with local differential privacy. arXiv preprint arXiv:1606.05053 (2016)
10. Papernot, N., Abadi, M., Erlingsson, U., Goodfellow, I., Talwar, K.: Semi-supervised knowledge transfer for deep learning from private training data. arXiv preprint arXiv:1610.05755 (2016)
11. Rendle, S., Freudenthaler, C., Gantner, Z., Schmidt-Thieme, L.: BPR: Bayesian personalized ranking from implicit feedback. In: Proceedings of the Twenty-Fifth Conference on Uncertainty in Artificial Intelligence, pp. 452–461 (2009)
12. Schafer, J.B., Frankowski, D., Herlocker, J., Sen, S.: Collaborative filtering recommender systems. In: Brusilovsky, P., Kobsa, A., Nejdl, W. (eds.) The Adaptive Web. LNCS, vol. 4321, pp. 291–324. Springer, Heidelberg (2007). https://doi.org/10.1007/978-3-540-72079-9_9
13. Shaked, S., Rokach, L.: Publishing differentially private medical events data. In: Buccafurri, F., Holzinger, A., Kieseberg, P., Tjoa, A.M., Weippl, E. (eds.) CD-ARES 2016. LNCS, vol. 9817, pp. 219–235. Springer, Cham (2016). https://doi.org/10.1007/978-3-319-45507-5_15
14. Vatsalan, D., Sehili, Z., Christen, P., Rahm, E.: Privacy-preserving record linkage for big data: current approaches and research challenges. In: Zomaya, A.Y., Sakr, S. (eds.) Handbook of Big Data Technologies, pp. 851–895. Springer, Cham (2017). https://doi.org/10.1007/978-3-319-49340-4_25
15. Yin, C., Ju, X., Yin, Z., Wang, J.: Location recommendation privacy protection method based on location sensitivity division. EURASIP J. Wirel. Commun. Netw. **2019**(1), 266 (2019)

Simultaneous Customer Segmentation and Behavior Discovery

Siqi Zhang[1], Ling Luo[2], Zhidong Li[1(✉)], Yang Wang[1], Fang Chen[1], and Richard Xu[1]

[1] School of Software, The University of Technology Sydney, Sydney, NSW 2006, Australia
siqi.zhang-3@student.uts.edu.au,
{Zhidong.Li,Yang.Wang,Fang.Chen,Richards.Xu}@uts.edu.au
[2] School of Computing and Information Systems, The University of Melbourne, Melbourne, VIC 3010, Australia
ling.luo@unimelb.edu.au

Abstract. Customer purchase behavior segmentation plays an important role in the modern economy. We proposed a Bayesian non-parametric (BNP)-based framework, named Simultaneous Customer Segmentation and Utility Discovery (UtSeg), to discover customer segmentation without knowing specific forms of utility functions and parameters. For the segmentation based on BNP models, the unknown type of functions is usually modeled as a non-homogeneous point process (NHPP) for each mixture component. However, the inference of these models is complex and time-consuming. To reduce such complexity, traditionally, economists will use one specific utility function in a heuristic way to simplify the inference. We proposed to automatically select among multiple utility functions instead of searching in a continuous space. We further unified the parameters for different types of utility functions with the same prior distribution to improve efficiency. We tested our model with synthetic data and applied the framework to real-supermarket data with different products, and showed that our results can be interpreted with common knowledge.

Keywords: Customer behavior · Bayesian non-parametric model · Utility function · Segmentation

1 Introduction

Customer segmentation is a common technique that allows a business to make better use of their resources and make more profits by studying the activities associated with the purchase behavior [4,9]. The traditional framework of customer segmentation is based on their demographic data. There are two drawbacks to this setting: 1) the collection of demographic data is wandering between the balance of completion and customer's privacy, and the missing of key attributes leads to unreliable segmentation. 2) The utility functions need to

© Springer Nature Switzerland AG 2020
H. Yang et al. (Eds.): ICONIP 2020, CCIS 1332, pp. 122–130, 2020.
https://doi.org/10.1007/978-3-030-63820-7_14

be determined before segmentation, whilst in our provided framework, we jointly estimate the segmentation of customers and the form and parameters of utility functions at the same time. Without explicitly setting the number of clusters, we employ the Bayesian non-parametric (BNP) framework to conduct the segmentation. Several challenges are hampering the inference when we jointly estimate the utility functions, parameters, and segmentation in the BNP framework. First, the optimization of utility function is a functional problem requiring modeling of stochastic process. In the previous work, Luo et al. describe customer purchase behavior by non-homogeneous point process (NHPP) [4,9], using a base measure of the polynomial and trigonometric functions. Such models are usually mathematically complex, requiring careful design for compatibility, robustness, and scalability. Instead, we proposed an approximation model, but it can still keep the flexibility to model the utility functions with different parameters in different types. Second, parameters for different types of utility functions are inconsistent for both of their prior and likelihood, given the diversity of their meanings. The inconsistency of posteriors can cause enormous amount of heuristic work, as the modeling heavily relies on expert knowledge. The re-parametric solution is to wrap up the identity of utility function with a parameter-free nonlinear function to keep the consistency of parameters. Such designation drastically reduces the inconvenience of designing utility functions by assuming all the parameters are generated from the same posterior distribution. As a result, the model has higher generalizability and is easier to interpret.

There are three main **contributions** of this work. First, we proposed an automatic and generalizable framework based on the BNP model, which can simultaneously segment the customers considering their behavior, discover their utility type, and how their purchase behavior is influenced by the product price (more external factors can be directly involved). Second, our framework overcomes the complex modeling and inefficient inference for NHPP. We unify the parameter estimation for different utility functions so that the predefined conjugate priors can be used to drastically simplify the inference. At last, we conduct case studies on the real-world supermarket data and show the patterns discovered using our method.

2   Related Work

To group customers, there are different segmentation or clustering approaches, which include decision tree, K-means, mixture model, and density peaks. Using decision trees for customer behavior research is easy to understand but the main drawback is that it must be learned with labeled data. The other methods are unsupervised but their generalizability is limited by parameter setting. Hence, we focus on the BNP model.

The NHPP can naturally fit the problem of describing events (e.g. purchase) based on observations, with different types of utility functions. However, the inference of NHPP under the BNP framework is an extremely complicated task. Previous research focused on the inference of intensity function without considering grouping at the same time. The tractable inference was proposed in [1], then the major research is to find faster ways to infer the intensity function [6,12]. There are also some models [7] considering the change of customer segmentation over time. The requirement of inference design is also the main obstacle to generalize these models. We propose a effective model to approximate NHPP with a unified framework to generalize.

Exploring purchase behavior based on price sensitivity is a common topic of customer analysis. Similar problem attracts research in a variety of applications, such as tourism and airline industry [8] . The utility function is the main assumption used in such studies to assess customer purchase behavior [13] to describe the relationship between price and purchase. The model determines one utility function for each customer, then analyses/segments customers according to the assumed utility function.

3 Methodology

3.1 Problem Definition

Given a customer $i = \{1...N\}$, we know a series of their purchase events y_i, where $y_i = \{y_{i,j}|y_{i,j} \in \mathbb{N}^+\}$ is the number of products that customer i purchased for their j^{th} purchase. The corresponding price is $x_i = \{x_{i,j}|x_{i,j} \in \mathbb{R}^+\}$. We assume that there are M_i observations for i in total. Here we use discount rate as the price to normalize the price value of different types of products. Details will be shown in the data pre-processing in Sect. 5.3. Our target is to segment customers into unknown number of groups, so that a group index k_i needs to be obtained for i. The grouping is based on the function f_i that can map price $x_{i,j}$ with purchase behavior $y_{i,j}$.

Considering the efficiency and generalizability, we covert the problem into the semi-parametric model but it can approximately cover the space that a full BNP model can cover. Here we assume that three utility functions can represent most types of relationships between customers' purchase behavior and price. As we do not know which function should be used for each customer, we use a latent variable $u_i \in \{1, 2, 3\}$ to denote the function selected for customer i. We hope to jointly estimate group index k_i and utility function type u_i, without heuristically selecting for each customer, by the *integration of a Bayesian semi-parametric model for utility function selection and BNP model for grouping*.

The flow of our work is that all the customers will be compared with different utility functions. Then our algorithm will determine the best latent utility function used to describe the customer behavior and customer group. Suppose two people are associated with utility function 1, and one person is associated with utility function 2. The customers in the same group have the same parameters in their utility functions. Since we have the unified utility function, the parameters for different forms of utility functions can still have the same parameter values.

3.2 Utility Functions

These three functions can explain most of the relation between purchase behavior and price [2]. The traditional way to represent different functions is based on different parameters. This will cause many heuristic settings, which requires domain knowledge to determine what priors are needed for each different setting, and what likelihood function is suitable for each parameter, otherwise, it could cause intractability with non-conjugated priors. This setting limits the generalizability and scalability of the system.

To overcome such an obstacle, we use $y = ag(x) + b$ as a general representation of any relation between demand and price change. The parameters a and b are unified, which can be interpreted in the same way in different utility functions, such as a as the coefficient and b as adjustment. Then we can represent such setting with fixed prior functions. The common utility functions can be reduced to our general representation, and directly fit our model. Such a setting provides the generalization capability so that it can be easily extended to incorporate a variety of utility functions. Specifically, the utility functions explored in this work are: f_i^1: $y_i = a_{i,1}x_i + b_{i,1}$, f_i^2: $y_i = a_{i,2}\log(x_i) + b_{i,2}$, f_i^3: $y_i = a_{i,3}e^{x_i} + b_{i,3}$.

The utility function is selected based on the negative log-likelihood loss function. It is a common way to measure if the utility function can fit the data points well or not.

3.3 Simultaneous Customer Segmentation and Utility Estimation Model

This section describes the details of the Simultaneous Customer Segmentation and Utility Estimation (UtSeg) model and introduces the generative process of parameters, latent variables, and observations of UtSeg. The model is mainly used for cluster customers into groups and infer their utility functions.

In the UtSeg, α_0 is the hyperparameter for the CRP. Then, each customer i will get $a_i = [a_{i1}, a_{i2}, a_{i3}]$ and $b_i = [b_{i1}, b_{i2}, b_{i3}]$ by using curve fitting function based on price and purchase information. We assume that a_i and b_i follow Gamma distribution. This is because of the Poisson distribution used to estimate the purchase number, given by $N_i(x_i) \sim Poi(y_i(x_i))$. The Poisson distribution can be decomposed as a superposition of multiple Poisson distributions with the summation of frequencies as the overall frequency. Therefore, b_i is also the parameter of a Poisson distribution.

This is the first property that can drastically reduce the complexity of inference, because the conjugated prior can be set for both gamma distribution, without sampling in high dimension space for stochastic process.

For each customer i, the generative process of UtSeg can be represented as follows:

$$k_i \sim CRP(\alpha_0), u_i \sim Mul(u_0), \alpha_{k_i} \sim Gam(\theta_a), a_{i,u_i} \sim Gam(\alpha_{k_i}),$$
$$\beta_{k_i} \sim Gam(\theta_b), b_{i,u_i} \sim Gam(\beta_{k_i}), l_{i,u_i} \sim N(\mu_{i,u_i}, \sqrt{M_i}\sigma_0)$$
$$\mu_{i,u_i} = \sum_{j=1\cdots M_i} a_{i,u_i}g_{u_i}(x_i) + b_{i,u_i} - y_i \tag{1}$$

– We generate table index k_i based on CRP, using the hyperparameter α_0;

- For utility function selection, an function index u_i is generated for customer i with Multinomial distribution parameterized by u_0;
- We generate a latent variable for each table k_i, for both coefficient variable α_{k_i} and offset variable β_{k_i} with the base measure parameterized by $gamma(\theta_a)$ and $gamma(\theta_b)$[1];
- a_i and b_i are generated based on α_{k_i} and β_{k_i} using Gamma distributions;
- The selected function should fit the observations, so the minimised loss l_{iu_i} can be learned based on Sect. 3.2. l_{iu_i} is assumed to be Gaussian distributed[2] loss, with variance σ_0, mean $\mu_{i,u_i} = \sum_j a_{i,u_i} g_{u_i}(x_i) + b_{i,u_i} - y_i$, based on a_i and b_i as a_{i,u_i} and b_{i,u_i} respectively.

Therefore, the joint probability of the model is:

$$P(k_{1\cdots n}, u_{1\cdots n}, \alpha_0, \theta_a, \theta_b, l_{1\cdots n,1\cdots 3}, a_{1\cdots n,1\cdots 3}, b_{1\cdots n,1\cdots 3})$$

$$\propto \prod_i P(k_i|\alpha_0)P(\alpha_{k_i}|\theta_a)P(\beta_{k_i}|\theta_b)P(u_i|u_0)P(a_{i,u_i}|\alpha_{k_i}, k_i) \cdot$$

$$P(b_{i,u_i}|\beta_{k_i}, k_i)P(l_{i,u_i}|u_i, a_{i,u_i}, b_{i,u_i}, g_{u_i}, x_i, y_i, \sigma_0, M_i) \qquad (2)$$

$$= \prod_i CRP(k_i|\alpha_0)Gam(\alpha_{k_i}|\theta_a)Gam(\beta_{k_i}|\theta_b)Mul(u_i|u_0)Gam(a_{i,u_i}|\alpha_{k_i})$$

$$Gam(b_{i,u_i}|\beta_{k_i})N(l_{i,u_i}|\mu_{i,u_i}, \sqrt{M_i}\sigma_0)$$

4   Inference: Gibbs Sampling for UtSeg Model

Gibbs Sampling is a Markov Monte Carlo method (MCMC) [1,4], which is widely used in the inference. In the UtSeg model, each customer is assigned to a utility function based on the multinomial prior and Gaussian likelihood for the loss function. The parameters θ_a and θ_b are randomly initialized and u_i from the last step is used. The possible sampling result can be any existing table or starting a new table. For each customer i, the posterior probability to select a table k_i. Where k_{i-} represents the current table assignments except for customer i. Similarly we sample the form of utility u_i by: Eq. (4). By sampling all the k_i and u_i iteratively, we can get the utility function allocation for all customers.

$$p(k_i = k|k_{i-}, u_{1\cdots n}, \alpha_0, \theta_a, \theta_b, l_{1\cdots n,1\cdots 3}, a_{1\cdots n,1\cdots 3}, b_{1\cdots n,1\cdots 3})$$

$$\propto CRP(k|k_{i-}, \alpha_0)Gam(\alpha_k|\theta_a)Gam(\beta_k|\theta_b)Gam(a_{i,u_i}|\alpha_k) \qquad (3)$$

$$Gam(b_{i,u_i}|\beta_k)N(l_{i,u_i}|\mu_{i,u_i}, \sqrt{M_i}\sigma_0).$$

$$p(u_i = u|k_{1\cdots n}, u_{i-}, \alpha_0, \theta_a, \theta_b, l_{1\cdots n,1\cdots 3}, a_{1\cdots n,1\cdots 3}, b_{1\cdots n,1\cdots 3})$$

$$\propto Mul(u|u_0)Gam(\alpha_k|\theta_a)Gam(\beta_k|\theta_b)Gam(a_{i,u_i}|\alpha_k) \qquad (4)$$

$$Gam(b_{i,u_i}|\beta_k)N(l_{i,u_i}|\mu_{i,u_i}, \sqrt{M_i}\sigma_0).$$

---

[1] For a Gamma distribution, we simplify both actual parameters into one parameter.
[2] This can be determined by the loss used. We use the quadratic loss, but Gaussian distribution is used to approximate the Chi-square distribution when data volume is large.

5 Experiments

5.1 Experiment Setup

Baseline Models

UtSeg-(1-3): This is a simplified model from UtSeg, which is based on CRP and one utility function to describe customer purchase behavior. Each method corresponds to one of the utility functions [2].

CRP-GM: This baseline is CRP with Gaussian mixture component [1]. We use $x_{i,j}$ and $y_{i,j}$ to compute the likelihood of CRP.

NHPP: This model is based on [3], which assumes that the mixture component is NHPP with different types of intensity functions.

Clustering: This model is parametric segmentation, which includes classic clustering models **K-Means (KM)** and **Density Peak (DP)** [5].

Evaluation Measurements

Confusion matrix: With ground truth data, we can use the confusion matrix (CM) to show the true and learned grouping.

Clustering distance: The average distance inside groups (ADIG) and the average distance between groups(ADBG) are used. The ADIG refers to the average distance between sample points of the same group, *lower* is better. The ADBG refers to the distance between groups, which the *greater* distance means the larger difference between groups.

Segmentation Log-Likelihood (LL): Segmentation LL can compare the fitness of different models. A *higher* log-likelihood value means the model fits better. To compare all models, we use the obtained group index. The likelihood is obtained by the Poisson distribution parameter on the average of the selected coefficients in each group. For CRP-GM, we double the likelihood as it only has one parameter [6].

5.2 Synthetic Data Set

We follow (1) to generate synthetic data for experiment. We generated pairs of purchased number and price for 100k customers. The evaluation results are shown in Table 1. Firstly, UtSeg has the best result for both distances. Naturally, using the parametric method can obtain better results when the chosen parameters happen to be similar to the true parameter. However, without special design or knowledge, the parameters are unknown, which is the largest obstacle to use those parametric methods. On the contrary, our method can be generalized to unseen cases without such settings. In terms of computation time, the UtSeg model is compared with the optimized NHPP model as implemented in

Table 1. Evaluation results on synthetic data.

	ADIG	ADBG	Segmentation LL	CM accuracy
UtSeg	0.563	0.670	−1321500	0.383
UtSeg-1	0.626	0.616	−1523572	0.372
UtSeg-2	0.856	0.709	−2651849	0.301
UtSeg-3	1.077	0.816	−3247918	0.193
CRP-GM	0.687	0.532	−1650943	0.348
NHPP	0.572	0.730		0.427
K-means K = 5	0.696	0.616		0.533
K-means K = 7	0.580	0.690		0.394
Density peak k = 5	0.670	0.689		0.405
Density peak k = 7	0.665	0.765		0.376

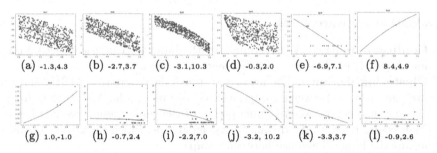

(a) -1.3,4.3   (b) -2.7,3.7   (c) -3.1,10.3   (d) -0.3,2.0   (e) -6.9,7.1   (f) 8.4,4.9

(g) 1.0,-1.0   (h) -0.7,2.4   (i) -2.2,7.0   (j) -3.2, 10.2   (k) -3.3,3.7   (l) -0.9,2.6

Fig. 1. Utility functions for different data sets: (a)–(d) are for synthetic data, (e)–(i) are parts for four product types. 5 utility functions and observed points are shown for each type. The learned parameters α_k and β_k are under the plots.

5.3   Case Study

In this section, we present a case study on a real data set of 1,529,057 purchase transaction records collected by an Australian national supermarket chain in 2014 and we use 41,210 of them. Base on the variation of customer purchase quantities (normalized according to product volume) and purchase price (normalize as a discount rate, which is in the range of [0, 1]). We run the algorithm on 4 products separately to see how the customers are segmented for their behavior. Our result can support the product providers to set promotion or stimulation. In the prepossessing, we further normalize quantity by purchased quantity per week subtracting the average amount throughout the year. This normalization can remove the influence of demand levels.

The results are given in Table 2. In the study, the UtSeg model provides better results in most cases, without setting functions and parameters using domain knowledge. The results are consistent with what we observed in the synthetic data.

Table 2. Evaluation results on real data.

	Measure	UtSeg	UtSeg-1	UtSeg-2	UtSeg-3	NHPP
Milk	ADIG	0.61	0.74	0.86	1.08	0.65
	ADBG	0.90	0.88	0.86	0.67	0.83
	Segment LL	−1.3E+05	−1.5E+05	−1.9E+05	−2.5E+05	
Chips	ADIG	0.63	0.73	0.83	1.01	0.68
	ADBG	0.80	0.67	0.71	0.76	0.82
	Segment LL	−1.1E+05	−2.1E+05	−2.4E+05	−2.6E+05	
Chocolate	ADIG	0.55	0.59	0.71	0.75	0.58
	ADBG	0.83	0.79	0.74	0.77	0.79
	Segment LL	−4.5E+04	−1.8E+05	−2.0E+05	−2.4E+05	
Softdrinks	ADIG	0.56	0.69	0.74	0.83	0.54
	ADBG	0.67	0.62	0.57	0.52	0.59
	Segment LL	−6.9E+04	−1.4E+05	−1.9E+05	−2.1E+05	
	Measure	CRP-GM	KM-3	KM-7	DP-3	DP-7
Milk	ADIG	0.90	1.06	0.55	1.07	0.59
	ADBG	0.83	0.60	0.72	0.79	0.89
	Segment LL	−2.0E+05	−	−	−	−
Chips	ADIG	0.73	0.97	0.78	0.95	0.67
	ADBG	0.61	0.88	0.53	0.89	0.54
	Segment LL	−1.8E+05	−	−	−	−
Chocolate	ADIG	0.66	0.83	0.55	1.31	0.69
	ADBG	0.75	0.58	0.72	0.58	0.81
	Segment LL	−1.8E+05	−	−	−	−
Softdrinks	ADIG	0.79	0.93	0.49	1.34	0.70
	ADBG	0.53	0.56	0.77	0.53	0.90
	Segment LL	−1.6E+05	−	−	−	−

6 Conclusion

In this paper, we propose a BNP framework to segment customers without knowing their utility functions of purchase behavior. Using the semi-parametric method, we unify the parameters of different types of utility functions into the same representation so they can be generated by the same distribution. This proposed technique significantly saved the effort to design a special inference algorithm so that we can efficiently learn the latent variables. The setting also makes it easier to generalize our method to comply with more utility functions.

References

1. Adams, R.P., Murray, I., MacKay, D.J.: Tractable nonparametric Bayesian inference in Poisson processes with Gaussian process intensities. In: Proceedings of the 26th Annual International Conference on Machine Learning, pp. 9–16 (2009)
2. Akaike, H.: Information theory and an extension of the maximum likelihood principle. In: Parzen, E., Tanabe, K., Kitagawa, G. (eds.) Selected Papers of Hirotugu Akaike. Springer Series in Statistics (Perspectives in Statistics), pp. 199–213. Springer, Heidelberg (1998). https://doi.org/10.1007/978-1-4612-1694-0_15
3. Griffiths, T.L., Jordan, M.I., Tenenbaum, J.B., Blei, D.M.: Hierarchical topic models and the nested Chinese restaurant process. In: Advances in Neural Information Processing Systems, pp. 17–24 (2004)
4. Kamakura, W.A., Russell, G.J.: A probabilistic choice model for market segmentation and elasticity structure. J. Market. Res. **26**(4), 379–390 (1989)
5. Kamen, J.M., Toman, R.J.: Psychophysics of prices. J. Market. Res. **7**(1), 27–35 (1970)
6. Lloyd, C., Gunter, T., Osborne, M., Roberts, S.: Variational inference for Gaussian process modulated Poisson processes. In: International Conference on Machine Learning, pp. 1814–1822 (2015)
7. Luo, L., Li, B., Koprinska, I., Berkovsky, S., Chen, F.: Discovering temporal purchase patterns with different responses to promotions. In: Proceedings of the 25thACM International on Conference on Information And Knowledge Management, pp. 2197–2202. ACM (2016)
8. Masiero, L., Nicolau, J.L.: Tourism market segmentation based on price sensitivity: finding similar price preferences on tourism activities. J. Travel Res. **51**(4), 426–435 (2012)
9. McDonald, M., Christopher, M., Bass, M.: Market segmentation. In: McDonald, M., Christopher, M., Bass, M. (eds.) Marketing, pp. 41–65. Springer, Heidelberg (2003). https://doi.org/10.1007/978-1-4039-3741-4_3
10. Porteous, I., Newman, D., Ihler, A., Asuncion, A., Smyth, P., Welling, M.: Fast collapsed Gibbs sampling for latent Dirichlet allocation. In: Proceedings of the 14th ACM SIGKDD International Conference on Knowledge Discovery and Data Mining, pp. 569–577. ACM (2008)
11. Rodriguez, A., Laio, A.: Clustering by fast search and find of density peaks. Science **344**(6191), 1492–1496 (2014)
12. Samo, Y.L.K., Roberts, S.: Scalable nonparametric Bayesian inference on point processes with Gaussian processes. In: International Conference on Machine Learning, pp. 2227–2236 (2015)
13. Sirvanci, M.B.: An empirical study of price thresholds and price sensitivity. J. Appl. Bus. Res. (JABR)**9**(2), 43–49 (1993)
14. Smyth, P.: Clustering sequences with hidden Markov models. In: Advances in Neural Information Processing Systems, pp. 648–654 (1997)

Structural Text Steganography Using Unseen Tag Attribute Values

Feno H. Rabevohitra[1] and Yantao Li[2(✉)]

[1] School of Big Data and Software Engineering, Chongqing University,
Chongqing 401331, China
`fenoheriniaina@cqu.edu.cn`
[2] College of Computer Science, Chongqing University, Chongqing 400044, China
`yantaoli@cqu.edu.cn`

Abstract. Apart from an effective steganography scheme, it is vital to have an abundance of cover medium while considering the practicability of a stego-system. Aside from images, document files are one of the most exchanged attached content via electronic mailings. In this paper, we present a structural steganographic scheme based on unseen tag attribute values using office documents as the medium. Specifically, we use the XML file that builds the core of the file documents to vehiculate the message. The secret is not visible within the text content, and the stego file size is not far from the cover size. We are among the first to investigate the unseen tag identifier within the cover document to hide the secret message. We assess the performance of the proposed scheme in terms of the invisibility, embedding capacity, robustness, and security. The performance results show the advantage of a higher capacity embedding and a better flexibility while keeping high practicability in terms of accessibility and implementation.

Keywords: Structural text steganography · Covert communication · Modern text hiding

1 Introduction

In work environments, office documents in the form of electronic files for writing notes, manuscripts, essays, reports, presentations, etc., are shared consistently between co-workers and collaborators. The content of those generated files can be heavily mixed and diverse, as they are not just limited to text. These text files can be embedded with formatting, images, audio files, and video files. Text content formatting is a basic functionality used in different steganographic schemes, such as font color manipulations [1], and font size and word spacing variations [2].

Text steganography can be split into a natural language (semantic and syntactic methods) or a structurally based (open space methods). The structural text steganographic methods focus on hiding the existence of the secret communication by exploiting the structure of the cover medium. The secret is written within the content, but is not visible to the human eyes (e.g., spaces, invisible characters, and tab) [3,4].

© Springer Nature Switzerland AG 2020
H. Yang et al. (Eds.): ICONIP 2020, CCIS 1332, pp. 131–139, 2020.
https://doi.org/10.1007/978-3-030-63820-7_15

Despite the early work is initiated by Khairullah et al. in 2009 [5] in this regard, and later are investigated by Por et al. in 2012 [6], Bhaya et al. in 2013, Rabevohitra in 2019 [1], all the recorded steganography techniques based on the same type of cover medium, to the best of our knowledge, are making drastic changes to the cover medium. They focus on the cover's visual appearance, and the lack of scientifically sounded methods to prove these schemes' resistance to steganalysis is missing. However, in this work, we focus entirely on using the unseen tag attribute within the core of the cover medium. Furthermore, we focus not only on the visual attack, but also statistical attacks; thus we use the tag attribute values location to hide the secret data.

In reviewing the works of literature, the most recent and most referred to steganographic techniques are mainly on digital images [7,8]. The common trait is that they all propose an embedding technique that generates a new image file, also known as a stego file. When hiding the secret message, care is made so that the stego file can withstand specific steganalysis techniques. The authors who use office work documents as a cover medium are [9–12]. These researchers build various steganographic schemes that mainly rely on human visual undetectability of the difference between the cover and the stego file. This has become a standard for most works treating the topic where the schemes' effectiveness is evaluated based on the visual interpretation of what a non-savvy user would see when inspecting the stego [13].

The main contributions of this work are summarized as follows:

- We present a structural text steganographic scheme based on unseen tag attribute values.
- We are among the first to investigate the unseen tag identifier within the cover document to hide the secret message.
- We assess the performance of the proposed scheme in terms of the invisibility, embedding capacity, robustness, and security. The results show the advantage of a higher capacity embedding and better flexibility while keeping high practicability in terms of accessibility and implementation.

The rest of this work is organized as follows: we introduce the office file structure in Sect. 2. We present the steganographic scheme in Sect. 3, and assess it in Sec. 4. Section 5 is devoted for a short discussion and Sect. 6 concludes this work.

2   Office File Structure

Office documents (docx, xlsx, and pptx), despite their appearance of being a single file, are actually compressed package archives. Their content can be extracted and modified. To illustrate the case, we create a new docx document file using the Office software, write the text "Hello, this is a test.", and then save it as test.docx. Since this test.docx file is a package, we can extract its content and obtain the file tree shown in Fig. 1.

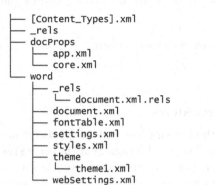

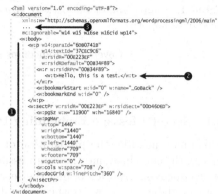

Fig. 1. A tree of the files that constitute the Word package.

Fig. 2. document.xml extracted from a
Word file document.

After unpacking the test.docx file, the file document.xml inside the folder
word is where the string 'Hello, this is a test.' is stored. To further understand the document.xml structure when extracted from the Word file document
package, we have the illustration shown in Fig. 2. Arrows 1, 2, and 3 indicate:

1. The block that specifies what is within the Word document when displayed
   to a typical user. Every text visible in the document is referred to within this
   block. The body element specifies the contents of the body of the document.
   It has no attributes but can contain several elements, most related to tracking
   changes and adding custom XML. Among the core elements are p and sectPr,
   where p specifies a paragraph within the content, and sectPr indicates the
   section properties for the final section.
2. The text 'Hello, this is a test.' is within the element paragraph
   $< w : p >$, the non-block region of text $< w : r >$, and the text element
   $< w : t >$.
3. The three-dot is used as a place holder for further document specification
   which we removed due to space limitations.

All the research in the literature using a structural text hiding technique
based on Word documents focuses on using the content presented to the regular
users, thus being limited to the body element and its inner elements.

3 Steganographic Scheme Based on Unseen Tag
Attribute Values

We illustrate the following scenario based on a Word file created with the
Microsoft Office software with a .docx extension.

Table 1. Comparison of the package size (in KB) generated based on weather compression is applied

Cover	Stego uncompressed	Stego compressed
40	420	29

3.1 Secret Message Embedding Procedures

This phase includes the preparation of the corpora (for text based secret messages), the encoding, and the compression. We use the `tags attributes values` of the `document.xml` for hiding the secret. For our experiment, we use the corpora available at https://github.com/dragona/english-words. Then, we generate a list of unique `identifiers` for mapping each word in the corpora. These `identifiers` are used as the secret in the cover during embedding. Not all the original `attribute values` from the `document.xml` are replaceable. Thus, we create the following exclusion rules where the `values` of all the `tag attributes` can be used for hiding the `identifiers` if the following conditions are fulfilled: 1) the attribute starts with `w` and ends with " or " >; 2) the attribute contains the two characters `id` in either lower or upper cases; and 3) the attribute is not `rsidRDefault`, `rsidDel` or just `id`. Finally, the encoding stage consists of extracting the content of the cover package and writing the secret message using their `identifiers`, in replacement of the original `attributes` value of the cover's `document.xml`. The initial `document.xml` will be replaced with the new `document.xml` encoded with the secret message. We then need to repackage what was previously extracted from the cover into a single `docx` file to build the `stego`. Everything within the package remains the same as the cover's original content, except for the `document.xml`. Compression should be applied when creating the package. The difference in size between the compressed and uncompressed package files is drastic, as illustrated in Table 1, where the same secret message and cover are used, but only the compression phase is added or ignored.

An impression of pseudo randomness can further be achieved by improving the generation of the unique `identifiers` for mapping each word in the corpora.

3.2 Secret Message Extraction

During the encoding phase, we repackage the content of the Word document to create the stego file. Based on the proposed scheme, the only required file from the Word document to extract the secret message is the `document.xml`. The other elements needed are the corpora and the reverse mapping table for getting the secrets from the `identifiers`.

4 Performance Assessment

Aligning with the requirements of a good steganographic scheme as described in the literature [14], we assess the proposed scheme based on the following criteria: invisibility, embedding capacity, robustness, and security.

4.1   Invisibility

The literature has defined different types of invisibility requirements for steganography: resistance to visual attack, structural attack, retyping attack, and statistical attack [15].

Visual Attack. The embedding of the secret in this proposed method is focused on the use of the `attributes value` of cover's `document.xml`, which is not visible from the Word file content when the document is opened by a standard way. Assuming that `Eve` gets access to the `document.xml` content and scans through the material to detect anomalies, the modifications during the encoding should go un-noticed and be considered as a standard content formatting. This is a pure assumption, as we cannot measure its full effectiveness, and we are not able to find an appropriate method, nor do we find such reference in the literature. The least we can do is to have a few tech-savvy participants from our lab, without knowing anything from the core purpose of the research, to find any anomalies from the `document.xml` file we extracted from a stego file. Out of 8 participants who take part in this process, no one is able to find apparent differences or is even close to noticing that the `attribute values` are not the original.

Structural Attack. A formatting attack is an example of a structural attack. It consists of changing the formatting or typesetting of a stego file content and then assessing the percentage of the secret message that is kept retrievable. This vanilla version of the proposed steganography scheme is the most resistant to aggressive structural attack. However, this remains an area of exploration as, during all our experimental phases, the same steps user manipulation resulted in a different outcome.

Retyping Attack. If we define a retyping attack as `Eve` creates a new file and retypes the content of the stego file into it, none of the secret messages embedded in the stego file within the `document.xml` will be ported to the new document. The new document will have new `attribute values`. Thus, this is one of the most aggressive attacks to the proposed scheme.

Statistical Attack. Many papers in the literature [16–18] have also introduced and kept as standard the use of Jaro Similarity for measuring the degree of invisibility. It consists of comparing the words from the cover, and the stego then measures their similarity. Yet, the proposed scheme does not change the contextual content of the stego file created compared to the cover. Thus the Jaro-Winkler Distance will equal to 1, meaning a high similarity between the cover and stego.

Most of the records in the literature related to text steganography focus on the core content of the text document to measure secrecy and the proposed work resistance to attacks. Steganalysis technique for general structural text steganography is still non-existent, and thus further solicits our interests in this area.

Unlike [1] and all similar works that are entirely relying on the structural modifications not having explicit visual modification on the content of the Word file cover, drastic changes are often noticed being applied to the document.xml file. These changes, frequently not being unnoticed to the eyes of an expert (like Eve), have not been considered in most of the previous works. We insist on the importance of allowing Eve to have access to all components of the stego file during her manipulations. Thus, in our experiment, we automate this task and build a classifier that makes an inference of the degree of suspiciousness of a Word file as to whether being a stego file. The outcome is promising; however, we will not elaborate on this in this manuscript.

4.2   Embedding Capacity

The embedding capacity of the proposed scheme depends heavily on the structure of the document.xml. The tags are auto-generated by the file processor when the document is created, and additional tags are added when the content is extended. The arrangement of the data and text in the document defines the structure of the content of the document.xml. In contrast to [1], the number of tags available for secret message encoding does not forcefully increase as the number of words in the document grows. Table 2 reports the embedding capacity of two covers of different sizes.

Comparing the available spaces for hiding the secret in [1] and this proposed method, we report the summary in Table 4. We note that for the same cover document which contains 4374 words, there are 4168 available locations for hiding data when using the method in [1] whereas ours has 1901. However, given the secret message "hello world", [1] would require the allocation of 12 chunks for hiding this secret, and the proposed method only requires the replacement of two tag values (2 chunks).

Table 2. Embedding capacity.

Cover (KB)	Corpora (# words)
40	1360
93	1901

Table 3. Robustness comparison

Methods	P_{rem}	P_{dist}
[1]	0.952903521	0.047096479
ours	0.434613626	0.565386374

Table 4. Available space and removing probability comparison

	Words	Places for embedding	Removing probability	"Hello world"
[1]	4374	4168	0.95	12 places
xml	4374	1901	0.43	2 places

4.3   Robustness

The robustness of a stego system corresponds to the degree of manipulation that can be applied to the stego file and how good it can keep the secret message fully extractable. A metric to measure this is by quantifying the lost portion probability of the secret message from the stego file.

$$P_{rem} = Emb_{location}/Cover_{length}$$
$$P_{dist} = [1 - P_{rem}]$$
$$1 < Emb_{location} < Cover_{length}$$

where P_{rem} denotes the removing probability, $Emb_{location}$ denotes the number of embeddable location in the cover, $Cover_{length}$ denotes the length of the cover message (text content), and P_{dist} denotes the probability of distortion robustness. Compared with [1], the proposed scheme provides higher P_{dist} and lower P_{rem} (Table 3).

4.4   Security

Resistance to Currently Known Attack. Document inspector feature for removing hidden data: Office documents have been designed to be shareable and with that in mind, Document Inspector has been made available so that the created files can be cleaned from the existence of: 1) properties and personal information, 2) headers, footers, and watermarks, 3) hidden text (text formatted as hidden text, also known as hidden characters), 4) document server properties, and 5) custom XML data (that is not visible in the document itself).

We put the presented scheme into the test and use Document Inspector on the stego file. The cleaning has no damaging effect on the stego file, and the embedded secret message is left intact.

5   Discussion

The original data format for embedding in the cover document's `document.xml` has eight values from 0 to 9 and A to F (which also refers to hexadecimal values). However, an *identifier* composed of eight digits is more than enough to uniquely identify each word from the dictionary (502,597 words). More accurately, only six values are needed to map each word uniquely. Considering that each word can be re-used in the secret message, to avoid redundancy of the *identifiers* in the created stego file, we allocate the six values for each word's mapping table element and two values to uniquely identify each repetition or the re-use of the same word. By doing so, each *identifier* is now a composition of a word identifier ID_{word} and a repetition counter rep. Our aim with this was to avoid statistical redundancy tracing of ID_{word} re-use, which could be exploited during a steganalyser's statistical attack.

6   Conclusion

In this paper, we presented a structural steganographic scheme based on unseen tag attribute values using office documents as the medium. Our comprehensive experiments verify the feasibility of building a general steganalysis classifier for structural text steganography given enough data, and demonstrate that the method is effective for a wide range of similar steganography scheme using unseen structural content of the cover medium.

Acknowledgement. This work was supported in part by the National Natural Science Foundation of China under Grant 62072061.

References

1. Rabevohitra, F.H., Li, Y.: Text cover steganography using font color of the invisible characters and optimized primary color-intensities. In: 2019 IEEE 19th International Conference on Communication Technology. IEEE Press, New York (2019)
2. Bender, W., Gruhl, D., Morimoto, N., Lu, A.: Techniques for data hiding. IBM Syst. J. **35**, 313–336 (1996)
3. Mei, Q., Wong, E.K., Memon, N.D.: Data hiding in binary text documents. In: Proceedings of SPIE 4314, Security and Watermarking of Multimedia Contents III (2001)
4. Artz, D.: Digital steganography: hiding data within data. IEEE Internet Comput. **5**, 75–80 (2001)
5. Khairullah, M.: A novel text steganography system using font color of the invisible characters in Microsoft word documents. In: 2009 2D International Conference on Computer and Electrical Engineering, Dubai, United Arab Emirates, p. 484 (2009)
6. Por, L., Wong, K., Chee, K.O.: UniSpaCh: a text-based data hiding method using Unicode space characters. J. Syst. Soft. **85**, 1075–1082 (2012)
7. Taburet, T., Bas P., Sawaya, W., Fridrich J.: A natural steganography embedding scheme dedicated to color sensors in the JPEG domain. In: Electronic Imaging 2019, Burlingame, United States (2019)
8. Taburet, T., Bas P., Fridrich J., Sawaya, W.: Computing dependencies between DCT coefficients for natural steganography in JPEG domain. In: Proceedings of ACM Workshop Information Hiding and Multimedia Security Workshop, pp. 57–62. ACM, New York (2019)
9. Bhaya, W., Rahma, A.M., AL-Nasrawi, D.: Text steganography based on font type in MS-word documents. J. Comput. Sci. **9**, 898–904 (2013)
10. Chang, C.-Y., Clark, S.: Practical linguistic steganography using contextual synonym substitution and a novel vertex coding method. Comput. Linguist. **40**, 403–448 (2014)
11. Mahato, S., Khan, D.A., Yadav, D.K.: A modified approach to data hiding in Microsoft Word documents by change-tracking technique. J. King Saud Univ. Comp. Info. Sci. **32**, 216–224 (2020)
12. Khadim, U., Khan, A., Ahmad, B., Khan, A.: Information hiding in text to improve performance for word document. Int. J. New Technol. Res. **3**, 50–55 (2015)
13. Shi, S., Qi, Y., Huang, Y.: An approach to text steganography based on search in Internet. In: 2016 International Computer Symposium, Chiayi, Taiwan, pp. 15–17 (2016)

14. Morkel, T., Eloff, J.H.P.: An overview of image steganography. In: Annual Information Security South Africa Conference, pp. 1–11 (2005)
15. Ahvanooey, T., Li, Q., Hou, J., Rajput, A.R., Chen, Y.: Modern text hiding, text steganalysis, and applications: a comparative analysis. Entropy **21**, 1–29 (2019)
16. Agarwal, M.: Text steganographic approaches: a comparison. Int. J. Net. Sec. Apps. **5** (2013)
17. Kingslin, S., Kavitha, N.: Evaluative approach towards text steganographic techniques. Indian J. Sci. Tech. **8**, 1–8 (2015)
18. Banerjee, I., Souvik B., Gautam, S.: Novel text steganography through special code generation. In: International Conference on Systemics, Cybernetics and Informatics, pp. 298–303 (2011)

Trajectory Anomaly Detection Based on the Mean Distance Deviation

Xiaoyuan Hu[1], Qing Xu[1(✉)], and Yuejun Guo[2]

[1] College of Intelligence and Computing, Tianjin University, Tianjin, China
qingxu@tju.edu.cn
[2] Graphics and Imaging Laboratory, Universitat de Girona, Girona, Spain

Abstract. With the development of science and technology and the explosive growth of data, there will be a lot of trajectories every day. However, how to detect the abnormal trajectory from many trajectories has become a hot issue. In order to study trajectory anomaly detection better, we analyze the Sequential conformal anomaly detection in trajectories based on hausdorff distance (SNN-CAD) method, and propose a new measurement method of trajectory distance Improved Moved Euclidean Distance (IMED) instead of Hausdorff distance, which reduces the computational complexity. In addition, we propose a removing-updating strategy to enhance the conformal prediction (CP). Then, we also put forward our Non-conformity measure (NCM), Mean Distance Deviation. It can enlarge the difference between trajectories more effectively, and detect the abnormal trajectory more accurately. Finally, based on the technical measures mentioned above and under the framework of enhanced conformal prediction theory detection, we also build our own detector called Mean Distance Deviation Detector (MDD-ECAD). Using a large number of synthetic trajectory data and real world trajectory data on two detectors, the experimental results show that MDD-ECAD is much better than SNN-CAD in both accuracy and running time.

Keywords: Conformal prediction · Non-conformity measure · Trajectory distance

1 Introduction

With the rapid proliferation of closed circuit television cameras, satellites and mobile devices, massive trajectory based on different kinds of moving objects such as people, hurricanes, animals and vehicles [11] have been generated (Fig. 1). Undoubtedly trajectory data analysis plays a vital role and abnormal trajectory detection is one of the most key issues for this topic. There are more mature

This work has been funded by Natural Science Foundation of China under Grants No. 61471261 and No. 61771335. The author Yuejun Guo acknowledges support from Secretaria dUniversitats i Recerca del Departament dEmpresa i Coneixement de la Generalitat de Catalunya and the European Social Fund.

© Springer Nature Switzerland AG 2020
H. Yang et al. (Eds.): ICONIP 2020, CCIS 1332, pp. 140–147, 2020.
https://doi.org/10.1007/978-3-030-63820-7_16

methods based on distance similarity [10]. Although it is relatively high in complexity in terms of large-scale data, it works well in small and medium-scale trajectory anomaly detection. The more famous method, Sequential conformal anomaly detection in trajectories based on hausdorff distance (SNN-CAD) method, is proposed by Laxhammar et al. [6]. Their detection method is mainly based on the conformal prediction (CP) theory [8]. Firstly, the Hausdoff distance [1] is used to calculate the distance between the trajectories as the trajectory similarity. Then Non-conformity Measure (NCM) [9] is given in the light of K-Nearest Neighbor [2], and finally uses conformal prediction detection theory to determine whether the trajectory is abnormal. However, the NCM can not distinguish the abnormal trajectory very well, and the detection accuracy is not high.

Fig. 1. A display of aircraft trajectories (left) and synthetic tracjectories (right). Red trajectories are abnormal and black trajectories are normal. (Colour fiugre online)

In the view of this, we take into account the new NCM, Mean Distance Deviation (MDD), and present a removing-updating strategy to enhance conformal anomaly detection. Accordingly we propose the Mean Distance Deviation based on Enhanced Conformal Anomaly Detector (MDD-ECAD), which can deal with trajectory anomaly detection very well.

Also imporantantly, in this paper, we propose a new distance measure by improving Euclidean Distance (ED), which is called Improved Moved Euclidean Distance (IMED). It can characterize the trajectory distance efficiently. What is more, IMED does not require that the length of the trajectories must be same and its computational complexity is small.

The rest of this paper is organized as follows. Section 2 introduces the relevant background knowledge of our work. Section 3 presents the details of our method MDD-ECAD. Experimental data and results are described in Sect. 4. Finally, the paper is concluded in the Sect. 5.

2   Background

In this section, we will introduce the basic concept of trajectory and the specific details of CP theory.

2.1 Trajectory Type

In general, a trajectory data we study in this paper is a sequence of coordinate points in Cartesian coordinate system. Speaking ahead of time, a trajectory can be simply represented as $T = (a_1, a_2, \cdots, a_n)$.

2.2 Conformal Prediction

Conformal prediction (CP) makes use of the past of experience to determine precise levels of confidence in new prediction. Generally speaking, assume a training data $\{(x_1, y_1), (x_2, y_2), \cdots, (x_l, y_l)\}$ where x_i $(i = 1, \cdots, l)$ is the input data, that is some data observed or collected by some means. And y_i $(i = 1, \cdots, l)$ is the output data, that is the label predicted by some method. For exame, x_i is a trajectory data collected by sensor and y_i is the label with only abnormal or normal type in the trajectory anomaly detection. Given a new observed data x_{l+1}, the basic idea of conformal prediction to estimate the p-value p_{l+1} of x_{l+1} by designed NCM according to training data. Finally, the p_{l+1} is compared with the pre-defined threshold ϵ to determine the label of x_{l+1}.

If $p_{l+1} < \epsilon$, x_{l+1} is identified as conformal anomaly. Otherwise, x_{l+1} is determined as normal. However, the key to estimate the p-value of the new example is how to design effective NCM. Next, we will introduce the concept of a Non-Conformity Measure (NCM) whose purpose is to measure the difference between the new example and a set of observed data.

Formally, NCM is a mathematical function. We can get a score α_i about the difference between the example x_i and the rest of dataset by a certain NCM. The score of x_i is given by

$$\alpha_i = A\left(X_{j \neq i}, x_i\right) \tag{1}$$

where X is a set of data; x_i is a example of dataset X; $A(.)$ is a form of NCM.

Based on formula (1), the score $(\alpha_1, \alpha_2, \cdots, \alpha_{l+1})$ is gained. Then the p-value of x_{l+1}, p_{l+1}, is determined as the ratio of the number of trajectories that have greater or equal nonconformity scores to x_{l+1} to the total number of trajectories. The p-value is defined as follows:

$$p_{l+1} = \frac{|\{\alpha_i | \alpha_i \geq \alpha_{l+1}, 1 \leq i \leq l+1\}|}{l+1} \tag{2}$$

where $|\{\cdot\}|$ computers the number of elements in the set. CP will estimate a set of p-value to predict the lable of the new example and work excellently by using an effective NCM, especially when ϵ is close to the proportion of abnormal data in the dataset.

The Sequential Hausdorff Nearest Neighbor Conformal Anomaly Detector (SNN-CAD) method was developed by laxhammar et al. [6]. Their main contribution is to use Hausdorff distance to calculate the trajectory distance and use k-nearest neighbor as NCM. Suppose there are two sets of $T_a = \{a_1, a_2, \cdots, a_m\}$,

$T_b = \{b_1, b_2, \cdots, b_n\}$. The Hausdorff distance can refer to this article. As for NCM, it is defined as follows:

$$\alpha_i = \sum_{T_b \in Neig(T_a)} d\left(T_a, T_b\right) \tag{3}$$

Where d(.) is a kind of tracjectory distance, Neig (T_a) represents the k-nearest neighbor of T_a.

3   Our Method

3.1   Improved Moved Euclidean Distance

In order to measure the distance between two trajectories effctively, researchers have put forward various methods to calculate the distance. The most commonly used and famous ones are ED, HD, and DTW. However, comparing the advantages and disadvantages of the above three distances, we come to the following conclusions: (1) DTW and HD can handle the unequal length trajectory data, but the computational complexity is too high to deal with large and medium-sized data. (2) ED calculates the trajectory distance quickly with the simple implementation, but it can not do anything for the unequal trajectory data.

After our discussion, we can't help thinking about how to calculate quickly and deal with unequal data. For this purpose, based on ED, we propose a new distance measure Improved Moved Euclidean Distance (IMED) to enlarge the difference between trajectories for better performing trajectory anomaly detection. The proposed distance measure can manage both equal and unequal length trajectories. The basic idea is to fix the longer tracjectory, moving the shorter tracjectory backward until the longer tracjectory is completely matched. Given two trajectories, $T_a = \{a_1, a_2, \cdots, a_m\}$, $T_b = \{b_1, b_2, \cdots, b_n\}$. Assuming $n \geq m$, the IMED is defined as follows:

$$d_{IME}(T_a, T_b) = \frac{\sum_{j=0}^{n-m} \sqrt{\sum_{i=1}^{m} \|b_{i+j} - a_i\|^2}}{n - m + 1} \tag{4}$$

especially, when n = m, T_a and T_b have the same trajectory length.

3.2   Mean Distance Deviation

An appropriate NCM is very critical and widely used for general anomaly detection. Generally, if a trajectory is similar to its neighboring trajectories, we can think that it is normal. Otherwise, if a trajectory is not the same as the trajectories around it, we can judge that the trajectory is abnormal. Actually, the employment of the local neighborhood is a fundamental consideration widely used in many anomaly detection methods, such as the classic KNN. In SNN-CAD, they use the sum of k-nearest neighbors of a trajectory as an indicator of comparison with other trajectories. The larger the value of KNN, the greater

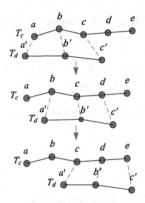

Fig. 2. An example of our IMED for unequal lengths.

the difference between the behavior of the trajectory and the surrounding trajectories. However, it is not ideal to use KNN to judge whether the trajectory
is abnormal. For this reason, we propose a new NCM, Mean Distance Deviation
(MDD). It is proved by the later experimental data (Sect. 5) that this method
is much better than KNN in trajectory anomaly detection. Now we will give its
specific definition (Fig. 2):

$$\alpha\left(T_a\right) = \sqrt{\frac{\sum_{T_b \in Neig(T_a)} (MD(T_a) - MD(T_b))^2}{k}} \tag{5}$$

where

$$MD = \frac{\sum_{T_b \in Neig(T_a)} d(T_a, T_b)}{k} \tag{6}$$

3.3   Removing-Updating Strategy

The process of anomaly detection based on CP is to calculate the p-value of each
data, and then compare with the given threshold value ϵ to determine whether
the trajectory is abnormal. Because the abnormal data detected last time will
interfere with this detection, we propose a removing-updating strategy to CP.

Specifically, when calculating the p-value of all data, the most abnormal data
will be removed. Then update the threshold and repeat the above process with
the remaining data until the threshold is 0.

4   Experiment

In this section, in order to evaluate the effect of MDD-ECAD and IMED, we
compared MDD-ECAD algorithm with SNN-CAD algorithm, as well as several
distances IMED, HD and DTW based on the synthetic data and real life data.

4.1 Data Sets

Synthetic tracjectories I [5] presented for anomaly detection is created by lax-hammar et al. [6] using the trajectory generator software. It includes 100 datasets with 2000 trajectories in each dataset, about 1% of which are abnormal trajectories. In addition, each trajectory is composed of a series of two-dimensional coordinate points. To expand the dataset for experiment, we use another **Synthetic tracjectories** [3] including **synthetic trajectories II, synthetic trajectories III, synthetic trajectories IV.** The three synthetic trajectories each contain 100 trajectory datasets with ϵ equal to 0.05, 0.01, and 0.02. And each dataset has 2000 trajectories with the number of sample points ranging from 20 to 100.

Aircraft trajectories [7] has in all 470 two-dimensional trajectories, involving 450 normal and 20 abnormal ones. And the trajectory length in the set varies from 12 to 171 sampling points.

4.2 Performance Measure

Trajectory anomaly detection is also two classification problem. Therefore, we can use the following evaluation indicators: true positive (TP), false positive (FP), false negative (FN), and true negative (TN). Precison (P), Recall (R) and F1 are used to test the classification accuracy. F1 score is used to evaluate the effect of all experiments. The larger F1 value is, the better the algorithm effect is.

$$P = \frac{TP}{TP + FP}, \; R = \frac{TP}{TP + FN}, \; F1 = \frac{2 * P * R}{P + R} \tag{7}$$

4.3 Experimental Results and Analysis

Table 1. The F1 results (%) of synthetic trajectory datasets with two methods.

Synthetic trajectory datasets	Approaches	P	R	F1
Synthetic trajectories I	SNN-CAD	87.15	77.48	79.80
	MDD-ECAD	88.65	91.83	**89.11**
Synthetic trajectories II	SNN-CAD	83.82	65.04	69.40
	MDD-ECAD	85.8	91.09	**86.35**
Synthetic trajectories III	SNN-CAD	89.31	74.31	79.31
	MDD-ECAD	92.45	90.96	**90.76**
Synthetic trajectories IV	SNN-CAD	87.47	83.88	84.62
	MDD-ECAD	91.37	94.61	**92.31**

In the experiment, we mainly compare the performance of SNN-CAD and MDD-ECAD. It can be seen from Table 1 that the F1 of MDD-ECAD is 89.11%,

Table 2. The F1 results (%) of real-life trajectory datasets with differnt methods.

Trajectory datasets	MDD-ECAD	SNN-CAD	iVAT+
Aircraft trajectories	**95**	75	90

86.35%, 90.76% and 92.31% respectively, higher than that of SNN-CAD. For testing our method on complex real life data, Table 2 shows MDD-ECAD still outperforms SNN-CAD and iVAT+ [4]. The F1 of MDD-ECAD is as high as 95%, while the SNN-CAD is only 75% and iVAT+ is 90%. The reason why SNN-CAD doesn't perform excellent may be that its NCM can't amplify the abnormal tracjectory behavior greatly, and the MDD we used can make up for this defect very well. In addition to the problem of detection framework, we use the removing and updating strategy to avoid the secondary interference of obvious abnormal trajectories to others.

Table 3. The F1 results (%) of MDD-ECAD with different distance measures.

Trajectory datasets	IMED	HD	DTW
Synthetic trajectories I	**89.11**	89.30	79.58
Synthetic trajectories II	**86.35**	84.80	71.86
Synthetic trajectories III	**90.76**	82.43	80.01
Synthetic trajectories IV	**92.31**	90.96	82.65
Aircraft trajectories	**95**	85	90

Table 4. Runtimes (s) of MDD-ECAD with differnt distance measuers.

	IMED	HD	DTW
Synthetic trajectories I	**0.591**	6.22	11.86
Synthetic trajectories II	**16.88**	85.53	97.43
Synthetic trajectories III	**17.03**	109.06	100.49
Synthetic trajectories IV	**17.72**	89.03	100.84
Aircraft trajectories	**2.39**	19.55	18.97

In order to compare the performance of IMED, HD and DTW, we use the three distances in MDD-ECAD method. Table 3 shows that the F1 of IMED is higher than HD and DTW, which indicates that IMED can measure the distance between trajectories better. In addition, the running time of IMED, HD and DTW is given (see Table 4), and it is obvious that the running time of IMED is fewer. From the theoretical analysis, IMED has the minimal computational complexity and no doubt runs the fastest. The experiment just verifies this point.

5   Conclusion

In this paper, in order to improve performance of SNN-CAD, we propose a new method to calculate the trajectory distance. An excellent Non-conformal measurment and a removing-updating strategy are also used for our anomaly detector. Large number of experimental data shows that our detector is better than SNN-CAD.

References

1. Dubuisson, M.P., Jain, A.K.: A modified Hausdorff distance for object matching. In: Proceedings of 12th International Conference on Pattern Recognition, vol. 1, pp. 566–568. IEEE (1994)
2. Güting, R.H., Behr, T., Xu, J.: Efficient k-nearest neighbor search on moving object trajectories. VLDB J. **19**(5), 687–714 (2010)
3. Guo, Y., Bardera, A.: SHNN-CAD+: An improvement on SHNN-CAD for adaptive online trajectory anomaly detection. Sensors **19**(1), 84 (2019)
4. Kumar, D., Bezdek, J.C., Rajasegarar, S., Leckie, C., Palaniswami, M.: A visual-numeric approach to clustering and anomaly detection for trajectory data. Vis. Comput. **33**(3), 265–281 (2015). https://doi.org/10.1007/s00371-015-1192-x
5. Laxhammar, R.: Synthetic trajectories (2013)
6. Laxhammar, R., Falkman, G.: Sequential conformal anomaly detection in trajectories based on Hausdorff distance. In: 14th International Conference on Information Fusion, pp. 1–8. IEEE (2011)
7. Leader, D.S.G.: Aircraft trajectories. https://c3.nasa.gov/dashlink/resources/132/
8. Shafer, G., Vovk, V.: A tutorial on conformal prediction. J. Mach. Learn. Res. **9**(March), 371–421 (2008)
9. Smith, J., Nouretdinov, I., Craddock, R., Offer, C., Gammerman, A.: Anomaly detection of trajectories with kernel density estimation by conformal prediction. In: Iliadis, L., Maglogiannis, I., Papadopoulos, H., Sioutas, S., Makris, C. (eds.) AIAI 2014. IAICT, vol. 437, pp. 271–280. Springer, Heidelberg (2014). https://doi.org/10.1007/978-3-662-44722-2_29
10. Toohey, K., Duckham, M.: Trajectory similarity measures. Sigspatial Special **7**(1), 43–50 (2015)
11. Zheng, Y.: Trajectory data mining: an overview. ACM Trans. Intell. Syst. Technol. (TIST) **6**(3), 1–41 (2015)

Tweet Relevance Based on the Theory of Possibility

Amina Ben Meriem$^{(\boxtimes)}$, Lobna Hlaoua, and Lotfi Ben Romdhane

SDM Research Group, MARS Research Lab ISITCom, University of Sousse, Sousse,
Tunisia
amina.benmaryem@gmail.com, lobna.hlaoua@essths.u-sousse.tn,
lotfi.ben.romdhane@gmail.com

Abstract. The popularity and the great success of social networks are
due to their ability to offer Internet users a free space for expression
where they can produce a large amount of information. Thus the new
challenges of information research and data mining are to extract and
analyze this mass of information which can then be used in different
applications. This information is characterized mainly by incompleteness,
imprecision, and heterogeneity. Indeed the task of analysis using models
based on statistics and word frequencies is crucial. To solve the problem
of uncertainty, the possibility theory turns out to be the most adequate.
In this article, we propose a new approach to find relevant short texts
such as tweets using the dual possibility and necessity. Our goal is to
translate the fact that a tweet can only be relevant if there is not only a
semantic relationship between the tweet and the query but also a synergy
between the terms of the tweet. We have modeled the problem through a
possibility network to measure the possibility of the relevance of terms in
relation to a concept of a given query and a necessity network to measure
the representativeness of terms in a tweet. The evaluation shows that
using the theory of possibilities with a set of concepts relevant to an
initial query gives the best precision rate compared to other approaches.

Keywords: Possibility logic · Social networks · Social information
retrieval

1 Introduction

The emergence of the Web, from a static Web to the social web, presents a
main factor in the continuous and significant growth in the amount of information produced on the web. Indeed, in the static web, users could only consume
information, while in the social web, users are also able to consume and produce information thanks to the ease of communication on social networks which
encourages humans of different interests to share and communicate more and
more [12]. Adding to the ambiguity and noise of natural language used in social
network (SN) textual publications, generally, SN users do not respect grammatical rules, which makes it difficult to decide whether a post is relevant or not

© Springer Nature Switzerland AG 2020
H. Yang et al. (Eds.): ICONIP 2020, CCIS 1332, pp. 148–156, 2020.
https://doi.org/10.1007/978-3-030-63820-7_17

for a specific given query. The use of conventional information retrieval (IR) techniques [10,11] applied to documents may be a solution in some cases, that is why a new subtype of IR has been proposed, namely social information retrieval that adapts IR techniques in social networks [2,4]. Social information retrieval is defined as the incorporation of information on social networks and relationships in the process of information retrieval [7]. Indeed, SN publications are characterized by imprecision, heterogeneity (users with different interests and backgrounds), and incompleteness due to their small size, so we cannot effectively guarantee the analysis of these texts. To remedy this problem, the use of the theory of possibility is a better solution because it is known for its solid theoretical basis to model the incompleteness and uncertainty of information [12]. Short queries used by the users are insufficient to model their needs, so in our proposed model we have added a preprocessing step at during which allows us to develop the query and create a concept for each word of the initial one. Then we have used it in the calculation of the relevance score which is based on the two basic metrics of possibility theory: Possibility and Necessity. We assume that a text is plausible to be relevant for a query if it shares concepts with the query and it is necessarily relevant if its terms are possibly representative. This paper is organized as follows: Sect. 1 briefly explains how some related works in IR and SIR have interpreted relevance. Then Sect. 2 describes our proposed approach for assigning relevance scores and constructing concepts. The last Sect. 3 presents some results obtained and a comparison with some of the existing models.

2   Related Works

An information retrieval system (IR) is capable of retrieving high quality information and aims to maximize user satisfaction by providing responses that meet their needs [2]. To have the best IR system, several approaches have been proposed using different technologies and methods. The basic approaches for calculating the relevance of the query and document content in IR systems are: BM25 [10] (which is based on Okapi BM25) and VSM [11] (based on vector space). Given the uncertainty and vagueness of natural language, several authors choose to use the theory of possibilities to calculate relevance in IR systems thanks to its ability to solve these problems using two metrics which are possibility and necessity. These two measures are used to estimate the relevance of the concepts representing the document. Boughanem et al. [15] and Brini et al. [16] proposed to use a possibilistic network in information retrieval in order to exploit the dependencies between terms and documents. As the volume of textual information increases rapidly with the increase in the use of social media, it is increasingly difficult to find relevant information. However, conventional information retrieval (IR) models are not able to adapt to this social context that surrounds both users and resources; that is why an IR sub-branch, which is the social information retrieval SIR, is proposed [2]. The goal of ad-hoc microblog search task is similar to the classic search of documents. It concists of responding to a specific query via a microblog index and select those that are likely to be relevant to the user's information need. Classic IR models which, in general, are based on factors such as the frequency of terms in documents, their lexical normalization and the length of documents, are limited by the short length of microblogs, where terms do not appear more than once. Thus, the short size of the tweet increases the difficulty of textual search by keywords in microblogs. Authors in [14] used a language modeling based approach which estimate of the probability of a term for a given microblog post in the collection. To estimate relevance, they only used the presence or absence of the term in the language model instead of its frequency in microblog posts (documents)in the collection. Authors in [13] studied the impact of term frequency weighting and document length normalisation in microblog retrieval. The results with BM25 model indicate that incorporating document length normalization and term frequency statistics degrade the retrieval performance. To solve the problem of term frequency and normalization with short text, authors in [8] proposed a term similarity graph based on the cooccurrence of terms for microblog retrieval. In the weighted graph, the nodes represent terms and the links represent their co-occurrences in the collection of tweets. To deal with these limitations, different retrieval approaches proposed to integrate social network features in relevance score, in addition to content features. Others focused on improving the representation of terms in queries or microblogs. Duan et al. [4] proposed a method to rank tweets based on their relevance using a query to rank approach based on the authority of the tweet writer and the content relevance of the tweet using BM25. Sendi et al. [12] have proposed algorithm using possibilistic logic and semantic resources to determine the interest of SN users to decide on the textual relevance of publications in a SN.

3 Possibilistic Approach for Tweet Retrieval

In order to solve the problems raised in the literature namely heterogeneity as well as the mass of information available in social networks, we propose an approach based on the theory of possibilities which allows us to filter tweets at two levels: In a first level we select the plausibly relevant tweets according to our hypothesis: "a tweet is plausibly relevant if it shares certain concepts with the user query". Indeed at this level do not consider a set of words to represent the query but rather the main concepts that can translate the user's need in a more exhaustive way. We thus widen the field of research since each word can belong to more than one concept. This selection will be made through a measure of possibility. The second level allows us to select the necessarily relevant tweets according to our hypothesis: "a tweet is necessarily relevant if its topics include the terms of the query". This will be expressed by a degree of necessity.

In the documents retrieval, the frequencies of terms are generally used to assign a weight to the document which will subsequently decide its rank in the list of returned documents. Since this factor can no longer be applied in the case of social retrieval, we therefore propose to consider the representativeness of the terms in the tweet using the WordRank algorithm.

3.1   Model Architecture

In order to be able to explain the different stages, we start with the adapted modeling throughout this article (Fig. 1).

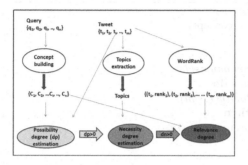

Fig. 1. Proposed model

Let Q be a user query and T a tweet composed respectively of n and m terms so that $Q = \{q_1, q_2, ..., q_i, ..., q_n\}$ and $T = \{t_1, t_2, .., t_i, ...t_m\}$.

In order to extend the initial query, we have chosen to use a set of concepts C to which the terms composing the initial query belong. With $C = c_1, c_2, ..c_i, c_n$ where c_i is the set of the considered concepts for term q_i. we note the im_{ij} the similarity between the qth term and the jth concept. A query can be represented as follows: $Q = (q_i, sim_{ij})i = 1..n$ and $j = 1..k$(k = number of concepts considered). In order to overcome the problem of representativeness of terms in tweet, we used the WordRank algorithm which allows to generate for each term t_i of the tweet a rank $rank_i$. We thus propose a model composed of 3 stages:

1. Estimation of possibility degree which takes as input the extended query as well as the terms of a tweet in order to calculate a similarity S. Tweets will be considered relevant based on S.
2. Estimation of Necessity degree which takes as input the topics of plausibly relevant tweets and the terms of the initial query and calculates a similarity S 'to decide which tweets are necessarily relevant.
3. Ranking based on relevance degree takes into account the $rank_i$ of the terms of the tweets as well as the similarities of these with the concepts c_j

3.2   Estimation Possibility Degree

Generally, most people use a few terms to search for microblogs that are insufficient to model their needs, which is why, before calculating the relevance of a text, we suggest a preprocessing step at during which we will develop the query and create a concept for each word of the initial one. A concept is a collection of words that are to a certain degree similar to a specific word. Our final goal is to have relevant tweets not only for the original query Q but also for all the words of concept C (see Algorithm 1).

Algorithm 1. Concept building

Input: Q (A query)
Output: *Concept* (A concept)
  $Concept \leftarrow list()$
  for $I \in Q$ **do**
    $synsets \leftarrow getSynonyms(I)$
    for $syn \in synsets$ **do**
      $sim \leftarrow similarity(I, syn)$
      if $sim > R$ **then**
        $concept.append((syn, sim))$
      end if
    end for
  end for

Our final goal is to filter the irrelevant tweets to an initial entered item denoted by Q. Our proposed approach is based on two hypotheses: as a first hypothesis, we assume that a tweet can only be classified as relevant if it shares concepts with the query, in other words, let t_j be a tweet term and $c_i k$ a concept term q_i, $\Pi(t_j|c_{ik})$ is the possibility that t_j is relevant to c_{ik}. $\sum \Pi(t_j|c_{ik})/m > 0$ if $Tweet \cap query \neq \varnothing$. We use the cosine [9] as similarity to estimate$\Pi(t_j|c_{ik})$. This method takes as input two vectors, so we converted each word in the tweet and in the concept into vectors using the word2vec [5] algorithm.

3.3 Estimation of Necessity Degree

Having a tweet T, a concept C, word $w_j \in T$, item denoted $c_i \in C$ and topics is a set of word representing the context of T. As mentioned in hypothesis 2, we assume a tweet is necessarily relevant if its terms are possibly representative, having a relevant word t_j, now we will calculate $N(t_j|T)$ to find out if it is almost certain that t_j is representative of T or not, in another word, to find out if t_j belongs to the topics or the context of the tweet T. To decide if a word is representative of the tweet we created a context of the tweet using TextRazorAPI [3] to extract topics, ie, $N(t_j|T) > 0$ if $t_j \subset topics\ of\ the\ tweet \neq \varnothing$. In our case $N(t_j|T) > 0$ if the similarity between t_j and the tweet topics, to calculate it we used the jaccard similarity.

3.4 Ranking Based on Relevance Degree

As input, we have a concept resulting from the previous step we will assign a relevance score to the tweet. We use the WordRank algorithm proposed by Ji et al. [6]in order to give a rank to each word in the tweet, that is $t_j \in T$ and $rank_j$ is the rank obtained for the word j using similarities. The ranking gives us an initial importance decision for each word in the tweet. A tweet will be representing like a set of $(t_j, rank_j)$. We normalized all rank values to have values between 0 and 1. In our case, if the similarity between a tweet word t_j and a concept item > 0 then the rank of this word and the degree of importance of the concept item c_i will be taken into account in the calculation of the relevance score. If a word t_j is both relevant to c_i and representative to the tweet T, it will contribute to the calculation of the overall relevance score of T with a certain degree depending on its rank $rank_j$ and the sim value of c sim_i.

4   Experimentation

Our final goal is to determine the list of relevant tweets with a high precision rate. In the rest of the experimentation part, we detailed the data sets and metrics used, then we assessed the impact or importance of using the theory of possibilities in having great precision, in the end, we compared our approach to others proposed. To evaluate our approach, we used two sets of data: the first contains 3011 (1386 relevant and 1625 irrelevant) tweets about the Queensland flood [1], the second data set contains 3503 (1660 relevant and 1843 irrelevant) tweets about the Nepal earthquake [1]. To evaluate our approach of tweet relevance decision based on the theory of possibility, we use the three best-known measures: precision, recall, and F-measure. Where Precision shows how many selected items are relevant, recall shows how many relevant items are selected, and F-measure is the synthetic indicator, which combines precision and recall measures. As mentioned above, our proposed approach is based on two main steps: the construction of a concept in which we are going to create a set of terms similar to the given query to some measure, then we will calculate the relevance of the tweets using the possibility of theory as detailed in Sect. 3.4.

For the concept building to each of our data sets we specify a query Q: for the first data set $Q = $ "QueensLand flood", and for the second data set $Q = $ "Nepal earthquake" (Table 1).

Table 1. Concept building results

Q	Queensland flood			Nepal earthquake		
R	0.5	0.7	0.9	0.5	0.7	0.9
Number of words	2983	367	7	2983	455	7

4.1   Evaluation

To evaluate our approach we used the three metrics detailed above: Precision, Recall, and F-measure. First, we tried to calculate relevance without taking into account the concept to see how well our algorithm for estimating the relevance score is performing, then we varied the size of the concept R to find what is approximately the best radius or size which will be considered in the comparison with other approaches. The result obtained are detailed in Table 2.

Table 2. Resulted evaluation metrics

Q	Queensland flood			Nepal earthquake		
R	0.5	0.7	0.9	0.5	0.7	0.9
Precision	91.87%	95.4%	98.3%	59.17%	58.63%	65%
Recall	75.05%	71.4%	72%	51.98%	51.64%	60%
F-measure	82.6%	81.7%	83.2%	55.3%	54.91%	62.4%

As we can notice in Table 2, having a small concept can reduce the recall rate but it improves the precision rate because it is free of noise and all the words it contains are very relevant. The best size of the concept found is when R is around 0.9, we only consider the closely related concepts to have a good precision for the rest of the evaluation, while 0.5 allows us to have a more interesting recall rate. To find out the impact of using possibility theory, we tried to compare our approach using the concept with R = 0.9 once by calculating the textual similarity only between a tweet and the concept, then using possibility only and finally using possibility and necessity (our approach), as shown in the Table 3.

Table 3. The impact of the possibility theory use

	Queensland flood			Nepal earthquake		
	Precision	Recall	F-measure	Precision	Recall	F-measure
With text similarity only	97.95%	90.78%	94%	58.3%	54.3%	56.2%
Using the possibility	98.16%	83.66%	90.3%	59.4%	53.4%	56.24%
Using possibility and necessity(our approach)	**98.3%**	72%	83.2%	**65%**	60%	62.4%

By observing the Table 3, we notice that the measure of necessity allows to reach a high rate of precision (98.3%). This confirms that the choice of the measure of necessity allows us to return more certain tweets and therefore it reduces noise but it is less effective in reducing silence unlike the measure of possibility.

4.2 Comparison

To test the performance of our approach, we compared it to a supervised approach based on labeled data and two semi-supervised approaches the first based on self-training and the second based on a graph proposed by Alam et al. [1].

As the Table 4 shows, our approach goes beyond the three approaches in precision rate which is our initial goal, and it also shows that, regardless of the query, our possibilistic approach is benefic in precision.

Table 4. Comparative table

	Queensland flood			Nepal earthquake		
	Precsion	Recall	F-measure	Precsion	Recall	F-measure
Supervised	80.08%	80.16%	80.16%	62.42%	62.31%	60.89%
Self training	80.78%	80.84%	81.08%	61.53%	61.53%	61.26%
Graph based approach	92.6%	94.49%	93.54%	64.58%	64.63 %	65.11%
Our approach	**98.3%**	72%	83.2%	**65%**	60%	62.4%

5 Conclusion

The tweets are proof of incompleteness since they are short, therefore, the information which it expresses is incomplete, because they are written in a non-grammatical language which is full of ambiguity and noise. This makes it difficult to decide whether a tweet is relevant to a topic, to solve that we proposed an approach based on the possibility theory to decide the relevance of a tweet to a given topic since the logic of possibilities presents a trustworthy theoretical base for modeling uncertain information. Our proposed approach consists of two phases, the first aims to extend the given query to have a larger set of words similar to a certain degree to the initial query, to the second phase, we proposed two possibilistic networks to calculate the degree of relevance of a tweet assuming that a tweet is plausible to be relevant if it shares concepts with the query, and it is necessarily relevant if its terms are possibly representative. In the experimental part, we have shown that the use of the theory of possibilities with a reduced concept of relevant terms gives a high rate of precision. In future work, we suggest using machine learning techniques with the theory of the possibility of obtaining better recall values, and we propose to use fuzzy logic to classify the relevance score, in which a tweet could be relevant and irrelevant, at the same time, to a certain degree, and the decision will be made using the inference.

References

1. Alam, F., Joty, S., Imran, M.: Domain adaptation with adversarial training and graph embeddings (2018)
2. Bouadjenek, M.R., Hacid, H., Bouzeghoub, M.: Social networks and information retrieval, how are they converging? a survey, a taxonomy and an analysis of social information retrieval approaches and platforms. Inf. Syst. **56**, 1–18 (2016)
3. Crayston, T.: Textrazor: Technology
4. Duan, Y., Jiang, L., Qin, T., Zhou, M., Shum, H.Y.: An empirical study on learning to rank of tweets. In: Proceedings of the 23rd International Conference on Computational Linguistics, pp. 295–303. Association for Computational Linguistics (2010)
5. Goldberg, Y., Levy, O.: word2vec explained: deriving mikolov et al'.s negative-sampling word-embedding method. arXiv preprint arXiv:1402.3722 (2014)
6. Ji, S., Yun, H., Yanardag, P., Matsushima, S., Vishwanathan, S.: WordRank: learning word embeddings via robust ranking. arXiv preprint arXiv:1506.02761 (2015)

7. Kirsch, S.M.: Social information retrieval (2005)
8. Lin, Y., Li, Y., Xu, W., Guo, J.: Microblog retrieval based on term similarity graph. In: Proceedings of 2012 2nd International Conference on Computer Science and Network Technology, pp. 1322–1325, December 2012. https://doi.org/10.1109/ICCSNT.2012.6526165
9. Nguyen, H.V., Bai, L.: Cosine similarity metric learning for face verification. In: Kimmel, R., Klette, R., Sugimoto, A. (eds.) ACCV 2010. LNCS, vol. 6493, pp. 709–720. Springer, Heidelberg (2011). https://doi.org/10.1007/978-3-642-19309-5_55
10. Robertson, S.E., Jones, K.S.: Relevance weighting of search terms. J. Am. Soc. Inf. Sci. **27**(3), 129–146 (1976)
11. Salton, G., Wong, A., Yang, C.S.: A vector space model for automatic indexing. Commun. ACM **18**(11), 613–620 (1975). https://doi.org/10.1145/361219.361220
12. Sendi, M., Omri, M.N., Abed, M.: Possibilistic interest discovery from uncertain information in social networks. Intell. Data Anal. **21**(6), 1425–1442 (2017)
13. Ferguson, P., O'Hare, N., Lanagan, J., Phelan, O., McCarthy, K.: An investigation of term weighting approaches for microblog retrieval. In: Baeza-Yates, R., et al. (eds.) ECIR 2012. LNCS, vol. 7224, pp. 552–555. Springer, Heidelberg (2012). https://doi.org/10.1007/978-3-642-28997-2_62
14. Massoudi, K., Tsagkias, M., de Rijke, M., Weerkamp, W.: Incorporating query expansion and quality indicators in searching microblog posts. In: Clough, P., et al. (eds.) ECIR 2011. LNCS, vol. 6611, pp. 362–367. Springer, Heidelberg (2011). https://doi.org/10.1007/978-3-642-20161-5_36
15. Boughanem, M., Brini, A., Dubois, D.: Possibilistic networks for information retrieval. Int. J. Approximate Reasoning **50**(7), 957–968 (2009)
16. Brini, A.H., Boughanem, M., Dubois, D.: A model for information retrieval based on possibilistic networks. In: Consens, M., Navarro, G. (eds.) SPIRE 2005. LNCS, vol. 3772, pp. 271–282. Springer, Heidelberg (2005). https://doi.org/10.1007/11575832_31

Healthcare Analytics-Improving Healthcare Outcomes using Big Data Analytics

A Semantically Flexible Feature Fusion Network for Retinal Vessel Segmentation

Tariq M. Khan[1(✉)], Antonio Robles-Kelly[1], and Syed S. Naqvi[2]

[1] School of IT, Deakin University, Waurn Ponds, VIC 3216, Australia
{tariq.khan,antonio.robles-kelly}@deakin.edu.au
[2] Department of Electrical and Computer Engineering, COSMATS University,
Islamabad, Pakistan
saud_naqvi@comsats.edu.pk

Abstract. The automatic detection of retinal blood vessels by computer aided techniques plays an important role in the diagnosis of diabetic retinopathy, glaucoma, and macular degeneration. In this paper we present a semantically flexible feature fusion network that employs residual skip connections between adjacent neurons to improve retinal vessel detection. This yields a method that can be trained employing residual learning. To illustrate the utility of our method for retinal blood vessel detection, we show results on two publicly available data sets, *i.e.* DRIVE and STARE. In our experimental evaluation we include widely used evaluation metrics and compare our results with those yielded by alternatives elsewhere in the literature. In our experiments, our method is quite competitive, delivering a margin of sensitivity and accuracy improvement as compared to the alternatives under consideration.

Keywords: Image segmentation · Retinal vessels · Deep neural networks · Medical image analysis

1 Introduction

The diagnosis of Diabetic Retinopathy (DR) has attracted significant attention recently due to the pathology being linked to long term diabetes, being one of the main causes of preventable blindness worldwide [1,2]. Moreover, DR is one of the main sources of vision impairment especially in the working age population [3]. The initial signs/symptoms of DR are lesions, a general term that connects microaneurysms (MA), exudates (hard and soft), inter-retinal microvascular abnormalities, hemorrhages (dot and blot) and leakages [4]. As a result, the condition and diagnosis of the disease is based on the number and type of lesions developed on the surface of the retina. Thus, the performance of an automated system for large scale public screening is expected to rely upon the accuracy of the segmentation of retinal blood vessels, optic cup/disc and retinal lesions. Along these lines, the retinal blood vessel detection has been broadly accepted as the main challenge and is often considered to be the most significant part

© Springer Nature Switzerland AG 2020
H. Yang et al. (Eds.): ICONIP 2020, CCIS 1332, pp. 159–167, 2020.
https://doi.org/10.1007/978-3-030-63820-7_18

of the automated diagnostic system [2]. This is since the characteristics of the vessels in the retina, such as their tortuosity, density, diameter, branching and shape makes them difficult to detect. The detection gets further complicated by the centerline reflex and the numerous constituent parts of the retina, *i.e.* the optic cup/disc, macula, the hard exudates, the soft exudates, etc., which may exhibit lesions or imperfections. Finally, the acquisition process and the camera calibration parameters can also introduce variability in the imaging process.

Unsupervised techniques segment blood vessels by labelling pixels on an image so as to assign these to either of two clusters, one of these being the vessels under consideration and the other one the background of the retina. One of the most popular approaches here is to identify the blood vessels in the retinal fundus images based on tracing techniques [5]. Matched filter methods [6], which use 2D filter kernels tuned to precisely map the vessels in the given retinal image, are also a popular choice. The main drawback with these methods is that they tend to exhibit a high false positive rate which leads to performance degradation [7]. Moreover, since the width of blood vessels is maximum at the optic disk and decreases gradually outward, multi-scale methods can often better analyse the shape and intensity of the blood vessels. This is since they operate at various scales for extracting the width, size and orientation of the vessels under consideration [1].

Blood vessel detection methods are supervised in nature, whereby a machine learning model is trained based on a database of manually segmented images. These methods have been applied to the detection of retinal vessels for diagnosing critical diseases such as glaucoma [8], diabetic retinopathy (DR) [9], retinal vascular occlusions [10], age-related macular degeneration (AMD) [11] and chronic systematic hypoxemia [12]. Moreover, deep learning based methods have achieved state of the art accuracy in tasks such as optic cup/disc detection [13] and vessels detection [14]. This has seen supervised machine learning models become the first choice for the development of retinal diagnostics systems. Despite their great success, blood vessel detection is still a challenging task where there are significant contrast variations and lesions. It is even more challenging where, added to these, the diameter of the vessels is small.

To overcome these conditions, in this paper, we present a semantically flexible feature fusion network which improves vessel detection accuracy making use of flexible feature learning. To do this, we employ residual skip connections in a pyramidal multi-scale architecture devoid of deep supervision. As a result, our network improves detection accuracy by providing a series of nested, dense skip pathways that allow for a flexible feature fusion at multiple scales. The detection accuracy and sensitivity is further improved by residual learning. Residual learning also allow to better preserve important vessel information and to speed-up the training process.

2   Semantically Flexible Feature Fusion Network

The architecture of our semantically flexible feature fusion network is somewhat reminiscent of that presented in [15], *i.e.* UNET++. It is worth noting, however,

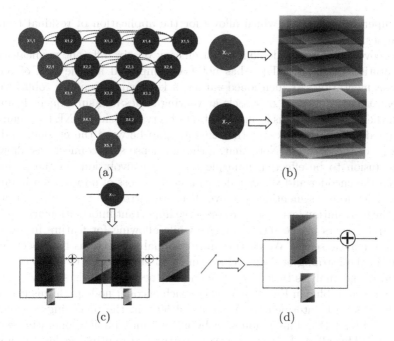

Fig. 1. Architectural detail of our retinal blood vessel detection network. (a) Diagram of the network proposed here showing the various connections between nodes and layers; (b) Layer-level architecture of the two kind of nodes used in our network; (c) Residual skip connections between adjacent nodes shown with horizontal blue arrows overlaid on the layer-level architecture of the residual connections; (d) Upsampling scheme in the decoder network shown with oriented green arrows and the layer-level architecture shown in detail. (Color figure online)

that there are several important differences between the architecture used here and that of UNet++. Firstly, the proposed network replaces the typical skip connections between adjacent nodes with the residual skip connections shown with blue arrows in Fig. 1 (a). The detailed architecture of the proposed residual skip connections is shown in Fig. 1 (c). From the figure, it can be observed that these convolutional layers are better suited for residual learning rather than deep supervision, thus enabling more flexible information flow between adjacent nodes and ease of the learning process. This also allows for a flexible feature fusion between different scales. The up-sampling of the feature maps is also performed with residual learning as shown in Fig. 1 (d). This allows the proposed network to learn up-sampled features in a more flexible manner, thus reducing training time without comprising accuracy. It is worth noting in passing, that U-Net++ uses these skip connections to connect the feature maps of encoders and decoders directly, which results in fusing semantically dissimilar feature maps. This dissimilarity makes the optimisation computationally costly, whereby deep supervision is added for model pruning so that the model complexity is adjusted. This also delivers a balance between performance and speed. In our network, no deep supervision is used, which allows for the application of residual training techniques.

Moreover, despite its demonstrated efficacy on six different medical image segmentation tasks, UNET++ has not been employed for the task of retinal vessel segmentation. As mentioned earlier, a key requirement for robust vessel segmentation is detection of vessels at varying scales and subsequent fusion to obtain the final result. This is an important observation since UNET++ employs redesigned skip paths to cover the semantic gap between the encoder and the subpaths of the decoder. Note that, although dense skip connections allow for feature fusion to be effected, multiple repeated convolutions in the pathways between the encoder and the decoder can result in loss of information in deeper layers. Therefore, as mentioned above, here we introduce residual connections along the convolution layers so as to preserve important information arising from edges and corners in the retinal images while allowing for feature fusion from varying semantic scales. We do this since residual connections have been found to help in the learning of deep architectures [16] and proven to be successful in medical image analysis tasks [17]. The encoder network consists of five encoder nodes (shown in blue in Fig. 1 (a)), where each encoder node performs two 3×3 convolutions with intermediate dropouts of 50% in the preceding convolution layer, see Fig. 1 (b). This is followed by a 2×2 max-pooling operation with a stride of 2. This allows for the recovery of features at multiple scales. Filter sizes of 32, 64, 128, 256, 512 are employed in the five encoder blocks, respectively. The decoder nodes are depicted in light brown color in Fig. 1 (a). Each decoder node consists of a 2D transpose convolution layer with a kernel size of 2×2 and a stride of 2. This results in half the number of feature channels. Residual learning is incorporated in the up-sampling process for ease of training as depicted in Fig. 1 (d).

The resulting feature maps are fused with the corresponding features from the encoder through a concatenation layer. The rest of the convolution and dropout layers are set to be consistent with the encoder nodes where residual learning pathways are introduced in the convolutional layers. This is in contrast with the encoder nodes, see Fig. 1 (c). Finally we have used the cross entropy loss so as to penalise the "disimilarity" between the detection output and the hand labelled data. The loss is given by $\mathcal{L} = \sum_{i=1}^{C} x_i \log(y_i)$ which, for the binary case, i.e. $C = 2$, becomes $\mathcal{L} = -y_1 \log(x_1) - (1 - y_1) \log(1 - x_1)$. Where, as usual, x_i denotes the output of the network for the ith class, i.e. the score yielded by the CNN, and y_i the corresponding ground truth label.

3   Results

3.1   Experimental Setup

All our experiments were performed using eight NVIDIA GTX1080 Ti GPUs with 11 GB memory each. The network has been implemented on Keras with a

Tensorflow back-end. For the training, an early stopping criteria on the loss function was employed to avoid over-fitting on an Adam optimizer with a learning rate of $2e - 4$ and $\beta_1 = 0.5$.

For our evaluation, we have employed two publicly available retinal image databases. The first of these is the Digital Retinal Images for Vessel Extraction (DRIVE)[1]. This database covers 400 diabetic patients taken from a retinopahty screening program in the Netherlands over a wide range of age groups between 25 and 90 years old [18]. Here, we have kept with the original grand challenge and used the training and testing splits specified therewith. The second dataset is the one corresponding to the Structured Analysis of the Retina (STARE) project. This is a project aimed at developing a system to automatically diagnose diseases or the human eye funded by the National Institute of Health [19]. The project contains a dataset of blood vessel segmentation images that have been hand-labelled[2]. For our experiments, we have used half of these images for testing and half for training.

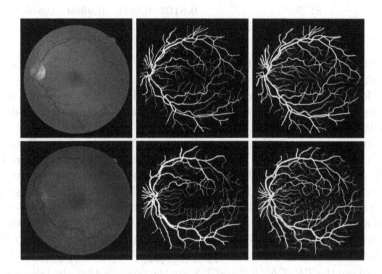

Fig. 2. Sample results on two images in the DRIVE dataset. From left-to-right we show the input image, the ground truth hand-labelled vessel map and the blood vessels detected by our network.

3.2   Evaluation and Comparison

We commence by illustrating the utility of our method for vessel detection in retinal images showing qualitative results for our network in Fig. 2. In the figures, from left-to-right, we show the input image to our network, the hand-labelled

---

[1] The dataset is widely available at https://drive.grand-challenge.org/.

[2] The dataset can be accessed at https://cecas.clemson.edu/~ahoover/stare/probing/index.html.

Table 1. Selectivity (Se), Specificity (Sp), Accuracy (Acc) and the Area Under the ROC Curve (AUC) yielded by our method and the alternatives when applied to the Digital Retinal Images for Vessel Extraction (DRIVE and STARE) dataset.

Dataset	Methods	Se	Sp	Acc	AUC
DRIVE	Dasgupta et al. [22]	0.7691	0.9801	0.9533	0.9744
	Yan et al. [23]	0.7653	**0.9818**	0.9542	0.9752
	Jiang et al. [24]	0.7839	0.9890	0.9709	**0.9864**
	Adapa et al. [25]	0.6994	0.9811	0.945	N.A
	SF³N	**0.8112**	0.9795	**0.9651**	0.9830
STARE	Li et al. [20]	0.7726	**0.9844**	0.9628	**0.9879**
	Orlando et al. FC [21]	0.7680	0.9738	N.A	N.A
	Orlando et al. UP [21]	0.7692	0.9675	N.A	N.A
	Yan et al. [23]	0.7581	0.9846	0.9612	0.9801
	Soomro et al. [27]	0.8010	0.9690	0.9610	0.9450
	SF³N	**0.8107**	0.9811	**0.9689**	0.9815

ground truth and the detection results delivered by our network. Note that the results delivered by our network are in good accordance with the ground truth. Moreover, our network recovers the fine detail as well as the broader blood vessels, being able to cope with varying contrast, lessions and different positioning of the retinal disk.

We now turn our attention to providing a quantitative analysis. To this end, we have compared the results yielded by our semantically flexible feature fusion network (SF^3N) with those delivered by methods elsewhere in the literature. These are those proposed by Li *et al.* [20], Orlando *et al.* [21,21], Dasgupta *et al.*[22], Yan *et al.* [23], Jiang *et al.* [24] and Adapa *et al.* [25]. In order to evaluate the performance of our vessel detection method and that of the alternatives, we have followed [26] and used the accuracy (Acc), sensitivity (Se) and specificity (Sp). These are given by $Acc = \frac{TP+TN}{TP+FN+TN+FP}$, $Se = \frac{TP}{TP+FN}$ and $Sp = \frac{TN}{TN+FP}$ where the TP, FN, FP and TN are the true positive, the false negative, the false positive and the true negative rates, respectively. These rates can be computed, in a straightforward manner by comparing the results yielded by our approach and the alternatives with the ground truth imagery which has been manually annotated by expert ophthalmologists in both datasets. Additionally, for all our experiments, we have also computed the Area Under the ROC Curve (AUC). Recall that the ROC curve is given by the true positive rate as a function of the false positive one. Thus, the larger the AUC, the better the detection ability of the network.

In Table 1, we show the area under the ROC curve, accuracy, sensitivity and specificity for our method and the alternatives when applied to the DRIVE dataset. In Table 1, we show the results for the STARE dataset. In both tables, the overall best is shown in bold font and, for the reference of the reader, we also show the year of publication for each of the methdos under consideration. For the DRIVE database, the sensitivity and accuracy of our network is higher than that of the methods under consideration. The sensitivity of [21] and [22] are the second and third highest, respectively. The specificity of the method in [23] is the highest in Table 1, with that yielded by our network being still quite competitive. The method of Jiang *et al.* [24] yields the best AUC on the DRIVE dataset, with ours being the second best. For the STARE dataset, and following the results in Table 1, our approach is, again, the best performing in terms of sensitivity and accuracy for all the methods under consideration. Our method is the third in terms of specificity and AUC, being only marginally behind that for the approaches of Li *et al.* [20] and Yan *et al.* [23] for the specificity and overall second best for the AUC.

4 Conclusions

In this paper, we have presented a network capable of semantically fuse features in a flexible manner in order to detect blood vessels on retinal images. Our network employs residual skip connections while making use of a multi-scale architecture devoid of deep supervision. In this manner, our network is designed to boost detection accuracy by providing a series of nested, dense skip pathways. The detection accuracy and sensitivity is improved by residual learning. This effectively allows our network to learn up-sampled features and cope with lesions, small vessels, large variations in image contrast and different positioning of the retinal disk. We have illustrated the utility of our network for purposes of retinal vessel detection on two widely available data sets. We have also compared our results with those recovered using several alternatives elsewhere in the literature. Our network is consistently the best performing in terms of selectivity and accuracy. It is also quite competitive in terms of area under the ROC curve and specificity as compared to the alternatives.

References

1. Khawaja, A., Khan, T.M., Khan, M.A.U., Nawaz, S.J.: A multi-scale directional line detector for retinal vessel segmentation. Sensors **19**(22), 4949 (2019)
2. Khawaja, A., Khan, T.M., Naveed, K., Naqvi, S.S., Rehman, N.U., Junaid Nawaz, S.: An improved retinal vessel segmentation framework using frangi filter coupled with the probabilistic patch based denoiser. IEEE Access **7**, 164344–164361 (2019)
3. Klein, R., Klein, B.E., Moss, S.E.: Visual impairment in diabetes. Ophthalmology **91**(1), 1–9 (1984)
4. Soomro, T.A., Khan, T.M., Khan, M.A.U., Gao, J., Paul, M., Zheng, L.: Impact of ICA-based image enhancement technique on retinal blood vessels segmentation. IEEE Access **6**, 3524–3538 (2018)
5. Zhang, J., Li, H., Nie, Q., Cheng, L.: A retinal vessel boundary tracking method based on Bayesian theory and multi-scale line detection. Comput. Med. Imag. Graph. **38**(6), 517–525 (2014)

6. Memari, N., Saripan, M.I.B., Mashohor, S., Moghbel, M.: Retinal blood vessel segmentation by using matched filtering and fuzzy c-means clustering with integrated level set method for diabetic retinopathy assessment. J. Med. Biol. Eng. 1–19 (2018)
7. Almotiri, J., Elleithy, K., Elleithy, A.: Retinal vessels segmentation techniques and algorithms: a survey. Appl. Sci. **8**, 01 (2018)
8. Thakoor, K.A., Li, X., Tsamis, E., Sajda, P., Hood, D.C.: Enhancing the accuracy of glaucoma detection from oct probability maps using convolutional neural networks. In: International Conference of the IEEE Engineering in Medicine and Biology Society, pp. 2036–2040 (2019)
9. Zeng, X., Chen, H., Luo, Y., Ye, W.: Automated diabetic retinopathy detection based on binocular siamese-like convolutional neural network. IEEE Access **7**, 30 744–30 753 (2019)
10. Muraoka, Y., et al.: Morphologic and functional changes in retinal vessels associated with branch retinal vein occlusion. Ophthalmology **120**(1), 91–99 (2013)
11. Cicinelli, M.V., et al.: Optical coherence tomography angiography in dry age-related macular degeneration. Surv. Ophthalmol. **63**(2), 236–244 (2018)
12. Traustason, S., Jensen, A.S., Arvidsson, H.S., Munch, I.C., Søndergaard, L., Larsen, M.: Retinal oxygen saturation in patients with systemic hypoxemia. Invest. Ophthalmol. Vis. Sci. **52**(8), 5064 (2011)
13. Jiang, Y., Tan, N., Peng, T.: Optic disc and cup segmentation based on deep convolutional generative adversarial networks. IEEE Access **7**, 64 483–64 493 (2019)
14. Jiang, Y., Zhang, H., Tan, N., Chen, L.: Automatic retinal blood vessel segmentation based on fully convolutional neural networks. Symmetry **11**, 1112 (2019)
15. Zhou, Z., Siddiquee, M.M.R., Tajbakhsh, N., Liang, J.: Unet++: redesigning skip connections to exploit multiscale features in image segmentation. IEEE Trans. Med. Imaging **39**(6), 1856–1867 (2020)
16. Szegedy, C., Ioffe, S., Vanhoucke, V., Alemi, A.A.: Inception-v4, inception-resnet and the impact of residual connections on learning (2017)
17. Ibtehaz, N., Rahman, M.S.: Multiresunet: rethinking the u-net architecture for multimodal biomedical image segmentation. Neural Netw. **121**, 74–87 (2020)
18. Staal, J., Abramoff, M.D., Niemeijer, M., Viergever, M.A., van Ginneken, B.: Ridge-based vessel segmentation in color images of the retina. IEEE Trans. Med. Imaging **23**(4), 501–509 (2004)
19. Hoover, A.D., Kouznetsova, V., Goldbaum, M.: Locating blood vessels in retinal images by piecewise threshold probing of a matched filter response. IEEE Trans. Med. Imaging **19**(3), 203–210 (2000)
20. Li, Q., Feng, B., Xie, L., Liang, P., Zhang, H., Wang, T.: A cross-modality learning approach for vessel segmentation in retinal images. IEEE Trans. Med. Imaging **35**(1), 109–118 (2016)
21. Orlando, J.I., Prokofyeva, E., Blaschko, M.B.: A discriminatively trained fully connected conditional random field model for blood vessel segmentation in fundus images. IEEE Trans. Biomed. Eng. **64**(1), 16–27 (2016)
22. Dasgupta, A., Singh, S.: A fully convolutional neural network based structured prediction approach towards the retinal vessel segmentation. In: International Symposium on Biomedical Imaging, pp. 248–251 (2017)
23. Yan, Z., Yang, X., Cheng, K.T.: Joint segment-level and pixel-wise losses for deep learning based retinal vessel segmentation. IEEE Trans. Biomed. Eng. 1 (2018)
24. Jiang, Y., Tan, N., Peng, T., Zhang, H.: Retinal vessels segmentation based on dilated multi-scale convolutional neural network. IEEE Access **7**, 76 342–76 352 (2019)

25. Adapa, D., et al.: A supervised blood vessel segmentation technique for digital fundus images using zernike moment based features. PLOS ONE **15**(3), 1–23 (2020)
26. Zhang, J., Dashtbozorg, B., Bekkers, E., Pluim, J.P.W., Duits, R., Romeny, B.M.: Robust retinal vessel segmentation via locally adaptive derivative frames in orientation scores. IEEE Trans. Med. Imaging **35**(12), 2631–2644 (2016)
27. Soomro, T.A., Afifi, A.J., Gao, J., Hellwich, O., Zheng, L., Paul, M.: Strided fully convolutional neural network for boosting the sensitivity of retinal blood vessels segmentation. Expert Syst. Appl. **134**, 36–52 (2019)

Automatic Segmentation and Diagnosis of Intervertebral Discs Based on Deep Neural Networks

Xiuhao Liang[1], Junxiu Liu[1(✉)], Yuling Luo[1,2], Guopei Wu[1],
Shunsheng Zhang[1], and Senhui Qiu[1,3(✉)]

[1] School of Electronic Engineering, Guangxi Normal University, Guilin, China
`j.liu@ieee.org, qiusenhui@gxnu.edu.cn`
[2] Guangxi Key Lab of Multi-source Information Mining and Security, Guilin, China
[3] Guangxi Key Laboratory of Wireless Wideband Communication
and Signal Processing, Guilin, China

Abstract. Lumbar disc diagnosis belongs to Magnetic Resonance Imaging (MRI) segmentation and detection. It is a challenge for even the most professional radiologists to manually check and interpret MRI. In addition, high-class imbalance is a typical problem in diverse medical image classification problems, which results in poor classification performance. Data imbalance is a typical problem in medical image classifications. Recently computer vision and deep learning are widely used in the automatic positioning and diagnosis of intervertebral discs to improve diagnostic efficiency. In this work, a two-stage disc automatic diagnosis network is proposed, which can improve the accuracy of training classifiers with imbalanced dataset. Experimental results show that the proposed method can achieve 93.08%, 95.41%, 96.22%, 89.34% for accuracy, precision, sensitivity and specificity, respectively. It can solve the problem of imbalanced dataset, and reduce misdiagnosis rate.

Keywords: Intervertebral discs · MRI · Imbalanced dataset ·
Two-stage disc automatic diagnosis network

1 Introduction

Lumbar slipped disc is a frequent orthopedic disease and the most common cause of low back pain. Lumbar slipped disc is clinically caused by the nucleus pulposus of lumbar disc protruding annulus fibrosus. The high prevalence of slipped disc spine disease is usually among working-age people. The disease involves related treatment and disability, which causes huge social costs and social burdens, as well as patient suffering. A significant portion of these costs come from medical imaging. In medical treatment, medical imaging can be used for initial diagnosis and subsequent evaluation. It enables radiologists to determine the location according to the sagittal and coronal planes. The radiologist analyses the severity for lumbar of the spine and generates a detailed diagnosis report,

© Springer Nature Switzerland AG 2020
H. Yang et al. (Eds.): ICONIP 2020, CCIS 1332, pp. 168–175, 2020.
https://doi.org/10.1007/978-3-030-63820-7_19

which is used for radiologist to communicate with patients and other physicians. Radiologists spend a lot of time observing the generated images for diagnosis via Magnetic Resonance Imaging (MRI). In this process, physicians need to do meticulous and patient work, which has the risk of missing diagnosis or misdiagnosis due to long-term high-pressure work. In addition, although MRI is the preferred imaging method and has a much higher resolution for soft tissues than Computed Tomography (CT), and can detect small lesions at an early stage, the interpretation of MRI is very time-consuming. Unfortunately, the lack of universally accepted diagnostic standards for disc-based discs has led to differences in diagnosis among experts, which has reduced the value of their diagnostic reports. Recently, automatic detection, localization and segmentation of medical image abnormalities are important tasks to support medical clinical decision-making. Artificial neural network [1–3] is the combination of brain science [4] and artificial intelligence. The extensive development of artificial neural networks has enabled the emergence of Convolutional Neural Networks (CNNs). Deep learning tutoring medical diagnosis also plays an important role. Research on spine image diagnosis is beneficial to the development of assistive technology to support physicians to reduce work pressure and the time of spine diagnosis, so that physicians have abundant time to research the coping strategies of the disease, moreover, also decrease the probability of misdiagnosis and missed diagnosis.

There are many researches on the image analysis of the spine, including the segmentation, location, detection and labelling of vertebral bodies (involving 2D and 3D) and intervertebral discs. Some researchers have studied the positioning and labelling problems in CT [5] and MRI [6,7] images. To address the challenges of spinal imaging interpretation, in the past decade, researchers have continuously used computer technology to explore medical imaging in order to find an optimal algorithm. Many previous works have used computer vision technology and some inspiring learning. The greedy Non-Maximum Suppression algorithm was used by [8] to remove most false positive detections in each slice. Robust vertebra localization and recognition based on supervised classification forest was proposed by [9]. An automatic disc scoring method based on supervised distance metric learning was proposed by [10] to solve serious class overlap problems. Driven by the ever-increasing computing power and Graphics Processing Unit (GPU) technology, the application of deep learning technology in medical imaging has been expected. In particular, the characteristics of convolutional neural networks have created deep learning methods in [11]. The algorithm can automatically learn representative features from data at different levels of abstraction and perform classification tasks at high capability levels. The transfer learning method was applied by [6] to detect MRI lumbar vertebrae. The CNN method was used by [7] to classify and qualitatively locate multiple abnormalities of T2-weighted sagittal lumbar MRI.

The purpose of this work is to improve the diagnostic efficiency of intervertebral discs and relieve physicians from the tedious manual diagnosis. This work uses the sliding window method to locate and diagnose the intervertebral discs by a two-stage disc diagnostic network, and three loss function schemes were used for experiments. Experiments show that the selected loss function scheme and the two-stage disc diagnostic network have good results, which can be used for clinical MRI diagnosis of intervertebral discs. The contribution of this work has two aspects: (1) a two-stage disc automatic diagnosis network is proposed, which increases the probability of transplantation to mobile devices, and (2) a high classification accuracy is obtained under the imbalanced dataset. The rest of the paper is organised as follows: Sect. 2 presents the research methods and Sect. 3 provides the experimental results and analysis. The conclusion and future work are given in Sect. 4.

2   Methodology

2.1   Datasets

The dataset is a human spine MRI image dataset including 1,112 herniated disc, 2,508 normal disc and 810,000 background images. In this work, the background images are background of the intervertebral discs. At the beginning, continuous background images were used as part of the dataset, but the trained model did not work well. After experiment, the background images generated from all the spine MRI images are randomly selected. The deep learning model trained by this method has strong generalization performance. 810,000 background images are obtained by the method. The dataset is cleaned by correcting erroneous data, consistency checking and clearing invalid images. Similar to the two-stage target detection method, the entire network framework includes a disc detector and a disc classifier. The disc detector is two-class classifier and the disc classifier is three-class classifier. The dataset is used to train the detector and disc classifier. Data used to train the disc detector includes disc and background images. Data used to train the disc classifier includes normal, herniated disc and moderate background images (10860 images). In addition, the testset of the overall system excluded the poor quality of MRI scans from the provided dataset, using only T2 sagittal scans, for a total of 50 cases.

2.2   Two-Stage Disc Diagnosis Network

Two-stage disc automatic diagnosis network is used in this paper to locate and diagnose lumbar slipped disc. The input to the processing pipeline is T2 sagittal MRI, and the outputs are a predicted picture with bounding boxes and labels (normal or herniation). The sliding window is responsible for performing a complete search for the entire input slice by using the window with the set size (44×44) and aspect ratio. The generated slices with the same size as the window are sent to the disc detector. After disc slices and a small number of background slices misinterpreted by the detector are generated. These slices are sent to the disc classifier to output the candidate normal and herniated disc slices. The Non-Maximum Suppression (NMS) algorithm is used to remove the duplicate discs, leaving the highest score. After the results are marked with grey rectangular bounding boxes and labels according to the recorded coordinates. Figure 1 shows that the whole process. The overall network framework is shown in Fig. 2. The overall network framework is including the disc detection network and disc classifier network. Two-dimensional convolution is used in the disc detector and disc classifier. The numbers in the blue convolution block indicate the size and number of kernels. The input for the disc detection is the slice generate from the sliding window. Outputs of the disc detection are BG slices (representing background slices) and disc slices (mixed with BG). After the disc slices mixed with BG continue to be send to the disc classifier. The probability of normal, herniated discs and BG are generated by activating softmax.

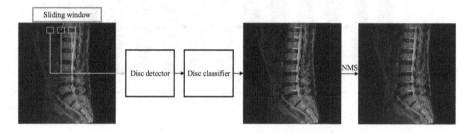

Fig. 1. Overview of the system.

2.3   Location of Intervertebral Disc-Levels

To be able to diagnose the disc area, it is necessary to locate the six disc-levels (T2-L1 to L5-S1) or more. The disc detection network is composed of three convolutional layer and head of two fully-connected layers. The first layer having 32 3×3 kernels to learn features and max-pooling of 2×2 pooled size. The second layer having 64 3×3 kernels and max-pooling of 2×2. The three layer having 128 1×1 kernels and max-pooling of 2×2. The disc detection network consisted of two fully-connected layers with 128 neurons in the first layer, 512 neurons in the second. The disc detection network is shown in Fig. 2. The input size is 16×16 and the channel is one. Epoch is set to 150. The disc detector is trained with SGD optimizer and the initial learning rate is set to 0.01. The weight decay is 0.0001, and momentum is 0.9. The dropout rate is 0.2. The dataset mentioned in Sect. 2.1 is randomly splited into training (70%), validation (15%) and test (15%). Since the dataset is an imbalanced dataset, three loss function schemes are used for validation and the best performance is selected as the loss function of the disc dection. The three loss functions include binary cross-entropy loss function, weighted cross-entropy loss function, and focal loss function. The binary cross-entropy loss function and the weighted cross-entropy loss function are calculated by $L_{bin} = -\sum_{i=1}^{n} y^i \log \hat{y}^i + \left(1 - y^i\right) \log \left(1 - \hat{y}^i\right)$ and $L_{\text{weight}} = -\sum_{i=1}^{n} \alpha y^i \log \hat{y}^i + \left(1 - y^i\right) \log \left(1 - \hat{y}^i\right)$, where y^i represent the ith ground truth label with one-hot encoding, $\hat{y}^i$ is the network sigmiod output

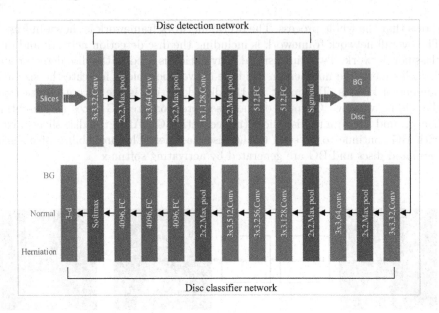

Fig. 2. Overall network framework.

of the ith label, n is the total number of image in the training data, α is a weighting factor and $\alpha \in [0,1]$.

The focal loss function is calculated by $FL(p_t) = -\alpha_t (1 - p_t)^\gamma \log(p_t)$, where α_t is a weighting factor, $\alpha_t \in [0,1]$, γ is a modulating factor, $\gamma \in [0,5]$. When y equal to one, $p_t = p$, otherwise $p_t = 1 - p$, $y \in \{\pm 1\}$ specifies the ground-truth class and $p \in [0,1]$ is the network model's estimated probability for the class with label y equal to one.

2.4   Classifying for Intervertebral Disc-Levels

After the disc slice is extracted through the disc detection network, the slice is resized 44×44 and delivered to the disc classifier network for grading normal, herniation and BG. The network is based on Alexnet, and kernel of the convolutional layers and pooling layers are all changed to 3×3 and 2×2, respectively. The disc classifier network is shown in Fig. 2. The channel is one and the disc detector is trained with SGD optimizer and the initial learning rate is 0.01. Epoch is set to 300. The weight decay is 0.0001, and momentum is 0.9. The fully-connected layer uses a regularization of dropout rate of 0.2. The network performs three classification tasks: normal, herniation and BG. The standard softmax activation function is used to predict the probability of each type. The dataset mentioned in Sect. 2.1 is randomly splited into training (70%), validation (15%) and test (15%). Since the classifier is three-class, the loss function uses multi-class cross entropy is calculated by $L_{\log}(Y,P) = -\frac{1}{N} \sum_{i=0}^{N-1} \sum_{k=0}^{K-1} y^{i,k} \log p^{i,k}$, where y is the one-hot ground truth label vector, N is the total number of image in the training data, K is the number of label values, $p^{i,k}$ is the probability that the ith sample is predicted to be the kth label.

3 Experiment Results

In this paper, the prediction results include true positive result (TP), false positive results (FP), true negative results (TN) and false negative results (FN). If a disc with a normal label is predicted to be normal, the result of prediction is considered to be TP. Predicted normal disc and actually herniated disc, which is considered to be FP. Predicted herniated disc and actually herniated disc, which is considered to be TN. Predicted herniated disc and actually normal disc, which is considered to be FN.

Accuracy, precision, specificity, sensitivity, recall, and F1-Score are used in experiments as evaluation metrics. They are defined by $A = (TP + TN)/(TP + TN + FN + FP)$, $P = TP/(TP + FP)$, $S_p = TN/(TN + FP)$, $S_e = TP/(TP + FN)$, $R = TP/(TP + FP)$ and $F = 2 * P * R/(P + R)$, where accuracy is the difference between the predicted value of a quantity and its actual value. Precision is predicted to be the correct proportion in the positive sample. Specificity represents the recognition rate of the actual negative. Sensitivity represents the recognition rate of the actual value. Recall is the measure of number of positive class predictions made with the all positive predictions. F1-Score is the measure which balances both the precision and recall.

The disc detector and disc classifier are trained utilizing the Tensorflow deep learning library on NVIDIA with 2080 super GPUs. In the disc dection network, for the solution to the imbalanced dataset, experiment with the three loss functions are mentioned in Sect. 2.3. For the binary classification loss function experiment, each mini-batch is 64. For the weighted cross-entropy loss function experiment, each mini-batch is 64 and the value of α is automatically adjusted according to the training dataset. For the focal loss function, each mini-batch is 64. The optimal value of α_t and γ is 0.25 and 2, respectively. In data science, evaluating the performance of the classifier is crucial. Precision, recall and F1-Score are used to evaluate the classifiers of the three loss functions, shown in Table 1. For disc's precision, the focal loss in this work is slightly worse than the binary cross-entropy loss and the weighted cross-entropy loss. For disc's recall, the focal loss is higher than the binary cross-entropy loss and the weighted cross-entropy loss with the increment is 3% and 3%, respectively. For disc's F1-Score, the focal loss is higher than the binary cross-entropy loss and the weighted cross-entropy loss with the increment is 1.55% and 1.45%, respectively.

For the overall performance test of the system, the focal loss function scheme with the best performance is used and evaluated in this work. The overall system test data uses 50 cases mentioned in Sect. 2.1. The testing process of the system is the same as that of Sect. 2.2. The results and the results of other methods are shown in Table 2. For accuracy, the result in this work is higher than supervised distance learning[10] with the increment is 0.824%, and less than CF[9] with the

Table 1. Comparison with evaluation indexes of three loss functions

Loss function	Image classes	Precision	Recall	F1-Score	Support
Binary cross-entropy loss	Background	1.0	1.0	1.0	121474
	Disc	0.981	0.9	0.9388	569
Weighted cross-entropy loss	Background	1.0	1.0	1.0	121474
	Disc	0.981	0.9	0.9398	569
Focal loss (This work)	Background	1.0	1.0	1.0	121474
	Disc	0.98	0.93	0.9543	569

Table 2. Comparison with experimental evaluation indexes of previous methods.

Approaches	Accuracy	Precision	Specificity	Sensitivity
Supervised distance learning [10]	0.92265	-	0.9665	0.9083
CF [9]	0.939	0.937	0.947	0.929
This work	0.9308	0.9541	0.8934	0.9622

reduction is 0.82%. For precision, the result is higher than [9] with the increment is 1.71%. Specificity is slightly worse than [10] and [9]. For sensitivity, the result is higher than [10] and [9] with the increment is 5.39% and 3.32%, respectively.

4 Conclusion

In this paper, a full-automatic two-stage diagnostic method for clinical treatment of intervertebral discs is proposed, and a feasibility plan for imbalanced dataset is provided. Through the experiments of 50 cases, the superiority of this method in diagnosis was verified. Therefore, the method is effective, automatic and accurate for clinical diagnosis of intervertebral discs. Results show that it achieves 93.08% disc locating and marking accuracy. Precision, specificity and sensitivity are 95.41%, 89.34% and 96.22%, respectively. The focal loss is used as a loss function for disc detection and a special training method. Compared with the binary classification cross loss and weighted cross-entropy loss, its performance is significantly improved. In future work, the degree of diagnosis of lumbar slipped disc can be further classified in detail.

Acknowledgments. This research was partially supported by the National Natural Science Foundation of China under Grant 61976063, the funding of Overseas 100 Talents Program of Guangxi Higher Education under Grant F-KA16035, the Diecai Project of Guangxi Normal University, 2018 Guangxi One Thousand Young and Middle-Aged College and University Backbone Teachers Cultivation Program, research fund of Guangxi Key Lab of Multi-source Information Mining & Security (19-A-03-02), research fund of Guangxi Key Laboratory of Wireless Wideband Communication and Signal Processing, and the Young and Middle-aged Teachers' Research Ability Improvement Project in Guangxi Universities under Grant 2020KY02030.

References

1. Liu, J., Huang, X., Luo, Y., Cao, Y.: An energy-aware hybrid particle swarm optimization algorithm for spiking neural network mapping. In: Liu, D., Xie, S., Li, Y., Zhao, D., El-Alfy, E.S. (eds.) International Conference on Neural Information Processing, ICONIP 2017, LNCS, vol. 10636, pp. 805–815, Springer, Cham (2017). https://doi.org/10.1007/978-3-319-70090-8_82
2. Fu, Q., et al.: Improving learning algorithm performance for spiking neural networks. In: 2017 17th IEEE International Conference on Communication Technology (ICCT 2017), pp. 1916–1919 (2018)
3. Luo, Y., et al.: Forest fire detection using spiking neural networks. In: CF 2018: Proceedings of the 15th ACM International Conference on Computing Frontiers, pp. 371–375 (2018)
4. Liu, J., et al.: Exploring self-repair in a coupled spiking astrocyte neural network. IEEE Trans. Neural Netw. Learn. Syst. **30**(3), 865–875 (2019)
5. Siewerdsen, J.H., et al.: Automatic vertebrae localization in spine CT: a deep-learning approach for image guidance and surgical data science. In: Medical Imaging 2019: Image-Guided Procedures, Robotic Interventions, and Modeling, pp. 1–8 (2019)
6. Zhou, Y., Liu, Y., Chen, Q., Gu, G., Sui, X.: Automatic lumbar MRI detection and identification based on deep learning. J. Digit. Imag. **32**(3), 513–520 (2019)
7. Jamaludin, A., Kadir, T., Zisserman, A.: SpineNet: automated classification and evidence visualization in spinal MRIs. Med. Image Anal. **41**(1), 63–73 (2017)
8. Lootus, M., Kadir, T., Zisserman, A.: Vertebrae Detection and Labelling in Lumbar MR Images. In: Yao, J., Klinder, T., Li, S. (eds.) Computational Methods and Clinical Applications for Spine Imaging. LNCVB, vol. 17, pp. 219–230. Springer, Cham (2014). https://doi.org/10.1007/978-3-319-07269-2_19
9. Glocker, B., Zikic, D., Konukoglu, E., Haynor, D.R., Criminisi, A.: Vertebrae localization in pathological spine CT via dense classification from sparse annotations. In: Mori, K., Sakuma, I., Sato, Y., Barillot, C., Navab, N. (eds.) MICCAI 2013. LNCS, vol. 8150, pp. 262–270. Springer, Heidelberg (2013). https://doi.org/10.1007/978-3-642-40763-5_33
10. He, X., Landis, M., Leung, S., Warrington, J., Shmuilovich, O., Li, S.: Automated grading of lumbar disc degeneration via supervised distance metric learning. In: Proceedings of SPIE, vol. 10134(1), pp. 1–7 (2017)
11. Liu, J., et al.: Financial data forecasting using optimized echo state network. In: Cheng, L., Leung, A.C.S., Ozawa, S. (eds.) ICONIP 2018. LNCS, vol. 11305, pp. 138–149. Springer, Cham (2018). https://doi.org/10.1007/978-3-030-04221-9_13

Detecting Alzheimer's Disease by Exploiting Linguistic Information from Nepali Transcript

Surendrabikram Thapa[1], Surabhi Adhikari[1], Usman Naseem[2], Priyanka Singh[3], Gnana Bharathy[4], and Mukesh Prasad[3(✉)]

[1] Department of Computer Science and Engineering,
Delhi Technological University, Delhi, India
[2] School of Computer Science, The University of Sydney, Sydney, Australia
[3] School of Computer Science, FEIT, University of Technology Sydney, Sydney, Australia
mukesh.prasad@uts.edu.au
[4] School of Information, Systems and Modelling, University of Technology
Sydney, Sydney, Australia

Abstract. Alzheimer's disease (AD) is the most common form of neurodegenerating disorder accounting for 60–80% of all dementia cases. The lack of effective clinical treatment options to completely cure or even slow the progression of disease makes it even more serious. Treatment options are available to treat the milder stage of the disease to provide symptomatic short-term relief and improve quality of life. Early diagnosis is key in the treatment and management of AD as advanced stages of disease cause severe cognitive decline and permanent brain damage. This has prompted researchers to explore innovative ways to detect AD early on. Changes in speech are one of the main signs of AD patients. As the brain deteriorates the language processing ability of the patients deteriorates too. Previous research has been done in the English language using Natural Language Processing (NLP) techniques for early detection of AD. However, research using local languages and low resourced language like Nepali still lag behind. NLP is an important tool in Artificial Intelligence to decipher the human language and perform various tasks. In this paper, various classifiers have been discussed for the early detection of Alzheimer's in the Nepali language. The proposed study makes a convincing conclusion that the difficulty in processing information in AD patients reflects in their speech while describing a picture. The study incorporates the speech decline of AD patients to classify them as control subjects or AD patients using various classifiers and NLP techniques. Furthermore, in this experiment a new dataset consisting of transcripts of AD patients and Control normal (CN) subjects in the Nepali language. In addition, this paper sets a baseline for the early detection of AD using NLP in the Nepali language.

1 Introduction

Alzheimer's disease (AD) is a neurodegenerative disease that has affected more than 50 million people worldwide. With someone developing the disease every three seconds, the AD renders to be the most common form of dementia [1]. Currently, there are no any approved drugs available to cure or stop the progression of AD. However, there are

© Springer Nature Switzerland AG 2020
H. Yang et al. (Eds.): ICONIP 2020, CCIS 1332, pp. 176–184, 2020.
https://doi.org/10.1007/978-3-030-63820-7_20

some drugs that help patients who are diagnosed in the earlier stages of AD. Hence, the early detection of AD is of extreme necessity to our aging society. The AD patients show a wide range of symptoms due to the changes in cortical anatomy [2]. One of the most important initial symptoms of AD is cognitive impairment. The biological factors like atrophies in the various regions of the brain bring out such cognitive impairments. For example, atrophies in the left anterior temporal lobe bring impairment in naming tasks, such as picture description problems [3]. Such atrophies in the regions of the brain can be detected only by Magnetic Resonance Imaging (MRI) images or Computed Tomography (CT) scans of the brain. Analysis of such imaging modalities helps to delineate AD patients from control normal subjects, but this technique should be hugely intervened by medical personnel. In the other hand, the cognitive impairment in patients can also be evidenced by aphasia or an impaired ability to understand or produce speech in day to day tasks [4]. Faber-Langendoen et al. [5] in the study of aphasia in AD patients found out that 100% of the AD patients and 36% of the patients with mild cognitive impairment (MCI) had a problem of aphasia whose severity increased with increased severity of dementia. Such anomalies in linguistic features of speech can be leveraged to build AI models for the early detection of AD.

Natural Language Processing (NLP) can hence be a very handy tool for the analysis and interpretation of the patient's speech. With rapid advancements in the field of computation, the speech narratives of subjects under study can be processed using NLP to detect AD. The prospects of NLP are being explored for mental illnesses such as depression. NLP can thus be significantly useful in improving the care delivery system.

The main contributions of the paper are:

- A new dataset that has been prepared for the Nepali language by translating the existing Dementia Bank in the English language.
- The work in detection of AD using linguistics in Nepali language is first of its kind.
- Baseline has been created for future researchers to further proceed in similar works.

The rest of the paper organised as follows: Sect. 2 of the paper describes the works that have been done to detect AD from the linguistic features of the speech. Similarly, Sect. 3 describes the methodology that has been used in this paper. The experimental results are discussed in Sect. 4 and the Sect. 5 is the conclusion section that summarizes the findings of the paper along with the future works that need to be done.

2   Related Works

Various research has been carried for the early detection of AD from speech and transcripts of the patients. Over the past decade or so, a lot of research are being conducted to detect AD using speech and language features since the deterioration of speech is one of the earliest symptoms of AD or Mild Cognitive Impairment (MCI). Thus, machine learning (ML) techniques were used to detect anomalies in narratives of patients with AD. Orimaye et al. [6] took syntactic, lexical as well as n-gram features to build the model. The n-gram models which performed better as compared to models that used syntactic and lexical features alone gave AUC of 0.93. To overcome drawbacks that might occur due to hand-picked features using ML algorithms for automated classification of AD using speech, researchers have used deep learning models that can learn the complexities of the language to automatically identify the linguistic features that reflect in narratives of AD patients with multiple levels of abstraction. Fritsch et al. [7] used a neural network language model (NNLM) with Long Short-Term Memory (LSTM) cells to enhance the statistical approach of n-gram language models. The model was evaluated by measuring its perplexity which resulted in the accuracy of 0.86. Chen et al. [8] proposed an attention-based hybrid network for automatic detection of AD which was able to categorize the transcripts with an accuracy of 0.97. The paper suggests that the attention mechanism helped to emphasize on decisive features.

In the English language, a lot of work has been done and some of the experiments have resulted into the state-of-the-art (SOTA) models. Apart from English, a lot of work has been done in other prominent languages like Mandarin Chinese, German, etc. but there has not been any research done in the fields of regional languages in South Asia. For a low resource language like Nepali where there is very little work in the field of NLP, this work in the detection of AD using linguistic features is the first of its kind.

3   Methodology

The flow diagram of the proposed approach for the classification of AD and CN patients using speech transcripts is shown in Fig. 1. The process starts with collection of data and goes through steps of pre-processing, feature extraction, and training of classifiers. The performance is evaluated after the models are trained and validated on the data.

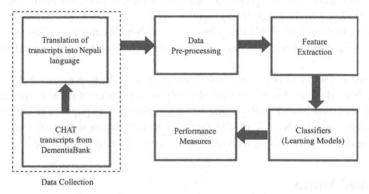

Data Collection

Fig. 1. Flowchart for the proposed methodology

3.1   Data Collection

The Dementia Bank's Pitt Corpus is audio files and text transcripts that include the narratives of the participants who participated in the research conducted by Becker et al. [9]. The participants were made to describe the kitchen scene in cookie theft picture and

Table 1. Demographic information of subjects from Dementia Bank

Attributes	Control Normal (CN)	Alzheimer's Disease (AD)
No. of participants	168 CN subjects	98 AD patients
Gender	31 M/67F	55 M/113F
Age	64.7 (7.6)	71.2 (8.4)
Education	14.0 (2.3)	12.2 (2.6)
MMSE	29.1 (1.1)	19.9 (4.2)

transcripts were obtained [9]. The demographic information about subjects under study can be shown in Table 1 where mean and standard deviation are also mentioned.

Originally, the text was in the English language which was translated into Nepali language for this study. The translations were made by two native Nepali language speakers who had at least 13 years of formal education in Nepali. The translations were later verified by a linguistic expert who's currently working in the University of Auckland. While translating, the words such as *uhm, uhh* were translated as it is. Such filter sounds like *uhm, uhh*, etc. are used by almost everybody but it is hypothesized that they are used more often by AD subjects. Similarly, the translation has been done in such a way that the repetitions, confusing syntax, linguistic errors are retained as it is to retain the originality. The dataset is made publicly available.

3.2 Data Preprocessing

The preprocessing step usually includes the removal of noise, filter words, and unwanted information that does not add any value to the semantics of the text [10]. In the English language, all the words are made either uppercase or lowercase in the preprocessing step. Nepali language, being a case insensitive language does not require any such operations. The punctuation marks like commas, semicolons, etc. that do not add semantic meaning to the text are removed.

3.3 Feature Extraction

In this experiment, vectorization techniques and word embeddings are used for feature extraction. The two methods for vectorization have been used, namely, CountVectorizer [11] and Term Frequency Inverse Document Frequency (TF-IDF) [11]. Similarly, this study makes use of the two most efficient word embeddings viz. Word2Vec and fastText. Both the pretrained and domain-specific word2vec [13] and fastText [14] models are trained to produce embeddings. For the domain-specific embeddings, 300-dimensional embeddings have been used for both Word2Vec and fastText embeddings, and the maximum length is set to 270. For pre-trained Nepali Word2Vec model, the model created by Lamsal [15] is used in the study. Similarly, for the pre-trained fastText embeddings, the pre-trained word vectors trained on Common Crawl and Wikipedia using fastText were used [14]. Both are 300-dimensional vectors.

3.4 Learning Models (Classifiers)

In this paper, both machine learning models and deep learning models were used to find the better model, which would classify the transcripts with greater accuracy. Since the work of the classification of AD vs CN in the Nepali language is the first of its kind, machine learning baselines are taken to evaluate the performance of machine learning algorithms. In this study, machine learning, ensemble learners as well as deep learning algorithms were employed.

The machine learning algorithms like Decision Tree (DT), K-Nearest Neighbors (KNN), Support Vector Machines (SVM) and Naïve Bayes (NB) as well as ensemble learners like Random Forest (RF), AdaBoost (ADB), and XGBoost (XGB) were employed in this study.

In addition, we have applied deep learning models, as, the deep learning models provide more accurate results for text classification especially when the classification task deals with subtle details of the linguistic components [12]. In this study, three deep learning models have also been applied, viz, Convolutional Neural Network (CNN), Bidirectional Long Short-Term Memory (BiLSTM), and a combination of CNN and BiLSTM. Also, the famous Kim's CNN architecture [16] has been used. For all the architectures, the number of epochs and batch size has been fixed to 20 and 50 respectively for all embeddings. For kernel regularization, L2 has been used whereas the optimizer is Adam. The summary of the architecture of the models is discussed in Table 2.

Table 2. Summary of the parameters of Deep Learning Models

Models	No. of Convolutional layers	No. of BiLSTM Layers	No. of Maxpool layers of Filter Size 3	Dropout Rate	No. of Dense Layers
Kim's CNN	3	–	3	0.5	1
CNN (1D)	4	–	2	–	3
BiLSTM	–	4	–	0.5,0.25	2
CNN + BiLSTM	4	2 + Batch Normalization	2	–	3

3.5 Performance Measures

In all the above-mentioned architectures, binary cross-entropy has been used as the loss function. The validation has been done using stratified 10-fold cross-validation. The performance of the proposed architectures has been measured using the evaluation metrics, accuracy (Acc), precision (Pre), recall (Rec), and F1-score.

4   Experimental Results

The baseline is established with various machine learning algorithms. TF-IDF and CountVectorizer (CV) were used to convert the text document into a matrix of token counts for the experiment. The results of the machine learning baselines with the TF-IDF and CountVectorizer are shown in Table 3. For machine learning models, the Naive Bayes classifier performed the best for both the vectorization techniques. The Naive Bayes classifier had F1-scores of 0.94 for both Count Vectorizer as well as the TF-IDF.. Overall, as can be seen from Fig. 2, the baseline machine learning models have comparable performance for both Count Vectorizer and TF-IDF. It can be deciphered from here that the vocabulary consists of many unique words, that are not repeated frequently and hence both techniques have similar vocabulary.

Table 3. Performance of ML algorithms with CV and TF-IDF

ML Classifier	TF-IDF				Count Vectorizer (CV)			
	Acc	Pre	Rec	F1-score	Acc	Pre	Rec	F1-score
DT	0.90	0.90	0.90	0.90	0.85	0.86	0.85	0.85
KNN	0.91	0.92	0.91	0.91	0.87	0.89	0.87	0.87
SVM	0.94	0.94	0.94	0.94	0.90	0.91	0.90	0.90
NB	0.94	0.94	0.94	0.94	0.94	0.95	0.94	0.94
RF	0.93	0.94	0.93	0.93	0.94	0.94	0.94	0.94
ADB	0.89	0.89	0.89	0.89	0.90	0.91	0.90	0.90
XGB	0.93	0.93	0.93	0.93	0.92	0.92	0.92	0.92

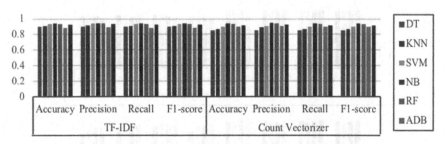

Fig. 2. Performance of ML models with TF-IDF and Count vectorizer

When the deep learning models are compared with the baseline models, it is found that the deep learning models with domain-specific word2vec embeddings outperform the baseline models. Among the discussed architectures as shown in Table 4, with domain-specific Word2Vec embeddings, Kim's CNN architecture and the combination of CNN and BiLSTM models show the best performance with the F1-score of 0.96 for both deep learning algorithms.

Table 4. Performance of Deep learning with word Embeddings

Deep Learning Models		Word2Vec				fastText			
		Acc	Pre	Rec	F1-score	Acc	Pre	Rec	F1-score
Pretrained	Kim's CNN	0.83	0.83	0.83	0.83	0.87	0.88	0.87	0.87
	CNN	0.86	0.87	0.86	0.86	0.87	0.88	0.87	0.86
	BiLSTM	0.87	0.88	0.87	0.87	0.89	0.89	0.89	0.89
	CNN + BiLSTM	0.87	0.88	0.87	0.87	0.76	0.84	0.76	0.73
Domain-Specific	Kim's CNN	0.96	0.97	0.96	0.96	0.94	0.94	0.94	0.94
	CNN	0.95	0.95	0.95	0.95	0.93	0.93	0.93	0.93
	BiLSTM	0.95	0.95	0.95	0.95	0.90	0.91	0.90	0.90
	CNN + BiLSTM	0.96	0.96	0.96	0.96	0.93	0.93	0.93	0.93

On the other hand, with pre-trained embeddings, BiLSTM model with fastText embeddings had higher F1-score of 0.89 as compared to all the models with different embedding. Figure 3 shows the performance of various deep learning architectures various embedding. The highest F1-score of 0.96 is given by Kim's CNN architecture for domain-specific Word2Vec model which outperforms NB, the best baseline classifier.

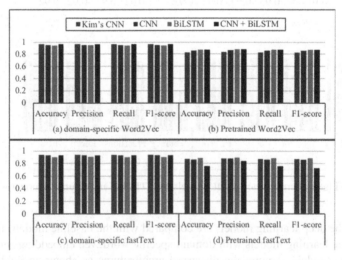

Fig. 3. Performance of deep learning models with different embeddings

The above-mentioned deep learning models can have different architectures. Kim's with 4 convolutional layers performed the best. This also gives us an idea that since a max pooling is used after each convolutional layer in the Kim's architecture, there is a reduction in the dimension, which implies using just the relevant features. Also, it is seen that domain-specific word embeddings perform better than pretrained word embeddings. The pre-trained word embeddings are more generic. Since the transcripts are pertaining to the cookie theft picture, there are unique words that are specifically related to the cookie theft picture. Due to this reason, domain-specific embeddings have better performance as they are more robust with regard to the vocabulary used in the transcripts.

5 Conclusion

The early detection of Alzheimer's disease in the Nepalese community is important considering aging population and limited health resource to cater the growing need in the country. This study introduces a novel dataset for the Nepali language with transcripts of the AD patients as well as CN participants. Also, the study creates a foundation for research using NLP techniques for the prediction of AD in the Nepali language. The comparative analysis in this study with different models is essential in terms of visualizing the effectiveness of different algorithms with regard to AD classification. In addition to greater accuracy in the classification of AD from the CN group, the process of classification is quick. Thus, it helps in reducing the costs and time associated with the diagnosis of the disease. The work can further be improved by developing techniques that are able to predict the different stages of AD. For further improvements, Nepalese patients should be included in the study to be able to understand the local Nepalese linguistic cues more practically. In addition to relying on English translations from Dementia Bank, Nepalese or other linguistically and culturally similar contexts can be employed in data collection to augment the data further. This study is expected to build a motivation among the researchers to work in this area for further developments in early detection of AD.

References

1. Zhou, X., Ashford, J.W.: Advances in screening instruments for Alzheimer's disease. Aging Med. **2**, 88–93 (2019)
2. Bakkour, A., Morris, J.C., Wolk, D.A., Dickerson, B.C.: The effects of aging and Alzheimer's disease on cerebral cortical anatomy: specificity and differential relationships with cognition. Neuroimage **76**, 332–344 (2013)
3. Domoto-Reilly, K., Sapolsky, D., Brickhouse, M., Dickerson, B.C., Initiative, Alzheimer's Disease Neuroimaging.: Naming impairment in Alzheimer's disease is associated with left anterior temporal lobe atrophy. Neuroimage **63**, 348–355 (2012)
4. Thapa, S., Singh, S., Jain, D.K., Bharill, N., Gupta, A., Prasad, M.: Data-driven approach based on feature selection technique for early diagnosis of Alzheimer's disease. In: 2020 International Joint Conference on Neural Networks (IJCNN). IEEE (2020)
5. Faber-Langendoen, K., Morris, J.C., Knesevich, J.W., LaBarge, E., Miller, J.P., Berg, L.: Aphasia in senile dementia of the Alzheimer type. Ann. Neurol. **23**, 365–370 (1988)

6. Orimaye, S.O., Wong, J.S., Golden, K.J., Wong, C.P., Soyiri, I.N.: Predicting probable Alzheimer's disease using linguistic deficits and biomarkers. BMC Bioinform. **18**, 34 (2017)

7. Fritsch, J., Wankerl, S., Nöth, E.: Automatic diagnosis of Alzheimer's disease using neural network language models. In: 2019 IEEE International Conference on Acoustics, Speech and Signal Processing (ICASSP), pp. 5841–5845. IEEE (2019)

8. Chen, J., Zhu, J., Ye, J.: An attention-based hybrid network for automatic detection of Alzheimer's disease from narrative speech. In: Proceedings of Interspeech, pp. 4085–4089 (2019)

9. Becker, J.T., Boiler, F., Lopez, O.L., Saxton, J., McGonigle, K.L.: The natural history of Alzheimer's disease: description of study cohort and accuracy of diagnosis. Arch. Neurol. **51**, 585–594 (1994)

10. Naseem, U., Musial, K.: DICE: deep intelligent contextual embedding for Twitter sentiment analysis. In: 15th International Conference on Data Analysis and Recognition (ICDAR 2019), pp. 953–958. IEEE (2019)

11. Singh, P.: Natural language processing. Machine Learning with PySpark, pp. 191–218. Springer, Heidelberg (2019). https://doi.org/10.1007/978-1-4842-4131-8

12. Naseem, U., Khan, S.K., Razzak, I., Hameed, I.A.: Hybrid words representation for airlines sentiment analysis. In: Liu, J., Bailey, J. (eds.) AI 2019. LNCS (LNAI), vol. 11919, pp. 381–392. Springer, Cham (2019). https://doi.org/10.1007/978-3-030-35288-2_31

13. Mikolov, T., Sutskever, I., Chen, K., Corrado, G.S., Dean, J.: Distributed representations of words and phrases and their compositionality. In: Advances in Neural Information Processing Systems, pp. 3111–3119 (2013)

14. Grave, E., Bojanowski, P., Gupta, P., Joulin, A., Mikolov, T.: Learning word vectors for 157 languages. arXiv preprint arXiv:1802.06893 (2018)

15. Lamsal, R.: 300-Dimensional Word Embeddings for Nepali Language. IEEE Dataport (2019)

16. Kim, Y.: Convolutional neural networks for sentence classification. arXiv preprint arXiv:1408.5882 (2014)

Explaining AI-Based Decision Support Systems Using Concept Localization Maps

Adriano Lucieri[1,2]($\boxtimes$) (iD), Muhammad Naseer Bajwa[1,2](iD), Andreas Dengel[1,2](iD), and Sheraz Ahmed[2](iD)

[1] Department of Computer Science, Technische Universität Kaiserslautern, Erwin-Schrödinger-Straße 52, 67663 Kaiserslautern, Germany
{adriano.lucieri,naseer.bajwa,andreas.dengel}@dfki.de
[2] Smart Data and Knowledge Services (SDS), German Research Center for Artificial Intelligence GmbH (DFKI), Trippstadter Straße 122, 67663 Kaiserslautern, Germany
sheraz.ahmed@dfki.de

Abstract. Human-centric explainability of AI-based Decision Support Systems (DSS) using visual input modalities is directly related to reliability and practicality of such algorithms. An otherwise accurate and robust DSS might not enjoy trust of domain experts in critical application areas if it is not able to provide reasonable justifications for its predictions. This paper introduces Concept Localization Maps (CLMs), which is a novel approach towards explainable image classifiers employed as DSS. CLMs extend Concept Activation Vectors (CAVs) by locating significant regions corresponding to a learned concept in the latent space of a trained image classifier. They provide qualitative and quantitative assurance of a classifier's ability to learn and focus on similar concepts important for human experts during image recognition. To better understand the effectiveness of the proposed method, we generated a new synthetic dataset called Simple Concept DataBase (SCDB) that includes annotations for 10 distinguishable concepts, and made it publicly available. We evaluated our proposed method on SCDB as well as a real-world dataset called CelebA. We achieved localization recall of above 80% for most relevant concepts and average recall above 60% for all concepts using *SE-ResNeXt-50* on SCDB. Our results on both datasets show great promise of CLMs for easing acceptance of DSS in clinical practice.

Keywords: Explainable Artificial Intelligence · Decision Support System · Concept Localization Maps · Concept Activation Vectors

1 Introduction

Inherently inquisitive human nature prompts us to unfold and understand the rationale behind decisions taken by Deep Neural Network (DNN) based algorithms. This curiosity has led to the rise of Explainable Artificial Intelligence

© Springer Nature Switzerland AG 2020
H. Yang et al. (Eds.): ICONIP 2020, CCIS 1332, pp. 185–193, 2020.
https://doi.org/10.1007/978-3-030-63820-7_21

(XAI), which deals with making AI-based models considerably transparent and building trust on their predictions. Over the past few years, AI researchers are increasingly turning their attention to this rapidly developing area of research not only because it is driven by human nature but also because legislations across the world are mandating explainability of AI-based solutions [6,18].

The applications of XAI are at least as widespread as AI itself including in medical image analysis for disease predictions [12], text analytics [13], industrial manufacturing [14], autonomous driving [5], and insurance sector [9]. Many of these application areas utilize visual inputs in the form of images or videos. Humans recognize images and videos by identifying and localizing various concepts that are associated with objects – for example concepts of shape (bananas are long and apples are round) and colour (bananas are generally yellow and apples are mostly red or green). XAI methods dealing with images also employ a similar approach of identifying and localizing regions in the input space of a given image that correspond strongly with presence or absence of a certain object, or concept associated with the object.

In this work we build upon Concept Activation Vectors (CAVs) proposed in [10] and extend it by introducing visual Concept Localization Maps (CLMs), which are generated to locate human-understandable concepts, as learnt and encoded by a classifier in its latent space, in the input image. These CLMs validate that the AI-based algorithm learned to focus on pertinent regions in the image while understanding relevant concepts. Furthermore, we develop a new synthetic dataset, called Simple Concept DataBase (SCDB), of geometric shapes with annotations for 10 concepts and their segmentation maps. This dataset mimics complex relationships between concepts and classes in real-world medical skin lesion analysis tasks and can assist researchers in classification and localization of complex concepts. We evaluate CLMs qualitatively and quantitatively using three different model architectures trained on SCDB dataset and provide a qualitative evaluation of CLMs on the real-world CelebA dataset.

2   Datasets

2.1   SCDB: Simple Concept DataBase

Attribution methods proved to work well in simpler detection tasks where entities are spatially easy to separate [8,15] but often fail to provide meaningful explanations in more complex and convoluted domains like dermatology, where concepts indicative of the predicted classes are spatially overlapping. Therefore, we developed and released SCDB[1], a new synthetic dataset of complex composition, inspired by the challenges in skin lesion classification using dermatoscopic images. In SCDB, skin lesions are modelled as randomly placed large geometric shapes (base shapes) on black background. These base shapes are randomly rotated and have varying sizes and colours. The *disease biomarkers* indicative of the ground truth labels are given as combinations of smaller geometric shapes

---

[1] https://github.com/adriano-lucieri/SCDB.

within a larger base shape. These *biomarkers* can appear in a variety of colours, shapes, orientations and at different locations. Semi-transparent fill colour allows *biomarkers* to spatially overlap. The dataset has two defined classes, C1 and C2, indicated by different combinations of *biomarkers*. C1 is indicated by joint presence of concepts *hexagon* ∧ *star* or *ellipse* ∧ *star* or *triangle* ∧ *ellipse* ∧ *starmarker*. C2 is indicated by joint presence of concepts *pentagon* ∧ *tripod* or *star* ∧ *tripod* or *rectangle* ∧ *star* ∧ *starmarker*. In addition to the described combinations, additional *biomarkers* are randomly generated within the base shape without violating the classification rules. Two more *biomarkers* (i.e. *cross* and *line*) are randomly generated on the base shape without any relation to target classes. Finally, random shapes are generated outside of the base shape as noise.

The dataset consists of 7 500 samples for binary image classification and is divided into train, validation and test splits of 4 800, 1 200, 1 500 samples respectively. Another 6 000 images are provided separately for concept training. Along with each image, binary segmentation maps are provided for every concept present in the image in order to evaluate concept localization performance. Segmentation maps are provided as the smallest circular area enclosing the *biomarker*. Figure 1 shows examples of dataset samples.

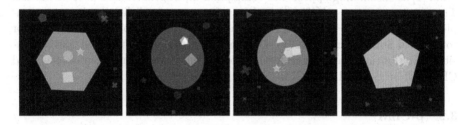

Fig. 1. Training samples from the proposed dataset. Large hexagons, ellipses, and pentagons are examples of base shapes, akin to skin lesions, and small squares, stars, and triangles etc. represent disease-related concepts.

2.2 CelebA

CelebA [11] is a dataset containing 202 599 face images each annotated with regards to 40 binary attributes. The dataset is split into train, validation, and test splits of 129 664, 32 415 and 40 520 samples, evenly divided with respect to gender labels. We chose CelebA for qualitative evaluation because the gender annotation allows for solving a non-trivial, high-level classification task that relies on some of the fine-grained face-attributes like *baldness*, *mustache*, and *makeup*.

3   Concept Localization Maps: The Proposed Approach

The CLM method obtains a localization map m_{Cl} for a concept C learnt on DNN's layer l, that locates the relevant region essential for the prediction of a concept classifier $g_C(f_l(x; \theta))$ given an input image $x \in X$. The linear concept classifier g_C generates a concept score for concept C given a latent vector of trained DNN $f_l(x; \theta)$ with optimal weights θ at layer l. The resulting map m_{Cl} corresponds to the region in the latent space of DNN that encodes the concept C.

3.1 g-CLM

To apply gradient-based attribution methods for concept localization we must find a binary mask m_{binC} that filters out latent dimensions which contribute least to the classification of concept C. For each concept we determine those dimensions by thresholding the concept classifier's weight vector v_C, also known as CAV. High absolute weight values imply a strong influence of the latent feature dimension to the concept prediction and shall thus be retained. Therefore, a threshold value T_C is computed automatically based on 90th percentile of weight values in v_C.

Gradient-based attribution methods are applied once the latent feature dimension is masked and the concept-relevant latent subset $f_{lC}(x, \theta)$ is obtained. The methods evaluated in our work apply SmoothGrad^2 [16] (SG-SQ) and Var-Grad [1] as ensembling approaches using plain input gradients as base-estimator. The noise vector $g_j \sim \mathcal{N}(0, \sigma^2)$ is drawn from a normal distribution and sampling is repeated $N = 15$ times. SG-SQ and VarGrad were proven to be superior to classical SmoothGrad (SG) in [7] in terms of trustworthiness and spatial density of attribution maps. Henceforth, all experiments referring to gradient-based CLM will be denoted by g-CLM.

3.2 p-CLM

The application of perturbation-based attribution methods requires local manipulation of the input image to observe changes in prediction output. In the case of CLM, the output is the predicted score of the concept classifier instead of image classifier. The systematic occlusion method from [19] is used in all experiments with a patch-size of 30 and stride of 10 since it provides a good trade-off between smoothness of obtained maps and localization performance. Occluded areas are replaced by black patches. Experiments referring to the perturbation-based CLM method are denoted as p-CLM.

4 Experiments

4.1 Experimental Setup

Three DNN types, namely *VGG16*, *ResNet50* and *SE-ResNeXt-50* are examined using CLM in order to study the influence of architectural complexity on concept representation and localization. All models were initialized with weights pre-trained on ImageNet [2]. Hyperparameter tuning on optimizer and Initial Learning Rate (ILR) provided best results for optimization using RMSprop [17] with ILR of 10^{-4}. Experiments were conducted for maximum of 100 epochs using learning rate decay with factor 0.5 and tolerance of 5 epochs, and early stopping after 10 epochs without improvement in validation loss.

VGG16, *ResNet50* and *SE-ResNeXt-50* achieved 97.5%, 93.5% and 95.6% image classification accuracy and 85.7%, 81.1% and 72.8% concept classification accuracy, respectively. Surprisingly, the simplest and shallowest architecture achieved the highest test accuracy. However, the average concept classification accuracies on the architectures' last pooling layers (*pool5*) indicate that complex architectures posseses more informed representations of concepts. Figure 2 shows some examples of SCDB along with generated CLMs. Rows two and three correspond to g-CLM (SG-SQ) and p-CLM, respectively. The examples presented in this figure reveal that g-CLMs can be used to localize concepts in many cases. However, it appears that the method often highlights additional *biomarkers* that do not correspond to the investigated concept. For some concepts, localization failed for almost all examples. Furthermore, the generated maps appear to be sparse and distributed, which is typical for methods based on input gradients. The heatmaps obtained from p-CLM are extremely meaningful and descriptive, as shown in the last row of Fig. 2. The granularity of these heatmaps is restricted by the computational cost (through chosen patch-size and stride) as well as the average concept size on the image. It is evident that the method is able to separate the contributions of specific image regions to the prediction of a certain concept. This even holds true if shapes are overlapping.

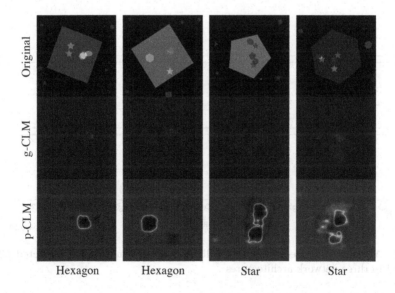

Fig. 2. Example images from proposed SCDB dataset shown in first row along with corresponding concept localization maps from *SE-ResNeXt-50* on layer *pool5*. Middle row and bottom row show corresponding g-CLM (SG-SQ) and p-CLM, respectively. The respective concept for the CLM computation is given below each column.

Quantitative Evaluation: To quantify CLMs performance, we compute average Intersection over Union (IoU), precision and recall between predicted CLMs and their respective ground truth masks for all images in the validation set of SCDB dataset. Therefore, the predicted CLMs are binarized using a per-map threshold from the 98th percentile. The metrics are computed for all images with a positive concept ground truth which means that images with incorrect concept prediction are included as well. Average results over all 10 concepts for all networks and variants are presented in Fig. 3. Concept localization performance of all methods increased with model complexity. This suggests that concept representations are most accurate in *SE-ResNeXt-50*. Results also clearly show that both variants of g-CLM are outperformed by p-CLM over all networks. p-CLM achieved best average localization recall of 68% over all 10 concepts, followed by g-CLM (SG-SQ) with 38% and g-CLM (VarGrad) with 36%. Most concepts relevant to the classification achieved recalls over 80% with p-CLM. The best IoU of 26% is also scored by p-CLM. It needs to be noted that IoU is an imperfect measure considering the sparsity of gradient-based CLMs and the granularity of p-CLMs.

Both qualitative and quantitative analyses suggest that the performance of CLM and thus the representation of concepts is improved with the complexity of the model architecture.

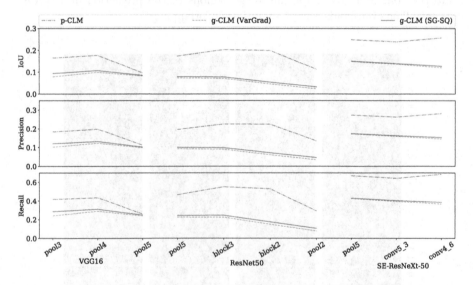

Fig. 3. Average IoU, precision and recall over all 10 concepts for predicted CLMs applied to three network architectures.

4.2   Evaluation on CelebA Dataset

Learning from our experiments on SCDB, we trained only *SE-ResNeXt-50* model on the binary gender classification task in CelebA. The resulting network achieved 98.6% accuracy on the test split. Concepts that achieved highest accuracies are often strongly related to single classes like facial hair (e.g. *goatee, mustache, beard* and *sideburns*) or makeup (e.g. *heavy makeup, rosy cheeks* and *lipstick*). Figure 4 shows images with their corresponding CLMs generated with our method. Due to the absence of ground truth segmentation masks in this dataset, results are only discussed qualitatively below.

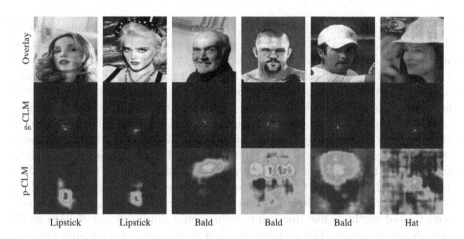

Lipstick   Lipstick   Bald   Bald   Bald   Hat

Fig. 4. Examples for CLMs generated from *SE-ResNeXt-50* trained on binary classification of gender with CelebA dataset. First row shows the original image with the heatmap overlay of p-CLM, second row shows g-CLM (SG-SQ) and the last row shows p-CLM. The respective concept for the CLM computation is given below each column.

First two columns in Fig. 4 show examples of CLMs for the *lipstick* concept. Although it is quite likely that the network learnt a more abstract notion of female and male lips for the classification, the robust localization indicates that the network indeed encodes a lip related concept in the learnt CAV direction. It is striking that g-CLM often fails, highlighting the cheeks as well.

All concepts related to facial hair achieved concept accuracies exceeding 80%. However, inspecting the generated CLMs reveals that the CAVs do not properly correspond with the nuances in concept definitions. The localization maps reveal that the concept *sideburns* never actually locates sideburns but beards in general. For the *goatee* and *mustache* it can be observed that a distinction between both is rarely made. It is thus very likely that the network learned a general representation of facial hair instead of different styles, as it would not aid solving the target task of classifying males versus females.

The *bald* concept produces almost perfect p-CLMs focusing on the forehead and bald areas as can be seen in columns 3 and 4 of Fig. 4. It perfectly demonstrates how the network learnt an intermediate-level feature from raw input that is strongly correlated to a target class. An intriguing finding is that often times, hats are confused with baldness as seen in the CLM for *baldness* in the second last column. However, g-CLM consistently failed to locate this concept. In addition to being sometimes mistaken for baldness, the CLM for *hat* in the last column shows that the network struggled to learn correct representation of a hat. Additional evaluation material for the proposed method is provided on our public repository[2].

5   Conclusion

We introduced the novel direction of concept localization for explanation of AI-based DSS and proposed a robust perturbation-based concept localization method (p-CLM) that has been evaluated on a synthetically generated dataset as well as a publicly available dataset of natural face images. p-CLM considerably outperformed two gradient-based variants (g-CLM) in qualitative and quantitative evaluation. Our initial results are promising and encourage further refinement of this approach. The computational efficiency and quality of heatmaps can be greatly improved by utilizing optimization-based perturbation methods like [3] and [4]. Not only will they reduce the number of network propagations by optimizing the prediction score, but also the flexible shape of masks would be beneficial for the quality of CLMs. Perturbation-based methods always introduce some distribution shift which might distort predicted outcomes. However, more sophisticated methods like image inpainting could minimize distribution shifts through perturbation. The method of CLM is another step towards explainable AI that could help break the barriers in the way of practical utilization of AI-based solutions. Our SCDB dataset is also publicly available for research community to advance XAI using concept based interpretation.

Acknowledgments. Partially funded by National University of Science and Technology (NUST), Pakistan through Prime Minister's Programme for Development of PhDs in Science and Technology and BMBF projects ExplAINN (01IS19074) and DeFuseNN (01IW17002).

References

1. Adebayo, J., Gilmer, J., Muelly, M., Goodfellow, I., Hardt, M., Kim, B.: Sanity checks for saliency maps. In: Advances in Neural Information Processing Systems, pp. 9505–9515 (2018)
2. Deng, J., Dong, W., Socher, R., Li, L.J., Li, K., Fei-Fei, L.: ImageNet: a large-scale hierarchical image database. In: 2009 IEEE Conference on Computer Vision and Pattern Recognition, pp. 248–255. IEEE (2009)
3. Fong, R., Patrick, M., Vedaldi, A.: Understanding deep networks via extremal perturbations and smooth masks. In: Proceedings of the IEEE International Conference on Computer Vision, pp. 2950–2958 (2019)
4. Fong, R.C., Vedaldi, A.: Interpretable explanations of black boxes by meaningful perturbation. In: Proceedings of the IEEE International Conference on Computer Vision, pp. 3429–3437 (2017)

---

[2] https://git.opendfki.de/lucieri/clm-supplement.

5. Glomsrud, J.A., Ødegårdstuen, A., Clair, A.L.S., Smogeli, Ø.: Trustworthy versus explainable AI in autonomous vessels. In: Proceedings of the International Seminar on Safety and Security of Autonomous Vessels (ISSAV) and European STAMP Workshop and Conference (ESWC) 2019, pp. 37–47. Sciendo (2020)
6. Guo, W.: Explainable Artificial Intelligence (XAI) for 6G: Improving Trust between Human and Machine. arXiv preprint arXiv:1911.04542 (2019)
7. Hooker, S., Erhan, D., Kindermans, P.J., Kim, B.: A benchmark for interpretability methods in deep neural networks. In: Advances in Neural Information Processing Systems, pp. 9734–9745 (2019)
8. Jolly, S., Iwana, B.K., Kuroki, R., Uchida, S.: How do convolutional neural networks learn design? In: 2018 24th International Conference on Pattern Recognition (ICPR), pp. 1085–1090. IEEE (2018)
9. Kahn, J.: Artificial Intelligence Has Some Explaining to Do (2018). https://www.bloomberg.com/news/articles/2018-12-12/artificial-intelligence-has-some-explaining-to-do
10. Kim, B., et al.: Interpretability beyond feature attribution: quantitative testing with concept activation vectors (TCAV). In: ICML (2017)
11. Liu, Z., Luo, P., Wang, X., Tang, X.: Deep learning face attributes in the wild. In: Proceedings of International Conference on Computer Vision (ICCV), December 2015
12. Lucieri, A., Bajwa, M.N., Braun, S.A., Malik, M.I., Dengel, A., Ahmed, S.: On interpretability of deep learning based skin lesion classifiers using concept activation vectors. In: IJCNN (2020)
13. Qureshi, M.A., Greene, D.: EVE: explainable vector based embedding technique using Wikipedia. J. Intell. Inf. Syst. **53**(1), 137–165 (2018). https://doi.org/10.1007/s10844-018-0511-x
14. Rehse, J.-R., Mehdiyev, N., Fettke, P.: Towards explainable process predictions for Industry 4.0 in the DFKI-smart-lego-factory. KI - Künstliche Intelligenz **33**(2), 181–187 (2019). https://doi.org/10.1007/s13218-019-00586-1
15. Selvaraju, R.R., Das, A., Vedantam, R., Cogswell, M., Parikh, D., Batra, D.: Grad-CAM: Why did you say that? arXiv preprint arXiv:1611.07450 (2016)
16. Smilkov, D., Thorat, N., Kim, B., Viégas, F., Wattenberg, M.: Smoothgrad: removing noise by adding noise. arXiv preprint arXiv:1706.03825 (2017)
17. Tieleman, T., Hinton, G.: Lecture 6.5–RmsProp: divide the gradient by a running average of its recent magnitude. COURSERA: Neural Netw. Mach. Learn. (2012)
18. Waltl, B., Vogl, R.: Explainable artificial intelligence the new frontier in legal informatics. Jusletter IT **4**, 1–10 (2018)
19. Zeiler, M.D., Fergus, R.: Visualizing and understanding convolutional networks. In: Fleet, D., Pajdla, T., Schiele, B., Tuytelaars, T. (eds.) ECCV 2014. LNCS, vol. 8689, pp. 818–833. Springer, Cham (2014). https://doi.org/10.1007/978-3-319-10590-1_53

Learning from the Guidance: Knowledge Embedded Meta-learning for Medical Visual Question Answering

Wenbo Zheng[1,3], Lan Yan[3,4], Fei-Yue Wang[3,4], and Chao Gou[2(✉)]

[1] School of Software Engineering, Xi'an Jiaotong University, Xi'an, China
zwb2017@stu.xjtu.edu.cn
[2] School of Intelligent Systems Engineering, Sun Yat-sen University,
Guangzhou, China
gouchao@mail.sysu.edu.cn
[3] The State Key Laboratory for Management and Control of Complex Systems,
Institute of Automation, Chinese Academy of Sciences, Beijing, China
Yanlan2017@ia.ac.cn, feiyue.wang@ia.ac.cn
[4] School of Artificial Intelligence, University of Chinese Academy of Sciences,
Beijing, China

Abstract. Traditional medical visual question answering approaches require a large amount of labeled data for training, but still cannot jointly consider both image and text information. To address this issue, we propose a novel framework called **Knowledge Embedded Meta-Learning**. In particular, we present a deep relation network to capture and memorize the relation among different samples. First, we introduce the embedding approach to perform feature fusion representation learning. Then, we present the construction of our knowledge graph that relates image with text, as the guidance of our meta-learner. We design a knowledge embedding mechanism to incorporate the knowledge representation into our network. Final result is derived from our relation network by learning to compare the features of samples. Experimental results demonstrate that the proposed approach achieves significantly higher performance compared with other state-of-the-arts.

Keywords: Visual question answering · Meta-learning · Knowledge graph

1 Introduction

Visual Question Answering (VQA) aims to provide a correct answer to a given question such that the answer is consistent with the visual content of a given image. In medical domain, VQA could benefit both doctors and patients. For example, doctors could use answers provided by VQA system as support materials in decision making, while patients could ask VQA questions related to their medical images for better understanding their health. Obviously, medical data

© Springer Nature Switzerland AG 2020
H. Yang et al. (Eds.): ICONIP 2020, CCIS 1332, pp. 194–202, 2020.
https://doi.org/10.1007/978-3-030-63820-7_22

for VQA are mostly multi-modal data composed of images, text. Recently, most methods for medical visual question answering (Med-VQA) are proposed and directly apply deep learning-based models to Med-VQA. However, there is the main challenge for Med-VQA using deep learning:

- The lack of training samples limits the success of deep-learning-based methods in this task, as small data sets typically exist in most medical imaging studies.
- In the meantime, multi-modal information of patients' data must be jointly considered to make accurate inferences about Med-VQA.

To tackle the aforementioned issue, we propose a novel relational network via meta-learning to address the problem of Med-VQA. We propose an effective feature fusion approach to combine the visual and textual features. Further, we present the construction of our knowledge graphs that relate image with text. We introduce a gated mechanism to embed knowledge into fusion representation learning. We build the two-branch relation network via meta-learning. In particular, first, we introduce the embedding approach to perform feature fusion representation learning. Then, we incorporate the knowledge representation into the feature fusion of our network. Finally, we design a relation model to capture and memorize the relation among different samples for final results. Experimental results show that our model performs better than similar works.

In summary, our main contributions are as follows:

✡ We propose a novel medical visual question answering approach. *To the best of our knowledge, this is the first attempt to study the medical visual question answering approach based on knowledge embedded meta-learning.*

✡ We design a novel feature fusion network to model fine and rich interactions between image and textual modalities.

✡ We present a novel meta-learning-based approach to effectively learn the discriminative feature extraction on unseen new samples.

✡ We design a novel knowledge embedding mechanism to unify knowledge graph with deep networks to facilitate medical VQA.

2 Methodology

2.1 Problem Setup

We consider the problem of Med-VQA as few-shot classifier learning, which consists of two phases: meta-training and meta-testing. In meta-training, our training data $\mathcal{D}_{\text{meta-train}} = \{(x_i, y_i)\}^n_{i=1}$ from a set of classes $\mathcal{C}_{train}$ are used for training a classifier, where x_i is a image and corresponding question, $y_i \in \mathcal{C}_{train}$ is the corresponding answer, and n is the number of training samples. In meta-testing, a support set of v labeled examples $\mathcal{D}_{\text{support}} = \{(x_j, y_j)\}^v_{j=1}$ from a set of new classes $\mathcal{C}_{test}$ is given, where x_j is a image and corresponding question for testing, and $y_j \in \mathcal{C}_{test}$ is the corresponding answer. The goal is to predict the labels of a query set $\mathcal{D}_{\text{query}} = \{(x_j)\}^{v+q}_{j=v+1}$, where q is the number of queries. This split strategy of training and support set aims to simulate the support and query set that will be encountered at test time. Further, we use the meta-learning on the training set to transfer the extracted knowledge to the support set. The model is shown in Fig. 1.

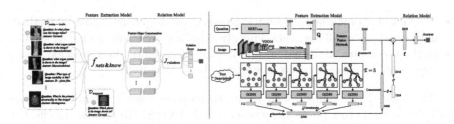

Fig. 1. Our Relation Network. Left: the framework of our relation network. Right: the architecture of our relation network.

2.2 Knowledge Graph Construction and Representation

Principle of GGNN GGNN is an end-to-end trainable network architecture that can learn features for arbitrary graph-structured data by iteratively updating node representation in a recurrent fashion. Formally, the input is a graph represented as $\mathcal{G} = \{\mathbf{V}, \mathbf{A}\}$, in which $\mathbf{V}$ is the node set and $\mathbf{A}$ is the adjacency matrix denoting the connections among these nodes. We define t as the time step of conducting the knowledge graph. At $t = 0$, input feature vectors $\mathbf{x_v}$ that depends on the special task is initialized as the hidden state. Then, at time-step t, we define $\mathbf{h}_v{}^t$ as the hidden state. For each node $v \in \mathbf{V}$, the basic propagation recurrent process is formulated as

$$
\begin{aligned}
\mathbf{h}_v{}^0 &= \mathbf{x}_v \\
\mathbf{a}_v{}^t &= \mathbf{A}_v{}^{\mathfrak{T}}[\mathbf{h}_1{}^{t-1} \cdots \mathbf{h}_{|\mathbf{V}|}{}^{t-1}]^{\mathfrak{T}} + \mathbf{b} \\
\mathbf{h}_v{}^t &= gate(\mathbf{a}_v{}^t, \mathbf{h}_v{}^{t-1})
\end{aligned}
\tag{1}
$$

where $\mathbf{A}_v$ is a sub-matrix of $\mathbf{A}$ represents the connections of node v with its neighbors, and *gate* denotes gated update mechanism, which is defined as:

$$
\begin{aligned}
\mathbf{z}_v{}^t &= \sigma(\mathbf{W}^z\mathbf{a}_v{}^t + \mathbf{U}^z\mathbf{h}_v{}^{t-1}) \\
\mathbf{r}_v{}^t &= \sigma(\mathbf{W}^r\mathbf{a}_v{}^t + \mathbf{U}^r\mathbf{h}_v{}^{t-1}) \\
\tilde{\mathbf{h}}_v^t &= \tanh(\mathbf{W}\mathbf{a}_v{}^t + \mathbf{U}(\mathbf{r}_v{}^t \odot \mathbf{h}_v{}^{t-1})) \\
\mathbf{h}_v{}^t &= (1 - \mathbf{z}_v{}^t) \odot \mathbf{h}_v{}^{t-1} + \mathbf{z}_v{}^t \odot \tilde{\mathbf{h}}_v^t
\end{aligned}
\tag{2}
$$

where $\odot$, σ and $\tanh$ are the element-wise multiplication operation, the logistic sigmoid and hyperbolic tangent functions, respectively.

The propagation process is repeated until iteration $\mathfrak{T}$. During this process, we update the representation of each node based on its history state and the message sent by its neighbors. Thus, we can obtain the final hidden states $\{\mathbf{h}_1{}^{\mathfrak{T}}, \mathbf{h}_2{}^{\mathfrak{T}}, \ldots, \mathbf{h}_{|\mathbf{V}|}{}^{\mathfrak{T}}\}$. All in all, the computation process of Eq. (1) can be reduced to $\mathbf{h}_v{}^t = \mathrm{GGNN}(\mathbf{h}_1{}^{\mathfrak{T}}, \mathbf{h}_2{}^{\mathfrak{T}}, \ldots, \mathbf{h}_{|\mathbf{V}|}{}^{\mathfrak{T}}; \mathbf{A}_v)$. Similar to [6], we employ an output network that is implemented by a fully-connected layer o, to compute node-level feature, expressed by

$$\mathbf{o}_v = o([\mathbf{h}_v{}^{\mathfrak{T}}, \mathbf{x}_v]), v = 1, 2, 3, \cdots |\mathbf{V}| \tag{3}$$

Constructing Image-Question GGNN. By observation, we consider the nouns and adjectives in the text description to be key information. We use the Natural Language Toolkit (NLTK) to get the nouns and adjectives of a question. We define these words as the keywords of this question. Distinctly, we need to construct one knowledge graph which relates images with keywords. Given dataset that covers n images and k keywords of questions, the graph has a node set $\mathbf{V}$ with $n + k$ elements. We define the $n \times k$ matrix $\mathbf{S}_{I\&Q}$ that denotes the confidence that this image has the keywords and its value range is $[0, 1]$. Then, we can get the adjacency matrix $\mathbf{A}_{I\&Q}$ expressed as

$$\mathbf{A}_{I\&Q} = \begin{bmatrix} \mathbf{0}_{n \times n} & \mathbf{S}_{I\&Q} \\ \mathbf{0}_{n \times k} & \mathbf{0}_{k \times k} \end{bmatrix} \tag{4}$$

where $\mathbf{0}.$ is a zero vector with dimension.

Finally, by this way, we can get the knowledge graph $\mathcal{G}_{I\&Q} = \{\mathbf{V}_{I\&Q}, \mathbf{A}_{I\&Q}\}$.

Knowledge Graph Representation. After building the knowledge graph, we employ the GGNN to propagate node message through the graph and compute a feature vector for each node. All the feature vectors are then concatenated to generate the final representation for the knowledge graph. We count the probabilities of all possible relationships given images and keywords from questions in dataset, which are denoted $\mathbf{S}_{I\&Q} = \{s_0, s_1, \cdots, s_{k-1}\}$. We initialize the node refers to the image i with s_i, and the node refers to each keyword with a zero vector. Thus, we can get the input feature for each node represented as

$$\mathbf{x}_v = \begin{cases} [s_i, \mathbf{0}_{n-1}] & \text{if node } v \text{ refers to one image} \\ [\mathbf{0}_n] & \text{if node } v \text{ refers to one keywords} \end{cases} \tag{5}$$

where $\mathbf{0}.$ is a zero vector with dimension $\cdot$. After $\mathfrak{T}$ iteration in Fig. 1, according to the principle of the GGNN, we can get the node-level feature $\mathbf{o}_v{}^{I\&Q}$ computed by Eq. (3). Finally, these features are concatenated to produce the final knowledge representation $\mathbf{f}^{knowledge}$. For the GGNN model, the dimension of the hidden state is set as 4098 and that of the output feature is set as 512. The iteration time $\mathfrak{T}$ is set as 5. GGNN is trained with ADAM following [10]. Therefore, we can get the 2560 (512 × 5) -D knowledge embedding vector $\mathbf{f}^{knowledge}$.

2.3   Feature Fusion Network

Image Feature Extraction. In order to extract the feature of medical image, we propose a new convolution network that based on VGG16 network [12] (pretrained on ImageNet) and Global Average Pooling (GAP) [9] strategy. We remove all the fully-connected layers in the VGG16 network and the convolution outputs of different feature scales are concatenated after global average pooling to form a 1984 -dimensional (-D) vector $\mathbf{I}$ to represent the image. The architecture is shown in Fig. 1.

Question Semantic Encoder. We propose a question encoder based on the Bidirectional Encoder Representation from Transformers (BERT) [4] to get the semantic feature of question. BERT is a pre-trained language representation model proposed by Google. Unlike the context-free model such as Glove which generates a "word embedding" for each word, BERT emphasizes more on the relationships between a word and the other words in a sentence that can effectively avoid polysemy. The model we used is a large version of BERT which includes 24 layers, 1024 hidden variables with a total of 340M parameters. To represent each sentence, we average the last and penultimate layer to obtain a 1024-D question feature vector. To better fit our fusion network, we fill and copy this vector. That is, we fill this vector with the same vector. Finally, we get the 2048-D question feature vector $\mathbf{Q}$.

Multimodal Fusion. We want to include question features within visual features. We use the bilinear fusion model [2] based on the Tucker decomposition of third-order tensors. This model learns to focus on the relevant correlations between input dimensions. It models rich and fine-grained multimodal interactions, while keeping a relatively low number of parameters. Each input vector $\mathbf{I}$ is fused with the question embedding $\mathbf{Q}$ using the same bilinear fusion:

$$\mathbf{f}^{network} = B(\mathbf{I}, \mathbf{Q}; \Theta) \tag{6}$$

where $B(\cdot)$ means the function of bilinear fusion, and Θ means the trainable parameters of our fusion network. Each dimension of $\mathbf{f}^{network}$ can be written as a bilinear function in the form $\sum w_{\mathbf{I},\mathbf{Q},\mathbf{f}^{network}}\mathbf{IQ}$. Thanks to the Tucker decomposition, the tensor $w_{\mathbf{I},\mathbf{Q},\mathbf{f}^{network}}$ is factorized into the list of parameters Θ. According to the principle of Tucker decomposition, we set the number of dimensions in $\mathbf{f}^{network}$ to 2048 to facilitate the use of residual connections throughout our architecture. All in all, in our fusion network, the local multimodal information is represented within a richer vectorial form $\mathbf{f}^{network}$ which can encode more complex correlations between both modalities.

2.4   Knowledge-Based Representation Learning

We introduce the gated mechanism that embeds the knowledge representation to enhance the representation learning, considering suppressing non-informative features and allowing informational features to pass under the guidance of the our knowledge graph, we introduce a gated mechanism expressed as

$$\mathbf{f} = \sigma(g(\mathbf{f}^{network}, \mathbf{f}^{knowledge})) \odot \mathbf{f}^{network} \tag{7}$$

where σ is the logistic sigmoid, $\odot$ denotes the element-wise multiplication operation, g is a neural network that takes the concatenation of the feature of the final knowledge embedding and the feature of extracting by using the feature fusion network. It is implemented by two stacked fully connected layers in which the first one is 4608 (2048 + 2560) to 1024 followed by the hyperbolic tangent function while the second one is 1024 to 2048.

2.5 Meta-learning Model

Meta-learning Based Classifier: As illustrated in Fig. 1, our matching network consists of two branches: a feature extraction model (feature fusion network and our knowledge graph) and a relation model during the training of our network. We define the function $f_{nets\&know}$ represents feature extraction function using feature fusion network and our knowledge graph, i.e., the output of $f_{nets\&know}$ is $\mathbf{f}$, and the function C represents feature concatenation function.

Relation Model. Suppose sample $x_j \in \mathcal{D}_{support}$ and sample $x_i \in \mathcal{D}_{meta\text{-}train}$, the concatenated feature map of the training and testing sets is used as the relation model $J_{relation}(\cdot)$ to get a scalar in range of 0 to 1 representing the similarity between x_i and x_j, which is called relation score. Suppose we have one labeled sample for each of n unique classes, our model can generate n relation scores $Judge_{i,j}$ for the relation between one support input x_j and training sample set examples x_i:

$$Judge_{i,j} = J_{relation}(C(\overbrace{f_{nets\&know}(x_i)}^{\text{The } \mathbf{f} \text{ of } x_i}, \overbrace{f_{nets\&know}(x_j)}^{\text{The } \mathbf{f} \text{ of } x_j})) \tag{8}$$
$$i = 1, 2, \cdots, n$$

Furthermore, we can do the operation of element-wise sum over our feature extraction model outputs of all samples from each training class to form this class's feature map. And this pooled class-level feature map is concatenated with the feature map of the test image and corresponding question as above.

Objective Function. We use mean square error (MSE) loss to train our model, regressing the relation score $Judge_{i,j}$ to the ground truth: matched pairs have similarity 1 and the mismatched pair have similarity 0.

$$Loss = \arg\min \sum_{i=1}^{n} \sum_{j=1}^{m} (Judge_{i,j} - (y_i == y_j))^2 \tag{9}$$

We design the two fully-connected layers to relation model. We use two fully-connected layers to have 8 and 1 outputs, respectively, followed by a sigmoid function to get the final similarity scores mentioned in Eq. (9). For all components in our all model, we use Adam optimizer with a learning rate of 0.001 and a decay for every 50 epochs. We train 800 epochs when the loss starts to converge.

3   Experimental Results

Dataset. The VQA-Med-2019 dataset [1] focuses on radiology images. The training set includes 3200 images and 12792 question-answer (QA) pairs. The validation set includes 500 medical images with 2000 QA pairs. The test set consists of 500 medical images and 500 questions. The test set is manually validated by two medical doctors.

Quantitative Evaluation. To quantitatively compare our model with others, on VQA-Med-2019 dataset, we used the accuracy, precision, recall, F-Measure, and BLEU, as performance metrics.

Baseline. We compare against various state-of-the-art baselines for VQA, including MUREL [3], CTI [5], DFAF [7], MLI [8], CC [11], MCAN [13]. Note that "**Ours w/o GGNN**" means a variant of Ours, which only using feature fusion network and not using knowledge graph and knowledge-based representation learning.

Comparison on the VQA-Med-2019 Dataset. Figure 2(a) shows the performance comparison of our model to ten top ranking results in the VQA-Med-2019 leaderboard[1]. Figure 2(b) shows the performance comparison of our model to baselines and SFN. Ours is 0.176 and 0.314 higher than best baseline (CTI) and best ranking (#1) in term of accuracy, respectively. *This suggests that our model is more robust than the state-of-the-arts on the VQA-Med-2019 dataset.* It also shows that knowledge embedded meta-learning strategy makes a significant contribution to the higher performance of our model, compared with baselines without meta-learning. These shows that our model achieves better performance over the state-of-the-art methods in term of accuracy, precision, recall, F-Measure, and BLEU. *From above, our approach is more effective and robust than the state-of-the-arts on the VQA-Med-2019 dataset.*

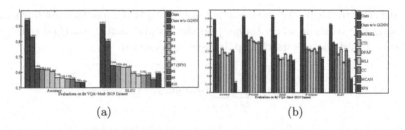

(a)   (b)

Fig. 2. Comparison Results. (a) Performance of Our Model to Ten Top Ranking Results in The Leaderboard on VQA-Med-2019; (b) Comparison of Our Model to Baselines and SFN on VQA-Med-2019.

---

[1] https://www.crowdai.org/challenges/imageclef-2019-vqa-med/leaderboards.

4   Conclusion and Future Work

In this paper, we propose a relational network based on meta-learning with knowledge embedding to address medical visual question answering. Our model can learn the knowledge representation and the feature fusion representation to compare the features of different samples. Our results show that our model achieves the state-of-the-art performance in the medical visual question answering task. In future research, we consider the investigation of the meta-learning and knowledge distillation for medical visual question answering.

Acknowledgment. This work is supported in part by the Key Research and Development Program of Guangzhou (202007050002), in part by the National Natural Science Foundation of China (61806198, 61533019, U1811463), and in part by the National Key Research and Development Program of China (No. 2018AAA0101502).

References

1. Ben Abacha, A., Hasan, S.A., Datla, V.V., Liu, J., Demner-Fushman, D., Müller, H.: VQA-Med: overview of the medical visual question answering task at Image-CLEF 2019. In: CLEF2019 Working Notes. CEUR Workshop Proceedings (2019)
2. Ben-Younes, H., Cadene, R., Thome, N., Cord, M.: Block: bilinear superdiagonal fusion for visual question answering and visual relationship detection. In: The Thirty-Third AAAI Conference on Artificial Intelligence (2019)
3. Cadene, R., Ben-younes, H., Cord, M., Thome, N.: Murel: multimodal relational reasoning for visual question answering. In: The IEEE Conference on Computer Vision and Pattern Recognition (CVPR), June 2019
4. Devlin, J., Chang, M.W., Lee, K., Toutanova, K.: BERT: pre-training of deep bidirectional transformers for language understanding. In: Proceedings of the 2019 Conference of the North American Chapter of the Association for Computational Linguistics: Human Language Technologies, pp. 4171–4186. Minneapolis, Minnesota, June 2019
5. Do, T., Do, T.T., Tran, H., Tjiputra, E., Tran, Q.D.: Compact trilinear interaction for visual question answering. In: The IEEE International Conference on Computer Vision (ICCV), October 2019
6. Fu, J., Zheng, H., Mei, T.: Look closer to see better: recurrent attention convolutional neural network for fine-grained image recognition. In: The IEEE Conference on Computer Vision and Pattern Recognition (CVPR), July 2017
7. Gao, P., et al.: Dynamic fusion with intra- and inter-modality attention flow for visual question answering. In: The IEEE Conference on Computer Vision and Pattern Recognition (CVPR), June 2019
8. Gao, P., You, H., Zhang, Z., Wang, X., Li, H.: Multi-modality latent interaction network for visual question answering. In: The IEEE International Conference on Computer Vision (ICCV), October 2019
9. Lin, M., Chen, Q., Yan, S.: Network in network. In: 2nd International Conference on Learning Representations, ICLR 2014, Banff, AB, Canada, 14–16 April 2014, Conference Track Proceedings (2014)
10. Marino, K., Salakhutdinov, R., Gupta, A.: The more you know: using knowledge graphs for image classification. In: The IEEE Conference on Computer Vision and Pattern Recognition (CVPR), July 2017

11. Shah, M., Chen, X., Rohrbach, M., Parikh, D.: Cycle-consistency for robust visual question answering. In: The IEEE Conference on Computer Vision and Pattern Recognition (CVPR), June 2019
12. Simonyan, K., Zisserman, A.: Very deep convolutional networks for large-scale image recognition. In: International Conference on Learning Representations, May 2015
13. Yu, Z., Yu, J., Cui, Y., Tao, D., Tian, Q.: Deep modular co-attention networks for visual question answering. In: The IEEE Conference on Computer Vision and Pattern Recognition (CVPR), June 2019

Response Time Determinism
in Healthcare Data Analytics
Using Machine Learning

Syed Abdul Baqi Shah[(✉)][iD] and Syed Mahfuzul Aziz[iD]

UniSA STEM, University of South Australia, Adelaide, SA, Australia
syed_abdul_baqi.shah@mymail.unisa.edu.au

Abstract. IT is revolutionizing the healthcare industry. The benefits
being realized could not be imagined a few decades ago. Healthcare Data
Analytics (HDA) has enabled medical practitioners to perform prescriptive, descriptive and predictive analytics. This capability has rendered
the practitioners far more effective and efficient as compared to their previous generations. At the same time, humankind is being served by the
more meaningful diagnosis of diseases, better healthcare, more effective
treatments and earlier detection of health issues. However, healthcare
practitioners still rely on their expert judgement during emergency situations because there is no assurance of response time determinism (RTD)
in current HDA systems. This paper addresses this problem by proposing
the inclusion of RTD in HDAs using a recent technique developed in the
field of real-time systems. An experiment was conducted simulating a
life-saving scenario of this technique to demonstrate this concept. Time
gains of up to 17 times were achieved, exhibiting promising results.

Keywords: Healthcare Data Analytics · Genetic algorithm ·
Determinism · Worst-case execution time · Response time determinism

1 Introduction

Information technology (IT) has contributed significantly to the advancement
of the field of healthcare during recent years [9,14]. This contribution has come
in many ways, for example, technology has assisted in prevention, identification, diagnosis, response, treatment of diseases, improvement of quality of life
and management of health records [10]. Besides improving the medical practice,
specialized devices and systems have been developed, which help the medical
practitioners. Similarly, mainstream technology domains are joining hands to
facilitate better healthcare. Artificial intelligence (AI), machine learning (ML),
data science, big data, cloud, data mining, information and communication technologies (ICT) and mobile applications are solving together the challenges in
healthcare which were not possible in the past [16]. The salient examples are: (i)
outdoor patient department (OPD) through telemedicine [22], (ii) health record

H. Yang et al. (Eds.): ICONIP 2020, CCIS 1332, pp. 203–210, 2020.
https://doi.org/10.1007/978-3-030-63820-7_23

management by digitalization [13], (iii) remote patient care [18], (iv) efficient hospital management through automation of workflows [16], (v) improved longevity assisted by cardio pacemakers [9], (vi) forensics powered by DNA analysis and bioinformatics [13], (vii) remote or robot-assisted surgery [12], and (viii) fighting pandemic by mass training of healthcare practitioners through virtual and augmented reality [20].

ML and Big Data synergize together to deliver value to applications in healthcare, which were not possible in the past [3]. An example application is the diagnosis of complicated diseases by AI-based healthcare applications using Big Data Analytics (BDA), which has increased the accuracy and reduced the efforts to diagnose health conditions. This significant concordance of ML and BDA has given rise to a new field called Healthcare Data Analytics (HDA).

No doubt that HDA is doing wonders, a review of the literature suggests that the healthcare industry is slow in leveraging the potential of ML and BDA [14]. There are so many life-saving and time-critical scenarios which can be helped further by the synergy between ML and BDA. For example, during COVID-19 days, the success rate from the application of mechanical ventilators on the patients in the USA has been very disappointing, i.e., less than 20%. That is why the European doctors are indecisive about the situations where the mechanical ventilators can be applied [11]. The AI, BDA and the doctor triumvirate are still helpless because there is no guarantee of response time determinism (RTD) from the technology available today. This paper aims to address the problem of lack of response time determinism in time-critical life-saving scenarios by posing the following research questions:

RQ1. How critical is the RTD for healthcare practice using HDA?
RQ2. How real-time systems research can help to enhance RTD in HDA?

This paper introduces response time determinism in HDA applications. It highlights the need for RTD in ML-based HDA applications, which is a novel contribution to knowledge because this need is not sufficiently focused in the previous literature on HDA applications. This paper leverages a recently developed worst-case execution time (WCET) analysis technique in real-time systems [19]. To the best of our knowledge, it is the first attempt to utilize this state-of-the-art technique in HDA. The HDA applications, once equipped with the RTD concept proposed in this paper, can help to improve the decision-making of the practitioners in life-saving time-critical situations.

2   Related Work

2.1   Healthcare Data Analytics

The healthcare sector has experienced unprecedented transformation during the past two decades, mainly driven by the disruption in IT [20]. A prominent, newly emerged field is HDA, resulting from the concordance of ML and BDA, the two emerging fields in IT [16]. However, researchers are of the opinion that the healthcare industry is slow in the adoption of HDA [14].

2.2   Applications of ML and Big Data in HDA

ML is helping healthcare practice in several ways. Table 1 presents a few example scenarios, which were not possible a few decades earlier when ML and BDA did not exist [16,21]. According to Mehta and Pandit [14], the major applications of MLA in HDA researched in healthcare are: (i) monitoring desirable attribute values (data) about patients [2], (ii) predicting the performance of patients' organs, e.g., heart failures of the patients [1], (iii) gaining insights into the diseases through data mining [6], (iv) evaluating the root cause of healthcare incidents by simulating the variation of influencing factors [5], and (v) reporting the data or its aggregation to the varying needs of healthcare users [9].

Table 1. Example scenarios for applications of ML and Big Data in HDA.

Scenario	How ML is helping?	Ref.
Brain stroke	Identifying blockages in brain vessels	[16,21]
Amputated limbs	Accurate 3D printing of artificial limbs	[7]
Robotic surgery	Pattern matching and aiding decision during surgery	[12]
Eye diseases	Accurate treatment and validating the efficacy	[3]
Heart disease	Diagnosing root-cause from sensory data, e.g., ECG	[9,16]
Stress disorder	Displaying virtual reality scenes to pacify the stress	[17]
Skin cancer	Accurate diagnosis and evaluation of treatment	[8]

2.3   Data Sources for the Training of ML in HDA

The top applications of HDA are decision support, operations optimization and reduction of costs in healthcare [14]. The ML models in HDA need to be trained before they can be used in healthcare practice. This training essentially requires sufficient data, which is in the form of (input, defined output: labels) datasets [9]. The sources of those datasets are: (i) clinical, (ii) patient behavior and sentiment, (iii) administrative and financial, and (iv) pharmaceutical data.

2.4   Response-Times in Healthcare Systems

Previous studies on HDA focus on predictive, prescriptive and descriptive analysis. Commonly used techniques in HDA are presented in Fig. 1 [9,10]. The BDAs available today are robust on analytics but are not deterministic in their response times. For example, while treating heart-attack of a patient, the doctor has a very short time to diagnose the root-cause and treat accordingly. However, the initial tests such as echocardiogram only give a clue, but the detailed tests like coronary catheterization (angiogram), Cardiac CT or Magnetic Resonance Imaging (MRI) require some time before giving more accurate root-causes of

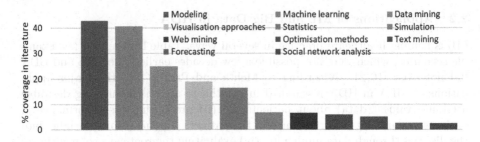

Fig. 1. Techniques in HDA used by previous studies.

the issues [9,16]. Therefore, the immediate steps for treatment of a patient in an emergency situation depend on the initial but incomplete diagnosis and more on the expert judgement of the doctor. Recent research in real-time systems has developed a technique to introduce determinism, which can be applied in several applications and across industries [19]. However, the scenarios for the application of this technique need to be investigated in the healthcare sector, which is the focus of this study.

3   Experimental Design and Validation

3.1   The Context of the Experiment

A patient, Mr P, is under a heart attack. His family brought him to the cardiology emergency. Dr D is attending Mr P. The electrocardiogram (ECG) can help Dr D in identifying whether it is a heart attack. Often, the information from ECG alone is not enough to pinpoint the exact issue. In such situations, the doctor refers to other types of tests, not all of which can be done instantly, and take time to provide deducible conclusions. Examples of those tests are echocardiogram, coronary catheterization (angiogram), Cardiac CT or Magnetic Resonance Imaging (MRI). Since, for Mr P, the ECG results are not conclusive of the exact problem, Dr has to base the decision about the next steps on his expert judgement, whether to start a medical procedure on Mr P or refer him to subsequent tests. Historically, several patients do not sustain for a later test, for example, angiogram. Although HDA is helping the medical practitioners in all those steps, for example, accurately identifying the issue and its root-cause in later steps, but it would have been instrumental, had Dr D be helped with deducible advice right during the heart attack situation. Hence, time-criticality in such situations is of paramount importance.

3.2   Design and Experimental Setup

Dr D has access to the HDA system, which is equipped with a response time determinism controller (RTDC), as shown in Fig. 2. This controller takes in the

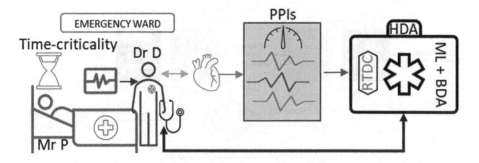

Fig. 2. Response-time determinism in a life-saving situation.

patient's performance indicators (PPIs), which are the selected parameters representing the patient's state. PPI is a matrix with (n × m) dimensions, where m is the number of time-points over which the data is captured, and n is the number of parameters observed for the patient.

When a matrix of PPIs is captured, it is fed to HDA for processing in the form of a batch. Each column value represents a distinct parameter. For example, from an ECG test at a specific time-point, a P-wave value representing atrial depolarization and a Q-wave value denoting the normal left-to-right depolarization of the interventricular septum can be two distinct columns in the PPI matrix.

For the experiment in this study, 32 parameters (columns) in the PPI matrix were included in the scope. The HDA system collects the PPI values at time-points (rows in the matrix) distanced at 1 millisecond each. Hence, the PPI matrix for the first processing batch is a matrix of (n time-points × 32 parameters). On receiving PPI matrix as input, the HDA system processes the data from its BDA component. It is a functionality similar to that described in the literature discussed in Sect. 2 and using the techniques presented in Fig. 1. However, to include time assurance of the response of HDA, a subsystem of HDA called RTDC is utilized, as shown in Fig. 2. The RTDC is described in the next subsection.

3.3   Implementation of RTDC and the Results

RTDC is a system which takes in arrays of parameters as inputs and estimates the WCET for the processing of those arrays. The input matrix can be considered an array of PPI vectors. A critical property of RTDC is that irrespective of the length of the input arrays, the estimated WCET of the array processing is provided within a deterministic time. RTDC is a specialized component, and it achieves high accuracy of estimates without actually executing those arrays in the BDA. This property makes RTDC a popular choice in the field of real-time systems [15, 19]. RTDC achieves determinism by using GA for estimating the time execution of the benchmarks (the input arrays). GA uses an artificial

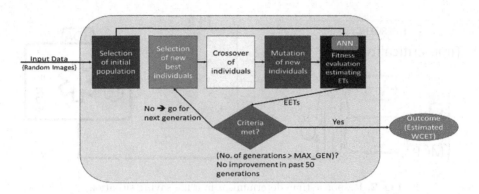

Fig. 3. Evolution process of GA through inferencing from the trained ANN.

neural network (ANN)-based prediction model. The input dataset for this experiment, $DataSet_{initial}$, was generated through Execution Time Profiler (ETP), a simulation, which was developed separately. The experiment was implemented in MATLAB 2020b. The ANN was first trained using $DataSet_{initial}$. After completing the training, the ANN utilizes the GA technique to estimate the WCET of benchmarks (the input arrays). This process is illustrated in Fig. 3.

The steps in this process are: (1) Selection of initial population, which is a one-time activity in the process. (2) Fitness evaluation using estimation of execution times (ETs). (3) Checking whether the stopping criteria has been met. If yes, the WCET estimation is complete and the process stops. If not, then (4) new best chromosomes (individuals) are selected. (5) A crossover of chromosomes is computed. (6) The new individuals are mutated. This process goes on until the stopping criteria are met.

The technique of Shah et al. [19] was used to estimate the WCET without actually processing the arrays in BDA. The efficiency of this experiment is reported as time gain ratio of actual time taken by BDA to process an array of inputs to the time taken by RTDC to process it. The experiment was run for

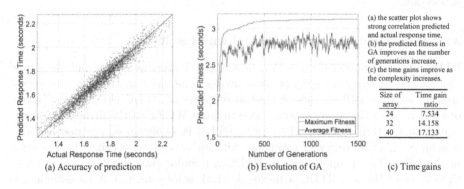

Fig. 4. Results of the experiment.

array sizes of 24, 32 and 40. The results are presented in Fig. 4, which prove a significant improvement in response times as compared to actual processing times in HDA. Figure 4 (a) demonstrates a strong correlation between predicted and actual response times. Figure 4 (b) shows that the predicted fitness in GA improves as the number of generations increase. Figure 4 (c) reveals that the time gains improve as the complexity increases.

4   Discussion and Conclusion

HDA has been very effective in helping healthcare practice [16]. Using HDA, medical practitioners are much more effective in their services than their previous generations. They can perform more in-depth analyses to diagnose the diseases, innovatively find treatments looking into the efficacy of similar treatments, efficiently manage their patients and their records [10]. However, there are emergency scenarios where RTD becomes critical. But the contemporary HDAs are still not designed to provide a response in a deterministic timeframe [4]. It is because the realization for the need of RTD in healthcare is still in the early stages, and the healthcare industry has not yet placed emphasis on demanding RTD from the designers of HDA. This paper explores the time-criticality challenges faced by practitioners in applying HDA. It also answers a key question about the ways the learning from other domains, mainly real-time systems, can help in assuring determinism in response times of HDA. A proof of concept experiment was done following a recent technique of introducing determinism in applications of real-time systems. The study faced limitations due to the unavailability of real-life datasets giving timing analysis classification from the healthcare industry to train the ANN-based ML model used in this experiment. The experiment yielded significant time gains in the processing of data. This experiment and the study lay the foundation for future research for implementing RTD in healthcare scenarios, assisted by HDA. Future studies are recommended to generate datasets with timing analysis classification in the healthcare industry for the training of ML models. Future researchers are also recommended to explore more life-saving scenarios where RTD makes a difference. They are also recommended to highlight the need for implementing RTD in the existing HDA and BDA solutions so that healthcare practitioners can be more effective in treatments during emergency situations.

References

1. AbdelRahman, S.E., et al.: A three-step approach for the derivation and validation of high-performing predictive models using an operational dataset: congestive heart failure readmission. BMC Med. Inform. Decis.-Making **14**(1), 41 (2014)
2. Althebyan, Q., et al.: Cloud support for large scale e-healthcare systems. Ann. Telecommun. **71**(9–10), 503–515 (2016). https://doi.org/10.1007/s12243-016-0496-9
3. Balyen, L., Peto, T.: Promising artificial intelligence-machine learning-deep learning algorithms in ophthalmology. Asia-Pac. J. Ophthalmol. **8**, 264–272 (2019)

4. Basanta-Val, P., et al.: Architecting time-critical big-data systems. IEEE Trans. Big Data **2**(4), 310–324 (2016)
5. Catlin, A.C., et al.: Comparative analytics of infusion pump data across multiple hospital systems. Am. J. Health-Syst. Pharm. **72**(4), 317–324 (2015)
6. Chen, H., et al.: Relational network for knowledge discovery through heterogeneous biomedical and clinical features. Sci. Rep. **6**, 29915 (2016)
7. Edwards, A.L., et al.: Application of real-time machine learning to myoelectric prosthesis control: a case series in adaptive switching. Prosthet. Orthot. Int. **40**(5), 573–581 (2016)
8. Esteva, A., et al.: Dermatologist-level classification of skin cancer with deep neural networks. Nature **542**(7639), 115–118 (2017)
9. Galetsi, P., Katsaliaki, K.: A review of the literature on big data analytics in healthcare. J. Oper. Res. Soc. **70**, 1511–1529 (2019)
10. Galetsi, P., Katsaliaki, K., Kumar, S.: Big data analytics in health sector: theoretical framework, techniques and prospects. Int. J. Inf. Manag. **50**, 206–216 (2020)
11. Gattinoni, L., et al.: Covid-19 does not lead to a "typical" acute respiratory distress syndrome. Am. J. Respir. Crit. Care Med. **201**(10), 1299–1300 (2020)
12. Huang, E.Y., et al.: Telemedicine and telementoring in the surgical specialties: a narrative review. Am. J. Surg. **218**(4), 760–766 (2019)
13. Kulynych, J., Greely, H.T.: Clinical genomics, big data, and electronic medical records: reconciling patient rights with research when privacy and science collide. J. Law Biosci. **4**(1), 94–132 (2017)
14. Mehta, N., Pandit, A.: Concurrence of big data analytics and healthcare: a systematic review. Int. J. Med. Inform. **114**, 57–65 (2018)
15. Rashid, M., Shah, S.A.B., Arif, M., Kashif, M.: Determination of worst-case data using an adaptive surrogate model for real-time system. J. Circuits Syst. Comput. **29**(01), 2050005 (2020)
16. Razzak, M.I., Imran, M., Xu, G.: Big data analytics for preventive medicine. Neural Comput. Appl. **32**, 4417–4451 (2019)
17. Reger, G.M., Smolenski, D., Norr, A., Katz, A., Buck, B., Rothbaum, B.O.: Does virtual reality increase emotional engagement during exposure for PTSD? Subjective distress during prolonged and virtual reality exposure therapy. J. Anxiety Disord. **61**, 75–81 (2019). https://doi.org/10.1016/j.janxdis.2018.06.001
18. Sajjad, M., et al.: Mobile-cloud assisted framework for selective encryption of medical images with steganography for resource-constrained devices. Multimed. Tools Appl. **76**(3), 3519–3536 (2016). https://doi.org/10.1007/s11042-016-3811-6
19. Shah, S.A.B., Rashid, M., Arif, M.: Estimating WCET using prediction models to compute fitness function of a genetic algorithm. Real-Time Syst. 1–36 (2020)
20. Wang, Y., Kung, L., Byrd, T.A.: Big data analytics: understanding its capabilities and potential benefits for healthcare organizations. Technol. Forecast. Soc. Chang. **126**, 3–13 (2018)
21. Yedurkar, D.P., Metkar, S.P.: Big data in electroencephalography analysis. In: Kulkarni, A.J., et al. (eds.) Big Data Analytics in Healthcare. SBD, vol. 66, pp. 143–153. Springer, Cham (2020). https://doi.org/10.1007/978-3-030-31672-3_8
22. Zobair, K.M., Sanzogni, L., Sandhu, K.: Telemedicine healthcare service adoption barriers in rural Bangladesh. Australas. J. Inf. Syst. **24** (2020)

Human Activity Recognition

A Landmark Estimation and Correction Network for Automated Measurement of Sagittal Spinal Parameters

Guosheng Yang[1], Xiangling Fu[1(✉)], Nanfang Xu[2], Kailai Zhang[3], and Ji Wu[3]

[1] School of Software Engineering, Beijing University of Posts
and Telecommunications, Beijing, China
`fuxiangling@bupt.edu.cn`
[2] Peking University Third Hospital, Beijing, China
[3] Department of Electronic Engineering, Tsinghua University, Beijing, China

Abstract. Recently, deep learning for spinal measurement in scoliosis achieved huge success. However, we notice that existing methods suffer low performance on lateral X-rays because of severe occlusion. In this paper, we propose the automated Landmark Estimation and Correction Network (LEC-Net) based on a convolutional neural network (CNN) to estimate landmarks on lateral X-rays. The framework consists of two parts (1) a landmark estimation network (LEN) and (2) a landmark correction network (LCN). The LEN first estimates 68 landmarks of 17 vertebrae (12 thoracic vertebrae and 5 lumbar vertebrae) per image. These landmarks may include some failed points on the area with occlusion. Then the LCN estimates the clinical parameters by considering the spinal curvature described by 68 landmarks as a constraint. Extensive experiment results which test on 240 lateral X-rays demonstrate that our method improves the landmark estimation accuracy and achieves high performance of clinical parameters on X-rays with severe occlusion. Implementation code is available at https://github.com/xiaoyanermiemie/LEN-LCN.

Keywords: Scoliosis · Convolutional neural network · Lateral X-rays

1 Introduction

Scoliosis is the most common spinal disorder where the percentage is 0.47–5.2% in adolescents [9]. The Cobb method [5] is considered as a classical and efficient way to quantitatively measure the angle of scoliosis both on the coronal and the sagittal plane. Previous studies demonstrated the use of deep learning in automated determination of the Cobb angle [3] on the coronal plane with better performance than the current gold standard of manual measurement. In the clinical evaluation of patients with scoliosis, sagittal plane parameters, especially thoracic kyphosis (TK) angle and lumbar lordosis (LL) angle measured on lateral (LA) X-rays are instrumental in the determination of surgical levels.

© Springer Nature Switzerland AG 2020
H. Yang et al. (Eds.): ICONIP 2020, CCIS 1332, pp. 213–221, 2020.
https://doi.org/10.1007/978-3-030-63820-7_24

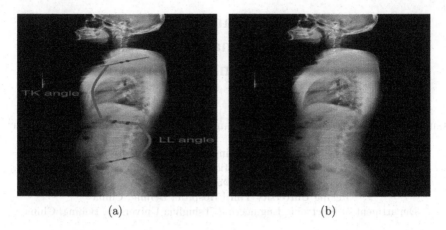

Fig. 1. (a) A lateral X-ray with TK angle and LL angle. The blue points are 1st, 2nd, 47th, 48th, 49th, 50th, 67th and 68th landmarks respectively. (b) The 68 landmarks of 17 vertebrae labeled by experts. (Color figure online)

The TK angle and LL angle are defined as the angle from 1st to 12th thoracic vertebra (T1-T12) and from 1st to 5th lumbar vertebra (L1−L5) shown in Fig. 1, respectively. However, manual assessment is time-consuming.

Recent studies have proposed some effective methods for automated angle measurement on anterior-posterior (AP) and LA X-rays. Such as landmarks are predicted by a structured multi-output regression network in [14]. A series of methods (like MVC-Net, MVE-Net) which combine features of multi-view (AP and LA) X-rays to use 3D space information were proposed [16,18]. The authors in [4] use 3D reconstructed X-rays which include AP and LA X-rays to predict landmarks. These two kinds of methods rely on a pair of AP and LA X-rays.

Some methods predict landmarks and angles based on segmentations. Such as an automatic DU-Net based on U-Net [13] to segment the spine, and a 6th polynomial to fit spinal curvature [15]. The Mask RCNN [6] is used to segment vertebrae and the centers of segmentation are used to calculate the Cobb angle [12]. An MBR-Net using a minimum bounding rectangle according to the segmented vertebral contour to measure the Cobb angle by considering the rectangle as the vertebra [8]. Lumbar vertebrae are segmented by U-Net to measure the LL angle on LA X-rays in [2]. The Mask RCNN to segment vertebrae and a small network to estimate landmarks on AP X-rays [19].

In these studies, most methods base on only AP X-rays to measure the parameters. Other methods base on combined AP and LA X-rays or a part of LA X-rays. Because of the severe occlusion as shown in Fig. 1, these methods perform low accuracy rates on only LA X-rays, particularly on thoracic vertebrae.

In this paper, we propose an automated Landmark Estimation and Correction Network (LEC-Net) which reduces measurement error on LA X-rays. Specifically, we propose a landmark estimation network (LEN) which is trained in an end-to-end way. The LEN bases on the hourglass architecture [11] to estimate 68 landmarks on LA X-rays. The output is optimized to the heatmap generated by Gaussian distribution. Accordingly, we propose a landmark correction network (LCN) which considers spinal curvature as a constraint and estimates clinical angles using 68 landmarks. The clinical parameters are the TK angle and LL angle in our experiments. The experiment results show that our method achieves higher performance on landmark estimation and smaller error on clinical parameters.

2   Methods

2.1   Overview

Related methods perform low accuracy rate on only LA X-rays, particularly on thoracic vertebrae. For example, we use the Mask RCNN (a state-of-the-art model for object detection and segmentation) to segment vertebrae on LA X-rays. We calculate the precision, recall and F1-score of vertebrae segmentation while segmentation is considered 'correct segmentation' if it has IoU (intersection over union) with a ground-truth box of at least 0.5 and 'failed segmentation' otherwise. The results are shown in Table 1.

Table 1. The results of segmentation on LA X-rays using the Mask RCNN. The results are expressed as a percentage.

	Precision	Recall	F1-score
Thoracic vertebrae	97.3	66.9	79.3
Lumbar vertebrae	98.8	97.2	98.0

The results show that it is challenging to use the methods on LA X-rays directly because of the severe occlusion, which work well on AP X-rays. For achieving high performance on LA X-rays, the intuitive idea is using unobscured vertebrae to correct obscured vertebrae by considering spinal curvature as constraints. Therefore, the LEC-Net consists of two cascade networks. The two cascade networks are: (1) the LEN which learns the features between LA X-rays and landmarks, however, the estimated landmarks may include some failed landmarks. (2) the LCN which corrects the failed landmarks to estimate the angles.

2.2   Landmark Estimation Network

The stack hourglass network (SHN) achieves high performance for human pose estimation. One of its advantages is to find key points on human images. We assume that landmarks are key points for vertebrae, therefore we modify the SHN as the backbone of the LEN for adapting our task better. For evaluation of

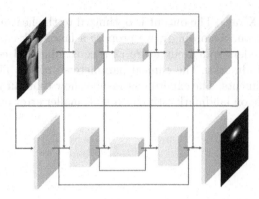

Fig. 2. The architecture of LEN. The LEN takes stack hourglass network as the backbone and modifies it to be more suitable for our task. Blue arrows mean concatenate operation. (Color figure online)

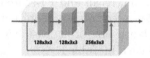

Fig. 3. The residual module that we use in the LEN.

our metric, the LEN does not process features down to a low resolution at the beginning of the network. In addition, considering the memory of our GPU and the size of our data set, the LEN uses 2-stack models and combines different level features. The LEN architecture is shown in Fig. 2. The layer implementation is residual module [7] as shown in Fig. 3. Every residual module includes 3 normal convolutions. We connect more features in different layers in Fig. 2 Inputting an LA X-ray, the LEN outputs a pixel-wise heatmap where the number of channels is equal to the number of landmarks:

$$LEN : I \rightarrow h \tag{1}$$

where I means an image and h means an estimated heatmap. Ground-truth heatmaps are constructed by modeling a landmark position as Gaussian peaks. We use C to define a heatmap and C_i the heatmap of the ith landmark. For a position(x, y) of C_i, $C_i(x, y)$ is calculated by

$$C_i(x, y) = exp(-\|(x, y) - (x_i^r, y_i^r)\|_2^2/\sigma^2) \tag{2}$$

where (x_i^r, y_i^r) is the ground-truth position of the ith landmark, $\sigma = 5$ is a constant to control the Gaussian distribution variance and the number of channels is 68 in our experiments. A Mean Squared Error (MSE) loss is used for comparing predicted heatmaps to ground-truth heatmaps.

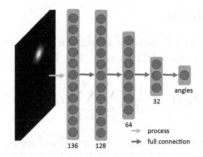

Fig. 4. The architecture of LCN. The LCN processes predicted heatmaps and outputs angles.

2.3 Landmark Correction Network

The LCN calculates the coordinates $[x_i^t, y_i^t]$ of the maximum in a heatmap C_i as input and outputs 2 angles (the TK angle and the LL angle). The landmark correction network architecture is shown in Fig. 4. In the training stage, we normalize coordinates and angles to $[0–1]$. The Coordinates of input are normalized by $CT = [x_1^t/w, y_1^t/h, ..., x_{68}^t/w, y_{68}^t/h]$ where w, h are the width and height of the image size. The estimated angles are normalized by a sigmoid function $y = \frac{1}{1+e^{-x}}$ and the ground-truth angles are normalized by $AG = [tk/180°, ll/180°]$. A Mean Squared Error (MSE) loss is used for comparing predicted angles to ground-truth angles.

3 Experiments

3.1 Dataset

Our dataset consists of 1200 spinal LA X-rays and the size is 957×491. We resize them to be 256×256. These images were provided by a local hospital and the ground-truth landmarks and angles were labeled by two clinical experts with cross-validation. Each of them has eight years of experience. The range of the TK angle is distributed from $0°$ to $75.53°$ and the range of the LL angle is distributed from $0.32°$ to $93.37°$ in our dataset. We also evaluate our method on the public dataset of 609 spinal anterior-posterior x-ray images [17].[1]

3.2 Training Details

The networks are implemented using the Pytorch backend. The experiments are running on NVIDIA 1080Ti. Both networks use the stochastic gradient descent (SGD) optimizer with momentum. The learning rate and momentum are 0.001 and 0.9 in both networks. The 1200 X-rays are divided into train set, validation set and test set randomly, where the proportion is 6:2:2. The results are the average performance of 5-folds validation.

---

[1] http://spineweb.digitalimaginggroup.ca/, Dataset 16.

3.3   Performance Metric

For landmark estimation, we use the landmark mean absolute error (LMAE) given by [16] to describe the relative error. The LMAE is defined as:

$$LMAE = \frac{1}{M}\frac{1}{N}\sum_{j=1}^{M}\sum_{i=1}^{N}|CT_i - CG_i| \tag{3}$$

where CG are ground-truth coordinates normalized as the same as the CT, M is the number of images and N is the number of coordinates per image, 136 (68 x-coordinates and 68 y-coordinates) in our experiments. For angle estimation, we use the angle mean absolute error (AMAE) and Symmetric Mean Absolute Percentage Error (SMAPE) given by [16] to describe the relative error. They are defined as:

$$AMAE = \frac{1}{M}\sum_{j=1}^{M}|Angle_i^{pre} - Angle_i^{gt}| \tag{4}$$

$$SMAPE = 100\% \times \frac{1}{M}\sum_{j=1}^{M}\frac{|Angle_i^{pre} - Angle_i^{gt}|}{(|Angle_i^{pre}| + |Angle_i^{gt}|)} \tag{5}$$

where $Angle_i^{pre}$ mean angles predicted or calculated by predicted landmarks and $Angle_i^{gt}$ mean ground-truth angles. The method of angles calculate by landmarks is like manual process shown in Fig. 1:

$$Angle_{tk} = |\arctan\frac{y_1^t - y_2^t}{x_1^t - x_2^t} - \arctan\frac{y_{47}^t - y_{48}^t}{x_{47}^t - x_{48}^t}| \tag{6}$$

$$Angle_{ll} = |\arctan\frac{y_{49}^t - y_{50}^t}{x_{49}^t - x_{50}^t} - \arctan\frac{y_{67}^t - y_{68}^t}{x_{67}^t - x_{68}^t}| \tag{7}$$

where $Angle_{th}$ and $Angle_{ll}$ mean the TK angle and the LL angle.

4   Results and Discussion

We compare our framework with other methods. We also compare the LEN with the SHN for landmark estimation. The results are shown in Table 2 and Table 3. We do not compare the methods which segment vertebrae on thoracic vertebrae because of low recall of segmentation in Table 2. We do not calculate the LMAE of the methods which segment vertebrae in Table 3. From the results, our method achieves high performance both for landmark and angle estimation. We also evaluate our method on the public dataset of 609 spinal anterior-posterior x-ray images. Since the public dataset are AP X-rays, we just evaluate the 68 key landmarks using the LEN. The results are shown in Table 4.

The LEN achieves high performance due to two parts: based on a state-of-the-art network (SHN) and combined different level features. Existing methods which directly estimate landmarks are mostly to output landmarks formatted

Table 2. Comparison with existing methods on thoracic vertebrae of LA X-rays.

		LMAE	AMAE(°)	SMAPE(%)
Related works	MVE-Net [16]	0.0197 ± 0.0112	12.72 ± 7.63	26.58 ± 20.96
	Sun et al. [14]	0.0259 ± 0.0216	15.51 ± 7.35	33.26 ± 26.67
	SHN [11]	0.0157 ± 0.0109	8.97 ± 4.77	17.47 ± 17.24
Ours	LEN (Only T1, T12)	0.0154 ± 0.0101	8.37 ± 4.12	17.09 ± 17.19
	LEN+LCN	**0.0139 ± 0.0091**	**4.48 ± 2.80**	**11.28 ± 12.85**

as $[x_i, y_i]$ by full connection layer. However, the mapping from images to vector landmarks leads to a loss of information even a simple task in [10]. We adapt the SHN to estimate landmarks, which is from images to images using CNN. The LEN combines more shallow feature and deep semantic information by more dense feature connection. This leads to more efficient information utiliztion.

The LCN considers spinal curvature described by 68 landmarks as a constraint. The angles are estimated by spinal curvature which uses more landmark information. The results demonstrate that our method is more accurate and robust both for landmark and angle estimation on LA X-rays.

Table 3. Comparison with existing methods on lumbar vertebrae of LA X-rays.

		LMAE	AMAE(°)	SMAPE(%)
Related works	Pan et al. [12]	–	11.76 ± 6.22	24.56 ± 27.59
	Horng et al. [8]	–	8.94 ± 5.68	19.73 ± 21.03
	Zhang et al. [19]	–	5.42 ± 4.93	13.87 ± 16.57
	MBR-Net [8]	–	9.96 ± 3.74	19.91 ± 12.11
	MVE-Net [16]	0.0159 ± 0.0130	7.28 ± 4.69	16.58 ± 17.01
	Sun et al. [14]	0.0147 ± 0.0083	8.64 ± 4.06	18.21 ± 19.30
	SHN [11]	0.0082 ± 0.0062	4.96 ± 2.74	11.84 ± 11.96
Ours	LEN (only L1, L5)	0.0078 ± 0.0061	4.25 ± 2.93	11.12 ± 10.43
	LEN+LCN	**0.0069 ± 0.0054**	**3.77 ± 2.26**	**10.31 ± 11.57**

Table 4. Evaluation on the public dataset of 609 spinal anterior-posterior x-ray images.

		LMAE	AMAE(°)	SMAPE(%)
Related works	MVE-Net [16]	0.0229 ± 0.0148	11.08 ± 8.41	26.00 ± 18.62
	Sun et al. [14]	0.0317 ± 0.0257	16.71 ± 9.91	36.79 ± 16.02
	SHN [11]	0.0152 ± 0.0151	8.32 ± 5.97	21.13 ± 17.87
Ours	LEN (T1, T12, L1, L5)	**0.0148 ± 0.0149**	**7.58 ± 6.05**	**20.03 ± 18.36**

5   Conclusion

In this paper, we notice that existing methods for clinical angle estimation on X-rays suffer from low accuracy on LA-rays. To address the issue, we first propose an end-to-end network based on a state-of-the-art network to estimate landmarks on LA X-rays. Then we propose a correction network which utilizes extra landmarks as constraints to estimate the angles. The error of calculated angles with 8 landmarks is reduced by estimating angles with spinal curvature. Extensive experiments demonstrated that our method improves the angle estimation accuracy on LA X-rays. In addition, this framework can also be used for landmark estimation or other parameters based on landmarks of other domain images with severe occlusion.

Acknowledgments. This study was supported by the National Key Research and Development Program of China (No.2018YFC0116800), by Beijing Municipal Natural Science Foundation (No. L192026), by the Young Scientists Fund of the National Natural Science Foundation of China (No.2019NSFC81901822) and by the Peking University Fund of Fostering Young Scholars' Scientific & Technological Innovation (No. BMU2018PYB016).

References

1. Al Okashi, O., Du, H., Al-Assam, H.: Automatic spine curvature estimation from X-ray images of a mouse model. Comput. Methods Programs Biomed. **140**, 175–184 (2017)
2. Cho, B.H., et al.: Automated measurement of lumbar lordosis on radiographs using machine learning and computer vision. Glob. Spine J. **10**, 611–618 (2019)
3. Cobb, J.: Outline for the study of scoliosis. Instr. Course Lect. AAOS **5**, 261–275 (1948)
4. Galbusera, F., et al.: Fully automated radiological analysis of spinal disorders and deformities: a deep learning approach. Eur. Spine J. **28**(5), 951–960 (2019). https://doi.org/10.1007/s00586-019-05944-z
5. Harrison, D.E., Harrison, D.D., Cailliet, R., Troyanovich, S.J., Janik, T.J., Holland, B.: Cobb method or Harrison posterior tangent method: which to choose for lateral cervical radiographic analysis. Spine **25**(16), 2072–2078 (2000)
6. He, K., Gkioxari, G., Dollár, P., Girshick, R.: Mask R-CNN. In: Proceedings of the IEEE International Conference on Computer Vision, pp. 2961–2969 (2017)
7. He, K., Zhang, X., Ren, S., Jian, S.: Deep residual learning for image recognition. In: IEEE Conference on Computer Vision & Pattern Recognition (2016)
8. Horng, M.H., Kuok, C.P., Fu, M.J., Lin, C.J., Sun, Y.N.: Cobb angle measurement of spine from X-ray images using convolutional neural network. Comput. Math. Methods Med. (2019)
9. Konieczny, M.R., Senyurt, H., Krauspe, R.: Epidemiology of adolescent idiopathic scoliosis. J. Child. Orthop. **7**(1), 3–9 (2012). https://doi.org/10.1007/s11832-012-0457-4
10. Liu, R., et al.: An intriguing failing of convolutional neural networks and the coordconv solution. In: Advances in Neural Information Processing Systems, pp. 9605–9616 (2018)

11. Newell, A., Yang, K., Deng, J.: Stacked hourglass networks for human pose estimation. In: Leibe, B., Matas, J., Sebe, N., Welling, M. (eds.) ECCV 2016. LNCS, vol. 9912, pp. 483–499. Springer, Cham (2016). https://doi.org/10.1007/978-3-319-46484-8_29

12. Pan, Y., et al.: Evaluation of a computer-aided method for measuring the cobb angle on chest X-rays. Eur. Spine J. **28**(12), 3035–3043 (2019)

13. Ronneberger, O., Fischer, P., Brox, T.: U-Net: convolutional networks for biomedical image segmentation. In: Navab, N., Hornegger, J., Wells, W.M., Frangi, A.F. (eds.) MICCAI 2015. LNCS, vol. 9351, pp. 234–241. Springer, Cham (2015). https://doi.org/10.1007/978-3-319-24574-4_28

14. Sun, H., Zhen, X., Bailey, C., Rasoulinejad, P., Yin, Y., Li, S.: Direct estimation of spinal cobb angles by structured multi-output regression. In: Niethammer, M., et al. (eds.) IPMI 2017. LNCS, vol. 10265, pp. 529–540. Springer, Cham (2017). https://doi.org/10.1007/978-3-319-59050-9_42

15. Tu, Y., Wang, N., Tong, F., Chen, H.: Automatic measurement algorithm of scoliosis cobb angle based on deep learning. In: Journal of Physics: Conference Series, vol. 1187. IOP Publishing (2019)

16. Wang, L., Xu, Q., Leung, S., Chung, J., Chen, B., Li, S.: Accurate automated cobb angles estimation using multi-view extrapolation net. Med. Image Anal. **58** (2019)

17. Wu, H., Bailey, C., Rasoulinejad, P., Li, S.: Automatic landmark estimation for adolescent idiopathic scoliosis assessment using BoostNet. In: Descoteaux, M., Maier-Hein, L., Franz, A., Jannin, P., Collins, D.L., Duchesne, S. (eds.) MICCAI 2017. LNCS, vol. 10433, pp. 127–135. Springer, Cham (2017). https://doi.org/10.1007/978-3-319-66182-7_15

18. Wu, H., Bailey, C., Rasoulinejad, P., Li, S.: Automated comprehensive adolescent idiopathic scoliosis assessment using MVC-Net. Med. Image Anal. **48**, 1–11 (2018)

19. Zhang, K., Xu, N., Yang, G., Wu, J., Fu, X.: An automated cobb angle estimation method using convolutional neural network with area limitation. In: Shen, D., et al. (eds.) MICCAI 2019. LNCS, vol. 11769, pp. 775–783. Springer, Cham (2019). https://doi.org/10.1007/978-3-030-32226-7_86

Facial Expression Recognition with an Attention Network Using a Single Depth Image

Jianmin Cai[1], Hongliang Xie[1], Jianfeng Li[1(✉)], and Shigang Li[1,2]

[1] School of Electronic and Information Engineering, Chongqing Key Laboratory of Nonlinear Circuit and Intelligent Information Processing, Southwest University, Chongqing, China
`2462129728@qq.com`, `2678847664@qq.com`, `popqlee@swu.edu.cn`
[2] Graduate School of Information Sciences, Hiroshima City University, Hiroshima, Japan
`shigangli@hiroshima-cu.ac.jp`

Abstract. In the facial expression recognition field, RGB image-involved models have always achieved the best performance. Since RGB images are easily influenced by illumination, skin color, and cross-databases, the effect of these methods decreases accordingly. To avoid these issues, we propose a novel facial expression recognition framework in which the input only relies on a single depth image since depth image performs very stable in cross-situations. In our framework, we pretrain an RGB face image synthesis model by a generative adversarial network (GAN) using a public database. This pretrained model can synthesize an RGB face image under a unified imaging situation from a depth face image input. Then, introducing the attention mechanism based on facial landmarks into a convolutional neural network (CNN) for recognition, this attention mechanism can strengthen the weights of the key parts. Thus, our framework has a stable input (depth face image) while retaining the natural merits of RGB face images for recognition. Experiments conducted on public databases demonstrate that the recognition rate of our framework is better than that of the state-of-the-art methods, which are also based on depth images.

Keywords: Facial expression recognition · Depth face image · Synthesized RGB face image

1 Introduction

Facial expression recognition is one of the most important tasks in computer vision and plays an important role in many applications, such as healthcare and human-computer interactions. During the early days of automatic facial expression recognition, many methods based on RGB facial expression databases were collected in laboratory environments. These methods have made a significant

H. Yang et al. (Eds.): ICONIP 2020, CCIS 1332, pp. 222–231, 2020.
https://doi.org/10.1007/978-3-030-63820-7_25

contribution to the field but have also exposed the natural defects of RGB face images. Obviously, an RGB face image is easily influenced by illumination and skin color, and different features can be obtained even on the same subject using the same feature extraction method but under different environments. At present, with the invention of high-resolution 3D imaging equipment, depth image-based facial expression recognition (FER) using static dynamic 3D face scans has attracted increasing attention. The main advantages of using depth images are two-fold: 1) Expressions are the results of facial deformations generated by facial muscles, and such information is directly recorded in the depth images; 2) 3D face scans are naturally robust to lighting and pose changes, and RGB face images obtained in different databases may have quite different imaging situations, while the depth image may not. Therefore, depth images contribute to facial expression recognition but perform much more stable in cross-databases [1]. However, in the facial expression recognition field, the RGB-based channel still achieves better performance than the depth-based channel. It is noticeable that RGB face images have natural merits over depth face images for final recognition because the RGB imaging situation is unified in each public database. To utilize the robustness of depth face images and the recognition of RGB face images, in this paper, we propose a facial expression recognition framework in which the input only relies on a single depth image. First, we pretrain an RGB face image synthesized model by a generative adversarial network (GAN) given pairs of depth face images and RGB face images. Then, we use the pretrained model as the first step in our framework. After inputting a depth image, we can easily obtain a synthesized RGB image under the training imaging standard. Considering that the expression is generated from facial muscle movements, the variation is focused on key facial parts (eyebrow, eye, mouth). An attention-based CNN with facial landmarks is proposed for the final recognition. The main contributions of this paper are threefold. (1) We propose a solution for the problem of different RGB imaging situations. We use a pretrained GAN model to synthesize an RGB face image under a unified imaging situation from a depth face image input. (2) We propose an attention-based CNN with facial landmarks for facial expression recognition. (3) On two public databases for facial expression recognition, the proposed framework achieves a superior performance compared with the previous depth-based methods.

2   Related Works

Until now, depth face images for expression recognition have been the main approach in 3D channels; many related studies have been reported. Li et al. [2] used a pretrained deep convolutional neural network to generate a deep representation of 3D geometric attribute maps, including a depth map, predicted by training linear SVMs. Then, Oyedotun et al. [3] proposed a learning pipeline for the depth map, which used a DCNN from scratch on the depth map images. At the same time, Yang et al. [1] also trained a CNN model for the depth map channel, while a landmark map was introduced for attention purposes.

Jan et al. [4] used shape attribute maps to represent 3D face scans and then cropped these maps into different facial parts according to facial landmarks. Finally, nonlinear SVMs were used for expression prediction. Recently, Zhu et al. [5] proposed a VGG16-BN model, which also used an attention-based CNN. This model proves that the attention mechanism is efficient when used in FER. On the other hand, some researchers have started to use the GAN to solve some problems for facial expression recognition. Zhang et al. [6] proposed an end-to-end deep learning model by jointly exploiting different poses and expressions for simultaneous facial image synthesis and pose-invariant facial expression recognition. Yang et al. [7] proposed recognizing facial expressions by extracting information of the expressive component through a de-expression learning procedure. Yang et al. [8] presented a novel approach to alleviate the issue of subject variations by regenerating expressions from any input facial images. Ali et al. [9] proposed a novel disentangled expression learning generative adversarial network (DE-GAN) to explicitly disentangle a facial expression representation from identity information. Cai et al. [10] proposed a novel identity-free conditional generative adversarial network (IF-GAN) to explicitly reduce inter-subject variations for facial expression recognition. Obviously, the synthesized image has merit for cross-databases.

3   Proposed Framework

Figure 1 shows the entire framework of the proposed approach. We pretrained a GAN model based on given pairs of depth images and RGB images from a unified imaging situation, so the model can synthesize the RGB image according to the training imaging situation. Then, the image is fed into Resnet-18 for classification. At the same time, we crop four key parts from the face based on the landmark. The key parts are fed into an attention block to produce local feature maps. These feature maps are pasted back into the global feature map directly after an intermediate layer.

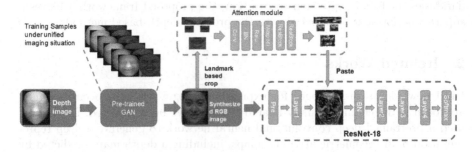

Fig. 1. Entire framework of the proposed approach.

3.1   Pretrain GAN

Pix2pix [11] is a famous framework based on conditional GANs for image-to-image translation tasks, in which it can condition on an input image and generate a corresponding output image. In this paper, we use pix2pix to generate the synthesized RGB image from the depth image. As we know, GAN learns features from training sample pairs and uses the learned features for unseen subjects. Therefore, the synthesized image for unseen subjects is highly consistent with the training target image. In the facial expression recognition field, the task is quite homogeneous, recognizing six basic facial expressions; although people conduct almost the same facial expression all over the world, the RGB imaging situation is different. To reduce the imaging difference, we only use one public database (Bosphorus database [13]) for training. This database takes samples under a unified imaging situation and provides us with 3D points and corresponding registered 2D RGB images. Given the point cloud data, we perform projection procedures using the 3D face normalization method proposed in [12] to achieve normalized 2D range images with x, y, and z coordinates (depth image). The input image pairs, e.g., $\langle Iinput, Itarget \rangle$, are used to train the pix2pix model. $Iinput$ is a depth map, while $Itarget$ is an RGB image of the same subject. Thus, we obtain a pretrained model under the training imaging situation.

3.2   Attention-Based CNN with Landmarks

Using the pretrained model, a synthesized RGB image is generated from a given depth image.

$$I_{category=depth}^{exp=E} = G(I_{category=RGB}^{exp=E}),\qquad(1)$$

where G is the generator and E belongs to any six basic prototypic facial expressions. RGB refers to RGB face image, and depth means depth image. From the above equation, a depth image with expression (E) becomes a synthesized RGB image of the same subject. It is reasonable to conclude that the generation process must be in accordance with the learned features under the training imaging situation. Since facial expressions are produced by facial muscle movements, the key parts naturally contribute to FER. To stress these parts, we crop four subimages from the synthesized image $I_s(size : 256 \times 256)$ based on the landmark. These subimages are the eyebrow $I_{eyebrow}$, the left eye I_{Leye}, the right eye I_{Reye}, and the mouth I_{mouth} (Fig. 2). Taking eyebrow cropping as an example, given the eyebrow landmark set as $P_i(x_i, y_i) = P_1, P_2, \ldots, P_{10}$, to locate the cropping edge, we calculate the maximum and minimum of x_i, y_i respectively: $T_{MaxX} = Max(x_i)$; $T_{MinX} = Min(x_i)$; $T_{MaxY} = Max(y_i)$; and $T_{MinY} = Min(y_i)$. Then, four vertexes are decided, as below, considering margins.

$$P_{UpLeft} = (T_{MinX} - 5, T_{MinY} - 5),\qquad(2)$$

$$P_{DownLeft} = (T_{MinX} - 5, T_{MaxY} + 5),\qquad(3)$$

$$P_{UpRight} = (T_{MaxX} + 5, T_{MinY} - 5),\qquad(4)$$

$$P_{DownRight} = (T_{MaxX} + 5, T_{MaxY} + 5), \qquad (5)$$

The other three key parts follow the same cropping principle. Next, to extract expression-related features from the synthesized RGB image, we build a network combining ResNet-18 [14], batch normalization (BN) [15], and the attention module. The structure of the attention module is displayed in Fig. 2. Each subimage is fed into each attention module to learn local features, and the input size is resized to 64×64. Then, to learn the high-level features, a convolution layer with stride $= 2$, kernel size $= 7$, filter numbers $= 64$, a BN layer, a ReLU layer, and a pooling layer follow. Considering the good performance of residual learning, two residual blocks are used while keeping the same number of filters and the same feature map size. The final output local feature size is 16×16, and the filter number is 64. At the same time, the synthesized image is fed into a ResNet-18 for learning the global features. After layer 1 of ResNet-18, the global feature size is 64×64, and the filter number is 64. Then, to strengthen the local features in the following layers, we resize four local feature maps to the appropriate size, double the local feature map value, and paste them back to the global feature map in the supposed position (Fig. 2). Finally, a BN layer is used for normalization. As a result, in this neural network, the key parts of the face have been fully strengthened, while the remainder of the parts with less information are not lost.

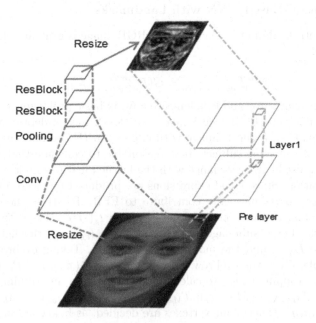

Fig. 2. Attention module.

4   Experiments

In this section, we evaluate the performance of our proposed framework on widely used 3D facial expression databases: the Bosphorus database and the BU-3DFE database. All experiments are conducted on the PyTorch deep learning framework. The Adam optimizer is used as the optimization method, the learning rate is set to 0.001, and the batch size is set to 64. The epoch is 200.

4.1   Database

To evaluate the effectiveness of our proposed framework, we use a standard 10-fold cross-validation experimental setting (9 training sessions and one test session) for Bosphorus database [13] and BU-3DFE database [16]. Similar to the common protocol [5,19], 60 subjects are selected, which are fixed throughout the experiment. Then, the subjects are divided into 10 subsets: 54 subjects for training and 6 subjects for testing. To avoid overfitting, a data augmentation method is applied to generate more data, including five crops and 7 rotations $[-9°, -6°, -3°, 0°, 3°, 6°, 9°]$. Finally, datasets that are 12 times larger than the original dataset are obtained.

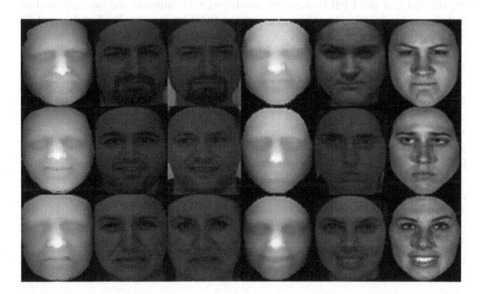

Fig. 3. Left three columns: input depth image, synthesized RGB image, and ground truth, from Bosphorus database. Right three columns: input depth image, synthesized RGB image, and ground truth, from BU-3DFE database.

4.2   Training GAN

In our framework, we only use the Bosphorus database for training the GAN model. Inserting the depth image and the corresponding RGB image pairs of the training set into pix2pix, a pretraining model can be trained. Then, we only input the depth image of the test set, and a synthesized RGB image is obtained. As Fig. 3 shows, the first column is the input depth image, the second column is the synthesized RGB image, and the third column is the ground truth. Even though there are some minor differences, the facial expression performed well. We also used the pretrained model for cross-validation and testing on the BU-3DFE samples. As the last three columns of Fig. 3 shows, the synthesized RGB image retained the facial expression perfectly, while the imaging situation is in accordance with the Bosphorus database. In particular, the shading in the ground truth disappears in the synthesized RGB image, which proves that our strategy can eliminate the differences between the databases.

4.3   Results

To optimize our recognition framework, we conduct the experiment on the Bosphorus database first. We use the pretrained model trained by the training set and test the FER on the test set. First, we compared the two approaches as follows: 1) directly input the synthesized RGB image into ResNet-18; and 2) use the proposed framework. The results are shown in Table 1. Then, we test the structure of the proposed network, combining local feature maps and global feature maps after each layer of ResNet-18. As shown in Table 2, the best recognition is combining local feature maps with the global feature map after layer 1. Finally, we used the Bosphorus-trained GAN model to synthesize the RGB image and demonstrate a 10-fold cross-validation. Table 3 shows the comparison with recent work on the Bosphorus database. Since one goal of this paper is focusing on cross-validation, we compare it with a recent study regarding the BU-3DFE database. The recent studies are mostly multi-channel-based methods, while their methods all use depth image as one of multiple channels; thus, we can compare them with the depth channels. Table 4 shows that our proposed depth image-based method performs the best over the other depth channels, even better than their best single channel. Moreover, their reports are all validated inside the BU-3DFE, while our synthesized RGB image is generated from Bosphorus, which is more robust.

Table 1. Compare different input on Bosphorus database.

Input	Accuracy
Synthesized RGB image + ResNet18	65.89%
Synthesized image + Proposed framework	77.80%

Table 2. Combining local and global maps on Bosphorus database.

Layer of ResNet18	Accuracy
Pre layer	75.32%
Layer1	77.80%
Layer2	72.56%

Table 3. Comparison of different methods on Bosphorus database.

Method	Setting	Accuracy
Li et al. [17]	3D-channel	75.83%
Li et al. [19]	3D-channel	76.11%
Fu et al. [20]	3D-channel	75.93%
Our method	depth-based	77.80%

Table 4. Comparison of different methods on BU-3DFE database.

Method	Depth channel accuracy	Best single channel accuracy
Yang et al. [18]	70.6%	83.4%
Li et al. [19]	80.21%	83.06%
Jan et al. [4]	81.83%	81.83%
Zhu et al. [5]	82.58%	82.74%
Our method	84.23%	84.23%

5   Conclusion

In this paper, to avoid the issues of natural RGB images, we propose a novel facial expression recognition framework in which the input only relies on a single depth image and synthesizes an RGB face image under a unified imaging situation from a depth face image input. Then, an attention-based CNN with facial landmarks for facial expression recognition is proposed.

References

1. Yang, H., Yin, L.: CNN based 3D facial expression recognition using masking and landmark features. In: 2017 Seventh International Conference on Affective Computing and Intelligent Interaction (ACII), pp. 556–560. IEEE, October 2017
2. Li, H., Sun, J., Wang, D., Xu, Z., Chen, L.: Deep representation of facial geometric and photometric attributes for automatic 3D facial expression recognition. arXiv preprint arXiv:1511.03015 (2015)
3. Oyedotun, O.K., Demisse, G., El Rahman Shabayek, A., Aouada, D., Ottersten, B.: Facial expression recognition via joint deep learning of RGB-depth map latent representations. In: Proceedings of the IEEE International Conference on Computer Vision, pp. 3161–3168 (2017)

4. Jan, A., Ding, H., Meng, H., Chen, L., Li, H.: Accurate facial parts localization and deep learning for 3D facial expression recognition. In: 2018 13th IEEE International Conference on Automatic Face & Gesture Recognition (FG 2018), pp. 466–472. IEEE, May 2018

5. Zhu, K., Du, Z., Li, W., Huang, D., Wang, Y., Chen, L.: Discriminative attention-based convolutional neural network for 3D facial expression recognition. In: 2019 14th IEEE International Conference on Automatic Face & Gesture Recognition (FG 2019), pp. 1–8. IEEE, May 2019

6. Zhang, F., Zhang, T., Mao, Q., Xu, C.: Joint pose and expression modeling for facial expression recognition. In: Proceedings of the IEEE Conference on Computer Vision and Pattern Recognition, pp. 3359–3368 (2018)

7. Yang, H., Ciftci, U., Yin, L.: Facial expression recognition by de-expression residue learning. In: Proceedings of the IEEE Conference on Computer Vision and Pattern Recognition, pp. 2168–2177 (2018)

8. Yang, H., Zhang, Z., Yin, L.: Identity-adaptive facial expression recognition through expression regeneration using conditional generative adversarial networks. In: 2018 13th IEEE International Conference on Automatic Face & Gesture Recognition (FG 2018), pp. 294–301. IEEE, May 2018

9. Ali, K., Hughes, C.E.: Facial expression recognition using disentangled adversarial learning. arXiv preprint arXiv:1909.13135 (2019)

10. Cai, J., Meng, Z., Khan, A.S., Li, Z., O'Reilly, J., Tong, Y.: Identity-free facial expression recognition using conditional generative adversarial network. arXiv preprint arXiv:1903.08051 (2019)

11. Isola, P., Zhu, J.Y., Zhou, T., Efros, A.A.: Image-to-image translation with conditional adversarial networks. In: Proceedings of the IEEE Conference on Computer Vision and Pattern Recognition, pp. 1125–1134 (2017)

12. Mian, A., Bennamoun, M., Owens, R.: Automatic 3D face detection, normalization and recognition. In: Third International Symposium on 3D Data Processing, Visualization, and Transmission (3DPVT 2006), pp. 735–742. IEEE, June 2006

13. Savran, A., et al.: Bosphorus database for 3D face analysis. In: Schouten, B., Juul, N.C., Drygajlo, A., Tistarelli, M. (eds.) BioID 2008. LNCS, vol. 5372, pp. 47–56. Springer, Heidelberg (2008). https://doi.org/10.1007/978-3-540-89991-4_6

14. He, K., Zhang, X., Ren, S., Sun, J.: Deep residual learning for image recognition. In: 2016 IEEE Conference on Computer Vision and Pattern Recognition (CVPR). IEEE Computer Society (2016)

15. Ioffe, S., Szegedy, C.: Batch normalization: accelerating deep network training by reducing internal covariate shift (2015)

16. Yin, L., Wei, X., Sun, Y., Wang, J., Rosato, M.J.: A 3D facial expression database for facial behavior research. In: 7th International Conference on Automatic Face and Gesture Recognition, FGR 2006. IEEE (2006)

17. Li, H., Chen, L., Huang, D., Wang, Y., Morvan, J.M.: 3D facial expression recognition via multiple kernel learning of multi-scale local normal patterns. In: Proceedings of the 21st International Conference on Pattern Recognition (ICPR2012), pp. 2577–2580. IEEE, November 2012

18. Yang, X., Huang, D., Wang, Y., Chen, L.: Automatic 3D facial expression recognition using geometric scattering representation. In: 2015 11th IEEE International Conference and Workshops on Automatic Face and Gesture Recognition (FG). IEEE (2015)

19. Li, H., Sun, J., Xu, Z., Chen, L.: Multimodal 2D+ 3D facial expression recognition with deep fusion convolutional neural network. IEEE Trans. Multimed. **19**(12), 2816–2831 (2017)
20. Fu, Y., Ruan, Q., Luo, Z., Jin, Y., An, G., Wan, J.: FERLrTc: 2D+3D facial expression recognition via low-rank tensor completion. Signal Process. **161**, 74–88 (2019)

Fast and Accurate Hand-Raising Gesture Detection in Classroom

Tao Liu, Fei Jiang$^{(\boxtimes)}$, and Ruimin Shen

Department of Computer Science and Engineering, Shanghai Jiao Tong University,
Shanghai, China
{liutaw,jiangf,rmshen}@sjtu.edu.cn

Abstract. This paper proposes a fast and accurate method for hand-raising gesture detection in classrooms. Our method is based on a one-stage detector, CenterNet, which significantly reduces the inference time. Meanwhile, we design three mechanisms to improve the performance. Firstly, we propose a novel suppression loss to prevent easy and hard examples from overwhelming the training process. Secondly, we adopt a deep layer aggregation network to fuse semantic and spatial representation, which is effective for detecting tiny gestures. Thirdly, due to less variation in aspect ratios, we only regress single width property to predict whole bounding box. Thus achieving a more accurate result. Experiments show that our method achieves 91.4% mAP on our hand-raising dataset and runs at 26 FPS, 6.7× faster than the two-stage ones.

Keywords: Hand-raising detection · CenterNet · Suppression loss

1 Introduction

The current hand-raising detection algorithms are mainly solved as object detection tasks based on a large-scale real dataset. However, 257ms inference time for each frame hinders its wide applications [11]. In this paper, we design a fast and accurate hand-raising detector for hand-raising gesture detection. Recently, one-stage detection-based algorithms like CornerNet [3] and CenterNet [14] have been gaining more attention due to their high inference speed. However, one-stage detectors encounter a severe easy-hard imbalance problem [8], which still have a performance gap compared with the two-stage ones.

The real hand-raising dataset encounters various hard examples: the obstruction of environments like curtain and mop stick, and the unconscious activities of students, as shown in Fig. 1(c). Those examples are quite similar to hand-raising gestures, which aggravate the imbalance problem. Several solutions are proposed to solve the above imbalance problem. Focal Loss [6] and GHM Loss [4] alleviate

---

F. Jiang—The work was supported by National Nature Science of Science and Technology (No. 61671290), China Postdoctoral Science Foundation (No. 2018M642019), Shanghai Municipal Commission of Economy and Information (No. 2018-RGZN-02052).

H. Yang et al. (Eds.): ICONIP 2020, CCIS 1332, pp. 232–239, 2020.
https://doi.org/10.1007/978-3-030-63820-7_26

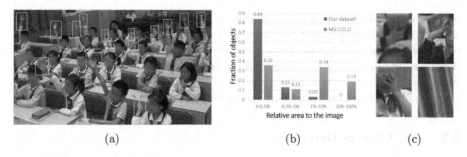

Fig. 1. Hand-raising gesture detection. (a) Examples of hand-raising gestures. (b) Fraction of objects vs. Relative area to the image. (c) Various hard examples including unconscious behaviors of students and backgrounds (curtain).

such problem from adjusted classification losses. Motivated by GHM loss [4], which also solves the imbalance problem from the aspect of regression loss, we propose a novel loss to suppress hard and easy examples simultaneously.

Besides, our hand-raising dataset contains plenty of tiny ones where nearly 84% of the objects occupy less than 0.5% area of the whole image, as shown in Fig. 1(b). Deep layer aggregation (DLA) [12] network uses a hierarchical and an iterative structure to fuse semantic and spatial representation, which performs well in detecting tiny objects. Such network is also incorporated into our detector.

Motivated by the fixed aspect ratio used in pedestrian detection tasks [2,13], we calculate the aspect ratio and only regress the width property. The heights can be automatically generated by the aspect ratio. Experimental results shows that more accurate bounding boxes are obtained. Our main contributions are summarized as follows:

(1) We propose a novel regression loss called suppression loss to alleviate the imbalance problem in the real hand-raising dataset.
(2) We utilize a deep layer aggregation network to detect tiny hand-raising gestures.
(3) We get more accurate bounding boxes by regressing only width with a fixed aspect ratio.
(4) Our method achieves 91.4% mAP on the real hand-raising dataset with 26 FPS inference speed, which can satisfy the practical use.

2 Related Works

We briefly introduce the related works on the imbalance problem, small objects detection method, and single property prediction for specific detection tasks.

2.1 Imbalance Problems of Object Detection Algorithm

Comparing with a fixed region proposal ratio in two-stage detectors, one-stage detectors need to enumerate all possible locations across the whole image. Therefore, one-stage detectors suffer from a severe easy-hard imbalance problem. Balanced L1 Loss [9] rebalances easy and hard examples by improving the gradient of easy examples and clips the large gradients produced by outliers. GHM Loss [4] down-weights both easy examples and outliers simultaneously. Inspired by previous methods, we down-weight gradients of easy and hard examples to prevent those examples from overwhelming the training process.

2.2 Tiny Objects Detection

Detecting objects in small size is still a challenge. Several methods are proposed. Feature Pyramid Network (FPN) [5] uses a bottom-up and top-down structure to fuse different levels of features, which improves the performance in detecting small and medium-sized objects. Deep layer aggregation (DLA) [12] uses iterative deep aggregation (IDA) and hierarchical deep aggregation (HDA) structure to fuse both semantic and spatial representation. The IDA module of DLA iteratively integrates layers from the shallowest to the deepest, and brings semantic information from deep layers to shallower layers. This iterative architecture makes DLA detect tiny objects well.

2.3 Single Property Prediction for Specific Detection Tasks

In object detection tasks, the width and height of a bounding box need to be predicted simultaneously due to the various aspect ratios of a single object from different angles. But for some specific tasks like pedestrian and our hand-raising detection, the aspect ratio of bounding boxes is fixed. Pedestrian detection algorithms like CSP [7] only predict the height and multiply by a fixed aspect ratio 0.41 to get the width. For the hand-raising dataset, the ratio of length to width is also fixed. Therefore, we only predict the width value.

3   Our Approach

We first introduce the overall architecture of the proposed algorithm for hand-raising detection. Then we illustrate three designed strategies in detail.

3.1   Overall Architecture

The overall architecture is shown in Fig. 2. To speed up the inference, our architecture is based on CenterNet [14], a one-stage detector. Firstly, we change the regression loss function to our suppression loss, which prevents both easy and hard samples from dominating the training process. Secondly, we use DLA [12] as the backbone to iteratively bring semantic information to different stages. Thirdly, we change the detection head to only regress the value of width. In the inference stage, the height of the bounding box is directly generated by a prior aspect ratio parameter for more accurate locating.

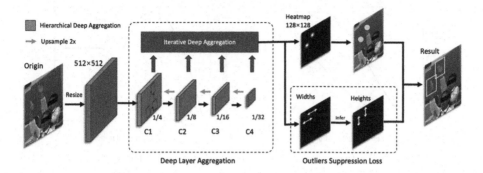

Fig. 2. Overall architecture of our method. Our method is based on CenterNet, a one-stage detector. Then we adopt DLA as the backbone and modify the detection head to a single branch which only regresses the width. The newly proposed suppression loss is added to improve performance.

3.2 Suppression Loss

Followed by CenterNet [14], we use a multi-task loss to solve classification and localization problems simultaneously:

$$L_{det} = L_{center} + \lambda_{size}L_{size} + \lambda_{off}L_{off} \tag{1}$$

The classification loss, L_{center}, is Focal loss [6]. L_{size} and L_{off} are localization losses to regress center points offsets, width and height. λ_{size} and λ_{off} are tuned weights of localization loss.

For regression loss, we design a novel loss function as follows:

$$L(\delta) = \begin{cases} -2|\delta|^3 + 3\delta^2, & -1 < \delta < 1 \\ 1, & \text{else} \end{cases} \tag{2}$$

Its corresponding gradient function is derived as:

$$L'(\delta) = \begin{cases} -6\delta^2 + 6\delta, & 0 < \delta < 1 \\ 6\delta^2 + 6\delta, & -1 < \delta < 0 \\ 0, & \text{else} \end{cases} \tag{3}$$

where δ is the deviation between detection and ground truth coordinates. The comparison with Smooth L1 is shown in Fig. 3. The errors (x-axis) closing to zero are defined as easy examples while larger than one as hard examples. Easy examples are in the majority, which are usually backgrounds and easy to determine but contribute little to the convergence of the model. The hard examples stay stable during the training process, which significantly hinders the generalization of a model. By designing a convex function, we suppress both easy and hard examples' gradients in a uniform way as shown in Fig. 3(b).

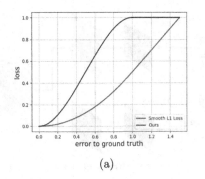 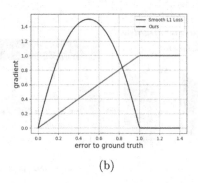

(a)   (b)

Fig. 3. Comparison of our loss and gradient function to Smooth L1 loss. Our loss function suppresses easy and hard examples simultaneously.

3.3 Deep Layer Aggregation

DLA [12] is adopted as the backbone to extract both semantic and spatial features, which has two basic structures: iterative deep aggregation (IDA) and hierarchical deep aggregation (HDA). HDA merges channels and depths using a tree structure to fuse semantic information for each stage. IDA iteratively merge scales and resolutions across different stages using projection and upsampling operations. Since 95% examples in our hand-raising datasets occupy less than 1% area to the whole image, DLA is efficient to detect those tiny objects.

3.4 Single Property Prediction Structure

Most of the detection tasks regress two properties: height and width, while our approach only regresses one property: height or width. In inference time, another property is directly calculated by multiplying a ratio parameter. In our hand-raising dataset, regressing width is better than height, which may be attributed to less horizontal labeling noise. Inspired by [10], we use k-means clustering with the Intersection over Union (IoU) metric to calculate the anchor box. The anchor box value is [113,78] with a ratio value 1.45.

4   Experiment Results

We have conducted extensive experiments on the real hand-raising datasets. The widely used evaluation criterion, mAP with IoU 0.5, for detection tasks is adopted. All experiments were tested on NVIDIA RTX-2080TI.

4.1   Our Hand-Raising Dataset

Our dataset contains 22k images with 76k bounding box annotations. All photos were labeled from 1K (1920 × 1080) cameras in real classrooms from primary and middle schools in China. We randomly divide our dataset into two parts: 80% of images for training and the rest for testing. During training, we use data augmentation of random shifting, cropping, and scaling.

Table 1. Backbone network comparison

Backbone	FPS	MACs(G)	Params(M)	mAP(%)
ResNet-101	**26**	**16**	48.67	78.0
Hourglass	14	46	191.24	82.4
DLA-34	**26**	25	**20.17**	**88.9**

4.2 Our Method vs. Previous Hand-Raising Detector

We compare our method with a previous hand-raising method [11] based on R-FCN [1], a typical two-stage detector. This improved R-FCN method spends 257 ms for each frame and gets 90.0% mAP. Our proposed method is based on CenterNet, a one-stage detector, which only costs 38 ms for each frame, 6.7× faster than the previous based method. Moreover, our method achieves 91.4% mAP.

4.3 Deep Layer Aggregation vs. Other Backbones

We conduct several different backbones to balance precision and speed, which is often negatively correlated. Table 1 shows the details of our experiment. The FPS (frames per second) of ResNet-101 and DLA-34 are more than 20, while Hourglass only 14. Comparing with the ResNet-101 backbone, DLA-34 improves mAP significantly with fewer parameters. The number of multiply and accumulate operations (MACs) is a measurement to evaluate the computation complexity. The MACs of DLA-34 is similar to ResNet-101 and nearly 46% less than the Hourglass one. Therefore, DLA-34 is utilized as the basic backbone.

4.4 Suppression Loss vs. Other Regression Losses

We conduct several experiments to compare our loss function to L1 Loss and Smooth L1 Loss. We use the L1 Loss function and get an mAP of 88.9%. If we change the loss function to Smooth L1 loss and GHM-R loss, the result gets 88.7% and 89.4% separately. When changing the loss function to our suppression loss, we get an improvement in mAP by 2% compared with Smooth L1 loss.

4.5 Single vs. Original Property Prediction

We compare single property prediction with original width-height prediction. Firstly, to find the optimal aspect ratio, we use k-means clustering with IoU metric [10] to calculate the aspect ratio of bounding boxes in our hand-raising datasets. The clustering result of the height-width value is [113,78], which has a fixed aspect ratio 1.45. Then we modify the architecture of CenterNet and only predict the width or height. We find that only adding a width channel achieves more accurate results. Predicting only height can obtain 0.1% improvements, while 0.4% improvements with width prediction only. In the inference stage, the width value is directly multiplied by the aspect ratio 1.45 to get the height value.

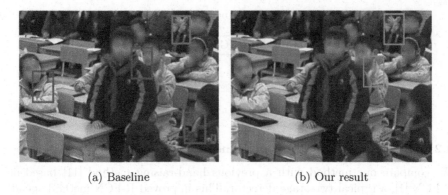

(a) Baseline   (b) Our result

Fig. 4. Experiment results. Detection results comparison of baseline (a) and our algorithm (b). Image (a) has detected several false positives marked with red bounding boxes. Image (b) is the result of our proposed method, which shows that our method can avoid false-positive examples (Color figure online)

Table 2. Overall improvement in summary

	Ablations				Ours
CenterNet (ResNet)	✓				
CenterNet (DLA)		✓	✓	✓	✓
Single-width head			✓		✓
Outliers suppression loss				✓	✓
mAP(%)	78.0	88.9	89.3	90.7	**91.4**

4.6 Overall Improvement

Table 2 shows all experiments in summary. Our proposed method gets a final mAP of 91.4%, which significantly improves by 13.4% compared to the baseline. Figure 4 shows two detection results from real classrooms.

5 Conclusion

We propose an improved one-stage detector based on CenterNet to detect hand-raising in classrooms. One-stage detectors are fast but poor in performance. Therefore, we offer three ways to improve performance. Suppression loss is proposed to prevent easy and hard examples from overwhelming the training process. Then DLA network is adopted to detect tiny hand-raising gestures. Moreover, we only predict the width value with a fixed aspect ratio. Experiments show that our classroom hand-raising detection is both fast and accurate.

References

1. Dai, J., Li, Y., He, K., Sun, J.: R-FCN: object detection via region-based fully convolutional networks. In: Advances in Neural Information Processing Systems, pp. 379–387 (2016)
2. Dollár, P., Wojek, C., Schiele, B., Perona, P.: Pedestrian detection: a benchmark (2009)
3. Law, H., Deng, J.: CornerNet: detecting objects as paired keypoints. In: Ferrari, V., Hebert, M., Sminchisescu, C., Weiss, Y. (eds.) Computer Vision – ECCV 2018. LNCS, vol. 11218, pp. 765–781. Springer, Cham (2018). https://doi.org/10.1007/978-3-030-01264-9_45
4. Li, B., Liu, Y., Wang, X.: Gradient harmonized single-stage detector. In: Proceedings of the AAAI Conference on Artificial Intelligence, vol. 33, pp. 8577–8584 (2019)
5. Lin, T.Y., Dollár, P., Girshick, R., He, K., Hariharan, B., Belongie, S.: Feature pyramid networks for object detection. In: Proceedings of the IEEE Conference on Computer Vision and Pattern Recognition, pp. 2117–2125 (2017)
6. Lin, T.Y., Goyal, P., Girshick, R., He, K., Dollár, P.: Focal loss for dense object detection. In: Proceedings of the IEEE International Conference on Computer Vision, pp. 2980–2988 (2017)
7. Liu, W., Liao, S., Ren, W., Hu, W., Yu, Y.: High-level semantic feature detection: a new perspective for pedestrian detection. In: Proceedings of the IEEE Conference on Computer Vision and Pattern Recognition, pp. 5187–5196 (2019)
8. Oksuz, K., Cam, B.C., Kalkan, S., Akbas, E.: Imbalance problems in object detection: A review. arXiv preprint arXiv:1909.00169 (2019)
9. Pang, J., Chen, K., Shi, J., Feng, H., Ouyang, W., Lin, D.: Libra R-CNN: towards balanced learning for object detection. In: Proceedings of the IEEE Conference on Computer Vision and Pattern Recognition, pp. 821–830 (2019)
10. Redmon, J., Farhadi, A.: Yolov3: An incremental improvement. arXiv preprint arXiv:1804.02767 (2018)
11. Si, J., Lin, J., Jiang, F., Shen, R.: Hand-raising gesture detection in real classrooms using improved r-fcn. Neurocomputing (2019)
12. Yu, F., Wang, D., Shelhamer, E., Darrell, T.: Deep layer aggregation. In: Proceedings of the IEEE Conference on Computer Vision and Pattern Recognition, pp. 2403–2412 (2018)
13. Zhang, S., Benenson, R., Schiele, B.: Citypersons: a diverse dataset for pedestrian detection. In: Proceedings of the IEEE Conference on Computer Vision and Pattern Recognition, pp. 3213–3221 (2017)
14. Zhou, X., Wang, D., Krähenbühl, P.: Objects as points. arXiv preprint arXiv:1904.07850 (2019)

Identifying Anger Veracity Using Neural Network and Long-Short Term Memory with Bimodal Distribution Removal

Rouyi Jin$^{(\boxtimes)}$, Xuanying Zhu, and Yeu-Shin Fu

Research School of Computer Science, Australian National University, Canberra,
ACT 2600, Australia
{rouyi.jin,xuanying.zhu,guyver.fu}@anu.edu.au

Abstract. Anger is an important emotion in social interactions. People can be angry from the feeling, or by acting, with an aim to turn situations to their advantage. With advances in affective computing, machine learning based approaches make it possible to identify veracity of anger through physiological signals of observers. In this paper, we examine time-series pupillary responses of observers viewing genuine and acted anger stimuli. A Fully-Connected Neural Network (FCNN) and an Long-Short Term Memory (LSTM) are trained using pre-processed pupillary responses to classify genuine anger and acted anger expressed from the stimuli. We also adopt the Bimodal Distribution Removal (BDR) technique to remove noise from the dataset. We find that both FCNN and LSTM can recognise veracity of anger with an accuracy of 79.7% and 89.7% respectively. The use of BDR is beneficial in providing an early stopping for LSTM to avoid overfitting and improve efficiency.

Keywords: Anger detection · Artificial neural network · Bimodal Distribution Removal · Classification · Deep learning · LSTM · Physiological signals · Pupillary response

1 Introduction

Emotions are complex internal states that lead to physical and physiological changes of human beings which can subsequently affect their behaviours, reactions and thoughts [5]. One of the most common emotions, anger, is often considered as an intense and most destructive emotion [2]. Since people are able to express emotions even when they are not genuinely feeling the emotions, it is important to recognise the veracity of these emotions. It is been found in [1,3] that the recognition rate was significantly improved when computation approaches were adopted. Therefore, this study aims to examine if veracity of anger can be identified better using computational approaches.

In 2008, Kim and André [6] found that physiological signals of observers who viewed the expression of an emotion are valid indicators of emotions expressed by others. More recently, Hossain and Gedeon [3] used observers physiological

© Springer Nature Switzerland AG 2020
H. Yang et al. (Eds.): ICONIP 2020, CCIS 1332, pp. 240–247, 2020.
https://doi.org/10.1007/978-3-030-63820-7_27

signals to classify the real and posed smiles by training a Fully Connected Neural Network (FCNN) which achieved a high accuracy of 93.7%. Chen et al. [1] conducted an anger detection experiment by studying the pupillary responses from those who perceive the genuine or the acted anger. A high accuracy of 95% was obtained using an FCNN trained with statistical pupillary features. However, the models provided in [1,3] require manual feature extraction, which could be time consuming. In this paper, we explore whether a Long-Short Term Memory (LSTM) model taking time-series raw pupillary signal is able to identify anger veracity. As a comparison, we also train a FCNN with different parameter setting using pupillary features. We apply Mini-batch method to avoid local minimum and use 5-fold cross-validation to fully use the dataset. Moreover, the Bimodal Distribution Removal (BDR) technique, an outlier detection algorithm, is implemented, so that some outliers can be removed without further influence in the training. Lastly, the effectiveness of BDR on both networks is demonstrated.

2   Methods

The recognition of genuine and acted anger is formulated into a time series classification task and we explore this problem with FCNN and LSTM with different settings. We aim to figure out the effectiveness of these networks and the influence of removing outliers during training. A detailed network architecture is shown in Fig. 1. The raw data was preprocessed before normalization. When training the model, we applied BDR as an outlier detection technique, which provides an early stopping of the training process when the loss function converges.

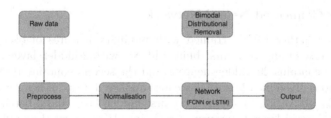

Fig. 1. The overall architecture of the networks implemented in anger detection

2.1   Dataset Description

We used a dataset collected in [1], which recorded left and right pupillary diameters on 22 participants watching videos of individuals expressing genuine and acted anger. Pupillary diameters were sampled at 60 Hz. There are 20 videos in total, half of which expressed genuine anger and the other half displayed acted anger. Among the 22 observer participants, 15 were females and 7 were males. Two were excluded due to the faulty of eye tracker and glasses wearers with intermittent data loss [1].

To train our FCNN, we used six features extracted by the raw pupillary diameters described in [3]: mean and standard deviation of the pupillary diameter of both eyes, means of the absolute values of the first and second differences of the pupillary diameter of both eyes, and Principle Component Analysis of the first and the second differences. To train LSTM, we used the raw pupillary diameters for two eyes. There were 10 samples less as these videos had a number of short term data recording errors during the experiment, so it was possible to calculate statistical features but the sequence was too broken up for meaningful use as a sequence of signals.

2.2 Data Preprocessing

Since the raw data used in our LSTM have varying lengths due to different durations of videos, we applied zero padding to shorter sessions to keep each sequence equal in length. The mean pupillary diameter of left and right eyes is used. However, it was noticed that sometimes only the left eye was recorded while sometimes only the right eye was recorded. We used the left data to fill the right and vice versa because there is a large difference in pupillary diameter among participants from multicultural background and the data collected from the same person in the meantime should not lead to large difference.

All the raw data are numerical, enabling the normalization process, which reduces the effect of data in different ranges. We adopted the z-score normalization, which considers the influence from outliers but does not produce with the exact same scale.

2.3 Fully Connected Neural Network

To examine whether FCNN trained with pupillary features of observers can identify veracity of anger, we first built a FCNN with 2 hidden layers. The first hidden layer contains 20 hidden neurons and the second contains 10. Following the suggestions given in [12] and [4], we also applied a dropout layer with rate = 0.15 after the activation function of the first hidden layer and a batch norm for the fully connected layer to prevent overfitting. We trained the model for 500 epochs, where the error was converged.

2.4 Long-Short Term Memory (LSTM)

Our data is eye tracking data and the changes of pupillary diameter are considered to be closely related to the time of the video. The raw data are collected in a time series, which indicates the data has dependencies. Thus, a recurrent neural network should be considered. However, it is noticed that the dimension of data is large and RNN is involved in gradient vanishing and exploding problem [10]. An LSTM can greatly avoid these issues and therefore considered as a suitable model for this anger detection classification problem.

In our LSTM model, we applied one hidden layer and 35 hidden dimensions for the network. Considering the largest input has a length of 186, and the time interval is $\frac{1}{60}$ s, the input size was set as 31. In this model, we used a 4 batch size and trained the model for 100 epochs because it converges quickly.

2.5 Loss Function and Optimizer

Loss function calculates the difference between the expected output and the predicted result. [8] mentioned that cross-entropy is usually used in classification tasks and therefore, we applied cross-entropy in both models.

An optimizer is closely tied with the loss function to update the model in response to the output of the loss function. Adam was adopted as our optimizer because it only requires the first-order derivative that cost much less memory [7]. The learning rate was set as 0.01.

2.6 Bimodal Distribution Removal Technique

Bimodal distribution removal (BDR) is one of the methods that can clean up noisy training sets during the training and provide a halting criterion to prevent overfitting [11]. The idea of BDR comes from the frequency distributions of errors for all the training patterns and usually there will be a large variance in the beginning [11]. With the training moves on, most of the errors drop very quickly while a small amount of the errors remain, which are considered as outliers.

The BDR is not started until the normalised variance of errors over the training set is below 0.1. Then we take those data points whose error has a value higher than the average error (δ_{ts}) as a subset and calculate the mean (δ_{ss}) and the standard deviation (σ_{ss}) of this subset. The criterion of permanently remove the recognized noisy data is the patterns from the subset with an error $\geq \delta_{ss} + \alpha\sigma_{ss}$ where α is in a closed interval between 0 and 1. The removal is repeated every 50 training epochs until the normalised variance of errors is less than 0.01. And thus the whole training will be halted [11].

2.7 5-Fold Cross-Validation and Mini-Batch

K-fold validation enables each data point to have a chance to be validated against through crossing over the training set and validation sets in a successive mode [9]. In this paper, 5-fold cross-validation is applied to both networks.

Mini-batch avoids local minima and enables a more computationally efficient process with robust convergence. Thus, it is used in both models.

3 Results and Discussion

This section firstly evaluates a FCNN trained on the same feature selected by [1] but with different parameters. Then an LSTM model is used to train the raw data. Lastly we will discuss the effectiveness of the BDR on FCNN and LSTM.

3.1   Evaluation of FCNN

As can be seen from Table 1, on average FCNN obtained an accuracy of 63.7% and F1-score of 58.9% over 10 runs while adding mini-batch method gives an accuracy and F1-Score at 79.7% and 78.7% respectively.

Table 1. Accuracy and F1-score for FCNN and FCNN with Mini-Batch

Model	Accuracy	F1-Score	Standard deviation of accuracy
FCNN	63.7%	58.9%	0.03
FCNN + Mini-batch	79.7%	78.7%	0.03

In order to analyse the difference statistically, we conducted two paired sample t-test on the accuracy and F1-Score. This test is to analyse the differences of the average accuracy and F1-Score between FCNN and FCNN + Mini-batch. The p-values were both smaller than 0.001, indicating that the improvement achieved using Mini-Batch was statistically significant.

The noteworthy improvement from mini-batch can be explained by the sufficient avoidance of local minimum. The normal training method can be stuck in a local minimal and some noisy gradients are required to jump out of a local minimum of the loss function and heading to the global minimum.

3.2   Evaluation of LSTM

As shown in Table 2, the average accuracy and F1-Score of LSTM are 89.7% and 91.5% respectively. It means the LSTM model can identify the genuine and acted anger at 89.7% correct. It is apparent that the LSTM has a remarkable improvement with an accuracy of around 10% and 12% F1-Score increment on average compared with FCNN. LSTM does not only increase the accuracy and f1 score, but also stabilizes the evaluation, because the standard deviation of the accuracy in FCNN is 0.03 while in LSTM, it is 0.007.

Two paired sample t-test on the accuracy and F1-Score were conducted to analyse whether there is a large difference between the two models. The p-values were both smaller than 0.001, indicating that LSTM performances statistically significantly better than FCNN with Mini-batch. The reason for this rapid increase can be the dependencies of the input playing an important role in training.

3.3   Importance of BDR

FCNN and BDR. As demonstrated in Table 3, in FCNN, the use of BDR technique does not improve the accuracy. On the contrary, the result is reduced by 5%, at the rate of 75.1%. Additionally, no early stopping is observed during the experiments in spite of the converged error. Both of the results reject the expectation that the result would be improved while the training would be stopped once the loss function is converged. However, the BDR did remove some noisy data points in this model.

Table 2. Accuracy and F1-score for FCNN with Mini-Batch and LSTM

Model	Accuracy	F1-Score	Standard deviation of accuracy
FCNN + Mini-batch	79.7%	78.7%	0.03
LSTM	89.7%	91.5%	0.007

As can be seen in Fig. 2, in the early stages of FCNN, the FCNN has a bimodal distribution as [11] stated that the BDR is employed in a training set whose error distribution in the early training (0–100 epochs) is almost bimodal. Figure 3 presented the error distribution at epoch 450 and showed that the error distribution after training was still bimodal, but the second peak is much smaller than that in Fig. 2, indicating the BDR removes some data points.

To figure out the reasons that BDR is not providing an early stopping, we investigated the variance changes. Variances during the training are always between 0.01 and 0.1 and converges at 0.03, which means that the training will not be halted and the training will always step into outlier detection until the end of training.

Table 3. Accuracy and F1-score for FCNN + Mini-Batch and LSTM with BDR by 5-fold Cross Validation

Model	Accuracy	F1-Score	Standard deviation of accuracy
FCNN + Mini-batch + BDR	75.1%	72.5%	0.02
LSTM + BDR	89.3%	91.1%	0.01

LSTM with BDR. In LSTM, firstly, it is inspected that there is no removal of noisy points during the training process. Secondly, there is no big improvement in accuracy by adding the BDR as shown in Table 3. To further analyse the importance of the BDR, we conducted a t-test on the results achieved by LSTM with and without BDR and the p value was not smaller than 0.01. This indicates statistically BDR does not improve our LSTM in terms of accuracy.

The BDR technique is triggered when the variance is between 0.01 and 0.1. During the evolvement of LSTM, the variance is decreasing overall during the training until the error is converged after about 30 epochs, where the variance is very close to 0 and the training is halted.

However, considering the error distribution in the beginning shown in Fig. 4, we did not observe a bimodal distribution. This violates the description in [11]. Though in the end there are a few peaks in the error distribution, the error is converged and those small peaks do not lead to large variance (Fig. 5).

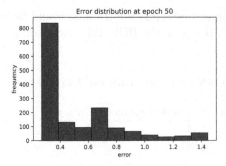

Fig. 2. Error Distribution at epoch 50 when training with FCNN

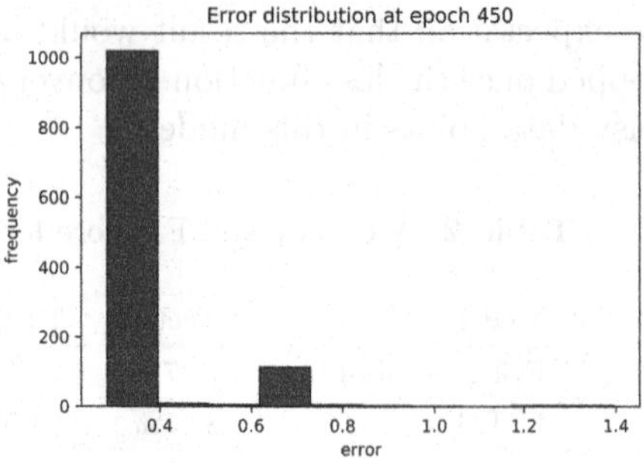

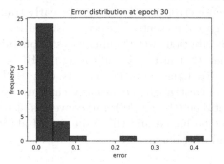

Fig. 3. Error Distribution at epoch 450 when training with FCNN

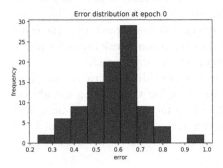

Fig. 4. Error Distribution at epoch 0 when training with LSTM

Fig. 5. Error Distribution at epoch 30 when training with LSTM

4   Conclusion and Future Work

This paper evaluates the effectiveness of a two-hidden layer FCNN and a LSTM network with the help of an outlier detection technique named BDR in a time series classification task. We choose the 5-fold cross-validation to make the results more generalised and also determine whether the mini-batch would improve the overall performance. It is shown that LSTM performs much better than the FCNN. Lastly, we concentrate on the performance of BDR.

The mini-batch is proved to be advantageous in improving the accuracy. From the comparisons of two networks, LSTM stands out with a high accuracy at 90%. However, compared with the higher accuracy (95%) in previous research [1], more techniques can be employed to improve the current accuracy in the future. For example, the 0 padding could be replaced by packing the padded sequence where the actual length of data is used. Moreover, input dimension could be changed to from the mean (1-D) to (left, right) (2-D).

In the last experiment, BDR does not show any accuracy enhancement in both models. It removes some noisy data points in FCNN but no early stopping is observed. Applying LSTM to eye tracking data with BDR leads to more efficient training while not affecting the accuracy. In the future, more complicated model can be trained faster for better accuracy hence better anger detection.

References

1. Chen, L., Gedeon, T., Hossain, Md.Z., Caldwell, S.: Are you really angry? Detecting emotion veracity as a proposed tool for interaction. In: Proceedings of the 29th Australian Conference on Computer-Human Interaction, OZCHI 2017, pp. 412–416. Association for Computing Machinery, New York (2017)
2. Ellis, A.: Anger: How to Live with and Without It. Hachette, UK (2019)
3. Hossain, Md.Z., Gedeon, T.: Classifying posed and real smiles from observers' peripheral physiology. In: Proceedings of the 11th EAI International Conference on Pervasive Computing Technologies for Healthcare, PervasiveHealth 2017, pp. 460–463. Association for Computing Machinery, New York (2017)
4. Ioffe, S., Szegedy, C.: Batch normalization: accelerating deep network training by reducing internal covariate shift. arXiv preprint arXiv:1502.03167 (2015)
5. Kim, C.J., Chang, M.: Actual emotion and false emotion classification by physiological signal. In: 2015 8th International Conference on Signal Processing, Image Processing and Pattern Recognition (SIP), pp. 21–24 (2015)
6. Kim, J., André, E.: Emotion recognition based on physiological changes in music listening. IEEE Trans. Pattern Anal. Mach. Intell. **30**(12), 2067–2083 (2008)
7. Kingma, D.P., Ba, J.: Adam: a method for stochastic optimization. arXiv preprint arXiv:1412.6980 (2014)
8. Kline, M., Berardi, L.: Revisiting squared-error and cross-entropy functions for training neural network classifiers. Neural Comput. Appl. **14**(4), 310–318 (2005)
9. Refaeilzadeh, P., Tang, L., Liu, H.: Cross-validation **5**, 532–538 (2009)
10. Santamaria-Granados, L., Munoz-Organero, M., Ramirez-González, G., Abdulhay, E., Arunkumar, N.: Using deep convolutional neural network for emotion detection on a physiological signals dataset (amigos). IEEE Access **7**, 57–67 (2019)
11. Slade, P., Gedeon, T.D.: Bimodal distribution removal. In: Mira, J., Cabestany, J., Prieto, A. (eds.) IWANN 1993. LNCS, vol. 686, pp. 249–254. Springer, Heidelberg (1993). https://doi.org/10.1007/3-540-56798-4_155
12. Srivastava, N., Hinton, G., Krizhevsky, A., Sutskever, I., Salakhutdinov, R.: Dropout: a simple way to prevent neural networks from overfitting. J. Mach. Learn. Res. **15**(1), 1929–1958 (2014)

Learning and Distillating the Internal Relationship of Motion Features in Action Recognition

Lu Lu, Siyuan Li, Niannian Chen[✉], Lin Gao, Yong Fan, Yong Jiang, and Ling Wu

Southwest University of Science and Technology, Mianyang, China
chenniannian@swust.edu.cn

Abstract. In the field of video-based action recognition, a majority of advanced approaches train a two-stream architecture in which an appearance stream for images and a motion stream for optical flow frames. Due to the considerable computation cost of optical flow and high inference latency of the two-stream method, knowledge distillation is introduced to efficiently capture two-stream representation while only inputting RGB images. Following this technique, this paper proposes a novel distillation learning strategy to sufficiently learn and mimic the representation of the motion stream. Besides, we propose a lightweight attention-based fusion module to uniformly exploit both appearance and motion information. Experiments illustrate that the proposed distillation strategy and fusion module achieve better performance over the baseline technique, and our proposal outperforms the known state-of-art approaches in terms of single-stream and traditional two-stream methods.

Keywords: Action recognition · Knowledge distillation · Temporal modeling · 3D Convolution

1 Introduction

With the advent of convolutional neural networks (CNN) [11], great progress has been made in the research field of activity understanding [14]. Generally, video-based activity understanding is to analyze, recognize, and label the human movements appearing in existing videos. Through training the neural networks with large video datasets [7,10] and the technologies of transfer learning, the CNN-based approaches achieve superior generalization in the task of action recognition. At present, the popular action recognition approaches are mainly divided into two categories: (1) Two-stream Convolutional Networks [15,19] , and (2) Convolutional 3D Network (C3D) [12,21].

In this paper, we also train a dual-action model that only accepts RGB images but generates some feature representation similar to those obtained by a trained motion stream network. Our research denote the dual-action model as Dual-action Stream (DS). Notably, the Dual-action Stream in our research is optimized

© Springer Nature Switzerland AG 2020
H. Yang et al. (Eds.): ICONIP 2020, CCIS 1332, pp. 248–255, 2020.
https://doi.org/10.1007/978-3-030-63820-7_28

by mean absolute error of multi-level features and the $L1$ distance between the Gram matrixes of internal feature blocks. This optimization strategy better learns the motion representation among the middle layers of the motion stream. The evaluation on two well-known action recognition dataset demonstrates the proposed method outperforms the other known state-of-art approach.

In summary, this paper mainly has the following contributions:

- This paper proposes a novel knowledge distillation method that better learns the characteristics of the representation of motion stream network and the internal relationship of motion features, and it has double functions.
- We propose an efficient, low-memory attention-based fusion module to fuse the classification scores of two different streams, which can be applied to any action recognition approaches that have two more streams.

2   Simulation of Motion Stream

Inspired one of the distillation methods [2], we propose an optimized distillation solution that utilizes not only the explicit privileged knowledge of motion stream but also distillate latent information from the features of the pre-trained motion stream. Different from the MAR [2] approach, the proposed strategy discovers and mines more comprehensive motion information from the intermediate layers of the optical flow stream, which promotes the student network to learn from the teacher network more effectively. Furthermore, this work proposes a lightweight and effective fusion module to fuse the scores produced by the motion streams and the proposed Dual-action Stream.

2.1   Distilling Motion Information

At the beginning of the training phase, a 3D convolutional network is constructed and trained to classify the category of the inputted flow clips, i.e., the motion stream. Based on the trained motion steam, we can build a similar network to learn the representation and knowledge of the trained motion stream, where the second network acts as the role of the student. The student network inputs and processes RGB clips while mimicking the feature extraction functions of the trained motion stream. According to the past distillation strategies [2], the Motion-Augmented RGB Stream (MAR) adopts Mean Squared Error (MSE) loss to reduce the Euclidean distance of high-level features between the motion stream and targeted stream (i.e., MAR stream). The MSE is formalized as Eq. 1.

$$\mathcal{L}_{\mathrm{MSE}} = \left\| f_{\mathrm{MAR}(n-1)} - f_{\mathrm{FLOW}(n-1)} \right\|_2 \tag{1}$$

where the n represents the number of total layers of the network, $f_{\mathrm{MAR}(n-1)}$ refers to the features produced by the layer before the final linear layer of the motion-augmented stream. $f_{\mathrm{FLOW}(n-1)}$ refers to the feature generated by of $n-1$ layer of optical flow stream.

However, in the MAR approach, the significance of low-level features is ignored, and the latent information is not well exploited. To address these issues, we propose a novel distillation stragegy that comprehensively extracts the knowledge of motion stream into the proposed Dual-action Stream meanwhile learning the knowledge of RGB frames. In the proposed distillation strategy, there are three kinds of loss terms to guide network learning.

2.2 Learning Multi-level Knowledge

According to the literature [22], the deeper layers of neural networks produce high-level global representations, while the shallow layers stand for low-level local features. Therefore, the proposed Dual-action Stream adopts the Mean Absolute Error (MAE) loss to simultaneously learn multi-level features of the motion stream. Intuitively, the proposed distillation stragegy can be graphically shown in Fig. 1. Denote the $f_{DS(i)}$ as i'th layer features of Dual-action Stream network. $f_{FLOW(i)}$ refers to the feature of optical flow stream i'th layer. The multi-level MAE loss term of Dual-action Stream can be expressed as Eq. 2.

$$\mathcal{L}_{\text{MAE}} = \frac{1}{n-1} \sum_{i=1}^{n-1} \left\| f_{DS(i)} - f_{FLOW(i)} \right\|_1 \tag{2}$$

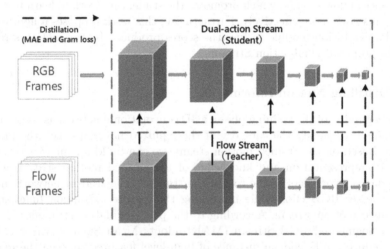

Fig. 1. The distillation strategy operating on multi-level features between the Dual-action Stream and motion stream.

This multi-level loss term distills the different level information of the trained motion stream into our proposed Dual-action Stream network that only operates on RGB frames. Besides, to utilize and exploit the existing appearance input in the training phase, the Dual-action Stream also adopts a categorical cross-entropy loss as the second loss term.

2.3 Learning Internal Relationship of Features

[5,9] adopt the distance of Gramian matrix of features to learn the texture and style of the input RGB images. The Gramian matrix is calculated by the inner product of flattened vectors of multi-channel features. It represents the characteristics and directionality between features, which can be thought of as texture and style information of RGB images in the case of [5,9]. Similar to these methodologies, the proposed work applies the Gramian matrix loss to the intermediate features of motion stream and proposed Dual-action Stream, which aims to capture and learn the characteristics and internal relationship of motion features. Let the C_i denote the channel number of features generated by i'th layer, $\overline{f}_{(i)}$ the flattened vectors of i'th features, the G the function of the inner product. The Gramian loss of Dual-action Stream is described as Eq. 3.

$$\mathcal{L}_G = \sum_i^{n-1} \frac{\left\| G\left(\overline{f}_{\mathrm{DS}(i)}\right) - G\left(\overline{f}_{\mathrm{FLOW}(i)}\right) \right\|_1}{(n-1)C_i T_i H_i W_i} \tag{3}$$

where the T_i, H_i, and W_i respectively refer to the temporal length, height, and width of feature block generated by i'th layer.

To aggregate and exploit the aforementioned useful knowledge, we propose a joint loss to backpropagate the Dual-action Stream network, which yields the network automatically integrate the motion representation and appearance information, and further improve the classification accuracy. The total loss of Dual-action Stream can be mathematically expressed as Eq. 4.

$$\mathcal{L}_{DS} = \mathrm{CrossEntropy}\left(h_{\mathrm{DS}}, y\right) + \alpha(\mathcal{L}_{\mathrm{MAE}} + \mathcal{L}_G) \tag{4}$$

where h_{DS} refers to the class prediction score of Dual-action Stream network, y is the groud truth label of multi-classification, α is a scalar weight that regulates the influence of all motion information. $\mathcal{L}_{\mathrm{MAE}}$ is multi-level MAE loss, $\mathcal{L}_G$ is the loss of gram function.

2.4 Attention-Based Fusion Module

Even though Dual-action Stream can identify the action category by itself, the two-stream prediction still can improve the final classification accuracy. For the exploratory studies and the scenarios where computing resources are not strictly required, the two-stream approach can still be used.

In this paper, we employ a linear neural module to replace the averaging fusion to integrate the scores produced by the trained two streams (e.g., Dual-action Stream and motion stream). The architecture of the proposed fusion module is displayed as Fig. 2.

In the fusion module, the outputs of two streams are concatenated and fed into a twin-layer linear model. After forwarding the two-dimensional output of the linear model (i.e., two full-connect layers) into the softmax layer, the importance weights of each stream are obtained. Finally, the weighted sum of

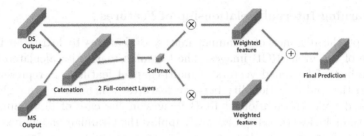

Fig. 2. The architecture of the proposed fusion module, DS output refers to the output of trained Dual-action Stream, the MS means the motion stream.

the scores of two streams is considered as the final prediction score. Because the parameters of motion stream and Dual-action Stream are frozen, through the backpropagating the cross-entropy loss, the designed fusion module can obtain the reasonable weights of each stream by updating the learnable parameters of the linear model.

3 Experiment

In this section, this paper describes the experimental details and results of the Dual-action Stream and the two-stream method with the new fusion module. First of all, we introduce the benchmark datasets and details of the implementation and training process. Afterward, we compare our approaches with the state-of-art approach over the two well-known datasets of action recognition. Finally, we explore the effectiveness of applying different components to our proposed Dual-action Stream.

3.1   The Details of Implementation and Training

In this article, networks are built and trained in the PyTorch framework using four GeForce GTX 1080Ti GPUs with a total of 44G memory. The optical flows that are used for training motion stream and fusion module are generated by the TV-L1 algorithm[13] with the default setting, all the RGB frames are extracted by the raw video at 25 fps, and all these initial features are resized to 256×256.

This paper selects the 3D ResNet-101 network [20] as the backbone of motion stream and Dual-action Stream. Similar to [8], We adopt a mini-batch stochastic gradient descent optimizer to train all models proposed in our approach, and the initial learning rate is set as 0.1, which will reduce by a weight decay of 0.0005 and the momentum of 0.9. In the training process, based on the previous experience [2], this paper set the hyperparameter α as 50 in Eq. 4.

Following [2,8], we conduct and evaluate the proposed approach on models with two kinds of input types, 16 consecutive frames clip (16f-clip) and 64 consecutive frames clip (64f-clip). At the training phase, a random clip of the given length (i.e., 16 or 64) is sampled from the video or optical flows, then the clip is cropped into the region of 112×112 and randomly apply horizontal flipping.

Table 1. The accuracy of experiment over UCF101 and HMDB-51 dataset

Methods	Pre-train dataset	UCF-101			HMDB-51		
		RGB	Flow	RGB+Flow	RGB	Flow	RGB+Flow
Two-stream Network [15]	ImageNet	73	83.7	88	40.5	54.6	59.4
ConvNet fusion [4]	ImageNet	82.6	86.2.7	90.6	47	55.2	58.2
DTPP [24]	ImageNet	89.7	89.1	94.9	61.5	66.3	75
TLE+Two-stream [3]	ImageNet	-	-	95.6	-	-	71.1
ActionVLAD [6]	ImageNet	-	-	92.7	49.8	59.1	66.9
C3D [16]	sports-1M	82.3	-	-	51.6	-	-
C3D [17]	sports-1M	85.8	-	-	54.9	-	-
R(2+1)D [18]	sports-1M	93.6	93.3	95	66.6	70.1	72.7
TSN [19]	ImageNet	85.7	87.9	93.5	-	-	68.5
I3D [1]	ImageNet	84.5	90.6	93.4	49.8	61.9	66.4
R(2+1)D [18]	ImageNet+Kinetics	96.8	95.5	97.3	74.5	76.4	78.7
TSN [19]	ImageNet+Kinetics	91.1	95.2	97	-	-	-
CCS + TSN [23]	ImageNet+Kinetics	94.2	95	97.4	69.4	71.2	81.9
Distillnation Methods	Pre-train dataset	Mimic	Mimic+RGB	Mimic+Flow	Mimic	Mimic+RGB	Mimic+Flow
MAR(16f) [2]	Kinetics	94.6	95.6	94.9	72.3	73.1	74.5
Dual-action Stream(16f)	Kinetics	95.2	95.6	95.6	73.7	73.5	76.8
MAR(64f) [2]	Kinetics	97.1	95.8	97.5	80.1	80.6	80.9
Dual-action Stream(64f)	Kinetics	97.2	97.6	97.7	80.3	80.8	81.2

3.2 Comparison, Ablation Study, and Analysis

So as to compare the proposed training strategy to the state-of-the-art action
recognition approaches, we report the performance over the split 1 test dataset
of UCF-101 and HMDB-51 in Table 1. Note that "Mimic" in the table refers
to Dual-action Stream/MAR stream [2], and the "Mimic+RGB/Flow" column
refers to the averaging fusion method used in the traditional two-stream methods
[15]. It's obvious that our proposed Dual-action Stream outperforms the other
state-of-art approaches on the 64 consecutive frames clip (64f-clip), and our
Dual-action Stream even exceeds some of the two-stream methods. On 16f-clip,
it shows that our results also have better advantages in the case of less sampling.
As for the comparison of the two-stream fusion method, our averaging fusion
approach with Dual-action Stream and flow stream is 9.7% better than the
original two-stream method [15] on UCF-101 dataset, and 21.8% on HMDB-51
dataset. For more benchmark, Our experimental results are 4.2% higher than
TSN[19] on UCF-101 and 12.7% higher on HMDB-51. Experiments show that

Table 2. The ablation study over the UCF101 dataset at split 1(16f-clips), the different
modules are gradually added to the baseline.

Methods	Accuracy
Baseline [MAR][2]	94.6
Dual-action Stream (Multi-level MAE Loss)	94.7
Dual-action Stream (Gram Loss)	94.8
Dual-action Stream (Multi-level MAE Loss+Gram Loss)	95.2
Dual-action Stream+Flow	95.6
Dual-action Stream+Flow+Attention-based Fusion	**95.7**

our method can better learn the features of the middle layers because we achieve state-of-the-art performance.

Compared with 64f-clip, 16f-clip have fewer input frames, which is more demanding for our method. Table 2 shows our ablation study over the UCF-101 dataset. All these studies are conducted on the 16f-clip input. Due to the [2] adopt the original MSE loss between the layers only before the last fully-connected layer, we consider it as our baseline. Based on the baseline, our ablation experiment evaluate the performance by adding multi-level MAE loss and Gram loss step by step. Finally, we evaluate the attention-based fusion module by integrating Dual-action Stream with the optical flow stream. Although the MAR [2] achieve amazing high performance, this table shows that the proposed Dual-action Stream and the attention-based fusion module can efficiently improve the performance.

4   Conclusion

In this paper, a novel distillation strategy is proposed to learn from the motion stream comprehensively, therefore it only receives RGB clips but hiddenly utilizes both appearance and motion information. The proposed gram loss and multi-level feature loss are proved to be able to learn motion information more effectively. The evaluation and comparison showed that our Dual-action Stream outperforms most of the two-stream approaches over the UCF101 and HMDB51 dataset.

Acknowledgment. This research is supported by The Foundation of Sichuan Provincial Education Department (NO. 18ZA0501).

References

1. Carreira, J., Zisserman, A.: Quo vadis, action recognition? A new model and the kinetics dataset. In: Proceedings of the IEEE Conference on Computer Vision and Pattern Recognition, pp. 6299–6308 (2017)
2. Crasto, N., Weinzaepfel, P., Alahari, K., Schmid, C.: MARS: motion-augmented RGB stream for action recognition. In: Proceedings of the IEEE Conference on Computer Vision and Pattern Recognition, pp. 7882–7891 (2019)
3. Diba, A., Sharma, V., Van Gool, L.: Deep temporal linear encoding networks. In: Proceedings of the IEEE conference on Computer Vision and Pattern Recognition, pp. 2329–2338 (2017)
4. Feichtenhofer, C., Pinz, A., Zisserman, A.: Convolutional two-stream network fusion for video action recognition. In: Proceedings of the IEEE Conference on Computer Vision and Pattern Recognition, pp. 1933–1941 (2016)
5. Gatys, L.A., Ecker, A.S., Bethge, M.: A neural algorithm of artistic style. arXiv preprint arXiv:1508.06576 (2015)
6. Girdhar, R., Ramanan, D., Gupta, A., Sivic, J., Russell, B.: ActionVLAD: learning spatio-temporal aggregation for action classification. In: Proceedings of the IEEE Conference on Computer Vision and Pattern Recognition, pp. 971–980 (2017)

7. Goyal, R., et al.: The "something something" video database for learning and evaluating visual common sense. In: ICCV, vol. 1, p. 3 (2017)

8. Hara, K., Kataoka, H., Satoh, Y.: Can spatiotemporal 3D CNNs retrace the history of 2D CNNs and ImageNet? In: Proceedings of the IEEE Conference on Computer Vision and Pattern Recognition, pp. 6546–6555 (2018)

9. Johnson, J., Alahi, A., Fei-Fei, L.: Perceptual losses for real-time style transfer and super-resolution. In: Leibe, B., Matas, J., Sebe, N., Welling, M. (eds.) ECCV 2016. LNCS, vol. 9906, pp. 694–711. Springer, Cham (2016). https://doi.org/10.1007/978-3-319-46475-6_43

10. Kay, W., et al.: The kinetics human action video dataset. arXiv preprint arXiv:1705.06950 (2017)

11. Kim, Y.: Convolutional neural networks for sentence classification. arXiv preprint arXiv:1408.5882 (2014)

12. Liu, H., Tu, J., Liu, M.: Two-stream 3D convolutional neural network for skeleton-based action recognition. arXiv preprint arXiv:1705.08106 (2017)

13. Pérez, J.S., Meinhardt-Llopis, E., Facciolo, G.: Tv-l1 optical flow estimation. Image Process. Line **2013**, 137–150 (2013)

14. Poppe, R.: A survey on vision-based human action recognition. Image Vis. Comput. **28**(6), 976–990 (2010)

15. Simonyan, K., Zisserman, A.: Two-stream convolutional networks for action recognition in videos. In: Advances in Neural Information Processing Systems, pp. 568–576 (2014)

16. Tran, D., Bourdev, L., Fergus, R., Torresani, L., Paluri, M.: Learning spatiotemporal features with 3D convolutional networks. In: Proceedings of the IEEE International Conference on Computer Vision, pp. 4489–4497 (2015)

17. Tran, D., Ray, J., Shou, Z., Chang, S.F., Paluri, M.: Convnet architecture search for spatiotemporal feature learning. arXiv preprint arXiv:1708.05038 (2017)

18. Tran, D., Wang, H., Torresani, L., Ray, J., LeCun, Y., Paluri, M.: A closer look at spatiotemporal convolutions for action recognition. In: Proceedings of the IEEE Conference on Computer Vision and Pattern Recognition, pp. 6450–6459 (2018)

19. Wang, L., Xiong, Y., Wang, Z., Qiao, Y., Lin, D., Tang, X., Van Gool, L.: Temporal segment networks for action recognition in videos. IEEE Trans. Pattern Anal. Mach. Intell. **41**, 2740–2755 (2018)

20. Xie, S., Girshick, R., Dollár, P., Tu, Z., He, K.: Aggregated residual transformations for deep neural networks. In: Proceedings of the IEEE Conference on Computer Vision and Pattern Recognition, pp. 1492–1500 (2017)

21. Xu, H., Das, A., Saenko, K.: R-C3D: region convolutional 3d network for temporal activity detection. In: Proceedings of the IEEE International Conference on Computer Vision, pp. 5783–5792 (2017)

22. Zeiler, M.D., Fergus, R.: Visualizing and understanding convolutional networks. In: Fleet, D., Pajdla, T., Schiele, B., Tuytelaars, T. (eds.) ECCV 2014. LNCS, vol. 8689, pp. 818–833. Springer, Cham (2014). https://doi.org/10.1007/978-3-319-10590-1_53

23. Zhang, J., Shen, F., Xu, X., Shen, H.T.: Cooperative cross-stream network for discriminative action representation. arXiv preprint arXiv:1908.10136 (2019)

24. Zhu, J., Zhu, Z., Zou, W.: End-to-end video-level representation learning for action recognition. In: 2018 24th International Conference on Pattern Recognition (ICPR), pp. 645–650. IEEE (2018)

SME User Classification from Click Feedback on a Mobile Banking Apps

Suchat Tungjitnob[1], Kitsuchart Pasupa[1]([⊠]) [iD], Ek Thamwiwatthana[2],
and Boontawee Suntisrivaraporn[2]

[1] Faculty of Information Technology, King Mongkut's Institute of Technology
Ladkrabang, Bangkok 10520, Thailand
62606062@kmitl.ac.th, kitsuchart@it.kmitl.ac.th
[2] Data Analytics, Chief Data Office, Siam Commercial Bank,
Bangkok 10900, Thailand
{ek.thamwiwatthana,boontawee.suntisrivaraporn}@scb.co.th

Abstract. Customer segmentation is an essential process that leads a bank to gain more insight and better understand their customers. In the past, this process requires analyses of data, both customer demographic and offline financial transactions. However, from the advancement of mobile technology, mobile banking has become more accessible than before. With over 10 million digital users, *SCB easy app* by Siam Commercial Bank receives an enormous volume of transactions each day. In this work, we propose a method to classify mobile user's click behaviour into two groups, *i.e.* 'SME-like' and 'Non-SME-like' users. Thus, the bank can easily identify the customers and offer them the right products. We convert a user's click log into an image that aims to capture temporal information. The image representation reduces the need for feature engineering. Employing ResNet-18 with our image data can achieve 71.69% average accuracy. Clearly, the proposed method outperforms the conventional machine learning technique with hand-crafted features that can achieve 61.70% average accuracy. Also, we discover a hidden insight behind 'SME-like' and 'Non-SME-like' user's click behaviour from these images. Our proposed method can lead to a better understanding of mobile banking user behaviour and a novel way of developing a customer segmentation classifier.

Keywords: Customer segmentation · Click feedback · Encoding click feedback as image · Mobile banking behaviour

1 Introduction

Mobile banking has become widely: with rapid improvement of smartphone technology, it is more accessible than before. Through mobile banking apps, bank customers can immediately make banking transactions, anywhere and anytime. These apps also enable banks to reach their customers more efficiently and reduce

© Springer Nature Switzerland AG 2020
H. Yang et al. (Eds.): ICONIP 2020, CCIS 1332, pp. 256–264, 2020.
https://doi.org/10.1007/978-3-030-63820-7_29

costs for expanding additional branches. Thus, the banking industry has rapidly shifted from traditional banking services to digital platforms.

Customer segmentation splits customers into distinct groups, based on similar characters and behaviours, for example, job, salary, age, etc [10]. Currently, big data technology and data science enables us to obtain many insights from the data. This helps banks to market products appropriately. Existing work has demonstrated that user feedback leads to a better understanding of user behaviour [11–13], but it requires more effort to process the data. Obviously, user feedback benefits the bank industry, Sunhem and Pasupa have used a smartphone's front-facing camera to track eye movements for user experience and user interface survey research for mobile banking app [14]. In addition to feedback from eye movements, user click are also relevant and easy to collect in a system log. With more than 250 million transactions each month, *SCB easy app* by Siam Commercial Bank allows collection of a large database, giving the bank many opportunities to understand customer lifestyle and their preferences.

Currently, SCB provides many products for Small and Medium-sized Enterprises (SME), which are registered businesses that maintain revenues, assets or have several employees below a certain threshold. SCB encourages its customers to use these products and reach out to the companies. However, many customers are natural persons, who not registration as a company. Here, we describe them as 'SME-like'. The bank wants to encourage the 'SME-like' organisations to use SME products as well. It is challenging for the bank to identify this group of customers, unless the customer notifies it. Mobile banking app is currently available only for personal account but not for business account. In this work, we showed how to classify *SCB easy app* users into two groups, *i.e.* 'SME-like' and 'Non-SME-like', based on behaviour on the apps, *e.g.* user clicks. We examined user click logs for some anonymous *SCB easy app* users, that were labelled as 'SME-like' and 'Non-SME-like'. So that the model would enable identification of unlabelled users and allow the bank to offer the right products or services to the right customers. The contributions of our work are:

1. We described a set of hand-crafted features extracted from *SCB easy app* click log data to distinguish between 'SME-like' and 'Non-SME-like' users. These features were evaluated with the existing, Extreme Gradient Boosting algorithm [1].
2. Click log data were visualised in a way that captured temporal information for click log data. These images were used to train a Convolutional Neural Network (CNN) model. This representation performed better than hand-crafted features.

2   Related Work

Now we can access big data and traditional methods have limitations facing very large amounts of data [4]. For this reason, machine learning techniques have been applied to the customer segmentation problem, due to their effectiveness and robustness. Numerous machine learning techniques, including classification, *i.e.*

decision tree [3], and clustering, *i.e.* *k*-means clustering [9] were used to segment customers in various industries. Kim *et al.* combined multiple classification methods to predict customer purchase propensity on an e-commerce website [7]. In the telecommunication industry, Dullaghan *et al.* analysed mobile customer behaviour and use by decision trees and Naïve Bayes algorithm [3].

Machine learning techniques have been used to segment customers in the banking industry as well. Li *et al.* segmented customer groups with credit card usage data by *k*-means clustering and then compared classification algorithms to train a forecasting model to separate unseen data according to those clusters [8]. Mihova *et al.* used *k*-means clustering to determine customer groups, based on their credit history [9].

Many works also showed that temporal data such as website click feedback can assist customer segmentation. Bock *et al.* trained a random forest classifier, with website visitor click feedback patterns. The classifier was able to form a demographic profile of a website visitor *i.e.* gender, age and occupation, to support an advertisement team [2].

Our click log data included time intervals, whereas most existing banking industry work did not consider this click data. Moreover, our click data came from a mobile banking application, whereas most previous work using temporal data came from website click data. Involving a usage time makes it possible to visualise these data in time and assist the management team to plan strategy.

3   Methods

3.1   Data Collection

The click log data come from a database of *SCB easy app*. They were flagged using data from user accounts as 'SME-like' and 'Non-SME-like'. The data was collected between 1–30 September, 2019. The raw log data labeled click events with a type and a timestamp. We collected data from 25,868 anonymous users, including 12,621 'SME-like' users and 13,247 'Non-SME-like' users, for 72,874,972 clicks. There were 535 unique events, which can divided into interface events and banking function events. Moreover, we wanted to select only events, that were essential to our task. So we created a matrix of our data by counting the number of usage times of each event of each user in one month, leading to a $25,868 \times 535$ matrix. This matrix represented the click event frequency in one month for each user. We used a random forest algorithm, using this matrix, to calculate an importance score for each event. We rank each event importance score and used an elbow method to determine a number of events that should be kept, based on its importance score: this led us to 56 events, including 21 banking function events and 35 interface events. We needed a small number of quality features to represent our target user and interface events did not represent mobile banking usage behaviour. Thus, we kept only 21 banking events and eliminated interface events. Then, we grouped the remaining 21 banking events into seven group of events, which we labeled 'primary events'. Events, that contained a keyword from one of the seven primary-events, were labeled as sub-events, *i.e.* transfer is a primary-event and transfer_slip was its sub-event. We also included additional sub-events, eliminated by the elbow method, to be part of a primary event. Finally, our click log data contained 17,133,290 clicks, separated into seven primary events and 57 sub events, see Fig. 1.

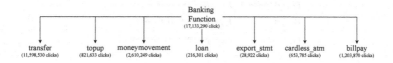

Fig. 1. Banking function primary events

3.2 Hand-Crafted Feature Extraction

In this step, we extracted a feature from a click log data to distinguish between an 'SME-like' and 'Non-SME-like' *SCB easy app* users. We found three groups of hand-crafted feature methods presented in Fig. 2.

1. Number of clicks for each primary event $\{F_1, F_2, \ldots, F_7\} \in \mathcal{F}_f$: We count a frequency for each primary event assuming that $\mathcal{F}_f$ should have a unique attribute, which can distinguish between 'SME-like' and 'Non-SME-like' users.
2. Number of clicks for each primary event within a period of time $\{F_8, F_9, \ldots, F_{28}\} \in \mathcal{F}_t$: We crafted a feature to included period of time due to the timestamp in our click log data. We counted each primary event frequency, using the timestamps, into three periods: 08:00 to 17:00, 17:00 to 24:00 and 24:00 to 08:00. This eight hour gap come from a standard working hour in Thailand, assuming that mobile banking application usage should be related to user working hour periods.
3. Combination of $\mathcal{F}_f$ and $\mathcal{F}_t$ ($\mathcal{F}_c$): We concatenated $\mathcal{F}_f$ and $\mathcal{F}_t$, assuming that a model would perform better when trained with more features.

3.3 Visualisation of the Log

Since the click log contained time stamps, when we extracted a feature with the hand-crafted method described above, we had to select the number of time intervals used to extract features. Since, there are many ways of designing features with these time intervals, we converted the click logs into an image, which could capture the attribute of those time stamps and enable us to visualise and identify the use behaviour trends found in the logs.

Based on 24 h days and 60 min hours, we created 'images' from each primary event with 24 × 60 pixels. These images were very sparse, so we rescaled from 60 (1 min per pixel) to 30 (2 min per pixel) leading to 24 × 30 pixel images. The steps for representing the log as an image are shown in Fig. 3.

$\mathcal{F}_f$		$\mathcal{F}_t$	
F_1	billpay	$F_8 - F_{10}$	billpay with time stamp
F_2	cardless atm	$F_{11} - F_{13}$	cardless atm with time stamp
F_3	export stmt	$F_{14} - F_{16}$	export stmt with time stamp
F_4	loan	$F_{17} - F_{19}$	loan with time stamp
F_5	money movement	$F_{20} - F_{22}$	money movement with time stamp
F_6	topup	$F_{23} - F_{25}$	topup with time stamp
F_7	transfer	$F_{26} - F_{28}$	transfer with time stamp

Fig. 2. Features extracted from click log data

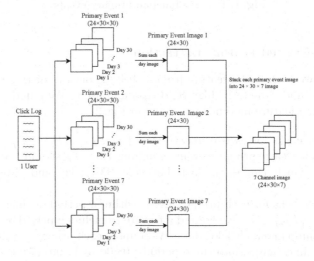

Fig. 3. Steps for encoding click log data in a seven channel image

The encoding led to seven 24×30 images, which represent use behaviour for each primary event of a single user. We stacked these seven images into one image, with seven channels—($24 \times 30 \times 7$) and refer them as $\mathcal{I}_{7c}$. Each channel of $\mathcal{I}_{7c}$ are describe in Fig. 4. We visualised $\mathcal{I}_{7c}$ by extracting each channel into seven grey scale images. Each image represented a primary event behaviour of that user. When viewing the image, we can see a different use pattern for each user. For example in Fig. 4, an 'SME-like' user did not use a cardless ATM function, so this image was all black, but a 'Non-SME-like' user used this event frequently, so this image tells us that this 'Non-SME-like' user frequently withdrew money, with the *SCB easy app* cardless ATM function.

Typical computer monitors can only basically output a three channel (RGB) image, but for $\mathcal{I}_{7c}$, we need to visualise each channel as a grey scale image. Thus, $\mathcal{I}_{7c}$ was still difficult for a human to visualise and we devised a method that converts $\mathcal{I}_{7c}$ into RGB images, which are easier to visualise.

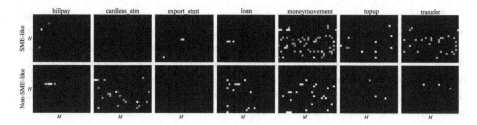

Fig. 4. Example of $\mathfrak{I}_{7c}$: each row represents a primary event. Each column represents $\mathfrak{I}_{7c}$ of one user example. H denote a 24 h (1 h per pixel). M denote a 30 intervals (2 min per pixel).

We selected only the top three frequency channels ('transfer' (11,598,530 clicks), 'moneymovement' (2,610,249 clicks) and 'billpays' (1,203,870 clicks)) from $\mathfrak{I}_{7c}$ to be represented as an RGB image (see Fig. 1). This led to RGB images ($24 \times 30 \times 3$), defined as $\mathfrak{I}_{rgb}$. Selection steps for the top three frequency channels, that convert $\mathfrak{I}_{7c}$ into $\mathfrak{I}_{rgb}$, are shown in Fig. 3. Instead of forcing us to distinguish seven grey levels from $\mathfrak{I}_{7c}$, $\mathfrak{I}_{rgb}$ enabled us to easily visualise a behaviour from one RGB image.

3.4 Models

XGBoost is an optimised version of tree based gradient boosting [5], designed to be efficient, flexible and more regularised to control over-fitting. XGBoost also trains faster with better performance than other gradient boosting implementations [1]. We used XGBoost to evaluate the performance of $\mathfrak{F}_f$, $\mathfrak{F}_t$ and $\mathfrak{F}_c$.

ResNet is a deep CNN architecture which was designed to eliminate the vanishing gradient problem. He *et al.* introduced a concept of 'skip connection', by adding an input value to the output after convolution block [6]. This enabled a network to stack more and deeper layers, without affecting training performance. We used an 18-layer version of ResNet, called ResNet-18. He *et al.*'s default settings [6] were used in an experiment on $\mathfrak{I}_{rgb}$. For $\mathfrak{I}_{7c}$, we modified ResNet-18 input layer settings to input a seven channel image, instead of the original three channel one.

4 Experiment Setting

Initially, we screened our data and found that many users were not very active and tended to provide noisy data, *i.e.* these users rarely used the *SCB easy app*. They not contribute useful information and their click log behaviours were difficult to distinguish.

Therefore, we only want to evaluate active users due to the reason that an active user is groups of users that are familiar to *SCB easy app* which can show a more meaningful usage behaviour. The question arose that where should we define this active threshold to discarded non-active users. We decided to sort our user usage frequency and discarded a user with lower than 50%, 55%, 60%, 65%, 70% and 75% percentile. The number of remaining users after discarding non-active users in each threshold are:

- 6,303 SME-like and 6,619 Non-SME-like for 50% threshold.
- 5,674 SME-like and 5,949 Non-SME-like for 55% threshold.
- 5,043 SME-like and 5,299 Non-SME-like for 60% threshold.
- 4,414 SME-like and 4,636 Non-SME-like for 65% threshold.
- 3,784 SME-like and 3,972 Non-SME-like for 70% threshold.
- 3,155 SME-like and 3,308 Non-SME-like for 75% threshold.

Finally, we conducted an experiment to evaluate our 5 set of inputs on SME-like classification task with 6 different discarded threshold.

Every input ($\mathcal{F}_f$, $\mathcal{F}_t$, $\mathcal{F}_c$, $\mathcal{I}_{7c}$ and $\mathcal{I}_{rgb}$) was first split into training and test sets with an 80:20 ratio. Then 20% of a training set was extracted as a validation set. The validation set was used for selecting a model with the lowest validation loss. We then evaluated the selected model on an unseen test set. All inputs were split with the same random seed to verify that every test set came from the same users, for the total of five random seeds.

For ResNet-18, the model settings were: batch size = 64; learning rate = 0.001 with the Adam optimisation algorithm; maximum number of epochs = 50.

5   Results and Discussion

Each input was trained with a different discarded threshold and the accuracy was evaluated on an unseen test set—see Table 1.

Table 1. 'SME-like' classification accuracy (as %)

Discarded threshold	Features				
	$\mathcal{F}_f$	$\mathcal{F}_t$	$\mathcal{F}_c$	$\mathcal{I}_{7c}$	$\mathcal{I}_{rgb}$
50	61.10 ± 0.79	61.10 ± 0.77	61.31 ± 0.89	69.43 ± 0.60	68.81 ± 0.99
55	60.92 ± 0.95	61.10 ± 0.93	61.49 ± 0.56	70.89 ± 0.55	68.59 ± 2.17
60	$\mathbf{62.29 \pm 0.80}$	$\mathbf{62.34 \pm 0.63}$	$\mathbf{62.37 \pm 1.08}$	71.96 ± 1.61	71.50 ± 1.39
65	61.29 ± 0.80	62.32 ± 0.91	62.31 ± 0.53	72.66 ± 0.93	72.54 ± 2.15
70	60.99 ± 0.31	61.69 ± 0.49	62.00 ± 0.58	73.41 ± 0.71	72.70 ± 1.28
75	61.48 ± 1.07	62.19 ± 1.19	62.26 ± 1.39	$\mathbf{73.46 \pm 2.43}$	$\mathbf{74.31 \pm 1.35}$
Average	61.35 ± 0.79	61.79 ± 0.82	61.95 ± 0.84	71.97 ± 1.14	71.41 ± 1.56

From Table 1, considering only hand-crafted features, it can be seen that $\mathcal{F}_c$ achieved the best performance at 61.95% average accuracy, followed by $\mathcal{F}_t$

SME User Classification from Click Feedback on a Mobile Banking Apps

at 61.79% and $\mathcal{F}_f$ at 61.35%. In addition, when considering each discarded threshold, $\mathcal{F}_c$ also performed better than $\mathcal{F}_t$ and $\mathcal{F}_f$. This showed that $\mathcal{F}_t$, to which we added click frequency with time intervals, delivered a better performing model than $\mathcal{F}_f$. Lastly, $\mathcal{F}_c$ showed that our classifier gained more benefit from combining the hand-crafted features, which provided the classifier with extra information.

From ResNet-18, trained with image inputs in Table 1, $\mathcal{I}_{7c}$ achieved the best performance at 71.97% average accuracy, followed by $\mathcal{I}_{rgb}$ at 71.41%. $\mathcal{I}_{7c}$ performed better than $\mathcal{I}_{rgb}$ at every threshold, except the 75 percentile. In general, $\mathcal{I}_{7c}$ gained more performance from its seven channel information compared to $\mathcal{I}_{rgb}$ with only three channels. However, $\mathcal{I}_{rgb}$ was more suitable for visualisation and these two performed similarly, differing by only $\sim 0.56\%$ in average accuracy. Lastly, at each discarded threshold, we can see that by discarding more inactive users, we gained more performance in $\mathcal{I}_{7c}$ and $\mathcal{I}_{rgb}$, $i.e.$ inactive users affected the model performance and need to be filtered out.

Overall, converting the click log data into $\mathcal{I}_{7c}$ and $\mathcal{I}_{rgb}$ improved the model performance: it outperformed $\mathcal{F}_f, \mathcal{F}_t$ and $\mathcal{F}_c$ at every threshold. The image captured better time-related features and reduced the need for hand-crafted features. Further, the image representation made visualisation of these logs much easier and helped display hidden patterns that lay in our click logs.

6   Conclusions

The click log data from a mobile banking application can lead to many opportunities for a bank to gain more knowledge of their customer. Converting these logs to images reduced the need for hand-crafted features and make it easier for understand user behaviour. Therefore, we proposed five sets of inputs, consisting of hand-crafted features ($\mathcal{F}_f, \mathcal{F}_t$ and $\mathcal{F}_c$) and images ($\mathcal{I}_{7c}$ and $\mathcal{I}_{rgb}$) to evaluate 'SME-like' classification. We found that using the images outperformed hand-crafted features, because it captured more time-related features. $\mathcal{I}_{rgb}$ performed better, when it come to visualisation and were suitable for helping the management team identify trends behind user click behaviour. We also investigated and provided some insights for the bank, which can help them able to reach more customer and increase their sales. Planned future work includes a multi-view approach generating another view of an image, for example, an image representation of behaviour in each business quarter and using this new image view, combined with the old one, to boost the performance of our 'SME-like' classifier.

References

1. Chen, T., Guestrin, C.: XGBoost: a scalable tree boosting system. In: Proceedings of the 22nd ACM SIGKDD International Conference on Knowledge Discovery and Data Mining (KDD 2016), San Francisco, CA, USA, pp. 785–794 (2016). https://doi.org/10.1145/2939672.2939785

2. De Bock, K., Van den Poel, D.: Predicting website audience demographics for web advertising targeting using multi-website clickstream data. Fundamenta Informaticae **98**(1), 49–70 (2010). https://doi.org/10.5555/1803672.1803677

3. Dullaghan, C., Rozaki, E.: Integration of machine learning techniques to evaluate dynamic customer segmentation analysis for mobile customers. Int. J. Data Mining Knowl. Manag. Process **7**, 13–24 (2017). https://doi.org/10.5121/ijdkp.2017.7102

4. Florez, R., Ramon, J.: Marketing segmentation through machine learning models: an approach based on customer relationship management and customer profitability accounting. Soc. Sci. Comput. Rev. **27**, 96–117 (2008). https://doi.org/10.1177/0894439308321592

5. Friedman, J.: Greedy function approximation: a gradient boosting machine. Ann. Stat. **29**, 1189–1232 (2001). https://doi.org/10.2307/2699986

6. He, K., Zhang, X., Ren, S., Sun, J.: Deep residual learning for image recognition. In: Proceedings of the International Conference on Computer Vision and Pattern Recognition (CVPR 2016), Las Vegas, NV, USA, pp. 770–778 (2016). https://doi.org/10.1109/CVPR.2016.90

7. Kim, E., Kim, W., Lee, Y.: Combination of multiple classifiers for customer's purchase behavior prediction. Decis. Support Syst. **34**, 167–175 (2003). https://doi.org/10.1016/S0167-9236(02)00079-9

8. Li, W., Wu, X., Sun, Y., Zhang, Q.: Credit card customer segmentation and target marketing based on data mining. In: Proceedings of the International Conference on Computational Intelligence and Security (CIS 2010), Nanning, China, pp. 73–76 (2011). https://doi.org/10.1109/CIS.2010.23

9. Mihova, V., Pavlov, V.: A customer segmentation approach in commercial banks. In: AIP Conference Proceedings, vol. 2025, p. 030003 (2018). https://doi.org/10.1063/1.5064881

10. Ngai, E., Xiu, L., Chau, D.: Application of data mining techniques in customer relationship management: a literature review and classification. Expert Syst. Appl. **36**, 2592–2602 (2009). https://doi.org/10.1016/j.eswa.2008.02.021

11. Pasupa, K., Chatkamjuncharoen, P., Wuttilertdeshar, C., Sugimoto, M.: Using image features and eye tracking device to predict human emotions towards abstract images. In: Bräunl, T., McCane, B., Rivera, M., Yu, X. (eds.) PSIVT 2015. LNCS, vol. 9431, pp. 419–430. Springer, Cham (2016). https://doi.org/10.1007/978-3-319-29451-3_34

12. Pasupa, K., Sunhem, W., Loo, C.K., Kuroki, Y.: Can eye movement information improve prediction performance of human emotional response to images? In: Liu, D., Xie, S., Li, Y., Zhao, D., El-Alfy, E.S. (eds.) ICONIP 2017. LNCS, vol. 10637, pp. 830–838. (2017). https://doi.org/10.1007/978-3-319-70093-9_88

13. Pasupa, K., Szedmak, S.: Utilising Kronnecker decomposition and tensor-based multi-view learning to predict where people are looking in images. Neurocomputing **248**, 80–93 (2017). https://doi.org/10.1016/j.neucom.2016.11.074

14. Sunhem, W., Pasupa, K.: A scenario-based analysis of front-facing camera eye tracker for UX-UI survey on mobile banking app. In: Proceedings of the 12th International Conference on Knowledge and Smart Technology (KST 2020), Pattaya, Thailand, pp. 80–85 (2020)

Image Processing and Computer Vision

3D Human Pose Estimation with 2D Human Pose and Depthmap

Zhiheng Zhou$^{(\boxtimes)}$, Yue Cao, Xuanying Zhu, Henry Gardner, and Hongdong Li

College of Engineering and Computer Science, Australian National University,
Canberra, ACT 2601, Australia
{zhiheng.zhou,Yue.Cao1,xuanying.zhu,Henry.Gardner,hongdong.li}@anu.edu.au

Abstract. Three-dimensional human pose estimation models are conventionally based on RGB images or by assuming that accurately-estimated (near to ground truth) 2D human pose landmarks are available. Naturally, such data only contains information about two dimensions, while the 3D poses require the three dimensions of height, width, and depth. In this paper, we propose a new 3D human pose estimation model that takes an estimated 2D pose and the depthmap of the 2D pose as input to estimate 3D human pose. In our system, the estimated 2D pose is obtained from processing an RGB image using a 2D landmark detection network that produces noisy heatmap data. We compare our results with a Simple Linear Model (SLM) of other authors that takes accurately-estimated 2D pose landmarks as input and that has reached the state-of-the-art results for 3D human pose estimate using the Human3.6m dataset. Our results show that our model can achieve better performance than the SLM, and that our model can align the 2D landmark data with the depthmap automatically. We have also tested our network using estimated 2D poses and depthmaps separately. In our model, all three conditions (depthmap+2D pose, depthmap-only and 2D pose-only) are more accurate than the SLM with, surprisingly, the depthmap-only condition being comparable in accuracy with the depthmap+2D pose condition.

Keywords: 3D Pose Estimation · Convolution Neural Network · Depthmap

1 Introduction

Human pose estimation has been a challenging topic computer vision area in recent years. The overall goal of pose estimation is to localize the positions of key points of the human body (e.g. chest, arms, legs, etc.). It is a crucial task in computer vision as it is heavily used in a range of application domains such as surveillance systems, gaming industry and so on.

This paper will focus on single-person pose estimation, in which there is only one person in a data sample. In the last century, most research has focused on single-person 2D pose estimation using traditional pixel-based computer

© Springer Nature Switzerland AG 2020
H. Yang et al. (Eds.): ICONIP 2020, CCIS 1332, pp. 267–274, 2020.
https://doi.org/10.1007/978-3-030-63820-7_30

vision methods [2]. But these methods cannot estimate human poses very accurately. With the development of deep learning and convolution neural networks, researchers have been able to achieve much better performance. Recently, deep convolutional neural networks (CNNs) such as the stacked hourglass model (SHGM) [12] and the deep high-resolution model (DHRM) [15] have been shown to generate reliable 2D poses based on RGB images. In particular the DHRM has reached state-of-the-art results on the MPII [1] and COCO [10] datasets and we incorporate this model into our system as discussed below.

For 3D pose estimation, the simple linear model (SLM) of [11] outperforms many 3D pose models on the Human3.6m [4,6] dataset. This model uses accurately-estimated 2D human pose landmarks to estimate 3D human pose. The estimated 2D human pose is generated by the stacked hourglass model (SHGM) based on an RGB image and the 3D pose is obtained using dictionary matching from 2D human poses to 3D human poses. Such a system cannot predict a reliable 3D pose when the 2D pose is complex for the dictionary mapping algorithm or when it maps to more than one possible 3D poses. In our model, we use the DHRM to obtain estimated 2D poses from an RGB image, and we process that information together with depthmap information to reliably estimate accurate 3D pose.

2   Related Work

As the field of deep learning and Convolution Neural Networks (CNNs) has developed, deep CNNs have been shown to provide much more dominant results than previous approaches [3,12,15–17]. Among lots of deep CNN-based pose estimation models, some have used arrays to represent the absolute position of keypoints (or "landmarks") [3,16], while others have chosen to represent the distribution of keypoints by heatmaps [12,15,17]. The heatmap representation models can have a better performance overall, but the array representation is more efficient.

For single-person 3D pose estimation, researchers tend to use array representation for 3D keypoints since three-dimension heatmaps are very computationally expensive. Among 3D pose estimation models, some of them use a single model to estimate 3D human pose directly from a single RBG image [7,13], while others are based on 2D poses to estimate 3D human pose [8,11]. Normally, the 2D poses are estimated by a 2D pose estimation model based on the original image. Among the 3D models based on 2D poses, the simple linear model [11] (SLM) reached the state-of-the-art results on Human3.6m dataset with a very simple structure. Typically, the input 2D pose and output 3D pose of the SLM are all in array representation.

3   Methodology

The input of our CNN model is an estimated 2D pose and a depthmap. The 2D pose is estimated from an RGB image containing a single person using the

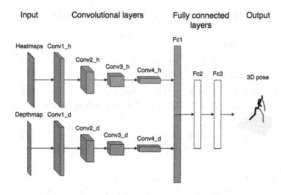

Fig. 1. The overall structure of our model.

deep high-resolution model (DHRM) of [15] based on an RGB image, and the depthmap contains the depth information corresponding to that RGB image. Since the estimated 2D poses of the deep high-resolution network are in heatmap representation, the 2D poses fed into our model are also represented by heatmaps. The target output of our model is the 3D pose expressed as an array (to save computational resources and increase efficiency). Typically, the human poses we used contained 16 human keypoints. Therefore, one 2D pose heatmap contained 16 2D heatmaps (one heatmap for the location distribution of each keypoint). In order words, the input 2D heatmaps contained 16 channels. The 3D poses were represented as 16×3 arrays (16 keypoints times 3 dimensions). Because each 2D pose has one corresponding depthmap, and the depthmap is a gray-scale image, the channel number of input depthmap is one.

3.1 Model Structure

Our model consists of two main parts, the first one is the feature extraction part which extracts features from inputs (2D pose heatmaps and depthmap), and the second one is the feature processing part which processes the features from previous part and predicts 3D poses. The feature extraction part contains multiple convolutional layers for extracting features. While the feature processing part contains multiple fully-connected layers for processing the features and predicting 3D pose. Figure 1 illustrates the structure of this model.

Feature Extraction Part. Since the input contains two different types of data (the 2D pose heatmap and the depthmap) we use two different CNNs to extract features simultaneously. Each CNN in this part contains four convolution layers as shown in Table 1. For the feature size of layers in the feature extraction part, the last two numbers stand for the feature size of the output of this layer, while the first number is the number of features, which is the channel. After each convolution layer (Conv1, Conv2, Conv3, Conv4), there is a ReLU layer (activation function) and a 2D batch normalization layer (normalizing the batch differences)

Table 1. Layers detail of our model.

Layers name	Detail	Feature/node size
Conv1_h & Conv1_d	3 × 3 conv. stride 1, ReLU, BatchNorm2D	32 × 64 × 64
Conv2_h & Conv2_d	3 × 3 conv. stride 1, ReLU, BatchNorm2D, 2 × 2 max-pooling stride 2	64 × 32 × 32
Conv3_h & Conv3_d	3 × 3 conv. stride 1, ReLU, BatchNorm2D, 2 × 2 max-pooling stride 2	128 × 16 × 16
Conv4_h & Conv4_d	3 × 3 conv. stride 1, ReLU, BatchNorm2D, 2 × 2 max-pooling stride 2	256 × 8 × 8
Fc1	fc., ReLU, BatchNorm1D	1024
Fc2	fc., ReLU, BatchNorm1D	1024
Fc3	fc	48 (16 × 3)

that follows the convolution layer sequentially. Except for layer Conv1 (Conv1_h and Conv1_d), each of the other convolution layers has one more layer which is a max-pooling layer (down-sampling the features to lower size and higher level) at the end of this layer.

Feature Processing Part. After getting features from heatmaps and depthmap, we flatten them from two dimensions to one dimension and concatenate them into one large feature. After that, we use three fully-connected layers to read the one dimension feature and estimate the 3D pose.

In Table 1, the feature/node size is the output node number for each fully connected layer. Typically, the output of the last fully connected layer (Fc3) is the model output, which is 48 numbers (16 keypoints times 3 dimensions). After the first and second fully connected layer (Fc1, Fc2), there is a ReLU layer and a batch normalization layer follow them sequentially. Typically, for Fc1, since it concatenates the features from two previous layers, which are Conv4_h and Conv4_d, the number of input nodes number is 32768 ($256 \times 8 \times 8 \times 2$).

3.2 Dataset

The dataset we used to evaluate our 3D models is UTD-Multimodal Human Action Dataset (UTD-MHAD) [5] collected by the University of Texas at Dallas. In this dataset, there are three kinds of data which are RGB video, depthmaps of the video, and 3D keypoints of the human in the video. The 3D keypoints are stored in array representation. Considering each frame in RGB videos as a sample, there are 58299 samples in total in this dataset.

3.3   Training Setup

Among all 58299 samples in the UTD-MHAD dataset, we used 53000 samples as training set, 2000 samples as validation set, and the remaining 3299 samples as testing set. For benchmarking purposes, we also retrained the simple linear model (SLM) [11] on the UTD-MHAD dataset. Typically, the input 2D pose and output 3D pose of the SLM are all in array representation. We also divided our model into two sub-models, the first one only takes 2D pose heatmaps as input, while the second one only takes depthmap as input. We tested these two sub-models to inspect the influence of the different types of input on performance. Before training the models, we fed all RGB images into a well-trained deep high-resolution model (DHRM) to get the estimated 2D poses heatmaps. Then the pixel values in heatmaps were normalized to the range [0, 1], and the values in depthmaps and 3D keypoints array were standardized to the range [−1, 1]. All the 3D models were trained by 200 epochs with the Adam optimizer, learning rate 0.001, on an 11G NVIDIA GeForce RTX 2080 Ti GPU.

3.4   Evaluation Metric

To evaluate our models, we use the Euclidean distance between the estimated 3D poses and the ground truth 3D poses as a metric. The formula is:

$$L = \frac{\sum_i (y_i - t_i)^2}{16} \tag{1}$$

where y_i is the predicted keypoint position, t_i is the real keypoint position, i is an iteration term of 16 keypoints of a 3D pose, the 16 in denominator stands for 16 keypoints. Since the keypoints values range between [−1, 1], the Euclidian distance will be too small to compare. Therefore, we used millimetres (by moving decimal points three digits to the right[1]) as the unit of the Euclidian distance.

4   Results

To conduct a comparative analysis of models with others, we ran the models five times to conduct a statistical analysis of the results. We used the two-way ANOVA test [14], as the results passed the Kolmogorov-Smirnov normality test [9], meaning that the results are not statistically different from a normal distribution.

Table 2 shows the results of the simple linear model and our models trained on the UTD-MHAD dataset. Our full model is the model with both heatmaps and depthmap as input. Our sub-model (Heatmaps only) takes only 2D pose heatmaps as input and our sub- model (Depthmap only) takes only depthmap as input.

From this table, our full model performance (32.5) is much better than the SLM performance (101.9) (p < 0.01). This is understandable because SLMs only

---

[1] Times original value with 1000.

Table 2. Results of three our proposed models.

Model	# Params	Error (mm)
Simple Linear Model [1]	6.29M	101.9
Our full model	35.44M	32.5
Our sub-model (Heatmaps only)	18.27M	67.0
Our sub-model (Depthmap only)	18.27M	41.7

use 2D keypoint arrays for prediction, while our model uses 2D heatmaps and a depthmap which carry much more information than a single 2D keypoints for prediction. However, the number of the parameters of the SLM is less than our model.

Our full model also has better performance (32.5) than the heatmaps-only sub-model (67.0) and the depthmaps-only sub-model (47.1) ($p < 0.05$). It means both heatmaps and depthmap have a contribution to the model performance. However, the depthmaps-only sub-model (47.1) performs better than the heatmaps-only sub-model (67.0) ($p < 0.05$). This could be because, we can observe human body shapes in depthmap, and the shape of a human can carry some information about the 2D human pose.

4.1   Sample Outputs

Figure 2 shows two critical sample outputs of our model and the simple linear model. The upper sample in this figure shows a walking pose, while the lower sample shows a basketball-shooting pose.

Walking Pose. When a human is walking, one of the hands will be in front of the human body, while the other one will be at the back. The pose with the left hand in front and the pose with the right hand in front are two different poses. Therefore, a reliable 3D pose estimation model should be able to distinguish these different poses. However, when the camera is in front of the human, which is the situation of the RGB image in this sample, the 2D poses for the left hand front pose and the right hand front pose could be quite similar. Therefore, in this situation, the model that only takes a 2D pose as input will have difficulty distinguishing these poses.

By observing the estimated 3D pose of the SLM in this sample, we can see that both of the hands in this estimated 3D pose are at the side of or slightly in front of the body, While the ground truth pose is a right hand front pose. Therefore, when the input 2D pose is ambiguous, the simple linear model may not estimate a reliable 3D pose. The estimated 3D pose of our full model is also a right hand front pose, and it is quite similar to the ground truth. Therefore, when the input 2D pose is ambiguous, our model can estimate a reliable 3D pose.

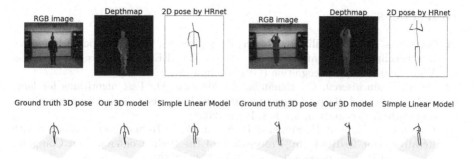

Fig. 2. Two sample outputs of simple linear model and our model.

Basketball Shooting Pose. Similar to the walking pose, when a human is shooting a basketball, the position of two hands will usually not be symmetric around the body. But the hands in this 2D pose taken in front of the human may appear to be symmetric to each other. In this situation, the simple linear model is less likely estimate a reliable 3D pose compared with a model that uses depth information.

However, this pose is more complex than the walking pose. By observing the estimated 3D pose of the SLM in this sample, we can see that the hands are around the human's shoulders. While the hands of the ground truth 3D pose are around the human's head (at least higher than the shoulders), and there is a large gap between the ground truth the 3D pose estimated by the SLM.

For the 3D pose estimated by our model, though there is a difference with the ground truth 3D pose we can still see that the 3D pose estimated by our model is similar to the ground truth 3D pose. The hands' position in our 3D pose is around the human's head. Therefore, when the input 2D pose is ambiguous and complex, our model still has a high probability of being able to estimate an accurate 3D pose.

5   Conclusion

In this paper, we have presented a reliable 3D human pose estimation model based on heatmaps of 2D pose information combined with a depthmap. The performance of our model is much better than the simple linear model on the UTD-MHAD dataset. In addition, our study of the two sub-models showed that the depthmap-only sub-model has a better contribution than the heatmaps-only sub-model. We also analyzed some failure situations for the simple linear model. When the input 2D pose is ambiguous and complex, the simple linear model cannot work well, while our model is robust in these situations.

References

1. Andriluka, M., Pishchulin, L., Gehler, P., Schiele, B.: 2D human pose estimation: new benchmark and state of the art analysis. In: IEEE Conference on Computer Vision and Pattern Recognition (CVPR), June 2014
2. Bo, L., Sminchisescu, C., Kanaujia, A., Metaxas, D.: Fast algorithms for large scale conditional 3D prediction. In: 2008 IEEE Conference on Computer Vision and Pattern Recognition, pp. 1–8. IEEE (2008)
3. Carreira, J., Agrawal, P., Fragkiadaki, K., Malik, J.: Human pose estimation with iterative error feedback. In: Proceedings of the IEEE Conference on Computer Vision and Pattern Recognition, pp. 4733–4742 (2016)
4. Ionescu, C., Li, F., Sminchisescu, C.: Latent structured models for human pose estimation. In: International Conference on Computer Vision (2011)
5. Chen, C., Jafari, R., Kehtarnavaz, N.: UTD-MHAD: a multimodal dataset for human action recognition utilizing a depth camera and a wearable inertial sensor. In: 2015 IEEE International Conference on Image Processing (ICIP), pp. 168–172. IEEE (2015)
6. Ionescu, C., Papava, D., Olaru, V., Sminchisescu, C.: Human3.6M: large scale datasets and predictive methods for 3D human sensing in natural environments. IEEE Trans. Pattern Anal. Mach. Intell. **36**(7), 1325–1339 (2014)
7. Li, S., Chan, A.B.: 3D human pose estimation from monocular images with deep convolutional neural network. In: Cremers, D., Reid, I., Saito, H., Yang, M.-H. (eds.) ACCV 2014. LNCS, vol. 9004, pp. 332–347. Springer, Cham (2015). https://doi.org/10.1007/978-3-319-16808-1_23
8. Lie, W.N., Lin, G.H., Shih, L.S., Hsu, Y., Nguyen, T.H., Nhu, Q.N.Q.: Fully convolutional network for 3D human skeleton estimation from a single view for action analysis. In: 2019 IEEE International Conference on Multimedia & Expo Workshops (ICMEW), pp. 1–6. IEEE (2019)
9. Lilliefors, H.W.: On the Kolmogorov-Smirnov test for normality with mean and variance unknown. J. Am. Stat. Assoc. **62**(318), 399–402 (1967)
10. Lin, T.-Y., et al.: Microsoft COCO: common objects in context. In: Fleet, D., Pajdla, T., Schiele, B., Tuytelaars, T. (eds.) ECCV 2014. LNCS, vol. 8693, pp. 740–755. Springer, Cham (2014). https://doi.org/10.1007/978-3-319-10602-1_48
11. Martinez, J., Hossain, R., Romero, J., Little, J.J.: A simple yet effective baseline for 3D human pose estimation. In: Proceedings of the IEEE International Conference on Computer Vision, pp. 2640–2649 (2017)
12. Newell, A., Yang, K., Deng, J.: Stacked hourglass networks for human pose estimation. In: Leibe, B., Matas, J., Sebe, N., Welling, M. (eds.) ECCV 2016. LNCS, vol. 9912, pp. 483–499. Springer, Cham (2016). https://doi.org/10.1007/978-3-319-46484-8_29
13. Pavlakos, G., Zhou, X., Derpanis, K.G., Daniilidis, K.: Coarse-to-fine volumetric prediction for single-image 3D human pose. In: Proceedings of the IEEE Conference on Computer Vision and Pattern Recognition, pp. 7025–7034 (2017)
14. Scheffe, H.: The Analysis of Variance, vol. 72. Wiley, Hoboken (1999)
15. Sun, K., Xiao, B., Liu, D., Wang, J.: Deep high-resolution representation learning for human pose estimation. arXiv preprint arXiv:1902.09212 (2019)
16. Toshev, A., Szegedy, C.: DeepPose: human pose estimation via deep neural networks. In: Proceedings of the IEEE Conference on Computer Vision and Pattern Recognition (CVPR), Columbus, OH, USA, pp. 24–27 (2014)
17. Wei, S.E., Ramakrishna, V., Kanade, T., Sheikh, Y.: Convolutional pose machines. In: Proceedings of the IEEE Conference on Computer Vision and Pattern Recognition, pp. 4724–4732 (2016)

A Malware Classification Method Based on Basic Block and CNN

Jinrong Chen[1,2](✉)

[1] Institute of Information Engineering, Chinese Academy of Sciences, Beijing, China
chenjinrong@iie.ac.cn
[2] School of Cyber Security, University of Chinese Academy of Sciences,
Beijing, China

Abstract. Aiming at solving the three problems ranging from considerable consumption of manpower in manual acquisition, to excessively high feature dimension and unsatisfying accuracy caused by manual feature acquisition, which will occur when using the current malware classification methods for feature acquisition. This paper proposes a malware classification method that is based on basic block and Convolutional Neural Network (CNN). The paper will firstly get the assembly code file of the executable malware sample, then extract the opcodes(such as "mov" and "add") of disassembled file of malware based on the label of basic block, and in the next, it will generate SimHash value vectors of basic blocks through these opcodes and a hash algorithm. Finally, the classification model is trained on the training sample set through using CNN. As we have carried out a series of experiments, and through these experiments, it is proved that our method can get a satisfying result in malware classification. The experiment showed that the classification accuracy of our method can achieve as highest as 99.24%, with the false positive rate being as low as 1.265%.

Keywords: Malware classification · Opcode · Basic block · Convolutional Neural Network

1 Introduction

The rapid development of information technology has not only brought a great deal of convenience to us, but has also brought potential security problems to networked computers. Among these problems, the most typical one is the attack and overflow of malicious code. Malware is a program or code that can spread through storage media and network, and can damage the integrity of computer system without our authorization and authentication [5]. Their types include viruses, worms, trojans, backdoors and spywares, etc. In recent years, the growth rate of malicious code is getting faster and faster, and the amount of malicious code is getting larger and larger. According to the threat report released by McAfee in August 2019 [9], more than 60 million cases of malicious code were

H. Yang et al. (Eds.): ICONIP 2020, CCIS 1332, pp. 275–283, 2020.
https://doi.org/10.1007/978-3-030-63820-7_31

added just in the first quarter of 2019. This has imposed great pressure on security vendors in analyzing and dealing with malicious code. And a fast and efficient method to classify malicious code could reduce the burden for many security vendors to analyze and deal with malicious code.

At present, there are still some problems exist in the malicious code classification technology. Firstly, when the malicious code classification technology uses machine learning to classify the malicious code, it needs to obtain the characteristics of the malicious code manually, and as a result, which will render the workload of obtaining the characteristics quite onerous. Secondly, because the classification model of malicious code relies on features acquired manually, which will lead to deficiencies in the comprehensiveness and effectiveness of feature acquisition, with the final classification accuracy being lower than expected. Therefore, we need to find a simple but effective method for malicious code classification, which could not only reduce the manual work in the process of obtaining classification features, but also ensure that the acquired features are conductive to the final classification accuracy. Aiming at solving problems existing in the current malicious code classification technology, this paper proposes a malicious code classification method that based on gray images that is generated through studying a large number of malicious codes and neural network technology. By considering basic blocks used by malware, we turn the malware classification problem into image recognition problem, then we prove its effectiveness through experiments. The main contributions of this paper are as follow:

(i) Proposed a basic block generation method and a reasonable method for generating gray image based on basic block;
(ii) Based on the gray image generating from malicious code, a suitable hash algorithm is found to generate basic block for classification of malicious code.

The paper is structured as follows. A survey on the related work is presented In Sect. 2. And in Sect. 3, we describe how we extract opcodes and generate the basic block. Then our experiments and discussion are presented in Sect. 4. Finally in Sect. 5 we conclude the paper.

2   Related Work

2.1   Malware Classification

Natalia Stakhanova et al. [16] proposed a malware classification method that is based on the value of network activity in 2011. And experimental study on a real-world malware collection demonstrated that their approach was able to group malware samples that behaved similarly. In 2012, Nikos Karampatziakis et al. [8] proposed a new malware classification system based on a graph induced by file relationships. Experiment showed that their method could be applied to other types of file relationships, and its detection accuracy can be significantly improved, particularly at low false positive rates. In 2013, Rafiqul Islam et al. [7] presented the first classification method of integrating static and dynamic features into a single test. Their approach had improved the previous results that was based on individual features and had reduced half the time that was needed to test such features separately. In 2016, Ke Tian et al. [17] proposed a new Android repackaged malware detection technique that was based on code heterogeneity analysis. They had performed experimental evaluation through over 7,542 Android apps, and their approach can achieve a false negative rate of 0.35% and a false positive rate of 2.97%. In 2019, Di Xue et al. [18] proposed a classification system Malscore that was based on probability scoring and machine learning. And by carrying out experiments, they proved that the system of combining static analysis with dynamic analysis can classify the malware very efficiently.

2.2 Deep Learning

The recent success in deep learning research and development has drawn a lot of our attention [15]. In 2015, Google released TensorFlow [1], which is a framework of realizing deep learning algorithm. Deep learning is a specific type of machine learning with a lot of work on it [6,10]. The most well-known deep networks is convolutional neural network (CNN). CNN is composed of hidden layers, fully connected layers, convolution layers, and pooling layers. The hidden layers are used to increase the complexity of the model. And CNN is now being widely applied to the image recognition, and has achieved a good performance [2–4,19].

3 Model Construction

3.1 Extracting Basic Block

In this part, we mainly describe how to extract the basic block from the disassembled file of malware.

loc_415A81:		sub_414076 proc near		__ismbbkalnum_1:	
33 C0	xor eax, eax	33 C0	xor eax, eax	8B FF	mov edi, edi
locret_415A83:		C3	retn	5D	pop ebp
C3	retn	Sub_414076 endp		C3	retn

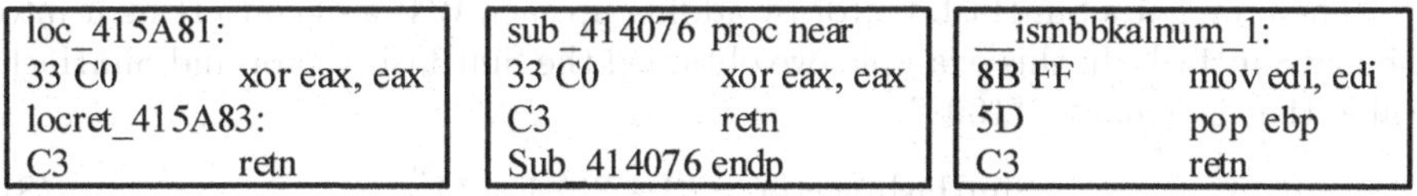

Fig. 1. Some labels of basic block

The malware we are studying is given by Microsoft [12]. And according to our study, a disassembled file of malware mainly contains multiple subroutines, and most of them start with "proc near", and end with "endp". Inside the subroutine, its branches are usually marked with "loc_" or "locret_ ". Outside the subroutine, the basic block is often marked with "XXX: "(X is a letter or symbol), as can be seen in Fig. 1.

We first extract these identifiers and opcodes that belong to them from the disassembled file according to the labels.

3.2 Applying Hash Algorithm to the Basic Block

We use SimHash algorithm to process the opcode to generate the basic block of malware. Simhash is a fingerprint generation algorithm or fingerprint extraction algorithm mentioned in [11]. And it is widely used by Google in the filed of removing duplicate pages. As a kind of locality sensitive hash, its main idea is to reduce dimension. Take the following popular case for an instance. After Simhash dimensionality reduction, a certain number of text content may only get a 32 or 64 bit binary string composed of 0 and 1.

For example in this paper(please see the right side of Fig. 1), we extract the opcodes that belong to a basic block of malware, then perform a 4-bit hash function h to explain the SimHash calculation process, Supposing this below:

$$D = (w_1 = \text{"mov"}, w_2 = \text{"pop"}, w_3 = \text{"retn"})^T \tag{1}$$

Then, we can get each above keyword's hash value as follow:

$$h(w_1) = (1, 0, 0, 0)^T \tag{2}$$
$$h(w_2) = (1, 0, 0, 1)^T \tag{3}$$
$$h(w_3) = (1, 0, 1, 0)^T \tag{4}$$

In the SimHash algorithm of our paper, the opcode of each instruction belonging to the basic block is regarded as keywords when being referred to SimHash. To achieve simplicity, we treated each opcode on the same footing. Therefore, all have the same weight of 1. Then, we can get the weight vector (WV) through weight and hash value as follows:

$$WV(w_1) = (1, -1, -1, -1)^T \tag{5}$$
$$WV(w_2) = (1, -1, -1, 1)^T \tag{6}$$
$$WV(w_3) = (1, -1, 1, -1)^T \tag{7}$$

Then, we got a SimHash vector by adding up each WV and converting it into binary SimHash. In this example, we obtained the SimHash vector and SimHash value that is equal to "1000".

$$\text{SimHash Vector} = (3, -3, -1, -1)^T \tag{8}$$

Finally, opcode sequence (OpcodeSeq) of each basic block of the malware is encoded to an n-bit SimHash value that has the same length relating to the selected hash algorithm.

According to the characteristics of the SimHash algorithm, each basic block will hash to similar SimHash values. Then we convert each SimHash bit into a pixel value $(0 \rightarrow 0, 1 \rightarrow 255)$. That is, when the bit value is 0, then the pixel value will be 0; and when the bit value is 1, then the pixel value will be 255. Then by arranging the n pixel dots in a matrix(each row of the matrix is a basic block), we convert the SimHash bits into a gray scale image. And in order to find out the appropriate hash algorithm for generating basic blocks of malicious code, we use some different hash algorithms (including multiple cascading hash functions) to generate the basic block, as shown in Table 1.

Table 1. Different hash algorithms versus image width

SimHash type	Cascading mode	Image width
SimHash128	MD5	128
SimHash256	SHA256	256
SimHash384	SHA384	384
SimHash512	SHA512	512
SimHash768	SHA512+SHA256	768
SimHash896	SHA512+SHA256+MD5	896
SimHash1024	SHA512+SHA384+MD5	1024

4   Evaluation

4.1   Malware Dataset

We use the dataset of [12], with each sample in the data set containing two files. Of which, one is hexadecimal file and the other is disassembled file. And as the disassembled file is generated from the IDA, we don't need to disassemble malware samples. The dataset has 10,868 disassembled files in 9 large malware families, and these samples have already been labelled the type of their families.

4.2   Evaluation Metrics

To evaluate the classifier's capability, True Positive Rate (TPR), False Positive Rate (FPR) and Accuracy are measured. TPR is the rate of malware samples correctly classified. FPR is the rate of malware samples falsely classified. The formulas of True Positive Rate (TPR), False Positive Rate (FPR) and Accuracy are given by Eq. 9, Eq. 10 and Eq. 11.

$$TPR = \frac{TP}{TP + FN} \tag{9}$$

$$FPR = \frac{FP}{FP + TN} \tag{10}$$

$$Accuracy(\%) = \frac{TP + TN}{TP + FN + FP + TN} * 100 \tag{11}$$

Where TP is the number of malware samples correctly classified in their class, FP is the number of malware samples incorrectly classified in another class, FN is the number of malware samples incorrectly classified in their class, and TN is the number of malware samples correctly classified in other classes.

4.3   Experimental Results and Discussion

The CNN structure [14] is demonstrated in Fig. 2. And it is clearly shown in Fig. 2, as an input, each malware image needs to go through three convolution layers, two subsampling layers and three full connection layers. And over the processes of convolutions (C1, C2, C3), each convolutional layer will involve 32 learnable filters of the size of 2×2. During the processes of subsamplings (S1, S2), the max pooling with window size 2×2, is applied to reducing training parameters. And after each max pooling, a dropout layer with probability 0.5 could avoid overfitting from happening. After the second subsampling layer (S2), we flatten the output feature map, then link it to other three fully connected layers of dimensions 512, 256, and 9 (number of malware categories) respectively. Then, the first two fully connected layers will take *tanh* as activation function with the last one utilizing *softmax* as activation function.

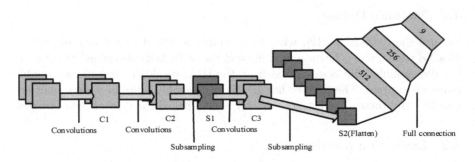

Fig. 2. CNN structure for malware image training

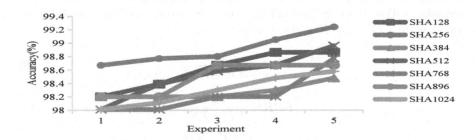

Fig. 3. Accuracy of hash algorithm

After preprocessing, 10,798 samples remained. 90% of them will be used for training, with the rest for testing. Experimental programs are written in Python, and the hardware environment is Intel®Xeon(R) CPU E5-2640 v3 @ 2.60GHz × 32 with 62.8 GB main memory. We repeat a number of times for each hash algorithm and select the top5 experimental results from them, as shown in Fig. 3, Fig. 4 and Fig. 5.

Table 2. Experimental results of SHA256

Experiment	Accuracy	TPR	FPR
1	98.67	99.17	**0.675**
2	98.77	99.61	0.740
3	98.80	99.59	1.718
4	99.05	99.60	1.290
5	**99.24**	**100**	1.265

From Fig. 3, we could know that in terms of accuracy, the best result is the hash algorithm SHA256, ranging from 98.6% to 99.3%, and the highest result is 99.24%. The experimental results of SHA256 are shown in Table 2. The worst result is the hash algorithm SHA768, and the accuracy of the rest of the hash algorithms(SHA128, SHA384, SHA512, SHA986 and SHA1024) are between 98% and 99%. According to our enlargement of Fig. 3, the order of the hash algorithms in terms of accuracy is as follows: $SHA256 > SHA128 > SHA512 > SHA896 > SHA1024 > SHA384 > SHA768$.

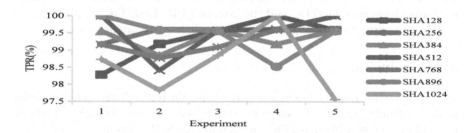

Fig. 4. True positive rate of hash algorithm

From Fig. 4, we could know that in terms of TPR, the best result seems to be achieved by hash algorithm SHA256, and the worst result is obtained by the hash algorithm SHA1024, and the TPR of other hash algorithms is between 98% and 100%. From Fig. 5, we could know that in terms of FPR, the best result is obtained by the hash algorithm SHA256, with its average FPR being 1.1376%. And the FPR of other hash algorithms is between 0.5% and 4%. From the analyses of Fig. 3, Fig. 4, and Fig. 5, we could know that SHA256 is the most suitable hash algorithm to generate the basic block of malicious code.

From Fig. 3, we could know that the difference between SHA256 and SHA384 is greater than that between SHA896 and SHA1024. From Table 1, we could know that the only difference between SHA896 and SHA1024 is that the former has cascaded SHA256, while the latter has cascaded SHA384. Therefore, it could be seen from Fig. 3 and Table 1, SHA256 is more negatively affected than SHA384 in the cascading hash function. A comparison of the gap between

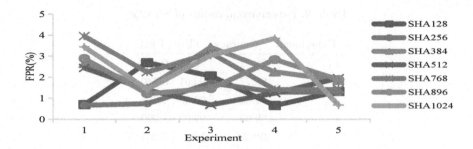

Fig. 5. False positive rate of hash algorithm

SHA256 and SHA768, as well as the comparison of the gap between SHA512 and SHA768 can also lead to this conclusion.

For comparison with our method, we choose the method proposed in Nataraj et al. [13] which has adopted GIST features of malware images and K-Nearest Neighbor (KNN, K = 3) classification. In the algorithm, GIST feature of 512 dimensions and KNN are used to classify these samples. The algorithm repeats 5 times for random sampling, and in the end, average accuracy of GIST-KNN algorithm on the test set of 9 families is 95.595%, the best accuracy of GIST-KNN algorithm gets 95.974%, and the average FPR of GIST-KNN algorithm is 4.31%. Compared with their method, ours is obviously more accurate.

5   Conclusion

Malware classification has become a major topic for research and concern owing to the continuing growth of malicious code in recent years. Aiming at tackling the problems caused by manual feature acquisition in the current malicious code classification method, we propose a method of malware classification that is based on basic block and convolutional neural network. Specifically, we propose a method for representing malware that relies on gray image that is generated from opcodes of the basic block. And experiments show that this method could achieve brilliant accuracy as high as 99.24%. Based on the method, the newly discovered malicious code samples can be accurately classified and their analysis efficiency can be improved.

References

1. Abadi, M., et al.: TensorFlow: a system for large-scale machine learning. In: 12th USENIX Symposium on Operating Systems Design and Implementation (OSDI 2016), pp. 265–283. USENIX Association, Savannah (2016)
2. Alex, K., Ilya, S., Hg, E.: ImageNet classification with deep convolutional neural networks, pp. 1097–1105, January 2012
3. Gibert, D., Mateu, C., Planes, J., Vicens, R.: Classification of malware by using structural entropy on convolutional neural networks. In: Thirty-Second AAAI Conference on Artificial Intelligence (2018)

4. Girshick, R., Donahue, J., Darrell, T., Malik, J.: Rich feature hierarchies for accurate object detection and semantic segmentation. In: IEEE Conference on Computer Vision and Pattern Recognition (2014)
5. Grimes, R.A.: Malicious Mobile Code. Oreilly & Associates Inc. (2001)
6. Heaton, J., Goodfellow, I., Bengio, Y., Courville, A.: Deep learning. Genet. Program. Evol. Mach. **19**(1–2), 1–3 (2017)
7. Islam, M.R., Tian, R., Batten, L., Versteeg, S.: Classification of malware based on integrated static and dynamic features. J. Netw. Comput. Appl. **36**, 646–656 (2013). https://doi.org/10.1016/j.jnca.2012.10.004
8. Karampatziakis, N., Stokes, J.W., Thomas, A., Marinescu, M.: Using File Relationships in Malware Classification. Springer, Heidelberg (2012)
9. Labs, M.: Mcafee labs threat report. McAfee Labs Threat Report (2019). https://www.mcafee.com/enterprise/en-us/assets/reports/rp-quarterly-threats-aug-2019.pdf
10. Lecun, Y., Bengio, Y., Hinton, G.: Deep learning. Nature **521**(7553), 436 (2015)
11. Manku, G.S., Jain, A., Das Sarma, A.: Detecting near-duplicates for web crawling. In: Proceedings of the 16th International Conference on World Wide Web, WWW 2007, pp. 141–150. Association for Computing Machinery, New York (2007). https://doi.org/10.1145/1242572.1242592
12. Microsoft: Microsoft malware classification challenge. Microsoft Malware Classification Challenge (2015). http://arxiv.org/abs/1802.10135
13. Nataraj, L., Karthikeyan, S., Jacob, G., Manjunath, B.: Malware images: visualization and automatic classification, July 2011. https://doi.org/10.1145/2016904.2016908
14. Ni, S., Qian, Q., Zhang, R.: Malware identification using visualization images and deep learning. Comput. Secur. **77**(AUG), 871–885 (2018)
15. Silver, D., et al.: Mastering the game of go with deep neural networks and tree search. Nature **529**(7587), 484–489 (2016)
16. Stakhanova, N., Couture, M., Ghorbani, A.A.: Exploring network-based malware classification. In: 2011 6th International Conference on Malicious and Unwanted Software (2011)
17. Tian, K., Yao, D., Ryder, B., Tan, G.: Analysis of code heterogeneity for high-precision classification of repackaged malware. In: 2016 IEEE Security and Privacy Workshops (SPW), pp. 262–271, May 016
18. Xue, D., Li, J., Lv, T., Wu, W., Wang, J.: Malware classification using probability scoring and machine learning. IEEE Access **PP**(99), 1 (2019)
19. Yan, Z., et al.: HD-CNN: hierarchical deep convolutional neural networks for large scale visual recognition. In: IEEE International Conference on Computer Vision (2016)

A Shape-Aware Feature Extraction Module for Semantic Segmentation of 3D Point Clouds

Jiachen Xu, Jie Zhou, Xin Tan$^{(\boxtimes)}$, and Lizhuang Ma

Shanghai Jiao Tong University, Shanghai, China
{xujiachen,lord_liang,tanxin2017}@sjtu.edu.cn, ma-lz@cs.sjtu.edu.cn

Abstract. 3D shape pattern description of raw point clouds plays an essential and important role in 3D understanding. Previous works often learn feature representations via the solid cubic or spherical neighborhood, ignoring the distinction between the point distributions of objects in various shapes. Additionally, most works encode the spatial information in each neighborhood implicitly by learning edge weights between points, which is not enough to restore spatial information. In this paper, a Shape-Aware Feature Extraction (SAFE) module is proposed. It explicitly describes the spatial distribution of points in the neighborhood by well-designed distribution descriptors and replaces the conventional solid neighborhood with a hollow spherical neighborhood. Then, we encode the inner pattern and the outer pattern separately in the hollow spherical neighborhood to achieve shape awareness. Building an encoder-decoder network based on the SAFE module, we conduct extensive experiments and the results show that our SAFE-based network achieves state-of-the-art performance on the benchmark datasets ScanNet and ShapeNet.

Keywords: Neural networks · Point clouds · Semantic segmentation · RGBD processing · Shape awareness

1 Introduction

Semantic segmentation of point clouds is a fundamental task in many 3D fields such as robotics and autonomous driving. Different from images or videos which are both regular grid data, 3D point clouds are hard to process because of its irregularity and sparsity, which hinders the development of semantic segmentation of 3D point clouds.

Impressively, PointNet [11] and PointNet++ [12] are the pioneer to process raw point cloud directly. But both PointNet and PointNet++ use the max-pooling to extract features for local regions, which destroys the spatial information and ignores the point distribution in each neighborhood. It is noteworthy that recognizing different kinds of point distributions could help recognize different shapes. For example, when recognizing a door, it is important to determine

© Springer Nature Switzerland AG 2020
H. Yang et al. (Eds.): ICONIP 2020, CCIS 1332, pp. 284–293, 2020.
https://doi.org/10.1007/978-3-030-63820-7_32

whether points are distributed on a plane. Therefore, PCNN [15] and Spider-CNN [18] utilize multi-layer perceptrons and the Taylor polynomial, respectively, to implicitly encode the relative positions, as well as the point distributions.

By contrast, to explicitly encode the point distribution of each local region and achieve shape awareness, we propose a more intuitive and shape-aware module, namely Shape-Aware Feature Extraction (SAFE), to explicitly describe the positional relations between points and retain the spatial information in each neighborhood. That is, each neighborhood is divided into several bins according to specific strategies and then descriptor, namely distribution descriptor, is generated based on the statistics of the number of points in each bin. Compared with previous works [15,17,18], this descriptor encodes spatial information explicitly because it directly describes the location of each point in the neighborhood.

Furthermore, a point cloud forms an underlying shape and the learned representation for each neighborhood should be of discriminative shape awareness [8]. However, in previous neighborhood-based works [8,12,17], local features are extracted from a solid spherical neighborhood which fails to distinguish objects with different point distributions. Therefore, we introduce a hollow spherical neighborhood and deal with inner and outer neighboring points separately, which makes full use of the difference between objects with different point distributions. Because different point distributions would show different patterns in the inner and outer neighborhoods. We will discuss about it in detail in Sect. 3.4.

Then, we build the SAFE-based encoder-decoder network and conduct experiments on ScanNet [3] and ShapeNet [2]. Results show that our SAFE-based network achieves the state-of-the-art results on both benchmark datasets.

2   Related Work

Regular Representation. To make full use of grid convolution, it is intuitive to convert irregular point clouds to regular representation [10]. Considering the high computational complexity and memory cost, SparseConvNet [4] proposed a novel way to store and index data so as to get rid of extra overhead. However, converting point clouds into regular representation inevitably destroys the inherent structure information.

Graph-Based Convolution Network. The point cloud itself could be seen as a graph as well as each local region. DGCNN [16] extracted edge features to describe the relation between a point and its neighbors so as to encode the local pattern of each neighborhood. Furthermore, HPEIN [6] proposed a novel edge branch to extract edge features in different scales and integrated edge features into the point branch to enhance the performance. GAC [14] used an attention convolution to tackle the problem that the extracted features incorporate points of different categories.

Point-Based Convolution Network. Instead of learning the edge weight by MLPs like most graph-based convolutions, InterpConv [9] imitated a 3D grid convolution and initialized a fixed number of learnable kernel points. Then,

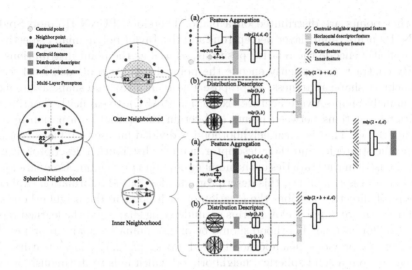

Fig. 1. Illustration of proposed Shape-Aware Feature Extraction (SAFE) module with the inner and outer neighborhoods. (a) Feature Aggregation and (b) Distribution Descriptor abstract features from both the inner and outer neighborhoods. d is the dimension of the input of SAFE module. (Color figure online)

neighboring points are interpolated to the kernel points so that each neighborhood could convolve with the kernel. Furthermore, KPConv [13] designed a deformable convolution kernel consisting of learnable points, that is, the position of each kernel point could be adjusted adaptively.

In aforementioned works, the local region is solid neighborhood. By contrast, our proposed SAFE module introduces hollow spherical neighborhood to achieve shape awareness. Besides, most existing works implicitly encode point distributions by positional relations between points. However, in the SAFE module, we propose the distribution descriptor to explicitly describe the point distribution.

3   Method

3.1   Hollow Spherical Neighborhood

To improve the ability of the SAFE module to distinguish objects with various point distributions, we replace the widely used solid neighborhood with a hollow spherical neighborhood. As shown in Fig. 1, a solid spherical neighborhood is partitioned into two parts with an inner radius of $R1$ and an outer radius of $R2$: the inner neighborhood (blue) and the outer neighborhood (orange). The distance between the centroid and each point in the inner neighborhood ranges from 0 to $R1$ while the distance of each point in the outer ranges from $R1$ to $R2$. For the inner and outer neighborhoods, local features that encode different patterns are abstracted separately and then integrated to form the shape-aware hollow spherical feature for each neighborhood.

3.2   Feature Aggregation

To make full use of the information of neighbors (i.e., features), for a certain point p_i in a point cloud, the SAFE module adopts a feature aggregation strategy to extract the local feature from its neighborhood, with p_i as the centroid and surrounding points as neighbors $p_{n_j} \in \mathcal{N}(p_i)$. Taking into account the distinctive positional relation between p_{n_j} and p_i, features of different neighbors are weighted differently according to the corresponding relation. As illustrated in Fig. 1(a), each weight is learnt from the relation between each neighboring point (blue) and the centroid (yellow). Therefore, the aggregated feature from neighbors is formulated as:

$$f_{aggr} = \max_{p_{n_j} \in \mathcal{N}(p_i)} \{\Psi(r_j) \cdot f_j\} \tag{1}$$

where f_{aggr} represents the aggregated feature for p_i. $\Psi(\cdot)$ is the multi-layer perceptron to learn the weight for each neighboring point. r_j is the relation between p_{n_j} and p_i, and f_j represents the feature of p_{n_j}. After aggregating the features of neighbors for p_i, Fig. 1(a) shows that the feature of centroid p_i (yellow) is directly concatenated to the aggregated feature (blue) followed by a shared multi-layer perceptron to form the extracted local feature for p_i. Therefore, the new feature keeps more information of the centroid than neighbors.

3.3   Distribution Descriptor

In addition to the features of neighbors themselves, the spatial information of neighborhood also matters. Therefore, we propose a distribution descriptor in SAFE module to describe the spatial distribution of points in each neighborhood. Intuitively, we divide the neighborhood into the 3D mesh grid and generate a vector as the descriptor based on the number of points in each cell. However, due to the sparsity of point clouds, many cells are empty so that there are many zeros in the descriptor and the distinguishing ability of the descriptor decreases. Instead, for a point p_i, its neighborhood $\mathcal{N}(p_i)$ is divided into b bins uniformly according to two strategies shown in Fig. 1(b). Compared with 3D mesh grid, they could improve the distinguishing ability while preserving spatial distribution information. As illustrated in Fig. 1(b), the first strategy captures the vertical spatial information. Additionally, because the objects in the scene can be rotated at any angle around the z axis, the second is enough to capture the horizontal spatial information and keep robust to objects with different directions of distribution as well.

The index of the corresponding bin that a certain neighboring point is located in could be formulated as:

$$idx = \lfloor \frac{arctan(v_z, \sqrt{v_x^2 + v_y^2})}{\Delta_d} \rfloor \tag{2}$$

where Δ_d denotes the angle between two sections and (v_x, v_y, v_z) represents the relative coordinate of the neighboring point to the centroid. Next, the number

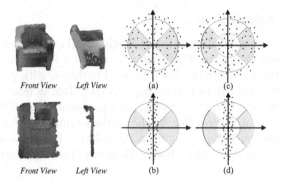

Front View   Left View   (a)   (c)

Front View   Left View   (b)   (d)

Fig. 2. The front view and left view of a chair and a door, which are selected from ScanNet dataset.

of neighboring points located in each bin is counted separately so that a b-dimensional distribution descriptor $l = \{l_i\}_{i=1}^{b}$ is then obtained.

3.4   Shape Awareness

As mentioned above, an important property of the SAFE module is shape awareness. To achieve that, we introduce the hollow spherical neighborhood into SAFE module instead of the solid spherical neighborhood so that it can learn local patterns from inner neighborhood and outer neighborhood separately to recognize the various point distributions, which usually have different local patterns in the outer neighborhood.

For simplicity, we take the chair and the door as examples, which represent two common types of point distributions. One type (e.g., chair) is that points are distributed uniformly in all directions. The other type (e.g., door) is that there exists a direction where points converge in a small scope. For example, points along the thin edge of the door converge in a small scope. As shown in Fig. 2, the top row is a 2D visualization of a chair and the bottom row visualizes a door (viewed towards the thin edge of the door). A solid spherical neighborhood is used in (a) and (b). It is noted that without the outer neighborhood, points are located in both yellow and white bins regardless of the shape. There is no significant difference between two distribution descriptors generated based on the number of points in each bin. But for the hollow spherical neighborhood used in (c) and (d), considering the outer neighborhood, points of the door are only located in white bins while points of the chair are in both white and yellow bins. Therefore, the difference between components of the descriptor of the door is obvious, that is, some components have large values while some are zero. While the difference of the descriptor of the chair is not obvious, that is, components of the corresponding descriptor would all have large or small values at the same time. Therefore, these shape-aware descriptors differ significantly for different shapes.

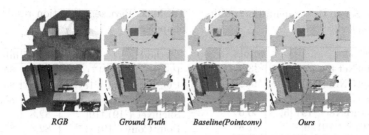

RGB   Ground Truth   Baseline(Pointconv)   Ours

Fig. 3. Visual results of ScanNet.

Although shaving off the inner neighborhood provides a shape-aware descriptor, there is still local information preserved in it. Therefore, we also keep the inner neighborhood and extract local features from these two neighborhoods separately.

3.5 Overall Architecture

Based on the proposed SAFE module, we build an encoder-decoder network. In the encoding stage, we utilize four sampling layers [12] to downsample the input point cloud hierarchically and the SAFE module is inserted after each encoding layer. The radius of the outer neighborhood R_2 is 0.1, 0.2, 0.4 and 0.8, respectively, and there are totally 32 points in the whole neighborhood (i.e., the inner and outer neighborhoods). In the decoding stage, we apply four corresponding interpolation layers [12] for upsampling. Then, we also insert SAFE module, which selects 16 points in the whole neighborhood, after each interpolation layer and the outer radius R_2 is 0.8, 0.4, 0.2 and 0.1, respectively. Although the distribution of points in the whole point cloud is not uniform, points in each neighborhood scatter uniformly. Therefore, in each neighborhood, we set the inner radius R_1 to be the half of R_2. Additionally, we divide each neighborhood into 18 to generate the descriptors.

4 Experiments

In this section, we first conduct experiments to prove the performance of the SAFE module in both semantic segmentation task and part segmentation task in Sect. 4.1 and Sect. 4.2, respectively. Furthermore, we validate the effectiveness of the hollow spherical neighborhood and prove that it could help achieve shape awareness in Sect. 4.3. Finally, we demonstrate the effectiveness of the distribution descriptor in Sect. 4.3.

4.1 Scene Semantic Segmentation on ScanNet

To show the performance of our SAFE module in scene semantic segmentation task, we conduct experiments on ScanNet v2 [3]. ScanNet totally contains 1,513

Table 1. Semantic segmentation results on ScanNet v2

Method	mIoU
PointNet++ ('17) [12]	33.9
PointCNN ('18) [7]	45.8
PointConv ('19) [17]	55.6
TextureNet ('19) [5]	56.6
HPEIN ('19) [6]	61.8
Ours	**62.6**

Table 2. Part segmentation results on ShapeNet

Method	mcIoU	mIoU
PointNet++ ('17) [12]	81.9	85.1
PCNN by Ext ('18) [1]	81.8	85.1
SpiderCNN ('18) [18]	82.4	85.3
ShellNet ('19) [19]	82.8	-
PointConv ('19) [17]	82.8	85.7
Ours	**82.9**	**85.9**

Table 3. Ablation study of SAFE module. "des." represents for distribution descriptors and "solid neigh." represents for solid spherical neighborhood

Method	SAFE w/o des.	SAFE w/solid neigh.	Ours
mIoU	60.4	60.8	62.4

annotated scans in which $1,201$ scans are used for training and 312 scans are used for validation. Additionally, there are still 100 test scans for online benchmarking. Follow [17], in training phase, we randomly sample $3m \times 1.5m \times 1.5m$ cubes in rooms and there are $4,096$ points per cube. Then, in testing phase, we test over the whole scene and submit the result to the official evaluation server.

Results. Table 1 shows the mean IoU (mIoU) over categories. Our method achieves 62.6% in mIoU and exceeds previous methods by a large margin. Moreover, in Fig. 3, we visualize the results of our method. Additionally, because we use the same backbone as PointConv [17], we also visualize the results of PointConv for comparison.

4.2 Part Segmentation on ShapeNet

To prove the generalization ability of our method to the part segmentation task, we conduct experiments on ShapeNet [2]. ShapeNet dataset is a collection of totally $16,681$ point clouds from 16 categories and each category has 2-6 part labels.

Results. Table 2 reports our result in terms of class average IoU (mcIoU) and instance average IoU (mIoU) for part segmentation. Our method achieves mcIoU of 82.9% and mIoU of 85.9%, and surpasses the state-of-the art methods on both mcIoU and mIoU.

4.3 Ablation Study

To further prove the effectiveness of our method, we conduct more ablation studies on ScanNet. However, because we can only submit the final result once to the online benchmark server of ScanNet, following PointConv [17], more ablation studies are conducted on the validation dataset of ScanNet.

Effectiveness of Distribution Descriptor. To demonstrate the effectiveness of distribution descriptors, we simply remove the two kinds of distribution descriptors, which are illustrated in Fig. 1(b), from our SAFE module. The result is reported in Table 3. We can learn from the table that SAFE module without the distribution descriptors would only achieve 60.4% in mIoU and lower the mIoU of the proposed SAFE module by 2.0%.

Table 4. IoUs of some objects in ScanNet using different kinds of neighborhoods in the SAFE module. "refrig." and "showercur." represent for refrigerator and show curtain.

Method	Chair	Desk	Refrig	Counter	Door	Window	Showercur	Wall
Solid neigh.	78.3	40.6	54.5	56.8	39.4	50.0	53.1	69.1
Hollow neigh.	**80.9**	**51.6**	**59.0**	**57.6**	**41.0**	**62.8**	**60.6**	**73.1**

Effectiveness of Hollow Neighborhood. To validate the effectiveness of hollow spherical neighborhood, we replace the proposed hollow neighborhood with conventional solid neighborhood in the SAFE module. Shown as Table 3, using the solid spherical neighborhood lowers the mIoU by 1.6%. As mentioned in Sect. 3.4, we introduce two common types of point distributions. One type includes chairs, refrigerators, etc. The other contains doors, windows, etc. To demonstrate that our proposed hollow neighborhood could be aware to these two distributions, we list the results on some objects in Table 4. It is proved that the hollow spherical neighborhood could enhance the performance of most objects and achieve the shape awareness.

5 Conclusion

In this paper, we propose a shape-aware feature extraction (SAFE) module. It adopts the hollow spherical neighborhood so as to separately encode the patterns of inner and outer neighborhoods, where two distribution descriptors are also introduced to explicitly retain the spatial information. Furthermore, the hollow neighborhood helps SAFE module distinguish various shapes. Then, we build an SAFE-basd encoder-decoder network, which can handle both semantic segmentation task and part segmentation task. Overall, our SAFE-based network achieves the state-of-the-art performance on both ScanNet and ShapeNet.

Acknowledgments. We thank for the support from National Natural Science Foundation of China (61972157, 61902129), Shanghai Pujiang Talent Program (19PJ1403100), Economy and Information Commission of Shanghai (XX-RGZN-01-19-6348), National Key Research and Development Program of China (No. 2019YFC1521104).

References

1. Atzmon, M., Maron, H., Lipman, Y.: Point convolutional neural networks by extension operators. ACM Trans. Graph. (TOG) **37**(4), 71 (2018)
2. Chang, A.X., et al.: Shapenet: an information-rich 3D model repository. arXiv preprint arXiv:1512.03012 (2015)
3. Dai, A., Chang, A.X., Savva, M., Halber, M., Funkhouser, T., Nießner, M.: Scannet: richly-annotated 3d reconstructions of indoor scenes. In: Proceedings of the IEEE Conference on Computer Vision and Pattern Recognition (CVPR), pp. 5828–5839 (2017)
4. Graham, B., Engelcke, M., van der Maaten, L.: 3D semantic segmentation with submanifold sparse convolutional networks. In: Proceedings of the IEEE Conference on Computer Vision and Pattern Recognition, pp. 9224–9232 (2018)
5. Huang, J., Zhang, H., Yi, L., Funkhouser, T., Nießner, M., Guibas, L.J.: Texturenet: consistent local parametrizations for learning from high-resolution signals on meshes. In: Proceedings of the IEEE Conference on Computer Vision and Pattern Recognition (CVPR), pp. 4440–4449 (2019)
6. Jiang, L., Zhao, H., Liu, S., Shen, X., Fu, C.W., Jia, J.: Hierarchical point-edge interaction network for point cloud semantic segmentation. In: Proceedings of the IEEE International Conference on Computer Vision, pp. 10433–10441 (2019)
7. Li, Y., Bu, R., Sun, M., Wu, W., Di, X., Chen, B.: Pointcnn: convolution on x-transformed points. In: Advances in Neural Information Processing Systems (NIPS), pp. 820–830 (2018)
8. Liu, Y., Fan, B., Xiang, S., Pan, C.: Relation-shape convolutional neural network for point cloud analysis. In: Proceedings of the IEEE Conference on Computer Vision and Pattern Recognition (CVPR), pp. 8895–8904 (2019)
9. Mao, J., Wang, X., Li, H.: Interpolated convolutional networks for 3D point cloud understanding. In: Proceedings of the IEEE International Conference on Computer Vision, pp. 1578–1587 (2019)
10. Maturana, D., Scherer, S.: Voxnet: a 3D convolutional neural network for real-time object recognition. In: 2015 IEEE/RSJ International Conference on Intelligent Robots and Systems (IROS), pp. 922–928 (2015)
11. Qi, C.R., Su, H., Mo, K., Guibas, L.J.: Pointnet: deep learning on point sets for 3D classification and segmentation. In: Proceedings of the IEEE Conference on Computer Vision and Pattern Recognition (CVPR), pp. 652–660 (2017)
12. Qi, C.R., Yi, L., Su, H., Guibas, L.J.: Pointnet++: deep hierarchical feature learning on point sets in a metric space. In: Advances in Neural Information Processing Systems (NIPS), pp. 5099–5108 (2017)
13. Thomas, H., Qi, C.R., Deschaud, J.E., Marcotegui, B., Goulette, F., Guibas, L.J.: KPConv: flexible and deformable convolution for point clouds. In: Proceedings of the IEEE International Conference on Computer Vision, pp. 6411–6420 (2019)
14. Wang, L., Huang, Y., Hou, Y., Zhang, S., Shan, J.: Graph attention convolution for point cloud semantic segmentation. In: Proceedings of the IEEE Conference on Computer Vision and Pattern Recognition (CVPR), pp. 10296–10305 (2019)
15. Wang, S., Suo, S., Ma, W.C., Pokrovsky, A., Urtasun, R.: Deep parametric continuous convolutional neural networks. In: Proceedings of the IEEE Conference on Computer Vision and Pattern Recognition, pp. 2589–2597 (2018)
16. Wang, Y., Sun, Y., Liu, Z., Sarma, S.E., Bronstein, M.M., Solomon, J.M.: Dynamic graph CNN for learning on point clouds. ACM Trans. Graphics (TOG) (2019)

17. Wu, W., Qi, Z., Fuxin, L.: Pointconv: deep convolutional networks on 3D point clouds. In: Proceedings of the IEEE Conference on Computer Vision and Pattern Recognition (CVPR), pp. 9621–9630 (2019)
18. Xu, Y., Fan, T., Xu, M., Zeng, L., Qiao, Y.: SpiderCNN: deep learning on point sets with parameterized convolutional filters. In: Ferrari, V., Hebert, M., Sminchisescu, C., Weiss, Y. (eds.) ECCV 2018. LNCS, vol. 11212, pp. 90–105. Springer, Cham (2018). https://doi.org/10.1007/978-3-030-01237-3_6
19. Zhang, Z., Hua, B.S., Yeung, S.K.: Shellnet: efficient point cloud convolutional neural networks using concentric shells statistics. In: Proceedings of the IEEE International Conference on Computer Vision (ICCV), pp. 1607–1616 (2019)

A Strong Baseline for Fashion Retrieval with Person Re-identification Models

Mikolaj Wieczorek[1]([✉]), Andrzej Michalowski[1], Anna Wroblewska[1,2][iD],
and Jacek Dabrowski[1]

[1] Synerise, Kraków, Poland
mikolaj.wieczorek@synerise.com
[2] Warsaw University of Technology, Warsaw, Poland

Abstract. Fashion retrieval is a challenging task of finding an exact match for fashion items contained within an image. Difficulties arise from the fine-grained nature of clothing items, very large intra-class and inter-class variance. Additionally, query and source images for the task usually come from different domains - street and catalogue photos, respectively. Due to these differences, a significant gap in quality, lighting, contrast, background clutter and item presentation exists. As a result, fashion retrieval is an active field of research both in academia and the industry. Inspired by recent advancements in person re-identification research, we adapt leading ReID models to fashion retrieval tasks. We introduce a simple baseline model for fashion retrieval, significantly outperforming previous state-of-the-art results, despite a much simpler architecture. We conduct in-depth experiments on *Street2Shop* and *DeepFashion* datasets. Finally, we propose a cross-domain (cross-dataset) evaluation method to test the robustness of fashion retrieval models.

Keywords: Clothes retrieval · Fashion retrieval · Quadruplet loss · Person re-identification · Deep learning in fashion.

1 Introduction

The aim of fashion retrieval is to find exact or very similar products from the vendor's catalogue (gallery) to the given query image. Creating a model that can find similarities between the content of the images is essential for the two visual-related products for the fashion industry: recommendations and search.

Visual recommendations (VR) – *In-shop retrieval* – visual similarity between a currently viewed product and other products from the catalogue.

Visual search (VS) – *Consumer-to-shop* – visual similarity between user taken/uploaded photo and the products' photos in the vendor's database. This case is a cross-domain retrieval problem.

This work was supported by the EU co-funded Smart Growth Operational Programme 2014–2020 (project no. POIR.01.01.01-00-0695/19).

H. Yang et al. (Eds.): ICONIP 2020, CCIS 1332, pp. 294–301, 2020.
https://doi.org/10.1007/978-3-030-63820-7_33

During work on VS solutions, we found that the task of clothes retrieval is in many ways analogous to person re-identification problem (ReID). Both problems must implicitly consider a common subset of clothes and materials deformations specific to human body poses and shapes. Moreover, both models have to deal with occlusion, lighting, angle and orientation differences. Finally, clothes are an essential factor in ReID task, especially when faces are not visible.

What makes ReID task different from VS, is the fact that ReID data can be deemed homogeneous in contrast to fashion datasets where images come from two domains. In ReID, the majority of pictures are taken with a comparable circumstance (e.g. a model's pose and a background). In contrast, user images in a fashion retrieval differ both in the alignment, orientation and content. Finally, ReID problems may use additional temporal information to narrow down the search space, e.g. [7], which adds an information stream unavailable in the fashion domain. The first two differences are addressed in fashion retrieval task by the right composition of training datasets, which contain examples from both domains (street/shop). Often the fashion product of interest is cropped, occluded or deformed as a person wears it (see Fig. 1).

Fig. 1. Examples of images from ReID dataset, *DeepFashion* and *Street2Shop*

We decided to investigate how and which ReID solutions can be effectively applied to the fashion retrieval task. Our main contributions are:

- Recognition of deep analogies between ReID and fashion retrieval tasks.
- A review of ReID models and their applicability to fashion retrieval tasks.
- Adjustments of ReID models for their application to the fashion domain.
- Thorough evaluation of the adapted ReID models on two fashion datasets.
- Our adapted model for fashion retrieval significantly outperforming state-of-the-art results for *DeepFashion* and *Street2Shop* datasets.
- A cross-domain (cross-dataset) evaluation to test the robustness of our approach.

2   Our Approach

Our work aimed to investigate if and how ReID models can be successfully applied to the fashion retrieval task. Based on our research on the performance of various models in person ReID task and their suitability for the fashion retrieval problem, we selected the most appropriate models.

First, [5] presents an approach that combines the most efficient training tricks and sets a strong baseline for other ReID researchers; hence its name: *ReID Strong Baseline* (RST). Through a thorough evaluation, it showed that by combining simple architecture, global features and using training tricks it could surpass SOTA performance in the ReID domain.

The second choice – *OSNet-AIN* [10] uses features extracted from different scales, which seems to be a well-suited approach in a fine-grained instance retrieval. The authors devised a flexible fusion mechanism that allows the network to focus on local or global features that improve performance. The whole neural architecture was purpose-built for the ReID task.

Loss Functions. While training the selected ReID models, we dealt with three loss functions. For the *OSNet-AIN*, we followed the training regime proposed by its authors, and we trained the model using only a classification loss. For the RST model, we used a loss function that consisted of three elements: a classification loss, a triplet loss [6] and a centre loss [8]. Additionally, we tested if by replacing the triplet loss with a quadruplet loss, one could improve the performance. Our implementation of the quadruplet loss follows the one found in [1].

Metrics. To evaluate the performance of our approach we used metrics that we found most often in the related papers. The most widely used metric in retrieval tasks is *Accuracy@k* (*Acc@k*). The metric measures if the retrieved item was among top-k proposals. The other metric that we encountered in the papers was *mAP*, which is a mean average precision, that shows how well the retrieval is done on average. Though *mAP* values were rarely reported in clothes retrieval papers, we decided to use this metric in our experiments along *Acc@k*.

2.1 SOTA Models for Fashion Retrieval Vs RST Model

To compare our results with the current SOTA, we found [4] to achieve the best results on *Street2Shop* dataset, while [3] seems to show SOTA performance on the *DeepFashion* retrieval task.

In Fig. 2, we present the RST model, which shows the pipeline and all parts of the architecture. It can be deemed as strikingly simple, yet it substantially exceeds current SOTA results. Apart from the architecture, it also utilizes several useful training tricks, which improve performance. RST model uses following tricks: warm-up learning rate, random erasing augmentation, label smoothing, last stride set to 1, BNNeck (normalization layer) and centre loss. A more detailed description of the base RST model can be found in [5].

3   Experiments

To allow a fair comparison of our model to the current SOTA results, we show the main settings used for training and evaluation in Table 1. Cropping images from

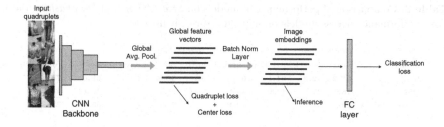

Fig. 2. RST model architecture

the dataset can be done either by using ground-truth (GT) or detected (DT) bounding boxes. For *Street2Shop* dataset, we use much smaller images than [4] and to make our task more challenging we compare our results to an ensemble model from [4]. Settings used in [3] for evaluation on *DeepFashion* dataset were not clearly specified, therefore we use question marks in Table 1 for some of them. Our assumptions about the settings used in [3] are based on the vague description in the paper mentioned above. We suppose that the model in [3] was trained with cropped images and human-curated dataset merged from *DeepFashion* and *Street2Shop*. Unfortunately, there is no code available to validate the results and experimentally confirm their settings.

Table 1. Comparison of the settings between the current SOTA and our model

	DeepFashion		Street2Shop	
	Current SOTA [3]	Our model	Current SOTA [4]	Our model
Backbone	GoogLeNet	GoogLeNet	ResNet-50	ResNet-50
Image size	224 × 224	224 × 224	800 × 800	320 × 320
Street photos crop	GT?	GT	GT	GT
Shop photos crop	GT?	GT	DT	✗
Data cleaning	✓?	✗	✗	✗
Ensemble model	✗	✗	✓	✗

ReID Models Comparison In the first experiment, we trained both ReID models to compare their performance on our datasets. For training, we used 256 × 128 input images. Table 2 contains the results of the models and current state-of-the-art metrics. The RST model (ResNet-50 backbone) surpasses the current SOTA model, and the *OSNet-AIN* performs worse than the other two approaches. The reason for the poor performance of *OSNet* may be the fact that it is a lightweight network and built specifically for ReID tasks. Due to the large performance gap between RST and *OSNet* models, we decided to conduct further experiments using only the more promising RST model.

Table 2. Comparison of performance of models on *Street2Shop* and *DeepFashion* data. Best performance across models on a given dataset is in bold

Model	Street2Shop				DeepFashion				
	mAP	Acc@1	Acc@10	Acc@20	mAP	Acc@1	Acc@10	Acc@20	Acc@50
RST	**37.2**	**42.3**	**61.1**	**66.5**	**35**	**30.8**	**62.3**	**69.4**	**78**
OSNet-AIN	18.9	25.3	40.8	45.4	20.1	17.5	40.2	46.9	53.8
Current SOTA	29.7	34.4	-	60.4	-	27.5	-	65.3	75

Backbone Influence. Next, we inspect the influence of the used backbone on results (Table 3). All runs were performed on input images of size 256×128, using an RST approach with all tricks enabled and using quadruplet loss. Our findings are in line with backbone performance presented by the authors in [5], i.e. *ResNet50-IBN-A* [9] is the best performing backbone. Such a large advantage in performance for *Resnet50-IBNs* may be caused by an instance normalization used, which reduces the impact of variations in contrast and lighting between street and shop photos.

Table 3. Results achieved by different backbones on *Street2Shop* and *DeepFashion*

Backbone	Street2Shop				DeepFashion				
	mAP	Acc@1	Acc@10	Acc@20	mAP	Acc@1	Acc@10	Acc@20	Acc@50
ResNet-50	32.0	36.6	55.3	60.6	32.4	28.1	58.3	65.5	74.2
SeResNet-50	30.5	34.6	53.1	58.7	31.3	27.0	57.8	65.4	74.4
SeResNeXt-50	31.9	36.9	54.5	59.7	32.2	27.8	58.5	66.0	74.6
ResNet50-IBN-A	**37.2**	**42,3**	**61.1**	**66.5**	**35.0**	**30.8**	**62.3**	**69.4**	**78.0**
ResNet50-IBN-B	36.9	41.9	60.6	65.1	32.2	28.1	58.4	65.8	74.7
EfficientNet-b1	28.8	35.1	52.1	56.7	28.5	23.4	49.8	56.8	66.1
EfficientNet-b2	29.4	34.0	50.8	56.2	24.1	20.4	45.9	53.2	62.6
EfficientNet-b4	31.8	38.2	55.6	60.2	26.8	23.1	59.1	57.4	66.7

Influence of Loss Functions. The results for the RST model using triplet and quadruplet loss are shown in Table 4. We can see that the quadruplet loss in our test settings performed marginally better than the triplet loss, yet it brings an improvement at almost no cost.

Influence of Input Image Size. In our fourth experiment, we tested if larger images would result in even higher performance. Outcomes of our experiments are presented in Table 5. Using larger images allows for boosting performance further. In our settings, we achieved the best results for input images of size 320×320. Using larger images (480×480) did not bring any advantage.

Comparison to the State-of-the-Art. In Table 6 we compare our results to the state-of-the-art on *Street2Shop* dataset [4]. For a fair comparison with [4]

Table 4. Our results on *Street2Shop* and *DeepFashion* datasets achieved with triplet and quadruplet loss functions

	Street2Shop				DeepFashion			
Loss function	mAP	Acc@1	Acc@10	Acc@20	mAP	Acc@1	Acc@10	Acc@20
Quadruplet	**37.2**	**42.3**	**61.1**	**66.5**	**35**	**30.8**	62.3	69.4
Triplet	37.1	41.8	60.4	65.7	34.8	30.5	**62.4**	**69.5**

Table 5. Comparison of performance of clothes retrieval with different input image sizes. All experiments were performed using *Resnet50-IBN-A*

	Street2Shop				DeepFashion				
Input size	mAP	Acc@1	Acc@10	Acc@20	mAP	Acc@1	Acc@10	Acc@20	Acc@50
256×128	38.6	44.5	62.5	67.2	35.0	30.8	62.3	69.4	78.0
224×224	42.4	49.2	66.2	70.9	40.5	35.8	68.5	75.1	82.4
320×320	**46.8**	**53.7**	**69.8**	**73.6**	**43.0**	**37.8**	**71.1**	**77.2**	**84.1**
480×480	46.6	53.5	69.0	72.9	42.4	37.3	69.4	75.4	82.2

we used settings presented in Table 1. Our best performing model was trained using the RST approach with *Resnet50-IBN-A* backbone, quadruplet loss and input image size 320×320.

Our model both in *SOTA* and *best* settings outperforms current state-of-the-art by a large margin, despite using much smaller images. In two categories our model performs marginally worse, but it may be attributed to the fact that the categories consist of small items such as eye-wear, where the fine-grained details cannot be adequately seen on smaller images we used.

It is important to note that the metrics reported by [4] as overall performance are just average values across all categories for each metric, meaning that the retrieval stage was limited to products only from a specific category, thus limiting the choice of the model and making retrieval less challenging. We also report the performance in these settings for our model and for [4] in the *Average over categories* row of Table 6 to allow fair comparison. Additionally, we propose an unconstrained evaluation, where we conduct retrieval from all gallery images, with no restrictions. These our results are in the *Unconstrained retrieval* row of Table 6. Probably better results from *Unconstrained retrieval* are due to class imbalance in the dataset; the best performing categories are the most numerous.

In Table 7 results on *DeepFashion* dataset are presented. For SOTA comparison model, we trained our model on cropped images using ground-truth bounding boxes. Our retrieval model slightly outperforms the results of [2] in SOTA settings. Our best performing model was trained using the RST approach with *Resnet50-IBN-A* backbone, quadruplet loss and input image size 320×320. It exceeds the current SOTA results significantly in all the reported metrics.

Table 6. Comparison of performance on *Street2Shop* dataset using mAP, Acc@1, and Acc@20 metrics. Best performance for each category is presented in bold per metric.

Category	Current SOTA			Our model SOTA settings			Our best model		
	mAP	Acc@1	Acc@20	mAP	Acc@1	Acc@20	mAP	Acc@1	Acc@20
Bags	23.4	36.0	62.6	29.2	39.9	71.7	**32.2**	**44.2**	**74.6**
Belts	9.4	9.5	42.9	**13.2**	**14.6**	**46.3**	11.3	12.2	**46.3**
Dresses	49.5	56.4	72.0	61.6	69.5	85.2	**65.8**	**73.7**	**85.9**
Eyewear	26.7	**36.2**	**91.4**	20.5	11.8	74.5	**27.0**	31.4	76.5
Footwear	11.0	14.8	34.2	27.9	32.5	62.2	**34.2**	**37.9**	**65.4**
Hats	32.8	30.8	70.8	34.0	**39.1**	73.4	**38.5**	37.5	**85.9**
Leggings	18.2	20.5	49.0	27.1	36.1	68.6	**30.8**	**37.3**	**70.7**
Outerwear	28.1	30.5	47.9	33.3	40.4	64.6	**36.8**	**43.5**	**68.0**
Pants	**28.2**	**33.3**	**51.5**	22.6	25.8	39.4	23.9	27.3	42.4
Skirts	62.3	68	80.2	63.1	69.7	**87.3**	64.5	**71.2**	86.5
Tops	36.9	42.7	61.6	42.5	48.7	69.4	**46.8**	**52.7**	**71.9**
Average over categories	29.7	34.4	60.4	34.1	38.9	67.5	**37.4**	**42.6**	**70.4**
Unconstrained retrieval	-	-	-	42.6	49.7	71	**46.8**	**53.7**	**73.6**

Table 7. Comparison of performance on *DeepFashion* dataset. Best performance for each metric is presented in bold

Current SOTA				Our Model SOTA settings				Our best model			
mAP	Top-1	Top-20	Top-50	mAP	Top-1	Top-20	Top-50	mAP	Top-1	Top-20	Top-50
-	25.7	64.4	75.0	31.8	27.4	66.2	75.3	**43.0**	**37.8**	**77.2**	**84.1**

Cross-Domain Evaluation. As the last experiment, we tested cross-domain evaluation, i.e. training a model on one dataset and then testing on the other [5]. The results (Table 8) are on a reasonable level when compared to the current SOTA, thus, indicating that the RST model with *Resnet50-IBN-A* backbone can learn a meaningful representation of garments that can be transferred between domains to a large extent.

Table 8. Comparison of the performance of the RST on cross-domain evaluation. DF → S2S means that the model was trained on *DeepFashion* dataset and tested on the *Street2Shop* test set.

DF → S2S				S2S → DF			
mAP	Acc@1	Acc@10	Acc@20	mAP	Acc@1	Acc@10	Acc@20
26.2	37.7	49.5	53.3	20.9	18.6	40.7	47.2

4   Conclusions

We examined a transferability and adjustability of ReID domain and models to fashion retrieval. Using the approach proposed by [5], several improvements and learning optimizations we achieved 54.8 mAP, 72.9 Acc@20 on *Street2Shop* and 47.3 Acc@1, 79.0 Acc@20 on *DeepFashion* dataset, establishing the new state-of-the-art results for both. The performance on *Street2Shop* seems particularly robust, compared to previous state-of-the-art as our results were achieved on images several times smaller than the previous top-scoring models. The auspicious results can also confirm the robustness with cross-domain evaluation. By analogy to [5], we consider the results achieved by our model as a stable and robust – strong – baseline for further fashion retrieval research.

References

1. Chen, W., Chen, X., Zhang, J., Huang, K.: Beyond triplet loss: a deep quadruplet network for person re-identification. In: CVPR. IEEE (2017)
2. Dodds, E., Nguyen, H., Herdade, S., Culpepper, J., Kae, A., Garrigues, P.: Learning embeddings for product visual search with triplet loss and online sampling. arXiv preprint arXiv:1810.04652 (2018)
3. Kuang, Z., et al.: Fashion retrieval via graph reasoning networks on a similarity pyramid. In: ICCV. IEEE (2019)
4. Kucer, M., Murray, N.: A detect-then-retrieve model for multi-domain fashion item retrieval. In: CVPR Workshops. IEEE (2019)
5. Luo, H., et al.: A strong baseline and batch normalization neck for deep person re-identification. IEEE Trans. Multimed. **22**, 2597–2609 (2019)
6. Schroff, F., Kalenichenko, D., Philbin, J.: FaceNet: a unified embedding for face recognition and clustering. In: CVPR. IEEE (2015)
7. Wang, G., Lai, J., Huang, P., Xie, X.: Spatial-temporal person re-identification. In: AAAI. AAAI Press (2019)
8. Wen, Y., Zhang, K., Li, Z., Qiao, Y.: A discriminative feature learning approach for deep face recognition. In: Leibe, B., Matas, J., Sebe, N., Welling, M. (eds.) ECCV 2016. LNCS, vol. 9911, pp. 499–515. Springer, Cham (2016). https://doi.org/10.1007/978-3-319-46478-7_31
9. Xingang, P., Ping Luo, J.S., Tang, X.: Two at once: enhancing learning and generalization capacities via IBN-Net. In: ECCV (2018)
10. Zhou, K., Yang, Y., Cavallaro, A., Xiang, T.: Learning generalisable omni-scale representations for person re-identification. arXiv preprint arXiv:1910.06827 (2019)

Adaptive Feature Enhancement Network for Semantic Segmentation

Kuntao Cao[1,2], Xi Huang[2], and Jie Shao[2,3(✉)]

[1] Guizhou Provincial Key Laboratory of Public Big Data, Guizhou University, Guiyang 550025, China
[2] Center for Future Media, School of Computer Science and Engineering, University of Electronic Science and Technology of China, Chengdu 611731, China
{caokuntao,xihuang}@std.uestc.edu.cn, shaojie@uestc.edu.cn
[3] Sichuan Artificial Intelligence Research Institute, Yibin 644000, China

Abstract. Semantic segmentation is a fundamental and challenging problem in computer vision. Recent studies attempt to integrate feature information of different depths to improve the performance of segmentation tasks, and a few of them enhance the features before fusion. However, which areas of the feature should be strengthened and how to strengthen are still inconclusive. Therefore, in this work we propose an Adaptive Feature Enhancement Module (AFEM) that utilizes high-level features to adaptively enhance the key areas of low-level features. Meanwhile, an Adaptive Feature Enhancement Network (AFENet) is designed with AFEM to combine all the enhanced features. The proposed method is validated on representative semantic segmentation datasets, Cityscapes and PASCAL VOC 2012. In particular, 79.5% mIoU on the Cityscapes testing set is achieved without using fine-val data, which is 1.1% higher than the baseline network and the model size is smaller. The code of AFENet is available at https://github.com/KTMomo/AFENet.

Keywords: Semantic segmentation · Feature enhancement · Attention mechanism

1 Introduction

Semantic segmentation is a most widely studied task in computer vision, and its purpose is to predict the semantic category of each pixel in an image. For vision-based applications, semantic segmentation has great values such as autonomous driving [18] and medical image segmentation [19]. However, the scale variability, partial occlusion, and illumination variation of objects make it challenging for parsing each pixel.

Fully Convolutional Network (FCN) [20] creates a new trend to use convolutional neural networks (CNN) to solve the semantic segmentation tasks, which greatly improves the accuracy of segmentation tasks. However, there are still some problems. Lacking suitable strategy to utilize global scene information results in that FCN based models cannot make more precise analysis of

© Springer Nature Switzerland AG 2020
H. Yang et al. (Eds.): ICONIP 2020, CCIS 1332, pp. 302–311, 2020.
https://doi.org/10.1007/978-3-030-63820-7_34

the complex scene. PSPNet [27] proves that the local and global information together make the prediction of semantic segmentation tasks more reliable. In deep networks, a high-level feature map contains more semantic meaning and less locational information, but the low-level is the opposite. Ideally, the final feature is looking forward to having a high resolution, which means that the feature includes more semantic and locational information. However, the resolution of high-level features obtained through frequent pooling and subsampling is very low. The dilated convolution is proposed to solve the problem in [25], above which can obtain contextual information of larger scale while maintaining feature resolution. Then, PSPNet [27] proposes Pyramid Pooling Module (PPM) composed of different sizes of pooling layers to capture multi-scale context. Referring to the pyramid structure, DeepLab V2 [2] uses different dilated convolution rates to form Atrous Spatial Pyramid Pooling (ASPP). Besides, UNet [19] does not use the dilated convolution, but obtains multi-scale information by fusing the features obtained by the subsampling to the features obtained from the up-sampling. Then, the encoder-decoder structure of the UNet is widely used for multi-level feature enhancement.

However, there is still a problem. Not all positions of low-level features need to be enhanced, but only the regions worthy of attention or needed in the low-level features should be strengthened. Inspired by this, we hope to enhance the context information of low-level features by fusing the adjacent two-level features before finally fusing the context information of all scales. In this paper, we propose an Adaptive Feature Enhancement Module (AFEM) that can enhance the semantic information of specific low-level features. Then, an Adaptive Feature Enhancement Network (AFENet) is designed to extract more contextual features using AFEM. The overall structure of AFENet as shown in Fig. 1 is simple and only connects the features of two adjacent parts in turn, which reduces the amount of computation and makes the model smaller. Our main contributions can be summarized as follows:

- We propose an Adaptive Feature Enhancement Module (AFEM) which can integrate the high-level features of specific regions into the low-level features to adaptively enhance the contextual information of the low-level features.
- With AFEM as the core, AFENet is designed to combine features of different layers in the form of intensive connections.
- Experiments on Cityscapes [5] and PASCAL VOC 2012 [7] validate the effectiveness of our proposed method.

2   Related Work

Semantic Segmentation. FCN [20] based approaches have achieved promising performance on semantic segmentation. Some works gather contextual information from various perspectives, and feature pyramid is a common way. PSP-Net [27] and DeepLab V2 [2] propose PPM (Pyramid Pooling Module) and ASPP (Atrous Spatial Pyramid Pooling) module to concatenate features with

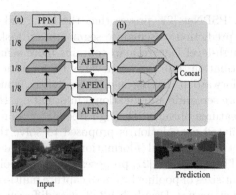

Fig. 1. Overview of the Adaptive Feature Enhancement Network (AFENet). (a) Backbone network: the part of PSPNet [27] from input to Pyramid Pooling Module (PPM). The network structure (b) integrates the enhanced features in the form of intensive connections. The detail of Adaptive Feature Enhancement Module (AFEM) is illustrated in Fig. 2.

multi-scale contextual information together for final prediction. DeepLab V3 [3] improves the ASPP module and adds the image pooling module to get global contextual information. By using long-range residual connections, RefineNet [13] exploits more semantic information. DenseASPP [22] encodes multi-scale information with large enough receptive fields by dense connection of multiple atrous convolutions. Considering that the features from the low level contain local information that the high level does not have, UNet [19] designs an encoder-decoder architecture to reuse low-level features. The encoder-decoder structure is used in [6,12] to enhance high-level features to obtain different scale context. Deeplab V3+ [4] adds a simple decoder module to combine low-level features. A versatile representation that encodes spatial structure information in distributed, pixel-centric relations is proposed in AAF [9]. BiSeNet [23] decouples the function of spatial information preservation and receptive field offering into two paths to improve the accuracy.

Attention Mechanism. Attention is a mechanism to mimic human vision habits, which tends to pay more attention to semantically more important regions and objects instead of the entire image. In particular, the self-attention mechanism is first proposed to draw global dependencies of inputs and applied in machine translation [21]. Attention mechanism has been applied in the field of semantic segmentation to improve the performance of segmentation [11,24,28]. PANet [11] selects the channel maps effectively by generating global attention with a global pooling. A smooth network is proposed by DFN [24] to enhance the intra-class consistence with the global context and the channel attention block. PSANet [28] believes that information flow in CNN is restricted inside the local region, so point-wise spatial attention is proposed to relax the constraint.

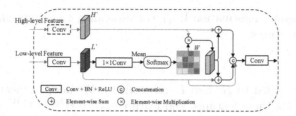

Fig. 2. Detail of Adaptive Feature Enhancement Module (AFEM). Feature enhancement is a widely used method. In view of the features of a certain layer, the common method is to strengthen from the perspective of the whole features. However, it is still uncertain which regions of the features should be strengthened and how to strengthen them. As shown in the figure, we collect the heat map W of the low-level features through the attention mechanism and then use W to process the high-level features to obtain the enhanced information needed by the low-level features. Finally, the enhanced features are obtained.

3 Adaptive Feature Enhancement

3.1 Adaptive Feature Enhancement Module

As mentioned above, high-level features contain more advanced contextual information. Because the network depth of the low-level features is not deep enough compared with the high-level features, the low-level features cannot get enough semantic features. We hope to enhance the semantic information of low-level features through high-level features. Different from the previous works, we design an adaptive enhancement strategy inspired by the attention mechanism so that the enhancement process can be learned through the convolution network. Meanwhile, the low-level information complemented by the high-level information is used to participate in segmentation prediction. The difficulty of effectively using the low-level features to enhance the segmentation effect lies in how to integrate high-level semantic information into low-level features to enhance the low-level features, that is to say, some pixels or regions need more advanced semantic information, while others may not. Therefore, the Adaptive Feature Enhancement Module (AFEM) is proposed as follows.

As shown in Fig. 2, AFEM is a simple and easy to understand structure. Given a high-level input feature map $H \in \mathbb{R}^{C_1 \times H_1 \times W_1}$ and a low-level input feature maps $L \in \mathbb{R}^{C_2 \times H_2 \times W_2}$, $H^{'} \in \mathbb{R}^{256 \times H_1 \times W_1}$ and $L^{'} \in \mathbb{R}^{256 \times H_1 \times W_1}$ are obtained by different 1×1 convolution layers, BN and ReLU. Among them, L is sampled to make the height and width of $H^{'}$ and $L^{'}$ consistent. Besides, both C_1 and C_2 are reduced to 256 channels. In order to obtain the locations of the low-level features which are to be enhanced, the position weight W through attention mechanism is defined as:

$$W = Softmax(\overline{conv_{1\times1}(L^{'})}), \tag{1}$$

where $\overline{conv_{1\times1}(L^{'})}$ is the result of where $\overline{conv_{1\times1}(L^{'})}$ is the result of $L^{'}$ first going through 1×1 convolution and then averaging all channels. Then, we can get the high-level semantic information W_{HL} corresponding to the specific locations of the low-level features:

$$W_H L = H^{'} \times W. \tag{2}$$

Next, W_{HL} is added to $H^{'}$ and $L^{'}$ respectively. We adopt concatenation operation to combine these features, and features $f_{cat} \in \mathbb{R}^{768 \times H_1 \times W_1}$ after concatenation can be defined as:

$$f_{cat} = cat(H^{'} + W_{HL},\ L^{'} + W_{HL},\ L^{'}), \tag{3}$$

where $cat(\cdot)$ is concatenation operation. Eventually, f_{cat} will be reduced to $(256 \times H_1 \times W_1)$ with 3×3 convolution layer, BN and ReLU. In this way, the robustness of output features can be enhanced, and more learning space can be given to the network to obtain more useful context information.

3.2   Network Architecture

The Adaptive Feature Enhancement Network (AFENet) is illustrated in Fig. 1. The purpose of the designed network is to make better use of AFEM to enhance multi-scale features and to fuse all enhanced features through sum and concatenation operations for final prediction. As shown in Fig. 1, three AFEMs are successively inserted between different adjacent blocks. Each AFEM has two inputs, one to receive high-level features and the other to receive low-level features. AFEM accepts the input of arbitrary number of channels, and finally outputs the feature maps of 256 channels. Feature maps from PPM [27] are reduced from 4096 channels to 256 channels with 3×3 convolution layers. From the bottom up, the output of AFEM and PPM [27] is denoted as X_1, X_2, X_3, X_4. Referring to the connection mode of features in FPN [15], we conduct intensive connection processing for the output features of PPM and AFEM. This process can be abstracted as:

$$(X_1, X_2, X_3, X_4) \longrightarrow (\widetilde{X}_1, \widetilde{X}_2, \widetilde{X}_3, \widetilde{X}_4), \tag{4}$$

where $\widetilde{X}_4 = X_4$, $\widetilde{X}_i = \widetilde{X}_{i+1} + X_i$, $i \in \{1, 2, 3\}$ and $\widetilde{X}_i$ is the result of processing. After that, all feature maps are concatenated and the concatenated feature is divided into 19 channels by two 3×3 convolution layers for final semantic segmentation. In addition, the auxiliary loss strategy in PSPNet [27] is still adopted, and the weight of the auxiliary loss is set to 0.4.

4   Experiments

4.1   Dataset

We evaluate our approach on two public datasets: Cityscapes [5] and PASCAL VOC 2012 [7]. The Cityscapes dataset [5] contains 5000 finely annotated images and 20000 coarsely annotated images with a high resolution of 2048 × 1024. In our experiment, we just use 5000 fine annotated images, which is divided into 2975, 500, and 1525 images for training (fine-train), validation (fine-val), and testing respectively. The PASCAL VOC 2012 segmentation dataset [7] contains 20 object classes and one background class. The original dataset is augmented by the Semantic Boundaries dataset [8], resulting in 10582, 1449, and 1456 images for training, validation and testing. The evaluation metric is mean Intersection over Union (mIoU).

4.2 Implementation Protocol

In our experiments, we employ the part of PSPNet [27] from input to PPM as the backbone. We use the SGD optimizer with the batch size 4 and 8 for Cityscapes and PASCAL VOC 2012, initial learning rate 0.01, weight decay 0.0001, and momentum 0.9 for training. The learning rate of the backbone is set to 0.001. Besides, our models are trained for 260 and 50 epochs for Cityscapes and PASCAL VOC 2012. For data augmentation, we use random scales in the range of [0.75, 2], random crop, and random horizontal flip for training. The cropped resolution is 768×768 for Cityscapes, and 480×480 for PASCAL VOC 2012. More implementation details can be found at https://github.com/KTMomo/AFENet.

4.3 Results

The comparison results with baseline are shown in Table 1. PSPNet [27] is the baseline method. AFEM is the proposed method, and MS denotes multi-scale inference. Here, all methods are trained only on the Cityscapes fine-train set. After adding AFEM, the new network is 0.42% mIoU higher than the baseline network. When multi-scale inference is added to both, the improvement of 0.22% mIoU is obtained by AFEM. This proves that the addition of AFEM makes the network get more semantic information, thus improving the performance of segmentation, which achieves our expected purpose.

The original PSPNet [27] is simplified. The specific operation is to directly reduce the output features of PPM [27] from 2048 channels to 256 channels, which greatly reduces the parameters of the model. Therefore, even if three AFEMs and some convolution layers are added, the new network is still smaller than PSPNet [27]. Table 2 shows that the model size is reduced by 2.47 MB.

Table 1. Simple ablation experiments on the Cityscapes validation set.

Method	mIoU (%)
PSPNet (baseline)	78.63
PSPNet+AFEM	79.05 (0.42↑)
PSPNet+MS	79.29
PSPNet+MS+AFEM	79.51 (0.22↑)

Table 2. Model size comparison.

Method	Model size (MB)
PSPNet [27] (baseline)	260.21
AFENet (ours)	257.74 (2.47↓)

Table 3. Experimental results compared on the Cityscapes testing set. † means only using the fine-train set for training. ‡ means both the fine-train and fine-val sets are used for training.

Method	mIoU (%)
PSPNet† [27]	78.4
PSANet† [28]	78.6
RefineNet‡ [13]	73.6
SAC‡ [26]	78.1
DepthSeg‡ [10]	78.2
AAF‡ [9]	79.1
BiSeNet‡ [23]	78.9
DFN‡ [24]	79.3
AFENet† (ours)	79.5

Table 4. Experimental results compared on the PASCAL VOC 2012 testing set. † means using multi-scale inference. Only VOC training data is used.

Method	mIoU (%)
FCN [20]	62.2
DeepLab† [1]	71.6
DeconvNet [17]	72.5
DPN [16]	74.1
Piecewise [14]	75.3
PSPNet† [27]	82.6
AFENet (ours)	78.9

In Table 3, we compare our method with other methods on the Cityscapes testing set. For a fair comparison, the test results predicted by the proposed method are submitted to the official server of Cityscapes [5] for verification. In particular, the more training data we use, the better the effect of the model. However, training with more data will take more time. In order to reduce the time cost, we only use the fine-train set for training. Compared with the baseline method PSPNet [27], our method is improved by 1.1% to 79.5%, and the experimental results of our method that only trains with the fine-train set are better than those of most methods trained with more data. It is worth mentioning that PSPNet [27] can achieve 80.2% mIoU by adding 20000 pieces of coarse data for training. Compared with the original 2975 training pictures, the amount of data is even larger, which will consume more training time. From the perspective of improving model accuracy, it is necessary. However, if it is only to verify the effectiveness of the method, the widely used 2975 pictures are enough.

As shown in Table 4, we achieve 78.9% mIoU on the PASCAL VOC 2012 dataset [7] with single scale inference. However, the result is 3.7% lower than the result of PSPNet [27] with multi-scale inference. One reason is that PSPNet uses multi-scale input for testing, which will generally make a great improvement. The other is the adaptability problems that may arise when different network structures are applied to different data sets.

In addition, some visual comparison results are shown in Fig. 3. As can be seen from the area marked by the red dotted box, the segmentation performance of our method is better than that of baseline method, which shows that the expression ability of semantic information at the low level is enhanced.

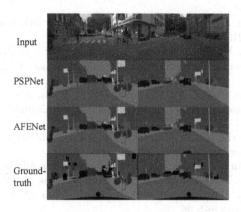

Fig. 3. Visualization of results on the Cityscapes validation set. Compared with PSP-Net [27], our method adaptively enhances the context of the low-level features, thus obtaining better segmentation results (see the area marked by the red dotted box, best viewed in color). (Color figure online)

5   Conclusion

In this paper, we propose an Adaptive Feature Enhancement Module (AFEM) to adaptively enhance the low-level features at specific locations. Meanwhile, Adaptive Feature Enhancement Network (AFENet) is designed to combine AFEM and backbone network to obtain richer contextual information. The validity of the method is proved on the Cityscapes dataset. In our future work, we are going to discuss the feasibility of AFEM in practical application scenarios. Finally, the code to reproduce the experimental results is available, hoping to help the relevant researchers.

Acknowledgments. This work was supported by Major Scientific and Technological Special Project of Guizhou Province (No. 20183002) and Sichuan Science and Technology Program (No. 2019YFG0535).

References

1. Chen, L., Papandreou, G., Kokkinos, I., Murphy, K., Yuille, A.L.: Semantic image segmentation with deep convolutional nets and fully connected CRFs. In: ICLR 2015 (2015)
2. Chen, L., Papandreou, G., Kokkinos, I., Murphy, K., Yuille, A.L.: DeepLab: semantic image segmentation with deep convolutional nets, atrous convolution, and fully connected CRFs. IEEE Trans. Pattern Anal. Mach. Intell. **40**(4), 834–848 (2018)
3. Chen, L., Papandreou, G., Schroff, F., Adam, H.: Rethinking atrous convolution for semantic image segmentation. CoRR abs/1706.05587 (2017)
4. Chen, L.-C., Zhu, Y., Papandreou, G., Schroff, F., Adam, H.: Encoder-decoder with atrous separable convolution for semantic image segmentation. In: Ferrari, V., Hebert, M., Sminchisescu, C., Weiss, Y. (eds.) ECCV 2018. LNCS, vol. 11211, pp. 833–851. Springer, Cham (2018). https://doi.org/10.1007/978-3-030-01234-2_49

5. Cordts, M., et al.: The cityscapes dataset for semantic urban scene understanding. CVPR **2016**, 3213–3223 (2016)
6. Ding, H., Jiang, X., Shuai, B., Liu, A.Q., Wang, G.: Context contrasted feature and gated multi-scale aggregation for scene segmentation. CVPR **2018**, 2393–2402 (2018)
7. Everingham, M., Gool, L.V., Williams, C.K.I., Winn, J.M., Zisserman, A.: The pascal visual object classes (VOC) challenge. Int. J. Comput. Vis. **88**(2), 303–338 (2010)
8. Hariharan, B., Arbelaez, P., Bourdev, L.D., Maji, S., Malik, J.: Semantic contours from inverse detectors. ICCV **2011**, 991–998 (2011)
9. Ke, T.-W., Hwang, J.-J., Liu, Z., Yu, S.X.: Adaptive affinity fields for semantic segmentation. In: Ferrari, V., Hebert, M., Sminchisescu, C., Weiss, Y. (eds.) ECCV 2018. LNCS, vol. 11205, pp. 605–621. Springer, Cham (2018). https://doi.org/10. 1007/978-3-030-01246-5_36
10. Kong, S., Fowlkes, C.C.: Recurrent scene parsing with perspective understanding in the loop. CVPR **2018**, 956–965 (2018)
11. Li, H., Xiong, P., An, J., Wang, L.: Pyramid attention network for semantic segmentation. In: BMVC 2018, p. 285 (2018)
12. Lin, D., Ji, Y., Lischinski, D., Cohen-Or, D., Huang, H.: Multi-scale context intertwining for semantic segmentation. In: Ferrari, V., Hebert, M., Sminchisescu, C., Weiss, Y. (eds.) ECCV 2018. LNCS, vol. 11207, pp. 622–638. Springer, Cham (2018). https://doi.org/10.1007/978-3-030-01219-9_37
13. Lin, G., Milan, A., Shen, C., Reid, I.D.: RefineNet: multi-path refinement networks for high-resolution semantic segmentation. CVPR **2017**, 5168–5177 (2017)
14. Lin, G., Shen, C., van den Hengel, A., Reid, I.D.: Efficient piecewise training of deep structured models for semantic segmentation. CVPR **2016**, 3194–3203 (2016)
15. Lin, T., Dollár, P., Girshick, R.B., He, K., Hariharan, B., Belongie, S.J.: Feature pyramid networks for object detection. CVPR **2017**, 936–944 (2017)
16. Liu, Z., Li, X., Luo, P., Loy, C.C., Tang, X.: Semantic image segmentation via deep parsing network. ICCV **2015**, 1377–1385 (2015)
17. Noh, H., Hong, S., Han, B.: Learning deconvolution network for semantic segmentation. ICCV **2015**, 1520–1528 (2015)
18. Pohlen, T., Hermans, A., Mathias, M., Leibe, B.: Full-resolution residual networks for semantic segmentation in street scenes. CVPR **2017**, 3309–3318 (2017)
19. Ronneberger, O., Fischer, P., Brox, T.: U-Net: convolutional networks for biomedical image segmentation. In: Navab, N., Hornegger, J., Wells, W.M., Frangi, A.F. (eds.) MICCAI 2015. LNCS, vol. 9351, pp. 234–241. Springer, Cham (2015). https://doi.org/10.1007/978-3-319-24574-4_28
20. Shelhamer, E., Long, J., Darrell, T.: Fully convolutional networks for semantic segmentation. IEEE Trans. Pattern Anal. Mach. Intell. **39**(4), 640–651 (2017)
21. Vaswani, A., et al.: Attention is all you need. NIPS **2017**, 5998–6008 (2017)
22. Yang, M., Yu, K., Zhang, C., Li, Z., Yang, K.: DenseASPP for semantic segmentation in street scenes. CVPR **2018**, 3684–3692 (2018)
23. Yu, C., Wang, J., Peng, C., Gao, C., Yu, G., Sang, N.: BiSeNet: bilateral segmentation network for real-time semantic segmentation. In: Ferrari, V., Hebert, M., Sminchisescu, C., Weiss, Y. (eds.) ECCV 2018. LNCS, vol. 11217, pp. 334–349. Springer, Cham (2018). https://doi.org/10.1007/978-3-030-01261-8_20
24. Yu, C., Wang, J., Peng, C., Gao, C., Yu, G., Sang, N.: Learning a discriminative feature network for semantic segmentation. CVPR **2018**, 1857–1866 (2018)
25. Yu, F., Koltun, V.: Multi-scale context aggregation by dilated convolutions. In: ICLR 2016 (2016)

26. Zhang, R., Tang, S., Zhang, Y., Li, J., Yan, S.: Scale-adaptive convolutions for scene parsing. ICCV **2017**, 2050–2058 (2017)
27. Zhao, H., Shi, J., Qi, X., Wang, X., Jia, J.: Pyramid scene parsing network. CVPR **2017**, 6230–6239 (2017)
28. Zhao, H., et al.: PSANet: point-wise spatial attention network for scene parsing. In: Ferrari, V., Hebert, M., Sminchisescu, C., Weiss, Y. (eds.) ECCV 2018. LNCS, vol. 11213, pp. 270–286. Springer, Cham (2018). https://doi.org/10.1007/978-3-030-01240-3_17

BEDNet: Bi-directional Edge Detection Network for Ocean Front Detection

Qingyang Li, Zhenlin Fan, and Guoqiang Zhong[✉]

Department of Computer Science and Technology, Ocean University of China,
Qingdao 266100, China
1194094543@qq.com, 916056589@qq.com, gqzhong@ouc.edu.cn

Abstract. Ocean front is an ocean phenomenon, which has important impact on marine ecosystems and marine fisheries. Hence, it is of great significance to study ocean front detection. So far, some ocean front detection methods have been proposed. However, there are mainly two problems for these existing methods: one is the lack of labeled ocean front detection data sets, and the other is that there is no deep learning methods used to locate accurate position of ocean fronts. In this paper, we design a bi-directional edge detection network (BEDNet) based on our collected ocean front data set to tackle these two problems. The labeled ocean front data set is named OFDS365, which consists of 365 images based on the gradient of sea surface temperature (SST) images acquired at every day of the year 2014. BEDNet mainly contains four stages, a pathway from shallow stages to deep stages, and a pathway from deep stages to shallow stages, which can achieve bi-directional multi-scale information fusion. Moreover, we combine the dice and cross-entropy loss function to train our network, obtaining the fine-grained ocean front detection results. In the experiments, we show that BEDNet achieves better performance on ocean front detection compared with other existing methods.

Keywords: Ocean front detection · BEDNet · Labeled data set

1 Introduction

Ocean fronts refer to narrow transition zones between water masses with different characteristics, such as temperature, salinity, density and others. Ocean front detection has been studied for many years. In recent years, deep learning has achieved excellent performance in many problems of pattern recognition and computer vision. Among them, edge detection benefits a lot from deep learning approaches, achieving a major breakthrough [1–3]. In this work, we solve the problem of ocean front detection from the perspective of edge detection owing to the strip shape of ocean fronts research.

Q. Li and Z. Fan—have equal contributions.

© Springer Nature Switzerland AG 2020
H. Yang et al. (Eds.): ICONIP 2020, CCIS 1332, pp. 312–319, 2020.
https://doi.org/10.1007/978-3-030-63820-7_35

Early ocean front detection methods mainly rely on gradient algorithms, but the performances of these algorithms remain low [4,5]. With the wide application of machine learning, some algorithms based on machine learning have been proposed. However, these methods only achieve a classification effect classifying a remote sensing image as front or non-front, not locating the accurate position of ocean fronts. Furthermore, there are no available labeled data sets for ocean front detection.

In order to solve the above problems, we propose a bi-directional edge detection network (BEDNet) based on our collected ocean front detection data set. Firstly, we built a labeled ocean front data set named OFDS365, which is composed of 365 images based on the gradient of SST images from every day of the year 2014. Gradient characterizes the degree of change between seawater at different temperatures. For the ground truth, we invite experts to label the positions of ocean fronts in each image. Secondly, we design a bi-directional deep model named BEDNet to detect ocean fronts. There are mainly four stages, a pathway from shallow stages to deep stages and a pathway from deep stages to shallow stages in BEDNet, which fuse bi-directional multi-scale feature information to improve the results of ocean front detection. Additionally, BEDNet assigns independent supervision to feature maps at different scales. Hence, each stage in BEDNet are trained by appropriate stage-specific supervision. Moreover, a loss function combining the dice and cross-entropy loss function is used for model training, which can achieve fine-grained ocean front detection to get accurate position of ocean fronts.

2   Related Work

Due to the significant effects of ocean fronts in marine environment and fisheries, scientists have built some methods for ocean front detection to date. In this section, ocean front detection methods are divide into two categories, which are methods based on gradient information and those based on machine learning.

2.1   Methods Based on Gradient Information

In the early days, experts mainly rely on gradient information to detect ocean fronts. Shaw and Vennell provided a front-tracking algorithm to describe the gradient and extract the structure of ocean fronts in SST images [6]. Belkin and O'Reilly proposed a method based on gradient information, which detected ocean fronts in chlorophyll (Chl) and SST satellite images [7]. Hopkins *et al.* introduced a new ocean front detection method, which took advantage of gradient local likelihood to detect and monitor ocean fronts from Advanced Very High Resolution Radiometer (AVHRR) SST satellite images [4]. Kirches *et al.* proposed a method named Gradhist, which combined and refined canny algorithm [8] and the histogram algorithm [9], achieving ocean front detection for remote sensing data [5]. However, these methods based on gradient information are not robust to noisy data, resulting in low accuracy in ocean front detection.

2.2   Methods Based on Machine Learning

With the wide application of machine learning, some methods of using machine learning to detect ocean fronts have been proposed. Sun *et al.* applied random forests to ocean front detection [10]. However, this method only classifies a SST image as front or non-front, not extracting the accurate position of ocean fronts from SST images. Lima *et al.* made use of deep convolutional neural network to detect ocean fronts from remote sensing images. Similar to [10], this method only performed classification of the remote sensing images [11].

3   Method

In this section, we introduce the bi-directional architecture of BEDNet and the loss function for the training of BEDNet.

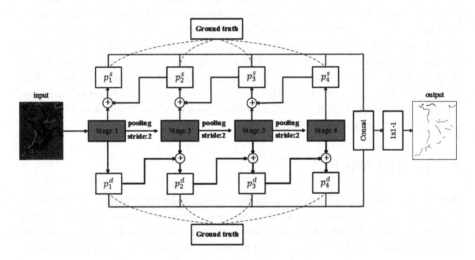

Fig. 1. The overall architecture of BEDNet.

3.1   BEDNet

The Overall Architecture of BEDNet: Considering the great success of bidirectional networks in edge detection [12], so we design a bi-directional edge detection network named BEDNet in this paper. Figure 1 shows the overall architecture of BEDNet. We use four stages to obtain multi-scale feature maps, bidirectional pathways to fuse bi-directional multi-scale information. In the pathway from shallow stages to deep stages, the prediction from deep stages can be obtained by adding the prediction from shallow stages. On the contrary, in the pathway from deep stages to shallow stages, the prediction from deep stages need to be added to the prediction from shallow stages.

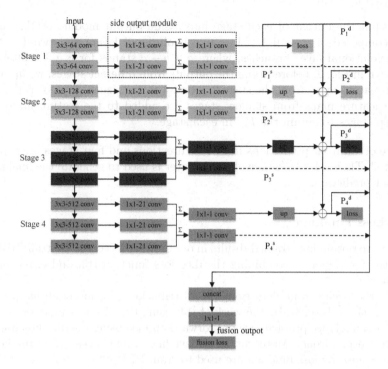

Fig. 2. The detailed architecture of BEDNet.

Because the scales of ocean front prediction from the four stages are different, we use different supervisory methods to train our network. Let Y is the ground truth annotated by experts. We define the supervision at stage s as follows:

$$Y_s^d = Y - \sum_{i<s} P_i^d,$$
$$Y_s^s = Y - \sum_{i>s} P_i^s, \tag{1}$$

where the P_i is the ocean front prediction at stage i. The superscript d denotes the pathway from shallow stages to deep stages, and s denotes the pathway from deep stages to shallow stages.

The Detailed Architecture of BEDNet: For clarity, Fig. 2 illustrates the detailed architecture of the four stages and the pathway from shallow stages to deep stages in BEDNet. In the following, we introduce the architecture of BEDNet in detail:

– There are 10 convolutional layers in the four stages of BEDNet, and a pooling layer following each stage is used to progressively enlarge the receptive fields.

– We put the output of each stage into a side output module (SOM), which is composed of several $1 \times 1 - 21$ convolutional layers and two $1 \times 1 - 1$ convolutional layer branches, where $a \times b - c$ stands for c $a \times b$ filters. As shown in Fig. 2, before fusing the outputs from different stages, we upsample the feature maps from the stage 2, 3 and 4 to the size of ground truth. Then the feature maps from shallow stages are added to the feature maps from deep stages to obtain the $P_s{}^d$ in each stage.

– The ocean front predictions from two directions and four stages are concatenated. Then a $1 \times 1 - 1$ convolutional layer is used to generate the final ocean front prediction.

3.2 Loss Function

In order to obtain fine-grained results in ocean front detection, we train BEDNet with the loss function combining the dice loss function [13] and cross-entropy loss function.

For the ocean front detection, the distribution of front/nonfront pixels is heavily biased. Inspired by the work of [14] using the dice loss function to solve the class-imbalance problem, we put forward an idea using the dice loss function to detect ocean fronts. Moreover, to achieve fine-grained ocean front prediction, the cross-entropy loss function are used to train BEDNet.

We combine the dice and cross-entropy loss function to minimize the difference between the prediction and the ground truth from image-level to pixel-level, getting fine-grained ocean front detection results. To the end, the loss function combining the dice loss function and cross-entropy loss function for each supervision is given by:

$$\mathcal{L}(P,Y) = \alpha L_d(P,Y) + \beta L_c(P,Y), \tag{2}$$

where $L_d(P,Y)$ and $L_c(P,Y)$ refer to the dice loss function and cross-entropy loss function, respectively. P and Y represent the prediction map and the ground truth. α and β are the parameters controlling the proportion of two loss functions.

Furthermore, each stage in BEDNet will generate two side edge predictions from two directions. We fuse the ocean front predictions from two directions and four stages with a fusion layer as the final output. Therefore, we define the overall loss function as:

$$\mathcal{L}_{final} = w_{side} \cdot \mathcal{L}_{side} + w_{fuse} \cdot \mathcal{L}_{fuse},$$
$$\mathcal{L}_{side} = \sum_{s=1}^{S} (\mathcal{L}(P_s^s, Y_s^s) + \mathcal{L}(P_s^d, Y_s^d)). \tag{3}$$

Here, w_{side} and w_{fuse} are weights of the side loss $\mathcal{L}_{side}$ and fusion loss $\mathcal{L}_{fuse}$, respectively, $\mathcal{L}_{fuse}$ is computed according to Eq. (2), and $S = 4$ denotes the number of stages.

4   Experiments

In this section, we introduce the conducted experiments in detail. In Sect. 4.1, we describe our collected ocean front detection data set named OFDS365 in detail. In Sect. 4.2, we demonstrate that our method achieves state-of-the-art performance in ocean front detection by comparing with other existing methods.

4.1   The Collected Ocean Front Data Set

One challenge of current ocean front detection research is the lack of available data sets, so that we collected and labeled an ocean front data set named OFDS365 to tackle this problem. There are 365 gradient images computed based on the SST images (from each day in 2014) in OFDS365, while the temperature range in each SST image is from $-5\,°C$ to $35\,°C$. In addition, the longitude range in each image is $118.025\,°E-130.975\,°E$, and the latitude range in each image is $23.025\,°\ N-39.975\,°\ N$. To attain the accurate ground truth, we have asked several experts to label the ocean fronts in each image of OFDS365.

We randomly select 5 images from each month to construct the test set, and the other 305 images are used as training set.

Table 1. The obtained F_1-score and standard deviation using different methods on the test set. The best results are highlighted in boldface.

Method	F_1-score(%)
Sobel	45.12 ± 2.97
HED	62.23 ± 3.32
RCF	66.18 ± 2.46
BEDNet	$\mathbf{74.78 \pm 1.82}$

4.2   Experimental Results

To evaluate BEDNet for ocean front detection, we compared it with other edge detection algorithms based on our collected OFDS365 data set. We chose edge detection algorithms Sobel detector [15], holistically-nested edge detection (HED) [16] and richer convolutional features (RCF) [17] as compared methods. Sobel detector is a traditional algorithm extracting edge information based on differentiation of neighboring pixels. HED and RCF are recent deep models for edge detection, which obtain excellent performance on edge detection. The obtained F_1-score and standard deviation using different methods on the test set are shown in Table 1. From Table 1, we can see that our BEDNet is much better than other compared methods.

In order to prove the superiority of our method qualitatively, we show the detection results using different methods on one image of the test set in Fig 3.

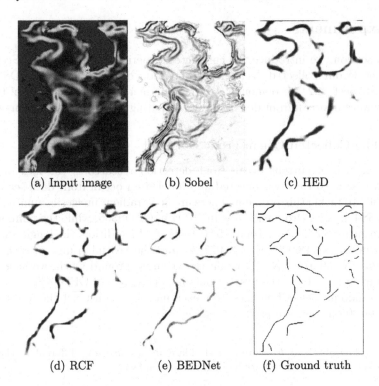

(a) Input image   (b) Sobel   (c) HED

(d) RCF   (e) BEDNet   (f) Ground truth

Fig. 3. The detection results using different methods on one image of the test set. (a) The input image. (b) (c) (d) (e) The detection results of Sobel detector, HED, RCF and our proposed BEDNet. (f) Ground truth.

As can be seen from Fig 3, BEDNet obtains the fine-grained ocean fronts, which locate the position of ocean fronts with sharper edges than other compared methods.

5   Conclusion

In this paper, we construct a novel labeled ocean front data set named OFDS365, which contains 365 images computed based on the gradient of the SST images from every day of 2014. Moreover, we design a novel bi-directional edge detection network named BEDNet, which mainly consists of four stages, a pathway from shallow stages to deep stages, and a pathway from deep stages to shallow stages. Furthermore, a fusing loss function combining the dice and cross-entropy loss function is used for the training of BEDNet to get fine-grained ocean fronts. Lastly, our experiments demonstrate that our method obtains better results than other compared methods on our collected ocean front detection data set.

Acknowledgments. This work was supported by the Major Project for New Generation of AI under Grant No. 2018AAA0100400, the National Natural Science Foundation of China (NSFC) under Grant No. 41706010, the Joint Fund of the Equipments Pre-Research and Ministry of Education of China under Grand No. 6141A020337, and the Fundamental Research Funds for the Central Universities of China.

References

1. Shen, W., Wang, X., Wang, Y., Bai, X., Zhang, Z.: DeepContour: a deep convolutional feature learned by positive-sharing loss for contour detection. In: CVPR, pp. 3982–3991 (2015)
2. Bertasius, G., Shi, J., Torresani, L.: DeepEdge: a multi-scale bifurcated deep network for top-down contour detection. In: CVPR, pp. 4380–4389 (2015)
3. Hwang, J., Liu, T.: Pixel-wise deep learning for contour detection. In: ICLR (2015)
4. Hopkins, J., Challenor, P., Shaw, A.G.: A new statistical modeling approach to ocean front detection from SST satellite images. J. Atmosp. Oceanic Technol. **27**(1), 173–191 (2010)
5. Kirches, G., Paperin, M., Klein, H., Brockmann, C., Stelzer, K.: GRADHIST-a method for detection and analysis of oceanic fronts from remote sensing data. Rem. Sens. Environ. **181**, 264–280 (2016)
6. Shaw, A., Vennell, R.: A front-following algorithm for AVHRR SST imagery. Rem. Sens. Environ. **72**(3), 317–327 (2000)
7. Belkin, I.M., O'Reilly, J.E.: An algorithm for oceanic front detection in chlorophyll and SST satellite imagery. J. Mar. Syst. **78**(3), 319–326 (2009)
8. Canny, J.F.: A computational approach to edge detection. IEEE Trans. Pattern Anal. Mach. Intell. **8**(6), 679–698 (1986)
9. Cayula, J.F., Cornillon, P.: Edge detection algorithm for SST images. J. Atmos. Oceanic Technol. **9**(1), 67–80 (1992)
10. Sun, J., Zhong, G., Dong, J., Saeeda, H., Zhang, Q.: Cooperative profit random forests with application in ocean front recognition. IEEE Access **5**, 1398–1408 (2017)
11. Lima, E., Sun, X., Dong, J., Wang, H., Yang, Y., Liu, L.: Learning and transferring convolutional neural network knowledge to ocean front recognition. IEEE Geosci. Rem. Sens. Lett. **14**(3), 354–358 (2017)
12. He, J., Zhang, S., Yang, M., Shan, Y., Huang, T.: Bi-directional cascade network for perceptual edge detection. In: CVPR, pp. 3828–3837 (2019)
13. Dice, L.: Measures of the amount of ecologic association between species. Ecology **26**(3), 297–302 (1945)
14. Milletari, F., Navab, N., Ahmadi, S.: V-Net: fully convolutional neural networks for volumetric medical image segmentation. In: 3DV, pp. 565–571 (2016)
15. Sobel, I.: Camera models and machine perception. Technical report, Computer Science Department, Technion (1972)
16. Xie, S., Tu, Z.: Holistically-nested edge detection. Int. J. Comput. Vis. **125**(1–3), 3–18 (2017)
17. Liu, Y., Cheng, M., Hu, X., Wang, K., Bai, X.: Richer convolutional features for edge detection. In: CVPR, pp. 5872–5881 (2017)

Convolutional Neural Networks and Periocular Region Image Recognition

Eliana Pereira da Silva, Francisco Fambrini$^{(\boxtimes)}$, and José Hiroki Saito

UNIFACCAMP - University Center of Campo Limpo Paulista,
Campo Limpo Paulista, Brazil
eliana.pereiras@gmail.com, ffambrini@gmail.com, saito@cc.faccamp.br

Abstract. There are some benefits in using periocular biometric traits for individual identification. This work describes the use of convolutional neural network Neocognitron, in this novel application, in individual recognition using periocular region images. Besides, it is used the competitive learning using the extreme points of lines detected in the preprocessing of the input images as winner positions. It was used Carnegie Mellon University - Pose, Illumination, and Expression Database (CMU-PIE), with 41,368 images of 68 persons. From these images, 57×57 periocular images were obtained as training and test samples. The experiments indicate results in the Kappa index of 0.89, for periocular images, and 0.91 for complete face images.

Keywords: Neocognitron · Periocular imaged · Face recognition · Individual identification

1 Introduction

The periocular region can be used to confirm or to contradict an identity. When parts of the faces, such as mouth and nose are occluded, the periocular region can be used to determine the identity of individuals. Several methods have been proposed, such as by Park et al. [1], using local binary patterns. Woodard et al. [2] used local appearance-based feature representation, dividing the image into spatially salient patches, and histograms of texture and color were computed for each patch. Tan and Kumar [3] used filters such as Leung-Mallik for simultaneously exploiting features of the iris and periocular region, recognition approach from the face images acquired at-a-distance. The surveys of Alonso-Fernandez and Bigun [4] and Rattani and Derakhshani [5] are very complete about traditional periocular region recognition, but they don't include any work using convolutional neural networks. Convolutional Neural Networks have been considered good alternative tools to solve different problems, such as recognition of handwritten characters and digits [6–8], and facial recognition [9]. This paper describes the use of Neocognitron, in recognition of individuals, using periocular images, which is discriminative by the great difference in details of this region in individuals. This text, after this introductory section, Sect. 2 refers to the

© Springer Nature Switzerland AG 2020
H. Yang et al. (Eds.): ICONIP 2020, CCIS 1332, pp. 320–326, 2020.
https://doi.org/10.1007/978-3-030-63820-7_36

description of the convolutional neural network Neocognitron used in the experiments; Sect. 3, description of the image database; in Sect. 4, it is presented the experimental results; and Sect. 5, is dedicated to the analysis of the results, and future works.

2 Neocognitron Convolutional Neural Network

The Neocognitron convolutional network was firstly proposed by Fukushima for the recognition of handwritten digit and letter [6]. In the Neocognitron a convolutional layer is denoted the Us, in which the S-cells are responsible for the attributes extraction, and the pooling layer is denoted Uc, in which the C-cells apply the averaging filter. The most simple attributes, such as edges and lines segments in several directions are extracted by the lower hierarchical stages, which are followed by stages designed to detect attributes such as angles, extreme points of the lines, and polygons.

An S-cell is calculated using Eq. (1), where the numerator of the first part of the argument has as first sum all the connected cell planes, and as the second sum, all the connections in the receptive field in one C-cells plane, or input image; and each input provided by a C-cell of preceding layer, uc, is multiplied by the weight a. At the denominator the variable Θ is a threshold responsible by the ability to extract attributes, b represents a weight, and vc is an output value of an auxiliary cell, V-cell.

$$u_s = \varphi[x] = \varphi \left[\frac{(1 + \sum_{planos} \sum_{recep} a \times u_c)}{1 + \Theta \times b \times v_c} \right] \tag{1}$$

After the argument x calculated, it is applied the activation function ϕ, defined by Eq. (2), also known as ReLU (*Rectified Linear Unit*):

$$\varphi[x] = \begin{cases} x, x \geq 0 \\ 0, x < 0 \end{cases} \tag{2}$$

It is noted that the argument x must be equal or higher than zero when the numerator $1 + \sum_{planos} \sum_{recep} a \times u_c$ is high or equal to the denominator $1 + \theta \times b \times v_c$. If the denominator is greater than the numerator, it inhibits the S-cell to fire, making us = 0, so it can be stated that the denominator has an inhibitory function. The weights a and b are variables and modified during the training. In general, these weights are greater or equal to zero.

A V-cell is calculated as a square root of the sum of the square of the input uc, multiplied with weight c, as shown in Eq. (3). The weight c is fixed, its value is normalized, and varies in the connections of the receptive field monotonically decreasing from the center to surrounding cells, in the radial direction.

$$v_c = \sqrt{(\sum_{planos} \sum_{recep} c \times u_c^2)} \tag{3}$$

The Eq. (4) refers to the C-cell, whose output is denoted uc, and is calculated as the sum of the receptive cells outputs us multiplied by the weight d, that decreases monotonically, such as weight c, in the radial direction, but the weights are not normalized.

$$u_c = \Psi\left[x\right] = \Psi\left[\sum\nolimits_{recep} d \times u_s\right] \tag{4}$$

The activation function Ψ is described by Eq. (5), and it corresponds to a normalization of the argument x.

$$\Psi[x] = \begin{cases} \frac{1}{1+x} & if\ x \geq 0 \\ 0, & othercase \end{cases} \tag{5}$$

2.1 Edge, Line and Extreme Point Detection

In Neocognitron, supervised training takes place when training the extractors for characteristics such as edges, lines, and extreme points. These feature extractors are described as follows.

Edge Detection

During edge extraction, the occurrences of edges in different directions are checked in the input images. Figure 1 (a) illustrates an edge extraction in the horizontal direction, and Fig. 1 (b), in the inclined direction. Note that the dashed squares represent the edge detection patterns and that the edges are checked on both sides of a line (side A, and side B), which are 180° out of phase. The dashed squares are filters in which the connections with weight 1 are highlighted in black and the other connections have weight 0.

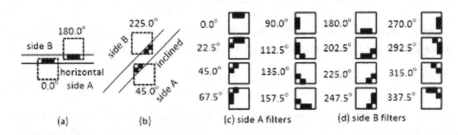

Fig. 1. Attributes recognized by the Neocognitron cells by the three stages of the network.

The 16 edge filters of size 5 × 5, divided into side A and side B are shown in Fig. 1(c), and Fig. 1(d), respectively. The filters corresponding to a 180° lag refer to the opposite sides of a line. These edge filters are used as input during supervised training to obtain edge detection S planes. Since the number of edges is fixed at 16, the number of cell planes S in the edge detection layer is fixed at 16, with one plane for each edge filter.

Line Detection

During the line detection procedure, three line thicknesses are considered, in addition to the eight edge directions, obtained in the previous layer. To obtain a given thickness, the parameters are varied as shown in Fig. 2(a). The two edges detected in the previous layer are represented by the variables kc, where $kc = 0$ for one edge and $kc = 1$ for the edge on the opposite side. The coordinates of the edge with kc = 0 are represented by the variables ix, deltax, and deltay, and the coordinates of the edge with $kc = 1$ are $ix + ixm$, deltax, and deltay. The deltax and deltay variables determine the direction of the line. With the variation of ix and ixm, the three thickness possibilities considered are verified. The coordinate (i, j) represents the position where the line is detected.

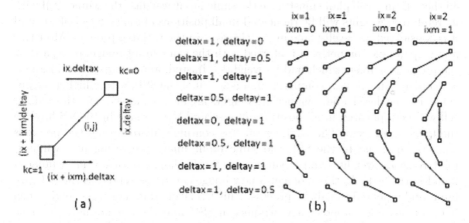

(a)   (b)

Fig. 2. (a) Parameters used to detect lines with different thicknesses, (b) thicknesses obtained varying parameters ix, ixm, deltax, and deltay.

Fig. 2(b) illustrates the thicknesses obtained by varying these values, where the length of the segment shown represents the thickness of the line.

Extreme Point Detection

Another pre-processing operation is the detection of extreme points, in the lines detected by layer U_{S2}, which pass through layer U_{C2} for convolutional smoothing operation. This detection of extreme points is carried out using special filters that detect the presence of line on one side and the absence on the other in several directions in which the lines are detected.

These pre-processing results input data for the later stages of the network, which normally consist of three more stages, beyond the output layer. The learning used in these later stages is competitive learning that will be described as follows.

2.2   Competitive Learning

As described, the weights a and b are adjusted, and the weights c and d are fixed so that the S-cells in the US layers must be trained. The training is competitive, non-supervised, and only the winner neuron have their weights adjusted. The competition occurs in a special cell plane, denoted Seed Selection Plane (SSP) [11,12]. The training of a US layer is started with no one trained cell plane, only with the SSP. When an input image is presented, the preceding C-cell layer of the training US layer presents its outputs. This preceding layer is the input image if the training layer is at the first stage. The inputs are computed by PSS S-cells, where all the cells have the same small weight greater than zero at the connections. These S-cells competes with the same weights but in different positions of SSP so that each S-cell results in different output value. The S-cell with higher output value is the winner, and its weights a and b are reinforced. If all the cells in a cell plane must have the same input weights, the winner cell with its reinforced weights will be replicated in all positions of a new S-cell plane, and it is considered an S-cell plane in the US layer in the training process. After this first step, a new competition is started with the same input image, disregarding the previous winner, which had its weights adjusted, and incorporated in a new S-cell plane. In this new competition, a new cell of the SSP, with a higher output value, is considered a new winner, its weights are also reinforced, and this winner cell will be replicated in all positions of a second S-cell plane in the US layer in the training process. The training process continues disregarding the previous winners, applying to the SSP the same input image, detecting new winners, reinforcing its weights, and creating new S-cell planes, until no one winner is found in the SSP. At this moment a new image can be presented to the network input and repeated the above process. This US layer training process ends when it is not possible to detect new winners in SSP, and there is no more any new input image for training. At this moment the training of the stage is finished and the next stage training is started with the same input images used in the training of the present stage.

Special Handling of the First Layer of Competitive Learning
In this Neocognitron implementation, the training of the first competitive learning layer, which takes place after the preprocessing layer of extreme point detection is treated in a special way. The SSP considers for competition only the S-cells in the positions where the extreme points were found. This showed better results in the detection of attributes for the recognition of the individuals by facial images and images of periocular regions.

3   Image Database

The images used in the experiments were extracted from the CMU-PIE database, which provides 41,368 images of 68 individuals. The individuals were photographed in 13 different poses, 43 illumination conditions, with and without the background illumination, 4 different expressions (smiling, talking, and winking), in 15 different positions, and 19 illumination conditions. For the acquisition of images of the periocular region, exclusive sub-images of the left eye of individuals from the CMU-PIE image database were captured. Figure 3 illustrates the two types of images used in the experiments: (a) periocular images with and without accessories; (b) face image with and without accessories.

(a) periocular
   images

(b) complete
    face
    images

Fig. 3. (a) Parameters used to detect lines with different thicknesses, (b) thicknesses obtained varying parameters ix, ixm, deltax, and deltay.

4 Experiments and Discussions

Table 1, it is shown results of five experiments with Neocognitron, for individual recognition. The first three experiments are of periocular region images, and the last two experiments are of complete face images. The number of individuals considered in each experiment is shown in the third row; the number of training samples is shown in fourth row; and the number of test samples is shown in fifth row. The last two rows show the kappa index proposed by Cohen [12], and the recognition rate, respectively. The threshold values (Θ in Eq. 1) which determine the input intensity values to the neuron fire, were: edge, 0.84, line, 0.84; US3, 0.8; U S4, 0.75; US5, 0.60 during training; and US3, 0.75, U S4, 0.70, and US5, 0.60, during the test. In all experiments it was used different samples for training and test, and the training was in sequence of classes, so that after all the training samples of the first class presented, all the second class samples were presented, and so on, until the training of the last class. For the result analysis, it was considered the recognition rate, TP/P, where TP represents the true positives, and P is the total of positive samples. The best result for the periocular image individual recognition, was 96.25%, and for the complete face image, was 96.75%, and 0.86, and 0.87 in the Kappa index, respectively. The best Kappa index was 0.89 for periocular images, and 0.91 for complete face images.

Table 1. Experiments using Neocognitron.

Experiment	1	2	3	4	5
Images	periocular	periocular	periocular	face	face
Class	10	10	12	10	12
Train	100	200	300	100	300
Test	100	200	200	100	200
Kappa	**0.89**	0.84	0.86	**0.91**	0.87
Rate	89.6%	86.15%	**96.25%**	91.50%	**96.75%**

5 Conclusions

In this work, it was used the Neocognitron network for individual recognition using a periocular image, compared to the recognition using a complete face image. This Neocognitron implementation uses extreme points to control the competition. Comparing the use of different image types: ocular region image, and complete face image, the results showed that the recognition rate using periocular region images and using complete face images was quite similar. Although the use of the CMU-PIE database, the image samples were resized because of the Neocognitron input image size. As future work, it is proposed to compare the obtained recognition rate using other types of CNNs.

Acknowledgements. The authors would like to thank Prof. Simon Baker from Carnegie Mellon University for the kindness of sending the PIE database, used in this work, and to acknowledge CAPES (Coordenação de Aperfeiçoamento de Pessoal de Nível Superior), Ministry of Education, Brazil, Financing Code 001.

References

1. Park, U., Jillela, R.R., Ross, A., Jain, A.K.: Periocular biometrics in the visible spectrum. IEEE Trans. Inf. Forensics Secur. **6**(1), 96–106 (2010)
2. Woodard, D.L., Pundlik, S.J., Lyle, J.R., Miller, P.E.: Periocular region appearance cues for biometric identification. In: 2010 IEEE Computer Society Conference on Computer Vision and Pattern Recognition-Workshops, pp. 162–169. IEEE, June 2010
3. Tan, C.W., Kumar, A.: Human identification from at-a-distance images by simultaneously exploiting iris and periocular features. In: Proceedings of the 21st International Conference on Pattern Recognition (ICPR 2012), pp. 553–556. IEEE, November 2012
4. Alonso-Fernandez, F., Bigun, J.: A survey on periocular biometrics research. Pattern Recogn. Lett. **82**, 92–105 (2016)
5. Rattani, A., Derakhshani, R.: Ocular biometrics in the visible spectrum: a survey. Image Vis. Comput. **59**, 1–16 (2017)
6. Fukushima, K., Miyake, S., Ito, T.: Neocognitron: a neural network model for a mechanism of visual pattern recognition. IEEE Trans. Syst. Man Cybern. **5**, 826–834 (1983)
7. LeCun, Y., Bottou, L., Bengio, Y., Haffner, P.: Gradient-based learning applied to document recognition. Proc. IEEE **86**(11), 2278–2324 (1998)
8. Bengio, Y., LeCun, Y.: Scaling learning algorithms towards AI. Large-Scale Kernel Mach. **34**(5), 1–41 (2007)
9. Saito, J.H., de Carvalho, T.V., Hirakuri, M., Saunite, A., Ide, A.N., Abib, S.: Using CMU PIE human face database to a convolutional neural network-neocognitron. In: ESANN, pp. 491–496 (2005)
10. Fukushima, K., Miyake, S.: Neocognitron: a new algorithm for pattern recognition tolerant of deformations and shifts in position. Pattern Recogn. **15**(6), 455–469 (1982)
11. Cardoso, Â., Wichert, A.: Neocognitron and the map transformation cascade. Neural Netw. **23**(1), 74–88 (2010)
12. Cohen, J.: A coefficient of agreement for nominal scales. Educ. Psychol. Measur. **20**(1), 37–46 (1960)

CPCS: Critical Points Guided Clustering and Sampling for Point Cloud Analysis

Wei Wang[1], Zhiwen Shao[2,3(✉)], Wencai Zhong[1], and Lizhuang Ma[1,4(✉)]

[1] Department of Computer Science and Engineering, Shanghai Jiao
Tong University, Shanghai, China
`ma-lz@cs.sjtu.edu.cn`
[2] School of Computer Science and Technology, China University of Mining
and Technology, Xuzhou, China
`zhiwen_shao@cumt.edu.cn`
[3] Engineering Research Center of Mine Digitization, Ministry of Education
of the People's Republic of China, Beijing, China
[4] School of Computer Science and Technology, East China
Normal University, Shanghai, China

Abstract. 3D vision based on irregular point sequences has gained increasing attention, with current methods depending on random or farthest point sampling. However, the existing sampling methods either measure the distance in the Euclidean space and ignore the high-level properties, or just sample from point clouds only with the largest distance. To tackle these limitations, we introduce the Expectation-Maximization Attention module, to find the critical subset points and cluster the other points around them. Moreover, we explore a point cloud sampling strategy to sample points based on the critical subset. Extensive experiments demonstrate the effectiveness of our method for several popular point cloud analysis tasks. Our module achieves the accuracy of 93.3% on ModelNet40 with only 1024 points for classification task.

Keywords: Point cloud · Attention mechanism · Expectation maximization · Sampling

1 Introduction

Recently, many works such as PointNet [9], PointNet++ [10] and DGCNN [15] use neural networks in point clouds, which demonstrate the success of processing irregular point cloud data in classification and segmentation. However, point cloud data is highly unstructured. This property results in two main problems: (i) There is no fixed neighbor in point cloud. (ii) The sensors introduce inevitable noise and nonuniform sampling into point cloud data. Therefore, the critical part of PointNet++ is the sampling and grouping layer, which uses farthest/random point cloud sampling to aggregate the local feature.

Since farthest/random sampling is based on the distance in the Euclidean space, as illustrated in Fig. 1, the sampled points may not represent the critical

© Springer Nature Switzerland AG 2020
H. Yang et al. (Eds.): ICONIP 2020, CCIS 1332, pp. 327–335, 2020.
https://doi.org/10.1007/978-3-030-63820-7_37

points that the network really pays attention to in the learning process. A more reasonable way is to adaptively find multiple critical points in network optimization process. However, most of the variants of PointNet++ are concerned about how to improve and extend convolution operator to point cloud more naturally, and disregard the limitations of farthest/random point sampling.

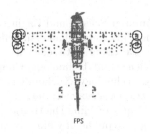

FPS

Fig. 1. Illustration of the FPS sampling algorithm. It may encounter some extreme conditions due to the distance measurement in Euclidean space.

Previous studies [8,20] have shown how to localize these critical points, and [20] demonstrates the effectiveness of critical points. Moreover, the previous work [8] proposes to map the point clouds to basis point sets.

In this work, we present a novel hierarchical clustering network for point cloud understanding. The key module of this work is called critical points set module (CPM). CPM utilizes a self-attention based expectation maximize process to localize the critical points set, and then fuses the clustered feature to the original input point clouds as synthetic semantic information. Moreover, we propose a novel point sampling mechanism (CPSM) with the critical points.

The major contributions of this paper are summarized below: (i) We propose to formulate critical point finding problem into EM process, and design a module for it. (ii) We propose a simple and replaceable way to gain semantice information without expensive annotation. (iii) We propose a critical point based sampling method.

2   Related Work

2.1   Deep Learning on 3D Data

Multi-view Based Methods. Su et al. [12] projects the 3D data into 2D images. Due to depth structure information is lost by projection, this kind of methods are sensitive to the number of views.

Voxel Based Methods. Maturana et al. [7] always convert point clouds into regular grids in order to use 3D convolution operators. However, the complexity of computation is high.

Point Cloud Based Methods. PointNet [9] and PointNet++ [10] proposes MLP and sampling, grouping modules (MSG and SSG). DGCNN [15] integrates EdgeConv into PointNet and captures the information of neighbors.

2.2   Critical Points and Sampling

Critical Points. Previous work [9] introduces a **Critical-Subset Theory**. We simply explain the definition of the theory in the following: For any point clouds X, there exists a subset $X_c \subseteq X$ called critical points. A deep architecture like PointNet can be formulated as $f = \gamma \circ u(X)$, where $u(X) = \underset{x_i \in X}{MAX}\{h(x_i)\}$, such that there exists a point set $T, X_c \subseteq T \subseteq X$, $f(X_c) = f(T)$. Obviously the performance of network depends on $u(X)$. While $u(X_c) = u(T)$, so the critical points X_c which contains the same element-wise maximums as T. In other words, the critical points X_c, has the same information capacity as T. If we extend T to its upper bound X, the critical points subset X_c could be viewed as a representation of X. We recommend the readers to find more details in [9,20].

Point Cloud Sampling. [1] proposes a progressive sampling method using the ranking score. [4] proposes novel differentiable approximation of point cloud sampling.

3   CPCS for Point Cloud Analysis

3.1   Critical Set Module

For the whole point cloud $X \in \mathbb{R}^{N \times d}$, there exists a set $X_c \in \mathbb{R}^{K \times d}$. We call the set X_c as the critical point. Note that X_c is initialized with the original input points, and X_c are updated dynamically in EM process after initialization.

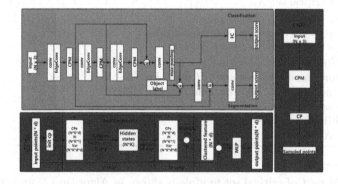

Fig. 2. The architecture of our work. The orange part shows the detailed structure of CPM and CPSM. The green part is the total network. N is the point number, K is the number of Gaussian distributions. d is the feature dimension. (Color figure online)

We denote X_c as the variable mean in Gaussian distribution, so the critical points selecting problem can be optimized like EM process. By using the conclusion of maximize likelihood estimation of GMM, we can formulate the problem in 2 steps. H is the hidden state of GMM, and we take Gaussian distribution as our kernel function G for hidden state (λ is a constant value):

$$G(X_j|X_{ci}, Var_i) = softmax(\lambda(X_j - X_{ci})Var_i^{-1}(X_j - X_{ci})^T), \quad (1)$$

$$H(X_j|X_{ci}, P_i, Var_i) = P_i G(X_j|X_{ci}, Var_i) / \sum_i^K P_i G(X_j|X_{ci}, Var_i). \quad (2)$$

The hidden states of X can be viewed as the probability for each point in X every Gaussian distribution. For E-step, we calculate the hidden states of point clouds X and the critical points X_c, as shown in Eq. (2). For M step, the critical points X_c, and the other two variables P and Var update in the following:

$$P_i = \sum_j^N H(X_j|X_{ci}, P_i, Var_i)/N, \quad (3)$$

$$X_{ci} = \sum_j^N H(X_j|X_{ci}, P_i, Var_i)X_j / \sum_j^N H(X_j|X_{ci}, P_i, Var_i), \quad (4)$$

$$Var_i = \sum_j^N H(X_j|X_{ci}, P_i, Var_i)(X_j - X_{ci})^T(X_j - X_{ci}) / \sum_j^N H(X_j|X_{ci}, P_i, Var_i). \quad (5)$$

Algorithm 1. Critical point set module.

Input: X, *Step*
Parameter: critical set X_c
Output: X_c
  1: Initialize X_c selected from X feature space.
  2: Initialize Var and P.
  3: **while** *Step* $\neq$ 0 **do**
  4:    E-step:Compute hidden state H using Eq. (2)
  5:    M-step:Update X_c, P, Var using Eq. (3)(4)(5)
  6:    Decrease *Step* by 1
  7: **end while**
  8: **return** X_c

The EM part of critical set module is shown in Algorithm 1, and the critical points set module (CPM) detail are illustrated in Fig. 2. In the module, the first "init cp" layer is to sample some initial critical points bases from the input points with different strategies. In our experiment, we initialize them in random selection. In order to achieve higher memory efficiency, we use a $d \times 1$ matrix to replace original $d \times d$ Var_i matrix by assuming the high dimensional features have no correlation.

3.2   Hierarchical Clustering in Network

By inserting the critical set module into the backbone, we implement the hierarchical clustering architecture for point clouds understanding. The backbone we choose for the architecture is based on PointNet and DGCNN. As show in Fig. 2, we implement a hierarchical clustering network by inserting our CPM modules into the backbone.

The output features of CPM can be viewed as the combination of critical points bases with soft weights. The number of clusters decreases with the stacked CPM modules in forward process, so that the receptive field of the network is expanded.

3.3   Synthetic Semantic Information Supervision

Since the clustering process is on feature space, the synthetic semantic labels are not restricted by the Euclidean distance, like the wings of plane. These synthetic semantic labels provide a different supervision signal from classification tasks, and are also beneficial to semantic segmentation. In other words, our CPM module can be viewed as a kind of unsupervised multi-task branch for point cloud learning without extra annotation.

3.4   Critical Point Sampling

As shown in Sect. 3.1, the critical points are determined by the expectation maximum process of the Self-attention. We extend the CPM module into the point clouds sampling method, called CPSM. Since the critical point are updated by EM process dynamically, we find that in most conditions, the critical point of a points cluster does not belong to this cluster actually. It is hard to visualize as the geometry based sampling methods. In order to compare with the other sampling methods, we designed quantitative experiment in Sect. 4.3. CPSM can be easily implemented in parallel. Compared with farthest point sampling, our CPSM does not require massive iteration, so it is computationally efficient.

4   Experiments

4.1   Point Cloud Classification

The results of point cloud classification on ModelNet40 [14] are shown in Table 1. Note that we only use 1024 points with 3D coordinates for each object. The iterator steps are all set to be 3 (determined by task and data complexity). We use Adam optimizer with an initial learning rate of 0.001. It can be seen that our method achieves state-of-the-art results on ModelNet benchmark. Compared with other published methods such as [5,7,13,16,18], etc. Our model achieves 93.3% with only 1024 points coordinates.

For the real scanned point clouds classification, we verify our method on the ScanObjectNN [19] dataset. Table 2 shows the results of our methods on

Table 1. ModelNet40 object classification accuracy. We compared results for CPM integrated in 2 different backbones. We plug 3 CPM modules in DGCNN with critical points (128-64-32), and 2 CPM modules in PointNet with critical points (64, 32)

Method	Input	Accuracy(%)
VoxNet	Voxel	85.9
Pointnet	1024 points	89.2
Pointnet++	1024 points	90.2
Pointnet++	5000 points + normal	91.9
SpiderCNN	1024 points + normal	92.4
PointConv	1024 points + normal	92.5
PointCNN	1024 points	92.5
KPConv	1024 points	92.9
DGCNN	1024 points	92.2
Ours (DGCNN)	1024 points	**93.3**
Ours (PointNet)	1024 points	90.9

ScanObjectNN. For two different backbones, our methods can achieves 1%–2% improvement to the original backbones. Both of the ModelNet and ScanObjectNN benchmarks verify the distinguished performance of our method in point cloud classification task. And these 2 kinds of data, including CAD and scanned point clouds, also demonstrate the adaptability of our methods.

Table 2. ScanObjectNN object classification accuracy. We plug 3 CPM modules in DGCNN with criticalpoints (128-64-32), and 2 CPM modules in PointNet with critical points (64, 32)

Method	OBJ_ONLY	OBJ_BG	PB_T25	PB_T25_R	PB_T50_R	PB_T50_RS
Pointnet	79.2	73.3	73.5	72.7	68.2	68.2
Pointnet++	84.3	82.3	82.7	81.4	79.1	77.9
SpiderCNN	79.5	77.1	78.1	77.7	73.8	73.7
DGCNN	86.5	82.8	83.3	81.5	80.0	78.1
PointCNN	85.5	**86.1**	83.6	**82.5**	78.5	78.5
Ours(DGCNN)	**86.7**	84.8	**83.8**	82.2	**81.2**	**79.8**
Ours(PointNet)	81.1	74.4	75.3	74.9	72.7	71.5

4.2 Point Cloud Part Segmentation

The architecture of part segmentation is shown in Fig. 2. We take a U-net structure network for part segmentation. We use Adam optimizer with initial learning rate of 0.001, and the number of critical points of each CPM is set as 64-32-16. In Table 3, we list mean IoU and IoU of each class of the proposed methods and [2,3,6,11] etc. The result suggests that our method achieves state-of-the-art performance. For some categories like lamp and chair, the performance of proposed model has distinct improvement.

Table 3. ShapeNet [17] part segmentation performance.

Method	KD-Net	Pointnet	KCNet	RSNet	Pointnet++	DGCNN	SpiderCNN	PointCNN	DPAM	Ours
Mean	82.3	83.7	84.7	84.9	85.1	85.1	85.3	86.1	86.1	85.9
Aero	80.1	83.4	82.8	82.7	82.4	84.2	83.5	84.1	84.3	84.3
Bag	74.6	78.7	81.5	86.4	79.0	83.7	81.0	86.5	81.6	84.8
Cap	74.3	82.5	86.4	84.1	87.7	84.4	87.2	86.0	89.1	89.3
Car	70.3	74.9	77.6	78.2	77.3	77.1	77.5	80.8	79.5	77.6
Chair	88.6	89.6	90.3	90.4	90.8	90.9	90.7	90.6	90.9	91.2
Earphone	73.5	73.0	76.8	69.3	71.8	78.5	76.8	79.7	77.5	75.9
Guitar	90.2	91.5	91.0	91.4	91.0	91.5	91.1	92.3	91.8	90.7
Knife	87.2	85.9	87.2	87.0	85.9	87.3	87.3	88.4	87.0	88.1
Lamp	81.0	80.8	84.5	83.5	83.7	82.9	83.3	85.3	84.5	86.7
Laptop	94.9	95.3	95.5	95.4	95.3	96.0	95.8	96.1	96.2	95.8
Motor	57.4	65.2	69.2	66.0	71.6	67.8	70.2	77.2	68.7	66.2
Mug	86.7	93.0	94.4	92.6	94.1	93.3	93.5	95.3	94.5	93.2
Pistol	78.1	81.2	81.6	81.8	81.3	82.6	82.7	84.2	81.4	81.4
Rocket	51.8	57.9	60.1	56.1	58.7	59.7	59.7	64.2	64.2	56.2
Skateboard	69.9	72.8	75.2	75.8	76.4	75.5	75.8	80.0	76.2	74.1
Table	80.3	80.6	81.3	82.2	82.6	82.0	82.8	83.0	84.3	84.0

4.3   Point Cloud Sampling

Although [1,4] can achieve sampling, they always need a pretrained task networks, and can be viewed as additional subnetworks. CPSM is quite different from [1,4]. It can be integrated into the network as a pooling functional layer. Due to the difference, we only compare CPSM with Farthest Point Sampling and Random Sampling, which can also be designed as pooling functional layer.

Single Stage Sampling. We add each of the 3 sampling layers after the 4th convolutional layer for comparison. Figure 3 shows the accuracy of different methods with multiple sampling ratio. When the sampling ratio is larger than $4\times$, CPSM performs best. Critical points can still keep vital information for point cloud understanding while the sampling ratio increases.

Cascaded Sampling. 2 cascaded sampling layers are added after the 3rd and 4th convolutional layer. For sampling ratio $4\times$, $8\times$ and $16\times$, they are separated as $(2\times, 2\times)$, $(4\times, 2\times)$, $(4\times, 4\times)$. The result shows in Fig. 4. Almost no performance degradation happens after cascaded modules for all 3 methods.

Table 4 suggests that CPSM performs more efficient than FPS, and makes a trade-off between FPS and Random on accuracy.

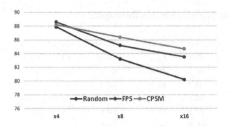

Fig. 3. The Single stage sampling results. The vertical axis is accuracy (%), the horizontal axis is the sampling ratio.

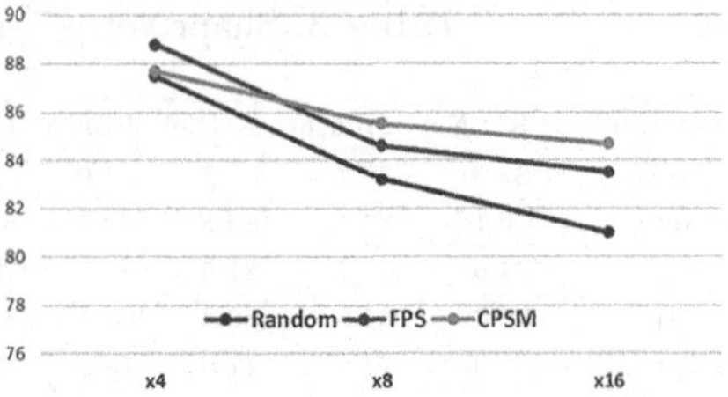

Fig. 4. Cascaded sampling results. The vertical axis is accuracy (%), the horizontal axis is the sampling ratio.

Table 4. A sampling time comparison between FPS and CPSM. The size of point cloud is 2048 and batch size is 32. The device is Nvidia 1080Ti. The time shorter is better.

Sample Ratio	FPS	CPSM
4×	0.58 s	0.15 s
8×	0.28 s	0.08 s
16×	0.14 s	0.04 s
32×	0.07 s	0.03 s

5   Conclusion

In this work, we formulate the critical points problem into EM process, and proposed the module (CPM) for finding the critical points. Moreover, we construct a critical points sampling module (CPSM) for point cloud sampling. Sufficient experiments show that our method achieves state-of-the-art performance on several benchmarks of point clouds analysis. The CPM provides an insight for exploring the relationship between critical set and the entire point cloud.

Acknowledgments. This work is supported by the National Natural Science Foundation of China (No. 61972157 and No. 61902129), the National Key R&D Program of China (No. 2019YFC1521104), the Shanghai Pujiang Talent Program (No. 19PJ1403100), and the Economy and Informatization Commission of Shanghai Municipality (No. XX-RGZN-01-19-6348).

References

1. Dovrat, O., Lang, I., Avidan, S.: Learning to sample. In: IEEE Conference on Computer Vision and Pattern Recognition, pp. 2760–2769 (2019)
2. Huang, Q., Wang, W., Neumann, U.: Recurrent slice networks for 3D segmentation of point clouds. In: IEEE Conference on Computer Vision and Pattern Recognition, pp. 2626–2635 (2018)

3. Klokov, R., Lempitsky, V.: Escape from cells: deep Kd-Networks for the recognition of 3d point cloud models. In: IEEE International Conference on Computer Vision, pp. 863–872 (2017)
4. Lang, I., Manor, A., Avidan, S.: SampleNet: differentiable point cloud sampling. arXiv preprint arXiv:1912.03663 (2019)
5. Li, Y., Bu, R., Sun, M., Wu, W., Di, X., Chen, B.: PointCNN: convolution on x-transformed points. In: Advances in Neural Information Processing Systems, pp. 820–830 (2018)
6. Liu, J., Ni, B., Li, C., Yang, J., Tian, Q.: Dynamic points agglomeration for hierarchical point sets learning. In: IEEE International Conference on Computer Vision, pp. 7546–7555 (2019)
7. Maturana, D., Scherer, S.: VoxNet: a 3D convolutional neural network for real-time object recognition. In: 2015 IEEE/RSJ International Conference on Intelligent Robots and Systems (IROS), pp. 922–928. IEEE (2015)
8. Prokudin, S., Lassner, C., Romero, J.: Efficient learning on point clouds with basis point sets. In: IEEE International Conference on Computer Vision Workshops (2019)
9. Qi, C.R., Su, H., Mo, K., Guibas, L.J.: PointNet: deep learning on point sets for 3D classification and segmentation. In: IEEE Conference on Computer Vision and Pattern Recognition, pp. 652–660 (2017)
10. Qi, C.R., Yi, L., Su, H., Guibas, L.J.: PointNet++: deep hierarchical feature learning on point sets in a metric space. In: Advances in Neural Information Processing Systems, pp. 5099–5108 (2017)
11. Shen, Y., Feng, C., Yang, Y., Tian, D.: Mining point cloud local structures by kernel correlation and graph pooling. In: IEEE Conference on Computer Vision and Pattern Recognition, pp. 4548–4557 (2018)
12. Su, H., Maji, S., Kalogerakis, E., Learned-Miller, E.: Multi-view convolutional neural networks for 3D shape recognition. In: IEEE International Conference on Computer Vision, pp. 945–953 (2015)
13. Thomas, H., Qi, C.R., Deschaud, J.E., Marcotegui, B., Goulette, F., Guibas, L.J.: KPConv: flexible and deformable convolution for point clouds. In: IEEE International Conference on Computer Vision, pp. 6411–6420 (2019)
14. Uy, M.A., Pham, Q.H., Hua, B.S., Nguyen, T., Yeung, S.K.: Revisiting point cloud classification: a new benchmark dataset and classification model on real-world data. In: IEEE International Conference on Computer Vision, pp. 1588–1597 (2019)
15. Wang, Y., Sun, Y., Liu, Z., Sarma, S.E., Bronstein, M.M., Solomon, J.M.: Dynamic graph CNN for learning on point clouds. ACM Trans. Graph. 38(5), 1–12 (2019)
16. Wu, W., Qi, Z., Fuxin, L.: PointConv: deep convolutional networks on 3D point clouds. In: IEEE Conference on Computer Vision and Pattern Recognition, pp. 9621–9630 (2019)
17. Wu, Z., et al.: 3D shapeNets: a deep representation for volumetric shapes. In: IEEE Conference on Computer Vision and Pattern Recognition, pp. 1912–1920 (2015)
18. Xu, Y., Fan, T., Xu, M., Zeng, L., Qiao, Y.: SpiderCNN: deep learning on point sets with parameterized convolutional filters. In: European Conference on Computer Vision, pp. 87–102 (2018)
19. Yi, L., et al.: A scalable active framework for region annotation in 3D shape collections. ACM Trans. Graph. 35(6), 1–12 (2016)
20. Zheng, T., Chen, C., Yuan, J., Li, B., Ren, K.: PointCloud saliency maps. In: IEEE International Conference on Computer Vision, pp. 1598–1606 (2019)

Customizable GAN: Customizable Image Synthesis Based on Adversarial Learning

Zhiqiang Zhang[1], Wenxin Yu[1(✉)], Jinjia Zhou[2], Xuewen Zhang[1], Jialiang Tang[1], Siyuan Li[1], Ning Jiang[1], Gang He[1], Gang He[3], and Zhuo Yang[4]

[1] Southwest University of Science and Technology, Mianyang, China
yuwenxin@swust.edu.cn, star_yuwenxin27@163.com
[2] Hosei University, Tokyo, Japan
[3] Xidian University, Xi'an, China
[4] Guangdong University of Technology, Guangzhou, Guangdong, China

Abstract. In this paper, we propose a highly flexible and controllable image synthesis method based on the simple contour and text description. The contour determines the object's basic shape, and the text describes the specific content of the object. The method is verified in the Caltech-UCSD Birds (CUB) and Oxford-102 flower datasets. The experimental results demonstrate its effectiveness and superiority. Simultaneously, our method can synthesize the high-quality image synthesis results based on artificial hand-drawing contour and text description, which demonstrates the high flexibility and customizability of our method further.

Keywords: Computer vision · Deep learning · Customizable synthesis · Generative adversarial networks

1 Introduction

In computer vision, image synthesis is always essential but challenging research. In recent years, with the development of deep learning, especially the introduction of generative adversarial networks (GAN) [1], image synthesis has made a significant breakthrough. However, the input of the original GAN is the noise vector of Gaussian distribution, resulting in image synthesis that cannot artificially control.

To make the image synthesis process more controllable, it is necessary to provide high-level control information. The current research is mainly from two aspects: one is to control the shape of the synthesis through the contour information, the other is to control the specific content of the synthesis through the text information. Some achievements [2] have been made in the aspect of shape control by contour, but the biggest problem in this aspect is that it can only control the shape information, not the specific content. The method of text control starts with image attributes or class labels [3], which can control the categories of synthetic content but cannot do anything for more specific details.

© Springer Nature Switzerland AG 2020
H. Yang et al. (Eds.): ICONIP 2020, CCIS 1332, pp. 336–344, 2020.
https://doi.org/10.1007/978-3-030-63820-7_38

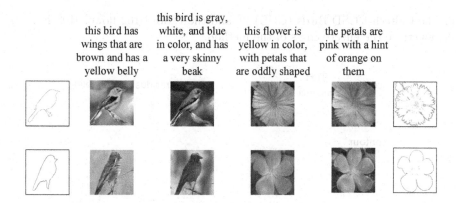

this bird has wings that are brown and has a yellow belly
this bird is gray, white, and blue in color, and has a very skinny beak
this flower is yellow in color, with petals that are oddly shaped
the petals are pink with a hint of orange on them

Fig. 1. The figure display the results of the corresponding birds and flowers under different texts and contours. The contours above are obtained by pre-processing the original dataset. The contours below are drawn by hand.

Furthermore, Reed *et al.* [4] proposed a method of synthesizing images based on the text description, which makes the whole synthesis process more flexible and better control the specific content of the synthesis. However, the synthesis method based on the text description can not control the shape information of the synthesized object. Subsequently, although many improvement text-to-image synthesis methods [5–7] have been put forward and achieved amazing results, the problem of unable to control the shape information of objects has not been solved.

To solve this problem, Reed *et al.* [8] proposed the Generative Adversarial What-Where Network (GAWWN), and realized the controllable image generation for the first time by combining the location information and text description. Although the method has achieved good control, on the one hand, the results of the method are not satisfactory. On the other hand, the bounding box and key points information used in this method belongs to the rough information, which can not realize the refined control of the object shape.

In order to achieve better control effect and synthesize more realistic results, a customizable synthesis method based on simple contour and text description is proposed. As shown in Fig. 1, the simple contour is used to determine the specific shape information for the object. The text description is then used to generate specific content. Finally, the high-quality images based on hand-drawn contour and artificial text description are obtained by using this method. It not only realizes fine-grained control but also completes the generation of the realistic image.

The main contributions of this paper are as follows: (1) an effective customizable image synthesis method is proposed, and it can achieve fine-grained control and high-quality image generation. (2) the whole process of image synthesis can be controlled manually, which makes our method most flexible. (3) experiments on the Caltech-UCSD Birds (CUB) [9] and the Oxford-102 flower [10] datasets demonstrate the effectiveness of the method.

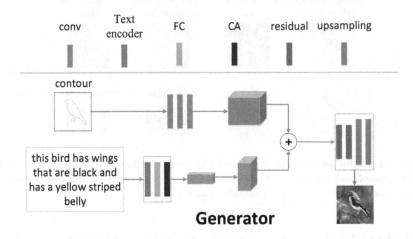

Fig. 2. The generator structure of the model. The generator synthesizes the corresponding image based on the text description and contour. The blue and brown cubes in the figure represent the corresponding extracted contour and text features. (Color figure online)

The rest of this paper is arranged as follows. Our method details are discussed in Sect. 2 and validated in Sect. 3 with promising experimental results. Section 4 concludes our work.

2   Customizable GAN

2.1   Network Architecture

The architecture of our approach is shown in Figs. 2 and 3. Figure 2 shows the network structure of the generator. In the generator, the simple contour and text description as the input is encoded in different ways and then combined. After that, the corresponding result is synthesized by de-convolution [11].

Specifically, in the generator, the contour is convoluted by a three-layer convolution neural network (CNN), followed by a ReLU activation operation. In addition to the first layer, each ReLU has a Batch Normalization (BN) operation [12] before it. The text description is first encoded as the text vector by a pre-trained text encoder [13], then expanded dimension by full connection layer. Finally, increase the number of text embeddings by condition augmentation (CA) [7] technology.

In order to effectively combine text embeddings with contour features, spatial replication is performed to expand the dimension of text embeddings. After the

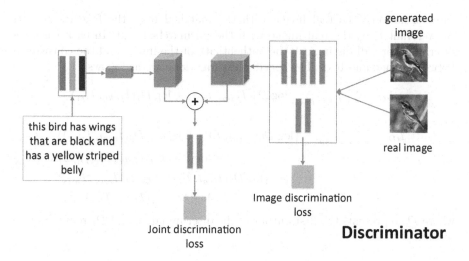

Fig. 3. The discriminator structure of the model. The discriminator judges whether the received image itself is true or fake and the matching degree between the image and text.

contour feature and text embeddings fusion, it will pass through two residual units, which are composed of residual blocks [14]. After that, the corresponding image results are synthesized by two up-sampling operations.

There are two parts of the content in the discriminator. One is to judge whether the input image is true or false; the other is to judge whether the input image and text match. Figure 3 shows the network structure of the discriminator. In the discriminator, the corresponding feature vector of the input image is obtained through the down-sampling operation. The down-sampling operation is divided into two types: one is to get the corresponding feature through two convolution layers and use it to judge whether the image is true or false; the other is to obtain the input image feature through five convolutions and then combine the extended dimension text vector to judge whether the image and the text match. In the image discrimination loss, the first convolution layer is followed by BN and leaky-ReLU [15] and the sigmoid function directly follows the second layer. In the joint discrimination loss, the combined image and text features are used to calculate the loss by two convolution layers. BN and leaky-ReLU operation follow the first convolution layer.

2.2 Adversarial Learning

There are three types of text input in the adversarial training process, that is, the matching text T, the mismatching text T_{mis}, and the relevant text T_{rel}. In the specific training, the generator synthesizes the corresponding image results through the simple contour and text description, and then the generated results will be sent to the discriminator. In the discriminator, it needs to distinguish three situations: the real image with the matched text, the fake image with the relevant text, the real image with the mismatched text. In each case, the discriminator will distinguish the authenticity of the image and the consistency between image and text. The specific loss functions are as follows:

$$L_G = \sum_{(I,T) \sim p_{data}} \log D_0(I_{fake}, T_{rel}) + \log D_1(I_{fake}, T_{rel}) \tag{1}$$

$$\begin{aligned} L_D = \sum_{(I,T) \sim p_{data}} \{&\log D_0(I_{real}, T) + [\log(1 - D_0(I_{real}, T_{mis})) \\ &+ \log(1 - D_0(I_{fake}, T_{rel}))]/2\} \\ + \{&\log D_1(I_{real}, T) + [\log D_1(I_{real}, T_{mis}) \\ &+ \log(1 - D_1(I_{fake}, T_{rel}))]/2\} \end{aligned} \tag{2}$$

where D_0 represents the first output of the discriminator, and D_1 represents the second.

2.3 Training Details

In the training process, the initial learning rate is set to 0.0002, and it decays to half of the original every 100 epochs. Adam optimization [16] with a momentum of 0.5 is used to optimize and update parameters. A total of 600 epochs are trained iteratively in the network, of which the batch size is 64.

3 Experiments

3.1 Dataset and Data Preprocessing

We validated our method on the CUB and the Oxford-102 flower datasets. The CUB dataset contains 11,788 images with 200 classes. The Oxford-102 dataset contains 8,189 images with 102 classes. Each image has ten corresponding text descriptions. Following Reed *et al.* [4], we split CUB dataset to 150 train classes and 50 test classes as well as Oxford-102 to 82 train classes and 20 test classes.

In order to experiment with customizable synthesis, it is necessary to pre-process the contour. For the processing of the bird dataset, we first download the corresponding binary image on its official website, then turn the black part of the background into white and retain the outermost contour lines. For the flower dataset, we use the Canny operator to process the flower foreground map, the official website provides the foreground map of the blue background, and pure foreground map can be obtained by turning the blue to white.

3.2 Qualitative Results

Compare our method with the existing controllable image synthesis (GAWWN), as shown in Fig. 4. There are two kinds of annotations in GAWWN: the bounding box, and the key points. In the figure, GAWWN_bb represents the GAWWN result based on the bounding box. GAWWN_kp represents the corresponding

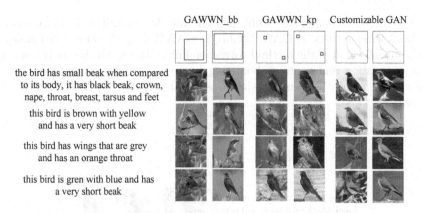

Fig. 4. The comparison between our method and GAWWN (including two results based on bounding box and key points).

result based on the key points. The synthesis results based on the bounding box, and key points generally have poor authenticity. By contrast, the results synthesized by our method have better authenticity as a whole. In detail processing, such as smoothness and texture, our results are also better than GAWWN. Besides, the resulting shape of GAWWN is rough, and the generated shape cannot be controlled accurately. Our method can control the specific shape precisely because it inputs contour information.

Table 1. The quantitative comparison results in the CUB dataset.

	GAWWN_bb	GAWWN_kp	Ours
Consistency	2.78	2.51	1.26
Text	2.46	2.28	1.44
Authenticity	2.67	2.34	1.42

3.3 Quantitative Results

For the evaluation of the controllable image synthesis model, Human Rank (HR) is used to quantify the comparison models. We employed 10 subjects to rank the quality of synthetic images by different methods. The text descriptions and contours corresponding to these results are all from the test set and are divided into 10 groups for use by 10 subjects. The subjects are asked to rank the results in the following ways: consistency, text, and authenticity. "Consistency" indicates whether the result is consistent with control information (the contour or bounding box or key points). "Text" denotes whether the result matches the text description. "Authenticity" represents the level of the authenticity of all results.

For the bird results, we established one way for quantitative comparison. It contains three results: 1) GAWWN_bb, 2) GAWWN_kp, 3) ours. The employers were not informed of the method corresponding to the result, but only knew the text description and contour, bounding box, and key points corresponding to the current result. The subjects were asked to rank the results (1 is best, 3 is worst).

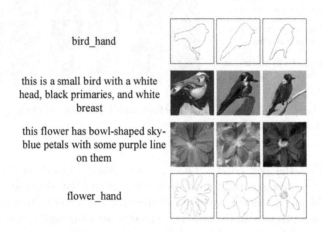

bird_hand

this is a small bird with a white head, black primaries, and white breast

this flower has bowl-shaped sky-blue petals with some purple line on them

flower_hand

Fig. 5. The text descriptions on the left are all artificial descriptions that do not exist in the dataset. The contours are also drawn manually.

Table 1 shows the comparison results with GAWWN in the CUB dataset. It is evident from the results that our method is considered to be the best in all respect. Our results have better authenticity and more conform to the text and control information.

3.4   Controllable Image Synthesis

The most important feature of our work is to realize fine-grained controllable image synthesis based on manual hand drawing and artificial text description. The relevant results are shown in Fig. 5. The contours in the figure are drawn by hand, and the text descriptions are also artificially described. These results reflect well the hand-drawn contour and artificial text description content, but also have high authenticity. This shows the effectiveness of our method in synthesizing high-quality images on the one hand. On the other hand, it reflects the high flexibility and controllability of our method because all inputs can be controlled artificially.

4   Conclusion

In this paper, we propose a fine-grained customized image synthesis method based on the simple contour and text description. The synthesis results demonstrate that our method not only maintains the basic shape of the contour but also conforms to the text description. Furthermore, we have evaluated the model on the Caltech-UCSD Birds and the Oxford-102 flower datasets. The experimental results show the effectiveness of our method. Besides, the high-quality image synthesis results based on hand-drawn contour and artificial description are also illustrated to prove that our method is highly controllable and flexible.

Acknowledgement. This research is supported by Sichuan Science and Technology Program (No. 2020YFS0307), National Natural Science Foundation of China (No. 61907009), Science and Technology Planning Project of Guangdong Province (No. 2019B010150002).

References

1. Goodfellow, I.J., et al.: Generative adversarial nets. In: Neural Information Processing Systems, vol. 27, pp. 2672–2680 (2014)
2. Isola, P., Zhu, J., Zhou, T., Efros, A.A.: Image-to-image translation with conditional adversarial networks. In: Computer Vision and Pattern Recognition, pp. 5967–5976 (2017)
3. Mirza, M., Osindero, S.: Conditional generative adversarial nets. arXiv:1411.1784 (2014)
4. Reed, S.E., Akata, Z., Yan, X., Logeswaran, L., Schiele, B., Lee, H.: Generative adversarial text to image synthesis. In: International Conference on Machine Learning, pp. 1060–1069 (2016)
5. Zhang, H., et al.: StackGAN: text to photo-realistic image synthesis with stacked generative adversarial networks. In: International Conference on Computer Vision, pp. 5908–5916 (2017)
6. Xu, T., et al.: AttnGAN: fine-grained text to image generation with attentional generative adversarial networks. In: Computer Vision and Pattern Recognition, pp. 1316–1324 (2018)
7. Zhu, M., Pan, P., Chen, W., Yang, Y.: DM-GAN: dynamic memory generative adversarial networks for text-to-image synthesis. In: Computer Vision and Pattern Recognition, pp. 5802–5810 (2019)
8. Reed, S.E., Akata, Z., Mohan, S., Tenka, S., Schiele, B., Lee, H.: Learning what and where to draw. In: Neural Information Processing Systems, vol. 29, pp. 885–895 (2016)
9. Wah, C., Branson, S., Welinder, P., Perona, P., Belongie, S.: The caltech-UCSD birds-200-2011 dataset. Technical report CNS-TR-2011-001, California Institute of Technology (2011)
10. Nilsback, M.-E., Zisserman, A.: Automated flower classification over a large number of classes. In: Indian Conference on Computer Vision, Graphics and Image Processing, pp. 722–729 (2008)
11. Zeiler, M.D., Fergus, R.: Visualizing and understanding convolutional networks. In: Fleet, D., Pajdla, T., Schiele, B., Tuytelaars, T. (eds.) ECCV 2014. LNCS, vol. 8689, pp. 818–833. Springer, Cham (2014). https://doi.org/10.1007/978-3-319-10590-1_53
12. Ioffe, S., Szegedy, C.: Batch normalization: accelerating deep network training by reducing internal covariate shift. In: International Conference on Machine Learning, pp. 448–456 (2015)

13. Reed, S.E., Akata, Z., Lee, H., Schiele, B.: Learning deep representations of fine-grained visual descriptions. In: Computer Vision and Pattern Recognition, pp. 49–58 (2016)
14. He, K., Zhang, X., Ren, S., Sun, J.: Deep residual learning for image recognition. In: Computer Vision and Pattern Recognition, pp. 770–778 (2016)
15. Xu, B., Wang, N., Chen, T., Li, M.: Empirical evaluation of rectified activations in convolutional network. arXiv:1505.00853 (2015)
16. Kingma, D.P., Ba, J.: Adam: a method for stochastic optimization. In: International Conference on Learning Representations (2015)

Declarative Residual Network for Robust Facial Expression Recognition

Ruikai Cui$^{(\boxtimes)}$, Josephine Plested, and Jiaxu Liu

Research School of Computer Science, Australian National University,
Canberra, Australia
{ruikai.cui,jo.plested,jiaxu.liu}@anu.edu.au

Abstract. Automatic facial expression recognition is of great importance for the use of human-computer interaction (HCI) in various applications. Due to the large variance in terms of head position, age range, illumination, etc, detecting and recognizing human facial expressions in realistic environments remains a challenging task. In recent years, deep neural networks have started being used in this task and demonstrated state-of-the-art performance. Here we propose a reliable framework for robust facial expression recognition. The basic architecture for our framework is ResNet-18, in combination with a declarative L_p sphere/ball projection layer. The proposed framework also contains data augmentation, voting mechanism, and a YOLO based face detection module. The performance of our proposed framework is evaluated on a semi-natural static facial expression dataset *Static Facial Expressions in the Wild* (SFEW), which contains over 800 images extracted from movies. Results show excellent performance with an averaged test accuracy of 51.89% for five runs, which indicates the considerable potential of our framework.

Keywords: Facial expression recognition · Deep declarative network · Deep learning · Data augmentation

1 Introduction

Facial expression detection and recognition, i.e. the task of automatically perceiving and recognizing human facial expressions based on vision inputs or other bio signals, is of great interest in the HCI research field. Although facial expression recognition under lab-controlled environments has been well addressed, it remains a challenging problem to recognize unconstrained expressions captured in realistic environments.

In recent years, researchers have focused more on recognize facial expressions in real-world scenarios. The *Static Facial Expressions in the Wild* (SFEW) dataset [2] was proposed, aiming to simulate the complex real-world environment. Over 800 images were extracted from 37 movies and it contains a total of 95 subjects. This real-world environment really poses a significant challenge to existing approaches. A number of methods which perform great on lad-controlled

© Springer Nature Switzerland AG 2020
H. Yang et al. (Eds.): ICONIP 2020, CCIS 1332, pp. 345–352, 2020.
https://doi.org/10.1007/978-3-030-63820-7_39

datasets like JAFFE, PIE, and MMI, yield significantly lower performance on this dataset [2].

To achieve good recognition performance, a method that robust to the influence factors is needed. Here, we introduce a novel deep learning method for facial expression recognition, the Declarative Residual Network, which is constructed based on ResNet [5], then improved by ideas distilled from deep declarative networks [4], and it demonstrates competitive performance. In addition, we describe a modelling framework consisting of a data augmentation method, voting mechanism, and a YOLO based face detection module, which behaves well when a dataset doesn't contain enough images. The performance of our framework was tested on the SFEW dataset.

This article is organized as follows. In Sect. 2, we provide details of our proposed framework. In Sect. 3, we give an experimental analysis of our framework. Section 4 presents the performance evaluation of our framework as well as comparison with methods proposed by other researchers on the SFEW dataset. Finally, we give a conclusion of our contribution.

2   Methodology

2.1   Architecture

Backbone. We use the ResNet-18 as the backbone architecture. The ResNet as well as its variations have been well examined on visual recognition tasks like the ImageNet Classification challenge. Therefore, we build our network upon ResNet-18. The structure of our network is shown in Fig. 1.

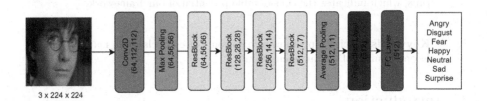

Fig. 1. Structure of bidirectional residual declarative network

For image input, it would first be downsampled by first a convolution layer and then a max-pooling layer. The output of the pooling layer would then be sent into the ResBlocks. The dimension of the last ResBlock's output is $(512, 7, 7)$. So, we first adopt average pooling and then flatten the output to change it into a vector of length 512. Different from conventional ResNet-18, we add a L_p sphere/ball projection layer to improve its robustness and generalization ability. The output of this layer would be sent to the fully connected (FC) layer and it would yield the prediction.

After each convolution and before activation, we adopt batch normalization (BN). Besides, BN would also be used before the projection layer. Since it doesn't contain learnable parameters, BN is not illustrated in the figures. We use ReLU for activation and Cross-Entropy for loss function. Stochastic Gradient Descent (SGD) with a mini-batch size of 256 is our choice for optimization. The learning rate starts from 0.1 and would be adjusted by dividing it by 10 every 30 epochs. We also apply a 0.0001 weight decay rate and 0.9 momentum rate.

Projection Layer. Proper normalization is critical for speeding up training and improving generalization performance. Rather than use some conventional normalization methods, we take advantage of a novel advance in the deep learning field, namely Deep Declarative Networks (DDN). The concept of DDN is proposed by Gould et al. [4], aiming to provide a general coherent framework for describing deep learning models that involve implicitly defined components.

Conventional approaches toward normalization would do the operation that for $x \in \mathbb{R}^n \mapsto y \in \mathbb{R}^n$, we have

$$y = \frac{1}{\|x\|_p} x \tag{1}$$

where $\|\cdot\|_p$ denotes the L_p-norm.

Instead of doing normalization in this way, we apply the declarative approach, which can be generalized as

$$y_p \in \underset{u \in \mathbb{R}^n}{\arg\min} \frac{1}{2}\|u - x\|_2^2, \text{ subject to } \|u\|_p = r \tag{2}$$

$$y_p \in \underset{u \in \mathbb{R}^n}{\arg\min} \frac{1}{2}\|u - x\|_2^2, \text{ subject to } \|u\|_p \leq r \tag{3}$$

for L_p-sphere projection and L_p-ball projection respectively. r denote the radius of the sphere or ball. We set it to 1 in our network, which could be interpreted as projection with a unit sphere or ball constrain.

2.2 Data Augmentation

Machine learning algorithms often suffer from the overfitting problem, and this is more significant when the dataset is small and the network is deep. To address this problem, we rely on data augmentation so that, in each iteration, the algorithm never sees the exact same set of images.

The face detector would crop a 256 × 256 region corresponding to the face region in a source image. We first horizontally flip it to create a mirror image and then expand these two images' width and height by 1.5 times respectively. By applying this augmentation strategy, we expand the original dataset by 6 times. This process is to mimic viewing subjects from different angles. As for training, the required input size is 224 × 224. We would randomly crop such a region from the preprocessed images with the per-channel mean [0.485, 0.456, 0.406] subtracted and divided by standard deviation [0.229, 0.224, 0.225]. This allows our model to learn from not only the whole face but also a partial region.

2.3 Face Detection

To learning meaningful representations of facial expressions, locating faces is the first step. We use the library *faced* [6] as our face detection module.

The *faced* library would do face detection in two stages. At stage one, a custom fully convolutional neural network (FCNN) implemented basing on YOLO would take a 288 × 288 RGB image and outputs a 9 × 9 grid where each cell can predict bounding boxes and the probability of one face. At stage two, a convolutional neural network (CNN) would be used to take the face-containing rectangle and predict the face bounding box. This module is trained on the WIDER FACE dataset [8]. In the end, we can get bounding boxes of a face and the probability of how likely it is really a face.

When setting the recognition threshold (probability) to 0.6, it yields 66 images that do not contain faces, which is 7.56% of the whole cropped images. Therefore, we can rely on these detected faces to train our network. We can observe a significant improvement as the network trained by cropped faces is over 45% in terms of recognition accuracy while the same network but trained with raw images only has an accuracy of around 20%.

2.4 Voting Mechanism

There are many scenarios for the output of the face detect module, i.e. faces detected, partial face detected, non-face detected, and their combinations. Figure 2 illustrates the situations where multiple possible faces are detected. Although they are different images, each pair is cropped from the same image. This is due to the complexity of the real-world environment and the limitation of our face detection module. To address this issue and take advantage of face probability, we introduce the voting mechanism to our framework.

Fig. 2. Scenarios of detection output. (a) partial face (left) (b) non face (middle) (c) desired face (right)

When detecting faces, the detection module would also give the probability of one face while our network would yield a 7-D vector as the probability of each expression. When we have more than one detected faces in the same image, instead of taking the image with the highest probability as the expression prediction evidence, we would average the 7-D vectors ($Pred \in \mathbb{R}^7$) for the same source image weighted by their face probability ($P \in \mathbb{R}^+$). More specifically, we apply the equation

$$Result = \sum_i P_i \cdot Pred_i \tag{4}$$

as voting, where the subscript i indicates the i-th images cropped from the same source.

3 Experimental Analysis

In this section, we provide experimental analysis of the Declarative Residual Network as well as the voting mechanism.

3.1 Evaluation Method

To evaluate the proposed architecture, we constructed the confusion matrix for prediction results and apply several evaluation metrics including accuracy, precision, recall, and F1-score. We would also consider the top 3 classification accuracy since some expressions are similar and even hard for humans to correctly identify. The mean average precision (mAP) is also a metric that we applied for evaluation.

We split the dataset into train, test, and validation sets. The performance results in Sect. 3.2 are evaluated on the validation set, and we would use the test set as the final evaluation of our model's performance.

3.2 Ablation Study on Projection Layer

In this section, we design an experiment to exam the performance improvement that the projection layer gives us as well as the effect of different projection types. We didn't apply voting in this experiment. Therefore, we manually deleted these non-face images in our test set.

As discussed in Sect. 2.1, we adopted six different projections, which are L_1-sphere(L1S), L_1-ball(L1B), L_2-sphere(L2S), L_2-ball(L2B), L_∞-sphere(LInfS), L_∞-ball(LInfB), respectively, combined with a network without projection. We trained 7 networks in total for 5 times each and average the results. The result is shown in Fig. 3.

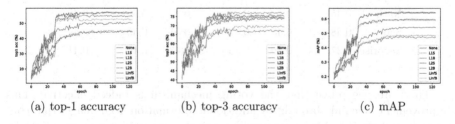

(a) top-1 accuracy   (b) top-3 accuracy   (c) mAP

Fig. 3. Model performance by epoch

From Fig. 3, we can observe that the network with L2S projection yields the best performance in terms of top-1 accuracy, and L2B projection is the best choice if we regard the top-3 accuracy as the most important metric. As for mean

Average Precision, the performance for the same norm (L_p) is similar, regardless of constrained by a sphere or ball.

The difference between networks with the projection layer and without the projection layer is significant. We can observe a nearly 10% top-1 accuracy improvement after adding the L2S projection. However, some projection types, such as L1S and L1B, would give a much worse performance with plain ResNet-18 in all aspects. For other projection types, they have a close performance on top-3 accuracy.

3.3 Voting Mechanism

We present the experiment result of the Voting Mechanism performance in this section. The experiment is conducted by training 5 different models using the training set and test them on the test set. The result below is an average of these 5 models. In order to achieve a fair comparison, we manually selected the correct face crop for models without voting if multiple faces are detected from the same image source. The model we trained here is a ResNet with L_2-sphere projection layer since we have proved that it has the best performance in terms of top-1 accuracy.

The detailed result is shown in Table 1. We can observe slight improvement for the voting model in almost every aspects. As for the averaged accuracy, it is 50.59% with the standard deviation equals 0.720 for models without voting and 51.89% with standard deviation equals 0.724 for models with voting.

Table 1. Performance comparison of declarative ResNet with and without voting

	Precision		Recall		F1-score	
	No voting	Voting	No voting	Voting	No voting	Voting
Angry	0.56	0.58	0.61	0.61	0.58	0.60
Disgust	0.48	0.51	0.51	0.51	0.49	0.51
Fear	0.62	0.60	0.65	0.68	0.63	0.64
Happy	0.57	0.59	0.51	0.55	0.54	0.57
Natural	0.45	0.49	0.30	0.32	0.36	0.38
Sad	0.48	0.48	0.51	0.51	0.49	0.49
Surprise	0.37	0.39	0.43	0.43	0.40	0.41

Therefore, we prove that the voting mechanism is indeed effective. This improvement is mainly brought by additional information from images that contains partial faces and even environments since some output neurons might be strongly activated by additional info and yield high confidence on some emotions, which may contribute to facial expression recognition. However, the improvement is not significant. The reason is that voting would only happen when there are multiple faces for a source image but we only have a small proportion of images that yield multiple cropped images.

4   Result and Discussion

We present and discuss our model's performance on the SFEW dataset. We would also compare it with approaches proposed in related work to determine whether it is a competitive framework for the robust facial expression recognition task.

4.1   Performance

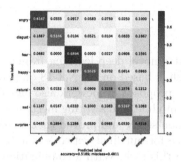

Fig. 4. Confusion matrix of recognition result

We present the confusion matrix in Fig. 4. The final accuracy for our model is 51.89%. According to this figure, the accuracy of Fear facial expression is the highest. The model misunderstands a number of natural and sad expression. However, for some images of these two classes, it is even hard for humans to identify the correct emotion.

4.2   Comparison

We compare our proposed framework with other approaches. The performance of the first approach is the SFEW baseline provided at [3]. They detect faces using Mixture of Pictorial Structures and then compute the Pyramid of Histogram of Gradients and Local Phase Quantisation features for the aligned faces. A support vector machine (SVM) was trained on the vector computed from feature fusion. The second approach is proposed in [1]. They proposed a new feature descriptor, namely Histogram of Oriented Gradients from Three Orthogonal Planes (HOG_TOP) and adopt Multiple Kernel Learning (MKL) to find an optimal feature fusion. The classifier for their approach is also a SVM but with multiple kernels. The third approach is Region Attention Networks (RAN) [7], which is the current state-of-the-art.

   The results of all the approaches are shown in Table 2. We can observe that our approach has a significantly better performance compared with the SFEW baseline, and surpass the MKL approach by 11%. Our method is still worse

Table 2. Comparison of different methods

Method	Baseline	MKL	Our method	RAN
Accuracy %	36.08%	40.21%	51.89%	56.40%

than the RAN approach. However, we only did little hyperparameter tuning and few additional techniques, such as face align and pre-training, are introduced. This indicates that our framework has a great potential on the real-world facial expression recognition task.

5 Conclusion

In this paper, we present a novel deep learning framework for facial expression recognition in wild, which is based on ResNet-18 and combined with a declarative projection layer. The proposed framework also includes a data augmentation method, a face detection module, and a voting mechanism. We examined the projection layer by an ablation study and proved that it indeed improves the backbone network. The choice for our final network is a L_2-sphere projection layer since it is most suited to this task. With a combination of these techniques, we achieved a competitive performance with 51.89% accuracy, which demonstrates the proposed framework is reliable and robust for facial expression recognition in a real-world environment.

References

1. Chen, J., Chen, Z., Chi, Z., Fu, H.: Emotion recognition in the wild with feature fusion and multiple kernel learning. In: Proceedings of the 16th International Conference on Multimodal Interaction, ICMI 2014, pp. 508–513. Association for Computing Machinery, New York (2014)
2. Dhall, A., Goecke, R., Lucey, S., Gedeon, T.: Static facial expression analysis in tough conditions: data, evaluation protocol and benchmark. In: 2011 IEEE International Conference on Computer Vision Workshops (ICCV Workshops), pp. 2106–2112. IEEE (2011)
3. Dhall, A., Goecke, R., Lucey, S., Gedeon, T.: The third emotion recognition in the wild challenge (emotiw 2015). https://cs.anu.edu.au/few/ChallengeDetails2015.html. Accessed 1 June 2020
4. Gould, S., Hartley, R., Campbell, D.: Deep declarative networks: a new hope. arXiv preprint arXiv:1909.04866 (2019)
5. He, K., Zhang, X., Ren, S., Sun, J.: Deep residual learning for image recognition. In: Proceedings of the IEEE Conference on Computer Vision and Pattern Recognition, pp. 770–778 (2016)
6. Itzcovich, I.: faced (2018). https://github.com/iitzco/faced
7. Wang, K., Peng, X., Yang, J., Meng, D., Qiao, Y.: Region attention networks for pose and occlusion robust facial expression recognition (2019)
8. Yang, S., Luo, P., Loy, C.C., Tang, X.: Wider face: a face detection benchmark. In: IEEE Conference on Computer Vision and Pattern Recognition (CVPR) (2016)

Deep Feature Compatibility
for Generated Images Quality Assessment

Xuewen Zhang[1], Yunye Zhang[1,2], Zhiqiang Zhang[1], Wenxin Yu[1(✉)],
Ning Jiang[1], and Gang He[1]

[1] Southwest University of Science and Technology,
Mianyang, Sichuan, China
yuwenxin@swust.edu.cn
[2] University of Electronic Science and Technology of China,
Chengdu, Sichuan, China

Abstract. The image quality assessment (IQA) for generated images main focuses on the quality of perceptual aspects. Existing methods for evaluating generated images consider the overall image distribution characteristics. At present, there is no practical method for a single generated image. To address this issue, this paper proposes a solution base on the deep feature compatibility (DFC), which first collects suitable comparison images by a collection model. Then it provides an individual score by computing the compatibility of target and pictures with good perceptual quality. This method makes up for the deficiency of Inception Score (IS) in a small number of results or/and a single image. The experiment on Caltech UCSD birds 200 (CUB) shows that our method performs well on the assessment mission for generated images. Finally, we analyze the various problems of the representative IQA methods in evaluating.

Keywords: Generated image · Image quality assessment · Single image

1 Introduction

The images generation via generative adversarial networks (GAN) [1] have shown unprecedented flexibility. The distortion of these sorts of pictures generally concerns with perception aspects rather than pure noise or blur. (eg. a poor generated image of a bird may not contain the head or wings) These kinds of distortions might be more obvious in some generation tasks beyond the form of image-to-image. For instance, pictures generated by natural language description [2] will fall into this problem due to the conversion process from less information (text description) to more information (images).

Finding an efficient quality assessment method for these kinds of images is significant and challenging. In recent literature, Inception Score (IS) [3] is used wildly as the indicator of the generation quality. Nevertheless, this method only measures the overall recognizability and diversity, which never focuses on

H. Yang et al. (Eds.): ICONIP 2020, CCIS 1332, pp. 353–360, 2020.
https://doi.org/10.1007/978-3-030-63820-7_40

a single image. Generally, IQA solutions are categorized into full-reference (FR) and no-reference (NR). FR-IQA methods are useless to the generated images because no pixel-level-based original image could be found. Consider the only feasible NR methods. They aren't very suitable for generated images either. Most NR methods concern the degradation distortion (e.g., blur or pure noise), which not fit the characteristics of the generated image. Inorder to ease this problem, this paper proposes a multi-stage evaluation solution based on the deep feature compatibility (DFC). DFC-IQA tries to find the target (single generated image) from a mixed-pictures set that contains itself and the images from the original pictures set. The image will be considered as splendid one if the process is laborious because that indicates the target image is close enough to real/good images. The main contribution of our work is shown as follows.

1. In the lack of an image quality assessment method suitable for a single generated image, we propose a new method DFC-IQA to obtain an individual score for the generated images' evaluation.
2. We offer a quantitative comparison method by introducing three quality-level images set, which suitable for discussing the efficiency of the generated images assessment.
3. We verify the effectiveness of our method by experimenting at Caltech-UCSD Birds 200 (CUB). Then the comparison with some available no-reference IQA methods shows that our proposal achieves the best result in evaluating the single generated images.

2   Related Work

For the evaluation task of image generation, Salimans et al. [3] introduce a method called Inception Score (IS). IS provides the score from two aspects: whether the whole feature distributions are distinct and diverse. Dowson et al. [4] propose a Fréchet distance between two multivariate normal distributions, which be used as Fréchet Inception Distance score (FID). The target of this method is the whole distribution, too. In other words, they are helpless to a single picture evaluation.

Full-reference IQA is limited due to the absence of the available full-reference image. Alternatively, no-reference ways generally try to get the representation of the target. Then it could predict the score after the regression training base on previous representation. There are many ways to get the features of an image, which main follows natural scene statistic (NSS) or convolution neural network (CNN). Mittal et al. [5] use the hand-crafted feature from an especially Gaussian distribution and the Support Vector Regression (SVR) to get the scores. Liu et al. [6] put the ranked image-pair into the neural network to learn the rank relationship between the high-quality image and the low one, then the score is obtained with fine-tunes at a human score set. The convolution neural networks (CNNs) achieves deep feature extraction. Bosse et al. [7] increase the depth of the network to extract the features to improve the performance of the assessment result further. These methods trend to concern pixel-level distortion like blur

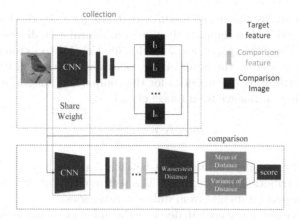

Fig. 1. The structure of the DFC-IQA method. The whole structure contains two essential components. One is a collection model that tells comparison components in which images to compare. Another is comparison components that could get the scoring base on the compatibility.

and noise, which may be challenging to detect the perception-level distortion of the generated image. However, Lu et al. [8] show the usage of CNNs in the aesthetic assessment task. The supplement of the human score images-set makes the parameter updating process dependent less on pre-training models. Talebi et al. [9] discuss the differences of three human-score datasets and employ CNNs to get the mapping relationship from the single input image to a score distribution. This method concern more with human subjective perception, which may better meet the evaluation requirements of generated images.

3   Deep Feature Compatibility for IQA

3.1   Preliminaries

Considering the high-flexibility and stochasticity of the generated image, we make a metaphor that it's a painting by small kids (computer). How do people score a painting by kids? We may firstly judge what kind of paintings are (a bird or a tree, et), then we recall the related object we have seen (that's what our collection model does) to give a score by comparing. But this comparative process might be very complicated. Thus, this paper introduces the concept of compatibility to simulate that. It can be described as if it is difficult for a computer to find the target picture after we put it into the images set with high quality. It's a high-quality image too.

The collection model aims to tell the comparison component which images to compare. These kinds of images with high quality in the perception aspect ought to have similar characteristics to the target. It can be noted that convolution neural network (CNN) perform well in the classify than traditional methods. Meanwhile, the image features that are got from the hidden layer of CNN could be utilized to compute the potential information diversity among the pictures [10]. Thus, this paper employs ResNet-152 [11] to extract the images' feature, which is used as the input of our collection model. And the output is a probability distribution of categories for the comparison images' selection. This component select n_i images from image class i.

$$n_i = N \times \frac{c_i}{\sum_{j=0}^{n_c} c_j} \tag{1}$$

Where N is the number of images to be compared with. c is the prediction probability distribution of categories. The softmax output determines how to collect the comparison images from different categories.

The distance of the feature can describe the differences among images. Therefore, the compatibility could be expressed by the distance's similarity degree between the features. The detail of how to compute the compatibility is shown in Sect. 3.2. In this paper, Wasserstein Distance [12] is employed to calculate two distribution of features.

$$W(P_1, P_2) = inf_{\gamma \sim \prod(P_1, P_2)} \mathbb{E}_{(x,y) \sim y}[||x - y||] \tag{2}$$

where P_1 and P_2 indicate two different distributions. And $\prod(P_1, P_2)$ indicates the whole joint distributions $\gamma(x, y)$ whose marginal are respectively Pr and Pg. And $\gamma(x, y)$ indicates the "mass cost" from x to y for the transformation from the distribution P_r to P_g.

3.2   Score Algorithm

The whole structure is shown (see Fig. 1). A single generated image as input of the network for getting the categories distribution to select comparison images. Then these images and the target image are together as the input of the features extraction net, which shares the weight with the previous one. Then these features are input into a Wasserstein Distance calculator. And the output which contains two distribution is utilized to compute the score.

This paper employs Wasserstein Distance (WD) of features to measure the differences among the pictures. We use the concept of compatibility to evaluate the image. The compatibility indicates the coordination of mixed image-set, which includes target image and images with high-score in perceptual aspect. In other words, a picture is going to get a high score if it's hard to find the target when it mixes with a good images-set. The following will describe how to represent compatibility from two aspects. And the final score could be provided by the value of compatibility.

A similarity between the target and the comparisons images directly determines whether we can quickly notice the odd one from plenty of good images. Thus, the point is how to represent the similarity. Even the real pictures (like photos) are sure to different from each other, so it seems not persuasive to only use features' distance to describe the compatibility. Instead, we represent the

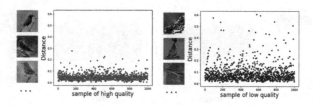

Fig. 2. Diversity distribution of high-quality images (left) and low-quality image (right). It could be noted that the diversity distance of the high-quality image is smaller and steady. This property contributes to the quality score.

similarity by the distance among each distance distribution within the mixed image-set which contain good pictures and target. We define it as diversity distribution(DD). Each image has a DD against other images in that set. In theory, this distance of DD could better measure whether a picture is strange than a simple feature distance. For the target, its compatibility (CP) is defined as the average distance of distance distributions against the comparison images.

$$CP = \frac{1}{n} \sum_{i=0}^{n} W(T, C_i) \tag{3}$$

$$T = (W(\hat{f}, f_1), W(\hat{f}, f_2), ..., W(\hat{f}, f_n)) \tag{4}$$

$$C_i = (W(f_i, f_1), W(f_i, f_2), ..., W(f_i, f_n) \tag{5}$$

Where W denotes the Wasserstein Distance between the two distribution. T and C_i are the diversity distribution concern about target-comparison and comparison-comparison, respectively. The length of features container of comparison images that include $f_1, f_2, ..., f_n$ is n. And $\hat{f}$ denotes the feature of the image which needs to be evaluated.

To describe the quality of the generated image more precisely, this paper introduces the stability of CP as a supplement for score computation. We observe that the DD of the grotesque images trend to unstable (see Fig. 2, we selected 1,000 high-quality and 1,000 low-quality pictures and computers for their DD distribution). Thus, the stability of DD could contribute the score processing. We use the variance of it to define stability.

$$Stb = varance(T) \tag{6}$$

$$score = f(CP, Stb) \tag{7}$$

Where f denotes a normalization function to compute the score. CP and Stb determine the compatibility of the target image. The less these two value, the higher score the image is going to get.

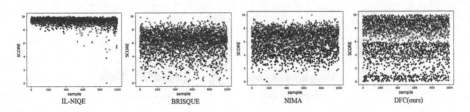

Fig. 3. The score scatter-plot of the testing images. These images from three different quality images set. Circle, cross, and triangle represent images from low, medium, and high-quality sets, respectively.

4 Experiments

4.1 Implementation

The testing images are selected from the results of Mirror-GANs [13] and DM-GANs [14] which realizes the image generation from the text description. The original training data set is Caltech UCSD birds 200 (CUB) which contains 11, 788 bird pictures, including 200 different classes. In order to quantify the comparison, we selected 3000 generated images with high, medium, and low subjective quality from the results and evaluate the effectiveness of the methods by verifying whether the score matches the quality level.

The score is provided by the two-component process. One of which is a collection model that consists of a convolutional neural network. ResNet 152 [11] is employed to extract the features, and we reset the parameter of the full connected layers. The softmax output is a category distribution, which could be utilized for the selection of comparison images. And Sinkhorn iterator is used to compute the Wasserstein Distance for the calculation of CP and Std. The final output distance indicates the compatibility, which endows a high score to the target image if the value close to 0. f is defined as $f(CP, Stb) = max\_score * 0.5 * ((1 - 10 * CP) + (1 - 100 * Std))$. We set all the values that smaller than 0 to 0.

4.2 Comparison

For the generated images, the main distortion is the unreasonable composition. Thus, the criterion for the assessment of generated images tends more to the perceptual aspects. To measure the effectiveness of the methods, this paper employ 2-class accuracy. Generally, comparing the score result with manual annotation can verify the effectiveness of the method. However, a fixed criterion for score (eg. Mean Opinion Score (MOS)) may not suitable for every evaluation requirement. And it's so time cost for people to give a certain score for every image assessment tasks. Thus, we use three quality levels to describe the score: high, medium, and low. For every sample, we annotate a quality-level.

Inception Score (IS) that be used wildly for generated images needs plenty of image results. It's not working for a single target. Therefore, we chose the no-reference IQA methods as the baseline. We select some representative NSS-based no-reference methods and aesthetics aspect methods with CNN, respectively. Our test-set compose with 3000 generated images of three quality levels to compare the effects of those different methods—the principle of selecting images of varying quality levels based on MOS. All the results are put together to show the sensitivity of different methods to different quality pictures (see Fig. 3).

Table 1. Two-class Accuracy (%), PLCC, and SROCC index on three different quality testing-set.

Method	acc (2Class)↑	PLCC↑	SROCC↑
IL-NIQE	0.5015	0.1130	0.1441
BRISQUE	0.6505	0.4284	0.4463
NIMA	0.8240	0.7076	0.7073
DFC (Ours)	**0.8654**	**0.7578**	**0.7567**

To further quantify the comparisons of the above results. Pearson linear correlation coefficient (PLCC) and Spearman rank-order correlation coefficient (SROCC) are adopted. Besides, we chose two classification accuracy [9] as a supplement. (see Table 1). We scored the images in high-quality and low-quality with sorts of methods. And the accuracy is provided according to the dividing line 5 (out of 10 points). It can be seen that our method achieves the best result in all indicators. The aesthetic-based method NIMA seems to be more suitable for generating image quality evaluation than the NSS methods (BRISQUE, IL-NIQE).

4.3   Discuss of Results

In general, the proposal of IQA is to detect the extent of distortion. And the distortion can be divided into many categories. For instance, a compression operation may hurt the pixel-level information of pictures. That's the evaluation requirement of one series of traditional IQA. Nevertheless, the distortion of generated images concerns more to human perception. A clean and no-noise generated picture of a bird that has no wings, eyes, beak may get a high score at pixel-level, though it's not good at all in human subjective cognition. NIMA considers the aesthetics within images, which closer to perceptual. And our method utilized the deep features compatibility to indicate whether the target will look strange in pictures set with good perceptual quality. It catches more information than only pixel-level distortion.

5   Conclusion

In the absence of a reasonable evaluation method for the singe generated images, we put forward DFC-IQA to evaluate it. Our approach contains two essential components. One is a collection model that tells comparison components in which images to compare. Another is comparison components that could get the scoring base on the compatibility between the target image and the images set with good quality to perceptual aspects. Experiments show that the DFC-IQA is more sensitive to different quality images, and our approach gets the best performance at two-class accuracy, PLCC, and SROCC.

Acknowledgement. This research is supported by Sichuan Provincial Science and Technology Program (No. 2020YFS0307).

References

1. Goodfellow, I.J., Pouget-Abadie, J., Mirza, M., Bing, X., Bengio, Y.: Generative adversarial nets (2014)
2. Reed, S.E., Akata, Z., Yan, X., Logeswaran, L., Schiele, B., Lee, H.: Generative adversarial text to image synthesis. CoRR abs/1605.05396 (2016). http://arxiv.org/abs/1605.05396
3. Salimans, T., Goodfellow, I.J., Zaremba, W., Cheung, V., Radford, A., Chen, X.: Improved techniques for training gans. In: Advances in Neural Information Processing Systems 29: Annual Conference on Neural Information Processing Systems 2016, Barcelona, Spain, 5–10 December 2016, pp. 2226–2234 (2016)
4. Dowson, D.C., Landau, B.V.: The fréchet distance between multivariate normal distributions. J. Multivar. Anal. **12**(3), 450–455 (1982)
5. Mittal, A., Moorthy, A.K., Bovik, A.C.: No-reference image quality assessment in the spatial domain. IEEE Trans. Image Process. Publ. IEEE Signal Process. Soc. **21**(12), 4695 (2012)
6. Liu, X., Weijer, J.V.D., Bagdanov, A.D.: Rankiqa: learning from rankings for no-reference image quality assessment. In: 2017 IEEE International Conference on Computer Vision (ICCV) (2017)
7. Bosse, S., Maniry, D., Muller, K.R., Wiegand, T., Samek, W.: Deep neural networks for no-reference and full-reference image quality assessment. IEEE Trans. Image Process. **27**(1), 206–219 (2017)
8. Xin, L., Zhe, L., Shen, X., Mech, R., Wang, J.Z.: Deep multi-patch aggregation network for image style, aesthetics, and quality estimation. In: IEEE International Conference on Computer Vision (2015)
9. Talebi, H., Milanfar, P.: Nima: neural image assessment. IEEE Trans. Image Process. **27**(8), 3998–4011 (2018)
10. Meena, Y., Monika, Kumar, P., Sharma, A.: Product recommendation system using distance measure of product image features (2018)
11. He, K., Zhang, X., Ren, S., Sun, J.: Deep residual learning for image recognition. In: 2016 IEEE Conference on Computer Vision and Pattern Recognition, CVPR 2016, Las Vegas, NV, USA, 27–30 June 2016, pp. 770–778. IEEE Computer Society (2016). https://doi.org/10.1109/CVPR.2016.90
12. Arjovsky, M., Chintala, S., Bottou, L.: Wasserstein gan (2017)
13. Qiao, T., Zhang, J., Xu, D., Tao, D.: Mirrorgan: learning text-to-image generation by redescription. In: IEEE Conference on Computer Vision and Pattern Recognition, CVPR 2019, Long Beach, CA, USA, 16–20 June 2019, pp. 1505–1514. Computer Vision Foundation/IEEE (2019). https://doi.org/10.1109/CVPR.2019.00160
14. Zhu, M., Pan, P., Chen, W., Yang, Y.: Dm-gan: dynamic memory generative adversarial networks for text-to-image synthesis (2019)

DRGCN: Deep Relation GCN for Group Activity Recognition

Yiqiang Feng, Shimin Shan, Yu Liu$^{(\boxtimes)}$, Zhehuan Zhao, and Kaiping Xu

School of Software, Dalian University of Technology, Dalian 116620, China
icicle4@mail.dlut.edu.cn, {ssm,yuliu,z.zhao}@dlut.edu.cn,
xkp13@tsinghua.org.cn

Abstract. Person to person relation is an essential clue for group activity recognition (GAR). And the relation graph and the graph convolution neural network (GCN) have become powerful presentation and processing tools of relationship. The previous methods are difficult to capture the complex relationship between people. We propose an end-to-end framework called Deep Relation GCN (DRGCN) for recognizing group activities by exploring the high-level relations between individuals. In DRGCN, we use a horizontal slicing strategy to layer each individual into smaller individual parts, then apply a deep GCN to learn the relation graph of these individual parts. We perform experiments on two widely used datasets and obtain competitive results that demonstrated the effectiveness of our method.

Keywords: Human activity recognition · Relation graph · DeepGCN

1 Introduction

Group activity recognition has gained much attention in recent years due to its essential role in the fields of video understanding and sports event analysis. Usually, we define group activity recognition as detecting activity in a scene that involves N individuals. When $N > 1$, it not only needs to focus on the appearance information of individuals but also relations between individuals.

The early study of group activity recognition mostly used probability graphical models with manually defined features, such as STL [1,4]. Ibrahim et al. RNN is also used to capture temporal dynamics [3,11,12]. CRM [2] learns to produce an intermediate spatial representation (activity map) based on individual and group activities. Many papers [7] use the structured model which integrates a variety of levels of detail. Hu et al. [6] propose a novel method based on deep reinforcement learning to refine the low-level features and high-level relations. Wu et al. [13] learn the Actor Relation Graph (ARG) to perform relational reasoning on graphs.

The essential features of the above methods are at the individual level. Although group activity is the product of individual interactions in the scene, the impact of group activity discrimination is a specific part of the human body. In

© Springer Nature Switzerland AG 2020
H. Yang et al. (Eds.): ICONIP 2020, CCIS 1332, pp. 361–368, 2020.
https://doi.org/10.1007/978-3-030-63820-7_41

addition, the blocked person may be confused with other people's parts. There-fore, we propose a slicing strategy to handle the features of each part more flexi-bly while reducing the interference caused by occlusion. Besides, we introduce a much deeper GCN with the layering strategy and learn more complex relation-ship between parts at a far distance. No prior knowledge is used to define the relation graph, which makes our model have fewer hyper-parameters and better generalization.

The main contributions of this article are:

1. DRGCN is proposed to focus on the relation between parts, not just individ-uals.
2. A much deeper GCN is introduced in the base of slicing strategy.
3. Our DRGCN achieves comparable results to the state-of-art models on the Volleyball and Collective datasets.

1.1 Overview

We use the pipeline shown in Fig. 1 for group activity recognition. The overall process has three stages: 1. Extract individual features by backbone and perform horizontal slicing. 2. Use DRGCN to learn the relation graph of individual parts. 3. Reconstruct and fuse features for group activity recognition. The above three stages will be described in the following subsections.

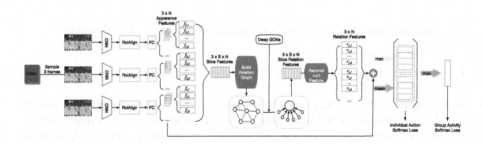

Fig. 1. An overview of our DRGCN method.

2   Our Method

2.1 Backbone

First, three frames was uniformly sampled from T consecutive frames. We employ the same feature extraction strategy as in ARG [13]. On the multi-scale feature map, we utilize RoIAlign (Region of Interest Align) with the bounding box of each individual to extract appearance features. Consider the proportion of human, the output size of RoIAlign is set to [8, 4]. After passing RoIAlign's output features through an fc (fully connected) layer, we obtain the individual's appearance feature $f_i \in \mathbb{R}^{1024}$, where i is the index of individuals in sampled frames. F_i is divided into S parts on average, and each component corresponds to a horizontal slice.

2.2 DeepGCN

The part features from the backbone will compose a relation graph. And Deep-GCN will optimize the relation graph. The optimized features are then fused by the max-mean fusion method to obtain the features suitable for group activity recognition.

Relation Graph. The input relation graph $\mathcal{G}$ of DeepGCN is composed of Q nodes $\mathcal{V}$ contain node features and a set of edges $\mathcal{E}$ representing the relations between features, where $Q = 3 \times S \times N$. The node of node v contains the appearance feature f_i^s and the center coordinate c_i^s. We concatenate two features as the node feature, $h_{v^q} = [f_i^s, c_i^s]$, where $q \in [1, Q]$. There are no pre-defined edges in the relation graph, and DRGCN learns dynamic structures of the relation graph.

DeepGCN Structure. Figure 2 shows our DeepGCN network structure. We use similar architecture as [9] to optimize the relation graph. The DeepGCN consists of a one-layer Head Module, a D-layers Body Module, and a Fusion Block. We will describe the structure of the ResGCN here in detail next.

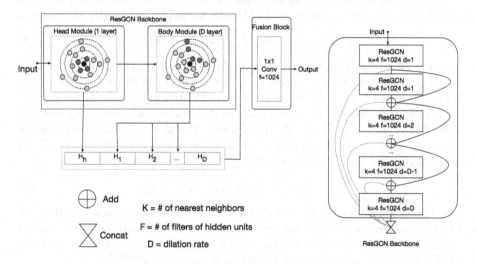

Fig. 2. DeepGCN architecture.

For the graph convolution of the l layer graph, its general formula is shown by formula 1,

$$\mathcal{G}_{l+1} = F(\mathcal{G}_l, W_l) = Update(Aggregate(\mathcal{G}_l, W_l^{agg}), W_l^{update}). \qquad (1)$$

$\mathcal{G}_l$ is the input graph of the l-th layer and $\mathcal{G}_{l+1}$ is the output graph of the l-th layer. W_l^{agg} and W_l^{update} respectively represent the parameters of aggregate and update functions. In the aggregation stage, each node updates its neighbor nodes according to the aggregation function. In the update phase, each node updates its features based on the features of itself and its neighbors.

We employ the k-NN (k-nearest neighbors) method as the aggregation function to build the neighbor set of each node. The Euclid distance in the 2D feature space is used as the distance metric and node v_l selects the k nodes which are nearest to v_l as neighbors $N(v_l)$. It can be considered that there is an edge between v_l and $u_l \in N(v_l)$.

We use max-pooling as the update function to pool the difference of features between the node and its neighbors. Our update function is represented by formula 2,

$$h_{u_l}^* = Conv_l(h_{u_l}, W_l^{update})$$
$$h_{v_l}^* = Conv_l(h_{v_l}, W_l^{update})$$
$$h_{v_{l+1}} = max(h_{u_l}^* - h_{v_l}^* | u_l \in N(v_l)), \tag{2}$$

where $h_{v_{l+1}}$ and h_{v_l} are the node features of the input graph at the $l+1$-th and l-th layer, respectively. $Conv_l(\cdot)$ is one convolution layer with one Relu layer at the l-th layer. It is worth mentioning that although the equation only updates the node features, the edges generated by the k-NN method have also changed. In this way, the relation graph has a dynamic structure in different layers.

We use the ResNet style skip-connection structure to build a deeper graph convolution network. So in the Body Module, formula 2 will update to formula 3

$$h_{v_{l+1}} = h_{v_l}^* + max(h_{u_l}^* - h_{v_l}^* | u_l \in N(v_l)). \tag{3}$$

Besides, we utilize Dilated k-NN in the Body Module, which can produce a larger field of view with more depth of the network. In the d-th layer of the Body Module, we use d as the dilation rate, Dilated k-NN returns the k nearest neighbors within the $k \times d$ neighborhood region by skipping every d neighbors. If $(u_1, u_2, ..., u_{k \times d})$ are the first sorted $k \times d$ nearest neighbors, nodes $(u_1, u_{1+d}, u_{1+2d}, ..., u_{1+(k-1)d})$ are the d-dilated neighbors of nodes. So the $N(v_l)$ of the node v in the $d - th$ layer is $N^d(v_l)$,

$$N_{(v_l)}^d = (u_1, u_{1+d}, u_{1+2d}, ..., u_{1+(k-1)d}). \tag{4}$$

Finally, we gather the node features of all nodes in the output graph of the l-th layer as the output H_l. Outputs of the Head Module and the Body Module are concatenated and sent to the fusion block. The fusion module consists of one CONV layer and outputs the slice relation feature $r_i^s \in \mathbb{R}^{1024/S}$.

2.3   Feature Reconstruction and Fusion

Features of the same individual from the same frame are concatenated as the individual relation feature $r_i = [r_i^1, r_i^2, ..., r_i^S]$. The individual appearance feature f_i and the individual relation feature r_i are element-wise added to get the fusion feature fu_i, $fu_i = f_i + r_i$. The time-significant feature f_{max} and the time-average feature f_{mean} is got by applying max-pooling and mean-pooling along the time dimension in the fusion feature fu, respectively. F_{max} is more sensitive, while f_{mean} has comprehensive information. The advantages of the two methods are combined by concatenating two features, the max-mean feature $M = [f_{max}, f_{mean}]$.

Finally, we apply the max-pooling along the individual dimension to get the group activity feature f_g. f_g and M_i are used respectively by two classifiers for group activity prediction and individual action prediction.

The loss functions are defined in formula 5,

$$\mathcal{L} = \mathcal{L}(y^G, \hat{y}^G) + w_A \sum_{1}^{N} \mathcal{L}(y_n^A, \hat{y}_n^A), \tag{5}$$

where $\mathcal{L}$ is the cross-entropy loss and y^G and y_n^I denote the ground-truth labels of group activity and individual action, $\hat{y}^G$ and $\hat{y}_n^I$ are the predictions to group activity and individual action, w_A is hyper-parameter to control the weight of group activity classification loss and individual action classification losses.

3   Experiments

3.1   Datasets

There are 4830 clips of 55 videos about volleyball matches in the Volleyball dataset [1]. Each clip is annotated with 8 group activity categories, and only its middle frame is annotated with 9 individual action labels. Following [8], we use 10 frames to train and test our model, which corresponds to 5 frames before the annotated frame and 4 frames after. To get the ground truth bounding boxes of unannotated frames, we use the tracklet data provided by [3]. We apply the metrics of the group activity accuracy and the single action accuracy to evaluate the performance following.

The collective dataset [4] contains 2481 activity clips of 44 videos. Unlike the volleyball dataset, the number of people participating in group activities is not fixed, and it considers the most frequent individual action label as the group activity label. We report the group activity accuracy to evaluate the performance.

3.2   Implementation Details

Our feature extraction backbones include the Inception-v3 network and the VGG19 network. Our model is trained in two stages: 1. The ImageNet pre-trained model is fine-tuned on a single frame without using the relation graph. 2. We fix the weights of backbone and further train the network with DeepGCN based on three frames.

We adopt stochastic gradient descent with ADAM to learn the network parameters with fixed hyper-parameters to $\beta_1 = 0.9$, $\beta_2 = 0.999$, $\epsilon = 10^{-8}$. For the Volleyball dataset, we train the network in 150 epochs using a mini-batch size of 1 and a learning rate ranging from $2e - 3$ to $1e - 5$. For the Collective Activity dataset, we use a mini-batch size of 4 with a learning rate ranging from $3e - 3$ to $1e - 3$ and train the network in 100 epochs. The individual action loss weight $w_A = 1$ is used.

3.3 Ablation Studies

In this subsection, ablation studies are performed on the Volleyball dataset and group activity accuracy is used as the evaluation metric to figure out the contribution of the proposed model components.

The first experiment is to study the impact of slicing strategy. Based on three frames, we use the model without DeepGCN as the baseline. We add a shallow GCN (4 layers) on the baseline and set the number of slice layers to 1, 2, 4, 8, respectively. The result is shown in Fig. 3a and the slicing strategy surpasses the non-layered strategy. It proves the effectiveness of the slicing strategy. When the layer number is 4, the accuracy yield the highest recognition accuracy of 91.02%. It is worth noting that when the number of layers is 8, its accuracy is even lower than the baseline results. It is because too much slicing makes the single part too small, and thus does not have valid features. In the following experiment, we fix the number of layers to 4.

We further compare the effect of different depths of GCNs on the model. Because the BodyModule part of GCN needs to do dilated-aggregate according to its depth, the depth of GCN is limited by the number of nodes in the graph, and the maximum depth is 36. We can observe in Fig. 3b that with the depth increases, models get better recognition accuracy. It proves the effectiveness of a deeper GCN.

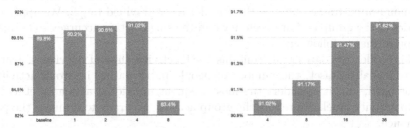

(a) Exploration of different number of slic- (b) Exploration of different number of GCN
ing parts number.   depth.

Fig. 3. Exploration of contribution of different components.

3.4 Comparison with Other Methods

In Table 1a, we show the results of our model using different backbones in the Volleyball Dataset. Our method outperforms recent methods using hierarchical

Table 1. Comparison of state of the art.

Method	Group Activity	Ind actions
StagNet [11]	89.3%	–
HRN [7]	89.5%	–
PRL [6]	91.4%	–
CRM-rgb [2]	92.07%	–
SSU [3]	90.6%	81.8%
ARG(Inc-v3) [13]	91.9%	83.1%
ARG(VGG19) [13]	**92.6%**	82.6%
DRGCN(Inc-v3)	91.6%	**83.3%**
DRGCN(VGG19)	92.2%	**83.1%**

(a) Comparison of SOTA on the Volleyball dataset.

Method	Accuracy
StagNet [11]	87.9%
SIM [5]	81.2%
SBGAR [10]	86.1%
CRM [2]	85.8%
ARG(vgg16) [13]	**90.1%**
DRGCN(vgg16)	89.6%

(b) Comparison of SOTA on the Collective dataset.

relational networks [7] or semantic RNN [11]. PRL [6] learns to progressively refine the low-level features and high-level relations of group activities based on deep reinforcement learning and CRM [2] learns to produce an intermediate spatial representation (activity map) based on individual and group activities. For a fair comparison, we only report the accuracy of CRM with only RGB. ARG [13] learns Actor Relation Graph (ARG) to perform relational reasoning on multi shallow graphs for group activity recognition. Our method outperforms PRL [6] and CRM [2]. Besides, our method achieves close accuracy to [13] in group activity accuracy and exceeds [13] in individual action recognition. Compared with the [13], our method applies the slicing strategy to enhance the most salient part features of individuals and suppresses the features of occlusions., thereby obtaining higher single action recognition accuracy.

In the Collective dataset experiment, we apply a set of depth GCNs with different parameters to process scenes with different numbers of individuals. The depth of the network is kept at 12, and as the number of people in the scene increases, we increase the kernel size of KNN to make it the same as the number of people in the scene. As shown in Table 1b, our method again obtains competitive results on the Collective dataset with an accuracy of 89.54%.

4   Conclusions

In this paper, we propose a slice-based relation learning framework called DRGCN for group activity recognition. We use a slicing strategy to get more detailed features and apply the Deep GCNs to learn higher-level relations between individuals. Experiment results on two popular datasets verify that our DRGCN can achieve comparable results to the state-of-art methods.

Acknowledgments. This work is supported by the National Natural Science Foundation in China (Grant: 61672128) and the Fundamental Research Fund for Central University (Grant: DUT20TD107).

References

1. Amer, M.R., Lei, P., Todorovic, S.: HiRF: hierarchical random field for collective activity recognition in videos. In: Fleet, D., Pajdla, T., Schiele, B., Tuytelaars, T. (eds.) ECCV 2014. LNCS, vol. 8694, pp. 572–585. Springer, Cham (2014). https://doi.org/10.1007/978-3-319-10599-4_37

2. Azar, S.M., Atigh, M.G., Nickabadi, A., Alahi, A.: Convolutional relational machine for group activity recognition. In: IEEE/CVF Conference on Computer Vision and Pattern Recognition, pp. 7884–7893 (2019)

3. Bagautdinov, T., Alahi, A., Fleuret, F., Fua, P., Savarese, S.: Social scene understanding: end-to-end multi-person action localization and collective activity recognition. In: Proceedings of the IEEE Conference on Computer Vision and Pattern Recognition, pp. 4315–4324 (2017)

4. Choi, W., Shahid, K., Savarese, S.: What are they doing?: collective activity classification using spatio-temporal relationship among people. In: 2009 IEEE 12th International Conference on Computer Vision Workshops, ICCV Workshops, pp. 1282–1289. IEEE (2009)

5. Deng, Z., Vahdat, A., Hu, H., Mori, G.: Structure inference machines: recurrent neural networks for analyzing relations in group activity recognition. In: Proceedings of the IEEE Conference on Computer Vision and Pattern Recognition, pp. 4772–4781 (2016)

6. Hu, G., Cui, B., He, Y., Yu, S.: Progressive relation learning for group activity recognition. ArXiv abs/1908.02948 (2019)

7. Ibrahim, M.S., Mori, G.: Hierarchical relational networks for group activity recognition and retrieval. In: Proceedings of the European Conference on Computer Vision, pp. 721–736 (2018)

8. Ibrahim, M.S., Muralidharan, S., Deng, Z., Vahdat, A., Mori, G.: A hierarchical deep temporal model for group activity recognition. In: Proceedings of the IEEE Conference on Computer Vision and Pattern Recognition, pp. 1971–1980 (2016)

9. Li, G., Muller, M., Thabet, A., Ghanem, B.: Deepgcns: can gcns go as deep as cnns? In: Proceedings of the IEEE International Conference on Computer Vision, pp. 9267–9276 (2019)

10. Li, X., Choo Chuah, M.: Sbgar: Semantics based group activity recognition. In: Proceedings of the IEEE International Conference on Computer Vision, pp. 2876–2885 (2017)

11. Qi, M., Qin, J., Li, A., Wang, Y., Luo, J., Van Gool, L.: stagnet: an attentive semantic rnn for group activity recognition. In: Proceedings of the European Conference on Computer Vision, pp. 101–117 (2018)

12. Shu, T., Todorovic, S., Zhu, S.C.: Cern: confidence-energy recurrent network for group activity recognition. In: Proceedings of the IEEE Conference on Computer Vision and Pattern Recognition, pp. 5523–5531 (2017)

13. Wu, J., Wang, L., Wang, L., Guo, J., Wu, G.: Learning actor relation graphs for group activity recognition. In: Proceedings of the IEEE Conference on Computer Vision and Pattern Recognition, pp. 9964–9974 (2019)

Dual Convolutional Neural Networks for Hyperspectral Satellite Images Classification (DCNN-HSI)

Maissa Hamouda[1,3]($\boxtimes$)(iD) and Med Salim Bouhlel[2,3](iD)

[1] Sousse University, ISITCom, Sousse, Tunisia
maissa_h@yahoo.fr
[2] Sfax University, ISBS, Sfax, Tunisia
[3] SETIT Laboratory, Sfax, Tunisia

Abstract. Hyperspectral Satellite Images (HSI) presents a very interesting technology for mapping, environmental protection, and security. HSI is very rich in spectral and spatial characteristics, which are nonlinear and highly correlated which makes classification difficult. In this paper, we propose a new approach to the reduction and classification of HSI. This deep approach consisting of a dual Convolutional Neural Networks (DCNN), which aims to improve precision and computing time. This approach involves two main steps; the first is to extract the spectral data and reduce it by CNN until a single value representing the active pixel is displayed. The second consists in classifying the only remaining spatial band on CNN until the class of each pixel is obtained. The tests were applied to three different hyperspectral data sets and showed the effectiveness of the proposed method.

Keywords: Hyperspectral satellite images · Feature extraction · Convolutional codes · Neural networks · Deep learning

1 Introduction

Remote sensing is the technique that, through the acquisition of images, aims to obtain information on the surface of the Earth. Remote sensing encompasses the entire process of capturing and recording the energy of emitted or reflected electromagnetic radiation, processing and analyzing the information, and then applying that information. The resulting images from Remote Sensing can be Monochromatic, Multispectral (2 to 10 spectral bands), or Hyperspectral (10 to 100 spectral bands).

Hyperspectral Satellite Imagery (HSI) is used in different fields such as astronomy, military security, and the environment [1,2]. The HSI is a series of images on the same scene but taken in several tens of wavelengths which correspond to as many colors. By increasing the dimensionality of images in the spectral domain, many problems can arise the high spectral dimensionality

© Springer Nature Switzerland AG 2020
H. Yang et al. (Eds.): ICONIP 2020, CCIS 1332, pp. 369–376, 2020.
https://doi.org/10.1007/978-3-030-63820-7_42

and the limited number of samples, the high computational cost, and the high spectral bands' correlation.

To classify a hyperspectral scene, you must: select the best (1) extraction method and (2) machine learning method. In Sect. 2, we present the different CNN architectures and the different data extraction methods, which we can apply in our work.

2   Related Works

Machine learning algorithms have been widely used in different fields (engineering, health, safety, etc.) [3,4]. More specifically, deep learning algorithms have revolutionized the field of extraction and classification of all objects. Deep learning methods [5,6], such as CNN (Convolutional Neural Networks), are highly recommended for classification of images, including HSI [7,8], due to their efficiency for cases of Heterogeneity, redundancy and strong correlation, and especially non-linearity.

2.1   CNN Architectures

Since its creation, the famous CNN model has undergone several changes in terms of its architecture, for example, the *LeNET* [9] (2 convolution layers, 2 pooling layers, and 3 Fullyconnected layers), the *ZFNet* [10] (5 convolution layers, 3 pooling layers, and 2 Fullyconnected layers), the *AlexNet* [11] (5 convolution layers, 3 pooling layers, and 2 Fullyconnected layers), the *GoogLeNet* [12] (64 convolutional layers, 16 pooling layers, and 11 Fullyconnected layers). All of these CNN models have been applied for the classification of non-satellite images. Furthermore, the *AdaNet* [2] and the *SFENet* [13] (3 convolution layers, 2 pooling layers, and 2 Fullyconnected layer) which have been applied on HSI images. The *SFENet* proposed a novel probabilistic method to reduce the spectral information, based on the Softmax function. The results obtained by both *AdaNet* and *SFENet* are very interesting, and the CNN model applied is very successful, which motivates us to make other optimizations.

2.2   Feature Extraction Methods

HSIs are made up of 3 dimensions: 2 spatial and 1 spectral. The extraction of HSI characteristics can be done in several ways: (1) the extraction by band, witch aims to extract each band apart, extract batches[1] of spatial data successively, and combine the results before classification. This method is very precise for classification, but it takes a long time for calculation [14,15]. (2) the extraction in depths, wich aims to extract the superimposed-spectral batches and to combine them together. This method is also precise for classification, but it takes a long

---

[1] Batch: Group of pixels containing the active pixel surrounded by its spatial neighbors.

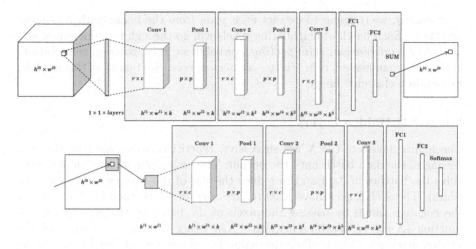

Fig. 1. The proposed CNN model

time for calculation too [16]. Finally, (3) the spectral band reduction, wich aims to apply a specific reduction method or even averaging. Generally, this method is not very precise for classification, and does not take much time for calculation [13, 17].

In this work, we propose a double CNN for the reduction and classification of HSI. This approach improves classification accuracy and reduces computation time compared to state of art methods. This approach is made up of two main CNN parts: The first is to extract the spectral data and reduce it by CNN until a single value representing the active pixel is displayed. The second consists in classifying the only remaining spatial plane (the result of the first step) on CNN until the class of each pixel is obtained. In the following section, we explain in detail the work carried out.

3 Proposed Approach

The proposed approach is based on the CNN algorithm (Fig. 1), which is used in two stages. The first step to reduce the spectral information. The second step to classify the image made up of the first step (spatial information).

Firstly, we will first extract spectral information. we extract from each band the corresponding pixel to obtain a vector of superimposed pixels representing the same spatial location but with different wavelengths. The vector obtained will then pass through the different stages of $CNN1$ (*convolution, relu, pooling, convolution, relu, pooling, convolution, relu, fully − connected, relu, fully − connected, relu, sum*). Instead of doing the classification task (Softmax) we calculate the sum of all the resulting neurons, to obtain a single output value. The previous steps will be applied to all the pixels of the image to obtain a new 2D image (reduced image).

Secondly, we're going to extract each pixel from the image with its spatial neighbors. Each batch of neighboring pixels will go through the different stages of $CNN2$ (*convolution, relu, pooling, convolution, relu, pooling, convolution, relu, fully − connected, relu, fully − connected, relu, Softmax*). of this module, we obtain a classified image.

3.1   CNN Hidden Layers

The hidden layers of CNN are successive, repetitive layers, allowing the processing of the data batch until the output: The *convolutionlayers* aims to convolve the batches of data and to reduce the size of the batches a little bit (the edges). The *Relulayers* have a corrective role, of which they aims to correct the negative values by passing the pixels of the batch by the positive or zero function ($Xout = max(0, Xin)$, with Xin being the input value). And the *subdivisionlayers* which allow the reduction of the size of the batches being processed. We choose from a group of pixels to be reduced, their maximums ($Xout = max(X1, X2, \ldots, Xn)$), with $X1, X2, \ldots, Xn$ the pixels to reduce and n the size of the subdivision filter).

3.2   CNN Output Layers

The output layers are composed of two $Fully − Connected$ layers and a Sum function for $CNN1$ or $Softmax$ function for $CNN2$: A fully connected layer is a layer where each neuron is connected to each neuron of the previous layer and at each connection has a weight. And a Softmax function is a generalized form of logistic regression; its output is equivalent to a categorical probability distribution, which indicates the probability that one of the classs is true.

4   Experiments and Results

In this section, we present the test data, the parameters of the CNN network and the results obtained by the proposed approach, by comparing them with other works.

4.1   Datasets

To validate our approach, we chose three public hyperspectral datasets: (1) $SalinasA$ are composed of 204 spectral bands, captured by the $AVIRIS$ sensor, in the Salinas Valley region of California. The size of Salinas is 86 × 83 pixels. It is composed of 6 classs, which are: green broccoli 1, corn, romaine lettuce 4, romaine lettuce 5, romaine lettuce 6, romaine lettuce 7. (2) $GulfofGabes$ is composed of 125 spectral bands. They were captured by $HyperionEO − 1$, in the region of Gabès in Tunisia, the spatial resolution of 30 m. Their sizes are from 100 × 100 pixels and are composed of 7 Class, namely: water, soil, hydrated soil and vegetation species. And, (3) $IndianPines$ are composed of 220 spectral

Table 1. Classification results of the "SalinasA" dataset

Class	(1)	(2)	(3)	(4)	(5)
1	0.8823	0.8823	0.8785	0.882	0.8823
2	0.6241	0.6243	0.6565	0.6317	0.6245
3	0.8298	0.8299	0.8263	0.8302	0.8299
4	0.5760	0.5760	0.5908	0.5762	0.5761
5	0.8143	0.8142	0.8111	0.8137	0.8142
6	0.7821	0.7820	0.7875	0.7826	0.7820
OA(%)	**93.1213**	**93.1353**	**77.1224**	**90.6556**	**93.1634**
AA	0.9337	0.9340	0.7917	0.9135	0.9342
K	0.9166	0.9168	0.7233	0.8867	0.9171
Sensitivity	0.9236	0.9239	0.7680	0.9026	0.9241
Specificity	0.9879	0.9879	0.9600	0.9836	0.9880
Time(s)*10^4	**14.879**	**10.046**	**0.0934**	**0.0816**	**0.2914**

Table 2. Classification results of the "Gulf Of Gabes" dataset

Class	(1)	(2)	(3)	(4)	(5)
1	0.1626	0.1627	0.1535	0.1517	0.1619
2	0.9362	0.9360	0.9367	0.9358	0.9360
3	0.8687	0.8687	0.8678	0.8671	0.8687
4	0.8731	0.8731	0.8719	0.8728	0.8730
5	0.8532	0.8532	0.8530	0.8525	0.8531
6	0.8867	0.8868	0.8869	0.8870	0.8867
7	0.8117	0.8116	0.8117	0.8118	0.8113
OA(%)	**88.9500**	**88.9800**	**87.8700**	**87.8600**	**88.9400**
AA	0.7881	0.7890	0.7725	0.7758	0.7891
K	0.8169	30.8174	0.7995	0.7995	0.8168
Sensitivity	0.7719	0.7722	0.7548	0.7551	0.7715
Specificity	0.9802	0.9803	0.9776	0.9774	0.9801
Time(s)*10^4	**24.592**	**20.945**	**0.15192**	**0.2942**	**0.5048**

bands, reduced to 200 by removing the water absorption region. It is captured by $AVIRIS$, in northwestern Indiana. The size of Indian Pines is 145 × 145 pixels. It is composed of 16 classs, which are: alfalfa. both types of corn, three different grass pastures, oat hay, several types of soybeans, and wood.

4.2 Experimental Setup

Before starting the tests, we set the parameters of our network (randomly chosen): Batch Size^2 = 15 × 15, Kernels Number = 10, Kernel Size^2 = 3 × 3, and

Table 3. Classification results of the "Indian Pines" dataset

Class	(1)	(2)	(3)	(4)	(5)
1	0.9956	0.9956	0.9969	0.9962	0.9956
2	0.8697	0.8696	0.8661	0.8633	0.8698
3	0.9319	0.9320	0.9144	0.9211	0.9320
4	0.9857	0.9858	0.9842	0.9838	0.9858
5	0.9648	0.9648	0.9619	0.9628	0.9648
6	0.9301	0.9305	0.9237	0.9265	0.9305
7	0.9973	0.9973	0.9979	0.9975	0.9973
8	0.9544	0.9546	0.9688	0.9631	0.9545
9	0.9981	0.9981	0.9971	0.9973	0.9981
10	0.9077	0.9074	0.9098	0.9098	0.9075
11	0.7662	0.7664	0.7473	0.7596	0.7664
12	0.9481	0.9479	0.9410	0.9408	0.9480
13	0.9804	0.9805	0.9772	0.9768	0.9805
14	0.8799	0.8796	0.9008	0.8967	0.8796
15	0.9635	0.9632	0.9618	0.9622	0.9632
16	0.9911	0.9911	0.9905	0.9897	0.9911
OA(%)	**95.6195**	**96.0048**	**71.7337**	**81.0131**	**96.0428**
AA	0.8949	0.8993	0.6146	0.7270	0.8995
K	0.9365	0.9420	0.6013	0.7298	0.9426
Sensitivity	0.9892	0.9949	0.6718	0.7451	0.9954
Specificity	0.9972	0.9976	0.9761	0.9842	0.9976
Time(s)*10^4	**186.61**	**27.885**	**0.41838**	**0.3418**	**2.3660**

Subdivision Filter$^2 = 3 \times 3$. The tests were carried out on an Intel (R) Core (TM) CPU i7-2670QM @ 2.20 GHz 2.20 GHz computer with a RAM of 8.00 GB.

4.3   Data Extraction Methods

The HSI is a multidimensional image, where it is often made up of several overlapping spectral bands. The processing is generally done band by band then merge the results, merge the bands to extract spectral and spatial information at the same time then classify, or even apply a reduction method, for the latter we tested two methods (reduction by the mean and probabilistic reduction). In this work, we tested the five following methods:

1. Extraction of spatial information only: We extract the spectral bands from the HSI. Then we treat band by band. Each band will be treated separately, then we merge the results. The results obtained by this first network are presented in *Column*1 of the three Tables 1, 2 and 3.

2. Extraction of spectral and spatial information at the same time: We extract the spectral and spatial information in batch surrounding each pixel of the HSI. The results obtained by this second network are presented in *Column*2 of the three Tables 1, 2 and 3.

3. Reduction of spectral bands (average): We reduce the spectral bands by merging their contents by the average. Then we extract the spatial information in batches surrounding each pixel of the HSI and classify it. The results obtained by this third network are presented in *Column*3 of the three Tables 1, 2 and 3.

4. Reduction of spectral bands (probability): We reduce the spectral bands by merging their contents by the Softmax function [13]. Then we extract the spatial information in batches surrounding each pixel of the HSI and classify it. The results obtained by this fourth network are presented in *Column*4 of the three Tables 1, 2 and 3.

5. Deep reduction of spectral bands (DCNN-HSI): We reduce the spectral bands by treating them in the CNN module, finished by the sum. Then we extract the spatial information in batches surrounding each pixel of the HSI and classify it. The results obtained by this fifth network are presented in *Column*5 of the three Tables 1, 2 and 3.

4.4   Results

In the three Tables 1, 2 and 3, we present the results obtained by the different methods: (1) Extraction of spatial information only (band by band), (2) Extraction of spectral and spatial information at the same time, (3) Reduction of spectral bands (average), (4) Reduction of spectral bands (probability), and (5) Proposed $DCNN - HSI$ approach. We tested and compared the results obtained by the proposed approach with other methods of classifying HSIs by CNN, using the same parameters. Thus, from the results obtained, we can conclude that the proposed approach improved the classification accuracy for the three datasets. In addition, the approach also made it possible to reduce the computation time by the other methods.

5   Conclusions

In this work, we have proposed a double application of Convolutional Neural Networks on Hyperspectral Satellite Images. The goal of this proposed method was to reduce at the beginning the enormous number of spectral information by a first modified CNN network. Then, the results data of the first part will be processed in a second CNN, to obtain a better classified image with a reduced computation time, compared to the other simple or reduction methods.

Acknowlegment. This contribution was supported by the Ministry of Higher Education and Scientific Research of Tunisia.

References

1. Wang, J., Gao, F., Dong, J., Du, Q.: Adaptive DropBlock-enhanced generative adversarial networks for hyperspectral image classification. IEEE Trans. Geosci. Remote Sensing 1–14 (2020)
2. Hamouda, M., Ettabaa, K.S., Bouhlel, M.S.: Hyperspectral imaging classification based on convolutional neural networks by adaptive sizes of windows and filters. IET Image Process. **13**(2), 392–398 (2018)
3. Chin, T.J., Bagchi, S., Eriksson, A., Van Schaik, A.: Star tracking using an event camera. In: 2019 IEEE/CVF Conference on Computer Vision and Pattern Recognition Workshops (CVPRW). IEEE, June 2019
4. Hamouda, M., Saheb Ettabaa, K., Bouhlel, M.S.: Adaptive batch extraction for hyperspectral image classification based on convolutional neural network. In: Mansouri, A., El Moataz, A., Nouboud, F., Mammass, D. (eds.) ICISP 2018. LNCS, vol. 10884, pp. 310–318. Springer, Cham (2018). https://doi.org/10.1007/978-3-319-94211-7_34
5. Haidar, A., Verma, B.K., Haidar, R.: A swarm based optimization of the xgboost parameters. Aust. J. Intell. Inf. Process. Syst. **16**(4), 74–81 (2019)
6. Hamouda, M., Ettabaa, K.S., Bouhlel, M.S.: Modified convolutional neural network based on adaptive patch extraction for hyperspectral image classification. In: 2018 IEEE International Conference on Fuzzy Systems (FUZZ-IEEE), pp. 1–7. IEEE (2018)
7. Feng, J., et al.: Attention multibranch convolutional neural network for hyperspectral image classification based on adaptive region search. IEEE Trans. Geosci. Remote Sensing 1–17 (2020)
8. Shen, Y., et al.: Efficient deep learning of nonlocal features for hyperspectral image classification. IEEE Trans. Geosci. Remote Sensing 1–15 (2020)
9. LeCun, Y., Bottou, L., Bengio, Y., Haffner, P., et al.: Gradient-based learning applied to document recognition. Proc. IEEE **86**(11), 2278–2324 (1998)
10. Zeiler, M.D., Fergus, R.: Visualizing and understanding convolutional networks. In: Fleet, D., Pajdla, T., Schiele, B., Tuytelaars, T. (eds.) ECCV 2014. LNCS, vol. 8689, pp. 818–833. Springer, Cham (2014). https://doi.org/10.1007/978-3-319-10590-1_53
11. Krizhevsky, A., Sutskever, I., Hinton, G.E.: Imagenet classification with deep convolutional neural networks. In: Advances in Neural Information Processing Systems, pp. 1097–1105 (2012)
12. Szegedy, C., et al.: Going deeper with convolutions. In: The IEEE Conference on Computer Vision and Pattern Recognition (CVPR), June 2015
13. Hamouda, M., Ettabaa, K.S., Bouhlel, M.S.: Smart feature extraction and classification of hyperspectral images based on convolutional neural networks. IET Image Process. **14**(10), 1999–2005 (2020)
14. Hang, R., Li, Z., Liu, Q., Ghamisi, P., Bhattacharyya, S.S.: Hyperspectral image classification with attention aided CNNs. arXiv preprint arXiv:2005.11977 (2020)
15. Hamouda, M., Ettabaa, K.S., Bouhlel, M.S.: Framework for automatic selection of kernels based on convolutional neural networks and ckmeans clustering algorithm. Int. J. Image Graph. **19**(04), 1950019 (2019)
16. Fang, J., Wang, N., Cao, X.: Multidimensional relation learning for hyperspectral image classification. Neurocomputing **410**, 211–219 (2020)
17. Azar, S.G., Meshgini, S., Rezaii, T.Y., Beheshti, S.: Hyperspectral image classification based on sparse modeling of spectral blocks. Neurocomputing **407**, 12–23 (2020)

Edge Curve Estimation by the Nonparametric Parzen Kernel Method

Tomasz Gałkowski[1,3](✉) and Adam Krzyżak[2,3]

[1] Institute of Computational Intelligence, Częstochowa University of Technology, Częstochowa, al. Armii Krajowej 36, 42-200 Częstochowa, Poland
tomasz.galkowski@pcz.pl

[2] Department of Computer Science and Software Engineering, Concordia University, Montreal, QC H3G 1M8, Canada
krzyzak@cs.concordia.ca

[3] Department of Electrical Engineering, Westpomeranian University of Technology, 70-310 Szczecin, Poland

Abstract. The article concerns the problem of finding the spatial curve which is the line of the abrupt or jump change in the $3d$-shape, namely: the edge curve. There are many real applications where such a problems play a significant role. For instance, in computer vision in detection of edges in monochromatic pictures used in e.g. medicine diagnostics, biology and physics; in geology in analysis of satellite photographs of the earth surface for maps and/or determination of borders of forest areas, water resources, rivers, rock cliffs etc. In architecture the curves arising as a result of intersecting surfaces often are also objects of interest. The main focus of this paper is detection of abrupt changes in patterns defined by multidimensional functions. Our approach is based on the nonparametric Parzen kernel estimation of functions and their derivatives. An appropriate use of nonparametric methodology allows to establish the shape of an interesting edge curve.

Keywords: Edge curve detection · Regression · Nonparametric estimation

1 Introduction

One of the most important problems in data analysis is to verify whether data observed or/and collected in time are genuine and stationary, i.e. the information

Part of this research was carried out by the second author during his visit of the Westpomeranian University of Technology while on sabbatical leave from Concordia University.

Research of the first author financed under the program of the Polish Minister of Science and Higher Education under the name "Regional Initiative of Excellence" in the years 2019–2022 project number 020/RID/2018/19, the amount of financing 12,000,000.00 PLN. Research of the second author supported by the Natural Sciences and Engineering Research Council of Canada under Grant RGPIN-2015-06412.

H. Yang et al. (Eds.): ICONIP 2020, CCIS 1332, pp. 377–385, 2020.
https://doi.org/10.1007/978-3-030-63820-7_43

sources did not change their characteristics. When the function observed is one-dimensional, the problem we are interested in is to find a point or moment where or when the change has arisen. From mathematical point of view this is an estimation problem of function discontinuity.

In multidimensional case the problem of change detection commonly consists of finding the curves in multidimensional space and it is obviously more complex task and needs more computer resources like processor power, memory space, and appropriate algorithms.

In this paper we propose the new concept of multidimensional function discontinuity detection based on nonparametric Parzen kernel estimation of functions and their derivatives. An application to estimation of edge curve for 3-dimensional surfaces is presented in details.

2   A Short Survey on Edge Curves Estimation Research

The abrupt change detection problem in one-dimensional case is called the edge detection problem. When the function severely changes the value its plot has the jump or discontinuity at this edge point. The problem is to determine when the change occurred. But when the function is two-dimensional the jump takes the form of a edge curve. Then the problem is to estimate the curve line in $3d$-space or its projection on the flat surface. The analogous general problem in multivariate space is to determine for instance, just a scatter plot of hyperspace curve line. An abrupt changes detection problem has several solutions. Various techniques concerning edge detection in $2d$-image processing are surveyed, e.g., in [3,13,24]. Let us mention only a few. Classical gradient-based methods using operations involving first order derivatives such as Sobel, Prewitt, Robert's [20] and Canny [4] edge detectors at which the distribution of intensity values in the neighborhood of given pixels determines the probable edges. Applying the Laplacian and Gaussian filtering and detecting of zero-crossing techniques analysis of the second derivative also allows edge detection in digital images [19]. In methods used with digital images the design points are equally spaced, for instance, as the regularly spaced pixels. The analysis is then based on neighboring observations, and the differences between regularly spaced neighboring pixels are used to determine derivatives.

In case of probabilistic data observed in time the natural general approach is to model data via distributions or densities. The problems are modelled by multidimensional probability density functions in continuous d-dimensional spaces, and distributions in the case of discrete series of random numbers representing statistical multidimensional processes. The representative templates like means and simple linear regression models the significant features could be compared using different sample sets. The detection of possible changes is based on some parameter deviation. More general criteria like mean square error can be also used to detect change. One of the most general measures of the distance between two distributions is the relative entropy known as the Kullback-Leibler distance [18]. For data streams for instance, cited methods are not usable directly. One possible way of detecting change is to compare likelihood between the subsequent examples using adjacent sliding time-windows, for previous elements in the stream and the further ones. The point of abrupt change p could be estimated when we observe a decreasing likelihood. The authors in [6] proposed an interesting solution applying the Kulback-Leibler divergence. If two distributions are identical the Kulback-Leibler divergence is close to 0, when they are substantially different the Kulback-Leibler divergence is close to 1.

When a parameter of the process is estimated the so-called parametric approach is applied. The nonparametric methodology is used when no assumptions on the functional form on the data have been made.

Edge detection technique based on Parzen kernel estimate has also been investigated by Qiu in [22,23].

In this paper, we focus our attention on the challenge of abrupt change detection, also called edge detection problem, by presenting the new original approach. The algorithms are developed for functions of two variables. Restricting our considerations to three-dimensional space allows to better understand the proposed approach, but by no means precludes its generalization to d-dimensional space. The main result is the method of edge detection derived from the nonparametric approach based on Parzen kernel algorithms for estimation of unknown regression functions and their derivatives from the set of noisy measurements. The method is applicable to calculation of edge curve where the abrupt change occurred and also how is the course of the subject function along this line. In our approach we compute the derivatives of the kernel itself which is a very simple and efficient process. Our algorithms performs in satisfactory manner in numerical experiments. Furthermore, our algorithm can scale up and it does not require the samples to be uniformly spaced.

The problem of detection of edge curves has been intensively studied in the recent years. The research efforts and results one may find, e.g., in [1,2,5,15–17,21,25,26]. Preliminary results on application of Parzen kernels to change detection have been shown in [10].

3   New Approach for Edge Detection

In general various phenomena can be mathematically described as a function $R(\cdot)$ of the d-dimensional vector variable $\mathbf{x}$. Then edge detection methods based on regression function analysing can be applied. In the case $d > 1$ the place of change (the edge) takes the form of a curve in d-dimensional space - across which R is discontinuous - its calculation is more difficult and is much more computationally demanding.

The main goal of this paper is to introduce a new simple method of edge detection derived from the nonparametric approach based on multidimensional Parzen kernel algorithms for estimating unknown functions and their derivatives from the set of noisy measurements. For theoretical analysis of Parzen and other nonparametric regression estimation techniques for so-called random design case we refer the reader to [14].

We consider the model of the object in the form:

$$y_i = R(\mathbf{x}_i) + \varepsilon_i, \, i = 1, ..., n \tag{1}$$

where $\mathbf{x}_i$ is assumed to be the d-dimensional vectors of deterministic input, $\mathbf{x}_i \in R^d$, y_i is the scalar random output, and ε_i is a measurement noise with zero mean and bounded variance. $R(.)$ is assumed to be completely unknown function. This is so-called fixed-design regression problem.

We start with estimator $\hat{R}_n(\mathbf{x})$ of function $R(\cdot)$ at point $\mathbf{x}$ based on the set of measurements y_i, $i = 1, ..., n$.

We use the Parzen kernel based algorithm of the integral type:

$$\hat{R}(\mathbf{x}) = h_n{}^{-d} \sum_{i=1}^{n} y_i \int_{D_i} \mathbf{K}\left(\frac{\|\mathbf{x} - \mathbf{u}\|}{h_n}\right) d\mathbf{u} \tag{2}$$

where $\|\mathbf{x} - \mathbf{u}\|$ denotes a norm or the distance function defined for points $\mathbf{x}$ and $\mathbf{u}$ in d-dimensional space and D_i's are defined below.

Factor h_n depending on the number of observations n is called the smoothing factor. The domain area D (the space where function R is defined) is partitioned into n disjunctive nonempty sub-spaces D_i and the measurements $\mathbf{x}_i$ are chosen from D_i, i.e.: $\mathbf{x}_i \in D_i$. For instance, in one-dimensional case let the $D = [0, 1]$, then $\cup D_i = [0, 1]$, $D_i \cap D_j = \emptyset$ for $i \neq j$, the points x_i are chosen from D_i, i.e.: $x_i \in D_i$.

The set of input values $\mathbf{x}_i$ (independent variable in the model (1) are chosen in the process of collecting data e.g., equidistant samples of ECG signal in time domain, or stock exchange information, or internet activity on specified TCP/IP port of the web or ftp server logs recorded in time. These data points should provide a balanced representation of function R in the domain D.

Let us mention that in nonparametric approach we impose no constraints on either the shape of unknown function (like e.g. in the spline methods or linear regression) or on any mathematical formula with a certain set of parameters to be found (like in so-called parametric approach). The standard assumption in theorems on convergence of (3) is that the maximum diameter of set D_i tends to zero when n tends to infinity (see e.g. [7, 8, 11]). We may assume that in the set of pairs $(\mathbf{x}_i, y_i)$ information (in some way *inscribed*) on essential properties of function R, like its smoothness is present.

The kernel function $\mathbf{K}$ in one-dimensional case $K(\cdot)$ satisfies the following conditions:

$$K(t) = 0 \quad for \quad t \notin (-\tau, \tau), \tau > 0$$
$$\int_{-\tau}^{\tau} K(t)dt = 1 \tag{3}$$
$$\sup_t |K(t)| < \infty$$

We will use the cosine kernel satisfying (3)

$$K(t) = \begin{cases} \frac{\pi}{4} \cos\left(\frac{\pi}{2}t\right) & for \ t \in (-1, 1) \\ 0 & otherwise \end{cases} \tag{4}$$

The algorithm for estimating the derivatives of order k is based on differentiation of the kernel function. Thus the kernel $K(\cdot)$ must be differentiable function of order k. The trigonometric cosine kernel (4) fulfils this condition. The estimate of $k-th$ derivative of the regression function in point x can be defined as follows:

$$\hat{R}^{(k)}(x) = h_n^{-1} \sum_{i=1}^{n} y_i \int_{D_i} K^{(k)} \left(\frac{x-u}{h_n} \right) du \tag{5}$$

The nonparameric approach in application to estimation of unknown functions and their derivatives was previously proposed and studied in univariate case in e.g. [9, 12].

The main idea of the paper is to deduce the dynamics of changes of any function by analyzing the course of the first derivative estimated from sample. The more rapidly the change occurs - the higher the first derivative (or speed). The steeper the slope - the larger the tangent referring to horizon surface at a given point. These facts motivate us to propose as a detector of abrupt changes the nonparametric estimator of the derivatives described previously.

The choice of the parameter h_n value plays an important role in the interpretation of results. The bigger the h_n the bigger the level of smoothness, but then detection at which point the jump has occurred is more difficult. On the other hand, a too small value of h_n causes higher oscillations of the estimates of the derivatives and consequently, the bigger number of sharp peaks of the first derivative. Optimal choice of smoothing sequence or bandwidth is rather difficult and it is often data dependent. Let us mention that the smoothing property of these algorithms makes it applicable when the observations are taken in the presence of random noise. Then the compromise choice of h_n parameter is crucial when derivatives of functions must be estimated from noised measurements. In the multidimensional case it is convenient to apply the product kernel given by:

$$\mathbf{K}(\mathbf{x}, \mathbf{u}, h_n) = \prod_{p=1}^{d} K \left(\frac{|x_p - u_p|}{h_n} \right) = \mathbf{K} \left(\frac{\|\mathbf{x} - \mathbf{u}\|}{h_n} \right) \tag{6}$$

The estimate of partial derivative of order k with respect to the coordinate variable x_j is given by:

$$\hat{R}_{x_j}^{(k)}(\mathbf{x}) = h_n^{-d} \sum_{i=1}^{n} y_i \int_{D_i} \frac{\partial^k}{\partial x_j^k} \mathbf{K} \left(\frac{\|\mathbf{x} - \mathbf{u}\|}{h_n} \right) d\mathbf{u} \tag{7}$$

It is clear that the estimation of particular derivative is obtained by the differentiation of the kernel function depending on the relative coordinate. Let us analyze the two-dimensional case.

The model of the object is now in the form:

$$y_i = R([x_1, x_2]_i) + \varepsilon_i, \, i = 1, ..., n \tag{8}$$

where the *2d*-vector of independent variable: $\mathbf{x}_i = [x_1, x_2]_i$.

The *2d* Parzen kernel based estimator is defined by:

$$\hat{R}([x_1, x_2]) = h_n^{-2} \sum_{i=1}^{n} y_i \cdot$$
$$\int_{D_i} K \left(\frac{x_1 - u_1}{h_n} \right) \cdot K \left(\frac{x_2 - u_2}{h_n} \right) du_1 du_2 \tag{9}$$

The integrals in (9) are easy to calculate analytically when using the cosine kernel defined by (4).

The points x_i should be chosen from D_i, i.e.: $x_i \in D_i$. Natural selection is an equally spaced grid, which is easy to construct, but the details are omitted here.

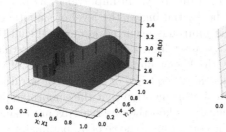

Original regression function

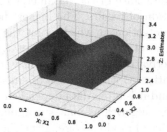

Regression function estimate

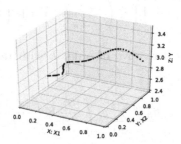

Estimated edge curve in 3*d*-space

Fig. 1. Estimation of edge curve without noise

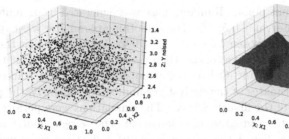
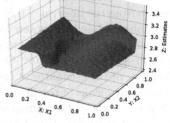

Noised measurements of function R   Regression function estimate

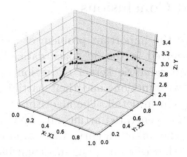

Estimated edge curve in 3d-space

Fig. 2. Estimation of edge curve using noised signal

4 Simulations Results

The function $R(\cdot)$ for simulation was defined as follows:

$$R([x_1, x_2]) = \begin{cases} 3 - 0.15 \cdot x_1 \cdot \sin(8 \cdot x_2 - 1) & for \ x_2 \leq L(x_1) \\ 2.8 - 0.15 \cdot x_1 \cdot \sin(8 \cdot x_2 - 1) & elsewhere \end{cases} \tag{10}$$

where

$$L(x_1) = 0.25 + 8 \cdot x_1 \cdot \sin\left((x_1 - 0.5)^2\right) \tag{11}$$

Two groups of tests were performed: at first, tests based on the sets of measurement pairs $\mathbf{x}, \mathbf{y}$ generated without measurement noise, and second, the sets of measurements with additive noise.

Test functions defined by (10) and (11) contain deep valleys and sharp slopes as can be seen in the figures. The task is to determine the curve along which the collapse has occurred. Figure 1 shows function without noise, its nonparametric estimation and (in the bottom) shows the 3d-view scatter plot of estimated edge curve, based on the concatenated set of points obtained from partial derivatives with respect to both coordinates x_1 and x_2. Figure 2 presents the results of simulations with additive noise. The initial probe set has been prepared as the set of

200×200 measurement points. Random noise was generated using uniform distribution from the interval $[-0.5, 0.5]$. The smoothing parameter was experimentally established and its chosen value was $h_n = 0.02$. Let us note that the greater h_n the greater the level of smoothness, then detection at which point the jump has occurred is more difficult. Otherwise, a too small value of h_n causes higher oscillations of the estimates of the derivatives and, simultaneously, the presence of more sharp peaks of the first derivative. The simulations were performed with application of the *python* programming language. The *scipy.signal.find_peaks* procedure was used to detect the local maxima of derivatives corresponding to function jumps.

5   Remarks and Conclusions

This paper considered the important problem of deciding whether the abrupt or sudden change occurred in the $3d$ space data. The proposed algorithm is derived from the nonparametric kernel regression estimation techniques with fixed-design of unknown functions and their partial derivatives. The proposed $2d$ algorithm is presented in detail. The algorithm is tested for jump detection in case of measurements generated artificially. The example test function with abrupt collapse along the unknown curve was examined.

Simulation results shown in the diagrams confirmed validity and usefulness of the proposed approach in practical cases. The method is applicable when the function is observed in presence of the measurement noise. Possible extension of the detection algorithm for estimation of the edge hyper-curves (in the meaning: in d-dimensional space) directly follows from the presented methodology.

We presented a new algorithm based on Parzen kernel estimate for detecting edges in three-dimensional images. Further extensions of the proposed approach will be investigated in the future research.

References

1. Alpert, S., Galun, M., Nadler, B., Basri, R.: Detecting faint curved edges in noisy images. In: Daniilidis, K., Maragos, P., Paragios, N. (eds.) ECCV 2010. LNCS, vol. 6314, pp. 750–763. Springer, Heidelberg (2010). https://doi.org/10.1007/978-3-642-15561-1_54
2. Bazazian, D., Casas, J.-R., Ruiz-Hidalgo, J.: Fast and robust edge extraction in unorganized point clouds. In: International Conference on Digital Image Computing: Techniques and Applications (DICTA), Adelaide, SA, pp. 1–8 (2015)
3. Bhardwaj, S., Mittal, A.: A survey on various edge detector techniques. In: 2nd International Conference on Computer, Communication, Control and Information Technology, pp. 220–226 (2012). Elseiver, SciVerse ScienceDirect, Procedia Technology 4
4. Canny, J.-F.: A computational approach to edge detection. IEEE Trans Pattern Anal. Mach. Intell. **8**(6), 679–698 (1986)
5. Dim, J.-R., Takamura, T.: Alternative approach for satellite cloud classification: edge gradient application. Adv. Meteorol. (11), 1–8 (2013)

6. Faithfull, W.-J., Rodríguez, J.-J., Kuncheva, L.I.: Combining univariate approaches for ensemble change detection in multivariate data. Inf. Fusion **45**, 202–214 (2019)
7. Gałkowski, T., Rutkowski, L.: Nonparametric recovery of multivariate functions with applications to system identification. Proc. IEEE **73**, 942–943 (1985)
8. Gałkowski, T., Rutkowski, L.: Nonparametric fitting of multivariable functions. IEEE Trans. Autom. Control **AC31**, 785–787 (1986)
9. Gałkowski, T.: On nonparametric fitting of higher order functions derivatives by the kernel method - a simulation study. In: Proceedings of the 5-th International Symposium on Applied Stochastic Models and data Analysis, Granada, Spain, pp. 230–242 (1991)
10. Gałkowski, T., Krzyżak, A., Filutowicz, Z.: A new approach to detection of changes in multidimensional patterns. J. Artif. Intell. Soft Comput. Res. **10**(2), 125–136 (2020)
11. Gasser, T., Müller, H.-G.: Kernel estimation of regression functions. In: Gasser, T., Rosenblatt, M. (eds.) Smoothing Techniques for Curve Estimation. LNM, vol. 757, pp. 23–68. Springer, Heidelberg (1979). https://doi.org/10.1007/BFb0098489
12. Gasser, T., Müller, H.-G.: Estimating regression functions and their derivatives by the kernel method. Scand. J. Stat. **11**(3), 171–185 (1984)
13. Gonzales, R.-C., Woods, R.-E.: Digital Image Processing, 4th edn. Pearson, London (2018)
14. Györfi, L., Kohler, M., Krzyzak, A., Walk, H.: A Distribution-Free Theory of Nonparametric Regression. Springer, Heidelberg (2002). https://doi.org/10.1007/b97848
15. Horev, I., Nadler, B., Arias-Castro, E., Galun, M., Basri, R.: Detection of long edges on a computational budget: a sublinear approach. SIAM J. Imaging Sci. **8**(1), 458–483 (2015)
16. Jin, Z., Tillo, T., Zou, W., Li, X., Lim, E.-G.: Depth image-based plane detection. Big Data Anal. 3(10) (2018). https://doi.org/10.1186/s41044-018-0035-y
17. Kolomenkin, M., Shimshoni, I., Tal, A.: On edge detection on surfaces. In: 2009 IEEE Conference on Computer Vision and Pattern Recognition, pp. 2767–2774 (2009)
18. Kullback, S., Leibler, R.-A.: On information and sufficiency. Ann. Math. Stat. **22**(1), 79–86 (1951)
19. Marr, D., Hildreth, E.: Theory of edge detection. Proc. R. Soc. London **B–207**, 187–217 (1980)
20. Pratt, W.-K.: Digital Image Processing, 4th edn. John Wiley Inc., New York (2007)
21. Ofir, N., Galun, M., Nadler, B., Basri, R.: Fast detection of curved edges at low SNR. In: 2016 IEEE Conference on Computer Vision and Pattern Recognition. CVPR), Las Vegas, NV (2016)
22. Qiu, P.: Nonparametric estimation of jump surface. Ind. J. Stat. Ser. A **59**(2), 268–294 (1997)
23. Qiu, P.: Jump surface estimation, edge detection, and image restoration. J. Am. Stat. Assoc. **102**, 745–756 (2007)
24. Singh, S., Singh, R. Comparison of various edge detection techniques. In: International Conference on Computing for Sustainable Global Development, pp. 393–396 (2015)
25. Steger, C.: Subpixel-precise extraction of lines and edges. ISPRS Int. Soc. Photogram. Remote Sensing J. Photogram. Remote Sensing **33**(3), 141–156 (2000)
26. Wang, Y.-Q., Trouve, A., Amit, Y., Nadler, B.: Detecting curved edges in noisy images in sublinear time. J. Math. Imaging Vis. **59**(3), 373–393 (2017)

Efficient Segmentation Pyramid Network

Tanmay Singha$^{(\boxtimes)}$, Duc-Son Pham, Aneesh Krishna, and Joel Dunstan

School of Electrical Engineering, Computing, and Mathematical Sciences,
Curtin University, Bentley, WA 6102, Australia
tanmay.singha@postgrad.curtin.edu.au

Abstract. Extensive growth in the field of robotics and autonomous industries, the demand for efficient image segmentation is increasing rapidly. Whilst existing methods have been shown to achieve outstanding results on challenging data sets, they cannot scale the model properly for real-world computational constraints applications due to a fixed large backbone network. We propose a novel architecture for semantic scene segmentation suitable for resource-constrained applications. Specifically, we make use of the global contextual prior by using a pyramid pooling technique on top of the backbone network. We also employ the recently proposed EfficientNet network to make our model efficiently scalable for computational constraints. We show that our newly proposed model - Efficient Segmentation Pyramid Network (ESPNet) - outperforms many existing scene segmentation models and produces 88.5% pixel accuracy on validation and 80.9% on training set of the Cityscapes benchmark.

Keywords: Scene segmentation · Pyramid pooling · EfficientNet

1 Introduction

Semantic segmentation is a process to label each pixel of an input image [1,2] with a class. To improve the performance, a common approach is to increase the size of the backbone network [7,18,19] such as from ResNet-18 to ResNet-200. However, all these deep convolutional neural networks (DCNNs) have balanced only one of these dimensions- depth, width and image resolution. Recently, a family of models, called EfficientNet has been proposed in [18] by exploiting an effective compound scaling technique to balance all the dimensions and optimise the architecture for a given computational constraint. Inspired by this, we use EfficientNet's B0 network as a feature extractor to develop an efficient scalable segmentation model for real-time computation. We also employ the pyramid pooling module (PPM) [5,22] to extract region-based global information from the feature map. Finally, we use a classifier module at the output stage.

We propose two models for semantic segmentation targetting real-time embedded devices, namely Base ESPNet and Final ESPNet, the latter includes an additional shallow branch to preserve the local context of the input. They both have comparably less parameters than many offline (e.g. DeepLab [2] and PSPNet [22]) and real-time segmentation models (e.g. SegNet [1]) and also produce better results on the Cityscapes data set [4].

H. Yang et al. (Eds.): ICONIP 2020, CCIS 1332, pp. 386–393, 2020.
https://doi.org/10.1007/978-3-030-63820-7_44

2 Related Work

Semantic segmentation typically follows an encoder and decoder design. Existing DCNNs, such as VGG [17], ResNet [6,19], or MobileNet [14] are used as the backbone network. To perform semantic segmentation, the fully connected layer of DCNN is replaced by a convolution layer, for example in Fully Convolution Network (FCN) [16], UNet [13], SegNet [1], Bayesian Segnet [9], and Deeplapv3+ [3]. Further improvement can also be made with techniques to encode and manage global context, such as the pooling module (PPM) [22], atrous spatial pyramid pooling (ASPP) [16] and Xiphoid Spatial Pyramid Pooling [15]. Recently, semantic segmentation research has started to address real-time low-resource constraints, such as ENet [10], ICNet [21] and ContextNet [11]. Many methods trades real-time inference speed for lower segmentation quality. To address this, DSMRSeg [20] introduced a dual-stage feature pyramid network with multi-range context aggregation module to achieve high speed with high accuracy, although this model does not accept high-resolution input images. FAST-SCNN [12] was proposed to handle high resolution. Whilst it is promising for resource-constrained applications, its accuracy is lower than state-of-the-arts.

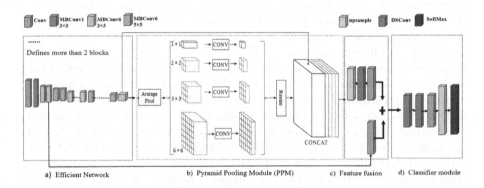

Fig. 1. Complete architecture of ESPNet

3 Proposed Methods

We propose the following two models- Base ESPNet and Final ESPNet. Our Base ESPNet is inspired by the encoder-decoder with skip connections [13,16]. In Final ESPNet, we introduce a new feature fusion module (FFM) after PPM to fuse local and global context. The detail is described next.

3.1   Network Architecture

The overall architecture of ESPNet is shown in Fig. 1 and consists of:

Backbone Network. We focus on MobileNet [7,14] to address resource constrained applications. We also adopt EfficientNet B0 [18] as our backbone network as it optimizes both accuracy and FLOPS. Its optimization objective is of the form $ACC(m) \times [FLOPS(m)/T]^w$ where $w = -0.07$ is a hyper-parameter to control the trade-off between accuracy ACC and FLOPS for model m. Figure 2 and Table 1 show the layer architecture of different MBConv blocks in EfficientNet B0.

The operations and connections of each block are determined by a per-block sub search space which involves the following: 1) Convolution operation: regular conv (Conv), depth-wise conv (DwConv), and mobile inverted bottleneck conv [14]; 2) Convolution kernel size: 3×3, 5×5; 3) Squeeze-and-excitation [8] ratio SERatio: 0, 0.25; 4) Skip operation: pooling, identity residual, or no skip; 5) Output filter size

Table 1. Stages of ESPNet

Stage (i)	Operators	Resolution	Channels	Layers
1	Conv, 3×3	256×256	32	1
2	MBConv1, k3×3	256×256	16	1
3	MBConv6, k3×3	128×128	24	2
4	MBConv6, k5×5	64×64	40	2
5	MBConv6, k3×3	32×32	80	3
6	MBConv6, k5×5	32×32	112	3
7	MBConv6, k5×5	16×16	192	4
8	MBConv6, k3×3	16×16	320	1
9	PPM	16×16	1600	1
10	FFM*	128×128	128	1
11	Classifier	512×512	20	1

*FFM is absent in base ESPNet.

F_i; and 6) Number of layers per block N_i. Convolution operation, kernel size, SERatio, skip operation and F_i determine the architecture of a layer whereas N_i controls the repetition of a layer inside the block. For example, Fig. 2 shows that each layer of block 4 has an inverted bottleneck 3×3 convolution and an identity residual skip path. The same layer is repeated N_4 times inside block 4. In the proposed models, two types of MBConv blocks of different layer architecture (MBConv1 and MBconv6) are used. We also introduce squeeze-and-excitation optimization each MBConv block to improve channel inter-dependencies at almost no computational cost. The filter size of each block is defined as {0.75, 1.0, 1.20, 1.25} of the size of filter in each block of MobileNetV2.

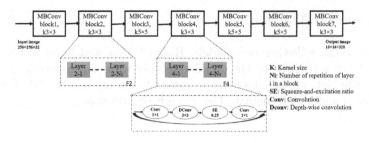

Fig. 2. Different Layers architecture of MBConv blocks

Shallow Branch. Inspired by down-to-sample technique in [12], we have introduced one shallow branch to our final ESPNet. The main motivation is to preserve the low-level features at high resolution. To ensure this, we establish this shallow connection after the stage 3 (Table 1) where image resolution becomes just a quarter of the original input size. As shown subsequently, this branch helps to improve the performance over the baseline model. Figure 1 shows the presence of this branch in final ESPNet.

Pyramid Pooling Module (PPM). The global contextual information is a key to successful semantic segmentation [5,11,22]. Therefore, a global scene-level reception is required by a deep network before sending the final feature map to the classifier module. We introduce PPM, which empirically proves to be an effective global contextual receptor. To reduce the loss of contextual information between different regions, our model separates the feature map into different sub-regions and forms pooled representation for different locations. After pooling, the feature maps of different sizes are fed into 1×1 convolution layer to reduce the dimension of context representation to $1/N$ of the original one where N represents the level size of pyramid. Then by re-sizing all low-dimension feature maps, we concatenate all to get the final global feature map (Fig. 1).

Feature Fusion Module. This section fuses the global and local feature maps to produce the final feature map. But due to lower size of global feature map, we use upsample method to scale up the resolution and then convolve both the features before final fusion. We adopt a simple addition technique like ICNet [21] and ContextNet [11] for fusion. Figure 1 shows the layer architecture of FFM.

Classifier. To assign a class to each pixel of an image, we design a classifier with two depth-wise separable convolutions (DSConv), one convolution (Conv), one upsampling and one softmax layer. DSConv not only convolves the input along all dimensions, but also reduces computational cost by reducing number of operations in convolution process. Here, we use 20 classes (including background) of the Cityscapes data set. Therefore, to generate a final output of 20 channels, we use one Conv layer followed a batch normalization and dropout layer. At last, we use softmax activation to generate final output of size $512 \times 512 \times 20$.

4   Experiment

Cityscapes Data Set. It is a large dataset for semantic understanding of urban street scenes. It consists of about 5000 fine and 20000 coarse annotated images. We used only the fine annotated images. Only the annotations for the training and validation sets are provided. We followed the standard split of the dataset.

Implementation. We conducted our experiments using a desktop computer with two Nvidia GeForce RTX 2080Ti GPU cards, each with 11GB GPU RAM. For parallel computing platform, we used CUDA 10.2. We developed our models based on tensorflow version 2.1 and keras 2.3.1. We also use the horovod framework to implement data-parallel distributed training. We set a batch size of 4 and use stochastic gradient decent (SGD) as the model optimizer with a momentum of 0.9. Inspired by [2,7,22], we use the 'poly' learning rate scheme which computes the current learning rate ($LR_{current}$) as $LR_{current} = LR_{base} \times (1 - iter/maxiter)^{power}$ where `iter` defines current iteration and `maxiter` defines maximum number of iterations in each epoch. We set LR_{base} to 0.045 and `power` to 0.9. This allow us to determine the optimal learning rate.

To overcome the limited training data, we apply various data augmentation techniques, such as random horizontal/vertical flip, random crop, re-sizing of image and many more. We use cross-entropy to calculate the model loss. Due to the limited size of physical memory of GPU cards, we use an input image size of 512×512 for training. Other existing models are also trained under the same configuration.

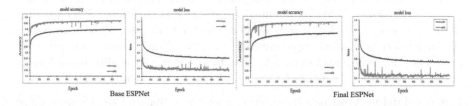

Fig. 3. Plot of model accuracy and loss

Model Evaluation. In this section, we study the performance of ESPNets on the Cityscapes data set. We consider both pixel-wise accuracy (Pi. Acc.) and mean of class-wise intersection over union (mIoU) on validation set. Figure 3 shows the performance of base and final ESPNet.

Table 2. Segmentation performance evaluation

Model	Input Size	Pi. Acc.	mIoU	Number of parameters (in Million)	Number of FLOPS (in Billion)	Train time per epoch (in Sec.)
Separable UNet	512×512	83%	29.5%	0.35	3.4	197
Bayesian SegNet	512×512	86.2%	49.4%	29.5	170.6	170
DeepLabV3+	512×512	72.9%	29.6%	37.7	33.4	53
FAST-SCNN	512×512	83.3%	43.3%	1.78	1.2	50
Base ESPNet S0	512×512	86.4%	55.1%	7.56	6.0	108
Base ESPNet S1	640×640	87.3%	58.3%	10.1	10.9	165
Base ESPNet S2	768×768	88.4%	59.5%	11.6	16.9	227
Final ESPNet	512×512	88.5%	60.8%	7.59	6.5	109

*All models are trained for 500 epochs under same system configuration.

Table 2 shows the quantitative performance of ESPNets after training all models for 500 epochs (no further improvement was observed for 1000 epochs). Here, we achieve 87.2% Pi. Acc. using base model and 88.5% Pi. Acc. using final model on the validation set. It clearly reflects that shallow branch in final model improves model performance by 1.3%. Likewise, the final model also achieves 60.8% val. mIoU which is 5.3% more than the base model mIoU. Table 2 also suggests that both proposed models provide the best overall balance between prediction time and segmentation accuracy. Whilst they are approximately as fast as FAST-SCNN, the performance in terms of mIoU is considerably superior. Note that offline training time is less critical in real-time applications.

For qualitative assessment, we generate the models' prediction on the validation and test set and show the prediction in Fig. 4. It can be seen that the edges of different objects such as car, bicycle, person, sidewalk are more accurately segmented by final ESPNet compared to baseline ESPNet. Even small tiny objects such as traffic signals are rightly detected by the final ESPNet whereas, base ESPNet misses few traffic signals.

Model Scaling. Our proposed model can be scaled up efficiently to adapt different resource constraints due to the scaling properties of EfficientNet. Doing so, we generate base ESPNet S0, S1 and S2 models which can tackle various input resolutions. Table 2 shows that S2 achieved 4.4% improvement on val. mIoU over S0 at the cost of 35% more FLOPS. Further scaling requires additional hardware resources and computational cost.

Performance Comparison. We compare the performance of some existing off-line and real-time segmentation models with ESPNets. To have a meaningful comparison among all, we trained FAST-SCNN, DeepLabV3+, Separable Unet, Bayesian SegNet under the same system configuration using 512×512px size of input. Note that the results in Table 2 are obtained after 500 epochs. Due to large size of parameters and FLOPS, DeepLabV3+ and Bayesian SegNet are used as off-line model whereas other models in Table 2 can be used for real-time computation. We replaced all standard Conv of UNet by DSConv layers to reduce computational cost, but performance of the model is still low. Comparably, FAST-SCNN performs better at full resolution whilst having less parameters. But if we compare FAST-SCNN's performance with our model under same configuration and input resolution, then both ESPNets perform better. For qualitative assessment, all models' prediction is shown in Fig. 5. The last two columns show the prediction by the proposed models. It can be seen that large objects such as road, vegetation, sky are segmented by both Separable UNet and DeepLabV3+. However, they fail to identify tiny objects such as pole, traffic lights whereas these tiny objects are not overlooked by FAST-SCNN and proposed ESPNets. Bayesian SegNet Identifies few tiny objects but fails to detect all and also unable to reconstruct few classes (e.g. sky). All these objects are correctly segmented by the ESPNets and FAST-SCNN. A closer inspection reveals that the segmentation quality of final ESPNet is better than that of FAST-SCNN: the edges of the objects are nicely segmented by final ESPNet and the appearance of tiny objects are generally sharper in the image.

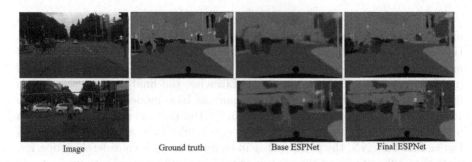

Fig. 4. Prediction by base and final ESPNet on validation (1st row) and test set (2nd row-no ground truth for test set)

Fig. 5. Prediction by all models on validation set

5   Conclusion

We have proposed efficient semantic segmentation models that provide the best overall balance for resource-constrained applications. Addition of a global pyramid prior provides rich contextual information whereas a shallow branch enriches the model performance by providing a local context. We have shown that the performance of ESPNets outperforms other competitive segmentation models. In future, we are planning to evaluate our models on other public benchmarks. Our implementation is available at https://github.com/tanmaysingha/ESPNet.

Acknowledgement. The authors would like to acknowledge Pawsey supercomputing centre for providing J. Dunstan the internship during which part of the work was done.

References

1. Badrinarayanan, V., Kendall, A., Cipolla, R.: Segnet: a deep convolutional encoder-decoder architecture for image segmentation. TPAMI **39**(12), 2481–2495 (2017)
2. Chen, L.C., Papandreou, G., Kokkinos, I., Murphy, K., Yuille, A.L.: Deeplab: semantic image segmentation with deep convolutional nets, atrous convolution, and fully connected crfs. TPAMI **40**(4), 834–848 (2017)
3. Chen, L.C., Zhu, Y., Papandreou, G., Schroff, F., Adam, H.: Encoder-decoder with atrous separable convolution for semantic image segmentation. In: Proceedings of ICCV, September 2018
4. Cordts, M., et al.: The cityscapes dataset for semantic urban scene understanding. In: Proceedings of CVPR, June 2016

5. He, K., Zhang, X., Ren, S., Sun, J.: Spatial pyramid pooling in deep convolutional networks for visual recognition. TPAMI **37**(9), 1904–1916 (2015)
6. He, K., Zhang, X., Ren, S., Sun, J.: Deep residual learning for image recognition. In: Proceedings of CVPR, June 2016
7. Howard, A.G., et al.: Mobilenets: efficient convolutional neural networks for mobile vision applications. arXiv preprint arXiv:1704.04861 (2017)
8. Hu, J., Shen, L., Sun, G.: Squeeze-and-excitation networks. In: Proceedings of CVPR, June 2018
9. Kendall, A., Badrinarayanan, V., Cipolla, R.: Bayesian segnet: model uncertainty in deep convolutional encoder-decoder architectures for scene understanding. arXiv preprint arXiv:1511.02680 (2015)
10. Paszke, A., Chaurasia, A., Kim, S., Culurciello, E.: Enet: a deep neural network architecture for real-time semantic segmentation. arXiv preprint arXiv:1606.02147 (2016)
11. Poudel, R.P., Bonde, U., Liwicki, S., Zach, C.: Contextnet: exploring context and detail for semantic segmentation in real-time. arXiv preprint arXiv:1805.04554 (2018)
12. Poudel, R.P., Liwicki, S., Cipolla, R.: Fast-scnn: fast semantic segmentation network. arXiv preprint arXiv:1902.04502 (2019)
13. Ronneberger, O., Fischer, P., Brox, T.: U-Net: convolutional networks for biomedical image segmentation. In: Navab, N., Hornegger, J., Wells, W.M., Frangi, A.F. (eds.) MICCAI 2015. LNCS, vol. 9351, pp. 234–241. Springer, Cham (2015). https://doi.org/10.1007/978-3-319-24574-4_28
14. Sandler, M., Howard, A., Zhu, M., Zhmoginov, A., Chen, L.C.: Mobilenetv 2: inverted residuals and linear bottlenecks. In: Proceedings of CVPR (June 2018)
15. Shang, Y., Zhong, S., Gong, S., Zhou, L., Ying, W.: DXNet: an encoder-decoder architecture with XSPP for semantic image segmentation in street scenes. In: Gedeon, T., Wong, K.W., Lee, M. (eds.) ICONIP 2019. CCIS, vol. 1143, pp. 550–557. Springer, Cham (2019). https://doi.org/10.1007/978-3-030-36802-9_59
16. Shelhamer, E., Long, J., Darrell, T.: Fully convolutional networks for semantic segmentation. TPAMI **39**(4), 640–651 (2017)
17. Simonyan, K., Zisserman, A.: Very deep convolutional networks for large-scale image recognition. arXiv preprint arXiv:1409.1556 (2014)
18. Tan, M., Le, Q.V.: Efficientnet: Rethinking model scaling for convolutional neural networks. arXiv preprint arXiv:1905.11946 (2019)
19. Targ, S., Almeida, D., Lyman, K.: Resnet in resnet: generalizing residual architectures. arXiv preprint arXiv:1603.08029 (2016)
20. Yang, M., Shi, Y.: DSMRSeg: dual-stage feature pyramid and multi-range context aggregation for real-time semantic Segmentation. In: Gedeon, T., Wong, K.W., Lee, M. (eds.) ICONIP 2019. CCIS, vol. 1142, pp. 265–273. Springer, Cham (2019). https://doi.org/10.1007/978-3-030-36808-1_29
21. Zhao, H., Qi, X., Shen, X., Shi, J., Jia, J.: ICNet for real-time semantic segmentation on high-resolution images. In: Proceedings of ECCV, September 2018
22. Zhao, H., Shi, J., Qi, X., Wang, X., Jia, J.: Pyramid scene parsing network. In: Proceedings of CVPR, July 2017

EMOTIONCAPS - Facial Emotion Recognition Using Capsules

Bhavya Shah[1], Krutarth Bhatt[1], Srimanta Mandal[2(✉)], and Suman K. Mitra[2]

[1] Institute of Technology, Nirma University, Ahmedabad, Gujarat, India
shahbhavyan12@gmail.com, krutarthbhatt.ml@gmail.com
[2] DA-IICT, Gandhinagar, Gujarat, India
{srimanta_mandal,suman_mitra}@daiict.ac.in

Abstract. Facial emotion recognition plays an important role in day-to-day activities. To address this, we propose a novel encoder/decoder network namely EmotionCaps, which models the facial images using matrix capsules, where hierarchical pose relationships between facial parts are built into internal representations. An optimal number of capsules and their dimension is chosen, as these hyper-parameters in the network play an important role to capture the complex facial pose relationship. Further, the batch normalization layer is introduced to expedite the convergence. To show the effectiveness of our network, EmotionCaps is evaluated for seven basic emotions in a wide range of head orientations. Additionally, our method is able to analyze facial images even in the presence of noise and blur quite accurately.

Keywords: Emotion recognition · Capsule networks · Batch-normalization

1 Introduction

Facial emotion recognition aims to classify human emotions like anger, fear, happy, sad, etc., based on expressions of faces. It has several real-world applications in the field of security, medical diagnosis, monitoring, and entertainment [5,23,24]. Several deep learning-based approaches [2,14,16,18] extract key features from the face for emotion classification. The performance is directly dependent on the extent of feature extraction. In classical approaches, feature extraction relies upon handcrafted techniques like Haar-cascade [20], histogram of oriented gradients [4] and Fisher method [10]. Such methods work efficiently for datasets with minimal occlusions. Images with partial faces, eyeglasses or other objects covering the face, are the possible challenges for these methods.

With the successful emergence of convolutional neural networks (CNNs) for several computer vision problems, several works model a variety of CNN architectures [9] to detect emotions. CNN is capable of automated feature extraction that captures all possible complex non-linear interactions among features. Some works [2,14,16,18] have shown the promising capabilities of CNNs for emotion

© Springer Nature Switzerland AG 2020
H. Yang et al. (Eds.): ICONIP 2020, CCIS 1332, pp. 394–401, 2020.
https://doi.org/10.1007/978-3-030-63820-7_45

classification. Some approaches focus on building feature extractors and on generating novel classifiers for emotion detection [1,2,14–16,21,22]. [18] replaces the softmax layer at the end of the deep learning model with support vector machine to exceed the fine-tuning of the lower level features. [2] reduces the number of parameters of the convolutional network by eliminating the fully connected layers and introducing depth-wise separable convolutions and residual modules. [14] uses attention based ten layered CNN architecture to capture specific facial regions, important for emotion detection. Attention has been captured via spatial transformer network which consists of two convolution layers (each followed by max-pooling and ReLU [1]), and two fully-connected layers. Authors of [16] address the emotion detection task by forming an ensemble of eight modern deep CNNs without requiring an auxiliary training data to achieve substantial performance improvement. More related works can be found in [6,11–13,19].

However, an internal data representation of a CNN does not take into account important spatial hierarchies between simple and complex objects and thus cannot achieve rotational invariance. Nevertheless, in facial emotion recognition, a face image can be translated or/and rotated. The MaxPooling layer in CNN notes the presence of a part, but not the spatial relation between the parts. Thus, the pose relationship between simpler features that make up a higher-level feature is absent. However, this relationship plays an important role in building strong high-level features that further aid the classification. The objective is to propose a network that can model hierarchical relationships of an image.

We propose an architecture based on capsule network, which was originally proposed in [17] to address the issues faced by CNNs like the inability to achieve translational and rotational invariance through the use of modified capsules. Capsules represent all the important information about the state of features in the form of a vector whose length represents the probability of detection of a feature and direction represents the state of the detected features. When detected feature moves around the image or its state somehow changes, the probability still stays the same as the length of a vector does not change, thus becoming pose invariant. Dynamic routing along with the reconstruction strategy in the capsule network helps in building a model that is invariant to rotation and can capture spatial hierarchy. We propose some vital changes to the architecture in [17]. The dimensionality of the capsule layers as well as their numbers are modified for encoding a large number of complex facial features along with their pose relationship. We introduce the batch-normalization layer in the network after activation, which leads to faster convergence of the model as compared to the conventional way of using batch normalization before activation as in [7].

2   Proposed Method

The overview of the architecture is shown in Fig. 1. The model is motivated by the shallow capsule network proposed in [17]. The network has a simple encoder/decoder architecture. The encoder takes in the input image and encodes it into a vector of instantiation parameters as capsules, which are then fed to the decoder that uses several fully connected layers for reconstruction.

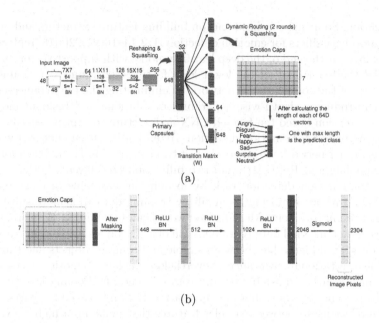

Fig. 1. Architecture of the proposed model: (a) The encoder network encodes the input image into a vector of pose parameters; (b) Decoder network uses this vector output to reconstruct the original image.

The design of encoder and decoder represents the first technical contribution of this work. As shown in Fig. 1(a), we use several convolution (CONV) layers at the beginning of our encoder to extract discriminative high-level features. The input layer is followed by two CONV blocks consisting of a single convolution layer whose output is fed into the ReLU activation function followed by the batch normalization layer. The first block is characterized by a CONV layer of 64 filters with kernel size as (7, 7) with a stride of (1, 1) and no padding. The second block uses a CONV layer with 128 filters of kernel size (11, 11) with a stride of (1, 1). The output of the second CONV block is fed to the primary capsules. The primary capsule is a convolutional capsule that begins with a CONV layer of 256 filters with kernel size (15, 15) and a stride of (2, 2) followed by the ReLU activation function and batch normalization. The obtained feature map is reshaped to (648, 1, 32) vector which is fed to 648 capsules to produce separate vector output of 32 dimension.

Capsules encapsulate information about the state of the features (size, orientation, etc.) in the form of a vector as compared to the scalar outputs of artificial neurons. The dimensions of these layers are carefully chosen to capture complex pose relationship that plays a crucial role in recognition. Length of each of the 648 output vectors is scaled to [0, 1] using a squashing function:

$$\mathbf{v}_j = \frac{||\mathbf{x}_j||^2}{1 + ||\mathbf{x}_j||^2} \cdot \frac{\mathbf{x}_j}{||\mathbf{x}_j||}, \tag{1}$$

where $\mathbf{v}_j$ is the vector output of capsule j and $\mathbf{x}_j$ is the input to j^{th} capsule. Note that, our architecture performs squashing twice. In the first case, $\mathbf{x}_j$ is 32 dimensional vector and in the second case, it's dimension becomes 64. The length of $\mathbf{v}_j$ denotes the probability of detection of features and the orientation of $\mathbf{v}_j$ denotes the internal state of the detected features. By considering the output vector of the first squashing operation as $\mathbf{u}_i$, we multiply it by a weight transformation matrix $\mathbf{W}$ to encode the important relative spatial relationship between the lower and higher-level facial features. $\hat{\mathbf{u}}_{j|i} = \mathbf{W}_{ij}\mathbf{u}_i$, where $\hat{\mathbf{u}}_{j|i}$ are the predicted vectors from capsule i (output of primary caps layer), which is obtained by multiplying the output $\mathbf{u}_i$ of a capsule in the layer below by $\mathbf{W}_{ij}$ that encodes the spatial relationship between capsule i in the lower level and capsule j at a layer above. During training, the network gradually learns $\mathbf{W}$ for each pair of capsules in lower and higher layers. The structure of $\mathbf{W}$ is such that it captures part-to-whole relationships between different objects in the image. All the predicted vectors $\hat{\mathbf{u}}_{j|i}$ are then combined with coupling coefficients c_{ij} to produce the total input for the next layer.

$$\mathbf{x}_j = \sum_i c_{ij}\hat{\mathbf{u}}_{j|i} \text{ where, } c_{ij} = \frac{exp(b_{ij})}{\sum_k exp(b_{ik})}. \tag{2}$$

c_{ij} incorporates the directional information used to route capsules between higher layers. Routing is done through the iterative dynamic routing algorithm [17] which considers simple agreement between lower and higher level capsule directions via softmax function. b_{ij} are the log prior probabilities for coupling between capsule i in the lower level and capsule j at a layer above. Initially, b_{ij} is set to 0 and with iterative dynamic routing process c_{ij} is estimated.

After the routing process, a 64-dimensional vector is generated. In the low-level capsules (primary caps layer), the location information is 'place coded' into active capsules. Moving to the higher-level capsules a certain shift from place coding to rate coding is seen because they represent complex entities with higher degrees of freedom. The problem requires careful analysis of numerous extracted features so we increase the dimensionality of higher-level capsules for efficient representation of such complex facial entities. At the end of the encoder, after applying the squashing function on the output vectors, the vector with maximum length becomes the final predicted class. The encoder loss L_c for class c is calculated as in [17] and the total margin loss obtained from all emotion classes is calculated as $L^M = \sum_c L_c$.

The decoder consists of deconvolutional layers that utilize the instantiation parameters of the 64D vector from the correct EmotionCaps capsule to reconstruct the input image. During training, only the capsule which corresponds to the correct emotion label is used for reconstruction while the others are masked with zero. While at the time of testing the capsule of the predicted class is used for reconstruction with all the others being masked with zero. The decoder network is used as a regularizer for capsule network. The network as shown in Fig. 1(b) comprises of four fully connected layers of dimension $448 \rightarrow 512 \rightarrow 1024 \rightarrow 2048 \rightarrow 2304$. The output of the last layer is reshaped to

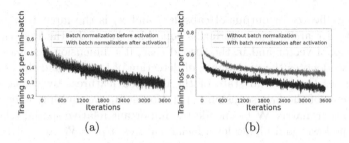

(a)   (b)

Fig. 2. Convergence rate: (a) with batch normalization layer before and after applying activation; (b) with and without considering the batch normalization layer (Color figure online)

the original image size (48 × 48). The decoder network is supervised by calculating the MSE loss (L^R). Since the architecture classifies an emotion class and reconstructs the input image, it is optimized with total loss $L^T = L^M + \alpha L^R$, where, L^R is the reconstruction loss (MSE), and L^M is the margin loss. $\alpha < 1$ ensures that margin loss dominates training.

2.1   Batch Normalization After Activation

The idea behind using batch normalization (BN) [7] is to address internal covariant shift (ICS) that arises when the input distribution to the layers of the neural network fluctuates. The BN layer helps the optimization algorithm to control the mean and variance of the output of the layer to overcome ICS. The BN layer normalizes the output activations y_i for layer i as $y_i = \gamma \hat{x}_i + \beta$. Here, γ and β are the hyper-parameters of the BN layer and $\hat{x}_i$ is the input data. The output of BN layer has a mean of β and a standard deviation of γ. These two hyper-parameters can control the statistics of a layer.

To gain a deeper insight into using the BN layer after activation function, we show the convergence rate graphs for the cases of using BN before (red color) and after the activation function (blue color) in Fig. 2(a). This suggests that the proposed usage of the BN layer leads to a faster convergence, as compared to the method [7], where BN has been applied before the activation. In the latter case, the BN layer cannot fully control the statistics of the input going into the next layer as the output of the batch norm layer has to go through an activation, whereas in the first case BN layer can control.

3   Experimental Results

We evaluate the proposed model on the Facial Expression Recognition 2013 (FER-2013) database [3] which contains grayscale images of 48 × 48 dimensions. The database contains a total of 35,887 labeled side and front face images of six basic expressions as well as the neutral expression. After random shuffling of the data, we use the first 29000 images for training and the remaining images

Table 1. Emotion recognition on FER-2013.   **Table 2.** Precision, recall and F1-score

Model	Accuracy
CapsNet [17]	47.17%
Arriaga et al. [2]	66.00%
Minaee et al. [14]	70.02%
Tang [18]	71.16%
Pramerdorfer et al. [16]	75.2%
CapsNet (Dimensional changes + no BN)	52.71%
EmotionCaps (Proposed Model)	**78.84%**

Emotion	Precision	Recall	F1-score
Angry	0.88	0.68	0.77
Disgust	1.00	0.35	0.52
Fear	0.92	0.61	0.73
Happy	0.72	0.95	0.82
Sad	0.80	0.76	0.78
Surprise	0.82	0.85	0.84
Neutral	0.76	0.81	0.79

for testing. We implement the network in PyTorch, where the model has been trained for 10 epochs at the learning rate of $5e-6$ with Adam optimizer. [8]. Two routing-by-agreement iterations were considered for this task. The model training can converge within 25 min with a single Tesla K80 GPU.

Table 1 lists the comparison of performances of different approaches [2, 14, 16–18], which consider FER-2013 dataset [3], with our proposed model. Our model produces average accuracy of 78.84% for five-fold validation. Observe that the proposed model outperforms all the existing models. Most of the approaches considered here for comparison are based on CNN and they fail to capture the pose relationships in the image. The proposed model encodes the spatial pose relationships of an image using capsules, as is the case for original CapsNet architecture [17], which we run on the dataset without any modification (the result of the 1st row) and after considering dimensional changes (result of the second last row). The improvement suggests that not only the capsules are important but their number and dimensions along with position of BN layer are very crucial for the task of emotion recognition. In Table 2 we share the precision, recall and F1-score values for each emotion class separately. From Table 2 we can infer that changes in F1-score of different emotions are small. This verifies the unbiased nature of our model across different emotions. The reconstructed images from the 64D output of the EmotionCaps are illustrated in Fig. 3(a) (second column). This is done to examine the efficiency of the encoder in encoding the internal pose parameters of the detected features. To further understand what the individual dimensions of 64D output vector has learned, we perturb only the 16D of vector of the output capsule and then reconstruct the image from this perturbed vector. The reconstructed images from the perturbed vectors are shown in columns 3–6. One can observe that different sets of dimensions reflect distinct facial features. Thus, we can infer that individual dimensions of corresponding emotion capsules are able to represent disparities in instantiation parameters such as facial attributes (intensity of eyes and mouth), head pose, etc.

BN layer which helps in overcoming the problem of ICS as proposed in [7] plays a key role in the model. As shown in Fig. 2(b), experiments performed without considering the use of BN results in a slower convergence rate as com-

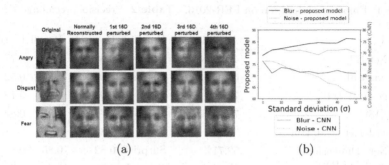

(a)   (b)

Fig. 3. Results Analysis: (a) The results of reconstruction using 64D and by perturbing different sets of 16D of activity vectors of emotion capsules; (b) Performance on Gaussian blurred and noisy images for different σ.

pared to the case where the batch normalization layer is used. This strengthens the aptness of BN layer in the model.

To measure the robustness of our model, several experiments are performed by introducing Gaussian blur and noise separately in the images. For the blur, the Gaussian kernel of size (5,5) is convolved with the images keeping the kernel standard deviation σ variable. Gaussian noise with different σ is added uniformly to the entire image. A comparison between the performance of our model and [2] on varying σ is shown in Fig. 3(b). One can observe that the proposed model works better than the CNN-based model in presence of blur and noise. Further, the performance does not degrade much with the increment of noise and blur strength. This behavior reflects the robustness of our method for facial emotion recognition. The reason behind considering the degradation in the system is that in a practical scenario, the imaging system often induces blur and noise into the image while capturing a facial image.

4   Conclusion

We proposed a novel capsule network-based facial emotion recognition model that uses an encoder/decoder architecture for emotion recognition. Experimental results show an upsurge in the accuracy compared to the existing methods. The results also demonstrated the significance of choosing the optimal number and dimensions of the layers. The suitable use of batch normalization and its effects have been depicted. Robustness of the model to blurring and noise has also been analyzed. This can be helpful for deploying such a model in real-world scenario.

References

1. Abien Fred, M.A.: Deep learning using rectified linear units (ReLU). Neural Evol. Comput. **1**, 7 p. (2018)
2. Arriaga, O., Valdenegro, M., Plöger, P.: Real-time convolutional neural networks for emotion and gender classification. In: ESANN, pp. 221–226 (2019)

3. Carrier, P.L., Courville, A., Goodfellow, I.J., Mirza, M., Bengio, Y.: Fer-2013 face database. Technical report (2013)
4. Dalal, N., Triggs, B.: Histograms of oriented gradients for human detection. In: CVPR, vol. 1, pp. 886–893 (2005)
5. Fasel, B., Luettin, J.: Automatic facial expression analysis: a survey. Pattern Recogn. **36**(1), 259–275 (2003)
6. Hosseini, S., Cho, N.I.: Gf-CapsNet: Using Gabor jet and capsule networks for facial age, gender, and expression recognition. In: FG, pp. 1–8 (2019)
7. Ioffe, S., Szegedy, C.: Batch normalization: accelerating deep network training by reducing internal covariate shift. In: ICML, ICML 2015, vol. 37, pp. 448–456. JMLR.org (2015)
8. Kingma, D.P., Ba, J.: Adam: a method for stochastic optimization (2014)
9. Ko, B.C.: A brief review of facial emotion recognition based on visual information. Sensors **18**(2), 401 (2018)
10. Liu, C., Wechsler, H.: Gabor feature based classification using the enhanced fisher linear discriminant model for face recognition. IEEE TIP **11**(4), 467–476 (2002)
11. Liu, P., Han, S., Meng, Z., Tong, Y.: Facial expression recognition via a boosted deep belief network. In: CVPR, pp. 1805–1812 (2014)
12. Lopes, A.T., de Aguiar, E., Souza, A.F.D., Oliveira-Santos, T.: Facial expression recognition with convolutional neural networks: coping with few data and the training sample order. Pattern Recogn. **61**, 610–628 (2017)
13. Marrero Fernandez, P.D., Guerrero Pena, F.A., Ing Ren, T., Cunha, A.: FERAtt: facial expression recognition with attention net. In: CVPR Workshops, pp. 1–10 (2019)
14. Minaee, S., Abdolrashidi, A.: Deep-emotion: facial expression recognition using attentional convolutional network. CoRR abs/1902.01019 (2019)
15. Mollahosseini, A., Chan, D., Mahoor, M.H.: Going deeper in facial expression recognition using deep neural networks. In: WACV, pp. 1–10 (2016)
16. Pramerdorfer, C., Kampel, M.: Facial expression recognition using convolutional neural networks:state of the art. CoRR abs/1612.02903 (2016)
17. Sabour, S., Frosst, N., Hinton, G.E.: Dynamic routing between capsules. In: NIPS, pp. 3856–3866 (2017)
18. Tang, Y.: Deep learning using linear support vector machines. In: ICML, pp. 1–6 (2013)
19. Tariq, U., Yang, J., Huang, T.S.: Multi-view facial expression recognition analysis with generic sparse coding feature. In: Fusiello, A., Murino, V., Cucchiara, R. (eds.) ECCV 2012. LNCS, vol. 7585, pp. 578–588. Springer, Heidelberg (2012). https://doi.org/10.1007/978-3-642-33885-4_58
20. Viola, P., Jones, M., et al.: Rapid object detection using a boosted cascade of simple features. In: CVPR(1), vol. 1, no. 511–518, p. 3 (2001)
21. Yu, Z., Zhang, C.: Image based static facial expression recognition with multiple deep network learning. In: ICMI, ICMI 2015, pp. 435–442. ACM, New York (2015)
22. Zeng, N., Zhang, H., Song, B., Liu, W., Li, Y., Dobaie, A.M.: Facial expression recognition via learning deep sparse autoencoders. Neurocomputing **273**, 643–649 (2018)
23. Zhang, F., Zhang, T., Mao, Q., Xu, C.: Joint pose and expression modeling for facial expression recognition. In: CVPR, pp. 3359–3368 (2018)
24. Zhang, T., Zheng, W., Cui, Z., Zong, Y., Yan, J., Yan, K.: A deep neural network-driven feature learning method for multi-view facial expression recognition. IEEE Trans. Multimed. **18**(12), 2528–2536 (2016)

End-to-end Saliency-Guided Deep Image Retrieval

Jinyu Ma and Xiaodong Gu[✉]

Department of Electronic Engineering, Fudan University, Shanghai 200433, China
xdgu@fudan.edu.cn

Abstract. A challenging issue of content-based image retrieval (CBIR) is to distinguish the target object from cluttered backgrounds, resulting in more discriminative image embeddings, compared to situations where feature extraction is distracted by irrelevant objects. To handle the issue, we propose a saliency-guided model with deep image features. The model is fully based on convolution neural networks (CNNs) and it incorporates a visual saliency detection module, making saliency detection a preceding step of feature extraction. The resulted saliency maps are utilized to refine original inputs and then compatible image features suitable for ranking are extracted from refined inputs. The model suggests a working scheme of involving saliency information into existing CNN-based CBIR systems with minimum impacts on the them. Some work assist image retrieval with other methods like object detection or semantic segmentation, but they are not so fine-grained as saliency detection, meanwhile some of them require additional annotations to train. In contrast, we train the saliency module in weak-supervised end-to-end style and do not need saliency ground truth. Extensive experiments are conducted on standard image retrieval benchmarks and our model shows competitive retrieval results.

Keywords: Content-based image retrieval · Saliency detection · Convolutional neural network · Weak-supervised

1 Introduction

The technology of content-based image retrieval (CBIR) has been attracting research interest due to the explosive increase of visual data from the internet and smart devices. Given a query image and an image database, CBIR returns database images ordered by their similarities with the query image.

CBIR systems usually start with representation learning, followed by image scoring and indexing, at last a search re-ranking can be performed. Quality of image representations is critical as it directly affects subsequent processes. Early work explores to represent images with hand-crafted features, either global ones [20] or local ones aggregated by BOW [12], VLAD [6] and Fisher Vector [5] etc. Since great success of CNN, deep features have been extensively explored for their impressive capability of discrimination and generalization. [13,14] propose

© Springer Nature Switzerland AG 2020
H. Yang et al. (Eds.): ICONIP 2020, CCIS 1332, pp. 402–409, 2020.
https://doi.org/10.1007/978-3-030-63820-7_46

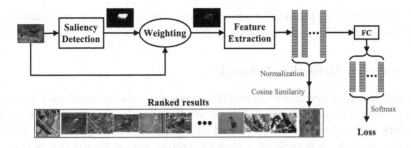

Fig. 1. Overview of the proposed SGDIR model.

different global pooling strategies as feature aggregation approaches. To make use of spatial information, [16] and [2] performs regional pooling and then aggregate local features into global ones. [9,10] incorporates attention mechanism in pooling to rule out interference of background noises.

Saliency detection is a fundamental task that helps with rapid discovering of informative and attractive parts from vision. In image retrieval, query images may contain more than what users want and retrieval with visual saliency tackles such problem by taking into account the semantic information of images. Given that, we propose a saliency-guided deep image retrieval model (SGDIR) in this paper. It extracts image features under guidance of predicted saliency maps and operates in an end-to-end manner. Saliency module of SGDIR will get trained along with the whole model and saliency ground truth is not required. Furthermore, the success of our model suggests a uniform scheme of involving saliency into CBIR, i.e. saliency detection networks can work as plug-and-play modules to assist existing CBIR models without additional structural modifications. Previous work like [1,17] has explored image retrieval with saliency, but they use hand-crafted features and rely on elaborately designed models.

We next illustrate the proposed SGDIR model in Sect. 2. Section 3 presents experiments conducted on different benchmarks. Finally, a brief conclusion of the paper is given in Sect. 4.

2   Proposed Approach

2.1   Overview

Figure 1 illustrates the overall structure of SGDIR. A network responsible for saliency detection is modularized as the first component of SGDIR. It takes in an image and generates a saliency map. Then, the original image is masked by its saliency map in a saliency-guided weighting module. Pixel values are adjusted according to the saliency value in corresponding spatial location. After that, the masked image is sent to feature extraction module, which is also a modularized network. Finally, it outputs a feature vector. For training, the feature will forward through a fully-connected layer that serves as classifier and a loss is then computed for optimization. For ranking, the feature is $l2$-normalized and pair-wise similarities are computed.

2.2 Saliency Detection Network

The saliency detection model in SGDIR serves as a relatively independent module and there is no need to refactor it, therefore, general saliency detection models will work. We choose a recent advanced model named PoolNet [8] as our saliency detection module. It is built on a U-shape architecture designed in a bottom-up and top-down manner, which shows strong ability to combine multi-level features. It is beyond the scope of this article to introduce this model in detail, yet it is suitable to embed the PoolNet in our model like a black box, of which only the input and output are parts of interest. It works end-to-end, i.e., when fed with natural images, it directly outputs saliency maps and does not need separate pre-processing or post-processing.

2.3 Saliency-Guided Weighting

The process of masking the original input by saliency map is named saliency-guided weighting. Let tensor $x \in \mathbb{R}^{H \times W \times C}$ be an input image where H, W, C are height, width and channel number, respectively, and function $S_\theta (\cdot)$ be the mapping of the whole PoolNet with parameter θ. The detected saliency map is represented as $S_\theta (x) \in \mathbb{R}^{H \times W \times 1}$. $S_\theta (\cdot)$ ends up with a sigmoid function, so pixel values of the saliency map ranges in $(0, 1)$. Then, saliency mask is given by:

$$m = (1 - \sigma) S_\theta (x) + \sigma, \tag{1}$$

where $\sigma \in (0, 1)$ is a hyperparameter to control the degree of weighting. Sometimes target objects are too small and most mask values are zero, which can cause abnormal statistics of masked images. By carefully setting the value of σ, mask values are clamped to no less than σ. Finally, masked image is given by:

$$x_m = x \circ m, \tag{2}$$

where the symbol $\circ$ represents element-wise-like production, i.e., C elements in a spatial location of x are respectively multiplied by the corresponding element in m.

Denote the final loss as L, gradient of parameter θ can be derived by chain rule as:

$$
\begin{aligned}
\frac{\partial L}{\partial \theta} &= \frac{\partial L}{\partial x_m} \cdot \frac{\partial x_m}{\partial m} \cdot \frac{\partial m}{\partial S_\theta (x)} \cdot \frac{\partial S_\theta (x)}{\partial \theta} \\
&= \frac{\partial L}{\partial x_m} \cdot x \cdot (1 - \sigma) \cdot \frac{\partial S_\theta (x)}{\partial \theta}.
\end{aligned} \tag{3}
$$

Given that cross entropy loss, feature extraction model and PoolNet is differentiable, parameter θ is trainable using end-to-end manner through backpropagation. The training process is weak supervised as we do not annotate saliency

Table 1. Datasets for training and testing.

Name	Total	Training	Testing	Categories
CUB-200-2011	11788	5994	5794	200
cars196	16185	8144	8041	196
flower102	6149	1020	6149	102

ground truth as training targets. Instead, since maximizing the accuracy of attention maps is consistent with maximizing retrieval accuracy, the attention block is directly trained with retrieval net together.

2.4 Representation Training

We adopt popular VGG16 and ResNet50 as feature extraction backbones. Outputs of them will be forwarded through softmax, then cross entropy losses are computed. In testing, outputs of classifiers are ignored and we instead use inputs of classifiers and normalize them.

3 Experiments

3.1 Experiment Settings

Implementation Details. We load pre-trained PoolNet model offered by its author, and pre-trained VGG16 and ResNet50 from ImageNet (except the last fully-connected layers, which are randomly initialized). Hyperparameter σ is set to 0.5. In each run we train 90 epochs with batch size of 8 using Adam optimizer. Initial learning rate is 10^{-5} and it decreases by a factor of 10 when reaching 1/3 and 2/3 of maximum number of epochs.

Datasets and Metrics. Experiments are carried out on three image retrieval datasets: CUB-200-2011, cars196 and flower102. Statistics of them are shown in Table 1. We adopt mAP and recall@k as evaluation metric. mAP is the mean value of average precisions over all queries. Recall@k is the mean value over individual recalls considering top k results.

3.2 Comparisons with Other Methods

Table 2 shows comparisons of retrieval results on CUB-200-2011 and flower102 in mAP. CroW aggregates deep convolutional features with cross-dimensional weighting. Selective is based on selective deep convolutional features. MAC parallelize a main stream and an auxiliary saliency detection stream and fuse their activation maps. Among them, SGDIR achieves the highest mAP on both datasets. In particular, SGDIR outperforms MAC, another saliency incorporated

406   J. Ma and X. Gu

Table 2. Retrieval results on CUB-200-2011 and flower102 in mAP metric. The best result for each dataset is in **bold**.

	Backbone	CUB-200-2011	flower102
CroW [7]	VGG16	0.15	0.34
Selective [4]	VGG16	0.05	0.40
MAC [18]	VGG16	0.28	0.59
*SGDIR	VGG16	**0.48**	**0.62**

Table 3. Retrieval results on CUB-200-2011 and cars196 in recall@k metric. The best result for each column is in **bold**, and the second best one is in *italic*.

	Backbone	CUB-200-2011				cars196			
		R@1	R@2	R@4	R@8	R@1	R@2	R@4	R@8
SCDA [19]	VGG16	0.622	0.742	0.832	0.901	0.585	0.698	0.791	0.862
CRL-WSL [21]	VGG16	0.659	0.765	0.853	0.903	0.639	0.737	0.821	0.892
LiftedStruct [11]	Inception	0.472	0.589	0.702	0.802	0.490	0.603	0.721	0.815
N-pairs [15]	Inception	0.510	0.633	0.743	0.832	0.711	0.797	0.865	0.916
A^3M [3]	Inception	0.612	0.724	0.818	0.892	0.800	*0.875*	*0.923*	*0.955*
DGCRL [22]	ResNet50	0.679	0.791	*0.862*	**0.918**	*0.759*	0.839	0.897	0.940
*SGDIR	VGG16	*0.702*	*0.793*	**0.867**	0.913	0.755	0.843	0.902	0.940
*SGDIR	ResNet50	**0.706**	**0.797**	**0.867**	*0.915*	**0.824**	**0.886**	**0.932**	**0.960**

weighting approach. In MAC, feature extraction and saliency detection are parallelized. In order to fuse output features of two streams, shape of them should be identical, thus MAC is defected in terms of flexibility when construct model. In contrast, SGDIR finds no necessity to consider dimensions of intermediate features. It picks an advanced saliency detection model and directly install it in a loosely coupled way.

Table 3 presents a comparison of retrieval results on CUB-200-2011 and cars196 in recall@k. SCDA proposes unsupervised learning that employs network saliency to generate discriminative features. CRL-WSL, LiftedStruct and N-pairs are metric learning methods with pair-wise ranking loss. A^3M trains an attribute-category reciprocal to help with key feature selection. DGCRL proposes to use decorrelated global centralized loss with normalize-scale layer. Although different backbones are used in different methods, SGDIR with VGG16 outperforms most methods, even some with deeper backbones. SGDIR with ResNet50 achieves the highest recall rate in 7 of the 8 columns.

3.3 Contribution of Saliency

Table 4 presents improvements of mAP on three datasets when saliency detection is enabled. Figure 2 shows that of recalls. From the results, saliency information does boost image retrieval performance, either simply combining it with off-the-shelf models or further training them. Also, such saliency-involving scheme will benefit both VGG16 and ResNet50, which suggests it may be widely applicable to various architectures as a handy and effective plug-in. There is an exception, that is, off-the-shelf ResNet50 downgrades performance when saliency detection is enabled. Nevertheless, after fine-tuning, the performance gets back to normal.

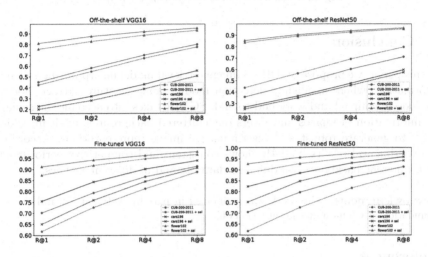

Fig. 2. Comparisons of recalls on three datasets when with or without saliency detection.

Table 4. Comparisons of mAPs on three datasets when with or without saliency detection.

		mAP w/o. → w. saliency		
		CUB-200-2011	cars196	flower102
Off-the-Shelf	VGG16	0.191 → 0.215	0.047 → 0.055	0.341 → 0.388
	ResNet50	0.185 → 0.127	0.055 → 0.057	0.415 → 0.428
Fine-tuned	VGG16	0.382 → 0.475	0.311 → 0.433	0.559 → 0.622
	ResNet50	0.361 → 0.475	0.403 → 0.467	0.547 → 0.621

3.4 Visualization of Saliency Maps

Figure 3 shows 6 groups of images, each includes an original image, a detected saliency map and a masked image. From images, cluttered backgrounds are basically blacked out.

Fig. 3. Visualization of detected saliency maps.

4 Conclusion

In this paper, we propose SGDIR, a image retrieval model incorporating saliency information, where a saliency detection module and a feature extract module are loosely coupled and work end-to-end. SGDIR takes into account the semantic information of images and filters out cluttered backgrounds in them, which helps to generate robust and discriminative image representations. According to experimental results, SGDIR shows consistent and competitive performance with different backbones, on different datasets and in different metrics.

Acknowledgments. This work was supported in part by National Natural Science Foundation of China under grant 61771145.

References

1. Bai, C., Chen, J., Huang, L., Kpalma, K., Chen, S.: Saliency-based multi-feature modeling for semantic image retrieval. J. Vis. Commun. Image Represent. **50**, 199–204 (2018). https://doi.org/10.1016/j.jvcir.2017.11.021
2. Gordo, A., Almazan, J., Revaud, J., Larlus, D.: End-to-end learning of deep visual representations for image retrieval. Int. J. Comput. Vis. **124**(2), 237–254 (2017). https://doi.org/10.1007/s11263-017-1016-8
3. Han, K., Guo, J., Zhang, C., Zhu, M.: Attribute-aware attention model for fine-grained representation learning. In: Proceedings of the 26th ACM International Conference on Multimedia, pp. 2040–2048 (2018)
4. Hoang, T., Do, T.T., Le Tan, D.K., Cheung, N.M.: Selective deep convolutional features for image retrieval. In: Proceedings of the 25th ACM International Conference on Multimedia, pp. 1600–1608 (2017)
5. Jegou, H., Perronnin, F., Douze, M., Sanchez, J., Perez, P., Schmid, C.: Aggregating local image descriptors into compact codes. IEEE Trans. Pattern Anal. Mach. Intell. **34**(9), 1704–1716 (2012). https://doi.org/10.1109/TPAMI.2011.235
6. Jégou, H., Douze, M., Schmid, C., Pérez, P.: Aggregating local descriptors into a compact image representation. In: CVPR 2010–23rd IEEE Conference on Computer Vision & Pattern Recognition, pp. 3304–3311. IEEE Computer Society (2010)
7. Kalantidis, Y., Mellina, C., Osindero, S.: Cross-dimensional weighting for aggregated deep convolutional features. In: Hua, G., Jégou, H. (eds.) ECCV 2016. LNCS, vol. 9913, pp. 685–701. Springer, Cham (2016). https://doi.org/10.1007/978-3-319-46604-0_48

8. Liu, J.J., Hou, Q., Cheng, M.M., Feng, J., Jiang, J.: A simple pooling-based design for real-time salient object detection. arXiv:1904.09569 [cs] (2019)
9. Ma, J., Gu, X.: Scene image retrieval with Siamese spatial attention pooling. Neurocomputing **412**, 252–261 (2020)
10. Noh, H., Araujo, A., Sim, J., Weyand, T., Han, B.: Large-scale image retrieval with attentive deep local features. In: 2017 IEEE International Conference on Computer Vision (ICCV), pp. 3476–3485. IEEE, Venice (2017). https://doi.org/10.1109/ICCV.2017.374
11. Oh Song, H., Xiang, Y., Jegelka, S., Savarese, S.: Deep metric learning via lifted structured feature embedding. In: Proceedings of the IEEE Conference on Computer Vision and Pattern Recognition, pp. 4004–4012 (2016)
12. Philbin, J., Chum, O., Isard, M., Sivic, J., Zisserman, A.: Object retrieval with large vocabularies and fast spatial matching. In: 2007 IEEE Conference on Computer Vision and Pattern Recognition, pp. 1–8. IEEE, Minneapolis (2007). https://doi.org/10.1109/CVPR.2007.383172
13. Radenovic, F., Tolias, G., Chum, O.: Fine-tuning CNN image retrieval with no human annotation. IEEE Trans. Pattern Anal. Mach. Intell. **7**, 1655–1668 (2018). https://doi.org/10.1109/TPAMI.2018.2846566
14. Razavian, A.S., Sullivan, J., Carlsson, S., Maki, A.: Visual instance retrieval with deep convolutional networks. ITE Trans. Media Technol. Appl. **4**(3), 251–258 (2016). https://doi.org/10.3169/mta.4.251
15. Sohn, K.: Improved deep metric learning with multi-class n-pair loss objective. In: Advances in Neural Information Processing Systems, pp. 1857–1865 (2016)
16. Tolias, G., Sicre, R., Jégou, H.: Particular object retrieval with integral max-pooling of CNN activations. arXiv:1511.05879 [cs] (2015)
17. Wang, H., Li, Z., Li, Y., Gupta, B., Choi, C.: Visual saliency guided complex image retrieval. Pattern Recogn. Lett. **130**, 64–72 (2020). https://doi.org/10.1016/j.patrec.2018.08.010
18. Wei, S., Liao, L., Li, J., Zheng, Q., Yang, F., Zhao, Y.: Saliency inside: learning attentive CNNs for content-based image retrieval. IEEE Trans. Image Process. **28**(9), 4580–4593 (2019)
19. Wei, X.S., Luo, J.H., Wu, J., Zhou, Z.H.: Selective convolutional descriptor aggregation for fine-grained image retrieval. IEEE Trans. Image Process. **26**(6), 2868–2881 (2017)
20. Wengert, C., Douze, M., Jégou, H.: Bag-of-colors for improved image search. In: Proceedings of the 19th ACM International Conference on Multimedia, pp. 1437–1440 (2011)
21. Zheng, X., Ji, R., Sun, X., Wu, Y., Huang, F., Yang, Y.: Centralized ranking loss with weakly supervised localization for fine-grained object retrieval. In: IJCAI, pp. 1226–1233 (2018)
22. Zheng, X., Ji, R., Sun, X., Zhang, B., Wu, Y., Huang, F.: Towards optimal fine grained retrieval via decorrelated centralized loss with normalize-scale layer. In: Proceedings of the AAAI Conference on Artificial Intelligence, vol. 33, pp. 9291–9298 (2019)

Exploring Spatiotemporal Features for Activity Classifications in Films

Somnuk Phon-Amnuaisuk$^{(\boxtimes)}$ ⓘ, Shiqah Hadi, and Saiful Omar

Universiti Teknologi Brunei, Jln Tungku Link, Gadong BE1410, Brunei
{somnuk.phonamnuaisuk,p20191012,saiful.omar}@utb.edu.bn

Abstract. Humans are able to appreciate implicit and explicit contexts in a visual scene within a few seconds. How we obtain the interpretations of the visual scene using computers has not been well understood, and so the question remains whether this ability could be emulated. We investigated activity classifications of movie clips using 3D convolutional neural network (CNN) as well as combinations of 2D CNN and long short-term memory (LSTM). This work was motivated by the concepts that CNN can effectively learn the representation of visual features, and LSTM can effectively learn temporal information. Hence, an architecture that combined information from many time slices should provide an effective means to capture the spatiotemporal features from a sequence of images. Eight experiments run on the following three main architectures were carried out: 3DCNN, ConvLSTM2D, and a pipeline of pre-trained CNN-LSTM. We analyzed the empirical output, followed by a critical discussion of the analyses and suggestions for future research directions in this domain.

Keywords: Activity classification · Spatiotemporal features · Hollywood2 dataset · 3DCNN · LSTM2D · CNN-LSTM

1 Introduction

The Hollywood2 dataset consists of short movie clips. The training movie clips and the testing movie clips are extracted from different films. Classifying human activities from movie clips is a challenging task for all appearance-based strategies as the model must learn the target activities, e.g., *Fight, Eat, Sit Down*, etc. from apparently highly uncorrelated images. To further elaborate, given two scenes with the same semantic label of *Kiss*, they may not share any common visual criteria except that the two humans in the scene are kissing each other. How could the semantic of *Kiss* be captured?

We investigated the effectiveness of deep learning in learning spatiotemporal features of target semantics. Given a model which has successfully learned the associations between the features and the semantic labels in the training data, could the model learn a deeper semantic and identify the correct semantic labels from different films, with different actors and different visual environments?

© Springer Nature Switzerland AG 2020
H. Yang et al. (Eds.): ICONIP 2020, CCIS 1332, pp. 410–417, 2020.
https://doi.org/10.1007/978-3-030-63820-7_47

The rest of the materials in this paper are organized into the following sections; Sect. 2 describes related works; Sect. 3 highlights the technicality of our approach; Sect. 4 describes the experimental designs and presents experimental results; and Sect. 5 provides the discussion and future direction.

2 Related Works

Although CNNs are designed to work with one input image at a time, CNNs can be extended to accept a sequence of images by stacking them into 3D input, i.e., width × height × frames. This approach could extend CNN to handle temporal information with minimum modifications to its standard CNN architecture.

Long Short-Term Memory (LSTM) [1] extends Recurrent Neural Network (RNN) by introducing the idea of gates: an *input gate*, an *output gate* and a *forget gate*. LSTM provides an elegant method to control which information to ignore and which to remember through its gating mechanism. LSTM allows feedback information from previous time steps to be included in its current input. Hence, it provides an effective means to handle temporal information.

In this work, we employ video clips from the Hollywood2 dataset [2]. The dataset is labelled with twelve classes of human actions taken from 69 movies. They are arranged into two disjointed sets with 33 movies in the train set and 36 movies in the test set. This means scenes from the train set and test set do not overlap since different films tend to have different cinematography, lighting conditions and props. In [2], the authors discussed the results from action recognition and scene recognition from the Hollywood2 dataset. Various models, trained using various features e.g., SIFT, HOG and HOF, were experimented with. The best average precision (AP) was reported at 0.326 for the action classification task.

The combination of CNN-LSTM were explored for action recognition tasks in recent works by [3,4] where LSTM handled temporal context. Since CNNs can learn good feature representations, CNN were employed to encode each image into a feature vector which would then be associated with natural language sentences from LSTM coupled with the CNN. In other words, image features were learned by CNNs and were associated with pre-labelled descriptive sentences of the image. After successful learning, the system would generate a description of previously unseen images [5–7].

3 Exploring Spatiotemporal Features

To deal with the complexity in human activity recognition such as temporal characteristics of activities, we experimented with three architectures: (i) 3D-CNN, (ii) ConvLSTM-2D, and (iii) CNN-LSTM. This is based on the intuition that spatial and temporal contexts are two important sources of information for activity classification tasks. In 3D-CNN, both spatial and temporal contexts are captured in the 3D-CNN architecture. In ConvLSTM-2D and CNN-LSTM, CNN offers deep spatial features while LSTM offers deep temporal contexts.

Table 1 presents the three main deep learning architectures employed in this work. All models present their output as a vector $O^{1\times12} \in [0,1]$. Since the problem is formulated as a multi-label classification, the loss function at the output layer is defined using *binary crossentropy loss*:

$$o_i = \frac{1}{1 + e^{-(WX+b)}} \tag{1}$$

$$L(T,O) = \frac{1}{N} \sum_{i=0}^{N} (t_i * log(o_i) + (1 - t_i) * log(1 - o_i)) \tag{2}$$

where $o_i \in O$ is the output from the sigmoid function. $L(T,O)$ is the average binary crossentropy loss from the predicted output vector $O^{1\times12}$ and the target binary vector $T^{1\times12} \in \{0,1\}$.

4   Experimental Design and Setup

We employed a total of 1704 video clips from the Hollywood2 dataset [2]. The dataset was compiled from two disjointed sets of films, forming the test set, and the training set containing 884 and 823 clips, respectively. Each video clip was labelled with the following actions: *answer phone, drive car, eat, fight, get out*

Table 1. Summary of the eight models employed in this work: Conv3D, ConvLSTM2D, and six models based on pre-trained CNN-LSTM. The number of trainable parameters give the readers an idea of model sizes.

3D-CNN based on Conv3D.

Layer Type	Output Shape	Remarks
Input	(8, 112, 264, 3)	
Conv3D	(8, 56, 132, 48)	ReLU
Conv3D	(8, 28, 66, 32)	ReLU
MaxPooling3D	(8, 14, 33, 32)	
Conv3D	(8, 7, 17, 16)	ReLU
MaxPooling3D	(8, 3, 8, 16)	
Flatten	(3072)	
Dense	(256)	ReLU
Dense	(12)	sigmoid

The model has 829,324 Trainable parameters

CNN-LSTM based on ConvLSTM2D.

Layer Type	Output Shape	Remarks
Input	(8, 112, 264, 3)	
ConvLSTM2D	(8, 56, 132, 48)	tanh, return seq
MaxPooling3D	(8, 28, 66, 48)	
ConvLSTM2D	(8, 14, 33, 36)	tanh, return seq
MaxPooling3D	(8, 7, 16, 36)	
ConvLSTM2D	(8, 7, 16, 16)	tanh, return seq
Conv3D)	(8, 7, 16, 4)	ReLU
Flatten	(3584)	
Dense	(256)	ReLU
Dense	(12)	sigmoid

The model has 1,148,968 Trainable parameters

CNN-LSTM based on Pretrained CNN and TimeDistributed Layer

	Input	TimeDistributed	LSTM	Dense	Dense	Trainable
Output Shape	(8, 112, 264, 3)	(8, 1024)	(256)	(512)	(12)	1,449,484
Activations		wrap DenseNet	tanh and sigmoid	ReLU	sigmoid	
Output Shape	(8, 112, 264, 3)	(8, 2048)	(256)	(128)	(12)	2,394,764
Activations		wrap InceptionV3	tanh and sigmoid	ReLU	sigmoid	
Output Shape	(8, 112, 264, 3)	(8, 4032)	(256)	(512)	(12)	4,529,676
Activations		wrap NASNet	tanh and sigmoid	ReLU	sigmoid	
Output Shape	(8, 112, 264, 3)	(8, 2048)	(256)	(512)	(12)	2,498,060
Activations		wrap ResNet50	tanh and sigmoid	ReLU	sigmoid	
Output Shape	(8, 112, 264, 3)	(8, 512)	(256)	(512)	(12)	925,196
Activations		wrap VGG16	tanh and sigmoid	ReLU	sigmoid	
Output Shape	(8, 112, 264, 3)	(8, 2048)	(256)	(512)	(12)	2,498,060
Activations		wrap Xception	tanh and sigmoid	ReLU	sigmoid	

Table 2. Top: summary of experimental designs. Bottom: summary of distributions of class instances in the train and test dataset.

Model Architectures

	3D-CNN	ConvLSTM2D	CNN-LSTM
Input	(8,112,264,3)	(8,112,264,3)	(8,112,264,3)
Output	12	12	12
Retrained all layers	Conv3D	ConvLSTM2D	-
Retrained LSTM	-	-	pretrained DenseNet, InceptionV3, NasNet, ResNet50, VGG16, Xception

Distribution of Class Instances in the Datasets

	Answer Phone	Drive Car	Eat	Fight	Get Car	Hand Shake	Hug	Kiss	Run	Sit Down	Sit Up	Stand Up
Set 1 (test, 884)	64	102	33	70	57	45	66	103	141	108	37	146
Set 2 (train, 823)	66	85	40	54	51	32	64	114	135	104	24	132

car, handshake, hug, kiss, run, sit down, sit up and *stand up*. Upon inspecting the clips and the labels, we learned that the majority of clips had a single label (approx 90%). However, some clips were labelled with more than one class (two classes, and a few three classes). Hence we decided to formulate the task as a multi-label classification task.

Conv3D, ConvLSTM2D, pretrained CNN, LSTM and TimeDistributed layers were the main components explored in the experiments. Input to all the experiments are a sequence of image frames[1]. Each image frame was scaled to an RGB with $(112 \times 264 \times 3)$ dimension. We devised eight experiments which are denoted as $E1, ..., E8$.

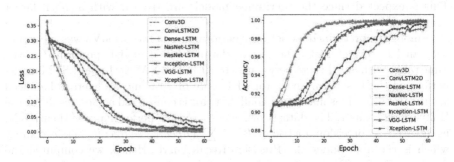

Fig. 1. Profiles of loss and accuracy of each model (E1 to E8) during the training stage.

$E1$ investigated spatiotemporal features using Conv3D. $E2$ explored the combination of CNN and LSTM using the ConvLSTM2D module from Keras. In both $E1$ and $E2$, the models were trained from scratch. The experiments $E3$ to $E8$ investigated spatiotemporal features using the following pretrained CNN:

---

[1] We chose eight frames from each clip. The frames were evenly pick from each clip. The number 8 was arbitrary decision.

DenseNet [8], InceptionV3 [9], NASNetLarge 0[10], ResNet50 [11], VGG16 [12] and Xception [13]. All models were pretrained with the imagenet dataset. Hence, our task here was to train the LSTM with output features from these pretrained models. Table 2 summarises the class instances in the datasets and the experimental design. Figure 1 shows the training loss and accuracy profiles.

Evaluation Criteria. The following standard metrics: Precision, Recall, Balanced accuracy and F1 score were employed to evaluate the results from the four experiments. Balanced accuracy and F1 score are expressed below for a quick reference:

$$Balanced\ accuracy = \frac{1}{2}(\frac{tp}{tp + fn} + \frac{tn}{tn + fp}) \tag{3}$$

$$F1\ score = \frac{Precision \times Recall}{Precision + Recall} \tag{4}$$

5   Experimental Results and Discussion

Table 3 tabulates the values of precisions, recalls, balanced accuracies, and F1 scores from all eight experiments. Figure 2 shows a graphical summary of the balanced accuracies and F1 scores from the test dataset.

The results show that the models are able to learn and can correctly classify movie clips from the training dataset (see Fig. 1). However, its performance deteriorated when tested using the test dataset. Models leveraged on transfer learning perform better than models that are trained from scratch in this work. This is expected since the pretrained models are trained with a much larger amount of data.

Among the pretrained models, the performance of InceptionV3 was the worst, with an F1 score of 14%. The rest of the pretrained models performed in the same range with an F1 score between 25 to 29%. The NASNetLarge-LSTM model performed the best with an average F1 score of 29% and an average balanced accuracy of 61%. This may seem small, but this is considered a good result for the Hollywood2 dataset. The dataset owner reported the performance of their model using average precision metric, $AP = \sum_n (Recall_n - Recall_{n-1})Precision_n$ which is the area under the Precision-Recall curve. Hence, we computed the AP from the NASNet model and compared it against the results from [2] in Table 3.

The model appears to learn from the training data successfully, but the performance with the test datasets can be further improved. The best model from NASNet yields a 61% balanced accuracy and a 29% F1 score. Although this may be explained as a consequence from the over fitting due to the relatively small training data size, a more profound implication can be argued and is discussed in the next subsection.

Table 3. Summary of precisions, recalls, balanced accuracies, and F1 scores from all experiments, from E1 to E8 (top to bottom). The model using pretrained NASNet and LSTM gives the best performance.

		Ans phone	Drive car	Eat	Fight	Get car	Hand shake	Hug	Kiss	Run	Sit down	Sit up	Stand up	Average
3DCNN	Bal ACC	0.48	0.53	0.53	0.58	0.49	0.50	0.50	0.51	0.60	0.51	0.55	0.52	0.52
	F1 score	0.02	0.15	0.11	0.25	0.00	0.00	0.02	0.09	0.32	0.07	0.00	0.22	0.10
Conv LSTM2D	Bal ACC	0.49	0.55	0.50	0.50	0.51	0.49	0.50	0.54	0.56	0.51	0.50	0.50	0.51
	F1 score	0.00	0.20	0.00	0.07	0.08	0.00	0.03	0.17	0.24	0.05	0.00	0.06	0.07
DenseNet LSTM	Bal ACC	0.71	0.86	0.54	0.50	0.66	0.65	0.49	0.69	0.59	0.54	0.55	0.62	0.61
	F1 score	0.36	0.75	0.15	0.00	0.44	0.20	0.00	0.46	0.30	0.16	0.17	0.36	0.28
Inception LSTM	Bal ACC	0.57	0.61	0.55	0.51	0.61	0.58	0.49	0.54	0.51	0.50	0.50	0.55	0.54
	F1 score	0.22	0.33	0.12	0.07	0.25	0.19	0.00	0.16	0.09	0.02	0.00	0.26	0.14
NASNet LSTM	Bal ACC	0.66	0.79	0.57	0.59	0.74	0.57	0.61	0.55	0.70	0.52	0.55	0.51	**0.61**
	F1 score	0.39	0.65	0.18	0.25	0.44	0.21	0.28	0.19	0.46	0.12	0.17	0.09	**0.29**
ResNet LSTM	Bal ACC	0.57	0.87	0.72	0.50	0.77	0.54	0.53	0.53	0.65	0.56	0.51	0.53	0.61
	F1 score	0.26	0.73	0.17	0.00	0.54	0.13	0.13	0.13	0.44	0.23	0.05	0.13	0.25
VGG LSTM	Bal ACC	0.56	0.83	0.53	0.50	0.63	0.51	0.56	0.67	0.70	0.52	0.51	0.59	0.59
	F1 score	0.22	0.72	0.10	0.03	0.38	0.04	0.20	0.49	0.52	0.12	0.05	0.31	0.27
Xception LSTM	Bal ACC	0.61	0.85	0.73	0.49	0.75	0.53	0.54	0.56	0.58	0.54	0.62	0.52	0.61
	F1 score	0.28	0.64	0.28	0.00	0.40	0.11	0.15	0.22	0.29	0.19	0.33	0.11	0.25

Comparing Average Precision (AP) metric to the values reported by the dataset owner.

		Ans phone	Drive car	Eat	Fight	Get car	Hand shake	Hug	Kiss	Run	Sit down	Sit up	Stand up	Average
SIFT-HOG -HOF [2]	AP	0.107	0.750	0.286	0.571	0.116	0.141	0.138	0.556	0.565	0.278	0.078	0.325	0.326
(our) NASNet	AP	0.348	0.676	0.118	0.261	0.373	0.148	0.226	0.213	0.436	0.230	0.250	0.220	0.292

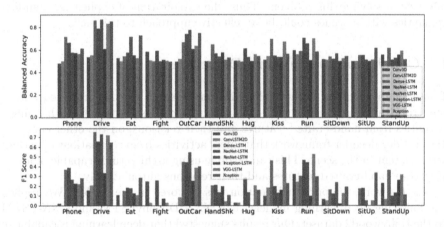

Fig. 2. A graphical summary of the *balanced accuracies* and the *F1 scores* from all four models. Combinations of transfer learning from NASNetLarge and LSTM provides the best result.

5.1 Critical Discussion

Learning desired semantics from the Hollywood2 dataset is a challenging problem. We are interested in exploiting the spatiotemporal features from a sequence of images to capture action-related semantics. Figure 3 highlights the challenges in this task. Each row represents a *SitUp* semantic label. Here, SitUp refers to the circumstance in which one of the female characters in the scene has raised her body from a laid-back position. This is a hard problem for any appearance-

Fig. 3. The three rows show a sequence of images from three different movies which represent the *SitUp* semantic label.

based technique [14] since different clips do not share common appearances. How could an equivalent computer representation that truthfully captures the semantic content of the scene be realized?

High-level visual analysis task involves challenges from explicit and implicit facial expressions, physical movements, non-verbal body languages, and context of the scene. Hence, the building of a complex table lookup model might not be effective in solving this problem. Thus, the exploitation of explicit and implicit semantics within scenes could be an effective approach to this task.

6   Conclusion and Future Directions

Contemporary human activity classification research can be projected onto a spectrum such that, on one end, it is a knowledge-based framework that infers activities from hand-crafted features and their relations; on the other end, it is the encoder-decoder framework that infers activities from correlations of actions with content in the scene. This can be done using architectures capable of learning those hand-crafted features and their relations automatically.

In this work, temporal information was explored in the models. We applied the following deep learning models: 3D-CNN, 2D-ConvLSTM and CNN-LSTM to the Hollywood2 dataset. Our results suggested that deep learning is capable of providing powerful automated feature extraction techniques. There are still many open research issues in the learning of spatiotemporal features. For example, the preparation of datasets to cover a wide range of semantics, and the computational approach that effectively capture the semantic of objects and their relations are still needed.

It has been pointed out in [7] that human 3D skeletal poses provides an effective means of inferring human activities. Exploiting skeletal information can be seen as providing extra attention to human objects. In future works, we look forward to exploring human poses and their relationships with other objects in the scene.

Acknowledgments. We wish to thank the Centre for Innovative Engineering, Universiti Teknologi Brunei for the financial support given to this research. We would also like to thank anonymous reviewers for their constructive comments and suggestions.

References

1. Hochreiter, S., Schmidhuber, J.: Long short-term memory. Neural Comput. **9**(8), 1735–1780 (1997)
2. Marszalek, M., Laptev, I., Schmid, C.: Actions in context. In: Proceedings of the IEEE Conference on Computer Vision and Pattern Recognition, (CVPR 2009), pp. 2929–2936 (2009)
3. Ullah, A., Ahmad, J., Muhammad, K., Sajjad, M., Baik, S.W.: Action recognition in video sequences using deep bi-directional LSTM With CNN features. IEEE Access **2018**(6), 1155–1166 (2018)
4. Varol, G., Laptev, I., Schmid, C.: Long-term temporal convolutions for action recognition. IEEE Trans. Pattern Anal. Mach. Intell. **2018**(40), 1510–1517 (2018)
5. Karpathy, A., Fei-Fei, L.: Deep visual-semantic alignments for generating image descriptions. In: Proceedings of the International Conference on Computer Vision and Pattern Recognition (CVPR). CoRR abs/1412.2306 (2015)
6. Vinyals, O., Toshev, A., Bengio, S., Erhan, D.: Show and tell: lessons learned from the 2015 MSCOCO image captioning challenge. IEEE Trans. Pattern Anal. Mach. Intell. **39**(4), 652–663 (2016)
7. Phon-Amnuaisuk, S., Murata, K.T., Pavarangkoon, P., Mizuhara, T., Hadi, S.: Children activity descriptions from visual and textual associations. In: Chamchong, R., Wong, K.W. (eds.) MIWAI 2019. LNCS (LNAI), vol. 11909, pp. 121–132. Springer, Cham (2019). https://doi.org/10.1007/978-3-030-33709-4_11
8. Huang, G., Liu, Z., van der Maaten, L., Weinberger, K.Q.: Densely connected convolutional networks. CoRR, abs/1608.06993 (2016). http://arxiv.org/abs/1608.06993
9. Szegedy, C., et al.: Going deeper with convolutions. In: Proceedings of the International Conference on Computer Vision and Pattern Recognition (CVPR), pp. 1–9 (2015)
10. Zoph, B., Vasudevan, V., Shlen, J., Le, Q.V.: Learning transferable architectures for scalable image recognition. In: Proceedings of the IEEE Conference on Computer Vision and Pattern Recognition (CVPR), pp. 8697–8710 (2018)
11. He, K., Zhang, X., Ren, S., Sun, J.: Deep residual learning for image recognition. CoRR, abs/1512.03385 (2015). http://arxiv.org/abs/1512.03385
12. Simonyan, K., Zisserman, A.: Very deep convolutional networks for large-scale image recognition. In: Proceedings of the International Conference on Learning representations (ICLR) CoRR, 1409.1556 (2015)
13. Chollet, F.: Xception: deep learning with depthwise separable convolutions. In: Proceedings of the IEEE Conference on Computer Vision and Pattern Recognition (CVPR), pp. 1251–1258 (2017)
14. Phon-Amnuaisuk, S., Ahmad, A.: Tracking and identifying a changing appearance target. In: Bikakis, A., Zheng, X. (eds.) MIWAI 2015. LNCS (LNAI), vol. 9426, pp. 245–252. Springer, Cham (2015). https://doi.org/10.1007/978-3-319-26181-2_23

Feature Redirection Network
for Few-Shot Classification

Yanan Wang[1], Guoqiang Zhong[1(✉)], Yuxu Mao[1], and Kaizhu Huang[2]

[1] Department of Computer Science and Technology, Ocean University of China,
Qingdao 266100, China
`ynwang63@163.com, gqzhong@ouc.edu.cn, 1369627028@qq.com`
[2] Department of Electrical and Eclectronic Engineering,
Xian Jiaotong-Liverpool University, SIP, Suzhou 215123, China
`Kaizhu.Huang@xjtlu.edu.cn`

Abstract. Few-shot classification aims to learn novel categories by giving few labeled samples. How to make best use of the limited data to obtain a learner with fast learning ability has become a challenging problem. In this paper, we propose a feature redirection network (FRNet) for few-shot classification to make the features more discriminative. The proposed FRNet not only highlights relevant category features of support samples, but also learns how to generate task-relevant features of query samples. Experiments conducted on three datasets have demonstrate its superiority over the state-of-the-art methods.

Keywords: Few-shot classification · Task-relevant · Feature redirection

1 Introduction

Inspired by humans' fast learning characteristic, few-shot classification aims at training a model with fast learning capability so that it can learn novel categories by giving limited amounts of samples. However, the task is more challenging due to the small amount of labeled data and the non-overlapping between the training set and test set.

Tackling few-shot classification problem requires training a classifier to generalize well with a few labeled examples in each class. Metric learning [1,10,14,15,19,20] is an effective approach to this problem. It mainly learns an appropriate feature space where different categories can be distinguished based on a distance metric. Meanwhile, meta-learning [2,8,12,17] aims to train a meta learner to learn how to predict gradient update or parameter initialization, so that the network can quickly adapt to new target tasks. All the above methods have made significant progresses in few-shot classification. However, most of them ignore the correlation between image classes, and just use monotonic feature extractors to independently extract the features of support samples and unlabeled data.

© Springer Nature Switzerland AG 2020
H. Yang et al. (Eds.): ICONIP 2020, CCIS 1332, pp. 418–425, 2020.
https://doi.org/10.1007/978-3-030-63820-7_48

In this work, we propose a novel feature redirection network, called FRNet. In contrast to previous approaches [2,9,14,15], our method considers the correlation between task and samples to extract features most relevant to the current task. As shown in Fig. 1, the feature redirection module is the key module of the whole network. It contains three parts, an SE adapter, a meta fusion block and a weight generator. The SE adapter learns the redirection information for each category simultaneously and generate class-aware features for support samples. The meta fusion block generates a set of class-sensitive weights and uses the redirection information to generate a task-relevant representation for each task. We train the weight generator to generate task redirection mask for query samples conditioned on the encoded task representation. After training, the feature redirection module can be used to find the task relevant features and make the features become more discriminative for few-shot classification.

Extensive experiments are conducted on multiple benchmarks to demonstrate the effectiveness of FRNet. The experimental results show that FRNet is on par with or exceeding the state-of-the-art few-shot classification methods in all experimental settings.

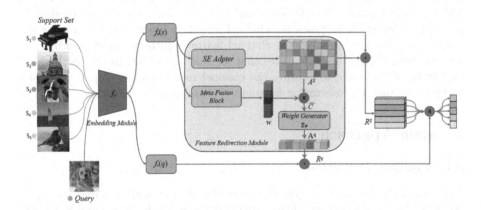

Fig. 1. The framework of FRNet on 5-way 1-shot classification problems.

2 Related Work

2.1 Few-Shot Learning

Current few-shot classification approaches can be roughly categorized into two main groups: metric-learning based and meta-learning based. The metric-learning based methods mainly learn a common feature space where different categories can be distinguished based on a distance metric. For example, Matching networks [15] model the relationship between inputs via biLSTM and attention. [14] learns a deep non-linear measure with neural network. [9] proposes an effective task-dependent metric space learning method, which can extract features according to different tasks. Our proposed method belongs to the metric-learning based method and exploits the correlation between category features to dynamically learn task-aware features of query samples.

The meta-learning based methods typically use a meta-learner to learn model different tasks by accumulating meta-knowledge. For instance, [2,12] enable the model to be quickly applied to new tasks by learning the initialization parameters of the model. [16] presents a meta-learning model equipped with external memory to predict parameters for meta-level learner and base-level learner. [17] uses an attention-based weight generator to get the classification weight vectors for novel category based on base categories. Our method also includes two parameter-generating layers, which can dynamically generate feature redirection parameters. The parameters generated are of lower dimension than that in previous works.

2.2 Attention

Attention mechanism can detect the relevant part that needs to be focused, which greatly improves the efficiency and accuracy of information processing. In particular, SENet [5] proposes the channel attention block, which can make the model pay more attention to the channel features with the most information, and suppress those channel features that are not important. In our method, we exploit the SE module to capture the channel relationship of support samples and provide task representation for query feature dynamic selection.

3   Main Approach

3.1   Problem Definition

The goal of the few-shot classification is to classify the unlabeled query samples according to the support set. If the support set contains K classes and N labeled samples in each class, the task can also be called K-way N-shot classification.

In this work, we adopt the episodic training mechanism to mimic the few-shot classification setting following the setting in [2,7,9]. For each episode, K classes and N samples per class are sampled from the training set D^{train} to form the support set, which is denoted as $S = \{(x_{k,n}^s, y_{k,n}^s) | k = 1, ..., K, n = 1, ..., N\}$; then the query set $Q = \{(x_i^q, y_i^q) | i = 1, ..., Q \times K\}$ consisting K classes and Q samples per class is sampled from the training set D^{train}.

3.2   Feature Redirection Module

In this work, we extend metric-learning by constructing a feature redirection module to obtain task-relevant features for each task. The overall structure of our model is shown in Fig. 1. In this section, we will first introduce the substructure of FRNet and then discuss the overall mechanism and training strategy.

SE Adapter. We adopt the SE module [5] as the adaptive unit, which called SE Adapter, to extract channel dependencies of support samples to form the category redirect masks.

Specifically, with the embedding module f_φ, the given support sample $s_{k,n}$ will be embedded as $f_\varphi(s_{k,n}) \in R^{C \times H \times W}$. The SE adapter computes the channel relevance of feature maps $\{f_\varphi(s_{k,n})\}_{k=1,n=1}^{K,N}$ to get the category redirection masks $A^s \in R^{NK \times C}$ as:

$$A_{k,n}^s = F_{SE}(F_{avg}(f_\varphi(s_{k,n}))), k = 1, ..., K, n = 1, ..., N, \qquad (1)$$

where F_{avg} is a global average pooling operator, and F_{SE} is the combination of FC+ReLU+FC layers.

Given the category redirect masks A^s, we then compute the class-aware features $R^s \in R^{NK \times C \times H \times W}$ for support set as follows:

$$R^s = A^s \odot f_\varphi(s), \qquad (2)$$

where $\odot$ denotes element-wise multiplication.

Meta Fusion Block. To dynamically obtain a task representation, we propose a meta fusion block. The meta fusion block is a convolutional module which takes the feature maps $f_\varphi(s)$ to calculate a class-sensitive set of weights $w \in R^{NK \times 1}$. The class-sensitive weights are then used to fuse the category redirect masks A^s into a task representation $\bar{C} \in R^C$ as follows:

$$w = W_2(\sigma(W_1(GAP(f_\varphi(s))))), \qquad (3)$$

$$\bar{C} = w^T A^s, \qquad (4)$$

where $W_1 \in R^{M \times \frac{M}{r}}$ and $W_2 \in R^{\frac{M}{r} \times 1}$ are the parameters of the meta fusion block, r is the reduction rate. σ refers to the ReLU function.

Weight Generator. Given the task representation $\bar{C}$ of a task, the weight generator is a parameter predictor that used to generate the task-relevant features for query samples. Let q_i be a query sample, where i is the index among all query samples. We denote the query feature map extracted from q_i as $f_\varphi(q_i) \in R^{C \times H \times W}$. For the query feature map $f_\varphi(q_i)$, a conditional single layer perceptron is constructed as the weight generator to produce redirection mask $A_q \in R^{C \times 1}$ as follows:

$$A_q = g_\phi(\bar{C}), \qquad (5)$$

where g_ϕ is the weight generator.

In order to constrain the weight scale for facilitating the training process, we apply the L_2 normalization to each generated mask. Finally, the query feature $R_i^q \in R^{C \times H \times W}$ can be formulated as

$$A_q = \frac{A_q}{||A_q||_2}, \qquad (6)$$

$$R_i^q = A_q \odot f_\varphi(q_i). \qquad (7)$$

3.3 Feature Redirection Network

As illustrated in Fig. 1, the overall FRNet architecture consists of three modules: an embedding module, a feature redirection module and a classification module. We employ ResNet-12 [3] as the backbone embedding module f_φ. For each episode, the embedding module f_φ first extracts the feature maps from both the support set S and the query sample q_i. The feature maps are then fed through the feature redirection module, which can mine the correlation between support set and query sample and dynamically redirect features to find task-relevant feature embeddings.

Finally, for the given query sample q_i in the few-shot classification task, the probability score [15] is computed as follows:

$$\widehat{P}_i = \sum_{k=1}^{K} \sum_{n=1}^{N} a(\widehat{x}_i, x_{k,n}) y_{k,n}, \tag{8}$$

$$a(\widehat{x}_i, x_{k,n}) = \frac{e^{d(R_i^q, R_{k,n}^s)}}{\sum_{k=1}^{K} \sum_{n=1}^{N} e^{d(R_i^q, R_{k,n}^s)}}, \tag{9}$$

where $d(R_i^q, R_{k,n}^s)$ is the cosine distance between the query and support sample embeddings.

We split the whole training procedure into 2 stages to maintain the consistency of the convergence of each part and provide extra transferability for the SE adapter. During the 1st training stage, we only learn the embedding module and the SE adapter. After that, we jointly train all the learnable parameters in the model. Given the few-shot classification task, we compute the predicted probability score for each query sample in Eq. 8. The loss function is then defined as the cross-entropy loss between the predicted probability P_i and the groundtruth y_i:

$$L = -\sum_{i=1}^{Q \times K} y_i log \widehat{P}_i. \tag{10}$$

4   Experiments

4.1   Datasets

We conduct experiments on two popular datasets: MiniImageNet [15] and TieredImageNet [11] to evaluate the proposed FRNet.

MiniImageNet. The miniImageNet dataset is a subset of ILSVRC-12 [6]. It consists of 100 different classes, each having 600 images. We follow the most common split in [9,12,14], with 64 classes for training, 16 for validation and 20 for test. All the images are resized to a resolution of 84 × 84.

TieredImageNet. The TieredImageNet dataet is a much larger subset of ILSVRC-12 [6]. It contains 34 categories, each of which has 10 to 20 classes. These are divided into 20 training (351 classes), 6 validation (97 classes) and 8 test (160 classes) categories, as in [2,12].

Table 1. Few-shot classification accuracies with 95% confidence intervals on the mini-ImageNet and tieredImageNet datasets. The best results are highlighted with boldface.

Model	Backbone	Type	miniImageNet		tieredImagenet	
			1-shot	5-shot	1-shot	5-shot
MAML [2]	ConvNet	Meta	48.70 ± 1.84	63.11 ± 0.92	51.76 ± 1.81	70.30 ± 1.75
SNAIL [4]	ResNet-12	Meta	55.71 ± 0.99	65.99 ± 0.58	–	–
adaNet [8]	ResNet-12	Meta	56.88 ± 0.62	71.94 ± 0.57	–	–
MTL [13]	ResNet-12	Meta	61.20 ± 1.80	75.50 ± 0.80	–	–
LEO [12]	WRN-28	Meta	61.76 ± 0.82	77.59 ± 0.12	66.33 ± 0.05	81.44 ± 0.09
RelationNet [14]	ConvNet	Metric	50.44 ± 0.82	65.32 ± 0.70	54.48 ± 0.93	71.32 ± 0.78
STANet [18]	ResNet-12	Metric	57.25 ± 0.40	69.45 ± 0.50	–	–
IDeMe-Net [1]	ResNet-18	Metric	57.71 ± 0.86	74.34 ± 0.76	–	–
TADAM [9]	ResNet-12	Metric	58.50 ± 0.30	76.70 ± 0.30	–	–
ECM [10]	ResNet-12	Metric	$59.00 \pm -$	$77.46 \pm -$	$63.99 \pm -$	$81.97 \pm -$
TPN [7]	ResNet-12	Metric	$59.46 \pm -$	$75.65 \pm -$	59.91 ± 0.94	73.30 ± 0.75
FRNet (ours)	ResNet-12	Metric	$\mathbf{63.57 \pm 0.26}$	$\mathbf{77.82 \pm 0.08}$	$\mathbf{68.67 \pm 0.86}$	$\mathbf{82.28 \pm 0.62}$

4.2 Comparison Results

To verify the effectiveness of the proposed method, we compare with other state-of-the-art methods on the above datasets. Specifically, five meta-learning based methods and six metric-learning based methods are picked for comparison. Table 1 shows the experimental results. It is noted that no matter whether compared with the meta-based methods or the metric-learning based methods, our method gets significant improvements on both 1-shot and 5-shot experiments. We attribute the observed improvements to the task adaptability learned by FRNet. In contrast to the existing metric learning based methods in which independently process category features, the features in FRNet are dynamically redirect calibration and then become more discriminative for classification.

4.3 Ablation Study

To verify the effectiveness of each component, we conduct ablation study on the miniImageNet dataset. The Matching Networks [15] is used as the baseline for comparison. To ensure a fair comparison, we re-implement it with ResNet-12 as feature extractor and report the results in Table 2.

Influence of Feature Redirection Module. By comparing our FRNet to Matching Networks, we can find significant improvements on both 1-shot and 5-shot scenarios. The performance gap provides evidence that feature redirection module can transform the target regions of support set into task-aware feature embeddings of the query samples. We can argue that the success of FRNet lies in the relevant features learned by feature redirection module.

Table 2. Ablation study on the miniImageNet dataset. * indicates the results reported in the original paper.

	1-shot	5-shot
Matching Networks [15]	54.44(43.77*)	66.70(60.60*)
FRNet (w/o pre-training)	57.49 ± 0.44	72.60 ± 0.35
FRNet (w/o meta fusion block)	63.07 ± 0.77	76.87 ± 0.22
FRNet (w/o weight generator)	62.87 ± 0.75	77.01 ± 0.58
FRNet	**63.57 ± 0.29**	**77.82 ± 0.58**

Influence of Pre-training. Here we estimate the importance of pre-training. By comparing the model trained from scratch with the one with pre-training, we observe that the model with pre-training gains 6.08% and 5.22% significant improvements on 1-shot and 5-shot respectively, which is shown in the second row of Table 2. These improvements are mainly due to the fact that pre-training enables SE adapter to learn more transferability than do scratch training.

Influence of Meta Fusion Block. To verify the effectiveness of the meta fusion block, we replace it by calculating the mean of redirection masks as the task representation. As can be seen in the third row of Table 2, there is no doubt that the performance has a slight decrease. We argue that the meta fusion block can learn the distribution of the relevant features in the latent space.

Influence of Weight Generator. If we train our network directly using task context to weight the query feature rather than using the weight generate layer, then the performance will be worse. The results are shown in the forth row of Table 2. This fact indicates that weight generator can learns to adaptively generate better weight for the query features and help improve the performance.

5   Conclusion

In this work, we present a metric-learning based model to extract task-relevant features for few-shot classification. The proposed FRNet has several advantages over the prior approaches. First, the SE adapter is used to adaptively activate useful features and perform feature filtering for support samples. In addition, a weight generator is introduced to learn task-aware feature representations. It utilizes the task representation to make the query features become more relevant for the current task. Furthermore, extensive experiments show that FRNet has matched or exceeded the state-of-the-arts.

Acknowledgments. This work was supported by the Major Project for New Generation of AI under Grant No. 2018AAA0100400, the National Natural Science Foundation of China (NSFC) under Grants No. 41706010 and No. 61876155, the Joint Fund of the Equipments Pre-Research and Ministry of Education of China under Grant No. 6141A020337, the Natural Science Foundation of Jiangsu Province under Grant No. BK20181189, the Key Program Special Fund in XJTLU under Grants No. KSF-A-01, KSF-T-06, KSF-E-26, KSF-P-02 and KSF-A-10, and the Fundamental Research Funds for the Central Universities of China.

References

1. Chen, Z., Fu, Y., Wang, Y.X., Ma, L., Liu, W., Hebert, M.: Image deformation meta-networks for one-shot learning. In: CVPR, pp. 8672–8681 (2019)
2. Finn, C., Abbeel, P., Levine, S.: Model-agnostic meta-learning for fast adaptation of deep networks. In: ICML, pp. 1126–1135 (2017)
3. He, K., Zhang, X., Ren, S., Sun, J.: Deep residual learning for image recognition. In: CVPR, pp. 770–778 (2016)
4. Mishra, N., Rohaninejad, M., Chen, X., Abbeel, P.: A simple neural attentive meta-learner. In: ICLR (2017)
5. Hu, J., Shen, L., Sun, G.: Squeeze-and-excitation networks. In: CVPR, pp. 7132–7141 (2018)
6. Krizhevsky, A., Sutskever, I., Hinton, G.E.: Imagenet classification with deep convolutional neural networks. In: NeurIPS, pp. 1097–1105 (2012)
7. Liu, Y., et al.: Learning to propagate labels: transductive propagation network for few-shot learning. In: ICLR (2019)
8. Munkhdalai, T., Yuan, X., Mehri, S., Trischler, A.: Rapid adaptation with conditionally shifted neurons. In: ICML (2017)
9. Oreshkin, B., López, P.R., Lacoste, A.: Tadam: task dependent adaptive metric for improved few-shot learning. In: NeurIPS, pp. 721–731 (2018)
10. Ravichandran, A., Bhotika, R., Soatto, S.: Few-shot learning with embedded class models and shot-free meta training. In: CVPR, pp. 331–339 (2019)
11. Ren, M., et al.: Meta-learning for semi-supervised few-shot classification. In: ICLR (2018)
12. Rusu, A.A., et al.: Meta-learning with latent embedding optimization. In: ICLR (2019)
13. Sun, Q., Liu, Y., Chua, T.S., Schiele, B.: Meta-transfer learning for few-shot learning. In: CVPR, pp. 403–412 (2019)
14. Sung, F., Yang, Y., Zhang, L., Xiang, T., Torr, P.H., Hospedales, T.M.: Learning to compare: relation network for few-shot learning. In: CVPR, pp. 1199–1208 (2018)
15. Vinyals, O., Blundell, C., Lillicrap, T., Wierstra, D., et al.: Matching networks for one shot learning. In: NeurIPS, pp. 3630–3638 (2016)
16. Munkhdalai, T., Yu, H.: Meta networks. In: ICML, pp. 2554–2563 (2017)
17. Gidaris, S., Komodakis, N.: Dynamic few-shot visual learning without forgetting. In: CVPR, pp. 4367–4375 (2018)
18. Yan, S., Zhang, S., He, X., et al.: A dual attention network with semantic embedding for few-shot learning. In: AAAI, pp. 9079–9086 (2019)
19. Huang, K., Hussain, A., Wang, Q., Zhang, R.: Deep Learning: Fundamentals, Theory, and Applications. Springer, Heidelberg (2019). https://doi.org/10.1007/978-3-030-06073-2. ISBN 978-3-030-06072-5
20. Yang, G., Huang, K., Zhang, R., Goulermas, J., Hussain, A.: Inductive generalized zero-shot learning with adversarial relation network. In: ECML (2020)

Generative Adversarial Networks for Improving Object Detection in Camouflaged Images

Jinky G. Marcelo[1,2]([⊠]) and Arnulfo P. Azcarraga[1]([⊠])

[1] De La Salle University, Manila, Philippines
jinky_marcelo@dlsu.edu.ph, arnie.azcarraga@delasalle.ph
[2] Central Mindanao University, Bukidnon, Philippines

Abstract. The effectiveness of object detection largely depends on the availability of large annotated datasets to train the deep network successfully; however, obtaining a large-scale dataset is expensive and remains a challenge. In this work, we explore two different GAN-based approaches for data augmentation of agricultural images in a camouflaged environment. Camouflage is the property of an object which makes it hard to detect because of its similarity to its environment. We leverage paired and unpaired image-to-image translation to create synthetic images based on custom segmentation masks. We evaluate the quality of synthetic images by applying these to the object detection task as additional training samples. The experiments demonstrate that adversarial-based data augmentation significantly improves the accuracy of region-based convolutional neural network for object detection. Our findings show that when evaluated on the testing dataset, data augmentation achieves detection performance improvement of 3.97%. Given the difficulty of object detection task in camouflaged images, the result suggests that combining adversarial-based data augmentation with the original data can theoretically be synergistic in enhancing deep neural network efficiency to address the open problem of detecting objects in camouflaged environments.

Keywords: Generative adversarial networks · Data augmentation · Camouflaged images

1 Introduction

Convolutional neural networks currently show impressive state-of-the-art performance on object detection; nonetheless, high accuracy depends mainly on the availability of large annotated datasets to successfully train the deep network [1,5,8,10]. Obtaining a large quantity of data samples is costly and highly challenging, particularly in the domain of agriculture [7,10]. To address this gap, data augmentation is an effective way to synthetically increase the size and add diversity to the training data [5]. Although geometric transformation techniques

© Springer Nature Switzerland AG 2020
H. Yang et al. (Eds.): ICONIP 2020, CCIS 1332, pp. 426–433, 2020.
https://doi.org/10.1007/978-3-030-63820-7_49

for data augmentation are useful, these approaches do not sufficiently address the diversity and variation in images, resulting in insufficient performance of the network model [7,8,10]. Generative adversarial networks (GAN) [6], which have demonstrated impressive image generation results for a variety of tasks [2–4], offer novel methods for data augmentation by generating plausible new samples from the learned distribution of data. Image-to-image translation is the task of translating one possible scene representation into another, provided adequate training data [3]. Several approaches have been proposed in image-to-image translation, some focusing on paired image samples, others on unpaired image samples.

Literature shows that the acquisition of agricultural data demands cost, time and professional diligence. As an alternative, generative adversarial networks have been used to produce synthetic images for data increase in agricultural dataset. Previous works have recognized that GAN demonstrates a compelling result in learning how to map images such as translating bell pepper images in the synthetic field to images in the empirical domain [1], creating artificial images on a small dataset of tomato plant disease images [5], enhancing the robustness of apple lesions detection model with the aid of generating lesions with new backgrounds, textures and shapes [11], conditioning leaf segmentation masks of plants to create corresponding and realistic images of potted plants in an isolated background [8], synthesizing images of greenhouse insect pest in sticky paper trap [10], and generating synthetic images that could be used in a plant disease classification training process [12].

Although there have been previous works on using adversarial networks for data augmentation, relatively little is known about creating artificial images in a complex scenario like a camouflaged environment. In the field of computer vision, camouflage is the property of an object which makes it difficult to detect due to the similarity to its surroundings [15]. The detection of camouflaged objects is useful in many applications such as surveillance systems, industrial applications, medical diagnosis, search and rescue missions, military applications and agricultural applications, among others. In agriculture, camouflaged images are cases whereby the objects are occluded because of a high resemblance of color to the foliage. Detecting objects from a similarly-colored background has been an open question in this field; however, camouflage detection has received less attention in literature due to the lack of standard dataset for this problem [16].

To explore further on this topic, we leverage adversarial-based data augmentation that differs from previous techniques by implementing image-to-image translation to produce synthetic images based totally on custom segmentation masks. The focus of this paper is two-fold. First, we randomly create custom segmentation masks and adopt generative adversarial networks to translate them into synthetic images in a camouflaged environment. This is the first work, to our knowledge, that uses an image mask as an input to generate synthetic images for data augmentation of an agricultural dataset in a camouflaged environment. Second, we evaluate if using generative adversarial networks is an effective app-

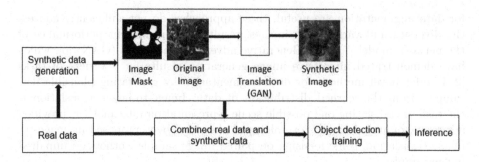

Fig. 1. Block diagram of our proposed method. The methodology includes data collection, generation of synthetic data using generative adversarial networks (paired image translation and unpaired image translation), evaluation of synthetic data by combining the real data and synthetic data for object detection, inference from the trained model of combined real data and synthetic data.

roach for data augmentation of small datasets by adding the synthetic images to real data for an object detection task.

2   Proposed Method

As shown in Fig. 1, the overall block diagram of the proposed system takes a binary custom mask and translates it into a synthetic photorealistic image of bell pepper in a camouflaged environment by training a generative adversarial network. The synthetic images are added to the real data for an object detection task to evaluate the effectiveness of adversarial-based data augmentation. The resulting model produces an image with a set of objects having rectangular bounding boxes and the associated probabilities. Pix2Pix [3] and Gaugan [4] were used for the task of image-to-image translation because these two conditional GANs showed promising performance in synthesizing input semantic layout into photorealistic images.

2.1   Dataset

As it is considered a high-value crop in the Philippines, images of bell pepper were selected as the sample dataset. The fruit of green bell pepper has heavy occlusion due to high color similarity with its foliage. When there is similarity of color, the fruits blend with their background foliage, resulting in difficult object detection. The samples for the green bell pepper dataset were collected in Impasugong, Bukidnon, Philippines. A total of 550 images were taken, using 400 images for training and 150 images for testing. The binary mask of an image was drawn by outlining the region of the objects into polygons and saved as mask image, i.e. the background of the image was segmented into black pixels and the bell peppers were segmented into white polygon pixels. The binary semantic masks with different sizes and number of polygons were randomly generated by a software.

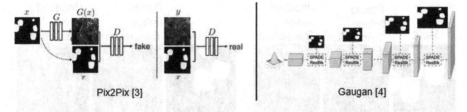

Fig. 2. *Left*: The image mask is given as input to the generator model. The discriminator classifies a given pair of images as the real pair or the generated pair. *Right*: The generator needs the mask to know what it should draw where, but the discriminator also needs to check that the generator puts the correct kind of object in the right place.

2.2 Paired Image Translation: Pix2Pix

One of the widely utilized algorithms for general-purpose image-to-image translation was designed with a training set of aligned pairs. Pix2pix, developed by Isola et al. [3], is a conditional adversarial generative network consisting of two models: the generator and the discriminator. The architecture consists of a generator model for creating an image, and the discriminator model for classifying an image, whether it is real or fake. As shown in Fig. 2 *(left)*, the discriminator, D, learns to classify between fake tuples (generator synthesized) and real tuples (mask, photo). The generator which is a convolutional network with U-net architecture, G, learns to fool the discriminator by producing images that look like those in the dataset. This technique demonstrated significant performance in translating a range of applications such as semantic labels into photo, shoe sketch into photo, and day into night photographs, among others [3]. Pix2Pix [3] requires aligned paired images, i.e. image mask-bell pepper image.

2.3 Unpaired Image Translation: Gaugan

Unlike the paired image translation, unpaired image translation maps the features and styles of an image from the source domain to the target domain using an unsupervised method [4]. Preparing the dataset using this approach is simpler, as it does not require aligned paired images as the training dataset. Gaugan, created by Park et al. [4], generates photorealistic images from a semantic segmentation map. As shown in Fig. 2 *(right)*, the generator is a fully convolutional decoder consisting of spade blocks which leads to more discriminative semantic information. Using spatially-adaptive normalization, it prevents the network from losing semantic information by allowing the image mask to control the parameters locally in each layer. The generator integrates this design into small residual blocks that get sandwiched between upsampling layers. Gaugan[4] requires two sets of unaligned examples from both domains, i.e. group image masks-group bell pepper images.

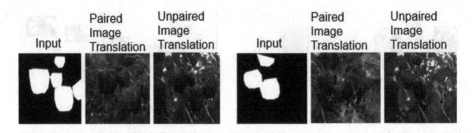

Fig. 3. Results of sample synthetic images generated by paired image translation (Pix2Pix [3]) and unpaired image translation (Gaugan [4])

3   Experiments and Results

3.1   GAN-Based Data Augmentation

In this section, we show experimental results from training paired image translation and unpaired image translation on the bell pepper dataset. We built the models using Tensorflow framework and trained our system using NVIDIA GeForce RTX2070. Figure 3 presents the sample images generated by inference after training the Pix2Pix [3] and Gaugan [4]. Qualitatively, it can be observed that samples which are clear and visually closer to the real images of bell peppers were generated during inference. The white pixels in the input image masks led the algorithms to synthesize the position, shapes and size of bell peppers in a camouflaged environment, resulting in synthetic bell peppers. Pix2Pix [3] and Gaugan [4] generated synthetic images with the same data distribution as the real bell pepper images. Most of the generated images proved to be of good quality despite the presence of camouflaged environment.

3.2   Empirical Evaluation

To evaluate our approach, we fed the generated synthetic images as additional dataset samples for object detection task. We finetuned and tested our updated datasets with the pre-trained model of Faster R-CNN Resnet-101 [9]. The majority of the pre-trained model's hyperparameters were applied. Each experiment was run with 5000 epochs on a batchsize of 1. The model was evaluated on the testing dataset using the mean average precision [13] at an intersection over union threshold (IoU) [14] of 0.75. A prediction is considered a true positive if the IoU score is greater than 0.75, which is considered an excellent prediction. Different object detection experiments were performed on different datasets to compare the data augmentation strategies, i.e. no data augmentation, traditional data augmentation approaches, paired image translation, unpaired image translation, combined paired and unpaired image translation, and combined traditional and GAN-based augmentation.

To determine the optimal quantity of synthetic images to be added to the original data, a series of experiments were performed by adding increments of 50 GAN-based images to the real data. As depicted in Fig. 4, the synthetic

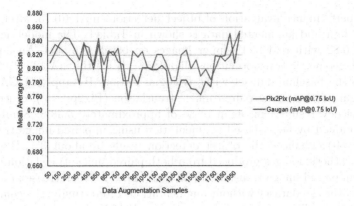

Fig. 4. Comparison of performance (mAP@0.75) of object detection system on combined real data and adversarial-based image translation, in increments of 50 synthetic images per experiment.

Table 1. Summary of performance of object detection (mAP@0.75) on training samples with various methods of data augmentation. The experiments reveal that combining real data, traditional data augmentation and GAN-based data augmentation achieve a performance improvement of 3.97%.

Experiments	Training samples	mAP@0.75
Without Data Augmentation	400	0.8200
With Geometric Transformations (rotation, translation, crop, shear)	2000	0.8399
With Adversarial-based Data Augmentation (Paired)	2400	0.8538
With Adversarial-based Data Augmentation (Unpaired)	2400	0.850
Combined real data and adversarial-based Data Augmentation (paired and unpaired)	4400	0.8456
Combined real data, geometric transformations and adversarial-based Data Augmentation (paired and unpaired)	6000	0.8597

images generated by paired image translation method outperformed the unpaired image translation. The graph also indicates that when adversarial-based synthetic images were added to the model, a relatively stable trend in object detection performance was observed; however, the saturation point on the number of synthetic samples when neural network stops learning cannot be determined yet in the graph pattern.

The performance evaluation of object detection, mAP@0.75, after training the real data and augmented data is shown in Table 1. The model achieved a mAP of 0.82 with real bell pepper images on baseline model. An augmentation with geometric transformations slightly increased the mAP by 1.99% compared to the baseline dataset without augmentation. By applying GAN-based data augmentation using paired image translation (Pix2pix [3]), object detection efficiency resulted in an increase of approximately 3.38%. Similarly, the result obtained by GAN-based augmentation using unpaired image translation (Gaugan [4]) enhanced the object detection result by about 3%. By combining the synthetic images produced from both paired image translation (Pix2Pix [3]) and unpaired image translation (Gaugan [4]), a 2.56% increase in mAP was achieved over the dataset without augmentation. Interestingly, the combination of real data, traditional data augmentation and GAN-based data augmentation achieved the highest improvement margin among the experiments we conducted, yielding a difference of 3.97%. The experimental results suggest that combining the adversarial-based data augmentation, traditional augmentation and the original data can theoretically be synergistic in enhancing deep neural network efficiency. Given the difficulty of object detection task in camouflaged images, an increase in performance from 82% to 85.97% is already a good start. The work of camouflage is still at its infancy. Hence, the result of this study will open up avenues for future research in camouflaged images.

4   Conclusion and Future Work

In this work, we presented methods for mapping out a data augmentation manifold based on generative adversarial networks. We leveraged paired and unpaired image translation synthesis network architectures to translate custom polygon masks into photorealistic images in camouflaged surroundings. Our findings show that adversarial generative networks exhibit great potential as an efficient technique for data augmentation. Both paired image translation (Pix2Pix) and unpaired image translation (Gaugan) techniques are capable of adding accurate, high quality images from polygon masks to synthetic agricultural dataset.

We trained and validated different object detection models using real data, incorporating augmented data based on geometric transformations, paired image translation and unpaired image translation, and integrating all datasets to thoroughly check and evaluate our approach. The experiments show that applying data augmentation based on paired image translation, unpaired image translation and geometric transformations to real data increased the mean average precision of object detection system resulting in overall improvement of 3.97% on testing dataset. This means that the use of an adversarial generative network is an effective approach for producing more data for training under multiple conditions. In future work, we will increase the complexity of the dataset while we ascertain the optimal mix of augmented samples with real image samples in camouflaged environment. Also, post-processing techniques to improve the quality of synthetic images by applying deblurring or other adversarial-based denoising approach include a direction for future work.

References

1. Barth, R., IJsselmuiden, J., Hemming, J., Van Henten, E.J.: Optimising realism of synthetic agricultural images using cycle generative adversarial networks. In: Proceedings of the IEEE IROS Workshop on Agricultural Robotics, pp. 18–22 (2017)

2. Zhu, J.Y., Park, T., Isola, P., Efros, A.A.: Unpaired image-to-image translation using cycle-consistent adversarial networks. In: Proceedings of the IEEE International Conference on Computer Vision, pp. 2223–2232 (2017)

3. Isola, P., Zhu, J.Y., Zhou, T., Efros, A.A.: Image-to-image translation with conditional adversarial networks. In: Proceedings of the IEEE Conference on Computer Vision and Pattern Recognition, pp. 1125–1134 (2017)

4. Park, T., Liu, M.Y., Wang, T.C., Zhu, J.Y.: Semantic image synthesis with spatially-adaptive normalization. In: Proceedings of the IEEE Conference on Computer Vision and Pattern Recognition, pp. 2337–2346 (2019)

5. Nazki, H., Lee, J., Yoon, S., Park, D.S.: Image-to-image translation with GAN for synthetic data augmentation in plant disease datasets. Smart Media J. 8(2), 46–57 (2019)

6. Goodfellow, I., et al.: Generative adversarial nets. In: Advances in Neural Information Processing Systems, pp. 2672–2680 (2014)

7. Nazki, H., Yoon, S., Fuentes, A., Park, D.S.: Unsupervised image translation using adversarial networks for improved plant disease recognition. Comput. Electron. Agric. 1(168), 105–117 (2020)

8. Zhu, Y., Aoun, M., Krijn, M., Vanschoren, J., HT Campus: Data augmentation using conditional generative adversarial networks for leaf counting in Arabidopsis plants. In: British Machine Vision Conference, pp. 3–24 (2018)

9. Ren, S., He, K., Girshick, R., Sun, J.: Faster R-CNN: towards real-time object detection with region proposal networks. In: Advances in Neural Information Processing Systems, pp. 91–99 (2015)

10. Lu, C.Y., Rustia, D.J., Lin, T.T.: Generative adversarial network based image augmentation for insect pest classification enhancement. IFAC-PapersOnLine 52(30), 1–5 (2019)

11. Tian, Y., Yang, G., Wang, Z., Li, E., Liang, Z.: Detection of apple lesions in orchards based on deep learning methods of CycleGAN and YOLOV3-Dense. J. Sens. 2019, 1–13 (2019)

12. Arsenovic, M., Karanovic, M., Sladojevic, S., Anderla, A., Stefanovic, D.: Solving current limitations of deep learning based approaches for plant disease detection. Symmetry 11(7), 9–39 (2019)

13. Zhu, M.: Recall, Precision and Average Precision. Department of Statistics and Actuarial Science, University of Waterloo (2004)

14. Gu, C., Lim, JJ., Arbeláez, P., Malik, J.: Recognition using regions. In: 2009 IEEE Conference on Computer Vision and Pattern Recognition, pp. 1030–1037. IEEE (2009)

15. Stevens, M., Merilaita, S.: Animal Camouflage: Mechanisms and Function. Cambridge University Press, Cambridge (2011)

16. Le, T.N., Nguyen, T.V., Nie, Z., Tran, M.-T., Sugimoto, A.: Anabranch network for camouflaged object segmentation. Comput. Vis. Image Underst. 184, 45–56 (2019)

Light Textspotter: An Extreme Light Scene Text Spotter

Jiazhi Guan and Anna Zhu$^{(\boxtimes)}$

School of Computer Science and Technology, Wuhan University of Technology,
Wuhan, China
guanjz@whut.edu.cn, annakkk@live.com

Abstract. Scene text spotting is a challenging open problem in computer vision community. Many insightful methods have been proposed, but most of them did not consider the enormous computational burden for better performance. In this work, an extreme light scene text spotter is proposed with a teacher-student (TS) structure. Specifically, light convolutional neural network (CNN) architecture, Shuffle Unit, is adopted with feature pyramid network (FPN) for feature extraction. Knowledge distillation and attention transfer are designed in the TS framework to boost text detection accuracy. Cascaded with a full convolution network (FCN) recognizer, our proposed method can be trained end-to-end. Because the resource consumption is halved, our method runs faster. The experimental results demonstrate that our method is more efficient and can achieve state-of-the-art detection performance comparing with other methods on benchmark datasets.

Keywords: Scene text spotting · Light architecture · Knowledge distillation · Attention transfer

1 Introduction

Scene text detection and recognition, a.k.a text spotting, has rapidly drawn growing attention from the computer vision community in the past few years. The ability to read text for scene understanding becomes essential for many services, such as auto cruise, visual impairment assistance, and so on. Deep neural network (DNN) becomes an indispensable choice in most previous works. However, to obtain better performance, a deeper and deeper network is designed without considering the complexity and resource consumption.

To overcome these challenges, we propose a light textspotter to reduce the model complexity while keeping the detection accuracy. It consists of a TS framework for text detection and a cascaded FCN recognizer. In the TS framework, attention transfer and knowledge distillation are designed to ensure the correct localization of text. Shuffle unit is adopted for feature extraction which heavily reduces the computational complexity. To achieve text spotting, we cascade the recognition branch of Mask Textspotter(MTS) [10] with our detector.

© Springer Nature Switzerland AG 2020
H. Yang et al. (Eds.): ICONIP 2020, CCIS 1332, pp. 434–441, 2020.
https://doi.org/10.1007/978-3-030-63820-7_50

Our network can be trained in end-to-end manner, which contributes to the overall performance. Our method achieves competitive detection performance on ICDAR2015 and TotalText dataset. Meanwhile, the computational speed increases by 18% compared with the second-fastest method. In end-to-end text spotting test, our proposed method also achieves comparable result.

In summary, our main contributions are concluded in three-folds: 1) Incorporating the extreme light CNN architecture, Shuffle Unit, with FCN into feature extractor to greatly reduce the complexity; 2) Improving the detection performance using knowledge distillation and attention transfer mechanism in the TS framework; 3) Boosting the scene text detection efficiency for practical usage.

2   Related Work

Scene Text Spotting includes two tasks, namely, scene text detection and recognition. Recently, more and more scholars held the opinion that the two tasks should be coupled to one model. Li et al. [5] proposed a unified model with an anchor base detector inspired by [8] and attention base encoder-decoder recognizer, but the model could not be trained end-to-end. Lyu et al. [10] proposed a novel text spotter, and it gets competitive performance in both rectangular and irregular text datasets. Their following work in [1] designed a spatial attention module to enhance universality. Busta et al. [7] adopt connectionist Temporal classification (CTC) with FCN structure into spotter to support end-to-end training. But, only the rectangular text can be well recognized in their model.

Light CNN is playing an increasingly important role in modern life, portable devices can not offer an adequate resource to applications requiring AI methods with DNN structure. Howard et al. proposed the idea of Depthwise Conv and Pointwise Conv in [4], which greatly reduce the number of parameters in CNN architectures while keeping competitive performance. Works in [2] proposed a novel idea to address the communication problem between channel groups, this work achieves the best performance in several tasks. In our work, we adopted Shuffle Unit defined in [2] to reduce the number of parameters.

3   The Proposed Method

Light Textspotter (LT) is an extremely light scene image text spotting model supporting end-to-end training. In this section, we present an elaborate illustration of our model, and the framework is shown in Fig. 1 (a). It mainly consists of a TS framework, the detail of the student pipeline is illustrated at the left of Fig. 1 (a), while the teacher one with similar architecture is simplified.

Within the TS framework, two pipelines run simultaneously in training. The feature extractor extracts four level features for multi-level text detection. Meanwhile, the sub-optimal network of student pipeline is guided by the teacher model using attention transfer mechanism. During detection, the anchor classification

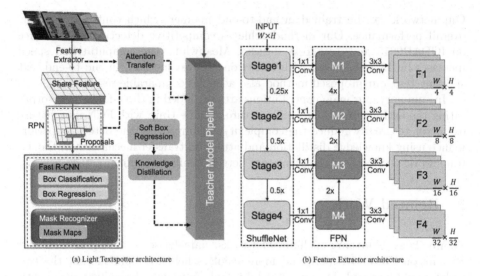

(a) Light Textspotter architecture   (b) Feature Extractor architecture

Fig. 1. (a) Two pipelines, left one for student, and another for teacher that provides extra materials to support the learning progress of the student. (b) Two pipelines in the opposite direction, one is up-down for feature extraction, another for feature merging. (Color figure online)

and box regression tasks are also influenced by the output of the teacher. Knowledge distillation assists the student to distinguish and locate text more accurately. After detection, Mask Recognizer outputs the final character sequence.

We use the extreme light CNN architecture in the student pipeline of our text detector. To obtain better performance in text detection task, we innovatively adopt an FPN network with ShuffleNet to cater varies size of text as shown in Fig. 1 (b). Every yellow box named Stage 1~4 are groups of Shuffle Unit [2]. An extra convolution layer is used after Stage4 to align the feature channels.

In the teacher pipeline, ResNet-50 is adopted as backbone. An attention transfer process is proposed to bridge both ends. The goal is to enhance the representation of student feature extractor by learning from teacher's semi-features.

The text Detector is based on Faster R-CNN [9], four sizes of anchors are generated, and the sizes are set to $\{32^2, 64^2, 128^2, 256^2, 512^2\}$. The aspect ratios are set to $\{0.3, 0.6, 1\}$ by considering the character shape.

The light CNN structure for text detection can boost the computational speed but impact accuracy. Inspired by [12], we propose to use knowledge distillation to improve the detection ability. The anchor classification distinction loss between TS framework is used, and the detail is described in Sect. 4. Cascaded with the mask recognizer proposed in [10], an end-to-end text spotter is built.

4   Optimization

LT is a multi-task learning model. All the losses designed in [10] are summarized as L_{mts}, and the losses involved in TS framework to update the student model are defined as L_{ts}. The holistic loss function can be defined as the following:

$$L = L_{mts} + \alpha L_{ts}, \tag{1}$$

$$L_{ts} = L_{at} + \delta_1 L_{kd} + \delta_2 L_{sreg}, \tag{2}$$

where α is set to 10^3 for training balance, δ_1 is set to 0.1 and δ_2 is set to 0.01 in this work.. As the sepia box is shown in Fig. 1 (a), L_{ts} consists of three parts: the attention transfer loss L_{at} calculated by the backbones of two sides in TS framework, the knowledge distillation loss L_{kd} and the soft box regression loss L_{sreg} calculated between the RPN of two pipelines.

Feature maps resolution alignment is required in most cases. With spacial design, the backbones in two pipelines are perfectly aligned in four stages. The mapping function F_{sum} [11] is used to merge all the channels:

$$F_{sum}(A) = \sum_{i=1}^{C} |A_i|, \tag{3}$$

where A is feature maps, C is the number of channels. With the mapping function, L_{at} can be calculated between the same size features from two sides of TS framework in the vector form by the following formula:

$$L_{at} = \sum_{j \in \Re} \left\| L_2(Q_S^j) - L_2(Q_T^j) \right\|_2, \tag{4}$$

$\Re$ is the set of feature pairs involved in the attention transfer process, $Q_S^j = vec(F_{sum}(A_S^j))$ and $Q_T^j = vec(F_{sum}(A_T^j))$ refer to the vector form of the j-th feature pair output at backbone of student and teacher pipeline respectively. As suggested in [11], we use l_2-normalized features to ensure successful learning.

The knowledge distillation loss L_{kd} reflects the gap in the anchor classification task. Leaning from soft-target is to calculate loss with the outputs of TS framework and soften the teacher output by temperature T before calculation. L_{kd} is defined from soft-target as following:

$$L_{kd} = \sum_{l \in \aleph} \sum_{\substack{s_i \in P_S^l \\ t_j \in P_T^l}} \frac{t_j}{T} \log \left(\frac{t_j}{T} / \frac{s_i}{T} \right), \tag{5}$$

where $\aleph$ is the set of features output from feature extractor of both ends of TS framework, $P_S^l = vec(A_S^l)$ and $P_T^l = vec(A_T^l)$ are the corresponding l-th vector form of cls layer output, respectively. They represent the probability of anchors being positive. In our work, T is set to 1. In box regression, we regard the teacher outputs as a judgment standard. L_{sreg} is defined as following:

$$L_{sreg} = \begin{cases} \|R_s - y\|_2^2, & \text{if } \theta \cdot \|R_s - y\|_2^2 > \|R_t - y\|_2^2, \\ 0, & \text{otherwise,} \end{cases} \tag{6}$$

where the θ is set to 1.2, y refers to the ground-truth regression label calculated identical to [8], R_s and R_t represent the box regression parameters predicted by teacher and student respectively.

5   Experiments

5.1   Datasets

SynthText is a synthetic dataset provided by [13], including more than 800,000 images labeled with rectangular text. It provides character-level labels. This dataset is used in both pretrain and finetune.

ICDAR2015 is a dataset including 1000 images in train set and 500 images in test set [3]. Most images in this dataset are blurred street view with slant and perspective text, some are hard to identify even for human. This dataset is part of the mixed dataset for network finetune.

TotalText is a comprehensive dataset provided by [6] using in text detection and recognition. It contains plentiful curved text. Images are labeled in character-level annotation. 1,255 images of train set are used in finetune, and 300 images of test set are used in performance evaluation.

Fig. 2. Text spotting results in ICDAR2015 (first row) and TotalText (second row).

5.2   Implementation Details

Thanks to the full-convolution design, our model supports end-to-end training. Following the training strategy used in [10], we use SynthText in pretrain and the mixed dataset in finetune.

In both pretrain and finetune, batch size is set to 4, the short side of input image is adjusted to 800 pixels while keeping the aspect ratio unchanged. The parameters of RPN and Fast R-CNN are set identical to [1]. SGD is adopted with weight decay of 1×10^{-4} and momentum of 0.9. In pretrain, initial learning rate is set to 1×10^{-2}, while 5×10^{-3} for finetune.

Three models are trained in step-by-step strategy. First one is the model with ShuffleNet-FPN structure named SFFPN. Then, TS framework is introduced and attention transfer is implemented, namely, SFFPN-AT. After convergence of SFFPN-AT, knowledge distillation losses are added into training and LT model is finetuned. Teacher model used in TS framework is the trained model provided by [10]. SFFPN is trained from scratch, in the first 100k iterations of pretrain, learning rate gradually decay to tenth, after another 140k iterations in pretrain and 200k iterations in finetune, the model converged. SFFPN-AT used exactly the same strategy of SFFPN, but with fewer iterations due to the implementation of attention transfer. In the finetune of LT, model is initialed with the parameters of SFFPN-AT. The initial learning rate is set to 5×10^{-4}.

All training processes are implemented on 4 NVIDIA TITAN GPUs with 24G memory. An NVIDIA Tesla T4 GPU with 16G memory is used in testing.

5.3   Qualitative Result

In order to evaluate our model, we implement testing on several aspects. By testing on ICDAR2015 and TotalText, we get plenty of well detected and recognized examples as exemplified in Fig. 2. For ICDAR2015, some text may even not be recognized by humans, but our model can successfully detect the text regions and correctly recognize the character sequence. For TotalText, most texts are curved. Our method can accurately detect and recognize the text as shown in the second row of Fig. 2, which clearly demonstrates the superiority of our model in irregular text spotting task.

Table 1. Performance of text detection and end-to-end task on ICDAR2015, 'P' refers to precision, 'R' refers to recall, 'FM' refers to F-measure, 'S' refers to the Strong lexicon, 'W' refers to the Weak lexicon and 'G' refers to the General lexicon.

Method	P(%)	R(%)	FM(%)	FPS	Method	FM(%)			FPS
						S	W	G	
Zhang et al. [14]	71.0	43.0	54.0	0.5	Karatzas, D. et al. [3]	13.8	12.0	8.0	–
Seglink [15]	73.1	76.8	75.0	–	Seglink [15]	67.9	–	–	–
EAST [16]	83.3	78.3	80.7	–	MTS [10]	81.9	75.7	70.3	3.3
TextSnake [17]	84.9	80.4	82.6	1.1	SFFPN (ours)	73.5	67.9	62.0	–
MTS [10]	91.6	81.0	86.0	5.15	SFFPN-AT (ours)	75.1	69.5	62.0	–
LT (ours)	94.5	70.7	80.0	9.09	LT (ours)	77.2	70.9	65.2	4.8

5.4   Rectangular and Irregular Text

To quantitatively demonstrate the performance of our model in rectangular scene text detection and recognition, we compare our model with several methods on ICDAR2015. In Table 1, the results show that our model gives satisfactory text detection performance with the highest precision of 94.5% and the fastest speed of 9.09 FPS. Comparing with the other methods, our method achieves state-of-the-art results. Comparing with the teacher model, end-to-end text reading speed is greatly improved by 45.5%.

To evaluate the irregular text detection performance, we conduct experiments on TotalText, the results are shown in Table 2. Comparing with state-of-the-art methods, our proposed is much better than most of them, which achieves the best recall of 78.8%. Taking the model size into consideration, our proposed method achieves almost the same overall detection performance as other methods while consuming only about half resources.

Table 2. Performance of text detection task on TotalText under Det-eval protocol and Ablation experiments. (* indicates the journal version of MTS, and the abbreviations have the same meaning as preceding)

Method	P(%)	R(%)	H(%)	Method	FM(%)			Improvement(%)		
EAST [16]	50.0	36.2	42.0							
MTS [10]	69.0	55.0	61.3		S	W	G	S	W	G
TextSnake [17]	82.7	74.5	78.4	SFFPN	73.5	67.9	62.0	–	–	–
MTS* [1]	80.9	76.2	78.5	SFFPN-AT	75.1	69.5	63.6	+1.6	+1.6	+1.6
LT (ours)	77.4	78.8	78.1	LT (ours)	77.2	70.9	65.2	+2.1	+1.4	+1.6

5.5   Model Size and Ablation

Because of the implementation of light CNN structure in our method, LT is therefore much smaller in model size than MTS [1]. Comparing with MTS, the parameters of LT reduced by 40%, meanwhile, the memory consumption and complexity earn an almost halve reduction.

Evaluating the effectiveness of each TS loss by comparing the three models trained step-by-step, we can summarize that both attention transfer and knowledge distillation contribute to the improvement of overall performance. Details are shown in Table 2.

6   Conclusion

In this paper, we creatively incorporated light CNN structure with TS framework, and designed three customized losses for detection task in scene text spotting. With the stepped training strategy, our proposed method achieves competitive performance on both rectangular and irregular datasets at the fastest speed. It is remarkable that our model only consumes about half the computational burden of most other state-of-the-art methods.

Acknowledgments. This work was supported by the National Natural Science Foundation of China under Grant 61703316.

References

1. Liao, M., Lyu, P., He, M., et al.: Mask textspotter: an end-to-end trainable neural network for spotting text with arbitrary shapes. IEEE Trans. Pattern Anal. Mach. Intell. (2019)
2. Zhang, X., Zhou, X., Lin, M., et al.: ShuffleNET: an extremely efficient convolutional neural network for mobile devices. In: Proceedings of the IEEE Conference on Computer Vision and Pattern Recognition, pp. 6848–6856 (2018)
3. Karatzas, D., et al.: ICDAR 2015 competition on robust reading. In: Proceedings ICDAR, pp. 1156–1160 (2015)
4. Sandler, M., Howard, A., Zhu, M., Zhmoginov, A., Chen, L.C.: Inverted residuals and linear bottlenecks: Mobile networks for classification, detection and segmentation. arXiv preprint arXiv:1801.04381 (2018)
5. Li, H., Wang, P., Shen, C.: Towards end-to-end text spotting with convolutional recurrent neural networks. In: Proceedings of IEEE International Conference on Computer Vision, pp. 5238–5246 (2017)
6. Ch'ng, C.K., Chan, C.S.: Total-text: a comprehensive dataset for scene text detection and recognition. In: International Conference on Document Analysis and Recognition (ICDAR), pp. 935–942 (2017)
7. Busta, M, Neumann, L,, Matas, J.: Deep textspotter: an end-to-end trainable scene text localization and recognition framework. In: Proceedings of the IEEE International Conference on Computer Vision, pp. 2204–2212 (2017)
8. Ren, S., He, K., Girshick, R., et al.: Faster R-CNN: towards real-time object detection with region proposal networks. In: Advances in Neural Information Processing Systems, pp. 91–99 (2015)
9. Lin, T.Y., Dollár, P., Girshick, R., et al.: Feature pyramid networks for object detection. In: Proceedings of the IEEE Conference on Computer Vision and Pattern Recognition, pp. 2117–2125 (2017)
10. Lyu, P., Liao, M., Yao, C., Wu, W., Bai, X.: Mask TextSpotter: an end-to-end trainable neural network for spotting text with arbitrary shapes. In: Ferrari, V., Hebert, M., Sminchisescu, C., Weiss, Y. (eds.) Computer Vision – ECCV 2018. LNCS, vol. 11218, pp. 71–88. Springer, Cham (2018). https://doi.org/10.1007/978-3-030-01264-9_5
11. Zagoruyko, S., Komodakis, N.: Paying more attention to attention: improving the performance of convolutional neural networks via attention transfer. arXiv preprint arXiv:1612.03928 (2016)
12. Hinton, G., Vinyals, O., Dean, J.: Distilling the knowledge in a neural network. arXiv preprint arXiv:1503.02531 (2015)
13. Gupta, A,, Vedaldi, A,, Zisserman, A.: Synthetic data for text localisation in natural images. In: Proceedings of the IEEE Conference on Computer Vision and Pattern Recognition, pp. 2315–2324 (2016)
14. Zhang, Z., Zhang, C., Shen, W., Yao, C., Liu, W., Bai, X.: Multi-oriented text detection with fully convolutional networks. In: Proceedings of CVPR, pp. 4159–4167 (2016)
15. Shi, B., Bai, X., Belongie, S.J.: Detecting oriented text in natural images by linking segments. In: Proceedings of CVPR, pp. 3482–3490 (2017)
16. Zhou, X., et al.: EAST: an efficient and accurate scene text detector. In: Proceedings of CVPR, pp. 2642–2651 (2017)
17. Long, S., Ruan, J., Zhang, W., He, X., Wu, W., Yao, C.: TextSnake: a flexible representation for detecting text of arbitrary shapes. In: Ferrari, V., Hebert, M., Sminchisescu, C., Weiss, Y. (eds.) ECCV 2018. LNCS, vol. 11206, pp. 19–35. Springer, Cham (2018). https://doi.org/10.1007/978-3-030-01216-8_2

LPI-Net: Lightweight Inpainting Network with Pyramidal Hierarchy

Siyuan Li[1][iD], Lu Lu[1], Kepeng Xu[1], Wenxin Yu[1(✉)], Ning Jiang[1],
and Zhuo Yang[2]

[1] Southwest University of Science and Technology, Mianyang, China
yuwenxin@swust.edu.cn
[2] Guangdong University of Technology, Guangzhou, China

Abstract. With the development of deep learning, there are a lot of inspiring and outstanding attempts in image inpainting. However, the designed models of most existing approaches take up considerable computing resources, which result in sluggish inference speed and low compatibility to small-scale devices. To deal with this issue, we design and propose a lightweight pyramid inpainting Network called LPI-Net, which applies lightweight modules into the inpainting network with pyramidal hierarchy. Besides, the operations in the top-down pathway of the proposed pyramid network are also lightened and redesign for the implementation of lightweight design. According to the qualitative and quantitative comparison of this paper, the proposed LPI-Net outperforms known advanced inpainting approaches with much fewer parameters. In the evaluation inpainting performance on 10–20% damage regions, LPI-Net achieves an improvement of at least 3.52 dB of PSNR than other advanced approaches on CelebA dataset.

Keywords: Image inpainting · Lightweight network · Deep convolution

1 Introduction

In recent years, with the rapid progress of deep convolution neural networks (DCNN), digital image inpainting technology has attracted extensive interest and achieve great progress. Up to now, most of these advanced approaches adopt the lengthy and complicated image inpainting generators. Therefore, these methods are greatly dependent on considerable computational resources and have a high inference latency. But in many popular vision applications, such as mobile applications, website tools, and batch image processing, the image inpainting tasks are expected to be carried out on small-scale platforms with limited computation.

This paper proposes an efficient pyramid network that is specifically designed for image inpainting and resource-constrained environments, which is named as Lightweight Pyramid Inpainting Network (LPI-Net). The proposed architecture

© Springer Nature Switzerland AG 2020
H. Yang et al. (Eds.): ICONIP 2020, CCIS 1332, pp. 442–449, 2020.
https://doi.org/10.1007/978-3-030-63820-7_51

combines the modified pyramid network with the novel lightweight ResBlock to adapt the image inpainting task. Due to the exquisite design of the pyramid network for the inpainting task, LPI network achieves excellent inpainting performance with a small number of parameters.

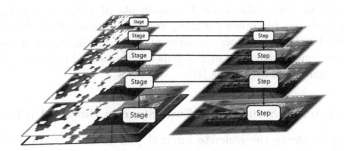

Fig. 1. The general design of the Lightweight Pyramid Inpainting Network, which consists of 5 stages in the bottom-up pathway (left half of the figure) and 4 steps in the top-down pathway (right half).

In addition, the proposed architecture is evaluated on Place2 [13] and CelebA [7] dataset. Compared with other inpainting methods, the proposed architecture obtains equivalent state-of-art performance in qualitative and quantitative aspects. In conclusion, the main contributions of this paper are as follows:

- We propose a tailored pyramid generator network specifically for image inpainting tasks. The structure and first layer of generator are specifically designed for inpainting.
- To reduce the parameters and computation of the designed model, the depthwise separable convolutions module and linear bottleneck module are embedded in the suitable position of the LPI-Net, the united layers are named as lightweight ResBlock.
- Experiments on two public datasets show that proposed LPI network achieves competitive inpainting results and only consumed little computing resources.

2   Proposed Method

2.1   Architecture of LPI-Net

The raw Feature Pyramid Networks (FPN) [5] consists of the bottom-up pathway, top-down pathway, and lateral connections, each pathway involves features at several scales with a scaling step of 2. At each feature block with the same scale, each pathway process the feature maps with more than three residual blocks. In order to facilitate the application of object detection, all stages in the top-down pathway maintain the dimension of features at 256. All these original designs for object detection make FPN a gigantic network, and it can not be directly applied to lightweight image inpainting.

In the paper, we proposed a lightweight inpainting network named Lightweight Pyramid Inpainting Network, which has a general architecture similar to the FPN but reduces some intricate and redundant designs. Moreover, the first layer and inside operations of LPI network are modified to better adapt to image inpainting, which can efficiently extract the high-resolution features.

As shown in Fig. 1, the general components of LPI network include the bottom-up pathway, top-down pathway, and lateral connections. Similar to the FPN [5], the bottom-up pathway consists of 5 stages, where each stage contains one standard convolution layer and N lightweight residual bottleneck layer with depthwise separable convolutions [10].

2.2   The Internal Structure of Each Stage in Bottom-Up Pathway

Figure 2 (Left) shows the concrete internal process of each stage in the LPI network, which includes a standard convolution layer and N novel lightweight residual bottlenecks (lightweight ResBlocks). The N is the number of superimposed lightweight blocks, and it is a hyperparameter that determines the scale of the LPI network.

The first convolution layer in each stage is designed to control the variation of resolution of all features in that stage, and it can expand the channel dimension of feature to a specific amount. In the lightweight ResBlock, the $tanh(x)$ activation function is adopted to deliver feature values into the range between -1 and 1, and the same paddings in each layer of lightweight ResBlock are used to maintain the same space dimension.

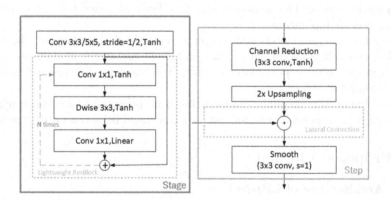

Fig. 2. Left: The forward process of each stage in the bottom-up pathway of the pyramid inpainting network, the 'Dwise' in the diagram refers to depthwise convolution [2]. Right: The forwarding process of lateral connections and detailed per step in the top-down pathway, the upsampling layer refers to bilinear interpolation.

To obtain the detailed information from the original image, we set the stride of the first convolution layer in the first stage of the bottom-up pathway as

1, so that the first stage adequately extracts and operates the full-resolution features from the corrupted image. This novel layer is specially designed for image inpainting tasks. Because the bottom-up pathway in the pyramid network aims to encode the image to compact features, the stride in other stages of the bottom-up pathway is set to 2, which gradually reduces the space dimension of features in the forwarding process.

2.3 Top-Down Pathway and Lateral Connections

The top-down pathway of LPI network reconstructs the high-resolution features by lateral connections, bilinear upsampling layer, and standard convolution layers.

The detailed operations of each step in the top-down pathway are shown in Fig. 2 (Right). The channel reduction layer reduces the dimension of features before the subsequent operations, the smooth layer maintain the channel of feature unchanged, which aims to process and fuse the upsampled features and the transferred features from the bottom-up pathway. Thus there are only two standard convolution layers in each step of the top-down pathway. These designs retrench a great deal of computation and space resources from the pyramid network.

2.4 Loss Function and Adversarial Learning

Similar to those advanced inpainting work [3,8,9,12], we also exploit the adversarial learning [1] to improve the inpainting performance. In this paper, the function of the LPI network (generator) and discriminator are respectively denoted as $G(x)$ and $D(x)$, and the design of $D(x)$ is similar to one of the recent advanced work [8].

The G and D play the two-player minimax game in adversarial learning, the adversarial loss is described in Eq. 1. The distribution p_{pred} is the generated data $(z = G(x))$ from the LPI network, and the p_{gt} is the ground truth image distribution that needs to be learned. The maximization of $\mathcal{L}_D$ makes the discriminator D better assign the correct label to both ground truth images and generated images as accurately as possible.

$$\max_{D} \mathcal{L}_D = \mathbb{E}_{x \sim p_{gt}(x)} \left[\log(D\left(x\right)) \right] + \mathbb{E}_{z \sim p_{pred}(z)} \left[\log\left(1 - D\left(z\right)\right) \right] \qquad (1)$$

Then the total loss function of the generator in LPI network can be formalized as Eq. 2, it only includes the l_{ℓ_1} distance between the inpainted image and truth image and the adversarial loss feedback from discriminator.

$$\min_{G} \mathcal{L}_G = \mathcal{L}_{\ell_1} + \mathcal{L}_D \qquad (2)$$

If respectively denote ground truth image and the inferred image as $\mathbf{I}_{gt}$ and $\mathbf{I}_{pred}$, the l_{ℓ_1} loss can be specifically interpreted as Eq. 3.

$$\mathcal{L}_{\ell_1} = \frac{1}{n} \sum_{i=1}^{n} \| \mathbf{I}_{gt}(i) - \mathbf{I}_{pred}(i) \|_1 \tag{3}$$

where the n refers to the total number of pixel in the image sample, and $\mathbf{I}(i)$ represents ith pixel value in image. For example, if the input image is a 256×256 RGB image, the denominator $n = 256 \times 256 \times 3 = 196,608$.

3   Experiments

3.1   Implementation Details

The performance evaluation of the proposed LPI network is based on two public image datasets - Places2 [13] and CelebA [7], and the resolution of samples in both datasets is 256×256. All the quantitative results in this section are based on the comparison between the real image sample $\mathbf{I}_{gt}$ and the processed composite sample $\mathbf{I}_{comp} = \mathbf{I}_{pred} \odot (1 - M) + \mathbf{I}_{gt} \odot M$. And in the evaluation stage, we measure the performance of $10,000$ randomly selected samples from the test data set.

The irregular mask maps used in the experiment are provided by work [6], which labeled the corrupted area with values 1. For the convenience of the direct use of masks in the training process, our experiment inverts the masks and resizes them into the resolution of 256×256. In this experiment, the generative loss (Eq. 2) and adversarial loss (Eq. 1) of LPI network are both updated and minimized by Adam [4] optimizers with the learning rate of 1×10^{-4} and 1×10^{-3} respectively.

Table 1. The comparison of 3 kinds of quantitative evaluation over the Places2 [13], these existing recorded data are taken from the literatures [6,8]. These data are calculated over 10,000 samples from Places2 test dataset, and the correspond mask maps are provided by PConv [6].

Method	10%–20% damage			20%–30% damage			30%–40% damage			40%–50% damage		
	PSNR	SSIM	ℓ_1(%)	PSNR	SSIM	ℓ_1(%)	PSNR	SSIM	ℓ_1(%)	PSNR	SSIM	ℓ_1(%)
GLCIC [3]	23.49	0.862	2.66	20.45	0.771	4.70	18.50	0.686	6.78	17.17	0.603	8.85
CA [11]	24.36	0.893	2.05	21.19	0.815	3.52	19.13	0.739	5.07	17.75	0.662	6.62
Pconv [6]	28.02	0.869	1.14	24.9	0.777	1.98	22.45	0.685	3.02	20.86	0.589	4.11
EdgeCnt [8]	27.95	0.920	1.31	24.92	0.861	2.26	22.84	0.799	3.25	21.16	0.731	4.39
LPI-Large	**30.55**	**0.951**	**0.71**	**26.44**	**0.900**	**1.51**	**23.78**	**0.842**	**2.47**	**21.54**	**0.775**	**3.79**
LPI	30.32	0.948	0.75	26.31	0.894	1.56	23.66	0.834	2.56	21.44	0.766	3.91

Table 2. The comparison of 3 kinds of quantitative evaluation over the CelebA [13], these existing recorded data are taken from the literature [8].

Method	10%–20% damage			20%–30% damage			30%–40% damage			40%–50% damage		
	PSNR	SSIM	$\ell_1(\%)$	PSNR	SSIM	$\ell_1(\%)$	PSNR	SSIM	$\ell_1(\%)$	PSNR	SSIM	$\ell_1(\%)$
GLCIC [3]	24.09	0.865	2.53	20.71	0.773	4.67	18.50	0.689	6.95	17.09	0.609	9.18
CA [11]	25.32	0.888	2.48	22.09	0.819	3.98	19.94	0.750	5.64	18.41	0.678	7.35
EdgeCnt [8]	33.51	0.961	0.76	30.02	0.928	1.38	27.39	0.890	2.13	25.28	0.846	3.03
LPI-Large	**37.03**	**0.978**	**0.33**	**32.00**	**0.952**	**0.76**	**28.75**	**0.920**	**1.31**	**25.74**	**0.874**	**2.19**
LPI	36.44	0.976	0.36	31.65	0.949	0.79	28.37	0.914	1.37	25.33	0.867	2.32

3.2 Quantitative Comparison and Analysis

To evaluate the inpainting performance on different degrees of image damage, we calculate the quantitative performance of the models under the four different damage ratios. In the following diagrams, the LPI-Larger is a large version of LPI network because it set the N (involved in Sect. 2.2) to 4, the standard LPI network set the N to 1.

Places2 [13] is a large-scale public dataset that collected numerous natural scenes, which contains millions of image samples. Compared to Places2, the scale of CelebA [7] is smaller, and it consists of 202,599 number of face images.

The performance comparison on test set of Places2 [13] is shown in Table 1, it can be observed that the proposed LPI network outperforms these state-of-art image inpainting approach in the listed four methods. And the Table 2 records equivalent inpainting comparison on the CelebA [7] of different advanced approaches, these data demonstrate that the excellent inpainting ability of LPI network on face completion task and medium-scale dataset.

Table 3 indicates the comparison of the parameters over these aforementioned approaches. It is noticeable that all these statistics only consider the generators in the whole network framework. Because in the real application of mobile devices, we can only deploy the pre-trained generators to accomplish the image inpainting task. Another point to note is that the CA [11] and EdgeConnect [8] are two-stage inpainting approaches, and thus we need to calculate the parameter number of two generators.

It can be observed that LPI-Large is a medium-scale network because it is only larger than the network of CA [11], the LPI is the most lightweight network and the parameters numbers is only 0.28 times of CA [11] and GLCIC [3]. Moreover, the inpainting performance of the LPI approximate LPI-Large and outperforms the other state-of-art inpainting approaches (observed from Tables 1 and 2).

3.3 Qualitative Comparison and Observation

As shown in Fig. 3, it illustrates the visual inpainting results of different methods on the test set of Places2 [13] and CelebA [7]. The images in the first three rows are sampled from CelebA [7], and the samples in the last three rows are

Table 3. The numbers of network parameters with involved methods, the 'M' in 'Parameters' column equal to 2^{20}. All the statistics only consider the generators. (*): The statistics of Pconv [6] is based on the unofficial implementation.

Method	Parameters	Occupied capacity of disk	Network type
GLCIC [3]	5.8M	46.3 MB	Two-Discriminator GAN
CA [11]	2.9M (×2)	13.8 MB	Two-stage GAN
Pconv [6]	31.34M*	393 MB*	Only Generator
EdgeCnt [8]	10.26M (×2)	41.1 MB	Two-stage GAN
LPI-Large	5.47M	22.0 MB	Generative Adversarial Network
LPI	**1.67M**	6.74 MB	Generative Adversarial Network

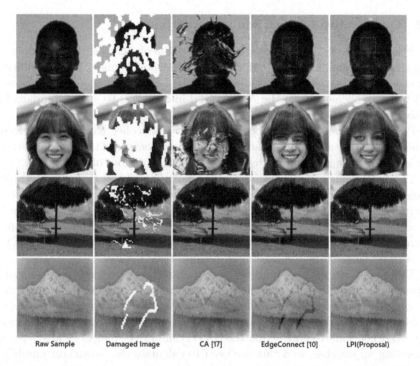

Raw Sample   Damaged Image   CA [17]   EdgeConnect [10]   LPI(Proposal)

Fig. 3. The qualitative comparison on test dataset of Places2 [13] and CelebA [7] over existing inpainting methods.

from Places2 [13]. The colored dotted rectangles display the detailed difference between our proposal and other approaches. The result demonstrates that the LPI network can produce more reasonable and legible results while occupying lower memory space.

4   Conclusions

To promote the application of image inpainting on mobile devices and embedded devices, this paper designs and proposes a lightweight pyramid inpainting network named LPI-Net. Benefited from the lightweight ResBlock and lightweight design of each step in the top-down pathway, the LPI network takes up at least 71.2% (CA [11] and GLCIC [3]) fewer parameters than these well-known state-of-art inpainting method.

Acknowledgements. This research is supported by Sichuan Provincial Science and Technology Program (No. 2020YFS0307), National Natural Science Foundation of China (No. 61907009), Science and Technology Planning Project of Guangdong Province (No. 2019B010150002). Supported by Postgraduate Innovation Fund Project by Southwest University of Science and Technology (No. 20ycx0002).

References

1. Goodfellow, I., et al.: Generative adversarial nets. In: Advances in Neural Information Processing Systems, pp. 2672–2680 (2014)
2. Howard, A.G., et al.: MobileNets: efficient convolutional neural networks for mobile vision applications. arXiv preprint arXiv:1704.04861 (2017)
3. Iizuka, S., Simo-Serra, E., Ishikawa, H.: Globally and locally consistent image completion. ACM Trans. Graph. (ToG) **36**(4), 107 (2017)
4. Kingma, D.P., Ba, J.: Adam: a method for stochastic optimization. arXiv preprint arXiv:1412.6980 (2014)
5. Lin, T.Y., Dollár, P., Girshick, R., He, K., Hariharan, B., Belongie, S.: Feature pyramid networks for object detection. In: Proceedings of the IEEE Conference on Computer Vision and Pattern Recognition, pp. 2117–2125 (2017)
6. Liu, G., Reda, F.A., Shih, K.J., Wang, T.C., Tao, A., Catanzaro, B.: Image inpainting for irregular holes using partial convolutions. In: Proceedings of the European Conference on Computer Vision (ECCV), pp. 85–100 (2018)
7. Liu, Z., Luo, P., Wang, X., Tang, X.: Deep learning face attributes in the wild. In: Proceedings of the IEEE International Conference on Computer Vision, pp. 3730–3738 (2015)
8. Nazeri, K., Ng, E., Joseph, T., Qureshi, F.Z., Ebrahimi, M.: EdgeConnect: generative image inpainting with adversarial edge learning. arXiv preprint arXiv:1901.00212 (2019)
9. Pathak, D., Krahenbuhl, P., Donahue, J., Darrell, T., Efros, A.A.: Context encoders: feature learning by inpainting. In: Proceedings of the IEEE Conference on Computer Vision and Pattern Recognition, pp. 2536–2544 (2016)
10. Sandler, M., Howard, A., Zhu, M., Zhmoginov, A., Chen, L.C.: MobileNetV2: inverted residuals and linear bottlenecks. In: Proceedings of the IEEE Conference on Computer Vision and Pattern Recognition, pp. 4510–4520 (2018)
11. Yu, J., Lin, Z., Yang, J., Shen, X., Lu, X., Huang, T.S.: Generative image inpainting with contextual attention. In: Proceedings of the IEEE Conference on Computer Vision and Pattern Recognition, pp. 5505–5514 (2018)
12. Yu, J., Lin, Z., Yang, J., Shen, X., Lu, X., Huang, T.S.: Free-form image inpainting with gated convolution. In: Proceedings of the IEEE International Conference on Computer Vision, pp. 4471–4480 (2019)
13. Zhou, B., Lapedriza, A., Khosla, A., Oliva, A., Torralba, A.: Places: a 10 million image database for scene recognition. IEEE Trans. Pattern Anal. Mach. Intell. **40**(6), 1452–1464 (2017)

MobileHand: Real-Time 3D Hand Shape and Pose Estimation from Color Image

Guan Ming Lim[1(✉)], Prayook Jatesiktat[2], and Wei Tech Ang[1,2]

[1] School of Mechanical and Aerospace Engineering,
Nanyang Technological University, 50 Nanyang Avenue,
Singapore 639798, Singapore
`guanming001@e.ntu.edu.sg, wtang@ntu.edu.sg`
[2] Rehabilitation Research Institute of Singapore, Nanyang Technological University,
11 Mandalay Road, Singapore 308232, Singapore
`prayook001@e.ntu.edu.sg`

Abstract. We present an approach for real-time estimation of 3D hand shape and pose from a single RGB image. To achieve real-time performance, we utilize an efficient Convolutional Neural Network (CNN): MobileNetV3-Small to extract key features from an input image. The extracted features are then sent to an iterative 3D regression module to infer camera parameters, hand shapes and joint angles for projecting and articulating a 3D hand model. By combining the deep neural network with the differentiable hand model, we can train the network with supervision from 2D and 3D annotations in an end-to-end manner. Experiments on two publicly available datasets demonstrate that our approach matches the accuracy of most existing methods while running at over 110 Hz on a GPU or 75 Hz on a CPU.

Keywords: End-to-end learning · 3D hand tracking · Efficient CNN

1 Introduction

Our hands play an important role in our interaction with the environment. Therefore, the ability to understand the hand shape and motion from color images is useful for a myriad of practical applications such as hand sign recognition, virtual/augmented reality, human-computer interaction, hand rehabilitation assessment and many more. New opportunities could also be realized if the hand tracking algorithm could run efficiently on mobile devices to take advantage of its portability and ubiquitous nature.

Although some methods are capable of tracking 2D or 3D hand joints on mobile devices [2,7], 3D hand shape and pose estimation is still restricted to devices with GPU hardware. As compared to sparse prediction of hand joint

Supported by Agency for Science, Technology and Research (A*STAR), Nanyang Technological University (NTU) and the National Healthcare Group (NHG). Project code: RFP/19003.

H. Yang et al. (Eds.): ICONIP 2020, CCIS 1332, pp. 450–459, 2020.
https://doi.org/10.1007/978-3-030-63820-7_52

Table 1. List of recent works on hand shape and pose estimation from color image

Authors (Publication)	Type of CNN used for feature extraction	Type/generation of hand model	Runtime
Baek et al. (CVPR'19) [1]	ResNet-50	MANO	Nil
Boukhayma et al. (CVPR'19) [3]	ResNet-50	MANO	Nil
Ge et al. (CVPR'19) [6]	Stacked hourglass, residual network	Graph CNN	50 Hz (GPU GTX 1080)
Hasson et al. (CVPR'19) [10]	ResNet-18	MANO	20 Hz (GPU Titan X)
Zhang et al. (ICCV'19) [20]	Stacked hourglass	MANO	Nil
Kulon et al. (CVPR'20) [14]	ResNet-50	Spatial mesh conv. decoder	60 Hz (GPU RTX 2080 Ti)
Zhou et al. (CVPR'20) [22]	ResNet-50	MANO	100 Hz (GPU GTX 1080 Ti)
This work	MobileNetV3-Small	MANO	110 Hz (GPU RTX 2080 Ti) 75 Hz (CPU 8-Core)

positions, dense recovery of 3D hand mesh is considerably more useful as it offers a richer amount of information. Therefore, the design of an efficient method for estimating 3D hand shape and pose remains an open and challenging problem.

In this work, we present an approach for real-time estimation of hand shape and pose, by using a lightweight Convolutional Neural Network (CNN) to reduce computation time. Although some tradeoff between speed and accuracy is unavoidable, our experiments on two datasets demonstrate that while the accuracy is comparable to most of the existing methods, the runtime of the proposed network is the fastest among all competitive approaches. We also proposed a simple joint angle representation to articulate a commonly used 3D hand model, which helps to improve accuracy. The video demonstrations and software codes are made available for research purposes at https://gmntu.github.io/mobilehand/.

2 Related Work

The advance in deep learning and ease of using a monocular RGB camera to capture hand motion, have motivated many previous works to use deep neural networks to estimate 3D hand pose from a single RGB image [4, 12, 16, 18, 24].

But recent works as listed in Table 1, are moving towards the estimation of hand shape together with pose because a 3D hand mesh is much more expressive. For example, it allows the computation of contact loss from mesh vertices during hand-object interaction [10], and also enables the rendering of 2D hand silhouette to refine hand shape and pose prediction [1, 3, 20]. As shown in Table 1, while two

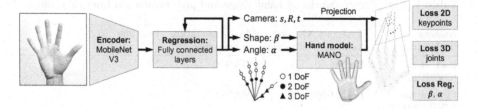

Fig. 1. Framework overview: a cropped image of a hand is passed through a CNN encoder to extract key features which are sent to an iterative regression module to infer a set of parameters. The shape and joint angles are used by the hand model to generate a 3D hand mesh which is projected to a 2D image plane using the camera parameters. By incorporating the generative and differentiable hand model as part of the deep learning architecture, the network can be trained end-to-end using both 2D keypoints and 3D joints supervision.

of the methods generate a 3D hand mesh using Graph CNN [6] or spatial mesh convolutional decoder [14], most of the methods employ a common parametric mesh model (MANO [17]) to exploit the inherent geometric priors encoded in the 3D hand model.

Although the runtimes of existing methods have achieved real-time rates on a GPU, we show that it is possible to further improve the computational performance and achieve real-time rates on CPU as well, making it suitable to be extended for mobile phone applications.

3   Method

The proposed method as illustrated in Fig. 1, is inspired by the work on end-to-end recovery of human body shape and pose [13]. To further improve the speed and accuracy of the method for hand shape and pose estimation, we proposed two key modifications: 1) an efficient CNN for image encoder and 2) a direct joint angle representation to articulate a 3D hand model. More details on the proposed framework are provided in the following sections.

3.1   Neural Network Architecture

The neural network architecture consists of two main parts: an image encoder and an iterative 3D regression module with feedback.

Image Encoder: We utilize MobileNetV3-Small [11] to extract image features as it is one of the latest generations of efficient and lightweight CNN targeted for mobile devices. The encoder takes in an RGB image (224 by 224 pixels) and the structure of MobileNetV3-Small is used up to the average pooling layer to output a feature vector $\phi \in \mathbb{R}^{576}$.

Iterative Regression: With the extracted feature vector $\phi \in \mathbb{R}^{576}$, it is possible to use a fully connected layer to directly regress the camera, hand shape and joint angle parameters $\Theta = \{s, R, t, \beta, \alpha\} \in \mathbb{R}^{39}$ [3]. However, it is challenging to regress Θ in one forward pass, due to large semantic gap [20] and especially when Θ includes rotation parameters R and α [13].

Thus, we use an iterative regression module [13,20] to make progressive changes to an initial estimate. This helps to simplify the learning problem as the module only needs to predict the change to move the parameters closer to the ground truth [5]. More specifically, the feature vector ϕ and current parameter vector Θ_t are concatenated and fed into a fully connected network that outputs the residual $\Delta\Theta_t$. The residual is then added to the current parameter to obtain a more accurate estimate $\Theta_{t+1} = \Theta_t + \Delta\Theta_t$. The initial estimate Θ_0 is set as a zero vector $\mathbf{0} \in \mathbb{R}^{39}$, and the number of iterations is kept at three as additional iteration has little effect on accuracy.

In this work, the regression block consists of an input layer with 615 nodes (576 features and 39 pose parameters), followed by two hidden layers with 288 neurons in each layer, and an output layer with 39 neurons. It is also important to insert dropout layers with a probability of 0.5 after the first and second layers to prevent overfitting.

3.2 3D Hand Model

The output parameters from the neural network are used by the 3D hand model MANO [17], to generate a triangulated hand mesh $M(\beta, \theta) \in \mathbb{R}^{3 \times N}$, with $N = 778$ vertices. The underlying 3D joints $J(\beta, \theta) \in \mathbb{R}^{3 \times K}$, where $K = 15$ joints, are obtained by linear regression from mesh vertices M.

MANO has been used in the majority of recent works on hand mesh recovery [1,3,10,20,22], as it offers simple control of the hand shape (finger length, palm thickness, etc.) and pose (3D rotation of the joints in axis-angle representation) with $\beta \in \mathbb{R}^{10}$ and $\theta \in \mathbb{R}^{3K}$ respectively.

However, pose $\theta \in \mathbb{R}^{45}$ contains redundant dimensions, resulting in infeasible hand pose (such as twisting of finger joint) if it is not constrained during the optimization process. This issue can be partially addressed by reducing the dimensionality of pose θ to $\theta_{PCA} \in \mathbb{R}^{10}$ [3] which is based on the Principal Component Analysis (PCA) of the pose database used to build MANO [17]. Nevertheless, θ_{PCA} may not be expressive enough and some works prefer the original pose representation, but manually define the pose limits [9] or impose geometric constraints [20].

Joint Angle Representation: Contrary to other methods, we propose a simple and effective joint angle representation $\alpha \in \mathbb{R}^{23}$ with a total of 23 degrees of freedom (DoF): four DoF for each finger and seven DoF for the thumb. In fact, joint angles have been used in other types of 3D hand model [15,21], where the rotation angles are bounded within a feasible range based on anatomical studies.

In order to maintain compatibility with MANO, we compute rotation matrices that transform our local joint angles to match MANO pose. By combining all the rotation matrices to form a sparse matrix $\mathbf{T} \in \mathbb{R}^{45 \times 23}$, all the joint angles $\alpha \in \mathbb{R}^{23}$ can be mapped to MANO pose $\theta \in \mathbb{R}^{45}$ in a single step:

$$\theta = \mathbf{T}\alpha \tag{1}$$

The advantage of using joint angle representation is further discussed in Sect. 4.1 which compares the results of using α, θ and θ_{PCA} representations.

Camera Model: The camera parameters $\{s, R, t\}$ represent the scaling $s \in \mathbb{R}^+$ in image plane, global rotation matrix $R \in SO(3)$ in axis-angle representation, and translation $t \in \mathbb{R}^2$ in image plane. A weak perspective camera model is used to project the 3D joints into the 2D image plane:

$$x = s\Pi(RJ(\beta, \theta)) + t, \tag{2}$$

where Π is simply an orthographic projection to remove the dependency on camera intrinsics for supervising with 2D keypoint annotations.

3.3 Loss Functions

The loss function consists of three main terms:

$$\mathcal{L} = \lambda_{2D}\mathcal{L}_{2D} + \lambda_{3D}\mathcal{L}_{3D} + \lambda_{reg}\mathcal{L}_{reg} \tag{3}$$

where the hyperparameters λ_{2D}, λ_{3D}, and λ_{reg}, are empirically set to 10^2, 10^2 and 10^3 respectively.

The first and second terms share a similar formulation to minimize the mean squared difference between the estimated 2D keypoints/3D joints and ground truth 2D/3D annotations:

$$\mathcal{L}_{2D/3D} = \frac{1}{n} \sum_{i=1}^{n} \|Estimated_i - Groundtruth_i\|_2^2 \tag{4}$$

where $n = 21$ includes the 15 hand joints J, with the addition of a wrist joint and five fingertips extracted from the mesh vertices M [3].

The last term acts as a regularizer to prevent mesh distortion by reducing the magnitude of shape β, where $\beta = \mathbf{0} \in \mathbb{R}^{10}$ is the average shape. The joint angle α is also constraint within a feasible range of upper $U \in \mathbb{R}^{23}$ and lower $L \in \mathbb{R}^{23}$ joint angle boundaries [15]:

$$\mathcal{L}_{reg} = \|\beta\|_2^2 + \sum_{i=1}^{23} [max(0, L_i - \alpha_i) + max(0, \alpha_i - U_i)] \tag{5}$$

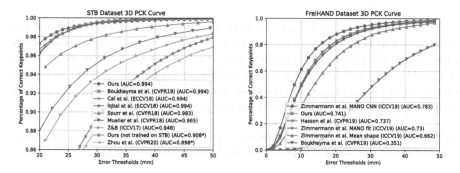

Fig. 2. (Left) Quantitative results on STB dataset, note that all the methods used the STB dataset for training, except for the last two methods with an "*" on the AUC score. (Right) Quantitative results on FreiHAND dataset.

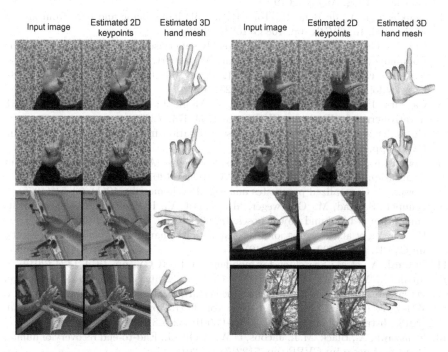

Fig. 3. Qualitative results: First two rows show the results on the STB dataset and the last two rows show the results on the FreiHAND dataset which contain hand-object interactions. The last row shows failure cases for challenging hand poses with the presence of another hand (bottom left) and extreme viewpoint where the hand is heavily occluded (bottom right).

5 Conclusion

In this paper, we present an efficient method to estimate 3D hand shape and pose that can achieve comparable accuracy against most of the existing methods, while the runtime of our method is the fastest on a GPU as well as a CPU. The proposed joint angle representation to articulate the hand model also helps to improve accuracy. Future works include increasing the robustness of the predictions and extending the method to run on mobile devices.

Acknowledgments. The computational work for this article was partially performed on resources of the National Supercomputing Centre, Singapore (https://www.nscc.sg).

References

1. Baek, S., Kim, K.I., Kim, T.: Pushing the envelope for RGB-based dense 3D hand pose estimation via neural rendering. In: CVPR, pp. 1067–1076 (2019)
2. Bazarevsky, V., Zhang, F.: On-device, real-time hand tracking with mediapipe. Google AI Blog, August 2019
3. Boukhayma, A., de Bem, R., Torr, P.H.S.: 3D hand shape and pose from images in the wild. In: CVPR, pp. 10835–10844 (2019)
4. Cai, Y., Ge, L., Cai, J., Yuan, J.: Weakly-supervised 3D hand pose estimation from monocular RGB images. In: Ferrari, V., Hebert, M., Sminchisescu, C., Weiss, Y. (eds.) ECCV 2018. LNCS, vol. 11210, pp. 678–694. Springer, Cham (2018). https://doi.org/10.1007/978-3-030-01231-1_41
5. Carreira, J., Agrawal, P., Fragkiadaki, K., Malik, J.: Human pose estimation with iterative error feedback. In: CVPR, pp. 4733–4742 (2016)
6. Ge, L., et al.: 3D hand shape and pose estimation from a single RGB image. In: CVPR, pp. 10825–10834 (2019)
7. Gouidis, F., Panteleris, P., Oikonomidis, I., Argyros, A.A.: Accurate hand keypoint localization on mobile devices. In: MVA, pp. 1–6 (2019)
8. Gower, J.: Generalized procrustes analysis. Psychometrika **40**(1), 33–51 (1975)
9. Hampali, S., Rad, M., Oberweger, M., Lepetit, V.: HOnnotate: a method for 3D annotation of hand and object poses. In: CVPR, pp. 3193–3203 (2020)
10. Hasson, Y., et al.: Learning joint reconstruction of hands and manipulated objects. In: CVPR, pp. 11799–11808 (2019)
11. Howard, A., et al.: Searching for mobilenetv3. In: ICCV, pp. 1314–1324 (2019)
12. Iqbal, U., Molchanov, P., Breuel, T., Gall, J., Kautz, J.: Hand pose estimation via latent 2.5D heatmap regression. In: Ferrari, V., Hebert, M., Sminchisescu, C., Weiss, Y. (eds.) ECCV 2018. LNCS, vol. 11215, pp. 125–143. Springer, Cham (2018). https://doi.org/10.1007/978-3-030-01252-6_8
13. Kanazawa, A., Black, M.J., Jacobs, D.W., Malik, J.: End-to-end recovery of human shape and pose. In: CVPR, pp. 7122–7131 (2018)
14. Kulon, D., Güler, R.A., Kokkinos, I., Bronstein, M., Zafeiriou, S.: Weakly-supervised mesh-convolutional hand reconstruction in the wild. In: CVPR (2020)
15. Lim, G.M., Jatesiktat, P., Kuah, C.W.K., Ang, W.T.: Camera-based hand tracking using a mirror-based multi-view setup. In: EMBC, pp. 5789–5793 (2020)
16. Mueller, F., et al.: Ganerated hands for real-time 3D hand tracking from monocular RGB. In: CVPR, pp. 49–59 (2018)

17. Romero, J., Tzionas, D., Black, M.J.: Embodied hands: modeling and capturing hands and bodies together. ACM TOG **36**(6) (2017)
18. Spurr, A., Song, J., Park, S., Hilliges, O.: Cross-modal deep variational hand pose estimation. In: CVPR, pp. 89–98 (2018)
19. Zhang, J., Jiao, J., Chen, M., Qu, L., Xu, X., Yang, Q.: A hand pose tracking benchmark from stereo matching. In: ICIP, pp. 982–986 (2017)
20. Zhang, X., Li, Q., Mo, H., Zhang, W., Zheng, W.: End-to-end hand mesh recovery from a monocular RGB image. In: ICCV, pp. 2354–2364 (2019)
21. Zhou, X., Wan, Q., Zhang, W., Xue, X., Wei, Y.: Model-based deep hand pose estimation. In: IJCAI, pp. 2421–2427 (2016)
22. Zhou, Y., Habermann, M., Xu, W., Habibie, I., Theobalt, C., Xu, F.: Monocular real-time hand shape and motion capture using multi-modal data. In: CVPR (2020)
23. Zimmermann, C., Ceylan, D., Yang, J., Russell, B., Argus, M.J., Brox, T.: Freihand: a dataset for markerless capture of hand pose and shape from single RGB images. In: ICCV, pp. 813–822 (2019)
24. Zimmermann, C., Brox, T.: Learning to estimate 3D hand pose from single RGB images. In: ICCV, pp. 4913–4921 (2017)

Monitoring Night Skies with Deep Learning

Yuri Galindo[1]([⊠]) [iD], Marcelo De Cicco[2,3,4] [iD], Marcos G. Quiles[1] [iD],
and Ana C. Lorena[5] [iD]

[1] Univ. Fed. São Paulo - UNIFESP, São José dos Campos, SP, Brazil
yurioliveiragalindo@gmail.com
[2] INMETRO, Divisão de Metrologia Cientifica, Rio de Janeiro, RJ, Brazil
[3] Observatório Nacional, Rio de Janeiro, RJ, Brazil
[4] EXOSS, Rio de Janeiro, RJ, Brazil
[5] Inst. Tecn. Aeronáutica - ITA, São José dos Campos, SP, Brazil

Abstract. The surveillance of meteors is important due to the possibility of studying the Universe and identifying hazardous events. The EXOSS initiative monitors the Brazilian sky with cameras in order to identify meteors, leading to a great quantity of non-meteor captures that must be filtered. We approach the task of automatically distinguishing between meteor and non-meteor images with the use of pre-trained convolutional neural networks. Our main contributions are the revision of the methodology for evaluating models on this task, showing that the previous methodology leads to an overestimation of the expected performance for future data on our dataset; and the application of probability calibration in order to improve the selection of most confident predictions, showing that apart from obtaining probabilities that better reflect the confidence of the model, calibration can lead to concrete improvements on both accuracy and coverage. Our method achieves 98% accuracy predicting on 60% of the images, improving upon the performance of the uncalibrated model of 94% accuracy predicting on 70% of the images.

Keywords: Deep learning · Computer vision · Uncertainty estimation

1 Introduction

Meteors, popularly known as "shooting stars", represent material remaining from the formation of the solar system that enter Earth's atmosphere at high speed, losing mass and producing light and ionisation. The observation of this process makes it possible to infer chemical and physical properties of the object. Meteor showers occur due to the passage of comets that produce a high quantity of debris, in an event that attracts the interest of human observers and can greatly increase the risk of hazard to spacecrafts [14].

Supported by FAPESP (2018/20508-2).

The non-governmental organization EXOSS (Exploring the Southern Sky) surveils the occurrence of meteors on the Brazilian sky based on the citizen science model, in which volunteers can install monitoring cameras at their properties. These cameras capture events of moving objects on the night sky with the UFOCapture software [13], populating the EXOSS database with captures of moving objects. These captures must then be filtered by the astronomers associated with the program for identifying meteor captures, averaging over 100 images per night to be visually analysed.

In this work we apply pre-trained Convolutional Neural Networks (CNNs) to the task of classifying the images captured by this meteor surveillance network as containing or not a meteor. We calibrate the likelihood given by our model on a separate partition to improve the confidence estimate of the predictions, and use this estimate to select the predictions with confidence above a certain threshold. With this strategy we are able to leave only images for which the CNN is not confident to be examined by the human experts, reducing their overload.

By employing this method we are able to achieve 98% of accuracy by predicting on 60% of the data, improving upon the baselines of 90% of accuracy without thresholding and of 94% of accuracy by predicting on 70% of the data with thresholding but no calibration. Our use of calibration increases the granularity of the choice of the confidence threshold, providing more freedom for setting the desired accuracy level. The identification of uncertain examples is especially relevant for surveillance systems such as the EXOSS network since novel events may be of interest for human inspection.

We also apply a different methodology for partitioning the dataset into training and test data that takes into account the station (location) of the captures, differing from previous work [3–5,9,12] that randomly selected images for composing the training and test partitions. We show that the previous methodology leads to overestimation of performance in our dataset: a model with estimated 97.7% of accuracy by predicting on randomly separated images actually obtains 90% of accuracy when predicting on unseen regions. Our proposed methodology provides a more reliable estimate of the performance of the model for new captures. This is specially relevant for contexts in which new capturing stations can be added at any time, such as EXOSS.

2 Related Work

Galindo and Lorena [5] employed pre-trained deep CNNs to a dataset of 1,660 images, achieving and accuracy of 96% and 0.94 of F1 score. Data augmentation based on image flipping and rotation were found to worsen accuracy, which may be related to the fact that the meteor trajectories produced are unlikely.

Marsola and Lorena [12] worked with a reduced subset of the dataset used in Galindo and Lorena [5], employing data augmentation and dropout. The achieved average accuracy was of 84.35%.

De Cicco et al. [4] employed a random forest classifier based on engineered features related to the trajectories of each object, achieving 90% of precision and

81% of recall. A small CNN was trained from scratch and used to classify images, reporting 88% precision and 90% recall. A Long Short Term Memory Network (LSTM) was also trained to classify pieces of the detected trajectory, achieving 90% of precision and 89% of recall. The dataset contained 200,000 CAMS (Cameras for Allsky Meteor Surveillance) captures of which approximately 3% contained meteors.

Gural [9] used Deep Learning techniques in a balanced dataset of 200,000 CAMS captures and reported up to 0.99 of F1 score, with 99.94% of precision and 99.6% of recall. Architectures which incorporated multiple frames of the video capture were experimented with but did not lead to an improvement of predictive performance.

Cecil and Campbell-Brown [3] achieved 99.8% of accuracy on a dataset of 55,960 images by identifying regions of interest and applying CNNs to the identified regions.

We contribute upon these works by showing that the methodology for training and testing the predictive model should be revised to take into account the region and date metadata, which may lead to overestimation of performance; and by applying calibration and confidence thresholding to identify uncertain examples that may lead to mistakes in automatic classification. The identification of uncertain examples makes it possible to identify novel events that may be of interest to astronomers, and was not previously explored.

3   Materials and Methods

3.1   The Dataset

Our dataset consists of 2,971 meteors and 2,649 non meteors images from the EXOSS initiative, taken by cameras from 52 different stations and recorded between January of 2016 and May of 2019. These images summarize a short video capture and are generated by the UFOCapture software [13]. The images provide enough information for a human classification in the vast majority of cases. Given the additional computational cost for training and prediction and the lack of performance gain reported by Gural [9] when using video information, we opted make our predictions based solely on this image information.

The two main sources of difficulty for this image classification task are the variety of non-meteor objects and uncontrolled environment. The automatic captures lead to images that may present occlusion, glitches, and various environment conditions such as rain and the presence of clouds. The non-meteor captures may come from a multitude of objects such as clouds, raindrops, insects, airplanes, birds, and artificial satellites. These objects may also be present on images that contain meteor captures. Figure 1 displays examples of meteor and non-meteor captures. Meteors are usually observed as small and straight white lines.

Fig. 1. Examples of a meteor (left) and non-meteor (right) image

3.2 Estimating Confidence

Deep Learning models for classification often adopt a softmax function in the last layer [2], which guarantees that the outputs are positive and sum up to 1, resembling probabilities. These models are generally trained using the Cross-Entropy loss function, that is minimized when the predicted probabilities correspond to the true likelihood of the predictions given the data.

This probabilistic interpretation of the output of Neural Networks for classification has led to the usage of confidence thresholds for estimating uncertainty in practical applications [7,15]. Classifications for which the largest predicted probability is under a threshold are deemed uncertain and are not output by the model. This approach can increase accuracy in the reduced set containing the examples with higher confidence.

Guo et al. [8] showed that the probabilities produced by modern high-capacity neural networks are miscalibrated: the confidence produced by the softmax function does not match the average accuracy of new predictions for that confidence level. The proposed solution is to use post-processing calibration methods that are trained on top of the model predictions on a calibration set. Among these methods are temperature scaling [8], consisting of the division by a constant before the softmax layer; and isotonic regression [1].

Isotonic regression refers to the problem of fitting a non-decreasing function that minimizes mean squared error. A common implementation fits a piecewise constant function by finding neighborhoods of points that violate the non-decreasing property and replacing them with their mean [16]. In the context of calibration, the ordering of the points is given by the uncalibrated probabilities, and the function is the true label of each data point. Since the calibrated score for regions with wrong predictions is replaced by the observed mean of positive examples, the isotonic fit serves as a binning algorithm.

We improve the use of confidence thresholds by calibrating the probabilities before applying the threshold. We found that the more reliable probabilities produced by calibration led to a better trade-off between the percentage of confident examples and accuracy.

4   Experiments

Our CNN model is based on the Resnet50 architecture [10], and was pre-trained in the ImageNet dataset. We fine-tune [6] the network to our data while maintaining the weights of the first 33 layers fixed. We selected this architecture and number of frozen layers through cross-validation on the task of predicting on new regions.

The CNN models were trained with cross-entropy loss for 30 epochs with the Adam algorithm [11]. A set of 500 random images separated from the training set was used to detect the epoch with best validation accuracy for early stopping. The following algorithm parameters were considered: $\beta_1 = 0.9, \beta_2 = 0.999$, a learning rate of 3e−4, and a learning rate decay of 0.99. The developed code is available at GitHub[1].

4.1   Effect of Data Splitting

Due to the automatic nature of the captures, a single object may trigger multiple captures. A common occurrence of this phenomena is due to storms, when the same group of clouds may be the focus of hundreds of videos captured on a given region. This causes a high correlation between images of similar time of capture.

Another relationship is caused by the differing frequencies of non-meteor objects between regions. For instance, cameras close to airports may have frequent captures of aircrafts that are rarely seen in other regions, while some regions have insects that do not appear on others.

We propose splitting the training and test data by different dates of capture or different regions in order to take these correlations into account. The date split prevents the presence of images from the same event in the training and test sets, and the region split also prevents this effect while measuring the generalization for unseen events and new camera and ambient conditions.

Table 1. Observed performance with different splitting criteria

Criteria for splitting the data	Accuracy	Precision	Recall
Random	$97.7 \pm 0.5\%$	$98 \pm 1\%$	$97.9 \pm 0.9\%$
Distinct dates	$95 \pm 1\%$	$94 \pm 1\%$	$97.7 \pm 0.7\%$
Distinct regions	$90 \pm 7\%$	$90 \pm 9\%$	$95 \pm 1\%$

The experiment in Table 1 is a comparison between the estimated performance using the methodologies of randomly splitting the data, separating images by date of capture, and separating by region. The separation between regions was performed by randomly selecting 10 regions (average of 1,620 images) for the test

---

[1] https://github.com/yurigalindo/DeepLearningMeteors.

set and using the images of the remaining 42 regions for training. For the methods of randomly separating the data and separating by regions, we evaluated performance on four different training and test splits with five different network initializations for each split, totaling 20 experiments for each methodology.

The separation between dates was performed by selecting six months across the three years of captures (1,417 images) for the test set. Due to the concentration of captures of some regions on specific periods, such as regions that had heightened activities on some periods or that were added or removed more recently, the months were selected as to have all regions present on both training and test sets, which prevented evaluation with different choices of months for testing. We evaluated this methodology with 15 different network initializations.

The accuracy estimated by testing the model on new date periods is of 95%, lower than the 97.5% of accuracy obtained when predicting on randomly selected new images. This is an evidence of the overestimation of performance due to the presence of images with similar timestamps on training and test data that may come from the same event. The lower estimated accuracy of 90% when predicting on new regions befits this hypothesis and suggests trouble with generalization to unseen objects and new station setups. The greater standard deviation of the region split when compared to the random split indicates that some separations of regions are harder than others due to greater dissimilarity between the training and test sets, whereas when randomly splitting the data the dissimilarity between the training and test set is more constant. This analysis cannot be extended to the date separation since only one split was evaluated, in face of the temporal constraints for splitting the data.

Separating training and test sets by region is the appropriate setup for our application, since new stations are constantly added to the EXOSS program and measuring the performance of the model when applied to new regions is more representative of how the model would be applied in practice. This approach might not be feasible in some cases, such as surveillance programs that have only a single station, in which case the separation by date should be used to prevent the presence of images of the same event on training and test sets. This methodology will be adopted on the following experiments and should be taken into account for future works regarding meteor surveillance.

4.2   Estimating Uncertainty

Our experimental setup consisted of separating three regions (average of 548 images) from the training set in order to create a calibration set. The calibration models are trained on the predictions made on this set, and evaluated at the region separated test set as described in Sect. 4.1. This experiment was performed 20 times, with four different test set splits and five different network initializations for each split.

Table 2 shows the performance of the different calibration methods operating at various confidence thresholds, in which the confidence is taken as the estimated probability of the predicted class. With the use of confidence thresholding, we only make predictions with confidence equal or greater than the threshold, and discard the remaining examples to be classified by humans afterwards. Coverage refers to the proportion of examples that are above the threshold and not discarded. The evaluated confidence thresholds for each model were 99%, 95%, 90%, 85%, 80%, 75% and 70%. Thresholds with performance similar to those displayed were omitted for brevity.

Table 2. Performance of thresholding strategies

Calibration method	Threshold	Accuracy	Coverage	Precision	Recall
None	99%	$94 \pm 8\%$	$70 \pm 20\%$	$92 \pm 10\%$	$98 \pm 1\%$
None	95%	$92 \pm 8\%$	$80 \pm 10\%$	$90 \pm 10\%$	$98 \pm 1\%$
None	None (50%)	$90 \pm 7\%$	100%	$90 \pm 9\%$	$95 \pm 1\%$
Temperature scaling	99%	$99.3 \pm 0.6\%$	$20 \pm 20\%$	$99 \pm 1\%$	$99.6 \pm 0.9\%$
Temperature scaling	90%	$98 \pm 2\%$	$60 \pm 30\%$	$98 \pm 3\%$	$99 \pm 1\%$
Temperature scaling	85%	$97 \pm 3\%$	$70 \pm 30\%$	$97 \pm 4\%$	$98 \pm 2\%$
Temperature scaling	75%	$95 \pm 6\%$	$80 \pm 20\%$	$94 \pm 7\%$	$97 \pm 2\%$
Isotonic regression	99%	$97 \pm 4\%$	$50 \pm 20\%$	$99 \pm 1\%$	$92 \pm 20\%$
Isotonic regression	85%	$94 \pm 5\%$	$80 \pm 10\%$	$96 \pm 5\%$	$93 \pm 5\%$

The use of thresholding was effective at improving performance at the cost of predicting on less examples. The uncalibrated model obtained 94% of accuracy at the highest confidence level, reducing the error rate without any threshold from 10% to 6% by predicting on 70% of the examples. Calibrating the model pushes this effect further, achieving 99.3% of accuracy and 99.6% of recall with 20% of coverage for the temperature scaled model and 97% of accuracy and 99% of precision with 50% of coverage for the model with isotonic regression.

The use of calibration led to a better control of the accuracy and coverage trade off. The 94% accuracy of the uncalibrated model at 99% confidence is similar to the temperature scaled model with 75% confidence and the isotonic regression model at 85% confidence. These models obtain 99.3% and 97% accuracy at the confidence level of 99% respectively, displaying performances that better reflect the high confidence. This indicates that the uncalibrated model was overconfident. Calibration also led to lower standard deviation of accuracy and precision, making the desired accuracy given a confidence level more reliable.

The temperature scaled model provides more advantageous choices and a more fine grained relationship between coverage and accuracy. It obtains better accuracy and precision when operating at the same confidence level of other models, displaying a more realistic estimate of confidence and making it possible to choose confidence levels with higher predictive performance.

For our application, the temperature scaled model operating at 90% of confidence provides a balanced and appropriate choice, maintaining accuracy and precision at 98% and recall at 99% while classifying 60% of the images.

5   Conclusion

In this work, we tackled the problem of classifying automatically captured images as containing or not meteors. We revised the methodology adopted on past work, demonstrating that training and test data should be properly separated, ideally by regions and alternatively by dates. We applied probability calibration in order to improve the selection of the most confident images, showing that aside from providing more reliable probabilities, calibration can lead to concrete improvements of coverage and predictive performance.

Acknowledgment. We thank FAPESP for funding this research (grant 2018/20508-2), the EXOSS organization for providing the data and astronomy expertise, and Pete Gural for discussions.

References

1. Barlow, R.E., Brunk, H.D.: The isotonic regression problem and its dual. J. Am. Stat. Assoc. **67**(337), 140–147 (1972)
2. Bishop, C.M.: Pattern Recognition and Machine Learning. Springer, New York (2006)
3. Cecil, D., Campbell-Brown, M.: The application of convolutional neural networks to the automation of a meteor detection pipeline. Planet. Space Sci. **186**, 104920 (2020)
4. De Cicco, M., et al.: Artificial intelligence techniques for automating the CAMS processing pipeline to direct the search for long-period comets. In: Proceedings of the IMC, Petnica (2017)
5. Galindo, Y.O., Lorena, A.C.: Deep transfer learning for meteor detection. In: Anais do Encontro Nacional de Inteligência Artificial e Computacional (ENIAC) (2018)
6. Girshick, R., Donahue, J., Darrell, T., Malik, J.: Rich feature hierarchies for accurate object detection and semantic segmentation. In: Proceedings of the IEEE Conference on Computer Vision and Pattern Recognition, pp. 580–587 (2014)
7. Goodfellow, I.J., Bulatov, Y., Ibarz, J., Arnoud, S., Shet, V.: Multi-digit number recognition from street view imagery using deep convolutional neural networks. arXiv preprint arXiv:1312.6082 (2013)
8. Guo, C., Pleiss, G., Sun, Y., Weinberger, K.Q.: On calibration of modern neural networks. In: Proceedings of the 34th International Conference on Machine Learning, vol. 70. pp. 1321–1330. JMLR.org (2017)
9. Gural, P.S.: Deep learning algorithms applied to the classification of video meteor detections. Mon. Not. Roy. Astron. Soc. **489**(4), 5109–5118 (2019)
10. He, K., Zhang, X., Ren, S., Sun, J.: Deep residual learning for image recognition. In: Proceedings of the IEEE Conference on Computer Vision and Pattern Recognition, pp. 770–778 (2016)
11. Kingma, D.P., Ba, J.: Adam: a method for stochastic optimization (2014)
12. Marsola, T.C., Lorena, A.C.: Meteor detection using deep convolutional neural networks. In: Anais do Simpósito Brasileiro de Automação Inteligente, vol. 1, p. 104260 (2019)
13. Molau, S., Gural, P.: A review of video meteor detection and analysis software. WGN J. Int. Meteor Organ. **33**, 15–20 (2005)

14. Moorhead, A.V., Cooke, W.J., Campbell-Brown, M.D.: Meteor shower forecasting for spacecraft operations (2017)
15. Norouzzadeh, M.S., et al.: Automatically identifying, counting, and describing wild animals in camera-trap images with deep learning. Proc. Natl. Acad. Sci. **115**(25), E5716–E5725 (2018)
16. Zadrozny, B., Elkan, C.: Transforming classifier scores into accurate multiclass probability estimates. In: Proceedings of the Eighth ACM SIGKDD International Conference on Knowledge Discovery and Data Mining, pp. 694–699 (2002)

MRNet: A Keypoint Guided Multi-scale Reasoning Network for Vehicle Re-identification

Minting Pan[1,2], Xiaoguang Zhu[2], Yongfu Li[1], Jiuchao Qian[2(✉)],
and Peilin Liu[2]

[1] Department of Micro-Nano Electronics and MoE Key Lab of Artificial Intelligence,
Shanghai Jiao Tong University, Shanghai, China
{Panmt53,yongfu.li}@sjtu.edu.cn
[2] Brain-Inspired Application Technology Center, Shanghai Jiao Tong University,
Shanghai, China
{zhuxiaoguang178,jcqian,liupeilin}@sjtu.edu.cn

Abstract. With the increasing usage of massive surveillance data, vehicle re-identification (re-ID) has become a hot topic in the computer vision community. Vehicle re-ID is a challenging problem due to the viewpoint variation, i.e. the different views greatly affect the visual appearance of a vehicle. To handle this problem, we propose an end-to-end framework called Keypoint Guided Multi-Scale Reasoning Network (MRNet) to infer multi-view vehicle features from a one-view image. In our proposed framework, besides the global branch, we learn multi-view vehicle information by introducing a local branch, which leverages different vehicle segments to do relational reasoning. MRNet can infer the latent whole vehicle feature by increasing the semantic similarity between incomplete vehicle segments. MRNet is evaluated on two benchmarks (VeRi-776 and VehicleID) and the experimental results show that our framework has achieved competitive performance with the state-of-the-art methods. On the more challenging dataset VeRi-776, we achieve 72.0% in mAP and 92.4% in Rank-1. Our code is available at https://github.com/panmt/MRNet_for_vehicle_reID.

Keywords: Vehicle re-identification · Relational reasoning · Multi-view features

1 Introduction

Vehicle re-identification (re-ID) is a task to retrieve all images with a specific vehicle identity captured by different cameras, which is useful to effectively locate vehicles of interest from a massive amount of video databases. In recent years, vehicle re-ID plays an important role in the video surveillance system and intelligent public security. An intuitive method is to use the information of license plates to identify vehicles [2,8], but the license plates cannot be clearly captured

© Springer Nature Switzerland AG 2020
H. Yang et al. (Eds.): ICONIP 2020, CCIS 1332, pp. 469–478, 2020.
https://doi.org/10.1007/978-3-030-63820-7_54

in many circumstances. As a result, learning the visual appearance of vehicles becomes the key to achieve a robust vehicle re-ID system.

Recently, Deep Convolutional Neural Network (DCNN) has been widely used in vehicle re-ID problem [9], where it is used to learn global features of an image; however, it is unable to capture detailed information from the vehicle's image. For example, two different vehicles with the same color and same model only can be distinguished by custom logos, tags in windows, etc. To leverage on neural network to extract detailed information from an image, it is feasible to design a local detector to recognize some specific regions [4]. [17] proposed a coarse-to-fine identification process to distinguish type of vehicles based on their vehicle models and color, and then carefully determine these vehicles by using subtle visual cues. However, the issue of viewpoint variation has not been effectively addressed in this work. In some situation, a vehicle shows great differences from different views due to the special 3D structure, causing that intra-class variability is higher than inter-class variability [15]. To tackle this challenge, Generative Adversarial Network (GAN) can be used to generate multi-view images [20], or to build viewpoint-invariant embedding feature space [19]. However, these works [19,20] did not take into consideration the relationship of different vehicle local regions within the vehicle's image, which is essential information to address the viewpoint variability problem.

Therefore, in this work, we propose a Keypoint Guided Multi-Scale Reasoning Network (MRNet) framework, to infer multi-view vehicle features from a one-view image. Our main contributions of this paper are as follows:

- **Neural Network.** MRNet performs simultaneously learning of the global representation and multi-view vehicle features in two branches, which effectively solves the practical viewpoint variability problem for vehicle re-ID. We divide a vehicle into several segments, and infer the multi-view features from a one-view image by creating an association between these segments.
- **Experimental Results.** We conduct comparison experiments and ablation studies on two benchmark datasets, and the results show that our proposed approach achieves competitive performance with the current state-of-the-art methods.

2   The Proposed MRNet Framework

As shown in Fig. 1, our proposed MRNet framework consists of two branches. In the global branch, we used the pretained ResNet-50 [5] as backbone and also adopt it as our baseline model.

2.1   Approach Overview

We define the training set as χ. Given three inputs x_a, x_p, and $x_n \in \chi$, where x_a and x_p belong to the same vehicle ID while x_a and x_n belong to the different vehicle IDs, we form a positive pair $P^+ = (x_a, x_p)$ and a negative pair

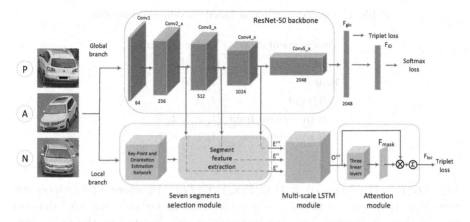

Fig. 1. Network architecture of the proposed MRNet, including global branch and local branch. In the global branch, the global features F_{glo} are extracted. The local branch is responsible for reasoning the multi-view vehicle features F_{loc} from a one-view image.

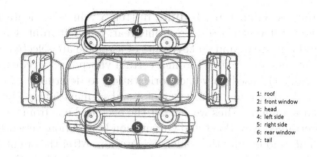

1: roof
2: front window
3: head
4: left side
5: right side
6: rear window
7: tail

Fig. 2. A vehicle is divided into seven segments, i.e. roof, front window, head, left side, right side, rear window and tail.

$P^- = (x_a, x_n)$. Let $f(\cdot)$ denote the feature extraction function, and $D(\cdot)$ denote the Euclidean distance in the feature space. We compute the distance of the positive pair by $D(P^+) = D(f(x_a), f(x_p))$ and the distance of the negative pair by $D(P^-) = D(f(x_a), f(x_n))$. Our goal is to design a robust function $f(\cdot)$ to reduce the positive distance $D(P^+)$ and increase the negative distance $D(P^-)$. In order to fully extract useful information from an image, we propose to divide a vehicle into seven segments (Fig. 2), and use the local branch to reason the relationship between them. A complete description of a vehicle is composed of a seven segments feature set $E = \{e_i \in R^D | i = (1, 2, ..., 7)\}$, and a feature set of an image captured by one view is a subset of the complete description, i.e. $E_{img} = \{e_j \in R^D | j = (1, 2, ..., m), m < 7\}$. Using the relational inference of each segment to obtain multi-view feature representation, we can cluster the same vehicle captured by different views in the semantic space,

472   M. Pan et al.

Table 1. Segment extraction based on vehicle orientation.

Vehicle orientation	Visible segments
Front	[1, 2, 3]
Rear	[1, 6, 7]
Left/right	[4, 5]
Left front/right front	[1, 2, 3, 4, 5]
Left rear/right rear	[1, 4, 5, 6, 7]

i.e. $D(G(T(x_a)), G(T(x_p))) < D(G(T(x_a)), G(T(x_n)))$, where $T(\cdot)$ denotes the transformation from an image to the seven segment features, and $G(\cdot)$ denotes the relational reasoning from the one-view vehicle features to the multi-view vehicle features.

2.2 Keypoint Guided Multi-scale Reasoning

Seven Segments Selection Module. In [16], a vehicle's orientation is annotated into eight different classes, i.e. front, rear, left, left front, left rear, right, right front and right rear, and 20 keypoints of a vehicle are selected. Considering that some segments are occluded from a certain viewpoint, we constructed eight groups (see Table 1) based on vehicle orientation to determine which segments are extracted. As shown in Fig. 2, segment 4 and segment 5 have similar features based on their symmetry, thus we can get the occluded one from the visible one. We utilize pretrained Key-Point and Orientation Estimation Network [7] to identify 20 keypoints and predict the vehicle orientation. After the orientation prediction, the visible segments can be selected according to Table 1. We project keypoints into the feature map $F \in R^{C \times H \times W}$ to mark the corresponding segments, and use the average pooling layer on the marked feature map to output segment feature vector $e_i \in R^C$. Therefore, the operation $T(\cdot)$ is constructed to represent all seven segments in an image x_i, i.e. $E = T(x_i) = \{e_i \in R^C | i = (1, 2, ..., 7)\}$, where e_i is equal to zero when its corresponding segment is occluded.

Multi-scale LSTM Module. In the Natural Language Processing (NLP), the Long Short-Term Memory network (LSTM) [6] is widely used to memory the information of the previous moment and predict the result of the next moment, building a connection of all inputs. Inspired by it, we adopt multi-scale LSTM to conduct the operation $G(\cdot)$, which utilizes the features of different scales to reduce the impact of inaccurate vehicle keypoint prediction. As shown in Fig. 1, we extract segment features from three deep blocks (conv2_x, conv3_x, conv4_x) of the global branch, resulting in feature $E' \in R^{7 \times 256}$, $E'' \in R^{7 \times 512}$ and $E''' \in R^{7 \times 1024}$, respectively. The Multi-scale LSTM module consists of three LSTM layers with different hidden sizes, and we use it to perform global semantic reasoning by putting the feature E, sequentially into each layer. The connection of the different layers can be unwrapped in Fig. 3. The feature set E' is input to

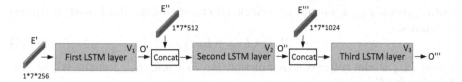

Fig. 3. The details of multi-scale LSTM module. Three LSTM layers with different hidden sizes are used to infer the multi-view vehicle features.

the first layer, and the output o' of this layer concatenated with the feature set E'' pass through the second layer. In the same way, we can obtain the output o''' of the third layer. The description of the whole vehicle will gradually grow and update in the memory cell during this reasoning process. The process can be formulated as follows:

$$o''' = V_3(V_2(V_1(E') * E'') * E'''), \tag{1}$$

where V_1, V_2 and V_3 are the parameters of each LSTM layer, and $*$ denotes the concatenation operation.

Attention Module. We leverage the Attention module to enhance the global multi-view feature representation by computing entire sequence length of output in the last LSTM layer. The attention map F_{mask} is calculated through three-layer linear transformation and the softmax function:

$$F_{mask} = softmax\left(f_{ReLU}\left(W_{fc}o''' + b_{fc}\right)\right), \tag{2}$$

where W_{fc} and b_{fc} are linear layer learnable parameters, and f_{ReLU} denotes the *ReLU* activation function. Finally, we can get the enhanced feature representation F_{loc} by applying F_{mask} to o''' as follow:

$$F_{loc} = \sum_{n=1}^{t} \left(F_{mask} \otimes o'''\right), \tag{3}$$

where $\otimes$ represents the element-wise multiplication.

2.3 Model Optimization

We combine triplet loss and softmax loss to train our model. The triplet loss is defined as follows:

$$L_{tri}(x^a, x^p, x^n) = max\left\{D(P^+) - D(P^-) + \alpha, 0\right\}, \tag{4}$$

where α serves as a margin parameter.

For the global branch, a 2048-dimensional feature vector F_{glo} from the global average pooling layer is then fed into a shallow multi-layer perception, and the feature vector F_{ID} is output for vehicle ID classification. This branch is trained as follows:

$$L_G = L_{sm} + L_{tri\_g}, \tag{5}$$

where L_{sm} is the softmax loss function for F_{ID} and L_{tri_g} is the triplet loss function for F_{glo}.

The local branch is trained with a triplet loss L_{tri_l}, and the overall objective function can be formulated as:

$$L_{total} = \lambda_1 L_{sm} + \lambda_2 L_{tri\_g} + \lambda_3 L_{tri\_l}, \tag{6}$$

where λ_1, λ_2 and λ_3 are weights to balance the losses used in model optimization.

3   Experimental Results

3.1   Datasets and Implementation Details

We train and evaluate our proposed framework on two benchmark datasets, namely, VeRi-776 [11] and VehicleID [9].

- **VeRi-776** consists of more than 50,000 images based on 776 vehicles, and it is separated into a training set and a test set, containing 37778 images of 576 IDs and 11579 images of 200 IDs, respectively. These images are captured by 20 non-overlapping cameras in real-world traffic surveillance environment, causing multi-view images of each vehicle.
- **VehicleID** is another benchmark dataset, containing 110,178 images of 13,134 vehicles for training and 111,585 images of 13,133 vehicles for testing. Each image is either captured from the front view or back view. There are six subsets of different sizes in the test set, of which three subsets (i.e. Small, Medium, Large) are usually used.

All inputs for training and testing are resized to 224×224. In the training phase, the batch size is set to 30, with 6 identities and 5 images for each ID. The margin of the triplet loss is set to 0.5. In VeRi-776 dataset, the AMSGrad [13] optimizer is used with an initial learning rate of 0.0001 for 100 maximum epochs, and the learning rate decays every 20 epochs by multiplying 0.1. In VehicleID dataset, the maximum epoch is set to 200, and the learning rate decays every 40 epochs by multiplying 0.1. The balance constants $\lambda_1, \lambda_2, \lambda_3$ in Eq. 6 are set to 0.4, 0.2, 0.4, respectively. During the test phase, we concatenate F_{glo} in the global branch and F_{loc} in the local branch to obtain final features. The mean Average Precision (mAP) as well as the Cumulative Match Curve (CMC) is adopted as the evaluation metric.

Table 2. Comparison of each component in the local branch on the VeRi-776. Att denotes the Attention module.

Methods	mAP	Rank-1	Rank-5	Rank-10
Baseline	60.1	88.4	95.5	97.0
MRNet (w/o Att)	70.4	91.8	96.9	97.9
MRNet	72.0	92.4	96.9	97.8

Table 3. Performance comparison of different number of scales in the Multi-scale LSTM module on the VeRi-776. Convn_x denotes the n-th block in the global branch.

Selected feature maps	mAP	Rank-1	Rank-5	Rank-10
Conv2_x	66.8	89.6	96.2	97.6
Conv3_x	65.7	89.1	96.0	97.2
Conv2_x + Conv3_x	66.8	90.6	96.1	97.9
Conv4_x	71.3	91.4	97.1	98.2
Conv3_x + Conv4_x	71.5	91.8	96.6	97.8
Conv2_x + Conv3_x + Conv4_x	72.0	92.4	96.9	97.8

3.2   Ablation Studies

Analyzing Each Component in the Local Branch. We incrementally evaluate the effectiveness of each component by starting from the baseline model to MRNet. The experimental results on VeRi-776 dataset are shown in Table 2. Compared with the baseline model, MRNet achieves an increase of around 12% in mAP and 4% in Rank-1, respectively. It indicates that the local branch generating multi-view features can pull the features of same vehicle captured by different views closer. When we remove the Attention module, the overall performance has decreased by 1.6% in mAP for the vehicle re-ID. This result shows that the Attention module further focuses efficiently on discriminative information and improves the matching performance.

Analyzing Different Number of Scales in the Multi-scale LSTM Module. We use different feature maps in the global branch as the input of the Multi-scale LSTM module, and test the effects of different number of scales in relational reasoning. As shown in Table 3, the performance gains consistently increase with more scales feature map available. We can find that multiple LSTM layers can reduce the influence of inaccurate keypoint prediction on reasoning multi-view vehicle features.

3.3   Comparisons with State-of-the-Art Methods

Experimental Results on VeRi-776 Dataset. The Rank-1, Rank-5 and mAP are adopted to evaluate the performance and the results are shown in

Table 4. Comparison of our proposed method with the state-of-the-art methods on VeRi-776 and VehicleID.

Veri-776				VehicleID						
Query = 1678, Test = 11579				Test size	Small		Medium		Large	
Methods	mAP	R-1	R-5	Methods	R-1	R-5	R-1	R-5	R-1	R-5
DGO [18]	17.9	50.7	67.5	VGG+CCL [9]	43.6	64.8	39.9	62.9	35.6	56.2
XVGAN [20]	24.6	60.2	77.0	VXGAN [20]	52.8	80.8	49.5	71.3	44.8	66.6
OIFE [16]	48.0	65.9	87.6	C2F [3]	61.1	81.7	56.2	76.2	51.4	72.2
VAMI [19]	50.1	77.0	90.8	VAMI [19]	63.1	83.2	52.8	75.1	47.3	70.2
FDA-Net [12]	55.4	84.2	92.4	FDA-Net [12]	–	–	59.8	77.0	55.5	74.6
RAM [10]	61.5	88.6	94.0	AAVER [7]	74.6	93.8	68.6	89.9	63.5	85.6
AAVER [7]	66.3	90.1	94.3	RAM [10]	75.2	91.5	72.3	87.0	67.7	84.5
VANet [1]	66.3	95.9	89.7	PRND [4]	78.4	92.3	75.0	88.3	74.2	86.4
PAMTRI [15]	71.8	92.8	96.9	VANet [1]	88.1	97.2	83.1	95.1	80.3	92.9
PRND [4]	74.3	94.3	98.7	–	–	–	–	–	–	–
MRNet (ours)	72.0	92.4	96.9	MRNet (ours)	76.2	93.7	73.5	91.3	67.9	88.5

Table 4. Among these methods, OIFE [16] uses the additional spatio-temporal information, and VANet [1] uses metric learning to address the viewpoint variation problem. Our method achieves 72.0% in mAP, 92.4% in Rank-1, which shows competitive performance compared to the state-of-the-art methods. Compared with VAMI [19], which also generates multi-view features of a vehicle, our network yields better results, a gain of 21.9% in mAP, 15.4% in Rank-1. It demonstrates that the proposed method can handle multi-view challenge of vehicle re-ID more effectively. Furthermore, we have comparable performance with PAMTRI [15], which utilizes randomized synthetic data for training model.

Experimental Results on VehicleID Dataset. Table 4 also presents the comparison results on VehicleID. We can find that our network outperforms AAVER [7] by 1.6% in Small size (Rank-1) and 4.9% in Medium size (Rank-1), which utilizes vehicle keypoint attention and a re-ranking pose-processing method. Our performance is also better than RAM [10], which focuses on more distinctive visual regions, implying that our framework successfully promotes the ranks of very hard samples.

Overall Performance on Two Datasets. Finally, we evaluate the overall performance on two datasets to prove the effectiveness of our method. As shown in Table 4, VANet [1] exceeds our method on VehicleID, but underperforms ours by around 5.7% in mAP on VeRi-776, mainly because it uses metric learning only, and discriminative information can not be learned well when there are many views. As for PRND [4], which uses YOLO [14] to generate the ROI of each vehicle part, it requires additional annotation work to train YOLO. On VehicleID dataset, PRND has good performance in Rank-1, but the value in

Rank-5 is low. This result shows that it is effective for simple samples, but it will fail with difficult samples. Comparing to state-of-the-art methods, the good performance in both datasets indicates the universality of our method.

4 Conclusions

In this paper, we proposed the Keypoint Guided Multi-Scale Reasoning Network (MRNet) to address the challenge of viewpoint variation on vehicle re-ID task. The MRNet uses the global branch to extract the global features of an input, and utilizes the local branch to do the relational reasoning from the one-view vehicle features to the multi-view vehicle features. Experiments are conducted on two benchmark datasets to evaluate the effectiveness of our proposed framework. Ablation studies show that each proposed technique helps enhance robustness and our network achieves competitive performance to the state-of-the-art methods.

References

1. Chu, R., Sun, Y., Li, Y., Liu, Z., Zhang, C., Wei, Y.: Vehicle re-identification with viewpoint-aware metric learning. In: Proceedings of the IEEE/CVF International Conference on Computer Vision (ICCV) (2019)
2. Du, S., Ibrahim, M., Shehata, M., Badawy, W.: Automatic license plate recognition (ALPR): a state-of-the-art review. IEEE Trans. Circ. Syst. Video Technol. **23**(2), 311–325 (2013)
3. Guo, H., Zhao, C., Liu, Z., Wang, J., Lu, H.: Learning coarse-to-fine structured feature embedding for vehicle re-identification. In: Thirty-Second AAAI Conference on Artificial Intelligence, pp. 6853–6860 (2018)
4. He, B., Li, J., Zhao, Y., Tian, Y.: Part-regularized near-duplicate vehicle re-identification. In: 2019 IEEE/CVF Conference on Computer Vision and Pattern Recognition (CVPR), pp. 3992–4000 (2019)
5. He, K., Zhang, X., Ren, S., Sun, J.: Deep residual learning for image recognition. In: Proceedings of the IEEE Conference on Computer Vision and Pattern Recognition (CVPR) (2016)
6. Hochreiter, S., Schmidhuber, J.: Long short-term memory. Neural Comput. **9**(8), 1735–1780 (1997)
7. Khorramshahi, P., Kumar, A., Peri, N., Rambhatla, S.S., Chen, J.C., Chellappa, R.: A dual-path model with adaptive attention for vehicle re-identification. In: Proceedings of the IEEE International Conference on Computer Vision (2019)
8. Lalimi, M.A., Ghofrani, S., Mclernon, D.: A vehicle license plate detection method using region and edge based methods. Comput. Electr. Eng. **39**(3), 834–845 (2013)
9. Liu, H., Tian, Y., Yang, Y., Pang, L., Huang, T.: Deep relative distance learning: tell the difference between similar vehicles. In: Proceedings of the IEEE Conference on Computer Vision and Pattern Recognition (CVPR) (2016)
10. Liu, X., Zhang, S., Huang, Q., Gao, W.: RAM: a region-aware deep model for vehicle re-identification. In: 2018 IEEE International Conference on Multimedia and Expo (ICME), pp. 1–6 (2018)

11. Liu, X., Liu, W., Mei, T., Ma, H.: A deep learning-based approach to progressive vehicle re-identification for urban surveillance. In: Leibe, B., Matas, J., Sebe, N., Welling, M. (eds.) ECCV 2016. LNCS, vol. 9906, pp. 869–884. Springer, Cham (2016). https://doi.org/10.1007/978-3-319-46475-6_53
12. Lou, Y., Bai, Y., Liu, J., Wang, S., Duan, L.: VERI-Wild: a large dataset and a new method for vehicle re-identification in the wild. In: Proceedings of the IEEE/CVF Conference on Computer Vision and Pattern Recognition (CVPR) (2019)
13. Reddi, S.J., Kale, S., Kumar, S.: On the convergence of adam and beyond. In: ICLR (2018)
14. Redmon, J., Divvala, S., Girshick, R., Farhadi, A.: You only look once: unified, real-time object detection. In: Proceedings of the IEEE Conference on Computer Vision and Pattern Recognition (CVPR) (2016)
15. Tang, Z., et al.: PAMTRI: pose-aware multi-task learning for vehicle re-identification using highly randomized synthetic data. In: Proceedings of the IEEE/CVF International Conference on Computer Vision (ICCV) (2019)
16. Wang, Z., et al.: Orientation invariant feature embedding and spatial temporal regularization for vehicle re-identification. In: 2017 IEEE International Conference on Computer Vision (ICCV), pp. 379–387 (2017)
17. Wei, X.-S., Zhang, C.-L., Liu, L., Shen, C., Wu, J.: Coarse-to-fine: a RNN-based hierarchical attention model for vehicle re-identification. In: Jawahar, C.V., Li, H., Mori, G., Schindler, K. (eds.) ACCV 2018. LNCS, vol. 11362, pp. 575–591. Springer, Cham (2019). https://doi.org/10.1007/978-3-030-20890-5_37
18. Xiao, T., Li, H., Ouyang, W., Wang, X.: Learning deep feature representations with domain guided dropout for person re-identification. In: Proceedings of the IEEE Conference on Computer Vision and Pattern Recognition (CVPR) (2016)
19. Zhou, Y., Shao, L.: Viewpoint-aware attentive multi-view inference for vehicle re-identification. In: 2018 IEEE/CVF Conference on Computer Vision and Pattern Recognition, pp. 6489–6498 (2018)
20. Zhou, Y., Shao, L.: Cross-view GAN based vehicle generation for re-identification. In: Proceedings of the British Machine Vision Conference (BMVC) (2017)

Multi-modal Feature Attention for Cervical Lymph Node Segmentation in Ultrasound and Doppler Images

Xiangling Fu[1], Tong Gao[1], Yuan Liu[3], Mengke Zhang[3], Chenyi Guo[2], Ji Wu[2], and Zhili Wang[3(✉)]

[1] School of Software Engineering,
Beijing University of Posts and Telecommunications, Beijing, China
[2] Department of Electronic Engineering, Tsinghua University, Beijing, China
[3] Department of Ultrasound,
Chinese People's Liberation Army General Hospital, Beijing, China
wzllg@sina.com

Abstract. Cervical lymph node disease is a kind of cervical disease with a high incidence. Accurate detection of lymph nodes can greatly improve the performance of the computer-aided diagnosis systems. Presently, most studies have focused on classifying lymph nodes in a given ultrasound image. However, ultrasound has a poor discrimination of different tissues such as blood vessel and lymph node. When solving confused tasks like detecting cervical lymph nodes, ultrasound imaging becomes inappropriate. In this study, we combined two common modalities to detect cervical lymph nodes: ultrasound and Doppler. Then a multimodal fusion method is proposed, which made full use of the complementary information between the two modalities to distinguish the lymph and other tissues. 1054 pairs of ultrasound and Doppler images are used in the experiment. As a result, the proposed multimodal fusion method is 3% higher (DICE value) than the baseline methods in segmentation results.

Keywords: Cervical lymph node · Segmentation · Multi-modal fusion · Ultrasound · Doppler

1 Introduction

Cervical lymph node (LN) enlargement is very common in clinical regions, and it is also one of the most frequently examined and diagnosed pathological lesions. The preferred diagnostic modality for identifying and characterizing cervical LNs is ultrasonography, combining with color Doppler sonography, owing to their non-invasive quality, easy accessibility, low cost, and non-radiation [18].

This work is supported by Beijing Municipal Natural Science Foundation (No. L192026).

Conventional ultrasound imaging, including B-mode ultrasound (US) and color Doppler, provide valuable information on the number, size, shape, boundary, internal echogenicity, and lymphatic and blood flow characteristics of lymph nodes [8].

However, sonography is much more operator dependent than other inspection methods. Reading ultrasound images requires relevant professional experience. Also, there are many causes of cervical lymph node enlargement [15]. Even well-trained experts may have a high rate of inter-observer bias. Therefore, an automatic segmentation algorithm has its potential to help radiologists in detection on LNs [5]. Based on the segmentation results, estimation of shapes, sizes, etc. could be extracted by algorithms.

Recently, in terms of semantic segmentation tasks, deep learning methods have achieved huge success. Region-based convolutional neural networks [4] proposed state-of-the-art accurate regions of interest (ROI). Fully convolutional networks (FCN) [10] also showed promising segmentation results. U-Net [12] is an FCN model for biomedical imaging tasks and its effectiveness has been tested in many researches. However, accurate US image segmentation tasks are different from normal images [6] due to various US artifacts and noises. Many researches focus on the segmentation of B-mode ultrasound in different body parts such as lymph node and breast. Gupta et al. [3] proposed a hybrid approach for accurate segmentation of the ultrasound medical images that is presented that utilizes both the features of kernel fuzzy clustering with spatial constraints and edge-based active contour method using distance regularized level set (DRLS) function. Lei et al. [7] proposed a boundary regularized deep convolutional encoder-decoder network (ConvEDNet) to address breast anatomical layers in the noisy Automated Whole Breast Ultrasound. Zhang et al. [19] proposed a method consists of multiple stages of FCN modules to segment lymph nodes. In the structure of their model, they trained the CFS-FCN model to learn the segmentation knowledge from a coarse-to-fine manner that performed better and requires fewer professional annotations.

The works above have achieved very good results in their datasets. But in terms of contents in images, their datasets were relatively simple because there were no other disturbance around the target tissue. Zhang et al. [19] also discussed that the performance of their model was not ideal for complex situations (with disturbance). In the cervical LN segmentation task, blood vessels and muscles are the main interference factors. These factors are rare in other body parts detection tasks such as breasts. Fortunately, Doppler provides blood flow information in addition to ultrasound-based on the Doppler effect. It has been proved that machine learning with multi-modal ultrasound including grayscale and Doppler can achieve high performance for breast cancer diagnosis [13]. Thus our natural thought was to take advantage of complementary information among multi-modal data.

In this paper, we proposed a feature attention method for multi-modal data fusion. Then tested our method in a siamese encoder structure. In comparison, different baselines and comparison methods were implemented to test the effectiveness of different single modality and combining methods.

2   Data Description

The study population was selected from patients with normal, reactive or malignant cervical LN who visited our hospital. 1054 pairs of ROIs including ultrasound images and doppler images were used to evaluate the diagnostic performance of a deep learning system for the segmentation of cervical LNs. The ROIs were extracted by professional doctors with over 5 years of clinical experience. The training, validation, and testing sets were randomly split on a scale of 6:2:2. According to the records in the ultrasound report, the long and short diameter distribution are shown in Table 1.

Table 1. Statistical characteristics of lymph node sizes

All	Training set	Validation set	Test set
Patients	634	211	209
Long diameter(cm)	1.904±0.871	1.878±0.881	1.810±0.821
Short diameter(cm)	0.956±0.372	0.972±0.428	0.900±0.304

3   Methodology

3.1   Data Preprocessing

Auto cropping: Usually, the pictures obtained from the ultrasonic machine will display some additional index information on the pictures. We manually cropped the ROI region showing only the B-mode ultrasound regions (or Doppler regions). Each ROI was resized to $256 \times 256 \times 3$ with Bilinear Interpolation. In addition, we trained a SSD [9] based auto cropping model with the cropped data for further prediction.[1]

Noise Reduction: Since ultrasound images were produced by ultrasound waves which were seriously affected by external noise, such as machine running noise, there are many gray points distributed in the image. To eliminate such noise, a 5×5 median filter was performed to patches.

Modalities Registration: During data allocation, there is a small deviation between ultrasound and doppler images. It is a common sense in clinical diagnose since ultrasound probes are hand-held. We applied a registration algorithm [14] to align each ultrasound and doppler image pair.

---

[1] Souce code for Auto Cropping SSD: https://github.com/RAY9874/Extract-us-region.

3.2 Multi-modal Model

We designed our network based on U-net but modified encoder part. The modified encoder is a siamese deep learning network that encodes ultrasound and doppler features, then decode masked images with combined multilevel features.

In terms of the encoder part, our model took ultrasound and doppler images as input, 5 downsample blocks were applied for each stream. Each downsample block contains 2 convolutional layers and 1 maxpooling layer. In each downsample block, we designed our dual stream encoder to reuse combined feature maps. 5 levels of reused feature maps are passed to the decoder.

In addition, inspired form Cross-stitch [11] and CBAM [17] module, a feature sharing module(FSM) Fig. 1 for multi-model fusion was applied. This module 'listens' from both streams and decide which part of 'message' to be passed from one stream to another. FSM takes ultrasound feature maps and doppler feature maps as input, returns 2 feature maps for each stream. Inside FSM, modality-wise attention and spatial-wise attention were applied to each feature map (Fig. 2).

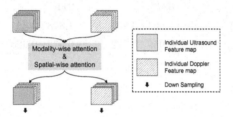

Fig. 1. Overview of feature sharing module structure. FSM receives two inputs, and apply the attention mechanism to the input feature map, which makes the fusion of the two modalities more effective. Inside FSM, modality-wise attention and spatial-wise attention is applied to each feature map from 2 streams

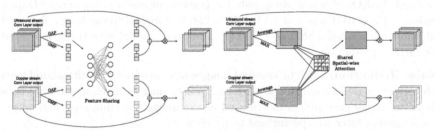

(a) Proposed modality-wise attention, GAP denotes global average pooling and GMP denotes global max pooling.

(b) Proposed spatial-wise attention, Average and Max operations are along the channel axis.

Fig. 2. Detail design of 2 attention modules proposed. For description of each component, please refer to Sect. 3.2.

For **modality-wise attention**, feature maps were compressed by two global pooling methods (max and average) to 1×1 but remain the channel dimension, which represents a feature that maximizes the response of a specific convolution kernel. Then a feature attention operation along channel dimension is applied among modalities. Feature attention was a 2 layer MLP that first reduces the dimension of inputs and then reconstructs to its original dimension. The output one-dimensional vector, as the attention between channels, scales the weight of the input feature map. For **spatial-wise attention**, feature maps were compressed to two 1-channel feature maps. Under the condition of using the shared convolution kernel, the two modalities focus on feature sharing in space. The output 1-channel feature map was used as the spatial attention map to scale the input.

Since this work discussed multi-modal fusion methods, the decoder part was not much modified except multi-level feature reuse.

3.3 Loss Function

In our experiment, we used DICE loss to optimize parameters. The target of the DICE loss was seeking parameters for maximizing DICE value between ground truth mask and predicted mask.

3.4 Model Training Details

The models were trained by using Keras 2.2.0 and tensorflow 1.4.0. Adam optimizer was used to train the network with a batch size of 12. The initial learning rate was set to 1e−4. The parameters of the network was randomly initialized. Finally, the model with the lowest validation loss was selected.[2]

4 Results and Discussion

In this section, we evaluated the segmentation performances of our method. To further discuss the effectiveness of multi-modal data and the proposed method, design of contrast experiment were based on 2 parts, modality-wise and model-wise experiments. All comparative experiments used the same training, validation and test set. The results of test set were presented.

We chose DICE value to evaluate the performance of each model. Mean DICE value of 3 classes was used to evaluate performance of models. At the same time, the accuracy of LN segmentation was also in our consideration (Fig. 3).

---

[2] Source code for the proposed method U-net-dual-steam + FSM: https://github.com/RAY9874/Multimodal-Feature-Attention-for-Cervical-Lymph-Node-Segmentation-in-Ultrasound-and-Doppler-Images.

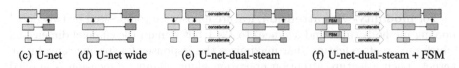

(c) U-net   (d) U-net wide   (e) U-net-dual-steam   (f) U-net-dual-steam + FSM

Fig. 3. An overview of several baselines designed. a) U-net b) U-net wide (double parameters) c) U-net-dual-stream d) proposed U-net-dual-stream+FSM.

4.1 Modality-Wise Comparison Experiments

There were 2 kinds of modalities in our task: ultrasound and Doppler. In this experiment, we fixed the algorithm model as U-net, and tested the results of two modalities.

4.2 Model-Wise Comparison Experiments

We designed several baseline models for comparison. These models all had similar architectures, but they had their own characteristics due to different data input or different targets. We hoped to discuss the influence of modalities and models on cervical lymph node segmentation task by comparing these models.

U-net-wide: In order to ensure the consistency of parameters, inspired from Unet++ [20], we doubled the parameters in encoder part for fair comparison.

U-net-dual-stream: Inspired from [1], we designed a siamese encoder U-net that encodes ultrasound and doppler image by 2 encoders as baseline model, denote as U-net-dual-stream. It concatenated feature maps in hidden layers. The concatenated feature maps were sent to decoder part.

U-net-dual-stream+FSM: Based on U-net-dual-stream, we applied the FSM module before all the concatenate operation of downsampling blocks. Thus at each stage of decoding, the decoder would receive the feature map processed by FSM.

CoarsetoFine FCN: We reproduced CoarsetoFine model proposed in paper [19] without post-processing (Boundary refinement). For fair evaluation, we concatenated ultrasound image and Dopper image as input of CoarsetoFine FCN (Table 2).

Table 2. Comparison of naive models and proposed models

Comparison methods	Data in use	Model name	Mean DICE	LN DICE
Modality wise comparison	Ultrasound	U-net	0.6586	0.725
	Doppler	U-net	0.6501	0.7179
	Ultrasound & Doppler	U-net	0.6983	0.7452
Model wise comparison	Ultrasound & Doppler	U-net	0.6983	0.7452
		U-net wide	0.7088	0.7651
		U-net-dual-stream	0.7193	0.7825
		CoarsetoFine FCN	0.6919	0.7596
		U-net-dual-stream+FSM	**0.7281**	**0.7863**

4.3 Effectiveness of Doppler Data

In the third and fourth example shown in Fig. 4, we could see that inside LN, only the lymphatic hilum has blood flow signals, but the blood flow of the blood vessel is full. In the ultrasound image, the manifestations of the lymph node and blood vessel were very similar, and the proposed model distinguished them accurately by comparing two modalities.

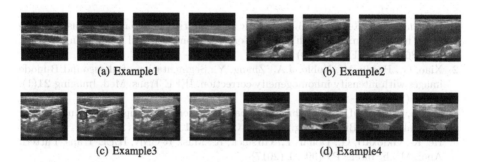

(a) Example1   (b) Example2

(c) Example3   (d) Example4

Fig. 4. Examples of proposed U-net-dual-stream+FSM segmentation results. All examples are from test set. From left to right: ultrasound image, Doppler image, prediction results, ground truth label, in each example, Color description: red for lymph node, blue for blood vessel, and green for muscle. (Color figure online)

4.4 Effectiveness of FSM

Through the last six experiments, we knew that the ultrasound + Doppler original image was the most suitable input mode for the two modalities. Here, we evaluated the proposed FSM module on the basis of dual-stream U-net. From the last experiment, after adding the FSM module, the mean DICE value and lymph DICE value have been improved. Different from encoding two modalities with the same encoder, we allowed two encoders to learn two modalities respectively, but the learned features must be exchanged to a certain extent. This kind of exchange was not only addictive but also subtractive to reduce the weight of some features. In this way, the two modalities made full use of complementary information and achieve better results.

5   Conclusion

In this paper, we proposed a multi-modal fusion method for semantic segmentation tasks in ultrasound images. This method makes full use of the complementary information between ultrasound and Doppler images, which are the two basic modalities in the clinical diagnosis of cervical lymph nodes, to realize a more accurate semantic segmentation. Through the feature sharing mechanism, the two modalities learn from each other and suppressed the useless features. Compared with the related work and some baselines, our proposed multi-modal fusion method segment the lymph region on the ultrasound image more precisely. In future work, this method could be provided as a better preprocessing for further lymph node classification tasks.

References

1. Farhangfar, S., Rezaeian, M.: Semantic segmentation of aerial images using FCN-based network. In: 2019 27th Iranian Conference on Electrical Engineering (ICEE), pp. 1864–1868. IEEE (2019)
2. Xiao, G., Brady, M., Noble, J.A., Zhang, Y.: Segmentation of ultrasound B-mode images with intensity inhomogeneity correction. IEEE Trans. Med. Imaging **21**(1), 48–57 (2002)
3. Gupta, D., Anand, R.: A hybrid edge-based segmentation approach for ultrasound medical images. Biomed. Sig. Process. Control **31**, 116–126 (2017)
4. He, K., Gkioxari, G., Dollar, P., Girshick, R.: Mask R-CNN. IEEE Trans. Pattern Anal. Mach. Intell. **PP**(99), 1 (2017)
5. Ikedo, Y., et al.: Automated analysis of breast parenchymal patterns in whole breast ultrasound images: preliminary experience. Int. J. Comput. Assist. Radiol. Surg. **4**(3), 299–306 (2009). https://doi.org/10.1007/s11548-009-0295-0
6. Noble, J.A., Boukerroui, D.: Ultrasound image segmentation: a survey. IEEE Trans. Med. Imaging **25**(8), 987–1010 (2006)
7. Lei, B., et al.: Segmentation of breast anatomy for automated whole breast ultrasound images with boundary regularized convolutional encoder-decoder network. Neurocomputing **321**, 178–186 (2018)
8. Li, Q., et al.: Controlled study of traditional ultrasound and ultrasound elastography on the diagnosis of breast masses. Ultrasound Q. **31**(4), 250 (2015)
9. Liu, W., et al.: SSD: single shot multibox detector. In: Leibe, B., Matas, J., Sebe, N., Welling, M. (eds.) ECCV 2016. LNCS, vol. 9905, pp. 21–37. Springer, Cham (2016). https://doi.org/10.1007/978-3-319-46448-0_2
10. Long, J., Shelhamer, E., Darrell, T.: Fully convolutional networks for semantic segmentation. IEEE Trans. Pattern Anal. Mach. Intell. **39**(4), 640–651 (2014)

11. Misra, I., Shrivastava, A., Gupta, A., Hebert, M.: Cross-stitch networks for multi-task learning. In: Proceedings of the IEEE Conference on Computer Vision and Pattern Recognition, pp. 3994–4003 (2016)
12. Ronneberger, O., Fischer, P., Brox, T.: U-Net: convolutional networks for biomedical image segmentation. In: Navab, N., Hornegger, J., Wells, W.M., Frangi, A.F. (eds.) MICCAI 2015. LNCS, vol. 9351, pp. 234–241. Springer, Cham (2015). https://doi.org/10.1007/978-3-319-24574-4_28
13. Sultan, L.R., Cary, T.W., Sehgal, C.M.: Machine learning to improve breast cancer diagnosis by multimodal ultrasound. In: 2018 IEEE International Ultrasonics Symposium (IUS), pp. 1–4. IEEE (2018)
14. Thurman, S.T., Fienup, J.R., Guizar-Sicairos, M.: Efficient subpixel image registration algorithms (2008). ol/33/2/ol-33-2-156.pdf
15. Turgut, E., Celenk, C., Tanrivermis, S.A., Bekci, T., Gunbey, H.P., Aslan, K.: Efficiency of B-mode ultrasound and strain elastography in differentiating between benign and malignant cervical lymph nodes. Ultrasound Q. **33**(3), 201 (2017)
16. Wells, P.N.T., Halliwell, M.: Speckle in ultrasonic imaging. Ultrasonics **19**(5), 225–229 (1981)
17. Woo, S., Park, J., Lee, J.-Y., Kweon, I.S.: CBAM: convolutional block attention module. In: Ferrari, V., Hebert, M., Sminchisescu, C., Weiss, Y. (eds.) ECCV 2018. LNCS, vol. 11211, pp. 3–19. Springer, Cham (2018). https://doi.org/10.1007/978-3-030-01234-2_1
18. Ying, M., Bhatia, K.S.S., Lee, Y., Yuen, H., Ahuja, A.: Review of ultrasonography of malignant neck nodes: greyscale, Doppler, contrast enhancement and elastography. Cancer Imaging **13**(4), 658–669 (2013). Official Publication of the International Cancer Imaging Society
19. Zhang, Y., Ying, M.T.C., Lin, Y., Ahuja, A.T., Chen, D.Z.: Coarse-to-fine stacked fully convolutional nets for lymph node segmentation in ultrasound images. In: IEEE International Conference on Bioinformatics & Biomedicine (2016)
20. Zhou, Z., Rahman Siddiquee, M.M., Tajbakhsh, N., Liang, J.: UNet++: a nested U-Net architecture for medical image segmentation. In: Stoyanov, D., et al. (eds.) DLMIA/ML-CDS -2018. LNCS, vol. 11045, pp. 3–11. Springer, Cham (2018). https://doi.org/10.1007/978-3-030-00889-5_1

MultiTune: Adaptive Integration of Multiple Fine-Tuning Models for Image Classification

Yu Wang[✉], Jo Plested, and Tom Gedeon

Research School of Computer Science, Australian National University,
Canberra, Australia
{yu.wang1,jo.plested,tom.gedeon}@anu.edu.au

Abstract. Transfer learning has been widely used as a deep learning technique to solve computer vision related problems, especially when the problem is image classification employing Convolutional Neural Networks (CNN). In this paper, a novel transfer learning approach that can adaptively integrate multiple models with different fine-tuning settings is proposed, which is denoted as *MultiTune*. To evaluate the performance of MultiTune, we compare it to SpotTune, a state-of-the-art transfer learning technique. Two image datasets from the Visual Decathlon Challenge are used to evaluate the performance of MultiTune. The FGVC-Aircraft dataset is a fine-grained task and the CIFAR100 dataset is a more general task. Results obtained in this paper show that MultiTune outperforms SpotTune on both tasks. We also evaluate MultiTune on a range of target datasets with smaller numbers of images per class. MultiTune outperforms SpotTune on most of these smaller-sized datasets as well. MultiTune is also less computational than SpotTune and requires less time for training for each dataset used in this paper.

Keywords: Transfer learning · Image classification · Convolutional neural networks

1 Introduction

Modern convolutional neural networks, such as AlexNet [7], VGG [12] and ResNet [5] have been proven to be very successful, and able to achieve extraordinary performance on well-known large-scale images datasets, for instance ImageNet [3]. However, due to the large amount of data and limitation of computation, it is usually hard to train a convolutional neural network on a large dataset from scratch. Transfer learning has been introduced to mitigate this issue.

Common machine learning algorithms are often designed to solve single and isolated tasks. However, the study of transfer learning aims to develop methods to transfer knowledge learnt from one or more source tasks and apply this knowledge to improve the learning process in a different but related target task [13]. There are two important concepts frequently used in transfer learning, which

© Springer Nature Switzerland AG 2020
H. Yang et al. (Eds.): ICONIP 2020, CCIS 1332, pp. 488–496, 2020.
https://doi.org/10.1007/978-3-030-63820-7_56

are freezing and fine-tuning. Freezing, or feature extraction, means to freeze the weights that are learnt from the source task and only update the weights in the last classification layer [2]. The frozen weights will act as a feature extractor to solve the target task. Fine-tuning is the opposite of freezing. It is performed where all or most of the weights learnt from the source task are retrained and updated to fit the target task. These pre-trained weights act as a regularizer that prevents overfitting during the learning process of the target task [1].

In this paper, we propose a novel technique that can be used in transfer learning to enable the adaptive integration of multiple fine-tuning models with different fine-tuning settings. It is denoted as *MultiTune* and will be mentioned by using this name in this paper.

2 Related Work

2.1 Transferability

There have been numerous researches studying the transferability of features in deep neural networks. One of the most thorough researches was done by Yosinski et al. [14]. They discussed the transferability of features when using convolutional neural networks. It is sated in their paper that features on the first layer seems to occur regardless of the exact loss function and natural image dataset, which can be considered as 'general'. The features on the last layer depend largely on the dataset and task, which can be considered as 'specific'. Their study quantified to which a particular layer is general or specific and found that even features transferred from distant tasks are better than random weights.

It is found that fine-tuning the transferred weights has better performance than freezing the transferred weights, in both cases when the source dataset is highly related to the target dataset and when the source dataset is not so related to the target dataset [6,9,14]. It is a common practice used in image classification to pre-train the model on the ImageNet [3] dataset. Then the learnt weights are transferred to the target dataset and fine-tuned during training. It has been shown that image classification by using this approach can achieve extraordinary results on different target datasets [6].

2.2 Adaptive Fine-Tuning: SpotTune

SpotTune is an adaptive fine-tuning method, which is able to determine which layers to be frozen and which layers to be fine-tuned per training example. The adaptive fine-tuning is achieved by training a policy network together with two parallel CNN models. One of the CNN models has all the layers to be frozen. The other CNN model has all its layers to be fine-tuned. The policy network outputs a decision vector containing 0 or 1 for each layer, where 0 means the image will go through the frozen layer, and 1 means the image will go through the fine-tuned layer. As a result, the optimal route of an image in terms of frozen or fine-tuning can be determined [4]. SpotTune could be considered as a state-of-the-art technique of transfer learning that achieved the highest score on the Visual Decathlon datasets [10] in 2019. It is used as a baseline to evaluate the performance of MultiTune proposed in this paper. Different to their work, MultiTune proposed by us involves two fine-tuning models with different settings instead of one freezing model and one fine-tuning model. Also, MultiTune does not contain a policy network to generate the routing decision, and therefore is less computational.

2.3   L2-SP Regularization

In transfer learning, it is assumed that the pre-trained model extracts generic features. These generic features are then fine-tuned to be more specific to fit the target task if fine-tuning is used. Thus, when using fine-tuning to solve a related target task, the neural network is initialized with pre-trained parameters (e.g. weights, bias) learnt from source task. However, it is found that some of these parameters may be tuned very far away from their initial values during the process of fine-tuning. This may cause significant losses of the initial knowledge transferred from the source task which is assumed to be relevant to the target task [8]. Li et al. proposed a novel type of regularization to reduce losses of the initially transferred knowledge. The pre-trained model is not only used as the starting point of the fine-tuning process but also used as the reference in the penalty to encode an explicit inductive bias. This novel type of regularization is called L2-SP regularization with SP referring to *Starting Point* of the fine-tuning process. Their results showed that L2-SP is much more effective than the standard L2 penalty that is commonly used in fine-tuning [8]. It can prevent overfitting and retain the knowledge learnt from the source task. So, the L2-SP is used as the regularizer when training the networks.

3   Proposed Approach

3.1   Network Architecture

The CNN architecture used in this paper is a type of ResNet with 26 layers, which is denoted as ResNet-26 [11]. There are 3 macro blocks of convolutional layers in this CNN. Each block has 64, 128, 256 output feature channels, respectively. Also, each macro block contains 4 residual blocks and every residual block consists of 2 convolutional layers with 3×3 filters and shortcut connection that usually used in ResNet. Average pooling with a stride of 2 is used to perform the downsampling and ReLU layers are used as the activation layers. It also contains a convolutional layer at the beginning and a fully connected layer at the end, which makes the total number of layers in this architecture to be 26.

3.2   MultiTune Implementation

The MultiTune is implemented by adding a single-layer neural network after the convolutional layers in the last block, which replaces the last fully connected

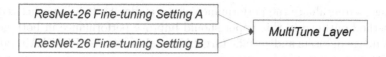

Fig. 1. Visualization of MultiTune.

Table 1. Settings of the two fine-tuning models.

Model	Reinitialization	Learning rate	Learning rate decay	LR decay rate
Fine-tuning A	Last block	0.1	[20, 50, 80]	0.1
Fine-tuning B	Last block	0.01 for last block, 0.1 for others	[20, 50, 80]	0.1

layer. This single fully connected layer is denoted as *MultiTune layer* here. In detail, the features extracted by the two ResNet-26 models after the last blocks are concatenated and then pass the MultiTune layer to be classified. Theoretically, the MultiTune layer should determine which features to take from these two different fine-tuning models. The MultiTune model proposed here can be expressed in Eq. 1, where Z represents the output of the MultiTune layer, W represents the weights of the MultiTune layer, X_1 and X_2 are the outputs after the last convolutional blocks of the first and second fine-tuning models, and η is a factor that controls what portion of each model to be used in the MultiTune layer. The presence of η enables an option to allocate more weights to one of the models. This factor η is set to be 0.5 here, which means these two ResNet-26 models are treated equally. Figure 1 is a visualization of MultiTune.

$$Z = W * concat[\eta X_1; (1 - \eta)X_2] \tag{1}$$

These two CNN models used here have different fine-tuning settings. For convenience, they are denoted as Fine-Tuning A and Fine-Tuning B. The settings of these two models are listed in the Table 1.

4 Experiments

4.1 Datasets

The datasets used in this paper are taken from the Visual Decathlon challenge. It contains 10 datasets from multiple visual domains. To reduce the computation burden of the evaluation process, the images in the Visual Decathlon Datasets are resized isotropically with a shorter side of 72 pixels [10]. Due to the computational limitations, it is hard to use all these 10 datasets to evaluate the performance of MultiTune. Inspired by Li et al.'s paper where they test their method with different target domains, the same approach is used for the selection of datasets to evaluate the performance of the model [8]. It is hypothesized that the method outlined in this paper should improve performance in both generic target image datasets and specific target image datasets. So, FGVC-Aircraft and CIFAR100 are used, which represents a more specific and a more generic dataset, respectively. Table 2 summarizes the details of these two datasets.

Table 2. Details of FGVC-Aircraft and CIFAR100 datasets

Dataset	Description	Mean	Standard deviation
FGVC-Aircraft	10,000 images of aircraft, 100 images per class. Training, validation and testing with around 3,333 images for each	[0.47983041, 0.51074066, 0.53437998]	[0.21070221, 0.20508901, 0.23729657]
CIFAR100	60,000 colour images for 100 object categories. 40,000 for training, 10,000 for validation, 10,000 for testing	[0.50705882, 0.48666667, 0.44078431]	[0.26745098, 0.25647059, 0.27607843]

4.2 Training of the Network

As SpotTune will be taken as the baseline in this paper, most of the settings used in MultiTune are set the same as SpotTune to keep consistency. Both of these methods are run with 110 epochs without early stopping. Cross Entropy loss is used because the target task is image classification. And, the optimizer used here is SGD with a momentum of 0.9. SpotTune uses a learning rate of 0.1 for the CNN models, and a learning rate of 0.01 for the policy network. The learning rate decay is set after the 40th, 60th and 80th epoch [4]. MultiTune does not include a policy network, and has different learning rates for each CNN model. The learning rate decay is also set to be different from SpotTune. Also, L2-SP regularization is used in MultiTune. Defining the weights of layers except for the last one as w and the weights of the last layer as $w_{\bar{s}}$, the L2-SP regularizer can be shown in Eq. 2 [8]. α and β in this equation are the factors that control the strength of the penalty, which are both set to 0.01 [8].

$$\Omega(w) = \frac{\alpha}{2}||w - w^0||_2^2 + \frac{\beta}{2}||w_{\bar{s}}||_2^2 \qquad (2)$$

The Cross Entropy loss is modified to add this L2-SP regularizer. Equation 3 shows the modified CE loss with L2-SP regularizer, where t_i is the ground truth and y_i is CNN's output for each class i in the dataset C.

$$L(y,t) = -\sum_i^C t_i log(y_i) + \frac{\alpha}{2}\sum_i^W ||w_i - w_i^0||_2^2 + \frac{\beta}{2}||w_{\bar{s}}||_2^2 \qquad (3)$$

5   Results and Analysis

The results of the SpotTune are taken as the baseline in this paper. To let the model see more images for better training and testing, the original code of SpotTune includes the validation set in the training set for each dataset. This means the model is trained on this larger combined training set but still evaluated by using the validation set which is a part of the training set. As a result, the validation accuracy reaches a large figure, almost 100%, after tens of epochs. It is very hard to evaluate the performance of the model in this case.

Table 3. Results of SpotTune and MultiTune on Aircraft and CIFAR100.

Dataset	SpotTune		MultiTune	
	Validation accuracy	Total time used (mins)	Validation accuracy	Total time used (mins)
Aircraft	55.15%	47.49	59.59%	38.19
Aircraft-20	45.60%	29.15	47.85%	22.50
Aircraft-15	39.20%	21.84	40.73%	16.88
Aircraft-10	30.70%	14.67	29.90%	11.51
Aircraft-5	17.40%	7.57	18.80%	5.91
CIFAR100	78.45%	454.80	79.31%	321.37
CIFAR100-20	59.15%	34.60	59.00%	22.80
CIFAR100-15	55.73%	23.74	56.40%	16.87
CIFAR100-10	49.10%	16.52	49.10%	11.37
CIFAR100-5	33.40%	8.96	29.20%	5.86

To address this issue, the validation set is removed from the training set when loading the datasets. Then the model can be trained only on the training set and evaluated by the unseen validation set.

The figures of results shown in Guo et al.'s paper are testing results obtained by submitting the results to the Visual Decathlon Challenge website [4]. Because only two datasets of the Visual Decathlon Datasets are used here, the results of them are not submitted to the website. The validation results instead of testing results are used to compare these methods.

The validation accuracy and training time of SpotTune and MultiTune on Aircraft and CIFAR100 datasets are listed in Table 3. Aircraft-20 means the smaller-sized Aircraft dataset with 20 images per class. Figure 2 shows the validation accuracy versus the number of epochs of SpotTune and MultiTune on these two datasets. To distinguish the results, the validation accuracy of Spot-Tune is illustrated by *blue* lines, the validation accuracy of MultiTune is shown by *red* lines.

The validation accuracy of MultiTune is consistently higher than that of SpotTune after 20 epochs, and the difference is around 4.5% for the Aircraft

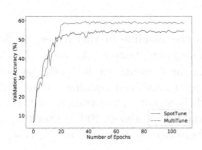

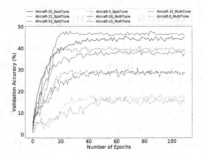

(a) Validation Accuracy versus No. of Epochs on Aircraft Dataset.

(b) Validation Accuracy versus No. of Epochs on Smaller Aircraft Datasets.

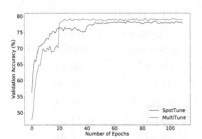

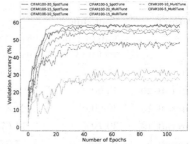

(c) Validation Accuracy versus No. of Epochs on CIFAR100 Dataset.

(d) Validation Accuracy versus No. of Epochs on Smaller CIFAR100 Datasets.

Fig. 2. Validation accuracy versus the number of epochs of SpotTune and MultiTune on aircraft, smaller aircraft, CIFAR100 and smaller CIFAR100 datasets. (Color figure online)

dataset and around 1% for the CIFAR100 dataset. The obtained results indicate that MultiTune has better performance than SpotTune on both a more specific dataset (Aircraft) and a more generic dataset (CIFAR100) when running these methods on the whole datasets. This higher performance achieved by MultiTune is due to the integration of two different fine-tuning models. This integration enables the model to extract more useful features from the image datasets. Reinitializing the last blocks lets the layers in the last blocks to learn from scratch, so that the features learnt can be more specific to the target dataset. Adjusting the learning rate in the last block of Fine-Tuning B reduces the update amount in the last block and facilitates the model to find the global minimum. The total training time is also taken as one of the considerations of the performance. As shown in Table 3, the percentage of reduction in the total training time by using MultiTune is 19.58% and 29.34% for Aircraft and CIFAR100.

Aircraft dataset has around 33 images per class, the number of images per class is roughly reduced by 43% and 60% for Aircraft-20 and Aircraft-15. In these two situations, the results of MultiTune are consistently better than SpotTune after 20 epochs. The difference is around 2.3% and 1.5%, respectively. But, when it comes to extremely small datasets, in the Aircraft-10 and Aircraft-5 datasets, the differences between these two methods are not so obvious. In Aircraft-10 and Aircraft-5, the number of images per class is roughly reduced by 70% and 85%. The inconspicuous differences in these two datasets may be due to the extremely small size of datasets. The significantly reduced size makes the model hard to learn enough knowledge to predict unseen data. It is clear in Fig. 2 that the smaller sized CIFAR100 datasets follow a similar pattern.

6 Conclusion

A novel transfer learning technique denoted as MultiTune is proposed, which can adaptively integrate multiple fine-tuning CNN models with different settings. It has been applied to image classification with two image datasets taken from the Visual Decathlon challenge. MultiTune is able to achieve a validation accuracy of 59.59% on the Aircraft dataset, which is around 4.5% higher than the result obtained by SpotTune. It outperforms SpotTune on the CIFAR100 dataset by around 1%. In addition, MultiTune achieves higher performance than SpotTune on most of the smaller-sized datasets. It also needs much less training time than SpotTune on all the datasets used in this paper. The results outlined in this paper indicate that the proposed MultiTune technique can improve the performance of transfer learning on the image classification problem. This makes MultiTune an excellent approach to be further adopted and applied in the fields of transfer learning and tasks related to image classification.

References

1. Agrawal, P., Girshick, R., Malik, J.: Analyzing the performance of multilayer neural networks for object recognition. In: Fleet, D., Pajdla, T., Schiele, B., Tuytelaars, T. (eds.) ECCV 2014. LNCS, vol. 8695, pp. 329–344. Springer, Cham (2014). https://doi.org/10.1007/978-3-319-10584-0_22
2. Azizpour, H., Razavian, A.S., Sullivan, J., Maki, A., Carlsson, S.: Factors of transferability for a generic convnet representation. IEEE Trans. Pattern Anal. Mach. Intell. **38**(9), 1790–1802 (2016)
3. Deng, J., Dong, W., Socher, R., Li, L.J., Li, K., Fei-Fei, L.: ImageNet: a large-scale hierarchical image database. In: CVPR 2009 (2009)
4. Guo, Y., Shi, H., Kumar, A., Grauman, K., Rosing, T., Feris, R.S.: SpotTune: transfer learning through adaptive fine-tuning. In: 2019 IEEE/CVF Conference on Computer Vision and Pattern Recognition (CVPR), pp. 4800–4809 (2019)
5. He, K., Zhang, X., Ren, S., Sun, J.: Deep residual learning for image recognition. CoRR. abs/1512.03385 (2015)
6. Kornblith, S., Shlens, J., Le, Q.V.: Do better imagenet models transfer better? In: Proceedings of the IEEE Conference on Computer Vision and Pattern Recognition, pp. 2661–2671 (2019)
7. Krizhevsky, A., Sutskever, I., Hinton, G.E.: ImageNet classification with deep convolutional neural networks. In: Advances in Neural Information Processing Systems, pp. 1097–1105 (2012)
8. Li, X., Grandvalet, Y., Davoine, F.: Explicit inductive bias for transfer learning with convolutional networks. CoRR (2018)

9. Plested, J., Gedeon, T.: An analysis of the interaction between transfer learning protocols in deep neural networks. In: Gedeon, T., Wong, K.W., Lee, M. (eds.) ICONIP 2019. LNCS, vol. 11953, pp. 312–323. Springer, Cham (2019). https://doi.org/10.1007/978-3-030-36708-4_26

10. Rebuffi, S., Bilen, H., Vedaldi, A.: Learning multiple visual domains with residual adapters. CoRR (2017)

11. Rebuffi, S., Bilen, H., Vedaldi, A.: Efficient parametrization of multi-domain deep neural networks. In: 2018 IEEE/CVF Conference on Computer Vision and Pattern Recognition (CVPR), pp. 8119–8127 (2018)

12. Simonyan, K., Zisserman, A.: Very deep convolutional networks for large-scale image recognition. In: International Conference on Learning Representations (2015)

13. Torrey, L., Shavlik, J.: Transfer learning. In: Handbook of Research on Machine Learning Applications. IGI Global (2009)

14. Yosinski, J., Clune, J., Bengio, Y., Lipson, H.: How transferable are features in deep neural networks? In: Advances in Neural Information Processing Systems, pp. 3320–3328 (2014)

No-Reference Quality Assessment Based on Spatial Statistic for Generated Images

Yunye Zhang[1,2], Xuewen Zhang[1], Zhiqiang Zhang[1], Wenxin Yu[1(✉)],
Ning Jiang[1], and Gang He[3]

[1] Southwest University of Science and Technology,
Mianyang, Sichuan, China
yuwenxin@swust.edu.cn
[2] University of Electronic Science and Technology of China,
Chengdu, Sichuan, China
[3] Xidian University, Xi'an, Shanxi, China

Abstract. In recent years, generative adversarial networks has made remarkable progress in the field of text-to-image synthesis whose task is to obtain high-quality generated images. Current evaluation metrics in this field mainly evaluate the quality distribution of the generated image dataset rather than the quality of single image itself. With the deepening research of text-to-image synthesis, the quality and quantity of generated images will be greatly improved. There will be a higher demand for generated image evaluation. Therefore, this paper proposes a blind generated image evaluator(BGIE) based on BRISQUE model and sparse neighborhood co-occurrence matrix, which is specially used to evaluate the quality of single generated image. Through experiments, BGIE surpasses all no-reference methods proposed in the past. Compared to VSS method, the surpassing ratio: SRCC is 8.8%, PLCC is 8.8%. By the "One-to-Multi" high-score image screening experiment, it is proved that the BGIE model can screen out best image from multiple images.

Keywords: Natural scene statistics · Generating adversarial networks · Generated images · No-Reference assessment · "One-to-multi" screening

1 Introduction

Methods for Image Quality Assessment(IQA) are composed of three types: full-reference, reduced-reference, and no-reference. As the performance of Generative Adversarial Networks(GANs) [1] improves, a good deal of generated images synthesized by models can be obtained. Considering that images synthesized by GANs with the method of text-to-image synthesis are random and unable to find reference samples, traditional metrics such as PSNR, SSIM are not noneffective.

This paper adopts no-reference evaluation for generated images. It is meaningful to propose an evaluation standard that is more relevant to generated

© Springer Nature Switzerland AG 2020
H. Yang et al. (Eds.): ICONIP 2020, CCIS 1332, pp. 497–506, 2020.
https://doi.org/10.1007/978-3-030-63820-7_57

images which will provide a backward verification idea for comprehensively evaluating the quality of networks. But the evaluation metrics for generated images are very scarce at present.

Statistics on pixel-level images alone will ignore the structural and spatial characteristics of the image. BRISQUE [2] first proposed statistics of pixel distribution features from the spatial domain. The neighborhood co-occurrence matrix(NCM) proposed by Zhou [3] can further obtain different entropy from the perspective of pixel pair-wise, but only using NCM for generated images does not perform a good quality evaluation. Therefore, this paper modifies and extends NCM to SCM, then combines it with the BRISQUE model to obtain a blind generated image evaluator(BGIE), which can get more complete spatial features as well as the statistical features of generated images. The evaluation results of generated images through this model is in line with human visual judgment.

The main contributions of this paper are as follows:

- A model named BGIE for evaluating the quality of single generated image synthesized by Generative Adversarial Networks is proposed.
- GMOS rule for generated images is proposed to standardize the scoring principles. SCM is proposed to extract more spatial features.
- The performance of BGIE surpasses previous models. This model can also select the best image among multiple generated images synthesized by the GANs through the scoring results, which meets the human eye visual judgment.

2   Related Work

For the past few years, GANs has accelerated the development of text-to-image synthesis which can correspondingly generate an image that matches a text description. Salimans et al. [4] proposed Inception Score (IS) to judge the overall distribution of generated images. However, Barratt et al. [5] pointed out that IS is sensitive and has some defects. FID [6] is an improvement of IS but aimed at computing the distacne between generated images' distribution and real images' distribution which is not for single image's evaluation. Therefore, this paper hopes to judge generated images' quality directly.

Some evaluation metrics based on statistical models have achieved good performance in no-reference quality evaluation. The BRISQUE model proposed by Mittal et al. [2] uses statistical methods to extract the MSCN coefficients in spatial domain. The VSS model proposed by Zhou et al. [3] obtains the structural entropy and information entropy of the image by performing spatial sequence statistics on the pair-wise level of the distorted image.

However, the above research is limited to the evaluation of traditional distortion images such as compression distortion, Gaussian blur, etc. These method can not be directly used to judge generated images. The high-quality generated image has the characteristics of clear foreground, enough texture details and

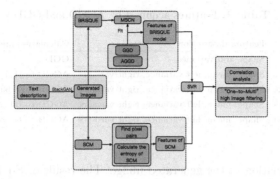

Fig. 1. Framework of evaluation model. The generated image obtained from a text description is used as the input of two feature extracting model: statistical model and the spatial model. SVR is used for regression prediction.

good spatial structure. Since generated images are not obtained by distorting from natural images, the traditional full-reference or reduced-reference evaluation methods are not suitable. Our previous work [7] is for generated images evaluation. But features extracted from this method are too simple to obtain more structural information and takes much time. Therefore, in the field of IQA, there is not yet a general method for single generated images evaluation.

3 Our Proposal

In view of the characteristics of generated images: uncertainty, no-reference, and large difference in image quality, the evaluation model should fully consider the statistical features of pixels and spatial distribution situation of the image. Therefore, a feature extraction method combining BRISQUE and spatial model is proposed. The specific model framework is shown in Fig. 1.

3.1 BRISQUE's First Application in Generated Images

The NSS (Natural Scene Statistics) method believes that natural scenes have certain statistical features that will be changed when the image is distorted. BRISQUE [2] proposes to fit MSCN (mean subtracted contrast normalization) coefficient from the perspective of the spatial domain to obtain the statistical characteristics of the image.

Normalize the local luminance of the generated image by [8]. The process is as follows:

$$\hat{I}(i,j) = \frac{I(i,j) - \mu(i,j)}{\sigma(i,j) + C}, \tag{1}$$

where $i \in 1, 2 \ldots M$, $j \in 1, 2 \ldots N$. M and N are width and length of the generated image, respectively. C is a constant used to keep the denominator from 0, usually taken as 1. μ is the average of the generated image and σ is

Table 1. Features acquired by AGGD and GGD

Feature ID	Feature description	Calculation method
$f1 - f2, f17 - 18$	Shape and variance	GGD
$f3 - f6, f9 - 12$	Shape, mean, left variance, right variance	AGGD to H pairwise products
$f7 - f10, f17 - 20$	Shape, mean, left variance, right variance	AGGD to V pairwise products
$f11 - 14, f25 - 28$	Shape, mean, left variance, right variance	AGGD to D1 pairwise products
$f15 - 18, f33 - 36$	Shape, mean, left variance, right variance	AGGD to D2 pairwise products

the stander deviation of the generated image. The result of Eq. 1 is the MSCN coefficient of the generated image I.

The 2 features obtained from generalized Gaussian distribution is as GGD (α, σ^2). There are 16 features extracted through asymmetric generalized Gaussian distribution from 4 directions, expressed as AGGD $(\eta, v, \sigma_l^2, \sigma_r^2)$. The specific parameters obtained by BRISQUE [2] are shown in Table 1, including features from the generated image and the reduced-resolution image.

3.2 SCM

The neighborhood co-occurrence matrix (NCM) [3] is proposed to describe the relationship between the co-occurrence pixel gray values at a given offset because structural information is an important influencing factor in the quality evaluation process.

Instead of accumulating pixel values, this paper find that sparse matrix has stronger characterization ability and lower amount of computation, so the NCM is modified to SCM(sparse neighborhood co-occurrence matrix) as Eq. 2. For the convenience of statistics, this paper does not taking different values of p from images in [3], but fixes the length and width of the sparse neighborhood co-occurrence matrix to $p = 256$.

$$S(i, j) = \begin{cases} 1, I(x, y) = i \ and \ u(x, y) = j \\ 0, \ otherwise \end{cases} \tag{2}$$

where $1 < x < m, 1 < y < n$. $u(x, y)$ refers to the average value of pixels in the neighborhood along a specific direction. To get $u(x, y)$, [3] computes the neighborhood mean of an image in the upper right and lower right directions. It extracts one-dimensional entropy and two-dimensional entropy of the distorted image and corresponding gradient map in two directions as the 6 features extracted by NCM.

Since sparse neighborhood co-occurrence matrix features are calculated according to pixel pairs, Fig. 2 shows how to extract pixel pairs in SCM from four directions: upper-left, upper-right, lower-right and lower-left.

Besides, using common gradient operators (such as Prewitt) to get the gray image gradient, like [3], this paper proposes to compute the gradient of the image from x direction and y direction, then compute the two-dimensional entropy of

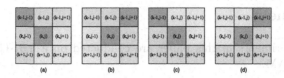

Fig. 2. Calculating the mean value of the neighborhood co-occurrence matrix.

Table 2. Detailed description of image entropy

Feature ID	Entropy	Feature description
$f37$	$e1$	One-dimensional entropy of the image
$f38 - f39$	$e2 - e3$	x, y gradient two-dimensional entropy
$f40 - f43$	$e4 - e7$	Two-dimensional entropy in four directions: upper right, lower right, upper left, and lower left
$f44$	$e8$	One-dimensional entropy of Prewitt gradient graph

the two gradient matrices. Since SCM is a 256×256 sparse matrix, which contains a few of elements of value 1, SCM map is binary.

In addition, in order to obtain more image structure entropy, all four directions in Fig. 2 are selected as the SCM in the experiment. One-dimensional entropy of the gradient image obtained by Prewitt operator is also added. A total of 8 features can be obtained by pair-wise pixels, as shown in Table 2.

By modifying and supplementing the NCM method, a new spatial model SCM is proposed. BGIE combines the two models of BRISQUE and SCM. In the experimental part, feature grouping experiments will be performed based on the BGIE model to obtain more representative features of the generated image.

3.3 GMOS

Mean opinion score (MOS) is used as a criterion for judging the quality of audio and video. Both absolute evaluation and relative evaluation in the subjective evaluation of human eyes, the quality of the image is divided into 5 scales: excellent 5 points, good 4 points, medium 3 points, poor 2 points, inferior 1 point. This paper proposes a generated mean opinion score (GMOS) for generated images, which is described in Table 3.

Table 3. GMOS for generated images

Score	Quality level	Generated image quality requirements
5	Excellent	There are clear birds with brilliant texture details
4	Good	There are foreground objects for birds, but the details are not enough
3	Medium	There are specific foreground objects, but the outline is deformed
2	Poor	The picture is messy, with irregular foreground objects
1	Inferior	The picture is messy and there is no foreground object

4   Experiment

All of the experiments in this paper are conducted on a 3.61-GHz 6-core PC
with 31G of RAM.

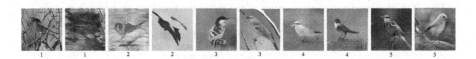

Fig. 3. Example of manual labeling. Messy generated images get low score, images
with incomplete foreground get middle score, images with clear foreground and full of
texture get high score.

4.1   Dataset

Generated Images Construction. The quality of the generated images synthesized by GANs is quite different. To make sure that the image dataset contains
balanced quality images, this paper selects StackGAN as basic network due to
easy reproduction and wide use. CUB [9] bird dataset is as the training dataset
of StackGAN, and 29,561 generated images are obtained. Since regression prediction is required when estimating the image score in the later stage, the image
quality in the dataset needs to be balanced. The proportion of low-quality or
high-quality images cannot be excessive. Because there are fewer vivid and high-
quality images that can be obtained by GANs. The 29,561 generated images will
be screened. Finally 1,100 generated images are selected as the experimental
dataset in this paper.

Manual Annotation. Invite 4 people as observers to mark 1,100 generated
images according to Table 3. Compute *zscore* of the manual score as the image
label. *zscore* is defined as follows:

$$zscore = (x - \bar{x})/std, \tag{3}$$

where x is some element of a set, $\bar{x}$ is the mean value of the elements in the set,
and *std* is the standard deviation of the set. An example of manual annotation
is shown in Fig. 3.

4.2   Feature Extraction and Grouping

According to BGIE model introduced in Sect. 3, feature extraction is performed
on 1,100 images. Low-resolution image is obtained by the downsampling with
step size of 2. Features $f1 - f4$ are gained according to GGD in the BRISQUE
model. Features $f5 - f36$ are gained according to AGGD in the BRISQUE from

four directions. This paper combines features in BRISQUE and SCM mentioned in Sect. 3.2 as follows:

$$BGIE\_with\_Prewitt = [f1, f2, \cdots, f42, f43, f44] \tag{4}$$

In the process of screening features that have the most impact on the generated image, the features are grouped for training, which can make use of fewer features to obtain better evaluation results and reduce computational overhead.

Fig. 4. Some examples of prediction results. The score is low when there is no target in generated image. But score is high when the bird posture is complete and clear.

The upper part of Table 4 shows the prediction results obtained by grouping features into groups. The lower part shows BGIE performs better than other algorithms. However, after adding the entropy of Prewitt gradient map as a feature, the prediction performance is affected. Therefore, f_{44} is removed from the final features of BGIE, so BGIE includes a total of 43 groups of features.

In this case, the proposed BGIE contains an appropriate amount of features with stronger performance capability, which ensures accurate prediction scores and a small amount of computation. After feature extraction, support vector regression(SVR) is used to perform regression experiment. In this part, LIBSVM toolbox is used for SVR. Figure 4 shows the result examples of using BGIE for feature extraction and regression prediction.

Fig. 5. "One-to-Multi" high resolution image filtering example. Each line corresponds to a sentence description of five images with different postures. The images with highest scores are marked with red borders. (Color figure online)

4.3 "One-to-Multi" High Score Image Screening

Several different components are proposed in StackGAN [10] to further verify the excellent performance. One of them is conditioning augmentation(CA). By CA component, StackGAN can obtain more diverse generated images under potential small disturbances. To verify the superiority of the BGIE, "One-to-Multi" high-score image screening verification experiment is added. By fixing 5 different bird poses, 5 corresponding pose generated images can be obtained from the same one text. In this experiment, a total of 1000 text descriptions are input, and 5000 generated images are obtained. The quality of these 5000 images is evaluated through BGIE. The best image in each group can be selected by highest score, like Fig. 5.

4.4 Correlation Analysis

Correlation analysis is a common used method to evaluate IQA metrics. By correlation analysis of the prediction score and the manual annotation, it proves whether the prediction score and the manual annotation are strongly correlated.

Table 4. Correlation analysis results comparison

Group	Method	PLCC ↑	SRCC↑
1	$f1-2$	0.553	0.551
2	$f3-4$	0.529	0.539
3	$f5-20$	0.671	0.674
4	$f21-36$	0.544	0.547
5	e_{NCM} [3]	0.321	0.301
6	e_{SCM}(ours)	0.325	0.305
7	IL_NIQE [11]	0.273	0.263
8	BRISQUE [2]	0.674	0.668
9	VSS [3]	0.717	0.707
10	BGIE_with_P(ours)	0.695	0.684
11	BGIE(ours)	**0.780**	**0.769**

In Table 4, methods started with "f" use the features in Table 1; methods started with "e" use the features in [3] and Table 2, respectively. In Table 4, upper part shows that some features in BRISQUE and SCM model can predict the generated images to some extent. Each group of experiment in Table 4 is repeated 10 times. The mean value is taken as the result.

Group 5 and Group 6 shows that features extracted from SCM has better correlation with labels than NCM. But SCM is not good enough because the structural entropy of the gradient image obtained by the Prewitt operator is included in SCM. Therefore, in BGIE, entropy of the Prewitt gradient map is eliminated. By comparing the data in Group 1, 2, 3 and 4, it shows that the parameters of the AGGD (in Table 1) of the generated image are more influential in the entire statistical model for quality evaluation.

In Group 7, [11] proposed an algorithm to evaluate images by using features of patches of images to fit MVG model. Although it works well in some public datasets, like LIVE [12], this model does not consider the diversity and complexity of the generated images. Therefore, the predicted results are very bad while taking large amount of time.

Comparing models in the lower part of Table 4, BGIE can obtain much better predicted results than previous methods while taking only 0.056 s/per image.

5   Discussion

This paper has many interesting innovations. *zscore* is used in manual annotation normalization and MSCN coefficient is used in image normalization, which makes labels and feature extraction theoretically uniform. On the basis of BGIE model, through grouping experiments on features, eliminate the features with poor expressiveness. Besides, the feature combination selects the best performance model—BGIE. From "One-to-Multi" high-score image screening experiments, it can be assumed that if BGIE is put into GANs as punishment mechanism, which can define a threshold to limit only saving high-quality images as output, the performance of the text-to-image synthesis method may be improved.

6   Conclusion

Due to the lack of evaluation metrics for generated images synthesized from text vector by GANs, this paper proposes an evaluation algorithm BGIE based on BRISQUE and sparse neighborhood co-occurrence matrix to judge single image quality. This method reaches PLCC of 0.780 and SRCC of 0.769, which proves that BGIE is in line with human vision. PLCC and SRCC of BGIE surpass other methods, especially surpass VSS to 8.8% and 8.8% respectively, which has the highest results among previous methods. "One-to-Multi" high-score image screening experiment verified that BGIE can screen out the best image of multiple images with different poses obtained by the same text description.

Acknowledgement. This research is supported by Sichuan Provincial Science and Technology Program (No. 2019YFS0146). Thank Prof. Wen Shiping for his valuable suggestion on the revision of this paper.

References

1. Goodfellow, I., et al.: Generative adversarial nets. In: Advances in Neural Information Processing Systems, pp. 2672–2680 (2014)
2. Mittal, A., Moorthy, A.K., Bovik, A.C.: No-reference image quality assessment in the spatial domain. IEEE Trans. Image Process. **21**(12), 4695–4708 (2012)

3. Zhou, Z., Lu, W., He, L., Gao, X., Yang, J.: Blind image quality assessment based on visuo-spatial series statistics. In: 2018 IEEE International Conference on Acoustics, Speech and Signal Processing (ICASSP), pp. 3161–3165. IEEE (2018)
4. Salimans, T., Goodfellow, I., Zaremba, W., Cheung, V., Radford, A., Chen, X.: Improved techniques for training GANs. In: Advances in Neural Information Processing Systems, pp. 2234–2242 (2016)
5. Barratt, S., Sharma, R.: A note on the inception score. arXiv preprint arXiv:1801.01973 (2018)
6. Heusel, M., Ramsauer, H., Unterthiner, T., Nessler, B., Hochreiter, S.: GANs trained by a two time-scale update rule converge to a local nash equilibrium (2017)
7. Zhang, Y., Zhang, Z., Yu, W., Jiang, N.: Cscore: a novel no-reference evaluation metric for generated images. In: Proceedings of the 2019 8th International Conference on Computing and Pattern Recognition, pp. 277–281 (2019)
8. Ruderman, D.L.: The statistics of natural images. Netw.: Comput. Neural Syst. 5(4), 517–548 (1994)
9. Wah, C., Branson, S., Welinder, P., Perona, P., Belongie, S.: The caltech-ucsd birds-200-2011 dataset (2011)
10. Zhang, H., et al.: StackGAN: text to photo-realistic image synthesis with stacked generative adversarial networks. In: Proceedings of the IEEE International Conference on Computer Vision, pp. 5907–5915 (2017)
11. Zhang, L., Zhang, L., Bovik, A.C.: A feature-enriched completely blind image quality evaluator. IEEE Trans. Image Process. 24(8), 2579–2591 (2015)
12. Sheikh, H.R.: Live image quality assessment database (2003). http://live.ece.utexas.edu/research/quality

Pairwise-GAN: Pose-Based View Synthesis Through Pair-Wise Training

Xuyang Shen$^{(\boxtimes)}$, Jo Plested, Yue Yao, and Tom Gedeon

Research School of Computer Science, Australian National University,
Canberra, Australia
{xuyang.shen,jo.plested,yue.yao,tom.gedeon}@anu.edu.au

Abstract. Three-dimensional face reconstruction is one of the popular applications in computer vision. However, even state-of-the-art models still require frontal face as inputs, restricting its usage scenarios in the wild. A similar dilemma also happens in face recognition. New research designed to recover the frontal face from a single side-pose facial image has emerged. The state-of-the-art in this area is the Face-Transformation generative adversarial network, which is based on the CycleGAN. This inspired our researchwhich explores two models' performance from pixel transformation in frontal facial synthesis, Pix2Pix and CycleGAN. We conducted the experiments on five different loss functions on Pix2Pix to improve its performance, then followed by proposing a new network Pairwise-GAN in frontal facial synthesis. Pairwise-GAN uses two parallel U-Nets as the generator and PatchGAN as the discriminator. The detailed hyper-parameters are also discussed. Based on the quantitative measurement by face similarity comparison, our results showed that Pix2Pix with L1 loss, gradient difference loss, and identity loss results in 2.72% of improvement at average similarity compared to the default Pix2Pix model. Additionally, the performance of Pairwise-GAN is 5.4% better than the CycleGAN, 9.1% than the Pix2Pix, and 14.22% than the CR-GAN at the average similarity. More experiment results and codes were released at https://github.com/XuyangSHEN/Pairwise-GAN.

Keywords: Face frontalization · Novel view synthesis · Image translation

1 Introduction

Three-dimensional face reconstruction from a single image is one of the popular computer vision topics over the past twenty years. Although end-to-end learning methods achieve the state-of-the-art in three-dimensional facial reconstruction [1,2], they still cannot infer the missing facial information if the input facial image is a side-pose at more than 30°. This issue not only happens on three-dimensional facial reconstruction tasks but also exists on other facial applications in computer vision. Face recognition is a widely used authentication and

© Springer Nature Switzerland AG 2020
H. Yang et al. (Eds.): ICONIP 2020, CCIS 1332, pp. 507–515, 2020.
https://doi.org/10.1007/978-3-030-63820-7_58

detection technique that currently requires front face images. However, this condition is challenging to fulfill in real life, especially for video surveillance which captures the object under any situation.

Inferring the missing facial information, known as frontal facial synthesis, is a good alternative for these applications to solve the issue raised by the side-pose facial image. From 2013, an increasing number of deep learning methods have been proposed to improve performance on frontal face synthesis problems [3,4]. With the publication of Two Pathways Generative Adversarial Network (TP-GAN) [5] and complete representations generative adversarial network (CR-GAN) [6], the focus of solving face synthesis problems was shifted into models based on GAN and CGAN [5–7]. The current state-of-the-art frontal facial synthesis is Pose-Invariant Generator Adversarial Network (FT-GAN) proposed by [7]. FT-GAN combines Cycle-Consistent Adversarial Networks (CycleGAN), considered state-of-the-art in pixel-to-pixel transformation [8,12,18], with key point alignment to generate frontal facial synthesis more realistically.

With these motivations, we begin our work by exploring two models, Pix2Pix and CycleGAN, from style transformation into frontal facial synthesis. The main contributions of this work are listed below:

- Five different loss functions were analyzed to improve the performance of the Pix2Pix in frontal facial synthesis. The best loss results achieved an 2.72% improvement compared to Pix2Pix, which is close to CycleGAN's performance.
- Pairwise-GAN which targets frontal facial synthesis is proposed as a new network architecture of CGAN. Pairwise-GAN reaches 44.3 average similarity and 74.22 maximum similarity between synthesis and ground truth. It gains 5.4% better results than the CycleGAN and 9.1% than the Pix2Pix. Compared to a 4% improvement over CycleGAN by the FT-GAN [7]. Pairwise-GAN is considered as SOTA in Color FERET dataset.
- A new quantitative measurement on face frontalization is introduced to evaluate the similarity between the generated frontal face and the ground-truth image.

2   Methods

2.1   Dataset and Pre-processing

We chose the Color FERET Database since it is free to access for research purposes. It was pre-processed by MTCNN to minimize the noise before training. In addition, we also restrict the angle of side-pose images to be at least 60° as synthesizing from side-image at a small angle is more accessible.

There are 3,135 images (2,090 pairs) in the training set and 369 (246 pairs) in the test set, where one pair contains one frontal image and one side-pose image. The size of input images in experiments is further resized into 256 by 256 pixel, due to the limitation of computation. The reason we chose 256 is that elaborate facial features can be reflected in the generated image from 256 to 512 pixels, such as hairstyle or detailed information on eyes [9].

2.2 Synthesis Loss Functions

We performed our first stage of experiments based on the train set and test set, which explored five different loss functions on Pix2Pix [14]. The overview of four different loss functions is shown in Fig. 1. This model was chosen because Pix2Pix and CycleGAN are two state-of-art models in style transformation where frontal facial synthesis also belongs. Additionally, the Pix2Pix is more applicable to experiment with different loss functions compared to the CycleGAN.

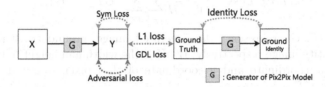

Fig. 1. Overview of loss functions used in the "exploring loss function" experiment. X and Y in the figure are the input image (side-pose facial image) and the generated frontal image. The ground identity is generated by applying the generator to the ground truth image

Adversarial loss aims to optimize the generator, which achieves a minimum Kullback-Leibler divergence (KL-divergence) between the generated data and ground truth data [10]. However, in practice, it commonly appears that the discriminator in the conditional adversarial network only focuses on whether the generated image is sharp and contains basic facial features or not, ignoring the input of the domain.

L1 Loss (Mean Absolute Loss) is employed to facilitate content consistency between the generated frontal image and the ground-truth frontal image. L1 loss also accelerates optimization in CGAN [5].

Gradient Difference Loss (GDL) aims to penalize the differences of image gradient predictions directly, where gradients are the differences between neighboring pixel values [11]. Since the facial images usually have continuous value within the neighboring, this formula can strengthen this relationship in the generated image, making it more realistic.

Symmetry Loss is based on the symmetric features in human faces [5], which encourages symmetrical structure generated by the generator.

Identity Loss first appeared in the implementation of CycleGAN [12] and was discussed in Cycada [13]. One intention of this function is to regularize the generator, which should not map the input image into a different domain image if it is already in the target domain. Our experiment found that this loss function helps preserve facial identity information from different people.

$$GDL\ Loss = \sum_{i,\ j}(||Y_{i,\ j} - Y_{i-1,\ j}| - |GT_{i,\ j} - GT_{i-1,\ j}||^{\alpha}+ \tag{1}$$

$$||Y_{i,\ j-1} - Y_{i,\ j}| - |GT_{i,\ j-1} - GT_{i,\ j}||^{\alpha})$$

$$Symmetry\ Loss = \frac{1}{W/2 \times H} \sum_{i=1}^{W/2} \sum_{j=1}^{H} |\ Y_{i,\ j} - Y_{W-(i-1),\ j}\ | \tag{2}$$

$$Identity\ Loss = \frac{1}{W \times H} \sum_{i=1}^{W} \sum_{j=1}^{H} |\ GT_{i,\ j} - GI_{i,\ j}\ | \tag{3}$$

where Y, GT, GI represents the generated image, ground truth image, and ground identity image respectively; W, H is the width and height of the images; i, j is the x coordinate and y coordinate of that pixel; $\alpha >= 1$, we tested $\alpha = 1\ and\ \alpha = 2$.

2.3 Network Architecture of Pairwise-GAN

During the experiments, we discovered that Pix2Pix and CycleGAN have outstanding achievements in general pixel-to-pixel transformation but gain ordinary performance on frontal facial synthesis. Notably, it was hard to balance the ratio of adversarial loss and other types of losses. If the proportion of adversarial loss is adjusted higher than the other, the generator can easily deceive the discriminator by generating a realistic image unrelated to the input domain. Alternatively, parts of the generated image are close to the original person but the entire image is not a real face; for example, the face may contain three eyes. As a result of further study of the network architecture, we developed Pairwise-GAN which is based on the network architecture of Pix2Pix and CycleGAN.

Generator. Unlike usual conditional adversarial networks and [5,16,17], Pairwise-GAN has two independent auto-encoders and weight sharing of the first two-layers of the decoder (Fig. 2). The layered architecture of U-Nets contains eight blocks in the encoder, eight blocks in the decoder, and skip connections between the encoder and decoder. In Pairwise-GAN, we use instance normalization instead of batch normalization to boost the performance of generator [15].

When training, Pairwise-GAN requires two side-pose images at the same angles from the same person but in a different direction as inputs(X_{left}, X_{right}). Left generator G_1 takes the side-pose image from the left direction, while another side-pose image will be passed into generator G_2. After different encoders extract facial features, two frontal facial images are generated through two decoders. As these two generators are independent, only one side-pose image is required to be input for prediction. This approach addresses affordability and the difficulties in pixel-to-pixel transformation inherent in the complexities of human faces.

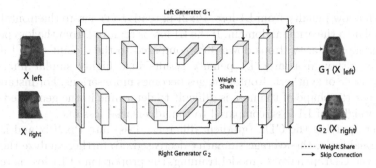

Fig. 2. Generator Architecture of Pairwise-GAN. X_{left} left-side facial input; X_{right} right-side facial input. Additionally, providing both sides faces is a common attribute for most facial datasets, such as Multi-PIE Face Database, CAS-PEAL Face Database, and Color FERET Database

Discriminator. We used the patch-based discriminator of GANs (Patch-GAN) [14] as the discriminator for Pairwise-GAN. In PatchGAN, one patch is the convolution result of one receptive field that the discriminator is sensitive to, such as, the ear, tooth, and eyes if the input image is a human face. The operation procedure is to cropping the input data into multiple overlapping patches, respectively discriminating the difference by the classifier (discriminator), and averaging the results.

Pair Loss. To reduce the difference of generated images between the left generator and right generator, we examined the weight sharing between two encoders and added the pair loss into the loss function.

$$Pair\ Loss = \frac{1}{W \times H} \sum_{i=1}^{W} \sum_{j=1}^{H} |\ YL_{i,\,j} - YR_{i,\,j}\ | \tag{4}$$

where YL and YR refer to the image generated by the left generator and right generator

3 Results and Evaluation

To measure the results quantitatively, we employed the facial similarity, structural similarity (SSIM), Frechet Inception Distance (FID), and Peak Signal-to-Noise Ratio (PSNR) by comparing the frontal facial synthesis and ground truths. Notably, The result of facial similarity (confidence) is provided by a commercial face comparison API (Face ++) based on face recognition.

3.1 Loss Function Analysis

In this experiment, a Pix2Pix with various loss functions was trained with 125 epochs, with one epoch taking 2,090 pairs of images. Additionally, both generator and discriminator were optimized with Adam and a learning rate of 0.0002.

With a low penalty from L1 loss, Pix2Pix tends to generate the frontal facial less similar to the original domain. If the L1 loss is removed from the loss penalty, the average similarity drops down 40% compared to the default one (Table 1). However, although a large L1 penalty results in a highly similar image, the blurring issue of synthetic frontal images becomes more serious. For instance, we found that the shape of the nose is difficult to determine in the generated image by 120 weights of L1 loss, compared to the adversarial loss one.

After applying the GDL (gradient difference loss) into Pix2Pix and keeping the original ratio, the average similarity decreased. To further analyze the influence of the GDL penalty to model training, the proportion of L1 loss is reduced below the adversarial loss; the ratio between L1 and GDL remains untouched. We noticed that the average similarity grows to 35. However, the obscured side of the input image is blurred in the synthesis, which we considered a drawback of the GDL penalty.

The behavior of symmetry loss resulted in a negative influence on the performance of Pix2Pix as the average similarity decreases into 31. It was also hard to converge during the training progress. As a result, we abandoned this loss in later experiments.

We explored identity loss which aims to regularize the generator. Compared to the L1 penalty and GDL penalty, identity loss leads to a significant improvement in the frontal facial of Pix2Pix, which the synthetic frontal face is most natural and sharp compared to others, notably, hairstyle and glasses were recovered in high quality. As a result, the identity penalty helped to preserve facial identity information; however, adding identity loss to GAN learning doubled the training time required in each epoch to calculate the ground identity image through the generator.

Table 1. Compare average similarity between ground truth and generated image on different loss configurations among 40 test images. Higher similarity is better

Hyper-parameters	Adv	L1	GDL	Sym	Id	Avgerage Similarity
Pix2Pix	1	0	0	0	0	25.68
Pix2Pix	1	40	0	0	0	33.11
Pix2Pix	1	120	20	0	0	31.17
Pix2Pix	20	3	0.5	0	0	34.89
Pix2Pix	20	3	0.1	0.05	0	31.07
Pix2Pix	20	3	0.1	0	5	**37.92**
Pix2Pix Default	*1*	*120*	*0*	*0*	*0*	*35.2*
CycleGAN Default	*1*	*0*	*0*	*0*	*5*	*38.7*

3.2   Pairwise-GAN Analysis

We trained each of the experiments of Pairwise-GAN for 250 epochs, with one epoch taking 1,045 images and used the same data distribution as previous experiments. We set the batch size to 1 and the learning rate to 0.0002. Additionally, Adam was selected as the optimizer for both generator and discriminator.

We expected the network architecture with weight sharing gains to achieve a better performance than using the loss penalty as the former is closer to a coercive specification. However, the results indicated another option which the pair loss helps to improve the average performance, and weight sharing contributes to refresh the peak performance (Table 2). If both weight sharing and pair loss are employed in the Pairwise-GAN, it decreased both peak and average performance, which results from the network is hard to converge.

Table 2. Results of different configurations on Pairwise-GAN (ablation study) and comparisons on Pairwise-GAN with Pix2Pix, CycleGAN, and CR-GAN

Hyper-parameters						Similarity Measure			Other Measure		
Adv	L1	GDL	Id	Pair	Weight Share	Avg	Max	Min	SSIM	FID	PSNR
10	0	0	5	10	Disable	44.23	79.14	22.02	0.576	102.141	13.968
10	3	0	5	10	Disable	44.30	74.22	**23.56**	**0.600**	91.517	**14.517**
10	3	0	5	0	Enable	42.34	**81.83**	17.16	0.550	**90.531**	14.199
10	0	0	10-5	10-2	Enable	42.79	70.61	16.43	0.515	93.433	13.987
10	0	0	0	10-2	Enable	**45.16**	71.95	20.07	0.505	119.211	13.209
CR-GAN Default [6]						30.08	47.16	12.9	0.362	171.28	10.916
Pix2Pix Default [14]						35.2	62.12	0	0.502	118.791	13.775
CycleGAN Default [12]						38.9	70.22	14.64	0.493	99.777	13.274
Groud Truth						100	100	100	1	0.0	+Inf

Fig. 3. Qualitative results of Pairwise-GAN in Color FERET database

Comparing with State-of-the-Art. FT-GAN, was the current state-of-the-art model in frontal facial generation used CMU Multi-PIE database, but did not release the codes [7]. Therefore, we compared our model with CycleGAN since FT-GAN is built on CycleGAN and within 4% better than it. Additionally, we also the CR-GAN in the comparison. Table 2 show Pairwise-GAN reaches 44.3 average similarity and 74.22 maximum similarity between synthesis and ground truth. In other words, the performance of Pairwise-GAN is around 5.4% better than the CycleGAN and 9.1% than the Pix2Pix, measured by the average similarity of synthesis and ground truth among 40 test images. It also obtains the best evaluation results from SSIM, FID, and PSNR. From the synthetic frontal images, we note that both CR-GAN and CycleGAN only generated the main facial features, and stacks onto the original side-pose image. On Pairwise-GAN, the field recovered is broader as it focuses on the facial features as well as other elements, such as hairstyle and neck (Fig. 3). Apart from that, Pairwise-GAN also requires less computation power in both training and prediction as it only consumes 224 s compared to CycleGAN requiring 315 s. The prediction can achieve 34 fps by using GPU, RTX 2060S.

4   Conclusion and Future Work

In this paper, we extend current work on synthesizing front face images based on side-pose facial images. Initially, we focused on the performance of Pix2Pix, which tests and analyses five different loss functions, including adversarial loss, L1 loss, gradient difference loss, symmetry loss, and identity loss. Since the improvement based on different loss penalty was minor, we continued our work to propose Pairwise-GAN. Through the analysis of experimental results on different loss functions, we concluded that L1 loss, GDL loss, and identity loss help alleviate the common issue existing in CGAN, where the output face is related to the input face. The ratio of these five-loss, achieving the highest score in our experiment, is 20:3:0.1:0:5 (adversarial:L1:GDL:symmetry:identity).

Our second experiment proved that Pairwise-GAN generated better frontal face results than the CR-GAN and CycleGAN in the Color FERET database by using fewer computation resources; specifically, it improves 5.4% and 14.22% on average compared to CycleGAN and CR-GAN in generated quality. Pairwise-GAN is considered as SOTA in Color FERET dataset. We also explored various configurations of Pairwise-GAN, which demonstrated that either, but not both, pair loss (soft penalty) or weight sharing (coercive specification) positively contribute to improvements. Further research on the network architecture is required to continue minimizing the difference of generated images by the two generators of Pairwise-GAN.

Acknowledgements. We thank Dawn Olley and Alasdair Tran for their invaluable editing advice.

References

1. Jackson, A.S., Bulat, A., Argyriou, V., Tzimiropoulos, G.: Large pose 3D face reconstruction from a single image via direct volumetric CNN regression. In: ICCV, pp. 1031–1039 (2017)

2. Feng, Y., Wu, F., Shao, X., Wang, Y., Zhou, X.: Joint 3D face reconstruction and dense alignment with position map regression network. In: Ferrari, V., Hebert, M., Sminchisescu, C., Weiss, Y. (eds.) Computer Vision – ECCV 2018. LNCS, vol. 11218, pp. 557–574. Springer, Cham (2018). https://doi.org/10.1007/978-3-030-01264-9_33

3. Kan, M., Shan, S., Chang, H., Chen, X.: Stacked progressive auto-encoders (SPAE) for face recognition across poses. In: CVPR, pp. 1883–1890 (2014)

4. Hassner, T., Harel, S., Paz, E., Enbar, R.: Effective face frontalization in unconstrained images. In: CVPR, pp. 4295–4304 (2015)

5. Huang, R., Zhang, S., Li, T., He, R.: Beyond face rotation: global and local perception GAN for photorealistic and identity preserving frontal view synthesis. In: ICCV, pp. 2439–2448 (2017)

6. Tian, Y., Peng, X., Zhao, L., Zhang, S., Metaxas, D.N.: CR-GAN: learning complete representations for multi-view generation. arXiv preprint arXiv:1806.11191 (2018)

7. Zhuang, W., Chen, L., Hong, C., Liang, Y., Wu, K.: FT-GAN: face transformation with key points alignment for pose-invariant face recognition. Electronics 8, 807 (2019)

8. Yao, Y., Zheng, L., Yang, X., Naphade, M., Gedeon, T.: Simulating content consistent vehicle datasets with attribute descent. In: ECCV (2020)

9. Karras, T., Laine, S., Aila, T.: A style-based generator architecture for generative adversarial networks. In: CVPR, pp. 4401–4410 (2019)

10. Goodfellow, I., et al.: Generative adversarial nets. In: NeurIPS, pp. 2672–2680 (2014)

11. Mathieu, M., Couprie, C., LeCun, Y.: Deep multi-scale video prediction beyond mean square error. arXiv preprint arXiv:1511.05440 (2015)

12. Zhu, J.Y., Park, T., Isola, P., Efros, A.A.: Unpaired image-to-image translation using cycle-consistent adversarial networks. In: ICCV, pp. 2223–2232 (2017)

13. Hoffman, J., et al.: Cycada: cycle-consistent adversarial domain adaptation. In: ICML, pp. 1989–1998 (2018)

14. Isola, P., Zhu, J.Y., Zhou, T., Efros, A.A.: Image-to-image translation with conditional adversarial networks. In: CVPR, pp. 1125–1134 (2017)

15. Ulyanov, D., Vedaldi, A., Lempitsky, V.: Instance normalization: The missing ingredient for fast stylization. arXiv preprint arXiv:1607.08022 (2016)

16. Liu, M.Y., Tuzel, O.: Coupled generative adversarial networks. In: NeurIPS, pp. 469–477 (2016)

17. Anoosheh, A., Agustsson, E., Timofte, R., Van Gool, L.: ComboGAN: unrestrained scalability for image domain translation. In: CVPR Workshops, pp. 783–790 (2018)

18. Yao, Y., Plested, J., Gedeon, T.: Information-preserving feature filter for short-term EEG signals. Neurocomputing (2020)

Pixel-Semantic Revising of Position: One-Stage Object Detector with Shared Encoder-Decoder

Qian Li[1,2] (ID), Nan Guo[1](✉) (ID), Xiaochun Ye[1,2] (ID), Dongrui Fan[1,2],
and Zhimin Tang[1,2]

[1] State Key Laboratory of Computer Architecture,
Institute of Computing Technology, Chinese Academy of Sciences, Beijing, China
{liqian18s,guonan,yexiaochun,fandr,tang}@ict.ac.cn
[2] University of Chinese Academy of Sciences, Beijing, China

Abstract. Recently, many methods have been proposed for object detection. However, they cannot detect objects by semantic features, adaptively. According to channel and spatial attention mechanisms, we mainly analyze that different methods detect objects adaptively. Some state-of-the-art detectors combine different feature pyramids with many mechanisms. However, they require more cost. This work addresses that by an anchor-free detector with shared encoder-decoder with attention mechanism, extracting shared features. We consider features of different levels from backbone (e.g., ResNet-50) as the basis features. Then, we feed the features into a simple module, followed by a detector header to detect objects. Meantime, we use the semantic features to revise geometric locations, and the detector is a pixel-semantic revising of position. More importantly, this work analyzes the impact of different pooling strategies (e.g., mean, maximum or minimum) on multi-scale objects, and finds the minimum pooling can improve detection performance on small objects better. Compared with state-of-the-art MNC based on ResNet-101 for the standard MSCOCO 2014 baseline, our method improves detection AP of 3.8%.

Keywords: Detection · Encoder-decoder · Attention mechanism · Pooling

1 Introduction

In recent years, CNNs have significantly improved performance of many computer vision tasks (classification, detection and segmentation). According to region proposals, object detection methods are divided into the two-stage [4, 7,8,21], and the one-stage [6,13,17,19]. The two-stage methods perform better than the one-stage because of multi-scale proposals, but the speed is much slower. According to anchor, detectors are divided into anchor-based [15,21,28] which they require more information related to objects, and the anchor-free detectors

© Springer Nature Switzerland AG 2020
H. Yang et al. (Eds.): ICONIP 2020, CCIS 1332, pp. 516–525, 2020.
https://doi.org/10.1007/978-3-030-63820-7_59

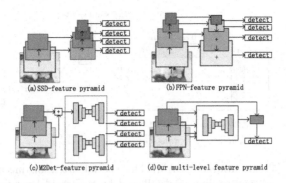

(a) SSD-feature pyramid

(b) FPN-feature pyramid

(c) M2Det-feature pyramid

(d) Our multi-level feature pyramid

Fig. 1. Illustration of the four feature pyramids, (a) illustrates the feature-based pyramid method [17] based on anchor for multi-scale objects detection, (b) fuses different horizontal features from top-to-bottom and bottom-to-top to detect multi-scale objects, (c) shows that M2Det [28] extracts features through many U-shape modules, then combines attention mechanisms to improve detection performance. (d) illustrates our multi-scale objects detection with a shared encoder-decoder module for learning shared features on multi-scale objects.

[11,14,16,18,20,27,29]. Based on these methods, we construct a detector with the shared encoder-decoder to improve detection performance.

However, there are many problems, such as lighting, size, overlapping, etc., resulting in the poor performance. Especially for multi-scale objects, [15,17, 24,28] exploit the attention mechanisms to improve the performance, but they require more cost. [15] changes anchors for different backbones to implement better. [10] proposes a new context-aware ROI pooling method. As shown in Fig. 1, for [15,17,28], parameters from different levels are independent. Inspired by them, we assume that a shared module can be implemented for multi-level features, extracting shared features.

The attention contains the spatial attention, the channel attention or both. [12] transforms distribution to retain the key information. [9] divides the attention into three parts. As shown in Fig. 2, [26] infers the attention map for two independent dimensions (channels and spatial), and multiplies the attention map with the input feature to improve performance. Therefore, can we assume different pooling operations have different detection performance? Our contributions are as follows:

- We propose a shared encoder-decoder with attention mechanism to improve the performance on multi-scale objects. And, we experiment the impact of the maximum, average, and minimum pooling methods for multi-scale objects. The minimum pooling improves the detection performance on small objects.
- We propose a semantic-revised method corresponding to geometric location to detect objects, adaptively, which is more flexible than state-of-the-state methods of just geometric prediction.
- Based on ResNet-50, our experiment achieves detection AP@0.5 of 49.8% on standard MSCOCO 2014 benchmark.

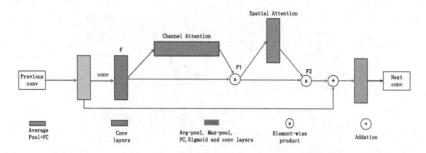

Fig. 2. ResNet [5] has utilized CBAM. The spatial attention mechanism exploits average-pooling and max-pooling, and followed by a sigmoid layer to normalize features, the channel attention only exploits average-pooling and a sigmoid layer.

2   Related Works

Feature Pyramid. As shown in Fig. 1, [17] directly predicts features from different levels, and solves the multi-scale problem to a certain extent. [28] uses U-shape module to extract high-level features, and the multi-level weights are independent, resulting in more cost and less correlation. [2] solves the problem by splitting feature into different modules, and the relationship becomes a challenge. Therefore, we use a shared module to obtain the multi-level shared features.

Encoder-Decoder. The traditional algorithms [5,23] learn more discriminative features by deeper network and the residual module. [1] uses an encoder-decoder for classification task. Therefore, we exploit a shared encoder-decoder to improve detection performance.

Attention Mechanism. Generally, attention mechanism can improve performance. [9] improves performance by the correlation between channels. A lightweight module [26] adopts the channel and spatial attention mechanisms to improve performance. We analyze the impact of the detection performance of different attention mechanisms on multi-scale objects and combing CBAM with minimum pooling can improve the detection performance on small objects.

3   Our Approach

In this section, as shown in Fig. 3, based on ResNet-50, our method includes a shared encoder-decoder module with the attention mechanism for feature pyramid, and a shared detector header with a classification prediction branch, a detection branch, a center-ness branch and a semantic-related center branch which revises regression prediction branch to make the detector more suitable for the actual application. Details as follow.

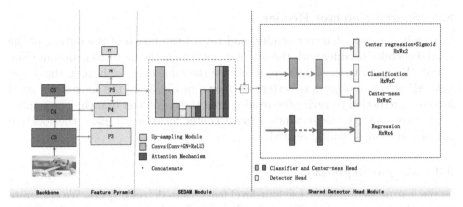

Fig. 3. An overview of the proposed anchor-free pixel-semantic revising of position. The architecture exploits the backbone and the shared encoder-decoder module with attention mechanism, obtaining more details for location. Then, the regression prediction produces the four distances (from top boundary to center, center to bottom, right to center, center to left). The semantic-related center prediction branch (center regression +sigmoid in figure) revises the pixel-level positions prediction (regression in figure).

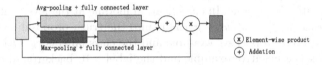

Fig. 4. Illustrations of our attention mechanism module, we use the average pooling and maximum pooling, followed by a fully connected layer, then, multiplied by the original features.

3.1   Shared Encoder-Decoder Module with Attention Mechanism (SEDAM)

As shown in Fig. 1, we propose a shared encoder-decoder module for multi-level feature pyramids. Since the semantic features within a category are similar, we present that the shared module learns the common features on multi-scale objects for a class, improving the generalization performance. The more the number of layers is, the more the discriminative features extracted are, on the contrary, losing more details about location. In addition, we analyze different attention mechanisms in the shared encoder-decoder, including a spatial attention with different pooling operations, a channel attention or the both.

Our Attention Mechanism. We use the channel attention to improve the detection AP, as shown in Fig. 4, the features pass two paths (an average-pooling followed by a fully connection layer, and a maximum-pooling followed by a fully connection layer) respectively. We fuse outputs from the two paths, then multiply with the features which are the input of paths to enhance the key information.

3.2   Shared Detector Header

We apply a shared detector header, and regard the fusion of the output of the shared encoder-decoder with the original features as the input to maintain more details. When features of different levels use the same detector header, the detection AP on small objects is better. As shown in Fig. 3, we use semantic-related location prediction to revise the results from the regression branch. The semantic feature can get the semantic-related center location to make the location prediction more semantic-related.

3.3   Margin Regression

In the feature pyramid, we use four-level features to detect objects. We elaborate the prediction processing of the i-level in detail, other levels are similar. Many candidates of bounding boxes are obtained at the level i. We define all candidates as D_i at the level i, where $D_i = (x^k{}_s, y^k{}_s, x^k{}_m, y^k{}_m, c_k) \in R^4 \times \{1, 2, 3, ..., C\}$. C is the number of categories, we set it to 80 on MSCOCO, c_k represents the class label in the k-th bounding box.

We propose a semantic-related location, as shown in the Eq. 1. For the semantic center, $B_i = (x^j{}_i, y^j{}_i)$ represents the j-th semantic-related center position prediction at the level i, the number of the semantic center B_i and the number of the candidates D_i is same. In classification module at the level i, if the center proposal position $(x^k_i + x^j_i, y^k_i + y^j_i)$ falls into the truth proposal at the level i, the bounding box is a positive example and the class label is c_k. Otherwise, the bounding box is a negative example and the label is 0 (background class).

$$x1 = (x^k_i + x^j_i) - x^k_s, y1 = (y^k_i + y^j_i) - y^k_s, x2 = x^k_m + (x^k_i + x^j_i), y3 = y^k_m + (y^k_i + y^j_i) \quad (1)$$

Where (x^k_i, y^k_i) denotes the k-th center proposal position at the level i. (x^j_i, y^j_i) represents the j-th semantic-related center prediction for revising the k-th center proposal position. (x^k_s, y^k_s) is the left-top margin of the k-th prediction, and (x^k_m, y^k_m) is the right-bottom margin of the k-th prediction. $(x1, y1)$ and $(x2, y2)$ represent the left-top position and right-bottom position of the k-th prediction at the level i, respectively.

3.4   Network Configures

Based on ResNet-50, as shown in Fig. 3, the encoder uses three down-sampling modules (a convolution, a group normalization and a ReLU), followed by a smooth layer, the decoder uses three up-sampling modules with the bilinear interpolation. The channel of the basis features is 256. We set the channel of SEDAM to 640 to improve efficiency of parameters. As shown in Fig. 3, we set the input size as 800×800.

Loss Function. As described in Eq. 2, we use three losses to optimize the classification, regression and center-ness. If a location prediction is closer to the center of the target, the probability value is closer to 1.0. Details are explained by [25].

$$L(p_{x,y}, d_{x,y}) = L_{cls}(p_{x,y}, c^*{}_{x,y}) + L_{reg}(d_{x,y}, d^*{}_{x,y}) + L_{center}(p_{x,y}, c^*{}_{x,y}) \quad (2)$$

Where $L_{cls}(p_{x,y}, c^*_{x,y})$ is the cross-entropy classification loss with an alpha 0.25 and a gamma 2 between predicted labels and truth labels. $L_{reg}(d_{x,y}, d^*_{x,y})$ denotes the regression loss (IOU-loss) with target center weights between the predicted locations and the target locations, and the weights are related to target margins (the left, the right, the top and the bottom). $L_{center}(p_{x,y}, c^*_{x,y})$ is the cross-entropy loss between center-ness predictions and target center weights.

4   Experiments and Results

In this section, we experiment different detection methods on large-scale standard MS COCO 2014 benchmark. We experiment 80 classes of training/validation, the training set includes 82783 images, and the validation set includes 40504 images. To compare with the state-of-the-art methods, we compare with traditional methods based on [15]. In our experiments, we experiment four methods, the A (without a shared encoder-decoder), the B (a shared encoder-decoders with CBAM), the C (a shared encoder-decoder combing CBAM with minimum pooling), and ours (a shared encoder-decoder with our attention mechanism).

Implementation Details. Based on ResNet-50, our network uses a random gradient descent method for $300k$ iterations, where an initial learning rate, a decay rate and momentum are 0.01, 0.0005, 0.9, respectively. We use 2 TITAN Xp GPUs, 8 batch size for training.

4.1   Ablation Studies

The Importance of the Shared Encoder-Decoder. As shown in Table 1, the A is poor on small objects. For example, the clock, the stop sign and bear achieve APs of 22.4%, 11.0% and 4.9%, respectively. For large objects, the person, the airplane, the fire hydrant and toilet achieve 5.9%, 8.6%, 7.3%, and 8.1% higher than the A, respectively. As shown in Table 2, ours with the semantic-related center is 1.0% higher on small object detection than the B with the semantic-revised. For small, medium and large objects, ours with semantic-revised module achieves 1.3%, 1.8% and 6.3% higher than the A without semantic-revised module, respectively. Therefore, the shared encoder-decoder with our attention mechanism performs on multi-scale objects better.

Comparison of Different Attention Mechanisms. As shown in Table 2, the A with semantic-revised module, the B with semantic-revised module, the C with semantic-revised module and ours with semantic-revised module achieve detection AP@0.5:0.95 of 25.3%, 27.4%, 27.8%, and 28.4%. According to different IOU values, the four methods with semantic-revised module achieve better. Therefore, the shared encoder-decoder module with our attention mechanism improves the detection performance. According to Table 2, we find that the minimum pooling performs better on small objects for detection task, and the channel attention mechanism is more suitable to detect multi-scale objects.

522   Q. Li et al.

Table 1. Comparison with using different attention mechanisms, there are four methods, the A (without a shared encoder-decoder), the B (a shared encoder-decoders with CBAM), the C (a shared encoder-decoder combing CBAM with minimum pooling), and ours (a shared encoder-decoder with our attention mechanism).

Method	SED	CBAM	IOU	Aera	Person	Airplane	Bus	Train	Fire hydrant	Stop sign	Cat	Elephant	Bear	Zebra	Giraffe	Toilet	Clock
A	–	–	0.5:0.95	S	18.8	23.7	6.66	6.96	20.7	11.0	11.3	21.6	4.9	29.1	24.9	11.0	22.4
B	✓	✓	0.5:0.95	S	19.4	23.2	9.02	7.07	22.5	12.0	10.1	24.0	8.11	28.6	26.2	12.0	22.9
C	✓	*	0.5:0.95	S	19.2	25.4	8.76	7.4	20.8	12.1	11.6	23.4	8.17	28.2	25.9	16.7	24.7
Ours	✓	–	0.5:0.95	S	19.6	23.8	8.26	7.23	21.9	12.3	9.68	23.4	9.41	29.8	26.6	13.6	24.0
A	–	–	0.5:0.95	M	44.3	40.4	31.9	25.3	52.4	55.6	43.4	44.5	58.9	50.8	54.9	41.7	48.6
B	✓	✓	0.5:0.95	M	45.2	41.4	34.5	25.5	55.2	56.3	44.5	47.4	62.0	50.6	54.6	44.9	50.2
C	✓	*	0.5:0.95	M	45.5	43.7	34.1	28.0	57.4	57.6	43.7	46.4	58.4	51.8	56.0	43.7	49.9
Ours	✓	–	0.5:0.95	M	45.2	43.1	34.8	23.8	57.5	56.5	43.6	47.3	59.9	51.5	54.8	44.3	48.8
A	–	–	0.5:0.95	L	52.5	51.1	63.1	54.3	62.0	77.7	49.4	57.0	59.4	56.4	54.0	49.0	50.5
B	✓	✓	0.5:0.95	L	55.4	56.4	67.9	57.8	67.8	80.5	55.3	63.3	63.0	58.0	59.8	54.3	53.0
C	✓	*	0.5:0.95	L	56.3	58.6	68.2	59.9	69.1	81.4	57.3	63.6	64.6	60.8	60.2	56.7	52.3
Ours	✓	–	0.5:0.95	L	**58.4**	**59.7**	**69.3**	59.5	**69.3**	80.6	57.1	**64.5**	**64.8**	**61.7**	**62.5**	**57.1**	**53.0**
A	–	–	0.5	–	64.1	70.0	69.1	76.9	74.2	66.8	77.7	76.4	81.8	81.5	80.7	70.3	67.2
B	✓	✓	0.5	–	68.9	74.0	73.2	80.0	77.5	69.4	81.7	81.2	84.9	83.9	84.8	74.1	69.0
C	✓	*	0.5	–	68.5	75.2	72.8	80.7	78.8	69.1	82.3	80.9	84.7	85.1	84.4	76.1	69.1
Ours	✓	–	0.5	–	69.3	73.5	72.9	79.1	79.0	69.9	81.9	81.0	84.5	83.9	85.0	75.1	68.1
A	–	–	0.75	–	33.7	42.6	55.1	54.0	56.2	57.7	52.6	51.9	65.9	52.4	53.6	49.0	36.8
B	✓	✓	0.75	–	34.5	45.2	59.0	57.2	61.0	59.1	58.1	56.9	72.2	53.2	56.1	53.8	38.4
C	✓	*	0.75	–	35.1	47.7	58.9	59.4	61.2	59.4	59.8	56.3	70.2	53.7	57.8	56.0	39.6
Ours	✓	–	0.75	–	36.3	47.7	59.4	58.7	61.9	58.7	59.8	57.9	70.9	56.1	58.3	56.9	38.9
A	–	–	0.5:0.95	–	35.1	40.5	47.9	48.5	48.6	50.4	47.5	47.9	57.7	49.8	50.5	44.6	37.3
B	✓	✓	0.5:0.95	–	36.9	43.4	52.1	51.6	53.0	52.2	52.4	52.8	61.2	50.7	53.8	49.2	38.7
C	✓	*	0.5:0.95	–	37.2	45.5	52.2	53.8	54.0	53.0	53.9	52.4	61.7	52.5	54.5	50.6	39.1
Ours	✓	–	0.5:0.95	–	**38.0**	45.4	**52.7**	52.7	54.0	52.4	53.8	**53.6**	**62.2**	**53.0**	**55.8**	**51.0**	**38.7**

The Importance of the Semantic-Revised. When the network without the semantic-revised center at an inference, the network performs worse on small objects. There are four methods without the semantic-revised, the method A, the method B, the method C, and ours, they are poor detection APs of 0.3%, 0.4%, 0.6% and 0.3% lower than methods with the semantic-revised center module, respectively. Therefore, we think that the semantic-revised branch makes detection performance better on multi-scale objects, adaptively.

Comparison with State-of-the-Art Detectors. As shown in Table 2, our method is better than [6] and MNC [3], and ours achieve detection APs of 0.4% and 3.8% higher than the others, respectively. More importantly, our method consumes less time and space. For MSCOCO benchmark, the four methods (the A, the B, the C and ours) are better than traditional detectors [3,4,17,21,22]. Therefore, ours performs better.

4.2   Discussion

As shown in Table 1 and Table 2, we believe that the minimum pooling optimizes the model toward features from small objects, so that the method C performs

Table 2. Comparisons of Detection APs(%) on MS COCO2014 benchmark.

Method	Backbone	Revise	Avg.Precision, IOU:			Avg.Precision, Area:		
			0.5:0.95	0.5	0.75	S	M	L
Faster R-CNN [21]	VGG-16	–	21.9	42.7	–	–	–	–
OHEM++ [22]	VGG-16	–	25.5	45.9	26.1	7.4	27.7	40.3
SSD [17]	VGG-16	–	25.1	43.1	25.8	6.6	25.9	41.4
SSD	MobileNet-v2	–	22.1	–	–	–	–	–
DSSD321 [6]	ResNet-101	–	28.0	46.1	29.2	7.4	28.1	47.6
R-FCN [4]	ResNet-50	–	27.0	48.7	26.9	9.8	30.9	40.3
MNC [3]	ResNet-101	–	24.6	44.3	24.8	4.7	25.9	43.6
A	ResNet-50	–	25.1	45.4	24.6	10.5	29.3	32.6
A	ResNet-50	✓	25.3	45.4	24.9	10.8	29.2	33.0
B	ResNet-50	–	27.3	49.4	26.5	11.1	30.7	36.8
B	ResNet-50	✓	27.4	49.2	26.7	11.5	30.6	36.6
C	ResNet-50	–	27.5	49.5	26.9	11.3	30.9	37.4
C	ResNet-50	✓	27.8	49.5	27.3	11.9	31.1	37.3
Ours	ResNet-50	–	28.4	49.9	28.1	11.5	31.2	39.0
Ours	ResNet-50	✓	**28.4**	**49.8**	28.1	**11.8**	31.1	38.9

better than the others on small objects. According to Table 1, the shared encoder-decoder can learn the similar semantic features on multi-scale objects. However, the semantic distribution between different categories may hurt performance because of the difference of distribution. According to these experiments, we find that our attention mechanism is more effective than the traditional attention mechanism for multi-scale objects.

5   Conclusions

We propose one-stage anchor-free detector with shared encoder-decoder with attention mechanism, exploiting SEDAM to detect multi-scale objects, adaptively. More importantly, the semantic-revised branch is more suitable for the actual scene. The attention mechanism with the minimum pooling improves performance on small objects detection better. Our approach reduces cost and performs better than traditional methods for multi-scale objects detection. We believe that our approach can be used to detect multi-scale objects in other basis structures to a certain extent.

References

1. Badrinarayanan, V., Kendall, A., Cipolla, R.: SegNet: a deep convolutional encoder-decoder architecture for image segmentation. IEEE Trans. Pattern Anal. Mach. Intell. **39**(12), 2481–2495 (2017)

2. Bae, S.H.: Object detection based on region decomposition and assembly
3. Dai, J., He, K., Sun, J.: Instance-aware semantic segmentation via multi-task network cascades
4. Dai, J., Yi, L., He, K., Jian, S.: R-FCN: object detection via region-based fully convolutional networks (2016)
5. Fei, W., et al.: Residual attention network for image classification (2017)
6. Fu, C.Y., Liu, W., Ranga, A., Tyagi, A., Berg, A.C.: DSSD: deconvolutional single shot detector. arXiv preprint arXiv:1701.06659 (2017)
7. Girshick, R.: Fast R-CNN. In: Computer Science (2015)
8. Girshick, R., Donahue, J., Darrell, T., Malik, J.: Rich feature hierarchies for accurate object detection and semantic segmentation. In: Computer Vision and Pattern Recognition (2014)
9. Hu, J., Shen, L., Sun, G.: Squeeze-and-excitation networks. In: Proceedings of the IEEE Conference on Computer Vision and Pattern Recognition, pp. 7132–7141 (2018)
10. Hu, X., Xu, X., Xiao, Y., Chen, H., Heng, P.A.: SINet: a scale-insensitive convolutional neural network for fast vehicle detection. IEEE Trans. Intell. Transp. Syst. **20**(3), 1010–1019 (2019)
11. Huang, L., Yi, Y., Deng, Y., Yu, Y.: DenseBox: unifying landmark localization with end to end object detection. In: Computer Science (2015)
12. Jaderberg, M., Simonyan, K., Zisserman, A., et al.: Spatial transformer networks. In: Advances in Neural Information Processing Systems, pp. 2017–2025 (2015)
13. Kong, T., Sun, F., Yao, A., Liu, H., Lu, M., Chen, Y.: RON: reverse connection with objectness prior networks for object detection. In: Proceedings of the IEEE Conference on Computer Vision and Pattern Recognition, pp. 5936–5944 (2017)
14. Law, H., Deng, J.: CornerNet: detecting objects as paired keypoints (2018)
15. Lin, T.Y., Dollár, P., Girshick, R., He, K., Belongie, S.: Feature pyramid networks for object detection (2016)
16. Lin, T.Y., Goyal, P., Girshick, R., He, K., Dollar, P.: Focal loss for dense object detection. IEEE Trans. Pattern Anal. Mach. Intell. **PP**(99), 2999–3007 (2017)
17. Liu, W., et al.: SSD: single shot multibox detector. In: Leibe, B., Matas, J., Sebe, N., Welling, M. (eds.) ECCV 2016. LNCS, vol. 9905, pp. 21–37. Springer, Cham (2016). https://doi.org/10.1007/978-3-319-46448-0_2
18. Redmon, J., Divvala, S., Girshick, R., Farhadi, A.: You only look once: unified, real-time object detection (2015)
19. Redmon, J., Farhadi, A.: YOLO9000: better, faster, stronger. In: IEEE Conference on Computer Vision & Pattern Recognition (2017)
20. Redmon, J., Farhadi, A.: YOLOv3: an incremental improvement (2018)
21. Ren, S., Girshick, R., Girshick, R., Sun, J.: Faster R-CNN: towards real-time object detection with region proposal networks. IEEE Trans. Pattern Anal. Mach. Intell. **39**(6), 1137–1149 (2017)
22. Shrivastava, A., Gupta, A., Girshick, R.: Training region-based object detectors with online hard example mining. In: IEEE 2016 IEEE Conference on Computer Vision and Pattern Recognition (CVPR), Las Vegas, NV, USA, 27–30 June 2016, pp. 761–769 (2016)
23. Simonyan, K., Zisserman, A.: Very deep convolutional networks for large-scale image recognition. In: Computer Science (2014)
24. Singh, B., Davis, L.S.: An analysis of scale invariance in object detection - snip
25. Tian, Z., Shen, C., Chen, H., He, T.: FCOS: fully convolutional one-stage object detection. In: Proceedings of the International Conference on Computer Vision (ICCV) (2019)

26. Woo, S., Park, J., Lee, J.Y., Kweon, I.S.: CBAM: convolutional block attention module (2018)
27. Yu, J., Jiang, Y., Wang, Z., Cao, Z., Huang, T.: UnitBox: an advanced object detection network (2016)
28. Zhao, Q., Sheng, T., Wang, Y., Tang, Z., Ling, H.: M2Det: a single-shot object detector based on multi-level feature pyramid network (2018)
29. Zhu, C., He, Y., Savvides, M.: Feature selective anchor-free module for single-shot object detection (2019)

Reduction of Polarization-State Spread in Phase-Distortion Mitigation by Phasor-Quaternion Neural Networks in PolInSAR

Kohei Oyama and Akira Hirose[✉]

Department of Electrical Engineering and Information Systems,
The University of Tokyo, 7-3-1 Hongo, Bunkyo-ku, Tokyo 113-8656, Japan
ahirose@ee.t.u-tokyo.ac.jp
http://www.eis.t.u-tokyo.ac.jp

Abstract. This paper presents that phasor-quaternion neural networks (PQNN) reduce not only the phase singular points (SP) in interferometric synthetic aperture radar (InSAR) but also the spread of polarization states in polarimetric SAR (PolSAR). This result reveals that the PQNN deals with the dynamics of transversal wave, having phase and polarization, in an appropriate manner. That is, the phasor quaternion is not just a formally combined number but, instead, an effective number realizing generalization ability in phase and polarization space in the neural networks.

Keywords: Polarimetric and interferometric synthetic aperture radar (PolInSAR) · Phase singular point (SP) · Phase singular unit (SU) · Phasor quaternion (PQ)

1 Introduction

Satellite-borne synthetic aperture radar (SAR) observes our planet earth to obtain information on the land shape and its movement, vegetation, ice and snow precisely, globally and frequently. The technology is going to contribute to various social-issue solutions by realizing prediction of volcano eruption, disaster monitoring of earthquakes and tsunamis, evaluation of land subsidence, monitoring of deforestation and glacier recession, and management of agricultural crops [1,2].

This work was supported in part by JSPS KAKENHI under Grant No. 18H04105, and also in part by Cooperative Research Project Program of the Research Institute of Electrical Communication, Tohoku University. The Advanced Land Observing Satellite (ALOS) original data are copyrighted by the Japan Aerospace Exploration Agency (JAXA) and provided under JAXA Fourth ALOS Research Announcement PI No. 1154 (AH).

© Springer Nature Switzerland AG 2020
H. Yang et al. (Eds.): ICONIP 2020, CCIS 1332, pp. 526–534, 2020.
https://doi.org/10.1007/978-3-030-63820-7_60

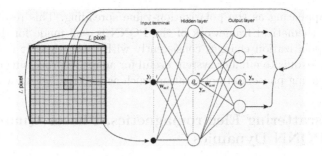

Fig. 1. Construction of the phasor quaternion neural network (PQNN) [45].

In this field, interferometric SAR (InSAR) has significant importance since its generation of digital elevation model (DEM) highly useful for watching land shape and movement. The DEM is based on observed phase information. There, the most serious issue is the existence of artificial phase singular points (SP), where the curvilinear integral of the phase-difference values around SP is not zero but $+2\pi$ or -2π, i.e., non-zero rotation, which leads to indeterminability of height. Hence we need to compensate the phase values of the SP-constructing four pixels (= singular unit (SU)) [2–15]. Usually, after a process of this compensation, we apply a phase unwrapping (PU) process to unwrap the $(-\pi, \pi]$-folded phase values. Many ideas have been reported to reduce the calculation cost and/or distortion [16–19].

In parallel, polarimetric SAR (PolSAR) is another important technology, where the polarization of scattered wave reflects the nature of vegetation and soil as well as artifacts such as buildings and roads, so that we can use the information to classify local land use [20–27]. The use of multiple frequencies is one of the performance improving techniques [28]. The authors have proposed quaternion neural networks (QNN) to deal with Poincare sphere information in three dimension [29, 30]. QNN was originally proposed by Matsui et al. to deal with three primary colors in three dimension [31]. The activation function used in QNN for such applications should be isotropic, i.e., independent of coordinate axes, to realize high generalization ability [32]. In this direction, we also proposed QNN auto-encoders [33] and QNN code-book generation [34].

In addition, polarimetric-interferometric SAR (PolInSAR) has also been investigated widely [35]. The authors proposed phasor quaternion neural networks (PQNN) as a combination of complex valued neural networks (CVNN) and QNN to treat the phase and the polarization of electromagnetic wave in a consistent manner [36–44]. PQNN achieved a high performance in the SP reduction [45]. The relationship between phase and polarization as physics has also been investigated [46]. Experiments revealed a high correlation between the phase and the polarization in the scattering phenomenon, based on which the authors proposed a new SP eliminating method [47, 48].

This paper shows experimentally that the phase-value compensation realizes not only the suppression of phase-value inconsistency but also the polarization distortion appearing as the polarization-value spreading. This result indicates that the mathematical framework of the PQNN is well made for dealing with phase and polarization changes consistently with each other. It is shown that PQNN is an exquisite number system useful for adaptive processing of transversal waves, having phase and polarization, such as electromagnetic wave.

2   Backscattering Electromagnetics, Phasor Quaternion and PQNN Dynamics

In this section, we briefly revisit the electromagnetics of backscattering, Stokes vector, Poincare sphere and phasor quaternion (PQ) in relation to PQNN neural dynamics. In general, the averaged Stokes vector g of electromagnetic wave backscattered at a earth surface point is calculated as

$$
g \equiv \begin{bmatrix} g_0 \\ g_1 \\ g_2 \\ g_3 \end{bmatrix} \equiv \begin{bmatrix} \langle |E_{\mathrm{H}}^{\mathrm{r}}|^2 \rangle + \langle |E_{\mathrm{V}}^{\mathrm{r}}|^2 \rangle \\ \langle |E_{\mathrm{H}}^{\mathrm{r}}|^2 \rangle - \langle |E_{\mathrm{V}}^{\mathrm{r}}|^2 \rangle \\ 2\mathrm{Re}\langle E_{\mathrm{V}}^{\mathrm{r}}(E_{\mathrm{H}}^{\mathrm{r}})^* \rangle \\ 2\mathrm{Im}\langle E_{\mathrm{V}}^{\mathrm{r}}(E_{\mathrm{H}}^{\mathrm{r}})^* \rangle \end{bmatrix} \tag{1}
$$

where $E^{\mathrm{r}} = [E_{\mathrm{H}}^{\mathrm{r}} \ E_{\mathrm{V}}^{\mathrm{r}}]^T$ is complex electric field of the observed scattered waves, H and V denote horizontal and vertical polarization components, respectively, $\langle \cdot \rangle$ is the mean, and $(\cdot)^*$ represents the complex conjugate or the complex conjugate transpose, respectively.

By normalizing the averaged Stokes vector by the total power g_0, we define a vector P consisting of the remaining three components uniquely representing a point on/in the Poincare sphere as

$$
P \equiv \begin{bmatrix} x \\ y \\ z \end{bmatrix} \equiv \begin{bmatrix} g_1/g_0 \\ g_2/g_0 \\ g_3/g_0 \end{bmatrix} \tag{2}
$$

In this paper, we name this vector Poincare vector. To express polarization and phase information simultaneously, we further define a vector p expressed as

$$
p \equiv \begin{bmatrix} x \exp(i \arg(S_{\mathrm{HH}})) \\ y \exp(i \arg(S_{\mathrm{HH}})) \\ z \exp(i \arg(S_{\mathrm{HH}})) \end{bmatrix} \equiv \begin{bmatrix} x \\ y \\ z \end{bmatrix} \exp(i \arg(S_{\mathrm{HH}})) \equiv P \, p^p
$$

that combines a unit phasor p^p, which represents its phase, and the Poincare vector P. We named this vector p phasor Poincare vector. The phase of the unit phasor p^p is an observed raw phase value. In this paper, we set it as the phase of the horizontal-horizontal scattering coefficient S_{HH}.

Figure 1 shows the construction of the PQNN with an input phasor-quaternion image data to be fed to the network. When the center four pixels (indicated in gray) construct a SP, we call them SU (singular unit as mentioned above).

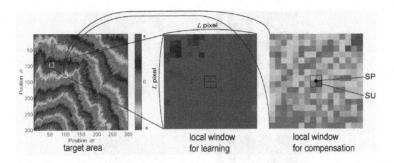

Fig. 2. (a) Total observed intergerogram data, (b) non-SU local window pixels to be fed to the network in the learning process, and (c) SU local window pixels to be fed in the compensation process. (For details, see Ref. [45]).

Here we describe the neural dynamics only briefly because of the limited pages. Please find the details including equations and neural-network parameters in Ref. [45]. In the learning process, the gray four pixels at the center of the input image in Fig. 1 have normal values (non-SP values) and shown to the output neurons as a set of output teacher signals. Other surrounding pixel values are fed to the input terminals. Then, the network learns the relationship of phase and polarization between the central four pixels and the surrounding pixels when they have no SP.

In the SP compensation process, the central four pixels in Fig. 1 are a SU, which constructs a SP. We compensate the SU pixel values as follows. We choose a SU and put a window so that the window center catches the SU. We feed the surrounding pixel values to the network to obtain a set of output signals, with which we overwrite the SU values. Every time we apply this elementary process, a positive or negative SP moves by a single pixel to its counterpart (= negative or positive one), and vanishes finally in the repetition.

In this presentation, we rather investigate the changes in polarization. Accordingly, we apply the above compensation process not only to SU but also to non-SU local areas in the following experiments (Fig. 2).

3   Experimental Results: Polarization Changes Through the Singular Point Compensation

Figure 3 shows an example of SP compensation results as reported already in Ref. [45]. Figure 3(a) presents the original interferogram phase, observed by Advanced Land Observing Satellite (ALOS) of the Japan Aerospace Exploration Agency (JAXA), for a region near Mt. Fuji in Japan, having 300×300 pixels with colors scaling $(-\pi, \pi]$, while (b) shows its singular points (SP) distribution (white: positive SP, black: negative SP). The number of the SPs is 2,613 in total. With such large number SPs, we cannot generate a high-quality DEM. Figure 3(c) shows the interferogram after PQNN compensation to reduce the

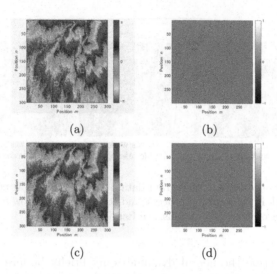

Fig. 3. (a) Original interferogram phase and (b) its singular points (SP) distribution (white: positive SP, black: negative SP, 2,613 in total), as well as (c) interferogram phase after PQNN compensation and (d) its SP (235 in total) [45].

SPs. The landscape (phase texture) is very similar to the original one shown in (a). However, the total number of SPs is 235 as shown in Fig. 3(d). The number is greatly reduced, leading to a high-accuracy DEM generation. Please refer to Ref. [45] for the details of the compensation and experimental parameters.

In this presentation, we rather pay attention to the changes in polarization. Figure 4 elucidate the effect of the phase-value compensation on the polarization states. Figure 4(a) plots the polarization states of the SU pixels in the original interferogram on the Poinacre shere. In this experiment, we focus on the single-pixel property without applying any spatial averaging, resulting in ever-unity degree of polarization so that all the points are found just on the Poincare sphere. The upper-left plot shows a skew view while other three plots show (x, y), (y, z) and (z, x)-direction views. The polarization states have a large spread. In contrast, Fig. 4(b) is the plot after the PQNN phase compensation. We find that their spread reduced very much.

Similarly, Fig. 4(c) is the plots of polarization states for non-SU pixels in the original interferogram. The spread is a little smaller than that of SU pixels. Figure 4(d) shows the plots after the PQNN phase compensation applied to non-SU pixels for comparison. Again, the spread has reduced greatly. The resulting spread is a little smaller than that of SU pixels in Fig. 4(b).

As the SP removal process, the PQNN compensation does not need to be adopted for non-SU areas. However, when we applied it, we have found that PQNN reduced the spread of polarization. This means that the PQNN compensation process makes the scattering mechanisms clearer. This result implies that the PQNN is useful not only for DEM generation in InSAR but also for land-

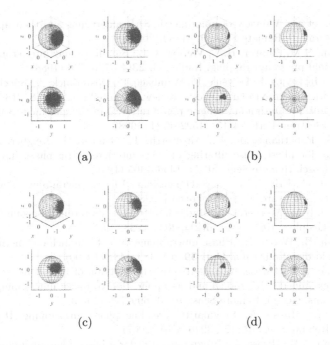

Fig. 4. Polarization state plots for SU (a) before and (b) after the PQNN phase compensation for SU pixels and those for non-SU (c) and (d).

use classification in PolSAR or, more appropriately, polarimetric-interferometric SAR (PolInSAR).

The above results in total reveals also that the PQNN framework deals with the electromagnetic wave consistently and effectively. PQNN is not just a formal combination of numbers (complex amplitude and Stokes vector) but, instead, a number system which gives appropriate treatment of coherent information having phase and polarization obtained by various coherent sensors and imagers.

4 Summary

This paper presented the fact that the PQNN phase compensation process is effective not only for SP reduction but also for polarization spread reduction. This result implies that the PQNN framework realizes high generalization ability in dealing with diverse coherent sensor and imager data.

References

1. Boerner, W.M.: Recent advances in extra-wide-band polarimetry, interferometry and polarimetric interferometry in synthetic aperture remote sensing and its applications. IEE Proc. - Radar Sonar Navig. **150**(3), 113–124 (2003)

2. Lee, J.S., et al.: A review of polarimetric SAR algorithms and their applications. J. Photogramm. Remote Sens. **9**, 31–80 (2004)
3. Goldstein, R.M., Zebker, H.A., Werner, C.L.: Satellite radar interferometry: two-dimensional phase unwrapping. Radio Sci. **23**(4), 713–720 (1988)
4. Lee, J.S., Jurkevich, I., Dewaele, P., Wambacq, P., Oosterlinck, A.: Speckle filtering of synthetic aperture radar images: a review. Remote Sens. Rev. **8**, 313–340 (1994)
5. Lombardini, F.: Optimum absolute phase retrieval in three-element SAR interferometer. Electron. Lett. **34**(15), 1522–1524 (1998)
6. Lee, J.S., Papathanassiou, K., Ainsworth, T., Grunes, M., Reigber, A.: A new technique for phase noise filtering of SAR interferometric phase images. IEEE Trans. Geosci. Remote Sens. **36**(5), 1456–1465 (1998)
7. Ghiglia, D.C., Pritt, M.D.: Two-Dimensional Phase Unwrapping: Theory, Algorithms, and Software. Wiley, Hoboken (1998)
8. Goldstein, R.M., Werner, C.L.: Radar interferogram filtering for geophysical applications. Geophys. Res. Lett. **25**(21), 4035–4038 (1998)
9. Gutmann, B., Weber, H.: Phase unwrapping with the branch-cut method: role of phase-field direction. Appl. Opt. **39**(26), 4802–4816 (2000)
10. Suksmono, A.B., Hirose, A.: Adaptive noise reduction of InSAR images based on a complex-valued MRF model and its application to phase unwrapping problem. IEEE Trans. Geosci. Remote Sens. **40**(3), 699–709 (2002)
11. Yamaki, R., Hirose, A.: Singularity-spreading phase unwrapping. IEEE Trans. Geosci. Remote Sens. **45**(10), 3240–3251 (2007)
12. Suksmono, A.B., Hirose, A.: Progressive transform-based phase unwrapping utilizing a recursive structure. IEICE Trans. Commun. **E89–B**(3), 929–936 (2006)
13. Oshiyama, G., Hirose, A.: Distortion reduction in singularity-spreading phase unwrapping with pseudo-continuous spreading and self-clustering active localization. IEEE J. Sel. Top. Appl. Earth Obser. Remote Sens. **8**(8), 3846–3858 (2015)
14. Cao, M., Li, S., Wang, R., Li, N.: Interferometric phase denoising by median patch-based locally optimal Wiener filter. IEEE Geosci. Remote Sens. Lett. **12**(8), 1730–1734 (2015)
15. Oyama, K., Hirose, A.: Adaptive phase-singular-unit restoration with entire-spectrum-processing complex-valued neural networks in interferometric SAR. Electron. Lett. **54**(1), 43–45 (2018)
16. Costantini, M., Malvarosa, F., Minati, F.: A general formulation for redundant integration of finite differences and phase unwrapping on a sparse multidimensional domain. IEEE Trans. Geosci. Remote Sens. **50**(3), 758–768 (2012)
17. Danudirdjo, D., Hirose, A.: InSAR image regularization and DEM error correction with fractal surface scattering model. IEEE Trans. Geosci. Remote Sens. **53**(3), 1427–1439 (2015)
18. Danudirdjo, D., Hirose, A.: Anisotropic phase unwrapping for synthetic aperture radar interferometry. IEEE Trans. Geosci. Remote Sens. **53**(7), 4116–4126 (2015)
19. Tomioka, S., Nishiyama, S.: Phase unwrapping for noisy phase map using localized compensator. Appl. Opt. **51**(21), 4984–4994 (2012)
20. Cloude, S.R., Pottier, E.: A review of target decomposition theorems in radar polarimetry. IEEE Trans. Geosci. Remote Sens. **34**, 498–518 (1996)
21. Cloude, S.R., Pottier, E.: An entropy based classification scheme for land applications of polarimetric SAR. IEEE Trans. Geosci. Remote Sens. **35**, 68–78 (1997)
22. Freeman, A., Durden, S.L.: A three-component scattering model for polarimetric SAR data. IEEE Trans. Geosci. Remote Sens. **36**, 963–973 (1998)

23. Touzi, R., Boerner, W.M., Lee, J.S., Lueneburg, E.: A review of polarimetry in the context of synthetic aperture radar: concepts and information extraction. Can. J. Remote Sens. **30**(3), 380–407 (2004)
24. Yamaguchi, Y., Moriyama, T., Ishido, M., Yamada, H.: Four component scattering model for polarimetric SAR image decomposition. IEEE Trans. Geosci. Remote Sens. **43**(8), 1699–1706 (2005)
25. Touzi, R., Raney, R.K., Charbonneau, F.: On the use of permanent symmetric scatterers for ship characterization. IEEE Trans. Geosci. Remote Sens. **42**(10), 2039–2045 (2004)
26. Wei, B., Yu, J., Wang, C., Wu, H., Li, J.: PolSAR image classification using a semi-supervised classifier based on hypergraph learning. Remote Sens. Lett. **5**(4), 386–395 (2014)
27. Sunaga, Y., Natsuaki, R., Hirose, A.: Land form classification and similar land-shape discovery by using complex-valued convolutional neural networks. IEEE Trans. Geosci. Remote Sens. **57**(10), 7907–7917 (2019)
28. Chen, K.S., Huang, W.P., Tsay, D.H., Amar, F.: Classification of multifrequency polarimetric SAR imagery using a dynamic learning neural network. IEEE Trans. Geosci. Remote Sens. **34**, 814–820 (1996)
29. Shang, F., Hirose, A.: Quaternion neural-network-based PolSAR land classification in poincare-sphere-parameter space. IEEE Trans. Geosci. Remote Sens. **52**(9), 5693–5703 (2014)
30. Shang, F., Naoto, K., Hirose, A.: Degree of polarization based data filter for fully polarimetric synthetic aperture radar. IEEE Trans. Geosci. Remote Sens. **57**(6), 3767–3777 (2019)
31. Matsui, N., Isokawa, T., Kusamichi, H., Peper, F., Nishimura, H.: Quaternion neural network with geometrical operators. J. Intell. Fuzzy Syst. **15**, 149–164 (2004)
32. Kinugawa, K., Fang, S., Usami, N., Hirose, A.: Isotropization of quaternion-neural-network-based PolSAR adaptive land classification in poincare-sphere parameter space. IEEE Geosci. Remote Sens. Lett. **15**(8), 1234–1238 (2018)
33. Kim, H., Hirose, A.: Unsupervised fine land classification using quaternion auto-encoder-based polarization feature extraction and self-organizing mapping. IEEE Trans. Geosci. Remote Sens. **56**(3), 1839–1851 (2018)
34. Kim, H., Hirose, A.: Unsupervised hierarchical land classification using self-organizing feature codebook for decimeter-resolution PolSAR. IEEE Trans. Geosci. Remote Sens. **57**(4), 1894–1905 (2019)
35. Cloude, S., Papathanassiou, K.: Polarimetric SAR interferometry. IEEE Trans. Geosci. Remote Sens. **36**(5), 1551–1565 (1998)
36. Hirose, A., Yoshida, S.: Generalization characteristics of complex-valued feedforward neural networks in relation to signal coherence. IEEE Trans. Neural Netw. Learn. Syst. **23**, 541–551 (2012)
37. Hirose, A., Yoshida, S.: Relationship between phase and amplitude generalization errors in complex- and real-valued feedforward neural networks. Neural Comput. Appl. **22**(7–8), 1357–1366 (2013). https://doi.org/10.1007/s00521-012-0960-z
38. Hirose, A., Yoshida, S.: Comparison of complex- and real-valued feedforward neural networks in their generalization ability. In: Lu, B.-L., Zhang, L., Kwok, J. (eds.) ICONIP 2011. LNCS, vol. 7062, pp. 526–531. Springer, Heidelberg (2011). https://doi.org/10.1007/978-3-642-24955-6_63
39. Mandic, D.P., Goh, V.S.L.: Complex Valued Nonlinear Adaptive Filters - Non circularity. Widely Linear and Neural Models, Wiley (2009)
40. Nitta, T. (ed.): Complex-Valued Neural Networks: Utilizing High-Dimensional Parameters. Information Science Reference, Pennsylvania (2009)

41. Aizenberg, I.: Complex-Valued Neural Networks with Multi-Valued Neurons. Studies in Computational Intelligence. Springer, Heidelberg (2011). https://doi.org/10.1007/978-3-642-20353-4

42. Hirose, A. (ed.): Complex-Valued Neural Networks: Advances and Applications. IEEE Press Series on Computational Intelligence. IEEE Press and Wiley, New Jersey (2013)

43. Hirose, A. (ed.): Complex-valued neural networks: theories and applications. Series on Innovative Intelligence, vol. 5. World Scientific Publishing, Singapore (2003)

44. Hirose, A.: Complex-Valued Neural Networks, 2nd edn. Springer, Heidelberg (2012). https://doi.org/10.1007/978-3-642-27632-3

45. Oyama, K., Hirose, A.: Phasor quaternion neural networks for singular-point compensation in polarimetric-interferometric synthetic aperture radar. IEEE Trans. Geosci. Remote Sens. **57**(5), 2510–2519 (2019)

46. Lee, J.S., Miller, A.R., Hoppel, K.W.: Statistics of phase difference and product magnitude of multi-look processed Gaussian signals. Waves in Random Media **4**(3), 307–319 (1994)

47. Shimada, T., Natsuaki, R., Hirose, A.: Pixel-by-pixel scattering mechanism vector optimization in high resolution PolInSAR. IEEE Trans. Geosci. Remote Sens. **56**(5), 2587–2596 (2018)

48. Otsuka, Y., Natsuaki, R., Hirose, A.: Consideration on singular-point generating mechanisms by analyzing the effect of phase-and-polarization optimization in PolInSAR. IEEE J. Sel. Appl. Earth Observ. Remote Sens. **13**(4), 1625–1638 (2020)

RoadNetGAN: Generating Road Networks in Planar Graph Representation

Takashi Owaki[✉] and Takashi Machida

Toyota Central R&D Labs., Inc., Nagakute, Japan
{t-owk,machida}@mosk.tytlabs.co.jp

Abstract. We propose RoadNetGAN, a road network generation method as an extension to NetGAN, a generative model that can generate graphs similar to real-world networks with the acquisition of similarity measure through learning. Our main contribution is twofold. Firstly, we added displacement attributes to the random walks to generate not only the sequence but also the spatial position of nodes as intersections within a road network to be generated, which increases the diversity of generated road network patterns including the shape of the city blocks. Secondly, we make the generator and discriminator neural networks conditional. This allows for learning of the specification of the initial node of random walks over a graph, which is especially important for interactive road network generation that is mostly used in the applications for urban planning of road networks. We demonstrate that the proposed method can generate road networks that mimic the real road networks with the desired similarity.

Keywords: Generative adversarial networks · Deep learning · Urban planning

1 Introduction

Real test driving in real road networks as well as virtual test driving in simulated road networks are employed for the validation of autonomous driving systems. In addition to these validations, test driving in road networks that mimic real road networks would further improve the reliability of autonomous driving systems. Apart from the validation of autonomous driving systems, creating road networks that are similar to those of the cities that have desirable aspects such as high comfort for the residents and the efficiency in energy consumption would help in designing cities that have the desired aspects. It is useful to automatically generate road networks that are similar to real road networks because manually designing such road networks is very costly.

We have four requirements for a road network generation method. Our first requirement is to generate a road network as a graph. It is because graph representation is often required in various processing concerning road networks such as visualization with computer graphics and path-finding. Our second requirement

© Springer Nature Switzerland AG 2020
H. Yang et al. (Eds.): ICONIP 2020, CCIS 1332, pp. 535–543, 2020.
https://doi.org/10.1007/978-3-030-63820-7_61

is to automatically acquire the similarity measures between real and generated road networks and evaluate the similarity. Devising the similarity measures and evaluating the similarity manually is often time-consuming and costly. Moreover, automatic acquisition of the similarity measures may find those that humans can hardly find. The second requirement can be fulfilled with generative adversarial networks (GAN) [1]. Our third requirement is a high, easily controllable dynamic range of the diversity of generated road networks. In the application of urban planning, such diversity would increase the degree of freedom in designing road networks. Our fourth requirement is to start road network generation from the desired node in a road network graph. This requirement is important for the interactive generation of road networks in applications for urban planning.

We propose a road network generation method that meets the four requirements described above as an extension to NetGAN [2], a generative model that generates graphs similar to real-world networks with GAN. To the best of our knowledge, there are no other published methods for generating road networks as graphs with GAN. Although NetGAN can synthesize large-scale real-world graphs from multiple generated random walks on the graphs, the original Net-GAN cannot be used for generating planar graphs, which are often used as road networks, owing to lack of consideration on the spatial arrangement of the nodes in the generated graph. We modify how the topology of resultant graphs is determined from generated random walks to obtain resultant road networks as planar graphs. With this modification, our first and second requirements are met.

We further extend NetGAN to meet our third and fourth requirements. The spatial positions of the nodes cannot be generated with the original NetGAN, which limits our third requirement for the wide range of the diversity of resultant road networks. We extend the neural networks used in the original NetGAN to generate not only the node sequences of random walks but also the spatial positions of the nodes, which increases the diversity of generated road network patterns such as the shape of the city blocks. For our fourth requirement, we introduce the approach used in conditional GAN [3] to specify the initial nodes of random walks because the initial nodes of random walks are randomly determined in the original NetGAN.

To summarize, our contributions are as follows:

1. We modified how the topology of resultant graphs is determined from generated random walks in NetGAN to obtain resultant road networks as planar graphs.
2. We extended the neural networks of NetGAN to generate not only node sequences but also the position of nodes with displacement attributes.
3. We made the generator and discriminator neural networks of NetGAN conditional to specify the initial nodes of random walks.

2   Related Work

Procedural Methods. There have been a lot of studies on procedural road network generation methods based on a set of rules. Parish and Muller [4] extended

L-system [5], which has been used to model the morphology of various organisms, to generate road networks as a part of a city generation system called CityEngine [6]. Chen et al. [7] proposed a procedural road network generation via underlying tensor fields guiding the generation of roads to enable intuitive user interaction. Benes et al. [8] proposed a method for growing road networks based on a simple traffic simulation among neighboring towns to enable not only the reduction of necessary user-defined parameters but also the simulation of city development over time. Although the above-mentioned procedural methods can greatly reduce the cost for designing road networks, a lot of tedious tasks such as tuning many parameters used in the methods are still required to design road networks that are similar to real road networks.

Deep Generative Methods. Recently, deep learning-based generative methods for graphs have gained increased attention. Some of the methods such as GraphVAE proposed by Simonovsky and Komodakis [9] and MolGAN proposed by De Cao et al. [10] directly generate $N \times N$ adjacency matrices for the number of nodes N, which leads to the computational cost of $O(N^2)$ and limits the application of the method to graphs that are by far smaller than city road networks such as molecular structure graphs. Instead of generating adjacency matrices, NetGAN generates graphs from many random walks in graphs, which suppresses the increase in computational costs for large-scale graphs and makes it possible to generate large-scale graphs that are similar to real-world graphs. Instead of directly generating adjacency matrices, GraphRNN proposed by You et al. [11] and DeepGMG proposed by Li et al. [12] recursively generate nodes and edges connecting generated nodes to generate resultant graphs. However, they are still computationally intensive due to a large amount of computation required to consider node ordering. Neural Turtle Graphics proposed by Chu et al. [13] is similar to our method in that it generates road networks represented in graphs with neural networks; it does not employ GAN, which might limit the novelty of generated road network patterns. StreetGAN proposed by Hartmann et al. [14] is also similar to our method in that the purpose of the method is to generate road networks and it employs GAN. However, it is difficult for StreetGAN to generate global patterns of road networks and avoid errors in transforming generated texture images into graphs as the post-processing since it is based on a texture image generation method called Spatial GAN [15].

3   Road Network Generation

The purpose of our proposed method is to generate road networks that are similar to a real road network. We refer the target real road network to the reference road network. Figure 1 shows the map data and road network graph of an example reference road network. The map data is based on the real map near Tokyo Station. We transform the map data into a road network graph by associating intersections and roads between intersections with nodes and links, respectively. Dead ends are also transformed into nodes. To simplify road network graphs, curved roads are transformed into straight roads. Motorways are exempted. Colored roads in Fig. 1A represent main roads.

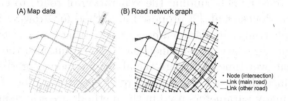

Fig. 1. Map and road network graph for an example reference road network near Tokyo station (Color figure online)

Our road network generation method, which is an extension to NetGAN, consists of the following two stages:

1. Training a generator neural network with a discriminator neural network to generate node sequences that are part of a whole road network graph.
2. Generating a whole road network graph from the node sequences generated with a generator neural network.

Details of these two stages will be described in Sect. 3.1 and 3.2, respectively.

3.1 Generative Adversarial Networks for Random Walk Generation in Road Networks

Figure 2 shows a schematic illustration of generative adversarial networks (GANs) for road network generation. The GANs consist of two neural networks, the generator, and the discriminator. The input of the generator is a vector whose elements are elementwise products between normally distributed random number vector and the embedding vector of initial nodes. Note that the embedding vector for each initial node is initialized with uniform random numbers and optimized in training. The output of the generator is a node sequence with displacement attributes. The displacement attributes consist of two elements, Δx and Δy, each representing displacements between consecutive nodes along x and y axes, respectively. Note that Δx and Δy are output as the result of classification, not regression. The displacement Δx is classified into one of the different Δxs of all the links in the reference road network. Similarly, the displacement Δy is classified into one of the different Δys of all the links in the reference road network. The input of the discriminator is among the node sequences connected in the reference road network (Real) or that generated as the output of the generator (Fake). The output of the discriminator is a classification result of the input node sequence (Real or Fake). The parameters of the generator are optimized in training so that the discriminator mistakenly classifies Fake as Real. The parameters of the discriminator are also optimized in training so

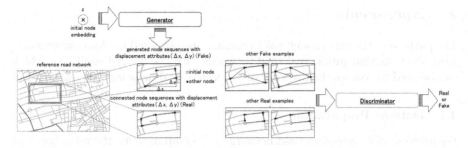

Fig. 2. Schematic illustration of our generator and discriminator networks conditioned on initial nodes of random walk generation with displacement attributes Δx and Δy

that it correctly classifies its input node sequence. Both of the generator and discriminator are variants of long-short term memory (LSTM) [16] networks. LSTM networks are widely employed in the processing of sequence data such as natural language processing (NLP) tasks. In NLP tasks, the input and/or output of LSTM networks are generally one-hot vectors of language components such as characters and words. The output of the generator and the input of the discriminator are a combination of one-hot vectors representing a node and two displacement attributes (Δx and Δy). The length of the one-hot vector representing a node is the number of nodes in the reference road network. The length of the one-hot vector representing Δx and Δy is the number of the classes for Δx and Δy described above, respectively.

3.2 Whole Road Network Generation from Generated Random Walks

The generator outputs random walks as node sequences that constitute a part of the whole road network to be generated. How the topology of a generated road network is determined from the generated random walks is changed from that of NetGAN to make it more suitable for road network generation. It is performed according to the following four steps:

1. Mark the nodes and links included in the main roads of the reference road network as determined.
2. Choose one of the determined nodes randomly and generate a node sequence from the node chosen as an initial node.
3. Starting from the initial node, mark nodes and links in the generated node sequence as determined one by one until the link intersects at least one of the links marked as determined.
4. Repeat steps 2 and 3 until the number of the links marked as determined reaches the number of the links in the reference road network.

We use edge overlap (EO), which is the ratio of the number of the links shared between the generated and reference road networks to that of all the links in the reference road network, as a similarity measure with which users can control the diversity of generated road networks as in NetGAN.

4   Experiments

The purpose of the experiment was to confirm the proposed method can generate road networks that mimic real road networks with the desired similarity, which can be used to control the diversity of generated road networks, specified as EO.

4.1   Dataset Preparation

We prepared four reference road networks. The map data for the reference road networks were near the main station of four cities: Tokyo, Osaka, Nagoya, and Kyoto. The area of each map was approximately 1.7 km × 1.7 km. As described in Sect. 3, we exempted motorways from the map data and transformed the remaining map data into a road network graph by associating intersections and roads between intersections with nodes and links, respectively. Dead ends were also transformed into nodes. To simplify road network graphs, curved roads were transformed into straight roads.

The length of the random walk was set to 16. The hyper-parameters of the generator and discriminator was as same as the reference implementation provided by the authors of NetGAN except for the number of parameter update steps of the discriminator (we used one instead of the three used in the reference implementation of NetGAN) for a single parameter update step of the generator: The number of dimensions for the input normally-distributed random number vector, z, was 16, and the number of the hidden units in the single hidden layer for the generator and discriminator was 40 and 30, respectively. Parameters p and q, which were used to bias random walk generation as in a node embedding method called node2vec proposed by Grover and Leskovec [17], were set to 1. We optimized the generator and discriminator with Adam. The learning rate was set to 0.0003. We evaluated EO for a whole road network generated with the procedure described in Sect. 3.2 every 100 training iterations. Accuracies of classifying displacements Δx and Δy were evaluated for 10,000 random walks. The parameters of the generator and discriminator were saved when EO reached 0.5, 0.6, 0.7, 0.8, and 0.9.

Figure 3A shows EO and accuracies for classifying displacements Δx and Δy against training iterations for the reference road network of Tokyo (Fig. 1). All the EO and accuracies reached 0.9 for 20,000 training iterations.

4.2   Whole Road Network Generation

Figure 3B shows the process of a whole road network generation with the target EO of 0.9 for the reference road network of Tokyo (Fig. 1). The first road network (Fig. 3B, the upper left map) corresponds to step 1 described in Sect. 3.2 where only the nodes and links included in the main roads of the reference road network were marked as determined. Finally, most of the node positions were reconstructed with the generated displacements Δx and Δy as in the reference road network (Fig. 3B, the lower middle map) except for some of the nodes enclosed by the double circles (Fig. 3B, the lower left map).

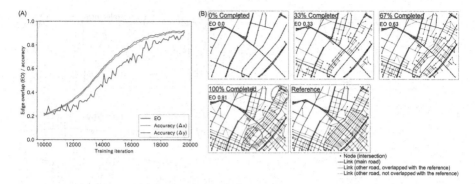

Fig. 3. (A) Edge overlap (EO) and accuracies for classifying displacement attributes Δx and Δy against training iteration (B) Whole road network generation from generated random walks for the reference road network of Tokyo

Figure 4 shows the result of road network generation for the target EO of 0.5 and 0.7 with the reference road networks. As expected, the difference between the generated and reference road networks was larger for the lower EOs. The double circles in the generated road networks show some regions where the differences in the node positions between the generated and reference road networks were large as in Fig. 3B.

Fig. 4. Generated road networks with the target EO of (A) 0.5 and (B) 0.7 for the reference road network of Tokyo

4.3 Applicability to Various Reference Road Networks

Figure 5 shows the results of road network generation with the target EO of 0.9 for the remaining three reference road networks of Osaka, Nagoya, and Kyoto with their reference road networks and map data. The double circles in the generated road networks show some regions where the differences in the node positions between the generated and reference road networks were large as in Fig. 3B and Fig. 4. The proposed method worked for the three diverse reference road networks as well. Although the number of training iteration required for the EO of 0.9 was within 20,000 for Osaka and Nagoya as well as Tokyo (Fig. 3A), that was over 30,000 for Kyoto. This might be because of characteristic patterns, such as the square-shaped city blocks in the reference road network of Kyoto.

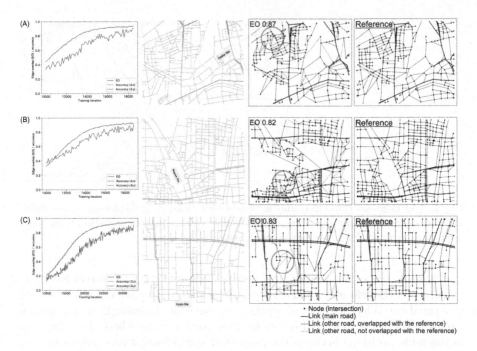

Fig. 5. Road network generation for the reference road networks of (A) Osaka, (B) Nagoya, and (C) Kyoto

5 Conclusion

This work introduced a deep generative method for road networks represented in planar graphs as an extension to NetGAN, a generative model that can generate graphs similar to real-world networks with the acquisition of similarity measure through learning. To enhance suitability of NetGAN for road network generation, (1) we modified how the topology of resultant graphs is determined from generated random walks to obtain resultant road networks as planar graphs, (2) we added displacement attributes to the random walks to generate not only the sequence but also the spatial position of nodes as intersections within a road network to be generated to increase the diversity of generated road networks, and (3) we made the generator and the discriminator conditional so that we can specify the initial node of random walks over a graph to be learned for interactive road network generation. We demonstrated that the proposed method can generate road networks that are similar to the four real road networks with the desired EO from 0.5 to 0.9.

Goals for future research will include more flexible road network generation such as addition and removal of nodes, which would further increase the diversity of generated road networks. Moreover, it would be useful to generate more attributes in addition to the displacement attributes introduced in this study.

To apply the proposed method to areas of various sizes, the scalability of the proposed method should be investigated.

References

1. Goodfellow, I.J., et al.: Generative adversarial nets. In: NIPS, pp. 2672–2680 (2014)
2. Bojchevski, A., Shchur, O., Zügner, D., Günnemann, S.: NetGAN: generating graphs via random walks. In: ICML, pp. 609–618 (2018)
3. Mirza, M., Osindero, S.: Conditional generative adversarial nets. arXiv preprint arXiv:1411.1784 (2014)
4. Parish, Y.I., Müller, P.: Procedural modeling of cities. In: SIGGRAPH, pp. 301–308 (2001)
5. Lindenmayer, A.: Mathematical models for cellular interactions in development I. Filaments with one-sided inputs. J. Theor. Biol. **18**(3), 280–299 (1968)
6. CityEngine.   https://www.esri.com/en-us/arcgis/products/esri-cityengine. Accessed 11 Sept 2020
7. Chen, G., Esch, G., Wonka, P., Müller, P., Zhang, E.: Interactive procedural street modeling. ACM Trans. Graph. **27**(3), 1–10 (2008)
8. Beneš, J., Wilkie, A., Křivánek, J.: Procedural modelling of urban road networks. Comput. Graph. Forum **33**(6), 132–142 (2014)
9. Simonovsky, M., Komodakis, N.: GraphVAE: towards generation of small graphs using variational autoencoders. In: Kůrková, V., Manolopoulos, Y., Hammer, B., Iliadis, L., Maglogiannis, I. (eds.) ICANN 2018. LNCS, vol. 11139, pp. 412–422. Springer, Cham (2018). https://doi.org/10.1007/978-3-030-01418-6_41
10. De Cao, N., Kipf, T.: MolGAN: an implicit generative model for small molecular graphs. In: ICML 2018 Workshop on Theoretical Foundations and Applications of Deep Generative Models (2018)
11. You, J., Ying, R., Ren, X., Hamilton, W.L., Leskovec, J.: GraphRNN: generating realistic graphs with deep auto-regressive models. In: ICML, pp. 5708–5717 (2018)
12. Li, Y., Vinyals, O., Dyer, C., Pascanu, R., Battaglia, P.: Learning deep generative models of graphs. In: ICLR Workshop Track (2018)
13. Chu, H., et al.: Neural turtle graphics for modeling city road layouts. In: ICCV, pp. 4522–4530 (2019)
14. Hartmann, S., Weinmann, M., Wessel, R., Klein, R.: StreetGAN: towards road network synthesis with generative adversarial networks. In: International Conference on Computer Graphics (2017)
15. Jetchev, N., Bergmann, U., Vollgraf, R.: Texture synthesis with spatial generative adversarial networks. arXiv preprint arXiv:1611.08207 (2016)
16. Hochreiter, S., Schmidhuber, J.: Long short-term memory. Neural Comput. **9**(8), 1735–1780 (1997)
17. Grover, A., Leskovec, J.: node2vec: scalable feature learning for networks. In: KDD, pp. 855–864 (2016)

Routing Attention Shift Network for Image Classification and Segmentation

Yuwei Yang[1], Yi Sun[2], Guiping Su[2], and Shiwei Ye[1]($\boxtimes$)

[1] School of Electronic, Electrical and Communication Engineering,
University of Chinese Academy of Sciences, Beijing 100049, China
yangyuwei18@mails.ucas.edu.cn
[2] School of Computer Science and Technology, University of Chinese Academy
of Sciences, Beijing 100049, China
{sunyi,sugp,shwye}@ucas.ac.cn

Abstract. Deep neural networks as fundamental tools of deep learning have evolved remarkably in various tasks; however, the computational complexity and resources costs rapidly increased when using deeper networks, which challenges the deployment of the resource-limited devices. Recently, shift operation is considered as an alternative to depthwise separable convolutions, using 60% fewer parameters compared spatial convolutions. Its basic block is composed by shift operations and 1×1 convolution in the intermediate feature maps. Previous works focus on optimizing the redundancy of the correlation between shift groups, making shift to be a learnable parameter, which yields more time to train and higher computation. In this paper, we propose a "dynamic routing" strategy to seek the best movement for shift operation based on attention mechanism, termed Routing Attention Shift Layer (RASL), which measures the contribution of channels to the outputs without back propagation. Moreover, the proposed RASL shows strong generalization to many tasks. Experiments on both classification and semantic segmentation tasks demonstrate the superior performance of the proposed methods.

Keywords: Deep neural networks · Shift operations · Dynamic routing · Attention mechanism

1 Introduction

Deep neural networks (DNNs) have achieve significant breakthroughs in many machine learning tasks, including computer vision, natural language processing, etc. However, deep learning models usually requires expensive storage and computing resources, which hinders the deployment of portable devices such as unmanned drones, mobile phones, etc.

In recent years, numbers of approaches have been proposed to solve this problem, such as low-bit quantization [1,2], network pruning [3,4], efficient architecture design [5–8]. Most of them focus on reducing the number of parameters

© Springer Nature Switzerland AG 2020
H. Yang et al. (Eds.): ICONIP 2020, CCIS 1332, pp. 544–553, 2020.
https://doi.org/10.1007/978-3-030-63820-7_62

but ignoring the FLOPs or model size. Wu et al. [7] present a shift operation as an alternative to spatial convolutions, saying zero FLOPs and zero parameters. A shift-based module combined shift and point-wise convolutions. In this module, shift direction is prefixed in numbers of channels of feature maps, according to the shift matrices, named shift group. Shift Networks show a convolution can be decomposed two components, shift operations make the spatial information aggregation, while point-wise convolutions provide channel information aggregation.

Shift operation is an efficient alternative over depthwise separable convolution. However, predetermined shift for number of channels is uninformed, which ignores the redundancy of the shift operation in one group and the difference of the contribution applied feature maps. Jeon et al. [9] suggest a depthwise shift layer that applies different shift values for each channel, formulating the shift value as a learnable function with additional shift parameters. To provide shift operation penalty during training, Spare shift layer [10] introduced a quantization-aware shift learning, finding only a few shift operations are sufficient to provide spatial information communication. Hacene et al. [11] use attention mechanism selects the best shift for each feature map of the architecture. Most of them proposed to ensure shift operation learnable but yield more time to run to learn the best movement.

In this paper, we seek to explore a new method to learn the best shift, which extends the dynamic routing algorithm [12], the main idea is comparing the similarity between input and output, measured by dot product. If the correlation between input and output is high that means the connection should be reinforced, the weight will be increased, otherwise, the weight will be decreased, finally we can obtain attention maps. In this approach, shift attention maps is easy get without assigning shift parameters to be learnable through back propagation. In particular, we called Route Attention Shift Layer to conduct how to shift. Our contributions are summarized as follows:

- We proposed a novel method named Routing Attention Shift Layer(RASL) to obtain the best movement of shift operation in Shift-Net without back-propagation.
- In our model, we design a light and fast network that greatly reduce the parameters and computational complexity, achieving the sate-of-the-art trade-off between accuracy and computational complexity.
- The proposed RASL has strong flexibility and can be easily extended to other tasks. To demonstrate the efficacy of our models, we evaluate RASL on CIFAR10/100 for image classification tasks, and medical image accurate semantic segmentation tasks.

2   Related Work

Network Quantization. A number of approaches have been proposed to quantize deep models to alleviate the billions of FLOPs with real-valued parameters. Among them, binarization [13] is an extreme quantization approach where both the weights and activations are represented by single bit, either +1 or −1. Moreover, the dot product can be computed by several XNOR-popcount bitwise operations. The XNOR operations can reduce hundreds units for floating point multi-plication.

Lightweight Networks. VGG16 [14] model has 16 layers and accounts for 138MB parameters after that wider and deeper network are designed to improve the performance with high FLOPs. To reduce the number of parameters and decrease architecture scale, several methods have been adopted to design lightweight networks. The most famous work is MobileNet [5], using depthwise separable convolution that split convolution layer into two subtasks: depthwise convolution and pointwise convolution that greatly speedup the running time. ShuffleNet [6] designed two operations: pointwise group convolution and channel shuffle that greatly reduce the parameters and complexity. Efficient model designs like SqueezeNet [15] adopts 1×1 convolution.

Attention Mechanism. Recently, attention models have been applied in many fields such as image analysis, natural language processing tasks. Specially, trainable attention can be categorized as hard attention [16] and soft attention [17,18]. Hard attention is a stochastic process, which often use Monte Carlo sampling and the training stage is non-differentiable. Contrarily,soft attention is probabilistic and utilizes standard back-propagation that is easy embedded in many models. In addition, self-attention techniques [19] have been proposed to find global, long-range dependencies within internal representation of image.

Convolutional Neural Networks (CNNs). CNNs rely on spatial convolutions with kernel sizes of 3×3 or lager to obtain enough information to learn the connections between input and output layers.Consider input tensor $X \in \mathbb{R}^{H \times W \times C}$ and the corresponding weight tensor $W \in \mathbb{R}^{k \times k \times C \times D}$, where $H \times W$ is the spatial dimension of the input; C is the number of input channels; D is the number of filters, k denotes the kernel's height and width. Then, we denote the output tensor $Y \in \mathbb{R}^{H \times W \times D}$, the convolution operation can be formulated as Eq. 1:

$$Y_{p,q,d} = \sum_{c=1}^{C} \sum_{i=-\lfloor \frac{k}{2} \rfloor}^{\lfloor \frac{k}{2} \rfloor} \sum_{j=-\lfloor \frac{k}{2} \rfloor}^{\lfloor \frac{k}{2} \rfloor} W_{i,j,d,c} X_{i+p,j+q,c} \tag{1}$$

Where p, q and i, j index along spatial dimensions and d, c index into channels. Every spatial convolution layer requires $C \times D \times k \times k$ parameters and $C \times D \times k \times k \times H \times W$ computational cost. As the network architecture using wider and deep convolution layer, the parameters of CNNs consume a considerable storage and run-time memory.

Shift Operation. Shift operation [7] can be regarded as a special case of depthwise convolution, kernel elements are assigned one value to decide the

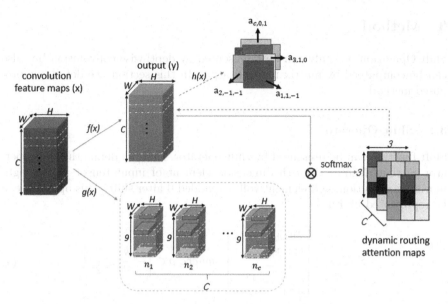

Fig. 1. Illustration of the proposed routing attention module for RASL. $f(x)$ is depth-wise separable convolution, owing to the number of shift directions is fixed by kernel size, we design the kernel size is 3, there exist 9 possible shift directions, $g(x)$ transfers each channel of the input feature maps into 9 possible directions. Every channel of output $f(x) \otimes 9$ possible shift directions respectively, getting a 3×3 matrix. The $\otimes$ denotes inner product. The softmax operation is performed on each channel. $h(x)$ is shift operation, and kernel is the final routing attention maps.

corresponding channel feature map which direction should be shifted. Shift function is represented in Eq. 2:

$$Y_{p,q,d} = \sum_{i=-\lfloor \frac{k}{2} \rfloor}^{\lfloor \frac{k}{2} \rfloor} \sum_{j=-\lfloor \frac{k}{2} \rfloor}^{\lfloor \frac{k}{2} \rfloor} W_{i,j,d} X_{i+p,j+q,d} \tag{2}$$

In work [7], there is a simple trick to decide shift directions: dividing the C channels of input feature maps evenly into $k \times k$ groups, Where each group has $\lfloor C/(k \times k) \rfloor$ channels assigned one shift. In Eq. 2, W are assigned by group values, the movement can be defined as follows:

$$W_{i,j,d} = \begin{cases} 1 & \text{if } i = \alpha_c, j = \beta_c \\ 0 & \text{otherwise} \end{cases} \tag{3}$$

Where α_c and $j = \beta_c$ denote the horizontal and vertical displacement assigned to cth filter.

3   Method

Shift Operation not only can be represented by depthwise convolution but also can be computeed by matrix multiplication. In this section, we detail our proposed method.

3.1   Shift Operator

Shift function can be presented by shift operator. Here we define the shift operator S_l that denotes the l-th dimension element of input tensor X has right moved one position, and element will be padded 0 after shift. This operator can be represented by Eq. 4

$$S^p(X) = \begin{bmatrix} x_{0+p,1,\cdots,c-1} \\ x_{0,1+p,\cdots,c-1} \\ \vdots \\ x_{0,1,\cdots,c-1+p} \end{bmatrix}, where\ p \in \left[-\lfloor \frac{k}{2} \rfloor, \lfloor \frac{k}{2} \rfloor \right] \tag{4}$$

Shift Operator has 4 properties as follows:
(1) $\forall p, q > 0, S_i^p S_i^q = S_i^{p+q}$
(2) $i \neq j, S_i^p S_j^q = S_j^q S_i^p$
(3) $x = (x_1, x_2, \cdots, x_n)^T, S_1^1 S_1^{-1} x = (I - e_1 e_1^T)x$
(4) $\forall S_i, S_i^T = S_i^{-1}$
To visualize the shift operator how work we take 2d input tensor X as example:

$$S_1^1 X = \begin{bmatrix} 0 & 1 & & \\ & 0 & \ddots & \\ & & \ddots & 1 \\ & & & 0 \end{bmatrix} X, S_1^{-1} X = \begin{bmatrix} 0 & & & \\ 1 & 0 & & \\ & & \ddots & \ddots \\ & & & 1 & 0 \end{bmatrix} X$$

$$S_2^1 X = X \begin{bmatrix} 0 & & & \\ 1 & 0 & & \\ & & \ddots & \ddots \\ & & & 1 & 0 \end{bmatrix}, S_2^{-1} X = X \begin{bmatrix} 0 & 1 & & \\ & 0 & \ddots & \\ & & \ddots & 1 \\ & & & 0 \end{bmatrix}$$

Consequently, Eq. 2 can be converted to matrix multiplication by shift operator:

$$Y_d = S_1^i S_2^j X_d, where\ i, j \in \left[-\lfloor \frac{k}{2} \rfloor, \lfloor \frac{k}{2} \rfloor \right] \tag{5}$$

3.2   Routing Attention Shift Layer

In shift operations, in order to simplify the method of allocating channels shift direction, the movement is fixed through kernel size. However, this heuristic assignment is lack task-driven, to solve this problem, we proposed routing attention shift layer (RASL). Compared to previous work [7,9,10] focused on learning channel shift as a parameter, relying on back propagation to get the best shift. The method we suggested RASL is based on attention mechanism and dynamic routing without applying back propagation, which reduces the computational complexity to learn the best shift.

Dynamic routing is first proposed by Hinton [12], the initial intention is measuring the agreement between the current output and the prediction by scalar product as if it was a log likelihood. Now we consider the kernel size is 3×3 (as shown in Fig. 1), there is 9 possible shift directions. The input image feature maps from previous hidden layer $X \in \mathbb{R}^{H \times W \times C}$ are first transformed into two feature space f, g, to calculate the attention, where $f(x) = W_f x$, $g(x) = S_1^i S_2^j x$, $f(x)$ is depthwise convolution, $g(x)$ applies the shift operator that transform each channel of features into 9 possible shift features.

Attention feature maps is denoted as $A_{c,i,j} = \frac{\exp(B_{c,i,j})}{\sum_{i,j} \exp(B_{c,i,j})}$, where $B_{c,i,j} = B_{c,i,j} + f(x)g(x)$, $B_{c,i,j}$ is initialized as 0 and all channels of output feature maps will make inner dot product to 9 possible shift features respectively. $B_{c,i,j}$ indicates the relation between $f(x)$ and $g(x)$, if the dot product of $f(x)g(x)$ is above the threshold, which means the relation should be reinforced for next layers. At the end of training process, the output of attention layer is $O = (o_1, o_2, \cdots, o_j, \cdots, o_c) \in \mathbb{R}^{H \times W \times C}$, each o_j will select the maximum value as 1, others set 0. In addition, we further multiply the output attention layer by a scale parameter α, β to balance the results of $f(x)g(x)$ and $B_{c,i,j}$.

Compared to vanilla shift layers divide the all channels into $\lfloor \frac{C}{k \times k} \rfloor$ groups and each group has one shift direction, RASL consider the agreement between output feature maps and inputs possible shifts, if the result of inner product is increased, the relation should be reinforced, finally we get attention maps. In this process, we do need make the shift as a learnable parameter updated by back propagation during training.

4 Experiments

In this section, we first conducted several ablation experiments on CIFAR10/CIFAR100 to demonstrate the performance of RASL for image classification. We also evaluated the proposed methods on medical image semantic segmentation. In these experiments, we have proved the effectiveness and better accuracy of proposed approach.

4.1 Implementation Details

In all CIFAR10/100 experiments, training images is cropped randomly or flipped horizontally. We do not use any further data augmentation in our implementation. we use Adam for optimization, an initial learning rate starts at 1e−2 and is decayed twice by multiplying 0.1 at the 32k and 48k iterations. We assign scale

Table 1. Comparison with the state-of-the art shiftNet models using ResNet20 on CIFAR-10/100. All the comparing results are directly cited from the original papers.

Model	Accurarcy CIFARR10/100	Params(Millions)	FLOPs
ResNet [20]	91.4%/66.3%	0.27	81M
ShiftNet [7]	90.6%/68.6%	0.16	53M
SparseShift [10]	91.7%/69.2%	0.16	53M
ActiveShift [9]	92.5%/70.7%	0.19	53M
RoutingAttentionShift(ours)	92.7%/70.6%	0.16	65M

scalar $\beta = 0.01$ and the training batch size is 128. We apply layer-reordering to the networks as: RASL->1 × 1 Conv ->BN->Relu.

In medical image segmentation, Unet [20] has proved the advantage of deep learning in medical images with long-distance cascade connection that captures the context information in the picture and accurately locate the areas where need to be focus on. Though, there exsit many approachs [21,22] to improve the performance of Unet, the basic architecture is not changed. Our segmentation experiments are based on the original Unet networks. Before liver segmentation, We also need to normalize the pixel of inputs by the max value and min value of the whole image. Besides, data augmentation is used to deal with the samll data size, and we geometrically rotated, flipped, cropped to enlarge our training dataset. Finally, use Dice coefficient to evaluate the performance of segmentation. Our simulation implementation is based on Pytorch.

4.2   Evaluation on CIFAR10/CIFAR100

CIFAR10/CIFAR100 dataset is contained 10 categories or 100 categories for image classification. Both of them consist 50k training and 10k test images with 32 × 32 resolution. Several representative networks are compared: ResNet, Shift-Net, ActiveShiftNet, RASNet. We report the results in Table 1.

As we can see in the Table 1, accuracy and parameters/FLOPs of our proposed method are compared to other related models, and the results show that our method achieves a better accuracy than other models. Owing to transforming inputs into $\mathbb{R}^{k \times k \times H \times W \times C}$ space, it will consume some computations, so in the Table 1 our method of FLOPs index is not the best result.

In addition, as mentioned in Sect. 3, group shift is prefixed by kernel size, which lacks flexibility and ignores the contribution of different channels displacement for outputs. In our classification experiments, the shift distributions in different layer depth are observed and the number of each position are counted. Specially, in some layers, the output attention matrix is fixed on 0 position that indicates the shift layers in these layers are unimportant. At the begining of training process, A is initialized as uniform distribution, after training, the value in attention maps is irregular, which enlarges the receptive fields. Generally, a large receptive field can leverage more context information and encode long-rang

Table 2. Quantitative metrics of liver segmentation results between our method and original Unet

Model	Dice	Hausdorff Distance	Parameters
Original Unet [20]	0.946	33.11	168M
RASL Unet(ours)	0.941	34.9	24.2M

relationship between pixels more effectively. Actually, a shift-based module inter-leaves shift operations with pointwise convolutions, which further mixes spatial information across channels.

4.3 Evaluation on Liver Tumor Segmentation

We evaluate the proposed methods on the public dataset liver tumor segmenta-tion (LiTS) which consists of 131 enhanced CT image sequences and the size of each CT slice is 512×512. The original dataset provides the ground truth of liver and liver tumors segmentation results. In order to train and test our method, we divided the dataset into 3 parts: 81 CT sequences as training dataset, 25 CT sequences as testing dataset, 25 CT sequences as validation set. The performance is measured in terms of quantitative metrics - Dice that is commonly used in medical imaged segmentation. Our experiments are based on the original Unet structure. During the training stage, we used the binary cross-entropy as loss function. And in the inference stage, we evaluated three quantitative metrics, including Dice, Hausdorff distance, and Parameters. Table 2 shows the mean value of quantitative metrics of liver segmentation results between normal Unet and based on RASL Unet.

In medical image segmentation, TP is true positive measures the proportion of actual positives that are correctly identified, FP is true negative measures the proportion of actual negatives that are correctly identified, FN is false negative denotes the error in which a test result improperly indicates no presence of a condition, FP is false positive denotes the error in which a test result improperly indicates presence of a condition.. Hausdorff distance $d(x, y)$ measures how far two subsets (x, y) of a metric space are from each other. In addition, d is the Euclidean distance, sup is suoermum, and inf is the infimum. Dice coefficient and Hausdorff distance is defined as following:

$$Dice = \frac{2TP}{2TP + FP + FN} \tag{6}$$

$$d_H(X, Y) = max\{\sup_{x \in X} \inf_{y \in Y} d(x, y), \sup_{y \in Y} \inf_{x \in X} d(x, y)\} \tag{7}$$

In this experiment, we apply binary cross loss function, which can be expressed as follows:

$$L(y_1^{(i)}, y_2^{(i)}) = -y_1^{(i)} \log y_2^{(i)} + (1 - y_1^{(i)}) \log(1 - y_2^{(i)}) \tag{8}$$

5 Conclusion

We have proposed a novel method to obtain the best shift direction based on dynamic routing algorithm. Specifically, we use shift operators to transform input feature maps, then inner dot with the depthwise convolutional output to get the relation among different shift directions. To demonstrate this procedure, we conducted experiments on image classification task. Moreover, we have generalized RASL from image classification task and achieved promising performance on LiTS2017 dataset.

References

1. Jacob, B., Kligys, S., Chen, B., et al.: Quantization and training of neural networks for efficient integer-arithmetic-only inference. In: Proceedings of the IEEE Conference on Computer Vision and Pattern Recognition, pp. 2704–2713 (2018)
2. Zhang, D., Yang, J., Ye, D., Hua, G.: Lq-nets: learned quantization for highly accurate and compact deep neural networks. In: Proceedings of the European Conference on Computer Vision (ECCV), pp. 365–382 (2018)
3. Han, S., Mao, H., Dally, W.J.: Deep compression: compressing deep neural networks with pruning, trained quantization and huffman coding. arXiv preprint arXiv:1510.00149 (2015)
4. Guo, Y., Yao, A., Chen, Y.: Dynamic network surgery for efficient dnns. In: Advances in Neural Information Processing Systems, pp. 1379–1387 (2016)
5. Howard, A.G., Zhu, M., Chen, B., et al.: Mobilenets: efficient convolutional neural networks for mobile vision applications. arXiv preprint arXiv:1704.04861 (2017)
6. Zhang, X., Zhou, X., Lin, M., Sun, J.: Shufflenet: an extremely efficient convolutional neural network for mobile devices. In: Proceedings of the IEEE Conference on Computer Vision and Pattern Recognition, pp. 6848–6856 (2018)
7. Wu, B., Wan, A., Yue, X., et al.: Shift: a zero flop, zero parameter alternative to spatial convolutions. In: Proceedings of the IEEE Conference on Computer Vision and Pattern Recognition, pp. 9127–9135 (2018)
8. Sandler, M., Howard, A., Zhu, M., Zhmoginov, A., Chen, L.-C.: Mobilenetv 2: inverted residuals and linear bottlenecks. In: Proceedings of the IEEE Conference on Computer Vision and Pattern Recognition, pp. 4510–4520 (2018)
9. Jeon, Y., Kim, J.: Constructing fast network through deconstruction of convolution. In: Advances in Neural Information Processing Systems, pp. 5951–5961 (2018)
10. Chen, W., Xie, D., Zhang, Y., Pu, S.: All you need is a few shifts: designing efficient convolutional neural networks for image classification. In: Proceedings of the IEEE Conference on Computer Vision and Pattern Recognition, pp. 7241–7250 (2019)
11. Hacene, G.B., Lassance, C., Gripon, V., Courbariaux, M., Bengio, Y.: Attention based pruning for shift networks. arXiv preprint arXiv:1905.12300 (2019)
12. Sabour, S., Frosst, N., Hinton, G.E.: Dynamic routing between capsules. In: Advances in Neural Information Processing Systems, pp. 3856–3866 (2017)
13. Hubara, I., Courbariaux, M., Soudry, D., El-Yaniv, R., Bengio, Y.: Binarized neural networks. In: Advances in Neural Information Processing Systems, pp. 4107–4115 (2016)
14. Simonyan, K., Zisserman, A.: Very deep convolutional networks for large-scale image recognition. arXiv preprint arXiv:1409.1556 (2014)

15. Iandola, F.N., Han, S., Moskewicz, M.W., Ashraf, K., Dally, W.J., Keutzer, K.: SqueezeNet: alexNet-level accuracy with 50x fewer parameters and < 0.5 MB model size. arXiv preprint arXiv:1602.07360 (2016)
16. Mnih, V., Heess, N., Graves, A.: Recurrent models of visual attention. In: Advances in Neural Information Processing Systems, pp. 2204–2212 (2014)
17. Jetley, S., Lord, N.A., Lee, N., Torr, P.H.S.: Learn to pay attention. arXiv preprint arXiv:1804.02391 (2018)
18. Vaswani, A., Lord, N.A., Lee, N., et al.: Attention is all you need. In: Advances in Neural Information Processing Systems, pp. 5998–6008 (2017)
19. Cheng, J., Dong, L., Lapata, M.: Long short-term memory-networks for machine reading. arXiv preprint arXiv:1601.06733 (2016)
20. Ronneberger, O., Fischer, P., Brox, T.: U-Net: convolutional networks for biomedical image segmentation. In: Navab, N., Hornegger, J., Wells, W.M., Frangi, A.F. (eds.) MICCAI 2015. LNCS, vol. 9351, pp. 234–241. Springer, Cham (2015). https://doi.org/10.1007/978-3-319-24574-4_28
21. Guan, S., Khan, A.A., Sikdar, S., Chitnis, P.V.: Fully dense UNet for 2D sparse photoacoustic tomography artifact removal. IEEE J. Biomed. Health inform. **24**(2), 568–576 (2019)
22. Alom, M.Z., Hasan, M., Yakopcic, C., Taha, T.M., Asari, V.K.: Recurrent residual convolutional neural network based on u-net (r2u-net) for medical image segmentation. arXiv preprint arXiv:1802.06955 (2018)

SpotFast Networks with Memory Augmented Lateral Transformers for Lipreading

Peratham Wiriyathammabhum[✉]

University of Maryland, College Park, MD, USA
peratham@umd.edu
http://www.cs.umd.edu/ peratham/

Abstract. This paper presents a novel deep learning architecture for word-level lipreading. Previous works suggest a potential for incorporating a pretrained deep 3D Convolutional Neural Networks as a frontend feature extractor. We introduce SpotFast networks, a variant of the state-of-the-art SlowFast networks for action recognition, which utilizes a temporal window as a spot pathway and all frames as a fast pathway. The spot pathway uses word boundaries information while the fast pathway implicitly models other contexts. Both pathways are fused with dual temporal convolutions, which speed up training. We further incorporate memory augmented lateral transformers to learn sequential features for classification. We evaluate the proposed model on the LRW dataset. The experiments show that our proposed model outperforms various state-of-the-art models, and incorporating the memory augmented lateral transformers makes a 3.7% improvement to the SpotFast networks and 16.1% compared to finetuning the original SlowFast networks. The temporal window utilizing word boundaries helps improve the performance up to 12.1% by eliminating visual silences from coarticulations.

Keywords: Lipreading · Deep learning · Memory augmented neural networks

1 Introduction

Lipreading or visual speech recognition is an impressive ability to recognize words from lip movements representing phonemes. Those lip movements are also named as visual speeches/sounds or visemes [2,13]. Visemes for different letters such as 'p' and 'b' can be very similar due to McGurk effect [9]. These letters are called homophones, which are ambiguous from visual cues but can be disambiguated using additional language cues such as neighboring characters. Lipreading has many useful real-world applications, such as surveillance or assistive systems. This paper focuses on word-level automatic lipreading, where the system tries to recognize a word being said given only a video sequence of moving lips without audio.

© Springer Nature Switzerland AG 2020
H. Yang et al. (Eds.): ICONIP 2020, CCIS 1332, pp. 554–561, 2020.
https://doi.org/10.1007/978-3-030-63820-7_63

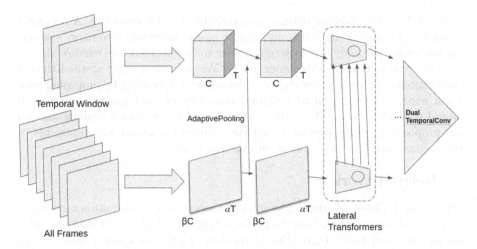

Fig. 1. SpotFast networks with lateral transformers utilize two pathways, consisting of a temporal window pathway and an all frame pathway. The temporal window pathway models fast-evolving actions. The all frame pathway models the whole video, which can incorporate more temporal contexts into the system. The adaptive average pooling layer reshapes the pre-fused features. The dual temporal convolution fuse both streams temporally and output final word-class prediction probabilities. The lateral transformers further model sequential information. C is the number of channels. T is the temporal resolution. α and β are hyperparameters.

The standard lipreading system pipeline includes mouth region cropping, mouth region compression, and sequence modeling. Recently, there have been significant improvements in automatic lipreading based on deep learning systems. The current state-of-the-art [10,17] consists of a 3D Convolutional Neural Networks (3DCNNs) as a front-end feature extractor and a 2-layered bidirectional Long-short Term Memory (biLSTM) as a back-end classifier. The system classifies the moving lips into 1-of-n words in a multi-class classification setting. Another approach [18] uses a transformer as a back-end instead of a biLSTM.

In this paper, we focus on the word-level lipreading and propose a temporal window as a hard attention mechanism to focus on the target word and eliminate the visual silence [14]. The visual silence is the visual signal that occurs during acoustic silence and is from coarticulation, where the lips are preparing for the next sound. Coarticulation [8] is a preference where humans adjust speech units based on neighboring units. The experiments in [14] indicates that eliminating the visual silence can significantly improve the performance. For the Lip-reading in the Wild (LRW) dataset [5], we hypothesize that eliminating the coarticulation at the beginning and the end of the short clips will help improve the performance and reduce computation cost. [11] investigates the usefulness of the boundary information of the target word and merely including the new feature set encoding, as a binary feature set indicating the inside-outside of the start and end frame numbers, can improve the performance a lot. However, some datasets may not have this labeled information available for this encoding. A temporal window is parametric modeling and can be easily integrated into many systems for any tasks with only one hyperparameter to be specified, the window size.

The contributions of this paper are (i) We propose a novel state-of-the-art deep learning architecture for end-to-end word-level lipreading by proposing temporal window sampling, dual temporal convolutions, and memory augmented lateral transformers. (ii) We evaluate the effect of the temporal window sizes on our proposed SpotFast networks. (iii) We compare the proposed components to the original SlowFast networks in an ablation study.

2   Related Work

Pretrained Video Models. The state-of-the-art action recognition models are primary choices when we want to perform transfer learning and finetune video models for other tasks. Lipreading in the deep learning era incorporates recent advancements in action recognition such as C3D (3D convolution) [15] or I3D (deep 3DCNNs) [3] as a better front-end and achieves state-of-the-art [12,17]. We further incorporate another recent advancement in action recognition, Slow-Fast networks [6], as our front-end feature extractor.

Transformers. As a recent promising alternative to biLSTMs and biGRUs in sequence modeling, a transformer model [16] is widely deployed in many state-of-the-art systems in various NLP tasks. A transformer consists of a stack of multi-head self-attention and feed-forward modules in an autoencoder setting. There is no recurrence in the model, so training a transformer can be easily paralleled. Lipreading also incorporates the transformer model and makes substantial improvements on many datasets [1,18]. We follow this direction and propose a lateral transformer for sequence modeling in our SlowFast-based architecture.

Memory. Incorporating memory is an approach to increase neural networks' capacity without increasing too much computation. Those memory augmented neural networks can be an efficient and effective way to represent variable-length inputs. A recently proposed product-key memory [7] is a promising neural network layer that can be incorporated into transformer-based models and significantly increase the capacity with only half computation. The memory holds a table of key-value entries with a multi-head mechanism which can be trained end-to-end. Each memory head has its query networks and sub-keys but shares the same values with other heads. For each head, an input query will be compared to all keys in the nearest neighbor setting, and the sparse weighted-sum of the corresponding memory values of the k nearest keys will be the output. The output of the memory layer will be the sum of all outputs from all heads.

3   Proposed Method

3.1   SpotFast Networks

SlowFast networks [6] consist of two pathways, slow and fast. The slow pathway is not suitable for lipreading since lip movements are fast evolving actions. We use the knowledge that the target word to be lipreaded for word-level lipreading is always keyword spotted. We then propose an alternative spot pathway to the slow pathway such that the networks will capture the fast-evolving action. The spot pathway is a temporal window centered at the keyword-spotted frame. We hope the spot pathway will focus more on the keyword. The idea of using word boundaries has been explored in [11]; however, we do not use the ground-truth boundaries as auxiliary inputs. Instead, it is only a hyperparameter in our networks. In [11], the test accuracy becomes 84.3% utilizing the precise word boundary information.

We keep the fast pathway as all frames in time. This is the same as the original SlowFast networks, except the inputs are instead the cropped lip sequences, not the whole frames. We hope the fast pathway will implicitly learn context which comes before or after the keyword. To fuse fast pathway to spot pathway via lateral connections, we use convolution fusion as in the original SlowFast networks with additional adaptive average pooling to temporally reshape the features from all frames into a fixed-length temporal window. We use the Spot-Fast networks as a front-end to extract spatio-temporal features depicted in Fig. 1.

3.2 Dual 1D Temporal Convolution Networks (TC)

We deploy a simple dual two-layered 1D temporal convolution to aggregate temporal information on each pathway with two different temporal scales for the back-end. The output from each pathway of the SpotFast networks is average-pooled to 3 modes, *[batch_size, feature_size, time_step]*. The first layer doubles the in_channel using a filter with a kernel size of 3 and a stride of 2 (temporal window) or a kernel size of 5 and a stride of 2 (all frames). We then apply a sequence of batchnorm, ReLU activation, and max pooling with a kernel size of 2 and a stride of 2. The second layer has the same parameters as the first layer while doubles the out_channel from the first layer to quadruple the initial in_channel. Next, the features from both pathways are averaged-pooled and fused using concatenation. Lastly, a linear feed-forward layer maps the fused feature into word-class probabilities.

3.3 Memory Augmented Lateral Transformers

To increase the back-end capacity, we put a transformer encoder on top of each pathway of the SpotFast networks to further learn features for classification. For each pathway, we use a 6-layer transformer encoder (base model) consisting of multi-head attention and a feed-forward module, which maps the input features in an autoencoder setting. We augment each transformer with the product-key memory at the layer before the last as in [7] (layer 5 for the base transformer model) to increase the capacity and stabilize training. The output feature after the feed-forward layer is fed into the memory and is added to the memory module's output via a skip connection. However, we empirically observe that independently putting the transformer on top of each pathway makes learning diffi-

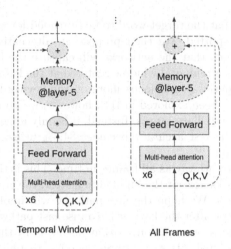

Fig. 2. Memory Augmented Lateral Transformers

cult. The loss does not go down at a reasonable rate or even diverged. To solve this problem, we add lateral connections to all layers (except the last layer) of both transformer encoders from the all frame pathway to the temporal window pathway (Fig. 2).

4   Experiments

4.1   Dataset, Preprocessing and Augmentations

We conduct the experiments using the Lip Reading in the Wild (LRW) dataset [5]. The LRW dataset consists of 488,766 training, 25,000 validation, and 25,000 testing short video clips. The video clips are talking face videos extracted from BBC TV broadcasts. There are 500 target words in this dataset. For each video clip, there are 29 frames. We use RGB frames in our experiments because the pretrained Kinetics models are in RGB. The dataset contains words with similar visemes such as 'SPEND' and 'SPENT' (tenses) or 'BENEFIT' and 'BENEFITS' (plural forms). The words are not totally isolated, and the word boundaries are not given. Those words are surrounded by irrelevant parts of the utterances which may provide contexts or are just noises.

The preprocessing consists of cropping mouth regions using fixed coordinates since the LRW dataset is already centered spatially. We then normalize all frames into $[0, 1]$, subtract them with 0.45 and divide them with 0.225, which are preprocessing parameters from the Kinetics pretrained models. The preprocessing is the same and consistent for both pathways.

We perform data augmentations like other previous works. The augmentations are done during training consisting of random upsampling ($[122, 146]$), random crop (crop to 112×112 pixels), and random horizontal flip (with a probability of 0.5). We augment the same way for every frame in both pathways. We upsample to 122×122 pixels and uniform crop to 112×112 pixels during the validation and testing phase. The data augmentations are the same and consistent for both pathways.

4.2 Comparisons with the State-of-the-Arts

We summarize the state-of-the-art methods in Table 1. Our final SpotFast with memory-augmented lateral transformers outperform previous state-of-the-art methods, including the one using optical flow information. Our proposed method makes an improvement over the prior state-of-the-art [17] by 0.3% and the prior RGB/grayscale state-of-the-art [18] by 0.7%.

Table 1. Top-1 test accuracies of the state-of-the-art methods on the LRW dataset.

Method	Accuracy
LRW [5]	61.1
WAS [4]	76.2
ResNet+biLSTMs [12]	83.0
ResNet+biGRUs [10]	83.4
ResNet+focal block+transformer [18]	83.7
I3D+biLSTMs [17]	84.1
SpotFast with lateral transformers (ours)	**84.4**

4.3 The Effects of the Window Sizes in SpotFast Networks

We determine the optimal temporal window size for the temporal window pathway using a grid search over 3 values, $\{15, 19, 23\}$. The validation and test accuracies are summarized in Table 2. The validation and test accuracies are comparable (SpotFast front-end increases the accuracy from 74.6% of ResNet+temporalConv [12].) with the window size of 23 being the best (6.1% increase in accuracy.). We then proceed with the SpotFast networks' training to the next phase, with the temporal window size of 23. The 3 values are heuristics from the word-boundary statistics estimated from the training partition of the LRW dataset. The word boundary distribution has the mean of 10.59 (We round it to 11.) and the standard deviation of 3.2 (We round it to 4.). For an approximately normal distribution, we use the 68-95-99.7 rule (three-sigma rule of thumb which follows the cumulative distribution function of the normal distribution. It will become 0-75-89 by Chebyshev's inequality for any distributions.) to create 3 values where the bands will cover 68-95-99.7 percents of the data population using $\{\mu + \sigma, \mu + 2\sigma, \mu + 3\sigma\}$ which becomes $\{15, 19, 23\}$. We can also observe from Table 2 that incorporating the lateral transformers into SpotFast networks and training the whole system end-to-end can further increase the test accuracy up to 3.7%.

Table 2. The top-1 accuracies of the SpotFast networks (without lateral transformers) varying the temporal window sizes.

Temporal window size	Validation	Test
SpotFast-15	81.3	80.6
SpotFast-19	81.2	80.4
SpotFast-23	**81.5**	**80.7**

4.4   Comparison with the SlowFast Networks

In this section, we compare our proposed method's performance with the original SlowFast networks in Table 3. For the vanilla SlowFast networks, we use the same inputs for both pathways as in the SpotFast networks. We finetune the SlowFast networks on the LRW dataset; however, the performance is low (68.3% test accuracy). Using the proposed temporal window sampling method, which changes the Slow pathway to the Spot pathway, the accuracy increases to 80.7%. This shows the proposed sampling's efficiency to eliminate the visual silence from coarticulations since the difference is massive (12.4%). When we add the lateral transformer with augmented memory, the accuracy further increases to 84.4%. This means, apart from the input sampling, which better models fast-evolving lip actions, the features of the deep 3DCNNs in both pathways can be further extracted using attention mechanisms in the lateral transformers with augmented memory.

Table 3. Comparisons of top-1 accuracies between the SlowFast networks and the SpotFast networks in ablation.

Method	Validation	Test	Improvements
SlowFast [6]	69.1	68.3	–
SpotFast-23	81.5	80.7	+12.4
SpotFast with lateral transformers	**84.9**	**84.4**	**+16.1**

5   Summary

We propose SpotFast networks with lateral transformers for word-level lipreading. We utilize a two-stream deep 3DCNNs, a temporal window pathway, and an all frame pathway. We evaluate a heuristics based on the 68-95-99.7 rule to select the optimal temporal window size. The temporal window utilizing word boundaries helps improve the performance up to 12.1% by eliminating visual silences from coarticulations. We show that incorporating a lateral transformer can improve the accuracy of 3.7%. We also show that our proposed model can outperform various state-of-the-art models. Some possible future directions include incorporating an optical flow input to the model and increasing the augmented-memory capacity.

References

1. Afouras, T., Chung, J.S., Senior, A., Vinyals, O., Zisserman, A.: Deep audio-visual speech recognition. IEEE Trans. Pattern Anal. Mach. Intell. (2018)
2. Bear, H.L., Harvey, R.: Phoneme-to-viseme mappings: the good, the bad, and the ugly. Speech Commun. **95**, 40–67 (2017)
3. Carreira, J., Zisserman, A.: Quo vadis, action recognition? a new model and the kinetics dataset. In: proceedings of the IEEE Conference on Computer Vision and Pattern Recognition, pp. 6299–6308 (2017)
4. Chung, J.S., Senior, A., Vinyals, O., Zisserman, A.: Lip reading sentences in the wild. In: 2017 IEEE Conference on Computer Vision and Pattern Recognition (CVPR), pp. 3444–3453. IEEE (2017)
5. Chung, J.S., Zisserman, A.: Lip reading in the wild. In: Lai, S.-H., Lepetit, V., Nishino, K., Sato, Y. (eds.) ACCV 2016. LNCS, vol. 10112, pp. 87–103. Springer, Cham (2017). https://doi.org/10.1007/978-3-319-54184-6_6
6. Feichtenhofer, C., Fan, H., Malik, J., He, K.: Slowfast networks for video recognition. In: Proceedings of the IEEE International Conference on Computer Vision, pp. 6202–6211 (2019)
7. Lample, G., Sablayrolles, A., Ranzato, M., Denoyer, L., Jégou, H.: Large memory layers with product keys. In: Advances in Neural Information Processing Systems, pp. 8546–8557 (2019)
8. Mann, V.A., Repp, B.H.: Influence of vocalic context on perception of the $[\int]$-[s] distinction. Percept. Psychophys. **28**(3), 213–228 (1980)
9. McGurk, H., MacDonald, J.: Hearing lips and seeing voices. Nature **264**(5588), 746 (1976)
10. Petridis, S., Stafylakis, T., Ma, P., Cai, F., Tzimiropoulos, G., Pantic, M.: End-to-end audiovisual speech recognition. In: 2018 IEEE International Conference on Acoustics, Speech and Signal Processing (ICASSP), pp. 6548–6552. IEEE (2018)
11. Stafylakis, T., Khan, M.H., Tzimiropoulos, G.: Pushing the boundaries of audio-visual word recognition using residual networks and LSTMs. Comput. Vis. Image Underst. **176**, 22–32 (2018)
12. Stafylakis, T., Tzimiropoulos, G.: Combining residual networks with LSTMs for lipreading. Proc. Interspeech **2017**, 3652–3656 (2017)
13. Taylor, S.L., Mahler, M., Theobald, B.J., Matthews, I.: Dynamic units of visual speech. In: Proceedings of the ACM SIGGRAPH/Eurographics Symposium on Computer Animation, pp. 275–284. Eurographics Association (2012)
14. Thangthai, K.: Computer lipreading via hybrid deep neural network hidden Markov models. Ph.D. thesis, University of East Anglia (2018)
15. Tran, D., Bourdev, L., Fergus, R., Torresani, L., Paluri, M.: Learning spatiotemporal features with 3d convolutional networks. In: Proceedings of the IEEE International Conference on Computer Vision, pp. 4489–4497 (2015)
16. Vaswani, A., et al.: Attention is all you need. In: Advances in Neural Information Processing Systems, pp. 5998–6008 (2017)
17. Weng, X., Kitani, K.: Learning spatio-temporal features with two-stream deep 3D CNNs for lipreading. BMVC (2019). https://bmvc2019.org/wp-content/uploads/papers/0016-paper.pdf
18. Zhang, X., Cheng, F., Wang, S.: Spatio-temporal fusion based convolutional sequence learning for lip reading. In: The IEEE International Conference on Computer Vision (ICCV), October 2019

Towards Online Handwriting Recognition System Based on Reinforcement Learning Theory

Ramzi Zouari[1](✉), Houcine Boubaker[1](✉), and Monji Kherallah[2](✉)

[1] National School of Engineers of Sfax, University of Sfax, Sfax, Tunisia
ramzi.zouari@gmail.com, houcine-boubaker@ieee.org
[2] Faculty of Sciences of Sfax, University of Sfax, Sfax, Tunisia
monji.kherallah@fss.usf.tn

Abstract. In this work, we formalize the problem of online handwriting recognition according to the reinforcement learning theory. The handwriting trajectory is divided into strokes and we extracted their structural and parametric features based on freeman codes, visual codes and beta-elliptic features respectively. The environments were trained using tabular q-learning algorithm in order to calculate the optimal sate-to-action values for each class of handwriting. The proposed model was evaluated on LMCA database and achieved very promising results for both structural and parametric representations.

Keywords: Stroke · Velocity · MPD · Reward · Policy · Episodes

1 Introduction

Handwriting recognition represents a very interesting part in the document analysis field. It can be classified into two categories: offline, where the image of the handwriting is acquired from a digitizer device, and online where the handwriting trajectory is captured using a touch screen and a stylus [1]. Due to the rapid growth of data entry devices, great interest was given to online handwriting processing during the past few decades. In fact, online mode allows recovering both static and dynamic information about the handwriting generation process such as temporal order, velocity and pressure. On the other hand, online handwriting processing faces several challenges like inter-variability and intra-variability. They relate respectively to the difference in writing style between writers and even for the same writer depending of its position and emotional states.

Online handwriting recognition includes two major steps: handwriting movement modeling that allows extracting kinematic and geometric proprieties of the handwriting, and a learning step which consists of calculating the optimal parameters that associate the extracted features with the different classes of handwriting [2]. In this work, we have applied three different modeling approaches using

H. Yang et al. (Eds.): ICONIP 2020, CCIS 1332, pp. 562–570, 2020.
https://doi.org/10.1007/978-3-030-63820-7_64

Reinforcement Learning in the learning stage. It has the objective of learning the action to be performed in each stroke of the handwriting.

The rest of this paper is organized as follow: the next section presents the related works. In Sect. 3, the proposed system is overviewed. The last section is dedicated for the experimental results and discussion.

2 Related Works

The first step in online handwriting recognition system consists of handwriting movement modeling. It allows understanding the phenomena related to the trajectory formation. In the literature, the proposed models can be classified into top-down and bottom-up categories. The top-down approaches consider the writing motion as a bio-motor act. It takes origin in the brain that activates the proper nerve and muscle pairs responsible of generating the movement of the desired shape. These approaches have to study the laws held between kinematic and geometric proprieties of perceptual-motor processes, like speed-accuracy trade-off [3] and speed-curvature trade-off [4]. The second class of approaches, called bottom-up, is interested in the analysis of the biomechanical processes. They proceed by studying the kinematic and geometric proprieties of the writing motion, and try to represent the neuromuscular impulses responsible of its production. These approaches include dynamic, space and kinematic oriented models. Dynamic-oriented models consider that handwriting movement is caused by a pair of antagonist muscles [5], while space-oriented models have the capability of describing the handwriting curve in space without considering the actual joints and muscles patterns [6]. Kinematic-oriented models allow representing the effect of neuromuscular impulses in the velocity domain. In fact, the velocity profile during acceleration-deceleration interval time is characterized by a bell-shaped curve shape. It can be fitted using Gaussian, delta lognormal and beta models [7]. Bezine et al. [8] presents an extended version of beta model, called beta-elliptic model, where geometric proprieties of the involved muscles were studied. In addition to the kinematic characteristics of the handwriting movement, each neuromuscular impulse delimited between two successive extrema speed times is represented in the spatial domain by an elliptic arc.

In the learning stage, the existing approaches are based on supervised learning methods like SVM [9], HMM [10], TDNN [11] and DBN [12]. They have the objective of finding the optimal parameters that correspond the input features to the desired outputs. Recently, RL begins to be applied for solving classification problems like document classification [13]. However, it is still rarely used for online handwriting recognition despite it arises from the cognitive reality of the learning evolution process. In fact, to adapt its reading skills in a multi-writer context with different and evolving writing styles, the subject proceeds with the qualification and the enhancement of its recognition process through RL model.

3   System Overview

3.1   Handwriting Movement Modeling

The handwriting trajectory is divided into segments according to the extremum velocity points. Thereafter, we extract their structural and parametric features.

Structural Features: We have applied Freeman and visual codes methods on the handwriting trajectory. In freeman codes, each stroke delimited between two successive extremums of velocity is represented by a numeric code between 0 and 7 depending of the incline angle of its endings points. In visual codes method [14], each stroke can be assigned into one of 12 possible numeric codes according to its shape and position related to baseline and median line. Figures 1a and 1b show the application of these methods on the Arabic handwriting letter "Ha".

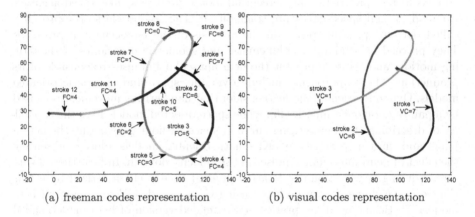

(a) freeman codes representation   (b) visual codes representation

Fig. 1. Structural representation of the Arabic letter "Ha"

Parametric Features: The kinematic and geometric proprieties of the writing motion was extracted according to the beta-elliptic model. In dynamic profile, the curvilinear velocity $V_\sigma(t)$ can be approximated by the algebraic sum of the overlapped beta functions (Fig. 2). They represent the result of the activation of N neuromuscular subsystems generated by the central neural system (Eq. 1).

$$V_\sigma(t) \approx \sum_{i=1}^{n} K_i \times \beta_i(t, q_i, p_i, t_{0i}, t_{1i}) \tag{1}$$

$$\beta_i(t, q_i, p_i, t_{0i}, t_{1i}) = \begin{cases} \left(\frac{t-t_{0i}}{t_{ci}-t_{0i}}\right)^{p_i} \left(\frac{t_{1i}-t}{t_1 t_{ci}}\right)^{q_i} & \text{if } t \in [t_{0i}, t_{1i}] \\ 0 & \text{elsewhere} \end{cases}$$

Where K_i is the amplitude of the ith beta impulse, (p_i, q_i) are intermediate parameters, and (t_{0i}, t_{1i}, t_{ci}) represent respectively the instants when the ith beta impulse reaches its starting, ending and culmination amplitude times. In geometric domain, each segment of trajectory delimited between two successive extrema speed times is assimilated to an elliptic arc. Thus, each stroke is defined by a vector of 9 parameters (Table 1).

Table 1. Beta-elliptic parameters

	Parameters	Explanation
Dynamic profile	K	Beta impulse amplitude
	$\delta t = (t_1 - t_0)$	Beta impulse duration
	$\frac{p_i}{p_i+q_i}$	Rapport of beta impulse asymmetry
	p_i	Beta shape parameters
	$\frac{K_i}{K_{i+1}}$	Rapport of successive Beta impulse amplitude
Geometric profile	a	Ellipse major axis half length
	b	Ellipse small axis half length
	θ	major axis inclination angle
	θ_p	incline angle of the tangents at the stroke endpoint

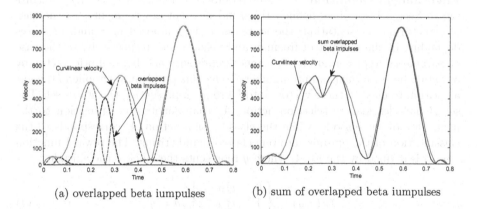

(a) overlapped beta iumpulses   (b) sum of overlapped beta iumpulses

Fig. 2. Velocity profile modeling

3.2   Reinforcement Learning Theory

RL is a class of machine learning where an agent has to act with its environment via a numerical reward signal [15]. The environment is typically formulated as a Markov Decision Process (MDP) defined by the 4-tuple $(\mathcal{S}, \mathcal{A}, \pi, r)$ where $\mathcal{S}$ is the state space, $\mathcal{A}$ represents a finite set of actions, π is a deterministic policy that maps states-to-actions and r is a numerical reward that reflects the quality of taking an action from a given state relative to the agent's ultimate goal. During the learning stage, the agent has to learn for each state $s \in \mathcal{S}$, the optimal policy π^* that maximizes the expected cumulative reward R (Eq. 2). The parameter $\gamma \in [0, 1]$ represents the discount factor for future rewards.

$$R = \mathbb{E}_\pi \left[\sum_{t=1}^{\infty} \gamma^{t-1} r_t | s_t = s, a_t = a \right] \tag{2}$$

In the environment simulation stage, we have applied q-learning algorithm [16]. It is off-policy method where the interaction between agent and environment was done independently of the policy π. In this case, the learning process breaks down into episodes, where all state-action pairs must be infinitely visited until reaching the optimal $Q(s, a)$ values. In each iteration, $Q(s, a)$ must be updated according to Eq. 3, where r_t is the immediate reward, $\gamma \in [0 : 1]$ represents a bias parameter and $\alpha \in [0 : 1]$ is a learning rate that denotes how much the difference between successive q-values is considered. The application of RL requires the environment definition, simulation and evaluation steps.

$$Q(s_t, a_t) = Q(s_t, a_t) + \alpha \left[r_t + \gamma max_{a_{t+1}} Q(s_{t+1}, a_{t+1}) - Q(s_t, a_t) \right] \tag{3}$$

Environment Definition: This step requires the definition of $\langle \mathcal{S}, \mathcal{A}, r \rangle$. According to Sect. 3.1, we have defined three independent environments. In the case of structural representation, the state set $\mathcal{S}$ is composed of 8 and 12 states depending of the number of freeman and visual codes respectively. In the case of parametric representation, we cannot represent each beta-elliptic vector by one state because their infinite number. To fix this problem, we applied k-means algorithm to classify these vectors into k groups representing the states set. The set $\mathcal{A}$ includes feature selection action $\mathcal{A}_f$ that denotes the transition to the next state of the episode, while the classification action $\mathcal{A}_c$ corresponds to the classification of the episode into one class of handwriting. The reward function $r(s, a)$ is defined by the Eq. 4, where y represents the label of the episode.

$$r(s, a) = \begin{cases} 0 & , if\, a \in \mathcal{A}_f \\ 1 & , if\, a \in \mathcal{A}_c, a = y \\ -1 & , if\, a \in \mathcal{A}_c, a \neq y \end{cases} \tag{4}$$

Environment Simulation: In each state of the epiqode, the agent executes an action a_t, receives an immediate reward r_t (Eq. 4) and moves to a new state. Therefore, the current $Q(s_t, a_t)$ value was updated according to Eq. 3. This algorithm is repeated until reaching the convergence criterion where $Q(s_t, a_t)$ at two successive instants are almost equals (Algorithm 1).

Algorithm 1: Environment simulation algorithm

Input: $\mathcal{S}$:states, $\mathcal{A}$: actions, $nb_{classes}$
Result: $Q_k^*(s,a)$ for each class of handwriting
initialize $Q_k(s,a)$ randomly for each class of handwriting;
for $k=1$: $nb_{classes}$ **do**
   repeat
      initialize $episode \subset \mathcal{S}$;
      repeat
         Take action (a_t), observe (r_t, s_{t+1}) ;
         Update $Q_k(s_t, a_t)$ (eq. 3);
         $s_t \leftarrow s_{t+1}$;
      until s *is terminal*;
   until $Q_k(t), \approx Q_k(t-1)$;
end

Environment Evaluation: Each class of handwriting is characterized by its proper Q_k^*-matrix. To classify an episode composed of a sequence of states, the agent has to compute this scores over the Q_k^*-matrices. These scores can be obtained by summing the $Q_k^*(s,a)$ transition values between states of the episode. Finally, the episode is classified into the class of higher score.

4 Experiments and Results

The experiments have been made on LMCA database [17]. It is a multi-writer database produced by 55 writers and containing 23141 online Arabic letters. The trajectory coordinates (x,y) are stored in txt files according to the UNIPEN format. LMCA includes a number of 56 classes corresponding to the different Arabic letter shapes. Two thirds of samples have been used for the environment simulation and the rest has been used for the evaluation. In the parametric representation, the number of states is fixed to 35 since it returns the minimum of distortion intra and inter clusters. Therefore, the Q-matrices size is relative to the number of states, where the rows represent the starting states and the columns the arrival ones. The last column corresponds to a terminal state that resulting from the classification action (Table 2). We note that each class of handwriting is defined by its proper Q-matrix. In the environment simulation step, Q-learning algorithm was applied with different hyper-parameter values. The below example shows the optimal Q_k^* matrix relative to the Arabic letter "Noun" when using freeman codes. The hyper-parameters α, γ and ϵ was fixed to 0.001, 0.6 and 10^{-6} respectively. In the environment evaluation step, the agent has to compute for each test sample X_{test} the sum of transitions between this different states over Q_k^* matrices. X_{test} is classified into the class of higher score (Eq. 5).

$$Q_k^* (s,a) = \begin{array}{c} \\ s_0 \\ s_1 \\ s_2 \\ s_3 \\ s_4 \\ s_5 \\ s_6 \\ s_7 \end{array} \begin{array}{ccccccccc} s_0 & s_1 & s_2 & s_3 & s_4 & s_5 & s_6 & s_7 & A_c \\ 0 & 0 & 0 & 0 & 0 & 0 & 0 & 0 & -1 \\ 0 & 0 & 0 & 0 & 0 & 0 & 0 & 0 & -1 \\ 0 & 0.2 & 1.6 & 0 & 0 & 0 & 0 & 0.2 & 10 \\ 0 & 0 & 4 & 4 & 0 & 0 & 0.6 & 0 & 7 \\ 0 & 0 & 4 & 4 & 1.6 & 0.6 & 0 & 0 & -1 \\ 0 & 0 & 4 & 0 & 1.6 & 1.6 & 0.6 & 0 & -1 \\ 0 & 0 & 0 & 0 & 1.6 & 1.6 & 0.6 & 0 & -1 \\ 0 & 0 & 0 & 0 & 0 & 0 & 0 & 0 & -1 \end{array}$$

Table 2. Environement configuration

Method	States	Q-matrices size
Freeman codes	8	$(8 \times 9 \times 56)$
Visual codes	12	$(12 \times 13 \times 56)$
Beta-elliptic	35	$(35 \times 36 \times 56)$

$$\begin{cases} X_{test} = s_6 \overset{0.6}{\curvearrowright} s_6 \overset{0.6}{\curvearrowright} s_5 \overset{1.6}{\curvearrowright} s_4 \overset{4}{\curvearrowright} s_3 \overset{4}{\curvearrowright} s_2 \overset{1.6}{\curvearrowright} s_2 \overset{10}{\curvearrowright} A_c \\ score\left(X_{test} | Q_k^*\right) = \sum_{i,j} Q_k^* \left(s_i, a_j\right) \\ C_{(X_{test})} = \arg\max_k \left[Score\left(X_{test} | Q_k^*\right) \right] \end{cases} \quad (5)$$

The experiment results demonstrate the effectiveness of the proposed approach which achieved the state-of-the-art performances on LMCA database. We attaigned the recognition rate of 98% (Tables 3 and 4) when applying beta-elliptic model. This can be explained by the relevance of the proposed methods where the trajectory is considered as a sequence of basic units over time. Furthermore, RL allows the agent to learn what action to be perform at each stroke of the trajectory, and not only for the whole trajectory shape. Furthermore, the trained $Q_k^* (s, a)$ matrices are not only useful for the classification task, but it represents also a support for the agent to simulate the handwriting generation process. We can conclude from the above $Q_k^* (s, a)$ matrix that all training samples of the Arabic handwriting letter "Noun" finish either with the strokes (s_3) or (s_4) from the freeman code representation, where the majority of them finish with the stroke (s_4). Moreover, all training samples do not contain the codes (s_0), (s_1) and (s_7) in their freeman codes representation. This information is very important in the field of handwriting trajectory modeling which may not be available when using supervised learning classifiers.

Table 3. Experiment results

	Method		
	Freeman codes	Visual codes	Beta-elliptic
Recognition rate (%)	96.48	97.23	98.33

Table 4. Results comparaison on LMCA database

System	Features	Method	Recognition rate (%)
[17]	Beta-elliptic	MLP	94.1
[11]	Beta-elliptic	TDNN	95.1
[14]	Visual codes	GA	96.2
[12]	Bottleneck features	DBN	96.1
Proposed system	Beta-elliptic	RL	**98.3**

5 Conclusions and Future Works

We presented a new framework for online handwriting recognition based on reinforcement learning theory. It consists of segmenting the handwriting trajectory into strokes and extracting their structural and parametric features based on freeman codes, visual codes and beta strokes respectively. Q-learning algorithm was applied to learn the optimal Q^* matrices for each environment.

As perspective, we intend to extend this work for the recognition of online handwriting words based on Deep Q-learning network. This allows estimating the Q-values using non linear models, instead of being stored into matrices.

References

1. Chaabouni, A., Boubaker, H., Kherallah, M., Alimi, A.M., El Abed, H.: Combining of off-line and on-line feature extraction approaches for writer identification. In: 12th International Conference on Document Analysis and Recognition, pp. 1299–1303. IEEE, China (2011)
2. Boubaker, H., El Baati, A., Kherallah, M., Alimi, A.M., Elabed, H.: Online Arabic handwriting modeling system based on the graphemes segmentation. In: 20th International Conference on Pattern Recognition, pp. 2061–2064. IEEE, Turkey (2010)
3. Plamondon, R., Alimi, A.M., Yergeau, P., Leclerc, F.: Modelling velocity profiles of rapid movements: a comparative study. Biol. Cybern. **69**(2), 119–128 (1993). https://doi.org/10.1007/BF00226195
4. Viviani, P., Flash, T.: Minimum-jerk, two-thirds power law, and isochrony: converging approaches to movement planning. J. Exp. Psychol. Hum. Percept. Perform. **21**(1), 32 (1995)
5. Hollerbach, J.M.: An oscillation theory of handwriting. Biol. Cybern. **39**(2), 139–156 (1981). https://doi.org/10.1007/BF00336740

6. Flash, T., Hogan, N.: The coordination of arm movements: an experimentally confirmed mathematical model. J. Neurosci. **5**(7), 1688–1703 (1985)
7. Plamondon, R.: A kinematic theory of rapid human movements. Part-I Movement representation and generation. Biol. Cybern. **72**(1), 309–320 (1995)
8. Bezine, H., Alimi, A. M., Sherkat, N.: Generation and analysis of handwriting script with the beta-elliptic model. In: 9th International Workshop on Frontiers in Handwriting Recognition, pp. 515–520. IEEE, Japan (2004)
9. Zouari, R., Boubaker, H., Kherallah, M.: Two staged fuzzy SVM algorithm and beta-elliptic model for online arabic handwriting recognition. In: Lintas, A., Rovetta, S., Verschure, P.F.M.J., Villa, A.E.P. (eds.) ICANN 2017. LNCS, vol. 10614, pp. 450–458. Springer, Cham (2017). https://doi.org/10.1007/978-3-319-68612-7_51
10. Tagougui, N., Boubaker, H., Kherallah, M., Alimi, A.M.: A hybrid MLPNN/HMM recognition system for online Arabic Handwritten script. In: World Congress on Computer and Information Technology, pp. 1–6. IEEE (2013)
11. Zouari, R., Boubaker, H., Kherallah, M.: A time delay neural network for online arabic handwriting recognition. In: Madureira, A.M., Abraham, A., Gamboa, D., Novais, P. (eds.) ISDA 2016. AISC, vol. 557, pp. 1005–1014. Springer, Cham (2017). https://doi.org/10.1007/978-3-319-53480-0_99
12. Tagougui, N., Kherallah, M.: Recognizing online Arabic handwritten characters using a deep architecture. In: 9th International Conference on Machine Vision, vol. 103410L, pp. 1–35, France (2017)
13. Dulac-Arnold, G., Denoyer, L., Gallinari, P.: Text classification: a sequential reading approach. In: Clough, P., Foley, C., Gurrin, C., Jones, G.J.F., Kraaij, W., Lee, H., Mudoch, V. (eds.) ECIR 2011. LNCS, vol. 6611, pp. 411–423. Springer, Heidelberg (2011). https://doi.org/10.1007/978-3-642-20161-5_41
14. Kherallah, M., Bouri, F., Alimi, A.M.: On-line Arabic handwriting recognition system based on visual encoding and genetic algorithm. Eng. Appl. Artif. Intell. **22**(1), 153–170 (2009)
15. Sutton, R.S., Barto, A.G.: Reinforcement learning: an introduction. MIT press (2018)
16. Watkins, C.J., Dayan, P.: Q-learning. Mach. Learn. **8**(3–4), 279–292 (1992)
17. Boubaker, H., Elbaati, A., Tagougui, N., El Abed, H., Kherallah, M., Alimi, A.M.: Online Arabic databases and applicationsOnline Arabic databases and applications. Guide to OCR for Arabic Scripts, pp. 541–557. Springer, Berlin (2012)

Training Lightweight yet Competent Network via Transferring Complementary Features

Xiaobing Zhang[1] , Shijian Lu[2(✉)] , Haigang Gong[1] , Minghui Liu[1] ,
and Ming Liu[1]

[1] University of Electronic Science and Technology of China, Sichuan, China
zhangxiaobing@std.uestc.edu.cn, {hggong,csmliu}@uestc.edu.cn,
minghuiliuuestc@163.com
[2] Nanyang Technological University, Singapore, Singapore
Shijian.Lu@ntu.edu.sg

Abstract. Though deep neural networks have achieved quite impressive performance in various image detection and classification tasks, they are often constrained by requiring intensive computation and large storage space for deployment in different scenarios and devices. This paper presents an innovative network that aims to train a lightweight yet competent student network via transferring multifarious knowledge and features from a large yet powerful teacher network. Based on the observations that different vision tasks are often correlated and complementary, we first train a resourceful teacher network that captures both discriminative and generative features for the objective of image classification (the main task) and image reconstruction (an auxiliary task). A lightweight yet competent student network is then trained by mimicking both pixel-level and spatial-level feature distribution of the resourceful teacher network under the guidance of feature loss and adversarial loss, respectively. The proposed technique has been evaluated over a number of public datasets extensively and experiments show that our student network obtains superior image classification performance as compared with the state-of-the-art.

Keywords: Knowledge distillation · Transfer learning · Model compression

1 Introduction

Deep neural networks (DNNs) have demonstrated superior performances in various research fields [2,15–17]. However, deeper and larger networks often come with high computational costs and large memory requirements which have impeded effective and efficient development and deployment of DNNs in various resource-constrained scenarios. In recent years, knowledge transfer has attracted increasing interest and several promising networks have been developed through

© Springer Nature Switzerland AG 2020
H. Yang et al. (Eds.): ICONIP 2020, CCIS 1332, pp. 571–579, 2020.
https://doi.org/10.1007/978-3-030-63820-7_65

knowledge distillation (KD) [5], attention transfer (AT) [11], factor transfer (FT) [6], etc. On the other hand, the aforementioned works share a common constrain of feature uniformity where the teacher network is trained with the task-specific objective alone and so learn (and transfer) unitary features and knowledge only. In addition, the *teacher-learned* features are usually optimal for the teacher's performance which may not be the case for the student network due to the large discrepancies in network architecture, network capacity and initial conditions between the teacher and student.

In this paper, we design an innovative network where a teacher network learns and transfers multifarious and complementary features to train a lightweight yet competent student network. The design is based on the observation and intuition that different vision tasks are often correlated and complementary and more resourceful and knowledgeable teachers tend to train more competent students. Our proposed network learns in two phases: 1) knowledge capture; and 2) knowledge transfer as illustrated in Fig. 1. In the first phase, the teacher network is trained under two very different tasks to capture diverse and complementary features. Specifically, an auxiliary image reconstruction task is introduced with which the teacher network can capture structural knowledge and generative latent representations beyond the task-specific features. In the second phase, the student network is trained under the image classification task in a supervised manner. Concurrently, its learned features are modulated and enhanced by feature loss and adversarial loss that facilitate to thoroughly assimilate both pixel-level and spatial-level distributions of the complementary knowledge distilled from the teacher network. With the transferred multifarious features, our teacher can empower a more competent student network in a more efficient manner, more details to be described in Experiments.

The contributions of this work can be summarized from three aspects. First, it designs an innovative knowledge transfer network where a teacher learns and transfers multifarious features to train a lightweight yet competent student. Second, it proposes a novel knowledge transfer strategy where the student is capable of absorbing multifarious features effectively and efficiently under the guidance of feature loss and adversarial loss. Third, our developed network outperforms the state-of-the-art consistently across a number of datasets.

2   Related Work

Knowledge transfer aims to train a compact student network by transferring knowledge from a powerful teacher. Cristian *et al.* [1] first uses soft-labels for knowledge transfer, and this idea is further improved by knowledge distilling by adjusting the temperature of softmax activation function [5]. On the other hand, knowledge distilling relies on label categories and it works only for softmax function. This constraint is later addressed in different ways, e.g. by transferring intermediate features [10, 14] or by optimizing the initial weight of student [4].

While the aforementioned methods obtain quite promising results, they train the teacher with a single task and objective and therefore can only transfer

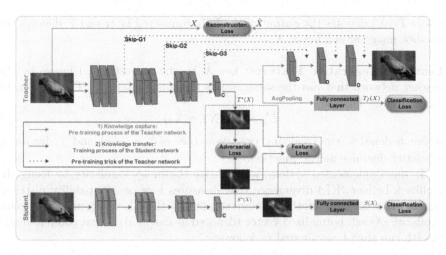

Fig. 1. Architecture of the proposed knowledge transfer network: 1) knowledge capture: a teacher network is first pre-trained with complementary objectives to learn multifarious features; 2) knowledge transfer: a student network is then trained to mimic both pixel-level and spatial-level distribution of the transferred features under the guidance of feature loss and adversarial loss, respectively. C and D denote the convolution operation and deconvolution module for feature alignment and image reconstruction.

task-specific unitary features. Our proposed method addresses this constraint by introducing a reconstruction task to the teacher network for learning and transferring the complementary and generative structural features beyond the task-specific features alone.

3 Proposed Methods

3.1 Learning Multifarious Features

Given a labeled dataset (X, Y), we first pre-train a teacher network T over the dataset for learning multifarious yet complementary features under a classification loss (CL) and a reconstruction loss (RL). The CL will drive T to learn discriminative classification features, whereas RL will drive T to learn generative reconstruction features, more details to be described in the following subsections.

Learning Discriminative Features: In the teacher network, we first include a convolution layer with batch normalization (denoted as 'C' in Fig. 1) for feature alignment. The convolution layer is followed by an averaged pooling and a fully connected layer that produces classification probabilities. Similar to the conventional metric in the classification task, we adopt the cross-entropy function E against labels Y for evaluating the classification result:

$$L_C^t = E(T_f(X), Y) \tag{1}$$

where $T_f(X)$ denotes the output of the fully connected layer and Y denotes the one-hot image-level label of X.

Learning Generative Features: Let $\tilde{X}$ be the reconstructed image by the teacher network that has the same size as the input image X. The RL can be formulated as follows:

$$L_R^t = f(\eta(\tilde{X}), \eta(X)) \tag{2}$$

where η denotes a normalizing operation (i.e. $\eta(\cdot) = \frac{\cdot}{\|\cdot\|_2}$) and f denotes a similarity distance metric function.

In our implemented system, we evaluate the image similarity by using the Kullback-Leibler (KL) divergence that measures how one probability distribution is different from another. Before computing the KL divergence, the cosine similarity of each normalized vector (denoted as $cos(\eta(.))$) is first computed and the RL can then be evaluated as follows:

$$L_R^t = KL(cos(\eta(\tilde{X})), cos(\eta(X))) = -\frac{1}{n} \sum_{i=1}^{n} cos(\eta(\tilde{X}_i)) \log(\frac{cos(\eta(X_i))}{cos(\eta(\tilde{X}_i))}) \tag{3}$$

Learning under the classification and reconstruction tasks alternately thus produces a resourceful and powerful teacher network, which is equipped with multifarious and complementary features for training a lightweight yet competent student network as to be described in the ensuing subsection.

3.2 Transferring Multifarious Features

Once the teacher network converges, we freeze its parameters and train the student network S to absorb the distilled knowledge that actually corresponds to the learned features before the fully connected layer of the teacher network. As illustrated in Fig. 1, the student network is trained with feature loss, adversarial loss and classification loss simultaneously.

For the feature loss, the transferred knowledge $T^*(X)$ from the teacher and the corresponding features $S^*(X)$ from the student are aligned and normalized (i.e. $\eta(\cdot) = \frac{\cdot}{\|\cdot\|_2}$) to calculate the feature metric as:

$$L_{Fea}^s = d(\eta(T^*(X)), \eta(S^*(X))) \tag{4}$$

Here, d can be evaluated by either L_1 or L_2 method to calculate the pixel-level absolute distance between features.

For the adversarial loss, a discriminator D is introduced to distinguish whether the input comes from teacher or student by maximizing the following objective:

$$L_D^s = \min_{S^*(X)} \max_D E_{S^*(X) \sim p_S}[log(1 - D(S^*(X)))] + E_{T^*(X) \sim p_T}[log(D(T^*(X)))] \tag{5}$$

where p_T and p_S correspond to the feature distribution of $T^*(X)$ and $S^*(X)$, respectively. Since the discriminator D is composed of fully connected layers with

Table 1. Comparison results of Top-1 mean classification error rate (%) with the unitary feature transferring methods on CIFAR10.

Student	Teacher	Student*	CL+RL					Teacher*
			W/o Skip	Skip-G1	Skip-G2	Skip-G3	Skip-G123	
ResNet20, 0.27M	ResNet56, 0.95M	7.18	6.24	5.92	6.22	6.13	**5.89**	5.78
ResNet20, 0.27M	WRN40-1, 0.66M	7.18	6.54	6.24	**6.10**	6.30	6.21	5.94
VGG13, 9.4M	WRN46-4, 11M	5.82	4.51	4.29	4.38	4.31	**4.21**	4.19
WRN16-1, 0.21M	WRN16-2, 0.97M	7.77	7.42	7.21	7.17	7.25	**7.15**	5.72
Student	Teacher	Student*	AT [11]	KD [5]	FT [6]	AB [4]	OFD [3]	Ours
ResNet20, 0.27M	ResNet56, 0.95M	7.18	7.13	7.19	6.85	6.49	6.32	**5.89**
ResNet20, 0.27M	WRN40-1, 0.66M	7.18	7.34	7.09	6.85	6.62	6.55	**6.10**
VGG13, 9.4M	WRN46-4, 11M	5.82	5.54	5.71	4.84	5.10	4.75	**4.21**
WRN16-1, 0.21M	WRN16-2, 0.97M	7.77	8.10	7.70	7.64	7.58	7.50	**7.15**

convolutional operations, adversarial loss can direct the student to assimilate and mimic the spatial-level relations in the transferred features.

The student network can thus be trained with the three losses as follows:

$$L_C^s = E(S(X), Y) \tag{6}$$

$$L^s = \alpha L_{Fea}^s + \beta L_D^s + L_C^s \tag{7}$$

Where α and β are balance weight parameters. During the student learning process, gradients are computed and propagated back within the student network, guiding it to learn the teacher's knowledge as defined in Eq. 7.

4 Experiments and Analysis

Our proposed network is evaluated over three datasets as follows: CIFAR10 [7] and CIFAR100 [8] are two publicly accessible datasets. They consist of 32×32 pixel RGB images that belong to 10 and 100 different classes, respectively. Both datasets have 50,000 training images and 10,000 test images. ImageNet refers to the large-scale LSVRC 2015 classification dataset, which consists of 1.2M training images and 50 K validation images of 1,000 object classes.

4.1 Implementation Details

During training process, SGD is employed as optimization and weight decay is set to 10^{-4}. On CIFAR dataset, the teacher network is pre-trained with 300 epoch. The learning rate of student drops from 0.1 to 0.01 at 50% training and to 0.001 at 75%. On ImageNet dataset, the student is trained for 100 epoch, with the initial learning rate 0.1 divided by 10 at the 30, 60 and 90 epoch, respectively.

Table 2. Comparison results with the adversarial learning based methods over CIFAR100 dataset.

Model	Top-1 error(%)
ResNet164,2.6M	27.76
ResNet20,0.26M	33.36
ANC [13]	32.45
TSCAN [18]	32.57
KSANC [12]	31.42
KTAN [9]	30.56
Ours	**29.28**

Table 3. Comparison results of Top-1 and Top-5 mean classification error (%) on ImageNet.

Student	Teacher	Test error(%)	
ResNet18	ResNet34	Top-1	Top-5
Student*		29.56	10.60
Teacher*		26.49	8.51
AT [11]		29.3	10.0
FT [6]		28.57	9.71
AB [6]		28.38	9.68
Ours		**28.08**	**9.49**

4.2   Comparisons with the State-of-the-Art

CIFAR10: Comparison results are shown in Table 1, where Student* and Teacher* provide Top-1 mean error rate of the student and teacher while trained from scratch. Two conclusions can be drawn: 1) In the top sub-table, the teacher pre-trained with skip connections 'Skip-G#' can empower the student to achieve the lowest classification error. It is attributed to the skip connection that can supplement the low-level information for the deconvolution modules, with which the teacher can extract and transfer more discriminative features to the student. 2) In the bottom sub-table, our proposed student network consistently outperforms both the original student network 'Student*' and the state-of-the-art results no matter whether the teacher and student networks are of different types. These outstanding performances are largely attributed to the fact that trained with different yet complementary tasks, our teacher network can effectively learn and transfer multifarious and complementary features to the student.

CIFAR100: To prove the generality of our technique, we compare it with the adversarial learning strategy applied methods on CIFAR100. This experiment involves ResNet164/ResNet20 with large depth gap to be teacher/student network pair. All the adversarial learning strategy applied methods obtain relatively good performance. Compared to the KTAN, our model makes noticeable performance with 1.28% improvement. It is largely due to our teacher which can learn multifarious knowledge by training with complementary tasks. As described above, our student acquires the lowest error with the same number of parameters, demonstrating that our model benefits from the multifarious knowledge learning method, as well as different level feature transferring strategy.

ImageNet: We also conduct a large-scale experiment over ImageNet LSVRC 2015 classification task to study its scalability. As results shown in Table 3, the proposed network outperforms the state-of-the-art methods consistently. In addition, our method helps improve the student's Top-1 accuracy by up to 1.48% as compared with the student trained from scratch in the Student* row. This

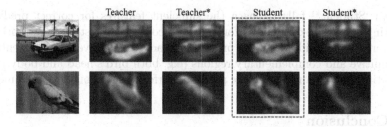

Fig. 2. Teacher and Teacher* columns represent the results from the teacher trained with both classification loss and reconstruction loss, or trained from scratch, respectively. Similarly, results in Student and Student* columns represent the outputs from the student network trained with our proposed teacher or trained from scratch.

Table 4. Ablation results of different transfer loss.

Transfer loss	Test Error(%)	
	CIFAR10	CIFAR100
L_C^s	7.18	31.04
$L_C^s + L_D^s$	6.42	29.62
$L_C^s + L_D^s + L_{L_2}^s$	6.17	28.97
$L_C^s + L_D^s + L_{L_1}^s$	**5.89**	**28.08**

clearly demonstrates the potential adaptability of our proposed method, making promising performance even on the more complex dataset.

4.3 Ablation Studies

Transfer Losses and Transfer Strategies: By comparing the first rows in Table 4, it indicates that adding adversarial loss L_D^s to absorb the shared features clearly improves the student's performance. This is largely attributed to the convolutional structure of the discriminator that can interpret the spatial information in features. In addition, by incorporating the feature loss to measure pixel-level distribution distance, either $L_{L_1}^s$ or $L_{L_2}^s$ shown in the last two rows, it can work as a complement to adversarial loss with distinct performance improvement. By using both adversarial loss and feature loss to capture different level distance between features, our student can assimilate the transferred multifarious features thoroughly with promising performance.

4.4 Discussion

Feature Visualization: As Fig. 2 shows, the teacher network 'Teacher' pre-trained with 'CL+RL' focuses on more multifarious features, whereas the same network trained from scratch 'Teacher*' focuses on targeted features only (e.g. bird's beak), leading to the loss of rich contour details. Additionally, the fully trained 'Student*' fails to learn the sufficient features for correct prediction, resulting in the sub-optimal performance. In contrast, the student network 'Student', under the guidance of the proposed 'Teacher', effectively pays attention to discrimitive and complementary regions (e.g. both bird's head and body parts), indicating and demonstrating the powerful performance of our proposed method.

5   Conclusion

This paper presents a novel knowledge transfer network for model compression in which the teacher can learn multifarious features for training a lightweight yet competent student. The learning consists of two stages, where the teacher is first trained with multiple objectives to learn complementary feature and the student is then trained to mimic both pixel-level and spatial-level feature distribution of the teacher. As evaluated over a number of public datasets, the proposed student network can learn richer and more useful features with better performance.

Acknowledgements. This work is supported in part by National Science Foundation of China under Grant No. 61572113, and the Fundamental Research Funds for the Central Universities under Grants No. XGBDFZ09.

References

1. Bucilua, C., Caruana, R., Niculescumizil, A.: Model compression. In: Proceedings of the 12th ACM SIGKDD International Conference on Knowledge Discovery and Data Mining, pp. 535–541 (2006)
2. Ghifary, M., Kleijn, W.B., Zhang, M., Balduzzi, D., Li, W.: Deep reconstruction-classification networks for unsupervised domain adaptation. In: Leibe, B., Matas, J., Sebe, N., Welling, M. (eds.) ECCV 2016. LNCS, vol. 9908, pp. 597–613. Springer, Cham (2016). https://doi.org/10.1007/978-3-319-46493-0_36
3. Heo, B., Kim, J., Yun, S., Park, H., Kwak, N., Choi, J.Y.: A comprehensive overhaul of feature distillation. In: Proceedings of the IEEE International Conference on Computer Vision, pp. 1921–1930 (2019)
4. Heo, B., Lee, M., Yun, S., Choi, J.Y.: Knowledge transfer via distillation of activation boundaries formed by hidden neurons. In: Proceedings of the AAAI Conference on Artificial Intelligence, vol. 33, pp. 3779–3787 (2019)
5. Hinton, G., Vinyals, O., Dean, J.: Distilling the knowledge in a neural network. arXiv preprint arXiv:1503.02531 (2014)
6. Kim, J., Park, S., Kwak, N.: Paraphrasing complex network: network compression via factor transfer. In: Advances in Neural Information Processing Systems, pp. 2760–2769 (2018)
7. Krizhevsky, A., Nair, V., Hinton, G.: Cifar-10 dataset
8. Krizhevsky, A., Nair, V., Hinton, G.: Cifar-100 dataset
9. Liu, P., Liu, W., Ma, H., Mei, T., Seok, M.: Ktan: knowledge transfer adversarial network. In: 2020 International Joint Conference on Neural Networks (IJCNN), pp. 1–7. IEEE (2018)
10. Romero, A., Ballas, N., Kahou, S.E., Chassang, A., Bengio, Y.: Fitnets: hints for thin deep nets. arXiv preprint arXiv:1412.6550 (2015)

11. Sergey, Z., Nikos, K.: Paying more attention to attention: improving the performance of convolutional neural networks via attention transfer. arXiv preprint arXiv:1612.03928 (2017)
12. Shu, C., Li, P., Xie, Y., Qu, Y., Dai, L., Ma, L.: Knowledge squeezed adversarial network compression. arXiv preprint arXiv:1904.05100 (2019)
13. Vasileios, B., Azade, F., Fabio, G.: Adversarial network compression. In: Proceedings of the European Conference on Computer Vision (ECCV) (2018)
14. Yim, J., Joo, D., Bae, J., Kim, J.: A gift from knowledge distillation: fast optimization, network minimization and transfer learning. In: Proceedings of the IEEE Conference on Computer Vision and Pattern Recognition, pp. 4133–4141 (2017)
15. Yoshihashi, R., Shao, W., Kawakami, R., You, S., Iida, M.: Classification-reconstruction learning for open-set recognition. In: Proceedings of the IEEE Conference on Computer Vision and Pattern Recognition, pp. 4016–4025 (2019)
16. Zhang, X., Gong, H., Dai, X., Yang, F., Liu, N., Liu, M.: Understanding pictograph with facial features: end-to-end sentence-level lip reading of Chinese. In: Proceedings of the AAAI Conference on Artificial Intelligence, vol. 33, pp. 9211–9218 (2019)
17. Zhang, X., Lu, S., Gong, H., Luo, Z., Liu, M.: AMLN: adversarial-based mutual learning network for online knowledge distillation. In: Vedaldi, A., Bischof, H., Brox, T., Frahm, J.-M. (eds.) ECCV 2020. LNCS, vol. 12357, pp. 158–173. Springer, Cham (2020). https://doi.org/10.1007/978-3-030-58610-2_10
18. Zheng, X., Hsu, Y., Huang, J.: Training student networks for acceleration with conditional adversarial networks. In: BMVC (2018)

TSGYE: Two-Stage Grape Yield Estimation

Geng Deng, Tianyu Geng$^{(\boxtimes)}$, Chengxin He, Xinao Wang, Bangjun He,
and Lei Duan

School of Computer Science, Sichuan University, Chengdu, China
dg_nikumata@163.com, {tygeng,leiduan}@scu.edu.cn, cxinhe@foxmail.com,
scdxwxa@gmail.com, bangjun_he@163.com

Abstract. Vision-based grapeyield estimation provides a cost-effective
solution for intelligent orchards. However, unstructuredbackground,
occlusionand dense berries make it challenging for grape yield estimation. We propose an efficient two-stage pipeline TSGYE: precise detection of grape clusters and efficient counting of grape berries. Firstly,
high-precision grape clustersaredetectedusing object detectors, such as
Mask R-CNN, YOLOv2/v3/v4. Secondly,based on the detected clusters, berry counted throughimage processing technology. Experimental
results showthat TSGYE with YOLOv4achieves 96.96% mAP@0.5 score
on WGISD, betterthan thestate-of-the-art detectors. Besides we manually annotateall test imagesof WGISD and make it publicwith a grape
berry counting benchmark. Our work is a milestone in grape yield estimation for two reasons: we propose an efficient two-stage grape yield
estimation pipeline TSGYE;we offer a public test set in grape berry
counting for the first time.

Keywords: Grape cluster detection · Berry counting · Computer
vision · Deep learning

1 Introduction

Combined with the Internet of Things, intelligent orchard deploys sensors and
software to control the fruit production process [1,2]. It mainly contains fruit
yield estimation [3], fruit disease detection [4] and fruit quality control [5], while
fruit yield estimation is the most critical component in them.

Vision-based fruit yield estimation mainly contains accurate fruit detection
and berry counting. Since the complex outdoor environment, such tasks are
challenging, mainly including: (1) Fruits and branches exist a lof of occlusion,
which requires high robustness detection algorithm [2]; (2) Fruit is plentiful but
small in shape, which requires an efficient counting algorithm [6]; (3) Few public
data in fruit yield estimation limits the application of deep learning [7].

Nevertheless, researchers achieved good results in mango, strawberry, apple
detection and yield estimation [5]. However, compared to apple and fruit with

© Springer Nature Switzerland AG 2020
H. Yang et al. (Eds.): ICONIP 2020, CCIS 1332, pp. 580–588, 2020.
https://doi.org/10.1007/978-3-030-63820-7_66

certain shape and color, the similarity of green color between grape and leaves, which make it challenging in grape yield estimation. Typically, vision-based grape yield estimation work mainly carried out from three aspects: (1) According to prior knowledge of grape berry circular shape, berry candidates are detected according to weights. However, taking weight as a measuring method exists errors and missed detection [3]; (2) Using 3D reconstruction technology, it can non-destructively count the grape clusters, but fail to count the number of grape berries [1]; (3) Using machine learning methods, grape clusters can be detected and instance segmented [6,7]. The above works indicate great research significance of grape yield estimation.

Therefore, this paper focuses on two aspects: precisely detecting grape clusters and efficiently counting grape berries. Specifically, YOLOv4 applied to detect labeled grape clusters on WGISD; geometric image counting is used for berry counting calculation.

The main contributions of this work are as follows:

- **Proposean efficient two-stagegrape yield estimationmethod based on detection and counting.** To our best knowledge, we are the firstto propose a two-stage grape yield estimation method. Firstly, high-precision grape clustersaredetectedusing detectors, such as Mast R-CNN, YOLOv2/v3/v4. Secondly,based on the detected clusters, berries counted throughimage processing technology.
- **Achieveideal experimental resultson WGISDdataset.** We conduct lots of experiments and demonstrate that TSGYE with YOLOv4achieves good detection performance on WGISD and offer a grape berry counting benchmark.
- **Providea public test set as ground truth for grape berry counting.** According to our knowledge, there is no public test set for grape berry counting. We manually annotatedall test imagesof WGISD on the ModelArt platform[1] and make it public[2].

2   Related Work

Computer vision is one of the mostly widely used technological tools in fruit recognition tasks, where Grape berry counting extensively attracted researchers' attentions. Recently proposed methods are two parts: (1) berry yield estimation; (2) grape detection and counting based on deep learning.

Berry Yield Estimation. Dunn *et al.* [8] presented one of the earliest works to employ image processing for berry detection. And Nuske *et al.* [3] presented a computer vision methodology to find berry candidates. Recently, several works on how to count berries in images. One of them counts berries in an image without detecting their exact location, such as method used in [9]. Instead, for each

---

[1] http://modelart.hu/.

[2] https://github.com/Nikumata/GrapeCounting.

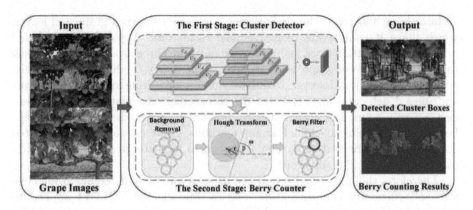

Fig. 1. The framework of TSGYE Pipeline. Firsily, grape clusters of original images will be located by Cluster Detector. Secondly, Berry Counter will calculate counting results based on detected cluster boxes.

image, they either output the sum of berries, or potential objects based on estimated density map. Moreover, evaluation of cluster yield by mobile applications has been proposed based on estimating the number of berries in a cluster [10]. These methods consider the background of images, which involves noise, causing inaccuracy in counting.

Grape Detection and Counting Based on Deep Learning. Using berry detection before counting has become a mainstream research direction, while deep learning based methods have achieved outstanding performance. Grape detection methods changed from traditional hand-crafted features to pixel-segmentation with CNNs as feature extractor. For example Nellithimaru *et al.* [11] applied Mask-RCNN to segment grapes and to reconstruct 3D images. Bargoti *et al.* [12] also employed the Faster R-CNN architecture for fruit detection. Based on this work, Liu *et al.* [13] integrated the fruit detection results in image sequences to perform object tracking. Although methods based on Mask R-CNN achieved excellent effects, they suffer from huge cost in labeling. Another group of architecture is the *singleshotdetector* (SSD), such as YOLO network, which predicting classes and bounding boxes in a single stage.

3 Methodology

The proposed methodology is divided into two parts. As shown in Fig. 1, firstly, locating the clusters in the images using detectors (Sect. 3.1). Secondly, exclude background information outside the detected boxes and count berries by Hough transform.

3.1 Grape Cluster Detector

YOLO network [14] is one of the state-of-the-art object detectors, we apply it to grape cluster detection. First, the image compressed into a fixed grid of

416 × 416 pixels, YOLO predicts its locations and its class in a single-step. A cell is responsible for performing a detection if a cluster center is over it. Each cell is associated to N boxes, and every box is composed of $(c_x, c_y, w, h, conf)$, where (c_x, c_y), w, s represents the cluster's center, witdth and height respectively, and $conf$ indicates the confidence that the detected box contains a cluster.

Next, extract features from the input image by feature extractor Cross-Stage Partial connections (CSP), to obtain a feature map, with size $S \times S$ pixels, and then divide the input image into $S \times S$ grid cells. Each cell predicts N boxes for C different grape classes, which forms a $(N \times 5 + C)$ vector. Then a $(N \times 5 + C) \times S \times S$ tensor will be generated. The training step tries to minimize a loss function defined over such a tensor, perform detection and classification in a single step.

3.2   Grape Berry Counter

We first convolve function with a Gaussian kernel for counting evaluation, the grape density should be

$$H(p) = \sum_{i=1}^{N} \delta(p - p_i) * G_{\sigma_p}, \sigma_p = \beta d^i$$

where β is the parameter, d^i is the Gaussian kernel proportional to the variance σ_p.

For the detected boxes predicted by cluster detection, we follow the method mentioned in [15], and determine sets of circles using circular Hough transform.

Detection of Reference Circles R. Reference grape berries are image patches showing distinct circular structures. Assuming that the most dominant circles in one image are berries.

Detection of Grape Berry Candidates C. Candidates for grape berry are all image patches which consist of at least a weak circular structure potentially showing one berry.

4   Experiment and Results

4.1   Experimental Settings

- **Datasets.** We train and test four networks on WGISD [7], which composed of 300 RGB images with 2048 × 1365 pixels, showing 4432 clusters from five different grape classes. Considering the limitation of computer memory, images are rescaled to 416 ∗ 416 pixels, and restored after predicting.
- **Parameter settings.** We employ the Keras-based implementation for Mask R-CNN[3]. For the YOLO networks, we employed Darknet[4].

---

[3] https://github.com/matterport/Mask_RCNN.
[4] https://github.com/AlexeyAB/darknet.

– **Setups.** Training is performed on a computer containing four NVDIA GeForce RTX GPUs (11 GB memory), a pair of Intel(R) Xeon(R) E5–2698 v3 CPUs, 192 GB RAM, and running Ubuntu 20.04 LTS.

Evaluation Metrics. In this paper, we use mean Average Precision (mAP) score to evaluate detection performance on grape images. mAP is default metric of precision in the PascalVOC Competition[5]. As shown in the 3 (b), Box^{TP} represents correctly detected boxes, Box^{FP}, Box^{FN} are similiar defintions. mAP was calculated under conditions of Intersection over Union (IoU) for a certain threshold from 0.3 to 0.8 step by 0.1, to evaluate the performance of the test set. IoU is specially important: higher value indicates better grape berries coverage, formaulated as follows:

$$IoU = \frac{|A \cap B|}{|A \cup B|} = \frac{Box^{TP}}{Box^{FP} + Box^{TP} + Box^{FN}}$$

where A $\cap$ B denotes the detected boxes and A $\cup$ B denotes the clusters respectively.

To evaluate the counting performance, we use Mean Absolute Error (MAE) [16], which defined as:

$$MAE = \frac{1}{N} \sum_{i=1}^{N} |C_i - C_i^{GT}|$$

where C_i is the estimated count and C_i^{GT} is the ground truth count associated to image i.

4.2   Result Discussion

Cluster Detection Results. Figure 2 (a) shows the training process of YOLOv4 network on WGISD. In order to prevent overfitting, we get weights from *Early Stopping Point*, which corresponds to the best performance point of the validation set.

Figure 2 (b) presents the results of cluster detection produced by four networks, considering the entire test set of 837 clusters in 58 images. YOLOv4 always keep the highest mAP score, especially better than the previous state-of-the-art method Mask R-CNN. Figure 3 (d) shows the predicted cluster boxes of YOLOv4 in Fig. 3 (a).

Compared to Mask R-CNN, YOLOv4 achieves better prediction results with less labeled data.

Grape Berry Counting Results. YOLOv4 enriched 96.96% cluster accuracy, which provides enough support for counting process.

---

[5] http://host.robots.ox.ac.uk/pascal/VOC/.

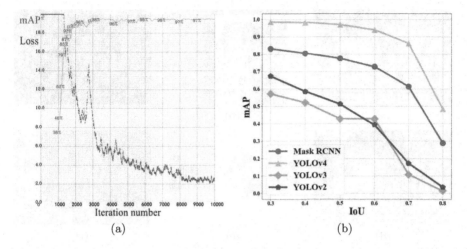

Fig. 2. Object Detection for test set of WGISD: Mask R-CNN, YOLOv4, YOLOv3, YOLOv2. (a) The iterative training process of YOLOv4. (b) The mAP score of four networks with the change of IoU threshold.

Since WGISD [7] only provides cluster detection labeling data, lacking of berry counting annotations. We manually annotated 58 images in test set using Huawei ModelArt. Considering the overlap of the same cluster of grapes in one image, we only label the berries, which expose more than three quarters of its size. The counting annotations are regarded as ground truth for evaluation.

In the berry counting experiments, we employ the Hough transform, setting with $minRad = 5$, $maxRad = 30$ and $sensitivity = 0.92$. We get berry candidates and introduce a simple classifier for each candidate, to estimate the probability of being berry.

Table 1. The counting results of WGISD test set.

Class	Images	Clusters	GroundTruth	Estimate	MAE	Overall MAE
CDY	15	180	3985	3688	**76.60**	297
CFR	10	159	4974	**4889**	168.30	85
CSV	9	111	3836	4350	128.44	514
SVB	14	283	5456	5774	137.86	318
SYH	10	117	3211	2413	142.80	798
Avg	11.6	170	**4292.4**	**4222.8**	149.41	614.4
Total	58	850	21462	21114	126.66	348

Table 1 results presents berries counting performance of our approach on WGISD test set. We report and analyze both the error per class and the overall error of 58 images.

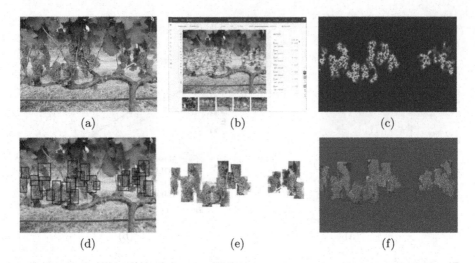

Fig. 3. Original images and corresponding grape berry density maps obtained by Gaussian kernels. (a) Original image. (b) Grape berry annotations on ModelArt platform. (c) The grape berry counting ground truth using density map. (d) Detected clusters from the original image. (e) Removing the pixels outside the detected clusters. (f) Grape berry counting results.

Considering the result that 4292.4 berries per image, our approach achieves 4222.8 MAE(1.621% the average accuracy gap), and the estimated counting results are shown in Fig. 3 (f). Compared with other four classes grape, the MAE error corresponding to SYH grape is 24.85%. The possible reason is that SYH grapes are small, the circle threshold C setting are too strict to identify berries with small radius. In contrast SVB grape, our method estimates 5774 berries, which is more than ground truth due to a certain missing error in labeling.

To be clear, there is no public dataset for evaluating grape counting. However, we manually annotated 58 images to verify the grape counting methods, and make it public with a benckmark. More researchers are welcome to improve the accuracy of grape counting.

5   Conclusions

In this paper, we presented an two-stage grape yield estimation method TSGYE. Through experimental comparison, we choose YOLOv4 as our grape cluster detector. In the second stage of berry counting, we manually annotated all test images of WGISD and made it public on github website with a benchmark method for grape berry counting.

More grape classes will be taken into consideration in further research, and deep learning berry counter will be also applied for improving counting accuracy.

Acknowledgements. This work was supported in part by the National Natural Science Foundation of China under grant No. 61972268 and No. 61906126, and is also supported by the project of Technology Innovation and Development of Chengdu Science and Technology Bureau (No.2019-YF05-01126-SN).

References

1. Nellithimaru, A.K., Kantor, G.A.: ROLS: Robust object-level SLAM for grape counting. In: Proceedings of the IEEE Conference on Computer Vision and Pattern Recognition Workshops, pp. 2648–2656 (2019)
2. Luo, L., Tang, Y., Lu, Q., Chen, X., Zhang, P., Zou, X.: A vision methodology for harvesting robot to detect cutting points on peduncles of double overlapping grape clusters in a vineyard. Comput. Ind. **99**, 130–139 (2018)
3. Nuske, S., Achar, S., Bates, T., Narasimhan, S.G., Singh, S.: Yield estimation in vineyards by visual grape detection. In: 2011 IEEE/RSJ International Conference on Intelligent Robots and Systems, pp. 2352–2358. IEEE (2011)
4. Barré, P., Herzog, K., Höfle, R., Hullin, M.B., Töpfer, R., Steinhage, V.: Automated phenotyping of epicuticular waxes of grapevine berries using light separation and convolutional neural networks. Comput. Electron. Agric. **156**, 263–274 (2019)
5. Naranjo-Torres, J., Mora, M., Hernández-García, R., Barrientos, R.J., Fredes, C., Valenzuela, A.: A review of convolutional neural network applied to fruit image processing. Appl. Sci. **10**(10), 3443 (2020)
6. Zabawa, L., Kicherer, A., Klingbeil, L., Töpfer, R., Kuhlmann, H., Roscher, R.: Counting of grapevine berries in images via semantic segmentation using convolutional neural networks. ISPRS J. Photogrammetry Remote Sens. **164**, 73–83 (2020)
7. Santos, T.T., de Souza, L.L., dos Santos, A.A., Avila, S.: Grape detection, segmentation, and tracking using deep neural networks and three-dimensional association. Comput. Electron. Agric. **170**, 105247 (2020)
8. Dunn, G.M., Martin, S.R.: Yield prediction from digital image analysis: a technique with potential for vineyard assessments prior to harvest. Aust. J. Grape Wine Res. **10**(3), 196–198 (2004)
9. Paul Cohen, J., Boucher, G., Glastonbury, C.A., Lo, H.Z., Bengio, Y.: Countception: counting by fully convolutional redundant counting. In: Proceedings of the IEEE International Conference on Computer Vision Workshops, pp. 18–26 (2017)
10. Aquino, A., Barrio, I., Diago, M.P., Millan, B., Tardaguila, J.: vitisBerry: an android-smartphone application to early evaluate the number of grapevine berries by means of image analysis. Comput. Electron. Agric. **148**, 19–28 (2018)
11. Nellithimaru, A.K., Kantor, G.A.: ROLS : robust object-level SLAM for grape counting. In: Proceedings of the IEEE Conference on Computer Vision and Pattern Recognition Workshops, pp. 2648–2656 (2019)
12. Bargoti, S., Underwood, J.: Deep fruit detection in orchards. In: 2017 IEEE International Conference on Robotics and Automation (ICRA), pp. 3626–3633. IEEE (2017)
13. Goodfelow, I., Bengio, Y., Courville, A.: Deep Learning (Adaptive Computation and Machine Learning Series). MIT Press (2016)
14. Bochkovskiy, A., Wang, C.Y., Liao, H.Y.M.: Yolov4: optimal speed and accuracy of object detection. arXiv preprint arXiv:2004.10934 (2020)

15. Roscher, R., Herzog, K., Kunkel, A., Kicherer, A., Töpfer, R., Förstner, W.: Automated image analysis framework for the high-throughput determination of grapevine berry sizes using conditional random fields. Comput. Electron. Agri. **100**, 148–158 (2017)
16. Coviello, L., Cristoforetti, M., Jurman, G., Furlanello, C.: In-field grape berries counting for yield estimation using dilated CNNS. arXiv preprint arXiv:1909.12083 (2019)

Unsupervised Reused Convolutional Network for Metal Artifact Reduction

Binyu Zhao[1], Jinbao Li[2]($\boxtimes$), Qianqian Ren[1]($\boxtimes$), and Yingli Zhong[1]

[1] Department of Computer Science and Technology, Heilongjiang University,
Harbin 150080, China
renqianqian@hlju.edu.cn
[2] Shandong Artificial Intelligence Institute, Qilu University of Technology
(Shandong Academy of Science), Jinan 250014, China
lijinb@sdas.org

Abstract. Nowadays computed tomography (CT) is widely used for medical diagnosis and treatment. However, CT images are often corrupted by undesirable artifacts when metallic implants are carried by patients, which could affect the quality of CT images and increase the possibility of false diagnosis and analysis. Recently, Convolutional Neural Network (CNN) was applied for metal artifact reduction (MAR) with synthesized paired images, which is not accurate enough to simulate the mechanism of imaging. With unpaired images, the first unsupervised model ADN appeared. But it is complicated in architecture and has distance to reach the level of existing supervised methods. To narrow the gap between unsupervised methods with supervised methods, this paper introduced a simpler multi-phase deep learning method extracting features recurrently to generate both metal artifacts and non-artifact images. Artifact Generative Network and Image Generative Network are presented jointly to remove metal artifacts. Extensive experiments show a better performance than ADN on synthesized data and clinical data.

Keywords: Metal artifact reduction · Convolutional Neural Networks · Medical imaging · Computed tomography

1 Introduction

Convolutional neural networks (CNNs) are becoming common means to solve metal artifact reduction (MAR) problems in recent years. While almost all CNN methods are supervised models training with paired images, which usually need to be synthesized [2,7]. Synthesizing paired images can not imperfectly simulate the physical mechanism of real clinical imaging and are not suitable for all CT images reconstructed by different CT devices. Performance degrading is inevitable when transferring the model to clinical images.

To avoid this trouble, Liao et al. introduce a novel unsupervised artifact disentanglement network (ADN) to disentangle metal artifacts from CT images in the latent space in a way of image translation [4]. But the architecture of ADN

© Springer Nature Switzerland AG 2020
H. Yang et al. (Eds.): ICONIP 2020, CCIS 1332, pp. 589–596, 2020.
https://doi.org/10.1007/978-3-030-63820-7_67

is complicated. Too many modules are introduced to assist to generate the target images. Thus the parameters of the total network are more than twice that of the target generators. Besides, their experimental results still show a certain gap comparing with supervised methods. It is more difficult to distinguish the whole metal artifacts and restore them with unpaired images.

In this paper, we propose a framework named Reused Convolutional Network (RCN) that attempts to narrow the gap between unsupervised methods with supervised methods with a simpler architecture. We transform the problem of removing metal artifacts to a generative problem by using CNNs to extract features to generate both metal artifacts and non-artifact images. We achieve it in unsupervised way by using our model twice, which also improves the utilization efficiency for the optimal model. We present the Artifact Generative Network to extract metal artifact information from artifact-affected images and the Image Generative Network to extract non-artifact information from both artifact-affected images and no-artifact-affected images. Compared to ADN, CNN modules can focus on single task which extracts the hidden features of the images.

The contributions of the paper is as followings:

(1) We propose an unsupervised network to achieve the task of metal artifact removal. Our network structure is simpler than ADN model.
(2) In order to achieve better performance in an unsupervised way, we propose two modules to extract artifact information and non-artifact information, respectively. Moreover we implement them twice to obtain optimal performance.
(3) We experiment out model in both synthesized dataset and clinical dataset, the experimental results show that we achieve a smaller gap between our unsupervised model with the existing advanced supervised models.

2 Related Work

Supervised Learning and Unsupervised Learning for MAR. Supervised methods are commonly proposed in recenrt years. Zhang et al. estimate a prior image in image domain to help the correction in the sinogram domain [7]. Gjesteby et al. include the NMAR-corrected CT as the input with a two-stream CNN to reduce secondary artifacts with perceptual loss [1]. Shen et al. use a recurrent and recursive network with dilation convolution and attention block to remove artifacts [3]. While, unsupervised method for MAR problem is in early stage. Liao et al. [4] propose the first unsupervised framework ADN last year. They disentangle metal artifacts from artifact-affected images, and fuse them with clean images to generate new artifact-affected CT images.

Generative Adversarial Networks for MAR. Though Generative adversarial networks (GANs) [8] might be hard to train, it generates clearer and more natural images. Conditional GAN (cGAN) and Markovian GAN (PatchGAN)

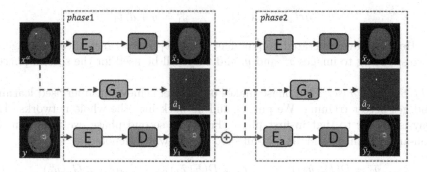

Fig. 1. Overview method. Modules with the same letters represent the same module.

have been applied to MAR recently. Wang et al. apply cGAN to reduce metal artifact in the CT image domain [5]. Liao et al. also introduce PatchGAN to discriminate whether the generative images is more likely a clean CT images [4]. After practice, we choose PatchGAN as part of our model, which is better than cGAN to sharper generated images and maintain image legibility in a high level under no-ground truth situation. Here the kernel size is three and the output size of discriminator is 40×40.

3 Reused Convolutional Network

Suppose that any artifact-affected image consists of an artifact component (metal artifacts, noises, etc.) and a non-artifact component (the anatomical structure). Based on this, Reused Convolutional Network (RCN) consists of an Artifact Generative Network (AGN) G_a to generate artifact-only images from the artifact-affected images, and an Image Generative Network (IGN), which contains two encoders E_a and E to learn non-artifact features from image space, and a decoder D to transform feature maps from the feature space back to the image domain to generate images more like a non-artifact image.

An overview is shown in Fig. 1. Given two unpaired images x^a and y, where x^a denotes a CT image with artifact, and y denotes a CT image without artifact. We need two different encoders to encode their own features. The procedure works in two phases:

The First Phase: When we put x^a and y into IGN, E_a and E encode their content components (or non-artifact features) as feature maps respectively. Then we consider to use a shared D to decode their non-artifact features and output artifact-free images $\hat{x}_1$ and $\hat{y}_1$. The E_a block and D block are key components since the clean CT images we expect rely on these two blocks to generate.

$$\hat{x}_1 = D(E_a(x^a)), \qquad \hat{y}_1 = D(E(y)) \qquad (1)$$

Moreover, we extract the artifact information from image $\hat{x}^a$ using AGN G_a, which is a U-Net like Pyramid network. Then the artifact-only image $\hat{art}_1$ will be combined with the image $\hat{y}_1$ to get a new artiact-affected image $\hat{y}_1^a$

$$\hat{art}_1 = G_a(x^a), \qquad \hat{y}_1^a = y + \hat{art}_1 \qquad (2)$$

Here we have generated non-artifact image $\hat{x}_1$ and artifact-affected image $\hat{y}_1^a$ corresponding to images x^a and y, and they will be used for the second phase.

The Second Phase: This phase makes out model achieve unsupervised learning and get better training. We put $\hat{x}_1$ and $\hat{y}_1^a$ back into the whole networks. The way is similar to that in first phase. From the second phase, we re-obtain the non-artifact image and artifact-affected image, which denoted as:

$$\hat{y}_2 = D(E_a(\hat{y}_1^a)), \qquad \hat{x}_2 = D(E(\hat{x}_1)), \qquad \hat{art}_2 = G_a(\hat{y}_1^a) \qquad (3)$$

Loss Function. Learning to generate two outputs $\hat{x}_1$ and $\hat{art}_1$ is crucial. Since there are no paired images, it is impossible to apply losses like L1 or L2 loss to minimize the difference between RCN's outputs and the ground truths. We introduce two discriminators D_a and D_i to adopt adversarial loss. These discriminators learn to distinguish whether an image is generated by RCN or sampled from dataset. Meanwhile, RCN learns to cheat D_a and D_i so that they cannot determine whether the outputs from RCN are generated images or real images. In this way, RCN can be trained without paired images.

$$\mathcal{L}_{adv}^a = \mathbb{E}[logD_a(x^a)] + \mathbb{E}[1 - logD_a(\hat{y}_1^a)] \qquad (4)$$

$$\mathcal{L}_{adv}^i = \mathbb{E}[logD_i(y)] + \mathbb{E}[1 - logD_i(\hat{x}_1)] \qquad (5)$$

Adversarial loss reduces metal artifacts but the images obtained in this way are only anatomically plausible not anatomically precise, i.e.,$\hat{y}_1$ and $\hat{y}_2$ may not be anatomically correspondent to y, the same problem also happens on x^a. There should be no information lost or model-introduced information during the encoding and decoding. We introduce two reconstruction losses to inherently encourage the encoders and decoders to preserve the original information. Here we use L1 loss to make outputs sharpener.

$$\mathcal{L}_{recx} = \mathbb{E}[||(\hat{x}_1 + \hat{art}_1) - x^a||_1 + ||(\hat{x}_2 + \hat{art}_2) - x^a||_1] \qquad (6)$$

$$\mathcal{L}_{recy} = \mathbb{E}[||\hat{y}_1 - y||_1 + ||\hat{y}_2 - y||_1] \qquad (7)$$

From two phases, we get two artifact images $\hat{art}_1$ and $\hat{art}_2$, and two artifact-free images $\hat{x}_1$ and $\hat{x}_2$. They should be same, we denote them as:

$$\mathcal{L}_{art} = \mathbb{E}[||\hat{art}_1 - \hat{art}_2||_1] \qquad (8)$$

$$\mathcal{L}_x = \mathbb{E}[||\hat{x}_1 - \hat{x}_2||_1] \qquad (9)$$

The total objective function is formulated as the weighted sum of these losses

$$\mathcal{L} = \lambda_{adv}(\mathcal{L}_{adv}^a + \mathcal{L}_{adv}^i) + \lambda_{art}\mathcal{L}_{art} + \lambda_x\mathcal{L}_x + \lambda_{recx}\mathcal{L}_{recx} + \lambda_{recy}\mathcal{L}_{recy} \qquad (10)$$

where λ's are the hyper-parameters that balance the weight of each loss.

4   Experiments

Dataset. We evaluate our proposed method on both synthesized dataset and clinical dataset. For synthesized dataset, we randomly select artifact-free CT images from DeepLesion [9], and to synthesize metal artifacts, we follow the method from CNNMAR [7]. We choose 1028 images used in the training set and 200 images used in the test set. All images are resized to 256×256. A total of 100 metal shapes are used in experiments and for each image 90 metal shapes used in the training set and 10 metal shapes used in the test set.

For clinical dataset, we choose the vertebrae localization and identification dataset from Spineweb. We split the CT images from this dataset into two groups, one with artifacts and the other without artifacts. The region HU values greater than 2,500 is identified as the metal regions. Then, CT images whose largest-connected metal regions have more than 400 pixels are selected as artifact-affected images. CT images with the largest HU values less than 2,000 are selected as artifact-free images. The size of each image is 256×256. After selection we get 734 images artifact-affected images and 3298 artifact-free images for training set. 183 artifact-affected images are retained as test set.

Implementation and Metrics. We implement out method under Pytorch [10] framework and use the Adam optimizer for training. The learning rate is initially set as 0.0001. As for hyperparameters, we use $\lambda_{adv} = 1.0$, $\lambda_{art} = \lambda_x = \lambda_{recx} = \lambda_{recy} = 10.0$ for both synthesized dataset and clinical dataset.

On synthesized dataset, we divide the training set into two parts with equivalent number of images, one part only use artifact-affected images and the other part only use artifact-free images. For supervised methods on clinical dataset, we need to synthesize metal artifacts using the way we approach in synthesized dataset for artifact-free images with clinical images. Then paired images are acquired for training the supervised methods. For unsupervised methods, each time we randomly select one artifact-affected image and one artifact-free image to solve the data imbalance problem.

For synthesized dataset, we choose Peak Signal-to-Noise Ratio (PSNR) and Structured Similarity Index (SSIM) for quantitative evaluations. For PSNR and SSIM, the higher the better. For clinical dataset, only qualitative evaluations are implemented since no ground truths are available.

Baselines. We compare the proposed method with five recent MAR methods. Three are supervised: MARGANs [6], cGANMAR [5], DuDoNet++ [12], and two methods, DeepMAR [11], ADN [4], are unsupervised. For ADN and cGANMAR, we train them with their officially released code. MARGANs, DuDoNet++ and DeepMAR are reimplemented by ourselves. Radon transform is used instead of Fanbeam transform when training DuDoNet++, therefore the performance may degrade.

Table 1. Quantitative evaluation on synthesized dataset (DeepLesion). Methods implemented by ourselves are marked with "*".

	Supervised			Unsupervised		
	MARGANs* [6]	cGANMAR [5]	DuDoNet++* [12]	DeepMAR* [11]	ADN [4]	Ours
PSNR	34.8	34.6	**35.7**	24.4	32.8	33.3
SSIM	88.4	92.9	**94.9**	44.5	91.1	91.5

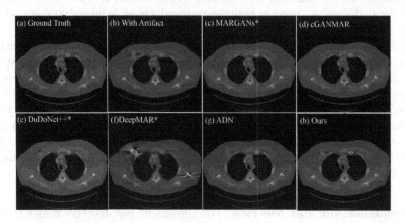

Fig. 2. Qualitative comparison with baseline methods on the synthesized dataset. The metal regions are segmented out through thresholding and colored in red. Methods implemented by ourselves are marked with "*".

Performance on Synthesized Dataset. Table 1 and Fig. 2 show the quantitative and qualitative evaluation results respectively. We observe that the performance of supervised methods cGANMAR and MARGANs are close. The structure of MARGANs and cGANMAR are both UNet-like, but using additional information to add conditions to the model to guide image generation makes cGANMAR perform better. While the performance of DuDoNet++ is better than these two GAN models, since it combines two domains, image domain and sinogram domain, to restore images. Though reducing metal artifact in sinogram introduces secondary artifact, Radon consistency loss and the following image enhancement network which input the output of sinogram enhancement network and original artifact-affected CT images makes the final images be corrected and better to retain the features of original non-artifact featrues.

DeepMAR delete the artifact-affected region to transform MAR problem to image inpainting. cGAN makes the output sharpener but the lack of the correction of secondary artifact makes the performance not well enough. When compared to the supervised method ADN, as a certain degree of error is inevitable, though the performance of two models might be in the same level, we have achieved a real improvement. The difference between these two methods is that ADN is based on the idea of image translation, while our model improves the utilization of the model and make the model only pay attention on the task of

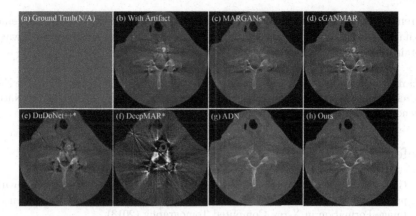

Fig. 3. Qualitative comparison with baseline methods on the clinical dataset. The metal regions are segmented out through thresholding and colored in red. Methods implemented by ourselves are marked with "*".

extraction. Therefore we achieve a progress. Besides, this also reflects that the performance training in larger dataset is better though the improvement is a little when referring to the experiment that Liao et al. [4] implemented.

Performance on Clinical Dataset. Here we analyze the performance on clinical dataset, which is shown in Fig. 3. Supervised methods MARGANs, cGAN-MAR and DuDoNet++ are trained with paired images synthesized from clean images of clinical dataset. We observe they can not output images well enough. MARGANs and cGANMAR reduce metal artifact only in image domain so the shadow and streak artifact is hard to remove. However DuDoNet++ reduce artifact also in sinogram domain, as the training metal artifact do not perfectly reconstruct the metal artifact from image, DuDoNet++ get into trouble with secondary artifact that conventional MAR method such as LI, NMAR, and CNN-MAR have. As for the unsupervised methods, DeepMAR has the same problems applied on synthesized dataset. In this no-label instance, ADN and our method show their capabilities suppressing metal shadows and removing artifact streaks. And we could observe closely that we restore the image information better.

5 Conclusion

In this paper, we present a two-phase method to produce clean images from metal artifact-affected images. Based on this method, we can remove metal artifact in an unsupervised way. To verify the efficiency of it, experimental evaluations have demonstrated a satisfying result narrowing the gap between our unsupervised learning and supervised learning methods for MAR problem. Our research further proves the feasibility of applying unsupervised methods to CT medical images, even perhaps other relevant or similar fields. Considering the limitations of removing metal artifacts only in image domain, we will try to combine remove artifact in image domain with in sinogram domain in an unsupervised way to obtain more clear images.

Acknowledgement. This work was supported in part by Heilongjiang Province Natural Science Foundation key project of China under Grant No. ZD2019F003, the Natural Science Foundation of Heilongjiang Province under Grant No. F2018028.

References

1. Gjesteby, L., et al.: Deep neural network for ct metal artifact reduction with a perceptual loss function. In: Proceedings of The Fifth International Conference on Image Formation in X-ray Computed Tomography (2018)
2. Sakamoto, M., et al.: Automated segmentation of hip and thigh muscles in metal artifact contaminated CT using CNN. In: International Forum on Medical Imaging in Asia 2019 (2019)
3. Shen, T., Li, X., Zhong, Z., Wu, J., Lin, Z.: R^2-Net: recurrent and recursive network for sparse-view CT artifacts removal. In: Shen, D., et al. (eds.) MICCAI 2019. LNCS, vol. 11769, pp. 319–327. Springer, Cham (2019). https://doi.org/10.1007/978-3-030-32226-7_36
4. Liao, H., Lin, W.-A., Yuan, J., Zhou, S.K., Luo, J.: Artifact disentanglement network for unsupervised metal artifact reduction. In: Shen, D., et al. (eds.) MICCAI 2019. LNCS, vol. 11769, pp. 203–211. Springer, Cham (2019). https://doi.org/10.1007/978-3-030-32226-7_23
5. Wang, J., Zhao, Y., Noble, J.H., Dawant, B.M.: Conditional generative adversarial networks for metal artifact reduction in CT images of the ear. In: Frangi, A.F., Schnabel, J.A., Davatzikos, C., Alberola-López, C., Fichtinger, G. (eds.) MICCAI 2018. LNCS, vol. 11070, pp. 3–11. Springer, Cham (2018). https://doi.org/10.1007/978-3-030-00928-1_1
6. Wang, Z., et al.: Deep learning based metal artifacts reduction in post-operative cochlear implant CT imaging. In: Shen, D., et al. (eds.) MICCAI 2019. LNCS, vol. 11769, pp. 121–129. Springer, Cham (2019). https://doi.org/10.1007/978-3-030-32226-7_14
7. Zhang, Y., Yu, H.: Convolutional neural network based metal artifact reduction in X-ray computed tomography. IEEE Trans. Med. Imaging **37**(6), 1370–1381 (2018)
8. Goodfellow, I.J., et al.: Generative adversarial networks. arXiv:1406.2661 (2014)
9. Yan, K., Wang, X., Lu, L., Summers, R.M.: DeepLesion: automated mining of large-scale lesion annotations and universal lesion detection with deep learning. J. Med. Imaging. **5**(3), 036501 (2018)
10. Paszke, A., et al.: Pytorch: an imperative style, high-performance deep learning library. In: Advances in Neural Information Processing Systems, pp. 8026–8037 (2019)
11. Ghani, M.-U., Karl, W.-C.: Fast enhanced CT metal artifact reduction using data domain deep learning. IEEE Trans. Comput. Imaging **6**, 181–193 (2020)
12. Lyu, Y., Lin, W.-A., Liao, H., Lu, J., Zhou, S.K.: Encoding metal mask projection for metal artifact reduction in computed tomography. In: Martel, A.L., et al. (eds.) MICCAI 2020. LNCS, vol. 12262, pp. 147–157. Springer, Cham (2020). https://doi.org/10.1007/978-3-030-59713-9_15

Visual-Based Positioning and Pose Estimation

Somnuk Phon-Amnuaisuk[1,2]([ID]), Ken T. Murata[3], La-Or Kovavisaruch[4],
Tiong-Hoo Lim[1], Praphan Pavarangkoon[3], and Takamichi Mizuhara[5]

[1] Media Informatics Special Interest Group, CIE, Universiti Teknologi Brunei,
Gadong, Brunei
{somnuk.phonamnuaisuk,lim.tiong.hoo}@utb.edu.bn
[2] School of Computing and Information Technology, Universiti Teknologi Brunei,
Gadong, Brunei
[3] National Institute of Information and Communications Technology, Tokyo, Japan
{ken.murata,praphan}@nict.go.jp
[4] National Electronics and Computer Technology Center (NECTEC), Khlong Luang,
Thailand
La-Or.Kovavisaruch@nectec.or.th
[5] CLEALINKTECHNOLOGY Co., Ltd., Kyoto, Japan
mizuhara@clealink.jp

Abstract. Recent advances in deep learning and computer vision offer
an excellent opportunity to investigate high-level visual analysis tasks
such as human localization and human pose estimation. Although the
performances of human localization and human pose estimation have significantly improved in recent reports, they are not perfect, and erroneous
estimation of position and pose can be expected among video frames.
Studies on the integration of these techniques into a generic pipeline
robust to those errors are still lacking. This paper fills the missing study.
We explored and developed two working pipelines that suited visual-
based positioning and pose estimation tasks. Analyses of the proposed
pipelines were conducted on a badminton game. We showed that the concept of tracking by detection could work well, and errors in position and
pose could be effectively handled by linear interpolation of information
from nearby frames. The results showed that the *Visual-based Positioning and Pose Estimation* could deliver position and pose estimations
with good spatial and temporal resolutions.

Keywords: Object detection · Visual-based positioning · Pose
estimation

1 Introduction

In this paper, a study of a badminton game analyses is discussed. The players' positions on the badminton court and their skeleton poses[1] were extracted

---

[1] Action analysis based on a skeleton figure, i.e., a stick man figure.

© Springer Nature Switzerland AG 2020
H. Yang et al. (Eds.): ICONIP 2020, CCIS 1332, pp. 597–605, 2020.
https://doi.org/10.1007/978-3-030-63820-7_68

from a sequence of images. This work proposed a pipeline of deep learning and computer vision tasks that extracted players' movements and actions from an image sequence. In summary, players' positions were detected and tracked using Mask R-CNN [1]. The positions were read from a 2D camera view coordinate and were transformed into 2D top-view positions in the world coordinate. The players' positions across a frame sequence would reveal their movements across time; analyzing each player's pose would then reveal their actions. These two sources of information could be employed in further high-level visual analytic tasks.

We coined the following two terms to facilitate the presentation and discussion in this paper: Outside-in Vision-based Positioning (OV-Positioning) workflow and Skeleton-based 3D Pose (S3D-Pose) estimation workflow. Outside-in referred to the fact that an external camera was used to track the agents in the scene. The term *outside-in* was borrowed from the augmented reality and virtual reality (AR/VR) community[2].

This paper reports our *work in progress* from the *ASEAN-IVO* project titled *Event Analysis: Applications of computer vision and AI in the smart tourism industry*. The techniques and findings reported in this study are applicable to scenes in airports, bus depots and museums. The contributions of this application paper are from: (i) the Outside-in Vision-based Positioning (OV-Positioning) workflow, and (ii) the Skeleton-based 3D Pose (S3D-Pose) estimation workflow. The rest of the materials in this paper are organized into the following sections; Sect. 2 describes related works; Sect. 3 describes the OV-Positioning, and the S3D-Pose workflows; Sect. 4 presents the evaluations, and Sect. 5 provides the conclusions and future direction.

2   Related Works

Human Activity Recognition (HAR) is a popular open research problem. Recognizing human activities from a 2D image is a challenging problem since further detailed distinctions of objects in the same class must be identified, i.e., to identify various humans' actions from the same human class. Since image data does not explicitly encode activity information, relevant discriminative features must be extracted from image data first. This makes vision-based HAR (VHAR) a complex problem in comparison to formulating and solving HAR using other types of sensors for example, using accelerometer data to track body or limb movements, or using radio frequency tag (RFID) to track where activities take place. Although the VHAR approach requires extra processing efforts to extract relevant discriminative features, it has many attractive points when its practicality is considered. Since humans recognize activities mainly from vision, the VHAR deployment often requires a minimum or no extra environmental preparation.

---

[2] AR/VR applications could either track the position of a head mounted display unit in a 3D world space using external sensors (outside-in) or using internal sensors (inside-out) equipped on the head-mounted display device.

VHAR problems are commonly formulated from an image recognition task perspective. Representing an image as a feature vector derived from the whole image is a common option. The original pixels information may also be preprocessed and transformed to enhance salient information: grayscale, binary silhouette for displaying the shape of an object, Histogram of Gradient (HOG), Scale Invariant Feature Transformation (SIFT); or be transformed to other representation schemes: space-time interest points (STIPs) [2], sparse representations and, representation extracted from CNN feature maps [3]. Recent works in this direction capture activities using techniques such as concept hierarchical of actions [4], action graph model and scene graph generation model [5].

Activities in a sports can be described based on the players' movements and actions. It seems intuitive that determining a player's position and skeletal pose should provide expressive information for the task. Object detection techniques such as Mask R-CNN [1] provide means to identify and track object instances in the scene.

Object detection technique can also be employed to detect key-points in the human body such as head, shoulders, elbows, knees, without markers. With advances of deep learning and computer vision techniques in the past decade, human pose estimation techniques have improved significantly [6,7]. CNNs were employed to identify 2D key-points of the human body [8–10] from unconstrained images. There are always many possible 3D interpretations of a 2D pose due to an extra dimension. Fortunately, physical constraints of human anatomy and intraframe information (in case of an image sequence) can be applied to filter out improbable 3D pose interpretations. In [11,12], the authors demonstrated approaches to transform human pose in 2D space to 3D space using deep learning techniques.

3   A Study of a Badminton Game Analyses

Traditional analyses of a badminton game were carried out manually by a human expert analyzing the movement of players, the opportunity to score and the errors made. Statistics of players' performance can reveal useful insights. Due to a lack of sophisticated video analysis techniques, this information is manually entered, and it is a bottleneck of the manual approach. By leveraging deep learning and computer vision techniques, players' movements and actions can be automatically extracted from video frames, overcoming the restriction of the manual approach.

A more in-depth insight of the badminton game may be revealed by associating the position and action of players to their scoring performance. In this section, we are going to discuss the proposed pipeline of tasks that automate the position and pose analysis from an image sequence: OV-Positioning and S3D-Pose.

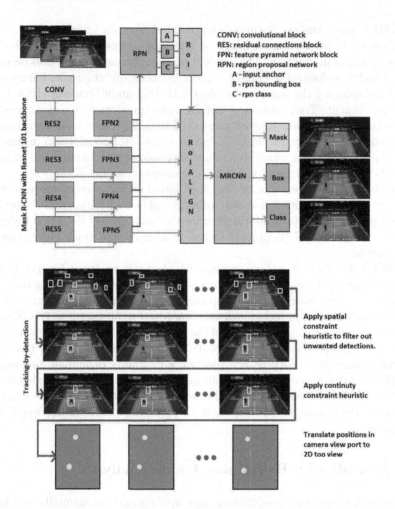

Fig. 1. Top pane: Image frames from a camera are processed by Mask R-CNN, players' positions and bounding boxes are determined. The three images on the right show output examples of the detection from Mask R-CNN. Bottom pane: Details the processing pipeline from 2D positions in camera view to a 2D top-view in the world space. Detection: Mask R-CNN detects multiple objects which could be noisy (top row). Tracking-by-detection: various heuristics are applied to filter out undesired boxes (row 2 & 3). At the final stage, players' positions are translated from the camera viewport into top-view in world space (bottom row).

3.1 Outside-In Vision-Based Positioning Workflow (OV-Positioning)

The OV-Positioning workflow consisted of the following tasks: object detection, tracking-by-detection, and translation to the positions in the world coordinates. Figure 1 shows a graphical summary of the OV-Positioning workflow.

Object Detection. A sequence of image frames, each with 852×472 (width $\times$ height in pixels), were passed through the object detection block. Here, Mask R-CNN with Resnet-101 backbone[3] was employed for human detection. ResNet is a convolutional neural network with skip connections. This seemingly simple modification improves learning and performance of the deep network significantly. Mask R-CNN is the current state-of-the-art semantic segmentation technique. It provides high-quality bounding box output of objects. This is achieved from the combination of Feature Pyramidal Network (FPN), Region Proposal Network (RPN) and RoIAlign, which effectively exploits information in the feature maps at different scales and with precise pixel alignment (than older techniques in Faster R-CNN [13]).

Tracking-by-Detection. Tracking-by-detection operates on the assumption that object tracking can be simply derived from object detection, provided that an effective object detector can detect objects with good spatial accuracy and high resolution in time. In real life applications, detection errors should be expected and dealt with. In this badminton game analysis task, the Mask R-CNN returned many detected objects. Here, the following heuristics were implemented: (i) a spatial constraint was applied to filter out all detected objects not in the badminton court. This heuristic ensured that only two players were detected; (ii) a continuity in spatial space was applied across frames. This heuristic filtered out erroneously detected boxes that resulted in a big jump in spatial space, and finally (iii) there were only two detected players in each frame. This heuristic dealt with extra detected boxes (false positive) or missing detected boxes (false negative). The missing detection or extra detections could be dealt with based on the information of the boxes from other frames.

Perspective Transformation Between Planes. The position of a human in the scene on the floor (x,y) coordinate (i.e., a virtual top-view camera) can be transformed from the position obtained from the camera view. This process is known as homography transformation. In the first stage, the players' positions $\mathbf{p}(x_c, y_c)$ were detected on the camera viewport. We apply the perspective transformation to transform the camera viewport plane to its corresponding 2D top-view in the world coordinate $\mathbf{p}(x_w, y_w)$ using the homography matrix H; $P_w = HP_c$. The homography matrix was estimated based on at least four known badminton court coordinates in the camera view and the corresponding coordinates in the world view.

3.2 Skeleton-Based 3D Pose Estimation Workflow (S3D-Pose)

A graphical summary of the S3D-Pose estimation workflow is shown in Fig. 2. The S3D-Pose estimation workflow consisted of the following tasks: object detection, tracking-by-detection, 2D pose estimation and 3D pose estimation from a

---

[3] Matterport.

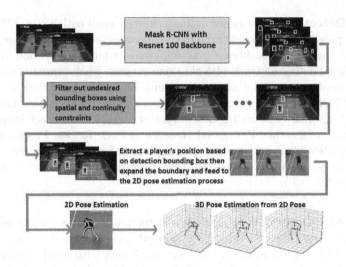

Fig. 2. The processing pipeline for 3D pose estimation: Mask R-CNN detects players location in the scene. The player bounding box is expanded, and key points in the 2D view are extracted. The 3D pose is estimated based on the 2D pose.

2D pose. It should be noted that the processing of Mask R-CNN, object detection, and tracking by detection processes were shared with the OV-Positioning discussed in the previous section.

The image patch of a player was then extracted with an extra 30-pixels expansion in all four directions, i.e., up, down, left and right. This was to ensure that the player's full body was captured as the bounding box from the object detection process is commonly designed to fit the object. We leverage on the implementation from [11], *Lifting from the Deep (LD)*, for the 2D and 3D pose estimation. LD fused probabilistic knowledge of 3D human poses with a multi-stage CNN architecture and used the knowledge of plausible 3D landmark locations to refine the search for better 2D locations.

The 3D poses extracted from 2D poses might not be consistent. It was possible for 3D poses to go missing or be misinterpreted in some frames. We applied (i) linear interpolation to fill in the 3D poses from any given two keyframes; and (ii) inter-frames continuity constraint to fix the abnormal jerking of positions between consecutive frames.

4   Evaluation of Position and Pose Estimation

We evaluated the output from the OV-Positioning workflow by comparing the projected top-view position obtained from the homography transformation against the footage obtained from a top-view camera. Fortunately, some games between the two players were also presented from a top-view camera. We manually marked the positions of the two players from the top-view camera as a

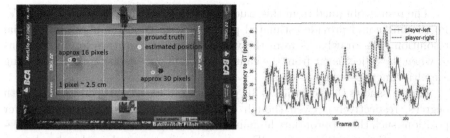

Fig. 3. The estimated positions obtained from the OV-Positioining process are compared with the ground truth positions. From the current setup, the discrepancy of one pixel is approximately 2.5 cm. The estimated positions of the player further from the camera are less accurate (the player on the right part of the frame).

ground truth. The comparison between the projected positions and the ground truth positions are shown in Figs. 3. We discovered that the estimated positions of players nearer to the camera had an average error of 13 pixels (equivalent to 32 cm. in our setup), and for players further from the camera, the average error was 25 pixels (62 cm). Erroneous results were correlated with fast movements which could easily be mitigated by a higher frame sampling rate.

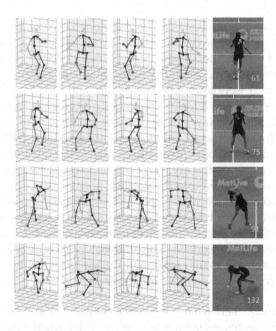

Fig. 4. The 3D skeleton lifted from the 2D skeleton which was interpreted from the 2D image on the rightmost column. Four skeletons are displayed at 30, 120, 210, and 300 azimuth degrees, respectively.

The results obtained from this study are very promising. We found that OV-Positioning could provide estimated positions with good temporal and spatial resolution. The drawbacks from the visual-based approach are from occlusions or when the object is far from the camera. These issues can be approached using a multi-camera system.

Figure 4 shows the skeletons in 3D positions (at 30, 120, 210, and 300 azimuth degrees, respectively). Even though OV-positioning provided accurate player positions such that appropriate human images were fed to the S3D-Pose for skeleton pose estimations, erroneous 3D poses were common and need to be cleaned up. We resorted to the *inbetweening* technique to fill in-between frames between any two keyframes. Firstly, outlier frames were identified as erroneous frames using handcrafted constraints. The outlier frame was the frame with an improbable movement of keypoints from the previous frame to the next frame. After good keyframes and erroneous keyframes were identified, two suitable frames were selected as the two keyframes. Subsequently, the keypoints of the sandwiched outlier frame were interpolated from the selected keyframes. In the case of multiple sandwiched frames, the interpolation was performed recursively. The process consisted of filling a frame from the middle point then repeating the process with newly added keyframes.

5   Conclusion and Future Directions

Activities in a badminton game can be described based on the players' actions in each image, e.g., the player serves the shuttlecock. In this context, analyzing physical activities from the skeletal poses is more effective than confabulating an image caption using the similarity of image labels [14].

We present two workflows: OV-Positioning and S3D-Pose for position and pose analysis, respectively. The OV-Positioning estimates a position using visual information. It offers many salient features compared to other positioning approaches such as traditional indoor positioning systems (IPS) using WiFi or Bluetooth beacon technology. As discussed above, the OV-Positioning performs visual analyses to extract the agents' positions in the scene. Therefore, an extra WiFi system is not required to estimate their positions. The estimated positions from OV-Positioning has a better spatial resolution and less latency than the estimation obtained from traditional wireless indoor position systems. S3D-Pose estimates human poses in 3D. This offers many salient features since human pose in 3D are invariant to viewpoints. The approach is effective for physical activity identification tasks and could enable multi-disciplinary studies in various areas such as sports science and enhance broadcasting experience.

Acknowledgments. This publication is the output of the ASEAN IVO (http:// www.nict.go.jp/en/asean_ivo/index.html) project titled *Event Analysis: Applications of computer vision and AI in smart tourism industry* and financially supported by NICT (http://www.nict.go.jp/en/index.html). We would also like to thank anonymous reviewers for their constructive comments and suggestions.

References

1. He, K., Gkioxari, G., Dollár, P., Girshick, R.: Mask R-CNN. arXiv:1703.06870v3 (2018)
2. Laptev, I., Lindeberg, T.: Space-time interest points. In: Proceedings of the 9th IEEE International Conference on Computer Vision, Nice, France, vol. 1, pp. 432–439 (2003)
3. Mo, L., Li, F., Zhu, Y., Huang, A.: Human physical activity recognition based on computer vision with deep learning model. In: Proceedings of the IEEE International Conference on Instrumentation and Measurement Technology, Taipei, Taiwan, pp. 1–6 (2016)
4. Kojima, A., Tamura, T., Fukunaga, K.: Natural language description of human activities from video images based on concept hierarchical of actions. Int. J. Comput. Vis. **50**(2), 171–184 (2002)
5. Xu, D., Zhu, Y., Choy, C.B., Li, F.F.: Scene graph generation by iterative message passing. In: Proceedings of the IEEE Conference on Computer Vision and Pattern Recognition, (CVPR 2017), pp. 5410–5419 (2017)
6. Shotton, J., et al.: Real-time human pose recognition in parts from single depth images. In: Proceedings of the IEEE Computer Society Conference on Computer Vision and Pattern Recognition (CVPR 2011), pp. 1297–1304 (2011)
7. Toshev, A., Szegedy, C.: Deeppose: human pose estimation via deep neural networks. In: Proceedings of the IEEE Computer Society Conference on Computer Vision and Pattern Recognition (CVPR 2014), pp. 1297–1304 (2011)
8. Tompson, J., Goroshin, R., Jain, A., LeCun, Y., Bregler, C.: Efficient object localization using convolutional networks. arXiv:1411.4280v3 (2015)
9. Wei, S.E., Ramakrishna, V., Kanade, T., Sheikh, Y.: Convolutional pose machine. In: Proceedings of the IEEE Computer Society Conference on Computer Vision and Pattern Recognition (CVPR 2016) (2016)
10. Newell, A., Yang, K., Deng, J.: Stacked hourglass networks for human pose estimation. In: Leibe, B., Matas, J., Sebe, N., Welling, M. (eds.) ECCV 2016. LNCS, vol. 9912, pp. 483–499. Springer, Cham (2016). https://doi.org/10.1007/978-3-319-46484-8_29
11. Tome, D., Russell, C., Agapito, L.: Lifting from the deep: convolutional 3D pose estimation from a single image. In: Proceedings of the IEEE Conference on Computer Vision and Pattern Recognition (CVPR 2017) (2017)
12. Kudo, Y., Ogaki, K., Matsui, Y., Odagiri, Y.: Unsupervised adversarial learning of 3D human pose from 2D joint locations. arXiv:1803.08244v1 (2018)
13. Ren, S., He, K., Girshick, R., Sun, J.: Faster R-CNN: towards real-time object detection with region proposal networks. In: Proceedings of the International Conference on Advances in Neural Information Processing Systems (NIPS), pp. 91–99 (2015)
14. Phon-Amnuaisuk, S., Murata, K.T., Pavarangkoon, P., Mizuhara, T., Hadi, S.: Children activity descriptions from visual and textual associations. In: Chamchong, R., Wong, K.W. (eds.) MIWAI 2019. LNCS (LNAI), vol. 11909, pp. 121–132. Springer, Cham (2019). https://doi.org/10.1007/978-3-030-33709-4_11

Voxel Classification Based Automatic Hip Cartilage Segmentation from Routine Clinical MR Images

Najini Harischandra[1]($\boxtimes$), Anuja Dharmaratne[1], Flavia M. Cicuttini[2], and YuanYuan Wang[2]

[1] School of IT, Monash University Malaysia, Bandar Sunway, Malaysia
{najini.arachchige,anuja}@monash.edu
[2] Department of Epidemiology and Preventive Medicine, Monash University, Melbourne, Australia
{flavia.cicuttini,yuanyuan.wang}@monash.edu

Abstract. Hip Osteoarthritis (OA) is a common pathological condition among the elderly population, which is mainly characterized by cartilage degeneration. Accurate segmentation of the cartilage tissue over MRIs facilitates quantitative investigations into the disease progression. We propose an automated approach to segment the hip joint cartilage as a single unit from routine clinical MRIs utilizing a voxel-based classification approach. We extracted a rich feature set from the MRIs, which consisting of normalized image intensity-based, local image structure-based, and geometry-based features. We have evaluated the proposed method using routine clinical hip MR images taken from asymptomatic elderly and diagnosed OA patients. MR images from both cohorts show full or partial loss of thickness due to aging or hip OA progression. The proposed algorithm shows good accuracy compared to the manual segmentations with a mean DSC value of 0.74, even with a high prevalence of cartilage defects in the MRI dataset.

Keywords: Cartilage segmentation · MRI · Hip osteoarthritis

1 Introduction

Osteoarthritis (OA) is the most common musculoskeletal disease which causes disability in the elderly population, especially in developed countries [7]. OA is a long-term chronic arthritic disease characterized by the deterioration of the cartilage in joints, pain, and swelling [13]. The disease affects large weight-bearing joints such as knee and hip, with a high prevalence of knee OA and more severe cases of hip OA. Magnetic Resonance Imaging (MRI) allows quantitative assessment of cartilage (e.g. cartilage volume, thickness), which leads to the diagnosis of OA in earlier stages. Accurate segmentation of cartilage provides a basis for quantitative analyses of OA and thus bring about great clinical interest in computer-assisted tools to quantitatively analyze cartilage morphology.

© Springer Nature Switzerland AG 2020
H. Yang et al. (Eds.): ICONIP 2020, CCIS 1332, pp. 606–614, 2020.
https://doi.org/10.1007/978-3-030-63820-7_69

There have been a few attempts to automatically segment the cartilage from hip MRIs utilizing traditional image processing algorithms, such as thresholding and edge detection [8, 11], multi-atlas [12], graph cut [16], shape priors [1] based methods. Some most recent studies have utilized machine learning based segmentation algorithms to extract femoral and acetabulum plates separately. An ensemble of neural networks has been trained on high-resolution MR images to segment the femoral and acetabular cartilage plates separately automatically [18]. A deep convolutional neural network, trained on 4530 MR image slices [5], show lower accuracy compared to the graph cut based method [16]. Most of these methods have utilized high-resolution MR image sequences (DESS, True-FISP, MEDIC, SPACE, and dGEMRIC) in training and testing phases [1, 16, 18]. Further, only the robust shape priors based algorithm has been evaluated over routine clinical MR images from a cohort representing the OA patients with cartilage deformities due to the disease progression. However, the study shows lower accuracy (mean DSC of 0.324) for routine clinical MR images from hip OA patients [10]. More studies are needed to evaluate the feasibility of segmenting hip cartilage tissue automatically from MRIs taken from adults with cartilage degeneration.

In this study, we propose a voxel classification based segmentation approach to extract the cartilage plane as a single unit from routine clinical hip MRIs from adults.

2 Materials and Methods

2.1 MRI Acquisition and Dataset

MR images were acquired from thirty-one healthy adults (aged 50–85, 13 males, 18 females) and nine diagnosed OA patients (aged 50–79, 5 males, 4 females). The dominant side of the hip (89% right-sided), had been imaged from healthy adults. The affected side of the hip was selected for imaging from the OA patients. All the hips were imaged on a 3.0-T whole-body magnetic resonance unit on the sagittal plane using a T2-weighted Fat-Suppressed 3D Gradient-Recalled Acquisition sequence in the Steady State (3D FS-GRASS) (repetition time 14.45 ms, echo time 5.17 ms, acquisition time 7 min 47 s, flip angle 25°, the field of view 16 cm, slice thickness 1.5 mm, slices 64, pixel matrix 320 × 320).

2.2 Manual Segmentation

The manual labeling of the cartilage area was done on every slice of the MR image sets by rater 1 under the guidance of an experienced radiologist. The obtained ground truth was validated using an inter- and intra-rater reliability assessment. Three image sets were randomly selected from both OA patients and non-OA participants cohorts and manually segmented by rater 2, to investigate inter-rater reliability. Further, these six MR images were re-segmented in a blinded fashion three months later by rater 1 for the evaluation of intra-rater reproducibility.

2.3   Automated Cartilage Segmentation

We propose a voxel classification-based approach to segment cartilage as a single unit combining the femoral and acetabulum planes from routine clinical hip MRIs. The cartilage is extracted The overall segmentation pipeline (Fig. 1) is described below, starting with pre-processing techniques.

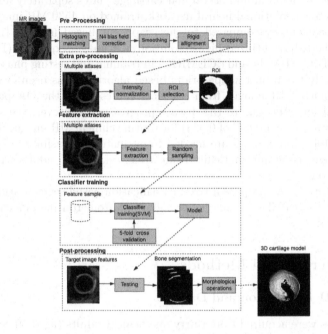

Fig. 1. Flowchart of the proposed voxel classification based cartilage segmentation pipeline

Pre-processing. All images were re-sampled to have isotropic (1 mm) pixels and pre-processed using below steps.

1. N4 bias field correction [14] (Truncate image intensity: [0.001 0.999], Shrink factor: 3, Convergence: [maximum number of iterations at each resolution = 200 × 150 × 100, convergence threshold = 0.001], B-spline fitting: [spline distance = 200, spline order = 3])
2. Smoothing using gradient anisotropic diffusion (10 iterations, time step: 0.02, conductance: 1.0)
3. Rigidly aligned to a reference image (ID = 165) using Insight segmentation and registration toolkit (ITK) [6]
4. Normalize intensity values of all images to [0, 1] followed by histogram matching

As the final step, we cropped the images to a targeted region of interest (ROI), focusing on the articular cartilage of the hip joint. For each MR image, the cropping size was calculated considering the center and the radius of the femoral head. The femoral head center was estimated using Hough transform and sphere fitting [8].

Solution to the Class-Imbalance Problem. Even after cropping, less than 1% of voxels belong to cartilage tissue. Training on a highly imbalanced dataset would result in a higher misclassification rate for the minority class. Thus, we added a step to extract the Bone Cartilage Interface (BCI) as the ROI for further processing. First, a cartilage probability map was created using all the manual cartilage segmentation. The initial BCI was extracted along the femoral head and acetabulum bone edges considering the voxels having a non-zero probability of being cartilage tissue. The final BCI was constructed by iteratively evolving the initial BCI along the profile normal to its surface and checking for cartilage tissue as proposed in [3].

Feature Extraction. Hip cartilage is located in the deep acetabulum socket of the hip joint and has a thin and round structure. Thus, cartilage can not be extracted by utilizing intensity-based features only for a binary classifier. Therefore, to increase the accuracy of the proposed segmentation approach, we incorporated three types of features: intensity-based, local image structure based, and geometric information based.

Normalized image intensity values were taken from the pre-processed images as the first feature. Local image structure based measurements were obtained by calculating image gradients using the central difference gradient operator. First, gradient values were calculated along the three axes (2D Gradient). Equation (1) shows the calculation of x derivative for a given image I. Next, 3D gradient magnitude based features were calculated over small cube-shaped neighborhoods with sizes 3, 5, and 7. The 3D gradient magnitude can be calculated using Eq. (2), where G_x, G_y, and G_z are directional gradients along each axis, respectively. Further, the mean and the variance were calculated for the obtained 3D gradient magnitude values over the small neighborhoods. The last local image structure based features were the three Eigenvalues of the Hessian image for each voxel [19].

$$dI/dx = \frac{I(x+1) - I(x-1)}{2} \tag{1}$$

$$mag(G_x, G_y, G_z) = \sqrt{G_x^2 + G_y^2 + G_z^2} \tag{2}$$

Next, three geometric based features were obtained considering the anatomical structure of the hip joint while relying on the pre-segmented proximal femur and acetabulum bone surfaces. We automatically segmented the proximal femur and the innominate bone surfaces from all MR images utilizing the work of [17]. We further manually refined the bone surfaces before incorporating them into this work. We estimated the femoral head center using hough transform and sphere fitting [8]. Then, relying on the obtained bone surfaces and the femoral head center, geometrical features per each voxel were calculated. Per each voxel, the closest Euclidean distance (3D) to the proximal femur surface, and the innominate bone and the angle between the main magnetic field direction of the MRI and the line connects the voxel to the femoral head center were calculated. Incorporating the manual bone segmentation helped to distinguish the cartilage from muscles and bone marrow lesions. The final set of features used in this study consists of normalized intensity value, 11 local image structure-based features, and three geometrical features. For further processing of the segmentation pipeline, each image voxel was represented using a 15-dimensional feature vector.

Classification Model. We utilized the Support Vector Machine (SVM) [9] as the binary classifier in the proposed segmentation pipeline. SVM is a supervised machine learning algorithm based on statistical learning theory. SVM is considered as a maximum margin classifier which has strong generalization properties and hence has been used in many medical image segmentation tasks.

3   Experiments and Results

3.1   Experimental Setup

We utilized the Gaussian RBF kernel in SVM and tuned the parameters, the regularization parameter C and the Gaussian RBF's variance σ using grid search approach. The grid range for C and σ was $\{2^{-20}, 2^{-18}, \cdots, 2^{18}, 2^{20}\}$ using a 5-fold cross-validation method. We conducted a leave one subject out validation approach to evaluate the performance of the proposed hip cartilage segmentation pipeline. For each MR image, the feature matrix was generated for the extracted BCI. Each test image was segmented using the model trained on the rest of 39 MR images. All the experiments were done on a four Intel Xeon E5-2640 v4 processor 4-core 2.4 GHz local cluster system. Accuracy of the cartilage segmentation was evaluated using five area overlap and distance-based metrics: Dice Similarity Coefficient (DSC) [2], sensitivity, specificity, Mean Absolute Surface Distance (MASD) [4], and Relative Absolute Volume Distance (RAVD) [15].

Table 1. Comparison of validation metrics between manual and automatic segmentation for different MR image cohorts (no. of MR image sets)

	All MR images (40)		OA patients cohort (9)		Non-OA participants cohort (31)	
	Mean	SD	Mean	SD	Mean	SD
DSC	0.740	0.052	0.676	0.062	0.759	0.031
Sensitivity	0.708	0.068	0.661	0.728	0.721	0.061
Specificity	0.997	0.001	0.997	0.001	0.998	0.001
MASD (mm)	1.418	0.207	1.657	0.284	1.349	0.110
RAVD (%)	12.286	8.887	13.76	9.772	11.85	8.73

3.2   Results

Inter- and Intra-rater Reliability. For the combined dataset, the intraclass correlation coefficient (ICC) yielded 0.908 (95% Confidence Interval CI: 0.537–0.982) for manual segmentation volumes from two raters. Intra-rater reliability analysis was conducted on manual segmentations done by rater1 after three months. For the combined dataset, ICC was recorded as 0.916(95% CI: 0.657–0.985) for the repeated manual segmentations by rater 1.

Automated Segmentation Accuracy. We compared the final automated cartilage segmentations obtained using the proposed voxel classification method with the manual labels, and Table 1 shows the summarized results of the volume and distance-based metrics. The proposed method showed a mean (±SD) DSC scores of 0.740 (±0.052) for the whole dataset (all 40 images). For the OA patients cohort, the automated cartilage segmentation recorded a mean DSC score of 0.676 (±0.062), which is slightly lower compared to the mean DSC value of 0.943 (±0.027) showed in the non-OA participants' cohort. The slight decline in DSC values for the OA patients cohort is due to the cartilage defects in the hip joint due to disease progression. Full cartilage thickness loss at femoral head central and superolateral subregions due to OA progression is visible on the MRIs from the OA patients cohort.

Representative examples of validation results of the cartilage segmentation for non-OA and OA participants cohort with maximum and median DSC values are shown in Fig. 2. Overall, there was good consistency between automatic and manual segmentations of the cartilages across the majority of the articulating surface. There were, however, specific areas where differences between automated and manual segmentations were consistently more apparent Such as around the femoral head fovea, the acetabular fossa.

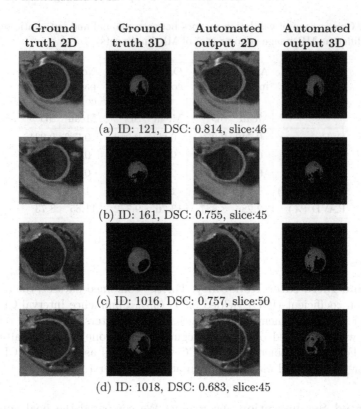

Ground truth 2D	Ground truth 3D	Automated output 2D	Automated output 3D

(a) ID: 121, DSC: 0.814, slice:46

(b) ID: 161, DSC: 0.755, slice:45

(c) ID: 1016, DSC: 0.757, slice:50

(d) ID: 1018, DSC: 0.683, slice:45

Fig. 2. Segmentation results for example slices with 3D visualization from non-OA and OA participants cohort (a) and (b) non-OA cohort, (c) and (d) OA cohort

4   Conclusion

In this paper, we presented an SVM based voxel classification method to automatically segment hip cartilage form routine clinical hip MRIs. Each voxel is represented as a high dimensional feature vector consisting of intensity-based, local image structure-based, and geometry-based features. Further, we evaluated the proposed segmentation technique on MRIs from two cohorts consisted of healthy adults and diagnosed OA patients. The accuracy of the automated segmentation is slightly low (DSC value: 0.676 ($\pm$0.062)) on OA patient's MR images due to cartilage degeneration with the progression of hip OA. The method performs better on the MRIs from healthy participants with a mean DSC value of 0.759 ($\pm$0.031).

References

1. Chandra, S.S., et al.: Automated analysis of hip joint cartilage combining MR T2 and three-dimensional fast-spin-echo images. Magn. Reson. Med. **75**(1), 403–413 (2016). https://doi.org/10.1002/mrm.25598

2. Dice, L.R.: Measures of the amount of ecologic association between species. Ecology **26**(3), 297–302 (1945)
3. Fripp, J., Crozier, S., Warfield, S.K., Ourselin, S.S.: Automatic segmentation of the bone and extraction of the bone & cartilage interface from magnetic resonance images of the knee. Phys. Med. Biol. **52**(6), 1617–1631 (2007). https://doi.org/10.1088/0031-9155/52/6/005
4. Gerig, G., Jomier, M., Chakos, M.: Valmet: a new validation tool for assessing and improving 3D object segmentation. In: Niessen, W.J., Viergever, M.A. (eds.) MICCAI 2001. LNCS, vol. 2208, pp. 516–523. Springer, Heidelberg (2001). https://doi.org/10.1007/3-540-45468-3_62
5. Girard, M., Pedoia, V., Norman, B., Rossi-Devries, J., Majumdar, S.: Automatic segmentation of hip cartilage with deep convolutional neural nets for the evaluation of acetabulum and femoral T1ρ and T2 relaxation times. Osteoarthritis Cartilage **26**, S439–S440 (2018). https://doi.org/10.1016/j.joca.2018.02.843
6. Johnson, H.J., McCormick, M.M., Ibanez, L.: The ITK Software Guide Book 2: Design and Functionality. Kitware Incorporated, New York (2015)
7. Lawrence, R.C., et al.: Estimates of the prevalence of arthritis and other rheumatic conditions in the united states. Arthritis Rheum. **58**(1), 26–35 (2008). https://doi.org/10.1002/art.23176
8. Nishii, T., Sugano, N., Sato, Y., Tanaka, H., Miki, H., Yoshikawa, H.: Three-dimensional distribution of acetabular cartilage thickness in patients with hip dysplasia: a fully automated computational analysis of MR imaging. Osteoarthritis Cartilage **12**(8), 650–657 (2004). https://doi.org/10.1016/j.joca.2004.04.009
9. Platt, J.: Sequential minimal optimization: a fast algorithm for training support vector machines (1998)
10. Ramme, A.J., et al.: Evaluation of automated volumetric cartilage quantification for hip preservation surgery. J. Arthroplasty **31**(1), 64–69 (2016). https://doi.org/10.1016/j.arth.2015.08.009
11. Sato, Y., et al.: A fully automated method for segmentation and thickness determination of hip joint cartilage from 3D MR data. Int. Congr. Ser. **1230**, 352–358 (2001). https://doi.org/10.1016/S0531-5131(01)00029-2
12. Siversson, C., Akhondi-Asl, A., Bixby, S., Kim, Y.J., Warfield, S.K.: Three-dimensional hip cartilage quality assessment of morphology and dGEMRIC by planar maps and automated segmentation. Osteoarthritis Cartilage **22**(10), 1511–1515 (2014). https://doi.org/10.1016/j.joca.2014.08.012
13. Sofat, N., Ejindu, V., Kiely, P.: What makes osteoarthritis painful? The evidence for local and central pain processing. Rheumatology **50**(12), 2157–2165 (2011). https://doi.org/10.1093/rheumatology/ker283
14. Tustison, N.J., et al.: N4ITK: improved N3 bias correction. IEEE Trans. Med. Imaging **29**(6), 1310–1320 (2010). https://doi.org/10.1109/TMI.2010.2046908
15. Van Ginneken, B., Heimann, T., Styner, M.: 3D segmentation in the clinic: a grand challenge, pp. 7–15 (2007)
16. Xia, Y., Chandra, S.S., Engstrom, C., Strudwick, M.W., Crozier, S., Fripp, J.: Automatic hip cartilage segmentation from 3D MR images using arc-weighted graph searching. Phys. Med. Biol. **59**(23), 7245–66 (2014). https://doi.org/10.1088/0031-9155/59/23/7245
17. Xia, Y., Fripp, J., Chandra, S.S., Schwarz, R., Engstrom, C., Crozier, S.: Automated bone segmentation from large field of view 3D MR images of the hip joint. Phys. Med. Biol. **58**(20), 7375–90 (2013). https://doi.org/10.1088/0031-9155/58/20/7375

18. Xia, Y., Manjon, J.V., Engstrom, C., Crozier, S., Salvado, O., Fripp, J.: Automated cartilage segmentation from 3D MR images of hip joint using an ensemble of neural networks. In: 2017 IEEE 14th International Symposium on Biomedical Imaging (ISBI 2017), pp. 1070–1073. IEEE (2017). https://doi.org/10.1109/ISBI.2017.7950701
19. Zhang, K., Lu, W., Marziliano, P.: Automatic knee cartilage segmentation from multi-contrast MR images using support vector machine classification with spatial dependencies. Magn. Reson. Imaging **31**(10), 1731–1743 (2013). https://doi.org/10.1016/j.mri.2013.06.005

Natural Language Processing

Active Learning Based Relation Classification for Knowledge Graph Construction from Conversation Data

Zishan Ahmad[1(✉)], Asif Ekbal[1], Shubhashis Sengupta[2], Anutosh Mitra[2], Roshni Rammani[2], and Pushpak Bhattacharyya[1]

[1] Indian Institute of Technology Patna, Patna, India
{1821cs18,asif,pb}@iitp.ac.in
[2] Accenture Technology Labs Bangalore, Bangalore, India
{shubhashis.sengupta,anutosh.maitra,roshni.r.ramnani}@accenture.com

Abstract. Creation of a Knowledge Graph (KG) from text, and its usages in solving several Natural Language Processing (NLP) problems are emerging research areas. Creating KG from text is a challenging problem which requires several NLP modules working together in unison. This task becomes even more challenging when constructing knowledge graph from a conversational data, as user and agent stated facts in conversations are often not grounded and can change with dialogue turns. In this paper, we explore KG construction from conversation data in travel and taxi booking domains. We use a fixed ontology for each of the conversation domain, and extract the relation triples from the conversation. Using active learning technique we build a state-of-the-art BERT based relation classifier which uses minimal data, but still performs accurate classification of the extracted relation triples. We further design heuristics for constructing KG that uses the BERT based relation classifier and Semantic Role Labelling (SRL) for handling negations in extracted relationship triples. Through our experiments we show that using our active learning trained classifier and heuristic based method, KG can be built with good correctness and completeness scores for domain specific conversational datasets. To the best of our knowledge this is the very first attempt at creating a KG from the conversational data that could be efficiently augmented in a dialogue agent to tackle the issue of data sparseness and improve the quality of generated response.

Keywords: Active learning · Knowledge Graph · Relation classification · Deep learning

1 Introduction

In recent years Knowledge Graphs (KG) have become popular across several applications like recommendation systems [5], web-search [10] etc. Knowledge graphs can also be used for Question Answering [2], query expansion [4] and

© Springer Nature Switzerland AG 2020
H. Yang et al. (Eds.): ICONIP 2020, CCIS 1332, pp. 617–625, 2020.
https://doi.org/10.1007/978-3-030-63820-7_70

co-reference resolution [7]. Although, most of the high-quality knowledge graph (KG) like Wikidata [9] are currently built by volunteers through crowd-sourcing, automated systems for building KG from factual texts are also being explored.

Conversational systems - where users and agents or machines interact - provide a rich source of deriving real-life and situational knowledge. Knowledge graphs derived and validated from conversational episodes in domains like customer support provide useful information on customer choice, preferences and other related information that can be used to serve customers better. However, building Knowledge Graph from conversational data presents a very different set of challenges than of those from deriving graphs from factual text and is largely unexplored. Unlike factual data, the beliefs in conversational data are not grounded. For example, *"Toronto is in Canada"* is a factual text, and a triple *isin(Toronto, Canada)* can be extracted from it. More texts supporting this fact can be found, thus increasing the confidence-weight in the belief. In conversations, beliefs can change over the conversational turns. For example, consider the following conversation snippet. The relation between the entities, *trip* and *Atlantis* is *destination(trip, Atlantis)* in the first *CUSTOMER* utterance. This relation changes to *destination(trip, Neverland)* at the second *CUSTOMER* utterance.

- CUSTOMER: *I'd like to book a trip to Atlantis from Caprica.*
- AGENT: *Hi...I checked a few options for you, and unfortunately, we do not currently have any trips that meet this criteria.*
- CUSTOMER: *Okay, I'd like to go to Neverland.*

From the above example, it can be seen that the relation triple extracted from the second *CUSTOMER* utterance is between *trip* and *Neverland*. However, there is no mention of the word *trip* in the second utterance. Thus, in conversations, implicit entities and relations can be present, making the task difficult. Another problem in constructing KG from conversations is that, since the facts are not grounded, methods using confidence-weights cannot be used for better triple extraction.

Knowledge graph from conversation data can have various practical applications. It has been shown that KG based generation helps in generating more coherent multi-sentence text [6]. Using KG for generating conversations can potentially help in grounding the conversation and making it coherent. Another application can be executing relational queries on conversation after conversation is complete. In a conversation between a user and a call-center agent (e.g. Travel Agency), the system could extract entities and relationships at each turn, and a final KG of these relation could be constructed by the end of the conversation. This final KG represents the final user requirements (travel booking details etc.) and queries could be executed to satisfy these requirements automatically (Query for ticket bookings etc).

In this paper, we explore KG construction from the conversational data. We begin by creating a KG ontology for a given dataset. Next, we device an active learning technique to train a BERT [3] based classifier for classifying relationships between the entities using minimal-supervision. Using these entities and

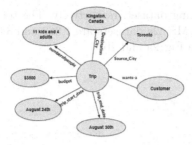

Fig. 1. Final knowledge graph populated with triples extracted from the conversation

their relationships, we build a heuristic for KG construction from conversational data. We evaluate our proposed methods on two different datasets. We show that using our BERT based active learning method, robust relation classifier can be built using minimal amount of training data. We also design a set of heuristics to build the KG from the extracted relation triplets.

1.1 Problem Definition

Given a conversation between a user and an agent, the task is to extract entity-relation triples, classify the triple relation to ontological relation types, and then construct a KG for the conversation. An example for the final task is given below:

- *user:* Hi, me and my family want to take a trip to Kakariko Village.
- *agent:* How many adults and how many children will you be bringing with you? Do you have a preferred departure location? What would be your maximum budget?
- *user:* We are four adults and 11 children departing from Godric's Hollow. $3500 is the most we are willing to spend.
- *agent:* I do not have any packages available from that departure location for that budget.
- *user:* Ok, do you have any travel packages to Kingston, Canada for 11 kids and 4 adults, $3500 or less, departing from Toronto?
- *agent:* Yes, I have a package available leaving Toronto on August 24th and returning to Toronto on August 30th.
- *user:* Yes, I'll take it. Thank you

All the changes in user request are accommodated in the final KG and only the final correct request is stored (c.f Fig. 1).

2   Dataset Description

Our system is built on two different datasets: (i). Microsoft Frames and (ii). Microsoft e2e taxi booking datasets. Both of these datasets are related to the booking services- MS Frames being from the travel domain while MS e2e dataset is from the taxi booking domain. Microsoft Frames and e2e datasets are goal trip

booking and taxi booking dataset, respectively. The total number of dialogues
in the MS Frames and MS e2e datasets are 1,369 and 3,094, respectively. Their
ontologies are shown in Fig. 2a and 2b.

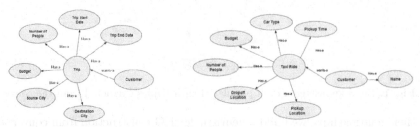

Knowledge Graph for Microsoft Frames   Knowledge Graph for Microsoft e2e taxi
dataset   booking dataset

Fig. 2. Knowledge Graph ontologies of MS Frames and MS e2e taxi dataset

3 Methodology

We use Open Information Extraction (OpenIE) [1] suite for extraction of entity-
relation triples. The OpenIE extracts propositions from a sentence, comprising
of a relation phrase and two or more argument phrases. The relation phrases
extracted from the OpenIE need to be classified into the relation types belonging to the KG ontology. Thus, extracting triples from the OpenIE and classifying them into the corresponding relation types (with respect to the KG of the
dataset) enables us to populate the KG with the appropriate entity-relationship
triples.

3.1 Relation Classification Model

We build a BERT [3] based model to classify the relation triples extracted by
OpenIE into the ontological relation types. To achieve this, we prepare the input
to the BERT model by enriching the statement from which the OpenIE triple is
extracted, with the extracted triple. This is done because, the triple alone does
not always provide sufficient information for relation classification. An example
of statement enrichment is shown below:

- **Statement:** I need to go to Denver Airport.
- **OpenIE triple extracted:** {'subject': 'I', 'relation': 'go to', 'object': 'Denver
  Airport'}
- **Enriched Statement:** <tok1>I</tok1> need to go to <tok2>Denver
  Airport</tok2>.
- **Relation Class:** *Dropoff_Location*

The enriched statement thus obtained is tokenized using BERT tokenizer, and
passed to the BERT encoder. At the final layer of BERT the representation
corresponding to the CLS token is extracted and passed through a softmax
layer, which classifies the enriched statement into different relation classes.

Table 1. Class distribution of Microsoft Frames and Microsoft e2e Taxi booking data

Microsoft frames		Microsoft e2e taxi booking	
Relation class	Number of samples	Relation class	Number of samples
Source_City	148	Pickup_Location	112
Destination_City	131	Dropoff_Location	110
Trip_Start_Date	102	Pickup_Time	74
Trip_End_Date	81	Car_Type	115
Number_of_People	77	Number_of_People	120
Budget	101	Budget	13
Other	360	Customer_Name	75
		Other	381

3.2 Active Learning

Since the datasets used for experiments are not annotated, we perform the following active learning process to train our BERT classifier using minimal supervision. To achieve this, we first run OpenIE on the entire dataset and extract the relation triples from all the dialogue utterances. Next, we sample a seed data of 300 instances (relation triples and their corresponding utterances) for the relation classification task. We prepare the ground truth (i.e. test set) by manually annotating a set of 300 samples to evaluate the performance of the classifier. We perform the following steps to train our classifier:

1. Train the classifier on seed data.
2. Run the trained classifier on un-annotated data.
3. Obtain the final class prediction and probabilities of prediction using the final Softmax layer of the classifier.
4. Calculate entropy of prediction probabilities using the following formula:

$$H(X) = -\sum_{i=1}^{n} p_i \log_2 p_i \tag{1}$$

Here, $H(X)$ is the entropy w.r.t the input X, n is the number of classes, p_i is the probability of prediction of the ith class.

5. From the annotated data obtained from classifier, add the samples with top k largest entropy to the seed sample.
6. if accuracy of the classifier increases by $\gamma\%$ and seed sample is less than α go-to step 1
7. else stop and save the final trained classifier

In the above active learning steps, we fix $\gamma\%$ to 1, and α to 700 samples. Using the aforementioned active learning steps, we build a high performing relation classifier using minimum supervision. The class distribution of the data after active learning in shown in Table 1.

Algorithm 1. Knowledge Graph Heuristic

```
 1: procedure KG_BUILD(conversation)
 2:     Initialize KG
 3:     SRL ← Semantic Role Labeller
 4:     C ← Pre-trained Relation Classifier
 5:     for utterance in conversation do
 6:         split utterance into sentences
 7:         for sentence in sentences do
 8:             OIE ← Get all the OpenIE triples from the sentence
 9:             C_Trip ← C(OIE)
10:             Add the C_Trip triples to the corresponding KG slot
11:             SRL_Sent ← SRL(sentence)
12:             if negation exists in SRL_Sent then
13:                 Arg ← Negated Argument
14:                 Remove all triples from KG containing Arg
15:     return KG                          ▷ Final Knowledge Graph of the conversation
```

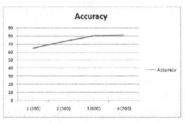
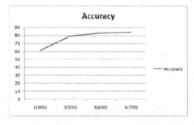

MS Frames Classifier   MS e2e taxi Booking Classifier

Fig. 3. Accuracy v/s Active learning steps

3.3 Heuristics for Knowledge Graph

Using OpenIE we extract propositions and relation phrase triples which are classified to their relation types using the trained classifier. However, to populate the KG of the conversation, we cannot just place the extracted triples to the KG based solely on their relation types. This is because, the extracted relations can be negated or updated as the conversations between the user and agent proceed. We use Semantic Role Labelling (SRL)[1] [8] to detect the negated verbs and their corresponding arguments. We look for the relations in KG that have entities matching any chunk in the negated argument of SRL, and remove it from the KG. When a relation is found in conversation for which the KG had already been populated with based on the previous utterances, we replace the old triple with the new triple. In doing so we assume that the user has changed their requirements for booking a trip or taxi. The detailed heuristic for KG construction is shown in Algorithm 1.

4 Experiments and Results

We conduct experiments for relation classification and KG construction. We test out methods on two datasets: MS Frames and MS e2e Taxi Booking. We train

---

[1] https://demo.allennlp.org/semantic-role-labeling.

Table 2. Final Precision (P), Recall (R) and F1-Score (F) of the Microsoft Frames and Microsoft e2e classifiers.

Microsoft frames classifier				Microsoft e2e classifier			
Relation class	P	R	F	Relation class	P	R	F
Source_City	0.88	0.90	0.89	Pickup_Location	0.80	0.61	0.69
Destination_City	0.85	0.90	0.88	Dropoff_Location	0.74	0.89	0.81
Trip_Start_Date	0.78	0.68	0.72	Pickup_Time	0.89	0.89	0.89
Trip_End_Date	0.83	0.74	0.79	Car_Type	0.69	0.76	0.72
Number_of_People	0.81	0.79	0.80	Number_of_People	0.95	0.91	0.93
Budget	0.78	0.80	0.79	Budget	1.0	0.75	0.86
Other	0.83	0.76	0.80	Customer_Name	0.90	0.94	0.92
				Other	0.83	0.84	0.84

the classifier for relation classification using the active learning steps mentioned in Sect. 3.2. The setups for the different experiments conducted are given below.

4.1 Results

Figure 3 shows that the relation classification accuracy of triples increases at each step of the active learning process for both MS Frames and MS e2e dataset. In case of MS Frames classifier the accuracy improves from 65% in the first step to 81% in the fourth step. For the classifier trained on MS e2e dataset the accuracy improves from 69% to 84% from first to the fourth step in active learning process.

Detailed evaluation results of the two classifiers are shown in Table 2 in terms of recall, precision and F1-score. We see that with a very minimal number of samples (i.e. with 700), the classifier attains a considerable performance increase for all the classes. Once the classifier is trained and we obtain good classification scores, we move on to building KG using the heuristic discussed in Sect. 3.3. The result obtained is measured in terms of 'Correctness' and 'Completeness'. Correctness is the percentage of correctly identified triples in the conversation. Completeness is the percentage of triples extracted out of total actual triples in the conversations. To compute this we manually select 50 random conversations and run the system on these conversations one by one. We observe the KG constructed from our proposed approach, and compare it against the actual KG constructed manually from the conversations. While for the MS Frames dataset our method obtains the 64% Correctness and 56% Completeness score, for MS e2e dataset the scores of 71% and 40% are obtained. From the result we can see that even by using a very simple heuristic on top of our method, we obtain the decent results in terms of correctness. The system, however, scores low in terms of completeness. Upon analysis it was observed that correctness is mostly affected by negations. The SRL often misses the negation, or is unable to associate negation with the negated triples. This causes the system to keep a triple in the KG when it had to be removed, thus increasing false positives. The completeness of the system is affected because of the inaccurate relation triple extraction by the OpenIE system. The system often misses triples in conversation, thus leaving the KG incomplete.

5   Conclusion

In this paper we have described a novel technique for building a Knowledge Graph from conversational data. First, we build a high performance relation triple classifier using active learning and minimal supervision. We then developed a KG construction heuristic that makes use of the trained classifier and SRL module. We have evaluated our method on two conversational datasets, MS Frames and MS e2e taxi booking. The experiments conducted in this paper show that a high performing classifier can be built using only 700 training samples through active learning.

In future we would like to explore better relation extraction methods for achieving better coverage. For example, the heuristic for building KG uses currently uses SRL for negation handling. This can be replaced by a better negation handling model.

Acknowledgement. The research reported in this paper is an outcome of the project "Autonomous Goal-Oriented and Knowledge-Driven Neural Conversational Agents", sponsored by Accenture LLP. Asif Ekbal acknowledges Visvesvaraya YFRF.

References

1. Angeli, G., Premkumar, M.J.J., Manning, C.D.: Leveraging linguistic structure for open domain information extraction. In: Proceedings of the 53rd Annual Meeting of the Association for Computational Linguistics and the 7th International Joint Conference on Natural Language Processing (Volume 1: Long Papers), pp. 344–354 (2015)
2. Bao, J., Duan, N., Yan, Z., Zhou, M., Zhao, T.: Constraint-based question answering with knowledge graph. In: Proceedings of COLING 2016, The 26th International Conference on Computational Linguistics: Technical Papers, pp. 2503–2514 (2016)
3. Devlin, J., Chang, M.W., Lee, K., Toutanova, K.: Bert: pre-training of deep bidirectional transformers for language understanding. arXiv preprint arXiv:1810.04805 (2018)
4. Graupmann, J., Schenkel, R., Weikum, G.: The spheresearch engine for unified ranked retrieval of heterogeneous xml and web documents. In: Proceedings of the 31st International Conference on Very Large Data Bases, pp. 529–540. VLDB Endowment (2005)
5. Guo, Q., et al.: A survey on knowledge graph-based recommender systems. arXiv preprint arXiv:2003.00911 (2020)
6. Koncel-Kedziorski, R., Bekal, D., Luan, Y., Lapata, M., Hajishirzi, H.: Text generation from knowledge graphs with graph transformers. arXiv preprint arXiv:1904.02342 (2019)

7. Ng, V., Cardie, C.: Improving machine learning approaches to coreference resolution. In: Proceedings of the 40th Annual Meeting on Association for Computational Linguistics, pp. 104–111. Association for Computational Linguistics (2002)
8. Shi, P., Lin, J.: Simple bert models for relation extraction and semantic role labeling. arXiv preprint arXiv:1904.05255 (2019)
9. Turki, H., et al.: Wikidata: a large-scale collaborative ontological medical database. J. Biomed. Inform. **99**, 103292 (2019)
10. Vu, T., Nguyen, T.D., Nguyen, D.Q., Phung, D., et al.: A capsule network-based embedding model for knowledge graph completion and search personalization. In: Proceedings of the 2019 Conference of the North American Chapter of the Association for Computational Linguistics: Human Language Technologies, (Volume 1: Long and Short Papers), pp. 2180–2189 (2019)

Adversarial Shared-Private Attention Network for Joint Slot Filling and Intent Detection

Mengfei Wu[1], Longbiao Wang[1(✉)], Yuke Si[1], and Jianwu Dang[1,2]

[1] Tianjin Key Laboratory of Cognitive Computing and Application,
College of Intelligence and Computing, Tianjin University, Tianjin, China
{wumf,longbiao_wang,siyuke}@tju.edu.cn
[2] Japan Advanced Institute of Science and Technology, Ishikawa, Japan
jdang@jaist.ac.jp

Abstract. Spoken language understanding plays an important role in the dialogue systems, and in such systems, intent detection and slot filling tasks are used to extract semantic components. In previous works on spoken language understanding, many ways that from traditional pipeline methods to joint models have been investigated. The features from these methods are usually extracted from one dataset that cannot jointly optimize databases with different distributions. In this paper, we propose a new adversarial shared-private attention network that learns features from two different datasets with shared and private spaces. The proposed adversarial network trains the shared attention network so that the shared distributions of two datasets are close, thereby reducing the redundancy of the shared features, which helps to alleviate the interference from the private and shared space. A joint training strategy between intent detection and slot filling is also applied to enhance the task relationship. Experimental results on public benchmark corpora, called ATIS, Snips and MIT, show that our proposed models significantly outperform other methods on intent accuracy, slot F1 measure and sentence accuracy.

Keywords: Spoken language understanding · Adversarial training · Self-attention mechanism

1 Introduction

Spoken language understanding (SLU) is a primary component of a conversation system and directly affects the performance of the whole spoken dialogue system. SLU aims to extract the semantic components by completing two tasks and expressing keywords and intentions in the semantic framework. These two tasks are named intent detection and slot filling, which engage in predicting the intent and semantic constituents respectively [1]. Table 1 shows an example from ATIS dataset [2]. For the sentence "Show me flights from Dallas to Pittsburgh", each word corresponds to a slot label and the whole sentence maps an intent category.

© Springer Nature Switzerland AG 2020
H. Yang et al. (Eds.): ICONIP 2020, CCIS 1332, pp. 626–634, 2020.
https://doi.org/10.1007/978-3-030-63820-7_71

Table 1. An example from ATIS dataset.

Sentence	Show	me	flights	from	Dallas	to	Pittsburgh
Slots	O	O	O	O	B-fromloc	O	B-toloc
Intent	atis_flights						

(a) Fully private   (b) Shared-private   (c) Adversarial shared-private

Fig. 1. Three schemes for two different datasets. The blue rectangles and black triangles represent features from the private space, while the green circles are shared features from two databases. (Color figure online)

Recently, due to the interdependency between slot filling and intent detection tasks, joint models, such as joint RNN-LSTM [3], attention-based Bidirectional-RNN (Bi-RNN) [4], have been widely applied for SLU tasks. Goo proposed a slot-gated model that focuses on learning the relationship between the intent and slot attention vectors [5]. However, most existing SLU models are trained by using the corresponding database and, ignoring the inner connection between different databases, as shown in the Fig. 1(a). Methods that exploit the relationship between databases [6] usually attempt to divide the features of different databases into private and shared spaces, as shown in the Fig. 1(b). However, for this framework, the shared feature space could contain some unnecessary private features, resulting in feature redundancy. The major limitation of this framework is that the shared feature space could contain some unnecessary private features, suffering from feature redundancy.

Due to the success of generative adversarial networks (GANs) in image generation tasks, adversarial learning is also applied to SLU tasks. Liu proposed a domain-general models that apply domain adversarial training in SLU tasks [7]. Lan proposed an adversarial multi-task learning method that merges a bidirectional language model (BLM) and a slot tagging model (STM) for semi-supervised training [8]. And Masumura proposed an adversarial training method for the multi-task and multi-lingual joint modeling needed for utterance intent classification [9].

In this paper, we extend the adversarial attention network to SLU tasks by using benchmark datasets. We propose an adversarial shared-private attention network (ASPAN) that generates features from shared and private spaces, as shown in Fig. 1(c). The features from shared space are trained by the adversarial attention network, which ensures that the shared feature space contains only common and task-invariant information. The adversarial network [10,11] targets at training the shared attention network to make the shared distributions of two datasets close, thus they can reduce the redundancy of the shared feature, which helps to alleviate the interference from private and shared spaces. Specifically,

these two databases are public benchmark corpora, and this paper is the first to attempt to train a model using the general features from these two datasets. In addition, we compare the experimental results of these different schemes and determine that the adversarial shared-private attention network performs better than other models.

The contributions of this work are summarized as follows: 1) We propose an adversarial shared-private attention network to exploit the relationship between two databases. 2) Furthermore, it's the first time to combine public benchmark corpora to learn the general features between databases. 3) The experimental results demonstrate the effectiveness of the proposed approaches.

2   Methodology

This section first explains the neural architecture of the adversarial shared-private attention model; then, the training strategy used for adversarial attention joint learning is introduced.

2.1   Neural Architectures

For a given utterance, the goal of intent detection is to identify the intent of the sentence, and the goal of the slot filling task is to match every word with a corresponding slot tag. We propose an adversarial shared-private attention model (ASPAN) that applies adversarial learning between two public benchmark corpora and can promote information sharing between two databases. Figure 2 shows the architecture of the adversarial shared-private attention model. In our work, the model has four main parts: the encoder module, which includes two different Bi-LSTM encoders that encode the utterance into a vector representation; the attention network module, which includes two independent self-attention layers and shared attention modules that map the input sequences x1 and x2 to

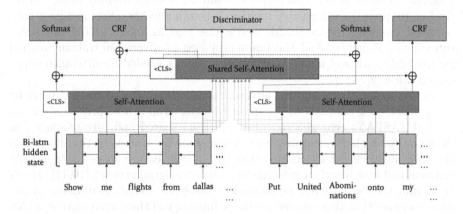

Fig. 2. The framework of the adversarial shared-private attention model.

different attention weights according to the database; classifiers, which are used to predict the intent labels; CRF layers, which are used to predict slot filling labels jointly when given the utterance representation from attention networks; and discriminator D, which calculates a scalar fraction that indicates whether the attention sequence x is from the ATIS or Snips dataset.

Bi-LSTM Encoder. Long short-term memory (LSTM) [12] can handle sequence information over time, and it has been demonstrated to perform well on text representation tasks. For a given utterance, we use the Bi-LSTM network to process every word vector in the utterance sequentially to generate sentence representations.

Self-attention. A self-attention mechanism is used to capture the dependencies between words in utterances and capture the internal structure of the sentence [13]. We add the attention layer after the Bi-LSTM layer. For the attention network, we can obtain the utterance representations that is calculated by different attention weights.

The intent representation Utt_i is calculated by summing up the product of attention score α_t and hidden state h_t along the time dimension, while the slot representation Utt_s is calculated by multiplying the attention score α_t and hidden state h_t.

Prediction Layer. For intent classifiers, we take the concatenation of intent attention output Utt_i and share attention output Utt_i^{share} and the concatenation of slot attention output Utt_s and share attention output Utt_s^{share} as inputs for predicting the intent and slot. Thus, the CRF layer [14] can capture this dependence and consider the neighbor slot tag relationship, which is beneficial to the model performance.

Discriminator. The discriminator is used to map the shared representations of sentences into a probability distribution that estimates what kinds of databases the encoded sentence comes from

$$D = D(Utt^{sh}, \theta_d) = Softmax(W_d Utt^{sh} + b^d) \tag{1}$$

where W_d and b^d represent the training parameters in the discriminator module.

2.2 Training

The goal of ASPAN is to train the shared attention network so that the distributions of the two corpora are as close as possible; thus, the model can learn the invariant features of the two databases to better leverage information sharing. The two different datasets are most commonly used benchmarks for spoken language understanding, and actually they are from different domains. The shared parts from two datasets include general features, such as grammar rule, pattern rules and colloquial types.

Adversarial training encourages the shared space to be purer and ensures that the shared representation is not impacted by private features. In this work, the cross-entropy loss functions of the main joint networks for each dataset are defined as follows:

$$Loss^1 = \sum_{k=1}^{N} \log(p_k^1|t_k^1, \theta_i^1) + \sum_{k=1}^{N}\sum_{r=1}^{R} \log(P_{kr}^1|T_{kr}^1, \theta_s^1) \tag{2}$$

$$Loss^2 = \sum_{k=1}^{N} \log(p_k^2|t_k^2, \theta_i^2) + \sum_{k=1}^{N}\sum_{r=1}^{R} \log(P_{kr}^2|T_{kr}^2, \theta_s^2) \tag{3}$$

where R and N represent the length of the utterance and the number of utterances, respectively, p_k is the intent prediction, t_k is the true intent label of the kth sentence, P_{kr} is the slot prediction, and T_{kr} is the true slot label of the rth word of the kth sentence. It is worthwhile to mention that the loss is the sum of the losses from intent detection and slot filling, as intent detection and slot filling are trained jointly to enhance the task relationship.

The adversary procedure is that when given an utterance, the shared attention layer generates a representation to mislead the discriminator while the discriminator attempts to correctly classify the source database of the sentence. We update the parameters of discriminator and shared-attention layer by maximizing the source tag cross-entropy loss, and update the parameters of shared-attention layer by adversarial fooling discriminator, as shown in (4):

$$Loss^{adv} = \min_{G} \max_{D} \sum_{k=1}^{K}\sum_{i=1}^{N_k} d_i^k log(D(E(Utt_k^{sh}))) \tag{4}$$

where d_i^k represents the label of the utterance database and Utt_k^{sh} denotes the output of the shared attention layer.

Finally, the total loss can be written as follows:

$$Loss = Loss^1 + Loss^2 + Loss^{adv} \tag{5}$$

The main joint networks and adversarial networks are trained via backpropagation, and the parameters are gradually updated by using the gradient reversal layers [15].

3   Experiments

3.1   Corpora

We conducted our experiments on three public benchmark corpora, i.e., ATIS (Airline Travel Information Systems) [2], Snips [16] and MIT datasets, which are widely used in SLU tasks.

- **ATIS:** The ATIS corpus is composed of the audio recordings of people making flight reservations. There are 4478, 500 and 893 sentences in the training, valid and test sets respectively.
- **Snips:** The Snips dataset contains crowdsourced user utterances, which are collected from Snips personal voice. There are 39 types of slots and 7 types of intents in the corpus, and each intent category contains 2000 sentences.
- **MIT:** The MIT corpus contains three datasets: the MIT Restaurant Corpus (MIT_R) and two MIT Movie Corpus(MIT_E, MIT_T). In our work MIT_R is used to conduct the experiments.

3.2   Experimental Setup

The hyperparameters are selected by tuning one hyperparameter at a time while keeping the others constant. Specifically, the word embedding size is set to 300, and it is initialized with pre-trained word embeddings based on the Word2Vec model [17]. The hidden size of the LSTM model is set to 200. During the training stage, we apply the Adam optimizer [18] for the models. We set the number of LSTM layers to 1, because with the increase in the number of layers, the accuracy of the model is reduced. Moreover, a learning rate of 0.001 and a dropout of 0.5 are effective, and the learning rate decay is set to 0.001 in the experiments.

3.3   Results and Analysis

Table 2 shows the performances on the ATIS and Snips datasets of each approach. There are three evaluation indicators: intent accuracy, slot F1 measure and sentence accuracy, where sentence accuracy represents the proportion of the sentences in which the intent and slot labels are both predicted correctly. The following baselines for SLU are implemented to ensure fairness of comparison.

- **RNN-LSTM:** An approach proposed by [3] that jointly models slot filling, intent determination, and domain classification in a single bi-directional RNN with LSTM cells.
- **Atten-BiRNN:** An attention-based bidirectional RNN model proposed by [4] for joint intent detection and slot filling tasks.
- **Slot-gated:** [5] proposed a slot gate that learns the relationship between the intent and slot attention vectors in order to obtain good semantic frame results based on global optimization.
- **SF-ID Network:** [19] proposed a novel bidirectional interrelated model which used an SF-ID network to establish direct connections for the tasks.
- **Fully private model (FP):** The structure of this model is similar to that of the proposed model without shared self-attention and discriminator module.
- **Shared-private model (SP):** The structure of this model is similar to that of the proposed model without discriminator module.

Excluding the intent accuracy on the ATIS corpus, the adversarial attention model that takes the ATIS and Snips datasets jointly as inputs achieves the best

Table 2. Experimental results of the compared models on the ATIS and Snips corpora.

Model	ATIS			Snips		
	Intent	Slot	Sent	Intent	Slot	Sent
RNN-LSTM	92.6	94.3	80.7	96.9	87.3	73.2
Atten-BiRNN	91.1	94.2	78.9	96.7	87.3	74.1
Slot-gated	94.1	95.2	82.6	97.0	88.8	75.5
SF-ID (SF First)	**97.76**	95.75	86.79	97.43	91.43	80.57
SF-ID (ID First)	97.09	95.80	86.90	97.29	92.23	80.43
FP(shared Bi-LSTM encoder)	95.88	95.32	86.01	98.54	95.84	90.42
FP(shared attention module)	96.08	95.69	86.11	98.57	96.08	90.57
SP(shared Bi-LSTM encoder)	96.08	95.48	86.21	98.62	96.15	90.60
SP(shared attention module)	96.21	95.77	86.54	98.72	96.35	90.87
ASPN (shared Bi-LSTM encoder)	96.41	95.76	87.01	98.81	96.75	90.68
ASPAN (shared attention module)	96.56	**95.92**	**87.22**	**99.00**	**96.90**	**92.00**

performance from Table 2, which proves that the information communication between the corpora can help to improve the performance of the model.

In addition, we compare the different schemes introduced in Fig. 1, including the fully private scheme the shared-private scheme and the proposed adversarial shared-private attention scheme. We observe that the adversarial shared-private model performs better than the other models, while the shared-private model has higher intent accuracy and slot F1 measure than the fully private model. The results show that generating the shared features between different datasets can improve performance; however, the results also confirm that adversarial training for the shared self-attention layer is very effective for extracting common features between datasets, possibly because adversarial training can prevent private features from entering the shared space and thereby alleviate interference from the private space to improve model performance. Thus, the general information is useful for learning better attention weights for sentence representation.

We conduct additional experiments to evaluate the case in which the attention module is removed and the shared Bi-LSTM is employed instead. The results in Table 2 show that the proposed adversarial model (ASPN) with the shared Bi-LSTM model performs better than the FP and SP models with the shared Bi-LSTM encoder. However, the performance of the model with the shared Bi-LSTM encoder is slightly worse than that of the model with the attention module, which reflects the effectiveness of the attention mechanism.

Next, we conduct an experiment on the relationship between model performance and the number of databases. Table 3 shows the experimental results when the MIT database is added as an input to the proposed model alongside ATIS and Snips; thus, in this case, there are three LSTM encoders and self-attention layers in our model. Since there is a single intent in the MITR dataset, the intent accuracy in Table 3 is not shown. Compared with Table 2, the results in Table 3

Table 3. Experimental results of the models on the ATIS, Snips and MIT corpora.

Model	ATIS			Snips			MIT_R		
	Intent	Slot	Sent	Intent	Slot	Sent	Intent	Slot	Sent
SF-ID (SF First)	**97.76**	95.75	86.79	97.43	91.43	80.57	–	74.23	53.70
SF-ID (ID First)	97.09	95.80	86.90	97.29	92.23	80.43	–	74.20	53.66
FP	96.08	95.69	86.11	98.57	96.08	90.57	–	74.36	53.80
SP	96.02	95.58	86.03	98.49	96.12	90.67	–	74.95	54.12
ASPAN	96.20	**95.76**	**86.80**	**98.61**	**96.58**	**91.27**	–	**75.74**	**54.55**

show that the performance of the ATIS and Snips datasets decrease only slightly when the MIT database is added for the shared-private model and adversarial shared-private attention model, possibly because the number of parameters of the model increased while the effective feature information extracted from these three databases did not, which may cause overfitting during training and greatly increase the difficulty of training.

Overall, the connection between these datasets with adversarial attention training can improve the performance of the method on SLU tasks. The adversarial training strategy benefits from shared feature extraction, thereby improving model performance.

4 Conclusion

In this paper, we proposed an adversarial shared-private attention model that can learn features from two datasets with shared and private spaces. For the adversarial dual attention network, the attention output distributions of the two databases should be similar to, better exploit the shared information. The experimental results confirm the better effectiveness of our model than of previous models. Compared with the previous models, the adversarial attention network has the best performance on the ATIS and Snips datasets. In addition, as the number of databases increases, the performance of the model worsens.

Acknowledgements. This work was supported in part by the National Natural Science Foundation of China under Grant 61771333, the Tianjin Municipal Science and Technology Project under Grant 18ZXZNGX00330.

References

1. Tur, G., De Mori, R.: Spoken Language Understanding: Systems for Extracting Semantic Information From Speech. Wiley, Hoboken (2011)
2. Tur, G., Hakkani-Tür, D., Heck, L.: What is left to be understood in ATIS. In: IEEE Spoken Language Technology Workshop, pp. 19–24. IEEE (2010)
3. Hakkani-Tür, D., et al.: Multi-domain joint semantic frame parsing using bidirectional RNN-LSTM. In: Interspeech, pp. 715–719 (2016)

4. Liu, B., Lane, I.: Attention-based recurrent neural network models for joint intent detection and slot filling. In: Interspeech, pp. 685–689 (2016)
5. Goo, C.-W., et al.: Slot-gated modeling for joint slot filling and intent prediction. In: Proceedings of the 2018 Conference of the North American Chapter of the Association for Computational Linguistics: Human Language Technologies, pp. 753–757 (2018)
6. Liu, P., Qiu, X., Huang, X.: Deep multi-task learning with shared memory for text classification. In: EMNLP, pp. 118–127 (2016)
7. Liu, B., Lane, I.: Multi-domain adversarial learning for slot filling in spoken language understanding. arXiv preprint arXiv:1711.11310 (2017)
8. Lan, O., Zhu, S., Yu, K.: Semi-supervised training using adversarial multi-task learning for spoken language understanding. In: IEEE International Conference on Acoustics, Speech and Signal Processing (ICASSP), pp. 6049–6053 (2018)
9. Masumura, R., Shinohara, Y., Higashinaka, R., et al.: Adversarial training for multi-task and multi-lingual joint modeling of utterance intent classification. In: Proceedings of the 2018 Conference on Empirical Methods in Natural Language Processing, pp. 633–639 (2018)
10. Ganin, Y., et al.: Domain-adversarial training of neural networks. J. Mach. Learn. Res. **17**, 2096–2030 (2016)
11. Tzeng, E., Hoffman, J., Saenko, K., Darrell, T.: Adversarial discriminative domain adaptation. In: Proceedings of the IEEE Conference on Computer Vision and Pattern Recognition, pp. 7167–7176 (2017)
12. Hochreiter, S., Schmidhuber, J.: Long short- term memory. Neural Comput. **9**(8), 1735–1780 (1997)
13. Vaswani, A., Shazeer, N., Parmar, N., et al.: Attention is all you need. In: Advances in Neural Information Processing Systems, pp. 5998–6008 (2017)
14. Raymond, C., Riccardi, G.: Generative and discriminative algorithms for spoken language understanding. In: Interspeech, pp. 1605–1608 (2007)
15. Ganin, Y., Lempitsky, V.: Unsupervised domain adaptation by backpropagation. In: Proceedings of the 32nd International Conference on Machine Learning, pp. 1180–1189 (2015)
16. Coucke, A., et al.: Snips voice platform: an embedded spoken language understanding system for private-by-design voice interfaces. arXiv preprint arXiv:1805.10190 (2018)
17. Goldberg, Y., Levy, O.: word2vec explained: deriving Mikolov et al'.s negative-sampling word-embedding method. arXiv preprint arXiv:1402.3722 (2014)
18. Bottou, L.: Large-scale machine learning with stochastic gradient descent. In: Lechevallier, Y., Saporta, G. (eds.) Proceedings of COMPSTAT 2010, pp. 177–186. Springer, Heidelberg (2010). https://doi.org/10.1007/978-3-7908-2604-3_16
19. Haihong, E., Niu, P., Chen, Z., Song, M.: A novel bi-directional interrelated model for joint intent detection and slot filling. In: Proceedings of the 57th Annual Meeting of the Association for Computational Linguistics, pp. 5467–5471 (2019)

Automatic Classification and Comparison of Words by Difficulty

Shengyao Zhang[1]([✉])(ID), Qi Jia[1](ID), Libin Shen[2](ID), and Yinggong Zhao[2](ID)

[1] Department of Computer Science and Engineering,
Shanghai Jiao Tong University, Shanghai, China
{sophie_zhang,jia_qi}@sjtu.edu.cn
[2] Leyan Technologies, Shanghai, China
{libin,ygzhao}@leyantech.com

Abstract. Vocabulary knowledge is essential for both native and foreign language learning. Classifying words by difficulty helps students develop better in different stages of study and gives teachers the standard to adhere to when preparing tutorials. However, classifying word difficulty is time-consuming and labor-intensive. In this paper, we propose to classify and compare the word difficulty by analyzing multi-faceted features, including intra-word, syntactic and semantic features. The results show that our method is robust against different language environments.

Keywords: Word difficulty · Multi-faceted features · Semantic features · Multi-language environments

1 Introduction

Vocabulary knowledge is important for second language (L2) learning. Vocabulary learning needs to define the word difficulty with its comprehensive characteristics and decide whether it is suitable for a person in certain level to learn. Targeting different groups of population, there exist a number of standards providing different difficulty levels of words, such as Common European Framework of Reference for Languages (CEFR) [1] and Hanyu Shuiping Kaoshi (HSK). However, the reference words cover only a part of the whole vocabulary. There emerge lots of new words in today's world, we hope a timely update and extension for the leveled vocabulary. Traditional word difficulty determination tasks manually done by linguistic experts are costly and time-consuming. Therefore, we aim to achieve automatic classification by learning the characteristics of words.

Most previous researches were restricted to using frequency as the only feature [2]. Although it is common sense that the word difficulty has negative correlation with its frequency, there are usually exceptions. For example, the frequency of word "ethnic" is 23752 in COCA[1] but its difficulty level is C1 in CEFR[2], while

---

[1] The Corpus of Contemporary American English: https://www.english-corpora.org/coca/.

[2] CEFR defines 6 difficulty levels {A1, A2, B1, B2, C1, C2} where A1 represents the minimum difficulty and C2 represents the highest difficulty.

© Springer Nature Switzerland AG 2020
H. Yang et al. (Eds.): ICONIP 2020, CCIS 1332, pp. 635–642, 2020.
https://doi.org/10.1007/978-3-030-63820-7_72

the frequency of word "jazz" is 26 but its difficulty is A2. Others attempted compound features, such as the combination of frequency, length, syllables, domain specificity, semantic relatedness and morphological relatedness [3–5]. Still, the above research focus on the linguistic theory but not developed effective ways to computationally predict word difficulties.

To address the technical challenges faced by previous approaches, we propose to extract features from large open-domain text corpora for representing word difficulty. We conduct experiments on English, German and Chinese to explore whether our method can be generalized to different corpus and language environments. We do experiments on both the word difficulty classification task and the word-pair difficulty ranking task to measure the effectiveness of extracted features for this task. Our main contributions are summarized as follows:

1. To the best of our knowledge, we are the first to automatically classify and compare words by difficulty using multi-faceted features. We discover that semantic features are most important in determining word difficulties.
2. Our multi-faceted features outperform the baselines and the performance are very close to human behavior.
3. Our method shows robustness against different corpora of the same language and is capable for predicting word difficulty in different languages, making it easier in updating the leveled vocabulary in new languages or environments.

2   Features

Given a leveled word list W, we aim at learning the multi-faceted features to represent the difficulty. We will describe these features covering several aspects.

Frequency and Length. Frequency (**Freq.**) is a common measurement calculated on a huge corpus to assess vocabulary difficulty. The frequency for word w is calculated as $f_w = \log_{10}(C\{w\} + 1)$, where $C\{w\}$ is counted in the corpus and constant 1 is used to take out-of-corpus words into computation.

The **Length** of a word is counted as the number of its characters.

Intra-word Features. We use a series of natural language processing approaches to obtain the intra-word features, including its spelling and pronunciation rules.

Phoneme. A pronunciation dictionary is chosen to generate the phonemes of an word. For example, the phonemes of word "cheese" are "CH", "IY" and "Z". A phoneme indicative vector $\mathbf{p}_w = [p_1, p_2, \dots]$ is set to represent a word's pronunciation. Set the phoneme $p_i = 1$ if it exists in a word, otherwise $p_i = 0$.

Character Level N-gram (BiProb & TriProb). Several linguists indicated that the spelling regulation of a word may influence its difficulty. Therefore we represent each word with its n-gram language model. We transform each word into its lower case and add the start and end token "$" to it to get the bigram and trigram froms of a word. For example, the bigram combination of word "the" is ("$t", "th", "he", "e$"). When n-gram model applied at character level, it can be regarded as the probability of forming a word. The greater probability is, the more fluent spelling will be. Suppose the word w is composed of the character sequence $c_1, c_2, \ldots, c_n$, the log probability of word w is computed as Formula 1, where $p(c_i|c_{i-1})$ and $p(c_i|c_{i-1}, c_{i-2})$ are estimated by Laplace Smoothing.

$$
\begin{aligned}
\log\left(p_{w_{Bi}}\right) &= \log\left(p(c_1|\text{``\$''})\right) + \log\left(p(c_2|c_1)\right) + \cdots + \log\left(p(\text{``\$''}|c_n)\right) \\
\log\left(p_{w_{Tri}}\right) &= \log\left(p(c_2|c_1, \text{``\$''})\right) + \log\left(p(c_3|c_2, c_1)\right) + \cdots + \log\left(p(\text{``\$''}|c_n, c_{n-1})\right)
\end{aligned}
\tag{1}
$$

N-gram Vector (BiVec & TriVec). We utilize binary indicative vector $\mathbf{N}_w = [n_1, \ldots, n_G]$ where G is the number of n-grams and each dimension represents the presence of a particular n-gram. To avoid sparse vectors, we only take the n-grams extracted from the given leveled word list W into computation.

Syntactic Features. The use of words can't be cut off from sentences. Intuitively, the difficulty of a word may be related to its role and the relation with other words. We use Stanford CoreNLP to extract these features [6,7].

POS. A binary indicative vector $\mathbf{t}_w = [t_1, \ldots, t_T]$ for word w is designed to represent the POS tag feature, where T is the number of different POS tags. The i-th element marked 1 indicates that the word w has the i-th POS in text.

Dep. We also use the binary indicative vector to indicate all universal dependencies of a word in the corpus. The vector of dependency is $\mathbf{d}_w = [d_1, d_2, \ldots, d_D]$ and D is the number of all the dependencies that words in W have in corpus. Figure 1 shows a parsing result obtained by Stanford CoreNLP. When representing the dependencies of each word into a vector, we add "_in" after the word's relationship which is pointed to this word and add "_out" after the relationship which is pointed out from the word. For example, word "man" has the dependencies of "amod_out", "det_out", "cop_out", "nsubj_out" and "punct_out".

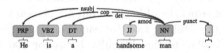

Fig. 1. Parsing result for sentence "He is a handsome man".

Semantic Features. The difficulty of a word is related to its meanings and the semantic knowledge is not only rely on one word but also reflected by its context. We obtain a comprehensive semantic representation of a word by learning its **Embedding** from the *Corpus* and the existing word embedding methods extract the features includes word similarity, synonym and topical information.

3   Dataset and Experiments

A dataset is made up of three parts: a reliable corpus (*Corpus*), a pronunciation dictionary (*Pdict*) and a standard leveled word list (W). *Corpus* and *Pdict* are the resource for extracting features, W is regarded as the ground truth. We select three languages to conduct the experiment. For **English**, we choose The New York Times Annotated Corpus [8] and Gutenberg Dataset [9] as *Corpus*. For *Pdict* selection, we choose the CMU Pronunciation Dictionary (CMUdict) [10]. The CEFR for British English is selected as W. For **German**, the German part of European Parliament Proceedings Parallel Corpus [11] is used as *Corpus*. A German pronunciation dictionary[3] modeled after CMUdict is chosen as *Pdict*. A three-level ground truth wordlist W based on CEFR standard is extracted from BerLiner Platz. For **Chinese**, we choose Chinese Wikipedia dump as *Corpus*. Mandarin Phonetic Symbols can be applied as *Pdict* and HSK can be regarded as W. More details of all the ground truth are shown in my GitHub[4].

For classification, the label for each word has annotated by CEFR or HSK. For ranking, we choose the pairs of words from any two different difficulty levels and each pair will be considered in both positive and negative directions. The training and test set are divided by a ratio of 9:1 and the average accuracy of 10 runs on test set are used as the metrics. In this task, we focus on the classification and ranking for word difficulty and ignore the phrases in W. We assign the lower levels for the 6.54% words with multi labels, since we assumpt that a L2 leaner will not recite a word again if it has been learned in a lower level.

4   Results

In this section, we discuss the results obtained by multi-faceted features and the ablation tests for feature selection.

4.1   Baseline Models

Human Baseline. To observe the limitation of human on classifying word difficulties, 5 people with educational background are chosen to do the classification and word-pair difficulty ranking task for each language. For classification, each person was asked to allocate the difficulty levels for 100 words. For difficulty ranking, each one was given 100 pairs of words to label their difficulty relations.

Random Baseline (Random). In classification task, we follow the original distribution of word levels and randomly assign a level for each word. In difficulty ranking task, each word pair will be randomly assigned with a difficulty relation.

Frequency-Only Baseline (FO). To construct the frequency-only baseline model, we calculate the word frequencies based on different corpora (Sect. 3).

Frequency-Clustering Baseline (FC). We apply K-means to divide the levels. The Euclidean distance between two words can be regarded as the difference on their frequencies: $dist(w_i, w_j) = |f_{w_i} - f_{w_j}|$.

---

[3] https://github.com/f-e-l-i-x/deuPD.
[4] https://github.com/LoraineYoko/word_difficulty.

Multi-features Baseline. The combination of frequency, length, syllables and the number of consonant clusters is used by Koirala and Culligan [4,5]. Hiebert et al. [3] used word frequency and POS tags together to measure word difficulty. Following these studies, we conduct the **FLSCP** (Freq, Length, #Syllables, #Consonant and #Phonemes) baseline and **FPOS** (Freq and POS) baseline. Since they are only theoretical research and lack of automatic classification experiments, we use MLP to make up the baselines.

4.2 Results for Multi-faceted Features

The results of word difficulty classification and word-pair difficulty ranking are shown in Table 1. MMF represents the Multi-faceted Features.

Table 1. The classification (CLS) and ranking (Rank) results using New York Times (E1), Gutenberg (E2), their combination (E1+E2), Parallel Corpus for German (GE) and Wikipedia for Chinese (CN) to extract the features. MFF is the multi-faceted features using Word2Vec to obtain word embeddings. (** indicates $p\text{-}value \leq 0.01$ compared with Random, FC, FO, FPOS and FLSCP baselines; †† indicates $p\text{-}value \leq 0.01$ compared with Random, FC, FO and FPOS.)

	E1		E2		E1+E2		GE		CN	
	CLS	Rank	CLS	Rank	CLS	Rank	CLS	Rank	CLS	Rank
Random	20.57	49.85	20.57	49.85	20.57	49.85	33.61	47.14	16.63	43.03
FC	8.23	67.50	17.53	30.36	22.41	55.00	34.93	49.24	33.84	40.87
FO	34.20	66.10	27.94	55.13	26.91	51.92	36.83	53.42	54.02	62.99
FPOS	33.18	52.06	29.14	52.55	28.19	54.87	37.69	50.88	53.34	63.61
FLSCP	33.78	68.49	28.70	62.06	26.56	60.56	39.22	52.07	55.16	67.26
MFF$_{\text{SVM}}$	40.84**	**75.59****	41.07**	73.63**	**43.85****	70.89**	42.39**	**70.47****	**57.80****	67.51††
MFF$_{\text{MLP}}$	**42.94****	74.91**	**41.18****	**74.88****	42.83**	**76.29****	**47.74****	67.91**	56.96**	**68.52**††
Human	49.28	88.89	49.28	88.89	49.28	88.89	44.44	65.85	60.82	81.16

Compared with the baselines, our proposed model takes more features into consideration, especially the syntactic and semantic features. In Table 1, we find that the results of English and German for both tasks implemented by MFF$_{\text{SVM}}$ and MFF$_{\text{MLP}}$ are better than all the baselines by T-test with $p\text{-}value \leq 0.01$. Although frequency plays an important role in Chinese, the result still shows the superiority of multi-faceted features. The performance on three languages indicates that multi-faceted features are effective for word difficulty classification. It is also relatively stable among different language environments, showing a strong generalization ability which can be used in diverse language environments.

Comparing the results with human baseline, it is observed that the performances of our models are close to human behavior. That is to say, it is a truly difficult task that even human can not achieve high accuracy with limited training. Our work is shown to be meaningful and there is still room for improvement.

4.3   Ablation Test and Feature Selection

Based on the extracted features, we use the multi-layer perceptron (MLP) to investigate the effectiveness of each single feature and their combination MFF.

Table 2. Classification ablation test of accuracy with each individual feature taken away. The embedding in this table is Word2Vec.

MFF	E1	E2	GE	CN	MFF	E1	E2	GE	CN
	42.94	41.18	47.74	56.96		42.94	41.18	47.74	56.96
MFF-Freq	40.81	40.51	47.12	51.64	MFF-Length	41.72	40.90	43.00	52.36
MFF-Phoneme	42.32	40.14	41.98	54.96	MFF-BiVec	42.85	40.77	43.00	56.70
MFF-TriVec	41.28	41.11	46.71	55.92	MFF-BiProb	42.04	38.98	45.06	56.10
MFF-TriProb	41.46	39.61	45.88	52.42	MFF-POS	40.70	40.93	43.21	55.32
MFF-Dep.	38.65	37.52	46.71	55.20	MFF-Embedding	34.22	33.78	41.36	45.16

Table 2 shows the classification results of MFF and each individual feature which are measured by removing it from MFF one at a time, then we find MFF has the best performance. The lower accuracy of a compound with certain individual feature taken away, the more effective this feature is. For all languages, word embedding is most effective, while other features behave differently in different languages. To investigate the effectiveness of features under different languages, we intuitively conduct the experiments on combination of features in different aspectsb (Table 3). This experiment makes an discovery that intra-word features play a very important role in German words, then frequency and length plays an important role in Chinese words. One reasonable explanation is that the pronunciation of German words is closely related to its difficulty (Table 2). For Chinese, the construction of HSK vocabulary fully considers the role of frequency. In addition, the length increases with difficulty level, following the statistical mapping {H1: 1.50, H2: 1.64, H3: 1.78, H4: 1.86, H5: 1.89, H6: 2.04}. For English, comparing the features extracted from E1 and E2, the relative strength of different feature aspects are similar, suggesting strong robustness of the model against different environments.

Table 3. Comparison of classification accuracy on different feature aspects on three languages. The embedding in this table is Word2Vec.

MFF	E1	E2	GE	CN	MFF	E1	E2	GE	CN
	42.94	41.18	47.74	56.96		42.94	41.18	47.74	56.96
Freq.+Length	34.13	29.55	36.05	**55.54**	Intra-word	28.14	28.45	**44.32**	41.82
Syntactic	31.51	30.56	39.34	52.28	Semantic	**39.40**	**36.82**	37.82	52.40

Due to obvious advantages of the results on word embeddings in Table 2 and 3, we further investigate the performances on different embeddings. Table 4 is the classification result for MFF with Word2Vec, GloVe and BERT. The best results appear between Word2Vec and BERT, but there is no obvious advantages on BERT. Although BERT model can capture the context of a word and clearly distinguish polysemy of a word in sentence-level tasks, when applying it to word level, each word is represented with a fixed vector which mixes all the contextual information together and the advantage of BERT model has been defeated.

Table 4. Classification results with the features including different embeddings.

	E1	E2	GE	CN
MFF[Word2Vec]	**42.94**	41.18	**47.74**	**56.96**
MFF[GloVe]	36.80	38.77	46.91	56.22
MFF[BERT]	42.11	**41.76**	46.30	53.78

5 Related Work

There are some previous papers [2,4] discussing the various features that influence word difficulty. However, most attempts takes the frequency as only feature for words. A typical example is an online language scoring API provided to check the word difficulty by ranking the frequencies in a huge corpus[5]. Other research talked about the feature combinations that influence word difficulty. Cesar Koirala [4] used the quantity difference between difficult words and easy words to show the function of word length, number of syllables and number of consonant clusters. Hiebert et al [3] chose statistic method to discuss the features of words that distinguish students' performances in various grades, including word frequency, part-of-speech and word morphological family size. Similarly, spelling rules and morphological features which consist of prefixes and suffixes are also considered in the study of difficulty in Japanese and German [12,13]. However, traditional research mostly focus on theoretical analysis individually, without a comprehensive analysis of all the features. They also ignore the importance of developing a effective approach to do the difficulty division task instead of long-term human labors. Our methods try to solve this bottleneck and use automatic classification to assign difficulty levels for words.

6 Conclusion

In this paper, we propose the word difficulty classification and word-pair difficulty ranking methods with multi-faceted features. Our model with multi-faceted features is significantly better than previous methods with limited features. The experiments further show the robustness of our approach against different languages and corpora, which indicates that it is a promising method in word difficulty level prediction.

---

[5] https://www.twinword.com/api/language-scoring.php.

In the feature, we will apply this method to more languages which may help to figure out the main discrepancy among different languages. This method can be also used to explore the word difficulty changes in different periods.

References

1. Little, D.: The common European framework of reference for languages: a research agenda. Lang. Teach. **44**(3), 381–393 (2011)
2. Breland, H.M.: Word frequency and word difficulty: a comparison of counts in four corpora. Psychol. Sci. **7**(2), 96–99 (1996)
3. Hiebert, E., Scott, J., Castaneda, R., Spichtig, A.: An analysis of the features of words that influence vocabulary difficulty. Educ. Sci. **9**(1), 8 (2019)
4. Koirala, C.: The word frequency effect on second language vocabulary learning. In: Critical CALL-Proceedings of the 2015 EUROCALL Conference, Padova, Italy, p. 318. Research-publishing.net (2015)
5. Culligan, B.: A comparison of three test formats to assess word difficulty. Lang. Test. **32**(4), 503–520 (2015)
6. Schuster, S., Manning, C.D.: Enhanced English universal dependencies: an improved representation for natural language understanding tasks. In: LREC, Portorož, Slovenia, pp. 23–28 (2016)
7. Toutanova, K., Klein, D., Manning, C.D., Singer, Y.: Feature-rich part-of-speech tagging with a cyclic dependency network. In: Proceedings of the 2003 Conference of the North American Chapter of the Association for Computational Linguistics on Human Language Technology, vol. 1, pp. 173–180. Association for Computational Linguistics (2003)
8. Evan, S.: The New York Times Annotated Corpus LDC2008T19. DVD. Linguistic Data Consortium, Philadelphia (2008)
9. Lahiri, S.: Complexity of word collocation networks: a preliminary structural analysis. In: Proceedings of the Student Research Workshop at the 14th Conference of the European Chapter of the Association for Computational Linguistics, pp. 96–105. Association for Computational Linguistics, Gothenburg, April 2014. http://www.aclweb.org/anthology/E14-3011
10. Kominek, J., Black, A.W.: The CMU arctic speech databases. In: Proceedings of the 5th ISCA Speech Synthesis Workshop (SSW5), Pittsburgh, PA, pp. 223–224 (2004)
11. Koehn, P.: Europarl: a parallel corpus for statistical machine translation. In: MT Summit, vol. 5, pp. 79–86. Citeseer (2005)
12. Hancke, J., Vajjala, S., Meurers, D.: Readability classification for German using lexical, syntactic, and morphological features. In: Proceedings of COLING 2012, pp. 1063–1080 (2012)
13. Nakanishi, K., Kobayashi, N., Shiina, H., Kitagawa, F.: Estimating word difficulty using semantic descriptions in dictionaries and web data. In: 2012 IIAI International Conference on Advanced Applied Informatics, pp. 324–329. IEEE (2012)

Dual-Learning-Based Neural Machine Translation Using Undirected Sequence Model for Document Translation

Lei Zhang and Jianhua Xu[✉]

School of Computer Science and Technology, Nanjing Normal University,
Nanjing 210023, Jiangsu, China
1922350320stu.njnu.edu.cn, xujianhua@njnu.edu.cn

Abstract. Document-level machine translation remains challenging owing to the high time complexity of existing models. In this paper, we propose a dual-learning-based neural machine translation (NMT) using undirected neural sequence model for document-level translation. Dual-learning mechanism can enable an NMT system to automatically learn from corpora through a reinforcement learning process. Undirected neural sequence models such as Bidirectional Encoder Representations from Transformers (BERT) have achieved success on several natural language processing (NLP) tasks. Inspired by a BERT-like machine translation model, we employ a constant-time decoding strategy in our model. In addition, we utilize a two-step training strategy. The experimental results show that our approach has much faster decoding speed than a previous document-level NMT model on several document-level translation tasks while the loss of our approach's translation quality is acceptable.

Keywords: Dual-learning · Neural machine translation · Undirected sequence model · Document-level

1 Introduction

During the past several years, the rapid development of NMT investigates the use of neural networks to model the translation process. The transformer model [1] has achieved the state-of-the-art performance in sentence-level translation tasks. However, when turning to document-level translation, the transformer model has a slow translation speed owing to its high time complexity. Different from sentence-level translation, document-level translation is in need of more time to train the models and translate the texts. Document-level NMT has attracted increasing attention from the community [2–4]. Some previous approaches propose to extend the transformer in order to improve the quality of document-level translation tasks over transformer. BERT [5] is an undirected neural sequence model that brought conspicuous improvements to a variety of discriminative language modeling tasks such as natural language inference. In undirected sequence models, every word in the sentence depends on the full left and right context

© Springer Nature Switzerland AG 2020
H. Yang et al. (Eds.): ICONIP 2020, CCIS 1332, pp. 643–650, 2020.
https://doi.org/10.1007/978-3-030-63820-7_73

around it. Mansimov et al. [6] propose a general framework that unifies decoding from both directed and undirected sequence models. Based on their work, we utilize a constant-time translation model using undirected sequence models on document-level translation. Our proposed model was also inspired by a translation-variant of BERT called a masked translation model [7]. Employing undirected models can support highly parallel decoding, which results in much faster training. In the constant-time decoding strategy, the number of iterations T is constant w.r.t. the length of a translation, i.e., $T = O(1)$. We utilize an optimistic decoding and length-conditioned beam search from a masked language model. In order to extract long contiguous sequences, we train the models with document-level corpora rather than only using shuffled sentence-level corpora.

Experimental results show that when compared to Zhang et al. [4], our approach offers a tradeoff between speed and performance, trading up to less than 3 BLEU scores in translation quality for an 7× speed-up during decoding. In many scenarios, this is an acceptable price to pay for a significant speedup by parallel decoding.

2   Related Work

Recent years have witnessed various translation models proposed for document-level translation. Most of existing studies aim to improve overall translation quality. Some of them [4,8] use extraction-based models to extract partial document context from previous sentences of the current sentence. For example, Zhang et al. [4] extend transformer translation model using multi-head self-attention [1] to compute the representation of document-level context. Tan et al. [3] propose a hierarchical model to capture the global document context for document translation. In addition, some studies concentrate on improving the translation speed of the NMT tasks. Ghazvininejad et al. [9] introduce conditional masked language models and a novel mask-predict decoding algorithm that leverages their parallelism to generate text in a constant number of decoding iterations.

3   Dual-Learning NMT Using Undirected Sequence Model

3.1   Dual-Learning for Neural Machine Translation (NMT)

The concept of dual learning was proposed by He et al. [10]. Machine translation always happen in dual directions, the forward translation and backward translation can provide quality feedback to the dual translation models. The dual-learning NMT can be described as the following process.

Consider a corpora of language A (D_A) and a corpora of language B (D_B). The two corpora are not necessarily aligned with each other. There are two translation models that can translate sentences from A to B and verse visa. By training with the dual learning NMT method, we can improve the accuracy of two translation models. We start from a sentence in a corpora D_A (or D_B)

and translate it forward to language B (or A) and then translate backward to language A (or B). By evaluating this two-hop translation results, we will get a sense about the quality of the two translation models mentioned above and be capable of improving them accordingly. This process can be iterated for many rounds until both translation models converge.

3.2 Decoding from Masked Language Models

An Undirected Sequence Model: BERT. BERT [5] is designed to pre-train deep bidirectional representations from unlabeled text by jointly conditioning on both left and right contexts in all layers and predict the original vocabulary only based on its left and right contexts. The word to be predicted is masked with a special [mask] symbol and the model is trained to predict $p(y_i|y_{<i}, [mask], y_{>i}, X)$. The y_i is the i-th vocabulary in the target sequence, and X is an input variable that denote the condition of sequence generation.

Optimistic Decoding and Beam Search from a MLM. MLM [5] is a BERT's pre-training task. It means that mask some percentage of the input tokens at random and predict those masked tokens. TLM (Translation Language Model) [7] is an extension of MLM, which concatenates parallel sentences, instead of considering monolingual text streams. The words are randomly masked in both the source and target sentences. There is a generation sequence G of pairs of an intermediate sequence $Y^t = (y_1^t, \ldots, y_L^t)$ and the corresponding coordinate sequence $Z^t = (z_1^t, \ldots, z_L^t)$, $y_i^t \in V$ and $z_i^t \in \{0, 1\}$, where V is a vocabulary, T is the number of generation steps, t is a number between 1 and T. The coordinate sequence indicates which of the current intermediate sequence are to be replaced. Consecutive pairs are related to each other by $y_i^{t+1} = (1 - z_i^{t+1})y_i^t + z_i^{t+1}\tilde{y}_i^{t+1}$, where $\tilde{y}_i^{t+1} \in V$ is a new symbol for the position i. This sequence of pairs G describes a procedure that starts from an empty sequence $Y^1 = ([mask], \ldots, [mask])$ and an empty coordinate sequence $Z^1 = (0, \ldots, 0)$, and then terminates with final target sequence Y^T after T steps. Mansimov et al. [6] model this procedure probabilistically as $p(G|X)$:

$$p(G|X) = p(L|X) \prod_{t=1}^{T} \prod_{i=1}^{L} p(z_i^{t+1}|Y^{\leq t}, Z^t, X) p(y_i^{t+1}|Y^{\leq t}, X)^{z_i^{t+1}} \quad (1)$$

The whole process can be conditioned on an input variable X, which indicates that the proposed model is applicable to both conditional and unconditional sequence generation. In the latter case, $X = \Phi$. Conditional MLMs [9] can train from the entire sequence in parallel, resulting in much faster training. Thus we employ conditional MLM in our experiments.

We first predict the length L of a target sequence Y according to $p(L|X)$ distribution to which we refer as length prediction. At each generation step t, we first select the next coordinates Z^{t+1} for which the corresponding symbols will be replaced according to $p(z_i^{t+1}|Y^{\leq t}, Z^t, X)$, to which we refer as coordinate selection. Once the coordinate sequence is determined, we replace the corresponding symbols according to the distribution $p(y_i^{t+1}|Y^{\leq t}, Z^t, X)$, leading to the next intermediate sequence Y^{t+1}. From this framework, we recover the sequence distribution $p(Y|X)$ by marginalizing out all the intermediate and coordinate sequences except for the final sequence Y^T.

Based on the adaptive Gibbs sampler [6], we utilize an inference procedure to approximately find the most likely sequence $\arg\max_Y p(Y|X)$ from the sequence distribution by exploiting the corresponding model of sequence generation. We exploit an optimistic decoding approach which is following Eq. (1):

$$
\begin{aligned}
\log p(G^*|X) = \underset{\substack{L, Y^1, \dots, Y^T \\ Z^1, \dots, Z^T}}{\arg\max} \ \log p(L|X) + \sum_{t=1}^{T} \sum_{i=1}^{L} (\log p(z_i^{t+1}|Y^{\leq t}, Z^t, X) \\
+ z_i^{t+1} \log p(y_i^{t+1}|Y^{\leq t}, X)
\end{aligned}
\tag{2}
$$

where G^* denotes the target sequence of pairs. The procedure is optimistic since we consider a sequence generated by following the most likely generation path to be highly likely under the sequence distribution obtained by marginalizing out the generation path. This optimism in the criterion admits a deterministic approximation scheme such as beam search. After iterating for T steps, beam search terminates with the final set of K generation hypotheses. Since much of the conditional MLM's computation can be batched, we can decode the same example into the K sequence generation hypotheses in parallel. Then we choose one of them according to Eq. (2) and return the final symbol sequence $\hat{Y}^T$.

3.3 Model Training

In document-level translation, the standard training objective is to maximize the log-likelihood of the training data:

$$
\hat{\theta} = \underset{\theta}{\arg\max}\{ \sum_{\langle X,Y \rangle \in D_d} \log P(Y|X; \theta) \}
\tag{3}
$$

where θ is a set of model parameters. Previous studies [4,8] employ two-step training strategies to make use of large-scale sentence-level parallel pairs. Following their work, we borrow large-scale corpora with sentence-level parallel pairs to pre-train our model first and use small-scale document-level corpora to fine-tune it.

4 Experiments

To examine the effect of our model, we conduct experiments on Chinese-to-English (Zh-En), Spanish-to-English (Es-En) and German-to-English (De-En) document-level translation. Our baseline model is the extended transformer model proposed by Zhang et al. [4]. We leverage a NMT system implemented by PyTorch for all experiments. We employ BLEU [11] (multi-blue) scores to measure the quality of the generated translations.

Table 1. Training, development and testing document-level parallel corpora. "sps" denotes sentence pairs and "docs" denotes documents

Language pairs	Training (sentence-level)	Training (document-level)	Development	Testing
Zh-En	2M sps	226K sps/1,906 docs	879 sps/8 docs	5.6K sps/67 docs
Es-En	–	4.2M sps/5,728 docs	1.8K sps/13 docs	5.7K sps/72 docs
De-En	–	172K sps/1,361 docs	1.2K sps/7 docs	2.3K sps/31 docs

Table 2. Evaluation of training and decoding speed. The speed is measured in terms of word/second (wps).

Model	Training	Decoding
Transformer	41K	873
Baseline	31K	364
Ours	106K	2635

Table 3. Performance (BLEU scores) comparison with other models on Zh-En document-level translation task.

Model	tst14	tst15	tst16	tst17	Avg
Transformer	15.49	17.37	16.09	17.81	16.69
Baseline	16.92	19.39	17.68	19.25	18.31
Ours	15.16	17.14	15.83	17.32	16.36

4.1 Experimental Settings

Datasets. In Zh-En translation task, we first use sentence-level parallel corpora LDC2004T07, LDC2003E14, LDC2004T08 and LDC2005T10, and then employ document-level parallel corpora Ted talks from the IWSLT 2017 [12]. In Es-En translation task, we carry out experiments on two different domains: talks and subtitles. TED Talks is part of the IWSLT 2014 and 2015 [12,13]. As for subtitles corpora, we use a subset of OpenSubtitles2018. For De-En translation, we use the document-level parallel corpora Ted Talks from the IWSLT 2014 [12]. Table 1 shows the statistics of corpora. In preprocessing, we use byte pair encoding [14] to segment words into sub-word units for all languages.

Model Settings. A transformer [1] with 1024 hidden units, 6 layers and 8 heads was utilized. We use pretrained models that were trained using a masked language modeling objective [7] on monolingual sentences from WMT NewsCrawl 2007–2008. We concatenate parallel Chinese and English sentences (or other language pairs' sentences), mask out a subset of the tokens in either the Chinese or English sentence (or other language pairs) and predict the masked tokens. As in Ghazvininejad et al. [9], 0–100% tokens were uniformly masked out. Other settings with the Adam [15] optimization and regularization methods are the same as the default transformer model. We train the models with an inverse square root learning rate schedule, learning rate of 10^{-4}, $\beta_1 = 0.9$, $\beta_2 = 0.98$. The beam size and dropout [16] rate are set to 4 and 0.1 respectively. Our models are trained on 8 GPUs and the batch size is set to 256. We use a fixed budget of $T = 20$, linearly annealing o_t from L to 1, and Least2Most decoding strategy [6,9], where o_t is the number of tokens predicted at the t-th iteration of generation. We utilize beam search and consider only one possible position

Table 4. Performance (BLEU scores) comparison with baseline model on Es-En document-level translation task.

Model	TED Talks	Subtitles
Baseline	36.97	36.54
Ours	34.65	34.08

Table 5. Performance (BLEU scores) comparison with baseline model on De-En document-level translation.

Model	tst13	tst14	Avg
Baseline	33.17	29.32	31.25
Ours	31.05	27.13	29.09

Table 6. Evaluation on pronoun translation of Zh-En document-level translation.

Model	tst14	tst15	tst16	tst17	Avg
Baseline	52.68	53.04	58.94	56.37	55.26
Ours	51.53	52.32	57.91	55.49	54.32

for replacing a symbol per hypothesis each time of generation. And we use four length candidates, which performs as well as using the ground-truth length [6].

4.2 Experimental Results

Evaluation of Efficiency. The training speed and decoding speed are shown in Table 2. Obviously, the decoding speed of our approach is nearly 7 times that of baseline.

Chinese-to-English Translation. We use the two-step training strategy to train the Zh-En translation models. We first train the models with sentence-level parallel corpora containing 2M sentence pairs, after that we utilize document-level parallel corpora that contains 226K sentence pairs to train the models. As shown in Table 3, using the same data, our model only losses 1.95 BLEU scores compared with baseline on Zh-En document-level translation.

4.3 Different Language Pairs

The BLEU scores of Es-En document-level translation task are shown in Table 4. For TED Talks, the BLEU scores are the average scores of the evaluation results on the test sets (tst2010, tst2011 and tst2012). Our model losses 2.39 BLEU scores (34.65 vs 36.97) compared with Zhang et al. [4], which is a relative decrease of less than 7% in translation quality. But our model speed up the decoding significantly. As for subtitles, the BLEU scores are the evaluation results on the test sets, and the result is similar to TED Talks'.

The results of De-En document translation are shown in Table 5. From the results, we can see that our proposed model reaches within 2.16 BLEU scores from baseline. Compared with baseline, our model is capable of improving translation speed while the loss of translation quality is acceptable.

Table 7. An example of noun translation in the Zh-En document-level translation.

Pre-context	... you 3D huanjing, nenggou zai shijie gedi denglu, cong **shouji** shang, **diannao** shang ...
Rear-context	... tamen xuanze le shijieshang qita diqu haitongmen yijing chuangzao de caipu ...
Source	**chengxu** limian you butong de bufen C wuli tiaojie, ganyingqi
Reference	There are different parts in the **application** – physical adjustment, sensors
Baseline	There are different parts of the **program** – physical regulation, sensors
Ours	There are different parts in the **program** – physical adjustment, sensors

4.4 Pronoun and Noun Translation

We conduct a further experiment on pronoun and noun translation. For the analysis of pronoun translation, we evaluate coreference and anaphora using the reference-based metric: accuracy of pronoun translation [17] in Zh-En translation. The experiment results are shown in Table 6. The source sentences are from tst2017. For the analysis of noun translation, as shown in Table 7, the word *chengxu* in source sentence is translated into *program* by baseline and our model. Our model catch the information such as the words *shouji* and *diannao* in the pre-context which provide essential evidence for an accurate translation of *chengxu*. This reveals that our model is capable of exploit some useful information in global context.

5 Conclusion

In order to improve document-level translation speed, we present a neural machine translation using undirected sequence model based on dual-learning, which is inspired by BERT and its translation variant. Our experiments on three language pairs corpora reveal that on document-level translation tasks, our approach with constant-time decoding strategy is much faster than the baseline [4] at a cost of less than 3 BLEU scores. In our future work, we will focus on optimizing our approach and train language models that have higher document-level translation quality.

References

1. Vaswani, A., et al.: Attention is all you need. In: Guyon, I., et al. (eds.) Advances in Neural Information Processing Systems 30, NIPS 2017, pp. 5998–6008. Curran Associates, New York (2017)
2. Bawden, R., Sennrich, R., Birch, A., Haddow, B.: Evaluating discourse phenomena in neural machine translation. In: Walker, M.A., Ji, H., Stent, A. (eds.) NAACL-HLT 2018, vol. 1, pp. 1304–1313. ACL, Stroudsburg (2018)

3. Tan, X., Zhang, L., Xiong, D., Zhou, G.: Hierarchical modeling of global context for document-level neural machine translation. In: Inui, K., Jiang, J., Ng, V., Wan, X. (eds.) EMNLP-IJCNLP 2019, pp. 1576–1585. ACL, Stroudsburg (2019)
4. Zhang, J., et al.: Improving the transformer translation model with document-level context. In: Riloff, E., Chiang, D., Hockenmaier, J., Tsujii, J. (eds.) The 2018 Conference on EMNLP, pp. 533–542. ACL, Stroudsburg (2018)
5. Devlin, J., Chang, M.W., Lee, K., Toutanova, K.: BERT: pre-training of deep bidirectional transformers for language understanding. In: Burstein, J., Doran, C., Solorio, T. (eds.) NAACL-HLT 2019, vol. 1, pp. 4171–4186. ACL, Stroudsburg (2019)
6. Mansimov, E., Wang, A., Cho, K.: A generalized framework of sequence generation with application to undirected sequence models. CoRR abs/1905.12790 (2019)
7. Lample, G., Conneau, A.: Cross-lingual language model pretraining. In: Wallach, H.M., Larochelle, H., Beygelzimer, A., d'Alché-Buc, F., Fox, E.B., Garnett, R. (eds.) Advances in Neural Information Processing Systems 32, NIPS 2019, pp. 7057–7067. Curran Associates, New York (2019)
8. Miculicich, L., Ram, D., Pappas, N., Henderson, J.: Document-level neural machine translation with hierarchical attention networks. In: Riloff, E., Chiang, D., Hockenmaier, J., Tsujii, J. (eds.) The 2018 Conference on EMNLP, pp. 2947–2954. ACL, Stroudsburg (2018)
9. Ghazvininejad, M., Levy, O., Liu, Y., Zettlemoyer, L.: Mask-predict: parallel decoding of conditional masked language models. In: Inui, K., Jiang, J., Ng, V., Wan, X. (eds.) EMNLP-IJCNLP 2019, pp. 6111–6120. ACL, Stroudsburg (2019)
10. He, D., et al.: Dual learning for machine translation. In: Lee, D.D., Sugiyama, M., von Luxburg, U., Guyon, I., Garnett, R. (eds.) Advances in Neural Information Processing Systems 29, NIPS 2016, pp. 820–828. Curran Associates, New York (2016)
11. Papineni, K., Roukos, S., Ward, T., Zhu, W.J.: Bleu: a method for automatic evaluation of machine translation. In: 40th Annual Meeting of the Association for Computational Linguistics, ACL 2002, pp. 311–318. ACL, Stroudsburg (2002)
12. Cettolo, M., Girardi, C., Federico, M.: Wit3: web inventory of transcribed and translated talks. In: 16th Conference of the European Association for Machine Translation (EAMT), Trento, Italy, pp. 261–268 (2012)
13. Cettolo, M., Jan, N., Sebastian, S., Bentivogli, L., Cattoni, R., Federico, M.: The IWSLT 2015 evaluation campaign. In: The International Workshop on Spoken Language Translation, Da Nang, Vietnam (2015)
14. Sennrich, R., Haddow, B., Birch, A.: Neural machine translation of rare words with subword units. In: 54th Annual Meeting of the Association for Computational Linguistics, ACL 2016, pp. 1715–1725. ACL, Stroudsburg (2016)
15. Kingma, D.P., Ba, J.: Adam: a method for stochastic optimization. In: Bengio, Y., LeCun, Y. (eds.) 3rd International Conference on Learning Representations, ICLR 2015, San Diego (2015)
16. Srivastava, N., Hinton, G., Krizhevsky, A., Sutskever, I., Salakhutdinov, R.: Dropout: a simple way to prevent neural networks from overfitting. J. Mach. Learn. Res. 15, 1929–1958 (2014)
17. Werlen, L.M., Popescu-Belis, A.: Validation of an automatic metric for the accuracy of pronoun translation (APT). In: Webber, B.L., Popescu-Belis, A., Tiedemann, J. (eds.) 3rd Workshop on Discourse in Machine Translation, EMNLP 2017, pp. 17–25. ACL, Stroudsburg (2017)

From Shortsighted to Bird View: Jointly Capturing All Aspects for Question-Answering Style Aspect-Based Sentiment Analysis

Liang Zhao, Bingfeng Luo, Zuo Bai, Xi Yin, Kunfeng Lai,
and Jianping Shen[✉]

Ping An Life Insurance of China, Ltd., Shenzhen, China
{zhaoliang425,luobingfeng981,
baizuo822,yinxi445,shenjianping324}@pingan.com.cn

Abstract. Aspect-based sentiment analysis (ABSA) aims to identify the opinion polarity towards a specific aspect. Traditional approaches formulate ABSA as a sentence classification task. However, it is observed that the single sentence classification paradigm cannot take full advantage of pre-trained language models. Previous work suggests it is better to cast ABSA as a question answering (QA) task for each aspect, which can be solved in the sentence-pair classification paradigm. Though QA-style ABSA achieves state-of-the-art (SOTA) results, it naturally separates the prediction process of multiple aspects belonging to the same sentence. It thus is unable to take full advantage of the correlation between different aspects. In this paper, we propose to use the global-perspective (GP) question to replace the original question in QA-style ABSA, which explicitly tells the model the existence of other relevant aspects using additional instructions. In this way, the model can distinguish relevant phrases for each aspect better and utilize the underlying relationship between different aspects. The experimental results on three benchmark ABSA datasets demonstrate the effectiveness of our method.

Keywords: Aspect-based sentiment analysis · Neural networks

1 Introduction

Aspect-based sentiment analysis (ABSA) [6,11] aims to identify the sentiment polarities of a specific aspect in a sentence. For example, *"The food is delicious, but the service can be improved."* delivers positive sentiment polarity on the *food* while negative sentiment polarity on the *service*, respectively. Apart from aspects, sometimes, the sentence may also contain multiple targets. For example, *"Spago and Indulge both have delicious food, but the service of Spago is better."* describes aspects *food* and *service* for two targets: *Spago* and *Indulge*. This necessitates the targeted aspect-based sentiment analysis (TABSA) [13],

© Springer Nature Switzerland AG 2020
H. Yang et al. (Eds.): ICONIP 2020, CCIS 1332, pp. 651–659, 2020.
https://doi.org/10.1007/978-3-030-63820-7_74

which aims to identify the opinion polarity towards a specific aspect associated with a given target.

Traditional (T)ABSA[1] models use specialized network structures to model the interaction between the aspect and the input sentence [9,10,13]. While these methods work well when trained from scratch, recent research [14] shows that it is hard for these architectures to take full advantage of the powerful pre-trained networks like BERT [3].

On the other hand, it is found that modeling the ABSA task as a question-answering (QA) task achieves new state-of-the-art (SOTA) results [14] because it introduces pre-trained language models using natural language instructions [1, 12]. Specifically, when classifying the sentiment polarity of *food*, we can compose a question like "What do you think of the food?" using templates and convert the original ABSA task into a question-answering (QA) task. This QA task can be natively supported by pre-trained language models like BERT using the *sentence-pair classification paradigm*. The model takes in the original sentence along with the generated question, and outputs the sentiment polarity of the aspect asked in the question[2].

However, the QA-style ABSA task naturally separates the prediction process of multiple aspects in the same sentence. Therefore, it is hard for the network to consider all aspects when making predictions, which are useful when the sentence mentions many aspects and targets.

In this paper, we build the bridge between different aspects by reformulating the question in the QA-style (T)ABSA. Instead of utilizing network architectures to incorporate multiple aspects, we inform the model the existence of other aspects in the question by providing additional instructions, which helps the model better distinguish the correspondence of aspects and phrases expressing sentiment polarities.

Extensive experiments are conducted and new SOTA results are presented on three benchmark ABSA datasets. It demonstrates the necessity of considering all aspects in (T)ABSA and the effectiveness of informing the model of the existence of other aspects in the question using natural language. In summary, the contribution is two-fold: 1) An easy-to-use method is proposed to consider all aspects in the QA-style ABSA task. 2) New SOTA results are achieved on three benchmark ABSA datasets, which demonstrate the effectiveness of our method.

2   Methodology

2.1   Task Definition

ABSA. In aspect-based sentiment analysis (ABSA), given a sentence s with m words, and a set of aspects $\{a_1, ..., a_k\} \in A$, we need to predict the sentiment polarity $y \in \{positive, negative, neutral, none\}$ for each aspect. There are two

---

[1] (T)ABSA refers to *ABSA or TABSA*.

[2] In this paper, the sentence-pair classification paradigm only refers to the QA-style ABSA task. These two terms are used exchangeably.

kinds of aspects: 1) When the aspects are pre-defined categories, the task is called aspect-category sentiment analysis (ACSA). 2) When the aspects are pre-identified terms in the sentence, the task is called aspect-term sentiment analysis (ATSA). The left side of Table 1 shows an example for the ACSA version of ABSA.

TABSA. In targeted aspect-based sentiment analysis (TABSA), the input sentence s contains m words, some of which are pre-identified targets $\{t_1, ..., t_l\}$. Given a fixed set of aspects $\{a_1, ..., a_k\} \in A$, we need to predict the sentiment polarity $y \in \{positive, negative, neutral, none\}$ expressed in the sentence s for each target-aspect pair. TABSA can also be split into two subtasks: 1) *Aspect detection* identifies if certain aspect a is expressed towards the target t. 2) *Sentiment classification* predicts the sentiment polarity for each (t, a) pair. The right side of Table 1 demonstrates an example for TABSA.

Table 1. Examples for ABSA and TABSA. Base questions are questions used in [14]. GP questions refer to the proposed global-perspective questions (see Sect. 2.3). It is assumed that the aspects and targets mentioned in the sentence are known in advance.

ABSA Example: The food is good, but the service can be improved	TABSA Example: LOCATION2 is central London so extremely expensive, LOCATION1 is often considered the coolest area of London		
Base Question (food): What do you think of the food?	**Base Question (LOCATION2, price):** What do you think of the price of LOCATION2?		
GP Question (food): What do you think of the food? Do not be confused with service	**GP Question (LOCATION2, price):** What do you think of the price of LOCATION2? Do not be confused with aspects like transit-location and general opinion, and do not be confused with targets like LOCATION1		
Aspect	**Polarity**		
ambience	none		
food	positive		
menu	none		
place	none		
price	none		
service	negative		
staff	none		
miscellaneous	none		

Target	**Aspect**	**Polarity**
LOC1	general	positive
LOC1	price	none
LOC1	safety	none
LOC1	transit-location	none
LOC2	general	none
LOC2	price	negative
LOC2	safety	none
LOC2	transit-location	positive

2.2 Base Question Construction

Since pre-trained language models are good at utilizing natural language questions and instructions [1], there is an emerging trend to cast natural language problems as question answering tasks [4,8]. In (T)ABSA, it is observed that composing a question for each aspect (or target-aspect pair) and converting

(T)ABSA into a sentence-pair classification problem significantly outperforms the traditional sentence classification setting when introducing pre-trained language models [14]. We follow their settings to compose our base question.

As shown in Table 1, in ABSA, given a sentence s and an aspect a_i, the generated base question is *"What do you think of the a_i?"*. In TABSA, given a sentence s, an aspect a_i, and a target t_j, we generate the base question using the template of *"What do you think of the a_i of t_j?"*.

Given the input sentence s and the generated question q, we classify the sentiment polarity for the aspect (or target-aspect pair) asked in q. As elaborated in Sect. 2.4, this task can be formulated as a sentence-pair classification problem that takes s and q as the input and produces the classification results.

2.3   Global-Perspective Question Construction

While producing promising results in several (T)ABSA datasets [14], using the base question in Sect. 2.2 in the sentence-pair classification paradigm naturally separates different aspects and targets into different prediction processes. Therefore, the model cannot collectively consider all the aspects and targets when predicting the sentiment polarity of an aspect (or target-aspect pair).

We argue that jointly considering all the aspects and targets is beneficial to (T)ABSA. First, bearing related aspects and targets in mind can help prevent the model from being misled by phrases describing other aspects or targets. Moreover, some aspects and targets are potentially related to each other. Modeling this correlation can bring extra information for the (T)ABSA model.

Specifically, in ABSA, given a sentence s, an aspect a_i and the aspect set A with size k, we generate the global-perspective (GP) question following the template of *"What do you think of the a_i? Do not be confused with a_1, ... a_{i-1}, a_{i+1}, ..., and a_k."*. The latter part informs the model of the existence of other potential distraction aspects in A and formulates the potential correlations between all aspects. Note that, in the situation where we already know the aspects mentioned in s (like ATSA or MAMS [5]), A which contains all the aspects except a_i is replaced with the aspects that we know are related to s.

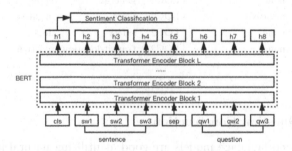

Fig. 1. Overview of our BERT-based sentence-pair classification model.

In TABSA, different from ABSA, the targets mentioned in the input sentence are included in the GP question. Given a sentence s, an aspect a_i along with the aspect set A of size k, and a target t_j along with the target set T of size l, the template is used to generate the GP question: *"What do you think of the a_i of T_j? Do not be confused with aspects like a_1, ... a_{i-1}, a_{i+1}, ..., and a_k, and do not be confused with targets like t_1, ..., t_{j-1}, t_{j+1}, ..., t_l."*. By informing the model of the existence of both related aspects and targets, the model can have a better understanding of the interaction of the phrase, aspects, and targets. Therefore, it leads to better prediction results.

2.4   Fine-Tuning with BERT

We use the sentence-pair classification paradigm of BERT to handle the (T)ABSA task. As shown in Fig. 1, [CLS], the input sentence s, [SEP] and the generated question q are fed into BERT, from which the output embedding **c** of [CLS] is extracted and used for sentiment classification.

3   Experiment

3.1   Datasets

SemEval14. SemEval14 [11] is a benchmark ABSA dataset. We use the restaurant domain, which contains 3608, 1120 for training and test. The sentiment polarities are expressed toward 5 pre-defined aspects[14].

MAMS. MAMS [5] is also an ABSA dataset. It contains more difficult cases where different aspects possess different sentiment polarities and is divided into two subtasks. Aspect category sentiment analysis (ACSA) is similar to SemEval14, which identifies the sentiment polarity of a fixed set of 8 pre-defined aspect categories. It contains 7090, 888, 901 for training, validation and test, respectively. Aspect term sentiment analysis (ATSA) picks certain phrases in the input sentence as aspect terms and contains 11186, 1332, 1336 data for training, validation and test, respectively.

SentiHood. SentiHood [13] is a TABSA dataset containing 3806, 955, 1898 sentences for train, validation and test, respectively. Each sentence contains several target-aspect pairs along with their sentiment polarities. Target mentions are replaced with special tokens like *LOCATION1* and *LOCATION2*. Following [14], the aspect set we consider is {*general, price, transit-location, safety*}.

3.2   Hyperparameters

Following [14], we use the pre-trained uncased BERT-base [3] for fine-tuning: 12 transformer layers, 768 hidden layer size, 12 self-attention heads, 0.1 dropout probability and 8 training epochs. The initial learning rate is 2e-5, and the batch sizes are 24, 24, 8 for SemEval-14, Sentihood, and MASA, respectively.

Table 2. ABSA Results on the SemEval-14 task 4 dataset.

Method	Precision	Recall	F1
XRCE [2]	83.23	81.37	82.29
NRC-Canada [7]	91.04	86.24	88.58
BERT [14]	92.78	89.07	90.89
BERT-QA [14]	92.87	90.24	91.54
BERT-QA-GP	**93.06**	**90.25**	**91.63**

Table 3. ACSA and ATSA results on the MAMS dataset.

Method	ACSA	ATSA
ATAE-LSTM [15]	70.63	77.05
GCAE [16]	72.10	77.59
CapsNet [5]	73.99	79.78
BERT [5]	78.29	82.22
CapsNet-BERT [5]	79.46	83.39
BERT-QA [14]	82.24	84.06
BERT-QA-GP	**83.57**	**84.21**

3.3 ABSA Results

We experiment our proposed GP question using two benchmark ABSA datasets: SemEval-14 task 4 and MAMS. The latter one is designed to include more difficult samples where different aspects possess different sentiment polarities. The baseline results are taken from [5,14] and BERT-QA for MAMS is implemented by the us because the original paper [14] does not include MAMS results.

BERT-QA achieves previous SOTA results in both datasets. And we also include other representative methods for a more comprehensive comparison.

Aspect Category Results. Aspect category sentiment analysis (ACSA) aims to identify sentiment polarities towards a fixed set of pre-defined categories. As shown in Table 2 and the ACSA column of Table 3, our proposed GP question (BERT-QA-GP) clearly improves the performance of the BERT-QA method, which was the previous SOTA method. Note that MAMS contains more difficult samples where different aspects possess different sentiment polarities. The proposed GP question achieves bigger improvement compared with the SemEval14 dataset. This shows that including the descriptions of other aspects in the question helps the model distinguish the correspondence between aspects and phrases expressing sentiment polarities.

Aspect Term Results. Different from ACSA, the aspects in aspect term sentiment analysis (ATSA) are phrases in the input sentence. As shown in the ATSA column of Table 3, while our proposed GP question (BERT-QA-GP) also improves the original BERT-QA, the improvement is not as significant as the one in ACSA. This conforms to the intuition that the pre-defined aspect categories often have different surface forms from the corresponding terms in the sentence. Therefore, in ACSA, the model is more easily misled by phrases describing other aspects. On the other hand, in ATSA, the aspect term is the word explicitly mentioned in the input sentence, thus less likely to be confused with others. Note that the model can still take advantage of the aspect correlation and deliver better results even though the confusion is less severe.

3.4   TABSA Results

Different from ABSA, sentences in TABSA may contain multiple targets. There-fore, we need to identify the sentiment polarity of an aspect towards a certain target. We follow the experimental settings in [14] and report both aspect detection and sentiment classification results. Aspect detection aims to find which aspects are mentioned for each target. And sentiment classification measures the accuracy and AUC of the predicted polarities given the gold results.

Table 4. TABSA results on the SentiHood dataset.

Method	Aspect		Sentiment	
	F1	AUC	Acc	AUC
LSTM-Loc [13]	69.3	89.7	81.9	83.9
SenticLSTM [10]	78.2	–	89.3	–
Dmu-Entnet [9]	78.5	94.4	91.0	94.8
BERT [14]	81.0	96.4	85.5	84.2
BERT-QA [14]	86.4	97.0	93.6	96.4
BERT-QA-GP	**86.6**	**97.3**	**93.8**	**96.8**

Table 4 shows the TABSA results in the SentiHood dataset. We can see that using the GP question (`BERT-QA-GP`) consistently improves the performance of `BERT-QA`. This shows that having a global view of relevant aspects and targets is also beneficial for the TABSA task. In the complicated multi-target multi-aspect sentences, taking relevant aspects and targets into consideration is beneficial fo the model to better pinpoint relevant phrases expressing sentiment polarity for certain aspects and targets.

3.5   Case Study

ABSA. The GP question can help the model ignore phrases irrelevant to the target aspect. In the sentence in the first row of Table 5, the phrase *not the best* describes *sushi*, yet `BERT-QA` mistakenly identifies the opinion towards *ambience* is neutral. However, with a global view of all the aspects, `BERT-QA-GP` correctly identifies a positive opinion towards the aspect *ambience*.

TABSA. Our GP question helps the model ignore distraction aspects and targets in both aspect detection and sentiment classification. In aspect detection, for example, `BERT-QA` predicts that aspect *transit-location* is expressed for *LOCA-TION2* in the sentence of the second row of Table 5. However, while phrases related to *transit-location* are near *LOCATION2*, *transit-location* is actually associated with *LOCATION1*. As for sentiment classification, as shown in the third row of Table 5, although `BERT-QA` correctly predicts that the *safety of*

LOLATION2 is negative, it erroneously outputs positive sentiment for the *general* aspect of *LOCATION2*. By telling the model not to be confused by distraction aspects and targets in the GP question, `BERT-QA-GP` pays more attention to the sentence structure and correctly outputs the right answer in both cases.

Table 5. Examples where GP questions help for both ABSA (the first line) and TABSA (the second and third line).

Sentence	Aspect	Target	BERT-QA	BERT-QA-GP	Gold
Certainly not the best sushi in New York, however, the place is very clean, sterile	Ambience	-	Neutral	Positive	Positive
The LOCATION1 is full of new apartment blocks, close to LOCATION2 and links to the London, yet the rent is cheap	Transit-location	LOCA-TION2	Positive	None	None
In general, anywhere on the LOCATION1 is ok, except LOCATION2 and Archway which are a bit dangerous	General	LOCA-TION2	Positive	Negative	Negative

4 Conclusion

Vanilla QA-style (T)ABSA task only considers one aspect (or target-aspect pair) at a time. In this paper, we propose to jointly consider all the aspects and targets in the QA-style (T)ABSA task by adding additional instructions to the original sentiment analysis question. Compared with considering each aspect and target independently, our method helps to prevent the model from being misled by phrases describing other aspects and targets. Besides, it also makes it possible for the model to take advantage of the correlations between different aspects and targets. The promising experimental results on three benchmark (T)ABSA datasets demonstrate the effectiveness of our proposed method.

References

1. Brown, T.B., et al.: Language models are few-shot learners. arXiv preprint arXiv:2005.14165 (2020)
2. Brun, C., Popa, D.N., Roux, C.: XRCE: hybrid classification for aspect-based sentiment analysis. In: SemEval@ COLING, pp. 838–842. Citeseer (2014)
3. Devlin, J., Chang, M.W., Lee, K., Toutanova, K.: BERT: pre-training of deep bidirectional transformers for language understanding. In: NAACL (2019)
4. Gardner, M., Berant, J., Hajishirzi, H., Talmor, A., Min, S.: Question answering is a format; when is it useful? arXiv preprint arXiv:1909.11291 (2019)
5. Jiang, Q., Chen, L., Xu, R., Ao, X., Yang, M.: A challenge dataset and effective models for aspect-based sentiment analysis. In: EMNLP-IJCNLP (2019)

6. Jo, Y., Oh, A.H.: Aspect and sentiment unification model for online review analysis. In: Proceedings of WSDM, pp. 815–824 (2011)
7. Kiritchenko, S., Zhu, X., Cherry, C., Mohammad, S.: NRC-Canada-2014: detecting aspects and sentiment in customer reviews. In: Proceedings of the 8th International Workshop on Semantic Evaluation (SemEval 2014), pp. 437–442 (2014)
8. Li, X., et al.: Entity-relation extraction as multi-turn question answering. In: ACL, pp. 1340–1350 (2019)
9. Liu, F., Cohn, T., Baldwin, T.: Recurrent entity networks with delayed memory update for targeted aspect-based sentiment analysis. In: NAACL, pp. 278–283 (2018)
10. Ma, Y., Peng, H., Cambria, E.: Targeted aspect-based sentiment analysis via embedding commonsense knowledge into an attentive LSTM. In: AAAI (2018)
11. Pontiki, M., Galanis, D., Pavlopoulos, J., Papageorgiou, H., Androutsopoulos, I., Manandhar, S.: SemEval-2014 task 4: aspect based sentiment analysis. In: Proceedings of the 8th International Workshop on Semantic Evaluation (SemEval 2014), pp. 27–35. Association for Computational Linguistics (2014)
12. Raffel, C., et al.: Exploring the limits of transfer learning with a unified text-to-text transformer. arXiv preprint arXiv:1910.10683 (2019)
13. Saeidi, M., Bouchard, G., Liakata, M., Riedel, S.: Sentihood: targeted aspect based sentiment analysis dataset for urban neighbourhoods. arXiv preprint arXiv:1610.03771 (2016)
14. Sun, C., Huang, L., Qiu, X.: Utilizing bert for aspect-based sentiment analysis via constructing auxiliary sentence. arXiv preprint arXiv:1903.09588 (2019)
15. Wang, Y., Huang, M., Zhu, X., Zhao, L.: Attention-based LSTM for aspect-level sentiment classification. In: Proceedings of EMNLP, pp. 606–615 (2016)
16. Xue, W., Li, T.: Aspect based sentiment analysis with gated convolutional networks. arXiv preprint arXiv:1805.07043 (2018)

Hierarchical Sentiment Estimation Model for Potential Topics of Individual Tweets

Qian Ji, Yilin Dai, Yinghua Ma, Gongshen Liu$^{(\boxtimes)}$, Quanhai Zhang$^{(\boxtimes)}$, and Xiang Lin

School of Electronic Information and Electrical Engineering, Shanghai Jiao Tong University, 800 Dongchuan RD, Shanghai 200240, China
{jeicy_good,lydai1108,ma-yinghua,lgshen,qhzhang,lionel}@sjtu.edu.cn

Abstract. Twitter has gradually become a valuable source of people's opinions and sentiments. Although tremendous progress has been made in sentiment analysis, mainstream methods hardly leverage user information. Besides, most methods strongly rely on sentiment lexicons in tweets, thus ignoring other non-sentiment words that imply rich topic information. This paper aims to predict individuals' sentiment towards potential topics on a two-point scale: positive or negative. The analysis is conducted based on their past tweets for the precise topic recommendation. We propose a hierarchical model of individuals' tweets (HMIT) to explore the relationship between individual sentiments and different topics. HMIT extracts token representations from fine-tuned Bidirectional Encoder Representations from Transformer (BERT). Then it incorporates topic information in context-aware token representations through a topic-level attention mechanism. The Convolutional Neural Network (CNN) serves as a final binary classifier. Unlike conventional sentiment classification in the Twitter task, HMIT extracts topic phrases through Single-Pass and feeds tweets without sentiment words into the whole model. We build six user models from one benchmark and our collected datasets. Experimental results demonstrate the superior performance of the proposed method against multiple baselines on both classification and quantification tasks.

Keywords: Sentiment analysis in Twitter · Hierarchical model · Deep learning

1 Introduction

Nowadays, the information exploited from tweets is abundant and useful, thus receiving great attention from researchers. The task in this paper is to predict individuals' sentiment towards potential topics on a two-point scale: positive or negative based on their past tweets. Generally, a user's attitudes towards different topics are closely related and won't change dramatically in a short time, so building models of individuals' tweets and estimating sentiment polarities towards potential topics are beneficial for precise topic recommendations for

© Springer Nature Switzerland AG 2020
H. Yang et al. (Eds.): ICONIP 2020, CCIS 1332, pp. 660–667, 2020.
https://doi.org/10.1007/978-3-030-63820-7_75

individuals, including related topics, advertisements and social circles. Earlier researchers [5] use a Support Vector Machines with part-of-speech features to categorize tweets. An adaptive recursive neural network for target-dependent classification is proposed, which propagates sentiment signals from sentiment-baring words to specific targets on a dependence tree [4].

All the methods mentioned above ignore potential sentiment relations within individuals' tweets but rely heavily on sentiment lexicons. Besides, the models mentioned above only focus on the classification task while more practical applications require a combination of extraction and classification. In this work, we propose a hierarchical model of individuals' tweets, which extracts topics with Single-Pass algorithm and models the relationship between individual sentiments and different topics. The main contributions of this paper are three-fold:

- Models are built on individuals' tweets and the topic phrase of each tweet is obtained through Single-Pass. Individuals' tweets without sentiment words, along with extracted topic and gold labels are inputs of HMIT. Based on the approach, it's possible to provide precise topic recommendations for individuals.
- We propose a novel topic-dependent hierarchical model, which extracts features from fine-tuned BERT and incorporates topic information through topic-level attention. CNN categorizes sentence representations into positive or negative.
- We build models on six users separately from one Twitter benchmark dataset and dataset collected by ourselves. We also create new test dataset, collecting neutral sentences from three general topics. In our experiments, the proposed method is able to outperform multiple baselines on both datasets in terms of classification and quantification.

2   Related Work

Target-based sentiment analysis aims to judge the sentiment polarity expressed for each target being discussed. To capture semantic relations flexibly, a target-dependent Long Short-Term Memory (TD-LSTM) is proposed [10]. As attention mechanism has been successfully applied to many tasks, a variety of attention-based RNN models have proven to be effective ways [12]. To our knowledge, we are the first to exploit target-individual relation for target-based sentiment analysis. Hierarchical models have been used predominantly for representing sentences. A hierarchical ConvNet to extract salient sentences from reviews is employed in [2]. Along with the wide use of pre-trained language models, there is a recent trend of incorporating extra knowledge to pre-trained language models as a different hierarchical model [1]. For BERT, it is difficult to be applied to downstream tasks which need to put emphasis on several specific words. We propose a hierarchical model that extracts overall information from fine-tuned BERT and then incorporates topic information. CNN categorizes the whole sentence representation into positive and negative.

3   Proposed Method

The HMIT architecture is shown in Fig. 1. We describe each component and how it is used in learning and inference in detail. For one user, $\{s_1, s_2, \ldots, s_m\}$ is a collection of his/her tweets, containing m tweets of various topics. A tweet s_i composed of n words is denoted as $s_i = \{x_1^{(i)}, x_2^{(i)}, \ldots, x_n^{(i)}\}$ with a gold sentiment label $y_i = \{POSITIVE, NEGATIVE\}$.

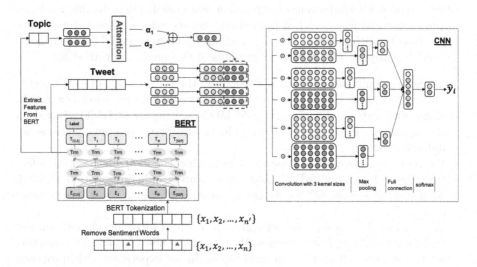

Fig. 1. The overall architecture of HMIT

3.1   Topic Phrases Extraction

To extract several topic phrases in each tweet, we employ Single-Pass algorithm. The core idea is to input texts continuously to determine the matching degree between the input text and an existing cluster. Texts whose maximum similarity to the cluster core are greater than the given threshold p_0 will be clustered as one category. After all texts are clustered, we set the most frequently occurred bi-gram as topic phrases for this cluster, so that every tweet is associated with a topic phrase $\{TP_1, TP_2\}$.

3.2   Fine-Tuned BERT with Non-sentiment Words

All sentiment words are removed from tweets first according to sentiment lexicons [6]. $\{x_1^{(i)}, x_2^{(i)}, \ldots, x_{n'}^{(i)}\}$ represents a tweet without sentiment words and is further fed into BERT tokenization. Each sentence is tokenized and padded to length N by inserting padding tokens. The embedding layer of BERT integrates word, position and token type embeddings where $E_j \in \mathbb{R}^K$ is the K-dimensional vector of the j-th word in the tweet. BERT is a multi-layer bidirectional Transformer encoder. In text classification, the decoder applies first token pooling to a full connection layer with softmax activation, returning a probability distribution on two categories. After fine-tuning BERT on our own dataset, we extract one layer of the latent vector from the encoder of fine-tuned BERT.

3.3 Topic-Level Attention

We use a topic-level attention mechanism over a topic phrase to produce a single representation. Since different tokens in a topic phrase may contribute to its semantics differently, we calculate an attention vector for a topic phrase. The hidden outputs corresponding to $\{TP_1^{(i)}, TP_2^{(i)}\}$ is denoted as $H^{(i)} = \{h_{TP1}^{(i)}, h_{TP2}^{(i)}\}$. We compute the aggregated representation of a topic phrase as

$$H^{(i)\prime} = \alpha^{(i)\mathsf{T}} H^{(i)} = \sum_{o \in \{1,2\}} \alpha_j^{(i)} h_{TPo}^{(i)} \tag{1}$$

where the topic attention vector $\alpha^{(i)} = \{\alpha_1^{(i)}, \alpha_2^{(i)}\}$ is distributed over topic phrase $H^{(i)}$. The attention vector $\alpha^{(i)}$ is a self-attention vector that takes the hidden outputs of a topic phrase as input and feeds them into a bi-layer perceptron. We concatenate each token representation and the aggregated topic representation $H^{(i)\prime}$ to obtain the final context-aware representation for each word.

3.4 CNN Classification

CNN has grabbed increasing attention in text classification tasks recently due to its strong ability to capture local contextual dependencies. Based on that, we propose to apply CNN to the final layer of classification. As shown in Fig. 1, convolution operation involves kernels with three different sizes. Suppose $w \in \mathbb{R}^{q \times 2K}$ is a filter of q tokens, a feature c_j is generated by:

$$c_j = f(w \circ h_{j:j+q-1}^{(i)\prime} + b) \tag{2}$$

Here $\circ$ denotes convolution, while $b \in \mathbb{R}$ is a bias term and f is ReLU activation function. This filter applies to whole possible tokens in the sentence to produce a feature map:

$$c = [c_1, c_2, ..., c_{N-q+1}] \in \mathbb{R}^{N-q+1} \tag{3}$$

Max-pooling layer take the maximum value $\hat{c} = \max\{c\}$ of c as the feature corresponding to filter w. $\hat{y}_i$ denotes the predicted label for the i-th tweet.

3.5 Inference and Learning

The objective to train topic-level attention and CNN classifier is defined as minimizing the sum of the cross-entropy losses of prediction on each tweet as follows:

$$\mathcal{L}_s = -\sum_{i=1}^{m} \hat{y}_i \log(y_i) + (1 - \hat{y}_i) \log(1 - y_i) \tag{4}$$

For inference, test news is first passed to the fine-tuned BERT to obtain its hidden vector. According to the topic-level attention mechanism, context-aware representations are incorporated with topic information and then fed to the CNN classifier. Finally, a prediction is obtained.

4   Experiments

4.1   Experimental Settings

Datasets. Table 1 shows the statistics of datasets. We select three users from Sentiment140 [9] to build models separately as $\mathbb{D}_{s1}$, $\mathbb{D}_{s2}$ and $\mathbb{D}_{s3}$. We also collect tweets from three talkative users and label them manually as $\mathbb{D}_{t1}$, $\mathbb{D}_{t2}$ and $\mathbb{D}_{t3}$. To verify the feasibility of the method in practical application, we collect 100 news for each of three topics: *health care, climate change, social security* as $\mathbb{T}_h$, $\mathbb{T}_c$ and $\mathbb{T}_s$.

Table 1. Dataset statistics

Datasets	Train			Test		
	Positive	Negative	Total	$\mathbb{T}_h$	$\mathbb{T}_c$	$\mathbb{T}_s$
$\mathbb{D}_{t1}$	1243	1038	2281	100	100	100
$\mathbb{D}_{t2}$	882	1044	1926	100	100	100
$\mathbb{D}_{t3}$	772	496	1268	100	100	100
$\mathbb{D}_{s1}$	119	119	238	–	–	–
$\mathbb{D}_{s2}$	98	183	281	–	–	–
$\mathbb{D}_{s3}$	66	210	276	–	–	–

Network Details. For Single-Pass, we set the threshold p_0 to 0.4. We tune pre-trained base uncased BERT which sets hidden size K as 768 with 12 hidden layers and 12 attention heads. Max sequence length N, batch size and learning rate are set to 128, 32 and 5×10^{-5} respectively. For the CNN classifier, we adopt three filter sizes: 2, 3 and 4 separately. 64 filters are used for each filter size and three pooling sizes are set to 4 in the task. We train the fine-tuned BERT for 3 epochs and the CNN classifier for 20 epochs.

Evaluation Metrics. We employ accuracy and F1 score as evaluation for classification. We regard evaluation of test sets as a quantification task, which estimates the distribution of tweets across two classes. We adopt Mean Absolute Error based on a predicted distribution $\hat{p}$, its true distribution p and the set $\mathcal{C}$ of classes. It's computed separately for each topic, and the results are averaged across three topics to yield the final score.

4.2   Models Under Comparison

We compare our proposed method with the methods that have been proposed for sentiment analysis (SA) and target-based sentiment analysis (TBSA).

- BERT [3]: BERT achieves state-of-the-art results in sentence classification, including sentiment classification.
- mem_absa [11]: Mem_absa adopts a multi-hop attention mechanism over an external memory to focus on the importance level of the context words and the given target.
- IAN [8]: IAN considers both attention mechanisms on the target and the full context. It uses two attention-based LSTMs to interactively capture the keywords of the target and its content.
- Cabasc [7]: Cabasc takes into account the correlation between the given target and each context word, composed of sentence-level content attention mechanism and content attention mechanism.

BERT^{-s}, mem_absa^{-s}, IAN^{-s} and Cabasc^{-s} are variant models of BERT, mem_absa, IAN and Cabasc respectively, removing sentiment words in training and testing.

4.3   Results and Analysis

Main Results. From Table 2, we observe that HMIT is able to significantly outperform other baselines in both classification and quantification tasks on our own dataset, which suggests that our proposed method is effective to capture the relationship between individual sentiments and different topics and succeed in sentiment estimation towards potential topics. We also find that BERT performs reasonably well on validation sets, which confirms its strong ability to represent a whole sentence and its feasibility as the first layer of our model. We compare HMIT with one SA model, three TBSA models and their variants. Table 2 shows that TBSA models display little advantage compared with SA models, which implies that current sentiment classification is mostly decided by sentiment lexicons or opinion words around the target instead of the target itself. Furthermore, the superior performance of the variants on both datasets indicates that removing sentiment words from tweets enables models to pay more attention to the topic in a tweet, thus constructing the relationship between topics and individual sentiments.

Table 2. Comparison results

Model	$\mathbb{D}_{t1}$		$\mathbb{D}_{t2}$		$\mathbb{D}_{t3}$		$\mathbb{D}_{s1}$		$\mathbb{D}_{s2}$		$\mathbb{D}_{s3}$	
	F1	MAE	F1	MAE	F1	MAE	Acc	F1	Acc	F1	Acc	F1
mem_absa	81.23	0.203	81.49	0.215	81.52	0.239	75.35	74.91	72.46	72.12	73.94	73.45
mem_absa^{-s}	80.28	0.183	80.72	0.186	78.37	0.192	73.91	73.92	71.93	71.47	72.03	72.01
IMN	83.42	0.168	82.04	0.167	82.26	0.170	76.89	75.94	74.92	74.32	74.78	74.50
IMN^{-s}	81.74	0.161	81.72	0.159	80.64	0.162	76.34	75.82	74.18	74.24	74.39	74.12
Cabasc	83.99	0.169	83.74	0.165	82.02	0.174	76.53	76.47	73.41	73.28	73.86	73.89
Cabasc^{-s}	82.31	0.163	82.66	0.160	81.32	0.169	75.99	75.61	73.99	73.84	73.35	73.70
BERT	81.79	0.161	83.11	0.153	82.65	0.172	77.35	77.11	**76.34**	**75.89**	75.32	74.29
BERT^{-s}	79.76	0.156	82.70	0.148	81.64	0.163	76.83	76.55	75.02	74.21	74.86	74.04
HMTI	**85.30**	**0.112**	**86.61**	**0.109**	**83.91**	**0.124**	**78.29**	**77.13**	75.96	74.08	**75.50**	**74.84**

Extract Features from BERT. We discover which encoding layer extracted from BERT is the most appropriate for further modification and classification. We extract features from -3, -2 and -1 encoding layer of BERT and simply add a CNN classifier after that. In Fig. 2, we report the accuracy and F1 score of cross-validation on $\mathbb{D}_{t2}$. It turns out that the penultimate layer is the most appropriate to make changes or incorporate external information. The last layer is too close to the target and the previous layers may not have been fully learned semantically. Therefore, we extract the penultimate layer in the method.

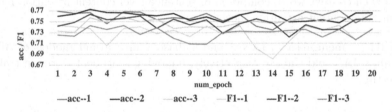

Fig. 2. Accuracy and F1 score on $\mathbb{D}_{t2}$ with different BERT layer

5   Conclusion

We have proposed a hierarchical model to make individual sentiment estimation of potential topics. The approach extracts topics automatically and models the relationship between individual sentiments and different topics. It takes as input tweets without sentiment words, extracts features first from fine-tuned BERT and then incorporates topic information in context-aware token representation through the topic-level attention mechanism. CNN further classifies the representation into positive or negative. The proposed architecture can potentially be applied for a precise individual recommendation or group sentiment estimation towards one topic.

Acknowledgment. This research work has been funded by the National Natural Science Foundation of China (Grant No. 61772337), the National Key Research and Development Program of China NO. 2016QY03D0604.

References

1. Bao, X., Qiao, Q.: Transfer learning from pre-trained bert for pronoun resolution. In: Proceedings of the First Workshop on Gender Bias in Natural Language Processing, pp. 82–88 (2019)
2. Denil, M., Demiraj, A., De Freitas, N.: Extraction of salient sentences from labelled documents. arXiv preprint arXiv:1412.6815 (2014)
3. Devlin, J., Chang, M.W., Lee, K., Toutanova, K.: Bert: pre-training of deep bidirectional transformers for language understanding. In: Proceedings of the 2019 Conference of the North American Chapter of the Association for Computational Linguistics: Human Language Technologies, Volume 1 (Long and Short Papers), pp. 4171–4186 (2019)
4. Dong, L., Wei, F., Tan, C., Tang, D., Zhou, M., Xu, K.: Adaptive recursive neural network for target-dependent Twitter sentiment classification. In: Proceedings of the 52nd Annual Meeting of the Association for Computational Linguistics (Volume 2: Short Papers), pp. 49–54 (2014)
5. Go, A., Bhayani, R., Huang, L.: Twitter sentiment classification using distant supervision. CS224N Project report, Stanford 1(12), 2009 (2009)
6. Liu, B., Hu, M.: Opinion lexicon (or sentiment lexicon) (2004). https://www.cs.uic.edu/~liub/FBS/sentiment-analysis.html
7. Liu, Q., Zhang, H., Zeng, Y., Huang, Z., Wu, Z.: Content attention model for aspect based sentiment analysis. In: Proceedings of the 2018 World Wide Web Conference, pp. 1023–1032. International World Wide Web Conferences Steering Committee (2018)
8. Ma, D., Li, S., Zhang, X., Wang, H.: Interactive attention networks for aspect-level sentiment classification. In: Proceedings of the 26th International Joint Conference on Artificial Intelligence, pp. 4068–4074. AAAI Press (2017)
9. Mohammad, S., Kiritchenko, S., Zhu, X.: NRC-Canada: building the state-of-the-art in sentiment analysis of Tweets. In: Proceedings of the Seventh International Workshop on Semantic Evaluation Exercises (SemEval-2013), Atlanta, Georgia, USA, June 2013
10. Tang, D., Qin, B., Feng, X., Liu, T.: Effective LSTMs for target-dependent sentiment classification. In: Proceedings of COLING 2016, The 26th International Conference on Computational Linguistics: Technical Papers, pp. 3298–3307 (2016)
11. Tang, D., Qin, B., Liu, T.: Aspect level sentiment classification with deep memory network. In: Proceedings of the 2016 Conference on Empirical Methods in Natural Language Processing, pp. 214–224 (2016)
12. Wang, J., et al.: Aspect sentiment classification with both word-level and clause-level attention networks. In: IJCAI, pp. 4439–4445 (2018)

Key Factors of Email Subject Generation

Mingfeng Xue, Hang Zhang, and Jiancheng Lv[✉]

Sichuan University, Yihuan Road, Chengdu 610065, China
mingfengxue@outlook.com, lvjiancheng@scu.edu.cn

Abstract. Automatic email subject generation is of great significance to both the recipient and the email system. The method of using deep neural network to solve the automatically generated task of email subject line has been proposed recently. We experimentally explored the performance impact of multiple elements in this task. These experimental results will provide some guiding significance for the future research of this task. As far as we know, this is the first work to study and analyze the effects of related elements.

Keywords: Email subject generation · Natural Language Processing · Hierarchical architecture

1 Introduction

Whether at work or in daily life, email is an extremely important way of communication. But not everyone maintains a good habit when it comes to writing emails – keeping the subject line precise and concise. This has caused a lot of trouble for both the recipient and the email system. The recipient needs to spend extra time reading spam and advertising emails, and the email system has difficulty classifying and sorting the emails quickly according to the subject. Therefore, it is of practical use to automatically generate a subject from the body of the email.

The email subject generation task is closely related to the abstraction and summarization task. However, compared with abstraction and summarization, the subject of an email is shorter and more abstract. Email, on the other hand, differs in form from the news data commonly used in summarization tasks, like the CNN/Daily Mail dataset, which always include key information in the first few sentences.

The difference between email subject generation and summary tasks makes it a problem worth studying. Carmel et al. first proposed the task of generating email subject lines automatically [5]. Unfortunately, no great research has been done since then. Until 2019, Zhang et al. had used deep learning to fulfil this task and provided data sets in a more complete way [18]. They applied the model, based on the work of Chen and Bansal [9], to the email data. For better study in this task, we improve the deep learning model on the basis of the existing research, propose several factors that might be effective in this task, and carry

© Springer Nature Switzerland AG 2020
H. Yang et al. (Eds.): ICONIP 2020, CCIS 1332, pp. 668–675, 2020.
https://doi.org/10.1007/978-3-030-63820-7_76

out experiments on them one by one. We apply a model of Extractor-Astractor structure, extracting the main information of the email hierarchically. We use transformer as abstractor and decode the context and the key words of email in decoder to figure out if they're effective. In addition, we verify the necessity of the hierarchical structure and the copy mechanism. Also, we explore the impact of precision and recall on results. These experimental results will provide some guiding significance for the future research of this task. At the same time, in the study of similar summarization tasks, our task also has a great reference significance.

Our contributions are threefold: (1) We study the effects of contextual information, keyword information and copy mechanism on email subject generation task. (2) We prove that the hierarchical architecture in email subject generation task is necessary. (3) We explore the impact of precision and recall of extraction step on performance.

2   Related Works

2.1   Email Subject Generation

The traditional tasks related to processing emails using NLP methods are mainly focused on abstraction [4,14,17] and classification [2,6,8]. The task of generating email subject lines was first proposed in 2016. Carmel et al. proposed an email system that could automatically generate subject recommendations and make comparative evaluations based on the email entered by users. In 2019, Zhang and Tetreault used a deep learning approach to solve this problem. They proposed a hierarchical structure consisting of an extractor and an abstractor. In the abstractor, the recurrent neural network and the copy mechanism are used, which mimicked the work in [9]. As far as we know, no other relevant research, other than these two, has been proposed on the task of email subject generation.

2.2   Summarization

Summarization and email subject generation have a lot in common. The early methods of summarization were mostly based on extractive methods. Aliguliyev proposed a generic document summarization method which is based on sentence clustering [1]. Filippova et al. presented an LSTM approach to deletion-based sentence compression where the task is to translate a sentence into a sequence of zeros and ones, corresponding to token deletion decisions [10]. This is a big step forward for deep learning in extractive summarization tasks. Zhong et al. sought to better understand how neural extractive summarization systems could benefit from different types of model architectures, transferable knowledge and learning schemas [19].

With the development of deep neural network, the abstractive models have been improved gradually. Nallapati et al. modeled abstractive text summarization using Attentional EncoderDecoder Recurrent Neural Networks [13].

Celikyilmaz et al. extended the CommNet model [15] and presented deep communicating agents in an encoder-decoder architecture to address the challenges of representing a long document for abstractive summarization [7].

Although there are many relevant studies, there is no relevant research to explore the effectiveness of different elements in related tasks, let alone analyze them, which is also the key significance of our work.

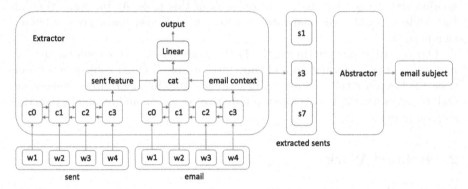

Fig. 1. The overall model architecture consists of an extractor and an abstractor. The extractor uses LSTM to encode the sentence and email body as sentence feature and email context representation, which then are inputted in linear layer to indicate if this sentence is a key sentence.

3   Methodology

In this section, we will introduce our experimental models and methods. We experimented with multiple elements, which intuitively worked for email subject generation, to explore how each element was critical to the task.

3.1   Architecture

The overall architecture we use is the hierarchical structure, which consists of an extractor and an abstractor. The extractor finds out key sentences from the email, and the abstractor then generates the final email subject based on these key sentences. Formally, given a training set of email-subject pairs $\{x_i, y_i\}_{i=1}^{N}$, which consist of sentences $\{s_{ij}^x\}$ and $\{s_{ij}^y\}$. The extractor indicates which sentences are the key ones as function $f : (S, X) \rightarrow \{0, 1\}$. The abstractor combines key sentences into long sentences S^k, then works as function $g : S^k \rightarrow Y$.

3.2   Extractor

The extractor works as a binary classification, that is, whether the sentence is a key sentence. We use bidirectional LSTM to encode the single sentence and the email where the sentence in and view the final hidden states as sentence feature and email context representation.

Given an email x which consists of $|x|$ sentences:

$$x = [s_1, s_2, ..., s_j, ..., s_{|x|}] \tag{1}$$

We first use two LSTM to encode the sentence feature c_j and the email context representation c:

$$\overrightarrow{c_j} = \overrightarrow{LSTM}(s_j), \overleftarrow{c_j} = \overleftarrow{LSTM}(s_j), c_j = [\overrightarrow{c_j}, \overleftarrow{c_j}] \tag{2}$$

$$\overrightarrow{c} = \overrightarrow{LSTM}(x), \overleftarrow{c} = \overleftarrow{LSTM}(d_j), c = [\overrightarrow{c}, \overleftarrow{c}] \tag{3}$$

Then we concatenate the sentence feature and email context representation as input to a linear layer which outputs the final classification results o_e (see Fig. 1):

$$o_e = softmax(linear([c_j, c])) \tag{4}$$

The extractor is trained to predict key sentences by minimizing the binary-cross-entropy loss.

3.3 Abstractor

Since transformer was introduced [16], it has achieved good results on a number of generation tasks. Compared with LSTM, one of its most important features is its ability to encode long sentences. We used transformer as the underlying

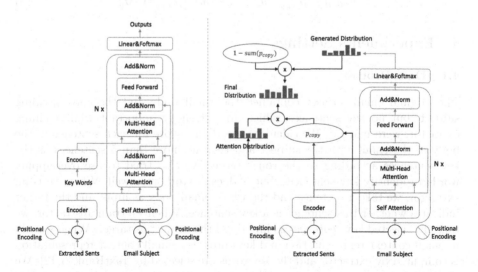

Fig. 2. The abstractor encode keywords using another encoder without positional encoding (left) and the multihead copy mechanism used in abstractor (right). The attention distribution and probability of copy is calculated at the last block.

abstractor and conducted different experiments on it. All kinds of abstractors are trained by minimizing the cross-entropy loss between subjects and output logits.

We used vanilla transformer as a benchmark to test the effect of each element on performance. On this benchmark, we added email context representation and keywords to observe performance changes, respectively. The email context representation has been obtained in extractor and we concatenate it with decoder output before the linear layer. Similarly, the keywords can be added to abstractor in the same way. We use another LSTM structure as the one calculated email context representation to obtain the representation of keywords. However, unlike the body of an email, there is no strict positional relationship between keywords. LSTM is not suitable for getting the representation. The second way to encode keywords is to use an additional transformer encoder, which does not require positional encoding (see Fig. 2).

When studying the influence of the copy mechanism, we take the subject's attention over encoder output as the copy distribution d_c. We concatenate the embedded subject emb, the subject's attention over encoder output $attn_{context}$ and the output of the decoder $output$ as input. Then we pass the input into a linear layer to get the copy probability, p_{copy}. Transformer uses multihead attention, which means the copy probability should also be multihead. For stable training, the final copy probability needs to be divided by the number of heads used:

$$p_{copy} = \sigma(linear([emb, attn_{context}, output]))/h \tag{5}$$

We use d_g denote the generation distribution, the final distribution is:

$$d_{final} = p_{copy} * d_c + (1 - sum(p_{copy})) * d_g \tag{6}$$

4   Experiments Settings

4.1   Data Process

The original email dataset contained the email body and the corresponding subject, but no key sentences, which are extremely important while training extractor, were marked. We calculate the Rouge score for each sentence in the body of the email with the subject and keep no more than 5 sentences as the key sentences according to the rouge score. We also tried to use overlapping words to identify key sentences, but it doesn't work very well. When we train extractor, we take a sentence and the whole email body as input and the target indicates whether this sentence is a key sentence. When we train abstractor, we take the selected key sentences as input and the subject as target. When we add in email context representation and keywords, the email context representation is computed by extractor and the keywords are selected by TextRank [3,12]. We also add the most extreme experiment, putting all the sentences into the training, which gives up the extactor-abstractor structure. This experiment would find out whether the hierarchical structure is effective or not.

4.2   Evaluation Metrics

On all the dataset we use standard ROUGE-1, ROUGE-2 and ROUGE-L [11] to measure the final generation quality. For the extractor, we pay attention to the precision and recall, which can be calculated further to get an F1 score.

5   Results and Analysis

5.1   Experiments Results and Analysis

We use the validation set to find the model with the highest score and then apply it to the test set. The experiments show that our extractor and abstractor both get good performance. After several rounds of training, the extractor's precision and recall hit 78.82% and 66.94%, which far exceeded [18], 74% and 42%. At the same time, in order to verify the validity of the email context representation, we try to use only sentences to train the extractor, which makes the precision and recall be 57.92% and 55.02%. Because some sentences in the email, such as a simple 'hello', are bound to be marked as non-critical. This result can be viewed as a near-random marking of normal sentences. Obviously, that can serve as evidence that the email context representation is valid.

In exploring the influence of the elements, transformer with email context added has the best performance, with ROUGE-1 score reaching 24.67, followed by vanilla transformer at 23.31. Both abstractor that add keywords are counterproductive for transformer. In our opinion, the email context contains information beyond the key sentences, so the addition slightly improves the performance of the abstract. Transformer is strong enough to abstract key sentences, which cover almost all the key words. In addition, the addition of LSTM or encoder makes the abstractor structure more complex, which increases the difficulty of training. This results in performance degradation. The copy mechanism is prominent in the previous Seq2Seq networks based on recurrent neural networks. This is because LSTM tends to forget previous words when encoding long sentences. The copy mechanism is actually a disguised reinforcement of the traditional attention, which makes networks get more chances to get access to previous words. The model that uses copy mechanism gets the highest score, which means copy mechanism is still necessary in this task. At the same time, the model that does not use extractor worked poorly, which means extraction step is indispensable even transformer has strong encoding ability in long sentences (Table 1).

5.2   Precision or Recall

At the end of extractor's training, it is difficult to improve the precision and recall simultaneously. We tried different ways of matching extractors with abstractors to test whether accuracy or recall is more important than the other. Two sets, two extractors each set, of extractors were selected for the experiment. The two extractors in the same set have similar F1 score but different precision and recall.

Table 1. Metric scores, which are influenced by different elements. Underlined: best.

	Dev			Test		
	R-1	R-2	R-L	R-1	R-2	R-L
Vanilla transformer	23.31	7.58	23.02	22.39	7.43	22.16
Keywords(cat)	20.89	6.57	20.71	20.32	5.98	20.17
Keywords(encoder)	21,25	7.03	19.96	20.18	6.38	19.96
Email context	24.67	7.98	24.42	23.55	8.03	24.37
Copy mechanism	24.89	8.49	24.46	23.94	8.27	23.88
No extractor	15.96	5.59	15.82	14.35	4.75	14.25

Table 2. Metric scores in different extractor sets.

Extractor Sets			Dev			Test		
F1 score	Precision	Recall	R-1	R-2	R-L	R-1	R-2	R-L
69.08	71.57%	66.77%	22.28	7.25	22.07	22.13	6.84	21.94
69.07	67.16%	71.10%	22.29	6.94	22.11	22.34	6.68	22.17
66.63	64.56%	68.85%	21.67	6.60	21.47	21.70	6.43	21.50
66.51	68.43%	64.69%	21.53	6.38	21.60	21.22	6.58	21.02

The experimental results show that F1 score has a great influence on the results. However, under similar F1 score conditions, slight changes in precision and recall had little impact on the results (See Table 2).

6   Conclusion

It is of practical use to automatically generate a subject from the body of the email. But there hasn't been a lot of research on it. We explored the importance of the related elements in the use of deep neural networks to generate subjects, which has directive significance to the related works. Hierarchical architecture and copy mechanism are necessary because of long email body and lots of overlapped words. Additional email context contributes to performance improvement but the keywords information do not. When using extract results, F1 score has a bigger impact on the performance, but slight variations in precision and recall have little effect on the results.

References

1. Aliguliyev, R.M.: A new sentence similarity measure and sentence based extractive technique for automatic text summarization. Expert Syst. Appl. 36(4), 7764–7772 (2009)
2. Bahgat, E.M., Rady, S., Gad, W., Moawad, I.F.: Efficient email classification approach based on semantic methods. Ain Shams Eng. J. 9(4), 3259–3269 (2018)

3. Barrios, F., López, F., Argerich, L., Wachenchauzer, R.: Variations of the similarity function of TextRank for automated summarization. In: Argentine Symposium on Artificial Intelligence (ASAI 2015)-JAIIO 44, (Rosario, 2015) (2015)
4. Carenini, G., Ng, R.T., Zhou, X.: Summarizing email conversations with clue words. In: Proceedings of the 16th International Conference on World Wide Web, pp. 91–100 (2007)
5. Carmel, D., Erera, S., Goldberg, I., Mizrachi, B.: Automatically generated subject recommendations for email messages based on email message content, US Patent 7,761,524, 20 July 2010
6. Carvalho, V.R., Cohen, W.W.: On the collective classification of email "speech acts". In: Proceedings of the 28th Annual International ACM SIGIR Conference on Research and Development in Information Retrieval, pp. 345–352 (2005)
7. Celikyilmaz, A., Bosselut, A., He, X., Choi, Y.: Deep communicating agents for abstractive summarization. In: Proceedings of the 2018 Conference of the North American Chapter of the Association for Computational Linguistics: Human Language Technologies, Volume 1 (Long Papers), pp. 1662–1675 (2018)
8. Chang, M., Poon, C.K.: Using phrases as features in email classification. J. Syst. Softw. **82**(6), 1036–1045 (2009)
9. Chen, Y.C., Bansal, M.: Fast abstractive summarization with reinforce-selected sentence rewriting. In: Proceedings of the 56th Annual Meeting of the Association for Computational Linguistics (Volume 1: Long Papers), pp. 675–686 (2018)
10. Filippova, K., Alfonseca, E., Colmenares, C.A., Kaiser, L., Vinyals, O.: Sentence compression by deletion with LSTMs. In: Proceedings of the 2015 Conference on Empirical Methods in Natural Language Processing, pp. 360–368 (2015)
11. Lin, C.Y.: Looking for a few good metrics: automatic summarization evaluation-how many samples are enough? (2004)
12. Mihalcea, R., Tarau, P.: TextRank: bringing order into text. In: Proceedings of the 2004 Conference on Empirical Methods in Natural Language Processing, pp. 404–411 (2004)
13. Nallapati, R., Zhou, B., dos Santos, C.N., Gülçehre, Ç., Xiang, B.: Abstractive text summarization using sequence-to-sequence RNNs and beyond. In: Goldberg, Y., Riezler, S. (eds.) Proceedings of the 20th SIGNLL Conference on Computational Natural Language Learning, CoNLL 2016, Berlin, Germany, 11–12 August 2016, pp. 280–290. ACL (2016). https://doi.org/10.18653/v1/k16-1028
14. Shrestha, L., McKeown, K.: Detection of question-answer pairs in email conversations. In: Proceedings of the 20th International Conference on Computational Linguistics, p. 889. Association for Computational Linguistics (2004)
15. Sukhbaatar, S., Szlam, A., Fergus, R.: Learning multiagent communication with backpropagation. In: Proceedings of the 30th International Conference on Neural Information Processing Systems, pp. 2252–2260 (2016)
16. Vaswani, A., et al.: Attention is all you need. In: Advances in Neural Information Processing Systems, pp. 5998–6008 (2017)
17. Zajic, D.M., Dorr, B.J., Lin, J.: Single-document and multi-document summarization techniques for email threads using sentence compression. Inf. Process. Manag. **44**(4), 1600–1610 (2008)
18. Zhang, R., Tetreault, J.: This email could save your life: introducing the task of email subject line generation. In: Proceedings of the 57th Annual Meeting of the Association for Computational Linguistics, pp. 446–456 (2019)
19. Zhong, M., Liu, P., Wang, D., Qiu, X., Huang, X.J.: Searching for effective neural extractive summarization: what works and what's next. In: Proceedings of the 57th Annual Meeting of the Association for Computational Linguistics, pp. 1049–1058 (2019)

Learning Interactions at Multiple Levels for Abstractive Multi-document Summarization

Yiding Liu⬤, Xiaoning Fan⬤, Jie Zhou⬤, and Gongshen Liu⁽✉⁾⬤

School of Electronic Information and Electrical Engineering, Shanghai Jiao Tong University, Shanghai 200240, China
{lydlovehdq,sanny02,fxn627,lgshen}@sjtu.edu.cn

Abstract. The biggest obstacles facing multi-document summarization include much more complicated input and excessive redundancy in source contents. Most state-of-the-art systems have attempted to tackle the redundancy problem, treating the entire input as a flat sequence. However, correlations among documents are often neglected. In this paper, we propose an end-to-end summarization model called *MLT*, which can effectively learn interactions at multiple levels and avoid redundant information. Specifically, we utilize a word-level transformer layer to encode contextual information within each sentence. Also, we design a sentence-level transformer layer for learning relations between sentences within a single document, as well as a document-level layer for learning interactions among input documents. Moreover, we use a neural method to enhance Max Marginal Relevance (MMR), a powerful algorithm for redundancy reduction. We incorporate MMR into our model and measure the redundancy quantitively based on the sentence representations. On benchmark datasets, our system compares favorably to strong summarization baselines judged by automatic metrics and human evaluators.

Keywords: Multi-document summarization · Multiple levels · MMR

1 Introduction

Multi-document summarization is currently one of the most important tasks in the world with increasing data and information on individual topics. It seeks to produce a brief and informative abstract from a collection of textual documents related to a specific topic. Generally, the salient information of a set of documents is determined by all the input rather than independently collecting key points in each document. Similarly, contextual information among sentences in each meta-document should not be ignored because sentences are not independent of each other. Thus, Learning interactions among input documents and contextual information within a meta-document is a crucial and challenging task for multi-document summarization.

© Springer Nature Switzerland AG 2020
H. Yang et al. (Eds.): ICONIP 2020, CCIS 1332, pp. 676–684, 2020.
https://doi.org/10.1007/978-3-030-63820-7_77

Since the source documents share the same underlying topic, multi-document summarization is also faced with excessive redundancy in source descriptions. Most state-of-the-art multi-document summarization frameworks are proposed to tackle the redundancy problem [2,3,11]. However, correlations among documents are often neglected.

To address the aforementioned issues, we propose a multi-level transformer model named *MLT*. As an end-to-end system, our model can effectively learn interactions at multiple levels and avoid redundancy while generating abstractive summaries. We design a sentence-level transformer layer for learning relations between sentences within a meta-document, as well as a document-level layer for learning interactions among input documents. To cope with the redundancy problem, we apply an MMR model like Fabbri et al. [6] did to measure the redundancy quantitively, taking the sentence presentations produced by the sentence-level transformer layer as input.

The key contributions of this paper can be summarized as follows:

- We propose an end-to-end abstractive model based on the Transformer structure that can effectively learn interactions at multiple levels.
- On benchmark datasets, our system compares favorably to strong summarization baselines judged by automatic metrics and human evaluators.

2   Related Work

Multi-document summarization has largely been performed on small-scale datasets. Thus, most previous systems are extractive, where summary-worthy sentences are directly extracted from source document clusters to form the final summary. Constructing sentence semantic relation graphs to obtain sentence representations is a popular method [1,19].

In addition to the methods mentioned above, recent works have attempted weakly supervised methods to generate abstractive summaries [11,20]. For large-scale datasets without annotation, performing unsupervised summarization is also considerable [4]. Due to some success achieved in dataset establishment, recent works have also seen considerable interest in training an abstractive model directly on parallel datasets [6,13,14].

3   Our Approach

In this section, we introduce the details of *MLT*. The encoder is a 7-layer network with 3 word-level transformer layers, 2 sentence-level transformer layers, and 2 document-level transformer layers from bottom to the top, learning interactions at multiple levels. Our decoder follows the original Transformer structure [18]. Moreover, we integrate an MMR model in the sentence-level transformer layers. Figure 1 provides a schematic view of the encoder.

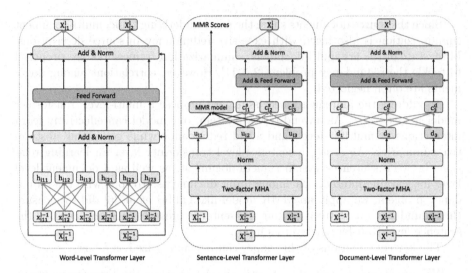

Fig. 1. A schematic view of the word-level, sentence-level, and document-level transformer layers. We integrate our MMR model into the sentence-level transformer layer to obtain MMR scores. We use the blue arrows to indicate the dependency among input sequences in the multi-head attention sublayer, and the green arrows to pack the output. Different colors indicate different modules. (Color figure online)

3.1   Embeddings

Let $\{d_1, d_2, \cdots, d_m\}$ denote a set of input documents. Each document d_i consists of a collection of sentences $\{s_{i1}, s_{i2}, \cdots, s_{in}\}$, where a given sentence s_{ij} is formed by several tokens $\{t_{ij1}, t_{ij2}, \cdots, t_{ijk}\}$. Since our encoder is a multi-layer network, we use x_{ijk}^l to denote the output of the l-th layer and the input of the next layer for token t_{ijk}.

Vanilla Transformer adds positional embeddings to word embeddings. In multi-document summarization, we argue that the order of the documents should not influence the summary. Therefore, we should not treat the input documents as a concatenated sequence and apply a global positional embedding to each token according to its position in this sequence. Instead, we utilize a local positional embedding to indicate the position of the token within its corresponding document. Following Vaswani et al. [18], we use the same sine and cosine functions to encode the positional information. Finally, the packed outputs of the embedding layer X^0 is the summation of the word embeddings **WE** and local positional embeddings **LPE**:

$$X^0 = \mathbf{WE} + \mathbf{LPE} \tag{1}$$

3.2 Word-Level Transformer Layer

A word-level transformer layer is used to learn interactions within each sentence. It is composed of two sub-layers:

$$H = \text{LN}(X^{l-1} + \text{MHA}(X^{l-1})) \tag{2}$$

$$X^l = \text{LN}(H + \text{FFN}(H)) \tag{3}$$

where LN is layer normalization, MHA is the self-attention sublayer, and FFN is a two-layer feed-forward network. In the word-level transformer layer, sentences are completely independent of each other. To satisfy the independence, we apply a special mask for each sentence in the MHA sublayer, which can avoid semantic attendance from other sentences. Specifically, tokens in sentence s_{ij} can only receive self-attention from t_{ij1} to t_{ijk} under the corresponding mask, as shown in Fig. 1.

3.3 Sentence-Level Transformer Layer

A sentence-level Transformer is used to learn relations between sentences within their corresponding document and compute the sentence representations. In this layer, input documents are thoroughly independent of each other. Here, we take document d_i as an example. For each sentence s_{ij}, its packed outputs $X_{ij}^{l-1} = [x_{ij1}^{l-1}; x_{ij2}^{l-1}; \cdots ; x_{ijk}^{l-1}]$ are fed to a two-factor multi-head attention sublayer (Two-factor MHA). We first transform X_{ij}^{l-1} into self-attention scores S_a^s and value vectors V_a^s at the sentence level, which are two main factors in this sublayer. Then, we compute the sentence-level attention distribution A_a^s over tokens within sentence s_{ij} based on S_a^s:

$$S_a^s = X_{ij}^{l-1} W_a^S \tag{4}$$

$$V_a^s = X_{ij}^{l-1} W_a^V \tag{5}$$

$$A_a^s = \text{Softmax}(S_a^s) \tag{6}$$

Specifically, $a \in \{1, 2, \cdots, h\}$ is one of the attention heads; $W_a^S \in \mathbb{R}^{d*1}$ and $W_a^V \in \mathbb{R}^{d*d_{head}}$ are weight matrices, where d is the dimension of the hidden states and d_{head} is the dimension of each head. Next, we compute the weighted summation of value vectors to get the sub-representation $head_a$ for each head a. And we obtain the sentence representation u_{ij} by concatenating sub-representations of all heads, and applying a linear transformation and a layer normalization afterward:

$$head_a = A_a^s V_a^s \tag{7}$$

$$u_{ij} = \text{LN}(W_c^w [head_1; head_2...; head_h]) \tag{8}$$

After that, we apply another multi-head attention sublayer to all sentence representations in document d_i. This sublayer allows the model to learn relations between sentences, taking the packed matrix $U_i = [u_{i1}; u_{i2}; \cdots ; u_{in}]$ as input, and yields a matrix $C_i^s = [c_{i1}^s; c_{i2}^s; \cdots ; c_{in}^s]$ stacked by the sentence-level context vectors. Finally, we add c_{ij}^s to each token in sentence s_{ij} using a broadcast mechanism, and apply another feed-forward network followed by a layer normalization to get the output of the sentence-level transformer layer:

$$C_i^s = \text{MHA}(U_i) \tag{9}$$

$$X_{ij}^l = \text{LN}(X_{ij}^{l-1} + \text{FFN}(c_{ij}^s + X_{ij}^{l-1})) \tag{10}$$

3.4 Document-Level Transformer Layer

A document-level transformer layer is used to learn correlations among documents. We still take document d_i as an example. Similar to the sentence-level transformer layer, we first pack the output of the last layer into a matrix X_i^{l-1}. Then, we use the same algorithm at the document-level to obtain self-attention scores S_a^d, value vectors V_a^d, the attention distribution A_a^d, the context vector c_i^d, and the output X_i^l, as shown in Fig. 1.

3.5 MMR Model

Maximal Marginal Relevance (MMR) [2] is a powerful extractive method and performs competitively compared with state-of-the-art systems. MMR selects a certain number of sentences from the source text iteratively based on their scores, considering relevance and redundancy jointly. We use a neural method to compute MMR scores, taking the sentence presentations produced by the sentence-level transformer layer as input. We refer readers to [6] for detailed information about computing MMR scores.

4   Experiments

4.1 Datasets

The choice of the dataset is vast but not the issue of interest in this paper. Here, we use Multi-News [6] and DUC 2004 for evaluation.

Multi-News is a large-scale news dataset for multi-document summarization, containing 44972 instances for training, 5622 for validation, and 5622 for inference. Statistics demonstrate that the gold summaries of source articles are highly abstractive [6]. DUC 2004 is a widely used standard test set. Since DUC 2004 contains only 50 document clusters, all abstractive models are trained on Multi-News to get test results.

4.2   Baselines

We compare our proposed model with several state-of-the-art systems:

LexRank [5] is a graph-based extractive summarizer which computes sentence importance based on eigenvector centrality.

TextRank [16] is also a graph-based ranking model. Compared with LexRank, TextRank uses a different method to compute sentence similarity.

MMR[2] is a powerful method combining query-relevance with information-novelty to extract summary-worthy sentences.

Pointer-Gen is the original model proposed by See et al. [17], which combines bidirectional LSTM with the pointer mechanism and coverage mechanism.

PG-MMR is the adapted pointer-generator model introduced by Lebanoff et al. [11], which mutes sentences that receive low MMR scores.

BaseTransformer, CopyTransformer are models formed by the Transformer structure. BaseTransformer is the vanilla Transformer model [18]. CopyTransformer utilizes the pointer mechanism used by Gehrmann et al. [7].

Hi-MAP [6] is based on bi-LSTM and incorporates the MMR module, learning all parameters simultaneously.

4.3   Experimental Settings

The encoder of MLT is stacked by 7 layers (with 3 word-level transformer layers at the bottom, 2 sentence-level transformer layers in the middle, and 2 document-level transformer layers at the top). The decoder is composed of a stack of 7 layers identical to vanilla Transformer. We train our model for 50000 steps using Adam [9] with learning rate of 0.7, $\beta_1 = 0.9$ and $\beta_2 = 0.998$. The learning rate is varied under a warmup strategy with warmup steps of 4000. We apply dropout with a rate of 0.2 and label smoothing of value 0.1. We set the model dimension $d = 512$, number of heads $h = 8$ and the feed-forward hidden size $d_{ff} = 2048$. We use $\lambda = 0.5$ and $\lambda = 0.3$ in Equation ?? to get results on Multi-News and DUC 2004 datasets respectively. For abstractive methods, we use beam search and apply length penalty and coverage penalty [7] to generate more fluent summaries at test time. We set all methods to give an output of 300 tokens for Multi-News and 100 tokens for DUC 2004 at most.

4.4   Results and Analysis

Automatic Evaluation. We evaluate all system summaries against human reference summaries using the pyrouge package, which is a Python implementation of the official ROUGE toolkit [12]. We utilize R-1, R-2, and R-SU4 to respectively measure the overlap of unigrams, bigrams, and unigrams and skip bigrams with a maximum distance of 4 words.

ROUGE scores on different models are shown in Table 1. We can observe that our proposed model outperforms other models by a large margin. Compared with

Table 1. Results on Multi-News and DUC 2004 datasets using ROUGE F_1.

Model	Multi-News			DUC-2004		
	R-1	R-2	R-SU4	R-1	R-2	R-SU4
ext-LexRank [5]	38.27	12.70	13.20	28.90	5.33	8.76
ext-TextRank [16]	38.44	13.10	13.50	33.16	6.13	10.16
ext-MMR [2]	38.77	11.98	12.91	30.14	4.55	8.16
abs-Pointer-Gen [17]	41.85	12.91	16.46	31.43	6.03	10.01
abs-PG-MMR [11]	40.55	12.36	15.87	36.42	9.36	**13.23**
abs-BaseTransformer [18]	41.08	12.49	15.78	26.11	4.86	7.20
abs-CopyTransformer [7]	43.57	14.03	17.37	28.54	6.38	7.22
abs-Hi-MAP [6]	43.47	14.89	17.41	35.78	8.90	11.43
abs-MLT (Our model)	**44.72**	**15.61**	**18.39**	**37.27**	**9.52**	12.31

Table 2. Human judgment results according to five dimensions. We computed the scores as the percentage of times selected as best minus the times selected as worst.

Model	Grammar	Non-redundancy	Referential clarity	Focus	Structure and Coherence
PG-MMR	−0.148	0.020	0.088	−0.280	−0.196
CopyTransformer	0.020	−0.380	−0.188	0.010	0.024
Hi-MAP	0.052	0.056	0.008	0.030	0.020
MLT	**0.076**	**0.304**	**0.092**	**0.240**	**0.152**

Transformer-based systems such as BaseTransformer and CopyTransformer, our model brings substantial improvements on all metrics, which demonstrates that our improvements made on the Transformer architecture are significantly effective. By exploiting the Transformer architecture and learning interactions at multiple levels, MLT outperforms Hi-MAP by (+1.25 ROUGE-1, +0.72 ROUGE-2, +0.98 ROUGE-SU4) points.

Human Evaluation. We randomly select 25 test instances from Multi-News and 25 from DUC 2004. Compared systems include PG-MMR, CopyTransformer, Hi-MAP, and our MLT. And we hired five well-educated evaluators to annotate which summary was the best and which was the worst according to five dimensions previously used in DUC-2005 [8]: Grammaticality, Non-redundancy, Referential clarity, Focus, and Structure and Coherence. We adopted Best-Worst Scaling [15], which requires fewer labors and has shown to be more reliable than rating scales [10]. The rating was computed as the percentage of times selected as best minus the times selected as worst, ranging from −1 to 1.

Table 2 shows human judgment results compared with different models. We can observe that our model is more frequently marked as the best system. We believe that learning interactions at multiple levels can help our MLT generate more fluent and coherent summaries.

5 Conclusion

In this paper, we extend the Transformer structure to encode contextual information at multiple levels and avoid redundancy while generating summaries. Specifically, our model can effectively learn interactions among input documents and relations between sentences within each document. We also integrate an MMR model to avoid redundancy. Our proposed model outperforms other models by a large margin on benchmark datasets.

Acknowledgments. This research work has been funded by the National Natural Science Foundation of China (Grant No. 61772337, U1736207) and the National Key R&D Program of China (2018YFC0830700).

References

1. Antognini, D., Faltings, B.: Learning to create sentence semantic relation graphs for multi-document summarization. EMNLP-IJCNLP **2019**, 32 (2019)
2. Carbonell, J.G., Goldstein, J.: The use of MMR, diversity-based reranking for reordering documents and producing summaries. In: SIGIR, pp. 335–336. ACM (1998)
3. Cho, S., Lebanoff, L., Foroosh, H., Liu, F.: Improving the similarity measure of determinantal point processes for extractive multi-document summarization. In: ACL, vol. 1, pp. 1027–1038. Association for Computational Linguistics (2019)
4. Chu, E., Liu, P.J.: MeanSum: a neural model for unsupervised multi-document abstractive summarization. In: ICML. Proceedings of Machine Learning Research, vol. 97, pp. 1223–1232. PMLR (2019)
5. Erkan, G., Radev, D.R.: LexRank: graph-based lexical centrality as salience in text summarization. J. Artif. Intell. Res. **22**, 457–479 (2004)
6. Fabbri, A.R., Li, I., She, T., Li, S., Radev, D.R.: Multi-news: a large-scale multi-document summarization dataset and abstractive hierarchical model. In: ACL, vol. 1, pp. 1074–1084. Association for Computational Linguistics (2019)
7. Gehrmann, S., Deng, Y., Rush, A.M.: Bottom-up abstractive summarization. In: EMNLP, pp. 4098–4109. Association for Computational Linguistics (2018)
8. Hao, T.: Overview of DUC 2005. In: Proceedings of the Document Understanding Conference (DUC 2005) (2005)
9. Kingma, D.P., Ba, J.: Adam: a method for stochastic optimization. In: ICLR (Poster) (2015)
10. Kiritchenko, S., Mohammad, S.: Best-worst scaling more reliable than rating scales: a case study on sentiment intensity annotation. In: ACL, vol. 2, pp. 465–470. Association for Computational Linguistics (2017)
11. Lebanoff, L., Song, K., Liu, F.: Adapting the neural encoder-decoder framework from single to multi-document summarization. In: EMNLP, pp. 4131–4141. Association for Computational Linguistics (2018)
12. Lin, C.Y.: ROUGE: a package for automatic evaluation of summaries. In: Text Summarization Branches Out, pp. 74–81 (2004)
13. Liu, P.J., et al.: Generating Wikipedia by summarizing long sequences. In: ICLR (Poster). OpenReview.net (2018)
14. Liu, Y., Lapata, M.: Hierarchical transformers for multi-document summarization. In: ACL, vol. 1, pp. 5070–5081. Association for Computational Linguistics (2019)

15. Louviere, J.J., Flynn, T.N., Marley, A.A.J.: Best-Worst Scaling: Theory, Methods and Applications. Cambridge University Press, Cambridge (2015)
16. Mihalcea, R., Tarau, P.: TextRank: bringing order into text. In: EMNLP, pp. 404–411. ACL (2004)
17. See, A., Liu, P.J., Manning, C.D.: Get to the point: summarization with pointer-generator networks. In: ACL, vol. 1, pp. 1073–1083. Association for Computational Linguistics (2017)
18. Vaswani, A., et al.: Attention is all you need. In: NIPS, pp. 5998–6008 (2017)
19. Yasunaga, M., Zhang, R., Meelu, K., Pareek, A., Srinivasan, K., Radev, D.R.: Graph-based neural multi-document summarization. In: CoNLL, pp. 452–462. Association for Computational Linguistics (2017)
20. Zhang, J., Tan, J., Wan, X.: Adapting neural single-document summarization model for abstractive multi-document summarization: a pilot study. In: INLG, pp. 381–390. Association for Computational Linguistics (2018)

Multitask Learning Based on Constrained Hierarchical Attention Network for Multi-aspect Sentiment Classification

Yang Gao[iD], Jianxun Liu$^{(\boxtimes)}$[iD], Pei Li$^{(\boxtimes)}$[iD], Dong Zhou[iD], and Peng Yuan[iD]

Hunan Key Lab for Services Computing and Novel Software Technology,
Hunan University of Science and Technology, Xiangtan 411201, China
`gyang330@163.com`, `ljx529@gmail.com`, `8992077@qq.com`,
`dongzhou1979@hotmail.com`, `mpenzlp@163.com`

Abstract. Aspect-level sentiment classification (ALSC) aims to distinguish the sentiment polarity of each given aspect in text. A user-generated review usually contains several aspects with different sentiment for each aspect, but most existing approaches only identify one aspect-specific sentiment polarity. Moreover, the prior works using attention mechanisms will introduce inherent noise and reduce the performance of the work. Therefore, we propose a model called Multitask Learning based on Constrained HiErarchical ATtention network (ML-CHEAT), a simple but effective method, which uses the regularization unit to limit the attention weight of each aspect. In addition, the ML-CHEAT uses the hierarchical attention network to learn the potential relationship between aspect features and sentiment features. Furthermore, we extend our approach to multitask learning to optimize the parameters update in the backpropagation and improve the performance of the model. Experimental results on SemEval competition datasets demonstrate the effectiveness and reliability of our approach.

Keywords: ALSC · ML-CHEAT · Hierarchical Attention · Regularization unit

1 Introduction

Aspect-level sentiment classification is a fine-grained sentiment analysis task that aims to identify the aspect-specific sentiment polarity from user-generated reviews [1,2]. For example, "Decor is nice though service can be spotty.", the sentiment polarity towards the aspect "ambiance" is positive, but the sentiment polarity towards the aspect "service" is negative. The review contains two

Supported by the National Natural Science Foundation of China (Grant Nos. 61872139, 61876062, 61702181), the Natural Science Foundation of Hunan Province (Grant No. 2018JJ3190) and the Scientific Research Fund of Hunan Provincial Education Department (Grant No. 18B199).

© Springer Nature Switzerland AG 2020
H. Yang et al. (Eds.): ICONIP 2020, CCIS 1332, pp. 685–692, 2020.
https://doi.org/10.1007/978-3-030-63820-7_78

aspects with different sentiment for each aspect, but most existing approaches only identify one aspect-specific sentiment polarity.

Previously, most existing approaches leverage the recurrent neural networks to extract the contextual information and the representations of aspect category which are usually led to mismatching of the sentiment polarity with the given aspect. Recently, with the wide application of attention mechanisms in NLP, we found that lots of ALSC models combine the attention mechanisms with recurrent neural networks and achieve great performance [2–6]. In particular, Ma et al. [3] proposed a model with bi-directional attention mechanisms for interactive learning context and attention weights of aspect terms respectively. However, the attention may inherently introduce noise and reduce performance. Because the attention weights will be assigned to the whole sentence, and a review usually contains multiple aspects. We can see that the distribution of opinion expression of each aspect is sparse.

Recently, some researchers used a hierarchical attention network to address ALSC tasks, which enables better learning the semantic relationship between sentiment words and the given aspect [7,8]. However, previous studies for multi-aspect sentiment analysis just use the attention layer to obtain the sentence representation under the guidance of the given aspect. They have not considered the potential relationship between aspect terms and sentiment terms.

To alleviate the above issue, we propose a novel Multitask Learning based on Constrained HiErarchical ATtention Network(ML-CHEAT). The rest of our paper is structured as follows: The detailed description of the model is given in Sect. 2. Section 3 presents extensive experiments to justify the effectiveness of our proposals. Finally, this work and its future direction are included in Sect. 4.

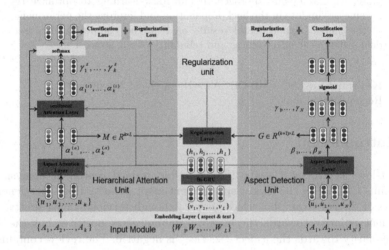

Fig. 1. An illustration of aspect-level sentiment classification based on Constrained HiErarchical ATtention network.

2   ML-CHEAT Network

2.1   Input Module

For the sentence $S = \{w_1, w_2, \ldots, w_n\}$ with K aspects: A_s^1 with popularity p_1, A_s^k with popularity p_k. We use an embedding matrix $\Phi_N \in R^{d \times N}$ to represent N predefined aspect categories. Φ_N is the set of aspects φ_i, the embedding vector φ_i represents aspect A_i, and d is the dimension of the embedding vector φ_i. Firstly, we convert the sentence to a sequence of vectors $V = \{v_1, v_2, \ldots, v_n\}$, then transform the K aspects of the sentence to vectors $U = \{u_1, u_2, \ldots, u_k\}$, which is a subset of N predefined aspect categories vectors. We take $\{V_n, \Phi_N, U_k, P_K\}$ as input of the ML-CHEAT model, where P_k is the collection of polarities. Then, we use BiGRU to extract the contextual information of each word in the sentence.

2.2   Constrained Hierarchical Attention Module

HiErarchical Attention Unit

Aspect Attention Layer. The key idea of multi-aspect sentiment classification is to learn different attention weights for different aspects, so that different aspects can concentrate on different parts of the sentence. Particularly, given the sentence S with K aspects, $A^s = \{A_1^s, A_2^s, \ldots, A_K^s\}$, for each aspect A_K^s, the weights of each word in expressing the aspect information in the sentence are calculated by:

$$g_{ki}^{(a)} = (u^{(a)})^T \tanh(W^{(a)} \left[\varphi_k; \overleftrightarrow{h}_i^{(a)}\right] + b^a), \quad (1)$$

where $W^{(a)} \in R^{d \times 3d}$ is the weight matrix parameter, φ_k is the embedding vector of aspect A_k^s, $\overleftrightarrow{h}_i^a$ is the contextual feature of the word w_i from the BiGRU of the input module, $b^{(a)} \in R^d$ is the bias vector parameter, $u^{(a)} \in R^d$ is the weight vector parameter, $(u^{(a)})^T$ is the transpose of $u^{(a)}$. The total weight of the contextual features of all the words in the sentence is 1. $\alpha_{ki}^{(a)}$ is the weight of word w_i contains information related to the given aspect A_k^s, it is defined as

$$\sum_{i=1}^{|T|} \alpha_{ki}^{(a)} = \sum_{i=1}^{|T|} \frac{\exp\left(g_{ki}^{(a)}\right)}{\sum_{j=1}^{|T|} \exp\left(g_{ki}^{(a)}\right)} = 1. \quad (2)$$

The aspect features $v_k^{(a)}$ extracted from the aspect attention layer are the weighted sum of the aspect features $\alpha_{ki}^{(a)}$ of all words of the input text,

$$v_k^{(a)} = \sum_{i=1}^{|T|} \alpha_{ki}^{(a)} \overleftrightarrow{h}_i^{(a)} \quad (3)$$

Location Mask Layer. To better compute the sentiment attention weights, we use a position matrix $M \in R^{|T| \times |T|}$ to represent the position relationship between a word and others in the text. The position relationship between two words is as

$$M_{ij} = 1 - \frac{|i-j|}{|T|},$$
(4)

where $i, j \in \{1, 2, \ldots, |T|\}$, the value M_{ij} increases as the distance of i, j gets closer. The position mask is calculated as

$$m = M\alpha$$
(5)

Sentiment Attention Layer. It uses the aspect features to capture the aspect-specific sentiment information by the sentiment attention layer. Similar to aspect attention, the input of sentiment attention is the contextual feature of each word from the BiGRU of the input module. The attention score $g_{ki}^{(s)}$ of word w_i in expressing the sentiment information of the aspect A_k^s is calculated by

$$g_{ki}^{(s)} = (u^{(s)})^T \tanh(W^{(s)} \left[\varphi_k; v_k^{(a)}; \overleftrightarrow{h}_i^{(s)}\right] + b^a),$$
(6)

where $W^{(s)} \in R^{d \times 3d}$ is the weight matrix parameter, $b^{(s)} \in R^d$ is the bias vector parameter, $u^{(s)} \in R^d$ is the weight vector parameter, $(u^{(s)})^T$ is the transpose of $u^{(s)}$. The total weight of the contextual features of all the words in the sentence is 1.

While calculating sentiment features, we take the positional relationship between the aspect term and the sentiment term into account, and introduce the position mask layer. The weight of sentiment attention is calculated as

$$\sum_{i=1}^{|T|} \alpha_{ki}^{(s)} = sum_{i=1}^{|T|} \frac{\exp\left(m_i g_{ki}^{(s)}\right)}{\sum_{j=1}^{|T|} \exp\left(m_i g_{ki}^{(s)}\right)} = 1.$$
(7)

The sentiment features $v_k^{(s)}$ extracted from the sentiment attention layer are the weighted sum of the sentiment features $\alpha_i^{(s)}$ of all words of the input text, $v_k^{(s)}$ is defined as

$$v_k^{(s)} = \sum_{i=1}^{|T|} \alpha_{ki}^{(s)} \overleftrightarrow{h}_i^{(s)}.$$
(8)

Aspect Detection Unit. We treat the ACD (Aspect Category Detection) task as a multi-label classification problem for the set of N aspect categories. It aims to checks the aspect $A_n \in A$ to see whether the sentence S mentions it. We use the same attention mechanisms with the aspect attention layer, they share parameters. For each aspect $A_n \in A$, the weights of each word in expressing the aspect information in the sentence are calculated by:

$$g_{ni}^{(a)} = (u^{(a)})^T \tanh(W^{(a)} \left[\varphi_n; \overleftrightarrow{h}_i^{(a)} \right] + b^a), \tag{9}$$

$$\sum_{i=1}^{|T|} \beta_{ni}^{(a)} = \sum_{i=1}^{|T|} \frac{\exp\left(g_{ni}^{(a)}\right)}{\sum_{j=1}^{|T|} \exp\left(g_{ni}^{(a)}\right)} = 1. \tag{10}$$

where φ_n is the embedding vector of aspect A_i. The total weight of the contextual features of all the words in the sentence is 1. $\beta_{ni}^{(a)}$ is the weight of word w_i contains information related to the given aspect A_n.

The aspect features $v_n^{(a)}$ extracted from the aspect detection attention layer are the weighted sum of the aspect features $\beta_{ni}^{(a)}$ of all words of the input text,

$$v_n^{(a)} = \sum_{i=1}^{|T|} \beta_{ni}^{(a)} \overleftrightarrow{h}_i^{(a)} \tag{11}$$

Sparse Regularization Unit. In this paper, we use the sparse regularization to compute the limit the allocation of aspect attention. Due to the aspects that are unknown in the inference stage. We should know that the regularization layer only uses in the training stage. For each aspect in the sentence, the sparse regularization constrains the attention weights (α_k or β_n) to focus on fewer words. In particularly, we use α_k as an example, $\alpha_k = \{\alpha_{k1}, \alpha_{k2}, \ldots, \alpha_{kL}\}$. To make α_k sparse, the sparse regularization is defined as:

$$R_s = \left| \sum_{i=1}^{L} \alpha_{ki}^2 - 1 \right|, \tag{12}$$

where L is the length of the sentence, α_{ki} is the is the weight of word w_i contains information related to the given aspect A_k^s. Mining the value R_s of can force the sparsity of α_k and constrain the attention weights to concentrate more less words than the traditional mechanisms.

2.3   Classification Module

Prediction of Sentiment Polarity. We take the target aspect category vector φ_k and the output $v_k^{(s)}$ of sentiment attention layer as the input of the sentiment classification module,

$$y_1 = softmax(w_1 \left[\varphi_k; v_k^{(s)} \right] + b_1) \tag{13}$$

Aspect Category Detection. We directly use the output of the aspect detection layer $v_n^{(a)}$ as the input of the aspect detection module,

$$y_2 = softmax(w_2 \times v_n^{(a)} + b_1). \tag{14}$$

2.4 Loss Function

In order to ensure the accuracy of aspect features extraction and aspect-specific sentiment features extraction, we use both supervision in the ACD task and ALSC task. The loss of ACDU task is

$$L^{(a)} = -\sum_{k=1}^{n}(\widehat{y}_{2k}\log(y_{2k}) + (1 - \widehat{y}_{2k})\log(1 - y_{2k})). \tag{15}$$

At last, the loss function is

$$L = \lambda L^{(a)} + (1 - \lambda)L^{(s)} + \lambda' \|\theta\|^{2} + 2R_{s} \tag{16}$$

where $\lambda \in (0,1)$ is a hyper parameter used to balance the aspect attention loss and the sentiment classification loss, λ' is the L2-regularization term, and θ is the parameter set.

3 Experiments

3.1 Datasets and Experiment Settings

We use the SemEval competition dataset Rest14 and Rest15 to evaluate the ML-CHEAT network at the sentence level of multi-aspect sentiment classification [8,9]. Each data set contains a target aspect and the aspect-specific sentiment polarity.

Experiment Settings. We train word embedding on the Yelp Challenge data set for the restaurant domain which contains 4.1M reviews on restaurants. Some parameters initialize by a uniform distribution $U(-0.01, 0.01)$. The dimension of word vectors, aspect embedding is 64 and the size of the hidden layer is 32. We train all models with a batch size of 64 examples, a momentum of 0.9, L2-regularization weight of 0.001, and the initial learning rate are 0.01.

3.2 Model for Comparison

AT-LSTM: It adopts the attention mechanisms in LSTM to generate a weighted representation of a sentence.

HEAT-BiGRU: The model captures the aspect information of a text and uses the aspect information to capture the aspect-specific sentiment information.

CAN-Rs: CAN-Rs is add sparsity regularization to AT-LSTM.

CHEAT-BiGRU-Rs: Add hierarchical attention unit and CAN-Rs.

To verify the vital role of the aspect detection in aspect-level sentiment classification, we introduces aspect detection unit and extend the regularization to the multi-task settings.

ML-AT-LSTM: This is the basic multi-task model without hierarchical attention and regularization.

ML-CHEAT-Rs: Add Rs to the ASLC task in ML-CHEAT-BiGRU.

ML-CHEAT-2Rs: Add Rs to both tasks in ML-CHEAT-BiGRU.

Table 1. Results of the ALSC task in terms of accuracy (%) and Macro-F1 (%).

Model	Rest14				Rest15			
	3-way		Binary		3-way		Binary	
	Acc	F1	Acc	F1	Acc	F1	Acc	F1
AT-LSTM	81.24	69.19	87.25	82.20	73.37	51.74	76.79	74.61
AT-CAN-Rs	82.28	70.94	88.43	84.07	75.62	53.56	78.36	76.69
HEAT-BiGRU	83.02	73.25	90.12	85.76	78.85	56.31	81.32	80.74
CHEAT-BiGRU-Rs	83.16	71.74	89.75	84.32	76.18	54.43	79.57	78.77
ML-AT-LSTM	82.60	71.44	88.55	83.76	76.33	51.64	79.53	78.31
ML-CHEAT-BiGRU-Rs	84.26	**74.13**	90.01	**85.92**	76.21	53.05	80.25	78.92
ML-CHEAT-BiGRU-2Rs	**83.42**	73.36	**90.08**	85.74	**79.74**	**56.24**	**82.33**	**80.64**

3.3 Evaluation and Analysis

Experimental results are shown in Table 1, "3-way" stands for 3-class classification (positive, neutral, and negative), and "Binary" for binary classification (positive and negative). The best scores are marked in bold. From the table we draw the following conclusions:

First, we observe that by using aspect features to assist sentiment features extraction and introducing position relationship between aspect term and sentiment term, our methods achieve competitive results. Second, we observe the model which by applying attention regularization(sparse regularization) to achieve better results. This verifies that introducing attention regularization will reduce the inherent noise of attention mechanisms and improve the performance of the work. Third, we observe that all multi-task method performs significantly better than the ones in single-task.

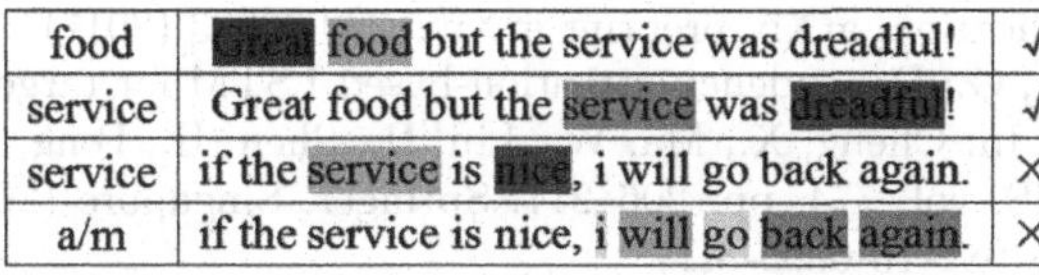

food	Great food but the service was dreadful!	√
service	Great food but the service was dreadful!	√
service	if the service is nice, i will go back again.	✕
a/m	if the service is nice, i will go back again.	✕

Fig. 2. Examples of ML-CHEAT. The colored word and the color depth illustrate the weight of word in sentiment attention layer. (Color figure online)

Case Studies. In Fig. 2, we list some examples of sentiment classification in the data sets. As shown in Fig. 2, the ML-CHEAT model could easily supervise the sentiment words and enable the model to concentrate more on the sentiment words corresponding to the given aspect. Especially, "Great" is the sentiment information towards food, and "dreadful" is the sentiment information towards service.

Error Analysis. We analyze error cases in the experiments. Some examples of error cases are shown in Fig. 2. We can find that ML-CHEAT-BiGRU-2Rs is hard to learn logical relationships in a sentence. For example, in "if the service is nice, i will go back again", it expresses negative feelings towards the service, but there are no obvious negative words, it is difficult to make a correct prediction. Our approach can easily extract the sentiment information "nice" but can not learn the word "if".

4   Conclusions and Future Work

In this paper, the ML-CHEAT network achieves a better performance on multi-aspect sentiment classification. It can learn the potential relationship between the aspect and sentiment more effectively. It can solve the problems that the sentiment mismatch caused by the incorrect aspect feature extraction. In addition, it uses the regularization layer to limit the attention weight of each aspect. However, there are still some logical relations we can not extract effectively and it can cause incorrect sentiment polarity prediction. In the future, we will consider how to use auxiliary information such as sentence structure, grammatical structure, logical relation, and semantic features to improve the accuracy of aspect-level sentiment classification.

References

1. Bakshi, R.K., Kaur, N., Kaur, R., et al.: Opinion mining and sentiment analysis. In: 2016 3rd International Conference on Computing for Sustainable Global Development (INDIACom), pp. 452–455. IEEE (2016)
2. Wang, Y., Huang, M., Zhu, X., et al.: Attention-based LSTM for aspect-level sentiment classification. In: Proceedings of the 2016 Conference on Empirical Methods in Natural Language Processing, pp. 606–615 (2016)
3. Ma, D., Li, S., Zhang, X., et al.: Interactive attention networks for aspect-level sentiment classification. arXiv preprint arXiv:1709.00893 (2017)
4. Wang, X., Chen, G.: Dependency-attention-based LSTM for target-dependent sentiment analysis. In: Cheng, X., Ma, W., Liu, H., Shen, H., Feng, S., Xie, X. (eds.) SMP 2017. CCIS, vol. 774, pp. 206–217. Springer, Singapore (2017). https://doi.org/10.1007/978-981-10-6805-8_17
5. Wang, J., Li, J., Li, S., et al.: Aspect sentiment classification with both word-level and clause-level attention networks. In: IJCAI, vol. 2018, pp. 4439–4445 (2018)
6. Nguyen, H.T., Le Nguyen, M.: Effective attention networks for aspect-level sentiment classification. In: 2018 10th International Conference on Knowledge and Systems Engineering (KSE), pp. 25–30. IEEE (2018)
7. Cheng, J., Zhao, S., Zhang, J., et al.: Aspect-level sentiment classification with heat (hierarchical attention) network. In: Proceedings of the ACM on Conference on Information and Knowledge Management, vol. 2017, pp. 97–106 (2017)
8. Gao, Y., Liu, J., Li, P., et al.: CE-HEAT: an aspect-level sentiment classification approach with collaborative extraction hierarchical attention network. IEEE Access **7**, 168548–168556 (2019)
9. Hu, M., Zhao, S., Zhang, L., et al.: CAN: constrained attention networks for multi-aspect sentiment analysis. arXiv preprint arXiv:1812.10735 (2018)

Neural Machine Translation with Soft Reordering Knowledge

Leiying Zhou[ID], Jie Zhou[ID], Wenjie Lu, Kui Meng[✉], and Gongshen Liu[✉][ID]

School of Electronic Information and Electrical Engineering, Shanghai Jiao Tong University, Shanghai 200240, China
{zhouleiying,sanny02,jonsey,mengkui,lgshen}@sjtu.edu.cn

Abstract. The Transformer architecture has been widely used in sequence to sequence tasks since it was proposed. However, it only adds the representations of absolute positions to its inputs to make use of the order information of the sequence. It lacks explicit structures to exploit the reordering knowledge of words. In this paper, we propose a simple but effective method to incorporate the reordering knowledge into the Transformer translation system. The reordering knowledge of each word is obtained by an additional reordering-aware attention sublayer based on its semantic and contextual information. The proposed approach can be easily integrated into the existing framework of the Transformer. Experimental results on two public translation tasks demonstrate that our proposed method can achieve significant translation improvements over the basic Transformer model and also outperforms the existing competitive systems.

Keywords: Neural machine translation · Reordering · Transformer · Self-attention

1 Introduction

The position information of words in both source and target sequence plays an important role in machine translation systems. Approaches to machine translation, including statistical machine translation (SMT) [2,5], recurrent neural network (RNN) [15], convolutional neural network (CNN) [7] and attention mechanism [1], incorporate information about the sequential position of words differently.

Recently, the Transformer model [16], which contains no recurrence and no convolution instead relies entirely on attention mechanism to draw global dependencies between input and output, has achieved a new state-of-the-art performance on multiple language pairs. The position information is explicitly incorporated into the model by a positional encoding mechanism [6]. However, this positional encoding method only focuses on encoding the sequential order relations of words in a sentence, and does not make full use of the position information of words, such as the word reordering information. Lack of explicit structures to

© Springer Nature Switzerland AG 2020
H. Yang et al. (Eds.): ICONIP 2020, CCIS 1332, pp. 693–700, 2020.
https://doi.org/10.1007/978-3-030-63820-7_79

exploit the word reordering knowledge may lead to attention faults and generate fluent but inaccurate or inadequate translations [17]. There are few works currently focusing on the reordering problem for Transformer.

In this paper, we present a simple but effective way of incorporating the reordering knowledge into the Transformer translation system. Specifically, we integrate an extra soft reordering sublayer into the existing system to model the word reordering information in a sentence. This paper primarily makes the following contributions:

- We propose a simple approach to incorporate the reordering knowledge into the Transformer translation system, which has not been studied extensively.
- The proposed method can be seen as an extension of the self-attention mechanism of Transformer to considering the reordering knowledge and it can be easily integrated into both the encoder and decoder of the Transformer.
- Experimental results on two public translation tasks demonstrate that our method is effective and outperforms both the basic Transformer model and several existing competitive models.

2   Related Work

Our work incorporates the reordering knowledge for NMT to improve the translation quality. There are two kinds of closely related studies, pre-reordering all the sentences in the source side before training the NMT models and incorporating the order information of words into NMT by modeling them with certain functions or mechanisms. Pre-reordering is a preprocessing step to modify the source-side word orders to be more close to these of the target side through word reordering models, which can be traced back to SMT. For end-to-end NMT, there are no explicit structures to exploit the word reordering knowledge. Thus, some researchers [8,11,18] try to incorporate the pre-reordering strategy of SMT into NMT models. Different from training models on pre-reordered data, there are a growing number of research works [13,16,17] modeling the order information of words with certain functions or mechanisms during the training process, which eliminates the complicated pre-reordering step. Our work is different from those works, as our approach explicitly captures word reordering knowledge through an extra soft reordering sublayer to tackle the reordering problem for Transformer.

3   Soft Reordering Mechanism

For the traditional SMT models, there are two common reordering methods, a preprocessing step for the source sentences or a postprocessing step for the predicted target translations. In either case, the order of each word is determined by its semantics and global contextual information, which is also consistent with human's habit of adjusting word orders when translating sentences. Inspired by this, our proposed approach obtains the reordering knowledge of each word based on its semantic and contextual information. But different from using reordering

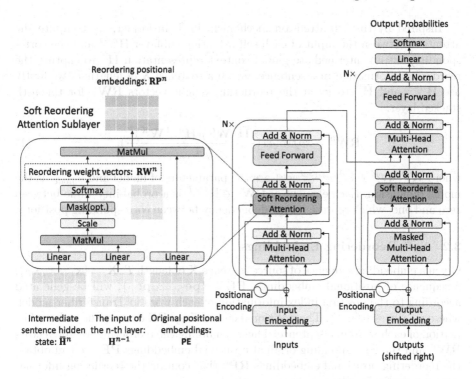

Fig. 1. The architecture of Transformer with soft reordering sublayer.

models to align words strongly in SMT models, we use a reordering-aware attention sublayer to gain the reordering information of sentences softly, which is the soft reordering knowledge. The soft reordering attention sublayer is then stacked with the other sublayers to learn a final reordering-aware sentence representation (as shown in Fig. 1).

3.1 Reordering-Aware Attention

The multi-head self-attention sublayers in the stacked encoder layers of Transformer allow each position to attend all positions in the previous layer of the encoder, which means each word can attend to all the related words in the source sentences. And the masked multi-head self-attention sublayers in the decoder layers encode the dependencies between words in the target sentences. Assuming that $\mathbf{H}^{n-1}$ is the input representation of the n-th stacked encoder or decoder layer, an intermediate representation vector $\overline{\mathbf{H}}^{n}$ can be obtained from the multi-head self-attention sublayer. And the outputs of these self-attention sublayers $\overline{\mathbf{H}}^{n}$ contain the contextual information for each position, which can be regarded as the expected global contextual representation vector. And the input of these self-attention sublayers $\mathbf{H}^{n-1}$, can be seen as the representation vector containing the semantic information of each position.

Inspired by the self-attention mechanism in Transformer, we compute the attention between the input of each self-attention sublayer $\mathbf{H}^{n-1}$ and the corresponding output intermediate global context representation $\overline{\mathbf{H}}^n$ to capture the reordering information in a sentence. Given a sentence $\mathbf{X}$ of length T, we firstly use $\mathbf{H}^{n-1}$ and $\overline{\mathbf{H}}^n$ to learn the reordering weight vectors $\mathbf{RW}^n$ for the n-th stacked layer:

$$\mathbf{RW}^n = softmax(\frac{(\overline{\mathbf{H}}^n \mathbf{W}^Q)(\mathbf{H}^{n-1}\mathbf{W}^K)^T}{\sqrt{d_{model}}}), \tag{1}$$

where $\mathbf{W}^Q, \mathbf{W}^K \in \mathbb{R}^{d_{model} \times d_{model}}$ are the parameters of model and d_{model} is the model dimension. Each element of $\mathbf{RW}^n \in \mathbb{R}^{T \times T}$ is a probability value between zero and one, which represents the dependency between corresponding positions.

3.2 Soft Reordering Embeddings

Given a embedding sequence of source sentence $\mathbf{X}$ of length T, $\mathbf{X} = \{\mathbf{x}_1, \ldots, \mathbf{x}_T\}$, a sequence of positional embeddings, $\mathbf{PE} = \{\mathbf{pe}_1, \ldots, \mathbf{pe}_T\}$, will be generated according to the position index information of each word in Transformer model, where $\mathbf{x}_j, \mathbf{pe}_j \in \mathbb{R}^{d_{model}}$. The positional embeddings $\mathbf{PE}$ contain the order information of each word in a sentence. Thus, combining the reordering weight vectors $\mathbf{RW}^n$ and the corresponding original positional embeddings $\mathbf{PE}$, we can obtain the reordering positional embeddings $\mathbf{RP}^n$ that contain the reordering information of a sentence. The calculation method is as:

$$\mathbf{RP}^n = \mathbf{RW}^n \cdot \mathbf{PE} \cdot \mathbf{W}^V, \tag{2}$$

where $\mathbf{W}^V \in \mathbb{R}^{d_{model} \times d_{model}}$ is the trainable weight matrix of the model. The dimensions of $\mathbf{RP}^n$ and $\mathbf{PE}$ are both $T \times d_{model}$. The learned reordering positional embeddings $\mathbf{RP}^n$ are further added to the current intermediate global context representation $\overline{\mathbf{H}}^n$ to achieve the soft reordering operation. Later, a layer normalization operation is employed on the calculation results:

$$\hat{\mathbf{H}}^n = LN(\mathbf{RP}^n + \overline{\mathbf{H}}), \tag{3}$$

where $\hat{\mathbf{H}}^n \in \mathbb{R}^{T \times d_{model}}$ is the intermediate representation that contains the reordering knowledge of a sentence. $\hat{\mathbf{H}}^n$ is then fed to the next sublayer to learn a new reordering-aware output representation $\mathbf{H}^n$ of this stacked layer. These processes are repeated until the final reordering-aware sentence representation $\mathbf{H}^N$ is generated.

4   Experiments

4.1   Datasets

We conducted experiments on the WMT 2019[1] English-Chinese (En-Zh) and the IWSLT 2016 [3] German-English (De-En) datasets. For WMT 2019 En-Zh task,

---

[1] http://www.statmt.org/wmt19/translation-task.html.

we used the casia2015 corpus as the training set, newsdev2017 as the validation set and newstest2017, newstest2018 and newstest2019 as test sets. For IWSLT 2016 De-En task, tst2013 was used as validation set and tst2010, tst2011, tst2012 and tst2014 were used as test sets.

4.2   Compared Methods

In our experiments, the baseline system is the vanilla Transformer model with absolute positional embedding. To validate the effectiveness of our proposed method, We also compare our work with the following models:

Additional PEs: the original absolute positional embeddings are used to enhance the position information of each word instead of the learned reordering positional embeddings.

Relative PEs [13]: a previously proposed approach incorporating relative position representations into the self-attention mechanism of the Transformer.

Reordering PEs [4]: a recently proposed method which learns positional penalty vectors of the sentence with the perceptron-based attention mechanism to penalize the original positional embeddings.

Besides, in order to show the performance of our method more intuitively, we compare our work with other three existing competitive models, RNNsearch [1], DTMT [10] and Evolved Transformer [14]. Since the datasets we used are different from these models, we used the source codes reported in these papers to experiment on our datasets and got the final comparative test results.

4.3   Setup

For both translation tasks, the byte pair encoding (BPE) algorithm [12] was used to encode the sentences in both source and target sides and the shared source-target vocabulary size is set to 32k tokens. And sentence pairs with either side longer than 100 tokens were dropped.

For all experiments, the embedding size was 512, the hidden size was 1024, and the number of heads was 8. The encoder and the decoder each had six layers. For training, we used the Adam optimizer [9] with a learning rate of 0.0001. The learning rate was varied under a warm-up strategy with warmup steps of 4,000. The value of label smoothing was set to 0.1, and the attention dropout and residual dropout were 0.3. For evaluation, we validated the model every epoch on the dev set. After all training epochs, the model with the highest BLEU score of the dev set was selected to evaluate the test sets. We used the multi-bleu.perl[2] as the evaluation metric for both translation tasks. We trained and evaluated all models on a single NVIDIA GeForce GTX 1080 Ti GPU.

---

[2] https://github.com/moses-smt/mosesdecoder/blob/master/scripts/generic/multi-bleu.perl.

Table 1. Evaluation results (BLEU) on WMT 2019 En-Zh dataset

System	dev17	test17	test18	test19	Average
RNNsearch	23.78	24.92	24.17	24.20	24.27
DTMT	26.35	28.07	26.10	27.34	26.97
Evolved Transformer	26.11	27.84	25.98	27.25	26.80
Transformer	25.04	26.37	25.09	25.76	25.57
+Additional PEs	25.15	26.21	25.36	25.89	25.65
+Relative PEs	25.51	26.86	25.46	26.09	25.98
+Reordering PEs	26.72	27.96	26.48	27.50	27.17
+Soft Reordering	**27.22**	**28.79**	**27.32**	**28.06**	**27.85**

Table 2. Evaluation results (BLEU) on IWSLT 2016 De-En dataset

System	tst13	tst10	tst11	tst12	tst14	Average
RNNsearch	25.12	24.46	28.06	24.92	22.94	25.10
DTMT	28.39	26.51	31.66	27.64	**26.02**	28.04
Evolved Transformer	28.17	26.33	31.45	27.28	25.36	27.72
Transformer	26.96	25.17	30.03	26.20	24.24	26.52
+Additional PEs	27.13	25.30	29.58	26.24	23.92	26.43
+Relative PEs	27.38	25.51	30.25	26.47	24.73	26.87
+Reordering PEs	28.42	26.39	31.37	27.63	25.78	27.92
+Soft Reordering	**29.23**	**27.28**	**32.06**	**27.93**	25.99	**28.50**

4.4   Results

Evaluation results for the En-Zh translation task and the De-En translation task are presented in Tables 1 and 2 respectively. From the results in the table, we can see that our proposed method +Soft Reordering outperforms both the baseline systems and the existing competitive systems on most test sets, which proves the validity of our approach.

Comparison to Baseline Systems. More concretely, our method significantly outperforms the vanilla Transformer model by 2.28 and 1.98 BLEU scores averagely for the En-Zh and De-En translation tasks, which shows that the learned soft reordering knowledge is beneficial for the Transformer model. Compared with the evaluation results of +Additional PEs, we can know that adding the original absolute positional embeddings has little or even negative impact on the improvement of the base model, which means the performance improvements of our method derive from the learned positional embeddings instead of the original absolute positional embeddings. Meanwhile, the results of +Soft Reordering are superior to +Relative PEs and +Reordering PEs, which indicates that our proposed reordering-aware attention mechanism can better capture the reordering knowledge of the sentences. Besides, our proposed model also outperforms the

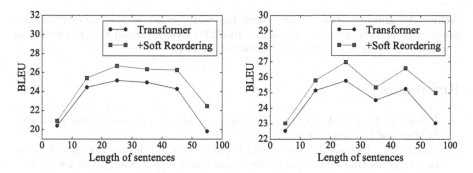

Fig. 2. Comparison of evaluation results of Transformer and +Soft Reordering on the test sets with different sentences length for En-Zh (left) and De-En (right) translation tasks.

three existing competitive systems for both translation tasks, which also proves the effectiveness of our method. Furthermore, the evaluation results in Tables 1 and 2 show that our proposed method has greater improvements for the En-Zh translation task than the De-En translation task, which conforms to the characteristics of the two language pairs and shows that the reordering knowledge is more important for the language pairs with large differences in word order.

Effect of Soft Reordering. Intuitively, the complexity of the dependency between words in a sentence increases with the length of the sentence, so the reordering information should have a greater impact on longer sentences. Therefore, to further explore the effect of incorporating the soft reordering knowledge into the Transformer, we grouped the sentence pairs of all test sets of each translation task according to the length of the BPE encoded source sentences. Then six new test sets were obtained for each task, in which the length of the source sentences is 0–10, 10–20, 20–30, 30–40, 40–50 and 50–100, respectively. Finally, these test sets were used to evaluate the vanilla Transformer model and our proposed method +Soft Reordering. The evaluation results are as shown in Fig. 2. We can observe that when the length of sentences gradually increases, the performance improvement of +Soft Reordering compared with Transformer also increases for both En-Zh and De-En translation tasks in general. This confirms our original intuition and indicates that the soft reordering knowledge has a greater effect on the promotion of long sentence translation performance.

5 Conclusion

In this paper, we proposed a reordering mechanism to incorporate the reordering knowledge into the Transformer translation system. The proposed approach can be easily integrated into both the encoder and decoder of the Transformer. The reordering knowledge is obtained by the additional soft reordering attention sublayers. And the experimental results on two public datasets demonstrate that our method is very effective and outperforms the Transformer baseline system and several existing competitive models.

Acknowledgments. This research work has been funded by the National Natural Science Foundation of China (Grant No. 61772337), the National Key Research and Development Program of China NO. 2016QY03D0604.

References

1. Bahdanau, D., Cho, K., Bengio, Y.: Neural machine translation by jointly learning to align and translate. In: ICLR (2015)
2. Brown, P.F., Pietra, S.D., Pietra, V.J.D., Mercer, R.L.: The mathematics of statistical machine translation: parameter estimation. Comput. Linguistics **19**(2), 263–311 (1993)
3. Cettolo, M., Girardi, C., Federico, M.: Wit3: Web inventory of transcribed and translated talks. In: Conference of European Association for Machine Translation, pp. 261–268 (2012)
4. Chen, K., Wang, R., Utiyama, M., Sumita, E.: Neural machine translation with reordering embeddings. In: ACL (1), pp. 1787–1799. Association for Computational Linguistics (2019)
5. Chiang, D.: A hierarchical phrase-based model for statistical machine translation. In: ACL, pp. 263–270. The Association for Computer Linguistics (2005)
6. Gehring, J., Auli, M., Grangier, D., Dauphin, Y.N.: A convolutional encoder model for neural machine translation. In: ACL (1), pp. 123–135. Association for Computational Linguistics (2017)
7. Gehring, J., Auli, M., Grangier, D., Yarats, D., Dauphin, Y.N.: Convolutional sequence to sequence learning. In: ICML. Proceedings of Machine Learning Research, vol. 70, pp. 1243–1252. PMLR (2017)
8. Kawara, Y., Chu, C., Arase, Y.: Recursive neural network based preordering for English-to-Japanese machine translation. In: ACL (3), pp. 21–27. Association for Computational Linguistics (2018)
9. Kingma, D.P., Ba, J.: Adam: a method for stochastic optimization. In: ICLR (Poster) (2015)
10. Meng, F., Zhang, J.: DTMT: a novel deep transition architecture for neural machine translation. In: AAAI, pp. 224–231. AAAI Press (2019)
11. Nakagawa, T.: Efficient top-down BTG parsing for machine translation preordering. In: ACL (1), pp. 208–218. The Association for Computer Linguistics (2015)
12. Sennrich, R., Haddow, B., Birch, A.: Neural machine translation of rare words with subword units. In: ACL (1). The Association for Computer Linguistics (2016)
13. Shaw, P., Uszkoreit, J., Vaswani, A.: Self-attention with relative position representations. In: NAACL-HLT (2), pp. 464–468. Association for Computational Linguistics (2018)
14. So, D.R., Le, Q.V., Liang, C.: The evolved transformer. In: ICML. Proceedings of Machine Learning Research, vol. 97, pp. 5877–5886. PMLR (2019)
15. Sutskever, I., Vinyals, O., Le, Q.V.: Sequence to sequence learning with neural networks. In: NIPS, pp. 3104–3112 (2014)
16. Vaswani, A., et al.: Attention is all you need. In: NIPS, pp. 5998–6008 (2017)
17. Zhang, J., Wang, M., Liu, Q., Zhou, J.: Incorporating word reordering knowledge into attention-based neural machine translation. In: ACL (1), pp. 1524–1534. Association for Computational Linguistics (2017)
18. Zhu, Z.: Evaluating neural machine translation in English-Japanese task. In: WAT, pp. 61–68. Workshop on Asian Translation (2015)

Open Event Trigger Recognition Using Distant Supervision with Hierarchical Self-attentive Neural Network

Xinmiao Pei[1], Hao Wang[1,2(✉)], Xiangfeng Luo[1,2(✉)], and Jianqi Gao[1]

[1] School of Computer Engineering and Science, Shanghai University,
Shanghai 200444, China
{peixinmiao,wang-hao,luoxf,gjqss}@shu.edu.cn
[2] Shanghai Institute for Advanced Communication and Data Science,
Shanghai 200444, China

Abstract. Event trigger recognition plays a crucial role in open-domain event extraction. To address issues of prior work on restricted domains and constraint types of events, so as to enable robust open event trigger recognition for various domains. In this paper, we propose a novel distantly supervised framework of event trigger extraction regardless of domains. This framework consists of three components: a trigger synonym generator, a synonym set scorer and an open trigger classifier. Given the specific knowledge bases, the trigger synonym generator generates high-quality synonym sets to train the remaining components. We employ distant supervision to produce instances of event trigger, then organizes them into fine-grained synonym sets. Inspired by recent deep metric learning, we also propose a novel neural method named hierarchical self-attentive neural network (HiSNN) to score the quality of generated synonym sets. Experimental results on three datasets (including two cross-domain datasets) demonstrate the superior of our proposal compared to the state-of-the-art approaches.

Keywords: Open-domain event extraction · Synonym set · Distant supervision · Neural network

1 Introduction

In event extraction, the discovery of unseen event triggers is one of the important and challenging tasks. It is also a fundamental pre-processing step for a wide range of natural language processing (NLP) applications, such as text summarization [8], question answering [3] and text mining [4]. Compared to a large number of studies carried out in mining entity synonyms, there is less attention that has been devoted to event trigger synonym extraction.

Problem Definition. Given an unstructured raw text data D, the task of event trigger recognition aims to discover all event trigger instances E then organize these triggers into synonym sets S so that each set is corresponding to

© Springer Nature Switzerland AG 2020
H. Yang et al. (Eds.): ICONIP 2020, CCIS 1332, pp. 701–708, 2020.
https://doi.org/10.1007/978-3-030-63820-7_80

one latent event type. However, open-domain synonym set generation of event trigger is challenging since determining the proper granularity of event synonym sets underlying different latent event types is difficult. Despite its importance, event trigger synonym extraction in the open domain remains an under-explored problem.

A straightforward way is supervised learning an event trigger detector. Prior studies mainly treat it as a multi-classification problem. Liu and Shulin [7] present a method to encode argument information in event detection via supervised attention mechanisms. Recently, Nguyen [9] and Sha [11] exploit syntactic information to enhance event detection. These models are typically trained on a small size of the human-annotated dataset in closed domains and thus subject to over-fitting.

However, rare research has been conducted for open event type identification. Most existing methods employ different graph clustering algorithms [2,10,13]. The problem is divided into two categories: (1) ranking methods based on similarity, and (2) detecting and organizing. However, this approach ignores intra-association among event triggers which may benefit the quality of discovered trigger synonym sets. Shen and Jiaming [12] attempts to model the interactions across entity synonym sets. This method is not suitable for event trigger synonym extraction where event triggers are usually domain-specified.

To address these issues, we introduce a novel framework based on distant supervision paradigm. Our method can be split into three phases: training instance and synonym set generation, synonym set quality evaluation and open event trigger classification. Our goal is to detect all probable event triggers and latent types without a specified event type list. Our contribution is as follows:

- We introduce a new framework of open event trigger extraction, whose goal is to detect all probable existing event triggers and latent types simultaneously.
- Human annotation of events in the open domain is substantially expensive. This method provides a universal solution to generate high-quality event trigger instances using distant supervision.
- A novel model, called HiSNN (Hierarchical Self-attentive Neural Network), is proposed as the score function for measuring intra-distance metric considering the hierarchical semantic relationship between trigger elements and trigger instances.

2   Our Model

We firstly give formal definitions for the existing notions in this paper. An event **trigger instance** is a phrasal representation, which includes the context information including the key event trigger word e and the complementary participant or destination c. Following the above definition, e and c are valid **trigger elements**.

This framework consists of three components: (1) a trigger synonym generator, which matches the unstructured raw text in the given knowledge base to event trigger instances; (2) a synonym set scorer, this phase build a neural model to score the trigger synonym set; and (3) an open trigger classifier to determine whether an unseen event trigger instance should be inserted into the existing event trigger synonym set or a new empty set.

2.1 Dataset Generation Using Distant Supervision

Given some known structural event instances, distant supervision provides a simple and effective way to discover more event triggers that are not in the knowledge base from raw text corpus by masking the trigger words. To automatically extend the annotation coverage, we assume that if a trigger synonym exists in one sentence, then this sentence is likely to be an event mention. For each event type existing in the base, we construct a synonym dictionary, so that we can successfully query unseen trigger words out of the pre-defined vocabulary of trigger words. As a result, we extract the training examples from the training data required for the next phase of open event type recognition.

Example 1. Given a sentence "Jia Yueting solved the problem of arrears of listed companies by selling assets to obtain funds.", "A company conducts asset auctions through judicial procedures." an entity linker may first map "asset sale" and "assent auction". Then, we found the trigger words "capital for debt payment", expanded from knowledge base. Finally, we get an trigger synonym set "asset sale", "assent auction", "capital for debt payment".

2.2 Trigger Synonym Set Scorer Architecture

In this subsection, we mainly explain how to score all trigger instances that are known to belong to a specific trigger synonym set. The right of Fig. 1 shows a high-level overview of the approach. The model is composed of four modules: 1) The input layer consists of two parts: a trigger synonym set and its corresponding trigger elements. 2) Instance representation learns instance feature in the trigger synonym set. 3) Element Representation extracts the corresponding element from instances in the known trigger synonym set. 4) Scorer layer makes a final representation of the synonym score.

Input Layer. The input consists of two parts: a trigger synonym set $S = \{s_1, s_2, s_3, \ldots, s_n\}$ and its corresponding trigger elements $W = \{w_1, w_2, w_3, \ldots, w_m\}$. For the trigger elements, we denote the dimension of element embeddings by $m \times R^d$, where m is the number of elements. For the trigger synonym set, we concatenate all argument vectors as the representation of the whole trigger instance, so the set embedding is represented by $l \times 5 \times R^d$, where l is the maximum number of instances in the set.

Instance Representation. We use a fully connected neural network with two hidden layers to extract the overall characteristics of trigger instances. Then, we sum all instance features and obtain the raw instance representation $v(S) =_{i=1}^{n} \phi(s_i)$.

Element Representation. The goal of this module is to produce the element represented. We employ bidirectional LSTM (BiLSTM), which consists of both

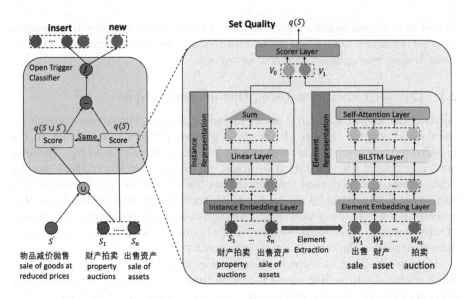

Fig. 1. Model architecture of the open event trigger classifier.

forward and backward networks to process the set. Then, we use the attention mechanism to learn dependence within the element and capture the internal structure of elements. The attention mechanism takes the wohle $LSTM$ hidden state H as input, and outputs a vector of weights $v(W)$.

$$\overrightarrow{h_t} = \overrightarrow{\text{LSTM}}(\overrightarrow{f_t}, \overrightarrow{h_{t-1}}) \tag{1}$$

$$\overleftarrow{h_t} = \overleftarrow{\text{LSTM}}(\overleftarrow{f_t}, \overleftarrow{h_{t+1}}) \tag{2}$$

$$H = [\overrightarrow{h_t}, \overleftarrow{h_t}] \tag{3}$$

$$v(W) = softmax(W_{s_2}tanh(W_{s_1}H)) \tag{4}$$

Scorer Layer. We first concatenate instance representation $v(S)$ and element representation $v(W)$ to obtain final set representation, then, we construct it using another fully connected neural network with three hidden layers to get our set score.

2.3   Learning Open Trigger Classifier

The right part of Fig. 1 shows a set scorer $q(\cdot)$ which takes a known trigger synonym set S as input, and returns a quality score S that measures how complete and coherent this set S is. Given this set S and an unseen trigger instance s', our open trigger classifier $f(S, s')$ first applies the set scorer to obtain input set score $S(i.e., q(S))$. Then, we add the unseen instance s' into the set and apply the set scorer again to obtain the quality score of $S \cup s'$. Finally, we calculate the difference between these two quality scores, and transform this score difference into the probability using a sigmoid unit as follows:

$$Pr(s' \in S) = f(S, s') = \phi(q(S \cup s') - q(S)) \tag{5}$$

Given a collection of k trigger set-instance pair $(S_i, s'_i)|_{i=1}^{k}$ with their corresponding labels $y_i|_{i=1}^{k}$, we learn the open trigger classifier using the log-loss as follows:

$$L(f) = \sum_{i=1}^{m} -y_i \log(f(S_i, s'_i)) - (1 - y_i) \log(1 - f((S_i, s'_i))) \tag{6}$$

where y'_i equals to 1 if $s' \in S$ equals to 0 otherwise.

2.4   Open Event Trigger Synonym Set Generation Algorithm

Inspired by [6], we design open event trigger synonym set generation algorithm for mine all event trigger set. This algorithm takes the above learned open trigger classifier model, all unseen triggers $T = s_1, s_2, s_3, \ldots, s_{|T|}$, and a probability threshold θ as input, and clusters all unseen triggers into trigger synonym sets. Specifically, this algorithm enumerates all unseen event trigger T once and maintains a pool of all detected synonym sets E. For each unseen trigger $s_i \in T$, it applies the open trigger classifier f to calculate the probability of adding this trigger into each detected set in E and finds the best trigger synonym set E_j that has the largest probability. If this probability value passes the threshold θ, and we will add s_i into set E_j. Otherwise, we create a new event trigger synonym set s_i with this single trigger and add it into the set S. The entire algorithm stops after one pass of the unseen triggers and returns all detected trigger synonym sets E. Note that we do not need to specify the number of sets, and our open event trigger synonym set generation algorithm will determine this value on its own. In this work, we simply set the probability threshold of θ to be 0.5 and study its Influence on clustering performance below.

3   Experiment

3.1   Datasets

In order to verify our model, we conduct our experiment on three datasets. The first dataset is financial domain[1], which is an event ontology corpus. It contains 303,363 news documents, including 2,648 event instances. To make the experiment more universal and validate the effectiveness of our proposal on cross-domain datasets, we construct two additional datasets based on THUCNews[2]. One dataset is in education and social domain which contains 278,649 news documents including 2,384 event instances, and the other dataset is in the entertaining and political domain which contains 186,102 news documents, including 1,845 events instances.

---

[1] https://github.com/Meow0727/Finance/upload.

[2] http://thuctc.thunlp.org/.

Table 1. Quantitative results of open event trigger recognition. We run all methods ten times and calculated their average score.

Method	Finance			Education&Society			Entertainment&Politics		
	ARI	FMI	NMI	ARI	FMI	NMI	ARI	FMI	NMI
Kmeans	27.62	27.88	84.26	43.66	44.95	86.01	40.91	43.10	83.81
Louvain [1]	31.74	32.15	88.64	40.31	43.98	81.27	42.07	52.11	83.59
Cop-Kmeans [14]	36.53	40.27	80.19	48.86	56.49	87.30	50.28	51.58	86.72
SVM+Louvain	9.59	14.53	69.27	8.86	9.37	51.33	12.98	16.80	70.27
L2C [5]	12.87	19.90	73.47	12.71	16.66	70.23	7.76	8.79	70.08
SynSetMine [12]	57.14	59.15	88.88	55.41	57.03	88.74	58.65	61.56	89.00
HiSNN	**64.77**	**65.41**	**88.28**	**62.79**	**65.57**	**89.99**	**65.86**	**67.28**	**90.25**
BERT-Instance	53.02	58.05	88.46	60.91	64.81	90.42	58.17	63.65	90.26
BERT-Element	67.26	69.87	91.75	74.99	76.27	93.26	75.38	78.00	93.52
BERT-HiSNN	**69.53**	**71.16**	**91.48**	**84.00**	**84.96**	**95.27**	**83.52**	**84.31**	**95.22**

3.2 Experimental Settings

For a fair comparison, we utilize pre-trained 50-dimensional word embedding vectors on different domain datasets. For HiSNN, we use a neural network with two hidden layers (of sizes 50, 250) as liner layer and another neural network with three hidden layers (of sizes 250, 500, 250) as scorer layer (c.f. Fig. 1). We optimize our model using Adam with an initial learning rate of 0.001 and apply dropout technique with a dropout rate of 0.3. For the generation algorithm, we set the probability threshold of θ to be 0.5. Following previous work [12], we measure ARI (Adjusted Rand Index), FMI (Fowlkes mallows score) and NMI (Normalized mutual information) to evaluate the results.

3.3 Results and Analysis

We first compare the performance of all methods for classifying event instances. As shown in Table 1, the results demonstrate that our method achieves an ARI of 64.77,FMI of 65.41 and NMI of 88.28 in finance domain. The main disadvantage of unsupervised methods (Kmeans and Louvain) and semi-supervised mothod(Cop-Kmeans) is that they cannot utilize supervision signals. The deficiency of SVM+Louvain and L2C does not have a holistic view of identifying event type due to they base on pairwise similarity. For SynSetMine, the relations between the elements is ignored. Therefore, our model HiSNN can capture event type-level features beyond pairwise similarity, besides, we take into account the importance among elements in determining event type. Furthermore, We utilize BERT pre-training vectors, we can see that the overall model performs better than BEAT-Instance and BEAT-Element. Besides, BERT-HiSNN performs better on the cross-domain dataset compared to the single-domain dataset due to BERT is more universal.

Then, we conduct more experiments to analyze each component of our HiSNN model in more details and show some detailed case studies.

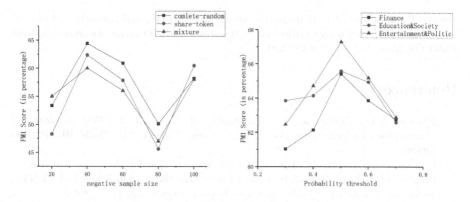

Fig. 2. Hyper-parameters analysis.

On the one hand, in order to train our classifier, we need to convert all event instances generated from distant supervision into event set-instance pair. Therefore,we study how different conversion strategy and negative sample sizes affect model performance on financial datasets. Results are shown in Fig. 2. We find that the complete-random strategy actually performs better than the share-token strategy easily. One possible explanation is that the complete-random strategy can generate more diverse negative samples and thus provide more supervision signals. On the other hand, in order to verify the influence of different thresholds on the algorithm, intuitively, the higher this threshold θ is, the more conservative our algorithm will be, and more event types will be generated. Therefore, we run our algorithm with fixed our model and different thresholds. The results are shown in Fig. 2. In all the above experiments, we set the threshold θ to be 0.5. we notice that the performance of our clustering algorithm is insensitive to θ and value within 0.4 and 0.6 is generally good for θ. Second, we find that setting θ to be 0.5 is robust and works well across all three cross-domain datasets.

4   Conclusion

This paper investigated mining unseen event triggers using distant supervision and distance metric learning. We presented a novel framework that effectively leverages Chinese knowledge bases to generate the training instances, then learn an open event trigger classifier to score trigger synonym sets, which allows detecting new event triggers and event types. We also proposed a hierarchical self-attentive neural network to score trigger synonym sets. In the future work, we will try to further automatically integrate prior knowledge into instance generation using scalable neural variational inference and learn this model in an end-to-end fashion.

Acknowledgment. The research reported in this paper was supported in part by the Natural Science Foundation of China under the grant No.91746203, National Natural

Science Foundation of China under the grant No.61991415, and Ministry of Industry and Information Technology project of the Intelligent Ship Situation Awareness System under the grant No. MC-201920-X01.

References

1. Blondel, V.D., Guillaume, J.L., Lambiotte, R., Lefebvre, E.: Fast unfolding of communities in large networks. J. Stat. Mech.: Theory Exp. **2008**(10), P10008 (2008)
2. Cybulska, A., Vossen, P.: Translating granularity of event slots into features for event coreference resolution. In: Proceedings of the the 3rd Workshop on EVENTS: Definition, Detection, Coreference, and Representation, pp. 1–10 (2015)
3. Feng, W., Wu, Y., Wu, W., Li, Z., Zhou, M.: Beihang-msra at semeval-2017 task 3: a ranking system with neural matching features for community question answering. In: Proceedings of the 11th International Workshop on Semantic Evaluation (SemEval-2017), pp. 280–286 (2017)
4. Ferracane, E., Marshall, I., Wallace, B.C., Erk, K.: Leveraging coreference to identify arms in medical abstracts: an experimental study. In: Proceedings of the Seventh International Workshop on Health Text Mining and Information Analysis, pp. 86–95 (2016)
5. Hsu, Y.C., Lv, Z., Kira, Z.: Learning to cluster in order to transfer across domains and tasks. arXiv preprint arXiv:1711.10125 (2017)
6. Kumar, A., Chatterjee, S., Rai, P.: Nonparametric bayesian structure adaptation for continual learning. arXiv preprint arXiv:1912.03624 (2019)
7. Liu, S., et al.: Exploiting argument information to improve event detection via supervised attention mechanisms (2017)
8. Nallapati, R., et al.: Abstractive text summarization using sequence-to-sequence rnns and beyond. arXiv preprint arXiv:1602.06023 (2016)
9. Nguyen, T.H., Grishman, R.: Graph convolutional networks with argument-aware pooling for event detection. In: Thirty-second AAAI Conference on Artificial Intelligence (2018)
10. Oliveira, H.G., Gomes, P.: ECO and onto. PT: a flexible approach for creating a portuguese wordnet automatically. Lang. Resour. Eval. 48(2), 373–393 (2014)
11. Sha, L., Qian, F., Chang, B., Sui, Z.: Jointly extracting event triggers and arguments by dependency-bridge RNN and tensor-based argument interaction. In: Thirty-Second AAAI Conference on Artificial Intelligence (2018)
12. Shen, J., Lyu, R., Ren, X., Vanni, M., Sadler, B., Han, J.: Mining entity synonyms with efficient neural set generation. Proceedings of the AAAI Conference on Artificial Intelligence, vol. 33, pp. 249–256 (2019)
13. Ustalov, D., Panchenko, A., Biemann, C.: Watset: Automatic induction of synsets from a graph of synonyms. arXiv preprint arXiv:1704.07157 (2017)
14. Wagstaff, K., Cardie, C., Rogers, S., Schrödl, S., et al.: Constrained k-means clustering with background knowledge. In: Icml, vol. 1, pp. 577–584 (2001)

Reinforcement Learning Based Personalized Neural Dialogue Generation

Tulika Saha[✉], Saraansh Chopra, Sriparna Saha, and Pushpak Bhattacharyya

Indian Institute of Technology Patna, Bihta, India
sahatulika15@gmail.com, saraansh.chopra@gmail.com,
sriparna.saha@gmail.com

Abstract. In this paper, we present a persona aware neural reinforcement learning response generation framework capable of optimizing long-term rewards carefully devised by system developers. The proposed model utilizes an extension of the recently introduced Hierarchical Encoder Decoder (HRED) architecture. We leverage insights from
Reinforcement Learning (RL) and employ policy gradient methods to
optimize rewards which are defined as simple heuristic approximations
that indicate good conversation to a human mind. The proposed model
is demonstrated on two benchmark datasets. Empirical results indicate
that the proposed approach outperforms their counterparts that do not
optimize long-term rewards, have no access to personas, standard models
trained using solely maximum-likelihood estimation objective.

Keywords: Natural language generation · Dialogue · Persona ·
Hierarchical encoder-decoder · Reinforcement learning

1 Introduction

Efficient communication between human and Virtual Agent (VA) in the form
of Natural Language Generation (NLG) has been a long-standing goal for any
conversational agent [2]. In recent times, two notable paradigms of research have
emerged pertaining to NLG. The first category includes open domain conversations typically nonchalant chit-chatting [4]. The second ones are goal-oriented
dialogue generation where the VA is required to interact with the user in natural language to solve a particular task of a domain [7]. Neural models such as
Bi-LSTMs or Memory Networks [10] recently had enough capacity and access to
large-scale datasets and seemed to produce meaningful responses in a chit-chat
environment. However, conversing with such generic chit-chat models for a while
exposes its weaknesses quickly. Also, to ensure that the VA provides a more natural, human-like and coherent conversational experience, it is imperative for the
VA to exhibit a persona and reciprocatively understand users persona to increase
users' engagement level and to gain its trust and confidence. Lately, researches
involving chit-chat VAs are classified into two broad categories: (i) first one is
implicit model where a user's persona is learnt implicitly from the dialogue data

© Springer Nature Switzerland AG 2020
H. Yang et al. (Eds.): ICONIP 2020, CCIS 1332, pp. 709–716, 2020.
https://doi.org/10.1007/978-3-030-63820-7_81

and is depicted as the user's spoken utterance embedding [5]; (ii) second is the explicit model where the user's persona is available explicitly, i.e., the produced responses from the VA are explicitly conditioned either on a given profile with various attributes [15] or on a text-described persona [13].

The challenges faced by these chit-chatting VAs hint the need of a conversational framework with the ability to (i) depict a consistent persona of the speaker (say A) and incorporate persona of the speaker (B) while generating responses in a dialogue and vice-versa; (ii) integrate carefully engineered rewards that mimic a human-like conversational experience as closely as possible; (iii) model long-term memory of generated utterances in the ongoing conversation. To realize these goals, we gather insights from Reinforcement Learning (RL) which has been used extensively in Dialogue Systems in various aspects [7]. In this paper, we propose a persona aware neural reinforcement learning response generation framework capable of optimizing long-term rewards carefully devised by system developers. The proposed model utilizes an extension of the recently introduced Hierarchical Encoder Decoder (HRED) architecture [9] and models conversation between two speakers conditioned on their respective personas to explore and examine the space of possible actions while simultaneously learning to maximize expected rewards. The simulated speakers need to learn an efficient persona aware dialogue policy from the ongoing dialogue simulations using well-known RL algorithm namely policy gradient methods [12] instead of employing the MLE (maximum likelihood estimate) objective used in traditional HRED models. The proposed model is demonstrated on two different datasets where personas are viewed in different ways, i.e., explicit and implicit (as stated above). Empirical results indicate that the proposed approach outperforms several strong baselines.

The key contributions of this paper are as follows : i. Propose a persona aware neural reinforcement learning response generation framework that utilizes an extension of the recently introduced HRED architecture tuned in accordance to the personas of the speaker; ii. The utility of RL helps optimize long-term rewards in the on-going dialogue resembling approximations that characterize a good conversation to a human mind; iii. Empirical results indicate that the proposed approach outperforms their counterparts that do not optimize long-term rewards, have no access to personas, standard models trained using solely MLE objective.

2 Related Works

There exist numerous works in the literature that have addressed the task of chit-chat based Dialogue Generation in different aspects. In [4], authors proposed the first-ever NLG framework that utilizes RL to optimize long-term rewards using the traditional SEQ2SEQ model. In [8], authors proposed an extension of the HRED model for dialogue generation that models hierarchy of sequences using two RNNs, i.e., one at word level and the other at the utterance level of a dialogue. However, none of these works models persona of the speaker while addressing the task of NLG. There are plenty of works that use persona of the speaker in implicit and explicit ways in the NLG framework. In [5], authors proposed a large-scale REDDIT dataset to model personas of the speaker by utilizing the SEQ2SEQ model for the task of dialogue generation. In [13], authors proposed a PERSONA-CHAT dataset with text-described persona for each speaker. In [14], authors proposed a PersonalDialogue dataset, where personas are available as a given profile with various attributes such as age, gender, location etc. In [15], authors proposed a personalized dialogue generation model that utilizes the encoder-decoder framework along with attribute embeddings to capture and incorporate rich persona. However, none of these works utilizes RL for optimizing long-term rewards as an approximations to different features of the human mind.

3   Proposed Approach

In this section, we will describe the different components of the proposed methodology.

Hierarchical Encoder Decoder. The overall architecture of the proposed framework is shown in Fig. 1, which is an extension of the recently introduced Hierarchical Encoder Decoder architecture [8,9]. Here, the conversational context or dialogue history is modelled using a separate RNN over the encoder RNN, thus forming a hierarchical structure known as the hierarchical encoder. The proposed network is built upon the HRED to include personas of the speaker involved in the conversation along with the other textual modalities. The main components of the HRED (in this paper) are *utterance encoder*, *context encoder*, *persona encoder* and *decoder* which are discussed as follows:

Utterance Encoder. Given a speaker utterance X_k, a Bidirectional Gated Recurrent Unit (Bi-GRU) [1] has been used to encode each of the words of the utterance, $x_{k,i}, i \in (1,n)$ depicted by a w dimensional word vector/embeddings.

Persona Encoder. For a speaker utterance, each persona sentence of the speaker is encoded separately. Each of the persona utterances is represented as a w dimensional word embedding with a linear layer on top of them. Finally, the representations across all the persona sentences are summed up to obtain the persona encoding. The encoded persona is passed through a 1-hop memory network [10] with a residual connection [13], using all the spoken utterances of the speaker as context and the persona representation as memory.

Context Encoder. The obtained representation from both the utterance and persona encoders are concatenated in every turn and fed as input to the context encoder which is a context GRU.

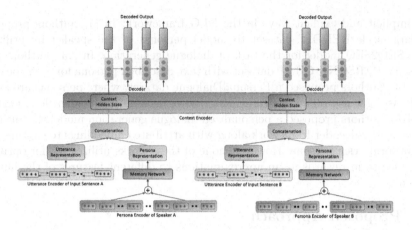

Fig. 1. The proposed persona aware HRED framework for a conversation with 2 turns

Decoder. The final hidden state representation of the context encoder is used as the initial state representation of the decoder. Similarly, a GRU unit has been employed for the decoder part. The decoder then generates word sequentially at every time step (say t) conditioned on the decoded words prior to t and final state representation of the context encoder. At each time-step t, decoder produces the probability of output token w using softmax. The HRED model explained above is initially trained with the negative log likelihood, i.e., the MLE objective function in a supervised manner to generate semantically plausible responses which will be used below for initialization.

3.1   Reinforcement Learning

A dialogue is typically represented as an alternating sequence between two speakers as $X_{a,1}, X_{b,1}, X_{a,2}, X_{b,2}, ..., X_{a,i}, X_{b,i}$. This sequence of utterances can be viewed as actions that are taken according to a policy learnt by the HRED model. Next, with the help of the MLE parameters, the model is tuned to learn a policy that maximizes long-term future rewards [4]. The components of the RL based training are discussed below.

State and Action. The state is denoted by the output of the hierarchical encoder (explained above) which represents the encoding of the current utterance conditioned on the persona of the speaker along with the dialogue history, $[S(H_X, H_{P,i}, H_C)]$. The action a, is the utterance to generate in the next time-step i.e., Y_t. The action space is infinite as the sequence generated can be of arbitrary length. So, the policy $\Pi(Y_t|S(H_X, H_{P,i}, H_C))$ learns the mapping from states to actions and is defined by its parameters.

Reward. Here, we will discuss few key factors that are attributed to the success of any dialogue and discuss how the approximations to these factors can be induced in computable reward function, r. Below are the reward functions used.

Cosine Triplet Loss. At each turn of the conversation, we expect speakers involved in the dialogue to keep adding new information and refrain from generating repetitive responses, i.e., we expect $X_{a,t}$ and $X_{a,t-1}$ to be diverse, thus, we penalize the semantic similarity between consecutive turns of the same speaker (say A here). Similarly, we also need to counter situations where the generated responses between the two speakers are highly rewarded but are not coherent in the sense of the topic being discussed, i.e., we expect that the conversation at a time-step t between two speakers, $X_{a,t}$ and $X_{b,t}$ be consistent and appropriate. Intuitively, this idea represents the triplet loss function [3] where the anchor is compared to two different inputs. We extend this idea to the semantic similarity between utterances. Let $X_{b,t}$ be the anchor (say). So, the goal is to minimize the semantic similarity between $X_{a,t}$ and $X_{a,t-1}$ and to maximize the semantic similarity between $X_{a,t}$ and $X_{b,t}$ and vice-versa with the speakers as the dialogue progresses. Let $H_{X,a,t}$, $H_{X,b,t}$ be hidden state encoder representations of two different speakers A and B at time-step t, respectively, and $H_{X,a,t-1}$ be the representation of speaker A at time-step $t-1$. Then the reward function is:

$$r_1 = (cos(H_{X,a,t}, H_{X,b,t}) - cos(H_{X,a,t}, H_{X,a,t-1}) - \gamma) \tag{1}$$

Negative Log Likelihood. The generated utterances by the speakers must pave way for the communication further, i.e., speakers should respond in a way that makes it easier for the other speaker to respond too. So, we penalize the generated response with the negative log likelihood if it is a dull response such as "*I don't know*", "*I have no idea*" and so on. A list L with such dull responses is manually created with 8 turns. So, the reward function is:

$$r_2 = -(1/N_L) \sum_{s \in L} (1/N_s) log_{X,t}(s|a) \tag{2}$$

where N_L represents the cardinality of L and N_s represents the number of tokens in the dull response s.

Thus, the final reward for an action a is the weighted sum of the rewards explained above:

$$r(a|S(H_X, H_{P,i}, H_C)) = \alpha r_1 + (1 - \alpha)r_2 \tag{3}$$

where α is 0.75. This reward is obtained after the end of each generated utterance. Policy Gradient algorithm [12] is used to optimize these rewards. The policy model Π is initialized using the pre-trained HRED model (using the MLE objective function).

4   Implementation Details

In this section, we first describe the details of the dataset used followed by the experimentation details.

4.1   Dataset

We perform experiments on two different datasets in which personas are represented in different ways i.e., explicit and implicit. For the explicit representation of the personas, we use the PERSONA-CHAT dataset [13]. This dataset contains 10,907 dialogues amounting to 1,62,064 utterances. For the implicit case, we use the REDDIT dataset [5] which contains 1.7 billion comments/utterances. This is a large-scale dataset with the utterances covering the persona profile of 4.6 million users. To extract persona utterances from this dataset, we follow the same method as used in the source paper.

4.2   Hyperparameters and Evaluation Metric

FastText embeddings of dimension 300 have been used to represent words of an utterance. The hidden size for all the GRU units is 512. The model is initialized randomly with a Gaussian distribution. For decoding, beam search with beam size of 5 is used. Adam optimizer is used to train the model. A learning rate of 0.0001 was found to be optimum. The models are automatically evaluated using standard metrics namely BLEU-1 score [6], perplexity and embedding based metric [9].

5   Results and Analysis

We compare our proposed approach with several baselines to highlight the contributions and gains of different components of the proposed approach in terms of performance. The different baselines are: **i. SEQ2SEQ**: This is the traditional sequence to sequence, i.e., encoder-decoder framework without the use of persona or RL based training; **ii. HRED-1**: This is the standard HRED model with a context of one without the usage of persona and RL; **iii. HRED-2**: HRED model with a context of two previous turns without the usage of persona and RL; **iv. HRED-3**: HRED model with a context of three previous turns without the usage of persona and RL; **v. HRED-3 + MN**: This model includes HRED-3 and Memory Network to model persona without the usage of RL based training; **vi. HRED-3 + MN + RL**: This is the proposed model that includes both the persona of the speakers along with RL based training to optimize long-term rewards.

Table 1 shows the results of all the baselines and the proposed models for both the datasets. As evident from the tables, all the HRED based models perform better than the traditional SEQ2SEQ model. Also, amongst the HRED models, conversational context of three turns gave the best results in terms of all the

Table 1. Results of all the baseline and proposed models. MN represents Memory Network, PPL represents perplexity.

Models	Dataset									
	PERSONA-CHAT					REDDIT				
	Embedding Metrics			PPL	BLEU-1	Embedding Metrics			PPL	BLEU-1
	Average	Extrema	Greedy			Average	Extrema	Greedy		
SEQ2SEQ	0.6084	0.3593	0.3999	84.779	0.0952	0.5918	0.2896	0.3013	106.371	0.0891
HRED-1 (context-1)	0.6042	0.3364	0.4014	47.633	0.1026	0.621	0.319	0.34	95.261	0.1047
HRED-2	0.6057	0.3367	0.4024	49.797	0.1014	0.588	0.299	0.315	103.186	0.1052
HRED-3	0.6060	0.3345	0.4043	47.739	0.1025	0.616	0.331	0.356	78.263	0.1059
HRED-3 + MN	0.6073	0.3387	0.4052	216.232	0.1096	0.621	0.337	0.369	111.150	0.1089
HRED-3 + MN + RL	**0.6200**	**0.3512**	**0.4162**	**96.474**	**0.1183**	**0.6311**	**0.325**	**0.384**	**150.851**	**0.1167**

metrics. This shows that long-term assimilation of memory across the dialogue helps produce better responses. In *HRED-3* model, memory network is incorporated to model the personas of the speaker to demonstrate a consistent persona in the conversation. Finally, in this model, we have incorporated the RL based training. As seen from the table, this model produces the best results amongst all the baseline models. Thus, each of these components aids the performance of the proposed model. All the reported results are statistically significant as we have performed Welch's t-test [11] at 5% significance level.

6 Conclusion and Future Work

In this paper, we propose a persona aware neural reinforcement learning response generation framework capable of optimizing long-term rewards carefully devised by system developers. The proposed model utilizes an extension of the HRED architecture and models conversation between two speakers conditioned on their respective personas to explore and examine the space of possible actions while simultaneously learning to maximize expected rewards. A thorough evaluation is carried out on two benchmark datasets with automated metrics as well as human evaluation. Empirical results indicate that the proposed approach outperforms several strong baselines. Future works include developing a more sophisticated and efficient end-to-end dialogue generation framework along with extending these approaches for creating end-to-end NLG models for low-resource language.

Acknowledgement. Dr. Sriparna Saha gratefully acknowledges the Young Faculty Research Fellowship (YFRF) Award, supported by Visvesvaraya Ph.D. Scheme for Electronics and IT, Ministry of Electronics and Information Technology (MeitY), Government of India, being implemented by Digital India Corporation (formerly Media Lab Asia) for carrying out this research.

References

1. Bahdanau, D., Cho, K., Bengio, Y.: Neural machine translation by jointly learning to align and translate. In: Bengio, Y., LeCun, Y. (eds.) 3rd International Conference on Learning Representations. ICLR (2015). http://arxiv.org/abs/1409.0473

2. Dušek, O., Novikova, J., Rieser, V.: Evaluating the state-of-the-art of end-to-end natural language generation: the e2e nlg challenge. Comput. Speech Lang. **59**, 123–156 (2020)
3. Hermans, A., Beyer, L., Leibe, B.: In defense of the triplet loss for person re-identification. CoRR abs/1703.07737 (2017). http://arxiv.org/abs/1703.07737
4. Li, J., Monroe, W., Ritter, A., Jurafsky, D., Galley, M., Gao, J.: Deep reinforcement learning for dialogue generation. In: Su, J., Carreras, X., Duh, K. (eds.) Proceedings of the 2016 Conference on Empirical Methods in Natural Language Processing, EMNLP (2016). https://doi.org/10.18653/v1/d16-1127
5. Mazaré, P., Humeau, S., Raison, M., Bordes, A.: Training millions of personalized dialogue agents. In: Riloff, E., Chiang, D., Hockenmaier, J., Tsujii, J. (eds.) Proceedings of the 2018 Conference on Empirical Methods in Natural Language Processing (2018). https://doi.org/10.18653/v1/d18-1298
6. Papineni, K., Roukos, S., Ward, T., Zhu, W.: Bleu: a method for automatic evaluation of machine translation. In: Proceedings of the 40th Annual Meeting of the Association for Computational Linguistics (2002). https://www.aclweb.org/anthology/P02-1040/
7. Saha, T., Gupta, D., Saha, S., Bhattacharyya, P.: Reinforcement learning based dialogue management strategy. In: Cheng, L., Leung, A.C.S., Ozawa, S. (eds.) ICONIP 2018. LNCS, vol. 11303, pp. 359–372. Springer, Cham (2018). https://doi.org/10.1007/978-3-030-04182-3_32
8. Serban, I.V., Sordoni, A., Bengio, Y., Courville, A.C., Pineau, J.: Building end-to-end dialogue systems using generative hierarchical neural network models. In: Schuurmans, D., Wellman, M.P. (eds.) Proceedings of the Thirtieth AAAI Conference on Artificial Intelligence (2016). http://www.aaai.org/ocs/index.php/AAAI/AAAI16/paper/view/11957
9. Serban, I.V., et al.: A hierarchical latent variable encoder-decoder model for generating dialogues. In: Singh, S.P., Markovitch, S. (eds.) Proceedings of the Thirty-First AAAI Conference on Artificial Intelligence, USA (2017). http://aaai.org/ocs/index.php/AAAI/AAAI17/paper/view/14567
10. Sukhbaatar, S., Szlam, A., Weston, J., Fergus, R.: End-to-end memory networks. In: Cortes, C., Lawrence, N.D., Lee, D.D., Sugiyama, M., Garnett, R. (eds.) Advances in Neural Information Processing Systems 28: Annual Conference on Neural Information Processing Systems (2015). http://papers.nips.cc/paper/5846-end-to-end-memory-networks
11. Welch, B.L.: The generalization ofstudent's' problem when several different population variances are involved. Biometrika (1947)
12. Zaremba, W., Sutskever, I.: Reinforcement learning neural turing machines-revised. arXiv preprint arXiv:1505.00521 (2015)
13. Zhang, S., Dinan, E., Urbanek, J., Szlam, A., Kiela, D., Weston, J.: Personalizing dialogue agents: i have a dog, do you have pets too? In: Gurevych, I., Miyao, Y. (eds.) Proceedings of the 56th Annual Meeting of the Association for Computational Linguistics, ACL (2018). https://www.aclweb.org/anthology/P18-1205/
14. Zheng, Y., Chen, G., Huang, M., Liu, S., Zhu, X.: Personalized dialogue generation with diversified traits. arXiv preprint arXiv:1901.09672 (2019)
15. Zheng, Y., Zhang, R., Huang, M., Mao, X.: A pre-training based personalized dialogue generation model with persona-sparse data. In: The Thirty-Fourth AAAI Conference on Artificial Intelligence, AAAI (2020). https://aaai.org/ojs/index.php/AAAI/article/view/6518

Sparse Lifting of Dense Vectors: A Unified Approach to Word and Sentence Representations

Senyue Hao[1] and Wenye Li[1,2(✉)]

[1] The Chinese University of Hong Kong, Shenzhen, China
116010062@link.cuhk.edu.cn, wyli@cuhk.edu.cn
[2] Shenzhen Research Institute of Big Data, Shenzhen, China

Abstract. As the first step in automated natural language processing, representing words and sentences is of central importance and has attracted significant research attention. Despite the successful results that have been achieved in the recent distributional dense and sparse vector representations, such vectors face nontrivial challenge in both memory and computational requirement in practical applications. In this paper, we designed a novel representation model that projects dense vectors into a higher dimensional space and favors a highly sparse and binary representation of vectors, while trying to maintain pairwise inner products between original vectors as much as possible. Our model can be relaxed as a symmetric non-negative matrix factorization problem which admits a fast yet effective solution. In a series of empirical evaluations, the proposed model reported consistent improvement in both accuracy and running speed in downstream applications and exhibited high potential in practical applications.

Keywords: Language representation · Bag of words · Sparse lifting

1 Introduction

With tremendous theoretical and practical values, the study of natural language processing (NLP) techniques has attracted significant research attention in computer science and artificial intelligence community for many years. A key step in NLP is to represent language and text elements (words, sentences, etc.) in a form that can be processed by computers. For this task, the classical vector space model, which treats the elements as vectors of identifiers, has been routinely applied in tremendous applications for decades [26].

As an implementation of the vector space model, the *one-hot* method encodes a word by a sparse vector with exactly one element being non-zero. Accordingly,

---

This work was partially supported by Shenzhen Fundamental Research Fund (JCYJ20170306141038939, KQJSCX20170728162302784), awarded to Wenye Li.

to represent a sentence, the *bag-of-words* scheme is naturally applied on *one-hot* vectors of words. Simple as it is, the representation scheme has reported good empirical results [10]. Besides, people have designed various representation methods, which try to encode each word into a low dimensional continuous space either as a dense vector or as a sparse one, such as the work of [22,23, 25,32]. With these methods, a sentence vector is typically built as an average, or a concatenation, of the vectors of all sentence words. All these methods have achieved quite successful results in a variety of applications.

Despite the successful results reported, all existing encoding methods face practical challenges. Motivated by both the success and the limitation of the existing methods, we designed a novel word representation approach, called the *lifting* representation. Our method projects dense word vectors to a moderately higher dimensional space while sparsifying and binarizing the projected vectors. Intuitively, comparing with *one-hot* word vectors, our encoding dimension is lower yet with generally more than one non-zero elements in each vector. Comparing with other word representation schemes, our encoding dimension is typically higher while most elements are zero. In this way, the proposed approach has the potential to encode the semantics of the words without bringing about much computational burden.

Based on the proposed *lifting* word representation method, representing a sentence is straightforward and natural. A sentence vector can be obtained in the way of *bag-of-words* which sums up the *lifting* vectors of all sentence words. In this way, the similarity and difference of any two sentences can also be easily obtained by calculating their vector similarity or Euclidean distance.

2   Related Work

2.1   Word and Sentence Representations

With *one-hot* representation model, each word is encoded as a binary vector [26]. Only one vector element is 1 and all other elements are 0. The length of the vector equals to the number of words in the vocabulary. The position of the 1 element in a vector actually gives an index of a specific word in the vocabulary. Accordingly, a sentence can be represented easily by the bag of its words, disregarding the grammar and word order. Simple as it is, this *bag-of-words* representation is commonly used in document classification and information retrieval, and has reported quite successful empirical results [10].

The distributional hypothesis [21] attracted much attention in designing word embedding methods. Starting from a summary statistics of how often a word co-occurs with its neighbor words in a large text corpus, it is possible to project the count-statistics down to a small and dense vector for each word [6,14], etc. More recent development focuses on the prediction of a word from its neighbors in terms of dense embedding vectors. Influential work includes the classical neural language model, [2], the *word2vec* (*Skip-gram* and *CBOW*) models [22], and the *GloVe* algorithm [25]. With such dense word vectors, a sentence is often processed as a concatenation of all sentence words [8,11]. However, measuring the similarity or difference between dense sentence representations is non-trivial. Specialized distance measures, such as the *WMD* distance [13], were designed, at the cost of significantly increased computation. Another approach is to represent a sentence by the weighted average of all its word vectors, and then use the average vectors to calculate the sentence similarities [1].

Recent research investigated the possibility of sparse representations. Some work starts from the co-occurrence statistics of words, including the NNSE method [23], the FOREST method [32], and the sparse CBOW model [28]. Some other work starts from the dense word vectors, including the work of [7] and [27]. In practice, such sparse word representations have been successfully applied and achieved quite good empirical results [29]. Similarly to the dense word vectors, to represent a sentence with these sparse vectors, people can resort to either the concatenation-based approach or the average-based approach.

2.2 Dimension Expansion

Biological studies revealed strong evidence of dimension expansion for pattern recognition. By simulating the fruit fly's odor detection procedure, a novel *fly* algorithm reported excellent performance in practical similarity retrieval applications [4]. Subsequent work along this line [17,18] designed a *sparse lifting* model for dimension expansion, which is more directly related to our work. The input vectors are lifted to sparse binary vectors in a higher-dimensional space with the objective of keeping the pairwise inner product between data points as much as possible. Then the feature values are replaced by their high energy concentration locations which are further encoded in the sparse binary representation. The model reported quite good results in a number of machine learning applications [20].

3 Model

3.1 Sparse Lifting of Dense Vectors

Our work leverages recent studies on dense word representations. It starts from a word representation matrix $X \in \mathcal{R}^{N \times d}$ from either the *word2vec* or the *GloVe* representation, with which each row gives a dense vector representation of a word in a vocabulary and has been zero-centered.

Motivated by the idea of sparse lifting, we seek a matrix $Z \in \{0,1\}^{N \times d'}$ which keeps the pairwise inner products between the row elements of X as much as possible while satisfying the requirement that $\sum Z_{ij} = Nk$ where k is the average number of non-zero elements in each row vector of Z.

The binary constraint on the desired matrix makes the problem hard to solve. To provide a feasible solution, we resort to the following model by relaxing the binary constraint and seeking a matrix $Y \in \mathcal{R}^{N \times d'}$ to minimize the difference between XX^T and YY^T in the Frobenius norm:

$$\min_{Y} \frac{1}{2} \left\| XX^T - YY^T \right\|_F^2, \tag{1}$$

subject to the element-wise constraint:

$$Y \geq 0. \tag{2}$$

This is a symmetric non-negative matrix factorization model [5]. In practice, the non-negativity constraint on each element of Y in Eq. (2) implicitly provides some level of sparsity on the solution Y^* [15]. When the solution Y^* is available, we can recover the desired matrix Z of *sparse-lifting* word vectors, or *lifting* vectors for short, trivially by setting $Z_{ij} = 1$ if Y_{ij}^* is among the topmost Nk elements of Y^*, and setting $Z_{ij} = 0$ otherwise.

The *lifting* word representation can be easily extended to represent a sentence, in a way that is much similar to that of *bag-of-words*. It leads to an attribute-value representation of sentences by representing each sentence roughly as a sum of the vectors of all its words [31]. With the *lifting* sentence representation, measuring the similarity or difference between two sentences becomes straightforward and trivial, which can be done just by calculating the inner product value or the Euclidean distance between the two sentence vectors.

3.2 Algorithm

The optimization model formulated in Eq. (1) subject to the constraint in Eq. (2) is a *symmetric non-negative matrix factorization* problem [5,15]. Different computational approaches are possible to tackle the problem [16]. We resort to a simple relaxation approach:

$$\min_{W,H \geq 0} \left\| XX^T - WH^T \right\|_F^2 + \alpha \left\| W - H \right\|_F^2. \tag{3}$$

Here we seek two matrices W, H of size $N \times d'$, and $\alpha > 0$ is a scalar parameter for the trade-off between the approximation error and the difference of W and H. With the relaxation, we force the separation of the unknown matrix Y by associating it with two different matrices W and H. Given a sufficiently large value of α, the matrix difference dominates the objective value and the solutions of W and H will tend to be close enough so that the word vectors will not be affected whether W or H are used as the result of Y.

The key to solving the problem in Eq. (3) is by solving the following two *non-negative least squares* (NLS) sub-problems [12]:

$$\min_{W \geq 0} \left\| \begin{bmatrix} H \\ \sqrt{\alpha}I_{d'} \end{bmatrix} W^T - \begin{bmatrix} XX^T \\ \sqrt{\alpha}H^T \end{bmatrix} \right\|_F^2, \text{ and } \min_{H \geq 0} \left\| \begin{bmatrix} W \\ \sqrt{\alpha}I_{d'} \end{bmatrix} H^T - \begin{bmatrix} XX^T \\ \sqrt{\alpha}W^T \end{bmatrix} \right\|_F^2,$$

where $I_{d'}$ is the $d' \times d'$ identity matrix. Solving the sub-problems in the two equations in an iterative way will lead to a stationary point solution, as long as an optimal solution is returned for every NLS sub-problem encountered.

4   Evaluations

4.1   General Settings

To evaluate the performance of the proposed word representation method, we carried out a series of evaluations. Our *lifting* vectors were generated from the dense word vectors released by the authors of *word2vec* and *GloVe*.

- *CBOW*: 300-dimensional word2vec vectors[1].
- *GloVe*: 300-dimensional word vectors[2].

We trained the *lifting* vectors with the 50,000 most frequent words out of the *CBOW* and *GloVe* word vectors respectively. The expanded dimension of the trained vectors were set to $d' = 1,000$. After training, on average 20 elements of each vector were set non-zero, i.e. the hash length $k = 20$. The results reported in this paper are just based on this setting. Besides, we have also varied different combinations of the parameters within the range of $d' = 1,000/2,000/5,000$ and $k = 10/20$. The evaluation results are quite similar and are therefore omitted.

In the evaluation, six benchmark datasets were used.

- CUSTREV: A set of 3,774 customers' positive or negative reviews [9].
- MPQA: A set of 10,606 articles with two opinion polarities [30].
- RT-POLARITY: A set of 10,662 movies' positive or negative reviews [24].
- STSA-binary: An extension of RT-POLARITY with 8,741 sentences [24].
- TREC: A set of 5,692 TREC questions with six question types [19].

In addition to the *one-hot*, *CBOW* and *GloVe* representations, our *lifting* vectors were compared with the following representations:

- *FOREST*: 52-dimensional word vectors[3].
- *NNSE*: 300-dimensional word vectors[4].
- *OVERCOMPLETE*: 1,000-dimensional sparse overcomplete word vectors[5].

For *one-hot* and *lifting* methods, each sentence vector is represented as *bag-of-words*. For other word vectors, we represent each sentence as an average of fifty word vectors with zero-padding [1]. A concatenation-based representation which treats each sentence vector as a concatenation of *CBOW* vectors was also included in the experiment, combined with the Word Mover Distance (*WMD*) to measure sentence similarities [13].

---

[1] https://code.google.com/archive/p/word2vec/.
[2] https://nlp.stanford.edu/projects/glove/.
[3] http://www.cs.cmu.edu/~ark/dyogatam/wordvecs/.
[4] http://www.cs.cmu.edu/~bmurphy/NNSE/.
[5] https://github.com/mfaruqui/sparse-coding/.

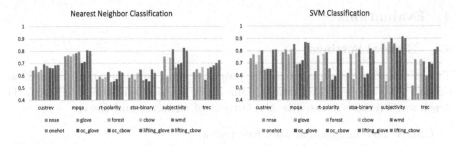

Fig. 1. Sentiment classification accuracies.

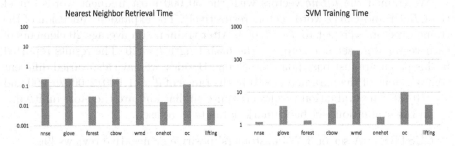

Fig. 2. Running time of NN classification and SVM classification on CUSTREV dataset.

4.2   Sentiment Analysis

We investigated the performance of the sparse-lifting vectors on sentiment analysis applications on the six benchmark datasets. On each dataset, we trained a classifier with different representations of sentences by the *nearest neighbors* (NN) algorithm and the *support vector machines* (SVM) algorithm respectively. For the SVM classification, we used the Gaussian radial basis function kernel, with the default kernel and cost parameters [3].

The comparison was made against with a number of representation schemes, including *NNSE*, *GloVe*, *FOREST*, *CBOW*, and *OVERCOMPLETE* (denoted by *oc_cbow* and *oc_glove* in the figure) representations with Euclidean distance measure. The classification accuracies are depicted in Fig. 1. Each result in the table is an average accuracy of 10-fold cross validations.

The *one-hot/bag-of-words* representation reported acceptable results when working with the SVM algorithm; but its results on NN classification were not as good. This result is consistent with the previous studies [10]. The *CBOW* and concatenation-based sentence vectors, when being combined with *WMD*, reported quite good accuracies. The performances of the averaged sentence representation with *Glove/CBOW/NNSE/FOREST* vectors, however, seemed not satisfactory, only slightly better than a random guess on some NN classification tasks.

Our proposed representations (denoted by *lifting_glove* and *lifting_word2vec* respectively) brought improved results in the experiments. Compared with *CBOW* and concatenation-based sentence vectors with the *WMD* measure, our proposed representations reported comparable (if not better) classification accuracies on most datasets; while on the TREC dataset which has six categories, both of our representations reported much better results.

4.3 Running Speed

We recorded the query time of the NN classifier with 90% of samples used in training and the rest 10% used in testing on CUSTREV dataset, which needs to compute the distances between each pair of testing and training samples. The experiment was performed in a computer server with 44 CPU cores. From Fig. 2, we can see that with highly sparse representations, the query time of the *lifting* representation and of the *one-hot/BOW* representation reported significantly superior results over other methods.

We recorded the training time of an SVM classifier with the libSVM package [3] with 90% of samples on CUSTREV dataset used as the training set. With a Gaussian kernel and the default setting of parameters, it took less than 10 seconds to train an SVM classifier with the *lifting* vectors and *bag-of-words* sentence representation. Similar results were found on SVM training with the *Glove*, *CBOW* and *OVERCOMPLETE* vectors and averaged sentence representations. All these results are tens of times faster than training with the *CBOW* vectors and concatenation-based sentence representation in *WMD* distance.

5 Conclusion

Our work designed a novel sparse lifting word representation method which projects given dense word vectors into a higher dimensional space while ensuring the sparsity and binarization of the projected vectors. Comparing with existing popular word and sentence vector representations, our proposed sparse-lifting representation has been shown to be an appropriate representation for distance-based learning tasks and has reported significantly improved results in sentiment analysis tasks. The improvement provides us with high confidence to apply the method in wider practical applications.

References

1. Arora, S., Liang, Y., Ma, T.: A simple but tough-to-beat baseline for sentence embeddings. In: ICLR 2017 (2017)
2. Bengio, Y., Ducharme, R., Vincent, P., Jauvin, C.: A neural probabilistic language model. J. Mach. Learn. Res. **3**, 1137–1155 (2003)
3. Chang, C.C., Lin, C.J.: LIBSVM: a library for support vector machines. ACM Trans. Intell. Syst. Technol. **2**(3), 27 (2011)

4. Dasgupta, S., Stevens, C., Navlakha, S.: A neural algorithm for a fundamental computing problem. Science **358**(6364), 793–796 (2017)
5. Ding, C., He, X., Simon, H.: On the equivalence of nonnegative matrix factorization and spectral clustering. In: SIAM SDM 2005, pp. 606–610 (2005)
6. Dumais, S.: Latent semantic analysis. Ann. Rev. Inf. Sci. Technol. **38**(1), 188–230 (2004)
7. Faruqui, M., Tsvetkov, Y., Yogatama, D., Dyer, C., Smith, N.: Sparse overcomplete word vector representations. arXiv:1506.02004 (2015)
8. Gehring, J., Auli, M., Grangier, D., Yarats, D., Dauphin, Y.: Convolutional sequence to sequence learning. arXiv:1705.03122 (2017)
9. Hu, M., Liu, B.: Mining and summarizing customer reviews. In: ACM SIGKDD 2004, pp. 168–177 (2004)
10. Joachims, T.: Text categorization with support vector machines: learning with many relevant features. In: ECML 1998, pp. 137–142 (1998)
11. Kim, Y.: Convolutional neural networks for sentence classification. arXiv:1408.5882 (2014)
12. Kuang, D., Yun, S., Park, H.: Symnmf: nonnegative low-rank approximation of a similarity matrix for graph clustering. J. Global Optim. **62**(3), 545–574 (2015)
13. Kusner, M., Sun, Y., Kolkin, N., Weinberger, K.: From word embeddings to document distances. In: ICML 2015, pp. 957–966 (2015)
14. Lebret, R., Collobert, R.: Word emdeddings through hellinger PCA. arXiv:1312.5542 (2013)
15. Lee, D., Seung, H.: Learning the parts of objects by non-negative matrix factorization. Nature **401**(6755), 788 (1999)
16. Lee, D., Seung, H.: Algorithms for non-negative matrix factorization. In: NIPS 2001, pp. 556–562 (2001)
17. Li, W.: Modeling winner-take-all competition in sparse binary projections. In: ECML-PKDD 2020 (2020)
18. Li, W., Mao, J., Zhang, Y., Cui, S.: Fast similarity search via optimal sparse lifting. In: NeurIPS 2018, pp. 176–184 (2018)
19. Li, X., Roth, D.: Learning question classifiers. In: COLING 2002, pp. 1–7 (2002)
20. Ma, C., Gu, C., Li, W., Cui, S.: Large-scale image retrieval with sparse binary projections. In: ACM SIGIR 2020, pp. 1817–1820 (2020)
21. McDonald, S., Ramscar, M.: Testing the distributional hypothesis: the influence of context on judgements of semantic similarity. In: CogSci 2001 (2001)
22. Mikolov, T., Chen, K., Corrado, G., Dean, J.: Efficient estimation of word representations in vector space. arXiv:1301.3781 (2013)
23. Murphy, B., Talukdar, P., Mitchell, T.: Learning effective and interpretable semantic models using non-negative sparse embedding. In: COLING 2012, pp. 1933–1950 (2012)
24. Pang, B., Lee, L.: Seeing stars: exploiting class relationships for sentiment categorization with respect to rating scales. In: ACL 2005, pp. 115–124 (2005)
25. Pennington, J., Socher, R., Manning, C.: Glove: global vectors for word representation. In: EMNLP 2014, pp. 1532–1543 (2014)
26. Salton, G., McGill, M.: Introduction to Modern Information Retrieval. McGraw-Hill Inc., New York (1986)
27. Subramanian, A., Pruthi, D., Jhamtani, H., Berg-Kirkpatrick, T., Hovy, E.: Spine: Sparse interpretable neural embeddings. In: AAAI 2018, pp. 4921–4928 (2018)
28. Sun, F., Guo, J., Lan, Y., Xu, J., Cheng, X.: Sparse word embeddings using l1 regularized online learning. In: IJCAI 2016, pp. 2915–2921 (2016)

29. Turney, P.: Leveraging term banks for answering complex questions: a case for sparse vectors. arXiv:1704.03543 (2017)
30. Wiebe, J., Wilson, T., Cardie, C.: Annotating expressions of opinions and emotions in language. Lang. Resour. Eval. **39**(2–3), 165–210 (2005)
31. Yang, J., Jiang, Y., Hauptmann, A., Ngo, C.: Evaluating bag-of-visual-words representations in scene classification. In: ACM SIGMM MIR 2007, pp. 197–206 (2007)
32. Yogatama, D., Faruqui, M., Dyer, C., Smith, N.: Learning word representations with hierarchical sparse coding. In: ICML 2015, pp. 87–96 (2015)

Word-Level Error Correction in Non-autoregressive Neural Machine Translation

Ziyue Guo, Hongxu Hou$^{(\boxtimes)}$, Nier Wu, and Shuo Sun

College of Computer Science-college of Software, Inner Mongolia University,
Hohhot, China
guoziyue08@126.com, cshhx@imu.edu.cn, wunier04@126.com, sunshuo07@126.com

Abstract. Non-Autoregressive neural machine translation (NAT) not only achieves rapid training but also actualizes fast decoding. However, the implementation of parallel decoding is at the expense of quality. Due to the increase of speed, the dependence on the context of the target side is discarded which resulting in the loss of the translation contextual position perception ability. In this paper, we improve the model by adding capsule network layers to extract positional information more effectively and comprehensively, that is, relying on vector neurons to compensate for the defects of traditional scalar neurons to store the position information of a single segment. Besides, word-level error correction on the output of NAT model is used to optimize generated translation. Experiments show that our model is superior to the previous model, with a BLEU score of 26.12 on the WMT2014 En-De task and a BLEU score of 31.93 on the WMT16 Ro-En, and the speed is even more than six times faster than the autoregressive model.

Keywords: Non-autoregressive neural machine translation · Word-level error correction · Capsule network

1 Introduction

Most neural machine translation (NMT) [1,2] models are sequentially autoregressive models (AT) such as RNNs, Transformer [3] which have state-of-the-art performance. The training process of Transformer is parallel, but in decoding phase, it exploit the generated sequence to predict the current target word which will cause severe decoding delay. In recent years, non-autoregressive neural machine translation model (NAT) [4] is proposed to effectively speed up the decoding process which exploits Knowledge Distillation [5] and fine-tuning to assist training. Subsequently, there are some novel-innovative improvements based on the NAT model, such as the work of regulating the similarity of hidden layer states by two auxiliary regularization terms [6], the model reconstruct generative translation through iterative refinement [7] and Ghazvininejad put forward to partially mask target translation through the conditional masked language model [8].

© Springer Nature Switzerland AG 2020
H. Yang et al. (Eds.): ICONIP 2020, CCIS 1332, pp. 726–733, 2020.
https://doi.org/10.1007/978-3-030-63820-7_83

In this work, we propose to utilize the Capsule Network [9] in the architecture which has a significant impact on extracting more deeply positional features and making the generated translation more advantageous in word order. Besides, we adopt the word-level error correction method to reconstruct the generated sentence which can alleviate the translation problems. Experiments show that our model is superior to the previous NAT models. On the WMT14 De-En task, the addition of the capsule network layers increases the BLEU score by more than 6. More significantly, our word-level error correction method brings 1.88 BLEU scores improvement. We also perform case study on WMT14 En-De and ablation study on IWSLT16 to verify the effectiveness of the proposed methods.

2 Background

2.1 Non-autoregressive Neural Machine Translation

Under the condition of given source sentence $S = (s_1, ..., s_K)$ and target sentence $T = (t_1, ..., t_L)$, the autoregressive model utilizes a sequential manner to predict the current word which will bring a certain degree of delay. Non-autoregressive neural machine translation model (NAT) [4] is proposed to improve the decoding speed which only predicts based on the source sequence and the target sequence length L_y predicted in advance:

$$P_{NAT}(T|S;\theta) = P(L_y|S;\theta) \cdot \prod_l^{L_y} P(t_l|S;\theta) \qquad (1)$$

where θ is a series of model parameters.

2.2 Neural Machine Translation with Error Detection

For error detection in NMT, the model first characterizes each word in the source sentence as a word embedding vector and then feeds it to the bidirectional LSTM. At each time step, the hidden state in both directions is combined and regarded as the final output. In addition, the error correction model also constructs mis-matching features, that is when there are wrong words in a output sequence, the pre-trained model will give the correct word prediction distribution and there will be a gap between their probability distributions. The model make the next prediction according to this gap feature, as shown in Eq. 2.

$$argmin \sum_{k=1}^{T} XENT \left(g_k, W \left[\overrightarrow{h_k}, \overleftarrow{h_k}, \overrightarrow{h_{k+1}}, \overleftarrow{h_{k+1}} \right] \right) \qquad (2)$$

where $XENT$ stands for cross-entropy loss, W represents the weight matrix, $\overrightarrow{h_k}, \overleftarrow{h_k}$ means the overall score of the sentence in the forward and backward directions and g_k is the gap label between k-th token and $k+1$st token.

3 Approach

3.1 Model Architecture

Since the NAT model ignores the target words and context information,
we use the Capsule Network [9] to
improve, the model architecture is
shown in Fig. 1 which also composed
of encoder and decoder. The hidden
layer state of the encoder is shown in
the Eq. 2.

$$h_j = \sum_i \alpha_{ij} F(e_i, w_{ij}) \qquad (3)$$

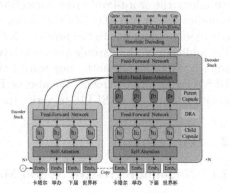

Fig. 1. The architecture of the proposed
NAT-CN model. The encoder use child
layer to capture location information and
the decoder integrate information by parent layer, then update the weights by
Dynamic Routing Algorithm (DRA).

where e_i is the output of the self-
attention layer, α represents the coupling coefficient of the capsule network, and the final output of this layer
is h_j.

Similar to the encoder side, we use
a child layer to extract source infor-
mation, but at decoder side we introduce an additional parent layer to integrate information extracted by the previous layer (ie, child layer), and map it to
another form that is consistent with the parent's representation:

$$s_j = \sum_i^M F(h_{ij}, w_{ij}) \qquad (4)$$

where M represents the number of child capsules in the child capsule layer.
Then use the Squashing function to compress the modulus of the vector into the
interval $[0, 1)$, each parent capsule will update the state as follows:

$$p_j = Squash(s_j) = \frac{\|s_j\|^2}{1 + \|s_j\|^2} \frac{s_j}{\|s_j\|} \qquad (5)$$

Integrate all the child capsules in the form described above to generate the
final parent capsule layer representation $P = [p_1, p_2, ..., p_N]$. After that, iterative
updating is used to determine what information in the N parent capsules will
be transmitted to the Multi-Head Inter-Attention sub-layer.

$$Attention(Q_p, K_p, V_p) = softmax(\frac{Q_p K_p^T}{\sqrt{d_k}}) \cdot V_p \qquad (6)$$

where Q_p is the output of the parent capsule layer, K_p, V_p are vectors from the
encoder, and they all contain rich position information.

Position-Aware Strategy. Since there is no direct target sequence information on the decoder side, we combine the extracted deeper information with the source information to get the final word vector representation and feed it to the next layer:

$$Emb_p(Q_p, K_p, V_p) = (e_1 + p_1, ..., e_n + p_n) \qquad (7)$$

where e_i represents the original source word embedding and p_i indicates the position vector extracted by the capsule network layers. Besides, to accomplish parallel decoding and advantage the decoder to infer, we calculate the ratio λ between target and source sentence lengths in the training set and given a bias term C. The target sentence length $+^*96$ $L_y = \lambda L_x + C$, then predict it from $[\lambda L_x - B, \lambda L_x + B]$, where B represents half of the searching window.

3.2   Training

Objective Function. We utilize teacher model to guide the training of NAT model to improve translation quality. In the capsule network layers, we update the parameters through an iterative dynamic routing algorithm:$b_{ij} = b_{ij} + p_j F(u_i, w_j)$, where u_i is the previous capsule network output, p_j is the parent capsule network layer output and $F(\cdot)$ denotes the calculation of the feed-forward neural network. We use cross-entropy to calculate the loss of NAT model with position awareness during the training phase, as shown in Eq. 8.

$$L_{NAT}(S; \theta) = -\sum_{l=1}^{L_y} \sum_{t_l} ((logP_{NAT}(t_l|L_y, S) \cdot logP_{AT}(t_l|t_1, .., t_{l-1}, S; \theta)) \qquad (8)$$

We utilize the Sequence-Level Interpolation Knowledge Distillation method [5] to assist training which makes the proposed NAT-CN model generate translations by selecting the output that is closest to the gold reference r but has the highest probability under the guidance of distilled data. The training process is shown in Eq. 9.

$$L_{IKD} = (1 - \alpha)L_{SEQ-NLL} + \alpha L_{SEQ-KD} = -(1 - \alpha)logp(r|s) - \alpha logp(\hat{t}|s) \qquad (9)$$

where α is a hyper-parameter and $\hat{t}$ is the output under the guidance of teacher model.

3.3   Word-Level Error Correction

Teacher Model. For the translation problem of the NAT model, we perform word-level error correction on the generated translation by use bilingual teacher model. As shown in Fig. 1, teacher model extracts features bidirectionally from source sequences and generates the latent variable $\overleftarrow{Z}$ and $\overrightarrow{Z}$, then integrates encoded potential variables to predict the probability distribution of candidate words as the gap feature. We use this gap to guide error correction and obtain the output of teacher model by maximizing the expected probability.

$$p(t|z) = \prod_l p(t_l|\overleftarrow{z_l}, \overrightarrow{z_l}); q(z|t, s) = \prod_l q(\overleftarrow{z_l}|s, t_{<l}, \overrightarrow{z_l}|s, t_{>l}) \qquad (10)$$

where z denotes latent variable, we only need to construct two probabilities of $p(\cdot)$ and $q(\cdot)$ by bidirectional transformer to get the maximum expectation.

Force Decoding. We can extract three kinds of matching features after training teacher model, which consists of latent variable z_l, token embedding E_p and categorical distribution $p(t_k|\cdot) \sim Categorical(softmax(I_k))$. Therefore, we can construct 4-dimensional mis-matching feature $f_k^{mis-match}$:

$$f_k^{mis-match} = (I_{k,m_k}, I_{k,i_{max}^k}, I_{k,m_k} - I_{k,i_{max}^k}, \Xi_{m_k \neq i_{max}}) \tag{11}$$

where m_k represents $k-th$ token in the NAT-CN model output, $i_{max}^k = argmax_i I_k$ is the gap feature. These four items respectively represent:the probability of forced decoding into the current output token m_k; the model does not use forced decoding but retains the probability information of the most likely word i_{max}^k; the difference between the first two items; the probability distribution used to indicate whether the current word is consistent with the predicted word.

Then we can use f_k to forcibly decode the current token into the token with highest probability. We modified the original NAT objective to get Eq. 12.

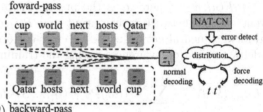

$$P_{NAT}(T|S, f_k; \theta) = P(L_y|S; \theta)$$

$$\cdot \prod_{l=1}^{L_y} P(t_l|S, Z, f_k; \theta) \tag{12}$$

Fig. 2. Use the output of the asynchronous bidirectional decoding model to perform word-level error correction on the translation of NAT-CN model.

As shown in Fig. 2, according to this mismatching feature, it can be decided whether the translation of the NAT-CN model is normally decoded to t or forcedly decoded to the reference translation t^*.

4   Experiments and Results

4.1   Datasets and Setting

We use the following three machine translation tasks: WMT14 En-De (4.5M pairs) and WMT16 En-Ro (610k pairs), IWSLT16 En-De (196k pairs). For WMT16, we utilize newsdev2016 as the verification set and newstest2016 as the test set. For IWSLT16, we employ test2013 as development set. For WMT14, we utilize newstest2013 and newstest2014 as the validation set and test set respectively. All datasets are tokenized by Moses[1] and segmented into sub-word units

---

[1] https://github.com/moses-smt/mosesdecoder.

Table 1. Evaluation of translation quality on select translation tasks including BLEU scores, decoding latency and training speed. Where "NAT-CN" represents the proposed model with capsule network and "EC" refers to the NAT-CN model combined with word-level translation error correction method. We use "KD" to empress the method of knowledge distillation and "i_{dec}" stands for the number of iterations.

Models	WMT14		WMT16		IWSLT16	Latency	Speedup
	En-De	De-En	En-Ro	Ro-En	En-De		
Transformer	27.41	31.29	33.12	33.86	30.90	607 ms	1.00×
NAT-FT	17.69	21.47	27.29	29.06	26.52	39 ms	15.6×
NAT-FT(+NPD $s = 10$)	18.66	22.41	29.02	30.76	27.44	79 ms	7.68×
NAT-IR($i_{dec} = 10$)	21.61	25.48	29.32	30.19	27.11	404 ms	1.5×
NAT-IR(*adaptive refinements*)	21.54	25.43	29.66	30.30	27.01	–	–
NAT-LV	25.10	–	–	–	–	89 ms	6.8×
FlowSeq-base(+KD)	21.45	26.16	29.34	30.44	–	–	–
FlowSeq-large(+KD)	23.72	28.39	29.73	30.72	–	–	–
CMLM-small($i_{dec} = 4$)	24.17	28.55	30.00	30.43	–	–	–
NAT-REG(*rescoring* 9)	24.61	28.90	–	–	27.02	40 ms	15.1×
NAT-CN(B = 0,1 candidates)	23.10	25.25	28.50	29.87	26.59	45 ms	13.47×
NAT-CN(B = 4,9 candidates)	24.92	27.47	29.69	30.31	27.05	72 ms	8.43×
NAT-CN(+EC, B = 4)	26.12	29.35	30.26	31.93	27.79	98 ms	6.18×

by BPE algorithm. We compare our model with strong baseline systems, including the NAT with fertility and noisy parallel decoding (NAT-FT+NPD) [4][2] and our model is modified on it, the NAT with iterative refinement (NAT-IR) [7], the NAT with discrete latent variables (NAT-LV) [11], the conditional sequence generation model with generative flow (FlowSep) [12], the Mask-Predict model (CMLM) [8] and the NAT with auxiliary regularization (NAR-REG) [6].

On the dataset WMT, our parameter settings are the same as Transformer [3] which are described in its paper. Because IWSLT is smaller, the word vector dimension set to 278, the number of hidden layer neurons set to 507, layer depth set to 5, and the attention head set to 2. We conduct experimental verification on the development set and finally select 0.6 as hyper-parameter α in Eq. 9 and the number of parent capsules N and child capsules M are both set to 6. Latency is calculated as the average decoding time of each sentence on entire test set without mini-batching and we test it on two NIVDIA TITAN X.

4.2   Analysis

Results. The experimental results are shown in Table 1. Specifically, on the WMT En→De task, our NAT-CN model get 24.92 BLEU[3] scores, which is an improvement of 6.26 BLEU scores compared to the NAT-FT(+NPD) model. After combining the word-level error correction method, we get 26.12 BLEU scores which is an improvement of 1.02 compared with the best baseline NAT-LV model and has a similar decoding speed, however, the difference is only

---

[2] Source code of this work is available at https://github.com/salesforce/nonauto-nmt.

[3] https://github.com/harpribot/nlp-metrics/tree/master/bleu.

Table 2. Translation case studies on WMT14 De→En task. In order to compare under the same conditions, we set B to 4 in the experiment.

Source	im jahr 2000 wurden weltweit etwa 100 milliarden fotos geschossen, aber nur ein winziger teil davon wurde ins netz geladen.
Reference	around 100 billion photographs were taken worldwide in 2000,but only a tiny part of them was uploaded.
AT	around 100 billion photos were taken worldwide in 2000, but only tiny part of them was uploaded.
NAT-FT	taken worldwide in 2000 about 100 billion photos photos , but uploaded only little part of them was was.
NAT-CN	about 100 billion photos photos taken worldwide in 2000, but only little part of them was was uploaded.
NAT-CN(+EC)	around 100 billion photos were taken worldwide in 2000, but only little part of them was [null] uploaded.

1.29 compared with the Transformer but the decoding speed is improved by 6.18 times. On the En-Ro task, the BLEU scores of 30.26 and 31.93 are finally obtained, and the word-level error correction method on Ro→En also brings 1.62 BLEU scores improvement.

Case Study and Ablation Study. A translation case on WMT14 De-En is shown in Table 2. We utilize Transformer [3] as AT model and set B to 4. Compared with the original NAT-FT model [4], our NAT-CN model has a better ability to capture the global position information, and the effect of the word-level error correction method is also significant. There is a gap in the word order between the NAT-FT model translation and the reference and there are also translation problems such as "photos photos" and "was was". However, our model corrects "photos" to "were" and "was" to "null", that is the target word at the current position is empty, and also corrects "about" to "around". We mark the corrected words in red font.

We perform ablation study on the IWSLT16 translation task to verify the impact of different methods. As shown in Table 3, after using the capsule network layers, the BLEU score of our model is increased by about 4 and the decoding speed also improved by 16.86 times. It is enough to see

Table 3. Ablation study performance on IWSLT16 development set.

Model variants	BLEU	Latency	Speedup
NAT-BASE	21.69	36 ms	16.86×
NAT-BASE(+CN)	25.61	59 ms	10.28×
NAT-BASE(+EC)	28.24	74 ms	8.20×
NAT-BASE(+Both)	28.81	93 ms	7.31×

the impact of the increase of the capsule network layers on the overall experimental results. After combining the word-level error correction method, the BLEU score improves 2.63 which also proves that this approach can make the translation close to the output of the autoregressive model.

5 Conclusion

We propose a novel NAT model architecture to extract the position feature and its context of the word embedding by adding capsule network layers to the vanilla NAT model. In addition, the word-level error correction method is used to reconstruct the translation of the NAT model, which reduces the degradation of the model while improving the decoding speed. Experiments show that our model has a significant effect compared to all non-autoregressive baseline systems.

References

1. Bahdanau, D., Cho, K., Bengio, Y.: Neural machine translation by jointly learning to align and translate. In: 3rd International Conference on Learning Representations, ICLR 2015, San Diego, CA, USA, 7–9 May 2015
2. Sutskever, I., Vinyals, O., Le, Q.V.: Sequence to sequence learning with neural networks. In: Advances in Neural Information Processing Systems 27: Annual Conference on Neural Information Processing Systems 2014, 8–13 December 2014
3. Vaswani, A., et al.: Attention is all you need. In: Advances in Neural Information Processing Systems 30: Annual Conference on Neural Information Processing Systems 2017, Long Beach, CA, USA, 4–9 December 2017, pp. 5998–6008 (2017)
4. Gu, J., Bradbury, J., Xiong, C., Li, V.O.K., Socher, R.: Non-autoregressive neural machine translation. In: 6th International Conference on Learning Representations, ICLR 2018, Vancouver, BC, Canada, 30 April–3 May 2018
5. Hinton, G.E., Vinyals, O., Dean, J.: Distilling the knowledge in a neural network. CoRR (2015). http://arxiv.org/abs/1503.02531
6. Wang, Y., Tian, F., He, D., Qin, T., Zhai, C., Liu, T.: Non-autoregressive machine translation with auxiliary regularization. In: The Thirty-Third AAAI Conference on Artificial Intelligence, AAAI 2019, The Ninth AAAI Symposium on Educational Advances in Artificial Intelligence, EAAI 2019, pp. 5377–5384 (2019)
7. Lee, J., Mansimov, E., Cho, K.: Deterministic non-autoregressive neural sequence modeling by iterative refinement. In: Proceedings of the 2018 Conference on Empirical Methods in Natural Language Processing, Brussels, Belgium, 31 October–4 November 2018, pp. 1173–1182. https://www.aclweb.org/anthology/D18-1149
8. Ghazvininejad, M., Levy, O., Liu, Y., Zettlemoyer, L.: Mask-predict: parallel decoding of conditional masked language models. In: Proceedings of the 2019 Conference on Empirical Methods in Natural Language Processing and the 9th International Joint Conference on Natural Language Processing, EMNLP-IJCNLP (2019)
9. Sabour, S., Frosst, N., Hinton, G.E.: Dynamic routing between capsules. In: Advances in Neural Information Processing Systems 30: Annual Conference on Neural Information Processing Systems 2017, pp. 3856–3866 (2017)
10. Zhou, L., Zhang, J., Zong, C.: Synchronous bidirectional neural machine translation. TACL **7**, 91–105 (2019)
11. Shu, R., Lee, J., Nakayama, H.: Latent-variable non-autoregressive neural machine translation with deterministic inference using a delta posterior. CoRR (2019)
12. Ma, X., Zhou, C., Li, X., Neubig, G.: Flowseq: non-autoregressive conditional sequence generation with generative flow. In: Proceedings of the 2019 Conference on Empirical Methods in Natural Language Processing and the 9th International Joint Conference on Natural Language Processing, EMNLP-IJCNLP (2019)

Recommender Systems

ANN-Assisted Multi-cloud Scheduling Recommender

Amirmohammad Pasdar[1]([✉]), Tahereh Hassanzadeh[2], Young Choon Lee[1],
and Bernard Mans[1]

[1] Department of Computing, Macquarie University, Sydney, Australia
amirmohammad.pasdar@hdr.mq.edu.au,
{young.lee,bernard.mans}@mq.edu.au
[2] School of Engineering and Information Technology,
University of New South Wales, Canberra, Australia
t.hassanzadehkoohi@student.unsw.edu.au

Abstract. Cloud computing has been widely adopted, in the forms of
public clouds and private clouds, for many benefits, such as availability
and cost-efficiency. In this paper, we address the problem of scheduling
jobs across multiple clouds, including a private cloud, to optimize cost
efficiency explicitly taking into account data privacy. In particular, the
problem in this study concerns several factors, such as data privacy of
job, varying electricity prices of private cloud, and different billing poli-
cies/cycles of public clouds, that most, if not all, existing scheduling algorithms do not 'collectively' consider. Hence, we design an ANN-assisted
Multi-Cloud Scheduling Recommender (MCSR) framework that consists
of a novel scheduling algorithm and an ANN-based recommender. While
the former scheduling algorithm can be used to schedule jobs on its own,
their output schedules are also used as training data for the latter recommender. The experiments using both real-world Facebook workload
data and larger scale synthetic data demonstrate that our ANN-based
recommender cost-efficiently schedules jobs respecting privacy.

Keywords: Recommender systems · Scheduling · Cloud computing

1 Introduction

Public clouds, such as Amazon Web Services (AWS), Google Cloud Platform
(GCP), and Microsoft Azure (Azure) have been increasingly adopted for cost
efficiency. They house millions of servers across the world powering nearly every
ICT service, such as social media, banking, and finance. These servers with vir-
tualization can be hired on-demand, and users only pay what they have used,
also known as the pay-as-you-go (PAYG) pricing. While the public cloud adoption has been successful in many cases, the use of private clouds is also common
due to various reasons including the privacy of jobs/data.

There have been many studies that address the problem of job scheduling to
exploit the PAYG pricing in whether public clouds alone or a hybrid cloud (a

© Springer Nature Switzerland AG 2020
H. Yang et al. (Eds.): ICONIP 2020, CCIS 1332, pp. 737–745, 2020.
https://doi.org/10.1007/978-3-030-63820-7_84

private cloud and a public cloud), e.g., [6,7,9,12]. However, the focus has been the selection and provisioning of servers with different prices in a particular public cloud, to offload jobs in a private cloud. Most, if not all, of previous studies, overlook data privacy and other important cost factors, such as varying electricity rates at the private cloud (e.g., off-peak, shoulder, and peak rates) and different billing cycles (e.g., in hours or in seconds) of public clouds.

In this paper, we study the problem of multi-cloud scheduling *collectively* considering the job's privacy and those two cost factors. To this end, we design an ANN-Assisted Multi-Cloud Scheduling Recommender (MCSR) framework that aims to cost-efficiently schedule jobs across multiple clouds including a private cloud. MCSR consists of a scheduler using simulated annealing (SA) and a recommender using artificial neural networks (ANNs). While the scheduler alone is capable of making good scheduling decisions in static environments, its capacity may not be as good with unseen workloads in more dynamic environments. The scheduler also produces training data for the recommender. MCSR leverages Recurrent Neural Network (RNN) and Long Short Term Memory (LSTM).

Experimental results show MCSR's scheduling recommendations for unseen workloads, made with RNN and LSTM, achieve up to 31% cost savings, in comparison with two state-of-the-art algorithms, Resource Management Service (RMS) [7] and an online cost-efficient scheduler (BOS) [6].

The paper is organized as follows. Related work is discussed in Sect. 2. Problem statement is given in Sect. 3 followed by Sect. 4 to detail MCSR. Section 5 and Sect. 6 state evaluation results and conclusion, respectively.

2   Related Work

The cost-efficiency of cloud computing has been extensively studied using various scheduling approaches [5,7,9,14]. However, most of these studies overlook privacy and the cloud energy cost and only focus on the trade-off between performance improvement and cost-saving. While some works [6,14] take into account energy costs, they overlook privacy and possible cost savings with different billing cycles.

A dynamic resource management system architecture is proposed [7] that considers jobs deadline, and uses regular and policy-driven deadline-sensitive queues that each of which holds available resources besides external resources. Bossche et al., [6] proposed an online hybrid scheduler to deal with workload offloading through the selection of most cost-efficient public resources. They designed a four-strategy scheduler that swaps the cheapest jobs in the private cloud queue with scheduled jobs for cloud bursting. In [9], authors referred to a cost evaluation for a workload bursting based approach overlooking privacy constraint.

Data-driven approaches are also gained attention for resource allocation [8, 10,11,15]. In [11] support vector machine (SVM) is used to profile and anticipate user activities for resource management in a multimedia cloud environment, and [15] proposes a framework that relies on the processing time estimations by statistical forecasting strategies to feasibly allocate resources to jobs. Champati et al., [8] discuss an online runtime estimation based algorithm to efficiently minimize makespan in the private cloud while keeping the offloading minimum. Cortez et al., in [10] present a system that provides predictions online to resource managers via a library and ML tools such as regression tree or random forest.

3   Problem Statement

The multi-cloud in this study consists of a private cloud and M public cloud platforms (CP) each of which has virtual machines (m). Each machine has computation capacities and the usage consumption is billed based on billing cycles (BC_{CP_i}). Also, there are duration-based low priorities resources and unused resource capacities (CP_i^{LP}). Available machine resources (m_i) can be used free of charge during its active cycle $(BC_{CP_i}^{active})$, otherwise, it incurs charges $(BC_{CP_i}^{new})$.

The private cloud has homogeneous machines that each of which has resource capacity (m_i^{res}) represented as CPU cores (m_i^{core}) and memory (m_i^{mem}). Each machine (m_i) uses energy in units of watts (ω) with respect to electricity rates per kilowatt-hour. Each machine (m_i) requires a wattage usage under different utilization levels $(m_i^{ut^l})$ [2]. Also, idle machines can be put into deep sleep mode leading to negligible power consumption.

The private cloud receives T jobs at time τ that each job (t_i) has a submission time (t_i^τ), privacy (t_i^p), and required resources (R_{t_i}) in terms of number of CPU cores and memory in resemblance to real-world traces [10]. Moreover, the private cloud processes a job if either it is privacy-sensitive or available cost-efficient resources exist. Otherwise, public clouds would execute the job.

The problem in our study is firstly how to schedule jobs within the multi-cloud such that the execution cost is minimized, and secondly, ANNs can facilitate the scheduling of unseen workload.

4   ANN-Assisted Multi-cloud Scheduling Recommender

In this section, we present MCSR as a dual-component configurable scheduling framework (Algorithm 1) that makes scheduling decisions assisted by a machine learning-based recommender component.

4.1   Scheduler

Algorithm 1 illustrates how workloads are scheduled across the multi-cloud. It considers the MCSR algorithm mode $(MCSR_{mode})$; in recommender (REC) mode, it sets jobs' recommended locations (loc_{t_i}) (line 1). Otherwise, the scheduler chooses cost-efficient machines of the multi-cloud based on either public cloud active cycles or comparison of their billing policies (lines 6–11). The scheduler seeks eligible active machines (m_{active}) of the private cloud and keeps idle machines (m_{idle}) list. Machines that satisfy each job (t_i) resource requirements

---

Algorithm 1: ANN-Assisted Multi-cloud Scheduling

Data: T, $char_T$, $m_{active/idle}$, BC_{CP}^{active}, Low-Priority machines BC_{CP}^{LP}, $loc_{LSTM/RNN}$, $MCSR_{mode}$, $W_{RNN/LSTM}$, η, and α

Result: s_0 (the cost-efficient state)

1 $\exists\, MCSR_{mode} = REC : \forall\, t_i \in T : loc_{LSTM/RNN}^{t_i} = ANN(char_{t_i}, W)$

2 **for** $t_i \in T$ **do**

3 $\quad \{m_{cnd}^{t_i}, m_{cnd_{bk}}^{t_i}\} \leftarrow EligibileMachines(t_i, m_{active})$

4 $\quad R_{t_i} \leftarrow \{R_{t_i}^{mem} \& R_{t_i}^{core}\} \& alter_{t_i}^{loc}(t_i, m_{cnd}^{t_i} = \emptyset)$

5 $\quad$ **if** t_i is a regular job $\&$ $m_{cnd}^{t_i} = \emptyset$ **then**

6 $\quad\quad \exists\, BC_{CP}^{active}(R_{t_i}) \& loc_{BC_{CP}^{active}} = loc_{LSTM/RNN}^{t_i} :$

7 $\quad\quad m_{cnd}^{t_i} \leftarrow BC_{CP}^{active}(R_{t_i})$

8 $\quad\quad$ **else**

9 $\quad\quad\quad m_{cnd}^{t_i} \leftarrow \min(Cost_{hour}^m, Cost_{sec}^m, Cost_{LP}^m)$

10 $\quad\quad\quad \exists\, m_{cnd}^{t_i} \neq Cost_{sec}^m \& loc_{LSTM/RNN}^{t_i} = \emptyset$: Update BC_{CP}^{active}

11 $\quad\quad\quad$ Otherwise : $m_{cnd}^{t_i} \leftarrow Estimate(BC_{CP}, loc_{LSTM/RNN}^{t_i}) \&$ Update BC_{CP}^{active}

12 $\quad\quad$ **end**

13 $\quad$ **end**

14 $\quad \exists\, m_{idle} : m_{active} \leftarrow m_{idle}.poll()$ Update m_{active}, $m_{cnd}^{t_i}$, and $m_{cnd_{bk}}^{t_i}$ $\&$ $s_0 \leftarrow createState(t_i, poll(m_{cnd}^{t_i}))$

15 **end**

16 $f_{s_0} \leftarrow fitness(s_0)$ and update m_{active}^{Res}

17 **while** $\eta \geq \eta_e$ **do**

18 $\quad s_{new} \leftarrow TRNS(s_0, m_{active}^{Res}, m_{cnd}^T)$, $f_{s_{new}} \leftarrow fitness(s_{new}) \& \eta \leftarrow \alpha * \eta$

19 $\quad$ **if** $(f_{s_{new}} - f_{s_0}) \geq 0$ OR $e^{-(f_{s_{new}} - f_{s_0})/\gamma} \geq rnd()$ **then**

20 $\quad\quad s_0 \leftarrow s_{new}$

21 $\quad$ **end**

22 **end**

---

are kept as the candidate (and back-up (bk)) list ($m_{cnd}^{t_i}$) (line 3). For privacy-sensitive jobs, only the private cloud machines (an *arbitrary* m_{idle}) are inquired but for regular jobs machines across the multi-cloud are explored (lines 6–11). If a regular job's candidate list is empty, the recommendation is altered regarding multi-cloud resources and the job resource requirement (R_{t_i}).

A transition is rejected due to either the transition probability controlled by γ or energy difference (i.e., how cost-efficient the state is) (line 19). SA maintains system temperature (η) in the metallurgy terminology (line 17–18) that is managed by $\alpha \in [0, 1]$. The SA-based scheduler aims to find a cost-efficient transition from a worse state to a state in which the temperature is below an expected temperature (η_e) and/or the cost-efficient state is found (line 17). A state's energy is determined by a fitness function (Eq. 1) that consists of four controlling parameters toward cost-efficiency.

$$fitness(state) = sign \times \frac{\theta \times Fit_{ratio}(state)}{EC(state)} \tag{1}$$

A state is assigned a *sign* to indicate the eligibility of jobs concerning the privacy constraint violation and/or missing expected deadlines. $Fit_{ratio}(state)$ shows how a state can lead to higher CPU and memory utilization (i.e., m_{active}^{Res}) in the private cloud. Also, it is assisted by $\theta \in [0,1]$ that has a higher value for the private cloud as the underutilized private cloud hurts cost-efficiency even it may be *cheaper* to offload jobs to the public clouds [13].

Finally, the state estimated cost ($EC(state)$) is computed with respect to the private cloud utilization which requires the expected wattage usage (ω_m), electricity rates and/or the public cloud estimated usage cost. The expected wattage (ω_m) is computed as $\frac{m_{ut}^{cur}-m_{ut}^{lb}}{m_{ut}^{ub}-m_{ut}^{lb}} \times (\omega_{m_{ut}^{ub}} - \omega_{m_{ut}^{lb}}) + \omega_{m_{ut}^{lb}}$ for the machine's current utilization (m_{ut}^{cur}) with the lower (lb) and upper (ub) bound utilization and the determined lower/upper bound of $\omega_{m_{ut}}$ for m_{ut}^{cur}. To make a transition from a state (s_0), each job's $m_{cnd}^{t_i}$ is permuted (line 18). When a machine (m_j) is chosen for job t_i, the corresponding machine resources are updated per each job if m_j is in the other jobs' candidate lists. Also, the state s_0 becomes ineligible when unavailability of resources in m_{active} (and non-existence of any m_{idle}) happens for privacy-sensitive jobs that is addressed by swapping jobs ($j^{swapped}$) and offloading directly to the cost-efficient public cloud.

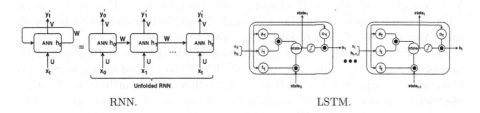

RNN.   LSTM.

Fig. 1. RNN and LSTM structure in which h_i represents the hidden layer. (a) U, V, and W are the input, output, and hidden weights, respectively. (b) LSTM gates; forget gate (f_t), activation gate (a_t), input gate (i_t), and output gate (o_t).

4.2   Recommender

The recommender is an ANN-based component and is proposed to assist the scheduler (Algorithm 1) with job location recommendations for scheduling by considering past scheduling decisions and their resource requirements.

ANNs are a collection of connected nodes called artificial *neurons* and are placed in different network *layers*. The *learning process* in ANNs is adjusting the network weights for a set of inputs (i.e., scheduling decisions and job resource requirements) and their corresponding outputs (i.e., the recommended cloud environment) known as *labels*. An input vector is fed to the network to produce a recommended output through the iterative-based *back propagation (BP)* algorithm in two phases; forward and backward to adjust weights accordingly. The conventional ANN starts over the learning process per each input that does not satisfy correlation among scheduling decisions during the time. Thus, RNN (and LSTM) is used for a recommendation in which learned information (i.e., adjusted weights) are passed to the next input through the time (Fig. 1a). It uses the stored information of past scheduling decisions and their resource requirements.

The MCSR recommender also leverages LSTM as RNN has the *vanishing gradient* issue. LSTMs as a special kind of RNNs have the chain structure shown in Fig. 1b. When jobs arrive at the private cloud, they are forwarded to the ANNs for job location recommendations.

5 Evaluation

In this section, we present experimental results for the MCSR scheduler and its recommender, respectively, for resource usage and execution cost. The performance of MCSR components is compared with RMS [7] and BOS [6].

5.1 Experimental Settings

Two sets of workloads are the input to our simulation: (1) Hadoop traces on a 600-machine cluster at Facebook [3] and (2) synthetic workload with ~11.6k jobs. Also, we set 0%–50% of jobs to be privacy sensitive.

The private cloud has 200 machines each of which has 8 vCPUs and 32GB memory with a computing capacity 3200MIPS. Power consumption is modeled based on the estimated load wattage under different CPU utilization [2]. Also, electricity rates vary and are categorized as off-peak, peak, and shoulder [4]. The modeled public clouds are AWS (and spot instances), GCP, and MS Azure.

Simulated annealing parameters for η, α, and γ are 100, 0.9, and 0.9, respectively. In every 60-s time interval, the RNN-based private cloud manager accepts standardized CPU, RAM, and overall machine utilization which belongs to a utilization category [10]. It is trained based on VM utilization traces [1] of a chosen distributed data center from Bitbrains composed of 1750 VMs.

The recommender has three layers and accepts standardized input features such as job submission time, length, required CPU cores and memory, privacy, deadline, and the electricity rates category. The output is one hot vector

Table 1. Job distribution across different clouds for Facebook workload.

Privacy	MCSR				RMS				BOS			
	Private	AWS	GCP	MS	Private	AWS	GCP	MS	Private	AWS	GCP	MS
0%	5668	202	17	8	5539	354	1	1	5759	124	9	3
10%	5738	137	17	2	5534	357	2	2	5780	106	8	2
20%	5747	140	7	1	5580	313	0	2	5792	101	3	0
30%	5779	106	9	0	5617	277	1	0	5829	64	3	1
40%	5763	114	11	7	5644	250	0	1	5803	82	8	3
50%	5777	103	13	2	5671	223	0	1	5819	69	7	1

based on the execution location. It is trained with a worth of 30 days workload submission (~177k jobs) considering privacy rates by MCSR under 100 epochs.

5.2 Results Without Recommender

This section presents the workload scheduling results for 24 h workload submission (~5.9k jobs). Job proportion in the multi-cloud (Table 1) shows that MCSR sent off fewer jobs to the private cloud and took advantage of public clouds (Algorithm 1, in particular, AWS). MCSR then used more GCP (and few MS) due to the per-second nature of the GCP billing cycle. In contrast, RMS and BOS ran approximately the same amount of jobs on the private cloud. MCSR used fewer machines (Fig. 2a) resulting in less cost (Figs. 2b and Fig. 2c) since it judiciously kept the number of active machines aligned with the workload.

Results show that MCSR compared to RMS and BOS achieves 78% and 74% cost saving in the multi-cloud. MCSR also improves resource utilization to 87% and 64% in comparison with RMS and BOS.

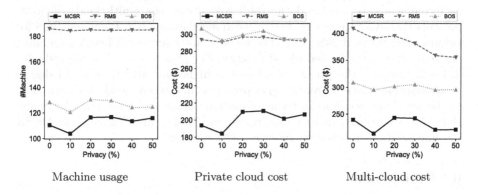

| Machine usage | Private cloud cost | Multi-cloud cost |

Fig. 2. Facebook workload (~5.9k jobs) results.

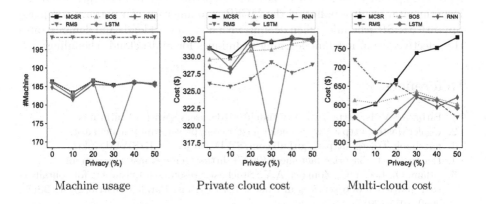

| Machine usage | Private cloud cost | Multi-cloud cost |

Fig. 3. Synthetic workload (~11.6k jobs) results.

Table 2. Job distribution across different clouds for ∼11.6k jobs.

(a) MCSR scheduler, RMS, and BOS.

	MCSR				RMS				BOS			
Privacy	Private	AWS	GCP	MS	Private	AWS	GCP	MS	Private	AWS	GCP	MS
0%	10511	447	618	2	10345	1227	6	0	10546	1026	5	1
10%	10329	655	590	4	10386	1184	5	3	10476	1096	3	3
20%	9954	990	618	16	10520	1053	4	1	10469	1105	2	2
30%	9454	1394	697	33	10602	974	0	2	10472	1101	2	3
40%	9113	1653	763	49	10681	894	3	0	10500	1072	5	1
50%	8974	1836	698	70	10790	787	1	0	10549	1023	4	2

(b) MCSR recommender.

	LSTM				RNN			
Privacy	Private	AWS	GCP	MS	Private	AWS	GCP	MS
0%	10534	400	643	1	10830	326	422	0
10%	10629	404	542	3	10662	395	520	1
20%	10175	652	750	1	10378	536	656	8
30%	8452	2408	679	39	9283	1231	1047	17
40%	9242	1291	1013	32	9496	1130	919	33
50%	9134	1421	983	40	8917	1504	1093	64

5.3   Results with Recommender

This section presents MCSR recommender results for a new trace with ∼0.025 as the average training error. ANNs' Performance efficiency is shown in Fig. 3 as recommendations reduced the total cost across the multi-cloud. Figure 3c presents that ANNs provided better recommendations than RMS and BOS for privacy rates 0% and 20%–40%. The recommender suggested better scheduling decisions due to the looked ahead functionality (Fig. 3c) which is aligned with Table 2, however, the private cloud cost is higher for MCSR (Fig. 3b) due to more machine usage. Figure 3a also presents that recommendations are close to the scheduler decisions in terms of machine usage and lower than RMS and BOS. MCSR utilized more public resources (Table 2 and Fig. 3c) and MCSR recommendations reached on average ∼32% cost saving.

6   Conclusion

This paper presented MCSR as a multi-cloud scheduling recommender framework with an online scheduler and a machine-learning based recommender. MCSR makes scheduling decisions taking full advantage of several cost-efficiency features in public clouds while respecting the privacy of jobs in the private cloud. Experimental results confirmed the MCSR recommender can perform comparably with MCSR scheduler when dealing with unseen workloads and demonstrates the effective use of machine learning techniques for multi-cloud scheduling.

References

1. Bitbrains VMs. http://gwa.ewi.tudelft.nl/datasets/gwa-t-12-bitbrains
2. CoolerMaster. https://www.coolermaster.com/power-supply-calculator/
3. Facebook Traces. https://github.com/SWIMProjectUCB/SWIM/wiki/
4. Energy Australia price fact sheet (2017). https://energyaustralia.com.au
5. Adam, O., Lee, Y.C., Zomaya, A.Y.: Stochastic resource provisioning for containerized multi-tier web services in clouds. IEEE Trans. Parallel Distrib. Syst. **28**(7), 2060–2073 (2017)
6. den Bossche, R.V., Vanmechelen, K., Broeckhove, J.: Online cost-efficient scheduling of deadline-constrained workloads on hybrid clouds. Fut. Gener. Comput. Syst. **29**(4), 973–985 (2013)

7. Calheiros, R.N., Buyya, R.: Cost-effective provisioning and scheduling of deadline-constrained applications in hybrid clouds. In: Wang, X.S., Cruz, I., Delis, A., Huang, G. (eds.) WISE 2012. LNCS, vol. 7651, pp. 171–184. Springer, Heidelberg (2012). https://doi.org/10.1007/978-3-642-35063-4_13
8. Champati, J.P., Liang, B.: One-restart algorithm for scheduling and offloading in a hybrid cloud. In: 2015 IEEE 23rd International Symposium on Quality of Service (IWQoS), pp. 31–40, June 2015. https://doi.org/10.1109/IWQoS.2015.7404699
9. Charrada, F.B., Tata, S.: An efficient algorithm for the bursting of service-based applications in hybrid clouds. IEEE Trans. Serv. Comput. **9**(3), 357–367 (2016)
10. Cortez, E., Bonde, A., Muzio, A., Russinovich, M., Fontoura, M., Bianchini, R.: Resource central: understanding and predicting workloads for improved resource management in large cloud platforms. In: Proceedings of the 26th Symposium on Operating Systems Principles (SOSP), pp. 153–167 (2017)
11. Daniel, D., Raviraj, P.: Distributed hybrid cloud for profit driven content provisioning using user requirements and content popularity. Cluster Comput. **20**(1), 525–538 (2017). https://doi.org/10.1007/s10586-017-0778-7
12. Farahabady, M.R.H., Lee, Y.C., Zomaya, A.Y.: Pareto-optimal cloud bursting. IEEE Trans. Parallel Distrib. Syst. **25**(10), 2670–2682 (2014)
13. Greenberg, A., Hamilton, J., Maltz, D.A., Patel, P.: The cost of a cloud: research problems in data center networks. SIGCOMM Comput. Commun. Rev. **39**(1), 68–73 (2008)
14. Lee, Y., Lian, B.: Cloud bursting scheduler for cost efficiency. In: 10th IEEE International Conference on Cloud Computing, pp. 774–777. IEEE (2017)
15. Zhu, J., Li, X., Ruiz, R., Xu, X.: Scheduling stochastic multi-stage jobs to elastic hybrid cloud resources. IEEE Trans. Parallel Distrib. Syst. **29**(6), 1401–1415 (2018)

Correlation-Aware Next Basket Recommendation Using Graph Attention Networks

Yuanzhe Zhang[1], Ling Luo[2(✉)], Jianjia Zhang[3], Qiang Lu[1], Yang Wang[3], and Zhiyong Wang[1]

[1] The University of Sydney, Sydney, NSW 2006, Australia
yzha9691@uni.sydney.edu.au, {steven.lu,zhiyong.wang}@sydney.edu.au
[2] The University of Melbourne, Melbourne, VIC 3010, Australia
ling.luo@unimelb.edu.au
[3] University of Technology Sydney, Sydney, NSW 2007, Australia
{Jianjia.Zhang,Yang.Wang}@uts.edu.au

Abstract. With the increasing number of commodities in our daily life, the recommender system plays a more and more important role in selecting items of users' interests. For the next basket recommendation task, in this work, we propose the first end-to-end correlation-aware model to predict the next basket considering intra-basket correlations using graph attention networks. Specifically, items and correlations between items are viewed as nodes and edges in a graph, respectively. By estimating and aggregating the intra-basket correlations using the attention layer of the self-attention model, the recommendation can be conducted at the basket level, instead of at the item level. We conduct comprehensive experiments on a real-world retailing dataset to show the improvement from state-of-the-art baselines using our proposed method.

Keywords: Recommender systems · Next basket recommendation · Graph convolutional neural networks

1 Introduction

People have been facing more and more options in their daily life, such as reading news, purchasing books, watching movies and listening to music. A recommender system is a powerful tool to feed people the items of their interests. However, few works have considered that, in many scenarios, multiple items are purchased together in one transaction. For example, when users go to a supermarket, they usually purchase a group of items instead of a single one. Such a group of items bought at the same time by the same user are referred to as a basket. The next basket recommendation is a task of recommending a basket of items when the historically purchased baskets are provided as input, which will be formally defined later.

© Springer Nature Switzerland AG 2020
H. Yang et al. (Eds.): ICONIP 2020, CCIS 1332, pp. 746–753, 2020.
https://doi.org/10.1007/978-3-030-63820-7_85

Figure 1 is an example of the next basket recommendation in the supermarket scenario. For each user, his transaction history consists of a sequence of baskets. The target is to predict what items belong to the next basket to be purchased in the future. In the transaction data, the size of baskets and the length of basket sequences are usually variable. As shown in Fig. 1, items in a particular basket are usually correlated and show a certain purpose. The first basket of *Cereal, Milk, Bread* and the last basket of *Tooth Paste, Tooth Brush* may imply a latent intention of preparing for breakfast and brushing teeth, respectively. Inspired by this observation, the next basket recommendation should involve related items, rather than independent items. In this way, modeling the intra-basket correlations between items are essential for the next basket recommendation.

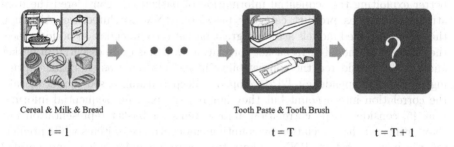

Cereal & Milk & Bread   Tooth Paste & Tooth Brush

t = 1   t = T   t = T + 1

Fig. 1. Illustration of the next basket recommendation task

To explore the correlation among items, a deep-learning-based model called Beacon [5] was recently proposed. In that model, the correlation among items is considered when encoding each basket. The correlation is firstly computed by counting the frequency of co-occurrences of item pairs and then fed into the basket encoder to create the correlation sensitive basket representation. However, in this work, the correlation estimation model and the main deep recommendation model are independent, i.e. the correlation among items needs to be computed externally. In order to better integrate the entire model, we propose an end-to-end graph deep learning model, in which nodes and edges represent items and correlations, respectively. Since there should exist an edge (correlation) between relevant items, in our model, the edge is estimated by self-attention from relevant item embeddings. The embeddings of relevant items are then aggregated with weights of correlations to form the correlation-aware basket representation.

Our main **contributions** are:

1. We explore the intra-basket correlation which is essential for basket analysis.
2. We propose an end-to-end model to estimate and aggregate correlations automatically during the training procedure.
3. We achieve better performance when comparing with state-of-the-art baselines for next basket recommendation.

2   Related Works

At an early age, the Markov chain was firstly proposed for this task [6]. In this work, matrix factorization was used to learn the general taste of a user, and Markov Chain modeled sequential behavior by learning a transition graph over items. [4] proposed to recommend the next basket based on K-nearest neighbors with the Wasserstein distance, but this model was difficult to apply on large scale datasets due to the huge computational cost. Recently, with emerging deep learning-based methods, a pioneering work [10] firstly used neural networks with fully-connected layers. The basket was represented as the average of item embeddings and they concatenated basket representations for basket sequence representations. After that, Recurrent Neural Networks [11] was proposed for better exploiting the sequential information of baskets. [1] considered the item attributes such as product category based on RNN's architecture. Although the aforementioned models achieved great basket recommendation performance, they ignored to model intra-basket correlation, which is quite essential in basket analysis. [9] considered the compatibility in baskets but was short for capturing long-term dependency. [2] developed a deep learning-based model to take the correlation into account but they ignored the plentiful sequential information. [5] considered the correlation among items for basket representation but they estimated the correlation by counting co-occurrence of items while predicting the next basket by RNNs. These two parts are independent and parallel which hurts the integration of the whole model. To bridge the research gaps, we propose to model the next basket recommendation task by graph attention networks so that the correlation among items could be estimated directly using the end-to-end deep learning model.

3   Methodology

3.1   Problem Formulations and Notations

The next basket recommendation problem is formally formulated as following. Assume there are m users $U = \{u_1, u_2, ..., u_m\}$ and n items $V = \{v_1, v_2, ..., v_n\}$. For each user, a basket B_t is a subset of V ($B_t \subseteq V$) consisting of several items purchased in his t^{th} transaction. The intra-basket correlation among items is estimated and stored in a matrix $C \in R^{n \times n}$, in which the entry c_{ij} is the correlation between v_i and v_j. The transaction history of a user is viewed as a sequence of baskets $< B_1, B_2, ... B_T >$. Note that the length of basket sequence T is different for different users. We aim to predict the next basket of each user B_{T+1} considering the intra-basket correlation among items.

3.2   Overview of the Model

Generally, our model use Graph Attention Network (GAT)[8] to model this problem. The items V are viewed as nodes in the graph and the correlations are items are viewed as edges in the graph which are estimated by the attention layer with scaled dot-product attention [7]. Figure 2 illustrates the overall structure of our model. Firstly, items are embedded into d-dimensional space as vector representations. After that, the item embeddings are fed to the attention layer to compute the correlation. Then we encode each basket for correlation-aware representation according to the embeddings of items inside the basket. For each user, there exists a sequence of baskets and we feed baskets into LSTM networks in terms of their chronological order. The output of LSTM is then used to compute the final probability of each item belonging to this basket.

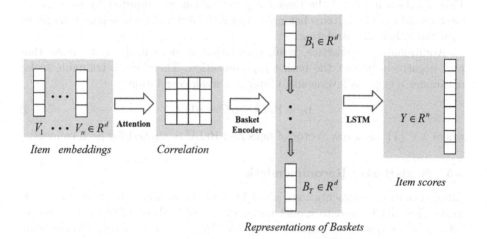

Fig. 2. Overall structure of our model

3.3   Item Embeddings and Correlation Estimation

We use a d-dimensional embedding vector $v_i \in R^d$ to represent each node (item) in the graph. Then the correlation among items can be estimated by the attention layer using the embedding vectors of items. Given the d-dimensional embedding vectors of n items $\{v_i\}_n$, a matrix $I \in R^{n \times d}$ can be generated to store the embeddings of all items. Correlation $\mathbf{C} \in R^{n \times n}$ between items is computed by the scaled dot-product attention [8] with normalization of $\sqrt{d}$ by

$$\mathbf{C} = \text{softmax}\left(\frac{IW_k(IW_q)^\top}{\sqrt{d}}\right), \tag{1}$$

where the $W_k \in R^{d \times d}$ and $W_q \in R^{d \times d}$ are learnable parameters for asymmetric item embeddings. The softmax is row-wise, i.e. conducted on each row of the matrix for normalization. This equation implies that the correlation between items is computed from the similarity between nodes.

3.4 Correlation-Aware Basket Encoder

In this section, we would introduce the basket encoder to get the correlation-aware representation of a basket from correlation C and item embeddings. For each basket B_t, a binary row vector $\mathbf{x}_t \in \{0,1\}^n$ is generated to indicate whether an item is inside this basket, where the ith value is 1 only when the ith item is inside the basket. The correlation-aware representation $\mathbf{b}_t$ of the basket B_t is a d-dimensional vector computed by:

$$\mathbf{b}_t = \mathbf{x}_t \mathbf{C} I. \tag{2}$$

This equation indicates the basket representation is computed by aggregating the embeddings of the items belonging to this basket and their neighboring nodes with the weight of correlation.

Additionally, in practice, weak correlation is more likely to be noise that may negatively impact the basket representation. Therefore, a trainable scalar parameter $\eta \in \mathbb{R}^+$ is leveraged to filter out weak correlation.

$$\mathbf{b}_t = \mathrm{ReLU}\left(\mathbf{x}_t \mathbf{C} - \eta \mathbf{1}\right) I, \tag{3}$$

where $\mathbf{1} \in \{1\}^n$ is a row vector of ones and ReLU is applied for each element.

3.5 Next-Basket Recommendation

After obtaining representations of all baskets, Long-Short Term Memory networks (LSTM) is used to model the sequence of baskets. Given the representations of a sequence of baskets $< B_1, B_2, ... B_T >$, the recurrent H-dimension hidden output $\mathbf{h}_t \in \mathbb{R}^H$ at step t is computed by

$$\mathbf{h}_t = \tanh\left(\mathbf{b}_t \Psi + \mathbf{h}_{t-1} \Psi' + \psi\right), \tag{4}$$

where $\Psi \in \mathbb{R}^{d \times H}$, $\Psi' \in \mathbb{R}^{H \times H}$ and $\psi \in \mathbb{R}^H$ are weight and bias parameters to be learned.

The item probability is then computed by the output of the final layer of LSTM $\mathbf{h}_T \in R^H$:

$$\mathbf{S} = \sigma(\mathbf{h}_T W), \tag{5}$$

where $W \in \mathbb{R}^{H \times n}$ and the σ is the sigmoid function to ensure the probability is in the range from 0 to 1. The output $\mathbf{S} \in R^n$ implies the probability of each item belonging to the predicted next basket.

Additionally, to get the correlation-aware output, we combine the output probability S with the correlation C with a hyperparameter α controlling the trade-off.

$$\mathbf{y} = \alpha(\mathbf{S}) + (1 - \alpha)(\mathbf{SC}), \tag{6}$$

The final recommendation is based on the predicted item scores $\mathbf{y}$. Since the size of the next basket is various and is often noncritical in the setting of previous works. In our work, we follow the traditional way of setting the basket size as a constant small number k. The final predicted next basket takes k items with the highest probability in $\mathbf{y}$.

3.6   Loss Function

Our goal is to make the predicted basket similar to the ground truth. The last basket B_{T+1} in each sequence is removed as ground truth and the remaining sequence $< B_1, B_2, ...B_T >$ is for training.

Generally, to make the predicted scores $\mathbf{y}$ closer to the ground truth B_{T+1}, we adopt weighted cross-entropy as the loss function.

$$\mathcal{L} = -\frac{1}{|B_{T+1}|} \sum_{i \in B_{T+1}} \log(\mathbf{y}_i) - \frac{1}{|V \backslash B_{T+1}|} \sum_{j \in V \backslash B_{T+1}} \log(1 - \mathbf{y}_j) \quad (7)$$

During training, the probability $\mathbf{y}$ of adopted items in the ground truth basket B_{T+1} is encouraged to increase (the first term) while the probability of other negative items in $V \backslash B_{T+1}$ is decreasing (the second term). The weights $|B_{T+1}|$ and $|V \backslash B_{T+1}|$ are used to fix the biases in the unbalanced data, i.e. the purchased items are much less than unpurchased ones.

4   Experiments

4.1   Dataset

The dataset used in our experiments is the TaFeng dataset[1], which is the most popular in the basket analysis research domain. TaFeng is a transaction dataset of a grocery store from November 2000 to February 2001 and each transaction can be viewed as a basket in our experiments. There are 32,266 users and 23,812 items with 817,741 transactions in total.

For preprocessing, as [5], users who bought at least 10 items and items which were bought by at least 10 users are selected for experiments. Additionally, each user must purchase at least 3 baskets to ensure a sequence of at least 2 baskets for training. In the preprocessed dataset, the average basket size is 5.9 and the average length of sequences of baskets is 7.0. To get the training, validation and test sets, we chronologically split the whole dataset. Specifically, since the TaFeng dataset spanned 4 months, the basket sequences in the first 3 months are considered for training. The baskets purchased from the 3 to 3.5 months and from the 3.5 to 4 months are for validation set and test set, respectively.

4.2   Evaluation Metrics

The evaluation metrics we use is the F1 score, which measures the similarity between the ground truth and the predicted basket. The F1 score combines the recall rate and precision rate. A large predicted basket hurts the precision rate because of including many irrelevant items outside the true basket while a small one is hard to include all relevant items, which hurts the recall rate. Since the average basket size is 5.9 in the TaFeng dataset, the F1 score at 5 is used in the experiments, which means the size of the predicted next basket is set as 5.

---

[1] https://www.kaggle.com/chiranjivdas09/ta-feng-grocery-dataset.

4.3 Baselines

We compare our model with a series of state-of-the-art baselines.

- POP takes the most popular items as the predicted basket.
- triple2vec[2] [9] considers the correlation among items in baskets without encoding the sequential information of baskets.
- DREAM[3] [11] is a basket recommendation model using recurrent neural networks without considering correlation.
- Beacon[4] [5] is a recent deep learning-based model. The basket representation employs correlation among items which is computed by counting the frequency of being purchased together.

4.4 Experimental Results

The experimental results are shown in Table 1. The final results on the test set are from the model with the best performance on the validation set after convergence. The optimizer we use is Adam [3]. Our model is trained for 50 epochs in total with batch size of 32. The hyperparameters are tuned by grid search, and the values used in our experiments are $d = 10$, $\alpha = 0.5$, $H = 16$ and learning rate $= 0.001$.

Table 1. Comparison of F1 score at 5 with baselines

Models	POP	triple2vec	DREAM	Beacon	**Our Model**
F1@5(%)	4.66	4.66	5.85	6.27	**6.44**

It is observed that our correlation-aware graph deep learning model performs better than other baselines[5]. The POP method naively takes the most popular items without modeling correlation and sequential information so that it achieves the lowest performance. The triple2vec takes the correlation into account but performs also poorly due to the lack of sequential information. DREAM leverages RNNs to encode the basket sequence information but ignores the correlation. Beacon considers both sequential information and correlation among items so that it gets improvement from DREAM's basic RNN structure. Note that the correlation in Beacon is estimated by counting the co-occurrence of item pairs. Benefit from the great expression ability of the attention model, our model can capture the correlations well with abundant transaction data. Even if our model does not leverage external correlation information, the prediction can still be more accurate. This implies that our end-to-end model can estimate and aggregate more helpful correlations automatically for the recommendation than the external items co-occurrence information.

---

[2] https://github.com/MengtingWan/grocery.
[3] https://github.com/LaceyChen17/DREAM.
[4] https://github.com/PreferredAI/beacon.
[5] Results of POP, triple2vec and DREAM are from [5].

5   Conclusion

In this paper, we present an end-to-end correlation-aware model for the next basket recommendation using graph attention networks. In our model, the correlation is estimated by the attention model directly during learning. The correlation-aware basket representation is then computed by aggregating embeddings of the items inside and their neighboring items with the weight of correlation. After that, the basket sequence is fed into LSTM for sequential information encoding. We compare our model with state-of-the-art baselines on a popular real-world basket grocery dataset and achieves the best performance, which demonstrates the benefits of taking the correlation between items into account for the next basket recommendation. In future work, we will make the size of the predicted basket adaptive for each user instead of a constant number.

References

1. Bai, T., Nie, J.Y., Zhao, W.X., Zhu, Y., Du, P., Wen, J.R.: An attribute-aware neural attentive model for next basket recommendation. In: ACM SIGIR (2018)
2. Gong, Y., et al.: Exact-k recommendation via maximal clique optimization. In: ACM Knowledge Discovery and Data Mining (KDD) (2019)
3. Kingma, D.P., Ba, J.L.: Adam: a method for stochastic optimization (2015)
4. Kraus, M., Feuerriegel, S.: Personalized purchase prediction of market baskets with Wasserstein-based sequence matching. In: ACM Knowledge Discovery and Data Mining (KDD) (2019)
5. Le, D.T., Lauw, H.W., Fang, Y.: Correlation-sensitive next-basket recommendation. In: International Joint Conference on Artificial Intelligence (IJCAI) (2019)
6. Rendle, S., Freudenthaler, C., Schmidt-Thieme, L.: Factorizing personalized Markov chains for next-basket recommendation. In: International World Wide Web Conference (WWW) (2010)
7. Vaswani, A., et al.: Attention is all you need. In: Conference on Neural Information Processing Systems (NIPS) (2017)
8. Veličković, P., Cucurull, G., Casanova, A., Romero, A., Lio, P., Bengio, Y.: Graph attention networks. The International Conference on Learning Representations (ICLR) (2018)
9. Wan, M., Wang, D., Liu, J., Bennett, P., McAuley, J.J.: Representing and recommending shopping baskets with complementarity, compatibility and loyalty. In: International Conference on Information and Knowledge Management (CIKM)(2018)
10. Wan, S., Lan, Y., Wang, P., Guo, J., Xu, J., Cheng, X.: Next basket recommendation with neural networks. In: ACM Conference on Recommender Systems (RecSys) (2015)
11. Yu, F., Liu, Q., Wu, S., Wang, L., Tan, T.: A dynamic recurrent model for next basket recommendation. International ACM SIGIR Conference on Research and Development in Information Retrieval (SIGIR) (2016)

Deep Matrix Factorization on Graphs: Application to Collaborative Filtering

Aanchal Mongia[1] , Vidit Jain[1], and Angshul Majumdar[2]([✉])

[1] Department of Computer Science and Engineering, IIIT-Delhi, Delhi, India
{aanchalm,vidit17121,angshul}@iiitd.ac.in
[2] Department of Electronics and Communications, IIIT-Delhi, Delhi, India

Abstract. This work addresses the problem of completing a partially filled matrix incorporating metadata associated with the rows and columns. The basic operation of matrix completion is modeled via deep matrix factorization, and the metadata associations are modeled as graphs. The problem is formally modeled as deep matrix factorization regularized by multiple graph Laplacians. The practical problem of collaborative filtering is an ideal candidate for the proposed solution. It needs to predict missing ratings between users and items, given demographic data of users and metadata associated with items. We show that the proposed solution improves over the state-of-the-art in collaborative filtering.

Keywords: Deep matrix factorization · Graph regularization · Collaborative filtering

1 Introduction

Today Collaborative Filtering (CF) is the de facto approach for recommender systems. The said problem can be modeled as matrix completion. Assuming that users and items are along the rows and columns of a matrix, the elements of the matrix are the ratings of users on items. In practice, the matrix is only partially filled. The objective of is to predict the missing ratings; in other words – completing the matrix. Initial studies on this topic relied on linear interpolation techniques to predict the ratings. User based techniques [3] take the user's ratings as the basis for interpolation and item based techniques [12] take the ratings of all users on the items as basis. There have been techniques like [18] to combine user and item based techniques. Such linear interpolation based techniques are easy to interpret, but do not always yield the best possible results. More powerful albeit abstract techniques have been used since the mid 2000s' For a survey of such interpolation techniques, the reader can peruse [2]. Currently latent factor modeling [6] is the de facto standard in collaborative filtering. It factors the ratings matrix into a users' latent factor matrix and items' latent factor matrix, thereby posing matrix completion as a factorization problem [8]. Another class of methods closely related to latent factor modeling, is the nuclear norm based

© Springer Nature Switzerland AG 2020
H. Yang et al. (Eds.): ICONIP 2020, CCIS 1332, pp. 754–762, 2020.
https://doi.org/10.1007/978-3-030-63820-7_86

matrix completion [13]. Theoretically the convex formulation [13] offers better guarantees compared to the non-convex factorization approach [8], however in [15] the limitations of the convex formulation were explicitly explained for the CF scenario. More recent techniques account for metadata associated with the users and items as graphs [5,11]. In [5] graph regularization is applied on the factorization based approach where as in [11] nuclear norm minimization was regularized by graph Laplacian. The success of deep learning led to deep matrix factorization model for CF [10]; note that [10] did not employ graph regularization and did not incorporate any metadata. In this paper, we propose to combine the graph regularization of [5,11] with the deep matrix factorization model of [10]. The goal is to improve the rating prediction performance compared to the state-of-the-art. Mathematically the resulting formulation leads to graph Laplacian regularized deep matrix factorization model. We solve it using alternating direction method of multipliers. Experiments of three benchmark movie recommendation datasets show that our proposed technique improves over the state-of-the-art approaches.

2   Literature Review

2.1   Basics of Latent Factor Model

The problem of collaborative filtering can be expressed in the following fashion

$$Y = R(X) + N \tag{1}$$

Here the matrix X is the ratings matrix; we assume that users are along the rows and items along the columns. R is the restriction operator, it passes the value of the available ratings from X to Y; Y is the partially filled matrix of observed ratings. The noise in the system N is assumed to be Normally distributed. The problem is to solve for X given Y and R. The latent factor model [6] assumes that the user's choice is determined by certain hidden factors. The items possess these factors to a certain extent. If there is a match between the user's propensity towards the factors, and the intensity with which these factors are present in the item, the user likes the item and rates it high. This phenomenon is modeled as an inner-product between the user's and item's latent factors. When all the users and items are considered, one can express the ratings matrix (X) in the following form –

$$X = UV \tag{2}$$

Here U^T denotes the users' latent factor matrix and V denotes the items' latent factor matrix. For collaborative filtering, the matrix factorization formulation is embedded in (1) giving rise to –

$$Y = R(UV) + N \tag{3}$$

The solution to (3) is posed as follows,

$$\min_{U,V} \|Y - R(UV)\|_F^2 + \lambda \left(\|U\|_F^2 + \|V\|_F^2 \right) \tag{4}$$

The first term is the data fidelity term; the Ridge type regularization on the latent factor matrices prevent over-fitting.

A more direct approach is to solve the original problem (1) by exploiting the inherent low-rank of the matrix X. This is posed as,

$$\min_X \|Y - R(X)\|_F^2 + \lambda \|X\|_* \tag{5}$$

In practice the convex surrogate of rank, i.e. the nuclear norm is used [4]

2.2   Matrix Completion on Graphs

The neighborhood based models of the yesteryears [3,12,18], although less accurate than the latent factor model were easily interpretable. Studies like [5] proposed combining the best of both worlds. They encoded the neighborhood information in graph Laplacians,

$$\min_{U,V} \|Y - R(UV)\|_F^2 + \lambda \left(Tr \left(U^T L_U U \right) + Tr \left(V L_V V^T \right) \right) \tag{6}$$

Here L_U and L_V are the graph Laplacians for the user and item latent factor matrices respectively. In [11] a similar idea was proposed for the nuclear norm minimization based completion problem.

$$\min_X \|Y - R(X)\|_F^2 + \mu \|X\|_* + \lambda \left(Tr \left(X L_U X^T \right) + Tr \left(X^T L_V X \right) \right) \tag{7}$$

2.3   Deep Matrix Factorization

Deep matrix factorization extends the standard matrix factorization into deeper layers [17],

$$\min_{U_1, U_2, U_3, V} \|X - U_1 U_2 U_3 V\|_F^2 + \lambda \left(\sum_i \|U_i\|_F^2 + \|V\|_F^2 \right) \tag{8}$$
$$\text{s.t.} U_2 \geq 0, \ U_3 \geq 0 \& V \geq 0$$

The non-negativity constraint ensures that the different layers do not collapse; it leads to ReLU type activation.

This model was incorporated into the matrix completion framework by [10].

$$\min_{U_1, U_2, U_3, V} \|Y - R(U_1 U_2 U_3 V)\|_F^2 + \lambda \left(\sum_i \|U_i\|_F^2 + \|V\|_F^2 \right) \tag{9}$$
$$\text{s.t.} U_2 \geq 0, U_3 \geq 0 \& V \geq 0$$

3   Proposed Formulation

In the past it has been seen that deep matrix factorization (9) improves the shallow models (in the absence of any auxiliary information). When auxiliary information is present, it has been elegantly introduced into the (shallow) matrix factorization framework (6) as graph regularization. This work shows that one can improve over either of these by combining graph regularization with deep matrix factorization.

The basic idea in graph regularized matrix factorization (6) is to regularize the user (U) and item (V) latent factors by their corresponding graph Laplacians. We follow the same idea here. The first task is to identify the user and item latent factors in the deep factorization framework. A 4 layer deep factorization model can be expressed as

$$X_{M \times N} = \underbrace{U_{M \times p}}_{user} F_{p \times q} G_{q \times r} \underbrace{V_{r \times N}}_{item} \tag{10}$$

Here X is the rating's matrix for M users and N products. It is factored into 4 latent factors – U, F, G and V. Looking at the dimensions of each, one can easily identify that U corresponds to the user latent factors and V the item latent factors; F and G are deep latent factors. Once the user and item latent factors are identified, the cost function to be solved can be expressed as –

$$\min_{U,F,G,V} \|Y - R(UFGV)\|_F^2 + \lambda \left(Tr \left(U^T L_U U \right) + Tr \left(V L_V V^T \right) \right)$$
$$\text{s.t.} F \geq 0, G \geq 0 \text{and} V \geq 0 \tag{11}$$

The said cost, incorporates only one type of similarity (each) for the users and items. One can compute multiple types of similarities, e.g. similarities can arise from different definitions, like cosine, correlation, Jaccard etc; it can also arise from different sources like users' demography and social network information; for items, different similarities can be computed based on product description. In order to model such differing possibilities, one needs to regularize deep matrix factorization from multiple graphs, in the fashion of [11]. This leads to our final formulation of deep matrix factorization on multiple graphs.

$$\min_{U,F,G,V} \|Y - R(UFGV)\|_F^2 + \lambda \left(\sum_i Tr \left(U^T L_{U_i} U \right) + \sum_j Tr \left(V L_{V_j} V^T \right) \right)$$
$$\text{s.t.} F \geq 0, G \geq 0 \& V \geq 0 \tag{12}$$

Ideally one needs different regularization parameters for each penalty term; but this would increase the tuning time drastically. To keep it simple, we have kept only one regularization parameter .

To solve (12), we first decouple it using the Majorization Minimization (MM) framework [16]. In an iterative fashion we solve the following,

$$\min_{U,F,G,V} \|B - UFGV\|_F^2 + \lambda \left(\sum_i Tr \left(U^T L_{U_i} U \right) + \sum_j Tr \left(V L_{V_j} V^T \right) \right)$$
$$\text{s.t.} F \geq 0, G \geq 0 \& V \geq 0 \tag{13}$$

where $B = (UFGV)_{k-1} + \frac{1}{\alpha} R^T \left(Y - R(UFGV)_{k-1} \right)$; α is the highest eigenvalue of $R^T R$. Here k denotes the iteration.

The solution for (13) proceeds by updating the variables in an alternating fashion. Here the super-script 'l' indicates the inner iterations (within k). Such an approach is called alternating direction method of multipliers (ADMM). The updates are shown as follows –

$$U \leftarrow \min_{U} \left\| B - U F^{(l-1)} G^{(l-1)} V^{(l-1)} \right\|_F^2 + \lambda \sum_i Tr \left(U^T L_{U_i} U \right)$$

$$F \leftarrow \min_{F} \left\| B - U^{(l)} F G^{(l-1)} V^{(l-1)} \right\|_F^2$$

$$G \leftarrow \min_{G} \left\| B - U^{(l)} F^{(l)} G V^{(l-1)} \right\|_F^2$$

$$V \leftarrow \min_{V} \left\| B - U^{(l)} F^{(l)} G^{(l)} V \right\|_F^2 + \lambda \sum_j Tr \left(V L_{V_j} V^T \right)$$

Here we have abused the notations slightly. We have not shown the positivity constraints explicitly. These will be incorporated during the updates of individual variables.

The solutions to the updates of F and G are given in [17],

$$F = \left(U^{(l)} \right)^\dagger B \left(G^{(l-1)} V^{(l-1)} \right)^\dagger \tag{14}$$

$$G = \left(U^{(l)} F^{(l)} \right)^\dagger B \left(V^{(l-1)} \right)^\dagger \tag{15}$$

Here $(\cdot)^\dagger$ denotes pseudoinverse. Once the variables F and G are updated given the formulae, non-negativity constraint is applied by forcing the negative entries in them to be zeroes.

For solving U, we take the derivative of the cost function and equate it to 0. This leads to –

$$\lambda L_U U + U F^{(l-1)} G^{(l-1)} V^{(l-1)} \left(F^{(l-1)} G^{(l-1)} V^{(l-1)} \right)^T = B \left(F^{(l-1)} G^{(l-1)} V^{(l-1)} \right)^T \tag{16}$$

where $L_U = \sum_i L_{U_i}$.

Note that (16) is actually a Sylvester's equation of the form $A_1 X + X A_2 = C$ with $\lambda L_U = A_1$, $A_2 = F^{(l-1)} G^{(l-1)} V^{(l-1)} \left(F^{(l-1)} G^{(l-1)} V^{(l-1)} \right)^T$ and $C = B \left(F^{(l-1)} G^{(l-1)} V^{(l-1)} \right)^T$. There are efficient solvers for the same. The solution for V can be similarly obtained.

Here we have shown the derivation for 4 layers; it can be easily generalized to N layers. In general, one needs N-2 Moore-Penrose pseudoinverses and 2 Sylvester's equations. The pseudo-inverse has a computational complexity of $O(n^w)$ where $n < 2.37$ and is conjectured to be 2. The complexity of the Sylvster's equation depends on the method used for solving it. It can be $O(n \log n)$ where $n > 2.37$ or $O(n^3)$.

In [17] it was mentioned that faster convergence to the algorithm is achieved when the variables are initialized properly. The initialization was easy in [17] since it was a fully observed system; ours is partially observed. To get a fully observed system we fill the partially observed ratings matrix by baseline prediction [7].

4   Experimental Results

4.1   Datasets

We have used three datasets. The first two are from Movielens[1] - the 100 K and 1M. The 100 K dataset consists ratings from 943 users on 1682 movies. The 1M dataset consists of 1 million ratings for 3900 movies by 6040 users. For both the datasets auxilliary information on user's age, gender, occupation and location is available; for the movies the genre information is available, along with its IMDB link, title, cast etc.

The third dataset is a new one called the Indian regional movie database (IRMD)[2]. It is collected from diverse range of Indian viewers with varying demographics. The complete description is available at [1]. It is a collection of approximately 10 K ratings, rated by 924 users on 2850 regional movies. The details of the dataset are provided in [1]. Out of the user metadata available, we have taken user age (derived from date of birth), gender, occupation and language. While, for the movie metadata only movie average rating, genre and language is considered.

For all the datasets, the multiple graph Laplacians are generated from different kinds of metadata; for users there will be one from age, another from gender, the third one on occupation and the last one on language. The graphs have been generated by the cosine distance of one hot encoded vectors from each kind of metadata. For the movies one can construct multiple graph Laplacians from genre and language (available for IRMD).

4.2   Benchmark Algorithms

Since our work combines concepts from multi-graph regularized matrix completion (MGRMC) [11] and deep latent factor model (DLFM) [10], it is natural that we compare against these two.

Along with these we compares with two recently published studies – deep heterogeneous autoencoders (DHA) [9] and deep collaborative filtering (DCF) [14]. The parameter values required for producing the results have been taken from the respective papers.

For all the datasets, we follow the standard protocol of 5 fold cross validation (the splits are fixed). For the proposed technique (MGRDMF), we have found out the value of (the only parameter) by 4 fold cross validation in the training set.

4.3   Results

The standard metrics for evaluation on these datasets are mean absolute error (MAE), precision and recall. MAE computes the deviation between predicted

---

[1] https://grouplens.org/datasets/movielens/.
[2] https://goo.gl/EmTPv6.

and actual ratings. For computing the precision (@10) and recall (@10) the ratings were binarized with the threshold of 3 on a 5 point scale, i.e. higher than 3 was considered good and lower than 3 was considered bad (Tables 1, 2 and 3).

Table 1. Results on 100K Movielens

Metric	Proposed	MGRMC	DLFM	DHA	DCF
MAE	.730	.735	**.726**	.819	.739
Prec@10	**.547**	.536	.522	.486	.528
Rec@10	**.663**	.658	.649	.574	.651

Table 2. Results on 1M Movielens

Metric	Proposed	MGRMC	DLFM	DHA	DCF
MAE	.621	.622	.678	.727	.705
Prec@10	.702	.691	.691	.614	.697
Rec@10	.650	.641	.635	.599	.643

Table 3. Results on IRMD

Metric	Proposed	MGRMC	DLFM	DHA	DCF
MAE	.620	.617	.623	.664	.624
Prec@10	.694	.689	.673	.607	.680
Rec@10	.639	.632	.627	.576	.631

The result shows that our method is not the best in terms of MAE, but is very close to the best results – less than 1% variation from the best results. In terms of precision and recall our method outperforms all others.

Our proposed technique is non-convex. With the proposed initialization, the method converges very fast. The empirical convergence plot the 100 K dataset is shown in Fig. 1. Note that we see jumps after every 5 iterations since we run the inner loop for those many iterations.

All the experiments were run on an Intel i7 processor with 32 GB RAM running a 64 bit Windows 10. The proposed technique (3 layers), MGRMC and DLFM were based on Matlab; DHA and DCF used Python. The run-times are shown in Table 4. We find that the DHA and DCF are slower than ours by almost an order of magnitude. MGRMC is that fastest; this is expected since it is a shallow technique. DLFM is slightly faster than ours since it does not have to solve Sylvester's equation in every iteration.

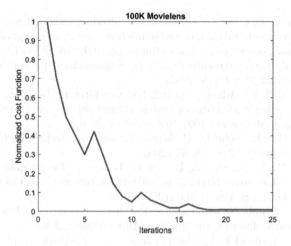

Fig. 1. Empirical convergence plot

Table 4. Comparison of runtimes (in minutes)

Dataset	Proposed	MGRMC	DLFM	DHA	DCF
100K	1:51	1:12	1:22	14:20	17:08
1M	11:29	4:53	7:39	101:33:00	132:48:00
IRMD	1:07	0:52	1:01	12:29	15:58

5 Conclusion

This work proposes a deep matrix factorization based matrix completion technique regularized by multiple graph Laplacians. The technique has shown been applied to the problem of collaborative filtering. Results show that the proposed model improves over the state-of-the-art.

Note that the technique is generic enough to be applied to other problems. Many problems in bioinformatics can be modeled thus; for example drug-target interactions, mRNA-miRNA interactions, protein-lipid interactions etc.

References

1. Agarwal, P., Verma, R., Majumdar, A.: Indian regional movie dataset for recommender systems. arXiv preprint arXiv:1801.02203 (2018)
2. Bobadilla, J., Ortega, F., Hernando, A., Gutiérrez, A.: Recommender systems survey. Knowl.-based Syst. **46**, 109–132 (2013)
3. Breese, J.S., Heckerman, D., Kadie, C.: Empirical analysis of predictive algorithms for collaborative filtering. arXiv preprint arXiv:1301.7363 (2013)
4. Candès, E.J., Tao, T.: The power of convex relaxation: near-optimal matrix completion. IEEE Trans. Inf. Theory **56**(5), 2053–2080 (2010)

5. Gu, Q., Zhou, J., Ding, C.: Collaborative filtering: weighted nonnegative matrix factorization incorporating user and item graphs. In: Proceedings of the 2010 SIAM International Conference on Data Mining, pp. 199–210. SIAM (2010)
6. Hofmann, T.: Latent semantic models for collaborative filtering. ACM Trans. Inf. Syst. (TOIS) **22**(1), 89–115 (2004)
7. Koren, Y., Bell, R.: Advances in collaborative filtering. In: Ricci, F., Rokach, L., Shapira, B. (eds.) Recommender Systems Handbook, pp. 77–118. Springer, Boston (2015). https://doi.org/10.1007/978-1-4899-7637-6_3
8. Koren, Y., Bell, R., Volinsky, C.: Matrix factorization techniques for recommender systems. Computer **42**(8), 30–37 (2009)
9. Li, T., Ma, Y., Xu, J., Stenger, B., Liu, C., Hirate, Y.: Deep heterogeneous autoencoders for collaborative filtering. In: 2018 IEEE International Conference on Data Mining (ICDM), pp. 1164–1169. IEEE (2018)
10. Mongia, A., Jhamb, N., Chouzenoux, E., Majumdar, A.: Deep latent factor model for collaborative filtering. Sig. Process. **169**, 107366 (2020)
11. Mongia, A., Majumdar, A.: Matrix completion on multiple graphs: application in collaborative filtering. Sig. Process. **165**, 144–148 (2019)
12. Sarwar, B., Karypis, G., Konstan, J., Riedl, J.: Item-based collaborative filtering recommendation algorithms. In: Proceedings of the 10th International Conference on World Wide Web, pp. 285–295 (2001)
13. Shamir, O., Shalev-Shwartz, S.: Collaborative filtering with the trace norm: learning, bounding, and transducing. In: Proceedings of the 24th Annual Conference on Learning Theory, pp. 661–678 (2011)
14. Shi, C., et al.: Deep collaborative filtering with multi-aspect information in heterogeneous networks. IEEE Trans. Knowl. Data Eng. (2019)
15. Shi, X., Yu, P.S.: Limitations of matrix completion via trace norm minimization. ACM SIGKDD Explor. Newsl. **12**(2), 16–20 (2011)
16. Sun, Y., Babu, P., Palomar, D.P.: Majorization-minimization algorithms in signal processing, communications, and machine learning. IEEE Trans. Sig. Process. **65**(3), 794–816 (2016)
17. Trigeorgis, G., Bousmalis, K., Zafeiriou, S., Schuller, B.W.: A deep matrix factorization method for learning attribute representations. IEEE Trans. Pattern Anal. Mach. Intell. **39**(3), 417–429 (2016)
18. Wang, J., De Vries, A.P., Reinders, M.J.: Unifying user-based and item-based collaborative filtering approaches by similarity fusion. In: Proceedings of the 29th Annual International ACM SIGIR Conference on Research and Development in Information Retrieval, pp. 501–508 (2006)

Improving Social Recommendations with Item Relationships

Haifeng Liu[1], Hongfei Lin[1($\boxtimes$)], Bo Xu[1], Liang Yang[1], Yuan Lin[1($\boxtimes$)], Yonghe Chu[1], Wenqi Fan[2], and Nan Zhao[1]

[1] Dalian University of Technology, Dalian, Liaoning, China
{liuhaifeng,yhchu,nanzhao}@mail.dlut.edu.cn,
{hflin,xubo,liang,zhlin}@dlut.edu.cn
[2] City University of Hong Kong, Kowloon, Hong Kong, China
wenqifan03@gmail.com

Abstract. Social recommendations have witnessed rapid developments for improving the performance of recommender systems, due to the growing influence of social networks. However, existing social recommendations often ignore to facilitate the substitutable and complementary items to understand items and enhance the recommender systems. We propose a novel graph neural network framework to model the multi-graph data (user-item graph, user-user graph, item-item graph) in social recommendations. In particular, we introduce a viewpoint mechanism to model the relationship between users and items. We conduct an extensive experiment on two public benchmarks, demonstrating significant improvement over several state-of-the-art models.

1 Introduction

Among the existing recommender systems approaches, Collaborative Filtering (CF) is one of the most popular and successful techniques for building advanced recommender systems. The basic idea of CF techniques is that users' preferences can be learned through their history behaviors towards items, such as ratings, clicks, and searching. The majority of CF-based recommender systems can achieve a great performance when huge amounts of history feedback between users and items are available. However, the prediction performance may drop significantly when there exists little interaction between users and items [3], given the fact that recommender systems cannot fully understand users and items through the limited interactions.

Recent studies have shown that social relations among users can provide another stream of potential information for understanding users' preferences, such that the sparse issue can be alleviated and the performance of recommender systems can be further improved. Those methods are known as social recommendations, which are proposed to integrate the information of social relations for enhancing the performance of recommender systems [2]. The rationale behind social recommendations is that users' preferences are similar or influenced by

© Springer Nature Switzerland AG 2020
H. Yang et al. (Eds.): ICONIP 2020, CCIS 1332, pp. 763–770, 2020.
https://doi.org/10.1007/978-3-030-63820-7_87

their social neighbors [3], such as friends and classmates, as suggested by social correlation theories [7]. These social relations have been proven to improve the prediction performance in recommender systems.

Although the aforementioned methods advance social recommendation with GNNs techniques, existing social recommendations methods are still far from satisfactory. Most of them only involve user-item interactions and user-user connections [2,8], while correlations among items could also be of great help. The reason behind this is because items are rather independent and some of them could be similar or related [8].

Moreover, item i_1 and item i_3 are likely to be related since they are co-purchased by user u_1, and item i_1 and i_2 are also likely to be connected or similar as they are bought by two connected social users u_1 and u_2. These relations among items can be formed as the third graph - item-item graph, which can be generated based on users' commonly purchased behaviors or social relations. Thus, it is quite desirable to consider the relations among items for learning better representations of items.

In this paper, we propose a graph neural network framework for the social recommendation (VMRec) by taking advantage of multi-graph and review information. Our major contribution can be summarized as follows,

- We introduce a principle way to utilize the review information to measure the strength among node (users/items) multi-graph (e.g., social graph, user-item graph, and item-item graph) for the social recommendation;
- We propose a GNN-based framework for a social recommendation (VMRec), which integrate review information and multi-graph to learn better user and item representations;

2   The Proposed Framework

In social recommendation systems, there are two set of entities: a user set $U(|U| = M)$ and an item set $I(|I| = N)$, where $M(N)$ is the number of users (items). We define the user-item interactions matrix $R \in \mathbb{R}^{N \times M}$ from user's implicit feedback, where the i, j-th element $r_{i,j}$ is 1 if there is an interaction between user u_i and item v_j, and 0 otherwise. The social graph between users can be described by $S \in \mathbb{S}^{M \times M}$, where $s_{i,j} = 1$ if there is a social relation between user u_i and user u_j, and 0 otherwise. The item-item graph can be denoted as $I \in \mathbb{I}^{N \times N}$, where $I_{i,j} = 1$ if there is a connection between item i_1 and item i_2, and 0 otherwise. Given an interactions matrix R, social graph S and item-item graph I, we aim to predict the unobserved entries (i.e., where $r_{i,j} = 0$) in R.

2.1   Model Architecture

There are three main components in our model, including embedding layer, graph modeling, and prediction modeling. The first component is embedding layer, which is proposed to combine review text and free embedding for users and items. The second component is graph modeling, which aims to learn the latent factors of users and items from different perspectives. The third component is prediction modeling for finalizing the user and item representation for prediction.

2.2 Embedding Layer

Users can provide their reviews towards items and these reviews can help characterize representations of users and items. Inspired by the Natural Language Processing, we employ the Word2Vec to initial the words in the review sentences, and then take the average of all words representation of reviews for users or items. They can be denoted as $p^r \in \mathbb{R}^{M \times D}$ for users text representation and $q^r \in \mathbb{R}^{N \times D}$ for items text representation with the dimension size D. In addition, we also introduce the free user and item representation, denoted as $p^g \in \mathbb{R}^{M \times D}$ for users and $q^g \in \mathbb{R}^{N \times D}$ for items.

Then, we introduce to fuse these two kinds of representation via neural networks to obtain user representation p_u^f and item representation q_i^f as follows,

$$p_u^f = g(W \times [p_u^r, p_u^g] + b) \tag{1}$$

$$q_i^f = g(W \times [q_i^r, q_i^g] + b) \tag{2}$$

where W and b are a transformation matrix and bias, and $g(*)$ is a non-linear function like ReLU. $[p_u^r, p_u^g]$ is the concatenation operation.

2.3 Graph Modeling

In addition to the user-item graph, the social graph and item-item graph provides a great opportunity to learn user and item representations from different perspectives. The GNNs-based social recommender systems employ graph neural networks to aggregate graph feature of neighboring nodes, which makes the aggravated representation more powerful. However, GNNs-based social recommender systems [3] only design for a single graph or two graphs, real-world scenarios often contain multiple interactive graphs. In this paper, we extend the graph neural network into a multi-graph with viewpoint mechanism for social recommender system.

User-Item Aggregation. To learn representations of users in the user-item graph, since different items contribute differently to user purchased behaviors, we introduce to incorporate the review information to differentiate the importance of items as follows,

$$p_u^p = Aggre_{user-item}\{\sum_{i \in R_u} v_{u,i} q_i^f\} \tag{3}$$

where $v_{u,i}$ is the important weight between user u and item i. In particular, $v_{u,i}$ can be calculated through user and item review information with viewpoint mechanism as follows,

$$v_{u,i} = \exp(-\gamma \|p_u^r - q_i^r\|^2) \tag{4}$$

where $\boldsymbol{p}_u^r$ and $\boldsymbol{q}_i^r$ are the user's review vector and item's review vector. γ is hyper-parameter.

Social Aggregation. The item-item aggregation is similar to social aggregation, here we ignored the item-item part for simply. As suggested by social theories [7], users are more likely to be influenced by their friends [2]. It is important to integrate social relations information into learning user representations. Moreover, tie strengths among users can differently influence users' behaviors. In particular, users in strong tie might share more similar preferences than users in weak tie. To consider these heterogeneous strengths of social relations, we introduce to differentiate users' local neighbors during aggregation operation in graph neural networks as follows,

$$\boldsymbol{p}_u^g = \sigma(\boldsymbol{W} \cdot Aggre_{social}\{\sum_{a \in S_u} v_{u,a}(\boldsymbol{p}_u^g \odot \boldsymbol{p}_a^g)\} + \boldsymbol{b}) \tag{5}$$

where S_u means social friends set of user u, and the $\odot$ denote the element-wise product. Similarly, $v_{u,a}$ is the important weight between user u and his friend a, and $v_{u,a}$ can be calculated through user and social friend review information with viewpoint mechanism as follows,

$$v_{u,a} = \exp(-\gamma\|\boldsymbol{p}_u^r - \boldsymbol{p}_a^r\|^2) \tag{6}$$

where $\boldsymbol{p}_u^r$ and $\boldsymbol{p}_a^r$ are the user's review vector and friend's review vector.

In addition to the directly connected neighbors, distant neighbors can also be beneficial, that is due to the fact that information can be diffused throughout the social network, and users might be affected by the k-hop neighbors. Therefore, we introduce to aggregate social information through k-layer aggregation as follows,

$$\boldsymbol{p}_u^{g^{k+1}} = \sigma(\boldsymbol{W} \cdot Aggre_{social}\{\sum_{a \in S_u} v_{u,a}(\boldsymbol{p}_u^{g^k} \odot \boldsymbol{p}_a^{g^k})\} + \boldsymbol{b}) \tag{7}$$

where $\boldsymbol{p}_u^{g^k}$ denotes the user u representation after k-layer aggregation operation. The user fusion representation $\boldsymbol{p}_u^f$ is equal to $\boldsymbol{p}_u^{g^k}$ when $k=0$.

2.4 Prediction Modeling

The last component in our proposed model is prediction modeling, which aims to finalize the user and item representation for prediction.

As the social graph and user-item graph provide important signals to understand users preferences, we propose to obtain the final user representation $\boldsymbol{p}_u$ as follows:

$$\boldsymbol{p}_u = \boldsymbol{p}_u^f \oplus \boldsymbol{p}_u^{g^{k+1}} \oplus \boldsymbol{p}_u^p \tag{8}$$

$$\boldsymbol{q}_i = \boldsymbol{q}_i^f \oplus \boldsymbol{q}_i^{g^{k+1}} \tag{9}$$

$$r_{ui} = \boldsymbol{p}_u^T \boldsymbol{q}_i \tag{10}$$

where $\oplus$ indicates summation operation. Likewise, we introduce to extract useful information from the item-item graph to enrich the representation of item as Eq. 9. With the user and item representation (e.g., $\boldsymbol{p}_u$ and $\boldsymbol{q}_i$), we perform score prediction via the inner product as Eq. 10.

2.5 Model Training

In order to learn the model parameters of our proposed model, we adopt the pair-wise loss as our objective for the Top-k recommendation task [8] as follows,

$$\min_{\theta} L = \sum_{u=1}^{M} \sum_{(i,j)\in R_u} -\sigma(r_{ui} - r_{uj}) + \lambda\|\theta\|^2 \tag{11}$$

where $\sigma(\cdot)$ is a sigmoid function. M denote the number of user-item pairs for training. θ denotes all trainable model parameters in our VMRec framework. λ is a regularization parameter that controls the complexity of user and item graph representation matrices. R_u denotes user u interactive items set. By optimizing the loss function, all parameters can be tuned via backward propagation.

3   Experiment Results and Discuss

3.1   Experimental Settings

Datasets. In our experiments, we choose two representative datasets Yelp and Flickr. In these two datasets, the user-item interactions can be seem as the user-item graph, and the user-user connections are regarded as a social graph. Table 1 summary the statistics the two datasets. Similar to many studies [8], we randomly select 90% of data for training, the rest of the data for testing. To tune the parameters, we randomly selected 10% of train data as the validation set.

Table 1. Statistics of the two datasets

Datasets	Yelp	Flickr
# Users	17,237	8,358
# Items	38,342	82,120
# Rating Density	0.031%	0.046%
# User-User Density	0.048%	0.268%
# Item-Item Density	0.001%	0.002%

Baselines. To evaluate the performance, we compared our proposed model VMRec with seven representative baselines, including traditional recommender system without social network information (BPR-MF [6] and SVD++ [4]), tradition social recommender systems (ContextMF [5]), deep neural networks based social recommender systems (TrustSVD [4]), and graph neural network based recommender system (DiffNet [8], GC-MC [1], PinSage [9]). Some of the original baseline implementations (BPR-MF and TrustSVD) are for rating prediction on recommendations. Therefore we adjust their objectives to pair-wise prediction with BPR loss using negative sampling.

Evaluation Metrics. We use two widely-used metrics [8] to evaluate the performance of recommender systems: NDCG@N and HR@N, where N is the number of recommended items. HR@N refers to the ratio of recovered items to the top-N recommended and NDCG@N measures the ranking performance of the recommender list in the testing data.

Table 2. Overall results of different algorithms.

Models	Yelp				Flickr			
	HR		NDCG		HR		NDCG	
	$N = 5$	$N = 10$	$N = 5$	$N = 10$	$N = 5$	$N = 10$	$N = 5$	$N = 10$
TrustSVD	0.1906	0.2915	0.1385	0.1738	0.1072	0.1427	0.0970	0.1085
ContextMF	0.2045	0.3043	0.1484	0.1818	0.1095	0.1433	0.0920	0.1102
GC-MC	0.1932	0.2937	0.1420	0.1740	0.0897	0.1182	0.0795	0.0956
PinSage	0.2099	0.3065	0.1536	0.1868	0.0925	0.1242	0.0842	0.0991
DiffNet	0.2276	0.3477	0.1679	0.2121	0.1210	0.1641	0.1142	0.1273
VMRec	**0.2445**	**0.3630**	**0.1772**	**0.2203**	**0.1410**	**0.1688**	**0.1252**	**0.1300**

Parameter Setting. To fairly compare the performance of models, we trained all of the models with the BPR loss for ranking recommendation. We randomly initialized user and item free representation with a Gaussian distribution, where the mean and standard deviation is 0 and 0.01. We used Adam optimizer to optimize all parameters with 0.001 learning rate. The latent factor dimension is set to 64, and $\gamma = \frac{1}{64}$. We used $Relu$ as the activation function in neural network. We set the depth parameter $K = 2$ for the two datasets.

3.2 Performance Comparison

The performance of different recommender system HR@N and NDCG@N is shown in Table 2. We can observe that TrustSVD, and ContextMF perform the worst performance among all the baselines across both datasets, that is due to the face that they model the user-item interactions via the linear inner product (MF-based methods). Meanwhile, GC-MC and PinSage, which is based on graph neural network architecture, can obtain much better performance than MF-based. Among baselines, DiffNet shows quite strong performance. Note that Diffnet is proposed to harness the power graph neural networks to learn representations in social recommendations. This performance gain implies once more the power of graph neural networks in recommender systems. Our proposed method VMRec consistently outperforms all the baseline methods. In particular, VMRec improves over DiffNet about 10% of HR on both datasets. Compared with Diffnet, we explicitly incorporate the relationships between items for learning items representation.

3.3 Detailed Model Analysis

The Effect of Viewpoint Mechanism. In this subsection, we analyze the effect of Viewpoint Mechanism on the performance of our model by comparing with two variants (VMRec-GCN and VMRec-One). The $v_{u,i}$ in VMRec-GCN is set to $\frac{1}{|R_u|}$ in Eq. (6), while $v_{u,i}$ in VMRec-One is set to 1 for all user-item pair. In VMRec-Viewpoint, we adopt viewpoint mechanism to calculate the $v_{u,i}$ from user and item reviews.

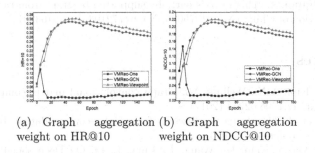

(a) Graph aggregation weight on HR@10   (b) Graph aggregation weight on NDCG@10

Fig. 1. Different graph representation process performance on Yelp

Figure 1 shows the performance of different graph aggregation weight on Yelp dataset. We can observe that VMRec-Viewpoint performs better that VMRec-GCN, which implies that user's review information is beneficial to enhance the performance of recommender system. In addition, We can see that VMRec-One without weight information, the performance of item prediction is deteriorated significantly, It justifies our assumption that users' review text can help to learn user or item latent factors and improve the performance of recommendation.

4 Related Work

Among recommender systems, collaborative filtering (CF) methods are the most popular techniques to model the user-item interactions. However, recent studies have shown that these models are limited to modeling the relationship between users and products in a linear space, and cannot capture the complex, non-linear relationship between users and items. To partially alleviate this issue, NeuMF is proposed to model the complex interactions between user and item representations via deep neural network. The GNNs techniques also applied to jointly user-item interactions and user-user connections in social recommendations [2,8]. Diffnet considers the social recommender systems from information propagation, and employs deep influence propagation model to aggregate users' influence in social graph [8].

5 Conclusion

In this paper, we integrated the relationships among items to enhance the performance of social recommendation with graph neural network techniques, In particular, we provided a principled approach to flexible integrate multi-graph (user-item graph, user social graph, and item-item graph). In addition, we introduced the viewpoint mechanism to distinguish the importance among users and items. Experimental results on two real-world datasets show that VMRec can outperform state-of-the-art baselines.

Acknowledgments. This work is partially supported by grant from the Natural Science Foundation of China (No. 61976036, No. 61772103, No. 61632011)

References

1. Berg, R., Kipf, T.N., Welling, M.: Graph convolutional matrix completion. arXiv preprint arXiv:1706.02263 (2017)
2. Fan, W., et al.: Graph neural networks for social recommendation. In: The World Wide Web Conference (2019)
3. Fan, W., Ma, Y., Yin, D., Wang, J., Tang, J., Li, Q.: Deep social collaborative filtering. In: ACM RecSys (2019)
4. Guo, G., Zhang, J., Yorke-Smith, N.: TrustSVD: collaborative filtering with both the explicit and implicit influence of user trust and of item ratings. In: Twenty-Ninth AAAI Conference on Artificial Intelligence (2015)
5. Jiang, M., Cui, P., Wang, F., Zhu, W., Yang, S.: Scalable recommendation with social contextual information. IEEE TKDE **26**, 2789–2802 (2014)
6. Rendle, S.: Factorization machines. In: 2010 IEEE International Conference on Data Mining, pp. 995–1000. IEEE (2010)
7. Tang, J., Chang, Y., Liu, H.: Mining social media with social theories: a survey. SIGKDD Explor. Newsl. **15**, 20–29 (2014)
8. Wu, L., Sun, P., Fu, Y., Hong, R., Wang, X., Wang, M.: A neural influence diffusion model for social recommendation. In: ACM SIGIR (2019)
9. Ying, R., He, R., Chen, K., Eksombatchai, P., Hamilton, W.L., Leskovec, J.: Graph convolutional neural networks for web-scale recommender systems. In: KDD (2018)

MCRN: A New Content-Based Music Classification and Recommendation Network

Yuxu Mao[1], Guoqiang Zhong[1(✉)], Haizhen Wang[1], and Kaizhu Huang[2,3]

[1] Department of Computer Science and Technology, Ocean University of China,
238 Songling Road, Qingdao 266100, China
gqzhong@ouc.edu.cn
[2] Department of Electrical and Electronical Engineering,
Xi'an Jiaotong-Liverpool University, Suzhou 215123, China
[3] Alibaba-Zhejiang University Joint Institute of Frontier Technologies,
Hangzhou 310058, China

Abstract. Music classification and recommendation have received widespread attention in recent years. However, content-based deep music classification approaches are still very rare. Meanwhile, existing music recommendation systems generally rely on collaborative filtering. Unfortunately, this method has serious cold start problem. In this paper, we propose a simple yet effective convolutional neural network named MCRN (short for music classification and recommendation network), for learning the audio content features of music, and facilitating music classification and recommendation. Concretely, to extract the content features of music, the audio is converted into "spectrograms" by Fourier transform. MCRN can effectively extract music content features from the spectrograms. Experimental results show that MCRN outperforms other compared models on music classification and recommendation tasks, demonstrating its superiority over previous approaches.

Keywords: Music classification and recommendation · Information retrieval · Convolutional neural networks · Music spectrogram dataset

1 Introduction

Deep learning has achieved great successes in many fields, such as object detection [5], natural language processing [12], and information retrieval [15]. Particularly, in recent years, there arises much interest in music classification and recommendation with deep learning models [2,16].

For music classification, its performance heavily relies on how effective the features are extracted from the audios. In light of this, most traditional music classification methods extract audio features manually or using feature engineering methods [1]. However, the discriminability of these features is not high enough, so that the music classification accuracy is relatively low. In recent years,

© Springer Nature Switzerland AG 2020
H. Yang et al. (Eds.): ICONIP 2020, CCIS 1332, pp. 771–779, 2020.
https://doi.org/10.1007/978-3-030-63820-7_88

more and more research tries to use deep learning models for music classification. For example, a deep convolutional neural network (CNN) with small filters for music classification was proposed in [7]. However, the CNN model was only applied on the raw waveform audios, where the potential capability of CNN models on 2D/3D image classification was not fully exploited.

For music recommendation tasks, an important problem is how to recommend music to users in line with their preferences. At present, although there is much research on recommendation systems, music recommendation is still a challenging and complicated problem, due to the diversity of music styles and genres. Among quite a few techniques, collaborative filtering is one of the most successful recommendation algorithms [10]. Herlocker et al. [6] first applied the collaborative filtering to music recommendation tasks. However, the collaborative filtering algorithm has the cold start problem, i. e. it is not effective when recommending new or unpopular items to users.

In this paper, we present a simple yet effective music classification and recommendation network called MCRN. To extract the audio content features, we convert audio signal into a spectrogram via the Fourier transformation, as input to MCRN. Since spectrogram contains the frequency distribution of music and vary in sound amplitude, MCRN can extract valuable content features from them. In addition, we collect a music spectrogram dataset containing nearly 200,000 images. It offers an excellent resource for music classification and recommendation research. The dataset is publicly available to facilitate further in-depth research[1]. With this dataset, we show that MCRN is superior to existing music classification and recommendation models.

2   Related Work

Music Classification. During the past few decades, audio recognition are generally realized based on traditional feature extraction on time series. For instance, in [8], MFCC was used to represent audio features for music classification, while Dario et al. [4] proposed to parameterize the short-time sequence features of music through the multivariate autoregressive coefficient. However, these feature extraction methods are based on feature engineering approaches, which may lead to the loss of valuable information in the audios. To overcome the shortcoming, a convolutional recurrent neural network for music classification was proposed in [3], where CNN and RNN were applied to extract and aggregate features, respectively. Frustratingly, this method only extract features in the time domain, while the frequency domain is not considered. Recently, some music classification methods based on 1D CNN have been explored [2]. These methods suppose that 1D CNN is effective for processing audio sequences in music classification.

Music Recommendation. The collaborative filtering has been widely applied in recommendation systems [9,17]. Particularly, some work used the collaborative filtering techniques for music recommendation [13]. They calculated user

---

[1] https://github.com/YX-Mao/Music-spectrogram-dataset.

Table 1. Music categories of the collected music spectrogram dataset.

Breakbeat	Deep House	Disco
Downtempo	Drum and Bass	Dubstep Grime
Electro House	Euro Dance	Trance

Fig. 1. A spectrogram obtained by Fourier transformation from a Deep_house type audio file.

preferences by constructing a music scoring matrix or recording playing coefficients. However, the collaborative filtering algorithms have a serious cold start problem, which is ineffective when recommending unpopular or new songs. To address it, an interesting music recommendation method was proposed by [14], where an attribute-based (i. e. mellow, unpretentious, sophisticated, intense and contemporary) method was used to characterize music content. Furthermore, with the development of deep learning, content-based music recommendation methods have been built based on CNNs [11,16]. Among others, the closest work to this paper is MusicCNNs [16]. Although the same data preprocessing method is adopted in MusicCNNs and this work, we propose a novel CNN architecture that is more effective than MusicCNNs in feature extraction of music content.

3   The Collected Dataset

To the best of our knowledge, there is currently no publicly available music spectrogram dataset. Thus, to facilitate the research of content-based music classification and recommendation, we have collected a new music spectrogram dataset.

We download 9,000 pieces of music from the JunoDownload website, including 9 types of music Table 1. To extract the audio content features, the audio signal is converted into an "image" by the Fourier transformation. The intensity of color on the spectrogram represents the amplitude of the sound at that frequency.

Concretely, the Sound eXchange (SoX) software and the Fourier transformation are adopt to convert the MP3 audio into a spectrogram. Figure 1 shows a partial spectrogram of a piece of music. To ease the training of CNN models, we crop the entire spectrogram to size 256×256 in this work, such that each piece of music is approximately split to 23 slices with a duration of 5 seconds. The image slices after cutting are shown in Fig. 2. To ensure the size of the data to be consistent, the edge parts that cannot be properly cropped in the spectrogram

Fig. 2. Spectrogram of a piece of music after split. The size of image is 256×256.

are ignored. Eventually, we obtain a total of 197,463 spectrograms, which can be used to train the models for music classification and recommendation.

4   Music Classification and Recommendation Network

4.1   Architecture of MCRN

MCRN is a simple yet effective convolutional neural network, which architecture is illustrated in Fig. 3. We describe the details of MCRN in the following.

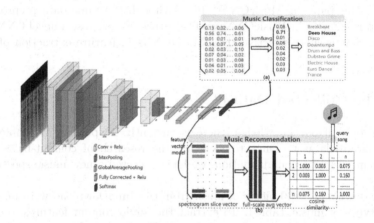

Fig. 3. The overview of MCRN. It can be used for (a) music classification and (b) music recommendation. For more details about the architecture of MCRN and its applications to music classification and recommendation, please refer to the text in Sect. 4.

The spectrogram is passed through a series of convolutional blocks, where seven convolutional layers and four pooling layers are divided into four blocks. Concretely, each of the first two blocks contains two convolutional layers and a max-pooling layer, where the size of the kernels is 3×3, and max-pooling is conducted over a 2×2 pixel window. The structure of the third block is highly similar to the previous two groups. It also contains two convolutional layers and a max-pooling layer, but rather than using the same size of convolutional kernels, we implement the receptive fields of the two convolutional layers using 5×5 and 3×3 kernels, respectively. In addition, the pixel window of the max-pooling is expanded to 4×4. The final block consists of a convolutional layer with 512 convolutional kernels of size 3×3 and a max-pooling layer. To regularize the entire network to prevent from overfitting, a global average pooling layer is followed. These convolutional layers are followed by two fully connected layers with 1024 and 512 dimensions, respectively, using RELU as the activation function.

4.2   Music Classification

The classification probability of spectrogram in each category can be obtained by MCRN, as shown in Fig. 3(a). Since a full-scale spectrogram was cut into multiple small fragments during the data preprocessing, we calculate the classification probability of the music in each category using spectrograms belonging to the same piece of music:

$$P_i^c = 1/T \sum_{t=1}^{T} a_{i,t}^c, \quad c \in \{Breakbeat, \ldots, Trance\}, \tag{1}$$

where T represents the number of spectrograms obtained by cutting a piece of music, and $a_{i,t}^c$ is the classification probability of the t-th slice of the i-th piece of music in category c. We predict the category C of the music by selecting the class with the highest probability:

$$C = \arg \max P_i^c. \tag{2}$$

The music classification method takes into account all spectrograms in a piece of music, i. e. each segment of music contributes to the final classification. Thus, the music classification results obtained by our proposed method are persuasive.

4.3   Music Recommendation

To represent music content, we integrate the spectrogram features extracted by MCRN together to create a full-scale music feature vector. Specifically, a feature vector is first created for each spectrogram based on MCRN. Please note that since each piece of song corresponds to about 23 spectrograms, 23 feature vectors can be obtained for a piece of music. Then, the feature vector of each piece of music is acquired by averaging the feature vectors of all spectrograms belonging to the music. Finally, our strategy for music recommendation is to calculate the similarity between music based on the cosine distance as follows:

$$\cos(X, Y) = \frac{\sum_{i=1}^{n}(x_i \times y_i)}{\sqrt{\sum_{i=1}^{n}(x_i)^2} \times \sqrt{\sum_{i=1}^{n}(y_i)^2}}, \tag{3}$$

where X and Y denotes two different pieces of music, x_i and y_i represent the feature values of the music, and n is the length of the feature vector. A full description of the music recommendation by MCRN is given in Algorithm 1.

Algorithm 1. Music Recommendation

Require: The music feature extractor M based on MCRN, the number of music N, the spectrogram number of a piece of music T, all music spectrogram slices after data preprocessing $D = \{d_{1,1}, d_{1,2}, \ldots, d_{N,T}\}$, the music for recommendation X

Ensure: The recommended music for X

1: Create feature vectors $F = \{f_{1,1}, f_{1,2}, \ldots, f_{N,T}\}$ from all music spectrogram slices in D according to feature extractor M

2: **for** music index $i = 1$ to N **do**

3:    **for** spectrogram index $j = 1$ to T **do**

4:       Select the feature vector of T spectrograms corresponding to the i-th music, $f_i = \{f_{i,1}, d_{i,2}, \ldots, d_{i,T}\}$

5:    **end for**

6:    Calculate the average feature vector of the i-th music: $F_i = 1/T \sum_{t=1}^{T} f_{i,t}$

7:    Add the average feature vector F_i of music to V: $V.append(F_i)$

8: **end for**

9: Calculate the cosine distance between music according to Equation (3)

10: The top 3 pieces of music with the highest similarity to X as its recommendations

---

5   Experiments

5.1   Implementation Details

We train MCRN 10 epochs with a batch size of 64. Each fully-connected layer follows a dropout with a drop rate of 0.5, and add L2 regularizers with the coefficient set to 0.001. An RMSprop optimizer with a learning rate $lr = 1e{-}3$ is adopted for parameter optimization. Since the 2D spectrogram cannot be directly applied to MLP and Softmax regression, we perform dimensionality reduction on the spectrogram to meet their input needs.

5.2   Experiments on Music Classification

To provide more reasonable evaluation, 9,000 pieces of music are divided into training set, validation set and test set according to the ratio of 0.65: 0.25: 0.1. The music of test set only used for the final evaluation of model.

Table 2 shows the classification results obtained by MCRN and some existing music classification approaches, including MLP, Softmax regression and some state-of-the-art deep learning methods. This table shows that MCRN achieves state-of-the-art performance on the music classification, and the total classification accuracy reaches 77.3%. Among 9 types of music, MCRN achieves excellent performance on 7 types of music. Taking the Dubstep Grime as an example, MCRN outperforms the competitors with the superiority result (83.84%). Such results demonstrate the superiority of MCRN on music classification.

5.3   Experiments on Music Recommendation

To verify the effectiveness of MCRN on music recommendation, we conduct recommendation experiments based on each piece of music in test set. The music

Table 2. Results of music classification accuracy by different models on test set.

Model	Breakbeat	Deep House	Disco	Down Tempo	Drum and Bass	Dubstep Grime	Electro House	Euro Dance	Trance	Total acc. (%)
MLP	11.01	41.41	33.00	69.07	61.00	13.03	12.86	53.81	9.09	33.81
Softmax regression	28.62	13.80	28.33	59.79	14.00	13.80	3.81	15.87	44.11	24.69
The model of [11]	75.16	54.25	**78.10**	71.28	89.65	65.06	62.26	58.25	86.53	71.18
The model of [2]	68.70	71.70	76.00	71.20	**92.00**	10.10	68.60	55.20	63.69	64.30
MusicCNNs [16]	67.72	72.86	62.85	58.97	90.42	75.79	**72.91**	57.33	82.87	71.30
MCRN(ours)	**76.77**	**79.80**	71.00	**73.20**	**92.00**	**83.84**	70.50	**60.00**	**89.90**	**77.30**

selected from test set each time is used as the recommendation item, namely query song. As long as the recommended music and query song belong to the same class, we consider that the recommendation is correct. For a fair comparison, similar to MusicCNNs [16], our recommendation experiment also uses cosine distance to measure the similarity between music. The comparison of MCRN with state-of-the-art methods are summarized in Table 3. The table shows that, for music recommendation, MCRN achieves excellent recommendation on top-1 and top-3, with the recommended accuracy is 71.50% and 84.65%, respectively.

Table 3. The comparison of recommendation accuracy of different models on the top-1 and top-3 metrics based on test set. MusicCNNs is an improvement of R-MusicCNNs, where the ReLU activation function in the R-MusicCNNs is replaced with ELU.

Model	top-1 acc.(%)	top-3 acc.(%)
MLP	34.15	60.67
Softmax regression	25.52	46.52
The model of [11]	67.28	82.98
R-MusicCNNs [16]	64.02	77.65
MusicCNNs [16]	64.75	78.01
MCRN (ours)	**71.50**	**84.65**

6 Conclusion

In this paper, a new deep convolutional neural network called MCRN is proposed, which is applied to content-based music classification and recommendation tasks. By learning the audio content features of music, MCRN overcomes the problem of the cold start for music recommendation applications. Importantly, to fully extract audio content features, we convert the audio signal into a form of spectrogram by Fourier transform. We collect a new music spectrogram dataset, which contains nearly 200,000 images. To the best knowledge, this is the first publicly available dataset of music spectrogram. On this dataset, we conduct extensive music classification and recommendation experiments. Experimental results show that MCRN attains new state-of-the-art results on music classification and recommendation tasks.

Acknowledgments. This work was supported by the Major Project for New Generation of AI under Grant No.2018AAA0100400, the National Natural Science Foundation of China (NSFC) under Grant No.41706010, the Joint Fund of the Equipments Pre-Research and Ministry of Education of China under Grant No.6141A020337, and the Fundamental Research Funds for the Central Universities of China.

References

1. Bergstra, J., Casagrande, N., Erhan, D., Eck, D., Kégl, B.: Aggregate features and AdaBoost for music classification. Mach. Learn. **65**(2–3), 473–484 (2006). https://doi.org/10.1007/s10994-006-9019-7
2. Bian, W., Wang, J., Zhuang, B., Yang, J., Wang, S., Xiao, J.: Audio-based music classification with DenseNet and data augmentation. In: Nayak, A.C., Sharma, A. (eds.) PRICAI 2019. LNCS (LNAI), vol. 11672, pp. 56–65. Springer, Cham (2019). https://doi.org/10.1007/978-3-030-29894-4_5
3. Choi, K., Fazekas, G., Sandler, M.B., Cho, K.: Convolutional recurrent neural networks for music classification. In: ICASSP, pp. 2392–2396 (2017)
4. Garciagarcia, D., Arenasgarcia, J., Parradohernandez, E., Diazdemaria, F.: Music genre classification using the temporal structure of songs (2010)
5. He, Y., Zhu, C., Wang, J., Savvides, M., Zhang, X.: Bounding box regression with uncertainty for accurate object detection. In: CVPR, pp. 2888–2897 (2019)
6. Herlocker, J.L., Konstan, J.A., Borchers, A., Riedl, J.: An algorithmic framework for performing collaborative filtering. SIGIR Forum **51**(2), 227–234 (2017)
7. Jongpil, L., Jiyoung, P., Keunhyoung, K., Juhan, N.: SampleCNN: end-to-end deep convolutional neural networks using very small filters for music classification. Appl. Sci. **8**(1), 150 (2018)
8. Kour, G., Mehan, N., Kour, G., Mehan, N.: Music genre classification using MFCC, SVM and BPNN. Int. J. Comput. Appl. **112**(6), 12–14 (2015)
9. Li, D., Lv, Q., Shang, L., Gu, N.: YANA: an efficient privacy-preserving recommender system for online social communities. In: CIKM, pp. 2269–2272 (2011)
10. Liu, X., Qiu, J., Hu, W., Huang, Y., Zhang, S., Liu, H.: Research on personalized recommendation technology based on collaborative filtering. In: ICSC, pp. 41–46 (2019)
11. Murray, M.: Building a music recommender with deep learning. http://mattmurray.net/building-a-music-recommender-with-deep-learning
12. Ren, S., Zhang, Z., Liu, S., Zhou, M., Ma, S.: Unsupervised neural machine translation with SMT as posterior regularization. In: AAAI, pp. 241–248 (2019)
13. Sánchez-Moreno, D., González, A.B.G., Vicente, M.D.M., Batista, V.F.L., García, M.N.M.: A collaborative filtering method for music recommendation using playing coefficients for artists and users. Expert Syst. Appl. **66**, 234–244 (2016)
14. Soleymani, M., Aljanaki, A., Wiering, F., Veltkamp, R.C.: Content-based music recommendation using underlying music preference structure. In: ICME, pp. 1–6 (2015)
15. Yang, X., Wang, N., Song, B., Gao, X.: BoSR: a CNN-based aurora image retrieval method. Neural Netw. **116**, 188–197 (2019)

16. Zhong, G., Wang, H., Jiao, W.: MusicCNNs: a new benchmark on content-based music recommendation. In: Cheng, L., Leung, A.C.S., Ozawa, S. (eds.) ICONIP 2018. LNCS, vol. 11301, pp. 394–405. Springer, Cham (2018). https://doi.org/10.1007/978-3-030-04167-0_36
17. Zhuang, F., Zheng, J., Chen, J., Zhang, X., Shi, C., He, Q.: Transfer collaborative filtering from multiple sources via consensus regularization. Neural Netw. **108**, 287–295 (2018)

Order-Aware Embedding Non-sampling Factorization Machines for Context-Aware Recommendation

Qingzhi Hou[1], Yifeng Chen[2,3,4], Mei Yu[2,3,4], Ruiguo Yu[2,3,4], Jian Yu[2,3,4], Mankun Zhao[2,3,4], Tianyi Xu[2,3,4], and Xuewei Li[2,3,4(✉)]

[1] School of Civil Engineering, Tianjin University, Tianjin, China
qhou@tju.edu.cn
[2] College of Intelligence and Computing, Tianjin University, Tianjin, China
{haichuang,yumei,rgyu,yujian,zmk,tianyi.xu,lixuewei}@tju.edu.cn
[3] Tianjin Key Laboratory of Cognitive Computing and Application, Tianjin, China
[4] Tianjin Key Laboratory of Advanced Networking (TANK Lab), Tianjin, China

Abstract. FM can use the second-order feature interactions. Some researchers combine FM with deep learning to get the high-order interactions. However, these models rely on negative sampling. ENSFM adopts non-sampling and gets fine results, but it does not consider the high-order interactions. In this paper, we add the high-order interactions to ENSFM. We also introduce a technique called Order-aware Embedding. The excellent results show the effectiveness of our model.

Keywords: Context-aware recommendation · Factorization machines · Non-sampling · The high-order interactions · Order-aware embedding

1 Introduction

ENSFM [1] achieves non-sampling, but only considers the second-order interactions. In this paper, we continue to use non-sampling. On this basis, the third-order and the fourth-order interactions are added. We also consider that the use of shared embedding may cause some problems. Therefore, we adopt a technique called Order-aware Embedding to solve these problems. Its main idea is to apply different embeddings to different orders for feature interactions.

The main contributions of this work are summarized as follows: (1)We consider that the high-order interactions have an important influence on performance, so the third-order and the fourth-order interactions are added. (2)We believe that the use of shared embedding will result in learned feature interactions less effective, so we adopt Order-aware Embedding.

2 Preliminaries

2.1 Factorization Machines (FM)

FM is a machine learning algorithm based on MF. The model uses a low-dimensional dense vector to represent the weight of a feature. The number of

H. Yang et al. (Eds.): ICONIP 2020, CCIS 1332, pp. 780–788, 2020.
https://doi.org/10.1007/978-3-030-63820-7_89

user features and item features are denoted by m and n, respectively. By using the factorized parameters, FM captures all interactions between features:

$$\hat{y}_{FM}(x) = w_0 + \sum_{i=1}^{m+n} w_i x_i + \sum_{i=1}^{m+n} \sum_{j=i+1}^{m+n} e_i^T e_j \cdot x_i x_j \tag{1}$$

2.2 Efficient Non-sampling Matrix Factorization

Although the performance of non-sampling matrix factorization is excellent, its shortcoming is also obvious—inefficiency. In order to solve this problem, researchers have proposed some effective solutions [2, 11, 12].

Theorem 1. *A generalized matrix factorization whose prediction function is:*

$$\hat{y}_{uv} = \mathbf{h}^T \left(\mathbf{p}_u \odot \mathbf{q}_v \right) \tag{2}$$

where $\mathbf{p}_u$ and $\mathbf{q}_v$ are representation vectors of user and item, respectively. And $\odot$ denotes the element-wise product of two vectors. Its loss function is:

$$\mathcal{L}(\Theta) = \sum_{u \in U} \sum_{v \in V} c_{uv} \left(y_{uv} - \hat{y}_{uv} \right)^2 \tag{3}$$

where c_{uv} is the weight of sample y_{uv}. It is completely equivalent to that of:

$$\tilde{\mathcal{L}}(\Theta) = \sum_{u \in U} \sum_{v \in V^+} \left(\left(c_{uv}^+ - c_{uv}^- \right) \hat{y}_{uv}^2 - 2 c_{uv}^+ \hat{y}_{uv} \right)$$
$$+ \sum_{i=1}^{d} \sum_{j=1}^{d} \left((h_i h_j) \left(\sum_{u \in U} p_{u,i} p_{u,j} \right) \left(\sum_{v \in V} c_{uv}^- q_{v,i} q_{v,j} \right) \right) \tag{4}$$

3   Our Model—ONFM

3.1   Overview

Using the FM form, ONFM is expressed as:

$$\hat{y}_{FM}(x) = w_0 + \sum_{i=1}^{m+n} w_i x_i + f_2(x) + f_3(x) + f_4(x) \tag{5}$$

$$f_2(x) = h_r \sum_{i=1}^{m+n} \sum_{j=i+1}^{m+n} \left(x_i e_i^2 \odot x_j e_j^2 \right) \tag{6}$$

$$f_3(x) = h_s \sum_{i=1}^{m+n} \sum_{j=i+1}^{m+n} \sum_{k=j+1}^{m+n} \left(x_i e_i^3 \odot x_j e_j^3 \odot x_k e_k^3 \right) \tag{7}$$

$$f_4(x) = h_t \sum_{i=1}^{m+n} \sum_{j=i+1}^{m+n} \sum_{k=j+1}^{m+n} \sum_{l=k+1}^{m+n} \left(x_i e_i^4 \odot x_j e_j^4 \odot x_k e_k^4 \odot x_l e_l^4 \right) \qquad (8)$$

where $f_2(x)$, $f_3(x)$ and $f_4(x)$ denote the second-order, the third-order and the fourth-order, respectively. Figure 1 shows the composition structure of ONFM.

There are five layers—Input, Order-aware Embedding, Feature Pooling, Fully-connected and Output. The input of Input are some high-dimensional sparse vectors obtained by one-hot encoding. We need to convert these special vectors into low-dimensional dense vectors. The role of Order-aware Embedding is to solve this problem. After Order-aware Embedding processing, we get three different sets of low-dimensional dense vectors. The embedding vectors of feature i for different orders can be formulated as [5]:

$$e_i^j = W_i^j X \left[start_i : end_i \right] \qquad (9)$$

Then these low-dimensional dense vectors directly enter Feature Pooling for feature interaction processing. The target of this layer is to reconstruct FM model in Eq. (5) into a completely equivalent generalized MF form:

$$\hat{y}_{FM}(\mathbf{x}) = \mathbf{h}_{aux}^T \left(\mathbf{p}_u \odot \mathbf{q}_v \right) \qquad (10)$$

where $\mathbf{p}_u$, $\mathbf{q}_v$ are two vectors obtained by Feature Pooling. They are only related to the corresponding user and item, not to the objects they interact with.

Finally, the two vectors are input to Fully-connected. Then, we obtain the final prediction $\hat{y}_{FM}$, which represents user u's preference for item v.

3.2   ONFM Theoretical Analysis

The basic theory of ONFM is that the FM model incorporating the high-order interactions in Eq. (5) can be transformed into a MF form in Eq. (10). Then we will prove the correctness of the theory.

Recalling Eq. (5), we consider three parts—$f_2(x)$, $f_3(x)$, $f_4(x)$, they can be transformed into the following form:

$$\begin{aligned} f_2(x) = h_1 & \left(\sum_{i=1}^{m} \sum_{j=i+1}^{m} \left(x_i^u e_i^{u,2} \odot x_j^u e_j^{u,2} \right) + \sum_{i=1}^{n} \sum_{j=i+1}^{n} \left(x_i^v e_i^{v,2} \odot x_j^v e_j^{v,2} \right) \right) \\ & + h_2 \left(\sum_{i=1}^{m} x_i^u e_i^{u,2} \odot \sum_{i=1}^{n} x_i^v e_i^{v,2} \right) \end{aligned} \qquad (11)$$

$$\begin{aligned} f_3(x) = h_3(a+b) + h_4 & \left(\sum_{i=1}^{m} \sum_{j=i+1}^{m} \left(x_i^u e_i^{u,3} \odot x_j^u e_j^{u,3} \right) \odot \sum_{i=1}^{n} x_i^v e_i^{v,3} \right) \\ & + h_4 \left(\sum_{i=1}^{m} x_i^u e_i^{u,3} \odot \sum_{i=1}^{n} \sum_{j=i+1}^{n} \left(x_i^v e_i^{v,3} \odot x_j^v e_j^{v,3} \right) \right) \end{aligned} \qquad (12)$$

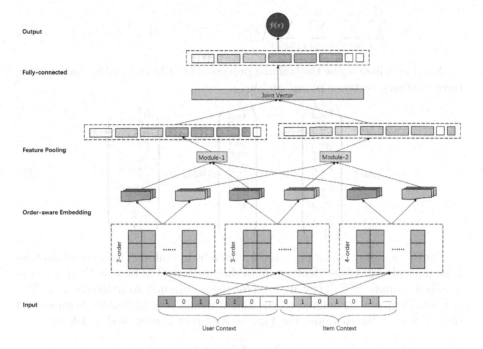

Fig. 1. The overall framework of ONFM.

$$a = \sum_{i=1}^{m} \sum_{j=i+1}^{m} \sum_{k=j+1}^{m} \left(x_i^u e_i^{u,3} \odot x_j^u e_j^{u,3} \odot x_k^u e_k^{u,3} \right) \tag{13}$$

$$b = \sum_{i=1}^{n} \sum_{j=i+1}^{n} \sum_{k=j+1}^{n} \left(x_i^v e_i^{v,3} \odot x_j^v e_j^{v,3} \odot x_k^v e_k^{v,3} \right) \tag{14}$$

$$
\begin{aligned}
f_4(x) &= h_5(c+d) \\
&+ h_6 \left(\sum_{i=1}^{m} \sum_{j=i+1}^{m} \sum_{k=j+1}^{m} \left(x_i^u e_i^{u,4} \odot x_j^u e_j^{u,4} \odot x_k^u e_k^{u,4} \right) \odot \sum_{i=1}^{n} x_i^v e_i^{v,4} \right) \\
&+ h_6 \left(\sum_{i=1}^{m} x_i^u e_i^{u,4} \odot \sum_{i=1}^{n} \sum_{j=i+1}^{n} \sum_{k=j+1}^{n} \left(x_i^v e_i^{v,4} \odot x_j^v e_j^{v,4} \odot x_k^v e_k^{v,4} \right) \right) \\
&+ h_7 \left(\sum_{i=1}^{m} \sum_{j=i+1}^{m} \left(x_i^u e_i^{u,4} \odot x_j^u e_j^{u,4} \right) \odot \sum_{i=1}^{n} \sum_{j=i+1}^{n} \left(x_i^v e_i^{v,4} \odot x_j^v e_j^{v,4} \right) \right)
\end{aligned}
\tag{15}
$$

$$c = \sum_{i=1}^{m} \sum_{j=i+1}^{m} \sum_{k=j+1}^{m} \sum_{l=k+1}^{m} \left(x_i^u e_i^{u,4} \odot x_j^u e_j^{u,4} \odot x_k^u e_k^{u,4} \odot x_l^u e_l^{u,4} \right) \tag{16}$$

$$d = \sum_{i=1}^{n} \sum_{j=i+1}^{n} \sum_{k=j+1}^{n} \sum_{l=k+1}^{n} \left(x_i^v e_i^{v,4} \odot x_j^v e_j^{v,4} \odot x_k^v e_k^{v,4} \odot x_l^v e_l^{v,4} \right) \qquad (17)$$

Next, we will describe the training process of ONFM in detail by constructing three auxiliary vectors—$\mathbf{p}_u$, $\mathbf{q}_v$ and $\mathbf{h}_{aux}$:

$$\mathbf{p}_u = \begin{pmatrix} p_{u,d}^{2,1} \\ p_{u,d}^{3,1} \\ p_{u,d}^{3,2} \\ p_{u,d}^{4,1} \\ p_{u,d}^{4,2} \\ p_{u,d}^{4,3} \\ p_{u,1} \\ 1 \end{pmatrix} ; \mathbf{q}_v = \begin{pmatrix} q_{v,d}^{2,1} \\ q_{v,d}^{3,2} \\ q_{v,d}^{3,1} \\ q_{v,d}^{4,3} \\ q_{v,d}^{4,2} \\ q_{v,d}^{4,1} \\ 1 \\ q_{v,1} \end{pmatrix} ; \mathbf{h}_{aux} = \begin{pmatrix} h_{aux,d}^{2} \\ h_{aux,d}^{4} \\ h_{aux,d}^{4} \\ h_{aux,d}^{6} \\ h_{aux,d}^{7} \\ h_{aux,d}^{6} \\ 1 \\ 1 \end{pmatrix} \qquad (18)$$

For the auxiliary vector $\mathbf{p}_u$, it is calculated by module-1. The input of module-1 are multiple sets of user feature embedding vectors. The first six elements have a unified format—$p_{u,d}^{x,y}$. They are used for the user-item feature interactions. The last two elements are related to the global weight, the first-order features and the self feature interactions. The form of each part is expressed as follows.

$$p_{u,d}^{2,1} = \sum_{i=0}^{m} x_i^u e_i^{u,2} \qquad (19)$$

$$p_{u,d}^{3,1} = \sum_{i=0}^{m} x_i^u e_i^{u,3} \qquad (20)$$

$$p_{u,d}^{3,2} = \sum_{i=0}^{m} \sum_{j=i+1}^{m} \left(x_i^u e_i^{u,3} \odot x_j^u e_j^{u,3} \right) \qquad (21)$$

$$p_{u,d}^{4,1} = \sum_{i=0}^{m} x_i^u e_i^{u,4} \qquad (22)$$

$$p_{u,d}^{4,2} = \sum_{i=0}^{m} \sum_{j=i+1}^{m} \left(x_i^u e_i^{u,4} \odot x_j^u e_j^{u,4} \right) \qquad (23)$$

$$p_{u,d}^{4,3} = \sum_{i=0}^{m} \sum_{j=i+1}^{m} \sum_{k=j+1}^{m} \left(x_i^u e_i^{u,4} \odot x_j^u e_j^{u,4} \odot x_k^u e_k^{u,4} \right) \qquad (24)$$

$$p_{u,1} = w_0 + \sum_{i=0}^{m} w_i^u x_i^u + h_1 \sum_{i=0}^{m} \sum_{j=i}^{m} \left(x_i^u e_i^{u,2} \odot x_j^u e_j^{u,2} \right)$$
$$+ h_3 \sum_{i=1}^{m} \sum_{j=i+1}^{m} \sum_{k=j+1}^{m} \left(x_i^u e_i^{u,3} \odot x_j^u e_j^{u,3} \odot x_k^u e_k^{u,3} \right) \qquad (25)$$
$$+ h_5 \sum_{i=1}^{m} \sum_{j=i+1}^{m} \sum_{k=j+1}^{m} \sum_{l=k+1}^{m} \left(x_i^u e_i^{u,4} \odot x_j^u e_j^{u,4} \odot x_k^u e_k^{u,4} \odot x_l^u e_l^{u,4} \right)$$

The second auxiliary vector $\mathbf{q}_v$ is similar to the first one, but the element position is adjusted accordingly. For the third auxiliary vector h_{aux}, $h^2_{\text{aux},d} = h_2$, $h^4_{\text{aux},d} = h_4$, $h^6_{\text{aux},d} = h_6$, $h^7_{\text{aux},d} = h_7$.

3.3 Optimization Method

Now, we will introduce some optimization methods for ONFM. Firstly, the theory we have proved shows that FM can be expressed as two uncorrelated vectors—$\mathbf{p}_u$ and $\mathbf{q}_v$. By precomputing the vectors, we can greatly improve the training efficiency. Secondly, after transforming FM into generalized MF, the prediction function of ONFM satisfies the requirements of Theorem 1, so the loss function it proposes is available for ONFM:

$$
\tilde{\mathcal{L}}(\Theta) = \sum_{u \in \mathbf{B}} \sum_{v \in \mathbf{V}^+} \left(\left(c_v^+ - c_v^- \right) \hat{y}(\mathbf{x})^2 - 2c_v^+ \hat{y}(\mathbf{x}) \right)
$$
$$
+ \sum_{i=1}^{d} \sum_{j=1}^{d} \left((h_{aux,i} h_{aux,j}) \left(\sum_{u \in \mathbf{B}} p_{u,i} p_{u,j} \right) \left(\sum_{v \in \mathbf{V}} c_v^- q_{v,i} q_{v,j} \right) \right)
$$

(26)

where $\mathbf{B}$ indicates a batch of users, and $\mathbf{V}$ indicates all items.

4 Experiments

4.1 Experimental Settings

Datasets. The two publicly available datasets used are ***Frapple*** and ***Last.fm***. For ***Frapple***, the number of user, item, feature and instance are 957, 4082, 5382, 96203. For ***Last.fm***, the number are 1000, 20301, 37358 and 214574.

Baseline. We compare ONFM with the following baseline:

- **PopRank**: This model returns Top-k most popular items.
- **FM** [9]: The original factorization machines.
- **NFM** [6]: Neural factorization machine uses MLP to learn nonlinear and high-order interactions signals.
- **DeepFM** [4]: This model combines FM and MLP to make recommendations.
- **ONCF** [7]: This model improves MF with outer product.
- **CFM** [10]: Convolutional Factorization Machine uses 3D convolution to achieve the high-order interactions between features.
- **ENMF** [3]: Efficient Neural Matrix Factorization uses non-sampling neural recommendation method to generate recommendations.
- **ENSFM** [1]: Efficient Non-Sampling Factorization Machines conducts non-sampling training by transforming FM into MF.

Table 1. The performance of different models on Frappe and List.fm.

Frappe	HR@5	HR@10	HR@20	NDCG@5	NDCG@10	NDCG@20
PopRank	0.2539	0.3493	0.4136	0.1595	0.1898	0.2060
FM	0.4204	0.5486	0.6590	0.3054	0.3469	0.3750
DeepFM	0.4632	0.6035	0.7322	0.3308	0.3765	0.4092
NFM	0.4798	0.6197	0.7382	0.3469	0.3924	0.4225
ONCF	0.5359	0.6531	0.7691	0.3940	0.4320	0.4614
CFM	0.5462	0.6720	0.7774	0.4153	0.4560	0.4859
ENMF	0.5682	0.6833	0.7749	0.4314	0.4642	0.4914
ENSFM	0.6094	0.7118	0.7889	0.4771	0.5105	0.5301
ONFM-1	0.6149	0.7198	0.7927	0.4778	0.5119	0.5305
ONFM-2	0.6468	0.7623	0.8485	0.4978	0.5354	0.5574
ONFM-3	**0.6743**	**0.7924**	**0.8703**	**0.5217**	**0.5601**	**0.5800**
Last.fm	HR@5	HR@10	HR@20	NDCG@5	NDCG@10	NDCG@20
PopRank	0.0013	0.0023	0.0032	0.0007	0.0011	0.0013
FM	0.1658	0.2382	0.3537	0.1142	0.1374	0.1665
DeepFM	0.1773	0.2612	0.3799	0.1204	0.1473	0.1772
NFM	0.1827	0.2678	0.3783	0.1235	0.1488	0.1765
ONCF	0.2183	0.3208	0.4611	0.1493	0.1823	0.2176
CFM	0.2375	0.3538	0.4841	0.1573	0.1948	0.2277
ENMF	0.3188	0.4254	0.5279	0.2256	0.2531	0.2894
ENSFM	0.3683	0.4729	0.5793	0.2744	0.3082	0.3352
ONFM-1	0.4400	0.5386	0.6294	0.3306	0.3625	0.3856
ONFM-2	0.5431	0.6220	0.6822	0.4190	0.4446	0.4601
ONFM-3	**0.5673**	**0.6457**	**0.6946**	**0.4478**	**0.4733**	**0.4858**

Evaluation Protocols and Metrics. ONFM adopts the leave-one-out evaluation protocol [8,10] to test its performance. For Frappe, we randomly choice one transaction as the test example for each specific user context because of no timestamp. For List.fm, the latest transaction of each user is held out for testing and the rest is treated as the training set. The evaluate metrics are Hit Ratio (HR) and Normalized Discounted Cumulative Gain (NDCG).

Parameter Settings. In ONFM, the weight of all missing data is set to c_0 uniformly, the batch size is set to 512, the embedding size is set to 64, the learning rate is set to 0.05, and the dropout ratio is set to 0.9. c_0 is set to 0.05 and 0.005 for Frappe and Lisr.fm, respectively.

4.2 Performance Comparison

Table 1 summarize the best performance of these models on Frappe and List.fm, respectively. In order to evaluate on different recommendation lengths, we set the length K = 5, 10, and 20 in our experiments. The experimental results show that our model achieves the best performance on all datasets regarding to both HR and NDCG. ONFM-1 adds the third-order interactions between features based on ENSFM. It is noted that ONFM-1 uses shared embedding. Compared with ENSFM, its performance is better, which indicates the effectiveness of the third-order interactions. On the basis of ONFM-1, ONFM-2 introduces the technique called Order-aware Embedding. The performance is improved, indicating that using order-aware embedding is a better choice. ONFM-3 is the final form of our model, which adds the third-order interactions and the fourth-order interactions meanwhile, and also use Order-aware Embedding. Compared with ENSFM, the performance of ONFM-3 is excellent.

5 Conclusion and Future Work

In this paper, we propose a novel model named Order-Aware Embedding Non-Sampling Factorization Machines. The key design of ONFM is to transform FM model incorporating the high-order interactions into a MF form through mathematical transformation. Then we can get three auxiliary vectors—$\mathbf{p}_u$, $\mathbf{q}_v$ and $\mathbf{h}_{aux}$. $\mathbf{p}_u$ and $\mathbf{q}_v$ are only related to the corresponding user and item. We also use Order-aware Embedding. Finally, through some optimization methods, we apply non-sampling to train ONFM. Extensive experiments on two datasets demonstrate that ONFM obtains effective feature information successfully.

Although the results of ONFM illustrate the importance of the high-order interactions, the way to calculate the high-order interactions is crude. In the future, we will design a more excellent method to calculate the high-order interactions. Moreover, different feature interactions have different influence on the accuracy of the final prediction. So in order to better extract feature information, we are also interested in applying attention mechanism to our model.

References

1. Chen, C., Zhang, M., Ma, W., Liu, Y., Ma, S.: Efficient non-sampling factorization machines for optimal context-aware recommendation. In: WWW (2020)
2. Chen, C., et al.: An efficient adaptive transfer neural network for social-aware recommendation. In: SIGIR (2019)
3. Chen, C., Zhang, M., Zhang, Y., Liu, Y., Ma, S.: Efficient neural matrix factorization without sampling for recommendation. ACM Trans. Inf. Syst. **38**(2), 14:1–14:28 (2020)
4. Guo, H., Tang, R., Ye, Y., Li, Z., He, X.: DeepFM: a factorization-machine based neural network for CTR prediction. In: IJCAI (2017)
5. Guo, W., Tang, R., Guo, H., Han, J., Yang, W., Zhang, Y.: Order-aware embedding neural network for CTR prediction. In: SIGIR (2019)

6. He, X., Chua, T.: Neural factorization machines for sparse predictive analytics. In: SIGIR (2017)
7. He, X., Du, X., Wang, X., Tian, F., Tang, J., Chua, T.: Outer product-based neural collaborative filtering. In: IJCAI (2018)
8. He, X., Liao, L., Zhang, H., Nie, L., Hu, X., Chua, T.: Neural collaborative filtering. In: WWW (2017)
9. Rendle, S.: Factorization machines. In: ICDM (2010)
10. Xin, X., Chen, B., He, X., Wang, D., Ding, Y., Jose, J.: CFM: convolutional factorization machines for context-aware recommendation. In: IJCAI (2019)
11. Xin, X., Yuan, F., He, X., Jose, J.M.: Batch IS NOT heavy: learning word representations from all samples. In: ACL (2018)
12. Yuan, F., et al.: f_{bgd}: learning embeddings from positive unlabeled data with BGD. In: UAI (2018)

The 13th International Workshop on Artificial Intelligence and Cybersecurity

A Deep Learning Model for Early Prediction of Sepsis from Intensive Care Unit Records

Rui Zhao[1], Tao Wan[1(✉)], Deyu Li[1], Zhengbo Zhang[2], and Zengchang Qin[3(✉)]

[1] School of Biological Science and Medical Engineering, Beijing Advanced Innovation Center for Biomedical Engineering, Beihang University, Beijing 100191, China
taowan@buaa.edu.cn
[2] Department of Biomedical Engineering, Chinese PLA General Hospital, Beijing 100853, China
[3] Intelligent Computing and Machine Learning Lab, School of ASEE, Beihang University, Beijing 100191, China
zcqin@buaa.edu.cn

Abstract. Early and accurate prediction of sepsis could help physicians with proper treatments and improve patient outcomes. We present a deep learning framework built on a bidirectional long short-term memory (BiLSTM) network model to identify septic patients in the intensive care unit (ICU) settings. The fixed value data padding method serves as an indicator to maintain the missing patterns from the ICU records. The devised masking mechanism allows the BiLSTM model to learn the informative missingness from the time series data with missing values. The developed method can better solve two challenging problems of data length variation and information missingness. The quantitative results demonstrated that our method outperformed the other state-of-the-art algorithms in predicting the onset of sepsis before clinical recognition. This suggested that the deep learning based method could be used to assist physicians for early diagnosis of sepsis in real clinical applications.

Keywords: Deep learning · BiLSTM · Sepsis · ICU

1 Introduction

Sepsis is a life-threatening condition in intensive care units (ICUs), and caused by a dysregulated host response to infection, which results in pathologic, physiologic, and biochemical abnormalities. Early identification of sepsis in ICU would allow faster administration of antibiotic treatment and improvement of clinical outcomes, as well as significantly reduce hospital expenses [1]. Recently, the increasing availability of electronic health records in clinical settings has inspired

This work was partially supported by the National Natural Science Foundation of China (61876197), and the Beijing Municipal Natural Science Foundation (7192105).

© Springer Nature Switzerland AG 2020
H. Yang et al. (Eds.): ICONIP 2020, CCIS 1332, pp. 791–798, 2020.
https://doi.org/10.1007/978-3-030-63820-7_90

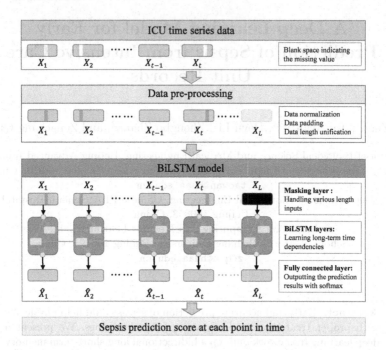

Fig. 1. Workflow of the presented BiLSTM based method. $\{X_1, ..., X_L\}$) are a set of multivariate time series after data padding and length unification, which are further processed via the masking layer of the BiLSTM model. The output of the filled data is the prediction score of the closest front point in time.

several attempts to identify sepsis patient conditions and trends through the automated analysis of electronic medical records (EMR), which has motivated our work in early prediction of sepsis onset through a computer-aided diagnostic method.

There are many computerized approaches emerging to detect and predict the onset of sepsis using EMR. These methods are mainly based on machine learning techniques, which involved the extraction of a great number of manual signatures. This might limit their applications to the complex ICU data, which contained time series with varying lengths and missing values. Deep learning has emerged as a promising tool to identify proper sepsis patients in ICU settings. Che et al. [2] developed a recurrent neural network (RNN) model to predict the onset of sepsis using the PhysioNet Challenge dataset. They took two representations of missing patterns via masking and time interval to cope with multivariate time series with missing values. Vicar et al. [3] in their latest work presented a long short term memory (LSTM) network with residual connections to perform the sepsis prediction task, in which the missing values were replaced with numerical representation from outside the normalized range of real data. The recent literature demonstrated that deep learning techniques could provide a powerful way to enhance the early prediction of sepsis onset in real clinical settings.

In this paper, we developed a deep learning framework using bidirectional LSTM (BiLSTM) networks to identify septic patients from the ICU records. The workflow is illustrated in Fig. 1. The clinical time series data were pre-processed through normalization, padding, and length unification. A fixed value padding method, was adopted to maintain the informative missingness from the missing values of sequential time steps. The multivariate series were unified with equal length to be sent to the BiLSTM model. During the training, a masking mechanism was devised to solve two key problems of data length variation and information missingness. This allowed the BiLSTM model not only to capture the long-term temporal dependencies over time through the bidirectional LSTM layers, but also to utilize the informative missing patterns to strengthen the prediction performance. The L2 regularization was integrated into the loss function to avoid overfitting in case of heavy class imbalance between septic and non-septic patients. Our deep learning method was quantitatively evaluated on the publicly available dataset from the PhysioNet Challenge 2019 [4].

2   Methodology

2.1   Data Pre-processing

Data Normalization. In order to reduce the variance of the data while preserving zero entries, all the clinical variables were normalized to lie between zero and one using the minimum-maximum scaling method. The process could not only eliminate the effect of singular samples, but also accelerate the speed of gradient descent for the subsequent training process of BiLSTM model.

Data Padding. The multivariate time series data collected from ICU records were characterized by a variety of missing values due to many reasons, such as medical events, anomalies, inconveniences and so on. It was noted that these missing values and their missing patterns provided rich information about target labels in time series prediction tasks [2]. In this work, we used a fixed value (-100) to replace the missing data, since this value was greatly different with the normalized ICU variables.

Data Length Unification. The BiLSTM model required that the input clinical time series had an unified data length. In this work, rather than cutting the data into the same size, we adopted a simple approach to search the maximum length L within the entire samples. All the data were lengthened to the length L by filling with zero values. The labels of the supplementary data were given the true label at the last time point of the original data.

2.2   BiLSTM Model Design

We established a deep learning method based on a BiLSTM model, in which a masking mechanism was adopted for better understanding and utilization of missing values in time series analysis. These informative missingness patterns could be incorporated into the bidirectional LSTM architecture and jointly trained with all the model components.

BiLSTM Network Architecture. The LSTM network is a popular model to deal with time series data. The main advantage is that the LSTM model shows a good capability to capture the long-range temporal dependencies due to its improved cell structure, thus alleviating the vanishing gradient problem that often occurs in classical RNN. Based on the LSTM, the BiLSTM model contains bidirectional LSTM layers and is trained in both forward and backward directions. The BiLSTM model addressed the gradient vanishing problem by incorporating gating functions into the cell state dynamics. A LSTM cell has four gates, including input gate i, forget gate f, control gate c, and output gate o, which can be defined as: $i_t = \sigma(W_i \cdot [h_{t-1}, x_t] + b_i)$, $f_t = \sigma(W_f \cdot [h_{t-1}, x_t] + b_f)$, $c_t = f_t \odot c_{t-1} + i_t \odot \tilde{c}_t$, $o_t = \sigma(W_o \cdot [h_{t-1}, x_t] + b_o)$, where $\tilde{c}_t = \tanh(W_c \cdot [h_{t-1}, x_t] + b_c)$, σ is the sigmoid function, $\{W_i, W_f, W_o, W_c\}$ and $\{b_i, b_f, b_o, b_c\}$ are the trainable parameters, x_t is the input vector of the current time step, tanh is used to scale the values into the range -1 to 1. h_t represents the hidden vector of LSTM, which can be expressed as $h_t = o_t \odot \tanh(c_t)$ ($\odot$ is the dot product function). The input gate i determines which information can be transferred to the cell. The forget gate f decides which information from input should be neglected from the previous memory. The control gate c controls the update of cell state from c_{t-1} to c_t. The output gate o is responsible for generating the output value of the LSTM cell. This special design allows the model to be effective and scalable to cope with complex ICU sequential data.

Masking Mechanism. In real clinical practice of sepsis detection and treatment, patients have different ICU lengths of stay and various conditions of disease. Thereby, the time series contained sequential time steps with a variety of lengths, and might suffer missing values due to the data acquisition. We utilized a masking mechanism to solve the data length variation and information missingness problems. In addition, the induced masking vector indicated the locations of the missing values, which were not considered during the model training. This allowed the BiLSTM model only take into account the missing patterns, but not the filled missing values. Given a set of time series $\{X_1, X_2, ..., X_{t-1}, X_t\}$, we assumed X_t is a missing time step. The training process at the time step t was skipped according to the defined masking vector. Thus, the output of the time step t was taken as the prediction score from its closest front time step $t - 1$ if it was a real data.

Cross Entropy Loss and L2 Regularization. We adopted the standard cross-entropy loss for sepsis prediction task, which could be used to accelerate model convergence during the training process. The cross-entropy loss function can be defined as: $\mathcal{L}_{CE} = -\sum_{l=1}^{M} y_{sl} \log(p_{sl})$, where M is the number of classes,

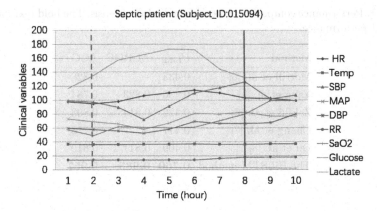

Fig. 2. An example of a septic patient with nine common variables in time, including heart rate (HR), temperature (Temp), systolic blood pressure (SBP), mean arterial pressure (MAP), diastolic blood pressure (DBP), respiration rate (RR), arterial oxygen saturation (SaO2), glucose, and lactate. The dotted green line indicates the early warning time of sepsis (six hours prior to its onset), and the red solid line indicates the onset of sepsis.

y_{sl} is the binary indicator (0 or 1) if the class label l is the correct classification for the observed sample s, p_{sl} is the predicted probability that the observed sample s belongs to the category l.

Class imbalance is one of the most challenging problems considering clinical time series data since the sepsis occurs at about 1.80% of all time points across all the patients [3]. To address this problem, we introduced a L2 regularization term in the loss function, to better control the model complexity and prevent overfitting during the model training in the case of heavy class imbalance. The loss function can be expressed as: $\mathcal{L} = \mathcal{L}_{CE} + \frac{\lambda}{2} \|W\|_2^2$, where W are the vector of weight coefficients, and λ is the regularization coefficient.

3 Experimental Results

3.1 Experimental Design

Data Description. The PhysioNet dataset [4] is a publicly available collection of multivariate clinical time series from 40,336 intensive care unit (ICU) patients. Each patient had a multivariate time series containing 36 clinical variables (8 vital sign variables, 26 laboratory variables, and 2 demographic variables). Figure 2 shows an example of a septic patient with nine common variables in time. We utilized the training set in our experiments since outcomes (such as sepsis labels) were available only for this subset. A total of 5118 patients, including 2932 sepsis patients, were extracted, of which 70% for training, 20% for validation, and the rest 10% for test.

Table 1. Performance comparison for early prediction of sepsis. The bold text indicates the best performance.

Method	U_{total}	AUROC	ACC
Morrill et al. [5]	0.433	–	0.828
Yang et al. [1]	0.430	0.823	0.784
Zabihi et al. [6]	0.422	0.814	0.803
Chang et al. [7]	0.417	–	0.778
Du et al. [8]	0.409	0.811	0.819
The BiLSTM method	**0.760**	**0.985**	**0.957**

Parameter Setting. The BiLSTM model was implemented under the deep learning framework of Keras (version 2.2.4) using NVIDIA Tesla V100 GPU on the high-performance computing platform (Huawei G5500). The clinical data were processed through Python 3.7.6. The maximum length of data was set as $L = 80$ time points. The learning rate was 0.001, the batch size was 64, and the epoch was assigned as 50. The parameter of the L2 regularization ($\lambda = 0.01$) was empirically tuned to obtain the best training stability.

Reference Methods. We compared our method with five reference approaches, which achieved the best prediction results in the PhysioNet Challenge 2019 [4]. Morrill et al. [5] derived a signature-based regression model in conjunction with a gradient booting machine. Yang et al. [1] developed a multi-feature fusion based XGBoost classification model. Zabihi et al. [6] presented an ensemble model consisting of five XGboost models. Chang et al. [7] applied temporal convolutional networks (TCN). Du et al. [8] introduced a classifier of gradient boosted decision tree (GBDT) to estimate the likelihood of sepsis onset. The original quantitative results reported in the publications were used for comparison.

Evaluation Metrics. For a fair comparison, the original evaluation metrics used in the PhysioNet, including utility (U_{total}), area under receiver operating characteristic curve (AUROC), and accuracy (ACC), were adopted in the experiments. The utility was a clinical utility-based scoring metric newly created for the challenge, which rewarded algorithms for early sepsis predictions and penalized them for late or missed sepsis predictions in both septic and non-septic patients. We also computed two more metrics of area under precision recall curve (AUPRC) and F-measure to evaluate detection performance of sepsis onset.

3.2   Prediction Performance

We conducted a prediction task to identify septic patients at least six hours prior to the onset time of sepsis according to the Sepsis-3 clinical criteria. The prediction performance was quantitatively evaluated using three popular measures

Table 2. Performance comparison using different data padding methods. The bold text indicates the best performance.

Method	U_{total}	AUROC	AUPRC	ACC	F-measure
Linear interpolation [9]	0.740	0.984	0.894	0.956	0.817
Mean filling [10]	0.687	0.979	0.859	0.952	0.791
Median filling [11]	0.713	0.976	0.847	0.945	0.775
K-NN filling [12]	0.643	0.978	0.855	0.948	0.769
Fixed value padding	**0.760**	**0.985**	**0.902**	**0.957**	**0.826**

(utility, AUROC, and accuracy). Table 1 shows the comparison results between our method and five reference approaches. We noted that the BiLSTM based method achieved the best performance in terms of all the metrics, especially the overall utility measure with up to 80% improvement. The prediction performance might degrade on the challenge's test dataset. Among the reference methods, Morrill et al. [5], Yang et al. [1], Zabihi et al. [6], and Du et al. [8]'s approaches used hand-crafted features, which could heavily depend on the feature extraction and selection, thus decreasing the predictive power. Yang et al. [1], Zabihi et al. [6], and Du et al. [8] employed the XGBoost or GBDT, which might have limited capability in handling high-dimensional features. Chang et al. [7] combined data imputation and TCN model, and obtained comparative results with the other four methods. The developed BiLSTM model was able to not only capture the long-term temporal dependencies in time series observations, but also utilize the missing patterns to further improve prediction performance.

3.3 Effect of Data Padding

In order to assess the effect of data padding on the prediction performance, we compared our method with four popular data imputation approaches, including linear interpolation [9], mean filling [10], median filling [11], and K-nearest neighbor (K-NN) filling [12]. The quantitative results are listed in Table 2. It can be seen that our fixed value method outperformed the other four approaches across all the evaluation metrics. Our padding method used fixed value that was much larger than the real data to fill in the missing values, serving as an indicator to inform the deep learning model which inputs were observed or missing. The informative missingness patterns could be learned through the deep learning model to improve predicative quality of sepsis, while avoiding redundant and erroneous information induced by the data padding process.

3.4 Effect of BiLSTM Model

We compared the predictive capability of the BiLSTM model and the conventional LSTM model in detecting onset of sepsis using clinical time series data in the ICU setting. In the prediction task, the BiLSTM model yielded the superior result with the AUC value of 0.98, approximately 29% improvement over the LSTM model, indicating that the BiLSTM architecture could effectively handle the complex ICU data containing multivariate time series with missing values.

4   Conclusion

We presented a deep learning framework to accurately predict the onset of sepsis in patients from the ICU records. A fixed value data padding method, replacing the conventional data imputation, provided a good preservation of informative missingness appearing in the data. These missing patterns could be learned via the deep learning model to improve the sepsis detection. The BiLSTM model incorporating the masking layer was built to perform early prediction of sepsis onset in the proceeding of six hours. The experiments demonstrated that the developed computerized method could be useful for early and reliable identification of sepsis in real-world clinical practice.

References

1. Yang, M., et al.: Early prediction of sepsis using multi-feature fusion based XGBoost learning and Bayesian optimization. In: The IEEE Conference on Computing in Cardiology (CinC), vol. 46, pp. 1–4 (2019)
2. Che, Z., Purushotham, S., Cho, K., Sontag, D., Liu, Y.: Recurrent neural networks for multivariate time series with missing values. Sci. Rep. **8**, 6085 (2018)
3. Vicar, T., Novotna, P., Hejc, J., Ronzhina, M., Smisek, R.: Sepsis detection in sparse clinical data using long short-term memory metwork with dice loss. In: The IEEE Conference on Computing in Cardiology (CinC), p. 19381144 (2019)
4. Reyna, M., et al.: Early prediction of sepsis from clinical data: the physionet/computing in cardiology challenge 2019. Criti. Care Med. **48**, 210–217 (2019)
5. Morrill, J., Kormilitzin, A., Nevado-Holgado, A., Swaminathan, S., Howison, S., Lyons, T.: The signature-based model for early detection of sepsis from electronic health records in the intensive care unit. In: The IEEE Conference on Computing in Cardiology (CinC), p. 19381156 (2019)
6. Zabihi, M., Kiranyaz, S., Gabbouj, M.: Sepsis prediction in intensive care unit using ensemble of XGboost models. In: The IEEE Conference on Computing in Cardiology (CinC), p. 19425736 (2019)
7. Chang, Y., et al.: A multi-task imputation and classification neural architecture for early prediction of sepsis from multivariate clinical time series. In: The IEEE Conference on Computing in Cardiology (CinC), p. 19381119 (2019)
8. Du, J., Sadr, N., Chazal, P.: Automated prediction of sepsis onset using gradient boosted decision trees. In: The IEEE Conference on Computing in Cardiology (CinC), p. 19381157 (2019)
9. Kreindler, D., Lumsden, C.: The effects of the irregular sample and missing data in time series analysis. Nonlinear Dyn. Psychol. Life Sci. **11**, 401–412 (2007)
10. Che, Z., Purushotham, S., Khemani, R., Liu, Y.: Interpretable deep models for ICU outcome prediction. In: AMIA Annual Symposium, vol. 10, pp. 371–380 (2016)
11. Kaji, D., et al.: An attention based deep learning model of clinical events in the intensive care unit. PLoS ONE **14**, e0211057 (2019)
12. Rahman, S., et al.: An attention based deep learning model of clinical events in the intensive care unit. J. Biomed. Inf. **58**, 198–207 (2015)

AdversarialQR Revisited: Improving the Adversarial Efficacy

Aran Chindaudom[1], Pongpeera Sukasem[1], Poomdharm Benjasirimonkol[1], Karin Sumonkayothin[1(✉)], Prarinya Siritanawan[2(✉)], and Kazunori Kotani[2]

[1] Mahidol University, Nakhonpathom 73170, Thailand
aran.chi@protonmail.com, pongpeera_sukasem@hotmail.com,
poomdharmbenjasirimongkol@gmail.com, karin.sum@mahidol.ac.th
[2] Japan Advanced Institute of Science and Technology, Ishikawa 923-1211, Japan
{prarinya,ikko}@jaist.ac.jp

Abstract. At present, deep learning and convolutional neural networks are currently two of the fastest rising trends as the tool to perform a multitude of tasks such as image classification and computer vision. However, vulnerabilities in such networks can be exploited through input modification, leading to negative consequences to its users. This research aims to demonstrate an adversarial attack method that can hide its attack from human intuition in the form of a QR code, an entity that is most likely to conceal the attack from human acknowledgment due to its widespread use at the current time. A methodology was developed to demonstrate the QR-embedded adversarial patch creation process and attack existing CNN image classification models. Experiments were also performed to investigate trade-offs in different patch shapes and find the patch's optimal color adjustment to improve scannability while retaining acceptable adversarial efficacy.

Keywords: Deep learning · Adversarial attack · Convolutional neural networks

1 Introduction

Neural Networks have been a foundation of everyone's daily lives and can be found anywhere, such as social media, analytical studies, customer base analysis, and software creation. However, should a malicious entity perform an adversarial attack against a deep learning model by adding perturbations to the model's input, a vulnerability in the model will be created, raising concerns regarding the invasion of user privacy. Even though there exist research projects with similar goals to deviate the results of a deep learning model through input modification, most of the perturbations created are still recognizable by humans as a form of attack.

This research intends to propose an attack pattern against deep learning models that can deviate their weights to provide desired outputs. Three major

© Springer Nature Switzerland AG 2020
H. Yang et al. (Eds.): ICONIP 2020, CCIS 1332, pp. 799–806, 2020.
https://doi.org/10.1007/978-3-030-63820-7_91

contributions of this work are: (1) create the scan-ready QR code symbols that contain features to be used as adversarial inputs, (2) examine the adversarial efficacy similarities or differences between square and circular adversarial QR patches, and (3) examine the optimal brightness values to enhance the adversarial QR patch's scannability while retaining its adversarial efficacy.

This paper contains five sections with various details regarding the research. The first section identifies the motivations and contributions of this research. The second section reviews the background knowledge and works related to this research. The third section explains the research methodology. The fourth section discusses the experiments conducted based on the methodology and their results. Finally, the fifth section summarizes the research, along with discussing the future works for the project.

2   Literature Review

Due to the nature of gradient descent in machine learning models, perturbations can be constructed from the gradient information and added into the input to deceive machine learning models. The process of adding perturbations is called an adversarial attack, and the perturbed input is called an adversarial example.

One of the earliest concepts of adversarial examples was proposed by Szegedy et al. [6]. They described adversarial examples as the example input images that are very slightly altered from the classified example images in the training dataset but can cause such deep learning models to classify them incorrectly.

Goodfellow et al. [3] suggested that image classification models are too linear. This property is due to high-dimensional dot products of linear functions. As a result, adding a perturbation to the input image in adversarial direction $sign\left(\nabla_x J\left(\theta\right)\right)$ can easily perturb the classification models. They also show that the current machine learning models consist mostly of similar functions, leading to adversarial examples' generalization, i.e., an adversarial example trained to target one particular model can be used to attack another model.

Regarding attacks in the physical world, Sharif et al. [4] proposed a method to attack facial biometric systems using a printed pair of eyeglass frames, which can be considered as a physically realizable accessory usually belonging to any person. However, this form of attack may only be used against facial recognition systems due to the limited usability of the printed eyeglasses.

Attacks in the form of adversarial patches were first introduced by Brown et al. [1] to create a generalized adversarial patch that can be added to any scene, causing the image classifier to output any class intended by the attacker. Xu et al. [7] proposed a method to create adversarial patches in the form of a t-shirt that can evade a real-time person detector when the person moves and wears it.

Since the adversarial patches are highly conspicuous to human perception, Chindaudom et al. [2] proposed a method to camouflage the adversarial patch into a scannable QR code by applying color modifications onto the trained patch. This paper is an expansion of the preliminary concepts in AdversarialQR, where the comparative analysis between different shapes of the Adversarial QR patch

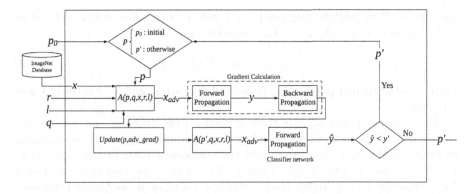

Fig. 1. The overview of the QR Adversarial Attack system

was performed, and the optimal color adjustment for improving the scannability while retaining acceptable efficacy was investigated.

3 Methodology

The adversarial patch creation and training processes are mostly identical to [2] with minor changes to support the circle QR shape.

3.1 System Architecture Overview

Figure 1 displays the architecture of the QR adversarial example creation and training system. Starting by initializing the target model using the pre-trained model (InceptionV3 [5]) using ImageNet ILSVRC2012 dataset. The dataset is split into training and testing images. Both have been resized to 299×299 pixels. Testing images are normalized using InceptionV3's mean and standard deviation, and filtering out incorrectly classified images. The initial patch is generated by the specifying shape (square or circle), and the ratio of patch size over image size. Finally, the patch is applied to a boolean matrix [2] to create a masked patch.

By maximizing the expectation of the equation extended from [1], the adversarial QR patch p' can be trained using the equation:

$$p' = \operatorname*{argmax}_{p} E_{x \sim X, r \sim R, l \sim L}[\log Pr(\hat{y}|A(p, q, x, r, l))] \tag{1}$$

where $\hat{y}$ represents the target class's confidence, the patch operator A is applied on each image x over the training set X. The rotation r (between 0, 90, 180, and 270°) and location l of the patch applied on a training image are varied over the distribution L and R to increase the patch's universality. q represents the string used to generate the QR code symbol.

After creating an adversarial example x_{adv} from the patch operator A, the target model performs forward propagation to obtain confidence value of the target class, and performs backward propagation to calculate the gradient adv_grad

that are used to update the pixels in patch p with an operator defined as $Update(p, adv\_grad)$, which can be described as:

$$p'_{new} = p' - \nabla_x J \tag{2}$$

where p' is the current patch, p'_{new} is the updated patch, and $\nabla_x J$ is the gradient adv_grad.

The updated patch p'_{new} is then applied on the training image using the same operator A, creating a new adversarial example x_{adv} which is evaluated by target model once again to obtain the confidence value of the target class $\hat{y}$ to be compared to the target value y'. The training process is stopped once the confidence score is higher than the target value, or if the training iteration reaches the maximum number specified from the parser. The adversarial QR patch p' is used in the next batch of training images. If the x_{adv} is successful in attacking the target model, it is saved into the file system for further usage.

One thing to note is that the ground truth is not concerned in the backward propagation process of the target classifier network, as the only objective is to alter the prediction values retrieved as the output from the target classifier network.

3.2   Implementation of QR Symbol on Circular Patch

According to the experimentation results shown in [2], the non-QR circular patches were able to retain their adversarial efficacy through updates better than their square counterpart. This led to the idea of implementing a new type of adversarial patch by applying the QR code data onto a circular-shaped patch.

The process to generate and train a circular QR patch is identical to the process used for the square QR shape. However, instead of directly using the QR code generated from the input string, it was embedded in the middle of circle at 85% of diameter to increase the area of adversarial perturbation. The size of the circle QR patch is slightly bigger (100×100 pixels) compared to the square QR patch (74×74 pixels) as the circle QR patch requires larger space to contain the QR code. Figure 2 shows the circular QR patch during the patch initialization process, and Fig. 3 shows the circular QR patch after the training process had completed (τ equal to 50). Note that the background color of the initial patch was randomized for each initialization and may not be the same color every time. The patch is also randomly rotated around 0, 90, 180, 270 degrees during the training process to ensure that the output adversarial QR patch is robust to the rotation. Figure 4 shows the trained square QR patch from [2] for comparison.

3.3   Scannability Improvement by Color Intensity Adjustment

It is challenging to generate a fully functional QR pattern (carrying an adversarial attack) from the original adversarial patch algorithm [1]. The problem is that the original adversarial patch algorithm sometimes produces black color patterns

Fig. 2. Initial circular QR patch

Fig. 3. Trained circular QR patch

Fig. 4. Trained square QR patch

Fig. 5. The process to make the trained QR patch visible to a QR scanner

that break the QR code. Thus, we introduced a new idea to constrain the patch by adjusting the patch's brightness around the black areas on the adversarial examples to solve the problem.

The color intensity of the trained patch's black (R:0, G:0, B:0) parts is increased with a value τ to create a quiet zone surrounding the QR symbol, making the patch more scannable to a QR code scanner device. The τ addition function can be defined as:

$$p'_{out}(u,v) = \begin{cases} p'(u,v) + \tau, & \text{if } p'(u,v) = [0,0,0] \\ p'(u,v), & \text{otherwise} \end{cases} \quad (3)$$

where u and v are the pixel's coordinates on the patch p' and τ is a small number. Figure 5 displays the steps to make the trained QR patch scannable, where the leftmost image is the QR symbol patched onto an image, the middle image is the black parts of the QR symbol from the left image, and the rightmost image is the area modified by the τ value.

4 Experiments

This section discusses the experiments to evaluate the circular QR patch's adversarial efficacy compared to its square counterpart and find the optimal value to modify the dark parts of the patch.

Figure 6 displays the evaluation of two example images before and after applying the circle QR adversarial patch, and also before and after applying color intensity modifications to the patch. After completing the circle QR patch creation and training process, the adversarial efficacy of the circle QR patch after

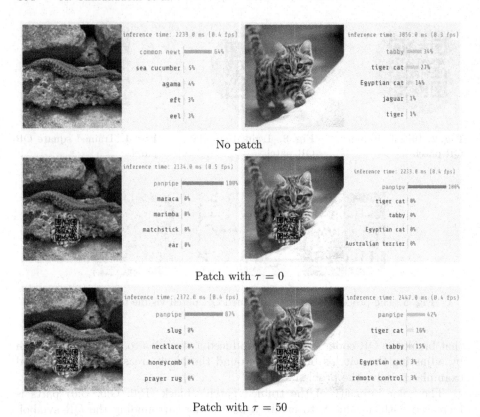

No patch

Patch with $\tau = 0$

Patch with $\tau = 50$

Fig. 6. Evaluations before and after embedding the circle QR adversarial patch

modification by the τ value was then evaluated and compared to the square QR patch. Both types of patches were evaluated by applying them onto 3,492 images from the ImageNet dataset at the same coordinates at $(u, v) = (80,160)$, and then calculate the average confidence score of image class "Panpipe" from varying τ values.

To evaluate and compare the circle QR patch's adversarial efficacy, the circular QR patches were generated and trained using the same configurations in [2] to maximize the accuracy of the comparison between the two patch shapes.

Figure 7 represents the average confidence score of the "Panpipe" image class over τ updates from 0 to 89, where the blue line is the confidence score from the circle QR patch, and the green line is from the square QR patch. The error bars of identical colors indicate the standard deviation of each patch shape. As a result, the circle QR patch was able to accumulate higher average confidence scores against the InceptionV3 model up to $\tau = 80$, where the average scores were almost zero. It can be derived that the circle QR patch can withstand τ modification while retaining its adversarial capabilities better than its square counterpart. Speculation was made that the cause of the circle QR patch's stronger

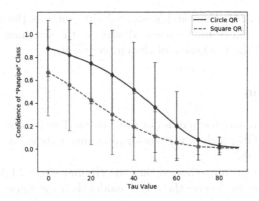

Fig. 7. Average confidence scores of the targeted "Panpipe" class for circle and square QR shapes over the varying τ from 0 to 89

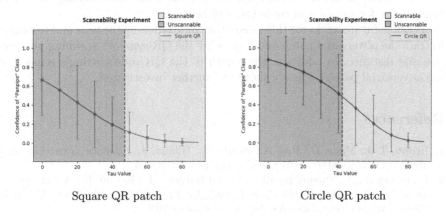

Square QR patch   Circle QR patch

Fig. 8. The scannability threshold experiments over the varying τ from 0 to 89

resistance to color intensity changes is similar to the comparison between the non-QR patches, where the edges and corners in a square QR patch contain salient features disrupting other features in the image, reducing the effectiveness of the patch.

The other experiment performed was to find the minimal τ value that allowed the QR adversarial patch to be scannable while still retaining the patch's adversarial efficacy at an acceptable level. The experiment was conducted by scanning the trained square and circle QR adversarial patch using a mobile phone's camera (Samsung Galaxy S10) to scan the QR symbol on a computer screen while also updating τ after every scanning attempts.

Figure 8 displays the results of the experiment, where the vertical blue dash line represents the minimal τ value needed to be able to scan by the device for each patch type. The minimal τ value to adjust the patch's color are approximately 48 for the square patch and 42 for the circle patch. However, various factors may also affect the patch's scannability, such as the scanning device's quality, the reflection from the scanned surface, the scanning device's distance to the patch, and the brightness of the environment.

5 Conclusion

In summary, this research expands our previous work to improve the performance of an adversarial QR patch in various forms against existing deep learning image classification models.

The experiment results showed that the circular-shaped QR patch yielded a better performance to deceive the target model than the square counterpart and is also more resistant to change in position and color intensity modifications. Another experiment was conducted to find the optimal τ value by adjusting the dark parts of the adversarial QR patches, with the values being 48 and 42 respectively for square and circle QR patches.

Possible future works for this research include reducing the time and resources to train the adversarial patch and improving the QR symbol's scanning perspective and distance. In addition, the length of the QR code's string's impact on the adversarial patch's efficacy should be further investigated.

References

1. Brown, T.B., Mané, D., Roy, A., Abadi, M., Gilmer, J.: Adversarial patch. CoRR abs/1712.09665 (2017). http://arxiv.org/abs/1712.09665
2. Chindaudom, A., Sumongkayothin, K., Siritanawan, P., Kotani, K.: Adversarialqr: an adversarial patch in QR code format. In: Proceedings of Imaging, Vision & Pattern Recognition. Fukuoka, Japan, September 2020
3. Goodfellow, I.J., Shlens, J., Szegedy, C.: Explaining and harnessing adversarial examples. In: Proceedings of International Conference on Learning Representations, (ICLR). San Diego, USA, May 2015
4. Sharif, M., Bhagavatula, S., Bauer, L., Reiter, M.K.: Accessorize to a crime: real and stealthy attacks on state-of-the-art face recognition. In: Proceedings of ACM SIGSAC Conference on Computer and Communications Security, pp. 1528–1540. Vienna, Austria (2016)
5. Szegedy, C., Vanhoucke, V., Ioffe, S., Shlens, J., Wojna, Z.: Rethinking the inception architecture for computer vision. In: Proceedings of IEEE Conference on Computer Vision and Pattern Recognition (CVPR). Las Vegas, USA, June 2016
6. Szegedy, C., et al.: Intriguing properties of neural networks. In: Proceedings of International Conference on Learning Representations (ICLR). Banff, Canada, April 2014
7. Xu, K., et al.: Adversarial t-shirt! evading person detectors in a physical world. In: Proceedings of European Conference on Computer Vision (ECCV), August 2020

Hybrid Loss for Improving Classification Performance with Unbalanced Data

Thanawat Lodkaew and Kitsuchart Pasupa[(✉)]

Faculty of Information Technology, King Mongkut's Institute of Technology
Ladkrabang, Bangkok 10520, Thailand
lodkaew.thanawat@gmail.com, kitsuchart@it.kmitl.ac.th

Abstract. Unbalanced data is widespread in practice and presents challenges which have been widely studied in classical machine learning. A classification algorithm trained with unbalanced data is likely to be biased towards the majority class and thus show inferior performance on the minority class. To improve the performance of deep neural network (DNN) models on poorly balanced data, we hybridized two well-performing loss functions, specially designed for learning imbalanced data, mean false error and focal loss. Since mean false error can effectively balance between majority and minority classes and focal loss can reduce the contribution of unnecessary samples, which are usually samples from the majority class, which may cause a DNN model to be biased towards the majority class when learning. We show that hybridizing the two losses can improve the classification performance of the model. Our hybrid loss function was tested with unbalanced data sets, extracted from CIFAR-100 and IMDB review datasets, and showed that, overall, it performed better than mean false error or focal loss.

Keywords: Class imbalance · Deep neural network · Loss function

1 Introduction

Class imbalance occurs when the samples of each class are not equally represented, $i.e.$ the numbers of representatives differ widely: many real-world datasets show this imbalance [8,13,17,18]. Since this is extremely common in practice, it has been widely studied in classical machine learning. Commonly, there are two types of imbalance—long-tailed imbalance [15] and step imbalance [3]. In step imbalance, classes are grouped into majority and minority classes. The two classes have different numbers of samples, but the number of samples is equal within majority classes and equal within minority classes. For long-tailed imbalance, the class frequency distribution is long-tailed, the samples of a few classes occupy most of the data, while samples of most classes rarely appear. In binary classification, when a dataset is imbalanced, it is a step imbalance. This paper focuses on binary classification.

Recently, deep neural networks (DNNs) have been used for various classification tasks, $e.g.$ image and text classification, and they have achieved excellent

© Springer Nature Switzerland AG 2020
H. Yang et al. (Eds.): ICONIP 2020, CCIS 1332, pp. 807–814, 2020.
https://doi.org/10.1007/978-3-030-63820-7_92

performance. However, DNNs perform poorly on imbalanced data due to ineffective learning [3,6]. In binary classification, when classification algorithms based on DNNs are trained with unbalanced data, classifiers will prefer the negative (majority) class and achieve high accuracy on it. However, it will show lower accuracy on the positive (minority) class.

Existing methods use two strategies for dealing with imbalanced data [9]— data sampling and algorithmic adjusting. There are two data sampling techniques—over-sampling the positive class and under-sampling the negative class. However, each techniques has disadvantages: over-sampling can easily cause model over-fitting, due to repeatedly duplicated samples, whereas under-sampling may throw away valuable information, and it is not practicable for extremely unbalanced data. Algorithmic adjusting changes the learning process, so that it can give higher importance to the positive class. One technique for adjusting the algorithm is cost-sensitive learning, which considers the misclassification costs [19]. If it is applied to a DNN model, the learning will jointly optimize the network parameters and misclassification costs, instead of optimizing the network parameters alone [10,21]. It will be difficult to simultaneously optimize the network parameters and misclassification costs, when the imbalance is large [7]. However, recent work has addressed the class imbalance problem, without adding additional parameters [14,22]. Solutions proposed in [14,22] allow the model to optimize just the network parameters. To clarify, they tried to solve the problem by modifying just the existing loss functions and did not alter the models. It was quite simple but effective. The essential advantage of this strategy for solving the problem is that it is easy to implement and use with existing DNN models.

Here, we studied two well-performing loss functions, namely mean false error (MFE) [22] and focal loss [14], specially designed to combat the imbalance problem. These two loss functions used different perspectives to make learning the model concentrate more on the positive class. Focal loss differentiates between easy samples (samples with low losses) and hard samples (samples with high losses), so that it can lower the weight of the loss contribution of easy samples and focus training on hard samples. This gives more importance to the positive class, because most easy samples are in the negative class. The mean false error technique changes the total error by summing the negative and positive sample errors separately. This effectively balances between the loss contributions of both classes and allows the positive class to have a substantial contribution in calculating the total loss.

There is a drawback for each loss. For focal loss, the contribution of the negative class (or easy samples class) to the total loss is reduced. However, the total loss is an average over the whole data, so losses from negative samples can still dominate it. For mean false error, although the total loss is calculated by summing the average losses of both classes, the loss from the negative class can still dominate the overall loss, because of the effect of the easy samples. Moreover, mean false error will work best, if every batch of training data contains at least one positive sample. If there is no positive sample in a batch, the total loss will be biased by the average of negative class, *i.e.* the easy samples.

To avoid the drawbacks, inspired by these two approaches, we formed a hybrid solution and defined a new loss function—the hybrid loss—so that advantages of each loss will compensate for the drawbacks of the other.

Our main contributions are: Firstly, we explored the ideas behind the mean false error and focal loss ideas, to understand how they perform, when the data is unbalanced. Secondly, we defined a hybrid loss function, a hybrid of mean false error and focal loss solutions, which combines advantages of the two ideas, and we showed that the two loss functions can be combined in an efficient way. Lastly, we tested our hybrid function with image and text datasets. For each dataset, a variety of imbalance levels was applied.

2   Related Works

2.1   Imbalanced Learning

Anand *et al.* [2] studied the effect of class imbalance and found that it adversely affects the backpropagation algorithm. The loss of the negative class rapidly decreased, whereas the positive class loss significantly increased in early iterations and the network would often converge very slowly. This occurred because the negative class completely dominated the network gradient used to update the weights. To deal with this, we need to increase the positive class contribution and correspondingly decrease the negative class contribution.

2.2   Focal Loss

Focal loss, $FL(p_t) = -\alpha_t(1 - p_t)^\gamma \log(p_t)$, was a modification of cross entropy loss [14]. A modulating factor $(1 - p)^\gamma$ was added to the cross entropy loss. For notational convenience, let p is the predicted probability and y is the ground-truth class. p_t will be p if $y = 1$ and be $1 - p$ for otherwise. By the equation of focal loss, $\gamma \geq 0$ is a tunable focusing parameter. In practice, α_t will be α, if the ground-truth class of sample is the positive class and be $1 - \alpha$ for otherwise.

The motivation for defining the focal loss is that cross entropy loss is not able to correctly balance the weights of positive and negative samples due to the imbalance. Although adding a weighting factor α partially addresses the problem, it cannot differentiate between easy samples and hard samples. Usually, most of easy samples are from negative class, and they hugely contribute to the total loss and dominate the network gradient. In general, hard samples add more discriminative information than easy samples [23], so that learning from hard samples is more effective than learning from easy ones. For this reason, the contribution of easy samples needs to be reduced while learning, so that the model can concentrate on learning hard samples.

Focal loss was designed to down-weight easy samples by adding a modulating factor to the cross entropy loss. This factor reduces the loss contribution from easy samples and focuses training on hard negative samples. Define

$l_{FL} = \frac{1}{n} \sum_{i=1}^{n} -\alpha_t^{(i)} (1 - p_t^{(i)})^\gamma \log(p_t^{(i)})$, as a total loss form of an α-balanced variant of focal loss, where n is the number of samples.

We considered focal loss as a reference for our improved method, described in the next section.

2.3 Mean False Error

Mean false error was derived from a mean squared error (MSE) [22], by separating the calculation of the total MSE for all samples to a sum of an average losses of negative and positive samples separately: $l_{MFE} = l_{MSE_-} + l_{MSE_+}$, where $l_{MSE_-} = \frac{1}{n_-} \sum_{i=1}^{n_-} \frac{1}{2}(y^{(i)} - p^{(i)})^2$ and $l_{MSE_+} = \frac{1}{n_+} \sum_{i=1}^{n_+} \frac{1}{2}(y^{(i)} - p^{(i)})^2$. Based on the equations, $y^{(i)}$ is the ground-truth class of sample i and n_- and n_+ are the numbers of negative or positive samples.

The motivation for introducing mean false error is that a MSE is not able to capture losses from the positive class effectively. That is, loss contributions from negative samples will overrule the contribution from positive samples, due to the higher volume of negative samples. Thus it computes the total loss from a sum of separate calculations of the average loss of each class. This allows the positive class to more fully contribute to updating weights of the network. In experiments on various benchmark datasets, Wang et al. [22] showed that mean false error performed better than a simple MSE approach. They further improved mean false error with mean squared false error (MSFE) [22]. Both of these variations were compared with our hybrid method—see Sect. 5.

3 Our Method

The principal advantage of focal loss is that it can control the difference between easy and hard samples and increase the loss contribution of the positive class by reducing the importance of easy samples. A weighting factor was added to the loss to balance the contribution of positive and negative samples. However, since the total loss is an average for both positive and negative classes, the negative class can still dominate the total loss. The mean false error solution diminishes this effect, because it can make positive class more important during training.

We showed that the advantage of each loss can address the drawback of the other. Hence, to more effectively learn unbalanced data, we mimicked the mean false error total loss calculation, by summing average separately computed losses from both classes: $l_{Hybrid} = l_{FL_-} + l_{FL_+}$, where $l_{FL_-} = \frac{1}{n_-} \sum_{i=1}^{n_-} -\alpha_t^{(i)} (1 - p_t^{(i)})^\gamma \log(p_t^{(i)})$ and $l_{FL_+} = \frac{1}{n_+} \sum_{i=1}^{n_+} -\alpha_t^{(i)} (1 - p_t^{(i)})^\gamma \log(p_t^{(i)})$. l_{FL_-} and l_{FL_+} are the average losses of the negative and positive classes.

To use the hybrid loss in back-propagation algorithm, we need their derivatives. For focal loss, let $p = \sigma(x) = \frac{1}{1+e^{-x}}$, be an output of a logistic function, and x is an input of the logistic function. [14] define a quality $x_t = xy$. Based on the definition of p_t in Sect. 2.2, $p_t = \frac{1}{1+e^{xy}}$. Using p_t, the derivative for focal loss

is: $\frac{\partial l_{FL}}{\partial x_t^{(i)}} = \frac{1}{n}\sum_{i=1}^{n} y^{(i)}(1-p_t^{(i)})^\gamma(\gamma p_t^{(i)}\log(p_t^{(i)}) + p_t^{(i)} - 1)$. For mean false error,
the derivative is: $\frac{\partial l_{MFE}}{\partial x^{(i)}} = \frac{\partial l_{MSE_-}}{\partial x^{(i)}} + \frac{\partial l_{MSE_+}}{\partial x^{(i)}}$, where

$$\frac{\partial l_{MSE_-}}{\partial x^{(i)}} = -\frac{1}{n_-}\sum_{i=1}^{n_-}(y^{(i)} - p^{(i)})p^{(i)}(1 - p^{(i)}), \tag{1}$$

$$\frac{\partial l_{MSE_+}}{\partial x^{(i)}} = -\frac{1}{n_+}\sum_{i=1}^{n_+}(y^{(i)} - p^{(i)})p^{(i)}(1 - p^{(i)}). \tag{2}$$

Note that the derivative in (1) is used for the negative sample, while (2) is used for the positive sample.

Using the mean false error derivative, we can define the derivative for the hybrid loss by combining the derivatives of focal loss for negative and positive classes: $\frac{\partial l_{Hybrid}}{\partial x_t^{(i)}} = \frac{\partial l_{FL_-}}{\partial x_t^{(i)}} + \frac{\partial l_{FL_+}}{\partial x_t^{(i)}}$, where

$$\frac{\partial l_{FL_-}}{\partial x_t^{(i)}} = \frac{1}{n_-}\sum_{i=1}^{n_-} y^{(i)}(1-p_t^{(i)})^\gamma(\gamma p_t^{(i)}\log(p_t^{(i)}) + p_t^{(i)} - 1), \tag{3}$$

$$\frac{\partial l_{FL_+}}{\partial x_t^{(i)}} = \frac{1}{n_+}\sum_{i=1}^{n_+} y^{(i)}(1-p_t^{(i)})^\gamma(\gamma p_t^{(i)}\log(p_t^{(i)}) + p_t^{(i)} - 1). \tag{4}$$

As in mean false error, these derivatives are used for the corresponding samples from each class.

Our hypothesis is that our hybrid loss function will perform better than mean false error and focal loss, because it allows the positive class to contribute in its full extent to the total loss and differentiate between easy and hard samples at the same time.

4 Experimental Framework

4.1 Datasets

We use two benchmark datasets, CIFAR-100 [12] and IMDB review [16]. Originally, both datasets were balanced, but we extracted various imbalanced sets from them: (1) Unbalanced Sets from CIFAR-100: CIFAR-100 has 100 classes and contains 600 images per class, including 500 training and 100 testing images. For fair comparison, we created three different sets of data, labeled Household, Tree 1 and Tree 2, by following the setting of Wang et al. [22]. Each set of data had two classes and the representation of one class was reduced to three different imbalance levels, 20%, 10% and 5%. (2) Unbalanced Sets from IMDB Review: IMDB review is for binary sentiment classification: it contains 25,000 movie reviews for training and 25,000 for testing, and each set includes 12,500 positive and 12,500 negative reviews. We created three different sets of data by leaving 20%, 10% and 5% of positive reviews.

Table 1. Performance of ResNet-50 with different loss functions. The high F_1-score and AUC demonstrate that the loss function was suited for image classification on unbalanced data

Dataset	Imb. level (%)	Metrics	Method			
			MFE	MSFE	FL	Hybrid
Household	20	F_1-score	38.02 ± 0.03	40.15 ± 0.06	41.77 ± 0.02	**43.38 ± 0.04**
		AUC	73.58 ± 0.01	74.86 ± 0.02	75.00 ± 0.02	**75.24 ± 0.01**
	10	F_1-score	13.06 ± 0.07	13.31 ± 0.06	22.01 ± 0.02	**25.40 ± 0.05**
		AUC	60.78 ± 0.02	60.80 ± 0.01	60.61 ± 0.03	**65.24 ± 0.02**
	5	F_1-score	2.87 ± 0.04	6.99 ± 0.01	9.02 ± 0.05	**10.06 ± 0.03**
		AUC	51.55 ± 0.03	55.74 ± 0.03	**57.72 ± 0.03**	54.80 ± 0.04
Tree 1	20	F_1-score	38.86 ± 0.05	42.69 ± 0.08	34.12 ± 0.05	**50.12 ± 0.06**
		AUC	**80.09 ± 0.01**	79.60 ± 0.02	78.98 ± 0.01	79.62 ± 0.02
	10	F_1-score	36.63 ± 0.10	40.63 ± 0.12	33.33 ± 0.13	**42.49 ± 0.11**
		AUC	73.32 ± 0.03	74.82 ± 0.04	70.80 ± 0.02	**76.08 ± 0.03**
	5	F_1-score	32.38 ± 0.02	30.48 ± 0.02	26.67 ± 0.13	**33.33 ± 0.05**
		AUC	**80.68 ± 0.05**	79.96 ± 0.04	72.20 ± 0.03	80.08 ± 0.03
Tree 2	20	F_1-score	56.38 ± 0.05	57.71 ± 0.03	58.76 ± 0.03	**61.66 ± 0.05**
		AUC	82.22 ± 0.02	82.46 ± 0.02	81.92 ± 0.02	**82.53 ± 0.01**
	10	F_1-score	53.48 ± 0.06	57.10 ± 0.08	57.13 ± 0.03	**61.86 ± 0.08**
		AUC	80.90 ± 0.01	81.08 ± 0.03	79.58 ± 0.03	**81.30 ± 0.03**
	5	F_1-score	47.59 ± 0.07	43.59 ± 0.10	50.95 ± 0.09	**55.71 ± 0.03**
		AUC	72.04 ± 0.07	**78.88 ± 0.08**	65.52 ± 0.09	71.88 ± 0.07

4.2 Experiment Settings

Each unbalanced data set was split into training, validation and test sets. All three sets have the same imbalance ratio. As both CIFAR-100 and IMDR review, already had training and test sets, we chose 20% of samples from the training set for the validation set. The obtained training and validation sets are used for training model, and the test set is used for evaluating the trained model. The experiment was run five times with different random splits.

We used ResNet-50 [5] for image classification, and Transformer [20], that is represented in Keras document for sentiment classification. Both models used the Adam Optimizer [11]. We ran the experiments using TensorFlow [1] and Keras [4].

5 Results and Discussions

Table 1 reports the classification performances of the methods used on the CIFAR-100 sets. Our hybrid loss function performed better than the other losses in most cases and achieved the highest F_1-score in all cases.

Table 2. Performances of Transformer on different loss functions. The high F_1-score and AUC demonstrated that the loss function is suited for the sentiment classification on imbalanced data.

Imb. level (%)	Metrics	Method			
		MFE	MSFE	FL	Hybrid
20	F_1-score	65.56 ± 0.01	67.14 ± 0.01	67.19 ± 0.02	**67.20 ± 0.05**
	AUC	91.67 ± 0.08	91.57 ± 0.09	91.68 ± 0.12	**92.16 ± 0.09**
10	F_1-score	52.57 ± 0.01	54.50 ± 0.01	53.77 ± 0.01	**54.83 ± 0.01**
	AUC	91.04 ± 0.03	90.80 ± 0.04	91.10 ± 0.02	**91.32 ± 0.06**
5	F_1-score	38.07 ± 0.01	40.48 ± 0.01	39.93 ± 0.01	**42.80 ± 0.02**
	AUC	88.93 ± 0.06	88.95 ± 0.02	88.71 ± 0.01	**89.52 ± 0.04**

We report the classification performances of Transformer trained using different loss functions in Table 2. The hybrid loss achieved the highest F_1-score and AUC at all imbalance levels.

6 Conclusion

We studied two loss functions, mean false error and focal loss for training deep neural networks on unbalanced data. As each of the two losses has advantages that can eliminate drawbacks of the other, we showed that hybridizing the two losses in a hybrid loss function that imitates the calculation procedures of mean false error's total loss to focal loss. Tests on this hybrid loss, on image and text classifications, at various imbalance levels, showed that the networks trained with it were superior to mean false error, mean squared false error and focal loss on the F_1-score, but worse in a few cases on the AUC.

This work focused on improving DNN performance for binary classification: future work will evaluate it on multi-class classification.

References

1. Abadi, M., et al.: Tensorflow: a system for large-scale machine learning. In: 12th USENIX Symposium on Operating Systems Design and Implementation (OSDI 16), pp. 265–283 (2016)
2. Anand, R., Mehrotra, K.G., Mohan, C.K., Ranka, S.: An improved algorithm for neural network classification of imbalanced training sets. IEEE Trans. Neural Netw. 4(6), 962–969 (1993)
3. Buda, M., Maki, A., Mazurowski, M.A.: A systematic study of the class imbalance problem in convolutional neural networks. Neural Netw. 106, 249–259 (2018)
4. Chollet, F., et al.: Keras (2015). https://keras.io
5. He, K., Zhang, X., Ren, S., Sun, J.: Deep residual learning for image recognition. In: Proceedings of the IEEE Conference on Computer Vision and Pattern Recognition, pp. 770–778 (2016)

6. Hensman, P., Masko, D.: The impact of imbalanced training data for convolutional neural networks. Degree Project in Computer Science, KTH Royal Institute of Technology (2015)
7. Huang, C., Li, Y., Chen, C.L., Tang, X.: Deep imbalanced learning for face recognition and attribute prediction. IEEE Trans. Pattern Anal. Mach. Intell. (2019)
8. Janowczyk, A., Madabhushi, A.: Deep learning for digital pathology image analysis: a comprehensive tutorial with selected use cases. J. Pathol. Inform. 7 (2016)
9. Johnson, J.M., Khoshgoftaar, T.M.: Survey on deep learning with class imbalance. J. Big Data 6(1), 1–54 (2019). https://doi.org/10.1186/s40537-019-0192-5
10. Khan, S.H., Hayat, M., Bennamoun, M., Sohel, F.A., Togneri, R.: Cost-sensitive learning of deep feature representations from imbalanced data. IEEE Trans. Neural Netw. Learn. Syst. 29(8), 3573–3587 (2017)
11. Kingma, D.P., Ba, J.: Adam: a method for stochastic optimization. arXiv preprint arXiv:1412.6980 (2014)
12. Krizhevsky, A.: Learning multiple layers of features from tiny images. Tech. rep. (2009)
13. Kudisthalert, W., Pasupa, K., Tongsima, S.: Counting and classification of malarial parasite from giemsa-stained thin film images. IEEE Access 8, 78663–78682 (2020)
14. Lin, T.Y., Goyal, P., Girshick, R., He, K., Dollár, P.: Focal loss for dense object detection. In: Proceedings of the IEEE International Conference on Computer Vision, pp. 2980–2988 (2017)
15. Liu, Z., Miao, Z., Zhan, X., Wang, J., Gong, B., Yu, S.X.: Large-scale long-tailed recognition in an open world. In: Proceedings of the IEEE Conference on Computer Vision and Pattern Recognition, pp. 2537–2546 (2019)
16. Maas, A.L., Daly, R.E., Pham, P.T., Huang, D., Ng, A.Y., Potts, C.: Learning word vectors for sentiment analysis. In: Proceedings of the 49th Annual Meeting of the Association for Computational Linguistics: Human Language Technologies, pp. 142–150. Association for Computational Linguistics, Portland, Oregon, USA, June 2011. http://www.aclweb.org/anthology/P11-1015
17. Pasupa, K., Kudisthalert, W.: Virtual screening by a new clustering-based weighted similarity extreme learning machine approach. PLoS ONE 13(4), e0195478 (2018)
18. Pasupa, K., Vatathanavaro, S., Tungjitnob, S.: Convolutional neural networks based focal loss for class imbalance problem: a case study of canine red blood cells morphology classification. arXiv preprint arXiv:2001.03329 (2020)
19. Sammut, C., Webb, G.I.: Encyclopedia of Machine Learning. Springer Science & Business Media, Berlin (2011)
20. Vaswani, A., et al.: Attention is all you need. In: Advances in Neural Information Processing Systems, pp. 5998–6008 (2017)
21. Wang, H., Cui, Z., Chen, Y., Avidan, M., Abdallah, A.B., Kronzer, A.: Predicting hospital readmission via cost-sensitive deep learning. IEEE/ACM Trans. Comput. Biol. Bioinform. 15(6), 1968–1978 (2018)
22. Wang, S., Liu, W., Wu, J., Cao, L., Meng, Q., Kennedy, P.J.: Training deep neural networks on imbalanced data sets. In: 2016 International Joint Conference on Neural Networks (IJCNN), pp. 4368–4374. IEEE (2016)
23. Zhu, X., Jing, X.Y., Zhang, F., Zhang, X., You, X., Cui, X.: Distance learning by mining hard and easy negative samples for person re-identification. Pattern Recogn. 95, 211–222 (2019)

Multi-scale Attention Consistency for Multi-label Image Classification

Haotian Xu, Xiaobo Jin, Qiufeng Wang, and Kaizhu Huang[✉]

Department of Intelligent Science, School of Advanced Technology,
Xi'an Jiaotong-Liverpool University, Suzhou, China
Haotian.Xu18@student.xjtlu.edu.cn,
{Xiaobo.Jin,Qiufeng.Wang,Kaizhu.Huang}@xjtlu.edu.cn

Abstract. Human has well demonstrated its cognitive consistency over image transformations such as flipping and scaling. In order to learn from human's visual perception consistency, researchers find out that convolutional neural network's capacity of discernment can be further elevated via forcing the network to concentrate on certain area in the picture in accordance with the human natural visual perception. Attention heatmap, as a supplementary tool to reveal the essential region that the network chooses to focus on, has been developed and widely adopted by CNNs. Based on this regime of visual consistency, we propose a novel end-to-end trainable CNN architecture with multi-scale attention consistency. Specifically, our model takes an original picture and its flipped counterpart as inputs, and then send them into a single standard Resnet with additional attention-enhanced modules to generate a semantically strong attention heatmap. We also compute the distance between multi-scale attention heatmaps of these two pictures and take it as an additional loss to help the network achieve better performance. Our network shows superiority on the multi-label classification task and attains compelling results on the WIDER Attribute Dataset.

Keywords: Image classification · Multi-label learning · Attention · Consistency

1 Introduction

Multi-label Classification task [1] has been a hot spot in the area of computer vision for many years. The main purpose of this task is to point out attributes and objects which are annotated in the pictures. Among all the approaches that try to solve this problem, deep neural networks are taking the leading role and have achieved remarkable results. Recent works [2,3] on classification and detection keep pushing the line forward, but multi-label classification still remains a challenging task due to its appearance complexities.

Human brains [4] are not sensitive to the spatial transformation of pictures and can still read the semantic details of the picture regardless of the operations

© Springer Nature Switzerland AG 2020
H. Yang et al. (Eds.): ICONIP 2020, CCIS 1332, pp. 815–823, 2020.
https://doi.org/10.1007/978-3-030-63820-7_93

made on images like rotation, scaling, cropping, and flipping. In this paper, we define the people's ability to consistently recognize objects in a picture without influenced by the spatial transformation as visual consistency. Through years of studies on convolutional neural networks, it is believed that visual consistency not only exists in human brains, but also in CNNs. Past studies on neuroscience [6] and CNN models [5] have uncovered the visual mechanism: when people see a picture, a high-level abstraction of visual representations is generated simultaneously. Further investigations find that the classification result of a picture mainly depends on a certain part of the visual representation. Such area that draws the notice of our brain is called the attention region. Consequently, we can introduce our core concept of visual attention consistency [7]: attention regions for the image classification follow the same transformation during both of the training and test stages.

Much work [8] has been done to locate attention regions of CNN classifiers. However, most of these work neglected the network's potential power of visual attention consistency. Guo et al. [7] firstly proposed a method which impels the original picture and its transformed counterpart to be noticed at the same attention region. Based on the previous works, we introduce our network structure which takes an original image and its flipped counterpart as inputs, which are then put into a standard Resnet50 with enhanced attention modules between blocks. The class activation mapping (CAM) [5] is leveraged to generate attention heatmaps for all labels on an image before the output layer, which is used to compute our new attention loss. The attention loss measures the distance between the attention heatmaps of the original image and its flipped counterpart on multiple scales. The experimental results show that our proposed approach achieves competitive results on the public multi-label WIDER Attribute dataset. In summary, our contributions are listed as follows: 1) We modify and integrate the light-weight attention module between blocks of Resnet to make the semantic information of the final attention heatmap abundant; 2) We measure the difference of three scale attention heatmaps of two input pictures to assist the training of the network.

2   Related Work

2.1   Multi-label Classification

As reviewed in [1], there has been extensive exploration studying the multi-label classification task. Label-separated and label-correlated methods are two mainstream approaches. The label-separated method tried to reduce the task of multi-label classification into multiple binary classification. As for the label-correlatd method, the probabilistic label enhancement [9] and matrix completion [10] were proposed to build the semantic correlations of labels. We propose a new loss using visual attention consistency to solve the problem from another perspective.

2.2 Attention Mechanism for Classification

It is broadly accepted that attention plays a significant role in human natural perception. Hu et al. [11] introduced the compact model to characterize inter-channel relationship, where a squeeze-and-excitation module with the global average was used to exploit channel-wise attention. Woo et al. [12] proposed a convolutional attention module which utilized both average pooling and max pooling on feature maps to achieve optimal performance. In our work, we try to approach the problem with the attention heatmaps, an indirect but workable way to locate label regions while forcing the attention to be consistent.

3 Proposed Method

In this section, we present backgrounds on the components that are adopted to facilitate the effectiveness of our network. Then we will specifically introduce the structure of our network (as shown in Fig. 1) and the visual attention consistency.

3.1 Class Activation Mapping

Class Activation Mapping (CAM) [5] has already become a popular tool for researchers to generate attention heatmaps. In most CNNs, fully connected layer after pooling layer takes in the feature map with weights $W \in \mathbb{R}^{L \times C}$ (L is the number of labels) and generate predictions for classification. CAM uses these weights to compute the attention heatmap at location (x, y) for label j as $M_j(x, y)$ shown in Eq. (1)

$$M_j(x, y) = \sum_{k=1}^{C} W(j, k) F_k(x, y), \tag{1}$$

where $W(j, k)$ and $F_k(x, y)$ represent the weight of label j at channel k and the feature map of channel k from the last convolution layer at spatial coordinate (x, y), respectively.

3.2 Multi-label Classification Loss

Although rank loss [14] has been widely used to facilitate performance of multi-label classification. For the purpose of simplicity, we adopt the weighted sigmoid cross entropy loss in [15]:

$$\ell_c = -\frac{1}{N} \sum_{i=1}^{N} \sum_{j=1}^{L} \omega_{ij} \left(y_{ij} \log \frac{1}{1 + e^{-x_{ij}}} + (1 - y_{ij}) \log \frac{e^{-x_{ij}}}{1 + e^{-x_{ij}}} \right), \tag{2}$$

$$\omega_{ij} = \begin{cases} e^{1-p_j}, & y_{ij} = 1 \\ e^{p_j}, & y_{ij} = 0 \end{cases}, \tag{3}$$

where N is the total count of images, L is the number of labels, $x_{ij} \in \mathbb{R}$ is the prediction of label j in image i and it is further modified to $1/\left(1 + e^{-x_{ij}}\right) \in [0,1]$, $y_{ij} \in \{0,1\}$ indicates whether the image i belongs to the label j, p_j is the fraction of the positive samples with label j within the training set and it is used to define weight ω_{ij} in the purpose of balancing training sample. This loss is adopted by all baselines we test and our method for fair comparison.

3.3   Attention Module

New findings indicate that given an intermediate feature map, we can take a further step to refine attention representations along two separate dimensions: channel attention and spatial attention. Our top priority is to retain more sufficient information and generate the feature map with stronger semantics at final layers of the CNN. To fulfill that purpose, we learn from many distinguished network structure designs [12]. Among all of them, BAM [16] is of great benefits. Bottleneck attention module, as a light-weight and effective module, learns what and where to focus or suppress through two separate pathways: channel and spatial.

We adopt both channel pathway and spatial pathway. For spatial attention, it is crucial to use a large receptive field to exploit contextual information of an image, where the dilated convolution can be a compute-efficient choice. Meanwhile, with respect to the channel attention, we sequentially conduct global pooling and average pooling on input channels in a channel-wise manner to extract the inter-channel relationship of features. Then we make an element-wise summation to merge the channel attentions with spatial attention. In practice, we make the minor justification of BAM by normalizing input features before sending them into the attention module. The attention module can be simply inserted between the blocks of Resnet.

3.4   Proposed Network

As illustrated in Fig. 1, our network takes two images as inputs: the original image I and its horizontally flipped image $T(I)$, which are put into a standard Resnet50 with the enhanced attention module. The module is inserted between blocks and acts like a 'bottleneck', where the attention module refines the information in a manner of residual learning. Given the channel attention $M_c(F) \in R^C$ and spatial attention $M_s(F) \in R^{H \times W}$ at two separate branches, our network transforms the blended output of both branches with the sigmoid function $\sigma(\cdot)$ as follows:

$$F' = F + F \otimes (\sigma(M_c(F) + M_s(F))), \tag{4}$$

where F and F' represent the input and the output respectively. Note that the $\otimes$ operator denotes the element-wise multiplication. Both channel attention and spatial attention are resized to $R^{C \times H \times W}$ before addition.

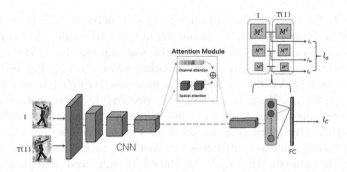

Fig. 1. Overall architecture of our proposed method: an attention module is inserted between each two blocks.

The final attention heatmap is generated for all labels by CAM. Specifically, we reshape the feature map F and the weights W of FC layer into $1 \times C \times H \times W$ and $L \times C \times 1 \times 1$, respectively. We conduct the channel-wise multiplications to sequentially combine feature maps for each label, and compute the summation over all dimensions of merged feature maps (see Eq. (1)). Then, we conduct a mean square difference between the attention heatmaps of the original image and the flipped image as shown in Eq. (5). Empirically, we resize the heatmap with three different scales to achieve a better classification result. We conduct our new loss on three different scales M_{small}, M_{medium} and M_{large} to obtain ℓ_s, ℓ_m and ℓ_l. The attention loss is a summation of these three losses

$$\ell_s = \frac{1}{NLHW} \sum_{i=1}^{N} \sum_{j=1}^{L} \left\| M_{ij}^s - M_{ij}^{s\prime} \right\|_2 , \qquad (5)$$

where ℓ_s indicates the attention loss for small-scale attention heatmap, M_{ij}^s represents the small-scale attention heatmap for image i and label j. $M_{ij}^{s\prime}$ indicates the small-scale attention heatmap of the flipped image. This new loss is then added up to the final loss with the multi-label classification loss. The final loss Eq. (6) is a linear combination of cross entropy loss (Eq. (2)) and attention loss

$$\ell = \ell_c + \lambda(\ell_s + \ell_m + \ell_l), \qquad (6)$$

where λ is a tradeoff coefficient between both items. In our work, λ is empirically set to 1.

4 Experiments

We evaluate our network on the WIDER Attribute Dataset [18], which is broadly used as a public dataset for the human attribute classification task. It contains 13,789 images from 30 scene categories, and 57,524 human bounding boxes with 14 binary attributes. The train-validation dataset includes 28,345 human bounding boxes while the test dataset includes 29,179 human bounding boxes.

To test the performance of our proposed network, we use pre-trained Resnet50 on ImageNet [13,17] as our backbone. All models are trained with the stochastic gradient descent at an initial learning rate 10^{-3}. We adopt label-based metrics to evaluate our model including mean Average Precision (mAP), mean accuracy (mA), macro and micro precision/recall/F1-score (denoted as P_{mac}, R_{mac}, $F1_{mac}$, P_{mic}, R_{mic}, $F1_{mic}$, respectively). Macro metrics are evaluated by averaging per-label metrics while micro metrics are the overall measures that count the true predictions for all images over all labels.

Our network mainly contributes two methods to improve the performance on multi-label classification task, we embed an enhanced attention module in Resnet and introduce a new loss to converge the network. In the following, we conduct an ablation analysis on our network to test the importance of each method.

Table 1. Performance (%) on WIDER Attribute dataset in terms of label-based metrics. The model marked with * uses both original and flipped inputs. AM means that the model embeds the attention module and ℓ_a represents multi-scale attention loss. The best results are highlighted in bold font.

Model	mAP	mA	Macro			Micro		
			$F1_{mac}$	P_{mac}	R_{mac}	$F1_{mic}$	P_{mic}	R_{mic}
R50	83.4	82.0	73.9	79.5	69.4	79.4	82.3	76.6
R50*	84.2	82.8	74.6	79.5	70.7	80.0	82.9	76.9
R50*+AM	84.6	83.4	75.4	79.1	72.4	80.4	82.2	78.7
R50*+ℓ_a	86.3	84.0	76.4	**80.9**	72.8	81.4	**83.7**	79.2
R50*+AM+ℓ_a	**86.6**	**84.6**	**76.6**	79.6	**74.4**	**81.7**	83.2	**80.2**

We run experiments on four combinations and try to compare the influence of each method on the output. Multi-label classification loss is adopted by all tests. We initially test our backbone Resnet50 with only original images as input. Then we gradually add our methods into the model. As illustrated in Table 1, the data augmentation with flipped inputs improves the results on all metrics and proves to be a good way to facilitate network training. But the attention module only has a slight improvement on mAP by 0.4% compared with Resnet50*. On the other hand, we can get a strong boost in performance when we add the attention loss to the network. Resnet50* with our scaled attention loss achieves roughly 2% of increase on all the metrics. Our ultimate model with all the methods receives the best performance on mAP and F1 score. Therefore, we can draw the conclusion that our attention loss is the key point of the network in contrast with the attention module.

To further verify the effectiveness and performance of our network, we compare our approach with the state-of-the-art methods on WIDER Attribute Dataset. Various CNN architectures are used as backbones of these models. Resnet101 [20] is trained with multiple data augmentation strategies.

Table 2. Comparisons of label-based metrics between our method and the state-of-the-art methods on WIDER Attribute dataset

Method	mAP	$F1_{mac}$	P_{mac}	R_{mac}	$F1_{mic}$	P_{mic}	R_{mic}
R-CNN [22]	80.0	–	–	–	–	–	–
DHC [18]	81.3	–	–	–	–	–	–
AR [19]	82.9	–	–	–	–	–	–
ResNet101 [20]	85.0	74.7	–	–	80.4	–	–
SRN [20]	86.2	75.9	–	–	81.3	–	–
VAA [21]	86.4	–	–	–	–	–	–
R50+ACf [7]	86.3	76.4	78.9	74.3	81.2	82.6	79.8
Ours	**86.6**	**76.6**	**79.6**	**74.4**	**81.7**	**83.2**	**80.2**

As we can see from Table 2, our method performs the best on all the metrics, leading on mAP by 0.3%, $F1_{mac}$ by 0.2%, P_{mac} by 0.7%, R_{mac} by 0.1%, $F1_{mic}$ by 0.5%, P_{mic} by 0.6%, R_{mic} by 0.4%. VAA [21] attains the second best result on mAP. Apart from our results, R50+ACf [7] achieves the best test result in general which takes the original and flipped images as input without other data augmentation as we do. For fair comparisons, we also mention that R50+ACfs [7] receives 86.8 on mAP which conducts both flipping and scaling for the data augmentation.

5 Conclusion

Inspired by the concept of visual attention consistency, we propose a method that forces the network to concentrate on the same attention region while the input images are spatially transformed. We conduct experiments on the WIDER Attribute dataset and achieve compelling results compared to the state-of-the-art methods. On account of the experimental results we achieve, we can come to the conclusion that such attention consistency does exist among hidden layers of the convolutional neural networks. Therefore we can generalize the property to other computer vision tasks such as zero-shot learning in the future work.

Acknowledgement. This study was funded by National Natural Science Foundation of China under no. 61876154, 61876155, and U1804159; Natural Science Foundation of Jiangsu Province BK20181189 and BK20181190; Key Program Special Fund in XJTLU under no. KSF-A-10, KSF-A-01, KSF-P-02, KSF-E-26 and KSF-T-06; and XJTLU Research Development Fund RDF-16-02-49 and RDF-16-01-57.

References

1. Zhang, M.L., Zhou, Z.H.: A review on multi-label learning algorithms. IEEE Trans. Knowl. Data Eng. **26**(8), 1819–1837 (2013)

2. Cao, Y., Wang, Q.-F., Huang, K., Zhang, R.: Improving image caption performance with linguistic context. In: Ren, J., et al. (eds.) BICS 2019. LNCS (LNAI), vol. 11691, pp. 3–11. Springer, Cham (2020). https://doi.org/10.1007/978-3-030-39431-8_1

3. Gao, Z., Liu, D., Huang, K., Huang, Y.: Context-aware human activity and smartphone position-mining with motion sensors. Remote Sens. **11**(21), 2531 (2019)

4. Lavie, N.: Distracted and confused? Selective attention under load. Trends Cogn. Sci. **9**(2), 75–82 (2005)

5. Zhou, B., Khosla, A., Lapedriza, A., Oliva, A., Torralba, A.: Learning deep features for discriminative localization. In Proceedings of the CVPR, pp. 2921–2929 (2016)

6. Desimone, R., Duncan, J.: Neural mechanisms of selective visual attention. Ann. Rev. Neurosci. **18**(1), 193–222 (1995)

7. Guo, H., Zheng, K., Fan, X., Yu, H., Wang, S.: Visual attention consistency under image transforms for multi-label image classification. In: Proceedings of the CVPR, pp. 729–739 (2019)

8. Stollenga, M.F., Masci, J., Gomez, F., Schmidhuber, J.: Deep networks with internal selective attention through feedback connections. In: Advances in Neural Information Processing Systems, pp. 3545–3553 (2014)

9. Li, X., Zhao, F., Guo, Y.: Multi-label image classification with a probabilistic label enhancement model. In: UAI, vol. 1, p. 3 (2014)

10. Cabral, R., De la Torre, F., Costeira, J.P., Bernardino, A.: Matrix completion for weakly-supervised multi-label image classification. IEEE Trans. Pattern Anal. Mach. Intell. **37**(1), 121–135 (2014)

11. Hu, J., Shen, L., Sun, G.: Squeeze-and-excitation networks. In: Proceedings of the CVPR, pp. 7132–7141 (2018)

12. Woo, S., Park, J., Lee, J.-Y., Kweon, I.S.: CBAM: convolutional block attention module. In: Ferrari, V., Hebert, M., Sminchisescu, C., Weiss, Y. (eds.) ECCV 2018. LNCS, vol. 11211, pp. 3–19. Springer, Cham (2018). https://doi.org/10.1007/978-3-030-01234-2_1

13. He, K., Zhang, X., Ren, S., Sun, J.: Deep residual learning for image recognition. In: Proceedings of the CVPR, pp. 770–778 (2016)

14. Dembczynski, K., Kotlowski, W., Hüllermeier, E.: Consistent multilabel ranking through univariate losses. arXiv preprint arXiv:1206.6401 (2012)

15. Li, D., Chen, X., Huang, K.: Multi-attribute learning for pedestrian attribute recognition in surveillance scenarios. In: 2015 3rd IAPR Asian Conference on Pattern Recognition (ACPR), pp. 111–115 (2015)

16. Park, J., Woo, S., Lee, J.Y., Kweon, I.S.: BAM: Bottleneck attention module. arXiv preprint arXiv:1807.06514 (2018)

17. Deng, J., Dong, W., Socher, R., Li, L.J., Li, K., Fei-Fei, L.: ImageNet: a large-scale hierarchical image database. In: Proceedings of the CVPR, pp. 248–255(2009)

18. Li, Y., Huang, C., Loy, C.C., Tang, X.: Human attribute recognition by deep hierarchical contexts. In: Leibe, B., Matas, J., Sebe, N., Welling, M. (eds.) ECCV 2016. LNCS, vol. 9910, pp. 684–700. Springer, Cham (2016). https://doi.org/10.1007/978-3-319-46466-4_41

19. Guo, H., Fan, X., Wang, S.: Human attribute recognition by refining attention heat map. Pattern Recogn. Lett. **94**, 38–45 (2017)

20. Zhu, F., Li, H., Ouyang, W., Yu, N., Wang, X.: Learning spatial regularization with image-level supervisions for multi-label image classification. In: Proceedings of the CVPR, pp. 5513–5522 (2017)

21. Sarafianos, N., Xu, X., Kakadiaris, I.A.: Deep imbalanced attribute classification using visual attention aggregation. In: Proceedings of the ECCV, pp. 680–697 (2018)
22. Girshick, R.: Fast R-CNN. In: Proceedings of the IEEE International Conference on Computer Vision, pp. 1440–1448 (2015)

Quantile Regression Hindsight Experience Replay

Qiwei He[1], Liansheng Zhuang[1(✉)], Wei Zhang[2,3], and Houqiang Li[1]

[1] University of Science and Technology of China, Hefei 230027, China
hqw1996@mail.ustc.edu.cn, lszhuang@ustc.edu.cn
[2] Peng Cheng Laboratory, Shenzhen 518000, China
[3] Science and Technology on Electronic Information Control Lab.,
Chengdu 610036, China

Abstract. Efficient learning in the environment with sparse rewards is one of the most important challenges in Deep Reinforcement Learning (DRL). In continuous DRL environments such as robotic manipulation tasks, Multi-goal RL with the accompanying algorithm Hindsight Experience Replay (HER) has been shown an effective solution. However, HER and its variants typically suffer from a major challenge that the agents may perform well in some goals while poorly in the other goals. The main reason for the phenomenon is the popular concept in the recent DRL works called intrinsic stochasticity. In Multi-goal RL, intrinsic stochasticity lies in that the different initial goals of the environment will cause the different value distributions and interfere with each other, where computing the expected return is not suitable in principle and cannot perform well as usual. To tackle this challenge, in this paper, we propose Quantile Regression Hindsight Experience Replay (QR-HER), a novel approach based on Quantile Regression. The key idea is to select the returns that are most closely related to the current goal from the replay buffer without additional data. In this way, the interference between different initial goals will be significantly reduced. We evaluate QR-HER on OpenAI Robotics manipulation tasks with sparse rewards. Experimental results show that, in contrast to HER and its variants, our proposed QR-HER achieves better performance by improving the performances of each goal as we expected.

Keywords: Deep reinforcement learning · Robotic manipulation · Multi-goal

1 Introduction

Reinforcement learning (RL) [10] is designed to predict and control the agent to accomplish different kinds of tasks from the interactions with the environment by receiving rewards. RL combined with Deep Learning [5] has been shown to be an effective framework in a wide range of domains. However, many great challenges still exist in Deep Reinforcement Learning (DRL), one of which is to

© Springer Nature Switzerland AG 2020
H. Yang et al. (Eds.): ICONIP 2020, CCIS 1332, pp. 824–831, 2020.
https://doi.org/10.1007/978-3-030-63820-7_94

make the agent learn efficiently with sparse rewards. In the environment with sparse rewards, rewards are zero in most transitions and non-zero only when the agent achieves some special states. This makes it extremely difficult for the policy network to inference the correct behavior in the long-sequence decision making. To tackle this challenge, Universal Value Function Approximator (UVFA)[9] is proposed to sample goals from some special states, which extends the definition of value function by not just over states but also over goals. This is equivalent to giving the value function higher dimensional states as parameters for the gain of extra information in different episodes. Lillicrap et al. developed the Deep Deterministic Policy Gradient (DDPG) [6] by utilizing Gaussian Noise for exploration, which significantly improves the performance in continuous control tasks such as manipulation and locomotion. Experience Replay (ER) [7] is a technique that stores and reuses past experiences with a replay buffer. Inspired by the above methods, Hindsight Experience Replay (HER) [1] replaces the desired goals of training trajectories with the sampled goals in the replay buffer and additionally leverage the rich repository of the failed experiences. Utilizing HER, the RL agent can learn to accomplish complex robotic manipulation tasks [8], which is nearly impossible to be solved with general RL algorithms.

Nevertheless, the above methods based on maximizing the expected return still has its problem called intrinsic stochasticity [2]. This phenomenon occurs because the return depends on internal registers and is truly unobservable. On most occasions, the return can be regarded as a constant value function over states, for instance, the maze. In this way, the optimal value of any state should also be constant after long time of training. However, in some occasions, different initial states of the environment will cause significantly different value functions that form the value distributions, which called parametric uncertainty [3]. Furthermore, the MDP process itself does not include past rewards for the current state so that it cannot even distinguish the predictions for different steps of receiving the rewards, which called MDP intrinsic randomness [3]. The above two reasons are the main sources of intrinsic stochasticity.

In the environment with sparse rewards, the intrinsic stochasticity exists mainly due to the parametric uncertainty. The initial goals in Multi-goal RL, as part of the environment, may be completely different from each other and the value distributions are significantly affected by the distribution of goals. However, from the perspective of the expected return, HER and its variants ignore the intrinsic stochasticity caused by the distribution of initial goals and mix the parameters of different value distributions in the training process. In principle, it may cause the instability and degradation of performance especially when the number of goals is large.

Inspired by the above insights, in this paper, we propose a novel method called Quantile Regression Hindsight Experience Replay (QR-HER) to improve the intrinsic stochasticity of the training process in Multi-goal RL. On the basis of Quantile Regression, our key idea is to reduce the interference between different goals by selecting the proper returns for the current goal from the similar goals in the replay buffer. We evaluate QR-HER on the representative OpenAI

Robotics environment and find that QR-HER can achieve better performance compared to HER and its state-of-the-art variant CHER [4]. Furthermore, we infer that the performance improvement of QR-HER is due to the enhancement of the policy for each goal.

2 Preliminary

2.1 Universal Value Function Approximators

UVFA [9] proposed utilizing the concatenation of states $s \in \mathcal{S}$ and goals $g \in \mathcal{G}$ as higher dimensional universal states (s, g) such that the value function approximators $V(s)$ and $Q(s, a)$ can be generalized as $V(s, g)$ and $Q(s, a, g)$. The goals can also be called goal states since in general $\mathcal{G} \subset \mathcal{S}$.

2.2 Multi-goal RL and HER

In Multi-goal RL, random exploration is unlikely to reach the goals. Even if the agent is lucky enough to reach a goal, it does not have enough experience to reach the next one. To address the challenge, [1] proposed Hindsight Experience Replay (HER) including two key techniques, *reward shaping* and *goal relabelling*. The key technique called *reward shaping* is to make the reward function dependent on a goal $g \in G$, such that $r_g : S \times A \times G \rightarrow R$. The formula is given by:

$$r_t = r_g\left(s_t, a_t, g\right) = \begin{cases} 0, & \text{if } |s_t - g| < \delta \\ -1, & \text{otherwise} \end{cases} \tag{1}$$

where we can figure out that this trick brings much more virtual returns to support the training. The other technique called *goal relabelling* is to replay each trajectory with different goals sampled from the intermediate states by special schemes. For the transition $(s_t \| g, a_t, r_t, s_{t+1} \| g)$, we will store its hindsight transition $(s_t \| g', a_t, r', s_{t+1} \| g')$ in the replay buffer instead.

3 Quantile Regression Hindsight Experience Replay

3.1 Distributional Mutil-Goal RL Objective

For convenience, we replace the state s with x, the Multi-goal Bellman operator is given as:

$$\mathcal{T}^\pi Q(x, a, g) = \mathbb{E}[R(x, a, g)] + \gamma \mathbb{E}_{P, \pi}\left[Q\left(x', a', g\right)\right]. \tag{2}$$

Using the above formula, the distributional Bellman operator is given as:

$$\mathcal{T}^\pi Z(x, a, g) \overset{D}{:=} R(x, a, g) + \gamma Z\left(x', a', g\right) \\ x' \sim P(\cdot | x, a, g), a' \sim \pi\left(\cdot | x', g\right), \tag{3}$$

where Z denotes the value distribution of Q, $Z \overset{D}{:=} U$ denotes equality of probability laws, that is the random variable Z is distributed according to the sam law as U.

3.2   The Wasserstein Metric

For different goals g, different value distributions Z will be produced. In order to minimize the gap among different value distributions, utilizing the inverse CDF (Cumulative Distribution Function) F^{-1}, we introduce the p-Wasserstein metric, which is written as:

$$W_p(Z_G, Z_{G'}) = \left(\int_0^1 \left| F_{(Z_G)}^{-1}(\omega) - F_{Z_{G'}}^{-1}(\omega) \right|^p d\omega \right)^{1/p}, \tag{4}$$

where we use G to represent the initial desired goals which are generated by the environments to be separated from the total sampled goals g, $G \subset g$. G is the main source of intrinsic stochasticity in Multi-goal RL while not the goals generated by hindsight replay. In the cases of RL with expected return, for the current state, we assume that there is only one value distribution and calculate the average probability of its different values. While in quantile distributional RL, we prefer to divide the probability space into different and identical small blocks. For each block, we find out all the corresponding returns of different value distributions utilizing the inverse CDF F^{-1}. Then when making action decisions, we consider all the return values in the blocks to select one from a comprehensive view rather than just averaging.

The quantile distributional parameters and corresponding inverse CDF are not available, so we introduce Quantile Regression network as the function to be learned from the samples. The number of blocks called Quant is fixed and the output of the regression network is the Z vector consisting of the returns of the quantiles. In the Bellman update, the Bellman operator continuously changes the value of the Z vector until convergence. In this way, we can use the Wasserstein Metric to calculate the Quantile Regression loss between the Z vectors of the current state and the next state for the network training, given by:

$$\mathcal{L}_{\text{QR}}^{\tau}(\theta) := \mathbb{E}_{\hat{Z} \sim Z} \left[\rho_{\tau}(\hat{Z} - \theta) \right], \text{ where} \tag{5}$$
$$\rho_{\tau}(u) = u \left(\tau - \delta_{\{u<0\}} \right), \forall u \in \mathbb{R}$$

where θ is the parameter to fit the unknown inverse CDF, for minimizing a step of Bellman update $\int_{\tau}^{\tau'} \left| F^{-1}(\omega) - \theta \right| d\omega$, it can be deduced mathematically that:

$$\left\{ \theta \in \mathbb{R} | F(\theta) = \left(\frac{\tau + \tau'}{2} \right) \right\}, \tag{6}$$

then if F^{-1} is continuous at $(\tau + \tau')/2$, we can use $\theta = F^{-1}((\tau + \tau')/2)$ as the unique minimizer.

However, the Quantile Regression loss is not smooth at zero, we will consider use the Huber loss $\rho_{\tau}^{\kappa}(u)$ to replace $\rho_{\tau}(u)$, given by:

$$\mathcal{L}_{\kappa}(u) = \begin{cases} \frac{1}{2}u^2, & \text{if } |u| \leq \kappa \\ \kappa \left(|u| - \frac{1}{2}\kappa \right), & \text{otherwise} \end{cases}, \rho_{\tau}^{\kappa}(u) = \left| \tau - \delta_{\{u<0\}} \right| \frac{\mathcal{L}_{\kappa}(u)}{\kappa} \tag{7}$$

3.3 Return Selection for Multi-goal RL

As demonstrated in the Introduction and Preliminary, the different initial goals mainly cause the intrinsic stochasticity in RL with sparse rewards. When updating the parameters for the current goal, we should exclude interference from other less relevant goals as much as possible. Hence, we propose using the Wasserstein Metric to eliminate the interference of the value distributions of goals with low correlation as the following formula:

$$Z_\theta(x, a, g, G) := \frac{1}{N} \sum_{i=1}^{N} \sum_{G_\epsilon} \delta_{\theta_i(x,a,g,G_\epsilon)}, G_\epsilon \subset G, \frac{W_p(Z_G, Z_{G_\epsilon})}{W_p(Z_G, 0)} < \epsilon, \quad (8)$$

where we only adopt G_ϵ as the subset of G for the return selection to update the value network. Therefore the value distributions significantly different from the current initial goal will not be selected in the replay buffer in a self-attention way. This method is somewhat similar to knowledge distillation in deep learning.

3.4 Algorithm

Utilizing the above derivations, we propose the algorithm for Quantile Regression Multi-goal RL as Algorithm 1.

4 Experiments

4.1 Environments

We evaluate QR-HER and compare QR-HER to HER and its SOTA variant on several challenging robotic manipulation tasks in simulated Mujoco environments Robotics [8] as the Fig. 1 shows, including two kinds of tasks, Fetch robotic arm tasks and Shadow Dexterous Hand tasks. Both two kinds of tasks have sparse binary rewards and follow a Multi-goal RL framework. We choose the most challenging tasks, FetchSlide and HandManipulatePen to carry out our experiments.

4.2 Implementation Details

We run the experiments using PyTorch on a machine with 2 14-cores Intel Xeon E5-2690 v4 CPUs and 4 TITAN X(Pascal) GPUs. To make a fair comparison, for all algorithms, each off-policy algorithm is implemented with identical hyperparameters. In the experiments, one epoch is equivalent to 500 episodes with a unique seed(one goal). 10 percent of the episodes are used for testing set to get the mean success rate. The seeds are different in different epochs. Both policy networks and value networks are using MLP with three hidden layers (256,256,256) and optimized using Adam optimizer with critic learning rate of 0.001 and actor learning rate of 3×10^{-4}. The replay buffer size is 10^6 and the batch size is 64. The γ for the Bellman backup is 0.97 and the polyak for target network updating is 0.95. The distributional parameters Quant is choosed from [20,50,100,200,500] and the range of return selection parameter ϵ is [0.1, 0.3].

4.3   Benchmark Performance

In the benchmark experiments, the better mean success rate represents for better performance to accomplish robotic manipulation tasks. Now we compare the mean success rates in Fig. 1, where the shaded area represents the standard deviation since we use different seeds. Actually, the training process is extremely unstable but we use filters to smooth the curve.

Algorithm 1. Quantile Regression Hindsight Experience Replay

1: Input: initial policy parameters θ, Q-function parameters ϕ_1, ϕ_2, V-function parameters ψ, empty replay buffer $\mathcal{R}$, a strategy $\mathcal{S}$ for sampling goals for replay, distributional parameter Quant(related to ρ_τ^κ), return selection parameter ϵ
2: Initialize replay buffer $\mathcal{R}$, Set target parameters equal to main parameters $\psi_{\text{targ}} \leftarrow$
   ψ
3: **for** episode $= 1, M$ **do**
4:    Sample an initial goal G, initial state s_0, $g = G$
5:    **for** $t = 0, T - 1$ **do**
6:       Sample an action from
         $a = \text{clip}\left(\mu_\theta(s_t, g) + \delta, a_{Low}, a_{High}\right)$, where $\delta \sim \mathcal{N}$
7:       Execute a_t in the environment and get next state s_{t+1}
8:    **end for**
9:    **for** $t = 0, T - 1$ **do**
10:      $r_t := r(s_t, a_t, g)$
11:      Store the transition $(s_t \| g, a_t, r_t, s_{t+1} \| g, G)$ in replay buffer $\mathcal{R}$
12:      Sample a set of additional goals for replay $\mathcal{G} := S$
13:      **for** $g' \in \mathcal{G}$ **do**
14:         $r' := r(s_t, a_t, g')$
15:         Store the transition $(s_t \| g', a_t, r', s_{t+1} \| g', G)$ in $\mathcal{R}$
16:      **end for**
17:   **end for**
18:   **for** $t = 1, N$ **do**
19:      Sample a minibatch B from the replay buffer $\mathcal{R}$
20:      **for** each transition in B **do**
21:         Calculate the return selection goals set G_ϵ from the initial goals set G
22:         **for** each goal in G_ϵ **do**
23:            Quantile Regression Q-targets updating
               $\mathcal{T} y_q(r, s', g, G) = \mathbb{E}[r(s, g, G_\epsilon)] + \gamma(1 - d)\mathbb{E}[V_{\psi_{\text{targ}}}(s', g, G)]$
24:            Quantile Regression Q-loss and π-loss gradient descent
               $\nabla_\psi \frac{1}{|B|} \sum_{s \in B} [\rho_\tau^\kappa (Q_\psi(s, g, G) - \mathcal{T} y_q(r, s', G))]^2$
               $\nabla_\theta \frac{1}{|B|} \sum_{s \in B} \rho_\tau^\kappa Q_{\phi,1}(s, g, \tilde{a}_\theta(s), G)$
25:            Target value network updating
               $\psi_{\text{targ}} \leftarrow \rho \psi_{\text{targ}} + (1 - \rho)\psi$
26:         **end for**
27:      **end for**
28:   **end for**
29: **end for**

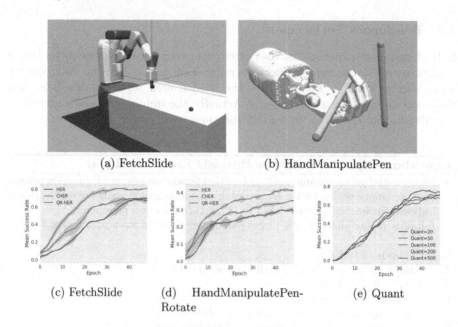

(a) FetchSlide   (b) HandManipulatePen

(c) FetchSlide   (d)   HandManipulatePen-   (e) Quant
                      Rotate

Fig. 1. The open AI robotics experiments for QR-HER

The agent trained with QR-HER shows the best benchmark performance at the end of the training. The value of Quant is the key hyper-parameter of QR-HER, as is shown in Fig. 1. The performance at Quant = 20 is 20% higher than at Quant = 200. Our conclusion is that the agent has its best performance when the Quant is about half of the number of goals(epochs).

4.4   Performance Analysis of Each Goal

According to our assumption, the quantile regression method with return selection is supposed to reduce the interference between different goals to improve the performance of each goal. The corresponding result is shown in Table 1. From the table, we can infer that QR-HER improves the overall performance through the optimization of the policy of each goal as we expected.

Table 1. Final success rates in HandManipulatePenRotate with different goals(seeds)

Method	seed = 0	1000	10000	20000	100000
HER	0.315	0.307	0.282	0.293	0.296
CHER	0.346	0.325	0.336	0.311	0.325
QR-HER (Ours)	**0.457**	**0.422**	**0.434**	**0.418**	**0.420**

5   Summary

The main contributions of this paper are summarized as follows: (1) We raise the issue of performance instability and performance degradation in Multi-goal RL, and attribute the cause to intrinsic stochasticity; (2) We introduce Wasserstein Metric and Quantile Regression into Multi-goal RL to derive QR-HER; (3) We show that QR-HER can exceed HER and its variants to achieve the state-of-the-art performance on OpenAI Robotics; (4) We show that QR-HER improves the performance of each goal to become the powerful evidence for the correctness of our theory.

Acknowledgments. This work was supported in part to Dr. Liansheng Zhuang by NSFC under Grant contract No. 61976199, in part to Dr. Houqiang Li by NSFC under Grant contract No. 61836011.

References

1. Andrychowicz, M., et al.: Hindsight experience replay. In: Advances in Neural Information Processing Systems, pp. 5048–5058 (2017)
2. Bellemare, M.G., Dabney, W., Munos, R.: A distributional perspective on reinforcement learning. In: Proceedings of the 34th International Conference on Machine Learning-Volume 70, pp. 449–458. JMLR. org (2017)
3. Dabney, W., Rowland, M., Bellemare, M.G., Munos, R.: Distributional reinforcement learning with quantile regression (2017)
4. Fang, M., Zhou, T., Du, Y., Han, L., Zhang, Z.: Curriculum-guided hindsight experience replay. In: Advances in Neural Information Processing Systems, pp. 12602–12613 (2019)
5. LeCun, Y., Bengio, Y., Hinton, G.: Deep learning. Nature **521**(7553), 436 (2015)
6. Lillicrap, T.P., et al.: Continuous control with deep reinforcement learning. arXiv preprint arXiv:1509.02971 (2015)
7. Lin, L.J.: Self-improving reactive agents based on reinforcement learning, planning and teaching. Mach. Learn. **8**(3–4), 293–321 (1992)
8. Plappert, M., et al.: Multi-goal reinforcement learning: challenging robotics environments and request for research. arXiv preprint arXiv:1802.09464 (2018)
9. Schaul, T., Horgan, D., Gregor, K., Silver, D.: Universal value function approximators. In: International Conference on Machine Learning, pp. 1312–1320 (2015)
10. Sutton, R.S., Barto, A.G.: Reinforcement learning: an introduction. MIT press (2018)

Sustainable Patterns of Pigeon Flights Over Different Types of Terrain

Margarita Zaleshina[1] ⓘ and Alexander Zaleshin[2(✉)] ⓘ

[1] Moscow Institute of Physics and Technology, Moscow, Russia
zaleshina@gmail.com
[2] Institute of Higher Nervous Activity and Neurophysiology, Moscow, Russia
terbiosorg@gmail.com

Abstract. Visual characteristics of terrain affect the properties of pigeon trajectories in medium-distance flights. Pigeon flight often provides a solution to the task of searching for food (foraging), returning home (homing), or exploring territory (surveying). In this work, we considered the flights of single pigeons and pigeon flocks, calculated flight characteristics such as direction, altitude and its deviations, and analyzed reactions to the boundaries between different areas. Based on remote sensing datasets, we identified visual characteristics of terrain, such as the density of surface fill and its distribution over the study terrain, boundaries of single objects, and boundaries between homogeneous areas. Applying spatial analysis, we compared the characteristics of pigeon GPS tracks and features of object distributions on terrain over which birds fly. Our analysis revealed which flight parameters are stable and which, on the contrary, are very sensitive to visually perceived terrain characteristics. We found that the properties of flight over an urbanized area often differ from the properties of flight over a natural landscape. Spatial data—pigeon GPS track records and open-access remote sensing datasets—were processed using the geographical information system QGIS. Our results show that adaptive visual perception can help solve navigation tasks when pigeons fly over mixed terrain. Knowledge of the characteristic features of bird flights can be used both for a better understanding of the spatial behavior of living creatures (humans and animals) and for optimization of artificial intelligence algorithms.

Keywords: Visual perception · Spatial navigation · Wayfinding · QGIS

1 Introduction

Studies of pigeon flights show that these birds are able to quickly respond to changes in the properties of the terrain over which they fly. For orientation, birds can use visual landmarks, such as noticeable single objects or extended lines (roads, rivers, coastlines), or homogeneous surfaces (forests, fields, lakes). Applied navigation algorithms for flying above land allow pigeons to change their trajectories depending on the perceived spatial environment during wayfinding over unfamiliar terrain, searching for

© Springer Nature Switzerland AG 2020
H. Yang et al. (Eds.): ICONIP 2020, CCIS 1332, pp. 832–839, 2020.
https://doi.org/10.1007/978-3-030-63820-7_95

feeding sites, or homing. Depending on the type of terrain—urban, natural, or mixed—the visual attributes of the surface change noticeably, including the density and distance between main types of surface elements. In contrast to a reaction to a landmark, which is always perceived as a visually significant object, a reaction to similar elements can differ: elements may be perceived as a unique object or as part of a texture pattern.

This paper shows the characteristic features of pigeon flights over medium distances (about 10 km) over various landscapes. Visual characteristics of surfaces were identified using remote sensing data obtained from open sources. We calculated and analyzed the following datasets: *i)* spatial features of types of terrain over which pigeon flights occur, *ii)* features of pigeon flights and their variation and sustainability, and *iii)* comparison of spatial features of terrain and features of pigeon flights.

2   Background and Related Works

The ability of pigeons (*Columba livia*) to orient themselves during flight (wayfinding) constantly attracts the attention of researchers. Modern researchers often use GPS records to examine pigeon navigational abilities. Pigeon flights provide a solution to the task of searching for food (foraging) or the task of returning home (homing). In addition, pigeons regularly make exploratory flights (surveying). Although the shortest distance through the air between two points is a straight line, excluding the effect of wind, birds never fly strictly "in a straight line". A real pigeon flight contains several components; the bird needs to follow the "straight line" direction, or to respond to landmarks.

In pigeon trajectories, the important components are: i) beeline path (straight line between start and finish points), ii) spontaneous deviations or deviations due to wind (Fig. 1). Deviations can be following: deviation from beeline direction, deviation from "mean direction" in a single time interval, returning to selected direction of flight in case of displacement, nearing to landmark, including "circular" flights around possible places of interest (landmarks), with a 360-degree turn.

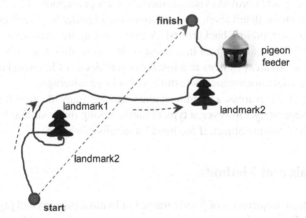

Fig. 1. Pigeon flight path in relation to external landmarks. Blue line shows pigeon's track, dashed gray line shows a beeline to final point in a straight direction, dashed red lines show typical direction in single time intervals. (Color figure online)

Blaser et al. [1] proved that pigeons are able to remember routes and fly to the objects which are important to them, such as home or feeding spots. The authors suggested that pigeons have their own spatial representation of their surroundings, a so-called "mental map", in which their own position, home loft and food spots are represented simultaneously.

A study of perception of the surrounding landscape during the flight and the influence of landscape on wayfinding and training demonstrated that memorized guidance control is likely to relate to local features of the landscape [2]. Lipp et al. [3] discovered that pigeons can select extended linear objects and use them as landmarks. Biro et al. [4] reported similar results: pigeons can fly home in a straight line, but more often they fly along well-known routes, preferring to be guided by familiar landmarks. Moreover, near their loft, pigeons mainly orient on familiar visual landmarks [5]. The significance of external landmarks and their influence on the change of direction does not only depend on the level of pigeon training. Vyssotski et al. [6] showed that pigeons move straight to the goal from the sea to the shore in good visibility conditions, but in bad visibility conditions they choose the direction of the closest landmark on the shore. Mann et al. [7] concluded that pigeons orient themselves better when flying above territory where landscape complexity is neither too high nor too low.

Visual perception of terrain is important when pigeons fly over medium distances [8]. At the same time, depending on the situation, the level of detail in perception can be changed (by changing the height of the flight, or the distance from objects of interest). That is, the scope of perception is co-scaled to the problem being solved. Visually recognizable extended boundaries between homogeneous textures are important spatial landmarks. Chan et al. [9] argued that extended surfaces or boundaries can act as landmarks by providing a frame of reference for encoding spatial information. In addition, the ability to perceive, distinguish, and respond rapidly to minor changes in textures can be very high in pigeons [10]. The reaction to extended boundaries between different homogeneous textures can be revealed by the flight of pigeons. The elements of a texture are defined as visually recognizable items that repeat along the surface. During motion, these elements provide visual information for perception [11].

Depending on the detail level, the same objects can either be perceived separately or merge with the surrounding background. A free-standing tree can serve as a landmark like a "beacon", but a similar tree in a forest or in a long alley will only be an element within a texture. An array of trees in a forest or even blocks of low-rise buildings can be perceived as a single homogeneous texture with a large coverage.

In the case of urban areas, a prominent house among many identical houses can often be perceived separately. However, a typical house among many similar houses can also be perceived as a unique object, if the need for details increases.

3   Materials and Methods

In this work flight trajectories of poorly trained individual pigeons and pigeons in flocks were studied. Pigeons flew *i)* over natural and agricultural areas (the typical distance between separate surface elements was assumed to be more than 100 m for fill patterns and less than 10 m for single elements), *ii)* over urban areas with low-rise buildings (the typical distance between separate surface elements was assumed to be from 10 m to 200 m), and *iii)* over boundaries between different areas. Pigeon flights were performed between two different points with a characteristic distance between them of about 10–15 km, and with departure from the selected starting points and arrival at the pigeon-lofts. Flight parameters were recorded using GPS-receivers mounted on pigeons and calculated using QGIS tools (http://qgis.org).

Spatial analysis of individual pigeon trajectories was performed based on Dryad data package (https://doi.org/10.5061/dryad.53f4b, [12]). Pigeons flew over natural and agricultural terrain and over urban terrain. Calculation was made for 102 flights of individual pigeons. Spatial analysis of flock trajectories was performed based on Dryad data package (https://datadryad.org/resource/doi:10.5061/dryad.f9n8t, [13]; three flocks with three, four, and five pigeons flew over mixed terrain near the seashore: sea coast, urban terrain and agricultural fields; GPS tracks points were taken five times per second) and on Movebank data package (https://www.datarepository.movebank.org/handle/10255/mov e.365, [14]; three flocks with eight, seven and eight pigeons flew over mixed terrain in the foothills: natural forests, agricultural fields and rural areas; GPS tracks points were taken four times per second).

Based on data from the open-access remote sensing datasets, we identified visual characteristics of the terrain, such as the density of surface fill and its distribution over the study area, the boundaries of distinct objects, and the boundaries between homogeneous areas. The following operations were performed:

– Step 1. Segregation of homogeneous textures and borders between textures.

The selection of a distinct homogeneous area was performed using the calculation of average density of texture elements of an area. Between selected areas with different textures, boundaries were constructed in form of isolines. Suitable average density parameters were identified for constructing isoline contours, that make it possible to

Fig. 2. Characteristic features. Blue graded color shows the trajectory of pigeons. Orange lines show the calculated isolines. Yellow circles show intersections of isolines and GPS tracks. (Color figure online)

distinguish forests and fields in form of extended homogeneous surfaces interspersed with separate inhomogeneous sections. The accuracy of the isolines was set within five meters or more (Fig. 2). With the same applied average density parameters, houses were distinguished as independent elements.

- Step 2. Calculating the surface fill density distribution and separation of territories by type of surfaces.

Calculation of the distribution of surface fill densities was performed on a layer of objects selected by isolines in step 1. Each selected object was presented as a centroid. According to the density of available centroids (the number of centroids per unit area), the territories over which the pigeons flew were divided into areas with different types of surfaces. The following factors were taken into account: the fill density of textures with similar repeating patterns, the characteristic sizes of simple objects included in these patterns and the typical distances between these simple objects. As a result, the surfaces were divided as follows: *i)* urban area with low-rise buildings; *ii)* extended boundaries of linear objects or boundaries between textures, with an average length of more than 300 m; *iii)* natural area (forest, grassland, fields); *iv)* other territories.

4   Results

In this study, 137 flights of pigeons were analyzed, including 25 flights in flocks of pigeons. The number of points in GPS records for individual pigeons ranged from 1,600 to 7,400. Pigeons flew over a mixed territory composed of forests, agricultural fields and urban territory with low-rise buildings.

The most widely presented ranges of parameter values for pigeon flights were identified by characteristics such as direction and altitude and their deviations. For each pigeon flight, the following characteristics were analyzed: instant flight direction, change in flight direction in an interval of five seconds, instant flight altitude, and change in flight altitude in an interval of five seconds. It was assumed that:

- Flight can be considered stable in direction if deviations from the direction within five seconds do not exceed 8 degrees.
- Flight can be considered highly variable in direction if deviations from the direction within five seconds exceed 20°.
- Flight can be considered low height-adjustable (with a stable perception scale) if the deviation in height for five seconds does not exceed 1 m.
- Flight can be considered high height- adjustable (with a change in the scale of perception) if the deviation in height for five seconds exceeds 2 m.

In particular, it was shown that there are characteristics in which flight can be considered stable in parameters for an interval of five seconds, and characteristics in which flight parameters change sharply. Then for each type of territory percentages were determined as the ratio of flight time with considered features to the total flight time with an interval of ten seconds. Thus, the combined indicators typical for flights over a certain type of territory were revealed. Based on the results of comparison for different types of territories (urban, natural, or border between different types of territories), characteristic distributions of localizations of variability or stability of flight parameters were identified.

Table 1 shows flight features calculated on the base of GPS tracks, such as stable direction (d_stab1,2), direction variability (d_var1,2), low height-adjustability (h_stab1,2) and high height-adjustability (h_var1,2), where preliminary data sources were GPS records from Movebank (MVB) and Dryad (DRD) packages.

Table 1. Comparison of characteristics of pigeon flights and terrain features

	Indicator	Urban	Field	Boundary	Forest
MVB	d_stab1	0,10	0,20	0,31	0,29
	d_var1	0,12	0,19	0,36	0,17
	h_stab1	0,26	0,23	0,21	0,34
	h_var1	0,14	0,24	0,25	0,28
DRD	d_stab2	0,07	0,18	0,38	0,26
	d_var2	0,10	0,16	0,34	0,12
	h_stab2	0,24	0,21	0,22	0,31
	h_var2	0,17	0,25	0,27	0,23

Using the methods of multi-factor analysis, it was found that the percent ratio was significantly differs for different types of territories and for flight features considered in Table 1. The analysis of variance (ANOVA) was used to detect significant factors in a multi-factor model. According to selected indicators, the dependence of flight characteristics on the terrain over which the flight takes place had a statistically significant effect ($F = 6.81$, $F_{Critical} = 3.07$, $p < .05$). At the same time, it was found that for single characteristics, it was impossible to reliably compare the flight parameters and the area over which pigeon flies. All factors were checked in pairs against each other on the full flight recording time for the absence of dependence.

For additional verification, according to GPS tracks for a control group of 15 pigeons, flight indicators were calculated with a sliding window of ten seconds. For each control point of the GPS tracks, a preliminary assumption was made about type of terrain over which pigeons flew. The results of determining the type of terrain by preliminary calculation were compared with data on the type of real terrain.

Each indicator from the list {d_stab, d_var, h_stab, h_var} was assigned a value of 0 if it is less than 0.21, or a value of 1 if it is more than 0.21. Depending on the total composition of the territory, i.e. on the ratio of different types of homogeneous and heterogeneous textures present in it, the algorithm for assigning 0 and 1 must be re-calculated. For future calculation we set for input arrays [d_stab d_var h_stab h_var] following output values: [0,0,1,0] = Urban; [0,0,1,1] = Field; [1] = Boundary; [1,0,1,1] = Forest. It was found that the accuracy of prediction of the type of terrain, over which the pigeons flew, according to the combined parameters of the flight of pigeons, is 38%. An example of forest identification is shown in Fig. 3.

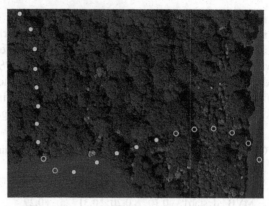

Fig. 3. Comparison of the predicted type of terrain and the actual type. Green dots show places that were identified as "forest" based on the properties of the pigeon's flight. Transparent dots show places that were identified as another type of terrain. (Color figure online)

5   Conclusions

Here we studied the typical tasks of finding a flight path over poorly familiar area. Visual spatial recognition can help in the basic formation and quick reconfiguration of flight paths. Based on the calculations made in this work, various cases were identified, for which the flight characteristics of pigeons are stable or sensitive to a change in external environment. Such methods can be applied to study the navigational mechanisms in pigeon flight over mixed terrains. Using the method of multi-factor analysis, it was found that in order to compare the flight characteristics of pigeons with the type of territory over which they fly, it is necessary to take into account four factors in GPS track sections: *i)* a stable direction for five or more seconds, *ii)* a high variability in direction or sharp change in direction, *iii)* stable height for five or more seconds, *iv)* high variability in height.

This study shows the roles of sustainability (return to the previous value after deviation), sensitivity (variations in flight features near lengthy linear objects or near boundaries of distinct areas), and scale perception (represent itself in change of flight height). The results obtained in this study can be used both for a better understanding of the spatial behavior of living creatures (humans and animals) and for optimization of artificial intelligence algorithms.

References

1. Blaser, N., Dell'Omo, G., Dell'Ariccia, G., Wolfer, D.P., Lipp, H.-P.: Testing cognitive navigation in unknown territories: homing pigeons choose different targets. J. Exp. Biol. **216**, 3123–3131 (2013)
2. Guilford, T., Biro, D.: Route following and the pigeon's familiar area map. J. Exp. Biol. **217**, 169–179 (2014)
3. Lipp, H.-P., et al.: Pigeon homing along highways and exits. Curr. Biol. England **14**, 1239–1249 (2004)

4. Biro, D., Freeman, R., Meade, J., Roberts, S., Guilford, T.: Pigeons combine compass and landmark guidance in familiar route navigation. Proc. Natl. Acad. Sci. **104**, 7471–7476 (2007)
5. Walcott, C.: Multi-modal orientation cues in homing pigeons. Integr. Comp. Biol. (2005)
6. Vyssotski, A.L., Dell'Omo, G., Dell'Ariccia, G., Abramchuk, A.N., Serkov, A.N., Latanov, A.V., et al.: EEG responses to visual landmarks in flying pigeons. Curr. Biol. **19**, 1159–1166 (2009)
7. Mann, R.P., Armstrong, C., Meade, J., Freeman, R., Biro, D., Guilford, T.: Landscape complexity influences route-memory formation in navigating pigeons. Biol. Lett. **10**, 20130885 (2014)
8. Zaleshina, M., Zaleshin, A.: Spatial features of terrain reflected in pigeon flights. In: Creem-Regehr, S., Schöning, J., Klippel, A. (eds.) Spatial Cognition 2018. LNCS (LNAI), vol. 11034, pp. 3–14. Springer, Cham (2018). https://doi.org/10.1007/978-3-319-96385-3_1
9. Chan, E., Baumann, O., Bellgrove, M.A., Mattingley, J.B.: From objects to landmarks: the function of visual location information in spatial navigation. Front. Psychol. **3**, 1–11 (2012)
10. Bovet, D., Vauclair, J.: Picture recognition in animals and humans. Behav. Brain Res. **109**, 143–165 (2000)
11. Zaleshina, M., Zaleshin, A., Galvani, A.: Visual perception of mixed homogeneous textures in flying pigeons. In: Nicosia, G., Pardalos, P., Giuffrida, G., Umeton, R. (eds.) MOD 2017. LNCS, vol. 10710, pp. 299–308. Springer, Cham (2018). https://doi.org/10.1007/978-3-319-72926-8_25
12. Pettit, B., Flack, A., Freeman, R., Guilford, T., Biro, D.: Not just passengers: pigeons, Columba livia, can learn homing routes while flying with a more experienced conspecific. Proc. R. Soc. B Biol. Sci. **280**, 20122160 (2012)
13. Watts, I., Pettit, B., Nagy, M., de Perera, T.B., Biro, D.: Lack of experience-based stratification in homing pigeon leadership hierarchies. R. Soc. Open Sci. **3**, 150518 (2016)
14. Santos, C.D., Neupert, S., Lipp, H.P., Wikelski, M., Dechmann, D.K.N.: Temporal and contextual consistency of leadership in homing pigeon flocks. de Polavieja GG, editor. PLoS One **9**, e102771 (2014)

Author Index